Heuristics

Heuristics

The Foundations of Adaptive Behavior

Edited by

Gerd Gigerenzer

Ralph Hertwig

Thorsten Pachur

OXFORD
UNIVERSITY PRESS

Oxford University Press, Inc., publishes works that further
Oxford University's objective of excellence
in research, scholarship, and education.

Oxford   New York
Auckland   Cape Town   Dar es Salaam   Hong Kong   Karachi
Kuala Lumpur   Madrid   Melbourne   Mexico City   Nairobi
New Delhi   Shanghai   Taipei   Toronto

With offices in
Argentina   Austria   Brazil   Chile   Czech Republic   France   Greece
Guatemala   Hungary   Italy   Japan   Poland   Portugal   Singapore
South Korea   Switzerland   Thailand   Turkey   Ukraine   Vietnam

Published by Oxford University Press, Inc.
198 Madison Avenue, New York, New York 10016

Library of Congress Cataloging-in-Publication Data

Heuristics : the foundations of adaptive behavior / edited by
Gerd Gigerenzer, Ralph Hertwig, and Thorsten Pachur.
p. cm.
Includes bibliographical references and index.
ISBN 978-0-19-974428-2
1. Adaptability (Psychology) I. Gigerenzer, Gerd. II. Hertwig, Ralph.
III. Pachur, Thorsten.
BF335.H428 2010
155.2'4–dc22   2010013592

9 8 7 6 5 4 3 2 1
Printed in the United States of America
on acid-free paper.

CONTENTS

LIST OF CONTRIBUTORS

C. Philip Beaman
School of Psychology & Clinical Language
    Sciences
University of Reading
Earley Gate
Whiteknights
Reading RG6 6A, United Kingdom
c.p.beaman@reading.ac.uk

Craig Bennell
Department of Psychology
Carleton University
B550 Loeb Building
1125 Colonel By Drive,
Ottawa, Ontario, K1S 5B6, Canada
craig_bennell@carleton.ca

Will M. Bennis
Department of Psychology
University of New York in Prague
Legerova 72
120 00 Prague
Czech Republic
wbennis@faculty.unyp.cz

Bryan F. Bergert
Max Planck Institute for Human
    Development
Center for Adaptive Behavior and
    Cognition (ABC)
Lentzeallee 94
14195 Berlin, Germany
bergert@mpib-berlin.mpg.de

Eduard Brandstätter
Institute of Education and Psychology
Johannes Kepler Universität Linz
Altenberger Straße 69
4040 Linz, Austria
eduard.brandstaetter@jku.at

Henry Brighton
Max Planck Institute for Human Development
Center for Adaptive Behavior and
    Cognition (ABC)
Lentzeallee 94
14195 Berlin, Germany
hbrighton@mpib-berlin.mpg.de

Arndt Bröder
Department of Psychology
University of Bonn
Kaiser-Karl-Ring 9
53111 Bonn, Germany
broeder@uni-bonn.de

Jennifer N. Davis
Applied Arts and Sciences
Lethbridge College
3000 College Drive South
Lethbridge, Alberta, T1K 1L6, Canada

Victor DeMiguel
Management Science and Operations
London Business School
Regent's Park
London NW1 4SA, United Kingdom
avmiguel@london.edu

Mandeep K. Dhami
Institute of Criminology
University of Cambridge
Sidgwick Avenue
Cambridge CB3 9DA, United Kingdom
mkd25@cam.ac.uk

Marianna Eddy
Department of Brain and Cognitive
    Sciences
Massachusetts Institute of Technology
Gabrieli Lab @ MIT
43 Vassar Street, 46-4033
Cambridge, MA 02139, USA
eddym@mit.edu

Malcolm R. Forster
Department of Philosophy
University of Wisconsin
5185 Helen C. White Hall
600 North Park Street
Madison WI 53706, USA
mforster@wisc.edu

Wolfgang Gaissmaier
Max Planck Institute for Human
    Development
Center for Adaptive Behavior and
    Cognition (ABC)
Lentzeallee 94
14195 Berlin, Germany
gaissmaier@mpib-berlin.mpg.de

Rocío Garcia-Retamero
Faculty of Psychology
University of Granada
Campus Universitario de Cartuja s/n,
18071 Granada, Spain
rretamer@ugr.es

Lorenzo Garlappi
Department of Finance
McCombs School of Business
University of Texas at Austin
Austin, TX 78712, USA
lorenzo.garlappi@mccombs.utexas.edu

Gerd Gigerenzer
Max Planck Institute for Human Development
Center for Adaptive Behavior and
    Cognition (ABC)
Lentzeallee 94
14195 Berlin, Germany
sekgigerenzer@mpib-berlin.mpg.de

Daniel G. Goldstein
Yahoo Research
111 W. 40th Street
New York, NY 10018, USA
dan@dangoldstein.com

Ralph Hertwig
Department of Psychology
University of Basel
Institut für Psychologie
Missionsstrasse 64a
4055 Basel, Switzerland
ralph.hertwig@unibas.ch

Stefan M. Herzog
Department of Psychology
University of Basel
Institut für Psychologie
Missionsstrasse 64a
4055 Basel, Switzerland
stefan.herzog@unibas.ch

Ulrich Hoffrage
Faculty of Business and Economics
University of Lausanne
Ecole des Hautes Etudes Commerciales (HEC)
Bâtiment Internef
1015 Lausanne, Switzerland
ulrich.hoffrage@unil.ch

Robin M. Hogarth
Department of Economics & Business
Pompeu Fabra University
Ramon Trias Fargas, 25 –27
08005 Barcelona, Spain
robin.hogarth@upf.edu

John M. C. Hutchinson
Senckenberg Museum für Naturkunde Görlitz
PF 300154
02806 Görlitz, Germany
majmch@gmail.com

Natalia Karelaia
INSEAD
Decision Sciences Area
Boulevard de Constance
77305 Fontainebleau, France
natalia.karelaia@insead.edu

Konstantinos V. Katsikopoulos
Max Planck Institute for Human Development
Center for Adaptive Behavior and
    Cognition (ABC)
Lentzeallee 94
14195 Berlin, Germany
katsikop@mpib-berlin.mpg.de

Timothy Ketelaar
Department of Psychology
New Mexico State University
Las Cruces, New Mexico 88003-8001, USA
ketelaar@nmsu.edu

Scott M. Krauchunas
Department of Psychology
Saint Anselm College

Michael D. Lee
Department of Cognitive Sciences
University of California, Irvine
3151 Social Science Plaza A
Mail Code: 5100
Irvine, CA 92697, USA
mdlee@uci.edu

Alejandro López-Rousseau
Amor de Dios 4 - 1L
28014 Madrid, Spain
lopezrousseau@yahoo.com

Natasha Loughlin
Department of Psychology
University of Adelaide
SA 5005, Australia

Ingrid B. Lundberg
Department of Psychology
University of Adelaide
SA 5005, Australia

Julian N. Marewski
Max Planck Institute for Human Development
Center for Adaptive Behavior and
    Cognition (ABC)
Lentzeallee 94
14195 Berlin, Germany
marewski@mpib-berlin.mpg.de

Laura Martignon
Institut für Mathematik und Informatik
Pädagogische Hochschule Ludwigsburg
Reuteallee 46
71634 Ludwigsburg, Germany
martignon@ph-ludwigsburg.de

Rui Mata
Department of Psychology
University of Basel
Institut für Psychologie
Missionsstrasse 64a
4055 Basel, Switzerland
ruimata@ruimata.com

Michael K. McBeath
Department of Psychology
Arizona State University
Tempe, AZ 85287-1104, USA
Michael.McBeath@asu.edu

Rachel McCloy
School of Psychology & Clinical Sciences
University of Reading
Earley Gate
Whiteknights
Reading RG6 6AL, United Kingdom
r.a.mccloy@reading.ac.uk

Ben R. Newell
School of Psychology
University of New South Wales
Sydney 2052, Australia
ben.newell@unsw.edu.au

Robert M. Nosofsky
Department of Psychological and Brain Sciences
Indiana University
1101 E. 10th Street
Bloomington, IN 47405, USA
nosofsky@indiana.edu

Philipp E. Otto
Faculty of Business Administration and
    Economics
European University Viadrina Frankfurt (Oder)
Postfach 1786
15207 Frankfurt (Oder), Germany
otto@euv-frankfurt-o.de

Thorsten Pachur
Department of Psychology
University of Basel
Missionsstrasse 64a
4055 Basel, Switzerland
thorsten.pachur@unibas.ch

Daniel Pichert
Max Planck Institute for Human Development
Center for Adaptive Behavior and Cognition
    (ABC)
Lentzeallee 94
14195 Berlin, Germany
danipu@gmx.de

Timothy J. Pleskac
Department of Psychology
282a Psychology
Michigan State University
East Lansing, MI 48824, USA
tim.pleskac@gmail.com

Markus Raab
German Sport University Cologne
Am Sportpark
Müngersdorf 6
50933 Cologne, Germany
raab@dshs-koeln.de

Torsten Reimer
Department of Communication
Purdue University
100 North University Street
West Lafayette, IN 47907-2098, USA
treimer@purdue.edu

Jörg Rieskamp
Department of Psychology
University of Basel
Institut für Psychologie
Missionsstrasse 62a
4055 Basel, Switzerland
joerg.rieskamp@unibas.ch

Benjamin Scheibehenne
Department of Psychology
University of Basel
Institut für Psychologie
Missionsstrasse 62a
4055 Basel, Switzerland
benjamin.scheibehenne@unibas.ch

Lael J. Schooler
Max Planck Institute for Human Development
Center for Adaptive Behavior and Cognition
    (ABC)
Lentzeallee 94
14195 Berlin, Germany
schooler@mpib-berlin.mpg.de

Ricarda I. Schubotz
Max Planck Institute for Neurological Research
Gleueler Straße 50
50931 Cologne, Germany
schubotz@nf.mpg.de

Dennis M. Shaffer
Department of Psychology
Ohio State University, Mansfield
352 Ovalwood Hall
1680 University Drive
Mansfield, OH 44906, USA
shaffer.247@osu.edu

David R. Shanks
Division of Psychology and Language Sciences
University College London
26 Bedford Way
London WC1H 0AP, United Kingdom
d.shanks@ucl.ac.uk

Jorge Simão
Department of Computer Science
University of Porto
R. do Campo Alegre, 823
4150-180 Porto, Portugal
jsimao@dcc.fc.up.pt

Philip T. Smith
School of Psychology & Clinical Sciences
University of Reading
Earley Gate
Whiteknights
Reading RG6 6AL, United Kingdom
p.t.smith@reading.ac.uk

Brent Snook
Psychology Department
Memorial University of Newfoundland
St. John's, NL, A1B 3X9, Canada
bsnook@play.psych.mun.ca

Frank J. Sulloway
Department of Psychology (IPSR)
University of California
Tolman Hall 4125
Berkeley, CA 94720-5050, USA
sulloway@berkeley.edu

Masanori Takezawa
Department of Psychology
Sophia University
Kioicho 7–1, Chiyoda,
Tokyo 102-8554, Japan
m.takezawa@sophia.ac.jp

Paul J. Taylor
Department of Psychology
Lancaster University
Fylde College
Lancaster LA1 4YF, United Kingdom
p.j.taylor@lancaster.ac.uk

Peter M. Todd
Program in Cognitive Science
Indiana University
1101 E. 10th Street
Bloomington, IN 47405, USA
pmtodd@indiana.edu

Raman Uppal
Institute of Finance and Accounting
London Business School
London NW1 4SA, United Kingdom
ruppal@london.edu

Oliver Vitouch
Department of Psychology
University of Klagenfurt
Universitätsstraße 65-67
9020 Klagenfurt, Austria
oliver.vitouch@uni-klu.ac.at

Kirsten G. Volz
Centre for Integrative Neuroscience
University of Tübingen
Neurocognition of Intuition Group
Paul-Ehrlich-Straße 17
72076 Tübingen, Germany
kirsten.volz@cin.uni-tuebingen.de

D. Yves von Cramon
Max Planck Institute for Human Cognitive and
    Brain Sciences
Stephanstraße 1A
04103 Leipzig, Germany
cramon@cbs.mpg.de

Florian von Wangenheim
Faculty of Business Administration
Technical University of Munich
Arcisstr. 21
80333 Munich, Germany
marketing@wi.tum.de

Nicola J. Weston
Faculty of Science and Technology
University of Plymouth
Link Block
Drake Circus
Plymouth PL4 8AA, United Kingdom
nicola.weston@plymouth.ac.uk

Jan K. Woike
Faculty of Business and Economics
University of Lausanne
Bâtiment Internef
1015 Lausanne, Switzerland
JanKristian.Woike@unil.ch

Markus Wübben
Faculty of Business Administration
Technical University of Munich
Arcisstr. 21
80333 Munich, Germany
markus@wuebben.net

Rational decision theory meets *Homo sapiens* in the Dilbert daily strip. Reprinted with permission of Kipka Komiks.

INTRODUCTION

Gerd Gigerenzer, Ralph Hertwig, and Thorsten Pachur

How do people make decisions when time is limited, information unreliable, and the future uncertain? On the basis of the work of Herbert A. Simon and with the help of colleagues around the world, the Adaptive Behavior and Cognition (ABC) Research Group at the Max Planck Institute for Human Development in Berlin has developed a research program on *simple heuristics*, also known as *fast-and-frugal heuristics*. Providing a fresh look at how the mind works as well as the nature of rational behavior, this program has stimulated a large body of research; led to fascinating applications in fields as diverse as law, medicine, business, and sports; and instigated controversial debates in psychology, philosophy, and economics. In a single volume, we have brought together key articles that have been previously published in journals across many disciplines. These articles present theory, applications, and a sample of the large number of existing experimental studies. We have shortened many of the articles, corrected errors, Americanized spelling, and updated references that were in press at the time.

What kinds of theories can provide insight into how people make decisions? Logic, probability, and heuristics are three answers to this question and, more generally, to the question of how the mind works. For Aristotle, logic was a theory of ideal human reasoning and inference. For Jean Piaget, logic became the guiding metaphor for cognitive development, with the mature mind operating like an intuitive logician. Probability theory emerged only late, in the mid-seventeenth century, renouncing logical cer-

tainty by acknowledging that humble humans live in the twilight of probability. Since the second half of the twentiethth century, the mind has been seen as an intuitive statistician and modeled by probabilistic accounts such as signal detection theory and Bayesian theories of cognition.

In contrast to logic and probability, *heuristics are processes that ignore information and enable fast decisions*. They are a comparatively recent means of understanding how the mind works. Albert Einstein used the term *heuristic* in the title of his 1905 Nobel Prize–winning article on quantum physics to indicate that he considered this view as incomplete, even false, but of great transitory use toward a more accurate theory. Max Wertheimer (a close friend of Einstein) and his fellow Gestalt psychologists spoke of heuristic methods in problem solving, such as "looking around." Herbert Simon replaced the somewhat vague terms of the Gestalt school with computational models for the "art of guided search." In artificial intelligence, heuristics were introduced for playing chess and problem solving with the goal of making computers "smart," whereas in psychology, "heuristics-and-biases" were introduced to explain why people are not so smart.

WHY HEURISTICS?

The classic answer to this question is that because of their cognitive limitations, humans are unable to perform rational calculations and instead rely on error-prone heuristics. A variant of this view says that even when people could optimize, that is, compute the best decision, they often rely on heuristics in order to save effort at the price of sacrificing some accuracy. The first answer assumes the inability to optimize, the second a pragmatic decision that it may not be worth spending the time. Both answers are based on the principle of an *accuracy–effort trade-off*: The less information, computation, or time one uses, the less accurate one's judgments will be. This trade-off is believed to be one of the few general laws of the mind.

The rationale for heuristics laid out in this book is entirely different from these classical views. Less effort can in fact lead to better or worse accuracy, depending on the environment in which a heuristic is used, that is, its *ecological rationality* (see later). We begin with two concepts fundamental to understanding the role and potential of heuristics: Savage's small worlds and Simon's scissors.

Savage's Small Worlds

Leonard Jimmie Savage is known as the creator of modern Bayesian decision theory, and his *Foundations of Statistics* (1954) counts as one of the most influential books on this topic. Savage carefully limited its applications to what he called "small worlds," simple and well-defined microcosms in which all relevant alternatives, consequences, and probability distributions are known and no surprises are allowed. A typical example for a small-world decision is the purchase of a lottery ticket. In a small world, it is always possible to "look before you leap," whereas in a large world, one can only "cross certain bridges once they are reached." In what we call a "large world" or, alternatively, an uncertain world, not all alternatives, consequences, and probabilities are known or knowable, and surprises can happen. Savage warned against both using his theory outside of small worlds and believing that Bayesian updating would be the general solution to the problem of induction. Yet his caveat is disregarded when theorists build optimization models for small worlds *and* leap to the conclusion that the results describe or prescribe how humans make decisions in the large world (see Binmore, 2009).

How should we make decisions in the large world—that is, when Bayesian theory or similar optimization methods are out of reach? The second half of Savage's (1954) *Foundations of Statistics* turns to this question, analyzing heuristics such as minimax (i.e., choosing the alternative that minimizes the greatest loss). Savage's distinction anticipates two research programs in the cognitive sciences. The first is to build complex models of behavior for small worlds; the second is to study the simple heuristics that perform well in large worlds. Ideally, these programs should progress in tandem, yet that is rarely the case. The limitation of optimization models to small worlds appears to be largely overlooked, and heuristics are relegated to mere shortcuts to optimal solutions.

In sum, the accuracy–effort trade-off indeed exists in a small world. In a large world, however, where there is no *general* accuracy–effort trade-off, heuristics can be more accurate than methods that use more information and computation, including optimization methods. Thus, one reason why people rely on heuristics is that these allow for decisions in both small and large worlds.

Simon's Scissors

Behavior has been explained by intentions, preferences, attitudes, personality traits, cognitive styles, risk aversion, altruism, egoism, and other internal causes. The common denominator is that these causes are located inside the mind, and overt action follows unless circumstances prevent it. This "internalistic" perspective still dominates in both cognitive and psychodynamic psychology. Herbert Simon proposed a different explanation, based on an *ecological* view of behavior (1990, p. 7):

> Human rational behavior (and the behavior of all physical symbol systems) is shaped by a scissors whose two blades are the structure of task environments and the computational capabilities of the actor.

Simon's scissors analogy implies that internal explanations are incomplete explanations of behavior because they ignore the influence of the physical or social environment. For instance, one of the foremost contributions of social psychology has been to demonstrate the power of social environments, as in Milgram's (1974) obedience experiments, in which the experimenter instructed the participant to administer electric shocks of increasing intensity to a person in another room every time the latter answered a question incorrectly. The degree to which people obeyed strongly depended on properties of the environment, such as whether the experiment was conducted in a nondescript office building rather than within the walls of a prestigiously ornate hall on Yale's old campus. It is impossible to understand why people's behavior in this and other situations is so intimately connected to the context if one looks for internal causes alone. Similarly, it is impossible to understand why a heuristic succeeds or fails by looking simply at the heuristic. The solution lies in the match between heuristic and environment, the two blades of Simon's scissors. Heuristics are not good or bad, rational or irrational per se, but only relative to an environment. The same holds for optimization methods. Thus, Simon's scissors analogy has given rise to a new question: In what environmental structures will a given heuristic fail, and in which will it succeed? We call this the study of ecological rationality. The structure of the environment, not the accuracy–effort trade-off, provides the key to understanding why and when it is rational to rely on heuristics.

RESEARCH PROGRAM

Research on fast-and-frugal heuristics has three goals: the first is descriptive, the second is normative, and the third is one of design or engineering.

(a) The adaptive toolbox. The descriptive goal is to analyze the content of the "adaptive toolbox," that is, the heuristics, their building blocks, and the evolved and learned core capacities on which heuristics operate. Examples of building blocks are search rules, stopping rules, and decision rules. Core capacities include, for instance, recognition memory, frequency monitoring, and the ability to imitate the behavior of others. Heuristics are simple because they take advantage of these capacities. The descriptive study of the adaptive toolbox examines its phylogenetic, ontogenetic, and cultural development, as well as the question of how heuristics

are selected in response to a goal. The main methods are observation and experimentation.

(b) Ecological rationality. The normative goal is to determine the environmental structures in which a given heuristic succeeds or fails, that is, the match between mind and environment. A heuristic is ecologically rational to the degree that it is adapted to the structure of an environment. Because ecological rationality dispenses with optimization, it can be applied to both small and large worlds. The study of ecological rationality results in statements about how well a heuristic functions (e.g., predicts faster, with less information, or more accurately) compared to competing strategies in a given environment. This analysis extends to the co-evolution of heuristics and environments. The main methods are computer simulation and mathematical analysis.

(c) Intuitive design. The engineering goal is to apply the results from *(a)* and *(b)* to design heuristics and/or environments for improving decision making in applied fields such as health care, law, and business. We refer to this goal as "intuitive design" because it relies on heuristics that reflect the way that the human mind works rather than on standard statistical software programs, which many professionals such as medical and legal decision makers find obscure.

To achieve these three goals, two requirements are indispensable.

1. *Process models, not only as-if models.* Optimization theories (such as Bayesian, expected utility maximization, cumulative prospect theory) typically imply complex estimations and computations and are thus presented as *as-if models*, that is, as models of the behavioral outcome, but not the cognitive process. The classical example of an as-if model is Ptolemy's theory in which planets move around the earth in circles and epicycles. Although few believed that this theory would describe the actual motions of planets, it was quite accurate in predicting their positions––provided that enough epicycles were included in the model. Kepler's theory in which planets move in ellipses around the sun, in contrast, was meant as a process

theory, that is, it described the actual motions of planets. The classical support for as-if models in the social sciences stems from the economist Milton Friedman (1953), who, like the psychologist B. F. Skinner, saw little value in modeling cognitive processes. In contrast, our aim is to understand actual decision processes, not only the outcomes. There is a good reason for this. Without modeling the cognitive blade of Simon's scissors, it is utterly impossible to determine in what environments heuristics succeed, that is, their ecological rationality.

2. *Computational models, not labels.* A crucial distinction is between models of heuristics and labels for them. Computational models include tit-for-tat, elimination-by-aspects, and the recognition heuristic, whereas "availability" and "representativeness" are often treated as vague one-word labels. Unlike labels, computational models enable the performance of heuristics in specific environments to be studied and can lead to novel predictions. None of the discoveries surveyed in this book, such as less-is-more effects, could have been made without computational models of heuristics.

The simple heuristics program is not the only one that aims to render more psychologically realistic theories of rational behavior. Two other influential ones are the heuristics-and-biases program and the optimization-under-constraints program. The heuristics-and-biases program (Kahneman, Slovic, & Tversky, 1982; Gilovich, Griffin, & Kahneman, 2002) shares with the simple heuristics program a focus on cognitive processes rather than as-if models, but differs in three important respects. First, the heuristics it describes are common-sense labels that have typically not been developed into computational models. Second, its definition of rationality—the benchmarks against which human judgment is evaluated—is not based on Simon's scissors; in it, rationality remains logical instead of ecological. Although it is sometimes said that the two research programs on heuristics differ by the amount of rationality they ascribe to humans, they already part ways

in their definitions of what counts as rational. Third, the heuristics-and-biases program assumes a general accuracy–effort trade-off and therefore also assumes that heuristics may be less effortful but can never be more accurate than more complex strategies. "Heuristics and biases" became inseparable twins and, in the words of economist Richard Thaler, biases or cognitive illusions are the "rule rather than the exception" (1991, p. 4). As a consequence, the role of heuristics is solely descriptive, and never normative as in the study of ecological rationality.

By introducing more realism into theories of rationality, the simple heuristics program also takes a drastically different approach from that of optimization under constraints. Optimization under constraints is a widely adopted modeling strategy in the cognitive sciences, neoclassical economics, behavioral economics, and optimal foraging theory. The idea is to make full rationality, or optimization without constraints, more psychologically realistic by adding psychological phenomena as free parameters to the utility framework (as in cumulative prospect theory or the inequality-aversion theory). This approach shares with the simple heuristics program an emphasis on computational models, but differs in three respects. First, it retains optimization—which becomes more demanding mathematically with each constraint added—and thus tends to generate complex as-if theories rather than process models. As Simon (1955) noted early in his career, "there is a complete lack of evidence that, in actual human choice situations of any complexity, these computations can be, or in fact are, performed" (p. 102). Second, like the heuristics-and-biases program, it assumes a general accuracy–effort trade-off, such as when computing the optimal stopping point at which the costs of further search exceed those of increasing accuracy. Finally, optimization with or without constraints requires known alternatives, consequences, and probability distributions, meaning that the domain of these theories is restricted to small worlds. This is why optimization models are of limited practical use for physicians, managers, politicians, and John Q. Public.

THE STUDY OF HEURISTICS ANSWERS BOTH DESCRIPTIVE AND NORMATIVE QUESTIONS

Whereas logic and probability have been interpreted as descriptive (how we actually reason) and normative (how we ought to reason), the role of heuristics in psychology was until now limited to the description of cognitive processes, with no claim to normative merits. This reflects a longstanding tradition in philosophy, where rationality is defined orthogonally to psychology. For instance, the laws of logic and probability typically define rational judgment in the heuristics-and-biases program, whereas psychology is relegated to explaining why people deviate from these laws. Although it was acknowledged that heuristics are often efficient, nearly every experimental illustration was designed to demonstrate the existence of ever-new judgmental errors, as measured by logical norms. The resulting opposition between the rational and the psychological has grown into an unquestioned article of faith. In this context, psychology was limited to the clinical explanation of bad reasoning, thus implying that if everyone were to become rational, psychological research could be abandoned because it is mute about the nature of good reasoning. As a famous economist once said with conviction, "Look, reasoning is either rational or it's psychological" (Gigerenzer, 2000, p. vii).

In the mid-1990s, when we began our research program, most of our scientific community took this schism for granted. A major contribution of our research to date, as shown in this book, has been to demonstrate that simple heuristics using limited search, stopping rules, and aspiration levels can lead to more accurate inferences or predictions than can algorithms based on the principles of logic, probability, or maximization (e.g., see Chapter 1). This puts psychological processes on a par with models that obey the classical maxims of rationality. More important, it brings a new question to the foreground: In which environments is a heuristic better than, say, a logistic regression or a Bayesian model, and in which is it not? Posing this question changes the nature of rationality and the discourse on it from logical to

ecological. Once it is understood that heuristics can be more accurate than more complex strategies, they are normative in the same sense that optimization methods such as multiple regression and Bayes' rule can be normative—in one class of environments, but not in all. Because heuristics ignore information or exploit forgetting, cognitive limitations can be rethought as properties that may enable good decisions, not merely hinder them (e.g., see Chapter 4).

Homo heuristicus is not the cognitive miser that previous research made him out to be. One of our first discoveries concerned a simple inference heuristic called take-the-best. This heuristic ignores dependencies between cues and relies on the first good cue that allows an inference to be made about the world. Whereas experimental evidence for the use of this kind of lexicographic rule has been documented for decades, for instance, in preferential choice (Ford, Schmitt, Schechtman, Hults, & Doherty, 1989), it was widely believed that a lexicographic rule "is naively simple" and "will rarely pass a test of 'reasonableness,'" to quote two eminent decision theorists, Ralph Keeney and Howard Raiffa (1993, pp. 77–78). Cognitive processes that ignore information cannot but be inferior, or such is the diehard belief of many decision theorists.

When we tested the take-the-best heuristic in a large world (where the order of cues was not known but had to be estimated from limited samples), however, the surprising result was that it could make *more* accurate predictions than strategies that use all information and computation, including optimization models (see Chapters 1 and 2). Hence, it is a conceptual error to equate complex models with rationality and to rate psychological heuristics as second-best or even liken them to irrationality. Which model is better is an empirical question and cannot be answered by an authoritative dictum. In this book, answers are provided by experiment, mathematical proof, and computer simulation.

A BRIEF HISTORY

The simple heuristics program has not evolved in a vacuum. Computational models of heuristics were proposed by Luce (1956), Simon

(1957), and Tversky (1972), among others, and the idea of an adaptive decision maker was advocated by Payne, Bettman, and Johnson (1993). In this earlier work, heuristics were still considered subject to an accuracy–effort trade-off. In the initial phase of our research program (featured in Part I), the focus was on showing that this deeply entrenched belief is not generally true. We demonstrated the existence of simple heuristics that can indeed be equally or even more accurate than complex strategies. Incredulous at first, we checked and double-checked the simulations. The results were reliable. The accuracy–effort trade-off is not an inevitable predicament of cognition: Looking beyond the individual into the mind–environment system, one begins to understand when and why the mind can have it both ways, achieving more accuracy with less effort.

The second phase of the research program focused on experiments. It began in an unexpected way. During decades of research on "heuristics and biases," few had doubted that people rely on heuristics. Yet once our research challenged the link between heuristics and reasoning errors, the argument was raised that there was little evidence that people actually use heuristics. We include two chapters by researchers who were highly skeptical of the use of fast-and-frugal heuristics such as take-the-best (see Chapters 17 and 18). In one of these, Arndt Bröder tells of how the experimental evidence finally convinced even him, one of the fiercest critics. He also points out how important it is to ask the right questions. For instance, the question is not "does everyone always use heuristic X?" but instead "in which environment do people use heuristic X, and is this use ecologically rational?" The second section of Part II features some of these enlightening experimental studies.

The third phase of research addressed the study of ecological rationality, asking: In which environment is a given heuristic more accurate than a strategy that needs more information and computation, and in which is it not? The study of ecological rationality is inspired by Simon's scissors analogy, with the mind and the environment as the two blades: In order to understand how a pair of scissors cuts, one needs to study how the two blades match and interact. Looking at just one blade and observing, for instance, that minds ignore dependencies between cues does not suffice for ascertaining whether this leads to rational or irrational behavior. As Egon Brunswik (1957) pointed out, the mind and the environment are like a husband and wife who have come to terms with each other by mutual adaptation. The question is how heuristics and environmental structures function in tandem. The first section of Part II features some answers to this question.

The most recent development in the simple heuristics program is the study of decision making "in the wild." Part III of this book features a sample of these exciting studies. They pose three questions that are related to the three goals of the program. The first question is descriptive: What strategies do experts and laypeople rely on in real-world decisions, outside the laboratory? Chapter 30 reports that when deciding on a location to break into (or establishing which one is likely to be burgled), experienced burglars and policemen follow the take-the-best heuristic, whereas inexperienced students in the laboratory appear to weight and add cues the "rational" way. The second question is both descriptive and prescriptive: How well does a heuristic perform compared to sophisticated statistical techniques developed for the same problem? Chapter 36 observes that experienced managers rely on only one reason to identify inactive customers and tests the accuracy of this heuristic compared to the accuracy of Pareto/NBD models that use more information and computation. Managers' heuristics use less information but predict actual customer behavior better. Yet this fascinating study does not tell us *in what world* relying on one good reason is better. The third question asks: How ecologically rational are the involved strategies? Chapter 34 shows that the $1/N$ heuristic—invest equally in N assets—can make more money than optimal investment models, including Markowitz's Nobel Prize-winning mean-variance portfolio. The point is not that simplicity can make you wealthier, but to understand both when the heuristic outperforms an optimization model and when optimization would pay. As in other ecological analyses, key properties of the environment include the predictability of the criterion, the sample size, and the number N of alternatives. With $N = 50$ assets and a window of 10 years of stock data (which is what many investment firms use), for example, $1/N$ would outperform the mean-variance portfolio, whereas around 500 years of stock data are needed to outperform $1/N$. The smaller the predictability and sample size and the larger the N, the greater the expected advantage of the heuristic over optimizing models.

TRANSPARENCY AND ROBUSTNESS

Last but not least, let us point out two methodological values that we have come to appreciate: transparency and robustness. Both are consequences of simplicity. Transparency can be reached by simple models that use zero free parameters (such as $1/N$ and the priority heuristic) or only few parameters (such as take-the-best, which needs to estimate the order of cues). It suffers when the number of adjustable parameters increases and when verbal labels are proposed instead of formal models. Of course, every model has parameters; the difference is whether they are free, adjustable within a range, or fixed. Unlike models of cognition that feature half-a-dozen adjustable parameters, those with zero adjustable parameters can be tested by hand. Thus, everybody can establish for themselves when a model does or does not predict the data. Transparency is essential for intuitive design. For instance, physicians tend to reject diagnostic systems based on logistic regression because they do not understand them. Yet a fast-and-frugal tree for coronary care unit allocation, as explained in Chapter 6, is transparent; a dozen years after being introduced, it was still used for predicting heart attacks by the doctors in the clinic under study and has been updated since for specific patient groups.

Robustness, a key feature of the evolved design of humans and other animals, concerns the ability of a mental strategy to operate successfully when the environment and inner states change. Robustness often follows from simplicity because simple models that have no or few free parameters are less vulnerable to overfitting (i.e., increasing the fit by fitting noise) and tend to be more robust. Robustness is not the same as optimization. An organism that is optimally adapted to its past may fail if the future changes. A robust design, in contrast, is one that is not optimally adapted to its past but has a good chance of performing well when the future holds surprises. As Chapter 1 explains, simplicity leads to bias, and bias often enhances robustness. Thus, in the simple heuristics program, the notion of *heuristics and biases* takes on a new, more favorable meaning. Rather than necessarily leading to biases in the sense of errors, heuristics have biases built in to enable good judgments. Without bias, a mind could not function well in our uncertain world.

How do people make decisions when optimization is out of reach? This is the central question this book addresses. Simon once said that this was the only question that he tried to pursue in his scientific life. Yet it is far from being solved. As Simon wrote in a letter to one of us (GG) late in his life, in 1999:

> I guess a major reason for my using somewhat vague terms—like bounded rationality—is that I did not want to give the impression that I thought I had "solved" the problem of creating an empirically grounded theory ... There still lies before us an enormous job of studying the actual decision processes.... .

This book presents some of the progress made in answering Simon's question. It conceives of the mind as a modular system, composed of heuristics, their building blocks, and evolved capacities. We thank all contributors and critics for carving out the details of this vision of adaptive rationality, and thus contributing, in the words of Herbert Simon (1999), "to this revolution in cognitive science, striking a great blow for sanity in the approach to human rationality." Yet the progress is far from complete, with many surprises generating new questions. In the search for answers to these, we look forward to the active help of our readers.

ACKNOWLEDGMENTS

We would like to thank Rona Unrau and Laura Wiles for helping at all stages of the development of this book; they provided wonderful and constructive support. We are grateful to Jürgen Rossbach and Marianne Hauser, who redesigned the figures and tables, and to Emina Canic, Florence Ettlin, Christel Fraser, Daniela Fromm, Eva Günther, Renate Hoffmann, Carmen Kaiser, Erna Schiwietz, Lea Schweizer, Sarah Turowski, and Françoise Weber for their help in compiling the reference list. We also thank the authors for taking the time to go through the shortened versions of their articles. Last not least, we express our gratitude to the Max Planck Society and the University of Basel, who provided the unique resources and the splendid intellectual atmosphere in which the science of heuristics could grow and mature.

Appetizer

CHAPTER 1

Homo heuristicus: Why Biased Minds Make Better Inferences

Gerd Gigerenzer and Henry Brighton

Abstract: Heuristics are efficient cognitive processes that ignore information. In contrast to the widely held view that less processing reduces accuracy, the study of heuristics shows that less information, computation, and time can in fact improve accuracy. We review the major progress made so far: (a) the discovery of less-is-more effects; (b) the study of the ecological rationality of heuristics, which examines in which environments a given strategy succeeds or fails, and why; (c) an advancement from vague labels to computational models of heuristics; (d) the development of a systematic theory of heuristics that identifies their building blocks and the evolved capacities they exploit, and views the cognitive system as relying on an "adaptive toolbox;" and (e) the development of an empirical methodology that accounts for individual differences, conducts competitive tests, and has provided evidence for people's adaptive use of heuristics. Homo heuristicus has a biased mind and ignores part of the available information, yet a biased mind can handle uncertainty more efficiently and robustly than an unbiased mind relying on more resource-intensive and general-purpose processing strategies.

As far as we can know, animals have always relied on heuristics to solve adaptive problems, and so have humans. To measure the area of a candidate nest cavity, a narrow crack in a rock, an ant has no yardstick but a rule of thumb: Run around on an irregular path for a fixed period while laying down a pheromone trail, and then leave. Return, move around on a different irregular path, and estimate the size of the cavity by the frequency of encountering the old trail. This heuristic is remarkably precise: Nests half the area of others yielded reencounter frequencies 1.96 times greater (Mugford, Mallon, & Franks, 2001). To choose a mate, a peahen similarly uses a heuristic: Rather than investigating all peacocks posing and displaying in a lek eager to get her attention or weighting and adding all male features to calculate the one with the highest expected utility, she investigates only three or four, and chooses the one with the largest number of eyespots (Petrie & Halliday, 1994). Many of these evolved rules of thumb are amazingly simple and efficient (for an overview, see Hutchinson & Gigerenzer, 2005).

The Old Testament says that God created humans in his image and let them dominate all animals, from whom they fundamentally differ (Genesis 1:26). It might not be entirely accidental that in cognitive science some form of omniscience (knowledge of all relevant probabilities and utilities, for instance) and omnipotence (the ability to compute complex functions in a split second) has shaped models of human cognition. Yet humans and animals have common ancestors, related sensory and motor processes, and even share common cognitive heuristics.

Consider how a baseball outfielder catches a ball. The view of cognition favoring omniscience and omnipotence suggests that complex problems are solved with complex mental algorithms: The player "behaves as if he had solved a set of differential equations in predicting the trajectory of the ball … At some subconscious level, something functionally equivalent to the mathematical calculations is going on" (Dawkins, 1989, p. 96). Dawkins carefully inserts "as if" to indicate that he is not quite sure whether brains actually perform these computations. And there is indeed no evidence that brains do. Instead, experiments have shown that players rely on several heuristics. The gaze heuristic is the simplest one and works if the ball is already high up in the air: Fix your gaze on the ball, start running, and adjust your running speed so that the angle of gaze remains constant (see Gigerenzer, 2007). A player who relies on the gaze heuristic can ignore all causal variables necessary to compute the trajectory of the ball—the initial distance, velocity, angle, air resistance, speed and direction of wind, and spin, among others. By paying attention to only one variable, the player will end up where the ball comes down without computing the exact spot. The same heuristic is also used by animal species for catching prey and for intercepting potential mates. In pursuit and predation, bats, birds, and dragonflies maintain a constant optical angle between themselves and their prey, as do dogs when catching a Frisbee (Shaffer, Krauchunas, Eddy, & McBeath, 2004).

The term *heuristic* is of Greek origin, meaning "serving to find out or discover." The mathematician George Polya distinguished heuristics from analytic methods; for instance, heuristics are indispensable for finding a proof, whereas analysis is required to check a proof's validity. In the 1950s, Herbert Simon (1955, 1991), whose collaborator Allen Newell studied with Polya, first proposed that people satisfice rather than maximize. *Maximization* means optimization, the process of finding the best solution for a problem, whereas *satisficing* (a Northumbrian word for "satisfying") means finding a good-enough solution. Simon used his term *satisficing*

both as a generic term for everything that is not optimizing as well as for a specific heuristic: In order to select a good alternative (e.g., a house or a spouse) from a series of options encountered sequentially, a person sets an aspiration level, chooses the first one that meets the aspiration, and then terminates search. The aspiration level can be fixed or adjusted following experience (Selten, 2001). For Simon, humans rely on heuristics not simply because their cognitive limitations prevent them from optimizing but also because of the task environment. For instance, chess has an optimal solution, but no computer or mind, be it Deep Blue or Kasparov, can find this optimal sequence of moves, because the sequence is computationally intractable to discover and verify. Most problems of interest are computationally intractable, and this is why engineers and artificial intelligence (AI) researchers often rely on heuristics to make computers smart.

In the 1970s, the term *heuristic* acquired a different connotation, undergoing a shift from being regarded as a method that makes computers smart to one that explains why people are not smart. Daniel Kahneman, Amos Tversky, and their collaborators published a series of experiments in which people's reasoning was interpreted as exhibiting fallacies. "Heuristics and biases" became one phrase. It was repeatedly emphasized that heuristics are sometimes good and sometimes bad, but virtually every experiment was designed to show that people violate a law of logic, probability, or some other standard of rationality. On the positive side, this influential research drew psychologists' attention to cognitive heuristics and helped to create two new fields: behavioral economics, and behavioral law and economics. On the negative side, heuristics became seen as something best to avoid, and consequently, this research was disconnected from the study of heuristics in AI and behavioral biology. Another negative and substantial consequence was that computational models of heuristics, such as lexicographic rules (Fishburn, 1974) and elimination-by-aspects (Tversky, 1972), became replaced by one-word labels: availability, representativeness, and anchoring. These were seen as the mind's substitutes for rational cognitive procedures. By the end of the 20th century, the use of heuristics became associated with shoddy mental software, generating three widespread misconceptions:

1. Heuristics are always second-best.
2. We use heuristics only because of our cognitive limitations.
3. More information, more computation, and more time would always be better.

These three beliefs are based on the so-called *accuracy-effort trade-off*, which is considered a general law of cognition: If you invest less effort, the cost is lower accuracy. Effort refers to searching for more information, performing more computation, or taking more time; in fact, these typically go together. Heuristics allow for fast and frugal decisions; thus, it is commonly assumed that they are second-best approximations of more complex "optimal" computations and serve the purpose of trading off accuracy for effort. If information were free and humans had eternal time, so the argument goes, more information and computation would always be better. For instance, Tversky (1972, p. 98) concluded that elimination-by-aspects "cannot be defended as a rational procedure of choice." More outspokenly, two eminent decision theorists, Keeney and Raiffa (1993), asserted that reliance on lexicographic heuristics "is more widely adopted in practice than it deserves to be," and they stressed that "it is our belief that, leaving aside 'administrative ease,' it is rarely appropriate" and "will rarely pass a test of reasonableness" (pp. 77–78). They did not, however, put their intuition to a test. A few years later, our research team conducted such tests, with surprising results. Contrary to the belief in a general accuracy-effort trade-off, less information and computation can actually lead to higher accuracy, and in these situations the mind does not need to make trade-offs. Here, a *less-is-more* effect holds.

That simple heuristics can be more accurate than complex procedures is one of the major discoveries of the last decades (Gigerenzer, 2008). Heuristics achieve this accuracy by successfully exploiting evolved mental abilities and environmental structures. Since this initial finding, a systematic science of heuristics has emerged, which we review in this article, together with the reactions it has provoked. Beginning with the standard explanation of why people rely on heuristics and the common assumption of a general accuracy-effort trade-off, we introduce less-is-more phenomena that contradict it. We then present the ecological rationality of heuristics as an alternative explanation and show how less-is-more phenomena emerge from the bias–variance dilemma that cognitive systems face in uncertain worlds. In the following sections, we make a case against the widespread use of vague labels instead of models of heuristics, review some of the progress made in the development of a systematic theory of the adaptive toolbox, and end with a discussion of proper methodology.

1. THE DISCOVERY OF LESS-IS-MORE

More information is always better. This has been argued both explicitly and implicitly. The philosopher Rudolf Carnap (1947) proposed the "principle of total evidence," the recommendation to use all the available evidence when estimating a probability. The statistician I. J. Good (1967) argued, similarly, that it is irrational to leave observations in the record but not use them. In the same way, many theories of cognition—from exemplar models to prospect theory to Bayesian models of cognition—assume that all pieces of information should be combined in the final judgment. The classical critique of these models is that in the real world, search for information costs time or money, so there is a point where the costs of further search are no longer justified. This has led to optimization-under-constraints theories in which search in the world (e.g., Stigler, 1961) or in memory (e.g., Anderson, 1991) is terminated when the expected costs exceed the benefits. Note that in this "rational analysis of cognition," more information is still considered better, apart from its costs. Similarly, the seminal analysis of the adaptive decision maker (Payne, Bettman, &

Johnson, 1993) rests on the assumption that the rationale for heuristics is a trade-off between accuracy and effort, where effort is a function of the amount of information and computation consumed:

> *Accuracy-effort trade-off:* Information and computation cost time and effort; therefore, minds rely on simple heuristics that are less accurate than strategies that use more information and computation.

Here is the first important discovery: Heuristics can lead to more accurate inferences than strategies that use more information and computation (see below). Thus, the accuracy-effort trade-off does not generally hold; there are situations where one attains higher accuracy with less effort. Even when information and computation are entirely free, there is typically a point where less is more:

> *Less-is-more effects:* More information or computation can decrease accuracy; therefore, minds rely on simple heuristics in order to be more accurate than strategies that use more information and time.

To justify the use of heuristics by accuracy-effort trade-offs means that it is not worth the effort to rely on more complex estimations and computations. A less-is-more effect, however, means that minds would not gain anything from relying on complex strategies, even if direct costs and opportunity costs were zero. Accuracy-effort trade-offs are the conventional justification for why the cognitive system relies on heuristics (Beach & Mitchell, 1978; Shah & Oppenheimer, 2008), which refrains from any normative implications. Less-is-more effects are a second justification with normative consequences: They challenge the classical definition of rational decision making as the process of weighting and adding all information. Note that the term *less-is-more* does not mean that the less information one uses, the better the performance. Rather, it refers to the existence of a point at which more information or computation becomes detrimental, independent of costs. In this article, when we refer to less information, we refer to ignoring cues, weights, and dependencies between cues. Our discussion of less-is-more effects begins with the seminal work of Robin Dawes and colleagues on ignoring weights.

1.1. Ignoring Weights to Make Better Predictions: Tallying

From sociologists to economists to psychologists, social scientists routinely rely on multiple linear regression to understand social inequality, the market, and individual behavior. Linear regression estimates the optimal beta weights for the predictors. In the 1970s, researchers discovered that equal (or random) weights can predict almost as accurately as, and sometimes better than, multiple linear regression (Dawes, 1979; Dawes & Corrigan, 1974; Einhorn & Hogarth, 1975; Schmidt, 1971). Weighting equally is also termed *tallying*, reminiscent of the tally sticks for counting, which can be traced back some 30,000 years in human history. These results came as a surprise to the scientific community. When Robin Dawes presented the results at professional conferences, distinguished attendees told him that they were "impossible." His paper with Corrigan was first rejected and deemed "premature," and a sample of recent textbooks in econometrics revealed that none referred to the findings of Dawes and Corrigan (Hogarth, in press).

In these original demonstrations, there was a slight imbalance: Multiple regression was tested by cross-validation (that is, the model was fitted to one half of the data and tested on the other half) but tallying was not. Czerlinski, Gigerenzer, and Goldstein (1999) conducted 20 studies in which both tallying and multiple regression were tested by cross-validation, correcting for this imbalance. All tasks were paired comparisons; for instance, estimating which of two Chicago high schools will have a higher dropout rate, based on cues such as writing score and proportion of Hispanic students. Ten of the 20 data sets were taken from a textbook on applied multiple regression (Weisberg, 1985). Averaged across all data sets, tallying achieved a higher predictive accuracy than multiple regression (Figure 1-1). Regression tended to overfit the data, as can be seen by the cross-over of lines: It had a higher fit than tallying but a lower predictive accuracy.

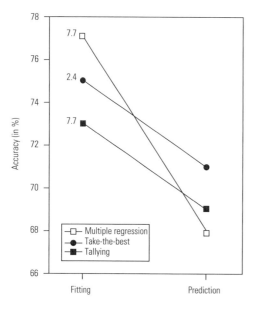

Figure 1-1. Less-is-more effects. Both tallying and take-the-best predict more accurately than multiple regression, despite using less information and computation. Note that multiple regression excels in data fitting ("hindsight"), that is, fitting its parameters to data that are already known, but performs relatively poorly in prediction ("foresight," as in cross-validation). Take-the-best is the most frugal, that is, it looks up, on average, only 2.4 cues when making inferences. In contrast, both multiple regression and tallying look up 7.7 cues on average. The results shown are averaged across 20 studies, including psychological, biological, sociological, and economic inference tasks (Czerlinski, Gigerenzer, & Goldstein, 1999). For each of the 20 studies and each of the three strategies, the 95% confidence intervals were ≤.4 percentage points.

The point here is not that tallying leads to more accurate predictions than multiple regression. The real and new question is in which environments simple tallying is more accurate than multiple regression, and in which environments it is not. This is the question of the *ecological rationality* of tallying. Early attempts to answer this question indicated that tallying succeeded when linear predictability of the criterion was moderate or small ($R^2 \leq .5$), the ratio of objects to cues was 10 or smaller, and the cues were correlated (Einhorn & Hogarth, 1975). The discovery that tallying can often match and even

outperform complex calculations is relevant to understanding the nature of adaptive cognition. Why should a mind waste time and effort in estimating the optimal weights of cues if they do not matter or even detract from performance? Note that the conditions under which tallying succeeds—low predictability of a criterion, small sample sizes relative to the number of available cues, and dependency between cues—are not infrequent in natural environments. Yet many models of cognition continue to assume that the weighting of cues is a fundamental characteristic of cognitive processing. Why is this discovery of a less-is-more effect neglected? According to the tools-to-theories heuristic (Gigerenzer, 1991), models of cognitive processes have often been inspired by new statistical tools. Thus, the scientific community would first have to rethink its routine use of multiple regression and similar techniques to facilitate accepting the idea that rational minds might not always weight but may simply tally cues. If this argument is correct, we will have to first teach better statistics to our future researchers in order to arrive at better models of mind.

1.2. Ignoring Cues to Make Better Predictions: Take-the-best

Consider again the canonical definition of rational inference as weighting and adding of all information (as long it is free). Yet, as illustrated in Figure 1-1, weighting and adding can lead to overfitting—that is, to excel in hindsight (fitting) but fail in foresight (prediction). The task of humans and other animals is to predict their world despite its inherent uncertainty, and in order to do this, they have to simplify. While tallying simplifies by ignoring the information required to compute weights, another way to simplify is to ignore variables (cues). The class of one-good-reason heuristics orders cues, finds the first one that allows a decision to be made, and then stops and ignores all other cues. Cues are ordered without paying attention to the dependencies between cues, but instead using a measure of the correlation between each cue and the criterion. This class of heuristic includes take-the-best (Gigerenzer & Goldstein, 1996), fast-and-frugal trees (Martignon, Katsikopoulos, & Woike,

2008), and the priority heuristic (Brandstätter, Gigerenzer, & Hertwig, 2006). For brevity, we focus here on take-the-best, but many of the results apply equally to the other heuristics.

The take-the-best heuristic is a model of how people infer which of two objects has a higher value on a criterion, based on binary cue values retrieved from memory. For convenience, the cue value that signals a higher criterion value is 1, and the other cue value is 0. Take-the-best consists of three building blocks:

1. Search rule: Search through cues in order of their validity.
2. Stopping rule: Stop on finding the first cue that discriminates between the objects (i.e., cue values are 1 and 0).
3. Decision rule: Infer that the object with the positive cue value (1) has the higher criterion value.

Take-the-best is a member of the one-good-reason family of heuristics because of its stopping rule: Search is stopped after finding the first cue that enables an inference to be made. Take-the-best simplifies decision making by both stopping after the first cue and by ordering cues unconditionally by validity, which for ith cue is given by:

$$v_i = \frac{\text{number of correct inferences using cue } i}{\text{number of possible inferences using cue } i}$$

Both these simplifications have been observed in the behavior of humans and other animals but routinely interpreted as signs of irrationality rather than adaptive behavior. In the late 1990s, our research group tested how accurately this simple heuristic predicts which of two cities has the larger population, using real-world cities and binary cues, such as whether the city has a soccer team in the major league (Gigerenzer & Goldstein, 1996, 1999). At the time, we were still influenced by the accuracy-effort trade-off view and expected that take-the-best might achieve a slightly lower predictive accuracy than multiple regression, trading off some accuracy for its simplicity. The unexpected result was that inferences relying on one good reason were more accurate than both multiple regression and

tallying. We obtained the same result, on average, for 20 studies (Figure 1-1). This result came as a surprise to both us and the rest of the scientific community. In talks given at that time, we asked the audience how closely they thought the predictive accuracy of take-the-best would approximate multiple regression. The estimates of experienced decision theorists were consistently that take-the-best would predict 5 to 10 percentage points worse than multiple regression, with not a single guess in favor of take-the-best. For instance, the late decision theorist Ward Edwards was so surprised that he wrote an amusing limerick in response (published in Gigerenzer et al., 1999, p. 188).

But there were more surprises to come. Chater, Oaksford, Nakisa, and Redington (2003) used the city population problem and tested take-the-best against heavy-weight nonlinear strategies: a three-layer feedforward connectionist network, trained using the backpropagation algorithm (Rumelhart, Hinton, & Williams, 1986); two exemplar-based models (the nearest-neighbor classifier [Cover & Hart, 1967] and Nosofsky's [1990] generalized context model); and the decision tree induction algorithm C4.5 (Quinlan, 1993). The predictive accuracy of the four complex strategies was rather similar, but the performance of take-the-best differed considerably. When the percentage of training examples (the sample size) was small or moderate (up to 40% of all objects), take-the-best outperformed or matched all the competitors, but when the sample size was larger, more information and computation seemed to be better. This was the first time that relying on one good reason was shown to be as accurate as nonlinear methods, such as a neural network. Yet, as Brighton (2006) showed in a reanalysis, Chater et al.'s method of fitting the models on the learning sample and then testing these models on the entire sample (including the learning sample) favored those models that overfit the data, especially at high sample sizes. When cross-validation was used, there was a new surprise: The predictive accuracy of take-the-best exceeded that of all rival models over the entire range of sample sizes (Figure 1-2). Cross-validation provides a far more reliable model selection criterion, and it is

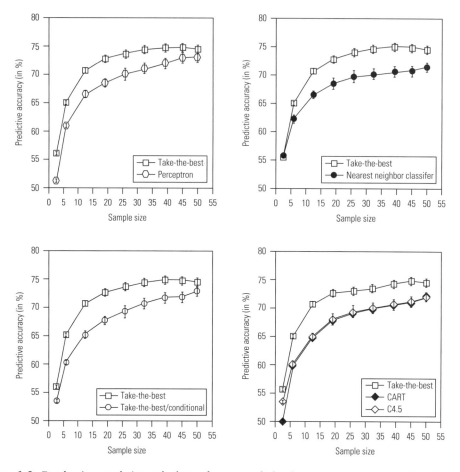

Figure 1-2. For the city population task, the performance of take-the-best was compared to five alternative models. Each panel plots the predictive accuracy of take-the-best and a rival model as a function of the number of objects used to train the model. Take-the-best outperforms (top left) a linear perceptron (essentially logistic regression); (top right) the nearest neighbor classifier; (bottom right) two tree induction algorithms, C4.5 and CART (classification and regression trees); and (bottom left) a variant of take-the-best that uses a more resource-intensive search rule that orders cues by conditional validity. Error bars are standard errors of means.

standard practice for assessing the relative performance of models of inductive inference (e.g., Hastie, Tibshirani, & Friedman, 2001; Stone, 1974). The same result was obtained for classification and regression trees (CART; Breiman, Friedman, Olshen, & Stone, 1984), which we thought might outperform take-the-best as a result of often inducing smaller decision trees than C4.5. An analysis of 20 data sets showed that the result in Figure 1-2 is the rule rather than the exception (Brighton, 2006).

Once again, another less-if-more effect was discovered, and a new question emerged: In which environments does relying on one good reason result in better performance than when relying on a neural network or on other linear and nonlinear inference strategies? We discuss this issue, the problem of understanding the ecological rationality of heuristics, in more detail in the next section. In short, the success of take-the-best seems to be due to the fact that it ignores dependencies between cues in what turns out to be an adaptive processing policy when observations are sparse. Whereas all the competitors in Figure 1-2 attempt to estimate the dependencies between cues in order to make better inferences, take-the-best ignores them by ordering the cues by validity. In fact, when one alters the search rule of take-the-best by carrying out the more resource-intensive process of ordering cues by conditional validity, performance drops to the level of the more resource-intensive algorithms (Figure 1-2, bottom left). Conditional validity takes into account the fact that when one cue appears before another in the cue order, this first cue is likely to affect the validity of the second cue and all subsequent ones. Ordering cues by conditional validity is a costly operation, which requires recomputing the predictive value of cues against multiple reference classes of observations. This policy is similar to the process of recursive partitioning used by the machine-learning algorithms C4.5 and CART.

1.3. More Information, Computation, and Time Is Not Always Better

These two results are instances of a broader class of less-is-more effects found in the last decades, both analytically and experimentally. We use *less-is-more* here as a generic term for the class of phenomena in which the accuracy-effort trade-off does not hold, although the individual phenomena differ in their nature and explanation. The conditions under which the recognition heuristic (discussed below) leads to a less-is-more effect have been derived analytically (Goldstein & Gigerenzer, 2002) as have the conditions in which a beneficial degree of forgetting improves accuracy in inference (Schooler & Hertwig, 2005). Studies on language acquisition indicate that there are sensitive phases in which a reduced memory and simpler input ("baby talk") speeds up language acquisition (Elman, 1993; Newport, 1990); experiments with experienced handball players indicate that they make better decisions with less time (Johnson & Raab, 2003); and expert golfers (but not novices) do better when they have only 3 s to putt than when they can take all the time they want (Beilock, Bertenthal, McCoy, & Carr, 2004; Beilock, Carr, MacMahon, & Starkes, 2002). Like the

surprising performance of equal weights, some less-is-more effects have long been known. For instance, in the (finitely repeated) prisoners' dilemma, two "irrational" players who play tit-for-tat can make more money than do two rational players who reason by backward induction and both defect (for an overview, see Hertwig & Todd, 2003; and Gigerenzer, 2007, 2008). The existence of these effects shows that there is more to heuristics than the accuracy-effort trade-off: The mind can use less information and computation or take less time and nevertheless achieve better performance.

Findings that show how less can be more have often been regarded as curiosities rather than as opportunities to rethink how the mind works. This is now changing. Most important, it has become clear that the discovery of less-is-more effects forces us to reassess our normative ideals of rationality. We turn now to the second step of progress made: the development of an understanding of *why* and *when* heuristics are more accurate than strategies that use more information and computation. The answer is not in the heuristic alone, but in the match between a heuristic and its environment. The rationality of heuristics is therefore ecological, not logical.

2. ECOLOGICAL RATIONALITY

All inductive processes, including heuristics, make bets. This is why a heuristic is not inherently good or bad, or accurate or inaccurate, as is sometimes believed. Its accuracy is always relative to the structure of the environment. The study of the ecological rationality asks the following question: In which environments will a given heuristic succeed, and in which will it fail? Understanding *when* a heuristic succeeds is often made easier by first asking *why* it succeeds. As we have shown, when analyzing the success of heuristics, we often find that they avoid overfitting the observations. For example, the ordering of cues chosen by take-the-best may not provide the best fit to the observations, but when predicting new observations, it often outperforms strategies that achieved a better fit. Indeed, all the models in Figure 1-2 achieved a better fit to the data than take-the-best did. The statistical concept of overfitting is part of the explanation for why heuristics succeed, but to gain a clearer understanding of how and when heuristics exploit the structure of the environment, this issue can be examined more closely.

2.1. Heuristics and Bias

The study of heuristics is often associated with the term *bias*. The heuristics and biases program of Kahneman and Tversky used the term with a negative connotation: Reasoning errors reveal human biases that, if overcome, would result in better decisions. In this view, a bias is defined as the difference between human judgment and a "rational" norm, often taken as a law of logic or probability, such as statistical independence. In contrast to this negative use of bias, simple heuristics are perhaps best understood from the perspective of pattern recognition and machine learning, where there are many examples of how a biased induction algorithm can predict more accurately than an unbiased one (Hastie et al., 2001). Findings such as these can be explained by decomposing prediction error into the sum of three components, only one of which is bias:

$$\text{Total error} = (\text{bias})^2 + \text{variance} + \text{noise}$$

The derivation of this expression can be found in many machine-learning and statistical inference textbooks (e.g., Alpaydin, 2004; Bishop, 1995, 2006; Hastie et al., 2001), but it is perhaps most thoroughly set out and discussed in a landmark article by Geman, Bienenstock, and Doursat (1992). The concepts of bias and variance can be understood by first imagining an underlying (true) function that some induction algorithm is attempting to learn. The algorithm attempts to learn the function from only a (potentially noisy) data sample, generated by this function. Averaged across all possible data samples of a given size, the bias of the algorithm is defined as the difference between the underlying function and the mean function induced by the algorithm from these data samples. Thus, zero bias is achieved if this mean function is precisely the underlying function. Variance captures how sensitive the induction algorithm is to the contents of these individual samples, and it is defined as the sum squared difference between the mean function, mentioned above, and the individual functions induced from each of the samples.

Notice that an unbiased algorithm may suffer from high variance because the mean function may be precisely the underlying function, but the individual functions may suffer from excess variance and hence high error. An algorithm's susceptibility to bias and variance will always depend on the underlying function and on how many observations of this function are available. The following example illustrates why seeking low bias will not always be functional for an organism, and how variance poses a significant problem when learning from finite data. The variance component of prediction error will prove essential to understanding why a less-is-more effect in heuristic inference can often be observed.

2.2. The Bias–Variance Dilemma

Figure 1-3A plots the mean daily temperature for London in 2000 as a function of days since January 1. In addition, the plot depicts two polynomial models attempting to capture the temperature pattern underlying the data. The first is a degree-3 polynomial model and the second a degree-12 polynomial model. As a function of the degree of the polynomial model, Figure 1-3B plots the mean error in fitting random samples of 30 observations. All models were fitted using the least squares method. Using goodness of fit to the observed sample as a performance measure, Figure 1-3B reveals a simple relationship: The higher the degree of the polynomial, the lower the error in fitting the observed data sample. The same figure also shows, for the same models, the error in predicting novel observations. Here, the relationship between the degree of polynomial used and the resulting predictive accuracy is U-shaped. Both high- and low-degree polynomials suffer from greater error than the best predicting polynomial model, which has degree-4.

This point illustrates the fact that achieving a good fit to observations does not necessarily mean we have found a good model, and choosing the model with the best fit is likely to result in

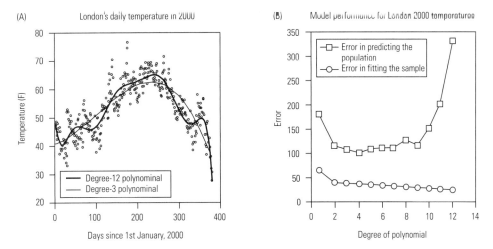

Figure 1-3. Plot (A) shows London's mean daily temperature in 2000, along with two polynomial models fitted with using the least squares method. The first is a degree-3 polynomial, and the second is a degree-12 polynomial. Plot (B) shows the mean error in fitting samples of 30 observations and the mean prediction error of the same models, both as a function of degree of polynomial.

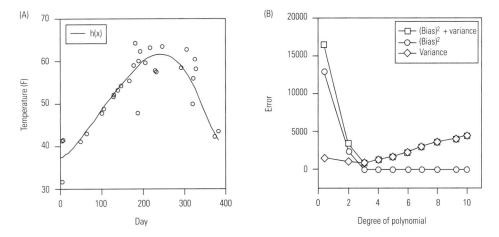

Figure 1-4. Plot (A) shows the underlying temperature pattern for some fictional location, along with a random sample of 30 observations with added noise. Plot (B) shows, as a function of degree of polynomial, the mean error in predicting the population after fitting polynomials to samples of 30 noisy observations. This error is decomposed into bias and variance, also plotted as function of degree of polynomial.

poor predictions. Despite this, Roberts and Pashler (2000) estimated that, in psychology alone, the number of articles relying on a good fit as the only indication of a good model runs into the thousands. We now consider the same scenario but in a more formal setting. The curve in Figure 1-4A shows the mean daily temperature in some fictional location for which we have predetermined the "true" underlying temperature pattern, which is a degree-3 polynomial, $h(x)$. A sample of 30 noisy observations of $h(x)$ is also shown. This new setting allows us to illustrate why bias is only one source of error impacting on the accuracy of model predictions.

The second source of error is variance, which occurs when making inferences from finite samples of noisy data.

As well as plotting prediction error as a function of the degree of the polynomial model, Figure 1-4B decomposes this error into bias and variance. As one would expect, a degree-3 polynomial achieves the lowest mean prediction error on this problem. Polynomials of degree-1 and degree-2 lead to significant estimation bias because they lack the ability to capture the underlying cubic function $h(x)$ and will therefore always differ from the underlying function. Unbiased models are those of degree-3 or higher, but notice that the higher the degree of the polynomial, the greater the prediction error. The reason why this behavior is observed is that higher degree polynomials suffer from increased variance due to their greater flexibility. The more flexible the model, the more likely it is to capture not only the underlying pattern but unsystematic patterns such as noise. Recall that variance reflects the sensitivity of the induction algorithm to the specific contents of samples, which means that for different samples of the environment, potentially very different models are being induced. Finally, notice how a degree-2 polynomial achieves a lower mean prediction error than a degree-10 polynomial. This is an example of how a biased model can lead to more accurate predictions than an unbiased model.

This example illustrates a fundamental problem in statistical inference known as the bias–variance dilemma (Geman et al., 1992). To achieve low prediction error on a broad class of problems, a model must accommodate a rich class of patterns in order to ensure low bias. For example, the model must accommodate both linear and nonlinear patterns if, in advance, we do not know which kind of pattern will best describe the observations. Diversity in the class of patterns that the model can accommodate is, however, likely to come at a price. The price is an increase in variance, as the model will have a greater flexibility, which will enable it to accommodate not only systematic patterns but also accidental patterns such as noise. When accidental patterns are used to make predictions, these predictions are likely to be inaccurate. This is

why we are left with a dilemma: Combating high bias requires using a rich class of models, while combating high variance requires placing restrictions on this class of models. We cannot remain agnostic and do both unless we are willing to make a bet on what patterns will actually occur. This is why "general purpose" models tend to be poor predictors of the future when data are sparse (Geman et al., 1992).

Our cognitive systems are confronted with the bias–variance dilemma whenever they attempt to make inferences about the world. What can this tell us about the cognitive processes used to make these inferences? First, cognitive science is increasingly stressing the senses in which the cognitive system performs remarkably well when generalizing from few observations, so much so that human performance is often characterized as optimal (e.g., Griffiths & Tenenbaum, 2006; Oaksford & Chater, 1998). These findings place considerable constraints on the range of potential processing models capable of explaining human performance. From the perspective of the bias–variance dilemma, the ability of the cognitive system to make accurate predictions despite sparse exposure to the environment strongly indicates that the variance component of error is successfully being kept within acceptable limits. Although variance is likely to be the dominant source of error when observations are sparse, it is nevertheless controllable. This analysis has important implications for the possibility of general-purpose models. To control variance, one must abandon the ideal of general-purpose inductive inference and instead consider, to one degree or another, specialization (Geman et al., 1992). Put simply, the bias–variance dilemma shows formally why a mind can be better off with an adaptive toolbox of biased, specialized heuristics. A single, general-purpose tool with many adjustable parameters is likely to be unstable and to incur greater prediction error as a result of high variance.

2.3. Explaining Less-is-more

The bias–variance dilemma provides the statistical concepts needed to further examine some of the less-is-more effects we have observed. First, from the perspective of bias, take-the-best offers no advantage over the alternative methods we have considered, because practically all models of inductive inference are capable of reproducing any response pattern that take-the-best can. Consequently, if a heuristic like take-the-best is to outperform an alternative method, it must do so by incurring less variance. Secondly, the variance component of error is always an interaction between characteristics of the inference strategy, the structure of the environment, and the number of observations available. This is why the performance of heuristic in an environment is not reflected by a single number such as predictive accuracy, but by a learning curve revealing how bias and variance change as more observations become available (Perlich, Provost, & Simonoff, 2003). Because the learning curves of two strategies—such as the pairs of curves in Figure 1-2—can cross, the superiority of one process over another will depend on the size of the training sample. Saying that a heuristic works because it avoids overfitting the data is only a shorthand explanation for what is often a more complex interaction between the heuristic, the environment, and the sample size.

To illustrate the point, we will perform a bias–variance decomposition of the error of take-the-best and a greedy version of take-the-best, which differs only in its use of a search rule that considers the cues in conditional validity order, discussed earlier (Martignon & Hoffrage, 2002). The following comparison between take-the-best and its greedy counterpart is insightful for two reasons. First, as Figure 1-2 suggests, the performances of the neural, exemplar, and decision tree models tend to be very similar to each other in paired comparison tasks, and in turn are very similar to the performance of the greedy version of take-the-best. Consequently, the performance of the greedy version of take-the-best provides a good proxy for the behavior of a number of alternative models of inductive inference. Second, Schmitt and Martignon (2006) proved that the greedy version of take-the-best is more successful in data fitting than take-the-best; yet when tested empirically, take-the-best nevertheless made more correct predictions (Martignon & Hoffrage, 2002). Comparing take-the-best and its greedy counterpart will allow us

to examine when consuming fewer processing resources is likely to be functional, while also fixing the class of models used, as the two strategies are both restricted to inducing cue orders, rather than some richer class of models.

Two artificially constructed environments will be used to compare the strategies, both of which are governed by a known underlying functional relationship between the cues and criterion. Knowing these functional relationships will allow us to perform a bias–variance decomposition of the prediction error of the two strategies. The first environment is an instance of the class of *binary environments*, where the validity of the cues follows a noncompensatory pattern, and all cues are uncorrelated. Noncompensatory environments are one example of a class of environments for which we have analytic results showing that take-the-best is unbiased and likely to perform well. Table 1-1 summarizes this result, along with two other studies that also aim to identify the environmental conditions favoring take-the-best. The second environment used in our comparison, however, is an instance of the class of *Guttman environments*, inspired by the Guttman scale (Guttman, 1944), where all the cues are maximally correlated with the criterion but vary in their discrimination rates. Formal definitions and illustrations of both these environments are provided in Appendix 1.

Figure 1-5A–D plots, for both of these environments, the prediction error achieved by take-the-best and its greedy counterpart. The performance of each model is shown separately in order to clearly distinguish the bias and variance components of error, which, when added together, comprise the total prediction error. Three important findings are revealed. First, in the binary environment, take-the-best performs worse than its greedy counterpart. This result illustrates that analytic results detailing when take-the-best is unbiased will not necessarily point to the cases in which take-the-best performs well. Second, in the Guttman environment, take-the-best outperforms its greedy counterpart. This result illustrates that proving that another strategy achieves a better fit than take-the-best is something quite different to proving that the strategy also achieves a higher

Table 1-1.   Three Examples of Environment Structure That Favor Take-the-best
The first two results are derived analytically and focus on the problem of achieving a good fit to the observations. From the perspective of bias and variance, these two results point to the cases in which take-the-best is unbiased. The third study addresses the case when performance refers to predictive accuracy and is based on simulation results and experiments with human participants.

Environment Structure	Result
Noncompensatory cue weights (Martignon & Hoffrage, 1999, 2002)	If (a) both the validities of the cues in take-the-best and the cue weights of a linear model have the same order; and (b) for each cue in this order, the weight of this cue is not exceeded by the sum of the weights of all subsequent cues; then (c) the inferences of take-the-best and the linear model will coincide.
Odds condition (Katsikopoulos & Martignon, 2006)	If (a) all cues are conditionally independent, and (b) an odds condition holds, then (c) take-the-best is optimal. Odds condition: When cues are ordered by validity, if the ith cue has validity v_i, then the odds condition holds if $$\log(o_i) > \sum_{k>i} \log(o_k), \quad \text{where } o_i = v_i/(1-v_i).$$
Cue redundancy (Dieckmann & Rieskamp, 2007)	If cues are highly correlated and therefore carry redundant information, then take-the-best rivals or exceeds the predictive accuracy of a heuristic using the confirmation rule, described in the main text.

predictive accuracy. Third, and perhaps most important, Figure 1-5 reveals that both of these behaviors are driven by the variance component of error and the relative ability of the two strategies to keep variance within acceptable limits. Bias plays almost no role in explaining the difference in performance between the models, and the less-is-more effect we demonstrated in Figure 1-2 can also be explained by the relative ability of the models to control variance. In short, this comparison tells us that take-the-best bets on the fact that ignoring dependencies between cues is likely to result in low variance. Model comparisons in natural environments show that this bet is often a good one. But as this comparison has revealed, the bet can also fail, even when take-the-best has zero bias.

At this point, it is important to note that the concepts of bias and variance have allowed us to move beyond simply labeling the behavior of an induction algorithm as "overfitting the data," or "suffering from excess complexity," because the relative ability of two algorithms to avoid these pathologies will always depend on the amount of data available. More generally, as the variance component of error points to the sensitivity of a learning algorithm to the particular contents of samples, the essence of our argument does not

hinge on the use of cross-validation as a model selection criterion. Adopting an alternative model selection criterion will not change the fact that the degree to which an algorithm is overly sensitive to the contents of the samples it learns from will depend on the size of the sample available. For example, very similar findings hold when the *minimum description length* principle is used as a model selection criterion (Brighton, 2006).

2.4. Biased Minds for Making Better Predictions

The relationship between mind and environment is often viewed from the perspective of bias, following the "mirror view" of adaptive cognition (Brighton & Gigerenzer, in press, set out the argument in more detail). In this view, a good mental model or processing strategy is assumed to be one that mirrors the properties of the world as closely as possible, preferably with no systematic bias, just as a linear model is assumed to be appropriate if the world is also linear. A cognitive system with a systematic bias, in contrast, is seen as a source of error and the cause of cognitive illusions. If this were true, how can cognitive heuristics that rely only on one good reason and ignore the rest make

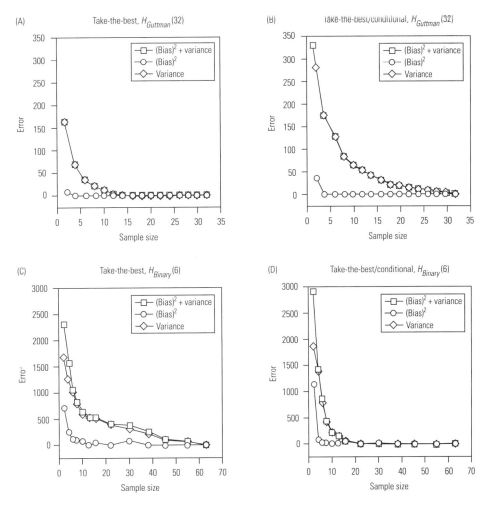

Figure 1-5. An illustration of the role played by variance in the performance of take-the-best. Plots (A) and (B) illustrate that, in Guttman environments, take-the-best outperforms the greedy variant of this heuristic, which orders cues by conditional validity. The performance difference is due to variance alone. Plots (C) and (D) illustrate that variance also explains why take-the-best is outperformed in binary environments. In both cases, take-the-best is unbiased and the relative performance of the models is explained almost entirely by variance.

more accurate inferences than strategies that use more information and computation do (as illustrated in Figure 1-2)? We have identified three reasons:

1. The advantage of simplicity is not because the world is similarly simple, as suggested by the mirror view. This is illustrated by the apparent paradox that although natural environments exhibit dependencies between cues

(such as the environment considered in Figure 1-2, where correlations between cues range between –.25 and .54), take-the-best can make accurate predictions by ignoring them so much so that it can outperform strategies that explicitly set out to model these dependencies. Superior performance is achieved by betting on lower variance, not lower bias.

2. As a consequence, if observations are sparse, simple heuristics like take-the-best are likely

to outperform more general, flexible strategies. It is under these conditions that variance will be the most dominant component of error.

3. Similarly, the more noise in the observations, the more likely a simple heuristic like take-the-best will outperform more flexible strategies. The greater the degree of noise, the more dominant the variance component of error is likely to be.

This argument is supported by a diverse set of related findings. First, consider how a retail marketing executive might distinguish between active and nonactive customers. Experienced managers tend to rely on a simple hiatus heuristic: Customers who have not made a purchase for 9 months are considered inactive. Yet there are more sophisticated methods, such as the Pareto/Negative Binomial Distribution model, which considers more information and relies on more complex computations. But when tested, these methods turned out to be less accurate in predicting inactive customers than the hiatus rule (Wübben & von Wangenheim, 2008). Second, consider the problem of searching literature databases, where the task is to order a large number of articles so that the most relevant ones appear at the top of the list. In this task, a "one-reason" heuristic (inspired by take-the-best) using limited search outperformed both a "rational" Bayesian model that considered all of the available information and PsychINFO (Lee, Loughlin, & Lundberg, 2002). Third, consider the problem of investing money into N funds. Harry Markowitz received the Nobel prize in economics for finding the optimal solution, the mean-variance portfolio. When he made his own retirement investments, however, he did not use his optimizing strategy, but instead relied on a simple heuristic: $1/N$, that is, allocate your money equally to each of N alternatives (see Table 1-2). Was his intuition correct? Taking seven investment problems, a study compared the $1/N$ rule with 14 optimizing models, including the mean-variance portfolio and Bayesian and non-Bayesian models (DeMiguel, Garlappi, & Uppal, 2009). The optimizing strategies had 10 years of stock data to estimate their parameters, and on that

basis had to predict the next month's performance; after this, the 10-year window was moved 1 month ahead, and the next month had to be predicted, and so on until the data ran out. $1/N$, in contrast, does not need any past information. In spite (or because) of this, $1/N$ ranked first (out of 15) on certainty equivalent returns, second on turnover, and fifth on the Sharpe ratio, respectively. Even with their complex estimations and computations, none of the optimization methods could consistently earn better returns than this simple heuristic.

Finally, similar results in pattern recognition and machine learning include the finding that the naïve Bayes classifier can often outperform more sophisticated methods, even though its assumption of independence is explicitly violated by the task environment (Domingos & Pazzani, 1997). A related example is ridge regression, which can often outperform unbiased methods by introducing bias as a result of shrinking or ignoring beta weights, but can more than offset this error by incurring a greater reduction in variance (Hastie et al., 2001, p. 59).

Why should experts and laypeople rely on heuristics? To summarize, the answer is not simply in the accuracy-effort dilemma but in the bias–variance dilemma, as higher accuracy can be achieved by more or less effort. For instance, in predicting daily temperature (Figure 1-4), the relevant trade-off is between reducing the variance component of error by expending "less effort," that is, using a simpler polynomial, and reducing the bias component of error by expending "more effort," that is, using a more complex polynomial. The bias–variance dilemma is one of several principles that characterize the ecological rationality of heuristics (Gigerenzer et al., 1999; Hogarth & Karelaia, 2005, 2006; Katsikopoulos & Martignon, 2006; Todd, Gigerenzer, & the ABC Research Group, in press). The more uncertain the criterion is, or the smaller the sample size available, the more a cognitive system needs to protect itself from one kind of error (variance) over the other (bias). A biased mind that operates with simple heuristics can thus be not only more efficient in the sense of less effort but also more accurate than a mind that bets only on avoiding bias. The specific

Table 1-2. Ten Well-Studied Heuristics for Which There Is Evidence That They Are in the Adaptive Toolbox of Humans
Each heuristic can be used to solve problems in social and nonsocial environments. See the references given for more information regarding their ecological rationality, and the surprising predictions they entail.

Heuristic	Definition	Ecologically Rational If	Surprising Findings (examples)
Recognition heuristic (Goldstein & Gigerenzer, 2002)	If one of two alternatives is recognized, infer that it has the higher value on the criterion.	Recognition validity >.5	Less-is-more effect if $\alpha > \beta$; systematic forgetting can be beneficial (Schooler & Hertwig, 2005).
Fluency heuristic (Jacoby & Dallas, 1981)	If both alternatives are recognized but one is recognized faster, infer that it has the higher value on the criterion.	Fluency validity >.5	Less-is-more effect; systematic forgetting can be beneficial (Schooler & Hertwig, 2005).
Take-the-best (Gigerenzer & Goldstein, 1996)	To infer which of two alternatives has the higher value: (a) search through cues in order of validity, (b) stop search as soon as a cue discriminates, and (c) choose the alternative this cue favors.	See Table 1-1 and main text	Often predicts more accurately than multiple regression (Czerlinski et al., 1999), neural networks, exemplar models, and decision tree algorithms (Brighton, 2006).
Tallying (unit-weight linear model, Dawes, 1979)	To estimate a criterion, do not estimate weights but simply count the number of positive cues.	Cue validities vary little, low redundancy (Hogarth & Karelaia, 2005, 2006).	Often predict equally or more accurately than multiple regression (Czerlinski et al., 1999).
Satisficing (Simon, 1955; Todd & Miller, 1999)	Search through alternatives and choose the first one that exceeds your aspiration level.	Number of alternatives decreases rapidly over time, such as in seasonal mating pools (Dudey & Todd, 2002).	Aspiration levels can lead to significantly better choices than chance, even if they are arbitrary (e.g., the secretary problem, see Gilbert & Mosteller, 1966; the envelope problem, see Bruss, 2000).
1/N; equality heuristic (DeMiguel et al., 2009)	Allocate resources equally to each of N alternatives.	High unpredictability, small learning sample, large N.	Can outperform optimal asset allocation portfolios.
Default heuristic (Johnson & Goldstein, 2003; Pichert & Katsikopoulos, 2008)	If there is a default, do nothing.	Values of those who set defaults match those of the decision maker; when the consequences of a choice are hard to foresee.	Explains why mass mailing has little effect on organ donor registration; predicts behavior when trait and preference theories fail.
Tit-for-tat (Axelrod, 1984)	Cooperate first and then imitate your partner's last behavior	The other players also play tit-for-tat; the rules of the game allow for defection or cooperation but not divorce	Can lead to a higher payoff than optimization (backward induction).
Imitate the majority (Boyd & Richerson, 2005)	Consider the majority of people in your peer group and imitate their behavior	Environment is stable or only changes slowly; info search is costly or time-consuming	A driving force in bonding, group identification, and moral behavior.
Imitate the successful (Boyd & Richerson, 2005)	Consider the most successful person and imitate his or her behavior	Individual learning is slow; information search is costly or time-consuming	A driving force in cultural evolution.

Note. For formal definitions, see references.

source of bias we identified lies in ignoring the dependencies between cues. The specific environmental structures that this bias can exploit are noisy observations and small sample sizes.

We turn now to a necessary precondition for understanding when, why, and how a given heuristic works.

3. FROM LABELS TO COMPUTATIONAL MODELS OF HEURISTICS

The development of computational models of heuristics over the last decades is another mark of progress, and without them, the analytic and simulation results on less-is-more could never have been discovered in the first place. Models need to be distinguished from labels. For instance, take similarity. On the one hand, there are models of similarity, including symmetric Euclidean distance and other Minkowski metrics (e.g., Shepard, 1974), as well as asymmetric similarity, such as Tversky's (1977) feature-mapping model. All of these are testable and some have been part of cognitive theories, such as Shepard's (1987) universal law of generalization. On the other hand, there is the label "representativeness," which was proposed in the early 1970s and means that judgments are made by similarity—but how similarity was defined is left open. A label can be a starting point, but four decades and many experiments later, representativeness has still not been instantiated as a model. As it remains undefined, it can account even for *A* and non-*A* (Ayton & Fisher, 2004), that is, everything and nothing. Consider the gambler's fallacy: After a series of *n* reds on the roulette table, expectation of another red *decreases*. This fallacy was attributed to people's reliance on the representativeness heuristic because "the occurrence of black will result in a more representative sequence than the occurrence of an additional red" (Tversky & Kahneman, 1974, p. 1125). Next consider the hot-hand fallacy, which is the opposite belief: After a basketball player scores a series of *n* hits, the expectation of another hit *increases*. This belief was also attributed to representativeness, because "even short random sequences are thought to be highly representative of their

generating process" (Gilovich, Vallone, & Tversky, 1985, p. 295). No model of similarity can explain a phenomenon and its contrary; otherwise it would not exclude any behavior. But a label can do this by changing its meaning: To account for the gambler's fallacy, the term alludes to a higher similarity between the series of *n* + 1 outcomes and the underlying chance process, whereas to account for the hot hand fallacy, it alludes to a similarity between a series of *n* and observation number *n* + 1 (Figure 1-6). Labels of heuristics cannot be proved or disproved, and hence are immune to improvement.

In a debate over vague labels, Gigerenzer (1996) argued that they should be replaced by models, whereas Kahneman and Tversky (1996, p. 585) insisted that this is not necessary because "representativeness (like similarity) can be assessed empirically; hence it need not be defined a priori." The use of labels is still widespread in areas such as social psychology, and it is therefore worth providing a second illustration of how researchers are misled by their seductive power. Consider the "availability heuristic," which has been proposed to explain distorted frequency and probability judgments. From the very beginning, this label encompassed several meanings, such as the number of instances that come to mind (e.g., Tversky & Kahneman, 1973); the ease with which the first instance comes to mind (e.g., Kahneman & Tversky, 1996); the recency, salience, vividness, and memorability, among others (e.g., Jolls, Sunstein, & Thaler, 1998; Sunstein, 2000). In a widely cited study

Figure 1-6. Illustration of the seductive power of one-word explanations. The gambler's fallacy and the hot hand fallacy are opposite intuitions: After a series of *n* similar events, the probability of the opposite event increases (gambler's fallacy), and after a series of similar events, the probability of the same event increases (hot hand fallacy). Both have been explained by the label "representativeness" (see main text).

designed to demonstrate how people's judgments are biased due to availability, Tversky and Kahneman (1973) had people estimate whether each of five consonants (K, L, N, R, V) appears more frequently in the first or the third position in English words. This is an atypical sample, because all five occur more often in the third position, whereas the majority of consonants occur more frequently in the first position. Two-thirds of participants judged the first position as being more likely for a majority of the five consonants. This result was interpreted as demonstration of a cognitive illusion and attributed to the availability heuristic: Words with a particular letter in the first position come to mind more easily. While this latter assertion may or may not be true, there was no independent measure of availability in this study, nor has there been a successful replication in the literature.

Sedlmeier, Hertwig, and Gigerenzer (1998) defined the two most common meanings of availability—ease and number—and measured them independently of people's frequency judgments. The number of instances was measured by the number of retrieved words within a constant time period (availability-by-number), and ease of retrieval was measured by the speed of the retrieval of the first word for each letter (availability-by-speed). The test involved a large sample of letters rather than the five consonants. The result was that neither measure of availability could predict people's actual frequency judgments. Instead, the judgments were roughly a monotonic function of the actual proportions, with a regression toward the mean, that is, an overestimation of low and an underestimation of high proportions. Moreover, the two definitions showed little correlation with one another. The basic flaw in the original research was to introduce a label after data were observed, rather than formulate a heuristic as a computational model that allows predictions to be expressed in a testable way.

One-word explanations such as the most recent "six general purpose heuristics identified (affect, availability, causality, fluency, similarity, and surprise)" (Gilovich & Griffin, 2002, p. 17) are not the only surrogates for theories. Others include redescription of the phenomenon[1] and so-called dual-process theories of thinking that postulate a System 1 and a System 2, each characterized by a list of general terms, such as rational versus heuristic, rule-based versus associative, and conscious versus unconscious, without formal and testable definitions of the two processes (e.g., Barbey & Sloman, 2007; Sloman, 1996; for a critique, see Gigerenzer & Regier, 1996). These surrogates for theories come close to black-box theorizing, and their popularity is an obstacle to progress in cognitive science.

In his essay "What is an 'explanation' of behavior?" Herbert Simon (1992, p. 155) wrote: "A running program is the moment of truth." A computational model can identify less-is-more effects, challenge the intuition that more information and computation are always better, and clarify which theories are psychologically implausible because they are computationally intractable in the real world. They also help us to derive, analytically, unexpected implications of a heuristic. For instance, violations of expected utility theory have been modeled by adding more and more adjustable parameters, as in cumulative prospect theory with its five adjustable parameters. The priority heuristic, a one-good-reason heuristic with no free parameters (Brandstätter, Gigerenzer, & Hertwig, 2008; Brandstätter et al., 2006) that has similar building blocks to take-the-best, has been shown to *imply* (not just have parameter sets that are *consistent with*) several of the major violations simultaneously, including the Allais paradox and the fourfold pattern (Katsikopoulos & Gigerenzer, 2008). The priority heuristic makes transparent and bold predictions about choice, and it has been demonstrated when it predicts well and when it does not (on the latter, see Birnbaum, 2008).

4. UNPACKING THE ADAPTIVE TOOLBOX

4.1. The Building Blocks of Heuristics

Although examples of rules of thumb in biology are not rare, they tend to be curiosities, partly because biology lacks a systematic theory of heuristics. Similarly, within cognitive science, there has been no such theory (although see Payne et al., 1993). The next step in progress we deal with is the beginning of a systematic study of heuristics and their building blocks. Research into the adaptive toolbox attempts to formulate such a theory by identifying the heuristics that humans and other animals use, the building blocks of heuristics that can be used to generate new ones, and the evolved capacities that these building blocks exploit (Gigerenzer & Selten, 2001). The gaze heuristic introduced earlier has three building blocks. As pointed out, it only works when the ball is already high in the air, and fails if the ball is at the beginning of its trajectory. To adjust to this new situation, a player does not need a new heuristic, but only to adapt the third building block. Instead of

1. Fix your gaze on the ball,
2. start running, and
3. adjust your running speed so that the angle of gaze remains constant,

the adapted heuristic is:

1. Fix your gaze on the ball,
2. start running, and
3. adjust your running speed so that the image of the ball rises at a constant rate.

One can intuitively see its logic. If the player sees the ball rising from the point at which it was hit with accelerating speed, the player should run backward, because the ball will hit the ground behind the player's position. If, however, the ball rises with decreasing speed, the player needs to run toward the ball instead. Just as there is a class of such tracking heuristics, there is a class of one-good-reason heuristics, of which take-the-best is one member. These heuristics also have three building blocks: search rules, stopping rules, and decision rules. Take-the-best is not a useful heuristic in every situation; more generally, no single strategy is always the best one—otherwise, the mind would resemble a mechanic with only one tool at hand. Consider the first building block of take-the-best:

Search rule: **Search through cues in order of their validity.**

This search rule can be followed if the cues are retrieved from memory, but situations exist in which the order of cues is dictated from outside.

Consider a red deer stag in rutting season that wants to enter the territory of a harem holder: In a fight with the rival over the females, which male is likely to win? For the stag, this question is a matter of genetic survival. Typically, the first cue is roaring. If the harem holder roars more impressively, the challenger may already give up and walk away. Otherwise, the next contest is initiated, parallel walking. It allows the competitors to assess each other's physical fitness and, potentially, confidence at a closer distance. If this contest also fails to produce a clear winner, the third contest is started: head-butting, the riskiest activity, as it can result in dangerous injuries (Clutton-Brock & Albon, 1979). This step-by-step heuristic is like take-the-best, but the search rule differs. The order of cues is not determined by (whatever the stag believes to be) the most valid cue, but by the cue that is first accessible. Sound can be encountered first in a forest environment where vision is restricted, visual stimuli next, and the most valid cue, head-butting, is last because it requires close contact. Thus, for the male deer, the adapted search rule is:

Search rule: **Search through cues in order of their environmental accessibility.**

The other building blocks remain the same. Consider now a situation where search by validity is not constrained. However, the task is new and the individual does not have the experience to come up with a good order. In this case, one can prove that it is of advantage to adjust the stopping rule and consequently, the decision rule (Karelaia, 2006):

Stopping rule: **Stop as soon as two cues are found that point to the same object.**
Decision rule: **Infer that this object has the higher criterion value.**

This stopping rule, termed a *confirmation rule*, works well in situations where (a) the decision maker knows little about the validity of the cues, and (b) the costs of cues are rather low (Karelaia, 2006). It is remarkably robust and insensitive to knowledge about cue ordering, and there is experimental evidence that a substantial proportion of people rely on this stopping rule as long as the problem is new (Gigerenzer, Dieckmann, &

Gaissmaier, in press). By adapting the building blocks of heuristics, organisms can react to new tasks and changing environments.

4.2. How Does the Mind Select Heuristics?

Table 1-2 shows 10 heuristics in the adaptive toolbox of humans. But how does the mind select a heuristic that is reasonable for the task at hand? Although far from a complete understanding of this mostly unconscious process, we know there are at least three selection principles. The first is that memory constrains the choice set of heuristics and thereby creates specific cognitive niches for different heuristics (Marewski & Schooler, 2010). Consider the choice between the first three heuristics in Table 1-2: the recognition heuristic, the fluency heuristic, and take-the-best. Assume it is 2003, and a visitor has been invited to the third round of the Wimbledon Gentlemen's tennis tournament and encouraged to place a bet on who will win. The two players are Andy Roddick and Tommy Robredo. First, assume that the visitor is fairly ignorant about tennis and has heard of Roddick but not of Robredo. This state of memory restricts the choice set to the recognition heuristic:

> If you have heard of one player but not the other, predict that the recognized player will win the game.

As it happened, Roddick won the match. In fact, this correct inference is not an exception: This simple heuristic predicted the matches of Wimbledon 2003 and 2005 with equal or higher accuracy than the ATP rankings and the seeding of the Wimbledon experts did (Scheibehenne & Bröder, 2007; Serwe & Frings, 2006). Now assume that the visitor has heard of both players but recalls nothing else about them. That state of memory limits the choice set to the fluency heuristic:

> If you have heard of both players, but the name of one came faster to your mind than the other, predict that this player will win the game.

Finally, assume that the visitor is more knowledgeable and can recall various facts about both players. That again eliminates the recognition heuristic and leaves a choice between the fluency heuristic and take-the-best. According to the experimental evidence, the majority of subjects switch to knowledge-based heuristics such as take-the-best when the values of both alternatives on relevant cues can be recalled (Marewski & Schooler, 2010), consistent with an analysis of the relative ecological rationality of the two heuristics in this situation. The general point is that memory "selects" heuristics in a way that makes it easier and faster to apply a heuristic when it is likely to yield accurate decisions. In the extreme case where the visitor has not heard of any of the players, none of the heuristics can be used. In this event, the visitor can resort to social heuristics, such as imitate the majority: Bet on the player on whom most others bet (Table 1-2).

The second known selection principle, after memory, is feedback. Strategy selection theory (Rieskamp & Otto, 2006) provides a quantitative model that can be understood as a reinforcement theory where the unit of reinforcement is not a behavior, but a heuristic. This model allows predictions about the probability that a person selects one strategy within a defined set of strategies. The third selection principle relies on the structure of the environment, as analyzed in the study of ecological rationality. For instance, the recognition heuristic is likely to lead to fast and accurate judgments if the recognition validity is high, that is, a strong correlation between recognition and the criterion exists, as is the case for tennis and other sports tournaments. There is experimental evidence that people tend to rely on this heuristic if the recognition validity is high but less so if the recognition validity α is low or at chance level ($\alpha = .5$). For instance, name recognition of Swiss cities is a valid predictor of their population ($\alpha = .86$), but not for their distance from the center of Switzerland, the city of Interlaken ($\alpha = .51$). Pohl (2006) reported that 89% of participants relied on the recognition heuristic in judgments of population, but only 54% in judgments of distance to Interlaken. Thus, the use of the recognition heuristic involves two processes: first, *recognition* in order to see whether the heuristic can be applied, and second, *evaluation* in order to judge whether it should be applied. Using functional magnetic resonance imaging (fMRI), Volz et al. (2006) reported specific neural activity that corresponded to these two processes. Similarly, the take-the-best heuristic is more accurate when the weights of cues vary widely, but less so when they are about equal. Rieskamp and Otto (2006) and Bröder (2003) reported that people adaptively select take-the-best when the environment has this property.

5. METHODOLOGY AND EMPIRICAL EVIDENCE

Since the Nobel prize-winning experiments of ethologist Niko Tinbergen (1958), biologists have experimentally studied rules of thumb in settings such as mate choice, patch leaving, and the coordination of individual behavior of social insects, among others (Hutchinson & Gigerenzer, 2005). Yet this beautiful work has had virtually no influence on cognitive science. After the cognitive revolution of the 1960s, psychologists focused on heuristics for choice under certainty, such as how to decide between two or more apartments, contraceptive pills, or jobs, described by a number of cues or attributes. An early review of process-tracing studies concluded that there is clear evidence for noncompensatory heuristics, whereas evidence for weighting and adding strategies is restricted to tasks with small numbers of alternatives and attributes (Ford, Schmitt, Schechtman, Hults, & Doherty, 1989). A heuristic is noncompensatory if it makes no trade-offs between cue values; examples are lexicographic rules such as take-the-best, elimination-by-aspects, conjunctive rules, and disjunctive rules. The work by Payne et al. (1993) additionally demonstrated that people tend to select the heuristics in an adaptive way.

The experimental study of heuristics for inference began to attract researchers relatively late, after we published *Simple Heuristics That Make Us Smart* in 1999. An important stepping stone was realizing that a test of a heuristic should satisfy three minimum criteria:

1. *Competitive tests:* Test multiple models of strategies and determine which ones predict (rather than fit) the data most accurately. Do not test one model and declare that the result appears to be good enough or not.

2. *Individual-level tests:* Test each model for each individual. Do not test what the average individual does, because systematic individual differences may make the average meaningless.

3. *Adaptive selection of heuristics:* Test whether people use a heuristic in situations where it is ecologically rational. Do not test whether everyone uses one heuristic all the time.

Several tests of heuristics exist that satisfy these criteria. For instance, Bergert and Nosofsky (2007) formulated a stochastic version of take-the-best and tested it against an additive-weighting model at the individual level. They concluded that the "vast majority of subjects" (p. 107) adopted the take-the-best strategy. Nosofsky and Bergert (2007) compared take-the-best with both additive-weighting and exemplar models of categorization, and concluded that "most did not use an exemplar-based strategy" but followed the response time predictions of take-the-best. This work deserves particular admiration, given that Nosofsky long promoted exemplar models but has adapted his viewpoint in keeping with the evidence. Similar comparative tests of models of heuristics or their building blocks have been conducted by Bröder (in press), Bröder and Gaissmaier (2007), Dieckmann and Rieskamp (2007), Rieskamp and Hoffrage (2008), Rieskamp and Otto (2006), Yee, Dahan, Hauser, and Orlin (2007), among others.

Why is comparative testing crucial for progress? There are two reasons. First, science is about finding better models than those that already exist; the task is not to test one single model in isolation and then proclaim that it fits the data or does not. Consider Newell, Weston, and Shanks (2003), who tested take-the-best in two experiments and found that in Experiment 1 "participants adhered to the search, stopping, and decision rules in 75%, 80%, and 89% of all possible cases, respectively. For Experiment 2 the figures are even more impressive: 92% for the search rule and 89% for the stopping and decision rules" (p. 93). Yet these results were disregarded by counting only those subjects who were consistent with the predictions in at least 90% of the cases, so that "only one-third (33%)

behaved in a manner completely consistent with TTB's search, stopping, and decision rules" (p. 82). This and similar results were later used to argue that finding evidence for take-the-best "has proved elusive" (Newell, 2005, p. 12). Here, an arbitrary criterion is set unrealistically high for the model one wants to disprove, whereas a proper evaluation would be competitive by comparing several models.

A second reason why competitive tests are necessary is that flaws in the experimental design will hurt all models tested, not only one. For instance, in Newell and Shanks (2003), the ecological validities were set to .80, .75, .70, and .69, and subjects were given 60 trials with feedback to learn the order. The authors reported that only three out of 16 participants sought information in this order. But the training sessions were clearly too short to learn the order of cues: Even with perfect memory, a participant would have needed at least 100 trials to learn the order of the two last cues (to find out that the third cue is better than the fourth only in one out of 100 times), and 20 trials each for the other cues.

Individual-level tests are essential because in virtually every task we find individual differences in strategies. This heterogeneity may be due to flat maxima, where several strategies are reasonable solutions to the same problem, or a kind of Darwinian variability that is rational if the world (or task) changes, or a strategic unpredictability that can be rational in competitive games. As a consequence, models need to be tested at the individual level, whereas conclusions from group averages are likely to be uninformative. Consider early tests of the recognition heuristic, a model of memory-based inferences. If a person uses this heuristic to infer which of two alternatives has a higher value on a criterion, they rely only on recognition information and ignore cue values about the recognized alternative in their memory. Richter and Späth (2006) reported three experiments. The third was the perfect test for the heuristic, whereas in the other two experiments the recognition validity was unknown or low. German participants were taught whether certain recognized American cities have international airports. They were also told the proportion of

cities in the reference class with airports, and that having an airport is highly predictive of population size. The task was to infer whether recognized cities with three kinds of associated information (airport, no airport, or no information) were more populous than unrecognized cities in paired comparisons.

The critical condition is the one where participants compare a recognized city with no airport and an unrecognized city. If participants follow the recognition heuristic, they will infer that the recognized city has the larger population, even if they know it has no airport. Because the mean adherence to the recognition heuristic was lower in the critical condition (.82) than in the other conditions (.95 and .98), Richter and Späth (2006, p. 159) concluded that "no evidence was found in favor of a noncompensatory use of recognition" but "clear evidence" for integration of recognition with additional knowledge. In Figure 1-7 we show a reanalysis of their data at the level of the individual participants. Even in the critical condition (Figure 1-7, bottom panel), the majority of participants consistently followed the recognition heuristic: nine participants followed it without a single exception (32 out of 32 times), and another eight followed it but for one single exception, whereas only a minority seemed to follow an alternative strategy. It is impossible to infer from means alone what proportion of individuals follow the recognition heuristic. Likewise, it is not possible to assert that there is clear evidence for an alternative noncompensatory model that has not even been formulated and tested. Marewski et al. (2010) formulated alternative models that integrate the additional information about the recognized information—the same models that Richter and Späth claimed to be supported by the fact that the recognition heuristic is not used all the time—and found that none of them were better than mere recognition at explaining the data. Similarly, individual-level analyses of several experiments showed that a majority of participants consistently followed the recognition heuristic in the presence of conflicting cues, while others employed, but less consistently, unidentified strategies (Pachur, Bröder, & Marewski, 2008).

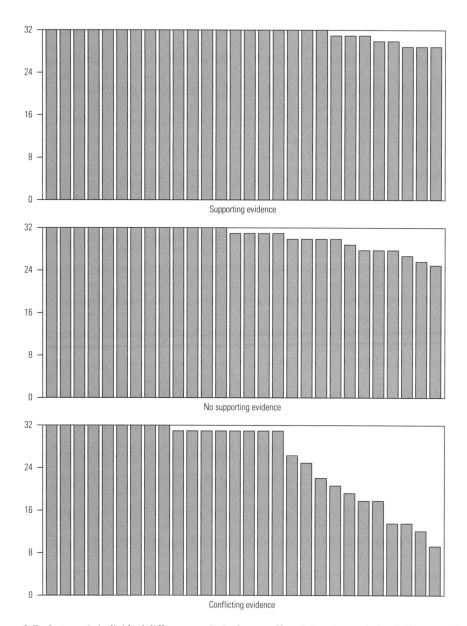

Figure 1-7. Systematic individual differences exist in the use of heuristics. A reanalysis of Richter and Späth (2006, Experiment 3) at the individual level reveals that even in the presence of conflicting information (bottom panel), the majority of participants still follow the recognition heuristic. Each bar represents one participant and its height the number of inferences out of a total of 32 that were consistent with the recognition heuristic. With supporting, no supporting, and conflicting evidence, the median participant followed the recognition heuristic in 100%, 97%, and 97% of inferences, respectively. We do not know which strategy the minority in the bottom panel (right side) followed, as no alternative strategies were tested. (Figure courtesy of Daniel G. Goldstein).

Finally, testing the adaptive selection of heuristics is essential to developing the theory of the adaptive toolbox as well as the earlier framework of the adaptive decision maker (Payne et al., 1993). As there is more than one heuristic, the question is not whether individuals always rely on a given heuristic, but whether they use heuristics in an adaptive way. Whereas some early papers set out to test whether people use a single heuristic all the time, later work asked whether people use several heuristics in an adaptive way (e.g., Bröder, in press). The study of ecological rationality of a heuristic provides the predictions for its adaptive use (e.g., Rieskamp & Otto, 2006).

6. HOMO HEURISTICUS

In this article, we presented a vision of human nature based on an adaptive toolbox of heuristics rather than on traits, attitudes, preferences, and similar internal explanations. We reviewed the progress made in developing a science of heuristics, beginning with the discovery of less-is-more effects that contradict the prevailing explanation in terms of accuracy-effort trade-offs. Instead, we argue that the answer to the question, "Why heuristics?" lies in their ecological rationality, that is, in the environmental structures to which a given heuristic is adapted. Using the bias–variance dilemma, we showed how the ecological rationality of heuristics can be formally studied, focusing on uncertain criteria and small samples that constitute environmental structures which fast-and-frugal heuristics can exploit. Homo heuristicus can rely on heuristics because they are accurate, not because they require less effort at the cost of some accuracy. We hope to have raised our readers' curiosity about the emerging science of heuristics and also hope that they might be inspired to solve some of the open questions, such as whether there is a system of building blocks of heuristics, similar to the elements in chemistry, and how a vocabulary for describing relevant environmental structures can be found. Let us end this article about the rationality of mortals from God's point of view.

How would a grand planner design a human mind? Consider three design perspectives. Design

1 would give the mind perfect memory. This would be ideal in a world that is absolutely certain and predictable, where what was observed in the past will also be observed in the future. This mind could remember, for instance, every day's temperature and thus could perfectly predict the future. In this world, perfect memory guarantees zero bias and zero variance, as every event has been observed and perfectly memorized. In fact, evolution has created something very close. A prominent example is a Russian named Shereshevsky, whom Luria (1968) studied for over three decades without finding the limits of his astounding memory. But this memory came at a price. For instance, Shereshevsky would read a page and recall it word for word, both forwards and backwards, but when he was asked to summarize the gist of what he read, he was more or less at a loss. Gist, abstraction, and other ways of going beyond the information given were not what this perfect memory buried in detail could deliver.

Design 2 accounts for the fact that the world is not absolutely predictable and fully observable, and therefore, a perfect memory would be a waste of energy. Instead, the goal is a mind that can make intelligent inferences from limited samples. The ideal is to have an infinitely flexible system of abstract representations to ensure zero bias, so that whatever structure the world has, it can be reproduced perfectly. As the content of the samples of observations in this world will vary, the induced representations are likely to be different, and this creates variance. Such a mind works best with large samples of observations and in a world that is relatively stable. Yet because this mind has no bias and must choose from an infinite space of representations, it is likely to require resource-intensive cognitive processing. This kind of design suggests general-purpose processing strategies such as exemplar models and neural networks as models of cognition (see Figure 1-2).

Design 3 aims at a mind that can make inferences quickly from a few observations, and it exploits the fact that bias can be adaptive and can help to reduce the estimation error (Figures 1-1 and 1-2). This design relies on several inference tools rather than a single universal tool. Each has a bias that can be offset by a greater reduction in variance. This design works well in a world where inferences have to be made from small samples, and where the future may change in unforeseen ways (Bookstaber & Langsam, 1985). Unlike in the previous cases, the creator of Design 3 need not assume omniscience, that is, knowledge of all relevant options, consequences, and probabilities both now and in the future. This corresponds to the world in which many experts live, such as the business managers using the hiatus heuristic and the Nobel laureate relying on $1/N$. After all, to build a mind with zero bias assumes that one knows the true state of the world and the representations needed to model it. Zero bias is neither possible nor always desirable for a real mind. Adopting the perspective of Design 3, the study of simple heuristics shows not only how a mind can make accurate inferences about an uncertain world efficiently but also how this efficiency is crucial to adapting the mind to its environment. Viewing humans as Homo heuristicus challenges widely held beliefs about the nature of cognitive processing and explains why less processing can result in better inferences.

ACKNOWLEDGMENTS

We are grateful to Julian Marewski, Shabnam Mousavi, Lael Schooler, and three anonymous reviewers for their helpful comments.

NOTES

1. Recall Moliere's parody of the Aristotelian doctrine of substantial forms: Why does opium make you sleepy? Because of its dormative properties. In the same way, explanation by redescription is alive today. Why does a specific problem representation improve reasoning? Because it makes the solution salient and transparent (for examples, see Gigerenzer, 1996, 2000). Why do people tend to share money equally in the ultimatum game? Because of a propensity for inequality avoidance (Fehr & Schmidt, 1999).

APPENDIX 1

Environments Used in the Bias–Variance Analysis

An environment is a collection of objects. Each object relates m binary cues to an integer criterion. The two classes of environment considered here are both parameterized by m. The first class of environment comprises *binary environments*, each of which has 2^m objects defined by

$$H_{\text{binary}}(m) = \left\{ \langle b_m(i), i \rangle : 0 \leq i \leq (2^m - 1) \right\}$$

where the function $b_m(i)$ maps integers onto their binary representations, coded using the binary cues (for example, $b_4(3) = (0, 0, 1, 1)$). Binary environments have noncompensatory weights, and the cues are uncorrelated. For example, $H_{\text{binary}}(3)$ defines the following environment:

Object	Cue1	Cue 2	Cue 3	Criterion
A	0	0	0	0
B	0	0	1	1
C	0	1	0	2
D	0	1	1	3
E	1	0	0	4
F	1	0	1	5
G	1	1	0	6
H	1	1	1	7

The second class of environment comprises *Guttman environments*, each of which has m objects given by

$$H_{\text{Guttman}}(m) = \left\{ \left\langle b_m\left(\sum_{j=0}^{i} 2^j \right), i \right\rangle : 0 \leq i \leq (m-1) \right\}$$

For example, $H_{\text{Guttman}}(5)$ defines the following environment:

Object	Cue 1	Cue 2	Cue 3	Cue 4	Cue 5	Criterion
A	0	0	0	0	1	0
B	0	0	0	1	1	1
C	0	0	1	1	1	2
D	0	1	1	1	1	3
E	1	1	1	1	1	4

In Guttman environments, all cues have validity 1.0 and are highly correlated with both other cues and the criterion. Binary and Guttman environments provide useful insights because they (a) elicit drastically different relative performances between take-the-best and alternative strategies that assess conditional dependencies between cues, and (b) are governed by a known underlying function, which allows us to perform a bias–variance decomposition of the error incurred by the different strategies.

PART I

Theory

Opening the adaptive toolbox

Introduction to Chapter 2

Reasoning the Fast and Frugal Way: Models of Bounded Rationality

This article by Gerd Gigerenzer and Dan Goldstein represents the "big bang" from which the research program on fast-and-frugal heuristics emerged. It demonstrated for the first time that the take-the-best heuristic, which ignores information, can be equally or more accurate than complex strategies that use all information in making inferences. Before its publication, the assumption had been that by using less information or computation, a person pays a price in terms of less accuracy (the "accuracy–effort trade-off"). Yet this article provided an existence proof that take-the-best does not have to trade off accuracy against effort. It also demonstrated less-is-more effects: that there is a point where more information can *decrease* accuracy—even when information is free. The implications for understanding the nature of cognition are fundamental: To make good inferences about the world, a cognitive system needs to ignore part of the available information. Cognitive limitations can enable, not just hinder, cognitive functioning.

Although heuristics had been studied before, the methodological novelty of this paper was that (*a*) inferences rather than preferences were analyzed and (*b*) a real-world environment rather than some hypothetical task was used. Consequently, researchers could test the accuracy of heuristics against external criteria, whereas preferences had often been evaluated against internal consistency criteria, such as transitivity. Moreover, when in this earlier work heuristics were tested in terms of their accuracy (e.g., in accuracy–effort trade-off analyses), *accuracy* did not mean success in the world but instead how closely a heuristic approximated a "gold standard," typically a weighting-and-adding strategy. The article by Gigerenzer and Goldstein, in contrast, showed that weighting and adding all information should not be blindly mistaken for the gold standard for making good inferences.

Based on earlier work on probabilistic mental models (Gigerenzer, Hoffrage, & Kleinbölting, 1991), this article uses the term *algorithm* to emphasize the importance of computational models of heuristics rather than verbal labels. In subsequent publications, the term *heuristic* was used to highlight the psychological principles of limited search and stopping rules that characterize the essence of these algorithms. Only with the help of computational models was it possible to discover that systematically ignoring information can lead to better inferences.

One of the article's limitations is that it underestimates the power of heuristics because accuracy was measured by the degree of fit to known data, rather than by predicting new data, as in cross-validation. When Czerlinski, Gigerenzer, and Goldstein (1999) subsequently tested the predictive accuracy, they discovered that two heuristics, take-the-best and tallying, were more accurate than multiple regression and other linear models in predicting across 20 problems (see Figure 1-1 in Chapter 1). How heuristics manage to overcome the accuracy–effort trade-off was not explained either. The bias-variance analysis in Chapter 1 indicates that take-the-best's ignoring of dependencies between cues is a decisive factor in its robustness. The study of the ecological rationality of take-the-best emerged as an attempt to answer this question (see Chapters 12 and 13).

The initial reaction to the result was disbelief, given the article's clash with the strongly held convictions that the accuracy–effort trade-off is inevitable and that complex problems demand complex solutions. Yet because the complete data were published in the appendix of the article, researchers were able to replicate the analysis. Nevertheless, it is noteworthy that virtually all researchers tried to find a more complex algorithm than take-the-best that might do better; nobody wanted to wager on even more simplicity. A second reaction was to suspect there was something strange about the real-world environment used, the population sizes of German cities. This suspicion was dispelled when a total of 20 environments were analyzed, with similar results (see Figure 1-1 in Chapter 1). Next, the Bayesian decision theorist Ward Edwards conjectured that although multiple linear regression was defeated, a real Olympian hero would throw any heuristic quickly into the sand. Yet when neural networks, classification-and-regression trees, and other vigorous warhorses were tested, take-the-best still competed very well, as illustrated by Figure 1-2 in Chapter 1. Edwards was so surprised that he composed a limerick in honor of take-the-best (Gigerenzer, Todd, & the ABC Research Group, 1999, p. 188). Only after the existence proof was accepted did the third and most important reaction emerge: attempts to find out in which environment—and why—a given heuristic outperforms a complex algorithm, and in which it lags behind. This is the study of the ecological rationality of a heuristic, an issue addressed in Chapters 1 and 12–16, and elsewhere, in this book.

CHAPTER 2

Reasoning the Fast and Frugal Way: Models of Bounded Rationality

Gerd Gigerenzer and Daniel G. Goldstein

Abstract: Humans and animals make inferences about the world under limited time and knowledge. In contrast, many models of rational inference treat the mind as a Laplacean Demon, equipped with unlimited time, knowledge, and computational might. Following Herbert Simon's notion of satisficing, the authors have proposed a family of algorithms based on a simple psychological mechanism: one-reason decision making. These fast-and-frugal algorithms violate fundamental tenets of classical rationality: They neither look up nor integrate all information. By computer simulation, the authors held a competition between the satisficing "take-the-best" algorithm and various "rational" inference procedures (e.g., multiple regression). The take-the-best algorithm matched or outperformed all competitors in inferential speed and accuracy. This result is an existence proof that cognitive mechanisms capable of successful performance in the real world do not need to satisfy the classical norms of rational inference.

Organisms make inductive inferences. Darwin (1872/1965) observed that people use facial cues, such as eyes that waver and lids that hang low, to infer a person's guilt. Male toads, roaming through swamps at night, use the pitch of a rival's croak to infer its size when deciding whether to fight (Krebs & Davies, 1987). Stockbrokers must make fast decisions about which of several stocks to trade or invest when only limited information is available. The list goes on. Inductive inferences are typically based on uncertain cues: The eyes can deceive, and so can a tiny toad with a deep croak in the darkness.

How does an organism make inferences about unknown aspects of the environment? There are three directions in which to look for

an answer. From Pierre Laplace to George Boole to Jean Piaget, many scholars have defended the now classical view that the laws of human inference are the laws of probability and statistics (and to a lesser degree, logic, which does not deal as easily with uncertainty). Indeed, the Enlightenment probabilists derived the laws of probability from what they believed to be the laws of human reasoning (Daston, 1988). Following this time-honored tradition, much contemporary research in psychology, behavioral ecology, and economics assumes standard statistical tools to be the normative and descriptive models of inference and decision making. Multiple regression, for instance, is both the economist's universal tool (McCloskey, 1985) and a model of inductive inference in multiple-cue learning (Hammond, 1990) and clinical judgment (B. Brehmer, 1994); Bayes's theorem is a model of how animals infer the presence of predators or prey (Stephens & Krebs, 1986) as well as of human reasoning and memory

(Anderson, 1990). This Enlightenment view that probability theory and human reasoning are two sides of the same coin crumbled in the early nineteenth century but has remained strong in psychology and economics.

In the past 25 years, this stronghold came under attack by proponents of the heuristics and biases program, who concluded that human inference is systematically biased and error prone, suggesting that the laws of inference are quick-and-dirty heuristics and not the laws of probability (Kahneman, Slovic, & Tversky, 1982). This second perspective appears diametrically opposed to the classical rationality of the Enlightenment, but this appearance is misleading. It has retained the normative kernel of the classical view. For example, a discrepancy between the dictates of classical rationality and actual reasoning is what defines a *reasoning error* in this program. Both views accept the laws of probability and statistics as normative, but they disagree about whether humans can stand up to these norms.

Many experiments have been conducted to test the validity of these two views, identifying a host of conditions under which the human mind appears more rational or irrational. But most of this work has dealt with simple situations, such as Bayesian inference with binary hypotheses, one single piece of binary data, and all the necessary information conveniently laid out for the participant (Gigerenzer & Hoffrage, 1995). In many real-world situations, however, there are multiple pieces of information, which are not independent, but redundant. Here, Bayes's theorem and other "rational" algorithms quickly become mathematically complex and computationally intractable, at least for ordinary human minds. These situations make neither of the two views look promising. If one would apply the classical view to such complex real-world environments, this would suggest that the mind is a supercalculator like a Laplacean Demon (Wimsatt, 1976)—carrying around the collected works of Kolmogoroff, Fisher, or Neyman—and simply needs a memory jog, like the slave in Plato's *Meno*. On the other hand, the heuristics-and-biases view of human irrationality would lead us to believe that humans are hopelessly lost

in the face of real-world complexity, given their supposed inability to reason according to the canon of classical rationality, even in simple laboratory experiments.

There is a third way to look at inference, focusing on the psychological and ecological rather than on logic and probability theory. This view questions classical rationality as a universal norm and thereby questions the very definition of "good" reasoning on which both the Enlightenment and the heuristics-and-biases views were built. Herbert Simon, possibly the best-known proponent of this third view, proposed looking for models of *bounded rationality* instead of classical rationality. Simon (1956, 1982) argued that information-processing systems typically need to *satisfice* rather than optimize. *Satisficing*, a blend of *sufficing* and *satisfying*, is a word of Scottish origin, which Simon uses to characterize algorithms that successfully deal with conditions of limited time, knowledge, or computational capacities. His concept of satisficing postulates, for instance, that an organism would choose the first object (a mate, perhaps) that satisfies its aspiration level—instead of the intractable sequence of taking the time to survey all possible alternatives, estimating probabilities and utilities for the possible outcomes associated with each alternative, calculating expected utilities, and choosing the alternative that scores highest.

Let us stress that Simon's notion of bounded rationality has two sides, one cognitive and one ecological. As early as in *Administrative Behavior* (1945), he emphasized the cognitive limitations of real minds as opposed to the omniscient Laplacean Demons of classical rationality. As early as in his *Psychological Review* article titled "Rational Choice and the Structure of the Environment" (1956), Simon emphasized that minds are adapted to real-world environments. The two go in tandem: "Human rational behavior is shaped by a scissors whose two blades are the structure of task environments and the computational capabilities of the actor" (Simon, 1990, p. 7). For the most part, however, theories of human inference have focused exclusively on the cognitive side, equating the notion of bounded rationality with the statement that humans are limited information processors, period. In a Procrustean-bed fashion, *bounded rationality* became almost synonymous with *heuristics and biases*, thus paradoxically reassuring classical rationality as the normative standard for both biases and bounded rationality (for a discussion of this confusion, see Lopes, 1992). Simon's insight that the minds of living systems should be understood relative to the environment in which they evolved, rather than to the tenets of classical rationality, has had little impact so far in research on human inference. Simple psychological algorithms that were observed in human inference, reasoning, or decision making were often discredited without a fair trial, because they looked so stupid by the norms of classical rationality. For instance, when Keeney and Raiffa (1993) discussed the lexicographic ordering procedure they had observed in practice—a procedure related to the class of satisficing algorithms we propose in this article—they concluded that this procedure "is naively simple" and "will rarely pass a test of 'reasonableness'" (p. 78). They did not report such a test. We shall.

Initially, the concept of bounded rationality was only vaguely defined, often as that which is not classical economics, and one could "fit a lot of things into it by foresight and hindsight," as Simon (1992, p. 18) himself put it. We wish to do more than oppose the Laplacean Demon view. We strive to come up with something positive that could replace this unrealistic view of mind. What are these simple, intelligent algorithms capable of making near-optimal inferences? How fast and how accurate are they? In this article, we propose a class of models that exhibit bounded rationality in both of Simon's senses. These satisficing algorithms operate with simple psychological principles that satisfy the constraints of limited time, knowledge, and computational might, rather than those of classical rationality. At the same time, they are designed to be fast-and-frugal without a significant loss of inferential accuracy, because the algorithms can exploit the structure of environments.

The article is organized as follows. We begin by describing the task the cognitive algorithms are designed to address, the basic algorithm itself, and the real-world environment on which the performance of the algorithm will be tested. Next, we report on a competition in which a satisficing algorithm competes with "rational" algorithms in making inferences about a real-world environment. The "rational" algorithms start with an advantage: They use more time, information, and computational might to make inferences. Finally, we study variants of the satisficing algorithm that make faster inferences and get by with even less knowledge.

THE TASK

We deal with inferential tasks in which a choice must be made between two alternatives on a quantitative dimension. Consider the following example:

> Which city has a larger population? (a) Hamburg (b) Cologne.

Two-alternative-choice tasks occur in various contexts in which inferences need to be made with limited time and knowledge, such as in decision making and risk assessment during driving (e.g., exit the highway now or stay on); treatment-allocation decisions (e.g., who to treat first in the emergency room: the 80-year-old heart attack victim or the 16-year-old car accident victim); and financial decisions (e.g., whether to buy or sell in the trading pit). Inference concerning population demographics, such as city populations of the past, present, and future (e.g., Brown & Siegler, 1993), is of importance to people working in urban planning, industrial development, and marketing. Population demographics, which is better understood than, say, the stock market, will serve us later as a "drosophila" environment that allows us to analyze the behavior of satisficing algorithms.

We study two-alternative-choice tasks in situations where a person has to make an inference based solely on knowledge retrieved from memory. We refer to this as *inference from memory*, as opposed to *inference from givens*. Inference from memory involves search in declarative knowledge and has been investigated in studies of, inter alia, confidence in general knowledge (e.g., Juslin, 1994; Sniezek & Buckley, 1993); the effect of repetition on belief (e.g., Hertwig, Gigerenzer, & Hoffrage, 1997); hindsight bias (e.g., Fischhoff, 1977); quantitative estimates of area and population of nations (Brown & Siegler, 1993); and autobiographic memory of time (Huttenlocher, Hedges, & Prohaska, 1988). Studies of inference from givens, on the other hand, involve making inferences from information presented by an experimenter (e.g., Hammond, Hursch, & Todd, 1964). In the tradition of Ebbinghaus's nonsense syllables, attempts are often made here to prevent individual knowledge from impacting on the results by using problems about hypothetical referents instead of actual ones. For instance, in celebrated judgment and decision-making tasks, such as the "cab" problem and the "Linda" problem, all the relevant information is provided by the experimenter, and individual knowledge about cabs and hit-and-run accidents, or feminist bank tellers, is considered of no relevance (Gigerenzer & Murray, 1987). As a consequence, limited knowledge or individual differences in knowledge play a small role in inference from givens. In contrast, the satisficing algorithms proposed in this article perform inference from memory, they use limited knowledge as input, and as we will show, they can actually profit from a lack of knowledge.

Assume that a person does not know or cannot deduce the answer to the Hamburg–Cologne question but needs to make an inductive inference from related real-world knowledge. How is this inference derived? How can we predict choice (Hamburg or Cologne) from a person's state of knowledge?

THEORY

The cognitive algorithms we propose are realizations of a framework for modeling inferences from memory, the theory of *probabilistic mental models* (PMM theory; see Gigerenzer, 1993; Gigerenzer, Hoffrage, & Kleinbölting, 1991). The theory of probabilistic mental models assumes that inferences about unknown states of the world are based on probability cues (Brunswik, 1955). The theory relates three

visions: (a) Inductive inference needs to be studied with respect to natural environments, as emphasized by Brunswik and Simon; (b) inductive inference is carried out by satisficing algorithms, as emphasized by Simon; and (c) inductive inferences are based on frequencies of events in a reference class, as proposed by Reichenbach and other frequentist statisticians. The theory of probabilistic mental models accounts for choice and confidence, but only choice is addressed in this article.

The major thrust of the theory is that it replaces the canon of classical rationality with simple, plausible psychological mechanisms of inference—mechanisms that a mind can actually carry out under limited time and knowledge and that could have possibly arisen through evolution. Most traditional models of inference, from linear multiple regression models to Bayesian models to neural networks, try to find some optimal integration of all information available: Every bit of information is taken into account, weighted, and combined in a computationally expensive way. The family of algorithms in PMM theory does not implement this classical ideal. Search in memory for relevant information is reduced to a minimum, and there is no integration (but rather a substitution) of pieces of information. These satisficing algorithms dispense with the fiction of the omniscient Laplacean Demon, who has all the time and knowledge to search for all relevant information, to compute the weights and covariances, and then to integrate all this information into an inference.

Limited Knowledge

A PMM is an inductive device that uses limited knowledge to make fast inferences. Different from mental models of syllogisms and deductive inference (Johnson-Laird, 1983), which focus on the logical task of truth preservation and where knowledge is irrelevant (except for the meaning of connectives and other logical terms), PMMs perform intelligent guesses about unknown features of the world, based on uncertain indicators. To make an inference about which of two objects, a or b, has a higher value, knowledge about a reference class R is searched, with $a, b \in R$. In our example, knowledge about the reference class "cities in Germany" could be searched. The knowledge consists of probability cues C_i $(i = 1,\ldots, n)$, and the cue values a_i and b_i of the objects for the ith cue. For instance, when making inferences about populations of German cities, the fact that a city has a professional soccer team in the major league (*Bundesliga*) may come to a person's mind as a potential cue. That is, when considering pairs of German cities, if one city has a soccer team in the major league and the other does not, then the city with the team is likely, but not certain, to have the larger population.

Limited knowledge means that the matrix of objects by cues has missing entries (i.e., objects, cues, or cue values may be unknown). Figure 2-1 models the limited knowledge of a person. She has heard of three German cities, *a*, *b*, and *c*, but not of *d* (represented by three positive and one negative recognition values). She knows some facts (cue values) about these cities with respect to five binary cues. For a binary cue, there are two cue values, positive (e.g., the city has a soccer team) or negative (it does not). *Positive* refers to a cue value that signals a higher value on the target variable (e.g., having a soccer team is correlated with high population). Unknown cue values are shown by a question mark. Because

she has never heard of *d*, all cue values for object *d* are, by definition, unknown.

People rarely know all information on which an inference could be based, that is, knowledge is limited. We model limited knowledge in two respects: A person can have (a) incomplete knowledge of the objects in the reference class (e.g., she recognizes only some of the cities), (b) limited knowledge of the cue values (facts about cities), or (c) both. For instance, a person who does not know all of the cities with soccer teams may know some cities with positive cue values (e.g., Munich and Hamburg certainly have teams), many with negative cue values (e.g., Heidelberg and Potsdam certainly do not have teams), and several cities for which cue values will not be known.

The Take-the-Best Algorithm

The first satisficing algorithm presented is called the "take-the-best" algorithm, because its policy is "take the best, ignore the rest." It is the basic algorithm in the PMM framework. Variants that work faster or with less knowledge are described later. We explain the steps of the take-the-best algorithm for binary cues (the algorithm can be easily generalized to many valued cues), using Figure 2-1 for illustration.

The take-the-best algorithm assumes a subjective rank order of cues according to their validities (as in Figure 2-1). We call the highest ranking cue (that discriminates between the two alternatives) the best cue. The algorithm is shown in the form of a flow diagram in Figure 2-2.

Step 1: Recognition Principle

The recognition principle is invoked when the mere recognition of an object is a predictor of the target variable (e.g., population). The recognition principle states the following: If only one of the two objects is recognized, then choose the recognized object. If neither of the two objects is recognized, then choose randomly between them. If both of the objects are recognized, then proceed to Step 2.

Example: If a person in the knowledge state shown in Figure 2-1 is asked to infer which of city *a* and city *d* has more inhabitants, the

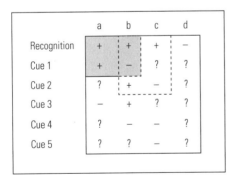

Figure 2-1. Illustration of bounded search through limited knowledge. Objects a, b, and c are recognized; object d is not. Cue values are positive (+) or negative (−); missing knowledge is shown by question marks. Cues are ordered according to their validities. To infer whether a > b, the take-the-best algorithm looks up only the cue values in the shaded space; to infer whether b > c, search is bounded to the dotted space. The other cue values are not looked up.

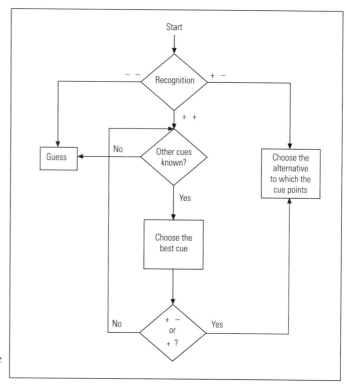

Figure 2-2. Flow diagram of the take-the-best algorithm.

inference will be city *a*, because the person has never heard of city *d* before.

Step 2: Search for Cue Values

For the two objects, retrieve the cue values of the highest ranking cue from memory.

Step 3: Discrimination Rule

Decide whether the cue discriminates. The cue is said to discriminate between two objects if one has a positive cue value and the other does not. The four shaded knowledge states in Figure 2-3 are those in which a cue discriminates.

Step 4: Cue-Substitution Principle

If the cue discriminates, then stop searching for cue values. If the cue does not discriminate, go back to Step 2 and continue with the next cue until a cue that discriminates is found.

Step 5: Maximizing Rule for Choice

Choose the object with the positive cue value. If no cue discriminates, then choose randomly.

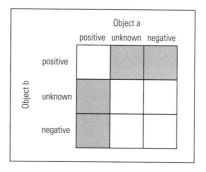

Figure 2-3. Discrimination rule. A cue discriminates between two alternatives if one has a positive cue value and the other does not. The four discriminating cases are shaded.

Examples: Suppose the task is judging which of city *a* or *b* is larger (Figure 2-1). Both cities are recognized (Step 1), and search for the best cue results with a positive and a negative cue value for Cue 1 (Step 2). The cue discriminates (Step 3), and search is terminated (Step 4).

The person makes the inference that city a is larger (Step 5).

Suppose now the task is judging which of city b or c is larger. Both cities are recognized (Step 1), and search for the cue values cue results in negative cue value on object b for Cue 1, but the corresponding cue value for object c is unknown (Step 2). The cue does not discriminate (Step 3), so search is continued (Step 4). Search for the next cue results with positive and a negative cue values for Cue 2 (Step 2). This cue discriminates (Step 3), and search is terminated (Step 4). The person makes the inference that city b is larger (Step 5).

The features of this algorithm are (a) search extends through only a portion of the total knowledge in memory (as shown by the shaded and dotted parts of Figure 2-1) and is stopped immediately when the first discriminating cue is found, (b) the algorithm does not attempt to integrate information but uses cue substitution instead, and (c) the total amount of information processed is contingent on each task (pair of objects) and varies in a predictable way among individuals with different knowledge. This fast and computationally simple algorithm is a model of bounded rationality rather than of classical rationality. There is a close parallel with Simon's concept of "satisficing": The take-the-best algorithm stops search after the first discriminating cue is found, just as Simon's satisficing algorithm stops search after the first option that meets an aspiration level.

The algorithm is hardly a standard statistical tool for inductive inference: It does not use all available information, it is noncompensatory and nonlinear, and variants of it can violate transitivity. Thus, it differs from standard linear tools for inference such as multiple regression, as well as from nonlinear neural networks that are compensatory in nature. The take-the-best algorithm is noncompensatory because only the best discriminating cue determines the inference or decision; no combination of other cue values can override this decision. In this way, the algorithm does not conform to the classical economic view of human behavior (e.g., Becker, 1976), where, under the assumption that all aspects can be reduced to one dimension (e.g., money), there exists always a trade-off between commodities or pieces of information. That is, the algorithm violates the Archimedian axiom, which implies that for any multidimensional object $a\,(a_1, a_2, \ldots, a_n)$ preferred to $b\,(b_1, b_2, \ldots, b_n)$, where a_1 dominates b_1, this preference can be reversed by taking multiples of any one or a combination of $b_2, b_3, \ldots, b_n$. As we discuss, variants of this algorithm also violate transitivity, one of the cornerstones of classical rationality (McClennen, 1990).

Empirical Evidence

Despite their flagrant violation of the traditional standards of rationality, the take-the-best algorithm and other models from the framework of PMM theory have been successful in integrating various striking phenomena in inference from memory and predicting novel phenomena, such as the confidence-frequency effect (Gigerenzer et al., 1991) and the less-is-more effect (Goldstein, 1994; Goldstein & Gigerenzer, 1996). The theory of probabilistic mental models seems to be the only existing process theory of the overconfidence bias that successfully predicts conditions under which overestimation occurs, disappears, and inverts to underestimation (Gigerenzer, 1993; Gigerenzer et al., 1991; Juslin, 1993, 1994; Juslin, Winman, & Persson, 1995; but see Griffin & Tversky, 1992). Similarly, the theory predicts when the hard–easy effect occurs, disappears, and inverts—predictions that have been experimentally confirmed by Hoffrage (1995) and by Juslin (1993). The take-the-best algorithm explains also why the popular confirmation-bias explanation of the overconfidence bias (Koriat, Lichtenstein, & Fischhoff, 1980) is not supported by experimental data (Gigerenzer et al., 1991, pp. 521–522).

Unlike earlier accounts of these striking phenomena in confidence and choice, the algorithms in the PMM framework allow for predictions of choice based on each individual's knowledge. Goldstein and Gigerenzer (1996) showed that the recognition principle predicted individual participants' choices in about 90% to 100% of all cases, even when participants were taught information that suggested doing otherwise (negative cue values for the recognized objects). Among the evidence for the empirical validity of the take-the-best algorithm are the tests of a bold prediction, the less-is-more effect, which postulates conditions under which people with little knowledge make better inferences than those who know more. This surprising prediction has been experimentally confirmed. For instance, U.S. students make slightly more correct inferences about German city populations (about which they know little) than about U.S. cities, and vice versa for German students (Gigerenzer, 1993; Goldstein 1994; Goldstein & Gigerenzer, 1996; Hoffrage, 1995). The theory of probabilistic mental models has been applied to other situations in which inferences have to be made under limited time and knowledge, such as rumor-based stock market trading (DiFonzo, 1994). A general review of the theory and its evidence is presented in McClelland and Bolger (1994).

The reader familiar with the original algorithm presented in Gigerenzer et al. (1991) will have noticed that we simplified the discrimination rule.[1] In the present version, search is already terminated if one object has a positive cue value and the other does not, whereas in the earlier version, search was terminated only when one object had a positive value and the other a negative one (cf. Figure 3 in Gigerenzer et al. with Figure 2-3). This change follows empirical evidence that participants tend to use this faster, simpler discrimination rule (Hoffrage, 1995).

This article does not attempt to provide further empirical evidence. For the moment, we assume that the model is descriptively valid and investigate how accurate this satisficing algorithm is in drawing inferences about unknown aspects of a real-world environment. Can an algorithm based on simple psychological principles that violate the norms of classical rationality make a fair number of accurate inferences?

THE ENVIRONMENT

We tested the performance of the take-the-best algorithm on how accurately it made inferences about a real-world environment. The environment was the set of all cities in Germany with

more than 100,000 inhabitants (83 cities after German reunification), with population as the target variable. The model of the environment consisted of 9 binary ecological cues and the actual 9×83 cue values. The full model of the environment is shown in the Appendix.

Each cue has an associated validity, which is indicative of its predictive power. The *ecological validity* of a cue is the relative frequency with which the cue correctly predicts the target, defined with respect to the reference class (e.g., all German cities with more than 100,000 inhabitants). For instance, if one checks all pairs in which one city has a soccer team but the other city does not, one finds that in 87% of these cases, the city with the team also has the higher population. This value is the ecological validity of the soccer team cue. The validity v_i of the ith cue is

$$v_i = p[t(a) > t(b) \mid a_i \text{ is positive and } b_i \text{ is negative}],$$

where $t(a)$ and $t(b)$ are the values of objects a and b on the target variable t and p is a probability measured as a relative frequency in R.

The ecological validity of the nine cues ranged over the whole spectrum: from .51 (only slightly better than chance) to 1.0 (certainty), as shown in Table 2-1. A cue with a high ecological validity, however, is not often useful if its discrimination rate is small.

Table 2-1 shows also the *discrimination rates* for each cue. The discrimination rate of a cue is the relative frequency with which the cue discriminates between any two objects from the reference class. The discrimination rate is a function of the distribution of the cue values and the number N of objects in the reference class. Let the relative frequencies of the positive and negative cue values be x and y, respectively. Then the discrimination rate d_i of the ith cue is

$$d_i = \frac{2x_i y_i}{1 - \frac{1}{N}},$$

as an elementary calculation shows. Thus, if N is very large, the discrimination rate is approximately $2x_i y_i$.[2] The larger the ecological validity of a cue, the better the inference. The larger the

Table 2-1.   Cues, Ecological Validities, and Discrimination Rates

Cue	Ecological Validity	Discrimination Rate
National capital (Is the city the national capital?)	1.00	.02
Exposition site (Was the city once an exposition site?)	.91	.25
Soccer team (Does the city have a team in the major league?)	.87	.30
Intercity train (Is the city on the Intercity line?)	.78	.38
State capital (Is the city a state capital?)	.77	.30
License plate (Is the abbreviation only one letter long?)	.75	.34
University (Is the city home to a university?)	.71	.51
Industrial belt (Is the city in the industrial belt?)	.56	.30
East Germany (Was the city formerly in East Germany?)	.51	.27

discrimination rate, the more often a cue can be used to make an inference. In the present environment, ecological validities and discrimination rates are negatively correlated. The redundancy of cues in the environment, as measured by pairwise correlations between cues, ranges between −.25 and .54, with an average absolute value of. 19.[3]

THE COMPETITION

The question of how well a satisficing algorithm performs in a real-world environment has rarely been posed in research on inductive inference. The present simulations seem to be the first to test how well simple satisficing algorithms do compared with standard integration algorithms, which require more knowledge, time, and computational power. This question is important for Simon's postulated link between the cognitive and the ecological: If the simple psychological principles in satisficing algorithms are tuned to ecological structures, these algorithms should not fail outright. We propose a competition between various inferential algorithms. The |contest will go to the algorithm that scores the highest proportion of correct inferences in the shortest time.

Simulating Limited Knowledge

We simulated people with varying degrees of knowledge about cities in Germany. Limited knowledge can take two forms. One is limited recognition of objects in the reference class.

The other is limited knowledge about the cue values of recognized objects. To model limited recognition knowledge, we simulated people who recognized between 0 and 83 German cities. To model limited knowledge of cue values, we simulated 6 basic classes of people, who knew 0%, 10%, 20%, 50%, 75%, or 100% of the cue values associated with the objects they recognized. Combining the two sources of limited knowledge resulted in 6 × 84 types of people, each having different degrees and kinds of limited knowledge. Within each type of people, we created 500 simulated individuals, who differed randomly from one another in the particular objects and cue values they knew. All objects and cue values known were determined randomly within the appropriate constraints, that is, a certain number of objects known, a certain total percentage of cue values known, and the validity of the recognition principle (as explained in the following paragraph).

The simulation needed to be realistic in the sense that the simulated people could invoke the recognition principle. Therefore, the sets of cities the simulated people knew had to be carefully chosen so that the recognized cities were larger than the unrecognized ones a certain percentage of the time. We performed a survey to get an empirical estimate of the actual covariation between recognition of cities and city populations. Let us define the *validity* α of the recognition principle to be the probability, in a reference class, that one object has a greater value on the target variable than another, in the cases where the one object is recognized and the other is not:

$$\alpha = p[t(a) > t(b) \mid a_r \text{ is positive and } b_r \text{ is negative}],$$

where $t(a)$ and $t(b)$ are the values of objects a and b on the target variable t, a_r and b_r are the recognition values of a and b, and p is a probability measured as a relative frequency in R.

In a pilot study of 26 undergraduates at the University of Chicago, we found that the cities they recognized (within the 83 largest in Germany) were larger than the cities they did not recognize in about 80% of all possible comparisons. We incorporated this value into our simulations by choosing sets of cities (for each knowledge state, i.e., for each number of cities recognized) where the known cities were larger than the unknown cities in about 80% of all cases. Thus, the cities known by the simulated individuals had the same relationship between recognition and population as did those of the human individuals. Let us first look at the performance of the take-the-best algorithm.

Testing the Take-the-Best Algorithm

We tested how well individuals using the take-the-best algorithm did at answering real-world questions such as, Which city has more inhabitants: (a) Heidelberg or (b) Bonn? Each of the 500 simulated individuals in each of the 6 × 84 types was tested on the exhaustive set of 3,403 city pairs, resulting in a total of 500 × 6 × 84 × 3,403 tests, that is, about 858 million.

The curves in Figure 2-4 show the average proportion of correct inferences for each proportion of objects and cue values known. The x axis represents the number of cities recognized, and the y axis shows the proportion of correct inferences that the take-the-best algorithm drew. Each of the 6 × 84 points that make up the six curves is an average proportion of correct inferences taken from 500 simulated individuals, who each made 3,403 inferences.

When the proportion of cities recognized was zero, the proportion of correct inferences was at chance level (.5). When up to half of all cities were recognized, performance increased at all

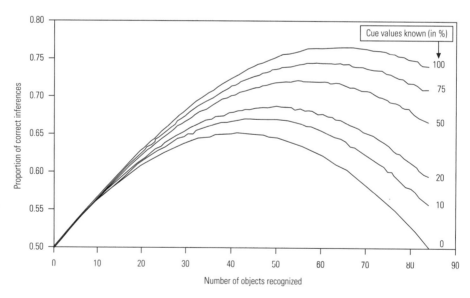

Figure 2-4. Correct inferences about the population of German cities (two-alternative-choice tasks) by the take-the-best algorithm. Inferences are based on actual information about the 83 largest cities and nine cues for population (see the Appendix). Limited knowledge of the simulated individuals is varied across two dimensions: (**a**) the number of cities recognized (x axis) and (**b**) the percentage of cue values known (the six curves).

levels of knowledge about cue values. The maximum percentage of correct inferences was around 77%. The striking result was that this maximum was not achieved when individuals knew all cue values of all cities, but rather when they knew less. This result shows the ability of the algorithm to exploit limited knowledge, that is, to do best when not everything is known. Thus, the take-the-best algorithm produces the *less-is-more* effect. At any level of limited knowledge of cue values, learning more German cities will eventually cause a decrease in proportion correct. Take, for instance, the curve where 75% of the cue values were known and the point where the simulated participants recognized about 60 German cities. If these individuals learned about the remaining German cities, their proportion correct would decrease. The rationale behind the less-is-more effect is the recognition principle, and it can be understood best from the curve that reflects 0% of total cue values known. Here, all decisions are made on the basis of the recognition principle, or by guessing. On this curve, the recognition principle comes into play most when half of the cities are known, so it takes on an inverted-U shape. When half the cities are known, the recognition principle can be activated most often, that is, for roughly 50% of the questions. Because we set the recognition validity in advance, 80% of these inferences will be correct. In the remaining half of the questions, when recognition cannot be used (either both cities are recognized or both cities are unrecognized), then the organism is forced to guess and only 50% of the guesses will be correct. Using the 80% effective recognition validity half of the time and guessing the other half of the time, the organism scores 65% correct, which is the peak of the bottom curve. The mode of this curve moves to the right with increasing knowledge about cue values. Note that even when a person knows everything, all cue values of all cities, there are states of limited knowledge in which the person would make more accurate inferences. We are not going to discuss the conditions of this counterintuitive effect and the supporting experimental evidence here (see Goldstein & Gigerenzer, 2002). Our focus is on how much better integration algorithms can do in making inferences.

Integration Algorithms

We asked several colleagues in the fields of statistics and economics to devise decision algorithms that would do better than the take-the-best algorithm. The five integration algorithms we simulated and pitted against the take-the-best algorithm in a competition were among those suggested by our colleagues. These competitors include "proper" and "improper" linear models (Dawes, 1979; Lovie & Lovie, 1986). These algorithms, in contrast to the take-the-best algorithm, embody two classical principles of rational inference: (a) complete search—they use all available information (cue values)—and (b) complete integration—they combine all these pieces of information into a single value. In short, we refer in this article to algorithms that satisfy these principles as "rational" (in quotation marks) algorithms.

Contestant 1: Tallying

Let us start with a simple integration algorithm: tallying of positive evidence (Goldstein, 1994). In this algorithm, the number of positive cue values for each object is tallied across all cues ($i = 1, \ldots, n$), and the object with the largest number of positive cue values is chosen. Integration algorithms are not based (at least explicitly) on the recognition principle. For this reason, and to make the integration algorithms as strong as possible, we allow all the integration algorithms to make use of recognition information (the positive and negative recognition values, see Figure 2-1). Integration algorithms treat recognition as a cue, like the nine ecological cues in Table 2-1. That is, in the competition, the number of cues (n) is thus equal to 10 (because recognition is included). The decision criterion for tallying is the following:

$$\text{If} \sum_{i=1}^{n} a_i > \sum_{i=1}^{n} b_i, \quad \text{then choose city } a.$$

$$\text{If} \sum_{i=1}^{n} a_i < \sum_{i=1}^{n} b_i, \quad \text{then choose city } b.$$

$$\text{If} \sum_{i=1}^{n} a_i = \sum_{i=1}^{n} b_i, \quad \text{then guess.}$$

The assignments of a_i and b_i are the following:

$$a_i, b_i = \begin{vmatrix} 1 \text{ if the } i\text{th cue value is positive} \\ 0 \text{ if the } i\text{th cue value is negative} \\ 0 \text{ if the } i\text{th cue value is unknown.} \end{vmatrix}$$

Let us compare cities a and b, from Figure 2-1. By tallying the positive cue values, a would score 2 points and b would score 3. Thus, tallying would choose b to be the larger, in opposition to the take-the-best algorithm, which would infer that a is larger. Variants of tallying, such as the frequency-of-good-features heuristic, have been discussed in the decision literature (Alba & Marmorstein, 1987; Payne, Bettman, & Johnson, 1993).

Contestant 2: Weighted Tallying

Tallying treats all cues alike, independent of cue validity. Weighted tallying of positive evidence is identical with tallying, except that it weights each cue according to its ecological validity, v_i. The ecological validities of the cues appear in Table 2-1. We set the validity of the recognition cue to .8, which is the empirical average determined by the pilot study. The decision rule is as follows:

$$\text{If } \sum_{i=1}^{n} a_i v_i > \sum_{i=1}^{n} b_i v_i, \text{ then choose city } a.$$

$$\text{If } \sum_{i=1}^{n} a_i v_i < \sum_{i=1}^{n} b_i v_i, \text{ then choose city } b.$$

$$\text{If } \sum_{i=1}^{n} a_i v_i = \sum_{i=1}^{n} b_i v_i, \text{ then guess.}$$

Note that weighted tallying needs more information than either tallying or the take-the-best algorithm, namely, quantitative information about ecological validities. In the simulation, we provided the real ecological validities to give this algorithm a good chance.

Calling again on the comparison of objects a and b from Figure 2-1, let us assume that the validities would be .8 for recognition and .9, .8, .7, .6, .51 for Cues 1 through 5. Weighted tallying would thus assign 1.7 points to a and 2.3 points to b. Thus, weighted tallying would also choose b to be the larger.

Both tallying algorithms treat negative information and missing information identically. That is, they consider only positive evidence. The following algorithms distinguish between negative and missing information and integrate both positive and negative information.

Contestant 3: Unit-Weight Linear Model

The unit-weight linear model is a special case of the equal-weight linear model (Huber, 1989) and has been advocated as a good approximation of weighted linear models (Dawes, 1979; Einhorn & Hogarth, 1975). The decision criterion for unit-weight integration is the same as for tallying, only the assignment of a_i and b_i differs:

$$a_i, b_i = \begin{vmatrix} 1 \text{ if the } i\text{th cue value is positive} \\ -1 \text{ if the } i\text{th cue value is negative} \\ 0 \text{ if the } i\text{th cue value is unknown.} \end{vmatrix}$$

Comparing objects a and b from Figure 2-1 would involve assigning 1.0 points to a and 1.0 points to b and, thus, choosing randomly. This simple linear model corresponds to Model 2 in Einhorn and Hogarth (1975, p. 177) with the weight parameter set equal to 1.

Contestant 4: Weighted Linear Model

This model is like the unit-weight linear model except that the values of a_i and b_i are multiplied by their respective ecological validities. The decision criterion is the same as with weighted tallying. The weighted linear model (or some variant of it) is often viewed as an optimal rule for preferential choice, under the idealization of independent dimensions or cues (e.g., Keeney & Raiffa, 1993; Payne et al., 1993). Comparing objects a and b from Figure 2-1 would involve assigning 1.0 points to a and 0.8 points to b and, thus, choosing a to be the larger.

Contestant 5: Multiple Regression

The weighted linear model reflects the different validities of the cues, but not the dependencies between cues. Multiple regression creates weights that reflect the covariances between predictors or cues and is commonly seen as an "optimal" way to integrate various pieces of information into an estimate (e.g., Brunswik, 1955; Hammond, 1966). Neural networks using the delta rule determine their "optimal" weights by the same principles as multiple regression does (Stone, 1986). The delta rule carries out the equivalent of a multiple linear regression from the input patterns to the targets.

The weights for the multiple regression could simply be calculated from the full information about the nine ecological cues, as given in the Appendix. To make multiple regression an even stronger competitor, we also provided information about which cities the simulated individuals recognized. Thus, the multiple regression used nine ecological cues and the recognition cue to generate its weights. Because the weights for the recognition cue depend on which cities are recognized, we calculated $6 \times 500 \times 84$ sets of weights: one for each simulated individual. Unlike any of the other algorithms, regression had access to the actual city populations (even for those cities not recognized by the hypothetical person) in the calculation of the weights.[4] During the quiz, each simulated person used the set of weights provided to it by multiple regression to estimate the populations of the cities in the comparison.

There was a missing-values problem in computing these $6 \times 84 \times 500$ sets of regression coefficients, because most simulated individuals did not know certain cue values, for instance, the cue values of the cities they did not recognize. We strengthened the performance of multiple regression by substituting unknown cue values with the average of the cue values the person knew for the given cue.[5] This was done both in creating the weights and in using these weights to estimate populations. Unlike traditional procedures where weights are estimated from one half of the data, and inferences based on these weights are made for the other half, the regression algorithm had access to all the information in the Appendix (except, of course, the unknown cue values)—more information than was given to any of the competitors. In the competition, multiple regression and, to a lesser degree, the weighted linear model approximate the ideal of the Laplacean Demon.

Results

Speed

The take-the-best algorithm is designed to enable quick decision making. Compared with the integration algorithms, how much faster does it draw inferences, measured by the amount of information searched in memory? For instance, in Figure 2-1, the take-the-best algorithm would look up four cue values (including the recognition cue values) to infer that a is larger than b. None of the integration algorithms use limited search; thus, they always look up all cue values.

Figure 2-5 shows the amount of cue values retrieved from memory by the take-the-best algorithm for various levels of limited knowledge. The take-the-best algorithm reduces search in memory considerably. Depending on the knowledge state, this algorithm needed to search for between 2 (the number of recognition values) and 20 (the maximum possible cue values: Each city has nine cue values and one recognition value). For instance, when a person recognized half of the cities and knew 50% of their cue values, then, on average, only about 4 cue values (that is, one fifth of all possible) are searched for. The average across all simulated participants was 5.9, which was less than a third of all available cue values.

Accuracy

Given that it searches only for a limited amount of information, how accurate is the take-the-best algorithm, compared with the integration algorithms? We ran the competition for all states of limited knowledge shown in Figure 2-4. We first report the results of the competition in the case where each algorithm achieved its best performance: when 100% of the cue values were known. Figure 2-6 shows the results of the simulations, carried out in the same way as those in Figure 2-4.

To our surprise, the take-the-best algorithm drew as many correct inferences as any of the other algorithms, and more than some. The curves for take-the-best, multiple regression, weighted tallying, and tallying are so similar that there are only slight differences among them. Weighted tallying performed about as well as

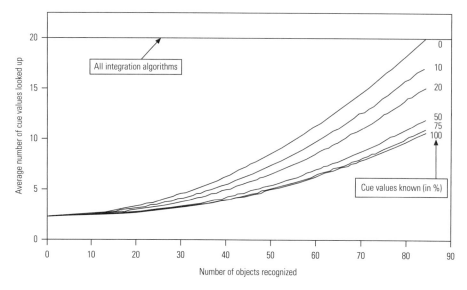

Figure 2-5. Amount of cue values looked up by the take-the-best algorithm and by the competing integration algorithms (see text), depending on the number of objects known (0–83) and the percentage of cue values known.

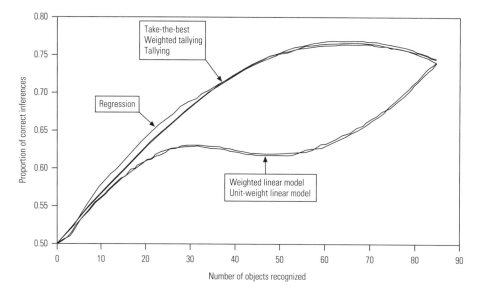

Figure 2-6. Results of the competition. The curve for the take-the-best algorithm is identical with the 100% curve in Figure 2-4. The results for proportion correct have been smoothed by a running median smoother, to lessen visual noise between the lines.

tallying, and the unit-weight linear model performed about as well as the weighted linear model—demonstrating that the previous finding that weights may be chosen in a fairly arbitrary manner, as long as they have the correct sign (Dawes, 1979), is generalizable to tallying. The two integration algorithms that make use of both positive and negative information, unit-weight and weighted linear models, made considerably fewer correct inferences.

By looking at the lower-left and upper-right corners of Figure 2-6, one can see that all competitors do equally well with a complete lack of knowledge or with complete knowledge. They differ when knowledge is limited. Note that some algorithms can make more correct inferences when they do not have complete knowledge: a demonstration of the less-is-more effect mentioned earlier.

What was the result of the competition across all levels of limited knowledge? Table 2-2 shows the result for each level of limited knowledge of cue values, averaged across all levels of recognition knowledge. (Table 2-2 reports also the performance of two variants of the take-the-best algorithm, which we discuss later: the minimalist and the "take-the-last" algorithm.) The values in the 100% column of Table 2-2 are the values in Figure 2-6 averaged across all levels of recognition. The take-the-best algorithm made as many correct inferences as one of the competitors (weighted tallying) and more than the others. Because it was also the fastest, we judged the competition goes to the take-the-best algorithm as the highest performing, overall.

To our knowledge, this is the first time that it has been demonstrated that a satisficing algorithm, that is, the take-the-best algorithm, can draw as many correct inferences about a real-world environment as integration algorithms, across all states of limited knowledge. The dictates of classical rationality would have led one to expect the integration algorithms to do substantially better than the satisficing algorithm.

Two results of the simulation can be derived analytically. First and most obvious is that if knowledge about objects is zero, then all algorithms perform at a chance level. Second, and less obvious, is that if all objects and cue values are known, then tallying produces as many correct inferences as the unit-weight linear model. This is because, under complete knowledge, the score under the tallying algorithm is an increasing linear function of the score arrived at in the unit-weight linear model.[6] The equivalence between tallying and unit-weight linear models under complete knowledge is an important result. It is known that unit-weight linear models can sometimes perform about as well as proper linear models (i.e., models with weights that are chosen in an optimal way, such as in multiple regression; see Dawes, 1979). The equivalence implies that under complete knowledge, merely counting pieces of positive evidence can work as well as proper linear models. This result clarifies one condition under which searching only for positive evidence, a strategy that has sometimes been labeled *confirmation bias* or *positive test strategy*, can be a reasonable and efficient inferential strategy (Klayman & Ha, 1987; Tweney & Walker, 1990).

Why do the unit-weight and weighted linear models perform markedly worse under limited

Table 2-2. Results of the Competition: Average Proportion of Correct Inferences

Algorithm	Percentage of Cue Values Known					
	10	20	50	75	100	Average
Take-the-best	.621	.635	.663	.678	.691	.658
Weighted tallying	.621	.635	.663	.679	.693	.658
Regression	.625	.635	.657	.674	.694	.657
Tallying	.620	.633	.659	.676	.691	.656
Weighted linear model	.623	.627	.623	.619	.625	.623
Unit-weight linear model	.621	.622	.621	.620	.622	.621
Minimalist	.619	.631	.650	.661	.674	.647
Take-the-last	.619	.630	.646	.658	.675	.645

Note. Values are rounded; averages are computed from the unrounded values. Bottom two algorithms are variants of the take-the-best algorithm.

knowledge of objects? The reason is the simple and bold recognition principle. Algorithms that do not exploit the recognition principle in environments where recognition is strongly correlated with the target variable pay the price of a considerable number of wrong inferences. The unit-weight and weighted linear models use recognition information and integrate it with all other information but do not follow the recognition principle, that is, they sometimes choose unrecognized cities over recognized ones. Why is this? In the environment, there are more negative cue values than positive ones (see the Appendix), and most cities have more negative cue values than positive ones. From this it follows that when a recognized object is compared with an unrecognized object, the (weighted) sum of cue values of the recognized object will often be smaller than that of the unrecognized object (which is −1 for the unit-weight model and −.8 for the weighted linear model). Here the unit-weight and weighted linear models often make the inference that the unrecognized object is the larger one, due to the overwhelming negative evidence for the recognized object. Such inferences contradict the recognition principle. Tallying algorithms, in contrast, have the recognition principle built in implicitly. Because tallying algorithms ignore negative information, the tally for an unrecognized object is always 0 and, thus, is always smaller than the tally for a recognized object, which is at least 1 (for tallying, or .8 for weighted tallying, due to the positive value on the recognition cue). Thus, tallying algorithms always arrive at the inference that a recognized object is larger than an unrecognized one.

Note that this explanation of the different performances puts the full weight in a psychological principle (the recognition principle) explicit in the take-the-best algorithm, as opposed to the statistical issue of how to find optimal weights in a linear function. To test this explanation, we reran the simulations for the unit-weight and weighted linear models under the same conditions but replacing the recognition cue with the recognition principle. The simulation showed that the recognition principle accounts for all the difference.

CAN SATISFICING ALGORITHMS GET BY WITH EVEN LESS TIME AND KNOWLEDGE?

The take-the-best algorithm produced a surprisingly high proportion of correct inferences, compared with more computationally expensive integration algorithms. Making correct inferences despite limited knowledge is an important adaptive feature of an algorithm, but being right is not the only thing that counts. In many situations, time is limited, and acting fast can be as important as being correct. For instance, if you are driving on an unfamiliar highway and you have to decide in an instant what to do when the road forks, your problem is not necessarily making the best choice, but simply making a quick choice. Pressure to be quick is also characteristic for certain types of verbal interactions, such as press conferences, in which a fast answer indicates competence, or commercial interactions, such as having telephone service installed, where the customer has to decide in a few minutes which of a dozen calling features to purchase. These situations entail the dual constraints of limited knowledge and limited time. The take-the-best algorithm is already faster than any of the integration algorithms, because it performs only a limited search and does not need to compute weighted sums of cue values. Can it be made even faster? It can, if search is guided by the recency of cues in memory rather than by cue validity.

The Take-the-Last Algorithm

The take-the-last algorithm first tries the cue that discriminated the last time. If this cue does not discriminate, the algorithm then tries the cue that discriminated the time before last, and so on. The algorithm differs from the take-the-best algorithm in Step 2, which is now reformulated as Step 2′:

Step 2′: Search for the Cue Values of the Most Recent Cue

For the two objects, retrieve the cue values of the cue used most recently. If it is the first judgment and there is no discrimination record available, retrieve the cue values of a randomly chosen cue.

Thus, in Step 4, the algorithm goes back to Step 2′. Variants of this search principle have been studied as the "Einstellung effect" in the water jar experiments (Luchins & Luchins, 1994), where the solution strategy of the most recently solved problem is tried first on the subsequent problem. This effect has also been noted in physicians' generation of diagnoses for clinical cases (Weber, Böckenholt, Hilton, & Wallace, 1993).

This algorithm does not need a rank order of cues according to their validities; all that needs to be known is the direction in which a cue points. Knowledge about the rank order of cue validities is replaced by a memory of which cues were last used. Note that such a record can be built up independently of any knowledge about the structure of an environment and neither needs, nor uses, any feedback about whether inferences are right or wrong.

The Minimalist Algorithm

Can reasonably accurate inferences be achieved with even less knowledge? What we call the "minimalist" algorithm needs neither information about the rank ordering of cue validities nor the discrimination history of the cues. In its ignorance, the algorithm picks cues in a random order. The algorithm differs from the take-the-best algorithm in Step 2, which is now reformulated as Step 2″:

Step 2″: Random Search

For the two objects, retrieve the cue values of a randomly chosen cue.

The minimalist algorithm does not necessarily speed up search, but it tries to get by with even less knowledge than any other algorithm.

Results

Speed

How fast are the fast algorithms? The simulations showed that for each of the two variant algorithms, the relationship between amount of knowledge and the number of cue values looked up had the same form as for the take-the-best algorithm (Figure 2-5). That is, unlike the integration algorithms, the curves are concave and

the number of cues searched for is maximal when knowledge of cue values is lowest. The average number of cue values looked up was lowest for the take-the-last algorithm (5.29) followed by the minimalist algorithm (5.64) and the take-the-best algorithm (5.91). As knowledge becomes more and more limited (on both dimensions: recognition and cue values known), the difference in speed becomes smaller and smaller. The reason why the minimalist algorithm looks up fewer cue values than the take-the-best algorithm is that cue validities and cue discrimination rates are negatively correlated (Table 2-1); therefore, randomly chosen cues tend to have larger discrimination rates than cues chosen by cue validity.

Accuracy

What is the price to be paid for speeding up search or reducing the knowledge of cue orderings and discrimination histories to nothing? We tested the performance of the two algorithms on the same environment as all other algorithms. Figure 2-7 shows the proportion of correct inferences that the minimalist algorithm achieved. For comparison, the performance of the take-the-best algorithm with 100% of cue values known is indicated by a dotted line. Note that the minimalist algorithm performed surprisingly well. The maximum difference appeared when knowledge was complete and all cities were recognized. In these circumstances, the minimalist algorithm did about 4 percentage points worse than the take-the-best algorithm. On average, the proportion of correct inferences was only 1.1 percentage points less than the best algorithms in the competition (Table 2-2).

The performance of the take-the-last algorithm is similar to Figure 2-7, and the average number of correct inferences is shown in Table 2-2. The take-the-last algorithm was faster but scored slightly less than the minimalist algorithm. The take-the-last algorithm has an interesting ability, which fooled us in an earlier series of tests, where we used a systematic (as opposed to a random) method for presenting the test pairs, starting with the largest city and pairing it with all others, and so on. An integration algorithm such as multiple regression cannot "find

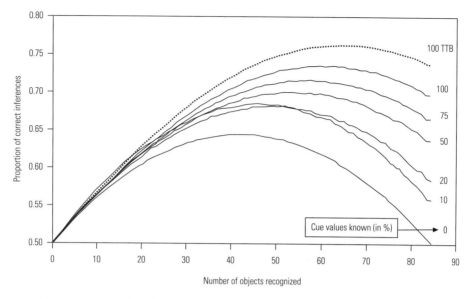

Figure 2-7. Performance of the minimalist algorithm. For comparison, the performance of the take-the-best algorithm (TTB) is shown as a dotted line, for the case in which 100% of cue values are known.

out" that it is being tested in this systematic way, and its inferences are accordingly independent of the sequence of presentation. However, the take-the-last algorithm found out and won this first round of the competition, outperforming the other competitors by some 10 percentage points. How did it exploit systematic testing? Recall that it tries, first, the cue that discriminated the last time. If this cue does not discriminate, it proceeds with the cue that discriminated the time before, and so on. In doing so, when testing is systematic in the way described, it tends to find, for each city that is being paired with all smaller ones, the group of cues for which the larger city has a positive value. Trying these cues first increases the chances of finding a discriminating cue that points in the right direction (toward the larger city). We learned our lesson and reran the whole competition with randomly ordered pairs of cities.

DISCUSSION

The competition showed a surprising result: The take-the-best algorithm drew as many correct inferences about unknown features of a real-world environment as any of the integration algorithms, and more than some of them. Two further simplifications of the algorithm—the take-the-last algorithm (replacing knowledge about the rank orders of cue validities by a memory of the discrimination history of cues) and the minimalist algorithm (dispensing with both) showed a comparatively small loss in correct inferences, and only when knowledge about cue values was high.

To the best of our knowledge, this is the first inference competition between satisficing and "rational" algorithms in a real-world environment. The result is of importance for encouraging research that focuses on the power of simple psychological mechanisms, that is, on the design and testing of satisficing algorithms. The result is also of importance as an existence proof that cognitive algorithms capable of successful performance in a real-world environment do not need to satisfy the classical norms of rational inference. The classical norms may be sufficient but are not necessary for good inference in real environments.

Cognitive Algorithms That Satisfice

In this section, we discuss the fundamental psychological mechanism postulated by the PMM family of algorithms: one-reason decision making. We discuss how this mechanism exploits the structure of environments in making fast inferences that differ from those arising from standard models of rational reasoning.

One-Reason Decision Making

What we call *one-reason decision making* is a specific form of satisficing. The inference, or decision, is based on a single, good reason. There is no compensation between cues. One-reason decision making is probably the most challenging feature of the PMM family of algorithms. As we mentioned before, it is a design feature of an algorithm that is not present in those models that depict human inference as an optimal integration of all information available (implying that all information has been looked up in the first place), including linear multiple regression and nonlinear neural networks. One-reason decision making means that each choice is based exclusively on one reason (i.e., cue), but this reason may be different from decision to decision. This allows for highly context-sensitive modeling of choice. One-reason decision making is not compensatory. Compensation is, after all, the cornerstone of classical rationality, assuming that all commodities can be compared and everything has its price. Compensation assumes commensurability. However, human minds do not trade everything; some things are supposed to be without a price (Elster, 1979). For instance, if a person must choose between two actions that might help him or her get out of deep financial trouble, and one involves killing someone, then no amount of money or other benefits might compensate for the prospect of bloody hands. He or she takes the action that does not involve killing a person, whatever other differences exist between the two options. More generally, hierarchies of ethical and moral values are often noncompensatory: True friendship, military honors, and doctorates are supposed to be without a price.

Noncompensatory inference algorithms—such as lexicographic, conjunctive, and disjunctive rules—have been discussed in the literature, and some empirical evidence has been reported (e.g. Einhorn, 1970; Fishburn, 1988). The closest relative to the PMM family of satisficing algorithms is the lexicographic rule. The largest evidence for lexicographic processes seems to come from studies on decision under risk (for a recent summary, see Lopes, 1995). However, despite empirical evidence, noncompensatory lexicographic algorithms have often been dismissed at face value because they violate the tenets of classical rationality (Keeney & Raiffa, 1993; Lovie & Lovie, 1986). The PMM family is both more general and more specific than the lexicographic rule. It is more general because only the take-the-best algorithm uses a lexicographic procedure in which cues are ordered according to their validity, whereas the variant algorithms do not. It is more specific, because several other psychological principles are integrated with the lexicographic rule in the take-the-best algorithm, such as the recognition principle and the rules for confidence judgment (which are not dealt with in this article; see Gigerenzer et al., 1991).

Serious models that comprise noncompensatory inferences are hard to find. One of the few examples is in Breiman, Friedman, Olshen, and Stone (1984), who reported a simple, noncompensatory algorithm with only three binary, ordered cues, which classified heart attack patients into high- and low-risk groups and was more accurate than standard statistical classification methods that used up to 19 variables. The practical relevance of this noncompensatory classification algorithm is obvious: In the emergency room, the physician can quickly obtain the measures on one, two, or three variables and does not need to perform any computations because there is no integration. This group of statisticians constructed satisficing algorithms that approach the task of classification (and estimation) much like the take-the-best algorithm handles two-alternative choice. Relevance theory (Sperber, Cara, & Girotto, 1995) postulates that people generate consequences from rules according to accessibility and stop this process when expectations of relevance are met. Although relevance theory has not been as formalized, we see its stopping rule as parallel to that of the take-the-best algorithm. Finally, optimality theory (Legendre, Raymond, & Smolensky, 1993; Prince & Smolensky, 1991) proposes that hierarchical noncompensation explains how the grammar of a language determines which structural description of an input best satisfies well-formedness constraints. Optimality theory (which is actually a satisficing theory) applies the same inferential principles as PMM theory to phonology and morphology.

Intransitivity

Transitivity is a cornerstone of classical rationality. It is one of the few tenets that the Anglo-American school of Ramsey and Savage shares with the competing Franco-European school of Allais (Fishburn, 1991). If we prefer *a* to *b* and *b* to *c*, then we should also prefer *a* to *c*. The linear algorithms in our competition always produce transitive inferences (except for ties, where the algorithm randomly guessed), and city populations are, in fact, transitive. The PMM family of algorithms includes algorithms that do not violate transitivity (such as the take-the-best algorithm), and others that do (e.g., the minimalist algorithm). The minimalist algorithm randomly selects a cue on which to base the inference; therefore, intransitivities can result. Table 2-2 shows that in spite of these intransitivities, overall performance of the algorithm is only about 1 percentage point lower than that of the best transitive algorithms and a few percentage points better than some transitive algorithms.

An organism that used the take-the-best algorithm with a stricter discrimination rule (actually, the original version found in Gigerenzer et al., 1991) could also be forced into making intransitive inferences. The stricter discrimination rule is that search is only terminated when one positive and one negative cue value (but not one positive and one unknown cue value) are encountered. Figure 2-8 illustrates a state of knowledge in which this stricter discrimination rule gives the result that *a* dominates *b*, *b* dominates *c*, and *c* dominates *a*.[7]

Biological systems, for instance, can exhibit systematic intransitivities based on incommensurability between two systems on one dimension (Gilpin, 1975; Lewontin, 1968). Imagine three species: *a, b,* and *c*. Species *a* inhabits both water and land; species *b* inhabits both water and air. Therefore, the two only compete in water,

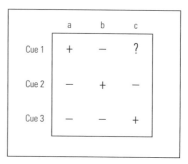

Figure 2-8. Limited knowledge and a stricter discrimination rule can produce intransitive inferences.

where species *a* defeats species *b*. Species *c* inhabits land and air, so it only competes with *b* in the air, where it is defeated by *b*. Finally, when *a* and *c* meet, it is only on land, and here, *c* is in its element and defeats *a*. A linear model that estimates some value for the combative strength of each species independently of the species with which it is competing would fail to capture this nontransitive cycle.

Cue Redundancy and Performance

Einhorn and Hogarth (1975) suggested that unit-weight models can be expected to perform approximately as well as proper linear models when (a) R^2 from the regression model is in the moderate or low range (around .5 or smaller) and (b) predictors (cues) are correlated. Are these two criteria necessary, sufficient, or both to explain the performance of the take-the-best algorithm? The take-the-best algorithm and its variants certainly can exploit cue redundancy: If cues are highly correlated, one cue can do the job.

We have already seen that in the present environment, $R^2 = .87$, which is in the high rather than the moderate or low range. As mentioned earlier, the pairwise correlations between the nine ecological cues ranged between −.25 and .54, with an absolute average value of .19. Thus, despite a high R^2 and only moderate-to-small correlation between cues, the satisficing algorithms performed quite successfully. Their excellent performance in the competition can be explained only partially by cue redundancy, because the cues were only moderately correlated. High cue redundancy, thus, does seem sufficient but is not necessary for the successful performance of the satisficing algorithms.

A New Perspective on the Lens Model

Ecological theorists such as Brunswik (1955) emphasized that the cognitive system is designed to find many pathways to the world, substituting missing cues by whatever cues happen to be available. Brunswik labeled this ability *vicarious functioning*, in which he saw the most fundamental principle of a science of perception and cognition. His proposal to model this adaptive process by linear multiple regression has inspired a long tradition of neo-Brunswikian research (B. Brehmer, 1994; Hammond, 1990), although the empirical evidence for mental multiple regression is still controversial (e.g., A. Brehmer & B. Brehmer, 1988). However, vicarious functioning need not be equated with linear regression. The PMM family of algorithms provides an alternative, nonadditive model of vicarious functioning, in which cue substitution operates without integration. This gives a new perspective of Brunswik's lens model. In a one-reason decision making lens, the first discriminating cue that passes through inhibits any other rays passing through and determines judgment. Noncompensatory vicarious functioning is consistent with some of Brunswik's original examples, such as the substitution of behaviors in Hull's habit–family hierarchy, and the alternative manifestation of symptoms according to the psychoanalytic writings of Frenkel-Brunswik (see Gigerenzer & Murray, 1987, chap. 3).

It has been reported sometimes that teachers, physicians, and other professionals claim that they use seven or so criteria to make judgments (e.g., when grading papers or making a differential diagnosis) but that experimental tests showed that they in fact often used only one criterion (Shepard, 1967). At first glance, this seems to indicate that those professionals make outrageous claims. But it need not be. If experts' vicarious functioning works according to the PMM algorithms, then they are correct in saying that they use many predictors, but the decision is made by only one at any time.

Can Reasoning Be Rational and Psychological?

At the beginning of this article, we pointed out the common opposition between the rational and the psychological, which emerged in the nineteenth century after the breakdown of the classical interpretation of probability (Gigerenzer et al., 1989). Since then, rational inference is commonly reduced to logic and probability theory, and psychological explanations are called on when things go wrong. This division of labor is, in a nutshell, the basis on which much of the current research on judgment under uncertainty is built. As one economist from the Massachusetts Institute of Technology put it, "either reasoning is rational *or* it's psychological" (Gigerenzer, 1994). Can reasoning not be both rational and psychological?

We believe that after 40 years of toying with the notion of bounded rationality, it is time to overcome the opposition between the rational and the psychological and to reunite the two. The PMM family of cognitive algorithms provides precise models that attempt to do so. They differ from the Enlightenment's unified view of the rational and psychological, in that they focus on simple psychological mechanisms that operate under constraints of limited time and knowledge and are supported by empirical evidence. The single most important result in this article is that simple psychological mechanisms can yield about as many (or more) correct inferences in less time than standard statistical linear models that embody classical properties of rational inference. The demonstration that a fast-and-frugal satisficing algorithm won the competition defeats the widespread view that only "rational" algorithms can be accurate. Models of inference do not have to forsake accuracy for simplicity. The mind can have it both ways.

ACKNOWLEDGMENTS

This research was funded by National Science Foundation Grant SBR-9320797/GG. We are deeply grateful to the many people who have contributed to this article, including Hal Arkes, Leda Cosmides, Jean Czerlinski, Lorraine Daston, Ken Hammond,

Reid Hastie, Wolfgang Hell, Ralph Hertwig, Ulrich Hoffrage, Albert Madansky, Laura Martignon, Geoffrey Miller, Silvia Papai, John Payne, Terry Regier, Werner Schubö, Peter Sedlmeier, Herbert Simon, Stephen Stigler, Gerhard Strube, Zeno Swijtink, John Tooby, William Wimsatt, and Werner Wittmann.

NOTES

1. Also, we now use the term *discrimination rule* instead of *activation rule*.

2. For instance, if $N = 2$ and one cue value is positive and the other negative ($x_i = y_i = .5$), $d_i = 1.0$. If N increases, with x_i and y_i held constant, then d_i decreases and converges to $2x_iy_i$.

3. There are various other measures of redundancy besides pairwise correlation. The important point is that whatever measure of redundancy one uses, the resultant value does not have the same meaning for all algorithms. For instance, all that counts for the take-the-best algorithm is what proportion of correct inferences the second cue adds to the first in the cases where the first cue does not discriminate, how much the third cue adds to the first two in the cases where they do not discriminate, and so on. If a cue discriminates, search is terminated, and the degree of redundancy in the cues that were not included in the search is irrelevant. Integration algorithms, in contrast, integrate all information and, thus, always work with the total redundancy in the environment (or knowledge base). For instance, when deciding among objects *a, b, c,* and *d* in Figure 2-1, the cue values of Cues 3, 4, and 5 do not matter from the point of view of the take-the-best algorithm (because search is terminated before reaching Cue 3). However, the values of Cues 3, 4, and 5 affect the redundancy of the ecological system, from the point of view of all integration algorithms. The lesson is that the degree of redundancy in an environment depends on the kind of algorithm that operates on the environment. One needs to be cautious in interpreting measures of redundancy without reference to an algorithm.

4. We cannot claim that these integration algorithms are the best ones, nor can we know a priori which small variations will succeed in our bumpy real-world environment. An example: During the proof stage of this article we learned that regressing on the ranks of the cities does slightly better than regressing on the city populations. The key issue is what are the structures of environments in which particular algorithms and variants thrive.

5. If no single cue value was known for a given cue, the missing values were substituted by .5. This value was chosen because it is the midpoint of 0 and 1, which are the values used to stand for negative and positive cue values, respectively.

6. The proof for this is as follows. The tallying score t for a given object is the number $n+$ of positive cue values, as defined above. The score u for the unit weight linear model is $n^+ - n^-$, where n^- is the number of negative cue values. Under complete knowledge, $n = n^+ + n^-$, where n is the number of cues. Thus, $t = n^+$, and $u = n^+ - n^-$. Because $n^- = n - n^+$, by substitution into the formula for u, we find that $u = n^+ - (n - n^+) = 2t - n$.

7. Note that missing knowledge is necessary for intransitivities to occur. If all cue values are known, no intransitive inferences can possibly result. The algorithm with the stricter discrimination rule allows precise predictions about the occurrence of intransitivities over the course of knowledge acquisition. For instance, imagine a person whose knowledge is described by Figure 2-8, except that she does not know the value of Cue 2 for object *c*. This person would make no intransitive judgments comparing objects *a, b,* and *c.* If she were to learn that object *c* had a negative cue value for Cue 2, she would produce an intransitive judgment. If she learned one piece more, namely, the value of Cue 1 for object *c,* then she would no longer produce an intransitive judgment. The prediction is that transitive judgments should turn into intransitive ones and back, during learning. Thus, intransitivities do not simply depend on the amount of limited knowledge but also on what knowledge is missing.

APPENDIX

The Environment

City	Population	Soccer Team	State Capital	Former East Germany	Industrial Belt	License Plate	Intercity Train Line	Exposition site	National Capital	University
Berlin	3,433,695	−	+	−	−	+	+	+	+	+
Hamburg	1,652,363	+	+	−	−	−	+	+	−	+
Munich	1,229,026	+	+	−	−	+	+	+	−	+
Cologne	953,551	+	−	−	−	+	+	+	−	+
Frankfurt	644,865	+	−	−	+	+	+	+	−	+
Essen	626,973	−	−	−	+	+	+	−	−	+
Dortmund	599,055	+	−	−	+	−	+	−	−	+
Stuttgart	579,988	+	+	−	−	+	+	−	−	+
Düsseldorf	575,794	−	+	−	−	+	+	−	−	+
Bremen	551,219	+	+	−	−	−	+	−	−	+
Duisburg	535,447	−	−	−	+	−	+	−	−	+
Hannover	513,010	−	+	+	−	+	+	−	−	+
Leipzig	511,079	−	−	+	−	+	+	+	−	+
Nuremberg	493,692	+	−	−	−	+	+	+	−	+
Dresden	490,571	+	−*	+	−	−	+	−	−	+
Bochum	396,486	+	−	−	+	−	+	−	−	+
Wuppertal	383,660	−	−	−	+	+	+	−	−	+
Bielefeld	319,037	−	−	−	−	−	+	−	−	+
Mannheim	310,411	−	−	−	−	+	+	−	−	+
Halle	310,234	−	−	+	−	−	−	−	−	−
Chemnitz	294,244	−	−	+	−	+	+	−	−	−
Gelsenkirchen	293,714	+	−	−	+	−	+	−	−	−
Bonn	292,234	−	−	−	−	−	+	−	−	+
Magdeburg	278,807	−	+	+	−	−	+	−	−	−
Karlsruhe	275,061	+	−	−	−	+	+	−	−	−
Wiesbaden	260,301	−	+	−	−	−	+	−	−	−
Münster	259,438	−	−	−	−	−	+	−	−	+
Mönchengladbach	259,436	+	−	−	−	−	−	−	−	−

(continued)

City	Population	Soccer Team	State Capital	Former East Germany	Industrial Belt	License Plate	Intercity Train Line	Exposition site	National Capital	University
Braunschweig	258,833	–	–	–	–	–	+	–	–	+
Augsburg	256,877	–	–	–	–	+	+	–	–	+
Rostock	248,088	–	–	+	–	–	+	–	–	–
Kiel	245,567	–	+	–	–	–	+	–	–	+
Krefeld	244,020	–*	–	–	–	–	–	–	–	–
Aachen	241,961	–	–	–	–	–	+	–	–	+
Oberhausen	223,840	–	–	–	+	–	+	–	–	–
Lübeck	214,758	–	–	–	–	–	+	–	–	–
Hagen	214,449	–	–	–	+	–	+	–	–	–
Erfurt	208,989	–	+	+	–	–	+	–	–	–
Kassel	194,268	–	–	–	–	–	+	–	–	+
Saarbrücken	191,694	+	+	–	–	–	+	+	–	+
Freiburg	191,029	–	–	–	–	–	+	–	–	+
Hamm	179,639	–	–	–	–	–	+	–	–	–
Mainz	179,486	–	+	–	+	–	+	–	–	+
Herne	178,132	–	–	–	+	–	–	–	–	–
Mülheim	177,681	–	–	–	+	–	–	–	–	–
Solingen	165,401	–	–	–	+	–	+	–	–	–
Osnabrück	163,168	–	–	–	+	–	+	–	–	–
Ludwigshafen	162,173	–	–	–	–	–	+	–	–	–
Leverkusen	160,919	+	–	–	–	–	–	–	–	–
Neuss	147,019	–	–	–	–	–	–	–	–	–
Oldenburg	143,131	–	–	–	–	–	+	–	–	+
Potsdam	139,794	–	+	+	–	+	+	–	–	–
Darmstadt	138,920	–	–	–	–	–	+	–	–	+
Heidelberg	136,796	–	–	–	–	–	+	–	–	+
Bremerhaven	130,446	–	–	–	–	–	+	–	–	–

City	Population									
Gera	129,037	−	+	+	−	+	+	−	−	−
Wolfsburg	128,510	−	−	+	−	−	−	−	−	−
Würzburg	127,777	−	−	−	−	+	+	+	−	+
Schwerin	127,447	−	+	+	+	+	+	−	−	+
Cottbus	125,891	−	+	+	−	−	−	−	−	−
Recklinghausen	125,060	−	−	−	+	+	−	−	−	−
Remscheid	123,155	−	−	+	−	+	−	−	−	−
Göttingen	121,831	−	−	−	−	+	−	−	−	+
Regensburg	121,691	−	−	+	−	+	−	−	−	+
Paderborn	120,680	−	−	+	−	−	−	−	−	+
Bottrop	118,936	−	−	−	−	−	−	−	−	−
Heilbronn	115,843	−	−	−	+	−	−	−	−	+
Offenbach	114,992	−	−	−	−	−	−	+	−	−
Zwickau	114,636	−	+	−	+	+	−	−	−	−
Salzgitter	114,355	−	−	−	−	+	−	−	−	−
Pforzheim	112,944	−	−	−	−	−	−	−	−	−
Ulm	110,529	−	−	−	−	+	+	−	−	+
Siegen	109,174	−	−	+	−	+	+	−	−	+
Koblenz	108,733	−	+	+	−	−	+	−	−	+
Jena	105,518	−	−	−	−	+	+	+	−	+
Ingolstadt	105,489	−	−	+	−	−	−	−	−	−
Witten	105,403	−	−	+	+	+	−	−	−	−
Hildesheim	105,291	−	−	+	−	+	+	−	−	+
Moers	104,595	−	−	−	+	−	−	−	−	−
Bergisch Gladbach	104,037	−	−	+	−	−	−	−	−	−
Reutlingen	103,687	−	−	−	−	−	−	−	−	−
Fürth	103,362	−	−	−	−	−	−	−	−	−
Erlangen	102,440	−	−	+	−	+	+	−	−	+

Note. City populations were taken from *Fischer Welt Almanach* (1993).
* The two starred minus values are, in reality, plus values. Because of transcription errors, we ran all simulations with these two minus values. These do not affect the rank order of cue validities, should not have any noticeable effect on the results, and are irrelevant for our theoretical argument.

Introduction to Chapter 3

Models of Ecological Rationality: The Recognition Heuristic

This article by Dan Goldstein and Gerd Gigerenzer turned to Gigerenzer and Goldstein's (1996) *recognition principle*, formulated as a building block of take-the-best, and investigated it as a stand-alone heuristic: the *recognition heuristic*. In reality, the recognition heuristic was not discovered in such a straightforward way: Serendipity assisted at its birth. Gigerenzer, Hoffrage, and Kleinbölting (1991, Prediction 4) had deduced a situation in which the "hard-easy" effect would disappear. After the article was published, Ulrich Hoffrage set out to test the prediction, for which one needed two sets of questions—one hard and one easy. He chose questions concerning the populations of American cities and German cities, which are hard and easy, respectively, for German students—or so everyone thought. Surprisingly, German students scored slightly higher when tested on American cities than on German ones. This result destroyed the experiment. How could people obtain more correct answers on a topic about which they knew less? The search for an explanation left Hoffrage and Gigerenzer sleepless for days. It took a sharp colleague, Anton Kühberger, to point out that the explanation was tucked away in the authors' own article, which mentioned recognition as a probabilistic cue. If you are semi-ignorant and have not heard of one city but have heard of the other, you will likely infer that the recognized city has the larger population. Because the authors had sampled all cities representatively, the recognition heuristic worked well in this environment. Consider Detroit versus Milwaukee. Many Germans had heard of Detroit (the larger city), but not of Milwaukee, and so they got it right. But with German cities, such as Hannover versus Bielefeld, this heuristic could no longer be used, because the German students recognized both—they knew too much. The recognition heuristic piggybacks on the evolved capacity of recognition memory; otherwise, it could not do its job.

This article used the cross-fertilizing "methodological trinity" of mathematical analysis, computer simulation, and experimentation. The mathematical analysis proves conditions under which less-is-more effects can be observed and determines their exact size. Whereas analysis rests on simplifying assumptions, computer simulations with actual recognition data test to what degree the analytic results can be replicated in a noisy world. Finally, experimentation tests to what degree people's inferences can be modeled by the recognition heuristic and whether less-is-more effects exist in practice.

Although vague labels such as "availability" had remained largely unquestioned for decades, the precise, testable model of the recognition heuristic led to a heated debate (e.g., Bröder & Eichler, 2006; Newell & Shanks, 2004; Pohl, 2006; Richter & Späth, 2006). Some have apparently mistaken the hypothesis to be that people rely on recognition indiscriminately, contrary to the concept of the adaptive toolbox. Most elementary, the recognition heuristic—like Bayes' rule—is a model of inference, not of situations where the answer is already known. For instance, when Oppenheimer (2003) asked students whether a well-known tiny town nearby was larger than an unknown and nonexistent city, he observed that most bet on the unknown city. He concluded from this and similar questions that there was little evidence for the recognition heuristic. Yet Gigerenzer et al. (1991) had clearly distinguished situations in which people have specific knowledge about target variables (local mental models) from those where heuristics are useful. Similarly, for the heuristic to be useful, the recognition validity needs to be larger than chance. With cities that do not exist, the recognition validity cannot be computed. At the same time, critical articles such as Oppenheimer's have helped to carve out the real questions: What are the triggering factors for the recognition heuristic? When is it likely that people resort to other strategies? And when they do, to which? These issues are discussed in Chapters 23 and 24.

In May 2009, the BBC, intrigued by the idea of less being more, decided to replicate the effect on their Radio 4 "More or Less" program. Listeners in New York and London were asked the Detroit–Milwaukee question. In his dissertation, Dan Goldstein had found that about 60% of American students answered correctly, compared to 90% of a corresponding class of German students. The BBC is not known for running tightly controlled studies, and so we were somewhat uneasy about what the outcome would be. Sixty-five percent of the New York listeners got the answer right, whereas in London, 82% did. This was as close as one can hope for an informal replication.

CHAPTER 3

Models of Ecological Rationality: The Recognition Heuristic

Daniel G. Goldstein and Gerd Gigerenzer

Abstract: One view of heuristics is that they are imperfect versions of optimal statistical procedures considered too complicated for ordinary minds to carry out. In contrast, the authors consider heuristics to be adaptive strategies that evolved in tandem with fundamental psychological mechanisms. The recognition heuristic, arguably the most frugal of all heuristics, makes inferences from patterns of missing knowledge. This heuristic exploits a fundamental adaptation of many organisms: the vast, sensitive, and reliable capacity for recognition. The authors specify the conditions under which the recognition heuristic is successful and when it leads to the counterintuitive less-is-more effect in which less knowledge is better than more for making accurate inferences.

In the statistical analysis of experimental data, missing data are an annoyance. However, outside of experimental designs—when data are obtained by natural sampling rather than systematic sampling (Gigerenzer & Hoffrage, 1995)—missing knowledge can be used to make intelligent inferences. We asked about a dozen Americans and Germans, "Which city has a larger population: San Diego or San Antonio?" Approximately two thirds of the Americans correctly responded that San Diego is larger. How many correct inferences did the more ignorant German group achieve? Despite a considerable lack of knowledge, 100% of the Germans answered the question correctly. A similar surprising outcome was obtained when 50 Turkish students and 54 British students made forecasts for all 32 English F. A. Cup third round

soccer matches (Ayton & Önkal, 1997). The Turkish participants had very little knowledge about (or interest in) English soccer teams, whereas the British participants knew quite a bit. Nevertheless, the Turkish forecasters were nearly as accurate as the English ones (63% vs. 66% correct).

At first blush, these results seem to be in error. How could more knowledge be no better—or worse—than significantly less knowledge? A look at what the less knowledgeable groups knew may hold the answer. All of the Germans tested had heard of San Diego; however, about half of them did not recognize San Antonio. All made the inference that San Diego is larger. Similarly, the Turkish students recognized some of the English soccer teams (or the cities that often make up part of English soccer team names) but not others. Among the pairs of soccer teams in which they rated one team as completely unfamiliar and the other as familiar to some degree, they chose the more familiar team in 627 of 662 cases (95%). In both these demonstrations, people used the fact that they did not recognize something as the basis for their predictions, and it turned out to serve them well.

The strategies of the German and Turkish participants can be modeled by what we call the *recognition heuristic.* The task to which the heuristic is suited is selecting a subset of objects that is valued highest on some criterion. An example would be to use corporate name recognition for selecting a subset of stocks from Standard and Poor's 500, with profit as the criterion (Borges, Goldstein, Ortmann, & Gigerenzer, 1999). In this article, as in the two preceding laboratory experiments, we focus on the case of selecting one object from two. This task is known as paired comparison or two-alternative forced choice; it is a stock-in-trade of experimental psychology and an elementary case to which many other tasks (such as multiple choice) are reducible.

The recognition heuristic is useful when there is a strong correlation—in either direction—between recognition and criterion. For simplicity, we assume that the correlation is positive. For two-alternative choice tasks, the heuristic can be stated as follows:

> *Recognition heuristic:* If one of two objects is recognized and the other is not, then infer that the recognized object has the higher value with respect to the criterion.

The recognition heuristic will not always apply, nor will it always make correct inferences. Note that the Americans and English in the experiments reported could not apply the recognition heuristic—they know too much. The recognition heuristic works exclusively in cases of limited knowledge, that is, when only some objects—not all—are recognized.

The effectiveness of the apparently simplistic recognition heuristic depends on its *ecological rationality:* its ability to exploit the structure of the information in natural environments. The heuristic is successful when ignorance, specifically a lack of recognition, is systematically rather than randomly distributed, that is, when it is strongly correlated with the criterion. (When this correlation is negative, the heuristic leads to the inference that the unrecognized object has the higher criterion value.)

The direction of the correlation between recognition and the criterion can be learned from experience, or it can be genetically coded. The latter seems to be the case with wild Norway rats. Galef (1987) exposed "observer" rats to neighbors that had recently eaten a novel diet. The observers learned to recognize the diet by smelling it on their neighbors' breath. A week later, the observers were fed this diet and another novel diet for the first time and became ill. (They were injected with a nauseant, but as far as they knew it could have been food poisoning.) When next presented with the two diets, the observer rats avoided the diet that they did not recognize from their neighbors' breath. Rats operate on the principle that other rats know what they are eating, and this helps them avoid poisons. According to another experiment (Galef, McQuoid, & Whiskin, 1990), this recognition mechanism works regardless of whether the neighbor rat is healthy or not when its breath is smelled. It may seem unusual that an animal would eat the food its sick neighbor had eaten; however, rats seem to follow recognition without taking further information (such as the health of the neighbor) into account. In this article, we investigate whether people follow the recognition heuristic in a similar noncompensatory way. If reasoning by recognition is a strategy common to humans, rats, and other organisms, there should be accommodations for it in the structure of memory. We explore this question next.

THE CAPACITY FOR RECOGNITION

As we wander through a stream of sights, sounds, tastes, odors, and tactile impressions, some novel and some previously experienced, we have little trouble telling the two apart. The mechanism for distinguishing between the novel and recognized seems to be specialized and robust. For instance, recognition memory often remains when other types of memory become impaired. Elderly people suffering memory loss (Craik & McDowd, 1987; Schonfield & Robertson, 1966) and patients suffering certain kinds of brain damage (Schacter & Tulving, 1994; Squire, Knowlton, &

Musen, 1993) have problems saying what they know about an object or even where they have encountered it. However, they often know (or can act in a way that proves) that they have encountered the object before. Such is the case with R. F. R., a 54-year-old policeman who developed such severe amnesia that he had great difficulty identifying people he knew, even his wife and mother. One might be tempted to say he had lost his capacity for recognition. Yet on a test in which he was shown pairs of photographs consisting of one famous and one nonfamous person, he could point to the famous persons as accurately as could a healthy control group (Warrington & McCarthy, 1988). His ability to distinguish between the unrecognized people (whom he had never seen before) and the recognized people (famous people he had seen in the media) remained intact. However, his ability to recall anything about the people he recognized was impaired. Laboratory research has demonstrated that memory for mere recognition encodes information even in divided-attention learning tasks that are too distracting to allow more substantial memories to be formed (Jacoby, Woloshyn, & Kelley, 1989). Because recognition continues to operate even under adverse circumstances, and it can be impaired independently from the rest of memory, we view it as a primordial psychological mechanism (for cases involving a selective loss of recognition, see Delbecq-Derousné, Beauvois, & Shallice, 1990).

Because the word *recognition* is used in different ways by different researchers, it needs to be precisely defined. Consider three levels of knowledge that an organism may have. First, one may have no knowledge of an object or event because one has never heard, smelled, touched, tasted, or seen it before. Such objects we call "unrecognized." Second are objects one has experienced before but of which one has absolutely no further knowledge beyond this initial sense of recognition. These we will call "merely recognized." (The Scottish verb "to tartle" gives a name to this state of memory; people tartle when they recognize another's face but cannot remember anything else about him or her.) The third

level of knowledge comprises mere recognition plus further knowledge; not only does one recognize the object, but one can provide all sorts of additional information about it, such as where one encountered it, what it is called, and so on. Thus, with the term *recognition*, we divide the world into the novel and the previously experienced.

This use of the term needs to be distinguished from another use, which might be characterized as "recognition of items familiar from a list" (e.g., Brown, Lewis, & Monk, 1977). Here the behavior of interest is a person's ability to verify whether a common thing (usually a word such as *house*) had been presented in a previous experimental session. Studies dealing with this meaning of recognition often fail to touch on the distinction between the novel and the previously experienced because the stimuli—mostly numbers or everyday words—are certainly not novel to the participant before the experiment. Experiments that use nonwords or never-seen-before photographs capture the distinction of interest here: that between the truly novel and the previously experienced.

Recognition also needs to be distinguished from notions such as availability (Tversky & Kahneman, 1974) and familiarity (Griggs & Cox, 1982). The availability heuristic is based on recall, not recognition. People recognize far more items than they can recall. Availability is a graded distinction among items in memory and is measured by the order or speed with which they come to mind or the number of instances of categories one can generate. Unlike availability, the recognition heuristic does not address comparisons between items in memory, but rather the difference between items in and out of memory (Goldstein, 1997). The term *familiarity* is typically used in the literature to denote the degree of knowledge (or amount of experience) a person has of a task or object. The recognition heuristic, in contrast, treats recognition as a binary, all-or-none distinction; further knowledge is irrelevant.

A number of studies demonstrate that recognition memory is vast, easily etched on, and remarkably retentive despite short presentation times. Shepard's (1967b) experiment with 612 pairs of novel photographs shown with unlimited presentation time resulted in participants correctly recognizing them with 99% accuracy. This impressive result was made to appear ordinary by Standing's experiments 6 years later. Standing (1973) increased the number of pictures (photographs and "striking" photographs selected for their vividness) to 1,000 and limited the time of presentation to 5 s. Two days later, he tested recognition memory with pairs of pictures in which one had been presented previously and one was novel. Participants were able to point to the previously presented picture 885 times of 1,000 with normal pictures and 940 times of 1,000 with "striking" pictures. Standing then outdid himself by a factor of 10. In perhaps the most extensive recognition memory test ever performed, he presented 10,000 normal pictures for 5 s each. Two days later participants correctly identified them in 8,300 of 10,000 pairs. When more and more pictures were presented, the retention percentage declined slightly, but the absolute number of pictures recognized increased.

Standing's participants must have felt they were making a fair number of guesses. Some research suggests that people may not rely on recognition-based inferences in situations in which they feel their memory is not reliable, such as when presentation times are short or when there are distractions at presentation (Strack & Bless, 1994). However, Standing's results, when adjusted by the usual guessing correction, come out well above chance. With respect to the performance with his "striking" pictures, Standing speculated, "If one million items could be presented under these conditions then 731,400 would be retained" (p. 210). Of course, presenting 1 million items is a feat no experimental psychologist is likely to try.

Recognition memory is expansive, sensitive, and reliable enough to serve in a multitude of inferential tasks. We now discuss how the accuracy of these recognition-based inferences relies not only on the soundness of memory but also on the relationship between recognition and the environment.

THEORY

Recognition and the Structure of the Environment

In this article, we investigate recognition as it concerns proper names. Proper name recognition is of particular interest because it constitutes a specialized domain in the cognitive system that can be impaired independently of other language skills (McKenna & Warrington, 1980; Semenza & Sgaramella, 1993; Semenza & Zettin, 1989). Because an individual's knowledge of geography comprises an incomplete set of proper names, it is ideal for recognition studies. In this article, we focus on two situations of limited knowledge: Americans' recognition of German city names and Germans' recognition of city names in the United States. The American students we have tested over the years recognized about one fifth of the 100 largest German cities, and the German students recognized about one half of the 100 largest U.S. cities. Another reason cities were used to study proper name recognition is because of the strong correlation between city name recognition and population.

It should be clear, however, that the recognition heuristic does not apply everywhere. The recognition heuristic is domain specific in that it works only in environments in which recognition is correlated with the criterion being predicted. Yet, in cases of inference, the criterion is not immediately accessible to the organism. How can correlations between recognition and inaccessible criteria arise? Figure 3-1 illustrates the ecological rationality of the recognition heuristic. There are "mediators" in the environment that have the dual property of reflecting (but not revealing) the criterion and being accessible to the senses. For example, a person may have no direct information about the endowments of universities, because this information is often confidential. However, the endowment of a university may be reflected in how often it is mentioned in the newspaper. The more often a name occurs in the newspaper, the more likely it is that a person will hear of this name. Because the newspaper serves as a mediator, a person can make

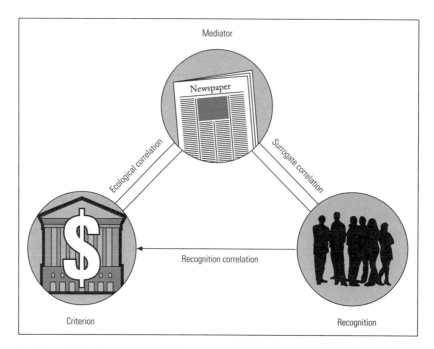

Figure 3-1. The ecological rationality of the recognition heuristic. An inaccessible criterion (e.g., the endowment of an institution) is reflected by a mediator variable (e. g., the number of times the institution is mentioned in the news), and the mediator influences the probability of recognition. The mind, in turn, uses recognition to infer the criterion.

an inference about the inaccessible endowment criterion. Three variables reflect the strength of association between the criterion, mediator, and recognition memory: the *ecological correlation,* the *surrogate correlation,* and the *recognition validity.*

The correlation between the criterion and the mediator is called the ecological correlation. In our example, the criterion is the endowment of a university and the mediator variable is the number of times the university is mentioned in the newspaper. The surrogate correlation is that between the mediator (a surrogate for the inaccessible criterion) and the contents of recognition memory, for instance, the number of mentions in the newspaper correlated against recognition of the names mentioned. Surrogate correlations can be measured against the recognition memory of one person (in which case the recognition data will be binary) or against collective recognition of a group, which we will examine later.

Figure 3-1 is reminiscent of Brunswik's lens model (e.g., Hammond, 1996). Recall that the lens model has two parts: environmental and judgmental. Figure 3-1 can be seen as an elaboration of the environmental part, in which recognition is a proximal cue for the criterion and the recognition validity corresponds to Brunswik's "ecological validity." In contrast to the standard lens model, the pathway from the criterion to recognition is modeled by the introduction of a mediator.

The single most important factor for determining the usefulness of the recognition heuristic is the strength of the relationship between the contents of recognition memory and the criterion. We define the recognition validity as the proportion of times a recognized object has a higher criterion value than an unrecognized object in a reference class. The recognition validity α is thus:

$$\alpha = R / (R + W),$$

where R is the number of correct (right) inferences the recognition heuristic would achieve, computed across all pairs in which one object is recognized and the other is not, and W is the number of incorrect (wrong) inferences under the same circumstances. The recognition validity is essential for computing the accuracy attainable through the recognition heuristic.

Accuracy of the Recognition Heuristic

How accurate is the recognition heuristic? What is the proportion of correct answers one can expect to achieve using the recognition heuristic on two-alternative choice tasks? Let us posit a reference class of N objects and a test whose questions are pairs of objects drawn randomly from the class. Each of the objects is either recognized by the test taker or unrecognized. The test score is the proportion of questions in which the test taker correctly identifies the larger of the two objects.

Consider that a pair of objects must be one of three types: both recognized, both unrecognized, or one recognized and one not. Supposing there are n recognized objects, there are $N - n$ unrecognized objects. This means there are $n(N - n)$ possible pairs in which one object is recognized and the other is not. Similarly, there are $(N - n)$ $(N - n - 1)/2$ pairs in which neither object is recognized. Both objects are recognized in $n(n-1)/2$ pairs. Dividing each of these terms by the total number of possible pairs, $N(N - 1)/2$, gives the proportion of each type of question in an exhaustive test of all possible pairs.

The proportion correct on an exhaustive test is calculated by multiplying the proportion of occurrence of each type of question by the probability of scoring a correct answer on questions of that type. The recognition validity α, it may be recalled, is the probability of scoring a correct answer when one object is recognized and the other is not. When neither object is recognized, a guess must be made, and the probability of a correct answer is 1/2. Finally, β is the knowledge validity, the probability of getting a correct answer when both objects are recognized. Combining terms in an exhaustive pairing of objects, the expected proportion of correct inferences, $f(n)$, is

$$f(n) = 2\left(\frac{n}{N}\right)\left(\frac{N-n}{N-1}\right)\alpha + \left(\frac{N-n}{N}\right)$$
$$\times \left(\frac{N-n-1}{N-1}\right)\frac{1}{2} + \left(\frac{n}{N}\right)\left(\frac{n-1}{N-1}\right)\beta. \tag{3-1}$$

Consider the three parts of the right side of the equation. The term on the left accounts for the correct inferences made by the recognition heuristic. The term in the middle represents the correct inferences resulting from guessing. The right-most term equals the proportion of correct inferences made when knowledge beyond recognition is used. Note that if $n = 0$, that is, no objects are recognized, then all questions will lead to guesses, and the proportion correct will be 1/2. If all objects are recognized ($n = N$), then the left-most two terms become zero and the proportion correct becomes β. The left-most term shows that the recognition heuristic comes into play most under "half ignorance," that is, when the number of recognized objects n equals the number of unrecognized objects $N - n$. (Note, however, that this does not imply that proportion correct will be maximized under these conditions.) Equation 3-1 specifies the proportion of correct inferences made by using the recognition heuristic whenever possible based on the recognition validity α, the knowledge validity β, and the degree of recognition (n compared with N). Next, we shall see how it leads to a curious state in which less recognition is better than more for making accurate inferences.

The Less-Is-More Effect

Equation 3-1 seems rather straightforward but has some counterintuitive implications. Consider the following thought experiment: Three Parisian sisters receive the bad news that they have to take a test on the 100 largest German cities at their lycée. The test will consist of randomly drawn pairs of cities, and the task will be to choose the more populous city. The youngest sister does not get out much; she has never heard of Germany (nor any of its cities) before.

The middle sister is interested in the conversations of grown-ups and often listens in at her parents' cocktail parties. She recognizes half of the 100 largest cities from what she has overheard in the family salon. The elder sister has been furiously studying for her baccalaureate and has heard of all of the 100 largest cities in Germany. The city names the middle sister has overheard belong to rather large cities. In fact, the 50 cities she recognizes are larger than the 50 cities she does not recognize in about 80% of all possible pairs (the recognition validity α is .8). The middle and elder sisters not only recognize the names of cities but also have some knowledge beyond recognition. When they recognize two cities in a pair, they have a 60% probability of correctly choosing the larger one; that is, the knowledge validity β is .6, whereas $\beta = .5$ would mean they have no useful further knowledge. Which of the three sisters will score highest on the test if they all rely on the recognition heuristic whenever they can? Equation 3-1 predicts their performance as shown in Figure 3-2.

The youngest sister can do nothing but guess on every question. The oldest sister relies on her knowledge (β) on every question and scores 60% correct. How well does the middle sister, who has half the knowledge of her older sister, do? Surprisingly, she scores the greatest proportion of correct inferences (nearly 68% correct, according to Equation 3-1). Why? She is the only one who can use the recognition heuristic. Furthermore, she can make the most of her ignorance because she happens to recognize half of the cities, and this allows her to use the recognition heuristic most often. The recognition heuristic leads to a paradoxical situation in which those who know more exhibit lower inferential accuracy than those who know less. We call such situations less-is-more effects. Figure 3-2 shows how less-is-more effects persist with other values of β.

Forecasting Less-Is-More Effects

In what situations will less-is-more effects arise? We first specify a sufficient condition in

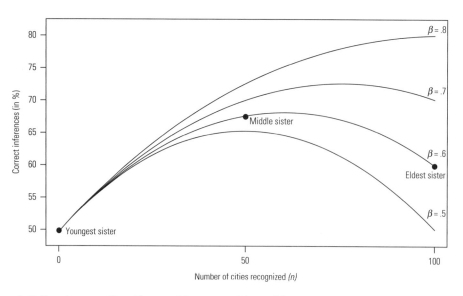

Figure 3-2. Less-is-more effects illustrated for a recognition validity $\alpha = .8$. When the knowledge validity β is .5, .6, or .7, a less-is-more effect occurs. A β of .5 means that there is no knowledge beyond recognition. When the knowledge validity equals the recognition validity (.8), no less-is-more effect is observed; that is, performance increased with increasing n. The performance of the three sisters is indicated by the three points on the curve for $\beta = .6$. The curve for $\beta = .6$ has its maximum slightly to the right of the middle sister's score.

idealized environments and then use computer simulation in a real-world environment.

Equation 3-1 models the accuracy resulting from using the recognition heuristic. The less-is-more effect can be defined as the state of affairs in which the value of $f(n)$ in Equation 3-1 at some integer from 0 to $N-1$ (inclusive) is greater than the value at N. For this to happen, the maximum value of $\phi(n)$, the continuous parabola connecting the discrete points, must occur closer to one of the points 0 to $N-1$ than to point N, that is, between 0 and $N-1/2$. Solving the equation $\phi'(n) = 0$, when $\phi'(n)$ is simply the first derivative of $\phi(n)$, one locates the maximum of $\phi(n)$ at

$$\frac{-\left(1 - 2\beta - 2N + 4\alpha N\right)}{2\left(1 - 4\alpha + 2\beta\right)} \qquad (3\text{-}2)$$

A simple calculation shows that when $\alpha = \beta$, the location of the maximum of $\phi(n)$ is equal to $N - 1/2$, exactly between the $N-1$st and Nth points. Either increasing α or decreasing β from this point causes the fraction (Equation 3-2), and thus the location of the maximum, to decrease. From this, we can conclude that there will be a less-is-more effect whenever $\alpha > \beta$, that is, whenever the accuracy of mere recognition is greater than the accuracy achievable when both objects are recognized.

This result allows us to make a general claim. Under the assumption that α and β are constant, any strategy for solving multiple-choice problems that follows the recognition heuristic will yield a less-is-more effect if the probability α of getting a correct answer merely on the basis of recognition is greater than the probability β of getting a correct answer using more information.

In this derivation, we have supposed that the recognition validity α and knowledge validity β remain constant as the number of cities recognized, n, varies. Figure 3-2 shows many individuals with different knowledge states but with fixed α and β. In the real world, the recognition and knowledge validities usually vary when one individual learns to recognize more and more objects from experience.[1] Will a less-is-more effect arise in a learning situation in which α and β vary with n, or is the effect limited to situations in which these are constant?

THE LESS-IS-MORE EFFECT: A COMPUTER SIMULATION

To test whether a less-is-more effect might arise over a natural course of learning, we ran a computer simulation that learned the names of German cities in the order a typical American might come to recognize them. How can one estimate this order? We made the simplifying assumption that the most well-known city would probably be learned about first, then the second-most well-known city, and so on. We judged how well-known cities are by surveying 67 University of Chicago students and asking them to select the cities they recognized from a list. These cities were then ranked by the number of people who recognized them.[2] Munich turned out to be the most well-known city, so our computer program learned to recognize it first. Recognizing only Munich, the program was then given an exhaustive test consisting of all pairs of cities with more than 100,000 inhabitants (the same 83 cities used in Gigerenzer & Goldstein, 1996). Next, it learned to recognize Berlin (the second-most well-known city) to make a total of two recognized cities and was tested on all possible pairs again. It learned and was tested on city after city until it recognized all of them. In one condition, the program learned only the names of cities and made all inferences by the recognition heuristic alone. This result is shown as the bottom curve in Figure 3-3 labeled *No Cues*. When all objects were unrecognized or all were recognized, performance was at a chance level. Over the course of learning, an inverse U shape, like that in Figure 3-2, reappears. Here the less-is-more curve is jagged because, as mentioned, the recognition validity was not set to be a constant but was allowed to vary freely as more cities were recognized.

Would the less-is-more effect disappear if the program learned not just the names of cities but information useful for predicting city populations as well? In other words, if there is recall of relevant facts, will this override the less-is-more effect and, therefore, the recognition heuristic?

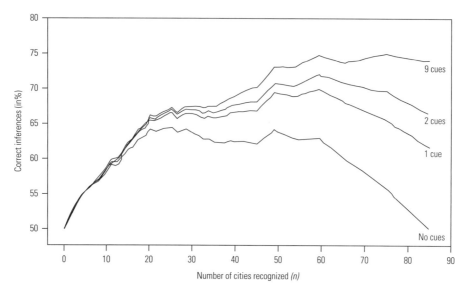

Figure 3-3. Less-is-more effects when the recognition validity is not held constant but varies empirically, that is, as cities become recognized in order of how well known they are. Inferences are made on recognition alone (no cues) or with the aid of one, two, or nine predictive cues and take-the-best (see Goldstein & Gigerenzer, 1999).

In a series of conditions, the program learned the name of each city, along with one, two, or nine predictive cues for inferring population (the same cues as in Gigerenzer & Goldstein, 1996). In the condition with one cue, the program learned whether each of the cities it recognized was once an exposition site, a predictor with a high ecological validity (.91; see Gigerenzer & Goldstein, 1996). The program then used a decision strategy called take-the-best (Gigerenzer & Goldstein, 1999) to make inferences about which city is larger. Take-the-best is a fast and frugal strategy for drawing inferences from cues that uses the recognition heuristic as the first step. It looks up cues in the order of their validity and stops search as soon as positive evidence for one object (e.g., the city was an exposition site) but not for the other object is found. It is about as accurate as multiple regression for this task (Gigerenzer & Goldstein, 1999).

Does adding predictive information about exposition sites wash out the less-is-more effect? With one cue, the peak of the curve shifted slightly to the right, but the basic shape persisted.

When the program recognized more than 58 cities, including information about exposition sites, the accuracy still went down. In the condition with two cues, the program learned the exposition site information and whether each city had a soccer team in the major league (another cue with a high validity, .87). The less-is-more effect was lessened, as is to be expected when adding recall knowledge to recognition, but still pronounced. Recognizing all cities and knowing all the information contained in two cues (the far right-hand point) resulted in fewer correct inferences than recognizing only 23 cities. Finally, we tested a condition in which all nine cues were available to the program, more information for predicting German city populations than perhaps any German citizen knows. We see the less-is-more effect finally flattening out; however, it does not go away completely. Even when all 83 cue values are known for each of nine cues and all cities are recognized, the point on the far right is still lower than 24 other points on that curve. A beneficial amount of ignorance can enable even higher accuracy than extensive knowledge can.

To summarize, the simplifying assumption that the recognition validity α and knowledge validity β remain constant is not necessary for the less-is-more effect to arise: It held as α and β varied in a realistic way. Moreover, the counter-intuitive effect even appeared when complete knowledge about several predictors was present. The effect appears rather robust in theory and simulation. Will the recognition heuristic and, thus, the less-is-more effect emerge in human behavior?

DOES THE RECOGNITION HEURISTIC PREDICT PEOPLE'S INFERENCES?

It could be that evolution has overlooked the inferential ease and accuracy the recognition heuristic affords. Do human judgments actually accord with the recognition heuristic? We test this question in an experiment in which people make inferences from limited knowledge.

Method

The participants were 22 students from the University of Chicago who were native speakers of English and who had lived in the United States for the last 10 years. They were given all the pairs of cities drawn from the 25 ($n = 6$) or 30 ($n = 16$) largest cities in Germany, which resulted in 300

or 435 questions for each participant, respectively. The task was to choose the larger city in each pair. Furthermore, each participant was asked to check the names of the cities he or she recognized off of a list. Half of the participants took this recognition test before the experiment and half after. (Order turned out to have no effect.) From this recognition information, we calculated how often each participant had an opportunity to choose in accordance with the recognition heuristic and compared this number with how often they actually did. If people use the recognition heuristic, they should predominantly choose recognized cities over unrecognized ones. If they use a compensatory strategy that takes more information into account, this additional information may often suggest not choosing the recognized city. After all, a city can be recognized for reasons that have nothing to do with population.

Results

Figure 3-4 shows the results for the 22 individual participants. For each participant, one bar is shown. The bar shows the proportion of judgments that agreed with the recognition heuristic among all cases in which it could be applied. For example, participant A had 156 opportunities to choose according to the recognition heuristic and did so every time, participant B did so 216 of

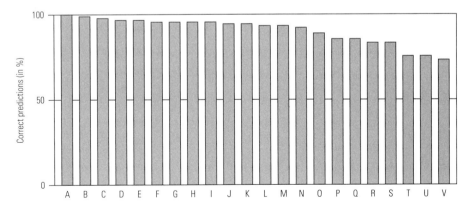

Figure 3-4. Recognition heuristic accordance. For each of 22 participants, the bars show the percentage of inferences consistent with the recognition heuristic. The individuals are ordered from left to right according to how often their judgments agreed with the recognition heuristic.

221 times, and so on. The proportions of recognition heuristic adherence ranged between 73% and 100%. The mean proportion of inferences in accordance with the recognition heuristic was 90% (median 93%).

This simple test of the recognition heuristic showed that it captured the vast majority of inferences.

TEST SIZE INFLUENCES PERFORMANCE

Equation 3-1 allows for a novel prediction: The number of correct inferences depends in a nonmonotonic but systematic way on the number of cities N included in the test. That is, for constant recognition validity α and knowledge validity β, the test size N (and n that depends on it) predicts various proportions of correct answers. Specifically, Equation 3-1 predicts when the deletion or addition of one object to the test set should decrease or increase performance.

Method

Using Equation 3-1, we modeled how the accuracy of the participants in the preceding experiment would change if they were tested on various numbers of cities and test these predictions against the participants' demonstrated accuracy. These predictions were made using nothing but information about which cities people recognize; no parameters are fit. With the data from the previous experiment, we looked at the participants' accuracy when tested on the 30 largest cities, then on just the 29 largest cities, and so on, down to the 2 largest. (This was done by successively eliminating questions and rescoring.) For each participant, at each test size, we could compute the number of objects they recognized and the recognition validity α from the recognition test. Assuming, for simplicity, that the knowledge validity β always was a dummy value of .5, we used Equation 3-1 to predict the change in the proportion of correct inferences when the number of cities N on the test varied.

Results

The average predictions for and the average actual performance of the individuals who took the exhaustive test on the 30 largest cities are shown in Figure 3-5. There are 28 predicted

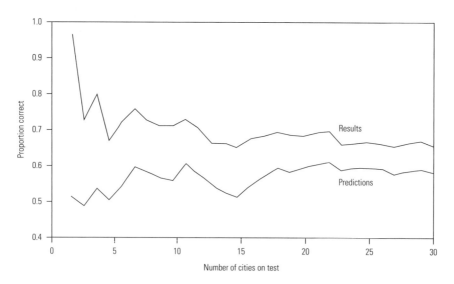

Figure 3-5. The use of the recognition heuristic implies that accuracy depends on test size (N) in an irregular but predictable way (Equation 3-1). The predictions were made with recognition information alone, and no parameters were fit. The knowledge validity used was a dummy value that assumes people will guess when both cities are recognized. The predictions mirror the fluctuations in accuracy in 26 of the 28 cases.

changes (up or down), and 26 of these 28 predictions match the data. Despite the apparent irregularity of the actual changes, Equation 3-1 predicts them with great precision. Note that there are no free parameters used to fit the empirical curve.

An interesting feature of Figure 3-5 is the vertical gap between the two curves. This difference reflects the impact of the knowledge validity β, which was set at the dummy value of .5 for demonstrative purposes. The reason this difference decreases with increasing N is that, as the tests begin to include smaller and smaller cities, the true knowledge validity β of our American participants tended toward .5. That is, it is safe to assume that when Americans are tested on the 30 (or more) largest German cities, their probability of correctly inferring which of 2 recognized cities is larger is only somewhat better than chance.

To summarize, the recognition heuristic predicts how performance changes with increasing or decreasing test size. The empirical data showed a strong, nonmonotonic influence on performance, explained almost entirely by the recognition heuristic.

NONCOMPENSATORY INFERENCES: WILL INFERENCE FOLLOW THE RECOGNITION HEURISTIC DESPITE CONFLICTING EVIDENCE?

People often look up only one or two relevant cues, avoid searching for conflicting evidence, and use noncompensatory strategies (e.g., Einhorn, 1970; Einhorn & Hogarth, 1981, p. 71; Fishburn, 1974; Hogarth, 1987; Payne, Bettman, & Johnson, 1993; Shepard, 1967a). The recognition heuristic is a noncompensatory strategy: If one object is recognized and the other is not, then the inference is determined; no other information about the recognized object is searched for and, therefore, no other information can reverse the choice determined by recognition. Noncompensatory judgments are a challenge to traditional ideals of rationality because they dispense with the idea of compensation by integration. For instance, when Keeney and Raiffa (1993) discussed lexicographic strategies—the prototype of noncompensatory rules—they repeatedly inserted warnings that such a strategy "is more widely adopted in practice than it deserves to be" because "it is naively simple" and "will rarely pass a test of 'reasonableness' "(pp. 77–78). The term *lexicographic* means that criteria are looked up in a fixed order of validity, like the alphabetic order used to arrange words in a dictionary. Another example of a lexicographic structure is the Arabic (base 10) numeral system. To decide which of two numbers (with an equal number of digits) is larger, one looks at the first digit. If the first digit of one number is larger, then the whole number is larger. If the first digits are equal, then one looks at the second digit, and so on. This simple method is not possible for Roman numerals, which are not lexicographic. Lexicographic strategies are noncompensatory because the decision made on the basis of a cue higher up in the order cannot be reversed by the cues lower in the order. The recognition heuristic is possibly the simplest of all noncompensatory strategies: It only relies on subjective recognition and not on objective cues. In this section, we are not concerned with the "reasonableness" of its noncompensatory nature (which we have analyzed in earlier sections in terms of α, β, n, and N), but with the descriptive validity of this property. Would the people following the recognition heuristic still follow it if they were taught information that they could use to contradict the choice dictated by recognition?

In this experiment, we used the same task as before (inferring which of two cities has the larger population) but taught participants additional, useful information that offered an alternative to following the recognition heuristic, in particular, knowledge about which cities have soccer teams in the major league (the German "Bundesliga"). German cities with such teams tend to be quite large, so the presence of a major league soccer team indicates a large population. Because of this relationship, we can test the challenging postulate of whether the recognition heuristic is used in a noncompensatory way. Which would participants choose as larger: an unrecognized city or a recognized city that they learned has *no* soccer team?

Method

Participants were 21 students from the University of Chicago. All were native English speakers who had lived in the United States for at least the last 10 years. The experiment consisted of a training session and a test session. At the beginning of the training session, participants were instructed to write down everything they were taught, and they were informed that after training they would be given a test consisting of pairs of cities drawn from the 30 largest in Germany. During the training session, participants were taught that 9 of the 30 largest cities in Germany have soccer teams and that the 9 cities with teams are larger than the 21 cities without teams in 78% of all possible pairs. They were also taught the names of 4 well-known cities that have soccer teams as well as the names of 4 well-known cities that do not. When they learned about these 8 cities, they believed they had drawn them at random from all 30 cities; in actuality, the computer program administering the experiment was rigged to present the same information to all participants. After the training, participants were asked to recall everything they had been taught without error. Those who could not do so had to repeat training until they could.

After participants passed the training phase, they were presented pairs of cities and asked to choose the larger city in each pair. Throughout this test, they could refer to their notes about which cities do and do not have soccer teams. To motivate them to take the task seriously, they were offered a chance of winning $15 if they scored more than 80% correct. To reiterate, the point of the experiment was to see which city the participants would choose as the larger one: a city they had never heard of before, or one that they had recognized beforehand but had just learned had no soccer team. From the information presented in the training session (which did not make any mention of recognition), one would expect the participants to choose the unrecognized city in these cases. The reason for this is as follows. An unrecognized city either does or does not have a soccer team. If it does (a 5-in-22 chance from the information presented), then there is a 78% chance that it is larger. If it does not, then soccer team information is useless and a guess must be made.

Any chance of the unrecognized city having a soccer team suggests that it is probably larger. Participants who do not put any value on recognition should always choose the unrecognized city.

Note that the role of recognition or the recognition heuristic was never mentioned in the experiment. All instruction concerned soccer teams. The demand characteristics in this experiment would suggest that, after passing the training session requirements, the participants would use the soccer team information for making the inferences.

Results

The test consisted of 66 pairs of cities. Of these, we were only interested in 16 critical pairs that contained one unrecognized city and one recognized city that does not have a soccer team. Before or after this task, we tested which cities each participant recognized (order had no effect). In those cases in which our assumptions about which cities the participants recognized were contradicted by the recognition test, items were eliminated from the analysis, resulting in fewer than 16 critical pairs.[3]

Figure 3-6 reads the same as Figure 3-4. Twelve of 21 participants made choices in accordance with the recognition heuristic without exception, and most others deviated on only one or two items. All in all, inferences accorded with the recognition heuristic in 273 of the 296 total critical pairs. Despite the presence of conflicting knowledge, the mean proportion of inferences agreeing with the heuristic was 92% (median 100%). These numbers are even a bit higher than in the previous study, which, interestingly, did not involve the teaching of contradictory information.

It appears that the additional information about soccer teams was not integrated into the inferences, consistent with the recognition heuristic. This result supports the hypothesis that the recognition heuristic was applied in a noncompensatory way.

WILL A LESS-IS-MORE EFFECT OCCUR BETWEEN DOMAINS?

A less-is-more effect can emerge in at least three different situations. First, it can occur between

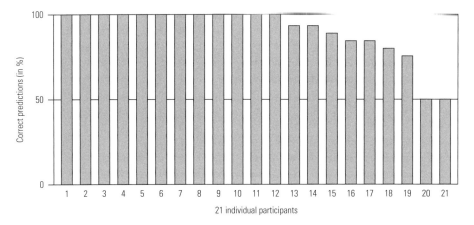

Figure 3-6. Recognition heuristic adherence despite training to encourage the use of information other than recognition. The bars show the percentage of inferences consistent with the recognition heuristic. The individuals are ordered from left to right by recognition heuristic accordance.

two groups of people, when a more knowledgeable group makes systematically worse inferences than a less-knowledgeable group in a given domain. An example was the performance of the American and German students on the question of whether San Diego or San Antonio is larger. Second, a less-is-more effect can occur between domains, that is, when the same group of people achieves higher accuracy in a domain in which they know little than in a domain in which they know a lot. Third, a less-is-more effect can occur during knowledge acquisition, that is, when the same group or individual makes more erroneous inferences as a result of learning. In this and the following experiment, we attempt to demonstrate less-is-more effects of the latter two types, starting with a less-is-more effect between domains.

The mathematical and simulation results presented previously show that less-is-more effects emerge under the conditions specified. However, the curious phenomenon of a less-is-more effect is harder to demonstrate with real people than by mathematical proof or computer simulation. The reason is that real people do not always need to make inferences under uncertainty; they sometimes have definite knowledge and can make deductions (e.g., if they know for certain that New York is the largest American city, they will conclude that every other city is

smaller). For this reason, even if there is a between-domains less-is-more effect for all items about which an inference must be made, this effect may be hidden by the presence of additional, definite knowledge.

In the following experiment, American participants were tested on their ability to infer the same criterion, population, in two different domains: German cities and American cities. Naturally, we expected the Americans to have considerably more knowledge about their own country than about Germany. Common sense (and all theories of knowledge of which we are aware) predicts that participants will make more correct inferences in the domain about which they know more. The recognition heuristic, however, could pull performance in the opposite direction, although its effect will be counteracted by the presence of certain knowledge that the Americans have about cities in the United States. Could the test scores on the foreign cities nevertheless be nearly as high as those on the domestic ones?

Method

Fifty-two University of Chicago students took two tests each: one on the 22 largest cities in the United States and one on the 22 largest cities in

Germany. The participants were native English speakers who had lived the preceding 10 years in the United States. Each test consisted of 100 pairs of randomly drawn cities, and the task was to infer which city is the larger in each pair. Half the subjects were tested on the American cities first and half on the German cities first. (Order had no effect.)

As mentioned, the curious phenomenon of a less-is-more effect is harder to demonstrate with real people than on paper because of definite knowledge. For instance, many Americans, and nearly all of the University of Chicago students, can name the three largest American cities in order. Knowing only the top three cities and guessing on questions that do not involve them led to 63% correct answers without making any inferences, only deductions. Knowing the top five in order yields 71% correct. No comparable knowledge can be expected for German cities. (Many of our participants believed that Bonn is the largest German city; it is 23rd.) Thus, the demonstration of a less-is-more effect is particularly difficult in this situation because the recognition heuristic only makes predictions about uncertain inference, not about the kinds of definite knowledge the Americans had.

Results

The American participants scored a mean 71.1% (median 71.0%) correct on their own cities. On the German cities, the mean accuracy was 71.4% (median 73.0%) correct. Despite the presence of definite knowledge about the American cities, the recognition heuristic still caused a slight less-is-more effect. For half of the participants, we kept track of which cities they recognized, as in previous experiments. For this group, the mean proportion of inferences in accordance with the recognition heuristic was 88.5% (median 90.5%). The recognition test showed that participants recognized a mean of 12 German cities, roughly half of the total, which indicates that they were able to apply the recognition heuristic nearly as often as theoretically possible (see Equation 3-1).

In a study that is somewhat the reverse of this one, a less-is-more effect was demonstrated with German students who scored higher when tested on American cities than on German ones (Hoffrage, 1995; see also Gigerenzer, 1993).

Despite all the knowledge—including certain knowledge—the Americans had about their own cities, and despite their limited knowledge about Germany, they could not make more accurate inferences about American cities than about German ones. Faced with German cities, the participants could apply the recognition heuristic. Faced with American cities, they had to rely on knowledge beyond recognition. The fast-and-frugal recognition heuristic exploited the information inherent in a lack of knowledge to make inferences that were slightly more accurate than those achieved from more complete knowledge.

WILL A LESS-IS-MORE EFFECT OCCUR AS RECOGNITION KNOWLEDGE IS ACQUIRED?

"A little learning is a dangerous thing," warned Alexander Pope. The recognition heuristic predicts cases in which increases in knowledge can lead to decreases in inferential accuracy. Equation 3-1 predicts that if $\alpha > \beta$, the proportion of accurate inferences will increase up to a certain point when a person's knowledge increases but thereafter decrease because of the diminishing applicability of the recognition heuristic. This study aims to demonstrate that less-is-more effects can emerge over the course of time as ignorance is replaced with recognition knowledge.

The design of the experiment was as follows. German participants came to the laboratory four times and were tested on American cities. As they were tested repeatedly, they may have gained what we lightheartedly call an "experimentally induced" sense of recognition for the names of cities they had not recognized before the experiment. This induced recognition is similar to that generated in the "overnight fame" experiments by Jacoby, Kelley, Brown, and Jasechko (1989), in which mere exposure caused nonfamous names to be judged as famous. Can mere exposure to city names cause people to infer that formerly unrecognized cities are large? If so, this should cause accuracy on certain questions to drop. For instance, in the first session, a German who has heard of Dallas but not Indianapolis would correctly infer that Dallas is larger. However, over the course of repeated testing, this person may develop an experimentally induced sense of recognition for Indianapolis without realizing it. Recognizing both cities, she becomes unable to use the recognition heuristic and may have to guess.

It is difficult to produce the counterintuitive effect that accuracy will decrease as city names are learned because it is contingent on several assumptions. The first is that recognition will be experimentally induced, and there is evidence for this phenomenon in the work by Jacoby, Kelley, Brown, & Jasechko (1989) and Jacoby, Woloshyn, & Kelley (1989). The second assumption is that people use the recognition heuristic, and there is evidence for this in the experimental work reported here. The third assumption is that, for these participants, the recognition validity α is larger than the knowledge validity β: a condition for a less-is-more effect. The simulation depicted in Figure 3-3 indicates that this condition might hold for certain people.

Method

Participants were 16 residents of Munich, Germany, who were paid for their participation. (They were not paid, however, for the correctness of their answers, because this would have encouraged them to do research on populations between sessions). In the first session, after a practice test to get used to the computer, they were shown the names of the 75 largest American cities in random order. (The first three, New York, Los Angeles, and Chicago, were excluded because many Germans know they are the three largest.) For each city, participants indicated whether they had heard of the city before the experiment, and then, to encourage the encoding of the city name in memory, they were asked to write the name of each city as it would be spelled in German. Participants were not informed that the cities were among the largest in the country, only that they were American cities. They were then given a test consisting of 300 pairs of cities, randomly drawn for each participant, and asked to choose the larger city in each pair.

About 1 week later, participants returned to the lab and took another test of 300 pairs of American cities randomly drawn for each participant. The third week was a repetition of the second week. The fourth week was the critical test. This time, participants were given 200 carefully selected questions. There were two sets of 100 questions each that were used to test two predictions. The first set of 100 was composed of questions taken from the first week's test. This set was generated by listing all questions from the first session's test in which one city was recognized and the other not (according to each participant's recognition in the first week) and randomly drawing (with replacement) 100 times. We looked at these repeated questions to test the prediction that accuracy will decrease as recognition knowledge is acquired.

A second set of 100 questions consisted of pairs with one "experimentally induced" city (i.e., a city that was unrecognized before the first session but may have become recognized over the course of repeated testing) and a new, unrecognized city introduced for the first time in the fourth session. All new cities were drawn from the next 50 largest cities in the United States, and a posttest recognition survey was used to verify whether they were novel to the participants. (Participants, however, did not know from which source any of the cities in the experiment were drawn.)

Which would people choose: an experimentally induced city that they had learned to recognize in the experiment or a city they had never heard of before? If people use the recognition heuristic, this choice should not be random but should show a systematic preference for the experimentally induced cities. This set of questions was introduced to test the hypothesis that recognition information acquired during the experiment would be used as a surrogate for genuine recognition information.

Results

If the assumptions just specified hold, one should observe that the percentage of times experimentally induced cities are inferred to be larger than recognized cities should increase and, subsequently, cause accuracy to decrease.

Table 3-1. A Less-Is-More Effect Resulting from Learning

Session	Mean % Correct	Median % Correct	Inferences (%)[a]
1	74.8	76	9.6
4	71.3	74	17.2

Note. The percentage of correct answers drops from the first to the fourth sessions. As German participants saw the same novel American city names over and over again in repeated testing, they began to choose them over cities that they recognized from the real world (column 4).
[a] Represents inferences in which an experimentally induced city was chosen over one recognized from before the experiment.

In the first week, participants chose unrecognized cities over recognized ones in 9.6% of all applicable cases, consistent with the proportions reported in Studies 1 and 3. By the fourth week, the experimentally induced cities were chosen over those that were recognized before the first session 17.2% of the time (Table 3-1). Participants' accuracy on the 100 repeated questions dropped from a mean of 74.8% correct (median 76%) in the first week to 71.3% correct (median 74%) in the fourth week, $t(15) = 1.82$, $p = .04$, one-tailed. To summarize, as unrecognized city names were presented over 4 weeks, participants became more likely to infer that these cities were larger than recognized cities. As a consequence, accuracy dropped during this month-long experiment. Surprisingly, this occurred despite the participants having ample time to think about American cities and their populations, to recall information from memory, to ask friends or look in reference books for correct answers, or to notice stories in the media that could inform their inferences.

How did participants make inferences in the second set of 100 questions, in which each question consisted of two unrecognized cities: one new to the fourth session and one experimentally induced? If the repeated presentation of city names had no effect on inferences, participants would be expected to choose both types of cities equally often (about 50% of the time) in the fourth session. However, in the fourth session, participants chose the experimentally induced cities over the new ones 74.3% of the time (median 77%). Recognition induced in the laboratory had a marked effect on the direction of people's inferences.

THE ECOLOGICAL RATIONALITY OF NAME RECOGNITION

What is the origin of the recognition heuristic as a strategy? In the case of avoiding food poisoning, organisms seem as if they are genetically prepared to act in accordance with the recognition heuristic. Wild Norway rats do not need to be taught to prefer recognized foods over novel ones; food neophobia is instinctual (Barnett, 1963). Having such a strategy as an instinct makes adaptive sense: If an event is life threatening, organisms needing to learn to follow the recognition heuristic will most likely die before they get the chance. Learning the correlation between name recognition and city size is not an adaptive task. How did the association between recognition and city population develop in the minds of the participants we investigated?

The recognition validity—the strength of the association between recognition and the criterion— can be explained as a function of the ecological and the surrogate correlations that connect an unknown environment with the mind by means of a mediator (see Figure 3-1). If the media are responsible for the set of proper names we recognize, the number of times a city is mentioned in the newspapers should correlate with the proportion of readers who recognize the city; that is, there should be a substantial surrogate correlation. Furthermore, there should be a strong ecological correlation (larger cities should be mentioned in the news more often). To test this postulated ecological structure, we analyzed two newspapers with large readerships: the *Chicago Tribune* in the United States and *Die Zeit* in Germany.

Method

Using an Internet search tool, we counted the number of articles published in the *Chicago Tribune* between January 1985 and July 1997 in which the words *Berlin* and *Germany* were mentioned together. There were 3,484. We did the same for all cities in Germany with more than 100,000 inhabitants (there are 83 of them) and checked under many possible spellings and misspellings. Sixty-seven Chicago residents were given a recognition test in which they indicated whether they had heard of each of the German cities. The proportion of participants who recognized a given city was the city's recognition rate.

The same analysis was performed with a major German language newspaper, *Die Zeit*. For each American city with more than 100,000 inhabitants, the number of articles was counted in which it was mentioned. The analysis covered the period from May 1995 to July 1997. Recognition tests for the American cities were administered to 30 University of Salzburg students (Hoffrage, 1995).

Results

Three measures were obtained for each city: the actual population, the number of mentions in the newspaper, and the recognition rate. Figure 3-7 illustrates the underlying structure and shows the correlations between these three measures. For the class of all German cities with more than 100,000 inhabitants, the ecological correlation (i.e., the correlation between the number of newspaper articles in the *Chicago Tribune* mentioning a city and its actual population) was .70; the number of times a city is mentioned in the newspaper is a good indicator of the city's population. The surrogate correlation, that is, the correlation between the number of newspaper articles about a city and the number of people recognizing it was .79; the recognition rates are more closely associated with the number of newspaper articles

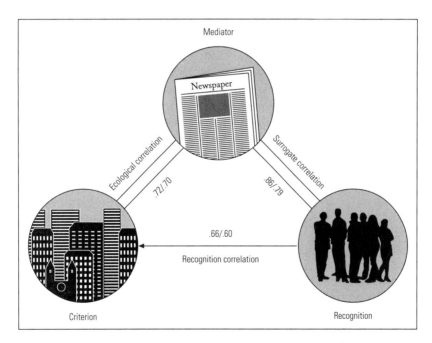

Figure 3-7. Ecological correlation, surrogate correlation, and recognition correlation. The first value is for American cities and the German newspaper *Die Zeit* as mediator, and the second value is for German cities and the *Chicago Tribune* as mediator. Note that the recognition validity is expressed, for comparability, as a correlation (between the number of people who recognize the name of a city and its population).

than with the actual populations. This effect is illustrated by large German and American cities that receive little newspaper coverage, such as Essen, Dortmund, and San Jose. Their recognition rates tend to follow the low frequency of newspaper citations rather than their actual population. Finally, the correlation between the number of people recognizing a city and its population—the recognition validity expressed as a correlation—was .60. Recognition is a good predictor of actual population but not as strong as the ecological and surrogate correlations.

Do these results stand up in a different culture? For the class of all American cities with more than 100,000 inhabitants, the ecological correlation was .72. The surrogate correlation was .86, and the correlation between recognition and the rank order of cities was .66. These results are consistent with those from the American data, with slightly higher correlations.

This study illustrates how to analyze the ecological rationality of the recognition heuristic. The magnitude of the recognition validity, together with n and N (Equation 3-1), specifies the expected accuracy of the heuristic but does not explain why recognition is informative. The ecological and surrogate correlations (see Figure 3-1) allow one to model the network of mediators that could explain why and when a lack of recognition is informative, that is, when missing knowledge is systematically rather than randomly distributed.

INSTITUTIONS, FIRMS, AND NAME RECOGNITION

For both the *Chicago Tribune* and *Die Zeit*, the surrogate correlation was the strongest association, which suggests that individual recognition was more in tune with the media than with the actual environment. Because of this, to improve the perceived quality of a product, a firm may opt to manipulate the product's name recognition through advertising instead of investing in the research and development necessary to improve the product's quality. Advertising manipulates recognition rates directly and is one way in which institutions exploit recognition-based inference.

One way advertisers achieve name recognition is by associating the name of their products with strong visual images. If the real purpose of the ad is to convey name recognition and not communicate product information, then only the attention-getting quality of the images, and not the content of the images, should matter. Advertiser Oliviero Toscani bet his career on this strategy. In his campaign for Bennetton, he produced a series of advertisements that conveyed nothing about actual Bennetton products but sought to induce name recognition by association with shocking images, such as a corpse lying in a pool of blood or a dying AIDS patient. Would associating the name of a clothing manufacturer with bloody images cause people to learn the name? Toscani (1997) reported that the campaign was a smashing success and that it vaulted Bennetton's name recognition into the top five in the world, even above that of Chanel. In social domains, recognition is often correlated with quality, resources, wealth, and power. Why? Perhaps because individuals with these characteristics tend to be the subject of news reporting as well as gossip. As a result, advertisers pay great sums for a place in the recognition memory of the general public, and the lesser known people, organizations, institutions, and nations of the world go on crusades for name recognition. They all operate on the principle that if we do not recognize them, then we will not favor them.

Those who try to become recognized through advertising may not be wasting their resources. As mentioned, the "overnight fame" experiments by Jacoby, Kelley et al. (1989) demonstrate that people may have trouble distinguishing between names they learned to recognize in the laboratory and those they learned in the real world. In a series of classic studies, participants read famous and nonfamous names, waited overnight, and then made fame judgments. Occasionally, people would mistakenly infer that a nonfamous name, learned in the laboratory, was the name of a famous person. The recognition heuristic can be fooled, and the previously anonymous can inherit the appearance of being skilled, famous, important, or powerful.

CAN COMPENSATORY STRATEGIES MIMIC THE RECOGNITION HEURISTIC?

So far we have dealt only with recognition and not with information recalled from memory. The recognition heuristic can act as a subroutine in heuristics that process knowledge beyond recognition. Examples are the take-the-last and take-the-best heuristics, which feature the recognition heuristic as the first step (Gigerenzer & Goldstein, 1996). These heuristics are also noncompensatory and can benefit from the information implicit in a lack of recognition but are also able to function with complete information. However, in cases in which one object is recognized and the other is not, they make the same inference as the recognition heuristic.

Do compensatory strategies exist that do not have the recognition heuristic as an explicit step but that, unwittingly, make inferences as if they did? It seems that only noncompensatory cognitive strategies (such as lexicographic models) could embody the noncompensatory recognition heuristic. However, it turns out that this is not so. For instance, consider a simple tallying strategy that counts the pieces of positive evidence for each of two objects and chooses the object with more positive evidence (see Gigerenzer & Goldstein, 1996). Such a strategy would be a relative of a strategy that searches for confirming evidence and ignores disconfirming evidence (e.g., Klayman & Ha, 1987). Interestingly, because there can be no positive evidence for an unrecognized object, such a strategy will never choose an unrecognized object over a recognized one. If this strategy, however, were, in addition, to pay attention to negative evidence and choose the object with the larger sum of positive and negative values, it would no longer make the same choice as the recognition heuristic. This can be seen from the fact that a recognized object may carry more negative than positive evidence, whereas an unrecognized object carries neither. As a consequence, compensatory strategies such as tallying that mimic the recognition heuristic will also mimic a less-is-more effect (Gigerenzer & Goldstein, 1999).

DOMAIN SPECIFICITY

The recognition heuristic is not a general purpose strategy for reasoning. It is a domain-specific heuristic. Formally, its domain specificity can be defined by two characteristics. First, some objects must be unrecognized ($n < N$). Second, the recognition validity must be higher than chance ($\alpha > .5$). However, what domains, in terms of content, have these characteristics? We begin with examples of recognition validities $\alpha > .5$, and then propose several candidate domains, without claims to an exhaustive list.

Table 3-2 lists 10 topics of general knowledge, ranging from the world's highest mountains to the largest American banks. Would the recognition heuristic help to infer correctly which of, for example, two mountains is higher? We surveyed 20 residents of Berlin, Germany, about which objects they recognized for each of the 10 topics and then computed each participant's recognition validity for each topic. Table 3-2 shows the average recognition validities. These validities are often high, and the topics in Table 3-2 can be extended to include many others.

Domains

Alliances and competition

Deciding whom to befriend and whom to compete against is an adaptive problem for humans and other social animals (e.g., Cosmides & Tooby, 1992; de Waal, 1982). Organisms need a way to assess quickly who or what in the world

Table 3-2. A Sample of Recognition Validities

Topic	Recognition Validity α
10 Largest Indian cities	0.95
20 Largest French cities	0.87
10 Highest mountains	0.85
15 Largest Italian provinces	0.81
10 Largest deserts	0.80
10 Tallest buildings	0.79
10 Largest islands	0.79
10 Longest rivers	0.69
10 Largest U.S. banks	0.68
10 Largest seas	0.64

has influence and resources. Recognition of a person, group, firm, institution, city, or nation signals its social, political, and economic importance to others of its kind that may be contemplating a possible alliance or competition. For instance, in the highly competitive stock market, the recognition heuristic has, on average, matched or outperformed major mutual funds, the market, randomly picked stocks, and the less recognized stocks. This result has been obtained both for the American and the German stock markets (Borges et al., 1999).

Risk avoidance A second domain concerns risky behavior when the risks associated with objects are too dangerous to be learned by experience or too rare to be learned in a lifetime (Cosmides & Tooby, 1994). Food avoidance is an example; the recognition heuristic helps organisms avoid toxic foods (Galef, 1987). If an organism had to learn from individual experience which risks to take (or foods to eat), it could be fatal. In many wild environments, novelty carries risk, and recognition can be a simple guide to a safe choice.

Social bonding Social species (i.e., species that have evolved cognitive adaptations such as imprinting on parents by their children, coalition forming, and reciprocal altruism) are equipped with a powerful perceptual machinery for the recognition of individual conspecifics. Face recognition and voice recognition are examples. This machinery is the basis for the use of the recognition heuristic as a guide to social choices. For instance, one author's daughter always preferred a babysitter whom she recognized to one of whom she had never heard, even if she was not enthusiastic about the familiar babysitter. Recognition alone cannot tell us whom, among recognized individuals, to trust; however, it can suggest that we not trust unrecognized individuals.

FAST-AND-FRUGAL HEURISTICS

The current work on the recognition heuristic is part of a research program to study the architecture and performance of fast-and-frugal heuristics (Gigerenzer & Goldstein, 1996;

Gigerenzer & Selten, 2001; Gigerenzer, Todd, & the ABC Research Group, 1999; Goldstein & Gigerenzer, 1999; Todd & Gigerenzer, 2000). The recognition heuristic is a prototype of these adaptive tools. It uses recognition, a capacity that evolution has shaped over millions of years that allows organisms to benefit from their own ignorance. The heuristic works with limited knowledge and limited time and even requires a certain amount of missing information. Other research programs have pointed out that one's ignorance can be leveraged to make inferences (Glucksberg & McCloskey, 1981); however, they refer to an ignorance of deeper knowledge, not ignorance in the sense of a mere lack of recognition.

Fast-and-frugal heuristics are formulated in a way that is highly transparent: It is easy to discern and understand just how they function in making decisions. Because they involve few, if any, free parameters and a minimum of computation, each step of the algorithm is open to scrutiny. These simple heuristics stand in sharp contrast to more complex and computationally involved models of mental processes that may generate good approximations to human behavior but are also rather opaque. For instance, the resurgence of connectionism in the 1980s brought forth a crop of neural networks that were respectable models for a variety of psychological phenomena but whose inner workings remained mysterious even to their creators (for alternatives, see Regier, 1996; Rumelhart & Todd, 1993). Whereas these models are precisely formulated but nontransparent, there also exist imprecisely formulated and nontransparent models of heuristics, such as "representativeness," "availability," and other one-word explanations (see Gigerenzer, 1996, 1998; Lopes, 1991). Transparent fast-and-frugal heuristics use no (or only a few) free parameters, allow one to make quantifiable and testable predictions, and avoid possible misunderstanding (or mystification) of the processes involved, even if they do sacrifice some of the allure of the unknown.

NOTES

1. When there are many different individuals who recognize different numbers of objects, as with

the three sisters, it is possible that each individual has roughly the same recognition validity. For instance, for the University of Chicago students we surveyed (Gigerenzer & Goldstein, 1996), recognition validity in the domain of German cities was about 80% regardless of how many cities each individual recognized. However, when one individual comes to recognize more and more objects, the recognition validity can change with each new object recognized. Assume a person recognizes n of N objects. When she learns to recognize object $n + 1$, this will change the number of pairs for which one object is recognized and the other is not from $n(N - n)$ to $(n + 1)(N - n - 1)$. This number is the denominator of the recognition validity (the number $R + W$ of correct plus incorrect inferences), which consequently changes the recognition validity itself. Learning to recognize new objects also changes the numerator (the number R of correct inferences); in general, if the new object is large, the recognition validity will go down, and if it is small, it will go up.

2. If several cities tied on this measure, they were ordered randomly for each run of the simulation.

3. Another precaution we took concerned the fact that unrecognized cities are often smaller than recognized ones, and this could work to the advantage of the recognition heuristic in this experiment. How can one tell whether people are following the recognition heuristic or choosing correctly by some other means? To prevent this confusion, the critical test items were designed so that the unrecognized cities were larger than the recognized cities in half of the pairs.

Introduction to Chapter 4

How Forgetting Aids Heuristic Inference

Psychological theory today is like a jigsaw puzzle with most pieces still unassembled. Allen Newell called for theorists to integrate rather than sideline existing theories of cognition (Newell, 1973). Unfortunately, many psychologists still tend to treat theories like toothbrushes—no self-respecting person wants to use anyone else's (Mischel, 2008; Watkins, 1984). There are different ways of instigating theory integration. The ACT-R research community strives to assemble the pieces into a unified theory of cognition (Anderson, 2007). One way the ABC Research Group at the Max Planck Institute for Human Development wagers that this integration can be achieved is by bringing together researchers with diverse theoretical backgrounds and having them work in close proximity. In the present case, it worked. Being office neighbors, Lael Schooler, whose intellectual mentor was J.R. Anderson, and Ralph Hertwig, whose mentor was Gerd Gigerenzer, quickly discovered how the heuristics program and the ACT-R cognitive architecture could be integrated.

Theory integration promises high payoffs, for instance, new, interesting, and sometimes counterintuitive insights. Schooler and Hertwig benefited twofold from these payoffs. The first payoff came when they implemented the recognition heuristic in ACT-R and thus "discovered" a heuristic that they had not considered earlier, the *fluency heuristic*. Although discussed for many years in social and cognitive psychology, few attempts had been made to define both fluency and the fluency heuristic precisely. The ACT-R architecture offers a precise definition using the concepts of activation strength and retrieval time for memory records, with the latter mapping one-to-one onto the former. In ACT-R, activation tracks environmental regularities, such as an object's frequency and recency of occurrence. Activation differences may thus partly reflect frequency differences, which in turn may be correlated with properties of the object, such as its size. By providing a key to unlock valuable encrypted information on environmental frequency, the fluency heuristic, like the recognition heuristic, can be used to make accurate inferences about the world. To what extent people actually used the fluency heuristic was not addressed in this investigation, which was based on computer simulations; Chapter 26 provides an answer to this question.

The second insight that resulted from Schooler and Hertwig's theory integration was how forgetting—a process often seen as a nuisance and a handicap—can be functional in the context of heuristic inference. After the authors had implemented the recognition heuristic and the fluency heuristic within the ACT-R cognitive architecture, they were able to analyze whether forgetting aids the two heuristics' accuracy. Indeed, it does. Less-is-more effects, as demonstrated in Chapter 3, thus describe not only the curious state in which less recognition is better than more in making accurate inferences but also instances in which some forgetting enables more accurate inferences than perfect memory would. More generally, Schooler and Hertwig's analysis challenges the common belief that cognitive limits, such as forgetting or limited working memory, inevitably pose a liability for the human mind. Their work points to the possibility that some cognitive limits may have evolved to foster specific cognitive processes, and at the same time that some cognitive processes may have evolved to exploit specific cognitive limits—as may be the case in the interplay of forgetting and heuristic inference.

CHAPTER 4

How Forgetting Aids Heuristic Inference

Lael J. Schooler and Ralph Hertwig

Abstract: Some theorists, ranging from W. James (1890) to contemporary psychologists, have argued that forgetting is the key to proper functioning of memory. The authors elaborate on the notion of beneficial forgetting by proposing that loss of information aids inference heuristics that exploit mnemonic information. To this end, the authors bring together two research programs that take an ecological approach to studying cognition. Specifically, they implement fast-and-frugal heuristics within the ACT-R cognitive architecture. Simulations of the recognition heuristic, which relies on systematic failures of recognition to infer which of two objects scores higher on a criterion value, demonstrate that forgetting can boost accuracy by increasing the chances that only one object is recognized. Simulations of the fluency heuristic, which arrives at the same inference on the basis of the speed with which objects are recognized, indicate that forgetting aids the discrimination between the objects' recognition speeds.

In *The Mind of a Mnemonist,* Luria (1968) examined one of the most virtuoso memories ever documented. The possessor of this memory— S. V. Shereshevskii, to whom Luria referred as S.— reacted to the discovery of his extraordinary powers by quitting his job as a reporter and becoming a professional mnemonist. S.'s nearly perfect memory appeared to have "no distinct limits" (p. 11). Once, for instance, he memorized a long series of nonsense syllables that began "ma, va, na, sa, na, va, na, sa, na, ma, va" (Luria, 1968, p. 51). Eight years later, he recalled the whole series without making a single error or omission. This apparently infallible memory did not come without costs. S. complained, for example, that he had a poor memory for faces: "People's faces are constantly changing; it is the different shades of expression that confuse me and make it so hard to remember faces" (p. 64).

"Unlike others, who tend to single out certain features by which to remember faces," Luria wrote, "S. saw faces as changing patterns, ... much the same kind of impression a person would get, if he were sitting by a window watching the ebb and flow of the sea's waves" (p. 64). One way to interpret these observations is that cognitive processes such as generalizing, abstracting, and classifying different images of, for example, the same face require ignoring the differences between them. In other words, crossing the "'accursed' threshold to a higher level of thought" (Luria, 1968, p. 133), which in Luria's view S. never did, may require the ability to forget.

Is forgetting a nuisance and a handicap or is it essential to the proper functioning of memory and higher cognition? Much of the experimental research on memory has been dominated by questions of quantity, such as how much information is remembered and for how long (see Koriat, Goldsmith, & Pansky, 2000). From this perspective, forgetting is usually viewed as a regrettable loss of information. Some have suggested, however, that forgetting may be functional. One of the first to explore this possibility was James (1890), who wrote, "In the practical use of our intellect, forgetting is as important a function as recollecting" (p. 679). In his view, forgetting is the mental mechanism behind the selectivity of information processing, which in turn is "the very keel on which our mental ship is built" (James, 1890, p. 680).

A century later, Bjork and Bjork (1988) argued that forgetting prevents out-of-date information—say, old phone numbers or where one parked the car yesterday—from interfering with the recall of currently relevant information. Altmann and Gray (2002) make a similar point that to be able to focus on current goals, it helps to forget previous goals. Forgetting prevents the retrieval of information that is likely obsolete. In fact, this is a function of forgetting that S. paradoxically had to do consciously. As a professional mnemonist, he committed thousands of words to memory. Learning to erase the images he associated with those words that he no longer needed to recall was an effortful, difficult process (Luria, 1968).

How and why forgetting might be functional has also been the focus of the extensive analysis conducted by Anderson and colleagues (Anderson & Milson, 1989; Anderson & Schooler, 1991, 2000; Schooler & Anderson, 1997). On the basis of their rational analysis of memory, they argued that much of memory performance, including forgetting, might be understood in terms of adaptation to the structure of the environment. The key assumptions of this rational analysis are that the memory system (a) meets the informational demands stemming from environmental stimuli by retrieving memory traces associated with the stimuli and (b) acts on the expectation that environmental stimuli tend to recur in predictable ways.

The rational analysis implies that memory performance reflects the patterns with which stimuli appear and reappear in the environment. To test this implication, Anderson and Schooler (1991) examined various environments that place informational demands on the memory system and found a strong correspondence between the regularities in the occurrence of information (e.g., a word's frequency and recency of occurrence) in these environments (e.g., conversation) and the classic learning and forgetting curves (e.g., as described by Ebbinghaus, 1885/1964). In a conversational environment, for instance, Anderson and Schooler (1991) observed that the probability of hearing a particular word drops as the period of time since it was last used grows, much as recall of a given item decreases as the amount of time since it was last encountered increases. More generally, they argue that human memory essentially bets that as the recency and frequency with which a piece of information has been used decreases, the likelihood that it will be needed in the future also decreases. Because processing unneeded information is cognitively costly, the memory system is better off setting aside such little needed information by forgetting it.

In what follows, we extend the analysis of the effects of forgetting on memory performance to its effects on the performance of simple inference heuristics. To this end, we draw on the research program on fast-and-frugal heuristics (Gigerenzer, Todd, & the ABC Research Group, 1999) and the ACT-R research program (Anderson & Lebiere, 1998). Both programs share a strong ecological focus. The fast-and-frugal heuristics program examines simple strategies that exploit informational structures in the environment, enabling the mind to make surprisingly accurate decisions without much information or computation. The ACT-R research program strives to develop an encompassing theory of cognition, specified to such a degree that phenomena from perceptual search to the learning of algebra might be modeled within the same framework. In particular, ACT-R offers a plausible model of memory that is tuned to the statistical structure of environmental events. This model of memory will be central to our implementation of the *recognition heuristic* (Goldstein & Gigerenzer, 2002) and *the fluency heuristic* (e.g., Jacoby & Dallas, 1981; Kelley & Jacoby, 1998), both of which depend on phenomenological assessments of memory retrieval. The former operates on knowledge about whether a stimulus can be recognized, whereas the latter relies on an assessment of the fluency, the speed, with which a stimulus is processed. By housing these memory-based heuristics in a cognitive architecture, we aim to provide precise definitions of heuristics and analyze whether and how loss of information—that is, forgetting—fosters the performance of these heuristics. We begin by describing the recognition heuristic, the fluency heuristic, and the ACT-R architecture.

HOW RECOGNITION OR LACK THEREOF ENABLES HEURISTIC INFERENCE: THE RECOGNITION HEURISTIC

Common sense suggests that ignorance stands in the way of good decision making. The recognition heuristic belies this intuition. To see how the heuristic turns ignorance to its advantage, consider the simple situation in which one must select whichever of two objects is higher than the other with respect to some criterion (e.g., size or price). A contestant on a game show, for example, may have to make such decisions when faced with the question, "Which city has more inhabitants, San Diego or San Antonio?" How she makes this decision depends on the information available to her. If the only information on hand is whether she recognizes one of the cities and there is reason to suspect that recognition is positively correlated with city population, then she can do little better than rely on her (partial) ignorance. This kind of ignorance-based inference is embodied in the recognition heuristic (Goldstein & Gigerenzer, 1999, 2002), which for a two-alternative choice can be stated as follows: If one of two objects is recognized and the other is not, then infer that the recognized object has the higher value with respect to the criterion.

Partial ignorance may not sound like much for a decision maker to go on. But because lack of recognition knowledge is often systematic rather than random, failure to recognize something may be informative. The recognition heuristic exploits this information.

Empirical Support

To find out whether people use the recognition heuristic, Goldstein and Gigerenzer (1999, 2002)

pursued several experimental approaches. In one, they presented University of Chicago students with pairs of cities randomly drawn from the 22 largest cities in the United States and in Germany, respectively. The task was to infer which city in each pair had the larger population. The Chicago students made a median of 71% correct inferences in the American city set. When quizzed on the German city pairs, they made a median of 73% correct inferences. If one assumes that more knowledge leads to better performance, these results are counterintuitive: Years of living in the United States gave these students ample opportunity to learn facts about American cities that could be useful for inferring city populations, whereas they knew little to nothing about the German cities beyond recognizing about half of them. Why would they perform slightly better on German city pairs? According to Goldstein and Gigerenzer (2002), the American students' meager knowledge about German cities is precisely what allowed them to infer that the cities they recognized were larger than the cities they did not recognize. The recognition heuristic was of no use to them when making judgments about American cities because they recognized them all. Goldstein and Gigerenzer referred to this surprising phenomenon as the *less-is-more effect* and showed analytically that recognizing an intermediate number of objects in a set can yield the highest proportion of correct answers. All else being equal, recognizing more than this many objects decreases inferential accuracy.

The following example, adapted from Goldstein and Gigerenzer (2002), provides an intuitive illustration of how the recognition heuristic gives rise to the less-is-more effect. Suppose that three brothers have to take a test on the 20 largest German cities. The youngest brother has never heard of any of the cities, the middle brother has heard of 10 of them, and the eldest brother has heard of them all. The middle brother tends to know the names of the larger cities. In fact, the 10 cities he recognizes are larger than the 10 cities he does not in, say, 80 of the 100 possible pairs to which he can apply his recognition knowledge (i.e., the 100 pairs in which he recognizes one city and does not recognize the other). Thus, his *recognition validity* (i.e., the proportion of times that a recognized object has a higher value on the criterion than does an unrecognized object in a given sample) is .80. Both the middle and the eldest brothers have some knowledge of German cities aside from recognition. When they recognize both cities in a pair, they have a 60% chance of correctly choosing the larger one on the basis of this other knowledge, so their *knowledge validity* is .60.

Suppose the tester randomly draws pairs from the 20 largest German cities and asks the three brothers to decide which member of each pair has the larger population. Who will score highest? The youngest brother guesses the answer to every question and thus gets 50% correct. The eldest brother relies on his knowledge about the cities to answer every question and scores 60% correct. Neither the youngest brother nor the eldest brother can use the recognition heuristic, the former because he fails to recognize any of the cities and the latter because he recognizes them all. The only one with partial ignorance to exploit, the middle brother, makes 68 correct inferences. He surpasses the inference accuracy of the eldest brother because his recognition validity of .80 exceeds the elder brother's knowledge validity of .60.[1]

How Recognition Exploits Environmental Correlations

How can people learn the association between recognition and a criterion when the criterion is not accessible? Goldstein and Gigerenzer (2002) proposed that there are "mediators" in the environment that both reflect the criterion and are accessible to the decision maker. For example, although a person may not know the population size of a German city, its size may be reflected in how often it is mentioned in the person's environment. This frequency of mention, in turn, is correlated with how likely the person is to recognize the city's name. This chain of correlations would enable people to make inferences about a city's size on the basis of whether they recognized it. To test the extent to which environmental frequencies operate as mediators between city recognition and city population, Goldstein and Gigerenzer (2002) computed the correlations among three measures for each of the 83 German

cities with more than 100,000 inhabitants: the actual population, the number of times the city was mentioned in the *Chicago Tribune* over a specific period, and the *recognition rate,* that is, the proportion of University of Chicago students who recognized the city (see upper portion of Figure 4-1).

The *ecological correlation,* that is, the correlation between how often a city was mentioned in the *Chicago Tribune* and its population, was .82. Does newspaper coverage of a city correlate with the number of people who recognized it? Yes, the *surrogate correlation,* that is, the correlation between how often a city was mentioned and the number of people recognizing it, was .66. Finally, the correlation between the number of people recognizing a city and its population, known as the *average recognition validity,* was .60. In other words, the cities' recognition rates were more closely associated with how often they were mentioned than with their actual populations. Because recognition tracks environmental frequency more closely than it tracks population size in this context, Goldstein and Gigerenzer (2002) suggested that environmental frequency is the mediator between recognition and population size.

The recognition heuristic relies on ignorance that is partial and systematic. It works because lack of recognition knowledge about objects such as cities, colleges, sports teams, and companies traded on a stock market is often not random. For Goldstein and Gigerenzer (2002), a lack of recognition comes from never having encountered something, dividing the "world into the novel and previously experienced" (p. 77). If human recognition were so exquisitely sensitive to novelty that it treated as unrecognized only those objects and events that one has never seen, then experience would eventually render the recognition heuristic inapplicable (see Todd & Kirby, 2001). Like the ignorance that comes from lack of experience, forgetting may maintain or even boost inferential accuracy by making the old, novel again. For illustration, consider the oldest brother in the three-brother scenario. If he were able to forget some of the city names, he could take advantage of the recognition heuristic. The resulting changes in his

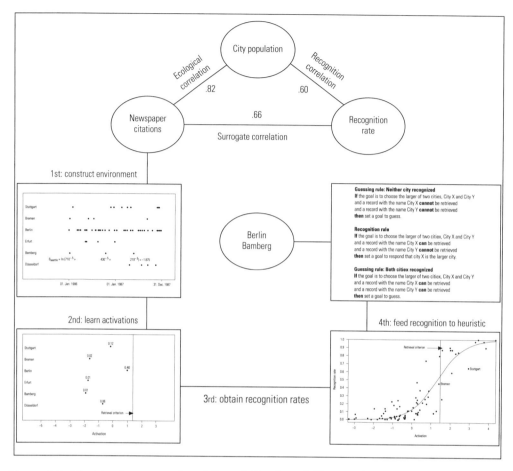

Figure 4-1. The triangle on top, adapted from Goldstein and Gigerenzer's (2002; Figure 7), shows the Pearson correlations between how often a German city was mentioned in the *Chicago Tribune*, its population, and its recognition rate. The lower portion outlines the steps in the simulation described in the text. 1st: Environments are constructed based on word frequency information from the *Chicago Tribune*. 2nd: The base level activations of the city name records were learned from the environment. 3rd: The model's recognition rates were obtained by fitting it to the students' recognition rates. 4th: The recognition heuristic was applied to the German city task, drawing on the simulated recognition rates.

performance would depend on which cities he no longer recognized. If his forgetting were random, he could not effectively exploit his "recovered" ignorance. If he tended to forget the names of smaller cities (of which he is likely to have heard about much less frequently), however, he could benefit from his ignorance. The recognition heuristic may not be the only inference strategy that could thus benefit from forgetting.

HOW RETRIEVAL FLUENCY ENABLES HEURISTIC INFERENCE: THE FLUENCY HEURISTIC

A key property of heuristics is that they are applicable under limited circumstances that, ideally, can be precisely defined. The recognition heuristic, for example, cannot be applied when both objects are either recognized or unrecognized. Thus, if a person's recognition rate is either very low or very high, he or she can rarely use the heuristic. When he or she does not recognize either object, use of the recognition heuristic gives way to, for instance, guessing. When he or she recognizes both objects, more knowledge-intensive strategies, such as the *take-the-best heuristic,* can be recruited (Gigerenzer, Todd, et al., 1999). Take-the-best sequentially searches for cues that are correlated with the criterion in the order of their predictive accuracy and chooses between the objects on the basis of the first cue found that discriminates between them (Gigerenzer & Goldstein, 1996).

Another, less knowledge-intensive, inference strategy that can be applied to a two-alternative choice when both objects are recognized is the *fluency heuristic* (see, e.g., Jacoby & Brooks, 1984; Toth & Daniels, 2002; Whittlesea, 1993). It can be expressed as follows: If one of two objects is more fluently processed, then infer that this object has the higher value with respect to the criterion.

Like the recognition heuristic, the fluency heuristic relies on only one consideration to make a choice; in this case, the fluency with which the objects are processed when encountered. In numerous studies, processing fluency mediated by prior experience with a stimulus has been shown to function as a cue in a range of judgments. For example, more fluent processing due to previous exposure can increase the perceived fame of nonfamous names *(the false fame effect;* Jacoby, Kelley, Brown & Jasechko, 1989) and the perceived truth of repeated assertions *(the reiteration effect;* Begg, Anas, & Farinacci, 1992; Hertwig, Gigerenzer, & Hoffrage, 1997).

As we show shortly, the ACT-R architecture offers the possibility of precisely defining fluency and how it depends on the past history of environmental exposure. As in the case of the recognition heuristic, the ACT-R architecture allows us to examine how forgetting may affect the fluency heuristic's accuracy. But unlike the recognition heuristic, the fluency heuristic seems to reflect the common intuition that more information is better (see Hertwig & Todd, 2003). To appreciate this, let us return to the oldest of the three brothers, who recognizes all the 20 largest German cities. If his history of exposure to the

cities, mediated by this history's effect on fluency, were indicative of their population size, he may now be able to match or even outdo the performance of the middle brother. To figure out which brother will do best, one needs to know the two heuristics' *validities* (the percentage of correct inferences that each yields in cases in which it is applicable) and *application* rates (to what proportion of choices can each heuristic be applied).

The fluency heuristic, in contrast to the recognition heuristic, does not exploit partial ignorance but rather graded recognition. Could it also benefit from forgetting? This is one of the key questions that we address in our analysis. Specifically, we investigate the role of forgetting in memory-based heuristics by modeling the relation between environmental exposure and the information in memory on which heuristics such as recognition and fluency feed. To lay the necessary groundwork, we now provide a brief introduction to the ACT-R architecture and describe how we implemented the recognition and fluency heuristics within it.

A BRIEF OVERVIEW OF ACT-R

ACT-R is a unified theory of cognition that accounts for a diverse set of phenomena ranging from subitizing (Peterson & Simon, 2000) to scientific discovery (Schunn & Anderson, 1998). A central distinction in ACT-R is between declarative knowledge *(knowing that)* and procedural knowledge *(knowing how).* ACT-R models procedural knowledge with sets of production rules (i.e., if-then rules) whose conditions (the "if" part of the rule) are matched against the contents of declarative memory. The fundamental declarative representation in ACT-R is the chunk, which we refer to here as a *record* to highlight the parallels between memory retrieval and information retrieval in library science. If all the conditions of a production rule are met, then the rule fires, and the actions specified in the "then" part of the rule are carried out. These actions can include updating records, creating new records, setting goals, and initiating motor responses. For example, Table 4-1 shows a set of colloquially expressed production rules that implement the recognition heuristic.

Table 4-1. The Production Set that Implements the Recognition Heuristic

Rule	Description
Guessing: Neither city recognized	**If** the goal is to choose the larger of two cities, City X and City Y, and a record with the name City X **cannot** be retrieved, and a record with the name City Y **cannot** be retrieved, **then** set a goal to guess.
Recognition	**If** the goal is to choose the larger of two cities, City X and City Y, and a record with the name City X **can** be retrieved, and a record with the name City Y **cannot** be retrieved, **then** set a goal to respond that City X is the larger city.
Guessing: Both cities recognized	**If** the goal is to choose the larger of two cities, City X and City Y, and a record with the name City X **can** be retrieved, and a record with the name City Y **can** be retrieved, **then** set a goal to guess.

Which of the rules in Table 4-1 will apply depends on whether records associated with City X and City Y can be retrieved. The overall performance of the recognition heuristic depends on (a) how often each of these rules applies and (b) when they do apply, how accurate the inferences are. Hereafter we refer to the complete set of rules in Table 4-1 as the *recognition heuristic* and to the second rule specifically as the *recognition rule.*

In ACT-R, declarative memory and procedural memory interact through retrieval mechanisms that assume that certain events tend to recur in the environment at certain times. In essence, the records that the system retrieves at a given point can be seen as a bet about what will happen next in the environment. In this framework, human memory functions as an information retrieval system, and the elements of the current context constitute a query to long-term memory to which the memory system responds by retrieving the records that are most likely to be relevant.

Many word processors incorporate a time-saving feature that, like ACT-R, takes advantage of forgetting. When a user goes to open a document file, the program presents a "file buffer," a list of recently opened files from which the user can select. Whenever the desired file is included on the list, the user is spared the effort of searching through the file hierarchy. For this device to work efficiently, however, the word processor must provide users with the files they actually want. It does so by "forgetting" files that are considered unlikely to be needed on the basis of the assumption that the time since a file was last opened is negatively correlated with its likelihood of being needed now. Similarly, the declarative retrieval mechanism in ACT-R makes more recently retrieved memory records more accessible on the assumption that the probability that a record is needed now depends in part on how long ago it was last needed.

Conducting Search

ACT-R makes the assumptions that information in long-term memory is stored in discrete records and that retrieval entails searching through them to find the one that achieves some processing goal of the system. The explanatory power of the approach depends on the system's estimates of the probability that each record in long-term memory is the one sought. In keeping with common usage in library science, we call this the *relevance probability.*[2] Any information retrieval system must strike a balance between the rate of recall, in this context the likelihood of finding the desired record (i.e., the proportion of hits), and the precision of recall, or the likelihood of retrieving irrelevant records (i.e., the proportion of false alarms). In ACT-R, this balance is achieved through a guided search process in which the records are retrieved in order of their relevance probabilities, with the most promising records looked up first.

Stopping Search

At some point, the information retrieval system must terminate search for further records. *If p* is the relevance probability, C is the cost of attempting to match a memory record against a condition of a production rule, and G is the gain associated with successfully finding the target, then according to ACT-R the memory system should stop considering records when:

$$pG < C. \qquad (4\text{-}1)$$

In other words, the system stops searching for more memory records when the expected value (pG) of the next record is less than the cost of considering it. If the next record to be considered has a relevance probability of less than $C \div G$, search will be stopped.

Activation Reflects Relevance

In ACT-R, the activation of a declarative memory record reflects its relevance probability. Specifically, the activation, A, equals the log odds (i.e., $\ln[p/(1-p)]$) that the record will be needed to achieve a processing goal (i.e., that it will match a condition of a production rule that fires). A record's activation is calculated by a combination of the base-level strength of the record, B_i, and the S_{ji} units of activation the record receives from each of the j elements of the current context:

$$A_i = B_i + \sum_j S_{ji}. \qquad (4\text{-}2)$$

A record's base-level strength is rooted in its environmental pattern of occurrence. Specifically, B_i is determined by how frequently and recently the record has been encountered in the past:

$$B = \ln(\sum_{j=1}^{n} t_j^d), \qquad (4\text{-}3)$$

where the record has been encountered n times in the past and the jth encounter occurred t_j time units in the past. Finally, d is a decay parameter that captures the amount of forgetting in declarative memory, thus determining how much information about an item's environmental frequency is retained in memory.[3] Typically, d is set to equal $-.50$, a value that has been shown to

fit a wide range of behavioral data (Anderson & Lebiere, 1998).

Consider, for illustration, the occurrence of American city names in the front-page headlines of the *New York Times*. Each circle in Figure 4-2 indicates a day on which a particular city appeared in the front-page headlines between January 1, 1986, and December 31, 1987. Clearly, there are drastic differences between cities in their frequency of occurrence. The national capital, Washington, DC, was mentioned 37 times during that period, first on January 14, 1986, and last on December 26, 1987. Seattle, in contrast, was mentioned merely 3 times—710, 430, and 219 days before January 1, 1988. Figure 4-2 also shows how these quantities were used to determine base-level activation on January 1, 1988. For this calculation, the parameter d, the decay rate, was set to $-.50$, and the resulting activation for Seattle, for example, is $\ln(710^{-.50} + 430^{-.50} + 219^{-.50}) = -1.87$.

Activation and Retrieval Probability

Whether a memory record's activation exceeds the retrieval criterion is determined by a noisy process. The sources of noise include momentary fluctuations in a record's estimated gain, estimated cost, and the activation it receives from the current constellation of context elements. These context elements could be part of our external environment, such as words on a sign, or internal, such as our mood or recently activated records. In the simulations reported below, we do not model the influence of contextual information, represented by the second term in Equation 4-2, in detail but rather assume that it contributes to the overall variance in activation. Because of its variability, the activation of a memory record is better represented by a distribution of activation values than by a single value, with B (see Equation 4-3) as the distribution's expected value. In ACT-R, activation is modeled as a logistic distribution, which approximates a normal distribution. Figure 4-3 shows these distributions around the expected value of the activation for the cities depicted in Figure 4-2.

The probability that a record will be retrieved, that is, that its activation will exceed the

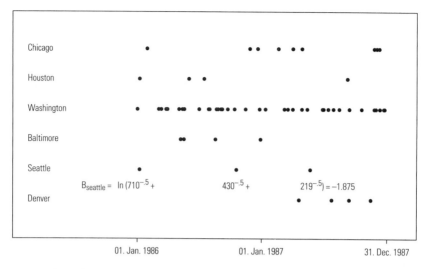

Figure 4-2. Number of days on which various city names were mentioned on the front page of the *New York Times* headlines.

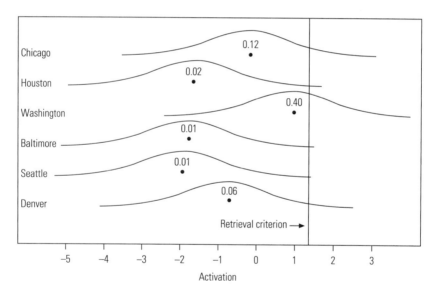

Figure 4-3. Activation distributions for the city name records that result from being mentioned in the front-page headlines of the *New York Times* headlines. The points correspond to the expected value of the distribution. The number at the center of each distribution shows the proportion of the distribution that lies to the right of the retrieval criterion τ (which to be consistent with subsequent simulations is set to 1.44). This proportion is the probability that the system will be able to retrieve the record and thereby recognize the city.

retrieval criterion, can be expressed as a logistic function:

$$\text{Probability of record retrieval} = \frac{1}{1 + e^{-(A - \tau)/s}}, \quad (4\text{-}4)$$

where s captures momentary and permanent fluctuations in the activation level of record i. Parameter τ equals $\ln C \div (G - C)$, a stopping rule that is equivalent to the $p < C \div G$-criterion from Equation 4-1 but transformed into the activation scale. The proportion of a record's activation distribution that is above the retrieval criterion, τ, gives the probability that the particular record will be retrieved. Retrieval of the memory record is crucial for our analysis of the recognition heuristic because we adopt Anderson, Bothell, Lebiere, and Matessa's (1998) assumption that retrieval of a record implies recognition of the associated word or, in this case, of the city name. The retrieval criterion τ is typically estimated by fitting models to data. The value of 1.44 used in Figure 4-3 is taken from the subsequent simulations. As Figure 4-3 shows, about 1/20 of the activation distribution for Denver, for example, lies to the right of the retrieval criterion, corresponding to a 6% chance that Denver will be recognized.

In brief, the relevance probability of each memory record is reflected in its distribution of activation. Records are searched in order of their activation until either a record is found that satisfies the current condition or the activation of the next record to be considered is so low that it is not worth considering.[4]

Activation and Retrieval Time

In ACT-R, retrieval time is an exponential function of activation:

$$\text{Retrieval time for a record} = Fe^{-A} \qquad (4\text{-}5)$$

where A is the activation for a particular record and F is a scale parameter. Anderson et al. (1998) found that values of F can be systematically estimated from the retrieval threshold, τ, using the equation $F = .348e^{\tau}$, so τ of 1.44 yields a value of 1.47 for F. Figure 4-4 plots Equation 4-5 for these parameter values, and the solid line represents the range of retrieval times that would be observed for activation values exceeding the retrieval threshold. As Figure 4-4 shows, the lower the activation, the more time it takes to retrieve a record. The open circle represents the retrieval time for a memory record whose activation falls just above τ. A memory record with activation below this point will fall short of the retrieval criterion and, because records with such low activations are unlikely to achieve processing goals, will fail to be retrieved at all.

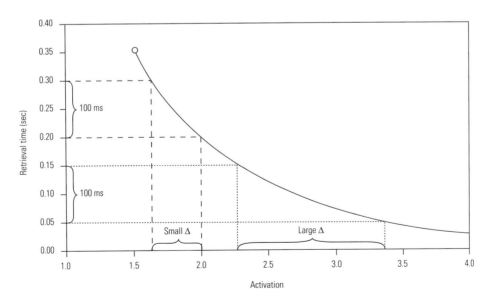

Figure 4-4. An exponential function relates a record's activation to its retrieval time. The open circle represents the retrieval time associated with τ, the retrieval criterion. Points to the left of τ are associated with low activation levels that result in retrieval failure.

As Figure 4-4 reveals, subsequent increases in activation lead to diminishing reductions in retrieval time, a property that, as we show shortly, is crucial to understanding how forgetting impacts the fluency heuristic. We now turn to the implementation of the recognition and fluency heuristics within ACT-R, which depend on the probability and speed of retrieval, respectively.

THE RECOGNITION AND FLUENCY HEURISTICS: KEYS TO ENCRYPTED ENVIRONMENTAL FREQUENCY

In ACT-R, activation tracks environmental regularities, such as an object's frequency and recency of occurrence. Therefore, activation differences partly reflect frequency differences, which, in turn, may be correlated with a characteristic of the object, such as the population of a city. Thus, it may seem that inferences could be based on activation values read off the records. However, applications of ACT-R have long assumed that, just as the long-term potentiation of neurons in the hippocampus cannot be tapped directly, subsymbolic quantities such as activation cannot be accessed directly. We nevertheless propose that the system can capitalize on differences in activation associated with various objects by gauging how it responds to them. Two responses that are correlated with activation in ACT-R are (a) whether a record associated with a specific object can be retrieved and (b) how quickly the record can be retrieved. The first, *binary* response underlies our implementation of the recognition heuristic, and the second, *continuous* response underlies our implementation of the fluency heuristic. We show that the heuristics can be understood as tools that indirectly tap the environmental frequency information locked in the activation values. The heuristics' effectiveness depends on the strength of the chain of correlations linking the criteria, environmental frequencies, activations, and responses. As we will demonstrate, forgetting strengthens this chain. Before we describe the simulations, a more general remark about the notion of recognition in ACT-R is in order.

ACT-R MODEL OF RECOGNITION

In modeling the recognition and fluency heuristics, we borrow from the Anderson et al. (1998) account of recognition. In an episodic recognition task, a person decides whether an item, typically a word, has been encountered in some specific context, say, in a newspaper article. The responses of the Anderson et al. model are determined by whether various memories are retrieved, thus the model assumes an all-or-none or a high-threshold notion of recognition, which is consistent with how Goldstein and Gigerenzer (2002) treat recognition.

In the literature on recognition memory, there is debate about whether such high-threshold models are compatible with the receiver operating characteristic (ROC) curves typically observed in recognition memory experiments (e.g., Batchelder, Riefer, & Hu, 1994; Kinchla, 1994; Malmberg, 2002). ROC curves, which are diagnostic of a participant's ability to distinguish between different kinds of stimuli, can be derived by manipulating participants' response bias. Specifically, in a recognition memory experiment, they are encouraged to be more or less liberal in their tendency to say that they recognize a stimulus. Based on these judgments, one can plot for each level of response bias a point that corresponds to the resulting hit rate and false alarm rate. The problem with standard implementations of discrete-state models is that they yield linear ROC curves. The curves participants generally produce, however, are curvilinear and are consistent with the more widely accepted signal detection theory (SDT) view of recognition, in which memory judgments are based on continuous information.

Does this property of high-threshold models by extension disqualify the Anderson et al. (1998) recognition model? In fact, their model does not produce ROC curves of any sort, simply because no mechanisms were specified to handle changes in response bias or to generate confidence ratings (which can also be used to generate ROC curves). Though straightforward modifications, such as varying the propensity of the model to respond so that it recognizes items, will not yield curvilinear ROC curves, one ought not jump to the conclusion that the Anderson et al. model cannot produce appropriate ROC curves. Malmberg (2002) demonstrated that whether a high-threshold model produces linear or curvilinear ROC curves depends critically on the assumptions made about the mechanisms that produce the confidence ratings. So though ACT-R belongs to the class of high-threshold models, its retrieved memory records rest on a continuous memory variable (i.e., activation). This variable, in turn, could be used to construct (curvilinear) ROC curves on the basis of confidence ratings.

To conclude, Anderson et al. (1998) did not consider basic ROC curves. Yet, the model has accounted quite successfully for many recognition memory effects, including the vexing list-strength effect (Ratcliff, Shiffrin, & Clark, 1990), which could not be handled by the mathematical models existing at the time. In addition, the same basic mechanisms have been applied to dozens of empirical results in a wide range of domains. All in all, we believe we are on solid theoretical ground by drawing on the Anderson et al. ACT-R account of recognition for modeling the recognition and the fluency heuristic. In the General Discussion section, we return to the distinction of binary versus continuous notions of recognition and consider a model that adopts a signal-detection view of recognition.

SIMULATIONS OF THE RECOGNITION AND FLUENCY HEURISTICS

Figure 4-1 illustrates the basic steps in our simulations that applied our ACT-R models of the recognition and fluency heuristics to the city population comparison task. First, we constructed environments that consisted of the names of German cities and the days on which they were encountered. Second, the model learned about each city from the constructed environments by strengthening memory records associated with each city according to Equation 4-3, ACT-R's base-level activation equation. Third, we determined the model's recognition rates by fitting Equation 4-4, the probability of retrieving a record given its activation, to the

rates at which the Goldstein and Gigerenzer (2002) participants recognized the cities. Fourth, these recognition rates were used to drive the performance of the recognition and fluency heuristics on the city population comparison task. We now describe these simulations in detail.

How the City Environments Were Constructed

In the simulations, the probability of encountering a German city name on a given day was proportional to its relative frequency in the *Chicago Tribune*. The frequencies were taken from the Goldstein and Gigerenzer (2002) counts of how often the 83 largest German cities were mentioned between January 1, 1985, and July 31, 1997. Thus, the probability of encountering city i on any given day was:

$$P(i) = \frac{f_i}{w}, \tag{4-6}$$

where f_i is the total number of citations for the ith city, and w is the total number days in the sample (the historical window). For example, Berlin, the largest city, was mentioned 3,484 times in the 4,747-day sample, so its daily encounter probability was .73. Duisburg, the 12th largest city, was mentioned 53 times, yielding a probability of .011. Based on these encounter probabilities, a historical environment was created for each city that consisted of a vector of 1s and 0s, where a 1 indicated that the city's name had been encountered on a particular day and 0 indicated that it had not. Because the size of the historical window is arbitrary, we set it to 4,747, the total number of days in the Goldstein and Gigerenzer analysis.

For this set of simulations, the probability of encountering a city on any given day was fixed according to Equation 4-6. That is, the probability of encountering a city was independent of when it was last encountered, though, of course, cities with higher probabilities would tend to have shorter lags between encounters than would less frequent cities. Later we report simulations that used environments with a more refined statistical structure, which led to comparable conclusions.

How the Activations for the Cities' Records Were Learned

As in the example illustrated in Figures 4-2 and 4-3, each city had an associated memory record that was strengthened according to Equation 4-3. When the end of each time window was reached, activation values for each city were calculated by averaging its activation across 500 constructed environments. The subsequent simulations are based on these average activation values. As one interprets the simulation results, however, it may be helpful to keep in mind Anderson's (1993) approximation to Equation 4-3:

$$B = k + \ln n - d \ln T, \tag{4-7}$$

where k is a constant, n is the number of times the item associated with the record has been encountered, and T is how long it has been since the record was first created. Taking the natural log compresses larger numbers more than smaller ones. Thus, because of this compression, each successive encounter with an item contributes less than the preceding encounter to the total activation. Similarly, activation decays quickly at first and more slowly thereafter, because each subsequent "tick" of the clock is compressed, and so subtracts less and less from the total activation.

Does Activation Capture the Correlation Between Environmental Frequency and the Criterion?

For the recognition and fluency heuristics to be useful inference strategies, activation needs to reflect the relation between objects' frequencies in the environment and their values on the criterion. Given that the ecological correlation between the raw citation counts and the city population size $(r = .82)$ is high, judgments of city size based on citation counts can reasonably be taken as an upper bound on inferential performance. Indeed, inferences about which of two cities is larger based on these counts (where a higher count implies a larger city) are accurate in 76.5% of city comparisons. In comparison, inferences based on a city's average activation (where a higher activation implies a larger city)

have an accuracy of 76.4%, just .1 percentage point below those based on the raw frequency information. Thus, activation seems to closely track the cities' environmental frequencies. With these bounds on accuracy in mind, we now examine the performance of the recognition and fluency heuristics.

An ACT-R Model of the Recognition Heuristic

The performance of the recognition and fluency heuristics depends on the cities' recognition rates. In line with Anderson et al. (1998), a city was recognized when the record associated with the city could be retrieved. A city's recognition rate was estimated by fitting Equation 4-4, which relates a record's activation to its probability of retrieval, to the empirical recognition rates that Goldstein and Gigerenzer (2002) observed. Equation 4-4's two free parameters were estimated using the nonlinear regression function from SPSS 11.0. These are τ, the retrieval criterion (estimated to be 1.44 units of activation), and s, the activation noise (estimated to be .728). The correlation between the estimated and empirical recognition rates was high $(r = .91)$. Figure 4-5 plots recognition as a function of activation. The points represent the empirical recognition rates, and the S-shaped curve shows the estimated recognition rates based on ACT-R's retrieval mechanisms (Equation 4-4).

To see how the Chicago students would be expected to do on the city comparison task, if they were to employ the recognition heuristic, we calculated the recognition heuristic's performance based on the empirical recognition rates recorded by Goldstein and Gigerenzer (2002). That is, if only one city was recognized, that city was chosen; otherwise, a guess was made. Performance of the recognition heuristic based on the empirical and model's recognition rates on all possible city pairs was .606 and .613, respectively. This indicates good agreement between the behavior of the ACT-R model of the recognition heuristic and that expected from the students.

Based on this correspondence, we can now pose novel questions concerning whether the recognition and fluency heuristics benefit from loss of information in memory.

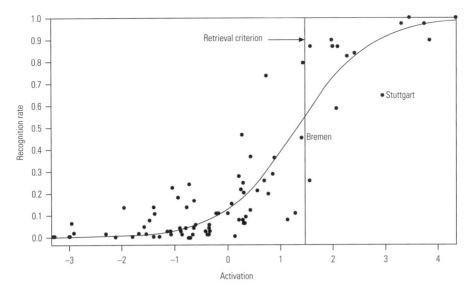

Figure 4-5. Recognition rate plotted as a function of activation. The points indicate the observed recognition rates of the 83 German cities. The S-shaped curve relates the activation of a city's record to its estimated recognition rate. For instance, Bremen has an observed recognition rate of .45, an activation of 1.39, and an estimated recognition rate of .48. Stuttgart has an observed recognition rate of .64, an activation of 2.89, and an estimated recognition rate of .88.

Does Forgetting Benefit the Recognition Heuristic?

To address this question, we varied the decay rate d (holding both the retrieval criterion, τ, and the activation noise, s, constant) and observed how the resulting changes in recognition affect inferences in the city population task.[5] The upper bound of the decay rate, 0, means no forgetting, the strength of a memory record is strictly a function of its frequency. Negative values of d imply forgetting, and more negative values imply more rapid forgetting. Using a step size of .01, we tested d values ranging from 0 to −1, the latter being twice the ACT-R default decay rate. In Figure 4-6, the solid line shows the recognition heuristic's average performance on pairwise comparisons of all German cities with more than 100,000 residents, including pairs in which it had to guess because both cities are recognized or unrecognized. Three aspects of this function are noteworthy. First, the recognition heuristic's performance assuming no forgetting (56% correct) is substantially worse than its performance assuming the "optimal" amount of forgetting (63.3% correct). Second, ACT-R's default decay value of −.50 yields 61.3% correct, only slightly below the peak performance level, which is reached at a decay rate of −.34. Third, the sensitivity curve has a flat maximum, with all decay values from −.13 to −.56 yielding performance in excess of 60% correct.

In other words, forgetting enhances the performance of the recognition heuristic, and the amount of forgetting can vary over a substantial range without compromising the heuristic's good performance. If there is too much forgetting (resulting in a situation in which most cities are unrecognized), however, the performance of the recognition heuristic eventually approaches chance level.

How Does Forgetting Help the Recognition Heuristic's Performance?

Two quantities shed more light on the link between forgetting and the recognition heuristic. The first is the proportion of comparisons in which the recognition rule can be used as the basis for making a choice, that is, the proportion

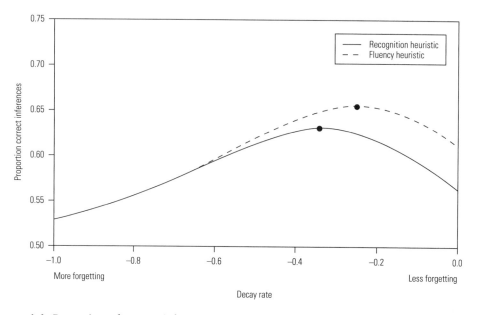

Figure 4-6. Proportion of correct inferences made by the recognition and fluency heuristics on all comparisons of the 83 largest cities in Germany. The amount of forgetting in the system was varied from 0, corresponding to no forgetting, to −1, a high forgetting rate. The peaks of each curve are marked with dots.

of comparisons in which only one of the cities is recognized. In Figure 4-7, the solid line shows that for the recognition rule this *application rate* peaks when d equals −.28, an intermediate level of forgetting. The second quantity is the proportion of correct inferences made by the recognition heuristic in those choices to which it is applicable. As shown in Figure 4-8, this recognition validity generally increases with the amount of forgetting, peaking when d equals −1. The performance (see Figure 4-6) and application rate (see Figure 4-7) peak at nearly the same forgetting rates of −.34 and −.28, compared to the peak of −1 for the validity curve (see Figure 4-8). So the decay rate of −.34 can be thought of as the optimal trade-off between the effects of forgetting on application rate and validity, with the application rate having the greater sway over performance. Thus, intermediate amounts of forgetting increase the performance of the recognition heuristic by sharply increasing its applicability and, to a lesser extent, by increasing its validity.

The results of the ACT-R simulations of the recognition heuristic suggest that forgetting serves to maintain the memory system's partial ignorance, a precondition for the heuristic's functioning. Loss of some information—a loss that is not random but a function of a record's environmental history—fosters the performance of the recognition heuristic. But how robust is this result and is it limited to the recognition heuristic that takes recognition to be all-or-one? To find out whether the phenomenon generalizes to memory-based inference strategies that make finer distinctions than that between recognition and nonrecognition, we now turn to the fluency heuristic.

An ACT-R Model of the Fluency Heuristic

The recognition heuristic exploits the correlation between recognizing an object and its environmental frequency, but when both objects are recognized this correlation is of no use. Yet, recognized objects could differ in their activation levels, indicating a difference in frequency. Although these activation differences cannot be assessed directly, Equation 4-5 raises the possibility that retrieval time, because of its one-to-one mapping with activation, could be used as a

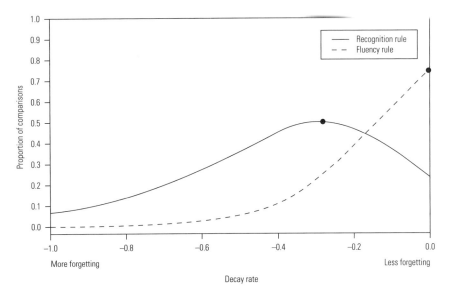

Figure 4-7. Application rate of the recognition rule and fluency rule. The application rate for the recognition rule is the proportion of all comparisons in which only one of the cities is recognized. The application rate for the fluency rule is the proportion of all comparisons in which both cities are recognized.

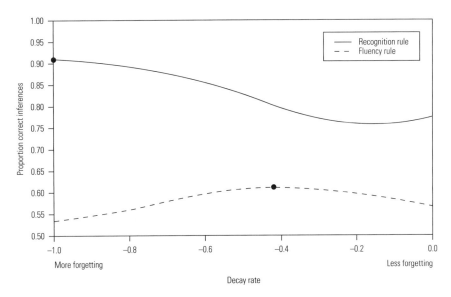

Figure 4-8. Validity of the recognition rule and fluency rule. The validity of a rule is the proportion of correct inferences that the rule makes when it can be applied.

proxy for activation. To see how this might be accomplished, let us assume that people are sensitive to differences in recognition times (i.e., retrieval times). Specifically, let us suppose that the University of Chicago students in the

Goldstein and Gigerenzer (2002) studies could tell the difference between instantaneously recognizing Berlin, for instance, and taking a moment to recognize Stuttgart. We suggest that such differences in recognition time partly reflect retrieval time differences, which, according to Equation 4-5, reflect the base-level activations of the corresponding memory records.

Moreover, retrieval time allows us to make the notion of fluency of reprocessing more precise. Operationalizing fluency as retrieval time, we now implement the fluency heuristic within the ACT-R framework. In Table 4-2, we specify the fluency heuristic for the two-alternative choice between two cities as a set of three production rules that build on the rules constituting the recognition heuristic presented in Table 4-1.

The first two rules embody the essential components of the recognition heuristic: Guess when neither alternative is recognized, and choose the recognized alternative when one is recognized and the other is not. Triggered only when both alternatives are recognized, the fluency rule sets a goal of comparing retrieval times. Hereafter we refer to the complete set of rules in Table 4-2 as

Table 4-2. The Production Set that Implements the Fluency Heuristic

Rule	Description
Guessing	If the goal is to choose the larger of two cities, City X and City Y, and a record with the name City X *cannot* be retrieved, and a record with the name City Y *cannot* be retrieved, then set a goal to guess.
Recognition	If the goal is to choose the larger of two cities, City X and City Y, and a record with the name City X *can* be retrieved, and a record with the name City Y *cannot* be retrieved, then set a goal to respond that City X is the larger city.
Fluency	If the goal is to choose the larger of two cities, City X and City Y, and a record with the name City X *can* be retrieved, and a record with the name City Y *can* be retrieved, then set a goal to compare retrieval times, and respond that the city retrieved fastest is larger

the *fluency heuristic* and to the third rule of the set specifically as the *fluency rule*.

In the interest of psychological plausibility, we built in limits on the system's ability to discriminate between retrieval times. Rather than assuming that the system can discriminate between minute differences in any two retrieval times, we assume that if the retrieval times of the two alternatives are less than a just noticeable difference (JND) apart, then the system must guess. Guided by Fraisse's (1984) conclusion, which was based on an extensive review of the timing literature, that durations of less than 100 ms are perceived as instantaneous, we set the JND to 100 ms rather than modeling the comparison of retrieval times in detail. We do not claim, however, that this value captures people's actual thresholds exactly.

Comparison of the Fluency and Recognition Heuristics

The fluency heuristic assumes that people compare the retrieval times for the two objects and choose the object that is more quickly recognized (the other object may be more slowly recognized or come up unrecognized). How accurate is this heuristic compared with the recognition heuristic? Surprisingly, using the default decay rate of −.50, the fluency heuristic (62.1%) performs only slightly better than the recognition heuristic (61.3%).

Let us analyze this performance in more detail. Recall that recognition validity is the probability of getting a correct answer when one object is recognized and the other is not. The recognition validity in our simulation was .82. The overall accuracy of the recognition heuristic is reduced, because the heuristic resorts to guessing in cases in which both cities are recognized (5.5% of all comparisons) or both cities are not recognized (58.2% of all comparisons). Analogous to the recognition validity, *fluency validity* (i.e., the validity of the fluency rule) is the probability of getting a correct answer when both objects are recognized. The fluency validity is .61, lower than the recognition validity but still higher than the recognition heuristic's chance-level performance when recognition does not discriminate between objects.

From this it follows that the fluency heuristic's competitive advantage over the recognition heuristic depends on the relative frequency of city pairs in which both objects are recognized. It is only in these comparisons that the performance of the two heuristics can differ; when one object is recognized and the other is not, the two heuristics behave identically, and when neither object is recognized, both must guess. This conclusion is illustrated by comparing the performance of the two heuristics on different subsamples of cities. For example, if comparisons are restricted to the 10 largest German cities (resulting mostly in pairs in which both objects are recognized), the fluency heuristic has about a 5% performance advantage over the recognition heuristic (63.8% vs. 58.8%). This advantage drops to 3% when the 20 largest cities are included (66.7% vs. 63.3%) and to less than 1% when all 83 of the largest cities are included. In short, the fluency heuristic compares most favorably with the recognition heuristic when the sample is dominated by large cities that tend to be easily recognized.

Does Forgetting Benefit the Fluency Heuristic?

Loss of information bolsters the performance of the recognition heuristic, but does it give a boost to the fluency heuristic as well? Indeed, the dashed line in Figure 4-6 shows that performance of the fluency heuristic peaks at a decay rate of −.25. How can it be that the fluency heuristic's performance peaks at intermediate levels of forgetting—a heuristic that feeds on recognition knowledge and not lack thereof (as the recognition heuristic does)? Is it possible that the peak in performance at intermediate levels of forgetting stems solely from the recognition rule within the fluency heuristic?

To investigate whether the fluency rule enjoys any independent benefit of forgetting, we analyzed the set of city comparisons in which both cities are recognized (to which the fluency rule applies) and the proportion of correct inferences that the fluency rule makes in this set as a function of forgetting. Figure 4-7 shows that the fluency rule's application rate drops as forgetting rises, as one would expect given that the fluency

rule applies only when both cities are recognized. When it applies, however, the fluency rule indeed benefits from intermediate levels of forgetting. As Figure 4-8 demonstrates, the fluency rule's validity peaks at the intermediate decay rate of −.42, though this peak is well below that of the recognition rule's validity. That is, the peak in the fluency heuristic's performance at intermediate levels of forgetting stems from benefits of forgetting that cannot be reduced to those for the recognition rule. But how does the fluency rule benefit from forgetting?

What Causes the Fluency Rule's Validity to Peak at Intermediate Decay Rates?

To understand how one important factor contributes to the shape of the fluency rule's validity curve, let us revisit the exponential function that relates activation to latency in Figure 4-4. Consider first retrieval times of 200 and 300 ms, which correspond to activations of 1.99 and 1.59, respectively. For these relatively low activations, only a small difference of .40 units of activation is required to exceed the 100-ms JND. In contrast, the 100-ms difference in retrieval time between 50 and 150 ms corresponds to a difference of 1.1 units of activation. Thus, by shifting the activation range downward, forgetting helps the system settle on activation levels corresponding to retrieval times that can be more easily discriminated. In the case of the fluency heuristic, memory decay prevents the activation of (retrievable) records from becoming saturated.

Less Is More—Even for the Fluency Heuristic

Intermediate amounts of forgetting benefit not only the recognition heuristic but the fluency heuristic as well. Generally, the application and validity rates of the recognition rule and the validity rate of the fluency rule profit from faster forgetting, whereas the application rate of the fluency rule pulls strongly toward slower forgetting. In short, three of the four quantities that determine the performance of the fluency heuristic peak at faster decay rates. This observation is akin to the less-is-more effect for the recognition heuristic (see Figures 2 and 3 in Goldstein & Gigerenzer, 2002). In the less-is-more context, decision makers who know less might exhibit greater inferential accuracy than do those who know more. In the present context, decision makers who have intermediate rates of memory decay can make more accurate inferences than those with little or no decay—whether they are using the recognition heuristic or the fluency heuristic.

IS THE BENEFICIAL EFFECT OF FORGETTING ROBUST IN ENVIRONMENTS WITH NATURAL CLUSTERING?

In the simulations reported thus far, the probability of a city's name being mentioned on a particular day was taken to be proportional to its overall citation rate and independent of when the city's name was last mentioned. This assumption ignores a potentially important aspect of the environmental structure, namely, that the occasions on which an item (e.g., a city name) is encountered tend to cluster temporally. Consider, for instance, the pattern for Chicago in Figure 4-2. The cluster in early 1987 relates to

stories about the mayoral election. The cluster toward the end of 1987 relates to the mayor dying in office. Even without knowing what a word means, one can predict well how likely it is to be mentioned in the future on the basis of how recently and frequently it has been mentioned in the past. The ACT-R activation equation was designed to be sensitive to just such patterns (Anderson & Schooler, 1991). To find out whether the benefits of forgetting generalize to a model of the environment that reflects the natural clustering of events, the models already presented were run again, but this time on environments that contained natural clustering. This was achieved by making the probability of encountering a city name dependent both on how long ago it was last encountered and how frequently it was encountered in the recent past. These dependencies were modeled on those found by Anderson and Schooler (1991) in their analysis of word usage in the *New York Times* headlines.

Figure 4-9 shows how the performance of the recognition and the fluency heuristics depends on the decay rate in this clustered environment.

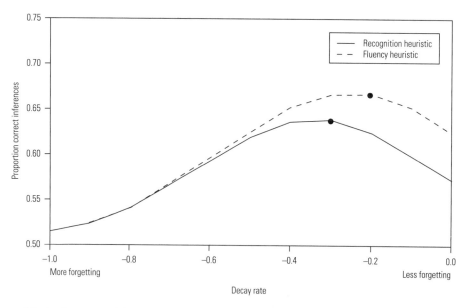

Figure 4-9. Performance of the recognition and fluency heuristics as the amount of forgetting varies, when activations are based on simulated environments that display more natural clustering of city mentions.

Although these curves are rough hewn because they are based on 11 decay values as opposed to the 101 decay values used to map out the other decay functions, the results are consistent with those of Figure 4-6 in which the probability of a word's being mentioned on a given day was proportional to its overall environmental frequency (see Equation 4-5). The similarity between the two sets of results suggests that learning over extended periods smoothes out the possible effects of clustering on performance.

GENERAL DISCUSSION

Some theorists have argued that forgetting is indispensable to the proper working of memory. Building on the notion of beneficial forgetting, we have demonstrated that ecologically smart loss of information—loss that is not random but reflects the environmental history of the memory record—may not only foster memory retrieval processes but can also boost the performance of inferential heuristics that exploit mnemonic information such as recognition and retrieval fluency. We did so by implementing inferential heuristics within an existing cognitive architecture, thus enabling us to analyze how parameters of memory such as information decay affect inferential accuracy. This analysis also revealed three distinct reasons for why forgetting and heuristics can work in tandem. In the case of the recognition heuristic, intermediate amounts of forgetting maintain the systematic partial ignorance on which the heuristic relies and increase somewhat the heuristic's validity, the probability that it correctly picks the larger city. In the case of the fluency heuristic, intermediate amounts of forgetting boost the heuristic's performance by maintaining activation levels corresponding to retrieval latencies that can be more easily discriminated. In what follows, we (a) discuss the robustness of the beneficial effects of forgetting, (b) investigate how the fluency heuristic relates to the availability heuristic, (c) discuss whether it is worthwhile maintaining the distinction between the fluency and recognition heuristics, and (d) conclude by examining whether forgetting plausibly could have evolved to serve heuristic inference.

A Signal-Detection View of Recognition: How Robust Are the Beneficial Effects of Forgetting?

We see the Goldstein and Gigerenzer (2002) recognition heuristic not so much as a model of recognition, but rather as a model of how the products of the recognition process could be used to make decisions. Given that the recognition heuristic starts where models of recognition leave off, it seems reasonable, for this purpose, to assume that items are either recognized or they are not, even if this is a simplification. However, as our interest was in the impact of forgetting on how the recognition heuristic operates, we needed to consider the details of the underlying recognition process. We adapted the Anderson et al. (1998) ACT-R model of episodic recognition, which is a high-threshold model that depends on the all-or-none retrieval of appropriate memory records. By adding fluency, our model is no longer strictly a high-threshold model because there is continuous information available for the retrieved items, though not for those items that failed to be retrieved. Models like this were considered by Swets, Tanner, and Birdsall (1961).

In what follows, we investigate whether our results are robust in the context of a signal-detection view of recognition memory, currently the most widely shared view of recognition. In this view, there is a potential for discriminability even among unrecognized items. Signal detection theory describes a decision maker who must choose between two (or more) alternatives—for instance, whether or not he or she has encountered a present stimulus previously—on the basis of ambiguous evidence (Green & Swets, 1966). This uncertain evidence is summarized by a random variable that has a different distribution under each of the alternatives (encountered vs. not encountered). The evidence distributions overlap, thus some events are consistent with each of the two alternatives. The decision maker establishes a decision criterion C that divides the continuous strength of evidence axis into regions associated with each alternative, for instance, the "recognized" versus the "unrecognized" region. If the evidence value associated with an event in question exceeds C, the decision maker will respond "recognized"; otherwise he or she will respond "unrecognized." On this view, though people's decisions are dichotomous (recognized vs. unrecognized), the underlying recognition memory and strength-of-evidence axis are not. Moreover, the unrecognized items are not of one kind but differ in gradation of strength, thus affording discrimination even if items are not recognized.

In the present ACT-R models of the fluency and recognition heuristic, the retrieval criterion, τ, doubles as a decision criterion for recognition. This dual role for τ is consistent with how it was used by Anderson et al. (1998). By decoupling τ's functions, we can now implement a version of the fluency heuristic that attempts to distinguish between unrecognized items. Specifically, if the retrieval criterion is assumed to be lower than the recognition decision criterion, then the fluency rule will apply to comparisons in which both objects exceed the modest retrieval criterion but remain unrecognized. The fluency heuristic can then capitalize on the fact that one unrecognized name is perhaps more fluently processed (i.e., has a higher activation value and faster retrieval time within ACT-R) than the other unrecognized name.

Will the benefits of forgetting generalize to this version of the fluency heuristic? To answer this question, we reran the simulations of the fluency heuristic but set τ so low that all memory records would be retrieved. As a result, all decisions were handled by the fluency rule. Figure 4-10 shows that forgetting also facilitates the performance of this version of the fluency heuristic. As in the previous simulations of the fluency heuristic, the reason for the performance boost is that loss of information lowers the range of activation to levels corresponding to more discriminable retrieval times. In other words, a given difference in activation in a lower part of the range results in a larger, more detectable difference in retrieval times than does the same-sized difference in a higher part of the range. Thus, the beneficial effects of forgetting also prove robust in a signal-detection view of recognition memory.

The Fluency and Availability Heuristics: Old Wine in a New Bottle?

The fluency heuristic feeds on environmental frequencies of occurrences that are related to criterion variables such as population size. It thus can be seen as another ecologically rational

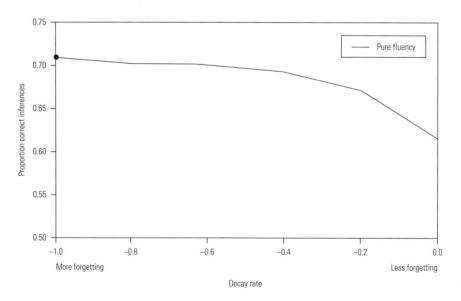

Figure 4-10. Performance of the fluency heuristic when continuous information is available for all city records.

cognitive strategy belonging to the *adaptive toolbox* of fast-and-frugal heuristics (Gigerenzer, Todd, et al., 1999). But is it new? Fluency shares an important property with one of the three major heuristics investigated in the heuristics-and-biases research program, namely, availability (Kahneman, Slovic, & Tversky, 1982). Both the availability heuristic and the fluency heuristic capitalize on a subjective sense of memory fluency. Tversky and Kahneman (1973) suggested that people using the availability heuristic assess the probability and the frequency of events on the basis of the ease or the frequency with which relevant instances of those events can be retrieved from memory. Thus, they proposed two notions of availability (Tversky & Kahneman, 1973, pp. 208, 210), one that depends on the actual frequencies of instances retrieved and one that depends on the ease with which the operation of retrieval can be performed (for more on the distinction between these two notions of availability, see Hertwig, Pachur, & Kurzenhäuser, 2005; Sedlmeier, Hertwig, & Gigerenzer, 1998).

If one understands availability to mean ease of retrieval, then the question arises regarding how ease should be measured. Sedlmeier et al. (1998), for example, proposed measuring ease in terms of speed of retrieval. Thus interpreted, availability becomes nearly interchangeable with fluency, although the fluency heuristic retrieves the event itself (e.g., the name of a city), whereas the availability heuristic retrieves instances from the class of events (e.g., people who died of a heart attack vs. people who died of lung cancer to estimate which of the two diseases has a higher mortality rate). We would have no objection to the idea that the fluency heuristic falls under the broad rubric of availability. In fact, we believe that our implementation of the fluency heuristic offers a definition of availability that interprets the heuristic as an ecologically rational strategy by rooting fluency in the informational structure of the environment. This precise formulation transcends the criticism that availability has been only vaguely sketched (e.g., Fiedler, 1983; Gigerenzer & Goldstein, 1996; Lopes & Oden, 1991). In the end, how one labels the heuristic that we have called fluency is immaterial because, as Hintzman (1990) observed, "the explanatory burden is carried by the nature of the proposed mechanisms and their interactions, not by what they are called" (p. 121).

The Fluency and Recognition Heuristics: Are They the Same Thing?

Heuristics, at their core, are models of cognitive processes. So, asking whether the fluency and recognition heuristics are the same thing amounts to asking whether they process information identically. In terms of our ACT-R implementation, the answer to this question is no. The recognition rule, once its conditions are matched, can proceed immediately to a decision. The fluency rule, in contrast, entails the additional steps required to compare the retrieval times for the respective objects. Having two distinct rules improves the overall efficiency of the system because information is processed only as much as is necessary to make a decision. But there is a second reason, independent of our implementation for keeping the heuristics separate. By assuming two heuristics, we can investigate situations in which one heuristic may be more applicable and effective than the other. For instance, the recognition heuristic may be more robust in the face of time pressure. When there is not enough time for distinctions in degrees of recognition, or for comparisons thereof, coarser information such as whether items are recognized may do the job. But even when people do have enough time to evaluate familiarity (or fluency), there may be factors that affect their sense of fluency but are less strongly related, unrelated, or even negatively related to recognition. For example, priming may be more likely to disrupt fluency assessments than recognition judgments. Moreover, if people had insight into the relative accuracy of recognition and fluency in a particular context, they might be able to select one heuristic over the other. By assuming two rather than one heuristic we retain the degrees of freedom to identify and model such situations.

What Came First: The Forgetting or the Heuristics?

One interpretation of the beneficial effect of forgetting as identified here is that the memory system loses information at the rate that it does in order to boost the performance of the recognition and fluency heuristics and perhaps other heuristics. On this view, an optimal amount of forgetting has evolved in the cognitive architecture in the service of memory-based inference heuristics. Though such a causal link may be possible in theory, we doubt that evolving inferential heuristics gave rise to a degree of forgetting that optimized their performance. The reason is that memory has evolved in the service of multiple goals. It is therefore problematic to argue that specific properties of human memory—for instance, forgetting and limited short-term memory capacity—have optimally evolved in the service of a single function. Although such arguments are seductive—for an example, see Kareev's (2000) thesis that limits on working memory capacity have evolved "so as to protect organisms from missing strong correlations and to help them handle the daunting tasks of induction" (p. 401)—they often lack a rationale for assuming that the function in question has priority over others.

On what anchors can one say that, for example, induction, object recognition, correlation detection, classification, or heuristic inference is the most important cognitive function? In the absence of an analysis that supports a principled ranking of these functions or a convincing argument as to why forgetting would have evolved in the service of one single function (and then later may have been co-opted by others), we hesitate to argue that memory loses information at the rate that it does in order to boost the performance of heuristics. We find it more plausible that the recognition heuristic, the fluency heuristic, and perhaps other heuristics have arisen over phylogenetic or ontogenetic time to exploit the existing forgetting dynamics of memory. If this were true, a different set of properties of memory (e.g., faster or slower forgetting rate) could have given rise to a different suite of heuristics.

Future Steps

By linking two research programs—the program on fast-and-frugal heuristics and the ACT-R research program—we were able to ground inference heuristics that exploit mnemonic information in a cognitive architecture. We believe that this synthesis opens potential avenues of research that go beyond those reported here. By implementing other heuristics, one could, for instance, investigate to what extent the benefits of forgetting may generalize to other heuristics, such as take-the-best, that rely on complexes of declarative knowledge (e.g., *Munich, Germany, has a professional soccer team*). In addition, such implementations may point toward other heuristics that have yet to be discovered.

We also believe that implementing heuristics within a cognitive architecture facilitates the investigation of questions that have been notoriously difficult to tackle within research on heuristics—issues such as how different heuristics are selected and how they are acquired. For example, Rieskamp and Otto (2006) have shown that associative learning mechanisms can capture how participants select between heuristics in ways that are adaptive for particular environments. Nellen (2003) found that associative learning mechanisms used in ACT-R can achieve an adaptive match between heuristics and environment structure as well. These investigations, however, presupposed the existence of a set of heuristics to select from. Stepping back even further, one may ask what are the "building blocks" of the fast-and-frugal heuristics, and what are the rules, the constraints, that govern the composition of the building blocks into new heuristics? Little progress, if any, has been made on this issue of the acquisition of heuristics. We believe that one promising place to look for building blocks and constraints on their composition is in the basic mechanisms of ACT-R. Building heuristics on an ACT-R foundation ensures, at the very least, that they are cognitively plausible. In addition, constructing heuristics in this way will enrich the understanding of the relation between the heuristics in the adaptive toolbox (see Gigerenzer, Todd, et al., 1999) and their basic cognitive foundations.

CONCLUSION

Analyses of cognitive limits, a well-studied topic in psychology, are usually underpinned by the assumption that cognitive limits, such as forgetting, pose a serious liability (see Hertwig & Todd, 2003). In contrast, we demonstrated that forgetting might facilitate human inference performance by strengthening the chain of correlations, linking the target criteria, environmental frequencies, and fundamental memory-retrieval processes. The recognition and fluency heuristics, we argued, use the response characteristics of these basic memory processes as a means to indirectly tap the environmental frequency information locked in the activations. In light of the growing collection of beneficial effects ascribed to cognitive limits (see Hertwig & Todd, 2003), we believe it timely to reconsider their often exclusively negative status and to investigate which limits may have evolved to foster which cognitive processes and which processes may have evolved to exploit specific limits—as we propose in the case of heuristic inference and forgetting.

ACKNOWLEDGMENTS

We thank John Anderson, Gerd Gigerenzer, Kenneth Malmberg, Carmi Schooler, Peter Todd, John Wixted, and the members of the ABC Research Group for their many constructive comments. We also thank Dan Goldstein for providing us with recognition rates and newspaper citation counts for the German cities.

NOTES

1. This score of correct inferences is derived as follows: There are a total of 190 comparisons. In 45 of them, the middle brother resorts to guessing because he recognizes none, thus scoring 50% correct inferences. In another 45, in which he recognizes both, he scores 60% correct (the validity of his additional knowledge). In the remaining 100 comparisons, he scores 80% correct inferences (due to the validity of his recognition knowledge). Thus, the total score of correct inferences equals $45 \times .5 + 45 \times .6 + 100 \times .8 = 129.5/190 = 68\%$.

2. In previous publications, Anderson and colleagues have called this *need probability*.

3. Within ACT-R time dependent forgetting is attributed to memory decay. In contrast, many memory researchers, beginning with McGeoch

(1932), have argued that tying forgetting to the passage of time through decay is simply a redescription of the empirical phenomenon rather than a description of an underlying process. As an alternative to decay, researchers have typically favored explanations that attribute time dependent forgetting to interference (e.g., Estes, 1955; Raaijmakers, 2003). On the interference view of forgetting, memory for a stimulus gets encoded in a particular context, consisting of myriads of internal and external elements. Those, in turn, have the potential to later act as retrieval cues. The context, however, "drifts" as cues (randomly) enter and leave it. As a consequence, fewer cues are shared between the original encoding and the retrieval contexts over time, thus lowering the probability of recall of the target stimulus. Within the ACT-R framework memory decay is claimed to be functional, but at the same time there is no commitment to the underlying causes of memory decay. Thus, ACT-R does not preclude explaining decay as the aggregate result of factors such as contextual drift process, neural degradation, or some other causes altogether. In addition, even the interference view of forgetting is not incompatible with ACT-R's premise that forgetting is instrumental in the organism meeting the informational demands posed by the environment. For instance, it is reasonable to assume that the rate at which new associations are strengthened influences the relative accessibility of older and newer memories. Specifically, to the extent that associations between cues and new memories are strengthened, the bonds between these cues and older memories will be weakened. Such a contingency leaves open the possibility that, over ontogenetic or phylogenetic times, the rate at which new associations are strengthened is set so as to tune the accessibility of older and newer memories to the informational demands posed by the environment.

4. For those who doubt the strictly serial nature of this search, Anderson and Lebiere (1998) have implemented a parallel connectionist model that yields the same result.

5. Alternatively, since τ and d trade off, we could have kept d constant and varied τ, but here we do not undertake an extensive analysis of the effect of this parameter on performance. In the General Discussion section, however, we do consider a model in which τ is set so low that all records can be retrieved.

Introduction to Chapter 5

Simple Heuristics and Rules of Thumb: Where Psychologists and Behavioural Biologists Might Meet

The ABC Research Group at the Max Planck Institute for Human Development is an interdisciplinary research community that has been working and publishing together for some 15 years now. In the social sciences, few interdisciplinary groups have been able to maintain functioning for such a continuous period, in our case despite high staff turnover. One of the reasons why interdisciplinarity works at the Institute is an important social institution: coffee time. Every afternoon at 4 PM, there is coffee and tea and, most important, time for exchange, learning, and trust. Researchers from roughly 10 disciplines share their knowledge to better understand decision making in an uncertain world. Two of these disciplines are psychology and behavioral biology.

This article by John Hutchinson, a biologist, and Gerd Gigerenzer, a psychologist by training, compares the ABC research program with the behavioral biology analysis of rules of thumb in animals. If we can find signs of the same rules of search, stopping, and decision making in several species, this might provide converging evidence for specific models of heuristics. Which heuristics can be found in both humans and other animals? For instance, biologists have argued that take-the-best might be in the adaptive toolbox of several species (e.g., Cross & Jackson, 2005; Shettleworth, 2005) and that the gaze heuristic (see Chapter 32) and its variants are used by baseball outfielders, bats, bees, and dogs to intercept prey, balls, or Frisbees (see Chapter 33). In food choice, Norway rats prefer food they recognize from having tasted or from having smelled on the breath of another rat. The recognition heuristic is followed even if the rat whose breath is smelled happens to be sick at the time (Galef, 1987; Galef, McQuoid, & Whiskin, 1990). Surprisingly, recognition dominates illness information, just as in humans, where brand-name recognition can dominate competing information from direct taste experience. For instance, when people taste two brands of peanut butter, a recognized brand and a no-name brand, they tend to find the recognized brand more tasty, even if they arrive at the opposite judgment when the products are not labeled (Hoyer & Brown, 1990). Thus, humans and other animals appear to share common heuristics.

Equally important is the question of which heuristics are not shared with other species. Evidence that two species solve a similar problem with different strategies may indicate different underlying cognitive capacities or different environments in which the species live. For instance, there is, at most, controversial evidence that even our closest relatives, primates, use *tit-for-tat*. Because heuristics depend on evolved or learned capacities, such as recognition memory and the ability to track moving objects against a noisy background, the absence of specific heuristics could be a clue to corresponding differences in core capacities.

We invite the reader to have a look at the 10 published reactions to the article, as well as the authors' reply to these (Hutchinson & Gigerenzer, 2005). Several commentators point to examples of animal behavior that appear to be based on heuristics similar to those used by humans; others ask whether the goal of general models of reinforcement learning might be to know what specific rules of thumb to use in what situation; and many emphasize the need for a more intense interdisciplinary exchange. The link between simple heuristics and complex worlds has been pointed out by John McNamara and Alasdair Houston (2009, p. 670): "Although behavioral ecologists have built complex models of optimal behavior in simple environments, we argue that they need to focus on simple mechanisms that perform well in complex environments."

CHAPTER 5

Simple Heuristics and Rules of Thumb: Where Psychologists and Behavioural Biologists Might Meet

John M.C. Hutchinson and Gerd Gigerenzer

Abstract: The Centre for Adaptive Behavior and Cognition (ABC) has hypothesized that much human decision making can be described by simple algorithmic process models (heuristics). This paper explains this approach and relates it to research in biology on rules of thumb, which we also review. As an example of a simple heuristic, consider the lexicographic strategy of take-the-best for choosing between two alternatives: Cues are searched in turn until one discriminates, then search stops and all other cues are ignored. Heuristics consist of building blocks, and building blocks exploit evolved or learned abilities such as recognition memory; it is the complexity of these abilities that allows the heuristics to be simple. Simple heuristics have an advantage in making decisions fast and with little information, and in avoiding overfitting. Furthermore, humans are observed to use simple heuristics. Simulations show that the statistical structures of different environments affect which heuristics perform better, a relationship referred to as ecological rationality. We contrast ecological rationality with the stronger claim of adaptation. Rules of thumb from biology provide clearer examples of adaptation because animals can be studied in the environments in which they evolved. The range of examples is also much more diverse. To investigate them, biologists have sometimes used similar simulation techniques to ABC, but many examples depend on empirically driven approaches. ABC's theoretical framework can be useful in connecting some of these examples, particularly the scattered literature on how information from different cues is integrated. Optimality modeling is usually used to explain less detailed aspects of behavior but might more often be redirected to investigate rules of thumb.

1. INTRODUCTION

We both work in a research group called the Centre for Adaptive Behavior and Cognition (ABC). Its main research topic is the cognitive mechanisms by which humans make decisions. We call these mechanisms *heuristics* and our thesis is that rather simple heuristics both work surprisingly well and are what humans

widely use. Simple heuristics correspond roughly to what behavioral biologists call rules of thumb. Our aim in this paper is to relate ABC's research to biological research on behavior. One of us (GG) is the director and founder of ABC, and, like most of the group, is a psychologist by training; the other (JMCH) is a behavioral ecologist who has worked in ABC for the last four years.

For a more thorough review of ABC's results and outlook, read the book *Simple Heuristics that Make Us Smart* (Gigerenzer, Todd, & the ABC Research Group, 1999). Another book, *Bounded Rationality: The Adaptive Toolbox*

(Gigerenzer & Selten, 2001), provides more of a discourse between ABC and other researchers. In the current paper, we seek to identify where behavioral biologists and ABC have used similar approaches or arrived at similar results, but also to clarify exactly where the two schools disagree or diverge on tactics. We thus hope to discover ways in which each discipline might learn from the other; we try to be open about potential limitations of ABC's approach. This paper is written to inform both biologists and psychologists.

Before making more general points, we start by giving some examples of the simple heuristics that ABC has studied, and then some examples of rules of thumb from biology. These will convey better than any definition the range of phenomena to which these terms are applied. The succeeding sections will deal more systematically with the principles behind ABC's research and contrast its techniques and findings with those from research on animal rules of thumb.

2. EXAMPLES OF FAST-AND-FRUGAL HEURISTICS IN HUMANS

2.1. Take-the-Best

Consider the task of which of two alternatives to choose given several binary cues to some unobservable criterion. An example is deciding which of two cities is the bigger, given such cues as whether each has a university or has a football team in the premier league. Gigerenzer and Goldstein (1996) proposed the following decision mechanism: (1) consider one cue at a time, always looking up the cue values for both alternatives; (2) if both cue values are identical examine the next cue, otherwise ignore all other cues and make a decision on the basis of this single cue; (3) if no cues are left to examine, guess. Such a process is called lexicographic because it resembles the obvious way to arrange two items into alphabetical order: First compare the first letters and only if they are identical consider the next letter. A hypothetical biological example might be a male bird that compares itself with a rival first on the basis of their songs; if the songs differ in quality the weaker rival leaves, and only

otherwise do both remain to compare one another on further successive cues, such as plumage or display.

We have not yet specified the order in which cues are examined. Intuitively it makes sense to try to look up the more reliable cues first, and also those that are most likely to make a distinction. Gigerenzer and Goldstein (1996) proposed to rank cues by validity; validity is defined as the proportion of correct inferences among all inferences that this cue, if considered in isolation, allows (a tie does not allow inference). With this cue order, the heuristic has been named "take-the-best." This order might have been individually estimated from a sample, or learned by instruction, or have evolved by natural selection.

Amazingly, the predictive accuracy of this heuristic, judged on a real-world dataset about German cities, was about equal to, or better than, that of multiple regression (Figure 5-1; Gigerenzer & Goldstein, 1999, p. 93). Figure 5-1 further compares the performance of take-the-best against two computationally sophisticated algorithms that also each construct a decision tree (H. Brighton, personal communication). Especially when the "learning" sample of cities used to construct the trees is small, take-the-best nearly always outperforms these methods in accurately comparing sizes of the remaining cities (i.e., in cross-validation). Chater, Oaksford, Nakisa, and Redington (2003) have performed a slightly different analysis for other sophisticated algorithms, including a three-layer feedforward neural network, and observed a similar pattern. These are surprising and striking results, especially as at least the comparison against multiple regression holds across 19 other such real-world comparison tasks besides the original city-size example (Czerlinski, Gigerenzer, & Goldstein, 1999).

Take-the-best is fast to execute and frugal in the information used, since usually not all cues are examined. It is simple in that it involves only comparisons of binary values, rather than the additions and multiplications that are involved in the standard statistical solutions to the task. This degree of frugality and simplicity applies to the execution of the procedure. If the prior

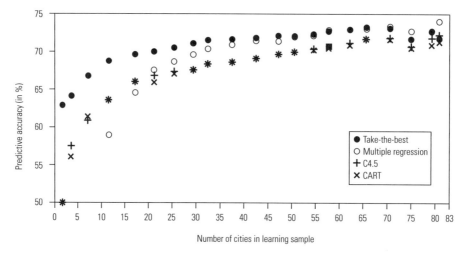

Figure 5-1. Predictive accuracy of take-the-best (TTB) compared to multiple regression and to two computationally intensive algorithms designed to generalize well to new samples: C4.5 (Quinlan, 1993) and CART (classification and regression tree: Breiman et al., 1984). Another such algorithm, MML (Buntine & Caruana, 1992), performed similarly to CART and C4.5. The task is judging which of two German cities has the larger population, based on nine cues (same dataset as Chater et al., 2003; Gigerenzer & Goldstein, 1999). The abscissa specifies the number of cities in the learning sample to which the regression equation or decision tree is fitted, and the ordinate specifies the predictive accuracy achieved in the test set (remaining cities of the 83). Results are averaged over 1,000 random selections of the learning set. Except for multiple regression, the strategies can each be expressed as decision trees. The intensive algorithms first grow a tree (for instance, in the case of C4.5, iteratively using reduction in entropy as a criterion for which cue to use for the next split), and then prune it so as to avoid overfitting. Results for multiple regression are not shown for learning sets involving fewer cities than the number of cues; the regression algorithm was not one that eliminated cues of low statistical significance. (Figure provided by H. Brighton.)

ranking of cues by validities must be individually learned, this requires counting, and prior experience of the task with feedback. Nevertheless, it is still relatively much simpler to gauge the rank order of validities than the cue weights in a multiple regression equation, partly because validities ignore the correlations between cues. Note, however, that ordering by validities is not necessarily optimal; finding the optimal order requires exhaustively checking all possible orders (Martignon & Hoffrage, 2002). In natural biological examples, a good ordering of cues could have been achieved by natural selection or by individual learning through trial and error; such an ordering might perform very well yet be neither ranked by validity nor optimal. Simulations

show that performance remains high if the ordering of cues only roughly matches validity (Martignon & Hoffrage, 2002), or if the ordering is generated by a simple learning algorithm, itself a simple heuristic (Dieckmann & Todd, 2004; Todd & Dieckmann, 2005).

Take-the-best was originally envisaged as a heuristic that processed information already in memory. However, when subjects are presented with the binary cues in written form, a variety of experiments have identified situations under which take-the-best and similar decision heuristics accurately describe how people sample and process the information (Bröder, 2000, 2003; Bröder & Schiffer, 2003; Newell & Shanks, 2003; Rieskamp & Hoffrage, 1999).

2.2. Comparing Heuristics in Structure and Performance

Take-the-best can be viewed as a sequence of three building blocks.

Search rule: Examine cues in order of validity, at each step comparing values between alternatives.

Stopping rule: Stop search when a cue discriminates.

Decision rule: Choose the alternative indicated by the discriminating cue.

This can be compared with a different class of heuristics based on tallying.

Search rule: Examine cues in arbitrary order, checking values of both alternatives but not necessarily consecutively.

Stopping rule: Stop search after m cues.

Decision rule: Tally these m cue values for each alternative and choose the alternative with the higher tally.

The amount of information used by take-the-best (its frugality) varies from decision to decision; the frugality of tallying is always m pairs of cue values. If m is all the cues available, tallying is called Dawes' rule (named after the pioneering work of Dawes, 1979). Tallying is also simple to execute in that it requires only counting. Unlike take-the-best, it does not require knowing an order of cues, just which direction each points (although the accuracy and frugality of tallying can benefit from more complex prior calculations to set m and eliminate cues likely to be uninformative). Like take-the-best, the predictive accuracy of Dawes' rule is as good as, or better than, multiple regression for the 20 real-world datasets (Czerlinski et al., 1999).

With some of these datasets take-the-best performed better than Dawes' rule, and with others worse. We now have some understanding of how the environment (i.e., the statistical structure of cues and criterion) determines this (Martignon & Hoffrage, 2002). Not surprisingly, in environments in which the weights from a multiple regression are roughly equal for all cues, Dawes' rule, which is equivalent to multiple regression with unit weights, performs better.

Take-the-best performs better when each cue weight is much greater than the next largest one. If each weight is greater than the sum of all smaller weights, and the order of weights matches that of validity, multiple regression must produce identical decisions to take-the-best. Such an environment is called noncompensatory because in the multiple regression an important cue cannot be outweighed by less important cues even if the latter all disagree with the former. It turns out that many of our 20 example environments tend towards having noncompensatory cue structures (Czerlinski et al., 1999): Most cues add little independent information to that provided by the most informative cues. Take-the-best and Dawes' rule can be viewed as each taking a bet on a different environment structure, whereas multiple regression tries to be a jack of all trades and computes its parameters to fit the structure (Martignon & Hoffrage, 2002).

It should now be clear that statements of the kind "This heuristic is good" are ill-conceived, or at least incomplete. A heuristic is neither good nor bad per se; rather, some are better than others in specified environments (e.g., compensatory or noncompensatory) on specified criteria (e.g., predictive accuracy or frugality). It follows that although ABC has an overall vision that simple heuristics are the solution that the brain uses for many tasks, we envisage that the heuristics used for different tasks will vary widely and not be special cases of one global all-inclusive model. This suggests a somewhat piecemeal research program, which need not be a weakness: The same piecemeal approach has certainly not held behavioral ecology back (Krebs, Stephens, & Sutherland, 1983). Incidentally, ABC also puts no general restrictions on the extent to which heuristics are innate or learned, or applied consciously or unconsciously. Nor has our research so far focused on categorizing specific instances of heuristic use along these dimensions. We expect that in different circumstances the same heuristic might fall into more than one category.

Formal models of heuristics like take-the-best and tallying have their roots in the work of Herbert Simon on satisficing and bounded rationality, but also in early models of heuristics for preferences, such as Tversky's (1972) elimination by aspects, and the work on the adaptive decision maker by Payne, Bettman, and Johnson (1993). Yet most recent work has abstained from formalizing heuristics or considering the conditions when they work well (Kahneman & Tversky, 1996). ABC's work also differs from those parts of cognitive psychology that are typically strong in modeling, yet rely on versions of expected utility (no search or stopping rules; e.g., prospect theory: Kahneman & Tversky, 1979) or on Wald's sequential analysis (which has stopping rules, but relies on optimization; Wald, 1947). Whereas ABC's research explores the benefits of simplicity, other schools of psychology try to explain complex behavior by building equally complex cognitive models.

Some very simple heuristics perform well not because of the method of combining cues but because they utilize a single "clever" cue. Loosely speaking, the heuristic lets the environment do much of the work. One example is the recognition heuristic (Goldstein & Gigerenzer, 2002): If one alternative is recognized and the other not, the recognized alternative is chosen independent of further information. It predicts the conditions for counterintuitive less-is-more effects: Americans made better inferences about German city sizes than about American ones, because with American cities they too often recognized both alternatives and could not apply the recognition heuristic.

Another example of a heuristic relying on a clever cue is how players catch a ball. To a Martian it might look like we are solving complex algebraic equations of motion to compute the trajectory of the ball. Studies have concluded instead that players might utilize a number of simple heuristics (e.g., McLeod & Dienes, 1996; Oudejans, Michaels, Bakker, & Davids, 1999). The gaze heuristic is the simplest candidate and works if the ball is already high in the air and traveling directly in line with the player: The player fixates his gaze on the ball, starts running, and adjusts his speed to ensure that the angle of the ball above the horizon appears constant (Gigerenzer, 2004). Another heuristic better describes actual behavior: it has the same first two building blocks (fixate and run) but the

third one is modified to keep the image of the ball rising at a constant speed. If players manage to follow either heuristic, they and the ball will both arrive at the same location when the ball reaches head height; the prediction is not that players run to a precomputed landing spot and wait for the ball. Neither heuristic is optimal, in the sense that they miss balls that would be catchable by running as fast as possible toward the point of impact (although the second heuristic would be optimal if the ball were not slowed by air resistance: see Brancazio, 1985). Note that players are typically unaware of using this sort of heuristic even though this accurately accounts for their behavior. Biologist readers will probably already be asking whether other animals might also use similar heuristics: Indeed, maintenance of a constant optical angle between pursuer and target has been found in a variety of animals besides humans, including bats, birds, fish, and insects (Shaffer, Krauchunas, Eddy, & McBeath, 2004). Surely, it is not the only heuristic that we share with animals.

3. SOME SIMPLE RULES OF THUMB FROM BIOLOGY

We now consider examples of rules of thumb from biology; there are many more that we could have chosen. Our aim in this section is to give a broad flavor of this area of biological research, and so we deliberately leave most comparisons with ABC's approach until later. The diversity of the biological examples and the lack of theoretical connections between many of them are parts of the picture that we wish to convey.

A recently described example is the method by which the ant *Leptothorax albipennis* estimates the size of a candidate nest cavity (Mallon & Franks, 2000; Mugford, Mallon, & Franks, 2001). Natural nest sites are narrow cracks in rocks, typically irregular in shape. The ants' solution is first to explore the cavity for a fixed period on an irregular path that covers the area fairly evenly. While doing this it lays down an individually distinct pheromone trail. It then leaves. When it returns, it again moves around but on a different irregular path. The frequency of encountering its old trail is used to judge size (rate ∝ 1/area). This "Buffon's needle algorithm" is remarkably accurate: Nests half the area of others yielded reencounter frequencies 1.96 times greater.

Another example concerns how the wasp *Polistes dominulus* constructs its nest (Karsai & Pénzes, 2000). The nest is a tessellation of hexagonal cells that grows as each new cell is added. Up to the 15-cell stage, only 18 arrangements of cells have been observed. These arrangements are all compact, which ensures that less new material is required and that the structure is strong. However, these optimality criteria are inadequate explanations of why just these 18 arrangements: Economy of material predicts 155 optimal arrangements, whereas not all the observed structures maximize compactness. A better explanation is a construction rule in which the wasp places each cell at the site where the sum of the ages of the existing walls is greatest. Age of wall might plausibly be judged by the concentration of pheromone added at the time of construction or the state of the larva inside. This rule explains all observed arrangements, with one exception that plausibly follows from a small mistake in execution of the rule. Further unexpected forms appear as the nest grows beyond 15 cells, but then it is plausible that the wasp does not visit all potential building sites, or that small differences in wall age get harder to judge as the structure gets older.

Social insects provide the richest source of rule-of-thumb examples (e.g., Camazine, Deneubourg, Franks, Sneyd, Theraulaz, & Bonabeau, 2001; Detrain & Deneubourg, 2002; Müller & Wehner, 1988; Sato, Saito, & Sakagami, 2003; Seeley, 1995). Some of these examples concern mechanisms that ensure that individual behavior is well integrated, when perhaps there is some particular advantage of each individual rigorously following simple rules. But other examples do not concern coordination. Perhaps it is just that social insects are small animals with small nervous systems. This might matter because they really can only follow simpler rules than higher animals, but it could be merely that biologists are readier to view them as robotically following simple rules than larger animals that more closely resemble ourselves. Instead, our

suspicion is that the plethora of good examples of rules of thumb in social insects is because this way of thinking about mechanisms happens to have become prevalent in this research community, with each new nice example stimulating similar interpretations of other phenomena. Perhaps then, rules of thumb will grow in prominence when researchers on other organisms realize the concept's usefulness. A more pessimistic explanation is that because social insects are small, studying their behavior is difficult, and our knowledge incomplete, which allows simple rules of thumb to be adequate explanations. According to this viewpoint (suggested to us by a social-insect worker responsible for some of the nicest examples of rules of thumb!), further research will lead to simple rules of thumb being rejected in favor of more complex mechanisms.

Some of the earliest analyses of rules of thumb came from considering the varied ways that simple animals locate stimuli (Fraenkel & Gunn, 1940). For instance, a copepod (a planktonic crustacean) faced with two light sources follows a trajectory as if it were pulled towards each source with a force proportional to source intensity/distance[2]. Such apparently complex behavior is explicable by the simple rule that the animal adjusts its orientation so as to maximize the amount of light falling on a flat eye. More recent research has examined how a female moth locates a pheromone-producing male (Kennedy, 1983). She applies the simple rule of heading upwind when the pheromone concentration lies above a particular threshold. This will not always get her to the male, because variation in wind direction creates a meandering plume of pheromone. When she breaks out of a plume, the lowered pheromone concentration triggers her to cast back and forth cross wind with increasing amplitude until she reencounters the plume. Analytic models have estimated the efficiency of different methods of taxis depending on aspects of environmental structure such as turbulence (Balkovsky & Shraiman, 2002; Dusenbery, 2001).

The two other areas of behavioral biology that make most frequent reference to rules of thumb are mate choice and patch-leaving.

A paper by Janetos (1980) seems responsible for a tradition in behavioral ecology of modeling mate choice as a process of sequential assessment of candidate males. The two most discussed rules are for a female to accept the first male above a preset threshold or for a female to view a preset number of N males and then return to the best ("best-of-N" rule). Janetos argued that animals follow simple rules that can achieve good but not optimal performance (Janetos & Cole, 1981). Other behavioral ecologists agreed that information constraints would restrict what sort of rule could be used but preferred to hypothesize that a rule's parameters were optimized for the environment (Real, 1990a). However, neither of these two rules explains adequately the patterns of return typically observed nor effects of the quality of previously encountered males on acceptance decisions, so somewhat more complex rules may be necessary (Hutchinson and Halupka, 2004; Luttbeg, 1996; Wiegmann, Real, Capone, & Ellner, 1996).

Patch-leaving rules represent more of a success for modeling. The idea is that food items occur in patches, and that they are depleted by the forager, which should thus at some stage move to another patch. The question is when. The number of food items remaining is unknown to the forager, but it is indicated by the rate at which it finds items. An elegant optimality model derives how the rule of thumb should depend on the environment (Iwasa, Higashi, & Yamamura, 1981). In an environment in which all patches are of similar quality, finding a food item should decrease the tendency to stay because the patch has been depleted. In an environment in which some patches are very poor and some very good, finding a food item should increase the tendency to stay, because the success suggests that it is a better patch. Later, it was realized that if an independent cue was available indicating initial patch quality, even in the second type of environment the decremental decision rule can be better (Driessen & Bernstein, 1999). This fits empirical research on the parasitoid wasp *Venturia canescens,* which lays its eggs in caterpillars: The concentration of host scent sets the tendency to stay, this decreases through some sort of habituation response, but the effect of finding a host further decreases the tendency to stay (Driessen & Bernstein, 1999). Between similar parasitoid species there is much variation in whether finding a host increases or decreases the tendency to stay, but we do not yet know enough about the environmental structure in most of these examples to judge whether the theory explains these differences (van Alphen, Bernstein, & Driessen, 2003; Wajnberg, Gonsard, Tabone, Curty, Lezcano, & Colazza, 2003).

Models of patch-leaving decision rules show a historical progression from unbounded rationality assuming omniscience towards more realistic assumptions of what information is available. At the omniscient end is the marginal value theorem (Charnov, 1976), specifying that the optimal switching point is when the instantaneous rate of the reward falls to the mean rate in the environment under the optimal policy. But how should the animal know this mean rate without knowing the optimal policy already? McNamara and Houston (1985) proposed a simple iterative algorithm by which this might be learned while foraging efficiently. Another problem is that when prey are discrete items turning up stochastically, the underlying rate (=probability) of reward is not directly observable. The optimality models of Iwasa et al. (1981) and others are one response to this situation, but another is the simpler rule, not derived from an optimality model, of giving up after a constant time without finding an item. If the giving-up time parameter is appropriate, the performance may come close to that of the optimum rule (Green, 1984). In the real world, in which environmental parameters are uncertain, it could be that the giving-up time rule works better than the optimum computed for a simple model of the environment. A more recent example concerns when a bee should leave one inflorescence for another; the problem is that bumblebees increasingly revisit flowers that they have just emptied because they can only remember the last few visited. Goulson (2000) proposed that a good solution that agreed with bumblebees' observed behavior is to leave once two empty flowers are found. Other workers have modified optimality models to incorporate characteristics of known or hypothesized psychological mechanisms, such as Weber's law, scalar expectancy theory, and rate-biased time perception (Hills & Adler, 2002; Kacelnik & Todd, 1992; Todd & Kacelnik, 1993).

4. HEURISTICS ARE PRECISE TESTABLE MODELS OF PROXIMAL MECHANISM

Having used specific examples to give a flavor first of the ABC program and then of biological research on rules of thumb, we now start to explain more about the principles and assumptions underlying the former. The ABC program has two interrelated components: the first is to study the heuristics that people actually use, and the second is to demonstrate in which environments a given heuristic performs well. We call the first the study of the "adaptive toolbox," the second the study of the "ecological rationality" of heuristics. The next two sections address how ABC models the adaptive toolbox.

ABC is concerned with the cognitive process of decision making, and in particular with which sources of information are considered and how they are processed in combination. Our concern is with mechanism, not merely with how behavior depends on cue values (what optimality modelers call the policy). Although observations of the policy can lead us to reject some candidate mechanisms, this is not a sufficient test because a variety of mechanisms can generate identical policies. For instance, take-the-best makes decisions indistinguishable from multiple regression if the cue weights are noncompensatory. They are, however, distinguishable if one can monitor how many cues are examined and in which order.

Much decision making depends on information already present in memory. We cannot rely on self-reports to know how we access such memories, but some information is obtainable from timing. For instance, one might hypothesize that humans rank two-digit numbers using the lexicographic strategy of first comparing the first digits alone, and only in the case of a tie looking at the second digit. In this example, the lexicographic heuristic must be rejected because experiments have shown that the timing

of the decision does depend on the second digit even if the first digits differ (Moyer & Landauer, 1967).

It is an open question whether the same heuristics are used when the information is external in the environment as when it is already in internal memory. The results of Bröder and Schiffer (2003) suggest a difference. But external search, besides being much more tractable to study, is of importance in its own right, and also of practical relevance in formulating advice about how Internet sites, for instance, should present information. Using the program Mouselab, it is possible to present information on a computer screen but require subjects to click on a button to read a cue value, so that we at least know the order in which they seek information and when they stop information search (Payne et al., 1993). Another potential approach is eye tracking.

Combining sources of information is a feature of decision making in not just animals but even bacteria and plants: For instance, for a seed to germinate in response to springtime warmth or photoperiod often requires weeks of winter chilling to remove dormancy (Bradbeer, 1988); this requirement prevents premature germination in autumn. Some insects show strikingly similar requirements before emerging (Tauber & Tauber, 1976). The mechanism in plants cannot be the same as what is known of the process in the insect brain (Williams, 1956), but in principle the same algorithm might describe how the cues interact. ABC's level of analysis is algorithmic, in the sense of Marr (1982). One advantage of this approach is that conclusions might apply across different decisions and different organisms; indeed, they also have relevance for programming computers. Another advantage is that algorithmic explanations are often simple enough to be readily comprehensible. To understand how computers perform a sorting task, for instance, it is natural to seek explanations at the algorithmic level, ignoring the chip's circuitry.

In some invertebrates remarkable progress has been made in explaining some aspects of cognition in terms of the underlying neurobiology, although gaps in our knowledge remain in even the best-known systems (e.g., olfactory learning in honeybees: Menzel, 2001; Menzel & Giurfa, 2001). There is no prospect in the near future of the kind of cognitive processes that ABC considers in humans becoming understandable in such terms. However, brain imaging does provide a window to test whether some of the hypothesized processes occur. Heuristics are assumed to exploit evolved abilities such as recognition memory (recognition heuristic), recollection memory (take-the-best), and object tracking (ball-catching heuristics). Therefore, one can test whether, in situations where people act as predicted by a given heuristic, brain areas that are known to specifically reflect the corresponding ability are activated. The first study of this kind has used functional magnetic resonance imaging (fMRI) to test whether decisions made when the recognition heuristic can be applied are indeed accompanied by activation of brain regions underlying recognition memory but not of those underlying guessing or recollection memory (Volz, Schooler, Schubotz, Raab, Gigerenzer, & von Cramon, 2006).

A complementary approach to testing the physical reality of a proposed heuristic is to attempt to model it using a framework such as ACT-R (Anderson, Bothell, Byrne, Douglass, Lebiere, & Qin, 2004). This is based on a restricted set of processing modules, the properties of which are constrained by numerous independent studies. Translating a heuristic into ACT-R both confirms that it is cognitively plausible and makes testable predictions about reaction times and fMRI results. ABC has made a start with using ACT-R, for a model of a version of the recognition heuristic (Schooler & Hertwig, 2005).

The heuristics that ABC describes may rely on input variables that require complex calculations to compute. For instance, the ball-catching heuristics rely on the ability to track a moving object against a noisy background, which is developing in two- or three-month-old infants (Rosander & von Hofsten, 2002), but which is extremely difficult to program computers to do. ABC's heuristics exploit these abilities but do not attempt to explain their mechanisms. The underlying assumption is of a hierarchical

organization of cognitive processing: heuristics on top of evolved or learned abilities. There is good evidence of a hierarchy in insects, because much of the processing is peripheral and electrodes can monitor what information is passed on to the central nervous system. It is less clear how well the assumption holds in vertebrates. ABC does not claim that algorithmic models are necessarily the best level of analysis for all that goes on in brains. The peripheral processing in retinas, for instance, can involve clever neuronal circuitry that perhaps is better analyzed with models of neural networks. The same argument may apply to some higher level capabilities in humans: Face recognition and language processing are possible instances. A computing analogy might be some time-critical task that has been written in machine code (or perhaps even outtasked to a special video chip) and thus remains opaque to another programmer who knows only higher level languages (cf. Todd, 1999).

Equally, ABC does not deny that humans can consciously perform highly complex calculations to compare options. The question is whether they trouble to do so for routine decisions, and also whether it is adaptive for them to bother.

The heuristics that ABC has proposed are highly specified; they are readily convertible to computer code and they yield bold quantitative predictions that are amenable to testing. This contrasts with most models of heuristics in cognitive psychology, which are often specified only at a level of detail described by block diagrams and arrows indicating that one quantity has some unquantified influence on another. Such models are typically so vague in their predictions that they are impossible to test. In order to facilitate rigorous testing, ABC tries to avoid heuristics with free parameters that must be fitted anew to each dataset or to each individual, unless they can be estimated independently. This is not because we necessarily deny that, for instance, there are individual differences in personality that might affect how or which heuristics are applied.

Given that real heuristics have not been written by a programmer but have evolved by the messy process of natural selection, and given that they are enacted by neurons, not silicon, ABC's precisely specified models seem likely to be simplifications capturing the broad principle but eventually requiring adjustments in the detail. Nevertheless, on the current evidence perhaps less adjustment will be necessary than one might suppose.

5. THE ATTRACTIONS OF SIMPLICITY

The heuristics studied by ABC are simple in comparison with standard statistical procedures applied to the same task. Proposals by other psychologists for how our minds tackle these tasks typically also involve more complex processes such as Bayesian probability updating. Part of the reason why ABC's heuristics can be simple is that they can utilize evolved or highly trained abilities, such as recognition memory, that may involve complex data processing.

It is not just Occam's Razor that has made ABC favor simple models. But we will start off by mentioning the weakest reason. That is that with simple heuristics we can be more confident that our brains are capable of performing the necessary calculations. The weakness of this argument is that it is hard to judge what complexity of calculation or memory a brain might achieve. At the lower levels of processing, some human capabilities apparently involve calculations that seem surprisingly difficult (e.g., Bayesian estimation in a sensorimotor context: Körding & Wolpert, 2004). So, if we can perform these calculations at that level in the hierarchy (abilities), why should we not be able to evolve similar complex strategies to replace simple heuristics?

One answer is that simple heuristics often need access to less information (i.e., they are frugal) and can thus make a decision faster, at least if information search is external. Another answer, and a more important argument for simple heuristics, is the high accuracy that they exhibit in our simulations (e.g., see Figure 5-1). This accuracy may be because of, not just in spite of, their simplicity. In particular, because they have few parameters they avoid overfitting data in a learning sample, and consequently

generalize better across other samples. The extra parameters of more complex models often fit the noise rather than the signal (MacKay, 1992; Hertwig & Todd, 2003). Of course we are not saying that all simple heuristics are good: Only some simple heuristics will perform well in any given environment.

Although we would argue strongly that ABC has made an important advance in demonstrating how well simple frugal heuristics can perform, we do not yet know how generally the claim of "simple is good" can be extended. In the hope of stimulating others to test our claims, we now play the devil's advocate and question the generality of our results. For instance, we cannot claim to have evidence that simple heuristics perform better than more complex ones for every task. Moreover, even in the tasks that we have investigated, we have inevitably not considered all possible heuristics, and the set considered is biased towards simplicity, so we cannot be sure that there are not other more complex heuristics that achieve equally impressive performance. For instance, although one strength of simple heuristics is that they generalize well by avoiding overfitting, other much more complex statistical procedures have also been designed to avoid overfitting (e.g., classification and regression trees, CART in Figure 5-1; Breiman, Friedman, Olshen, & Stone, 1984).

It is tempting to propose that since other animals have simpler brains than humans, they are more likely to have to use simple heuristics. But a contrary argument is that humans are much more generalist than most animals, and that animals may be able to devote more cognitive resources to tasks of particular importance. For instance, the memory capabilities of small food-storing birds seem astounding by the standards of how we expect ourselves to perform at the same task (Balda & Kamil, 1992). Some better examined biological examples suggest unexpected complexity: For instance, pigeons seem able to use a surprising diversity of methods to navigate, especially considering that they are not long-distance migrants (Wiltschko & Wiltschko, 2003; but cf. Wallraff, 2001). The greater specialism of other animals may also mean that the environments that they deal with are more predictable, and thus that the robustness of simple heuristics may no longer be such an advantage (cf. the argument of Arkes & Ayton, 1999, that animals in their natural environments do not commit various fallacies because they do not need to generalize their rules of thumb to novel circumstances).

A separate concern is that for morphological traits there are plenty of examples of evolution getting stuck on a local adaptive peak and not finding its way to the neatest solution. The classic example is the giraffe's recurrent laryngeal nerve, which travels down and then back up the neck because in all mammals it loops round the aorta. Nobody knows how common such a situation might be with cognitive traits. It could be that humans' ability to learn through experience makes them more readily adopt simple heuristics than other animals that are more rigidly programmed and where natural selection alone is responsible for the adaptation.

Another way to consider the recurrent laryngeal nerve is that it may be simple in terms of what is easy for existing embryological processes to engineer. We can only make plausibility arguments about what algorithms are difficult for an organism to build or evolve. Those that are simple to engineer need not be those that are simple to describe: A perfect linear response is simple to describe but perhaps often difficult to engineer physiologically. For instance, nectivorous insects judge meal volume with stretch receptors in their guts, but the way these receptors work results in a nonlinear response (Real, 1992). Artificial neural networks may provide some guidance about what sorts of processing are easy or hard to engineer (Real, 1992; Webb & Reeve, 2003). However, what is easy to hardwire need not be easy to calculate consciously. For humans acting consciously, a weighted-additive calculation is much harder than tallying (weights all unity), but for an insect specialized on a specific task, evolution can have hardwired the weights (for instance, by controlling sensitivity of the receptors for different cues); then the insect need simply tally these ready-weighted cues, yet it achieves what to us looks like a harder weighted-additive calculation

(Franks, Mallon, Bray, Hamilton, & Mischler, 2003).

6. ADAPTATION AND ECOLOGICAL RATIONALITY

The following sections deal with the fit of the heuristics to the environment, which ABC refers to as *ecological rationality*. In this section, we compare and contrast this with biologists' concern with adaptation. Adaptation is the assumption underlying optimality modeling, a technique that has dominated behavioral ecology, and the next section will consider how useful this might be in investigations of cognitive mechanism. We will then turn from mechanisms to the other blade of Simon's scissors (1990), the environment.

ABC's research program is very much concerned with heuristics working well in the environment in which they perform. Biologists mostly deal with rules of thumb that are adapted through natural selection, but the human heuristics that ABC studies have also been honed by individual or cultural learning of what works well. A likely possibility is that natural selection has set humans up with a set of heuristics (the adaptive toolbox: Gigerenzer, Todd, et al., 1999) each member of which we can readily learn to apply as appropriate to a specific environment. Or the building blocks of heuristics (such as when to stop search) might be readily recombined to create novel heuristics suitable for a novel task. These possibilities deal with the objection that humans have not had time to evolve heuristics to cope with today's environments. If two environments share a common statistical structure, the same heuristics will work well. We require only a mechanism for learning or reasoning which heuristic from our toolbox works best in a novel environment (Rieskamp & Otto, 2006).

The idea of adaptation is, of course, old hat to most biologists; they see no reason to believe that cognition is not adapted like everything else–hence, the field of cognitive ecology (Dukas, 1998; Shettleworth, 1998). Nevertheless, biologists face the same problem as psychologists that much behavior must be studied in the artificial environment of the laboratory where its adaptive significance need not be obvious. For instance, one result that has worried behavioral biologists is that in operant "self-control" experiments animals tend to forgo the option with a higher long-term reward rate in favor of one in which less food is delivered but with less delay (Logue, 1988). Recently, Stephens and Anderson (2001) suggested that a rule of thumb based on maximizing short-term gain rate makes adaptive sense when the same reward structure as in the self-control experiments is presented in a patch-leaving context. In that context, the difference in short-term rates between staying a short time or a long time in a patch agrees with, and even amplifies, the difference in long-term rates (see also Real, 1992; Stephens, 2002; and cf. Kareev, 2000). The argument is that the operant self-control task in which the decision rule had first been recognized, and in which it appeared dele-terious, is an artificial situation, which played no part in the rule's evolution or maintenance. Such a result mirrors some of ABC's work (and that of other psychologists) pointing out that what have been viewed as maladaptive biases in humans are the by-products of rules that make adaptive sense in an appropriate environment (e.g., Arkes & Ayton, 1999; Gigerenzer, 2000, Chapter 12; Hoffrage, Hertwig, & Gigerenzer, 2000).

The biologists' evolutionary perspective at least made them hanker for an adaptive explanation for the self-control results. Biologist readers may be amazed that adaptation is not at all a universal consideration in psychology. In fact, human psychologists do have a plausible defense. Many argue that our brain has evolved as a general-purpose calculating machine and that most of its capabilities, such as a facility at chess, are mere by-products, which have not been subject to direct selection. Allied to the general-purpose-calculating-machine viewpoint are the normative assumptions of the heuristics-and-biases school of Kahnemann and Tversky, that heuristics should be judged by whether they follow the rules of logic (Gilovich, Griffin, & Kahneman, 2002). Philosophically, ABC argues instead that what matters is not logic but performance, and that in real environments many so-called biases are adaptive (Gigerenzer, 2000,

Chapter 12). And empirically we have found it a highly illuminating research strategy to apply the working assumption that our decision-making heuristics fit the statistical structures in our environments.

By "adaptation" biologists imply not only that a trait fits the environment but that it has been shaped by the environment for that task. Therefore, claims of adaptation of heuristics are vulnerable to the arguments of the biologists Gould and Lewontin (1979), who were concerned about many claims of adaptation in biology being mere "just-so stories." Unfortunately, human psychologists are not able to utilize many of the lines of evidence that biologists apply to justify that a trait is adaptive. We can make only informed guesses about the environment in which the novel features of human brains evolved and, because most of us grow up in an environment very different to this, the cognitive traits that we exhibit might not even have been expressed when our brains were evolving (Dawkins, 1982, p. 38). Biologists use a more detailed fit of trait to environment as evidence for adaptation, but because simple heuristics have few characters (e.g., parameters), even this approach may be unavailable.

It thus would be a weak argument (which ABC avoids) to find a heuristic that humans use, then search for some environment in which that heuristic works well, and then claim on this basis alone that the heuristic is an adaptation to that environment. The heuristic may work well in that environment, but that need not be the reason why it evolved or even why it has survived. For instance, our colleagues Lael Schooler and Ralph Hertwig (2005) have constructed a model demonstrating that for a type of recognition heuristic it can be beneficial that we forget out-of-date information at a certain rate; but memory is used for a diversity of other purposes, so they rightly avoid claiming that this model explains the length of our memories. To claim adaptation, it is at least necessary to check that the heuristic is generally used only in environments in which it works well and better than other heuristics that we use in other contexts. ABC's empirical research program has yet to develop this far, although there is no barrier to it doing so.

ABC avoids the difficult issue of demonstrating adaptation in humans by defining ecological rationality as the performance, in terms of a given currency, of a given heuristic in a given environment. We emphasize that currency and environment have to be specified before the ecological rationality of a heuristic can be determined; thus, take-the-best is more ecologically rational (both more accurate and frugal) than tallying in noncompensatory environments, but not more accurate in compensatory ones. Unlike claiming that a heuristic is an adaptation, a claim that it is ecologically rational deliberately omits any implication that this is why the trait originally evolved, or has current value to the organism, or that either heuristic or environment occur for real in the present or past. Ecological rationality might then be useful as a term indicating a more attainable intermediate step on the path to a demonstration of adaptation. There is nevertheless a risk that a demonstration of ecological rationality of a given heuristic in a given environment will mislead someone who uses this evidence alone to infer adaptation. Think of the Victorian habit of noting the most fanciful resemblance of an animal to a part of its environment as an adaptation. This reached its apogee in such ridiculous illustrations as pink flamingos camouflaged against pink sunsets (Gould, 1991, Chapter 14; sexual selection is the real explanation for most bright plumage).

7. WHY NOT USE OPTIMALITY MODELLING?

Optimality modeling is used in behavioral ecology mostly as a test of whether a particular adaptive argument explains a particular phenomenon. The model is constructed to include the components of the explanation (maximized currencies, constraints, trade-offs, etc.) and often a deliberate minimum of anything else. The next stage is to calculate the optimal behavior given these assumptions. If these predictions match empirical data, one can claim to have a coherent explanation for why that behavior occurs. Sometimes

the match occurs only over a restricted range of a model parameter, in which case measuring or varying the corresponding characteristic in the real world offers a further empirical test. In the absence of a match, a new or modified explanation must be sought.

ABC's concern with adaptation to the environment might seem to ally it with optimality modeling. Much of ABC's research has involved finding what decision rules work *well* in a model environment; optimality modeling involves finding what decision rules work *best* in a model environment. In both instances good performance is the basis of predictions, or even expectations, about the rules actually used. Optimality modeling has the attractions that there is no arbitrariness in deciding whether a heuristic works well enough, and no uncertainty whether there might be another, better heuristic that one had not thought of. Moreover, it has proved its practical utility in dominating the successful fields of behavioral ecology and biomechanics, making testable predictions that have not only stimulated empirical research but also strikingly often been well supported by the data. So, why does ABC not take this road?

Typically one prediction of an optimality model is the policy, which describes what behavior is performed given any specified value of an individual's external environment and internal state. Although the policy can itself be viewed as a decision rule, it is the mechanisms generating policies that interest ABC and other psychologists. Behavioral ecologists do believe that animals are using simple rules of thumb that achieve only an approximation of the optimal policy, but most often rules of thumb are not their interest. Nevertheless, it could be that the limitations of such rules of thumb would often constrain behavior enough to interfere with the fit with predictions. The optimality modeler's gambit is that evolved rules of thumb can mimic optimal behavior well enough not to disrupt the fit by much, so that they can be left as a black box. It turns out that the power of natural selection is such that the gambit usually works to the level of accuracy that satisfies behavioral ecologists. Given that their models are usually deliberately schematic, behavioral ecologists are usually satisfied that they understand the selective value of a behavior if they successfully predict merely the rough qualitative form of the policy or of the resultant patterns of behavior.

But ABC's focus on process means that it is concerned with a much more detailed prediction of behavior. A good model of the process can lead to predictions of behavior that differ from standard optimization models or for which optimization models are mute. For instance, the ball-catching heuristics mentioned in Section 2 predict that the player catches the ball while running, the precise running speeds, and when players will run in a slight arc. All these predictions concern observable behaviors. The example of *Polistes* nest construction (see Section 3) also showed how much more specific process models can be.

Nevertheless, there are several ways in which optimality modeling can help to suggest what rules of thumb the animal uses.

(1) The optimal policy provides clues. It does at least indicate aspects of the environment to which decisions might usefully respond, although it may be indirect cues that are actually used. Conversely, optimality modeling is helpful in pointing out what aspects of the environment a decision heuristic should ignore. In certain cases the optimal policy may be so simple that it can be generated by a simple heuristic. For instance, if items are randomly (Poisson) distributed across patches, Iwasa et al. (1981) showed that the optimal leaving rule is to spend a constant time in each patch regardless of foraging success. In other cases an examination of the form of the optimal policy can suggest a heuristic that would come close to generating such a policy. Thus, for a different patch-leaving model, Green (1984) plotted against the time spent on the patch the critical number of prey items that must have been found to make it worthwhile to stay longer. The calculations required were computationally involved but the thresholds fell quite close to a straight line through the origin, suggesting a simple rule that would perform close to optimally.

(2) If enacting the optimal policy would require, say, unrealistically extensive knowledge or demanding memory requirements to be achievable, it is possible to introduce more realistic information constraints into an optimality model. Several optimality models examine the effects of a restricted memory on performance and behavior (e.g., Bélisle & Cresswell, 1997; Hutchinson, McNamara, & Cuthill, 1993; Roitberg, Reid, & Li, 1993). More common, and differing only in degree of specification, is to constrain the rule of thumb to be of a particular nonoptimal form but use optimality to specify the values of any parameters. The expectation is that an adapted heuristic lies on a local optimum. Such an approach has been used by both biologists and members of ABC for mate choice rules (Hutchinson & Halupka, 2004; Real, 1990b; Todd & Miller, 1999; Wiegmann & Mukhopadhyay, 1998), and Real (1990a) points out that in the appendix to Simon's classic paper on satisficing, Simon (1956) also uses optimality to set the threshold. As we learn more about an organism's sensory and cognitive capacities, and so can add ever more realistic constraints to an optimality model, one might hope that the different approaches converge in their predictions.

(3) Optimality modeling can be applied to the processes of gathering information and stopping search. Thus Fawcett and Johnstone (2003) calculated the optimal order of cues to examine given cues that differed in costs and informativeness. Luttbeg (1996) calculated how a female should concentrate sampling effort on those males that earlier had appeared the most promising.

(4) Optimality modeling may help us in providing a gold standard against which to compare performance of candidate heuristics. If a simple heuristic performs almost as well as the optimum, there is less need to search further for a better heuristic. An ABC paper in this spirit is Martignon and Laskey (1999), which computes a Bayesian network against which to compare the performance of take-the-best.

(5) Any fine-scale mismatch between optimality prediction and observation can be suggestive of what rule of thumb is being used (although there are other potential reasons for a lack of fit errors in model specification, evolutionary time lags, etc.). Even if the nature of the mismatch does not itself suggest the rule of thumb, it at least highlights a problem to which the solution may be the mechanism used by the animal. Thus, Müller and Wehner (1988) were stimulated by the systematic errors that ants make in path integration (i.e., their deviation from the optimal solution of heading straight back to the nest) to suggest a rule of thumb that explains these errors. This rule is to average the angles of each outward step, weighted by the distance moved. Another example is that the classic optimality models of diet choice predict a sudden switch from complete unselectivity to complete specialization as density increases. However, experiments typically find gradually increasing partial preferences instead (e.g., Krebs et al., 1977). This was the stimulus to suggest various refinements that would explain the difference, such as that the birds make discrimination errors, or that they have to estimate prey density or value with learning rules that are sensitive to runs of bad luck. Such constraints and mechanisms can be incorporated in a new generation of more realistic optimality models (e.g., Bélisle & Cresswell, 1997; McNamara & Houston, 1987a; Rechten, Avery, & Stevens, 1983). As long as the additional hypotheses are confirmed by testing further independent predictions, this process of successively improving models can progressively inform us about cognitive mechanisms (Cheverton, Kacelnik, & Krebs, 1985).

Thus we would encourage optimality modelers to consider decision processes to be interesting topics that their technique might address. Indeed, the rational analysis school of psychology has had some success with that approach (Anderson, 1990; Chater and Oaksford, 1999). However, there remains a more fundamental reason for ABC's objection to the routine use of the optimality approach. There are a number of situations where the optimal solution to a real-world problem cannot be determined. One problem is computational intractability, such as the notorious traveling salesman problem (Lawler, Lenstra, Rinnooy-Kan, & Shmoys, 1985). Another problem is if there are multiple criteria to optimize and we do not know the appropriate way to convert them into a common currency (such as fitness). Third, in many real-world problems it is impossible to put probabilities on the various possible outcomes or even to recognize what all those outcomes might be. Think about optimizing the choice of a partner who will bear you many children; it is uncertain what partners are available, whether each one would be faithful, how long each will live, etc. This is true about many animal decisions too, of course, and biologists do not imagine their animals even attempting such optimality calculations.

Instead, the behavioral ecologist's solution is to find optima in deliberately simplified model environments. We note that this introduces much scope for misunderstanding, inconsistency, and loose thinking over whether "optimal policy" refers to a claim of optimality in the real world or just in a model. Calculating the optima even in the simplified model environments may still be beyond the capabilities of an animal, but the hope is that the optimal policy that emerges from the calculations may be generated instead, to a lesser level of accuracy, by a rule that is simple enough for an animal to follow. The animal might be hardwired with such a rule following its evolution through natural selection, or the animal might learn it through trial and error. There remains an interesting logical gap in the procedure: There is no guarantee that optimal solutions to simplified model environments will be good solutions to the original complex environments. The biologist might reply that often this does turn out to be the case; otherwise, natural selection would not have allowed the good fit between the predictions and observations. Success with this approach undoubtedly depends on the modeler's skill in simplifying the environment in a way that fairly represents the information available to the animal. The unsatisfying uncertainty of how to simplify is often not appreciated. Bookstaber and Langsam (1985) argue that by choosing simple models with many of the uncertainties ignored, we introduce a bias in the optimal behavior predicted, favoring complex rules over coarser ones.

The same criticism about simplification of real environments can also be made of any simulation of a heuristic in a model environment, so much of ABC's research is as vulnerable to the argument as optimality modeling. ABC has tried to avoid the criticism by using data from a variety of real-world environments. (This technique is rare in biology, but an analogous example is Nakata, Ushimaru, and Watanabe's (2003) testing of web-relocation rules in spiders; rather than make assumptions about the temporal and spatial autocorrelations in prey capture rates, they used observed rates from sticky traps set out in the field.) ABC demonstrated the high performance of take-the-best on a diverse set of 20 real-world problems (Czerlinski et al., 1999). It was hoped that the environmental structures in these examples would be representative of problems in other domains. However, these supposedly real-world problems are still gross simplifications from the sorts of decisions that we really face. For instance, the performance criteria were just frugality and accuracy, it had already been determined which cues were available, and there were no search costs. Another limitation is that one can judge how far the performance results are general to other decision problems only by understanding what statistical structures in these environments influenced performance of the heuristics tested. The best way to prove that a statistical structure has the hypothesized effect on performance is to construct simple model environments.

8. ENVIRONMENT STRUCTURE

It should already be clear that ABC has an interest in identifying what statistical properties of the environment allow particular heuristics to perform well. Their identification enables us to predict in which environments a heuristic is used. We might then go on to ask whether such statistical properties are easy to recognize, and hence how a heuristic for selecting appropriate heuristics might work.

When describing the example of take-the-best, we have already mentioned two pertinent aspects of environment structure, whether the cues are noncompensatory and the size of the learning sample (see Figure 5-1). Another aspect is whether cues show many negative correlations with each other (specifying that high values of a cue always indicate, other things being equal, a better option; Johnson, Meyer, & Ghose, 1989; Shanteau & Thomas, 2000). Negative correlations might be typical of competing commercial products, because, for a product to survive in the market place, traits in which it is weak must be compensated by other desirable features (e.g., for cars, a low maximum speed may be associated with low price or high safety). This is a different environment structure from city sizes, and also perhaps from male traits used by females for mate choice, where quality variation might be expected to generate a positive correlation between all traits (which is observed in some examples, but others show no correlation: Candolin, 2003). Other aspects of environment structure that ABC has analyzed are "scarcity" (the number of objects relative to the number of cues in the learning sample; Martignon & Hoffrage, 2002) and the skewness of frequency distributions (Hertwig, Hoffrage, & Martignon, 1999).

Behavioral ecology has also considered what aspects of the environment favor different rules of thumb, but often by using analytic techniques in combination with the optimality approach. We have already mentioned Iwasa et al.'s (1981) derivation of optimal patch-leaving rules, showing that how evenly prey are spread among patches determines whether a prey capture should make the predator more or less likely to move. Another example is McNamara and Houston's (1987b) derivation of how the forgetting rate of a simple linear-operator memory rule should depend on the rate at which the environment changes.

Autocorrelation in food supply may be an important aspect of environment structure for animals. One would predict that nectar-feeders would avoid returning to a flower immediately after exploiting it, but return once it has had time to refill. Whereas bird species feeding on aggregated cryptic invertebrates remain in a good spot (win-stay), nectar-feeding birds indeed tend to "win-shift" in the short-term (Burke & Fulham, 2003). Even naive captive-reared honeyeaters *Xanthomyza phrygia* more easily learned to win-shift than win-stay with short delays between feeding sessions, but vice versa with long delays (Burke & Fulham, 2003). An easy rule to ensure returning at regular intervals to a resource is to follow the same route repeatedly; such traplining behavior is shown by nectar-feeding birds and insects as well as birds feeding on flotsam along stream edges (e.g., Davies & Houston, 1981; Thomson, 1996). Spatial, rather than temporal, autocorrelation may be the important statistical structure determining movement rules for species feeding on nonrenewing hidden food (e.g., Benhamou, 1992; Fortin, 2003).

9. SOCIAL RATIONALITY

For both humans and animals, an important component of their environment is social; that is, it is generated by other individuals. Even plants can be considered to show social heuristics: for instance, seeds may use cues such as daily temperature fluctuations to sense when competitors are absent (Thompson & Grime, 1983). A simple human example of an adaptive social heuristic is to copy the choice of meal of someone who is more familiar with the restaurant.

There has been much analysis in both the human and biological literature concerning when it pays to copy other individuals (e.g., Henrich & Boyd, 1998; Sirot, 2001). One specific example concerns escape flights in flocks of wading birds. Birds in a flock that see their neighbors flying up should immediately copy them if it was a predator that alarmed the first bird. But how to avoid numerous false alarms? Checking for the predator themselves may be unreliable and cause delay, so instead Lima (1994) suggested that they might use the simple rule of flying only if at least two other birds in the flock have flown up simultaneously. Modeling confirms that this is an efficient strategy except when flock size is small (Proctor, Broom, & Ruxton, 2001), and there is also empirical evidence of its use (Cresswell, Hilton, & Ruxton, 2000).

Not all social heuristics involve copying, and interaction may be only indirect. For instance, Thuijsman, Peleg, Amitai, and Shmida (1995) considered simple rules responding to nectar volume that bees might use to choose between alternative patches of flowers. Although these rules seemed maladaptive when applied to an individual foraging in isolation (they cause matching), they made good sense in an environment where there are competitors for the nectar (they then produce an ideal free distribution). With hummingbirds, sometimes an individual has a flower to itself, and sometimes competitors also visit (Gill, 1988). If a flower's nectar supply declines because of competition, the bird should decrease intervals between visits, but increase them if weaker production caused the decline.

In the case of many social situations, what heuristic is adaptive for one player depends on the heuristic used by another. If this is mutual, the obvious method of analysis is game theory, which is widely used in theoretical biology. Most biological game theory centers on finding the evolutionary stable state (Maynard Smith, 1982), where both players behave optimally given the strategy of their opponent. This takes us back to ABC's objections to routinely using an optimality approach, but many game-theoretic biological models are often so abstract that the lack of realism of strategies such as hawk and dove is not an issue. This does not mean that they need be useless in helping us understand rules of thumb; for instance, game-theoretic analysis of the handicap principle has transformed our expectations of what sorts of mate-quality cues are attended to (Grafen, 1990). Nevertheless, as game-theoretic models become tailored more closely to real situations, it can turn out to be critical how we model what information is available to each player, and thus how they can "negotiate" (e.g., Barta, Houston, McNamara, & Székely, 2002).

Computer tournaments between simple strategies were the original method of analysis of the iterated prisoner's dilemma game (Axelrod & Hamilton, 1981) in which one of the simplest strategies, tit-for-tat, was the victor. Tit-for-tat has stood up remarkably well to new challengers, although recently a more complex rule has been claimed as superior (Hauert & Stenull, 2002). More important is that this paradigm has been influential in getting both economists and biologists thinking in terms of simple algorithmic response strategies, with sometimes deliberately limited cognitive abilities (Hoffmann, 2000). Unfortunately, existing claims of animals using-tit-for-tat are unconvincing (Hammerstein, 2003); part of the problem is that real biological situations are much more complex than the iterated prisoner's dilemma game, so that other strategies become available.

Another aspect of social rationality that ABC has started to investigate is the mechanisms by which individuals in a group amalgamate their separate knowledge or judgments to make a group decision (Reimer & Katsikopoulos, 2004). Maybe there is something to be learnt in this regard from research on group decision-making in social insects. For instance, Seeley (2003) considers how honeybees use simple rules to compare the quality of different potential nest sites even though no individual need have visited more than one site. Scouts that have discovered an inferior nest site advertise it (dance) less vigorously and for less time. Recruits are consequently more likely to visit the better sites, and dancing for inferior sites dies out. Seeley and Visscher (2003, 2004) discuss why it is adaptive that the colony moves when a critical-sized quorum (10 to 15 individuals) agree on one site, rather than waiting for a consensus or majority. This sounds like satisficing in that the colony takes the first option exceeding a threshold, but it is not a case of ignoring all but the first acceptable site, because scouts may already have visited other sites and competed to recruit nestmates.

A similar quorum rule has evolved in ants (Pratt, Mallon, Sumpter, & Franks, 2002). Franks et al. (2003) argued that this and other voting methods restrict the sorts of heuristics that an ant colony can use to choose between nest sites.

They considered such models as satisficing, elimination by aspects, and lexicographic strategies, but produced firm evidence both that ants consistently select the best site and that even the least important cue could affect a decision. Thus, a weighted-additive model fitted best. They argued that such a mechanism may be inevitable in a parallel-processing superorganism in which the method of decision is roughly counting votes of individual workers weighted by their individual enthusiasm for their single site. This mechanism makes it infeasible that the colony could consider attributes successively in turn even if a noncompensatory environment structure would favor this.

10. HOW BIOLOGISTS STUDY RULES OF THUMB

Having now explained the principles behind the ABC program, we concentrate again on biological research on rules of thumb. In this section we contrast the techniques of the two disciplines.

Many behavioral ecologists are interested mostly in the ultimate function of behavior. To them, rules of thumb may mostly seem important in providing a possible excuse if their optimality models fit only approximately. Then there are rarer behavioral biologists who, very much like ABC, do have an interest in the adaptation of rules of thumb. They may use similar simulation techniques to compare the performance of different rules of thumb. For instance, Houston, Kacelnik, and McNamara (1982) considered how a forager should decide between two resources providing food items stochastically, each with an unknown reward rate (a "two-armed bandit"). Candidate rules of thumb included "win-stay, lose-shift," probability matching, and sampling each resource equally until one had yielded d more successes than the other. Which was the best rule depended on the environment, although the first two examples were generally the worst.

The simulation approach has the limitation that there is no guarantee that there are not simpler or better rules. One test is to give a real animal exactly the same task as the simulated agents and compare performance: Thus, Baum and Grant (2001) found that real hummingbirds did better in two of their three model environments than did any of the simulated simple rules of movement. Another check on the biological relevance of postulated rules of thumb is to compare behavior of the simulated agents with that of real animals. Some papers use the same simulation model to predict both behavior and performance (e.g., Wajnberg et al., 2000). In this example, the parameters of the patch-leaving rule were first estimated from experimental data, but then varied to examine which mattered for performance. Other papers use simulation only to check whether postulated decision rules can explain observed emergent behaviors (e.g., de Vries & Biesmeijer, 2002; Keasar, Rashkovich, Cohen, & Shmida, 2002; Ydenberg, 1982); ultimate function is not the main focus.

However, most biological research on rules of thumb has not involved computing but an experimental, bottom-up approach that starts by observing the animals and is usually not driven by anything but the most intuitive theoretical expectations of what rules would work well. The interest is in details of mechanism, maybe aiming down to the levels of neurons and molecules. ABC has emphatically not taken this approach, but much of human and animal psychology has this emphasis on discovering the details of the mechanism. Although research in this tradition usually starts by investigating the response to single cues, sometimes attention may later shift to examining how cues are integrated. With this approach, rules of thumb are not the testable hypotheses with which one starts an investigation but rather they emerge at the end of the process as broad summary descriptions of the more detailed patterns already discovered. The adaptive advantages of the observed mechanism over others may only appear as speculation in the discussion.

Some of the most elegant examples of this bottom-up approach come from the classic work of Tinbergen (1958), although for him ultimate function was certainly not always a peripheral issue. For instance, he was interested in how a digger wasp *Philanthus triagulum* finds its way back to its burrow. By building a circle of fir cones around the burrow and then moving them while it was away, he showed that wasps use such objects as landmarks. He went on to examine what sorts of objects are used as landmarks, at what point they are learned, and how close landmarks interact with more distant ones. He also became interested in how the wasps found their prey. Using a variety of carefully presented models hanging from a thread, he showed that what first alerted the wasps was the appearance of a smallish and moving object; they then approached closely downwind to check its scent, jumped on it, and then could use tactile or taste cues to further check its suitability. Although the right scent was necessary as a second stage, and although they could retrieve lost prey items by scent alone, without the initial movement stimulus a correctly smelling dead bee attracted no interest. Tinbergen was also surprised that, although homing wasps showed great sophistication in recognizing landmarks visually, hunting wasps were easily fooled into smelling a moving object that was visually very unlike their bee prey.

Some of this type of behavioral research has developed beyond the behavior to examine the neurological processes responsible. This can sometimes be uniquely illuminating with regards to rules of thumb. For instance, Römer and Krusch (2000) have discovered a simple negative feedback loop in the ear of bushcrickets, which adjusts the sensitivity of the ear according to the loudness of the signal. The consequence is that the female's brain is totally unaware of all but the loudest male cricket in the vicinity (or possibly two, if a different male is loudest in each ear). The consequence behaviorally is a rule of thumb for mate choice of simply heading towards the male that appears loudest (usually the closest). Whether this is adaptive has not been considered. Unfortunately, results at this almost physiological level of analysis are still largely restricted to perception, learning, and memory (e.g., Menzel & Giurfa, 2001; Menzel, Greggers, & Hammer, 1993; Shettleworth, 1998), not yet revealing much about cue integration or decision making.

Advances in molecular biology mean that other non-neural mechanisms of cue integration are also becoming accessible. For instance, recent work has established that there are three independent pathways influencing when an *Arabidopsis* plant flowers (one responds to photoperiod, one to chilling, and one is endogenous), and how these pathways interact is something molecular biologists now hope to answer (Simpson, Genadall, & Dean, 1999).

In summary, although some biologists study rules of thumb in the same way that ABC studies heuristics, most of the results derive from experiment that has not been driven by theory. Such work often throws up surprises in the particulars, which one hopes theory can explain. ABC relies on other schools of psychology, for instance the heuristics-and-biases school (Gilovich et al., 2002), to provide some of the empirical surprises that its theories explain.

11. HOW ANIMALS COMBINE INFORMATION FROM MULTIPLE CUES

Much of ABC's research has been on the integration of different cues, so a disappointment about the biological research is that most papers examine a single cue. Often all other cues are held constant. When the interactions between cues have been investigated, and lots of such studies exist, most often the results are not related to those of other such studies. Recently a few papers have reviewed how females integrate cues to male quality (Candolin, 2003; Fawcett, 2003, Chapter 3; Jennions & Petrie, 1997) but results from many other domains of decision making could be connected (e.g., Partan & Marler, 1999). This is certainly somewhere that ABC can contribute to behavioral biology, by providing testable theory of what statistical structures of cues favor what methods of cue integration.

This is not the place for a thorough review of the empirical results, but a general conclusion is the diversity of methods used to combine cues. For instance, Shettleworth (1998, Chapter 7) reviews how animals combine cues used in navigation (local and distant landmarks, path integration, sun compass, etc.). Experiments indicate clear cases both of a sequential application of cues and of averaging the locations pointed to by conflicting cues. However, even in those species that average, if there is too much conflict between cues, they tend to fall back on large-scale spatial cues, which in nature are the most constant and reliable. An interesting comparison is the rules for dealing with conflicting temporal cues (Fairhurst, Gallistel, & Gibbon, 2003).

We now focus in turn on sequential and nonsequential cue assessment, finding in each case that empirical results from biology might prompt new directions of research for ABC.

11.1. Sequential Cue Assessment

Most studies measure only how cue values and the availability of cues affect the outcome of choice, not the process, so we cannot readily tell whether assessment of cues is sequential. The exception is if there is an observable behavioral sequence in which different cues are seen to be inspected at each stage before others are available, or where different cues predict breaking off the process at different stages. For instance, female sage grouse first assess males in a lek on the basis of their songs, and then visit only those passing this test for a closer visual inspection of display rate (Gibson, 1996). Such a "layered" process of sexual selection seems extremely widespread (Bonduriansky, 2003) and clear sequences of cue inspection are similarly well known in navigation and food choice. Note, however, that a sequential process need not necessarily imply a fixed cue order, nor that cues observed at one stage are ignored in decisions at later stages. Thus, either visual or olfactory cues in isolation are sufficient to attract hawkmoths to a flower, but both cues must be present to stimulate feeding (Raguso & Willis, 2002).

Even where the sequential aspect is not apparent, a clear ranking of importance of cues is at least compatible with a decision rule like take-the-best. For instance, honeybees trained to identify model flowers decide on the basis of color only if the odors of two alternatives match, and on the basis of shape only if color and odor match (Gould & Gould, 1988, Chapter 8). Gould and Gould explained this order on the basis of validity: Odor was the most reliable cue to the species of flower, color varied more from flower to flower, and shape varied depending on the angle of approach. They also are clear that by the time the bee gets close enough to sense flower odor, all three cues are available.

However, other examples suggest that ABC's sequential cue assessment models may need to be extended. One complication is that most cues are quantitative rather than the binary cues on which take-the-best operates. A threshold can convert quantitative into binary, which might be applicable for categorization into species or sex (e.g., Vicario, Naqvi, & Raksin, 2001), but most tasks studied involve comparison of a continuous criterion such as quality. With quantitative characters, the distinction between compensatory and noncompensatory becomes muddied. If two individuals differ considerably on one cue, there may be no useful information to be gained by looking at further cues; but if they differ only a little, it may be useful to consider further cues without necessarily discarding the information from the first cue. With quantitative cues we may find that which cues predict choices depends on which exhibit the most variation in that habitat and that year (e.g., Lifjeld & Slagsvold, 1988). We might observe such a pattern even if the same method of cue integration were used in the different environments, but it would not be surprising if choosers learned not to trouble to examine the less informative cues in that environment. Another complication with quantitative traits is that intermediate cue values may be more attractive than either extreme (e.g., Calkins & Burley, 2003).

Whereas for search in memory or search on a computer screen examining cues in order of decreasing validity may make good sense, in the biological examples other factors seem more important. In mate choice, the more reliable cues to quality tend to be examined last. In locating resources, the cue giving the most exact location tends to be examined last. One reason is likely to be the cost of sampling each cue in terms of risk, energetic expenditure, or time. For instance, mock fighting another male may be the most reliable cue to which male would win a real fight, but mock fighting has considerable dangers of damage, and consequently is not attempted unless other safer displays have failed to make the difference in quality apparent (Enquist, Leimar, Ljungberg, Mallner, &

Sgerdahl, 1990; Wells, 1988). Morphological cues may be judged at a glance, whereas behavioral traits may require time to assess. Fawcett and Johnstone (2003) consider the optimal order to assess cues differing in informativeness and cost. The other related reason for less valid cues to be assessed earlier is that some cues must necessarily appear before others. For instance, a deer stag cannot help but see the size of its rival before it starts fighting it, and the deepness of a roar may be available as a cue to size even before the animals get close enough to judge size visually.

Paradoxically, in these situations a more noncompensatory environment may lead to examining cues in increasing order of validity (the reverse of take-the-best), at least in cases where the quantitative nature of cues means that cue values are unlikely to tie. As the chooser gets progressively closer or more willing to take risks, more cues become available; it should be adapted to read those new cues whose validities outweigh those of earlier cues, but less valid new cues are unlikely to provide useful additional information and so might be ignored. An interesting question is to what extent the orders in which cues are examined are adaptations. With sexual selection, it could often be that particular traits evolve as signals because of the stage of the assessment process in which they can be examined, rather than that the cue informativeness of pre-existing signals has favored an order of inspection.

11.2. Nonsequential Cue Assessment

There are striking examples of an additive effect of different cues. By manipulating realistic computer animations of sticklebacks *Gasterosteus aculeatus,* Künzler and Bakker (2001) showed that the proportion of choices for one image over another was linearly related to the number of cues in which it was superior (cf. tallying). Similarly, Basolo and Trainor (2002) showed in the swordtail fish *Xiphophorus helleri* that the time for a female to respond was explicable as the sum of the effects of each component of the sword (cf. weighted-additive). However, Hankinson and Morris (2003) pointed out an alternative explanation for such additive results, which depend on averaging the responses of many fish. An additive pattern need not be due to an additive interaction of the cues in all individuals, but to each individual responding to different single cues—each extra cue persuades another subset of the population. We do know of cases of different individuals in the same population attending to different cues (e.g., Hill, Enstrom, Ketterson, Nolan, & Ziegenfus, 1999). The method of processing may differ between individuals too; older female garter snakes demand males that are good on two cues, whereas either cue alone satisfies younger females (Shine, Phillips, Waye, LeMaster, & Mason, 2003).

More complex interactions between cues are also observed. For instance, in the guppy *Poecilia reticulata* color affected choice when both animations showed a low display rate, but not when they both showed a high rate; conversely, display rates mattered when both animations displayed color, but not an absence of color (Kodric-Brown & Nicoletto, 2001). Another complex pattern is suggested in the work of both Zuk, Ligon, and Thornhill (1992) and Marchetti (1998); female choice was unaffected by manipulations of single male traits that earlier observational studies had suggested females were utilizing. One interpretation is that if one signal disagrees with all the other signals, it is ignored, which might be adaptive if accidental damage to single morphological characters is not indicative of quality. Some traits that we can measure independently may well be treated by the animal as composite traits, implying that complex integration of cues may happen at an almost perceptual level (Calkins & Burley, 2003; Rowe, 1999; Rowe & Skelhorn, 2004). One cue may alert the receiver to the presence of another (e.g., Hebets, 2005), or one cue may act as an amplifier for another (Hasson, 1991; for instance, contrasting plumage coloration makes it easier for the receiver to judge display movements). The usual assumption is that amplifiers rely on constraints in the way perception works, but such multiplicative cue interactions arise through other mechanisms also (Patricelli, Uy, & Borgia, 2003) and so it might be an adaptation to some particular environment structures. A multiplicative interaction favors two traits both

being well developed over either one in isolation. Perhaps this is ecologically rational in negatively correlated environments (cf. Johnson et al.'s [1989] finding of the benefits of including interaction terms in choice models in such environments).

12. BREAKING DOWN DISCIPLINARY BOUNDARIES

In the preceding section, we showed how empirical results on rules of thumb and ABC's theoretical approach could mutually illuminate each other. This short section examines further ways to develop the interaction.

ABC has already published research on heuristics used by animals. For instance, Davis, Todd, and Bullock (1999) simulated various rules that a parent bird might use to allocate food amongst its chicks (feed them in turn, or feed the largest, or hungriest, etc.). Other ABC papers have dealt with rules of thumb for mate choice, which relate to both animals and humans (Hutchinson & Halupka, 2004; Simão & Todd, 2002; Todd & Miller, 1999). The resulting papers fitted comfortably into the biological literature, emphasizing the similarities in approaches of the two schools.

Another way to break down the interdisciplinary barriers is to test theory developed in one school on the organisms (human or animal) of the other. ABC is currently testing whether humans use the same patch-leaving rules known from animals (Wilke, Hutchinson, & Todd, 2004). One experimental context is a computer game modeled on a foraging task, but another consists of internal search in memory for solutions to a Scrabble-like word puzzle. It is known that different species use different patch-leaving rules, presumably in response to their environments (van Alphen et al., 2003; Wajnberg et al., 2003), but we will test whether, as a generalist species, individual humans can rapidly change the rule according to the environment structure encountered.

Equally valid a research strategy would be to move in the opposite direction, testing whether animals use the heuristics that ABC has proposed that humans use. Demonstrating the parallel evolution of human heuristics in other lineages facing similar environmental structures would provide more stringent tests of their status as adaptations. Studying humans has some advantages, such as the possibility to use introspection to formulate plausible hypotheses about our heuristics, but animals provide many other advantages. In most nonhuman animals it is clearer what is their natural habitat and it is possible still to study the animal's behavior and its consequences in that environment. Comparative studies can test whether the rules of thumb used by related species have adjusted to their differing environments. Analyzing the structure of the environment is usually easier than with humans because most species are more specialist. Shorter life cycles make it easier to relate the immediate consequences of a behavior to fitness. Practical considerations also allow far more complete manipulations of an animal's environment than in humans. Moreover, as Tinbergen found, it is often the case in animals that quite crude tricks suffice, itself perhaps a reflection of animals' greater reliance on simpler rules of thumb.

Of course calls for better communication between biologists and psychologists are not original, and behavioral ecology has always had some contacts with animal psychology (e.g., Fantino & Abarca, 1985; Kamil & Sargent, 1981; Rowe & Skelhorn, 2004). One link of some relevance to ABC is the investigation of animal models that duplicate the human "biases" emphasized by the heuristics-and-biases school (e.g., Bateson et al., 2003; Fantino, 1998; Shafir, Waite, & Smith, 2002). If these findings are related to the natural environments of these animals (not always done), this can be an avenue to test explanations of these biases as products of adaptive heuristics (e.g., Arkes & Ayton, 1999; Schuck-Paim, Pompilio, & Kacelnik, 2004).

13. CONCLUSIONS

ABC has demonstrated that simple heuristics can be a surprisingly effective way of making many decisions, both in terms of frugality and performance. Research has also started to show that humans really use these simple heuristics

in environments where they are ecologically rational. It lies ahead to discover how much of human cognition can be usefully understood in terms of ABC's algorithmic approach. Within psychology there is a wide range of opinion about the likely answer and thus about the importance of ABC's work. However, there is increasing interest from economists, who realize that their unboundedly rational optimality models often provide an inadequate prediction of human decisions.

How might ABC gain from a closer relationship with behavioral biology? Certainly biology considerably broadens the range of examples of heuristics, some of which will turn out to be shared between animals and humans. Some make particularly strong examples because they can be anchored in proven neurological mechanisms or because their adaptive value is less ambiguous than with humans. Animal examples may illuminate characteristics of natural environments that are less important to modern humans, but to which our cognitive mechanisms are still adapted: An example is our suggestion that cue orders may have as much to do with costs and accessibility of each cue as with validity. We have also discussed how the tools of optimality modeling might be reapplied to the study of heuristics.

What might biology gain from a broader knowledge of ABC's work? Rules of thumb are already part of behavioral biology's vocabulary. And biologists already use the usual ABC approach of simulating candidate heuristics to judge their performance. However, although biological examples of rules of thumb and of cue integration are not so rare, they tend to be isolated curiosities in the literature. Can some of these different rules be classified by shared building blocks, just as with ABC's simple heuristics? ABC's emphasis on simple algorithmic decision rules might provide a useful impetus both to interpret further animal behaviors in such terms, and then to expose commonalities between the examples. This is especially the case with cue integration, for which biology seems not to have developed an equivalent of ABC's theoretical framework explaining why particular methods of cue integration work well in particular types of information environments. Also largely missing from biology is the idea that simple heuristics may be superior to more complex methods, not just a necessary evil because of the simplicity of animal nervous systems (but see: Bookstaber & Langsam, 1985; Real, 1992; Stephens, 2002; Stephens and Anderson, 2001). The shared assumption that performance is what matters should facilitate communication between biologists and ABC.

One of the possible derivations of the phrase "rule of thumb" is from craftsmen using the size of their thumb as a measure instead of a ruler (Brewer, 1996). To finish with a pleasing parallel between humans and animals, consider this example. The sticky part of a spider's web is a spiral thread with each whorl evenly spaced from its predecessor, as one expects of a well-designed net. Just like the craftsman, the spider uses a part of its own body as a caliper. To demonstrate this, Vollrath (1987) cut off the spider's legs on one side; the legs regrew at the next molt, but smaller than before, and the spacing of the spiral was then proportionately closer.

ACKNOWLEDGMENTS

We thank Edmund Fantino, Konstantinos Katsikopoulos, Heike Reise, Lael Schooler, Masanori Takezawa, Peter Todd, and an anonymous referee for their comments on an earlier version of the manuscript and Henry Brighton for providing Figure 5-1. We also thank Randolph Grace for stimulating and facilitating this review.

Introduction to Chapter 6

Naive and yet Enlightened: From Natural Frequencies to Fast and Frugal Decision Trees

How do doctors classify patients into disease categories? Many psychological theories assume that doctors look up and integrate all evidence, as in exemplar models of categorization, but in reality much of decision making is sequential and frugal. For instance, in routine HIV screening, a physician begins with an ELISA test. If it is negative, testing is stopped and the diagnosis is "not infected." If it is positive, another ELISA test (preferably from a different manufacturer) will be performed. If this is negative, the diagnosis will be "not infected." If, however, the result is again positive, a Western blot test will be conducted. If this is negative, the diagnosis will be "not infected," and if positive, "infected." This sequential procedure, which may be repeated with another blood sample, does not correspond to a full tree with complete information. It is a "fast-and-frugal tree," which ignores part of the information. For instance, if the first ELISA test is negative, no other tests will be conducted, even though sometimes an infection is missed with an ELISA. A 36-year-old HIV-infected American construction worker who tested negative for HIV 35 times holds the world record in "misses" (Gigerenzer, 2002). Fast-and-frugal trees are a standard technique for classification, from HIV tests to cancer screening. Yet these heuristics have received too little attention in the psychology of categorization and decision making.

Written by a mathematician (Laura Martignon), two psychologists (Oliver Vitouch and Masanori Takezawa), and a philosopher (Malcom Forster), this article provides a case study in intuitive design, explaining how to construct medical decision-making systems that physicians can easily memorize and understand. Martignon et al. also explain the relation between simple heuristics and full decision trees expressed in terms of natural frequencies. A full tree corresponds to a Bayesian analysis. Observing that people cannot solve simple Bayesian problems, psychologists attributed this for many decades to the usual suspect—cognitive limitations. Today we know that the problem lies in the external representation: Conditional probabilities cloud the minds of laypeople and physicians alike, whereas natural frequencies are transparent and can turn innumeracy into insight (Gigerenzer & Hoffrage, 1995, 1999). The main source of error is outside the mind, not inside it. The term *natural frequencies* has been incorporated into the vocabulary of evidence-based medicine, and hundreds of doctors have been trained in using them to understand the outcomes of their screening tests (Gigerenzer, Gaissmaier, Kurz-Milcke, Schwartz, & Woloshin, 2007). However, when the number of cues or predictors grows, a Bayesian analysis—with or without natural frequencies—becomes computationally intractable or fraught with estimation error because one typically has too few data points to fill in the thousands of "leaves" of such a gigantic tree. For binary cues, a full tree has 2^n leaves and grows exponentially. A fast-and-frugal tree has only $n + 1$ leaves and thus can handle many cues.

Fast-and-frugal trees, which follow the template of take-the-best, are not the only heuristics used for classification. The alternative is to follow the template of tallying, as in von Helversen and Rieskamp's (2008) mapping model. Chapter 14 reports comparative tests of fast-and-frugal trees in many real-world situations. Fast-and-frugal trees have been proposed as models of the unconscious processes underlying British magistrates' bail decisions (see Chapter 28) and as tools for intuitive design, such as whether to allocate a patient with severe chest pain to the coronary care unit (see this article).

CHAPTER 6

Naive and yet Enlightened: From Natural Frequencies to Fast and Frugal Decision Trees

Laura Martignon, Oliver Vitouch, Masanori Takezawa, and Malcolm R. Forster

Abstract: The trees for classification and for decision that are introduced in this chapter are naïve, fast, and frugal. Why they are "naïve," that is, why they ignore conditional dependencies between cues, is extensively illustrated. Why they are "frugal," in the sense that they tend to use much fewer cues than those provided by the environment, is also explained in detail. The trees' "fastness" appears as a consequence of their frugality. The main property of these trees is that they implement one-reason classification/decision in analogy with heuristics for one-reason decision making. The lexicographic nature of these trees is shown with the help of a characterization theorem. As will also become clear, fast-and-frugal trees generalize take-the-best.

An evolutionary view of rationality as an adaptive toolbox of fast-and-frugal heuristics is sometimes placed in opposition to probability as the ideal of enlightened rational human inference. Indeed, this opposition has become the cornerstone of an ongoing debate between adherents to theories of normative as opposed to bounded rationality. On the one hand, it has been shown that probability provides a good approximation to human cognitive processing for tasks involving simple inferences, and humans actually are able to reason the Bayesian way when information is presented in formats to which they are well adapted (Gigerenzer & Hoffrage, 1995). On the other hand, it is clear that probabilistic inference becomes infeasible when the mind has to deal with too many pieces of information at once. Coping with resource

limitations, the mind—as Gigerenzer, Todd, and the ABC Research Group (1999) claim—adopts simple inference heuristics, often based on just one-reason decision making. Our aim is to present a unifying framework, based on the systematic use of trees for knowledge representation, both for fully Bayesian and for fast-and-frugal decisions.

Tree-structured schemes are ubiquitous tools for organizing and representing knowledge, and their history goes back to the third century, when Porphyry introduced a first version of the tree of life (Isagoge, around AD 305). We will show that both full Bayesian inference and one-reason decision making are processes that can be described in terms of tree-structured decision rules. A fully specified Bayesian model can be represented by means of the "full" or "maximal" tree obtained by introducing nodes for all conceivable conjunctions of events, whereas a one-reason decision rule can be represented by a "minimal" subtree of the maximal tree (with maximal and minimal reference to the number of paths connecting the root to the leaves). Subtrees of the full tree not containing any path from root to leaves are regarded as "truncated" since they necessarily truncate the access to available information; they will not be treated in this chapter. Minimal trees can be obtained by radically pruning the full tree. A minimal tree has a leaf at each one of its levels, so that every level allows for a possible decision. Indeed, when a radical reduction of complexity is necessary and when the environment is favorable, such a minimal tree will be extremely fast and frugal with negligible losses in accuracy. In this chapter, we introduce a name for such minimal trees, following the terminology used by Gigerenzer et al. (1999) for heuristics that very much resemble minimal trees. We will call them "fast-and-frugal trees."

While the construction by means of a radical pruning of the full tree serves theoretical purposes in order to understand the mathematical properties of fast-and-frugal trees, it seems unlikely that humans construct these trees in such a top-down fashion. Humans apparently use simple construction rules, without integrating information. They tend to ignore dependencies between cues, and their decision strategy is solely based on the ranking of these cues with respect to their "stand-alone" predictive usefulness.

We begin by describing how natural frequencies provide fully specified trees, which we will call "natural frequency trees," that carry and represent the statistical information required for Bayesian reasoning. We will then transform natural frequency trees into fully specified classification trees. We will proceed by describing how to prune radically a full classification tree, transforming it into a fast-and-frugal classification tree, which is then easily converted into a decision tree. We will show that fast-and-frugal trees are one-reason decision-making tools which operate as lexicographic classifiers.[1] Then we will approach the natural question: How do humans construct fast-and-frugal trees for classification and decision? We will propose simple construction rules, where all that matters is the ranking of cues. Once the ranking is established, the fast-and-frugal tree checks one cue at a time, and at each step, one of the possible outcomes of the considered cue is an exit node which allows for a

decision. Finally, we will compare fast and frugal trees with an "optimizing" model from the general linear model framework, namely, logistic regression.

TREE-STRUCTURED REPRESENTATIONS IN CLASSIFICATION TASKS

A classification (also called categorization) tree is a graphical representation of a rule—or a set of rules—for making classifications. Each node of the tree represents a question regarding certain features of the objects to be classified or categorized. Each branch leading out of the node represents a different answer to the question. It is assumed that the answers to the question are exclusive (nonoverlapping) and exhaustive (cover all objects). That is, there is exactly one answer to the question for each object, and each of the possible answers is represented by one branch out of the node. The nodes below a given node are called its "children," and the node above a node is called "parent." Every node has exactly one parent except for the "root" node, which has no parent, and which is usually depicted at the top or far left. The "leaf" nodes, or nodes having no children, are usually depicted at the bottom or far right. In a "binary" tree, all non-leaf nodes have exactly two children; in general, trees nodes may have any number of children. The leaf nodes of a classification tree represent a "partition" of the set of objects into classes defined by the answers to the questions. Each leaf node has an associated class label, to be assigned to all objects for which the appropriate answers are given to the questions associated with the leaf's ancestor nodes.

The classification tree can be used to construct a simple algorithm for associating any object with a class label. Given an object, the algorithm traverses a "path" from the root node to one of the leaf nodes. This path is determined by the answers to the questions associated with the nodes. The questions and answers can be used to define a "decision rule" to be executed when each node is traversed. The decision rule instructs the algorithm which arc to traverse out of the node, and thus which child to visit. The classification algorithm proceeds as follows:

Algorithm TREE-CLASS:

(1) Begin at root node.
(2) Execute rule associated with current node to decide which arc to traverse.
(3) Proceed to child at end of chosen arc.
(4) If child is a leaf node, assign to object the class label associated with node and STOP.
(5) Otherwise, go to (2).

NATURAL FREQUENCY TREES

Natural frequency trees provide good representations of the statistical data relevant to the construction of optimal classification trees. In this section, we begin by recalling how natural frequency trees for complex classification tasks— that is, tasks involving several pieces of information—were introduced by Krauss, Martignon, Hoffrage, and Gigerenzer (2001), by generalizing the results of Gigerenzer and Hoffrage (1995). Krauss et al. showed empirically that the following problem is solved with ease by most participants:

> 100 out of every 10,000 women at age 40 who participate in routine screening have breast cancer.
>
> 80 of every 100 women with breast cancer will get a positive mammography.
>
> 950 out of every 9,900 women without breast cancer will also get a positive mammography.
>
> 76 out of 80 women who had a positive mammography and have cancer also have a positive ultrasound test.
>
> 38 out of 950 women who had a positive mammography, although they do not have cancer, also have a positive ultrasound test.
>
> How many of the women who get a positive mammography and a positive ultrasound test do you expect to actually have breast cancer?

The frequencies in this task, for example, "38 out of 950," were called "natural frequencies" following Gigerenzer and Hoffrage (1995) and Kleiter (1994). In contrast, the traditional probability format of the task consisted of statements such as "For a woman with breast cancer, the probability of getting a positive mammogram is 80 percent." The important discovery was that the natural frequency format makes the task much easier to solve than the probabilistic format. The argument made by Gigerenzer and Hoffrage to explain the beneficial effects of natural frequencies was computational and evolutionary. Since humans are used to counting and automatically sampling frequencies (see also Hasher & Zacks, 1984), they are also at ease when having to form simple proportions with these sampled frequencies.[2] Krauss et al. (2001) observed that some participants in their experiments drew trees like that in Figure 6-1 as an aid in solving the task.

Such a tree was called a "natural frequency tree." The numbers in the nodes indicate that the two tests are conditionally independent, given cancer. This is obviously an assumption. The reality of medical tests is that neither combined sensitivities nor combined specificities are reported in the literature; it is a frequent convention to assume tests' conditional independence, given the disease.

Observe that this natural frequency tree is *causally* organized. That is, the top node divides the universe of patients into those with cancer and those free of cancer. Successive nodes represent tests which are useful for diagnosing cancer because their outcomes are *caused* by the presence or absence of cancer. Thus, the patient's classification on the top node is a cause of the patient's classification on the lower nodes. Causal organization is useful for scientific evaluation of causal claims, but is less useful if the purpose is to facilitate rapid diagnosis. When a patient arrives at the doctor's office, it is not known whether she has cancer. Thus, it is not possible to follow the TREE-CLASS algorithm described in the previous section. The first decision—whether to trace the "breast cancer" or the "no breast cancer" arc—cannot be made from the information available to the doctor. For example, suppose a woman gets a positive mammogram (M+) and a positive ultrasound (U+). We cannot tell whether to trace the "breast cancer" or the "no breast cancer" link. In the first case, we would follow the U+ and M+ links to place her among the 76 women in the leftmost leaf node. In the

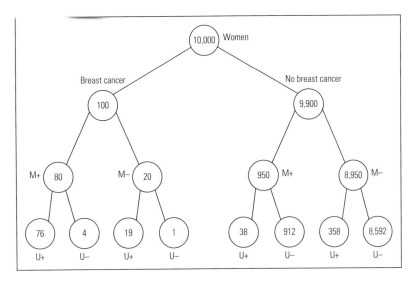

Figure 6-1. The natural frequency tree for classifying a patient as having or not having cancer, based on the results of a mammogram and an ultrasound test.

second case, we would again follow U+ and M+ to place her among the 38 women in the fifth leaf node from the left. To calculate the probability that she has cancer, we need to trace each of these paths in turn and combine the results to form the ratio 76/(38 + 76). This calculation requires us to use information stored in widely separated parts of the tree. There are more practical natural frequency trees for diagnosis. They are obtained by inverting the order followed for the sequential partitioning of the total population (10,000 women) in Figure 6-1. Consider the tree in Figure 6-2.

Organizing the tree in the *diagnostic* direction produces a much more efficient classification strategy. An example of a diagnostic tree for the cancer task is shown in Figure 6-2. This tree has two major advantages over the tree in Figure 6-1 for a diagnostic task. First, we can follow the TREE-CLASS algorithm for the first two steps before becoming stuck at the second-to-last level above the leaf nodes. For example, for the hypothetical woman with M+ and U+ described above, we would be able to place her among the 114 women at the leftmost node on the third level from the top. Second, once we have placed a patient at a node just above the bottom of the tree, we can compute the probability of placing

her at each of the two possible leaf nodes by using only local information. That is, the probability our hypothetical woman has cancer can be computed by looking at the cancer node just below, discovering that there are 76 exemplars associated with that node, and dividing it by the 114 exemplars at the third level.

Comparing the leaves of Figures 6-1 and 6-2 reveals that they are the same; that is, they contain the same numbers, although their ordering is different, as is the topology of their connection to the rest of the tree. One might question whether a natural sampler would partition the population in the causal or the diagnostic direction. Pearl (e.g., 1988; see also Fiedler, 2000) argues that knowledge tends to be organized causally, and diagnostic inference is performed by means of inversion strategies, which, in the frequency format, are reduced to inverting the partitioning order as above (in the probability format, the inversion is carried out by applying Bayes' theorem; Bayes, 1763). Others (e.g., Chase, 1999) argue that ecologically situated agents tend to adopt representations tailored to their goals and the environment in which they are situated. Thus, it might be argued that a goal-oriented natural sampler performing a diagnostic task will probably partition the original

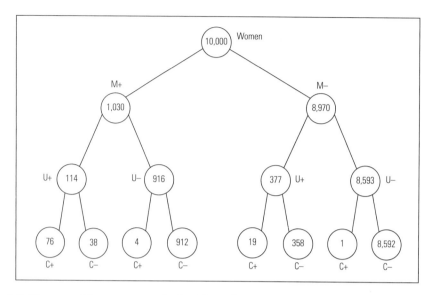

Figure 6-2. The natural frequency tree obtained from the tree in Figure 6-1, when the sampling order is mammogram → ultrasound →cancer(C).

population according to the cues first, and end by partitioning according to the criterion.

Now, consider another version of the diagnostic ordering of the cues, where, in the first phase, women are partitioned according to their ultrasound, and in the second phase, they are partitioned according to the mammograms and finally according to breast cancer. The tree is depicted in Figure 6-3.

Again, the numbers in the leaves coincide with those in the leaves of the trees in Figures 6-1 and 6-2. Partitioning is commutative: we obtain the same final cells no matter which partitioning order we follow.

FROM NATURAL FREQUENCY TREES TO CLASSIFICATION AND DECISION TREES

Remember that the decision maker has to decide what to do for each of the four combinations of cue values ([positive mammogram, positive ultrasound], [positive mammogram, negative ultrasound], [negative mammogram, positive ultrasound], [negative mammogram, negative ultrasound]). A fully specified classification tree would, for instance, look like the tree in

Figure 6-3, without the lowest level. Its leaves would be labeled by the four combinations of cue values listed above. If, based on the statistical information provided by the natural frequency tree, decision makers have to decide between "apply biopsy" or "send the patient home," they will try to reduce the number of *worst* errors, namely, sending women home who do have cancer, while trying to keep the number of biopsies on women without breast cancer low.

Radical Pruning

We now provide the construction rules for simple decision trees, starting from the fully specified natural frequency trees. There are, of course, many ways in which the complexity of the fully specified tree can be reduced. We will adopt the most radical one, by a sequential pruning which eliminates half of the remaining tree at every step. By observing the tree in Figure 6-2, we realize that if we send all women with a negative mammogram home with no further testing, we will miss 20 cancer cases out of the 10,000 women tested. This corresponds to pruning the children and grandchildren of the negative mammogram node in the tree. If we use ultrasound instead of mammogram as our "one-reason

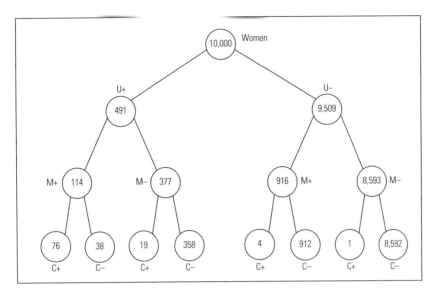

Figure 6-3. Natural sampling in the order ultrasound → mammography → cancer(C).

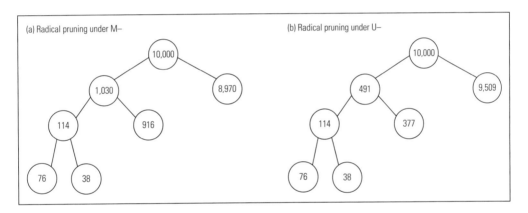

Figure 6-4. The trees resulting from radically pruning the fully specified tree.

decision rule," we will miss five patients with the disease out of the 10,000 women tested (cf. Figure 6-3). Simplifying our trees even further, we can eliminate all children nodes of "positive mammogram and negative ultrasound" in Figure 6-2, obtaining the radically pruned trees in Figure 6-4a and b. Our error has become larger: 24 women with cancer will be declared healthy. The same error would arise if we prune the children of "positive ultrasound and negative mammogram" in Figure 6-3. In fact, the leaves left after pruning are the same in both cases, as shown in Figure 6-5.

The medical reality of the diagnosis and treatment of breast cancer is very close to the decision strategy resulting from this pruning procedure. If a woman with no symptoms has a negative mammogram, the doctor "sends her home." In routine screening, the mammogram is the first test taken, followed—if positive—by the ultrasound test. If both are positive, the doctor will tend to recommend a biopsy. Biopsy will

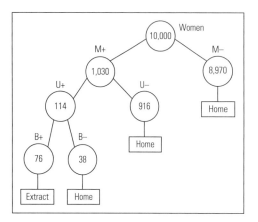

Figure 6-5. A fast-and-frugal decision tree in the "breast cancer" situation. The symbols B+ and B– stand for positive and negative biopsy.

(almost surely) detect the tumor if it exists and, after close laboratory examination, classify it as malignant or benign. A malignant tumor will be extracted "locally." In cases of extremely large tumors, amputation will be performed.

Medical decisions can usually not be based on the fully specified trees due to the costs involved in performing tests. These costs are not just in terms of the prices of the tests (mammograms and ultrasounds have comparable prices; modern biopsy can be twice as expensive); they are also to be seen as costs in time and, last but not least, in terms of the patient's health (Cousins, 1989; Gigerenzer, 2002). The medical tendency is to reduce the number of tests and biopsies to the minimum required for good diagnosis. When such constraints are taken into account, the radically simplified tree of Figure 6-5 becomes the viable strategy.

FAST-AND-FRUGAL TREES

A tree such as the one depicted in Figure 6-5 may be called a fast-and-frugal tree, according to the definition we present below. We formulate this definition for binary trees, that is, trees constructed with binary cues and a binary criterion. The generalization to other cases is straightforward. With the classification according to a binary criterion (for example, "cancer"

or "no cancer"), we associate two possible decisions, one for each possible classification (for example, "biopsy" or "no biopsy"). An important convention has to be applied beforehand: Cue profiles can be expressed as vectors of 0s and 1s, where a 1 corresponds to the value of the cue more highly correlated with the outcome of the criterion considered "positive" (for example, presence of cancer). The convention is that left branches are labeled with 1s and right branches with 0s. Thus, each branch of the fully specified tree can be labeled with a 1 or a 0, according to the cue value associated with the node at the end of the branch.

Definition

A fast-and-frugal binary decision tree is a decision tree with at least one exit leaf at every level. That is, for every checked cue, at least one of its outcomes can lead to a decision. In accordance with the convention applied above, if a leaf stems from a branch labeled 1, the decision will be positive (for example, "perform biopsy").

This definition cannot stand alone, that is, without a good characterization of fast-and-frugal trees as classifiers. Thus, the rest of this section is devoted to analytical characterizations that identify fast-and-frugal trees as very special types of classifiers. We begin by recalling that in any natural frequency tree organized in the diagnostic direction, as in Figures 6-2 and 6-3, each leaf represents the number of subjects in the population that have a given cue profile and have or do not have the disease. Again, according to our convention, we will encode "having the disease" with a 1, and "not having the disease" with a 0. If we have, say, three cues, the leaves of the full frequency tree will be labeled (111, 1), (111, 0), (101, 1), (101, 0), (100, 1), (100, 0), (011, 1), (011, 0), (010, 1), (010, 1), (001, 0), (000, 1), (000,0), where the binary vectors will appear in decreasing lexicographic order from left to right. Observe that we have separated the cue profile from the state of the disease by a comma.

Since this ordering is similar to the ordering of words in a dictionary, it is usually called "lexicographic." Lexicographic orderings allow for simple classifications, by establishing that all profiles larger (in the lexicographic ordering) than a certain fixed profile will be assigned to one class, and all profiles smaller than the same fixed profile will be assigned to the other class. Let us pin this definition down.

Given a set of *n* binary cues, we say that L is a "lexicographic classifier" on the set of all possible cue profiles if there is a cue profile α such that L classifies all cue profiles larger than α (in the lexicographic ordering) as members of one class and all profiles smaller than α as members of the other. The profile α will be called the "splitting profile" of the classification (cf. Figure 6-6). The splitting profile α is classified according to its last bit. If this is 1, it will be assigned the same class as all profiles larger than α; it will be assigned the alternative class, if its last bit is 0.

A "lexicographic decision rule" makes one decision, say, D, for all profiles larger than a given, fixed profile, and the alternative decision, $\neg$D, for all profiles smaller than that same profile. The profile itself is assigned decision D if it ends with a 1, and decision $\neg$D if it ends with a 0.

A fast-and-frugal decision tree makes decisions *lexicographically*. This is what we prove in the following theorem.

Theorem

Let T be the fast-and-frugal decision tree defined by the cue profile α. Denote by $\bar{\alpha}$ the profile that coincides with α in all but the last cue value. Assume that α ends with a 1. Then T makes exactly the same decisions as a lexicographic decision rule that assigns the same decision D assigned to α to every profile $\beta > \bar{\alpha}$, and the alternative decision $\neg$D assigned to $\bar{\alpha}$ to every $\beta < \alpha$ (cf. Figure 6-7).

Proof. Assume $\beta > \alpha$. This means, by definition of the lexicographic ordering, that for some *k* the first *k* cue values in the cue profile β coincide with those of α, but its $(k+1)$-st cue value is 1, while the $(k+1)$-st cue value of α is 0. By construction, this $(k+1)$-st cue value labels a branch which terminates in a leaf, and, by convention, such a leaf must necessarily lead to decision D. This proves our assertion. An analogous argument proves that if $\beta < \alpha$, β will be assigned decision $\neg$D. Q.E.D.

At this point, we want to make a connection between fast-and-frugal decision trees and a well-established simple heuristic for comparison called "take-the-best." Take-the-best, a heuristic for comparison proposed by Gigerenzer and

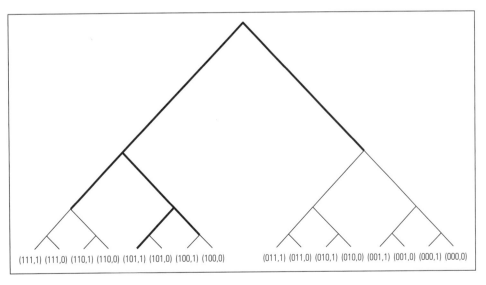

(111,1) (111,0) (110,1) (110,0) (101,1) (101,0) (100,1) (100,0)   (011,1) (011,0) (010,1) (010,0) (001,1) (001,0) (000,1) (000,0)

Figure 6-6. A lexicographic classifier determined by the path of profile (101), where the three bits are cue values and the last bit corresponds to the criterion (for example, having or not having the disease)

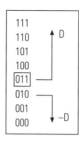

Figure 6-7. A lexicographic classifier that has the profile (011) as split.

Goldstein (1996), is a strategy for lexicographic comparison. In other words, if two objects have profiles of, say, (11101010) and (11110101), take-the-best will decide that the first one has a larger value on the criterion, simply because its cue profile is "larger" in the lexicographic sense.

The question is now: what makes a fast-and-frugal tree a "good" decision tree? In other words, given a set of cues, how do we know how to order them so as to minimize errors when constructing a fast-and-frugal tree? One thing is certain: The decision maker in a hurry does not have the time to construct the full tree and then choose the best ordering of cues by comparing the performances of possible orderings (see later). The naïve decision maker uses simple, naïve ways for obtaining good fast-and-frugal trees. In the next section, we will illustrate some simple methods for constructing good fast-and-frugal trees with a real-life example.

CONSTRUCTING FAST-AND-FRUGAL DECISION TREES

In order to illustrate the construction of a fast-and-frugal tree, we walk through an example extracted from the literature, where a simple tree—according to our definition, a fast-and-frugal tree—for medical diagnosis was constructed (Green & Mehr, 1997). Consider the following situation. A man is rushed into a hospital with severe chest pain. The doctors have to decide whether the patient should be assigned to the coronary care unit (CCU) or to a monitored

nursing bed (NB). The cues on which a doctor bases such a decision are the following:

(1) ST-segment elevation in the electrocardiogram (ECG)
(2) patient report of chest pain as most important symptom
(3) history of heart attack
(4) history of nitroglycerin use for chest pain
(5) pain in the chest or left arm
(6) ST-segment "barring"
(7) T-waves with peaking or inversion

Green and Mehr (1997) analyzed the problem of finding a simple procedure for determining an action based on this cue information. They began their project with the aim of implementing an existing logistic regression-based instrument proposed by Pozen, D'Agostino, Selker, Sytkowski, and Hood (1984), the Heart Disease Predictive Instrument, in a rural hospital. What they found was that by using the instrument, doctors quickly became sensitive to the important diagnostic cues (as opposed to pseudo-diagnostic or less valid ones). Even without the instrument with its exact beta weights at hand, they maintained the same level of performance. Inspired by the work of the ABC Research Group, this observation led Green and Mehr to construct a simple competitor. They reduced the seven cues to only three (creating a new cue formed by the disjunction of 3, 4, 6 and 7) and proposed the tree depicted in Figure 6-8.

Although Green and Mehr (1997) succeeded in constructing a fast-and-frugal decision tree with excellent performance, they did not reveal how they ended up with precisely this tree, nor did they provide any standard procedure to construct such trees. Our intention is to provide simple rules for their construction. Using the Green and Mehr task as an example, we will illustrate several methods for designing fast-and-frugal trees and then compare their performance.[3]

ORDERING OF CUES

Table 6-1 shows a data subset from the Green and Mehr (1997) study. In order to construct a fast-and-frugal tree, one can, of course, test all possible orderings of cues and shapes of trees on

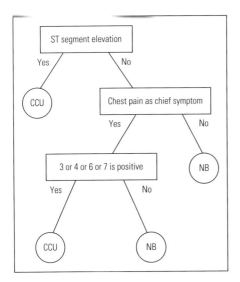

Figure 6-8. Green and Mehr (1997) tree for making decision D, "assign to CCU," or ¬D "assign to NB."

Table 6-1. Original Data from the Green and Mehr (1997) Study

C1,C2, C3	Infarction	No Infarction
111	9	12
110	1	1
101	3	5
100	0	2
011	2	15
010	0	10
001	0	19
000	0	10

C1 = ST-segment elevation; C2 = chest pain; C3 = any other cue of 3, 4, 6, 7. Columns 2 and 3 give the respective number of patients.

the provided data set and optimize fitting performance; in the general case, this requires enormous computation if the number of cues is large. Another approach is to determine the "best" cue according to some given rule, and then determine the "second best" cue conditional on the first, and so on. But this again requires a fairly large number of computations.

In conceptual analogy to naïve Bayes models, naïve decision makers will not look into conditional dependencies and/or correlations between cues. Our conjecture is that they will basically have a good feeling of how well each cue alone predicts the criterion. They will sample natural frequency trees for each of the three cues individually. These trees are simple enough as to be grasped/stored by our decision makers. They need a good feeling, however, of how the cues compare to each other (see Figure 6-9a–c). The question is: What is a good cue?

In what follows, we make a short digression to answer this question in detail. Let us consider the contingency table for an abstract criterion C over an abstract cue:

$$\begin{array}{ccc} & C & \neg C \\ \text{cue} & a & b \\ \neg\text{cue} & c & d \end{array}$$

Recall that a test can be good in more than one way. Its sensitivity, that is, the chances of obtaining a positive test result given that the patient has the disease [that is, $a/(a + c)$], can be very high. Or its specificity, that is, the chances of obtaining a negative result given that the patient does not have the disease [that is, $d/(d + b)$], can be very high. Another measure is based on the proportion of correct predictions. One can look at the correct predictions made by a positive test. This proportion [that is, $a/(a + b)$] is the "positive validity"—also called "positive predictivity"—of the test. Yet another measure is the proportion of correct predictions made by a negative test, or "negative validity" [that is, $d/(d + c)$], also called "negative predictivity." If, instead of separating into positive and negative parcels, we look at the global goodness of a test, we have diagnosticity (the average of sensitivity and specificity) and validity (the average of positive and negative validity). The diagnosticity of the cue is given by

$$\text{Diag(cue)} = P(\text{cue}\,|\,C)\,P(C) \\ + P(\neg\text{cue}\,|\,\neg C)\,P(\neg C)$$

The validity (or predictivity) of the cue is given by

$$\text{Val(cue)} = P(C\,|\,\text{cue})\,P(\text{cue}) \\ + P(\neg C\,|\,\neg\text{cue})\,P(\neg\text{cue})$$

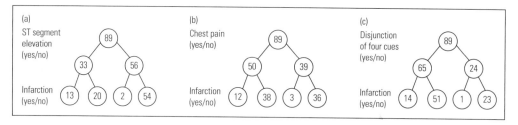

Figure 6-9. **a.** Natural frequency diagnostic tree for ST-segment elevation. **b.** Natural frequency diagnostic tree for chest pain. **c.** Natural frequency diagnostic tree for "disjunction of four cues."

Note that sensitivity and positive validity coincide only in the special case of equal marginals of the two-by-two table, as do specificity and negative validity. Their averages, however—validity and diagnosticity—necessarily coincide and are given by

$$P(C \cap cue) + P(\neg C \cap \neg cue)$$

where $\cap$ denotes conjunction.

Here, we will focus on two different types of orderings: orderings based on (1) either sensitivity or specificity and (2) either positive or negative validity.

THE SHAPE OF TREES

As shown in Figure 6-10, there are four possible shapes, or branching structures, of fast-and-frugal trees for three cues.

Trees of type 1 and 4 are called "rakes" or "pectinates." As defined here, rakes have a very special property. They embody a strict conjunction rule, meaning that one of the two alternative decisions is made only if all cues are present (type 1) or absent (type 4). Trees of types 2 and 3 are called "zig-zag trees." They have the property of alternating between positive and negative exits in the sequence of levels. Given a decision task and a set of cues, how can we choose one of these fast and-frugal trees? We now list some simple, naïve ways of ranking cues and deciding the shape of trees. Observe that all cues considered have the same technical cost once the electrocardiogram and the anamnesis have been performed; thus, procedural cost is not an issue when constructing the tree.

An important aspect is that, at least in the context of medical decision making, misses and false alarms differ in importance. Doctors' first priority is to reduce misses; their second priority is to reduce false alarms. This difference in gravity of errors will be discussed in more detail later, where we will focus on the performance of trees. This asymmetry will be reflected in the construction rules proposed, with the aim of achieving a large number of hits (correct assignments to coronary care unit) already at the first decisional level.

Let us first exhibit the contingency tables for the three cues in the Green and Mehr task (Table 6-2). Sensitivity and specificity of the cues are given in Table 6-3; positive and negative validities, in Table 6-4.

Now we make use of this information in four different approaches to constructing a fast-and-frugal tree.

(1) *Max(sens, spec)*. We begin by picking the cue with maximal sensitivity. All remaining cues are then ranked by the maximum of

Table 6-2. Contingency Tables for "ST-Segment Elevation," "Chest Pain," and "Any of 3, 4, 6, 7"

	Infarction	No Infarction
ST-segment = 1	13	20
ST-segment = 0	2	54
Chest pain = 1	12	38
Chest pain = 0	3	36
(Any of 3, 4, 6, 7) = 1	14	51
(Any of 3, 4, 6, 7) = 0	1	23

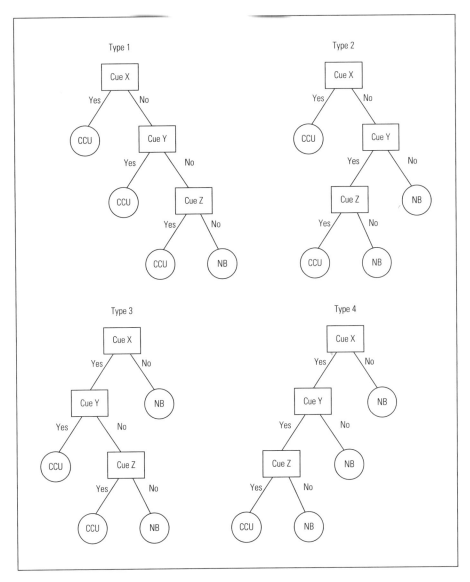

Figure 6-10. The four different shapes of fast-and-frugal trees with three cues.

Table 6-3. Sensitivity and Specificity of Each Cue

	ST-Segment	Chest Pain	Any of 3, 4, 6, 7
Sensitivity	.87	.80	.93
Specificity	.73	.49	.31

Table 6-4. Positive and Negative Validity of Each Cue

	ST-Segment	Chest Pain	Any of 3, 4, 6, 7
Val+	.39	.24	.22
Val−	.96	.92	.96

(sensitivity, specificity). At each level, the larger value will determine the terminal decision. If the cue has been selected due to its sensitivity, we assign positive terminal decision to those members of the population for which the cue value is 1 (if cue value is 0, we proceed to check the next cue). If the cue has been selected due to its specificity, we assign the negative terminal decision to those members of the population for which the cue value is 0 (if cue value is 1, we proceed to check the next cue). In the case of the Green and Mehr data, the ranking obtained is then <any of four cues> → <ST-segment > → <chest pain>. The resulting tree is of type 1.

(2) *Max (val+, val–).* We begin by picking the cue with maximal positive validity. All remaining cues are then ranked by the maximum of (positive validity, negative validity). At each level, the larger value will determine the terminal decision. The ranking obtained is <ST segment> → <any of four cues> → <chest pain>. The resulting tree is of type 2.

(3) *Zig-zag(sens, spec).* We begin by picking the cue with maximal sensitivity, just as in the Max(sens, spec) *case*. In the next step, however, we proceed in zig-zag and choose the cue with the highest specificity. We continue by switching directions again, producing an alternating sequence of (sens/spec) ruling the respective terminal decisions accordingly (for example, "sens" and cue value 1 ⇒ positive decision), until we have exhausted all cues. The ranking obtained is <any of four cues> → <ST segment> → <chest pain>. The resulting tree is of type 2.

(4) *Zig-zag(val+, val–).* We begin by picking the cue with maximal positive validity, just as in the Max(val+, val–) case. In the next step, we proceed in zig-zag and choose the cue with the highest negative validity. We *continue* by switching directions again, producing an alternating sequence of (val+/val–) ruling the respective terminal decisions accordingly (for example, "val+" and cue value 1 ⇒ positive decision), until we have exhausted all cues. The ranking obtained is

<ST segment> → <any of four cues> → <chest pain>. The resulting tree is of type 2.

The construction methods described above are simple. The first cue checked tends to guarantee a large number of hits from the very beginning. The rest is guided either by a strict maximum principle or by an alternating procedure that aims at counterweighting the previous decision at every new step. The "go for sensitivity and positive validity" prescription for the first level restricts the resulting trees (see Figure 6-10) to type 1 and type 2; it excludes, by design, types 3 and 4, which would start with a terminal negative decision.

A core property of all procedures described above is that they follow simple principles, disregarding intercorrelations and conditional dependencies between cues. Thus, they are "naïve" trees, in analogy to naïve Bayesian strategies. Another property is that they allow for a terminal decision at every level, often stopping at an early stage. Thus, they deserve to be called "fast-and-frugal" trees, according to the concept of fast-and-frugal heuristics.

PERFORMANCE OF FAST-AND-FRUGAL DECISION TREES

How do the classifications of our trees compare? In order to compute the performance of different rankings, we begin by listing {no. of misses, no. of false positives} of all possible cue orderings for all possible fast-and-frugal trees (Table 6-5). Note that "pectinates" (types 1 and 4) are, by design, commutative. The ranking of cues has

Table 6-5. The Performance of All Possible Trees

	Type 1	Type 2	Type 3	Type 4
Cue order 123	{0, 64}	{0, 35}	{2, 18}	{6, 12}
132	{0, 64}	{0, 35}	{2, 18}	{6, 12}
213	{0, 64}	{0, 35}	{3, 28}	{6, 12}
231	{0, 64}	{0, 43}	{3, 28}	{6, 12}
312	{0, 64}	{0, 52}	{1, 32}	{6, 12}

Entries correspond to {no. misses, no. false positives}.

Table 6-6. Performance of Decision Trees

	No. of Infarctions Sent to NB	No. of Healthy Patients Sent to CCU	Total No. of Errors
Max(sens, spec)	0	64	64
Max(val+, val−)	0	35	35
Zig-zag(sens, spec)	0	52	52
Zig-zag(val+, val−)	0	35	35
Green & Mehr, 1997	0	35	35
			Total no. of patients = 89

no influence on the partitioning and, hence, on their performance. Table 6-6 exhibits the performance of the decision trees constructed in the previous section. As intended, all resulting trees succeed in avoiding misses.

We now tackle the question of an adequate performance criterion. Theoretically, the costs of making misses and false positives might be identical. Looking at Table 6-5, we see that the best trees in this respect are different from those displayed in Table 6-6. If. misses and false alarms were equally costly, the type 4 trees with a performance of {6, 12} would be best, and the type 1 trees would be worst. But in the context discussed here, it is obviously worse to assign an infarction patient to the nursing bed than to assign a healthy patient to the coronary care unit. This is the typical situation in medical diagnosis. We therefore need a context-specific definition concerning the order relation of diagnostic trees.

Definition

Let S and T be decision trees. We say that S "dominates" T if S has fewer misses than T. If both trees have the same number of misses, then S dominates T if S has fewer false positives than T. If S dominates T, we write S > T. Two trees are "equivalent" if they have the same number of misses and the same number of false positives.

This definition can be somewhat relaxed to allow for more flexibility and/or penalize trees with an excessive number of false positives. One could, for instance, choose a positive threshold value α and establish T > S if $0 < [\text{sens}(S) - \text{sens}(T)] < \alpha$ and $\text{spec}(T) \gg \text{spec}(S)$. This means that a tree T would be chosen in favor of

a tree S with somewhat higher sensitivity as soon as the sensitivity difference is negligible and T is *clearly* preferable in terms of specificity.

As becomes evident from Tables 6-5 and 6-6, the Green and Mehr tree, whose performance coincides with Max(val+, val−) and zig-zag(val+, val−), dominates all other fast-and-frugal trees. This means that two of our construction rules succeeded in identifying a "locally optimal" solution (in the class of all possible trees) for our classification problem.

COMPARING FAST-AND-FRUGAL DECISION TREES TO TRADITIONAL MODELS

The next question arises here. Do fast-and-frugal trees perform well compared to rational and computationally demanding models? Let us compare the performance of logistic regression, a statistical tool widely used in expert systems of medical diagnostics. The performance of fitted logistic regression with various cutoff points compared to fast-and-frugal decision trees is illustrated in Figure 6-11.

We fitted a logistic regression model based on the three predictors exactly as used by the Green and Mehr tree (two single cues and the disjunction cue), and, for the sake of generality, we also fitted logistic regression with the whole set of the seven original cues. As evident from the graph, logistic regression with all seven cues performs better than the best fast-and-frugal trees. It also achieves maximal sensitivity (avoiding all misses), and at the same time has a better specificity (two false positives less).[4] Note that our performance analysis covers only the *fitting* case,

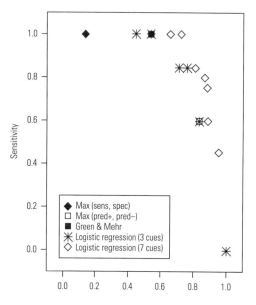

Figure 6-11. Performance (sensitivity and specificity) of logistic regression and the constructed fast-and-frugal trees.

that is, modeling known data. The predictive accuracy of competing models (generalization to new data) can systematically differ from their success in fitting. As a guideline, simpler models tend to generalize better (see Martignon, Katsikopoulos, & Woike, 2008).

CONCLUSION

Simple trees bet on a certain structure of the world, irrespective of the small fluctuations in a given set of available data. This can be a major advantage for generalization if the stable part of the process, which also holds for new data and new environments, is recognized and modeled. From a statistical point of view, it would, of course, be preferable to *test* empirically such assumptions instead of boldly implementing them in the model. But in real-life decision

making, we usually do not have large numbers of data that are representative of the concrete decisional setting of interest at our disposal. For instance, even for large epidemiological trials in medicine, it often remains unclear whether the resulting databases allow good generalization to the situation in a particular hospital (due to special properties of local patients, insufficient standardization of measurements and diagnostic procedures, etc.).

In many decisional domains, we may be better off trusting the robust power of simple decision strategies rather than striving for full knowledge of brittle details.

NOTES

1. This corresponds to a characterization of fast-and-frugal trees as linear classifiers with noncompensatory weights (cf. Martignon & Hoffrage, 1999).
2. An alternative account of the effect of the natural frequency format is that the correct way of doing the partitioning of information becomes transparent from the instruction (cf. Macchi & Mosconi, 1998; Fiedler, Brinkmann, Betsch, & Wild, 2000). Natural frequencies are a stable currency (80 cases equal 80 cases at every node of the tree), whereas 2% of A can be much more or much less than 2% of B.
3. In order to make the illustration simpler, we will treat the disjunction of cues (3, 4, 6, 7) as one cue instead of working with the four cues separately. Note that cue 5 (chest pain), which was included in the logistic regression model, is not included in the disjunctive cue (nor anywhere else in the tree), as it would be redundant with respect to the "higher-ranked" cue 2 (chest pain as chief symptom).
4. The same performance can actually be achieved by a much simpler linear model here, namely, "tally" (count the number of 1s) with a threshold of 2: Allocate all patients with two or more positive cue values to the CCU (cf. Table 6-1).

Introduction to Chapter 7

The Priority Heuristic:
Making Choices Without Trade-offs

Simple heuristics for modeling people's preferential choice had been investigated for some time before the research program represented in this book was launched (e.g., Luce, 1956; Payne, Bettman, & Johnson, 1993; Tversky, 1969, 1972). The common explanation for people's reliance on these heuristics centered on accuracy–effort trade-offs; that is, the importance that a person places on making an accurate decision versus saving cognitive effort. At its outset, the fast-and-frugal heuristics program focused on inference rather than on preference (see Chapter 2). The reason was that the program dispensed with the previous focus on coherence criteria (e.g., the laws of probability or the axioms of expected utility theory) and conceptualized heuristics as tools for adaptive and accurate decision making in the real world. But to demonstrate the accuracy of heuristics, one needs a clear and accepted benchmark. With respect to preference, accuracy of choice has been defined in many ways, ranging from coherence (e.g., transitivity) to "gold standards," such as the expected utility model or expected value model. Inference, in contrast, comes with the advantage of external criteria, thus enabling a clear-cut definition of accuracy. By looking at these external criteria, the research program could demonstrate that trading accuracy for effort is not the whole story. Less effort in terms of less information, time, and computation can actually lead to higher accuracy.

Despite the early work on preference heuristics, this modeling approach became more or less sidelined, possibly because of the dominance of prospect theory (Kahneman & Tversky, 1979) and other modifications of expected utility theory. For illustration, consider Amos Tversky's work. In a radical departure from the expected utility framework, Tversky (1972) developed a heuristic account of preferential choice, the elimination-by-aspect model. Notwithstanding this heuristic model, in Tversky's collaboration with Daniel Kahneman, the goal became to develop a descriptive account of risky choice based on minimal modifications of expected utility theory.

When simple heuristics frequently proved to be both descriptive and even prescriptive in inference, an often-voiced objection was that these would not generalize to preferences. The reason given was that preferential choice often takes place in environments in which cues, attributes, or reasons—say, low-priced consumer products and their quality—are correlated negatively. Negative correlations, in turn, cause conflict, and conflicts can only be reconciled by making trade-offs, which are incompatible with simple lexicographic heuristics and the psychological principle of one-reason decision making. Therefore, according to common wisdom, people do not use simple heuristics when making preferential choices.

There was much reluctance among researchers in the ABC Research Group to investigate the potential role of heuristics in preference. In the end, it fell to an external colleague, Eduard Brandstätter, to overcome this lack of enthusiasm for monetary gambles, resulting in the present article. Eduard Brandstätter, Gerd Gigerenzer, and Ralph Hertwig's research began with three key insights: First, they realized that a gamble, albeit lacking a cue structure, can be decomposed in terms of reasons that make a gamble more or less attractive (see Payne, 1973). Second, they realized that the framework of building blocks—search rules, stopping rules, and decision rules—developed in inference could be generalized to preference. Finally, they understood that the psychological principles of one-reason decision making and sequential search (embodied in the take-the-best heuristic; see Chapter 2) could also be applied to preferential choice, resulting in the priority heuristic.

Both in inference and in preference research, a model's performance depends on the structure of the environment. That is, depending on the gambles that researchers construct (i.e., whether the gambles stem from a model's region of good or bad performance), any model can be shown to be good or bad. Unlike inference research, however, preference research appears largely unfamiliar with the Brunswikian concept of "representative sampling" of stimuli (e.g., gambles) from a clearly defined reference class. The authors' solution to this problem was to abstain from designing their own choice problems. Instead, they compiled several existing data sets of problems into one large set of 260 problems, including those designed by the authors of competing theories. In addition, they took advantage of the method successfully used in research on inference, namely, the comparative testing of a large number of models; in fact, they pitted the priority heuristic against 13 other choice models.

This article sparked off a heated controversy that unfolded in a debate published in *Psychological Review* (Birnbaum, 2008; Johnson, Schulte-Mecklenbeck, & Willemsen, 2008; Rieger & Wang, 2008) as well as other journals. This debate centered on three issues that reach far beyond the priority heuristic: One issue is the clash between the ideal of building models with several adjustable parameters that allow good fits (as espoused by Birnbaum) and the ideal of building simple models without adjustable parameters (such as the priority heuristic) that, by necessity, result in lower fits but may result in better predictions of novel data (see also Blavatskyy & Pogrebna, 2008). The second issue is whether one should model cognitive processes in addition to outcomes, or whether fitting and predicting outcomes is the sole criterion in the design of psychologically plausible models. The third issue is whether there is experimental evidence that people sometimes make choices without trade-offs, thus challenging the widespread intuition that trade-offs are indispensable for various psychological processes, including motivation, moral sense, attitudes, and decision making.

One limit of this article is that it presents only a single newly discovered heuristic, which may create the impression that one and only one heuristic can predict choices across any kind of choice problem. This impression is, of course, counter to the notion of the adaptive toolbox of heuristics. In addition, the authors already highlighted one important boundary condition of the priority heuristic—namely, that the heuristic tends to be triggered in choice problems that are difficult (rather than those where the gambles' expected values are widely discrepant). Brandstätter, Gigerenzer, and Hertwig (2008) built on this boundary condition and proposed that people first seek a no-conflict solution by using heuristics such as Rubinstein's similarity heuristic. Only when this fails do people resort to heuristics that resolve conflicts such as the priority heuristic.

CHAPTER 7

The Priority Heuristic:
Making Choices Without Trade-offs

Eduard Brandstätter, Gerd Gigerenzer, and Ralph Hertwig

Abstract: Bernoulli's framework of expected utility serves as a model for various psychological processes, including motivation, moral sense, attitudes, and decision making. To account for evidence at variance with expected utility, the authors generalize the framework of fast-and-frugal heuristics from inferences to preferences. The *priority heuristic* predicts (a) the Allais paradox, (b) risk aversion for gains if probabilities are high, (c) risk seeking for gains if probabilities are low (e.g., lottery tickets), (d) risk aversion for losses if probabilities are low (e.g., buying insurance), (e) risk seeking for losses if probabilities are high, (f) the certainty effect, (g) the possibility effect, and (h) intransitivities. The authors test how accurately the heuristic predicts people's choices, compared with previously proposed heuristics and three modifications of expected utility theory: security-potential/aspiration theory, transfer-of-attention-exchange model, and cumulative prospect theory.

Conventional wisdom tells us that making decisions becomes difficult whenever multiple priorities, appetites, goals, values, or simply the attributes of the alternative options are in conflict. Should one undergo a medical treatment that has some chance of curing a life-threatening illness but comes with the risk of debilitating side effects? Should one report a crime committed by a friend? Should one buy an expensive, high-quality camera or an inexpensive, low-quality camera? How do people resolve conflicts, ranging from the prosaic to the profound?

The common denominator of many theories of human behavior is the premise that conflicts are mastered by making trade-offs. Since the Enlightenment, it has been believed that weighting and summing are the processes by which

such trade-offs can be made in a rational way. Numerous theories of human behavior—including expected value theory, expected utility theory, prospect theory, Benjamin Franklin's moral algebra, theories of moral sense such as utilitarianism and consequentionalism (Gigerenzer, 2004), theories of risk taking (e.g., Wigfield & Eccles, 1992), motivational theories of achievement (Atkinson, 1957) and work behavior (e.g., Vroom, 1964), theories of social learning (Rotter, 1954), theories of attitude formation (e.g., Fishbein & Ajzen, 1975), and theories of health behavior (e.g., Becker, 1974; for a review see Heckhausen, 1991)—rest on these two processes. Take how expected utility theory would account for the choice between two investment plans as an example. The reasons for choosing are often negatively correlated with one another. High returns go with low probabilities, and low returns go with high probabilities. According to a common argument, negative correlations between reasons cause people to experience conflict, leading them to make trade-offs (Shanteau & Thomas, 2000). In terms of expected utility, the trade-off between investment plans is performed by weighting the utility of the respective monetary outcomes by their probabilities and by summing across the weighted outcomes of each plan. The plan chosen is that with the higher expected utility.

Weighting and summing are processes that have been used to define not only rational choice but also rational inference (Gigerenzer & Kurz, 2001). In research on inference, weighting was the first to be challenged. In the 1970s and 1980s, evidence emerged that simple unit weights such as +1 and −1 often yield the same predictive accuracy—that is, the same ability to predict rather than simply "postdict," or fit—as the "optimal" weights in multiple regression (Dawes, 1979). According to these results, weighting does not seem to affect predictive accuracy as long as the weight has the right sign.

Next, summing was called into question. The 1990s brought evidence that the predictive accuracy of lexicographic heuristics can be as high as or higher than the accuracy of complex strategies that perform both weighting and summing. This was shown for both inferences (e.g., Gigerenzer & Goldstein, 1996; Gigerenzer, Todd, & the ABC Research Group, 1999) and preferences (e.g., Payne, Bettman, & Johnson, 1993). The heuristics in question order attributes—which can be seen as a simple form of weighting—but do not sum them. Instead, they rely on the first attribute that allows for a decision. These results suggest that summing is not always necessary for good reasoning. In addition, some of the environmental structures under which weighting (ordering) without summing is ecologically rational have been identified (Hogarth & Karelaia, 2005; Katsikopoulos & Martignon, 2006; Martignon & Hoffrage, 2002; Payne et al., 1993).

Here is the question that concerns us: If, as the work just reviewed demonstrates, both summing without weighting and weighting without summing can be as accurate as weighting and summing, why should humans not use these simpler heuristics? Specifically, might human choice that systematically contradicts expected utility theory be a direct consequence of people's use of heuristics? The success of a long tradition of theories seems to speak against this possibility. Although deviations between the theory of expected utility and human behavior have long since been experimentally demonstrated, psychologists and economists have nevertheless retained the weighting and summing core of the theory, but they have adjusted the functions to create more complex models such as prospect theory and security-potential/aspiration theory. In this article, we demonstrate that a simple heuristic that forgoes summing and therefore does not make trade-offs can account for choices that are anomalies from the point of view of expected utility theory. In fact, it does so in the very gambling environments that were designed to demonstrate the empirical validity of theories of risky choice that assume both weighting and summing. By extension, we suggest that other areas of human decision making that involve conflicting goals, values, appetites, and motives may likewise be explicable in terms of simple heuristics that forgo complex trade-offs.

THE BERNOULLI FRAMEWORK AND ITS MODIFICATIONS

Very few great ideas have an exact date of origin, but the theory of mathematical probability does. In the summer of 1654, the French mathematicians Blaise Pascal and Pierre Fermat exchanged letters on gambling problems posed by a notorious gambler and man-about-town, the Chevalier de Méré. This exchange resulted in the concept of mathematical expectation, which at the time was believed to capture the nature of rational choice (Hacking, 1975). In modern notation, the principle of choosing the option with the highest expected value *(EV)* is defined as

$$EV = \sum p_i x_i , \qquad (7\text{-}1)$$

where p_i and x_i are the probability and the amount of money, respectively, of each outcome $(i = 1, \ldots , n)$ of a gamble. The expected value theory was a psychological theory of human reasoning, believed to describe the reasoning of the educated homme éclairé.

Despite its originality and elegance, the definition of a rational decision by EV soon ran into trouble when Nicholas Bernoulli, a professor of law in Basel, posed the perplexing St. Petersburg paradox. To solve the paradox, his cousin Daniel Bernoulli (1738/1954) retained the core of the expected value theory but suggested replacing objective money amounts with subjective utilities. In his view, the pleasure or utility of money did not increase linearly with the monetary amount; instead, the increases in utility declined. This phenomenon entered psychophysics a century later in the form of the Weber-Fechner function (Gigerenzer & Murray, 1987), and it entered economics in the form of the concept of diminishing returns (Menger, 1871/1990). Daniel Bernoulli modeled the relation between objective and subjective value of money in terms of a logarithmic function. In modern terminology, the resulting expected utility *(EU)* is defined as

$$EU = \sum p_i u(x_i), \qquad (7\text{-}2)$$

where $u(x_i)$ is a monotonically increasing function defined on objective money amounts x_i. At the time of Daniel Bernoulli, the maximization of expected utility was considered both a description and prescription of human reasoning. The present-day distinction between these two concepts, which seems so obvious to researchers today, was not made, because the theory was identical with its application, human reasoning (Daston, 1988). However, the "rational man" of the Enlightenment was dismantled around 1840, when probability theory ceased to be generally considered a model of human reasoning (Gigerenzer et al., 1989). One motive for the divorce between expected utility and human reasoning was apparent human irrationality, especially in the aftermath of the French Revolution. Following the demise of expected utility, psychological theories of thinking virtually ignored the concept of expected utility as well as the laws of probability until the 1950s. The revival of expected utility began with von Neumann and Morgenstern (1947), who based expected utility on axioms. After their landmark book appeared, followed by influential publications such as Edwards (1954, 1962) and Savage (1954) on subjective expected utility, theories of the mind once again started to model human reasoning and choice in terms of probabilities and the expected utility framework (e.g., Fishbein & Ajzen, 1975; Heckhausen, 1991).

However, it was not long until the first experiments were conducted to test whether people's choices actually follow the predictions of expected utility. Evidence emerged that people systematically violated expected utility theory (Allais, 1953; Ellsberg, 1961; MacCrimmon, 1968; Mosteller & Nogee, 1951; Preston & Baratta, 1948), and this evidence has accumulated in the subsequent decades (see Camerer, 1995; Edwards, 1968; Kahneman & Tversky, 2000). Although specific violations of expected utility, including their normative status, are still under debate (Allais, 1979; Hogarth & Reder, 1986), there is widespread consensus among experimental researchers that not all of the violations can be explained away.

This article is concerned with how to react to these empirical demonstrations that human behavior often contradicts expected utility theory. So far, two major reactions have surfaced. The first is to retain expected utility theory, by arguing that the contradictory evidence will not generalize from the laboratory to the real world. The arguments for this assertion include that in most of the experiments, participants were not paid contingent on their performance (see Hertwig & Ortmann, 2001) or were not paid enough to motivate them to behave in accordance with expected utility and that outside the laboratory, market pressures will largely eliminate behavior that violates expected utility theory (see Hogarth & Reder, 1986). This position is often reinforced by the argument that even if one accepts the empirical demonstrations, no powerful theoretical alternative to expected utility exists, and given that all theories are false idealizations, a false theory is still better than no theory.

The second reaction has been to take the data seriously and, just as Bernoulli did, to modify the theory while retaining the original expected utility scaffolding. Examples include disappointment theory (Bell, 1985; Loomes & Sugden, 1986), regret theory (Bell, 1982; Loomes & Sugden, 1982), the transfer-of-attention-exchange model (Birnbaum & Chavez, 1997), decision affect theory (Mellers, 2000), prospect theory (Kahneman & Tversky, 1979), and cumulative prospect theory (Tversky & Kahneman, 1992). These theories are noteworthy attempts to adjust Bernoulli's framework to the new empirical challenges by adding one or more adjustable parameters. They represent a "repair" program that introduces psychological variables such as emotions and reference points to rescue the Bernoullian framework (Selten, 2001).

Despite their differences, all of these modifications retain the assumption that human choice can or should be modeled in the same terms that Bernoulli used: that people behave as if they multiplied some function of probability and value, and then maximized. Because of the complex computations involved in some of these modifications, they have often been interpreted to be *as-if* models. That is, they describe and ideally predict choice outcomes but do not explain the underlying process. The originators of prospect theory, for instance, set themselves the goal "to assemble the minimal set of modifications of expected utility theory that would provide a descriptive account of … choices between simple monetary gambles" (Kahneman, 2000, p. x). Prospect theory deals with empirical violations of expected utility by introducing new functions that require new adjustable parameters. For instance, a nonlinear function π was added to transform objective probabilities (assuming "regular prospects"):

$$V = \sum \pi(p_i) v(x_i) \qquad (7\text{-}3)$$

where V represents the value of a prospect. The decision weights $\pi(p_i)$ are obtained from the objective probabilities by a nonlinear, inverse S-shaped weighting function. Specifically, the weighting function π overweights small probabilities and underweights moderate and large ones (resulting in an inverse S shape). The value function $v(x_i)$ is an S-shaped utility function. Just as Bernoulli introduced individual psychological factors (diminishing returns and a person's wealth) to save the expected value

framework, Kahneman and Tversky (1979) postulated π and v to account for the old and new discrepancies. In the face of new empirical discrepancies and to extend prospect theory to gambles with more than three outcomes, Tversky and Kahneman (1992) further modified prospect theory into cumulative prospect theory.

The essential point is that the weighting function (defined by two adjustable parameters in cumulative prospect theory) and the value function (defined by three adjustable parameters) interpret people's choices that deviate from Bernoulli's framework within that very same framework. For example, the empirical shape of the weighting function is inferred by assuming a multiplication calculus. Overweighting small probabilities, for instance, is an interpretation of people's cognition within Bernoulli's framework—it is not the empirical phenomenon itself. The actual phenomenon is a systematic pattern of choices, which can be accounted for without reference to functions that overweight or underweight objective probabilities. We demonstrate this in the alternative framework of heuristics. The aim of models of heuristics is to both describe the psychological process and predict the final choice.

HEURISTICS IN RISKY CHOICE

In this article, we pursue a third way to react to the discrepancy between empirical data and expected utility theory: to explain choice as the direct consequence of the use of a heuristic. Unlike proponents of expected utility who dismiss the empirical data (e.g., de Finetti, 1979), we take the data seriously. In fact, we test whether a sequential heuristic can predict classic violations of expected utility as well as four major bodies of choice data. Heuristics model both the choice outcome and the process, and there is substantial empirical evidence that people's cognitive processes and inferences can be predicted by models of heuristics (e.g., Bröder, 2000; Bröder, 2003; Bröder & Schiffer, 2003; Dhami, 2003; Huber, 1982; Newell, Weston, & Shanks, 2003; Payne et al., 1993; Payne, Bettman, & Luce, 1996; Rieskamp & Hoffrage, 1999; Schkade & Johnson, 1989).

Which Heuristic?

Two classes of heuristics are obvious candidates for two-alternative choice problems: lexicographic rules and tallying (Gigerenzer, 2004). Lexicographic rules order reasons—probabilities and outcomes—according to some criterion, search through $m \geq 1$ reasons, and ultimately base the decision on one reason only. The second class, tallying, assigns all reasons equal weights, searches through $m \geq 2$ reasons, and chooses the alternative that is supported by most reasons. For choices between gambles, the empirical evidence suggests that people do not treat the reasons equally, which speaks against the tallying family of heuristics (Brandstätter & Kühberger, 2005; Deane, 1969; Loewenstein, Weber, Hsee, & Welch, 2001; Sunstein, 2003). This result was confirmed in the empirical tests reported below. We are then left with a heuristic from the class of lexicographic rules and two questions. First, what are the reasons and in what order are they examined? Second, when is examination stopped? Based on the empirical evidence available, our first task is to derive a candidate heuristic from the set of all possible heuristics.

Priority Rule: In What Order Are Reasons Examined?

First we consider simple monetary gambles of the type "a probability p to win amount x; a probability $(1 - p)$ to win amount y" $(x, p; y)$. Here, the decision maker is given four reasons: the maximum gain, the minimum gain, and their respective probabilities (for losses, see below). All reasons are displayed simultaneously; they are available at no cost. Thus, unlike in tasks for which information needs to be searched in memory (Gigerenzer & Goldstein, 1996) or in the environment (such as search in external information stores), all the relevant information is fully displayed in front of the participant. The resulting choices are thus "decisions from description" and not "decisions from experience" (Hertwig, Barron, Weber, & Erev, 2004). The *priority rule* refers to the order in which people go through the reasons after screening all of them once to make their decision.

Four reasons result in 24 possible orderings. Fortunately, there are logical and empirical constraints. First, in two-outcome gambles, the two probabilities are complementary, which reduces the number of reasons to three. This in turn reduces the number of possible orders from 24 to 6. The number can be further constrained by empirical evidence. What is perceived as more important, outcomes or probabilities?

The primacy of outcome over probability had already been noted in Arnauld and Nicole's (1662/1996) Enlightenment classic on the art of thinking. As an example, lottery buyers tend to focus on big gains rather than their tiny probabilities, which is historically grounded in the fact that winning the lottery was one of the very few ways to move upward socially in traditional European societies (Daston, 1988). Similarly, empirical research indicates that emotional outcomes tend to override the impact of probabilities (Sunstein, 2003). Loewenstein et al. (2001) suggest that, in the extreme, people neglect probabilities altogether and instead base their choices on the immediate feelings elicited by the gravity or benefit of future events. Similarly, Deane (1969) reported that anxiety (as measured by cardiac activity) concerning a future electric shock was largely influenced by the intensity of the shock, not by the probability of its occurrence. A series of choice experiments supports the hypothesis that outcome matters more than probability (Brandstätter & Kühberger, 2005).[1]

From these studies, we assume that the first reason for choosing is one of the two outcomes, not the probability. This reduces the number of orders once again, from six to four. But which outcome is considered first, the minimum or the maximum outcome? The empirical evidence seems to favor the minimum outcome. The frequent observation that people tend to be risk averse in the gain domain (Edwards, 1954) is consistent with ranking the minimum outcome first. This is because the reason for focusing on the minimum outcome is to avoid the worst outcome. In contrast, ranking the maximum outcome first would imply that people are risk seeking with gains—an assumption for which little empirical evidence exists. Further empirical support is given by research documenting that people try to avoid disappointment (from ending up with the worst possible outcome of the chosen gamble) and regret (from obtaining an inferior outcome compared with the alternative not chosen). This motivation to avoid winning nothing (or the minimum amount) is incorporated in regret theory (Loomes & Sugden, 1982), disappointment theory (Bell, 1985), and in the motivation for avoidance of failure (Heckhausen, 1991).

We conclude that the empirical evidence favors the minimum gain. This reduces the number of possible orders of reasons from four to two. To distinguish between the two remaining orders, we conducted an experiment in which the minimal outcome was held constant, and thus all decisions depended on maximum gains and the probabilities of the minimum gains. These two reasons always suggested opposite choices. Forty-one students from the University of Linz, Austria (22 women, 19 men; $M = 23.2$ years, $SD = 5.3$ years) were tested on four problems:

(500, .50) and (2,500, .10) [88%]
(220, .90) and (500, .40) [80%]
(5,000, .50) and (25,000, .10) [73%]
(2,200, .90) and (5,000, .40) [83%]

For instance, the first choice was between €500 (US$600) with $p = .50$, otherwise nothing, and €2,500 (US$3,000) with $p = .10$, otherwise nothing. Faced with this choice, 36 of 41 participants (88%) selected this first gamble, which has the smaller probability of the minimum gain but the lower maximum gain. On average, 81% of the participants chose the gamble with the smaller probability of the minimum gain. This result suggests the probability of the minimum gain—rather than the maximum gain—as the second reason. The same conclusion is also suggested by another study in which the experimenters held the minimum outcomes constant across gambles (Slovic, Griffin, & Tversky, 1990; Study 5). Thus, in the priority rule, below, we propose the following order in which the reasons are attended to:

Priority Rule. Consider reasons in the order: minimum gain, probability of minimum gain, maximum gain.

Stopping Rule: What Is a Good-Enough Reason?

Heuristic examination is limited rather than exhaustive. Limited examination makes heuristics different from expected utility theory and its modifications, which have no stopping rules and integrate all pieces of information in the final choice. A stopping rule defines whether examination stops after the first, second, or third reason. Again, we consult the empirical evidence to generate a hypothesis about the stopping rule.

What difference in minimum gains is good enough ("satisficing") to stop examination and decide between the two gambles solely on the basis of this information? Just as in Simon's (1983) theory of satisficing, in which people stop when an alternative surpasses an aspiration level (see also Luce, 1956), our use of the term *aspiration level* refers to the amount that, if met or exceeded, stops examination of reasons. Empirical evidence suggests that the aspiration level is not fixed but increases with the maximum gain (Albers, 2001). For instance, consider a choice between winning $200 with probability .50, otherwise nothing ($200, .50), and winning $100 for sure ($100). The minimum gains are $0 and $100, respectively. Now consider the choice between $2,000 with probability .50 ($2,000, .50) and $100 for sure ($100). The minimum gains still differ by the same amount, the probabilities are the same, but the maximum outcomes differ. People who select the sure gain in the first pair may not select it in the second. Thus, the difference between minimum gains that is considered large enough to stop examination after the first reason should be dependent on the maximum gain.

A simple way to incorporate this dependency is to assume that people intuitively define it by their cultural number system, which is the base-10 system in the Western world (Albers, 2001). This leads to the following hypothesis for the stopping rule:

Stopping Rule. Stop examination if the minimum gains differ by 1/10 (or more) of the maximum gain.

The hypothesis is that 1/10 of the maximum gain, that is, one order of magnitude, is "good enough." Admittedly, this value of the aspiration level is a first, crude estimate, albeit empirically informed. The aspiration level is a fixed (not free) parameter. If there is an independent measure of individual aspiration levels in further research, the estimate can be updated, but in the absence of such an independent measure, we do not want to introduce a free parameter. We refer to this value as the *aspiration level*. For illustration, consider again the choice between winning $200 with probability .50, otherwise nothing ($200, .50), and winning $100 for sure ($100). Here, $20 is "good enough." The difference between the minimum gains exceeds this value ($100 > $20), and therefore examination is stopped. Information concerning probabilities is not used for the choice.

What if the maximum amount is not as simple as 200 but is a number such as 190? Extensive empirical evidence suggests that people's numerical judgments are not fine-grained but follow prominent numbers, as summarized in Albers (2001). Prominent numbers are defined as powers of 10 (e.g., 1, 10, 100, …), including their halves and doubles. Hence, the numbers 1, 2, 5, 10, 20, 50, 100, 200, and so on, are examples of prominent numbers. They approximate the Weber-Fechner function in a culturally defined system. We assume that people scale the maximum gain down by 1/10 and round this value to the closest prominent number. Thus, if the maximum gain were $190 rather than $200, the aspiration level would once again be $20 (because $19 is rounded to the next prominent number).

If the difference between minimum gains falls short of the aspiration level, the next reason is examined. Again, examination is stopped if the two probabilities of the minimum gains differ by a "large enough" amount. Probabilities, unlike gains, have upper limits and hence are not subject to the Weber-Fechner property of decreasing returns (Banks & Coleman, 1981). Therefore, unlike for gains, the aspiration level need not be defined relative to the maximum value. We define the aspiration level as 1/10 of the probability scale, that is, one order of magnitude: The probabilities need to differ by at least 10 percentage points to stop examination.

This leads to the following hypothesis for the stopping rule:

> *Stopping Rule.* Stop examination if probabilities differ by 1/10 (or more) of the probability scale.

If the differences in the minimum outcomes and their probabilities do not stop examination, then finally the maximum outcome— whichever is higher—decides. No aspiration level is needed.

THE PRIORITY HEURISTIC

The priority and stopping rules combine to the following process model for two-outcome gambles with nonnegative prospects (all outcomes are positive or zero). We refer to this process as the *priority heuristic* because it is motivated by first priorities, such as to avoid ending up with the worst of the two minimum outcomes. The heuristic consists of the following steps:

> *Priority Rule.* Go through reasons in the order: minimum gain, probability of minimum gain, maximum gain.
>
> *Stopping Rule.* Stop examination if the minimum gains differ by 1/10 (or more) of the maximum gain; otherwise, stop examination if probabilities differ by 1/10 (or more) of the probability scale.
>
> *Decision Rule.* Choose the gamble with the more attractive gain (probability).

The term *attractive* refers to the gamble with the higher (minimum or maximum) gain and the lower probability of the minimum gain. The priority heuristic models difficult decisions, not all decisions. It does not apply to pairs of gambles in which one gamble dominates the other one, and it also does not apply to "easy" problems in which the expected values are strikingly different (see the General Discussion section).

The heuristic combines features from three different sources: Its initial focus is on outcomes rather than on probabilities (Brandstätter & Kühberger, 2005; Deane, 1969; Loewenstein et al., 2001; Sunstein, 2003), and it is based on the sequential structure of the take-the-best heuristic (Gigerenzer & Goldstein, 1996), which is a heuristic for inferences, whereas the priority heuristic is a model of preferential choices. Finally, the priority heuristic incorporates aspiration levels into its choice algorithm (Luce, 1956; Simon, 1983). The generalization of the priority heuristic to nonpositive prospects (all outcomes are negative or zero) is straightforward. The heuristic is identical except that "gains" are replaced by "losses":

Priority Rule. Go through reasons in the order: minimum loss, probability of minimum loss, maximum loss.

Stopping Rule. Stop examination if the minimum losses differ by 1/10 (or more) of the maximum loss; otherwise, stop examination if probabilities differ by 1/10 (or more) of the probability scale.

Decision Rule. Choose the gamble with the more attractive loss (probability).

The term *attractive* refers to the gamble with the lower (minimum or maximum) loss and the higher probability of the minimum loss. Next, we generalize the heuristic to gambles with more than two outcomes (assuming nonnegative prospects):

Priority Rule. Go through reasons in the order: minimum gain, probability of minimum gain, maximum gain, probability of maximum gain.

Stopping Rule. Stop examination if the gains differ by 1/10 (or more) of the maximum gain; otherwise, stop examination if probabilities differ by 1/10 (or more) of the probability scale.

Decision Rule. Choose the gamble with the more attractive gain (probability).

This priority rule is identical with that for the two-outcome gambles, apart from the addition of a fourth reason. In gambles with more than two outcomes, the probability of the maximum outcome is informative because it is no longer the logical complement of the probability of the minimum outcome. The stopping rule is also identical, except for the fact that the maximum gain is no longer the last reason, and therefore the same aspiration levels apply to both minimum and maximum gains. The decision rule is identical with that for the two-outcome case. Finally, the algorithm is identical for gains and losses, except that "gains" are replaced by "losses."

The priority heuristic is simple in several respects. It typically consults only one or a few reasons; even if all are screened, it bases its choice on only one reason. Probabilities are treated as linear, and a 1/10 aspiration level is used for all reasons except the last, in which the amount of difference is ignored. No parameters for overweighting small probabilities and underweighting large probabilities or for the value function are built in. Can this simple model account for people's choices as well as multiparameter models can? To answer this question, we test whether the priority heuristic can accomplish the following:

1. Account for evidence at variance with expected utility theory, namely (a) the Allais paradox, (b) risk aversion for gains if probabilities are high, (c) risk seeking for gains if probabilities are low (e.g., lottery tickets), (d) risk aversion for losses if probabilities are low (e.g., buying insurance), (e) risk seeking for losses if probabilities are high, (f) the certainty effect, (g) the possibility effect, and (h) intransitivities; and

2. Predict the empirical choices in four classes of problems: (a) simple choice problems (no more than two nonzero outcomes; Kahneman & Tversky, 1979), (b) problems involving multiple-outcome gambles (Lopes & Oden, 1999), (c) problems inferred from certainty equivalents (Tversky & Kahneman, 1992), and (d) problems involving randomly sampled gambles (Erev, Roth, Slonim, & Barren, 2002).

CAN THE PRIORITY HEURISTIC PREDICT VIOLATIONS OF EXPECTED UTILITY THEORY?

The Allais Paradox

In the early 1950s, choice problems were proposed that challenged expected utility theory as a descriptive framework for risky choice (Allais, 1953, 1979). For instance, according to the independence axiom of expected utility, aspects that are common to both gambles should not influence choice behavior (Savage, 1954; von Neumann & Morgenstern, 1947). For any three alternatives X, Y, and Z, the independence axiom can be written (Fishburn, 1979):

If $pX + (1 - p)Z > pY + (1 - p)Z$,
then $X > Y$ (7-4)

The following choice problems produce violations of the axiom (Allais, 1953, p. 527):

A:	100 million	$p = 1.00$
B:	500 million	$p = .10$
	100 million	$p = .89$
	0	$p = .01$

By eliminating a .89 probability to win 100 million from both A and B, Allais obtained the following gambles:

C:	100 million	$p = .11$
	0	$p = .89$
D:	500 million	$p = .10$
	0	$p = .90$

The majority of people chose A over B, and D over C (MacCrimmon, 1968), which constitutes a violation of the axiom.

Expected utility does not predict whether A or B will be chosen; it only makes predictions of the type "if A is chosen over B, then it follows that C is chosen over D." The priority heuristic, in contrast, makes stronger predictions: It predicts whether A or B is chosen, and whether C or D is chosen. Consider the choice between A and B. The maximum payoff is 500 million, and therefore the aspiration level is 50 million; 100 million and 0 represent the minimum gains. Because the difference (100 million) exceeds the aspiration level of 50 million, the minimum gain of 100 million is considered good enough, and people are predicted to select the sure gain A. That is, the heuristic predicts the majority choice correctly.

In the second choice problem, the minimum gains (0 and 0) do not differ. Hence, the probabilities of the minimum gains are attended to, $p = .89$ and .90, a difference that falls short of the aspiration level. The higher maximum gain (500 million vs. 100 million) thus decides choice, and

the prediction is that people will select gamble D. Again, this prediction is consistent with the choice of the majority. Together, the pair of predictions amounts to the Allais paradox.

The priority heuristic captures the Allais paradox by using the heuristic building blocks of order, a stopping rule with a 1/10 aspiration level, a lexicographic decision rule, and the tendency to avoid the worst possible outcome.

The Reflection Effect

The *reflection effect* refers to the empirically observed phenomenon that preferences tend to reverse when the sign of the outcomes is changed (Fishburn & Kochenberger, 1979; Markowitz, 1952; Williams, 1966). Rachlinski's (1996) copyright litigation problem offers an illustration in the context of legal decision making. Here, the choice is between two gains or between two losses for the plaintiff and defendant, respectively:

The plaintiff can either accept a $200,000 settlement [*] or face a trial with a .50 probability of winning $400,000, otherwise nothing.

The defendant can either pay a $200,000 settlement to the plaintiff or face a trial with a .50 probability of losing $400,000, otherwise nothing [*].

The asterisks in brackets indicate which alternative the majority of law students chose, depending on whether they were cast in the role of the plaintiff or the defendant. Note that the two groups made opposite choices. Assuming that plaintiffs used the priority heuristic, they would have first considered the minimum gains, $200,000 and $0. Because the difference between the minimum gains is larger than the aspiration level ($40,000 rounded to the next prominent number, $50,000), plaintiffs would have stopped examination and chosen the alternative with the more attractive minimum gain, that is, the settlement. The plaintiff's gain is the defendant's loss: Assuming that defendants also used the priority heuristic, they would have first considered the minimum losses, which are $200,000 and $0. Again, because the difference between these outcomes exceeds the aspiration level, defendants would have stopped examination and chosen the alternative with the more attractive minimum loss, that is, the trial. In both cases, the heuristic predicts the majority choice.

How is it possible that the priority heuristic predicts the reflection effect without—as prospect theory does—introducing value functions that are concave for gains and convex for losses? In the gain domain, the minimum gains are considered first, thus implying risk aversion. In the loss domain, the minimum losses are considered first, thus implying risk seeking. Risk aversion for gains and risk seeking for losses together make up the reflection effect.

The Certainty Effect

According to Allais (1979), the *certainty effect* captures people's "preference for security in the neighborhood of certainty" (p. 441). A simple demonstration is the following (Kahneman & Tversky, 1979):

A:	4,000 with	$p = .80$
	0 with	$p = .20$
B:	3,000 with	$p = 1.00$

A majority of people (80%) selected the certain alternative B.

C:	4,000 with	$p = .20$
	0 with	$p = .80$
D:	3,000 with	$p = .25$
	0 with	$p = .75$

Now the majority of people (65%) selected gamble C over D. According to expected utility theory, the choice of B implies that $u(3,000)/u(4,000) > 4/5$, whereas the choice of C implies the reverse inequality.

The priority heuristic starts by comparing the minimum gains of the alternatives A (0) and B (3,000). The difference exceeds the aspiration level of 500 (400, rounded to the next prominent number); examination is stopped; and the model predicts that people prefer the sure gain B, which is in fact the majority choice. Between C and D, the minimum gains (0 and 0) do not differ; in the next step, the heuristic compares the probabilities of the minimum gains (.80 and .75). Because this difference does not reach

10 percentage points, the decision is with the higher maximum gain, that is, gamble C determines the decision.

As the example illustrates, it is not always the first reason (minimum gain) that determines choice; it can also be one of the others. The priority heuristic can predict the certainty effect without assuming a specific probability weighting function.

The Possibility Effect

To demonstrate the possibility effect, participants received the following two choice problems (Kahneman & Tversky, 1979):

A:	6,000 with	$p = .45$
	0 with	$p = .55$
B:	3,000 with	$p = .90$
	0 with	$p = .10$

The majority of people (86%) selected gamble B.

C:	6,000 with	$p = .001$
	0 with	$p = .999$
D:	3,000 with	$p = .002$
	0 with	$p = .998$

In the second problem, most people (73%) chose gamble C. This problem is derived from the first by multiplying the probabilities of the nonzero gains with 1/450, making the probabilities of winning merely "possible." Note that in the certainty effect, "certain" probabilities are made "probable," whereas in the possibility effect, "probable" probabilities are made "possible." Can the priority heuristic predict this choice pattern?

In the first choice problem, the priority heuristic starts by comparing the minimum gains (0 and 0). Because there is no difference, the probabilities of the minimum gains (.55 and .10) are examined. This difference exceeds 10 percentage points, and the priority heuristic, consistent with the majority choice, selects gamble B. Analogously, in the second choice problem, the minimum gains (0 and 0) are the same; the difference between the probabilities of the minimum gains (.999 and .998) does not exceed 10 percentage points. Hence, the priority heuristic correctly predicts the choice of gamble *C*, because of its higher maximum gain of 6,000.

The Fourfold Pattern

The *fourfold pattern* refers to the phenomenon that people are generally risk averse when the probability of winning is high but risk seeking when it is low (as when buying lotteries) and risk averse when the probability of losing is low (as with buying insurance) but risk seeking when it is high. Table 7-1 exemplifies the fourfold pattern (Tversky & Fox, 1995).

Table 7-1 is based on certainty equivalents *C* (obtained from choices rather than pricing). Certainty equivalents represent that amount of money where a person is indifferent between taking the risky gamble or the sure amount *C*. For instance, consider the first cell: The median certainty equivalent of $14 exceeds the expected value of the gamble ($5). Hence, in this case people are risk seeking, because they prefer the risky gamble over the sure gain of $5. This logic applies in the same way to the other cells.

The certainty equivalent information of Table 7-1 directly lends itself to the construction of simple choice problems. For instance, from the first cell we obtain the following choice problem:

A:	100 with	$p = .05$
	0 with	$p = .95$
B:	5 with	$p = 1.00$

The priority heuristic starts by comparing the minimum gains (0 and 5). Because the sure gain

Table 7-1. The Fourfold Pattern

Probability	Gain	Loss
Low	$C(100, .05) = 14$	$C(-100, .05) = -8$
	Risk seeking	Risk aversion
High	$C(100, .95) = 78$	$C(-100, .95) = -84$
	Risk aversion	Risk seeking

Note. C(100, .05) represents the median certainty equivalent for the gamble to win $100 with probability of .05, otherwise nothing (based on Tversky & Fox, 1995).

of $5 falls short of the aspiration level of $10, probabilities are attended to. The probabilities of the minimum gains do not differ either (1.00 − .95 < .10); hence, people are predicted to choose the risky gamble *A*, because of its higher maximum gain. This is in accordance with the certainty equivalent of $14 (see Table 7-1), which implies risk seeking. Similarly, if the probability of winning is high, we obtain:

A:	100 with	$p = .95$
	0 with	$p = .05$
B:	95 with	$p = 1.00$

Here, the sure gain of $95 surpasses the aspiration level ($10) and the priority heuristic predicts the selection of the sure gain *B*, which is in accordance with the risk-avoidant certainty equivalent in Table 7-1 ($78 < $95). The application to losses is straightforward:

A:	−100 with	$p = .05$
	0 with	$p = .95$
B:	−5 with	$p = 1.00$

Because the minimum losses (0 and −5) do not differ, the probabilities of the minimum losses (.95 and 1.00) are attended to, which do not differ either. Consequently, people are predicted to choose the sure loss *B*, because of its lower maximum loss (−5 vs. −100). This is in accordance with the risk-avoidant certainty equivalent in Table 7-1. Similarly, if the probability of losing is high we obtain:

A:	−100 with	$p = .95$
	0 with	$p = .05$
B:	−95 with	$p = 1.00$

In this case, the minimum losses differ (0 − [−95] > 10) and the priority heuristic predicts the selection of the risky gamble *A*, which corresponds to the certainty equivalent of Table 7-1.

Note that in this last demonstration, probabilities are not attended to and one does not need to assume some nonlinear function of decision weights. As shown above, the priority heuristic correctly predicts the reflection effect, and consequently, the entire fourfold pattern in terms of one simple, coherent strategy.

Intransitivities

Intransitivities violate expected utility's fundamental *transitivity axiom*, which states that a rational decision maker who prefers X to Y and Y to Z must then prefer X to Z (von Neumann & Morgenstern, 1947). Consider the choice pattern in Table 7-2, which shows the percentages of choices in which the row gamble was chosen over the column gamble. For instance, in 65% of the choices, gamble A was chosen over gamble B. As shown therein, people prefer gambles $A > B$, $B > C$, $C > D$, and $D > E$. However, they violate transitivity by selecting gamble E over A.

If one predicts the majority choices with the priority heuristic, one gets gamble $A > B$ because the minimum gains are the same, their probabilities do not differ, and the maximum outcome of A is higher. Similarly, the heuristic can predict all 10 majority choices with the exception of the .51 figure (a close call) in Table 7-2. Note that the priority heuristic predicts gamble $A > B$, $B > C$, $C > D$, $D > E$, and $E > A$, which results in the intransitive circle. In contrast, cumulative prospect theory, which reduces to prospect theory for these simple gambles, or the transfer-of-attention-exchange model attach a fixed overall value V to each gamble and therefore cannot predict this intransitivity.

Table 7-2.   Violations of Transitivity

Gamble	B	C	D	E
A (5.00, .29)	**.65**	**.68**	.51	.37
B (4.75, .33)	–	**.73**	.56	.45
C (4.50, .38)		–	**.73**	.65
D (4.25, .42)			–	**.75**
E (4.00, .46)				–

Note. Gamble A (5.00, .29), for instance, offers a win of $5 with probability of .29, otherwise nothing. Cell entries represent proportion of times that the row gamble was preferred to the column gamble, averaged over all participants from Tversky (1969). Bold numbers indicate majority choices correctly predicted by the priority heuristic.

CAN THE PRIORITY HEURISTIC PREDICT CHOICES IN DIVERSE SETS OF CHOICE PROBLEMS?

One objection to the previous demonstration is that the priority heuristic has been tested on a small set of choice problems, one for each anomaly. How does it fare when tested against a larger set of problems? We tested the priority heuristic in four different sets of choice problems (Erev et al., 2002; Kahneman & Tversky, 1979; Lopes & Oden, 1999; Tversky & Kahneman, 1992). Two of these sets of problems were designed to test prospect theory and cumulative prospect theory, and one was designed to test security-potential/ aspiration theory (Lopes & Oden, 1999); none, of course, were designed to test the priority heuristic. The contestants used were three modifications of expected utility theory: cumulative prospect theory, security-potential/aspiration theory, and the transfer-of-attention-exchange model (Birnbaum & Chavez, 1997). In addition, we included the classic heuristics simulated by Thorngate (1980); the lexicographic and the equal-weight heuristic (Dawes, 1979) from Payne et al. (1993); and the tallying heuristic (see Table 7-3). The criterion for each of the four sets of problems was to predict the majority choice. This allows a comparison between the various heuristics, as well as between heuristics, cumulative prospect theory, security-potential/ aspiration theory, and the transfer-of-attention-exchange model.

The Contestants

The contesting heuristics can be separated into two categories: those that use solely outcome information and ignore probabilities altogether (outcome heuristics) and those that use at least rudimentary probabilities (dual heuristics).[2] These heuristics are defined in Table 7-3, in which their algorithm is explained through the following choice problem:

A:	80% chance to win 4,000
	20% chance to win 0
B:	3,000 for sure

Table 7-3. Heuristics for Risky Choice

Outcome Heuristics

Equiprobable: Calculate the arithmetic mean of all monetary outcomes within a gamble. Choose the gamble with the highest monetary average.
Prediction: Equiprobable chooses *B*, because *B* has a higher mean (3,000) than *A* (2,000).

Equal-weight: Calculate the sum of all monetary outcomes within a gamble. Choose the gamble with the highest monetary sum.
Prediction: Equal-weight chooses *A*, because *A* has a higher sum (4,000) than *B* (3,000).

Minimax: Select the gamble with highest minimum payoff.
Prediction: Minimax chooses *B*, because *A* has a lower minimum outcome (0) than *B* (3,000).

Maximax: Choose the gamble with the highest monetary payoff.
Prediction: Maximax chooses *A*, because its maximum payoff (4,000) is the highest outcome.

Better-than-average: Calculate the grand average of all outcomes from all gambles. For each gamble, count the number of outcomes equal to or above the grand average. Then select the gamble with the highest number of such outcomes.
Prediction: The grand average equals 7,000/3 = 2,333. Because both *A* and *B* have one outcome above this threshold, the better-than-average heuristic has to guess.

Dual Heuristics

Tallying: Give a tally mark to the gamble with (a) the higher minimum gain, (b) the higher maximum gain, (c) the lower probability of the minimum gain, and (d) the higher probability of the maximum gain. For losses, replace "gain" by "loss" and "higher" by "lower" (and vice versa). Select the gamble with the higher number of tally marks.
Prediction: Tallying has to guess, because both *B* (one tally mark for the higher minimal outcome, one for the higher probability of the maximum outcome) and *A* (one tally mark for the lower probability of the minimal outcome, one for the higher maximum outcome) receive two tally marks each.

Most-likely: Determine the most likely outcome of each gamble and their respective payoffs. Then select the gamble with the highest, most likely payoff.
Prediction: Most-likely selects 4,000 as the most likely outcome for *A* and 3,000 as the most likely outcome for *B*. Most-likely chooses *A*, because 4,000 exceeds 3,000.

Lexicographic: Determine the most likely outcome of each gamble and their respective payoffs. Then select the gamble with the highest, most likely payoff. If both payoffs are equal, determine the second most likely outcome of each gamble, and select the gamble with the highest (second most likely) payoff. Proceed until a decision is reached.
Prediction: Lexicographic selects 4,000 as the most likely outcome for *A* and 3,000 as the most likely outcome for *B*. Lexicographic chooses *A*, because 4,000 exceeds 3,000.

Least-likely: Identify each gamble's worst payoff. Then select the gamble with the lowest probability of the worst payoff.
Prediction: Least-likely selects 0 as the worst outcome for *A* and 3,000 as the worst outcome for *B*. Least-likely chooses *A*, because 0 is less likely to occur (i.e., with $p = .20$) than 3,000 $(p = 1.00)$.

Probable: Categorize probabilities as "probable" (i.e., $p \geq .50$ for a two-outcome gamble, $p \geq .33$ for a three-outcome gamble, etc.) or "improbable." Cancel improbable outcomes. Then calculate the arithmetic mean of the probable outcomes for each gamble. Finally, select the gamble with the highest average payoff.
Prediction: Probable chooses *A*, because of its higher probable outcome (4,000) compared with *B* (3,000).

Note. Heuristics are from Thorngate (1980) and Payne et al. (1993). The prediction for each heuristic refers to the choice between *A* (4,000, .80) and *B* (3,000).

Cumulative prospect theory (Tversky & Kahneman, 1992) attaches decision weights to cumulated rather than single probabilities. The theory uses five adjustable parameters. Three parameters fit the shape of the value function; the other two fit the shape of the probability weighting function. The value function is:

$$v(x) = x^\alpha \text{ if } x \geq 0, \text{ and} \tag{7-5}$$

$$v(x) = -\lambda(-x)^\beta \text{ if } x < 0 \tag{7-6}$$

The α and β parameters modulate the curvature for the gain and loss domain, respectively; the λ parameter ($\lambda > 1$) models loss aversion. The weighting function is:

$$w^+(p) = p^\gamma / (p^\gamma + (1-p)^\gamma)^{1/\gamma}, \text{ and} \tag{7-7}$$

$$w^-(p) = p^\delta / (p^\delta + (1-p)^\delta)^{1/\delta} \tag{7-8}$$

where the λ and δ parameters model the inverse S shape of the weighing function for gains and losses, respectively.

Another theory that incorporates thresholds (i.e., aspiration levels) in a theory of choice is security-potential/aspiration theory (Lopes, 1987, 1995; for details, see Lopes & Oden, 1999). Security-potential/aspiration theory is a six-parameter theory, which integrates two logically and psychologically independent criteria. The security-potential criterion is based on a rank-dependent algorithm (Quiggin, 1982; Yaari, 1987) that combines outcomes and probabilities in a multiplicative way. The aspiration criterion is operationalized as the probability to obtain some previously specified outcome. Both criteria together enable security-potential/aspiration theory to model people's choice behavior.

The third modification of expected utility theory entering the contests is the transfer-of-attention-exchange model (Birnbaum & Chavez, 1997), which was proposed as a response to problems encountered by prospect theory and cumulative prospect theory. This model has three adjustable parameters and is a special case of the more general configural weight model (Birnbaum, 2004). Like prospect theory, the transfer-of-attention-exchange model emphasizes how choice problems are described and

presented to people. Unlike prospect theory, it offers a formal theory to capture the effects of problem formulations on people's choice behavior.

In models with adjustable parameters, parameter estimates are usually fitted for a specific set of choice problems and individuals. Data fitting, however, comes with the risk of overfitting, that is, fitting noise (Roberts & Pashler, 2000). To avoid this problem, we used the fitted parameter estimates from one set of choice problems to predict the choices in a different one. For cumulative prospect theory, we used three sets of parameter estimates from Erev et al. (2002); Lopes and Oden (1999) and Tversky and Kahneman (1992). For the choice problems by Kahneman and Tversky (1979), no such parameter estimates exist. The three sets of parameter estimates are shown in Table 7-4. As one can see, they cover a broad range of values. Thus, we could test the predictive power of cumulative prospect theory with three independent sets of parameter estimates for the Kahneman and Tversky (1979) choice problems, and with two independent sets of parameter estimates for each of the other three sets of problems. In addition, for testing security-potential/aspiration theory, we used the parameter estimates from Lopes and Oden (1999); for testing the transfer-of-attention-exchange model, we used its prior parameters (see Birnbaum, 2004), which were estimated from Tversky and Kahneman (1992),

Table 7-4. Parameter Estimates for Cumulative Prospect Theory

Set of Problems	Parameter Estimates				
	α	β	λ	γ	δ
Erev et al. (2002)	0.33			0.75	
Lopes & Oden (1999)	0.55	0.97	1.00	0.70	0.99
Tversky & Kahneman (1992)	0.88	0.88	2.25	0.61	0.69

Note. The parameters α and β capture the shape of the value function for gains and losses, respectively; λ captures loss aversion; γ and δ capture the shape of the probability weighting function for gains and losses, respectively. See Equations 7-5 to 7-8 in the text. The Erev et al. (2002) set of problems is based on gains only.

to predict choices for the other three sets of choice problems.

Contest 1: Simple Choice Problems

The first test set consisted of monetary one-stage choice problems from Kahneman and Tversky (1979).[3] These 14 choice problems were based on gambles of equal or similar expected value and contained no more than two nonzero outcomes.

Results. Figure 7-1 shows how well the heuristics, cumulative prospect theory, security-potential/ aspiration theory, and the transfer-of-attention exchange model each predicted the majority response. The maximum number of correct predictions is 14. The white parts of the columns show correct predictions due to guessing. All heuristics, with the exceptions of the priority, equiprobable, and the lexicographic heuristics, had to guess in this set of problems.

The priority heuristic predicted all 11 choice problems correctly. In no instance did it need to guess. All other heuristics performed at or near chance level, except for the equiprobable and tallying heuristics: Equiprobable correctly predicted 10 of 14, whereas tallying predicted 4 of 11 choices correctly.[4] It is interesting that among the 10 heuristics investigated, those that used only outcome information performed slightly better than did those also using probability information.

For testing cumulative prospect theory, we used three different parameter sets. The first parameter set was from Lopes and Oden (1999) and resulted in 64% correct predictions. The second set was from Tversky and Kahneman (1992) and resulted in 71% correct predictions. The third was from Erev et al.'s (2002) randomly constructed gambles, which resulted in chance performance (50% correct).

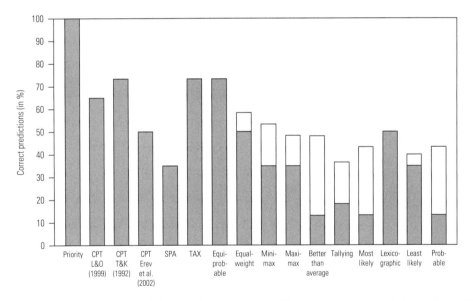

Figure 7-1. Correct predictions of the majority responses for all monetary one-stage choice problems (14) in Kahneman and Tversky (1979). The gray parts of the bars represent correct predictions without guessing; the union of the gray and white parts represents correct predictions with guessing (counting as 0.5). The Erev et al. (2002) set of problems consists of positive gambles; its fitted parameters allow only for predicting the choice behavior for positive one-stage gambles (making eight problems). Parameters for cumulative prospect theory (CPT) were estimated from Lopes and Oden (L&O; 1999); Tversky and Kahneman (T&K; 1992), and Erev et al., respectively. SPA = security-potential/aspiration theory; TAX = transfer-of-attention-exchange model.

On average, cumulative prospect theory correctly predicted 64% of the majority choices.[5] One might assume that each of the parameter sets failed in predicting the same choice problems. However, this was not the case; the failures to predict were distributed across 10 problems. This suggests that choice problems correctly predicted by one parameter set were incorrectly predicted by another set and vice versa. Finally, security potential/aspiration theory correctly predicted 5 of 14 choice problems, which resulted in 36% correct predictions, and the transfer-of-attention-exchange model correctly predicted 71% of the choice problems (i.e., 10 of 14).

Why did the heuristics in Table 7-3 perform so dismally in predicting people's deviations from expected utility theory? Like the priority heuristic, these heuristics ignore information. However, the difference lies in how information is ignored.

For gains, the priority heuristic uses the same first reason that minimax does (see Table 7-3). Unlike minimax, however, the priority heuristic does not always base its choice on the minimum outcomes, but only when the difference between the minimum outcomes exceeds the aspiration level. If not, then the second reason, the probability of the minimum outcome, is given priority. This reason captures the policy of the least-likely heuristic (see Table 7-3). Again, the priority heuristic uses an aspiration level to "judge" whether this policy is reasonable. If not, the maximum outcome will decide, which is the policy of the maximax heuristic (see Table 7-3). The same argument holds for gambles with losses, except that the positions of minimax and maximax are switched. Thus, the sequential nature of the priority heuristic integrates several of the classic heuristics, brings them into a specific order, and uses aspiration levels to judge whether they apply.

In summary, the priority heuristic was able to predict the majority choice in all 14 choice problems in Kahneman and Tversky (1979). The other heuristics did not predict well, mostly at chance level, and cumulative prospect theory did best when its parameter values were estimated from Tversky and Kahneman (1992).

Contest 2: Multiple-Outcome Gambles

The fact that the priority heuristic can predict the choices in two-outcome gambles does not imply that it can do the same for multiple-outcome gambles. These are a different story, as illustrated by prospect theory (unlike the revised cumulative version), which encountered problems when it was applied to gambles with more than two nonzero outcomes. Consider the choice between the multiple-outcome gamble A and the sure gain B:

A:		
	0 with	$p = .05$
	10 with	$p = .05$
	20 with	$p = .05$
	...	
	190 with	$p = .05$
B:	95 with	$p = 1.00$

The expected values of A and B are 95. According to the probability weighting function in prospect theory, each monetary outcome in gamble A is overweighted, because $\pi(.05) > .05$. For the common value functions, prospect theory predicts a higher subjective value for the risky gamble A than for the sure gain of 95. In contrast, 28 of 30 participants opted for the sure gain B (Brandstätter, 2004).

The priority heuristic gives first priority to the minimum outcomes, which are 0 and 95. The difference between these two values is larger than the aspiration level (20, because 19 is rounded to 20), so no other reason is examined and the sure gain is chosen.

The second set of problems consists of 90 pairs of five-outcome lotteries from Lopes and Oden (1999). In this set, the expected values of each pair are always similar or equal. The probability distributions over the five rank-ordered gains have six different shapes: Lotteries were (a) *nonrisk* (the lowest gain was larger than zero and occurred with the highest probability of winning), (b) *peaked* (moderate gains occurred with the highest probability of winning), (c) *negatively skewed* (the largest gain occurred with the highest probability of winning), (d) *rectangular* (all five gains were tied to the same probability, $p = .20$), (e) *bimodal* (extreme gains occurred with

Figure 7-2. A typical choice problem used in Contest 2, from Lopes and Oden (1999). Each lottery has 100 tickets (represented by marks) and has an expected value of approximately $100. Values at the left represent gains or losses. Reprinted from *Journal of Mathematical Psychology, 43,* L. L. Lopes & G. C. Oden, "The role of aspiration level in risky choice: A comparison of cumulative prospect theory and SP/A theory," p. 293. Copyright 1999 with permission from Elsevier.

the highest probability of winning), and (f) *positively skewed* (the largest gain occurred with the lowest probability of winning). An example is shown in Figure 7-2.

These six gambles yielded 15 different choice problems. From these, Lopes and Oden (1999) created two other choice sets by (a) adding $50 to each outcome and (b) multiplying each outcome by 1.145, making 45 (3 × 15) choice problems. In addition, negative lotteries were created by appending a minus sign to the outcomes of the three positive sets, making 90 choice problems. This procedure yielded six different choice sets (standard, shifted, multiplied—separately for gains and losses), each one comprising all possible choices within a set (i.e., 15).

Results. The priority heuristic yielded 87% correct predictions, as shown in Figure 7-3. All other heuristics performed around chance level or below. The result from the previous competition—that outcome heuristics are better predictors than the dual heuristics—did not generalize to multiple-outcome gambles.

The parameter values for cumulative prospect theory were estimated from two independent sets of problems. With the parameter estimates from the Tversky and Kahneman (1992) set of problems, cumulative prospect theory predicted 67% of the majority responses correctly. With the estimates from the Erev et al. (2002) set of problems, the proportion of correct predictions was 87%. With the second set of

parameter estimates, cumulative prospect theory tied with the priority heuristic, whereas cumulative prospect theory's performance was lower with the first set. Its average predictive accuracy was 73%. The fact that it did not perform better than the heuristic did is somewhat surprising, given that cumulative prospect theory was specifically designed for multiple-outcome gambles. Finally, the transfer-of-attention-exchange model correctly predicted 63% of the majority responses.

Lopes and Oden (1999) fitted cumulative prospect theory to their set of problems. We used these parameter estimates and "tested" cumulative prospect theory on the Lopes and Oden set of problems, which is known as "data fitting." The resulting fitting power with five adjustable parameters was 87%. A slightly higher result emerged for security-potential/aspiration theory, for which the fitting power with six parameters was 91%.

To sum up, the 90 five-outcome problems no longer allowed the priority heuristic to predict 100% correctly. Nevertheless, the consistent result in the first two contests was that the priority heuristic could predict the majority response as well as or better than the three modifications of expected utility theory or any of the other heuristics. We were surprised by the heuristic's good performance, given that it ignores all intermediate outcomes and their probabilities. It is no doubt possible that gambles can be deliberately constructed with intermediate outcomes

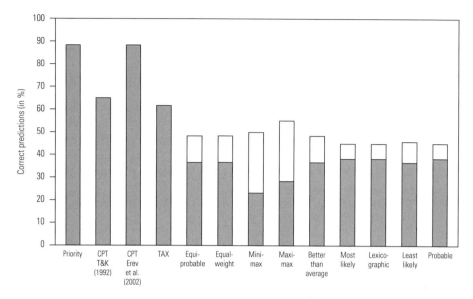

Figure 7-3. Correct predictions of the majority responses for the 90 five-outcome choice problems in Lopes and Oden (1999). The gray parts of the bars represent correct predictions without guessing; the union of the gray and white parts represents correct predictions with guessing (counting as 0.5). Tallying was not applicable (see Footnote 4). The parameters taken from Erev et al. (2002) predict gains only. Parameters for cumulative prospect theory (CPT) are from Tversky and Kahneman (T&K; 1992) and Erev et al., respectively. TAX = transfer-of-attention-exchange model.

that the priority heuristic does not predict as well. Yet in these six systematically varied sets of gambles, no other model outperformed the priority heuristic.

Contest 3: Risky Choices Inferred From Certainty Equivalents

The previous analyses used the same kind of data, namely choices between explicitly stated gambles. The next contest introduces choices inferred from certainty equivalents. The certainty equivalent, C, of a risky gamble is defined as the sure amount of money C, where a person has no preference between the gamble and the sure amount. Certainty equivalents can be translated into choices between a risky gamble and a sure payoff. Our third test set comprised 56 gambles studied by Tversky and Kahneman (1992). These risky gambles are not a random or representative set of gambles. They were designed for the purpose of demonstrating that cumulative prospect theory accounts for deviations

from expected utility theory. Half of the gambles are in the gain domain ($\$x \geq 0$); for the other half, a minus sign was added. Each certainty equivalent was computed from observed choices (for a detailed description, see Brandstätter, Kühberger, & Schneider, 2002). Consider a typical example from this set of problems:

$$C(\$50, .10; \$100, .90) = \$83$$

Because this empirical certainty equivalent falls short of the expected value of the gamble ($\$95$), people are called *risk averse*. We can represent this information as a choice between the risky gamble and a sure gain of equal expected value:

A:	10% chance to win 50
	90% chance to win 100
B:	95 for sure.

The priority heuristic predicts that the minimum outcomes, which are $50 and $95, are compared

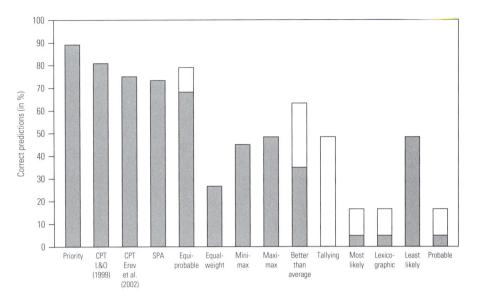

Figure 7-4. Correct predictions of the majority responses for the 56 certainty equivalence problems in Tversky and Kahneman (1992). The gray parts of the bars represent correct predictions without guessing; the union of the gray and white parts represents correct predictions with guessing (counting as 0.5). The parameters taken from Erev et al. (2002) predict gains only. Parameters for cumulative prospect theory (CPT) are from Lopes and Oden (L&O; 1999) and Erev et al., respectively. In the latter set of problems, predictions refer to gains only. SPA = security-potential/aspiration theory.

first. The difference between these two values is larger than the aspiration level ($10). No other reason is examined and the sure gain is chosen.

Results. The priority heuristic made 89% correct predictions (see Figure 7-4). The equiprobable heuristic was the second-best heuristic, with 79%, followed by the better-than-average heuristic. All other heuristics performed at chance level or below, and tallying had to guess all the time (see Table 7-3). The pattern obtained resembles that of the first competition; the outcome heuristics fared better than did those that also used probability information.

Cumulative prospect theory achieved 80% correct predictions with the parameter estimates from the Lopes and Oden (1999) set of problems, and 75% with the Erev et al. (2002) data set (see Figure 7-4). Thus, the average predictive accuracy was 79%. Security-potential/aspiration theory fell slightly short of these numbers and

yielded 73% correct forecasts. In contrast, when one "tests" cumulative prospect theory on the same data (Tversky & Kahneman, 1992) from which the five parameters were derived (i.e., data fitting rather than prediction), one can correctly "predict" 91% of the majority choices. The parameters of the transfer-of-attention-exchange model were fitted by Birnbaum and Navarrete (1998) on the Tversky and Kahneman (1992) data; thus, we cannot test how well it predicts the data. In data fitting, it achieved 95% correct "predictions."

Contest 4: Randomly Drawn Two-Outcome Gambles

The final contest involved 100 pairs of two-outcome gambles that were randomly drawn (Erev et al., 2002). Almost all minimum outcomes were zero. This set of problems handicapped the priority heuristic, given that it could rarely make use of its top-ranked reason. An example from this set is the following (units are points that correspond to cents):

A:	49% chance to win 77
	51% chance to win 0
B:	17% chance to win 98
	83% chance to win 0

These pairs of lotteries were created by random sampling of the four relevant values x_1, p_1, x_2, and p_2. Probabilities were randomly drawn from the uniform distribution (.00, .01, .02, … 1.00) and monetary gains from the uniform distribution (1, 2, 3, … 100). The constraint $(x_1 - x_2)$ $(p_1 - p_2) < 0$ eliminated trivial choices, and the sampling procedures generated choices consisting of gambles with unequal expected value.

Results. Although the priority heuristic could almost never use its top-ranked reason, it correctly predicted 85% of the majority choices reported by Erev et al. (2002). In this set, the outcome heuristics performed worse than those also using probability information did (see Figure 7-5). As a further consequence, the

performance of minimax was near chance level, because its only reason, the minimum gains, was rarely informative, and it thus had to guess frequently (exceptions were four choice problems that included a sure gain). Cumulative prospect theory achieved 89% and 75% correct predictions, depending on the set of parameters, which resulted in an average of 82% correct predictions. The security-potential/aspiration theory correctly predicted 88%, and the transfer-of-attention-exchange model achieved 74% correct forecasts. In the four contests, with a total of nine tests of cumulative prospect theory, three tests of security-potential/aspiration theory, and three tests of the transfer-of-attention-exchange model, these 89% and 88% figures were the only instances in which the two models could predict slightly better than the priority heuristic did (for a tie, see Figure 7-3).

Again, we checked the fitting power of cumulative prospect theory by the Erev et al. (2002) set of problems. This resulted in a fitting power of 99%. As in the previous analyses, a substantial discrepancy between fitting and prediction emerged.

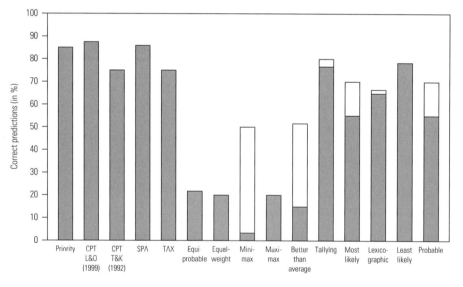

Figure 7-5. Correct predictions of the majority responses for the 100 random choice problems in Erev et al. (2002). The gray parts of the bars represent correct predictions without guessing; the union of the gray and white parts represents correct predictions with guessing (counting as 0.5). Parameters for cumulative prospect theory (CPT) are from Lopes and Oden (L&O; 1999) and Tversky and Kahneman (T&K; 1992), respectively. SPA = security-potential/aspiration theory; TAX = transfer-of-attention-exchange model.

THE PRIORITY HEURISTIC AS A PROCESS MODEL

Process models, unlike as-if models, can be tested on two levels: the choice and the process. In this article, we focus on how well the priority heuristic can predict choices, compared with competing theories. Yet we now want to illustrate how the heuristic lends itself to testable predictions concerning process. Recall that the priority heuristic assumes a sequential process of examining reasons that is stopped as soon as an aspiration level is met. Therefore, the heuristic predicts that the more reasons that people are required to examine, the more time they need for making a choice. Note that all three modifications of expected utility theory tested here (if interpreted as process models) assume that all pieces of information are used and thus do not imply this process prediction.

To illustrate the prediction, consider the following choice:

A:	2,500 with	$p = .05$
	550 with	$p = .95$
B:	2,000 with	$p = .10$
	500 with	$p = .90$

Given the choice between A and B, the priority heuristic predicts that people examine three reasons and therefore need more time than for the choice between C and D, which demands examining one reason only:

C:	2,000 with	$p = .60$
	500 with	$p = .40$
D:	2,000 with	$p = .40$
	1,000 with	$p = .60$

In summary, the prediction is as follows: If the priority heuristic implies that people examine more reasons (e.g., three as opposed to one), the measured time people need for responding will be longer. This prediction was tested in the following experiment for two-outcome gambles, for five-outcome gambles, for gains and losses, and for gambles of similar and dissimilar expected value.

Method. One hundred twenty-one students (61 females, 60 males; $M = 23.4$ years, $SD = 3.8$ years)

from the University of Linz participated in this experiment. The experimental design was a 2 (one reason or three reasons examined) × 2 (choice between 2 two-outcome gambles or choice between 2 five-outcome gambles) × 2 (gambles of similar or dissimilar expected value) × 2 (gains vs. losses) mixed-factorial design, with domain (gains vs. losses) as a between-participants factor and the other three manipulations as within-participants factors. The dependent variable, response time (in milliseconds), was measured from the first appearance of the decision problem until the moment when the participant indicated his or her choice by clicking either gamble A or B. Then the next choice problem appeared on the computer screen. Each participant responded to 40 choice problems, which appeared in random order within each kind of set (i.e., two-outcome and five-outcome set). The order was counterbalanced so that half of the participants received the five-outcome gambles before the two-outcome gambles, whereas this order was reversed for the other half of the participants. All 40 choice problems from the gain domain (gains were converted into losses by adding a minus sign) are listed in the Appendix.

Results and discussion. The prediction was that the response time is shorter for those problems in which the priority heuristic implies that people stop examining after one reason, and it is longer when they examine all three reasons. As shown in Figure 7-6, results confirmed this prediction.

This result held for both choices between two-outcome gambles (one reason: $Mdn = 9.3$, $M = 10.9$, $SE = 0.20$; three reasons: $Mdn = 10.1$, $M = 11.9$, $SE = 0.21$; $z = -3.8$, $p = .001$) and choices between five-outcome gambles (one reason: $Mdn = 10.3$, $M = 12.6$, $SE = 0.26$; three reasons: $Mdn = 11.8$, $M = 14.1$, $SE = 0.41$; $z = -2.9$, $p = .004$). It is not surprising that five-outcome gambles need more reading time than two-outcome gambles, which may explain the higher response time for the former. We additionally analyzed response times between the predicted number of reasons people examined (one or three) when the expected values were similar

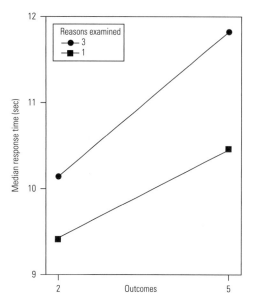

Figure 7-6. Participants' median response time dependent on the number of outcomes and the number of reasons examined.

(one reason: $Mdn = 9.8$, $M = 12.1$, $SE = 0.24$; three reasons: $Mdn = 11.1$, $M = 13.2$, $SE = 0.30$; $z = -4.5$, $p = .001$) and when expected values were dissimilar (one reason: $Mdn = 9.7$, $M = 11.5$, $SE = 0.22$; three reasons: $Mdn = 10.1$, $M = 12.1$, $SE = 0.26$; $z = -1.7$, $p = .085$); when people decided between two gains (one reason: $Mdn = 9.3$, $M = 11.5$, $SE = 0.22$; three reasons: $Mdn = 10.5$, $M = 12.7$, $SE = 0.27$; $z = -4.2$, $p = .001$) and when they decided between two losses (one reason: $Mdn = 10.2$, $M = 12.1$, $SE = 0.25$; three reasons: $Mdn = 10.5$, $M = 12.5$, $SE = 0.29$; $z = -1.7$, $p = .086$). In addition to our predictions, we observed that the effects are stronger for gambles from the gain domain than from the loss domain and when the expected values are similar rather than dissimilar.

The priority heuristic gives rise to process predictions that go beyond those investigated in this article. One of them concerns the order in which people examine reasons. Specifically, the priority heuristic predicts that reasons are considered in the following order: minimum gain, probability of minimum gain, and maximum gain. This and related predictions can be examined with process-tracing methodologies such as

eye tracking. Using mouse lab, for instance, Schkade and Johnson (1989) reported evidence for choice processes that are consistent with lexicographic strategies like the priority heuristic.

FRUGALITY

Predictive accuracy is one criterion for comparing models of choice between gambles; frugality is another. The latter has not been the focus of models of risky choice. For instance, expected utility theory and cumulative prospect theory take all pieces of information into account (exceptions to this are sequential search models such as heuristics and decision field theory; see Busemeyer & Townsend, 1993).

How to define *frugality*? All heuristics and modifications of expected utility theory assume a specific reading stage, in which all pieces of information are read and the relevant one (which varies from model to model) is identified. For instance, a person who relies on the minimax heuristic will read the text and determine what the minimal outcomes are. A person who relies on cumulative prospect theory will read the text and identify all relevant pieces of information from the point of view of this theory. This reading phase is common to all choice models and is not what we refer to in our definition of frugality. The frugality of a strategy refers to the processes that begin after the text is read.

We define frugality as the proportion of pieces of information that a model *ignores* when making a decision. Guessing, for instance, is the most frugal strategy; it ignores 100% of the information, and therefore its frugality is 100%. In a two-outcome gamble, the probabilities are complementary, which reduces the number of pieces of information from eight to six (the two minimum outcomes, their probabilities, and the two maximum outcomes). Minimax, for instance, ignores four of these six pieces of information; thus its frugality is 67%. The modifications of expected utility theory do not ignore any information (regardless of whether one assumes six or eight pieces of information), and thus their frugality is 0%.

Unlike heuristics such as minimax, which always derive their decision from the same pieces of information, the frugality of the priority heu ristic depends on the specific choice problem. For two-outcome gambles, the probabilities of the maximum outcomes are again complementary, reducing the number of pieces of information from eight to six. In making a choice, the priority heuristic then ignores either four pieces of information (i.e., the probabilities of the minimal outcomes and the maximal outcomes), two pieces of information (i.e., the maximal outcomes), or no information. This results in frugalities of 4/6, 2/6, and 0, respectively. However, for the stopping rule, the heuristic needs information about the maximum gain (or loss), which reduces the frugalities to 3/6, 1/6, and 0, respectively.[6]

For each of the four sets of choice problems, we calculated the priority heuristic's frugality score. In the first set of problems (see Figure 7-1; Kahneman & Tversky, 1979), the priority heuristic ignored 22% of the information. For the five-outcome gambles in Figure 7-3, the heuristic ignored 78%. As mentioned before, one reason for this is that the heuristic solely takes note of the minimum and maximum outcomes and their respective probabilities, and it ignores all other information. The modifications of expected utility theory, in contrast, ignored 0%. In other words, for five-outcome gambles, the heuristic predicted people's choices (87%) as good as or better than the modifications of expected utility theory with one fourth of the information. In the Tversky and Kahneman (1992) set of problems, the priority heuristic frugality score was 31%; for the set of randomly chosen gambles, the heuristic ignored 15% of the information. This number is relatively low, because as mentioned before, the information about the minimum gain was almost never informative. In summary, the priority heuristic predicted the majority choice on the basis of fewer pieces of information than multiparameter models did, and its frugality depended strongly on the type of gamble in question.

OVERALL PERFORMANCE

We now report the results for all 260 problems from the four contests. For each strategy, we calculated its mean frugality and the proportion of correct predictions (weighted by the number of choice problems per set of problems). As shown in Figure 7-7, there are three clusters of strategies: the modifications of expected utility and tallying, the classic choice heuristics, and the priority heuristic. The clusters have the following characteristics: The modifications of expected utility and tallying could predict choice fairly accurately but required the maximum amount of information. The classic heuristics were fairly frugal but performed dismally in predicting people's choices. The priority heuristic achieved the best predictive accuracy (87%) while being relatively frugal.

Security-potential/aspiration theory, cumulative prospect theory, and the transfer-of-attention-exchange model correctly predicted 79%, 77%, and 69% of the majority choices, respectively. With the exception of the least-likely heuristic and tallying, most classic heuristics did not predict better than chance. For instance, the performances of the minimax and lexicographic rules were 49% and 48%, respectively.

The four sets of problems allowed for 15 comparisons between the predictive accuracy of the priority heuristic and cumulative prospect theory, security-potential/aspiration theory, and the transfer-of-attention-exchange model.[7] The priority heuristic achieved the highest predictive accuracy in 12 of the 15 comparisons (Figures 7-1, 7-3, 7-4, and 7-5), and cumulative prospect theory and security-potential/aspiration theory in one case each (plus one tie).

DISCUSSION

The present model of sequential choice continues the works of Luce (1956), Selten (2001), Simon (1957), and Tversky (1969). Luce (1956) began to model choice with a semiorder rule, and Tversky (1969, 1972) extended this work, adding heuristics such as "elimination by aspects." In his later work with Kahneman, he switched to modeling choice by modifying expected utility theory. The present article pursues Tversky's original perspective, as well as the emphasis on sequential models by Luce, Selten, and Simon.

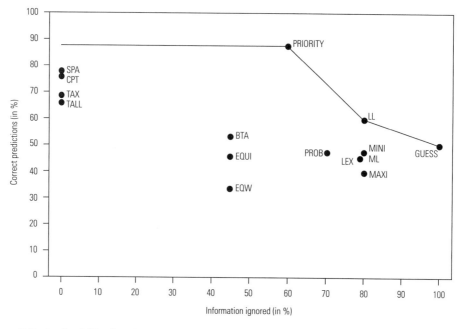

Figure 7-7. Predictability-frugality trade-off, averaged over all four sets of problems. The percentage of correct predictions refers to majority choices (including guessing). PRIORITY = priority heuristic; SPA = security-potential/aspiration theory; CPT = cumulative prospect theory; TAX = transfer-of-attention-exchange model; TALL = tallying; LL = least-likely heuristic; BTA = better-than-average heuristic; PROB = probable heuristic; MINI = minimax heuristic; GUESS = pure guessing; EQUI = equiprobable heuristic; LEX = lexicographic heuristic; ML = most-likely heuristic; MAXI = maximax heuristic; EQW = equal-weight heuristic. For a description of the heuristics, see Table 7-3.

Limits of the Model

Our goal was to derive from empirical evidence a psychological process model that predicts choice behavior. Like all models, the priority heuristic is a simplification of real world phenomena. In our view, there are four major limitations: the existence of individual differences, low-stake ("peanuts") gambles, widely discrepant expected values, and problem representation.

Individual differences and low stakes. The priority heuristic embodies risk aversion for gains and risk seeking for losses. Even if the majority of people are risk averse in a particular situation, a minority will typically be risk seeking. Some of these risk lovers may focus on the maximum gain rather than on the minimum one as the first reason. Thus, the order of reasons is one potential source of individual differences; another one is the aspiration level that stops examination.

We propose order and aspiration as two sources of individual differences. Moreover, risk seeking can also be produced by the properties of the choice problem itself. For instance, low stakes can evoke risk seeking for gains. Thus, low stakes can lead to the same reversal of the order of reasons as postulated before for individual differences.

Discrepant expected values. Another limiting condition for the application of the priority heuristic is widely discrepant expected values. The set of random gambles by Erev et al. (2002) revealed this limitation. For instance, gamble A offers 88 with $p = .74$, otherwise nothing, and gamble B offers 19 with $p = .86$, otherwise nothing. The expected values of these gambles are 65.1 and 16.3, respectively. The priority heuristic predicts the choice of gamble B, whereas the majority of participants chose gamble A.

To investigate the relation between the ratio of expected values and the predictive power of the priority heuristic, we analyzed a set of 450 problems with a large variability in expected values (Mellers, Chang, Birnbaum, & Ordòñez, 1992). In this set, all minimal outcomes are zero; thus the priority heuristic could not use its top-ranked reason. We also tested how well cumulative prospect theory, security-potential/ aspiration theory, the transfer-of-attention-exchange model, and expected value theory predict the majority choices.

Figure 7-8 shows the proportion of correct predictions as a function of the ratio between expected values.[8] As was suggested by our analysis of the Erev et al. (2002) set of problems, the priority heuristic's accuracy decreased as the ratio between expected values became large. For instance, in the fourth quartile, its performance was only slightly above 50%. In the first quartile, however, the priority heuristic outperformed all other contestants by a minimum of 16 percentage

points (security-potential/aspiration theory) and a maximum of 40 percentage points (transfer-of-attention-exchange model). In the second quartile, the priority heuristic still outperformed the other modifications of expected utility theory. These performed better than the priority heuristic when the ratio between expected values exceeded about two. It is interesting, however, that expected value theory performed virtually as well as the best-performing modification for larger ratios. Tallying (not shown in Figure 7-8) performed identically to security-potential/ aspiration theory in the first two quartiles and worse than any other model when the ratios between expected values were larger. Thus, the results suggest that when choices become difficult—because of similar expected values—a simple sequential heuristic performs best. When choices become easy—because of widely discrepant expected values—expected value theory predicts choices as well as or better than the parameterized models. Both the priority heuristic

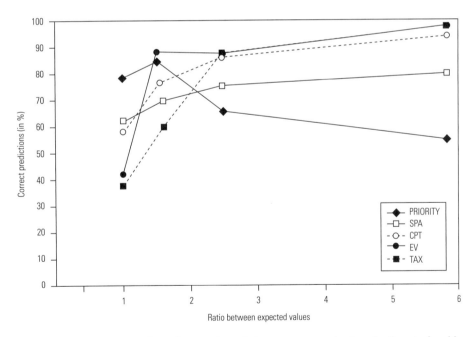

Figure 7-8. Correct predictions dependent on the ratio between expected values for the set of problems in Mellers et al. (1992). For parameter estimates, see Footnote 8. PRIORITY = priority heuristic; TAX = transfer-of-attention-exchange model; SPA = security-potential/aspiration theory; CPT = cumulative prospect theory; EV = expected value theory.

and expected value theory successfully predict behavior without transforming probabilities and outcomes.

Figure 7-8 suggests that people do not rely on the priority heuristic indiscriminately. How can we model when they rely on the heuristic and when they do not? One way would be to assume that people estimate the expected values, and if the ratio is smaller than two, they turn to the priority heuristic. But calculating expected values is not the only method. Alternatively, people may first look at the three (four) reasons, and if no difference is markedly larger than the others, they apply the priority heuristic. Screening the reasons for a large difference is akin to what Tversky, Sattath, and Slovic (1988) called "looking for a decisive advantage" (p. 372).

Problem representation. A final potential limitation refers to the impact of different representations of the same decision problems on people's choices. For illustration, consider the following two problems reported by Birnbaum (2004):

A marble will be drawn from an urn, and the color of the marble drawn blindly and randomly will determine your prize. You can choose the urn from which the marble will be drawn. In each choice, which urn would you choose?

Urn *A*:	85 red marbles to win $100
	10 white marbles to win $50
	5 blue marbles to win $50
Urn *B*:	85 black marbles to win $100
	10 yellow marbles to win $100
	5 purple marbles to win $7

The same participants were also asked to choose between the following two urns:

Urn *A'*:	85 black marbles to win $100
	15 yellow marbles to win $50
Urn *B'*:	95 red marbles to win $100
	5 white marbles to win $7

The Urn *A* versus Urn *B* problem is the same as the Urn *A'* versus Urn *B'* problem, except that the latter adds up the probabilities of the same outcomes (e.g., 10 white marbles to win $50 and 5 blue marbles to win $50 in Urn *A* are combined to 15 yellow marbles to win $50 in Urn *A'*).

According to Birnbaum (2004), 63% of his participants chose *B* over *A* and only 20% chose *B'* over *A'*. His transfer-of-attention-exchange model predicts this and other new paradoxes of risky decision making (see also Loomes, Starmer, & Sugden, 1991). The priority heuristic, in contrast, does not predict that such reversals will occur. The heuristic predicts that people prefer Urn *A* and *A'*, respectively (based on the minimum gains). In evaluating the validity of models of risky choice, it is important to keep in mind that it is always possible to design problems that elicit choices that a given model—be it the expected utility theory, prospect theory, cumulative prospect theory, the transfer-of-attention-exchange model, or the priority heuristic—can and cannot explain. For this reason, we refrained from opportunistic sampling of problems. Instead, we tested the priority heuristic on a large set of existing problems that were initially designed to demonstrate the validity of several of its contestants.

Process Models

The priority heuristic is intended to model both choice and process: It not only predicts the outcome but also specifies the order of priority, a stopping rule, and a decision rule. As a consequence, it can be tested on two levels: choice and process. For instance, if a heuristic predicts choices well, it may still fail in describing the process, thus falsifying it as a process model. Models of choice that are not intended to capture the psychological processes (i.e., as-if models), however, can only be tested at the level of choice. In discussions with colleagues, we learned that there is debate about what counts as a process model for choice. For instance, whereas many people assume that cumulative prospect theory is mute about the decision process, some think the theory can be understood in terms of processes. Lopes (1995) explicitly clarified that the equations in theories such as security-potential/aspiration theory are not meant to describe the process. She even showed that the outcomes of lexicographic processes—similar to those in the priority heuristic—can resemble those of modifications of subjective expected utility theories.

The priority heuristic can be seen as an explication of Rubinstein's (1988) similarity-based model (see also Leland, 1994; Mellers & Biagini, 1994). The role of "similarity" in his model is here played by the aspiration level, and the priority rule imposes a fixed order on the reasons. Unlike the algebra in expected utility theory and its modifications, which assume weighting, summing, and exhaustive use of information, the priority heuristic assumes cognitive processes that are characterized by order, aspiration levels, and stopping rules. In Rubinstein's (2003) words, "we need to open the black box of decision making, and come up with some completely new and fresh modeling devices" (p. 1215). We believe that process models of heuristics are key to opening this black box.

Predicting Choices: Which Strategies Are Closest?

Which of the strategies make the same predictions and which make contradictory ones? Table 7-5 shows the percentage of identical predictions between each pair of strategies tested on the entire set of 260 problems. The strategy that is most similar to the priority heuristic in terms of prediction (but not in terms of process) is not a heuristic, but rather cumulative prospect theory using the parameters from the Erev et al. (2002) set of problems. The least similar strategy in terms of prediction is the equal weight heuristic, which, unlike the priority heuristic, ignores probabilities and simply adds the outcomes.

A second striking result concerns models with adjustable parameters. The degree of overlap in prediction is not so much driven by their conceptual similarity or dissimilarity as by whether they are fitted to the same set of problems. Consider first the cases in which the parameters of different models are derived from the same set of problems. The transfer-of-attention-exchange model (with parameter estimates from Tversky & Kahneman, 1992) most closely resembles cumulative prospect theory

Table 7-5. Percentage of Same Predictions of Each Pair of Strategies

	Strategy	1	2	3	4	5	6	7	8	9	10	11	12	13	14	15	16
1.	PRIORITY	—															
2.	CPT; L&O (1999)	78	—														
3.	CPT; Erev et al. (2002)	89	92	—													
4.	CPT; T&K (1992)	68	80	60	—												
5.	TAX	65	77	57	96	—											
6.	SPA	72	91	81	77	76	—										
7.	MAXI	38	40	26	57	58	44	—									
8.	MINI	51	49	75	59	60	47	39	—								
9.	TALL	70	62	56	52	51	63	20	49	—							
10.	ML	51	57	48	42	41	62	39	43	60	—						
11.	LL	64	62	48	38	36	66	36	32	81	67	—					
12.	BTA	49	57	46	70	72	57	67	53	43	32	39	—				
13.	EQUI	43	43	51	64	70	41	77	59	19	22	19	74	—			
14.	EQW	31	27	32	62	65	27	77	58	19	32	19	69	84	—		
15.	PROB	51	57	48	42	41	62	39	43	60	89	67	32	22	32	—	
16.	LEX	50	53	44	44	42	60	44	44	51	89	62	33	28	37	89	—

Note. The numbers specify the percentage of problems in which two strategies made the same predictions. For instance, the priority heuristic (PRIORITY) and minimax (MINI) made the same predictions in 51 % of all problems and different predictions in 49% of them. Parameters for cumulative prospect theory (CPT) are estimated from Lopes and Oden (L&O; 1999), Erev et al. (2002), and Tversky and Kahneman (T&K; 1992), respectively. Italic numbers indicate the percentage of same predictions when the parameters of the same model are derived from different sets of problems. Bold numbers indicate the percentage of same predictions when the parameters of different models are derived from the same set of problems. TAX = transfer-of-attention-exchange model; SPA = security-potential/aspiration theory; MAXI = maximax heuristic; TALL = tallying; ML = most-likely heuristic; LL = least-likely heuristic; BTA = better-than-average heuristic; EQUI = equiprobable heuristic; EQW = equal-weight heuristic; PROB = probable heuristic, LEX = lexicographic heuristic. For a description of the heuristics, see Table 7-3.

when its parameters are estimated from the same set of problems (96% identical predictions). Similarly, security-potential/aspiration theory (with parameter estimates from Lopes & Oden, 1999) most closely resembles cumulative prospect theory when its parameters are estimated from the same problem set (91% identical predictions). Consider now the cases in which the parameters of the same model are derived from different sets of problems. There are three such cases for cumulative prospect theory, and the overlaps are 92%, 80%, and 60%. Thus, on average the overlap is higher (94%) when the same problem set is used rather when the same model is used (77%). This shows that the difference between problem sets has more impact than the difference between models does.

Can the Priority Heuristic Predict Choices in Gambles Involving Gains and Losses?

In the four contests, we have shown that the priority heuristic predicts choices by avoiding trade-offs between probability and outcomes; we have not investigated trade-offs between gains and losses. The priority heuristic can be generalized to handle gain-loss trade-offs, without any change in its logic. This is illustrated by the following choice between two mixed gambles (Tversky & Kahneman, 1992):

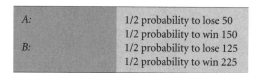

The heuristic starts by comparing the minimum outcomes (−50 and −125). Because this difference exceeds the aspiration level of 20 (1/10 of the highest absolute gain or loss: 22.5 rounded to the next prominent number), examination is stopped, and no other reasons are examined. The priority heuristic selects gamble A, which is the majority choice (inferred from certainty equivalents as in Contest 3). Applied to all six choice problems with mixed gambles in the Tversky and Kahneman (1992) set of problems, the priority heuristic predicted the majority choice in each case. We cross-checked this result

against the set of problems by Levy and Levy (2002), with six choices between mixed gambles with two, three, or four outcomes. Again, the priority heuristic predicted the majority choice in each case correctly. However, we did not test the proposed generalization of the priority heuristic against an extensive set of mixed gambles and thus cannot judge how appropriate this generalization is.

Choice Proportions

The priority heuristic predicts majority choices but not choice proportions. However, a rank order of choice proportion can be predicted with the additional assumption that the earlier the examination stops, the more extreme the choice proportions will be. That is, when examination is stopped after the first reason, the resulting choice proportions will be more unequal (e.g., 80/20) than when stopping occurs after the second reason (e.g., 70/30), and so on. To test this hypothesis, we analyzed two sets of problems (Kahneman & Tversky, 1979; Lopes & Oden, 1999) in which the priority heuristic predicted stopping after the first, second, or third reason (this was not the case for the Erev et al., 2002, choice problems, in which stopping after the first reason was not possible in almost all problems; the problems in the Tversky & Kahneman, 1992, data set were derived from certainty equivalents and hence do not contain choice proportions). Thus, the hypothesis implies that the predicted choice proportions should be higher when fewer reasons are examined. The results show that if examination stopped after the first, second, and third reason, the respective mean choice proportions are .85 ($SD = .06$; $n = 3$), .83 ($SD = .09$; $n = 4$), and .72 ($SD = .09$; $n = 7$) in the Kahneman and Tversky (1979) set of problems. Similarly, in the Lopes and Oden (1999) set of problems, these values are .75 ($SD = .10$; $n = 30$), .66 ($SD = .11$; $n = 48$), and .54 ($SD = .03$; $n = 12$), which supports the heuristic's capacity to predict a rank order of choice proportions.

We suggest that the number of reasons examined offers one account for the process underlying the observed relationship between choice proportion and response time. Our analysis showed that when fewer reasons were examined, the choice proportions became more extreme and the response times decreased. This implies, everything else being equal, that more extreme choice proportions should be associated with faster response times. Some support for this implication is given in Mosteller and Nogee (1951) and in Busemeyer and Townsend (1993).

Occam's Razor

Models with smaller numbers of adjustable parameters, which embody Occam's razor, have a higher posterior probability in Bayesian model comparison (MacKay, 1995; Roberts & Pashler, 2000). Consider an empirically obtained result that is consistent with two models. One of these predicts that behavior will be located in a small range of the outcome space, and the other predicts that behavior will be located in a wider range. The empirical result gives more support (a higher Bayesian posterior probability) to the one that bets on the smaller range. Consequently, if several models predict the same empirical phenomenon equally well, the simplest receives more support (Simon, 1977). We provided evidence that the priority heuristic (a) is simpler and more frugal than subjective expected utility and its modifications; (b) can predict choices equally well or better across four sets of gambles; (c) predicts intransitivities, which some modifications of expected utility theory have difficulty predicting; and (d) predicts process data such as response times.

Every model has parameters; the difference is whether they are free, adjustable within a range, or fixed. The parameters in modifications of expected utility theory are typically adjustable within a range, because of theoretical constraints. In contrast, most heuristics have fixed parameters. One can fix a parameter by (a) measuring it independently, (b) deriving it from previous research, or (c) deriving it theoretically. For modifications of expected utility theories, we used parameters measured on independent sets of problems. For the priority heuristic, we derived its order from previous research and obtained the 1/10 aspiration level from our cultural base-10 number system. These ways of fixing parameters can help to make more precise

predictions, thus increasing the empirical support for a model.

Fast-and-Frugal Heuristics: From Inferences to Preferences

By means of the priority heuristic, we generalize the research program on fast-and-frugal heuristics (Gigerenzer et al., 1999) from inferences to preferences, thus linking it with another research program on cognitive heuristics, the adaptive decision maker program (Payne et al., 1993). This generalization is not trivial. In fact, according to a widespread intuition, preference judgments are not likely to be modeled in terms of noncompensatory strategies such as the priority heuristic. The reason is that preferential choice often occurs in environments in which reasons—for example, prices of products and their quality—correlate negatively. Some researchers have argued that negative correlations between reasons cause people to experience conflict, leading them to make trade-offs, and trade-offs in turn are not conducive to the use of noncompensatory heuristics (e.g., Shanteau & Thomas, 2000). The priority heuristic's success in predicting a large majority of the modal responses across 260 problems challenges this argument.

The study of fast-and-frugal heuristics for inferences has two goals. One is to derive descriptive models of cognitive heuristics that capture how real people actually make inferences. The second goal is prescriptive in nature: to determine in which environments a given heuristic is less accurate than, as accurate as, or even more accurate than informationally demanding and computationally expensive strategies. In the current analysis of a fast-and-frugal heuristic for preferences, we focused on the descriptive goal at the expense of the prescriptive one for the following reason: When analyzing preference judgments in prescriptive terms, one quickly enters muddy waters because, unlike in inference tasks, there is no external criterion of accuracy. Moreover, Thorngate (1980) and Payne et al. (1993) have already shown that in some environments, preference heuristics can be highly competitive—when measured, for instance, against the gold standard of a weighted additive model. Notwithstanding our focus on the descriptive accuracy of the priority heuristic, we showed that it performed well on two criteria that have also been used to evaluate the performance of fast-and-frugal inference strategies, namely, frugality and transparency.

Perhaps one of the most surprising outcomes of the contest between the priority heuristic, the neo-Bernouillian models (i.e., those assuming some type of weighing and summing of reasons), and previously proposed heuristics, respectively, is the dismal performance of the latter. Why does the priority heuristic so clearly outperform the other heuristics? The key difference is that the classic heuristics (with the exception of the lexicographic heuristic) always look at the same piece or several pieces of information. The priority heuristic, in contrast, relies on a flexible stopping rule. Like the classic heuristics, it is frugal, but unlike them, it is adapted to the specific properties of a problem and its frugality is hence not independent of the problem in question. The sequential nature of the priority heuristic is exactly the same as that assumed in heuristics such as take-the-best, take-the-last, and fast-and-frugal trees (Gigerenzer, 2004). These heuristics, equipped with flexible stopping rules, are in between the classic heuristics that always rely on the same reason(s) and the neo-Bernoulli models that use all reasons. We believe this new class of heuristics to be of great importance. Its heuristics combine some of the advantages of both classic trade-off models and heuristics, thus achieving great flexibility, which enables them to respond to the characteristics of individual problems.

CONCLUSION

We have shown that a person who uses the priority heuristic generates (a) the Allais paradox, (b) risk aversion for gains if probabilities are high, (c) risk seeking for gains if probabilities are low (e.g., lottery tickets), (d) risk aversion for losses if probabilities are low (e.g., buying insurance), (e) risk seeking for losses if probabilities are high, (f) the certainty effect, and (g) the possibility effect. Furthermore, the priority heuristic is capable of accounting for choices that conflict with (cumulative) prospect theory, such as

systematic intransitivities that can cause preference reversals. We tested how well the heuristic predicts people's majority choices in four different types of gambles; three of these had been designed to test the power of prospect theory, cumulative prospect theory, and security-potential/aspiration theory, and the fourth was a set of random gambles. Nevertheless, despite this test in "hostile" environments, the priority heuristic predicted people's preference better than previously proposed heuristics and better than three modifications of expected utility theory. We also identified an important boundary of the priority heuristic. Specifically, the heuristic performed best when the ratio between expected values was about 2:1 or smaller. Finally, the heuristic specifies a process that leads to predictions about response time differences between choice problems, which we tested and confirmed.

We believe that the priority heuristic, which is based on the same building blocks as take-the-best, can serve as a new framework for models for a wide range of cognitive processes, such as attitude formation or expectancy-value theories of motivation. The heuristic provides an alternative to the assumption that cognitive processes always compute trade-offs in the sense of weighting and summing of information. We do not claim that people never make trade-offs in choices, judgments of facts, values, and morals; that would be as mistaken as assuming that they always do. Rather, the task ahead is to understand when people make trade-offs and when they do not.

ACKNOWLEDGMENTS

Ralph Hertwig was supported by Swiss National Science Foundation Grant 100013-107741/1. We thank Will Bennis, Michael Birnbaum, Jerome Busemeyer, Uwe Czienskowski, Ido Erev, Claudia Gonzalez Vallejo, Robin Hogarth, Eric Johnson, Joseph Johnson, Konstantinos Katsikopoulos, Anton Kühberger, Lola Lopes, Robin Pope, Drazen Prelec, and Lael Schooler for many helpful comments and fruitful discussions, and Uwe Czienskowski a second time for checking the statistical analyses. We are also grateful to Barbara Mellers for providing us with the opportunity to analyze her data and to Florian Sickinger for his help in running the response time experiment.

NOTES

1. The results depend on the specific set of gambles: When one of the reasons is not varied, it is not likely that people attend to this reason. For instance, in a "dublex gamble" (Payne & Braunstein, 1971; Slovic & Lichtenstein, 1968), one can win $x with probability p_1 (otherwise nothing), and lose $y with probability p_2 (otherwise nothing). Here, the minimum gain of the winning gamble and the minimum loss of the losing gamble are always zero, rendering the minimum outcomes uninformative. Similarly, Slovic et al. (1990) argued that probabilities were more important than outcomes, but here again all minimum outcomes were zero.

2. We did not consider three of the heuristics listed by Thorngate (1980). These are low expected payoff elimination, minimax regret, and low payoff elimination. These strategies require extensive computations.

3. These are the choice problems 1, 2, 3, 4, 7, 8, 3', 4', 7', 8', 13, 13', 14, 14' in Kahneman and Tversky (1979).

4. Note that tallying does not predict choice behavior for problems with more than two outcomes. Whereas it is easy to compare the highest and the lowest outcomes of each gamble as well as their respective probabilities, it is unclear how to evaluate the probabilities of an intermediate outcome.

5. As one can see from Table 7-4, the Erev et al. (2002) estimates of prospect theory's parameters only refer to gains. Therefore, only a subset of the problems studied by Kahneman and Tversky (1979) could be predicted, which was accounted for by this and the following means.

6. For two-outcome gambles, six instead of eight pieces of information yield a lower-bound estimate of the frugality advantage of the heuristics over parameter-based models such as cumulative prospect theory, which do not treat decision weights as complementary. For n-outcome gambles, with $n > 2$, all $4n$ pieces of information were used in calculating frugalities. Similarly, in the case of ambiguity, we calculated a heuristic's frugality in a way to give this heuristic the best edge against the priority heuristic.

7. For the first set of problems, there were 3 independent parameter sets for cumulative prospect theory, 1 for security-potential/aspiration theory, and 1 for the transfer-of-attention-exchange model, resulting in 5 comparisons. For the second set, these numbers were 2, 0, and 1; for the third set, 2, 1, and 0; and for the fourth set, 2, 1, and 1; resulting in 15 comparisons.

8. For each problem, we calculated the ratio between the larger and the smaller expected value. We then divided the ratios into four quartiles and calculated the mean ratio for each quartile, which were 1.0, 1.8, 2.6, and 5.8. We used the same parameter estimates as in the four contests. For cumulative prospect theory, Figure 7-8 shows the mean performance across the three analyses using the parameter estimates from Erev et al. (2002), Lopes and Oden (1999), and Tversky and Kahneman (1992).

APPENDIX

Choice Problems From the Gain Domain
Used in Response Time Experiment

Two-Outcome Gambles

One Reason Examined		Three Reasons Examined	
EV Similar	EV Dissimilar	EV Similar	EV Dissimilar
(2,000, .60; 500, .40)	(3,000, .60; 1,500, .40)	(2,000, .10; 500, .90)	(5,000, .10; 500, .90)
(2,000, .40; 1,000, .60)	(2,000, .40;1,000, .60)	(2,500, .05; 550, .95)	(2,500, .05; 550, .95)
(5,000, .20; 2,000, .80)	(6,000, .20; 3,000, .80)	(4,000, .25; 3,000, .75)	(7,000, .25; 3,000, .75)
(4,000, .50; 1,200, .50)	(4,000, .50; 1,200, .50)	(5,000, .20; 2,800, .80)	(5,000, .20; 2,800, .80)
(4,000, .20; 2,000, .80)	(5,000, .20; 3,000, .80)	(6,000, .30; 2,500, .70)	(9,000, .30; 2,500, .70)
(3,000, .70; 1,000, .30)	(3,000, .70; 1,000, .30)	(8,200, .25; 2,000, .75)	(8,200, .25; 2,000, .75)
(900, .40; 500, .60)	(1,900, .40; 1,500, .60)	(3,000, .40; 2,000, .60)	(6,000, .40; 2,000, .60)
(2,500, .20; 200, .80)	(2,500, .20; 200, .80)	(3,600, .35; 1,750, .65)	(3,600, .35; 1,750, .65)
(1,000, .50; 0, .50)	(2,000, .50; 1,000, .50)	(2,500, .33; 0, .67)	(5,500, .33; 0, .67)
(500, 1.00)	(500, 1.00)	(2,400, .34; 0, .66)	(2,400, .34; 0, .66)

Five-Outcome Gambles

One Reason Examined		Three Reasons Examined	
EV Similar	EV Dissimilar	EV Similar	EV Dissimilar
(200, .04; 150, .21; 100, .50; 50, .21; 0, .04)	(200, .04; 150, .21; 100, .50; 50, .21; 0, .04)	(200, .04; 150, .21; 100, .50; 50, .21; 0, .04)	(250, .04; 200, .21; 150, .50; 100, .21; 0, .04)
(200, .04; 165, .11; 130, .19; 95, .28; 60, .38	(250, .04; 215, .11; 180, .19; 145, .28; 110, .38)	(140, .38; 105, .28; 70, .19; 35, .11; 0, .04)	(140, .38; 105, .28; 70, .19; 35, .11; 0, .04)
(200, .04; 165, .11; 130, .19; 95, .28; 60, .38)	(250, .04; 215, .11; 180, .19; 145, .28; 110, .38)	(200, .20; 150, .20; 100, .20; 50, .20; 0, .20)	(250, .20; 200, .20; 150, .20; 100,.20; 0, .20)
(140, .38; 105, .28; 70, .19; 35, .11; 0, .04)	(140, .38; 105, .28; 70, .19; 35, .11; 0, .04)	(240, .15; 130, .30; 100, .10; 50, .30; 0, .15)	(200, .15; 150, .30; 100, .10; 50, .30; 0, .15)
(200, .20; 150, .20; 100, .20; 50, .20; 0, .20)	(200, .20; 150, .20; 100, .20; 50, .20; 0, .20)	(200, .32; 150, .16; 100, .04; 50, .16; 0, .32)	(250, .32; 200, .16; 150, .04; 100, .16; 0, .32)
(200, .04; 165, .11; 130, .19; 95, .28; 60, .38)	(250, .04; 215, .11; 180, .19; 145, .28; 110, .38)	(348, .04; 261, .11; 174, .19; 87, .28; 0, .38)	(348, .04; 261, .11; 174, .19; 87, .28; 0, .38)
(200, .04; 165, .11; 130, .19; 95, .28; 60, .38)	(250, .04; 215, .11; 180, .19; 145, .28; 110, .38)	(348, .04; 261, .11; 174, .19; 87, .28; 0, .38)	(398, .04; 311, .11; 224, .19; 137, .28; 0, .38)
(200, .32; 150, .16; 100, .04; 50, .16; 0, .32)	(200, .32; 150, .16; 100, .04; 50, .16; 0, .32)	(260, .15; 180, .15; 120, .15; 80, .20; 0, .35)	(260, .15; 180, .15; 120, .15; 80, .20; 0, .35)
(348, .04; 261, .11; 174, .19; 87, .28; 0, .38)	(348, .04; 261, .11; 174, .19; 87, .28; 0, .38)	(260, .15; 180, .15; 120, .15; 80, .20; 0, .35)	(310, .15; 230, .15; 170, .15; 130, .20; 0, .35)
(200, .04; 165, .11; 130, .19; 95, .28; 60, .38)	(250, .04; 215, .11; 180, .19; 145, .28; 110, .38	(200, .32; 150, .16; 100, .04; 50, .16; 0, .32)	(200, .32; 150, .16; 100, .04; 50, .16; 0, .32)

Note. EV = expected value.

Introduction to Chapter 8

One-Reason Decision-Making:
Modeling Violations of Expected Utility Theory

There is a difference between showing that a model is *consistent* with observed behavior and proving that a model *implies* this behavior: The latter is a much stronger result. Consider the finding that people often violate the predictions of expected utility theory. There are at least two ways to react to these violations. One is to rescue the basic framework of maximizing some function of utilities and probabilities by introducing additional adjustable parameters until the deviating behavior becomes consistent with the new theory. Cumulative prospect theory, for instance, represents such a repair program. It uses five adjustable parameters, which allow immense flexibility in finding parameter values that fit observed behavior. Yet this flexibility makes it hard to understand what behavior it predicts and what behavior it excludes. For instance, it is difficult to see that none of its parameter combinations are simultaneously consistent with gambling on low probability gains (e.g., people playing the lottery) and the Allais paradox behavior (Neilson & Stowe, 2002). That is, to account for each of these behaviors, one needs a different combination of parameters.

The other reaction is to dispose with defensive repairs, rethink the psychological processes, and formulate simple models. The priority heuristic introduced in Chapter 7 represents such a start from scratch and does not use a single adjustable parameter—nor do $1/N$ (equality heuristic, see Chapters 34 and 35) and the recognition heuristic (see Chapter 3). This article by Konstantinos Katsikopoulos and Gerd Gigerenzer proves that the priority heuristic logically *implies* well-established violations of expected utility theory such as the Allais paradox and the four-fold pattern, the reflection effect, and the certainty effect. This is an important analytical result, because it shows that unlike the expected utility repair program, a psychological framework can explain these phenomena in a more stringent way. Someone who relies on the priority heuristic will exhibit several violations of the expected utility theory. Thus, there is no longer any need to test this part of the argument empirically. In tandem with the previous article, this article demonstrates how experimental and analytical methods can go hand in hand.

CHAPTER 8

One-Reason Decision-Making: Modeling Violations of Expected Utility Theory

Konstantinos V. Katsikopoulos and Gerd Gigerenzer

Abstract: People violate expected utility theory and this has been traditionally modeled by augmenting its weight-and-add framework by nonlinear transformations of values and probabilities. Yet individuals often use one-reason decision-making when making court decisions or choosing cellular phones, and institutions do the same when creating rules for traffic safety or fair play in sports. We analyze a model of one-reason decision-making, the priority heuristic, and show that it simultaneously implies common consequence effects, common ratio effects, reflection effects, and the fourfold pattern of risk attitude. The preferences represented by the priority heuristic satisfy some standard axioms. This work may provide the basis for a new look at bounded rationality.

Most descriptive theories of decision making—and certainly those that are variants of expected value theory (EVT) or expected utility theory (EUT)—make the following psychological assumptions:

1. *Independent evaluations:* Every option has a value that is measured by a single number (options are not evaluated relative to other options).
2. *Exhaustive search:* The value of an option is calculated by using all available information (for gambles, the probabilities and values for all possible outcomes).
3. *Trade-offs:* To calculate an option's value, low values on one attribute (e.g., a value) can be compensated by high values on another attribute (e.g., a probability). EVT makes two additional assumptions for calculating an option's value.

4. *Objective probabilities:* The probabilities used to calculate an option's value are equal to the objective probabilities (the objective probabilities are not transformed in a nonlinear way).
5. *Objective values:* The outcome values used to calculate an option's value are equal to the objective monetary values (the objective values are not transformed in a nonlinear way).

To account for the St. Petersburg Paradox (Jorland, 1987), which violates EVT, Daniel Bernoulli (1738/1954) introduced EUT, which changes the *objective values* assumption 5. To account for further findings such as buying lottery tickets and insurance policies, the Allais paradox (Allais, 1952/1979), as well as the fourfold pattern of risk attitude (Tversky & Kahneman, 1992), modifications of EUT relax assumptions 4 and 5 by using nonlinear transformations with a number of free parameters.

In this paper we follow Selten's (2001) and others' call to develop and analyze a fundamental alternative approach to modeling choice. Specifically, we target the basic assumptions 1 to 3 but retain assumptions 4 and 5. In Section 1, we briefly review some of the empirical evidence for simple heuristics that do not retain assumptions 1 to 3. These heuristics are a way of implementing Simon's bounded rationality (1955, 1956), using the approach of Gigerenzer and Selten (2001), Leland (1994), and Rubinstein (1988).

In Section 2, we present the priority heuristic, proposed by Brandstätter et al. (2006), which is related to lexicographic semiorders (Luce, 1956; Tversky, 1969), and predicted empirical data better than modifications of EUT such as cumulative prospect theory did. In that paper, specific examples were used to numerically illustrate that the priority heuristic can account for major violations of expected utility theory (such as the Allais paradox and the fourfold pattern of risk attitude). But no mathematical conditions were derived under which the priority heuristic predicts these violations. In Section 3, we prove under which conditions the heuristic implies major violations of EUT. This facilitates understanding how the Allais paradox, the fourfold pattern of risk attitude, and other systematic patterns, may arise from cognitive processes that implement one-reason decision-making, rather than from probability weighting and utility functions.

For further understanding of the heuristic, in Section 4, we derive conditions under which the preferences represented by the heuristic satisfy standard axioms. In Section 5, we discuss the relation of the priority heuristic to Rubinstein's (1988) similarity model. We conclude that simple heuristics that make no trade-offs seem to be a promising approach to modeling bounded rationality.

1. WHY SIMPLE HEURISTICS?

Assumptions 1 to 3 are commonplace. Why do we propose they be reconsidered? In this section, we discuss two reasons: empirical evidence for people's use of heuristics that violate these assumptions and prescriptive reasons for why these heuristics can make quick and accurate predictions.

1.1. Empirical Evidence

People often do not evaluate options in isolation but instead relative to at least one other option.

For instance, when judging the value or size of objects, ratings are more inconsistent—both within and between individuals—when objects are evaluated independently rather than in comparison to other objects (e.g., Gigerenzer & Richter, 1990). Different choices are made depending on the other options in the choice set (Shafir et al., 1993) and on the other options preceding an option when these are sequentially presented (Schwarz, 1999; Schwarz et al., 1985). Regret theory (Loomes & Sugden, 1987) and range-frequency theory (Parducci, 1965) both model the relative evaluation of options. Based on this and other evidence, Luce and von Winterfeldt (1994, p. 267) conclude that "no theory that is based on separate evaluations of gambles can possibly work." Thus, psychologically, a class of situations exists in which an option has a value only relative to other options.

The second assumption is that the value of an option is calculated by searching for all available information. This assumption is unrealistic in many contexts, such as on the Internet, where there is too much information and limited search is necessary. Similarly, experimental research has shown that people do not search exhaustively but employ limited search, both in internal search (in memory) and in external search (e.g., in libraries; Payne et al., 1993). A number of theories have modeled limited search, both within the framework of optimization (Stigler, 1961) and satisfying (Simon, 1955, 1956). In the extreme, search could terminate after the first reason that allows for a decision, thus making no trade-offs. Bröder (2000, 2003; Bröder & Schiffer, 2003) report that under various conditions (e.g., time pressure, high information costs) a majority of people rely on lexicographic heuristics that look up one reason at a time and stop as soon as a reason allows them to do so. Rieskamp and Otto (2006) and Rieskamp and Hoffrage (1999) show that people adapt the length of search to the structure of the problem.

Third, the experimental evidence shows that people often do not make trade-offs but base their decisions on heuristics that are "noncompensatory," which means that low values on one attribute (value or probability) cannot be compensated by high values on others. These no-trade-off heuristics include lexicographic models, conjunctive rules, disjunctive rules, and elimination-by-aspects (see also Lilly, 1994). Consider this classic review of 45 studies in which the process of decision making was investigated by means of Mouselab, eye movement, and other process tracking techniques (Ford et al., 1989). Varying between studies, the choices to be made included apartments, microwaves, and birth control methods:

> "The results firmly demonstrate that noncompensatory strategies were the dominant mode used by decision makers. Compensatory strategies were typically used only when the number of alternatives and dimensions were small or after a number of alternatives have been eliminated from consideration" (p. 75).

Consistent with this result, most subsequent studies that reported trade-offs have used only a small number of attributes (typically only 2 to 4) and have fitted the data by means of conjoint analysis or other linear models without testing lexicographic or other no-trade-off models. Studies that investigated consumer choice on the Internet and in other situations with large numbers of alternatives and cues—and that tested models with stopping rules—concluded that a majority of participants followed noncompensatory processes. For instance, Yee et al. (2007) reported that when people had a choice between 32 SmartPhones that varied on six cues, noncompensatory models predicted their choices better than Bayesian and other models that assume trade-offs did. Similarly, when people chose between cameras varying on seven attributes with two to six levels each, noncompensatory strategies again provided the best prediction: 58% relied on one attribute only, 33% relied on two attributes, and only 2% used three attributes (Gilbride & Allenby, 2004). Experiments in which participants chose a product (such as an answering machine or toaster) from the Web sites CompareNet and Jango showed the same result: The larger the number of alternatives offered, the more customers relied on a no-trade-off strategy (Jedetski et al., 2002). Bröder and his colleagues (Bröder, 2000; Bröder &

Schiffer, 2003) conducted 20 studies, concluding that a lexicographic heuristic, take-the-best, is used under a number of conditions such as when information is costly and the variability of the validity of the attributes is high. Bröder and Gaissmaier (2007) and Nosofsky and Bergert (2007) showed that take-the-best predicts response times better than weighted additive and exemplar models. Thus, the experimental evidence strongly suggests that heuristics that rely on limited search and do not make tradeoffs are in people's "adaptive toolbox" (Gigerenzer and Selten, 2001), and that these heuristics are selected in a sensitive way according to the structure of the problem (Gigerenzer et al., 1999; Lopes, 1995; Payne et al., 1993).

1.2. Prescriptive Reasons

The empirical evidence cited above shows that people proceed differently from assumptions 1 to 3. Relying on limited search and foregoing trade-offs, however, does not generally imply that these decisions are inferior or irrational. First, institutions routinely apply lexicographic rules in designing environments in order to make them safer and more transparent and allow human minds to operate in an efficient way. Which vehicle has the right of way at a crossing is defined by a lexicographic rule, not by a trade-off between the police officer's hand signal, the color of the traffic light, the traffic sign, and where the other car is coming from. Similarly, in soccer and hockey, the national and international associations agreed on lexicographic rules to determine the final standing within a group of competing teams. The Arabic number system allows using a simple lexicographic rule to decide which of two numbers is larger, employing order and limited search unavailable in other systems.

Second, lexicographic heuristics can also be accurate. Under certain conditions, they are more accurate than multiple regression and other linear models that make tradeoffs (Gigerenzer et al., 1999; Martignon & Hoffrage, 2002; Hogarth & Karelaia, 2005, 2006; Baucells et al., 2008), as well as nonlinear models such as neural networks and classification and regression trees (Brighton, 2006). Lexicographic heuristics can even be optimal (Katsikopoulos &

Martignon, 2006). We would like to emphasize these results, given that ever since lexicographic rules were first proposed in economics by Carl Menger, decision researchers have often dismissed them as a form of irrationality (see also Fishburn, 1974). But how can it be that heuristics are accurate?

In fact, there are good mathematical reasons for their accuracy. First, the heuristics tend to be robust. That is, they do not lose much of their accuracy between fitting known data and predicting new data. In contrast, models with numerous free parameters tend to overfit the data and lose accuracy in prediction (Roberts & Pashler, 2000). Second, lexicographic heuristics can exploit a number of structural properties, such as the presence of cumulatively dominating options in the choice set (Baucells et al., 2008) or large differences in the statistical informativeness of attributes (Martignon & Hoffrage, 2002; Hogarth & Karelaia, 2005, 2006; Katsikopoulos & Fasolo, 2006; Katsikopoulos & Martignon, 2006). Simulation studies have shown that these properties are relatively common.

A major unresolved problem in the tradition of revising EVT and EUT by using free parameters is that none of the estimated sets of parameters in models such as cumulative prospect theory can *simultaneously* account for buying lottery tickets, buying insurance policies, the Allais paradox, and other choice patterns observed in the literature (Neilson & Stowe, 2002). For instance, the functions estimated by Camerer and Ho (1994) and Wu and Gonzalez (1996) imply that people will purchase neither lottery tickets nor insurance policies. Moreover, Neilson and Stowe (2002) concluded that the troubles run deeper; they showed that no parameter combinations allow for these two behaviors *and* a series of choices made by a large majority of participants and reasonable risk premia. Similarly, Blavatskyy (2005) showed that the conventional parameterizations of cumulative prospect theory do not explain the St. Petersburg paradox. Overall, the parameter values fitted to one set of data are unlikely to be robust, in the sense of generating accurate predictions for new sets of data. On the other hand, simple heuristics such as the priority heuristic have no free parameters and tend to be robust (Gigerenzer et al., 1999; Martignon & Hoffrage, 2002).

2. THE PRIORITY HEURISTIC

The priority heuristic specifies how people choose between two gambles by (1) evaluating the gambles in relation to each other (as opposed to independently), (2) relying on limited search (as opposed to using all information), and (3) without making trade-offs between attributes (values and probabilities). The priority heuristic specifies how values and probabilities are ordered according to a priority rule, how a stopping rule terminates the search for information, and how a decision is made based on the available information. Unlike the priority heuristic, prospect theory and other modifications of EUT assume exhaustive search and they have no stopping rules, and thus the order of attributes is assumed to be of no importance. The heuristic does not need nonlinear transformations of value and probability but takes attributes in their natural currencies (i.e., it uses objective values and objective probabilities). Finally, the priority heuristic does not have any free parameters.

For a couple of two-outcome gambles with non-negative values (hereafter referred to as *gains*), the priority heuristic implements the following sequential process:

Priority rule Go through attributes in the order: minimum gain, probability of minimum gain, maximum gain.

Stopping rule Stop information search if the minimum gains differ by one tenth (or more) of the maximum gain (across the two gambles); otherwise, stop search if probabilities of minimum gain differ by 0.1 (or more).

Decision rule Choose the gamble that is more attractive in the attribute (gain or probability) that stopped search.

We will refer to the one tenth of the maximum gain as the aspiration level for gains and to 0.1 as that for probabilities.[1] The more *attractive* gamble is the one with the higher (minimum or maximum) gain or with the lower probability of minimum gain. The first step of the priority heuristic—comparing minimum gains—is identical to the minimax heuristic except that there is an aspiration level that determines whether mini-max is followed or not. The last step—compar-ing maximum gains—is identical to the maximax heuristic.

For nonpositive values (hereafter called *losses*), the difference is that "gain" is replaced by "loss." The more attractive loss is the lower one and the more attractive probability of minimum loss is the higher one. In this paper, we do not consider gambles that obtain both gains and losses. If the gambles have more than two out-comes, the probability of the maximum gain (or loss) is the fourth attribute. If no attribute leads to a prediction, a gamble is picked randomly. The heuristic applies to "difficult" choices, that is, nondominated gambles and gambles where the expected values are relatively close (see below). If instead one alternative dominates the other, or the expected values are far apart, the assumption is that choice is made without going through the process.[2]

We now explain in more detail how the parameters of the priority heuristic were set a-priori according to empirical evidence and logical constraints. The priority heuristic has three fixed parameters: the order of attributes and the two aspiration levels for values and probabilities. Consider the order of attributes first, using the example of two-outcome gambles with non-negative values. A simple gamble with two outcomes has four attributes: minimum and maximum gains, and their respective probabili-ties. This amounts to 24 possible orderings. The logical constraint that the two probabilities are complementary reduces the number of attri-butes to three, and the number of orderings to six. Empirical evidence suggests that values are more important than probabilities (for a review, see Brandstätter et al., 2006). For instance, insur-ance buyers focus on the potential large loss rather than on the low probabilities; lottery ticket buyers focus on the big gains rather than small probabilities (Daston, 1988); emotional outcomes tend to override the impact of proba-bilities (Sunstein, 2003); and in the extreme, people neglect probabilities altogether and base their choices on the immediate feeling elicited by the gravity or benefits of future events

(Loewenstein et al., 2001). If gains are the first consideration, this reduces the possible number of orders from six to four. But which gain is con-sidered first, the minimum or the maximum gain? The empirical evidence seems to favor the minimum gain, consistent with the motivation to avoid the worst outcome and to avoid failure (Heckhausen, 1991). This further reduces the number of possible orders to two. Experiments indicate that for most people, the probability of the minimum gain is ranked second (Brandstätter et al., 2006; Slovic, Griffin, & Tversky, 1990, study 5). This results in the order: minimum gain, probability of minimum gain, maximum gain.

Which difference in minimum gains is large enough to stop the process and choose the gamble with the higher minimum gain? The existence and operation of aspiration levels has been long demonstrated in choice (Lopes, 1995). Empirical evidence suggests that this aspiration level is not fixed but increases with the maxi-mum gain, and it is defined by our cultural base-10 system (Albers, 2001). This leads to the hypothesis that the aspiration level is one tenth of the maximum gain. Furthermore, unlike the value scale, which has open ends, the probability scale is bounded at both ends. There are several reasons why the aspiration level for probabilities has to be a difference rather than a ratio (Leland, 2002). The most important is that probabilities, unlike gains, have complements, so that an increase from 0.10 to 0.15 is equivalent to a decrease from 0.90 to 0.85; this point is captured by differences but not by ratios. A simple hypoth-esis is that one tenth of the probability scale, that is, 10 percentage points difference, is large enough. Empirical evidence suggests that people typically do not make more fine-grained differ-ences except at the ends of the probability scale (Albers, 2001).

This is not to say that other parameter values would be impossible; given the consistent report of individual differences, they might in fact explain some of these. As the remainder of the paper will make clear, however, the intent is to show that a lexicographic model based on crude estimates of order and aspiration levels, that has been successful in predicting people's choice of gambles, can be shown to imply major "anomalies" in choice.

2.1. Predictive Power

To illustrate how the heuristic works, consider one of the problems posed by Allais (1952/1979), known as the Allais paradox, where people choose first between gambles A and B:

A: 100,000,000 with probability 1.00
B: 500,000,000 with probability 0.10
     100,000,000 with probability 0.89
     0 with probability 0.01

By subtracting a 0.89 probability to win 100 million from both gambles A and B, Allais obtained the following gambles, C and D:

C: 100,000,000 with probability 0.11
     0 with probability 0.89
D: 500,000,000 with probability 0.10
     0 with probability 0.90

The majority of people chose gamble A over B and D over C (MacCrimmon, 1968) which constitutes a violation of the independence axiom of EUT (see below). EUT does not predict whether A or B will be chosen; it only makes conditional predictions such as "if A is chosen, then C is chosen." The priority heuristic, in contrast, makes stronger predictions: It predicts whether A or B will be chosen, and whether C or D will be chosen. Consider the choice between A and B. The maximum gain is 500 million and therefore the aspiration level for gains is 50 million. The difference between the minimum gains equals $(100-0) = 100$ million that exceeds the aspiration level, and search is stopped. The gamble with the more attractive minimum gain is A. Thus the heuristic predicts the majority choice correctly.

In the choice between C and D, minimum gains are equal. Thus the next attribute is looked up. The difference between the probabilities of minimum gains equals $0.90-0.89 = 0.01$ which is smaller than the aspiration level for probabilities of 0.1. Thus the choice is decided by the last attribute, maximum gain, in which gamble D is more attractive. This prediction is again consistent with the choice of the majority. Thus the priority heuristic predicts the Allais paradox.

How well does this simple heuristic overall explain people's choices? Brandstätter et al. (2006) compared three modifications of EUT—cumulative prospect theory (Tversky & Kahneman, 1992), security-potential/aspiration theory (Lopes & Oden, 1999), and transfer-of-attention-exchange model (Birnbaum & Chavez, 1997)—with the priority heuristic on how well they could predict the majority choice in four published sets of gambles. The sets were from Kahneman and Tversky (1979), Tversky and Kahneman (1992), Lopes and Oden (1999), and Erev et al. (2002) and included various kinds of gambles: two-outcome gambles, choices based on certainty equivalence, five-outcome gambles, and randomly generated gambles. Across the 260 pairs of gambles, the priority heuristic predicted 87% of the choices correctly, followed by 79%, 77%, and 69% for security-potential/aspiration theory, cumulative prospect theory, and transfer-of-attention-exchange model, respectively. Ten other heuristics (including minimax and maximax) were also tested and all performed less well, with many at chance level.

The limits of the predictive power of the priority heuristic were analyzed using a set of 450 pairs of gambles. The priority heuristic was more predictive than the modifications of EUT when the problems were difficult in the sense that the expected values of the two gambles are close, with a ratio of at most 2. When the problems were easy (ratio is larger than 2), the modifications of EUT did better than the priority heuristic, but none of them could outperform EVT. Both the priority heuristic and EVT use objective monetary values and probabilities, and no modifications of EUT that uses nonlinear transformations were more predictive. This raises the possibility that objective values and probabilities may suffice for predicting people's choices.

In summary, the first limit of the priority heuristic is that it does not account better than EVT and modifications of EUT for easy problems. The second limit is that it does not model individual differences (unless one introduces free parameters for order and aspiration levels that, however, should be measured independently rather than fitted to the data). We now show that this simple heuristic, even without free parameters, implies major violations of EUT.

3. EXPLAINING VIOLATIONS OF EUT

For the remainder of this article, we denote values by x, y,..., probabilities by p, p',..., and gambles by G, G',.... Gambles are also symbolized explicitly, for example, for a simple gamble, $(x, p; 0, 1 - p)$. It is assumed that probabilities do not equal 0 or 1. A gamble where x occurs with probability 1 is denoted by $(x, 1)$. Compound gambles are symbolized by $(G, p; G', 1 - p)$. For our analyses, we assume that compound gambles are equivalent to their reduced simple-gamble form. This, however, does not mean that we also assume that people obey accounting axioms.

The relation "$>_h$" on the space of pairs of gambles is defined as follows: $G >_h G'$ if and only if the priority heuristic predicts that G is chosen over G' without using a random device. If the heuristic has to use such a device, we write $G =_h G'$. If $G >_h G'$ or $G =_h G'$, we write $G \geq_h G'$. To simplify, in the remainder of this article, we will use a version of the priority heuristic in which search is *not* stopped if the value and probability differences are equal to their respective aspiration levels. For example, if the probabilities of minimum gain equal 0.35 and 0.25, their difference, 0.10, is not large enough to stop search.

A core axiom of EUT is the independence axiom: for all gambles G, G', G'' and for all p, if G is preferred to G', then $(G, p; G'', 1 - p)$ is preferred to $(G', p; G'', 1 - p)$. Two kinds of empirical findings, common consequence effects and common ratio effects, violate the independence axiom (Starmer, 2000).[3] We start this section by characterizing the conditions on values and probabilities under which the priority heuristic predicts these effects.

The priority heuristic predicts *common consequence* (CC) effects if the following statement holds:

$$(y, 1) >_h (G, p, y, 1 - p)$$
$$\text{and } (G, p; 0, 1 - p) >_h (y, p; 0, 1 - p),$$
$$\text{where } G = (x, p'; 0, 1 - p') \text{ and } x > y > 0. \quad (CC)$$

The common consequence is y in the first pair of gambles and 0 in the second pair of gambles (occurring, in all cases, with probability $1 - p$). In the Allais paradox,[4] $y = 100,000,000$, $p = 0.11$, $x = 500,000,000$, and $p' = {}^{10}/_{11}$.

Result 1 (common consequence) Statement (CC) holds if and only if

$$y / x > 0.1 > p(1 - p')$$

Proof The reduced form of $(G, p; y, 1 - p)$ is $(x, pp'; y, 1 - p; 0, p(1 - p'))$. It is clear that $(y, 1)$ $>_h (x, pp'; y, 1 - p; 0, p(1 - p'))$ if and only if minimum gain stops search, that is, if and only if $y - 0 > (0.1)x$, or $y/x > 0.1$.

The reduced form of $(G, p; 0, 1 - p)$ is $(x, pp'; 0, 1 - pp')$. It holds that $(x, pp'; 0, 1 - pp')$ $>_h (y, p; 0, 1 - p)$ if and only if the probability of minimum gain does not stop search, that is, if and only if $(1 - pp') - (1 - p) < 0.1$, or $p(1 - p) < 0.1$.

Remark 1 In words, the priority heuristic implies common consequence effects whenever the minimum (nonzero) gain (of all gains in CC) is larger than one tenth of the maximum gain and the probability of a zero gain for the risky option in the first pair of gambles (in CC) is smaller than one tenth. These factors of one-tenth correspond to the aspiration levels in the priority heuristic. The condition in Result 1 is fulfilled in the Allais paradox: $y/x = 0.2$ and $p(1 - p') = 0.01$.

Common ratio effects can be modeled as follows (Starmer, 2000): people's choice between $(x, \lambda p; 0, 1 - \lambda p)$ and $(y, p; 0, 1 - p)$ where $x > y > 0$ and $\lambda > 0$ changes as p changes (x, y, and λ are held constant). For example, consider the following choice problem:

A: 6,000 with probability 0.45
    0 with probability 0.55
B: 3,000 with probability 0.90
    0 with probability 0.10

Kahneman and Tversky (1979) found that the majority of people (86%) chose gamble B. Now consider a second problem:

C: 6,000 with probability 0.001
    0 with probability 0.999
D: 3,000 with probability 0.002
    0 with probability 0.998

Here most people (73%) chose gamble C. This is a common ratio effect with $x = 6{,}000$, $y = 3{,}000$ and $\lambda = 1/2$. Note that the gambles have equal expected values (this need not be the case for all common ratio problems). This finding is referred to as a "possibility" effect to emphasize that choices change as gains change, from probable in the A-or-B problem, to merely possible in the C-or-D problem. The priority heuristic predicts that gamble B is chosen because minimum gains are equal (0) while probability of minimum gain stops search ($0.55 - 0.10 > 0.10$) and B is more attractive in it. The priority heuristic predicts that C is chosen because it is more attractive in maximum gain.

The priority heuristic predicts *common ratio* (CR) effects for gambles with equal expected values if the following statement holds:

$$\left(y,\ p;\ 0, 1-p \right) >_h \left(x,\ \lambda p;\ 0, 1-\lambda p \right)$$
$$\text{and } \left(x,\ \lambda cp;\ 0, 1-\lambda cp \right) >_h \left(y,\ cp;\ 0, 1-cp \right), \quad (CR)$$
$$\text{where } x > y > 0,\ \lambda = y/x, c > 0.$$

In the example above, $c = 1/450$.

In both problems in (CR) the gamble with lower maximum gain (y) is chosen if and only if search stops by the probability of minimum gain. This follows because the minimum gains are always equal to zero and do not stop search. Computing the differences between the probabilities of minimum gain and rearranging terms, we have:

Result 2 (common ratio) Statement (CR) holds if and only if $\left(1 - \lambda \right) p > 0.1 > \left(1 - \lambda \right) cp$.

Remark 2 In words, the priority heuristic implies common ratio effects (for gambles with equal expected values) if and only if the difference between the probabilities of minimum (zero) gain in the first pair of gambles (in CR) is larger than one tenth and the difference between the probabilities of minimum gain (zero) in the second pair of gambles is smaller than one tenth. This one tenth corresponds to the aspiration level for probabilities in the priority heuristic.

To model the next violation of EUT, we define, for any gamble G, its *opposite* $-G$ to be the gamble that obtains value $-x$ when G obtains x

(and with the same probability). For example, if $G = (5, 0.6; 0, 0.4)$, then $-G = (-5, 0.6; 0, 0.4)$.

Kahneman and Tversky (1979) found that choices are reversed when gambles are substituted by their opposites—these are called *reflection* effects. For example, 80% of their participants chose $(3{,}000, 1)$ over $(4{,}000, 0.8; 0, 0.2)$ but 92% chose $(-4{,}000, 0.8; 0, 0.2)$ over $(-3{,}000, 1)$. The priority heuristic predicts the choice of $(3{,}000, 1)$ based on minimum gain and the choice of $(-4{,}000, 0.8; 0, 0.2)$ based on minimum loss. More generally, it is easy to see that the following holds:

Result 3 (reflection) $G >_h G'$ if and only if $-G' >_h -G$.

Remark 3 Because the priority heuristic uses the same process for both gains and losses, it considers minimum gains and minimum losses first, respectively. Prioritizing minimum gains reflects the motivation to avoid the worst, while prioritizing minimum losses reflects the motivation to seek the best. The same reasoning applies to the other attributes, resulting in reflection effects.

The final violation of EUT we consider is the *fourfold pattern of risk attitude* (for comparing a gamble with one outcome to a gamble with two outcomes; Tversky & Kahneman, 1992). This finding challenges the assumption of universal risk aversion and expresses the purchase of both lottery tickets and insurance policies. People were found to be risk taking for losses: for example, Tversky and Fox (1995) found that people's median certainty equivalent (CE) for $(-100, 0.95; 0, 0.05)$ equals -84. But Tversky and Fox (1995) also found that people are risk taking for gains if the gain probability is low—the CE of $(100, 0.05; 0, 0.95)$ was 14. Conversely, people were found to be risk averse for high-probability gains such as $(100, 0.95; 0, 0.05; \text{CE} = 78)$ and for low-probability losses such as $(-100, 0.05; 0, 0.95; \text{CE} = -8)$.

The priority heuristic can predict this pattern. Result 4 below refers to the case where the risky gamble has one nonzero outcome and Result 5 is the generalization for two nonzero outcomes.

Result 4 (Fourfold Pattern) Let $x > 0$. It holds that (i) $(px, 1) >_h (x, p; 0, 1 - p)$ if and only if $p > 0.1$, and (ii) $(-x, p; 0, 1 - p) >_h (-px, 1)$ if and only if $p > 0.1$.

Proof 1. If $p > 0.1$, minimum gain stops search because $px - 0 = px > (0.1)x$. Thus $(xp, 1) >_h (x, p; 0, 1 - p)$. If $p \leq 0.1$, probability of minimum gain is also looked up but it does not stop search. The gamble $(x, p; 0, 1 - p)$ has more attractive maximum gain than $(px, 1)$, thus $(x, p; 0, 1 - p) >_h (xp, 1)$.

2. It suffices to combine (i) with Result 3. ∎

Result 5 (Fourfold Pattern) Let $x > y > 0$, $z = px + (1 - p)y$, and $p^* = (0.1)x/(x - y)$. It holds that (i) $(z, 1) >_h (x, p; y, 1 - p)$ if and only if $p > p^*$, and (ii) $(-x, p; -y, 1 - p) >_h (-z, 1)$ if and only if $p > p^*$.

   Proof 1. If $p > p^*$, minimum gain stops search because $z - y = px + (1 - p)y - y = p(x-y) > p^*(x-y) = (0.1)x$. Thus $(z, 1) >_h (x, p; y, 1 - p)$. If $p \leq p^*$, minimum gain does not stop search. The gamble $(x, p; y, 1 - p)$ has more attractive probability of minimum gain as well as maximum gain than $(z, 1)$. Thus, $(x, p; y, 1 - p) >_h (z, 1)$.

2. It suffices to combine (i) with Result 3. ∎

Remark 4 These proofs show that the fourfold pattern can be explained by the priority heuristic because of the following mechanism: In different choice problems, different attributes stop search.

Remark 5 In Result 4, a probability p is considered to be low whenever $p \leq 0.1$ and in Result 5, a probability is considered to be low whenever $p \leq p^*$. Note that $p^* = 0.1$ when $y = 0$.

Remark 6 If one stays within the EUT framework and retains assumptions 1–3, the fourfold pattern can be explained by using a probability weighting function. For example, Prelec (1998) used the probability weighting function $w(p) = \exp(-(-\ln p)^a)$. In recent years, some researchers have elevated probability weighting to the status of a self-standing empirical phenomenon. This appears to have been established mostly by thought experiments: "Is it not clear that an increase from 0.01 to 0.02 in the probability of winning a prize means much more than

an increase from 0.10 to 0.11?" We are not aware of direct evidence; rather, the empirical data requires nonlinear probability weighting functions if one wants to retain assumptions 2 and 3. In contrast, Results 1 to 5 show that weighting of either probabilities or values is not necessary for analytically deriving major deviations from EUT. As mentioned above, this analytical result is confirmed by experimental evidence (Brandstätter et al., 2006). Across a total of 710 monetary choice problems, two striking results were obtained. When the ratio of expected values was between 1 and 2 (difficult problems), the priority heuristic predicted majority choice better than modifications of EUT, including cumulative prospect theory and heuristics such as minimax. When the ratio was larger (easy problems), the classical theory of expected value predicted best. Models that relied on nonlinear weighting of probabilities, such as cumulative prospect theory, were in each case second-best to either priority or expected value. Neither the heuristic nor the theory of expected value uses nonlinear weighting.[5]

   Our results are compatible with the interpretation of the priority heuristic as a "tie-breaking rule" that applies to situations where the choice options look similar and no-conflict solutions such as dominance and Rubinstein's similarity rule (see Section 5) cannot be found (Brandstätter et al., 2006; Erev et al., 2008). The famous anomalies emerge in exactly these cases.

   In summary, in this section we have shown that the priority heuristic implies common consequence effects, common ratio effects, reflection effects, and the fourfold pattern of risk attitude (people are risk averse for gains if probabilities are high and for losses if probabilities are low, and risk taking for gains if probabilities are low and for losses if probabilities are high). Note that because the priority heuristic has no free parameters, it is also true that the heuristic predicts these phenomena simultaneously.

   We want to emphasize that it is a major strength of a model of risky choice to predict these phenomena rather than simply being potentially consistent with the phenomenon. Viscusi (1989) has made the same point when he showed that his prospective reference theory predicts, rather than assumes, violations of EUT such as the Allais paradox and the overweighting of low-probability events. For example, he derived the key property $P(p)/P(q) \leq P(ap) = P(aq)$ (for $p < q$ and $a < 1$) of the probability weighting function of prospect theory (Viscusi, 1989, pp. 249–250).

4. WHAT PREFERENCES DOES THE PRIORITY HEURISTIC REPRESENT?

The priority heuristic does not assume preferences on the space of gambles—it is a model for the process of comparison between two gambles. It is possible, however, to study which axioms the preferences, represented by the heuristic, satisfy. EUT is based on the axioms of *independence* and *transitivity*, together with the more technical axioms of *completeness* and *continuity*. We have already shown that independence[6] is not satisfied by the heuristic, consistent with experimental evidence. Does the heuristic allow for occasional intransitive preferences? The heuristic represents transitive (TR) preferences if the following holds:

For all $G >_h G'$ and $G' >_h G''$, it holds that $G >_h G''$. (TR)

(TR) would hold if the priority heuristic evaluated options independently and assigned a single numerical value to them. The heuristic, however, evaluates options relative to each other and can predict occasional intransitivities. Take, for example, $G = (3, 0.49; 0, 0.51)$, $G' = (2, 0.55; 0, 0.45)$, and $G'' = (1, 0.6; 0, 0.4)$. Then, by maximum gain, $G >_h G'$ and $G' >_h G''$, but, by probability of minimum gain, $G'' >_h G$. More generally, the following holds:

Result 6 (transitivity) Let G, G', and G'' be gambles with one zero and one nonzero outcome. (i) If $G >_h G'$ and $G' >_h G''$ both hold by probability of minimum gain, (TR) holds. In the other cases, it is possible that (TR) does not hold. (ii) If $G >_h G'$ and $G' >_h G''$ both hold by probability of minimum loss, (TR) holds. In the other cases, it is possible that (TR) does not hold.

Proof (1) For this proof, let $G = (x, p; 0, 1 - p)$, $G' = (x', p'; 0, 1 - p')$, and $G'' = (x'', p''; 0, 1 - p'')$. We assume that $G >_h G'$ and $G' >_h G''$.

If $G >_h G'$ and $G' >_h G''$ both hold by probability of minimum gain, it has to be that $G >_h G''$ because $p - p' > 0.1$ and $p' - p'' > 0.1$ imply $p - p'' > 0.1$.

Next we show that for the following three cases it can be that $G'' >_h G$.

If $G >_h G'$ by probability of minimum gain and $G' >_h G''$ by maximum gain, it holds that $p - p' > 0.1$, $|p' - p''| \leq 0.1$, and $x' > x''$. These do not exclude $|p - p''| \leq 0.1$ and $x'' > x$ which means that $G'' >_h G$ is possible (e.g., take $x = 1$, $x' = 3$, $x'' = 2$, $p = 0.51$, $p' = 0.4$, and $p'' = 0.45$).

If $G >_h G'$ by maximum gain and $G' >_h G''$ by probability of minimum gain, it holds that $|p - p'| \leq 0.1$, $x > x'$, and $|p - p''| > 0.1$. It can again be that $G'' >_h G$ because it is again possible that $|p - p''| \leq 0.1$ and $x'' > x$ (take, e.g., $x = 2$, $x' = 1$, $x'' = 3$, $p = 0.45$, $p' = 0.51$, $p'' = 0.4$).[7]

The last case, where $G >_h G'$ and $G' >_h G''$ both hold by maximum gain, also does not exclude that $G'' >_h G$. This is illustrated by the example preceding the result.

(2) It suffices to combine (i) with Result 3. ∎

Remark 7 Note that, according to the priority heuristic, the psychological reason for intransitivity is a threshold phenomenon, well known from psychophysics: when two differences (in the last case in the proof of Result 6 in probabilities of minimum gain), each below the aspiration level (in that case, 0.06 and 0.05) are combined, the result (0.11) can exceed the aspiration level, and this may result in an intransitivity. Note that such intransitivity due to thresholds should not be seen as a form of irrationality. Our sensory systems, visual or tactile, rely on such thresholds and produce intransitivity in rare occasions but that does not mean that these systems are inadequate. Every intelligent system produces systematic errors in an uncertain world (Gigerenzer, 2005). Note that others have also argued that transitivity may not be normatively compelling (Fishburn, 1991) or, more generally, have discussed the potential value of inconsistency (Engel & Daston, 2006). The result above can be extended as follows:

Result 7 (transitivity) Let G, G', and G'' be gambles with two nonzero outcomes. (i) If $G >_h G'$ and $G' >_h G''$ both hold by minimum gain or by probability of minimum gain, (TR) holds. In the other cases, it is possible that (TR) does not hold. (ii) If $G >_h G'$ and $G' >_h G''$ both hold by minimum loss or by probability of minimum loss, (TR) holds. In the other cases, it is possible that (TR) does not hold.

Proof In addition to the four cases that are consistent with $G >_h G'$ and $G' >_h G''$ for gambles with one nonzero outcome, there are five more to be considered for gambles with two nonzero outcomes: (a) $G >_h G'$ and $G' >_h G''$ both hold by minimum gain, (b) $G >_h G'$ holds by minimum gain and $G' >_h G''$ holds by probability of minimum gain, (c) $G >_h G'$ holds by minimum gain and $G' >_h G''$ holds by maximum gain, (d) $G >_h G'$ holds by probability of minimum gain and $G' >_h G''$ holds by minimum gain, and (e) $G >_h G'$ holds by maximum gain and $G' >_h G''$ holds by minimum gain.

For this proof, let $G = (x, p; y, 1 - p)$ $G' = (x',p';y', 1 - p')$ and $G'' = (x'', p''; y'', 1 - p'')$ with $x > y$, $x' > y'$, and $x'' > y''$

In (a), it holds that $y - y' > (0.1) \max \{x, x'\}$ and $y' - y'' > (0.1)\max \{x', x''\}$, and thus also $y - y'' > (0.1)(\max\{x, x'\}+ \max\{x', x''\})$. Because $\max\{x, x'\} + \max\{x', x''\} > \max\{x, x', x''\}$, it also holds that $G >_h G''$.

In (b), it holds that $y - y' > (0.1) \max\{x, x'\}$, $|y' - y''| \leq (0.1) \max\{x', x''\}$, and $p' - p''>0.1$. These do not exclude $|y - y''| \leq (0.1) \max\{x, x''\}$, $|p-p''|\leq 0.1$, and $x'' > x$, which means that $G'' >_h G$ is possible: for example, take $x = 5$, $x' = 6$, $x''= 11$, $p = 0.4$, $p' = 0.6$, $p'' = 0.45$, $y = 3$, $y' = 1$, and $y'' = 2$.

In (c), it holds that $y - y' > (0.1) \max\{x, x'\}$, $|y' - y''|\leq (0.1) \max\{x', x''\}$, $|p' - p''|\leq 0.1$, and $x' > x''$ These do not exclude $|y - y''|\leq (0.1) \max\{x, x''\}$, and $p'' - p > 0.1$, which means that $G'' >_h G$ is possible: for example, take $x = 11$, $x' - 6$, $x'' = 5$, $p = 0.4$, $p' = 0.55$, $p'' = 0.6$, $y = 3$, $y' = 1$, and $y'' = 2$.

In (d), it holds that $|y - y'| \leq (0.1) \max\{x, x'\}$, $p - p' > 0.1$, and $y' - y'' (0.1) \max \{x', x''\}$. These do not exclude $| y - y'' | \leq (0.1) \max\{x, x''\}, |p'' - p| \leq 0.1$, and $x'' > x$, which means that $G''_h > G$ is possible: for example, take $x = 11$, $x' - 5$, $x'' = 6$, $p = 0.6$, $p' = 0.4$, $p'' = 0.55$, $y = 2$, $y' = 3$, and $y'' = 1$.[8]

In (e), it holds that $|y - y'| \leq (0.1)\max \{x, x'\}$, $|p-p'|\leq 0.1$, $x > x'$, and $y' - y'' > (0.1)\max \{x', x''\}$. These do not exclude $|y - y'| \leq (0.1)\max \{x, x''\}$

and $p''- p > 0.1$, which means that $G'' >_h G$ is possible: for example, take $x = 11$, $x' = 5$, $x'' = 6$, $p = 0.45$, $p' = 0.4$, $p'' = 0.6$, $y = 2$, $y' = 3$, and $y'' = 1$.

(2) It suffices to combine (i) with Result 3. ∎

The independence axiom is often weakened to *betweenness*. Another commonly used axiom is *monotonicity*. In the remainder of this section, we examine whether the preferences represented by the priority heuristic satisfy completeness (CM), continuity (CN), betweenness (BE), and monotonicity (MO). That is, we check whether the following statements hold:

For all G, G', it holds that $G >_h G'$ or $G' >_h G$
  or $G =_h G'$.   (CM)
For all $G >_h G' >_h G''$, there exists $0 < p < 1$:
  $G' =_h (G, p; G'', 1 - p)$.   (CN)
For all $G >_h G'$ and $0 < p < 1$, it holds that
  $G >_h (G, p; G', 1 - p) >_h G'$.   (BE)
If, for $i = 1, \dots, n-1, \Sigma_{j=1,\dots,i}\, p_j \geq \Sigma_{j=1,\dots,i}\, q_j$ and
  $x_1 \geq \dots \geq x_n$,
  then $(x_1, p_1; \dots; x_n, p_n) \geq_h (x_1, q_1; \dots; x_n, q_n).$ (MO)

Result 8 (other axioms) Statements (CM) and (MO) hold. Statements (CN) and (BE) do not.

Proof By the definition of the relation $">_h"$, (CM) holds.

For (MO) to hold it suffices to show that (a) $p_1 \geq q_1$ and (b) $p_n \leq q_n$. To show (a), we set $i = 1$ in the condition $\Sigma_{j=1,\dots,i}P_j \geq \Sigma_{j=1,\dots,i}\, q_j$. To show (b), we set $i = n - 1$ in the condition $\Sigma_{j=1,\dots,i}P_j \geq \Sigma_{j=1,\dots,i}\, q_j$ (and also use that $\Sigma_{j=1,\dots,n}P_j = \Sigma_{j=1,\dots,n}q_j = 1$).

To show that (CN) does not hold, we construct the following counterexample:

Take $G = (10, 0.8; 0, 0.2)$, $G' = (5, 0.6; 0, 0.4)$ and $G'' = (10, 0.4; 0, 0.6)$. By the probability of minimum gain, $G >_h G' >_h G''$. For an arbitrary p, the reduced form of $(G, p; G'', 1 - p)$ is $(10, (0.8)$ $p + 0.4(1 - p); 0, (0.2)\, p + 0.6(1 - p))$. But it is impossible that $(10, (0.8)\, p + 0.4\,(1 - p); 0, (0.2)$ $p + 0.6(1 - p)) =_h (5, 0.6; 0, 0.4)$ because maximum gains are unequal.

To show that (BE) does not hold, we construct a counterexample where $G >_h G'$ and

$0 < p < 1$ but it does not hold that $G >_h (G, p; G', 1 - p)$: Take $G = (5, 0.6; 1, 0.4)$, $G' = (20, 0.4; 2, 0.6)$ and $p = 0.9$. By the probability of minimum gain, $G >_h G'$. The reduced form of $(G, p; G', 1 - p)$ is $(20, 0.04; 5, 0.54; 2, 0.06; 1, 0.36)$. By the maximum gain, $(20, 0.04; 5, 0.54; 2, 0.06; 1, 0.36) >_h (5, 0.6; 1, 0.4)$. ∎

Remark 8 As seen in (BE), given that $G > i, G'$ and $0 < p < 1$, the betweenness axiom makes two requests (see also Camerer & Ho, 1994): $G >_h (G, p; G', 1 - p)$ (called *quasi-convexity*) and $(G, p; G', 1 - p) >_h G'$ (called *quasi-concavity*). Because the priority heuristic predicts reflection effects, it is easy to see that the counterexample to quasi-convexity, that uses gains, immediately suggests a counterexample to quasi-concavity, that uses losses, that is, $G = (-20, 0.4; -2, 0.6)$, $G' = (-5, 0.6; -1, 0.4)$ and $p = 0.1$. It turns out, however, that the nonstrict version of quasi-convexity holds for losses and that the nonstrict version of quasi-concavity holds for gains.

Result 9 (*nonstrict quasi-concavity*) For all gambles $G >_h G'$ with gains and for $0 < p < 1$, it holds that $(G, p; G', 1 - p) \geq_h G'$.

Proof We show that, given gambles $G >_h G'$ with gains and $0 < p < 1$, $G' >_h (G, p; G', 1 - p)$ is impossible. To begin with, it is obvious that $G' >_h (G, p; G', 1 - p)$ cannot hold by maximum gain.

For this proof, let x_G and p_G be, respectively, the minimum gain of G and its probability. Also, let x_G' and p_G' be, respectively, the minimum gain of G' and its probability.

Minimum gain cannot stop search and imply $G' >_h (G, p; G', 1 - p)$ because then it would also hold that $x_G' > x_G$ and that $x_G' - x_G$ exceeds the aspiration level for gains which imply that $G' >_h G$.

For the probability of minimum gain, we distinguish three cases: (a) $x_G' = x_G$, (b) $x_G' < x_G$, and (c) $x_G < x_G'$. For (a), (b), and (c) we will show that the probability of minimum gain does not stop search or that it cannot imply $G' >_h (G, p; G', 1 - p)$.

If (a) holds, the difference between the probabilities of minimum gains of G' and $(G, p; G', 1 - p)$ equals $p\, p_G + (1 - p)\, p_G' - p_G' = p(p_G - p_G') < p_G - p_G' \leq 0.1$, where the last inequality holds because $p_G - p_G' > 0.1$ would, together with (a), imply $G' >_h G$.

If (b) holds, $(G, p; G', 1 - p)$ is more attractive in probability of minimum gain than G' (because $(1 - p)\, p_G' < p_G'$) and thus it cannot be that $G' >_h (G, p; G', 1 - p)$.

If (c) holds, we only need to consider the case where G' is more attractive in probability of minimum gain than $(G, p; G', 1 - p)$. Then the difference between these probabilities equals $p\, p_G - p_G'$. For this to exceed the aspiration level for probabilities, it must be that $p > (0.1 + p_G')/p_G$. Because $1 > p$, this implies that $p_G - p_G' > 0.1$. But $p_G - p_G' > 0.1$, together with (c), implies $G' >_h G$. ∎

Remark 9 The strict version of Result 9 does not hold: As a counterexample, take $G = (10, 0.5; 0, 0.5)$, $G' = (10, 0.34; 0, 0.66)$ and $p = 0.5$.

Remark 10 Quasi-concave preferences indicate a preference for randomization: A mixture of equally desirable gambles is preferred to any of the gambles (Camerer & Ho, 1994, p. 173). Graphically, quasi-concave preferences are represented by convex indifference curves in the Marchak-Machina triangle. Combining Result 9 and Result 3, yields the following:

Result 10 (nonstrict quasi-convexity) For all gambles $G >_h G'$ with losses and for $0 < p < 1$, it holds that $G \geq_h (G, p; G', 1 - p)$. ∎

In summary, the priority heuristic represents preferences that are complete, monotone, and (nonstrictly) quasi-concave for gains and (nonstrictly) quasi-convex for losses and are, under some conditions, transitive. The preferences do not embody continuity and betweeness. More generally, instead of being based on axioms, the priority heuristic models choice by incorporating psychological principles: relative evaluation, search stopped by aspiration levels, and avoiding trade-offs. These psychological principles underlie our conception of bounded rationality. Other researchers have modeled bounded rationality in different but related ways.

5. RELATION TO RUBINSTEIN'S (1988) SIMILARITY MODEL

Rubinstein's (1988) model presupposes two similarity relations, one in the space of values and one in the space of probabilities; both are defined by six axioms. These relations play a similar role to the aspiration levels of the priority heuristic. For example, the relation "~" that is defined by $p \sim p'$ if and only if $|p - p'| \leq 0.1$ satisfies the six axioms (p. 148). The two relations can be seen as free parameters; in fact, for any relation "~" and for any scalar $k > 1$, there exist a strictly increasing and positive function H on the unit interval so that $x \sim y$ if and only if $1/k \leq H(x)/H(y) \leq k$ (p. 149).

Rubinstein models the choice between $(x, p; 0, 1 - p)$ and $(y, p'; 0, 1 - p')$ where $0 < x, p, y, p' < 1$. We write $x \sim y$ to denote that the two gains x and y are similar and $p \sim p'$ to denote that the two probabilities p and p' are similar. In the first step of the model it is asked if $x > y$ and $p > p'$. If yes, $(x, p; 0, 1 - p)$ is chosen. If not, in the second step, it is asked if one of the conditions $\{p \sim p'$ and not $(x \sim y)$ and $x > y\}$ or $\{x \sim y$ and not $(p \sim p')$ and $p > p'\}$ holds. If yes, $(x, p; 0, 1 - p)$ is chosen. If not, the model makes no prediction. For extensions, see Aizpurua et al. (1993), Leland (1994), and Buschena and Zilberman (1995, 1999).

Like the priority heuristic, the similarity model attempts to describe the process of choice and does not transform values and probabilities. However, it differs in so far as it does not employ limited search (except for the dominance check) and is not lexicographic because it does not specify an order in which values and probabilities are considered. Furthermore, it has an EUT representation (Rubinstein, 1988, pp. 150–151) and in this sense it implements independent evaluations that make trade-offs. Note that other similarity models do not have EUT representations (Leland, 1994). Finally, the predictions of the similarity model can be tuned because it has adjustable parameters.

Can Rubinstein's model reproduce the predictions of the priority heuristic? In the simple case of dominance, i.e., $x > y$ and $p > p'$, the two models make identical predictions. Can the parameters of the similarity model be set so that it reproduces the predictions of the priority heuristic in cases of *conflict*, that is, $x > y$ and $p < p'$, as well? This is not the case: For example, assume $|p - p'| \leq 0.1$; the priority heuristic then predicts that $(x, p; 0, 1 - p)$ is chosen. To match this for all x and y, the similarity relation in the space of

maximum gains needs to be such that for all x and y with $x > y$ it does *not* hold that $x \sim y$. But this means that any maximum gain would not be similar to any different maximum gain, which contradicts the axiom of nondegeneracy (Rubinstein, 1988, p. 148).

In summary, the similarity model keeps assumptions (4) and (5) of EVT, as the priority heuristic does. On the other hand, the similarity model does not employ limited search, is not lexicographic, and uses free parameters. Consistent with these conceptual differences, the predictions of the two models differ. In fact, the two models can be seen as complementary in the sense that the priority heuristic is a candidate for the third, unspecified step of the similarity model, when the choice is "difficult."

6. BOUNDED RATIONALITY

The concept of bounded rationality has been often defined as optimization under constraints, such as information and deliberation costs (Conlisk, 1996; Sargent, 1993).

Yet it also has been understood in a different way, in terms of a "map" of cognitive illusions (or anomalies), as in Kahneman (2003). Note that the first involves optimization and emphasizes rationality whereas the second does neither and instead emphasizes irrationality.

The priority heuristic does not involve computing an optimum but deals with limited information and time by using simple stopping rules that make it fast and frugal. But the heuristic is not an instance of cognitive illusions either. There exists a third interpretation of bounded rationality. We see the priority heuristic in the bounded rationality framework proposed by Gigerenzer and Selten (2001): modeling how people actually make decisions based on an "adaptive toolbox" of heuristics that are fast and frugal without optimization computations.

The priority heuristic is a member of a class of models known as *one-reason decision making* (Gigerenzer, 2004), which also includes fast-and-frugal trees (Martignon et al., 2003) and take-the-best (Gigerenzer & Goldstein, 1996). These models implement limited search with stopping rules (in contrast to assumption 2), make no trade-offs (in contrast to assumption 3), do not transform the information given (following assumptions 4 and 5), and some assume that options are evaluated relatively (while others model independent evaluations as in assumption 1).

Since the codification of rational choice in the seventeenth century in terms of the maximization of the expected value, the dominant strand for dealing with discrepancies between theory and evidence has been the gradual transformation of the values and probabilities in the equation. For example, Daniel Bernoulli argued that rich men valued increases in their wealth less than poor men did and proposed that the utility of money is a logarithmic function.[9] The more general characteristics—that options are considered independently, that all pieces of information are used and that these are weighted and added—have remained largely unchallenged.

In this paper, we showed that a simple heuristic using relative evaluation, limited search, and no trade-offs implies common consequence effects, common ratio effects, reflection effects and the fourfold pattern of risk attitude (people are risk-averse for gains if probabilities are high, risk-taking for gains if probabilities are low (as in buying lottery tickets), risk-averse for losses when probabilities are low (as in buying insurance policies), and risk-taking for losses when probabilities are high). Because the heuristic has no free parameters, it predicts these phenomena simultaneously, rather than being potentially consistent with the phenomena. We also examined the kind of preferences represented by the heuristic and found conditions under which it obeys axioms such as transitivity, betweenness, and monotonicity. These analytical results, combined with the experimental results reviewed, contribute to the objective of constructing a descriptive theory of decision under risk in the spirit of bounded rationality.

NOTES

1. When we use the term "nonlinear" transformation in this paper, we refer to continuous functions as in the probability weighting function of prospect theory, not to a simple step-function as represented by the aspiration levels. For simplicity,

we do not deal here with the idea that aspiration levels for values are rounded to the closest prominent number (Brandstätter et al., 2006, p. 413).

2. If the expected values are relatively far apart (by a factor of more than 2; see below), people can often "see" that the choice is obvious. Similarly, one can see that 71×11 is larger than 18×13 without calculating the products. There are probably a number of simple heuristics that help us to see which is larger, such as Rubinstein's similarity rule (see Section 5) and cancellation: If two numbers are close, ignore them, and compare the other two numbers. In the example, 11 and 13 would be ignored.

3. Because we have assumed that the reduction of compound gambles holds, violations of independence come from violations of so-called preference axioms such as consequence monotonicity (Luce, 1990).

4. Another approach to studying the Allais paradox is to decompose it into axioms so that, if they all hold, the paradox disappears. Birnbaum (2004) identified three such axioms: transitivity, restricted branch independence, and coalescing. We derive conditions under which the priority heuristic predicts transitivity in the next section. It is possible to similarly study restricted branch independence—which is a weaker version of Savage's (1954) "sure thing" axiom—but the conditions become complicated and we do not report them here. Coalescing states that in a gamble with two outcomes that yield the same value with the same probability, the two outcomes can be combined into a single one. Just as we assumed that, for our analyses, reduction of compound gambles holds, we also assume that coalescing holds.

5. Peter Todd (December 2003, personal communication) suggested a way of connecting the priority heuristic to probability weighting. If one takes the one-tenth aspiration level for probabilities of the heuristic and makes the auxiliary assumption that a "subjective" probability is "weighted" to be the arithmetic mean of all probabilities from which it differs by less than 0.1, one gets what appears as underweighting and overweighting at the ends of the probability scale: For $p < 0.1$, the subjective probabilities are larger than the objective probabilities, which is the same effect as overweighting. For instance, the objective probability 0.05 differs by not more than 0.1 from all probabilities in the interval [0, 0.15], so the subjective probability would be

estimated as 0.075. Similarly, for $p > 0.9$, the subjective probabilities are smaller than the objective probabilities, which corresponds to underweighting. If p is in $[0.1, 0.9]$, there is no difference between objective and subjective probabilities.

6. There are many conceptualizations of independence (Marley & Luce, 2005). It is easy to see that the priority heuristic satisfies some of them such as branch independence (Marley & Luce, 2005, p. 98) and not others such as co-monotonic consequence monotonicity (Marley & Luce, 2005, p. 79), but we do not go into these details here.

7. Note that the counterexamples for these two cases are formally identical: in the second case, G' plays the role that G played in the first case, G'' plays the role that G' played in the first case, and G plays the role that G'' played in the first case.

8. Note that, as in the proof of Result 6, the counterexamples for the cases (c) and (d) are formally identical. This is also true for the counterexamples for the cases (b) and (e).

9. Note that Bernoulli has been recently accused of committing an error in his analysis: "Bernoulli's model of utility is flawed because it is reference independent: It assumes that the utility that is assigned to a given state of wealth does not vary with the decision maker's initial state of wealth" (Kahneman, 2003, p. 704). Kahneman continues, "I call this Bernoulli's error". We would like to vindicate Bernoulli from the charge. Contrary to Kahneman's assertion, Bernoulli was explicit about the impact of initial state of wealth on utility: "Thus there is no doubt that a gain of one thousand ducats is more significant to a pauper than to a rich man though both gain the same amount"(Bernoulli, 1738/1954, p. 24). And Bernoulli explicitly included initial wealth in his equations and diagrams: "... let AB represent the quantity of goods initially possessed" (p. 26). For general treatments of Bernoulli, see Daston (1988, pp. 70–77) and Jorland (1987).

Introduction to Chapter 9

Moral Satisficing: Rethinking Moral Behavior as Bounded Rationality

Rational and moral behavior appear, at first glance, to be strange bedfellows. Yet theories of rational expectation have served as a template for understanding morality, most prominently the theory of maximizing expected utility. This utilitarian approach to moral behavior, exemplified by John Stuart Mill, teaches that the best moral action is the one that maximizes some currency—utility, welfare, or the greatest happiness of the greatest number. Because it assumes a single common currency, less of one good can always be compensated for by more of something else. Yet making trade-offs does not always conform to our intuitions about justice, rights, or honesty. Honor, true love, and dignity are not for sale, at least for some of us. If you lied once, you may not be able to compensate by telling the truth the next time. Dangerous moral trade-offs have been the stuff of novels and movies, as the plot of Adrian Lyne's movie *Indecent Proposal* illustrates. Diana and David, a young financially troubled couple, take a chance at winning the money they need in Las Vegas. After losing at the tables, they are approached by a billionaire who is instantly attracted to Diana. He offers a million dollars for a night with her. The couple finally accept the offer, apparently making some utilitarian calculation. But after the night is over, they learn that trading off faithfulness and honor for money threatens to destroy their marriage.

The following essay offers a perspective on moral behavior based on satisficing rather than maximizing. Satisficing can mean basing a moral decision on only one reason and ignoring the rest, avoiding trade-offs, as in heuristic decisions. Yet this article makes a more specific proposal: Much of moral behavior is guided, consciously or unconsciously, by social heuristics rather than by virtue, moral reasoning, or maximization. Candidate social heuristics include imitate-your-peers, divide resources equally, tit-for-tat, and the default heuristic. Note how this perspective differs from assuming specific moral rules such as "don't kill," as in the Ten Commandments or in rule-utilitarianism. If everyone followed the rule "don't kill," more than 100 million people would not have been killed in the last century. Yet if people follow social heuristics, such terrible outcomes are less surprising. Note that social heuristics are not good or bad per se; they can lead to moral or immoral behavior, depending on the social environment. This approach helps to understand the inconsistencies that can be observed in almost every human's behavior and unifies moral with social behavior.

Moral satisficing is a descriptive and prescriptive perspective on moral behavior, not a normative one that declares what is good and bad. It aims at explaining how moral behavior results from the mind on the one hand and the environmental structure on the other. Based on that, one can prescribe how a given moral goal can be better realized, such as how to increase the number of potential organ donors. Moral satisficing connects with the heuristic structure of legal judgments (see Chapter 28), where bail decisions violate due process but make sense in the environment in which the lay judges act (they "pass the buck" to protect themselves). It also relates to Chapter 35 regarding how parents distribute their time and love across their children to achieve fairness and justice. Here, the success of the simple heuristic "divide your time equally between the children" can predictably lead to unequal results, depending on the structure of the environment—here, the number and temporal spacing of the children.

CHAPTER 9

Moral Satisficing: Rethinking Moral Behavior as Bounded Rationality

Gerd Gigerenzer

Abstract: What is the nature of moral behavior? According to the study of bounded rationality, it results not from character traits or rational deliberation alone, but from the interplay between mind and environment. In this view, moral behavior is based on pragmatic social heuristics rather than moral rules or maximization principles. These social heuristics are not good or bad per se, but solely in relation to the environments in which they are used. This has methodological implications for the study of morality: Behavior needs to be studied in social groups as well as in isolation, in natural environments as well as in labs. It also has implications for moral policy: Only by accepting the fact that behavior is a function of both mind and environmental structures can realistic prescriptive means of achieving moral goals be developed.

What is the nature of moral behavior? I will try to answer this question by analogy with another big question: What is the nature of rational behavior? One can ask whether morality and rationality have much to do with one another, and an entire tradition of moral philosophers, including Hume and Smith, would doubt this. Others, since at least the time of the ancient Greeks and Romans, have seen morality and rationality as two sides of the same coin, albeit with varying meanings. As Cicero (*De Finibus* 3, 75–76) explained, once reason has taught the ideal Stoic—the wise man—that moral goodness is the only thing of real value, he is happy forever and the freest of men, since his mind is not enslaved by desires. Here, reason makes humans moral. During the Enlightenment, the theory of probability emerged and with it a new vision of rationality, once again tied to

morality, which later evolved into various forms of consequentialism in ethics. In the twentiethth century, the notion of bounded rationality arose in reaction to the Enlightenment theory of (unbounded) rationality and its modern versions. In this essay, I ask: What vision of moral behavior emerges from the perspective of bounded rationality?

I will use the term *moral behavior* as short for behavior in morally significant situations, subsuming actions evaluated as moral or immoral. The study of bounded rationality (Gigerenzer, 2008a; Gigerenzer & Selten, 2001a; Simon, 1990) examines how people actually make decisions in an uncertain world with limited time and information. Following Herbert A. Simon, I will analyze moral behavior as a result of the match between mind and environment, as opposed to an internal perspective of character or rational reflection. My project is to use a structure I know well—the study of bounded rationality—and ask how it would apply to understanding moral behavior. I argue that *much* (not all) of moral behavior is based on heuristics. A heuristic is a mental process that ignores part of the available information and does not optimize, meaning that it does not involve the computation of a maximum or minimum. Relying on heuristics in place of optimizing is called *satisficing*. To prefigure my answer to the above question, the analogy between bounded rationality and morality leads to five propositions:

1. *Moral behavior is based on satisficing, rarely on maximizing.* Maximizing (finding the provably best course of action) is possible in "small worlds" (Savage, 1954) where all alternatives, consequences, and probabilities are known with certainty, but not in "large worlds" where nothing is certain and surprises can happen. Given that the certainty of small worlds is rare, normative theories that propose maximization can seldom guide moral behavior. But can maximizing at least serve as a normative goal? The next proposition provides two reasons why this may not be so.

2. *Satisficing can reach better results than maximizing.* There are two possible cases. First, even if maximizing is feasible, relying on heuristics can lead to better (or worse) outcomes than when relying on a maximization calculus, depending on the structure of the environment (Gigerenzer & Brighton, 2009). This result contradicts a view in moral philosophy that satisficing is a strategy whose outcome is or is expected to be satisfactory rather than optimal. "Everyone writing about satisficing seems to agree on at least that much" (Byron, 2004, p. 192). Second, if maximizing is not possible, trying to approximate it by fulfilling more of its conditions does not imply coming closer to the best solution, as the theory of the second-best proves (Lipsey, 1956). Together, these two results challenge the normative ideal that maximizing can generally define how people ought to behave.

3. *Satisficing operates typically with social heuristics rather than exclusively moral rules.* The heuristics underlying moral behavior are often the same as those that coordinate social behavior in general. This proposition contrasts with the moral rules postulated by rule consequentialism, as well as the view that humans have a specially "hardwired" moral grammar with rules such as "don't kill."

4. *Moral behavior is a function of both mind and the environment.* Moral behavior results from the match (or mismatch) of the mental processes with the structure of the social environment. It is not the consequence of mental states or processes alone, such as character, moral reasoning, or intuition.

5. *Moral design.* To improve moral behavior towards a given end, changing environments can be a more successful policy than trying to change beliefs or inner virtues.

This essay should be read as an invitation to discuss morality in terms of bounded rationality and is by no means a full-fledged theory of moral satisficing. Following Hume rather than Kant, my aim is to provide not a normative theory that tells us how we ought to behave but a descriptive theory with prescriptive consequences, such as how to design environments that help people to reach their own goals. Following Kant rather than Hume, moral philosophers have often insisted that the facts about human psychology should not constrain ethical reflection. I believe that this poses a risk of missing essential insights. For instance, Doris (2002) argued that the conception of character in moral philosophy is deeply problematic, because it ignores the evidence amassed by social psychologists that moral behavior is not simply a function of character, but of the situation or environment as well (e.g., Mischel, 1968). A normative theory that is uninformed of the workings of the mind or impossible to implement in a mind (e.g., because it is computationally intractable) is like a ship without a sail. It is unlikely to be useful and to help make the world a better place.

My starting point is the Enlightenment theory of rational expectation. It was developed by the great seventeenth-century French mathematician Blaise Pascal, who together with Pierre Fermat laid down the principles of mathematical probability.

MORAL BEHAVIOR AS RATIONAL EXPECTATION UNDER UNCERTAINTY

Should one believe in God? Pascal's (1669/1962) question was a striking heresy. Whereas scores of earlier scholars, from Thomas Aquinas to René Descartes, purported to give *a priori* demonstrations of the divine existence and the immortality of the soul, Pascal abandoned the necessity of God's existence in order to establish moral order. Instead, he proposed a calculus to decide whether it is rational to believe that God exists (he meant God as described by Roman Catholicism of the time). The calculus was for people who were convinced neither by the proofs of religion nor by the arguments of the atheists and who found themselves suspended between faith and disbelief. Since we cannot be sure, the result is a bet, which can be phrased in this way:

> *Pascal's Wager:* If I believe in God and He exists, I will enjoy eternal bliss; if He does not exist, I will miss out on some moments of worldly lust and vice. On the other hand, if I do not believe in God, and He exists, then I will face eternal damnation and hell.

However small the odds against God's existence might be, Pascal concluded that the penalty for wrongly not believing in Him is so large and the value of eternal bliss for correctly believing is so high that it is prudent to wager on God's existence and act as if one believed in God—which in his view would eventually lead to actual belief. Pascal's argument rested on an alleged isomorphism between decision problems where objective chances are known and those where the objective chances are unknown (see Hacking, 1975). In other words, he made a leap from what Jimmy Savage (1954), the father of modern Bayesian decision theory, called "small worlds" (in which all alternatives, consequences, and probability distributions are known, and no surprises can happen) to what I will call "large worlds," in which uncertainty reigns. For Pascal, the calculus of expectation served as a general-purpose tool for decisions under uncertainty, from games of chance to moral dilemmas: Evaluate every alternative (e.g., to believe in God or not) by its n consequences, that is, by first multiplying the probabilities p_i with the values x_i of each consequence i ($i = 1,\ldots, n$), and then summing up:

$$EV = \sum p_i x_i \qquad (9\text{-}1)$$

The alternative with the highest expected value (EV) is the rational choice.

This new vision of rationality emphasized risk instead of certainty and subsequently spread through the Enlightenment in many incarnations: as Daniel Bernoulli's expected utility, Benjamin Franklin's moral algebra, Jeremy Bentham's hedonistic calculus, and John Stuart Mill's utilitarianism, among others. From its inception, the calculus of expectation was closely associated with moral and legal reasoning (Daston, 1988). Today, it serves as the foundation on which rational choice theory is built.

For instance, Gary Becker tells the story that he began to think about crime in the 1960s after he was late for an oral examination and had to decide whether to put his car in a parking lot or risk getting a ticket for parking illegally on the street. "I calculated the likelihood of getting a ticket, the size of the penalty, and the cost of putting the car in a lot. I decided it paid to take the risk and park on the street" (Becker, 1995, p. 637). In his view, violations of the law, be they petty or grave, are not due to an irrational motive, a bad character, or mental illness but can be explained as rational choice based on the calculus of expectation. This economic theory has policy implications: Punishment works and criminals are not "helpless" victims of society. Moreover, city authorities should apply the same calculus to determine the optimal frequency of inspecting vehicles, the size of the fine, and other variables that influence citizens' calculations whether it pays to violate the law.

In economics and the cognitive sciences, full (unbounded) rationality is typically used as a methodological tool rather than as an assumption about how people actually make decisions. The claim is that people behave *as if* they maximized some kind of welfare, by calculating Bayesian probabilities of each consequence and multiplying these by their utilities. As a model of the mind, full rationality requires reliable knowledge of all alternative actions, their consequences, and the utilities and probabilities of these consequences. Furthermore, it entails determining the best of all existing alternatives, that is, being able to compute the maximum expectation.

The calculus of expectation provided the basis for various (act-)consequentialist theories of moral behavior, according to which actions are to be judged solely by their consequences, and therefore are not right or wrong per se, even if they use torture or betrayal. The best moral action is the one that maximizes some currency—the expected value, welfare, or the greatest happiness of the greatest number. Depending on what is being maximized, many versions of consequentialism exist; for instance, maximizing happiness may refer to the total amount of happiness, not the total number of people, or vice versa (Braybrooke, 2004). Whereas consequentialism sets up a normative ideal of what one should do (as opposed to observing what people actually do), the calculus of expectation has also influenced descriptive theories of behavior. Versions of Equation 9-1 have been proposed in theories of health behavior, consumer behavior, intuition, motivation, attitude formation, and decision making. Here, what *ought to be* provided the template for theories of *what is*. This ought-to-is transfer is a widespread principle for developing new descriptive theories of mind, as illustrated by Bayesian and other statistical optimization theories (Gigerenzer, 1991). Even descriptive theories critical of expected utility maximization, such as prospect theory, are based on the same principles: that people make decisions by looking at all consequences and then weighting and summing some function of their probabilities and values—differing only on specifics such as the form of the probability function (e.g., linear or S-shaped). Hence, the calculus of expectation has become one of the most successful templates for human nature.

Morality in Small Worlds

The beauty and elegance of the calculus of expectation come at a price, however. To build a theory on maximization limits its domain to situations where one can find and prove the optimal solution, that is, well-defined situations in which all relevant alternatives, consequences, and probabilities are known. As mentioned above, this limits the experimental studies to "small worlds" (Binmore, 2009; Savage, 1954). Much of decision theory, utilitarian moral philosophy, and game theory focuses on maximizing, and their experimental branches thus create small worlds in which behavior can be studied. These range from experimental games (e.g., the ultimatum game) to moral dilemmas (e.g., trolley problems) to choices between monetary gambles. Yet this one-sided emphasis on small-world behavior is somewhat surprising given that Savage spent the second half of his seminal book on the question of decision making in "large worlds," where not all alternatives, consequences, and probability distributions are known, and thus maximization is no longer possible. He proposed instead the use of heuristics such as minimax—to choose the action that minimizes the worst possible outcome, that is, the maximum loss. This part of Savage's work anticipated Herbert Simon's concept of bounded rationality, but few of Savage's followers have paid attention to his warning that his maximization theory should not be routinely applied outside small worlds (Binmore, 2009, is an exception).

Maximization, however, has been applied to almost everything, whether probabilities were known or not, and this overexpansion of the theory has created endless problems (for a critique, see Bennis, Medin, & Bartels, 2010). Even Pascal could not spell out the numbers needed for his wager: the prior probabilities that God exists, or the probabilities and values for each of the consequences. These gaps led scores of atheists, including Richard Dawkins (2006), to criticize Pascal's conclusion and propose instead numerical values and probabilities to justify that it is rational *not* to believe in God. None of these conclusions, however, follow from the maximization calculus per se, because both sides can always pick particular probabilities and utilities in order to justify their a priori convictions. The fact that maximization limits the domain of rationality and morality to small worlds is one of the motivations for searching for other theories.

When Conditions for Maximization Cannot Be Fulfilled, Should One Try to Approximate?

Many moral philosophers who propose maximization of some kind of utility as normative, concede that in the real world—because of lack of information or cognitive limitations—computing the best moral action turns out to be impossible in every single case. A standard argument is that maximization should be the ideal to aspire for, that is, to reach better decisions by more approximation. This argument, however, appears inconsistent with the *general theory of the second-best* (Lipsey, 1956). The theory consists of a general theorem and one relevant negative corollary. Consider that attaining an optimal solution requires simultaneously fulfilling a number of preconditions. The general theorem states that if one of these conditions cannot be fulfilled, then the other conditions, although still attainable, are in general no longer desirable. In other words, if one condition cannot be fulfilled (because of lack of information or cognitive limitations), the second-best optimum can be achieved by departing from all the other conditions. The corollary is (Lipsey, 1956, p. 12):

> Specifically, it is *not* true that a situation in which more, but not all, of the optimum conditions are fulfilled is necessarily, or is even likely to be, superior to a situation in which fewer are fulfilled. It follows, therefore, that in a situation in which there exist many constraints which prevent the fulfillment of the Paretian optimum conditions, the removal of any one constraint may affect welfare of efficiency either by raising it, by lowering it, or by leaving it unchanged.

Thus, the theory of the second-best does not support the argument that when maximization is unfeasible because some preconditions are not fulfilled, it should nevertheless be treated as an ideal to be approximated by fulfilling other conditions in order to arrive at better moral outcomes. The theory indicates that maximization cannot be a sound gold standard for large worlds in which its conditions are not perfectly fulfilled.

I now consider an alternative analogy for morality: bounded rationality.

MORAL BEHAVIOR AS BOUNDED RATIONALITY

How should one make decisions in a large world, that is, without knowing all alternatives, consequences, and probabilities? The "heresy" of the twentieth century in the study of rationality was—and still is considered so in many fields—to dispense with the ideal of maximization in favor of bounded rationality. The term *bounded rationality* is attributed to Herbert A. Simon, with the qualifier *bounded* setting his vision apart from that of "unbounded" or "full" rationality, as represented by the calculus of expectation and its modern variants. Bounded rationality dispenses with the idea that optimization is the sine qua non of a theory of rationality, making it possible to deal with problems for which optimization is unfeasible, without being forced to reduce these to small worlds that accommodate optimization. As a consequence, the bounds to information and computation can be explicitly included as characteristics of a problem. There are two kinds of bounds: those in our minds, such as limits of memory, and those in the world, such as noisy, unreliable samples of information (Todd & Gigerenzer, 2001).

When I use the term *bounded rationality*, I refer to the framework proposed by Herbert A. Simon (1955, 1990) and further developed by others, including Reinhard Selten and myself (Gigerenzer & Selten, 2001a, 2001b; Gigerenzer, Todd, & the ABC Research Group, 1999). In short, bounded rationality is the study of the cognitive processes (including emotions) that people actually rely on to make decisions in the large world. Before I explain key principles in the next sections, I would like to draw your attention to the fact that there are two other, very different interpretations of the concept of bounded rationality.

First, Ken Arrow (2004) argued that bounded rationality is ultimately optimization under constraints, and thus nothing but unbounded rationality in disguise—a common view among economists as well as some moral philosophers. Herbert Simon once told me that he wanted to sue people who misuse his concept for another form of optimization. Simon elsewhere (1955, p. 102) argued "that there is a complete lack of evidence that, in actual human choice situations of any complexity, these computations can be, or are in fact, performed." Second, Daniel Kahneman (2003) proposed that bounded rationality is the study of deviations between human judgment and full rationality, calling these cognitive fallacies. In Kahneman's view, although optimization is possible, people rely on heuristics, which he considers second-best strategies that often lead to errors. As a model of morality, Arrow's view is consistent with those consequentialist theories that assume the maximization of some utility while adding some constraints into the equation, whereas Kahneman's view emphasizes the study of discrepancies between behavior and the utilitarian calculus, to be interpreted as moral pitfalls (Sunstein, 2005). Although these two interpretations appear to be diametrically opposed in their interpretation of actual behavior as rational versus irrational, both accept some form of full rationality as the norm. However, as noted, optimization is rarely feasible in large worlds, and—as will be seen in the next section—even when it is feasible, heuristic methods can in fact be superior.

I now introduce two principles of bounded rationality and consider what view of morality emerges from them.

PRINCIPLE ONE: LESS CAN BE MORE

Optimizing means to compute the maximum (or minimum) of a function and thus determine the best action. The concept of *satisficing*, introduced by Simon, is a Northumbrian term for *to satisfy*, and is a generic term for strategies that ignore information and involve little computation. These strategies are called *heuristics*. Note that Simon also used the term *satisficing* for a specific heuristic: choosing the first alternative that satisfies an aspiration level. I will use the term here in its generic sense. The classical account of why people would rely on heuristics is the accuracy–effort trade-off: Compared to relying on a complex calculus, relying on a heuristic can save effort at the cost of some accuracy. Accordingly, in this view, a heuristic is second-best in terms of accuracy, because less effort can never lead to more accuracy. This viewpoint is still prevalent in nearly all textbooks today. Yet research on bounded rationality has shown that this trade-off account is not generally true; instead, the

heuristic can be both more accurate and less effortful (see Gigerenzer & Brighton, 2009):

> *Less-can-be-more*: If a complex calculus leads to the best outcome in a small world, the same calculus may lead to an outcome inferior to that of a simple heuristic when applied in a large world.

For instance, Harry Markowitz received his Nobel Prize for an optimal asset allocation method known as mean-variance portfolio (currently advertised by banks worldwide), yet when he made his own investments for retirement, he did not use his optimization method. Instead, he relied on an intuitive heuristic known as *1/N: Allocate your money equally to each of N alternatives* (Gigerenzer, 2007). Studies showed that $1/N$ in fact outperformed the mean-variance portfolio in terms of various financial criteria, even though the optimization method had 10 years of stock data for estimating its parameters (more than many investment firms use). One reason for this striking result is that estimates generally suffer from sampling error, unless one has sufficiently large samples, whereas $1/N$ is immune to this kind of error because it ignores past data and has no free parameters to estimate. For $N = 50$, one would need a sample of some 500 years of stock data in order for the optimization model to eventually lead to a better outcome than the simple heuristic (DeMiguel, Garlappi, & Uppal, 2009). This investment problem illustrates a case where optimization can be performed (the problem is computationally tractable), yet the error in the parameter estimates of the optimization model is larger than the error due to the "bias" of the heuristic. In statistical terminology, the optimization method suffers mainly from *variance* and the heuristic from *bias*; the question of how well a more flexible, complex method (such as a utility calculus) performs relative to a simple heuristic can be answered through the *bias–variance dilemma* (Geman, Bienenstock, & Doursat, 1992). In other words, the optimization method would result in the best outcome if the parameter values were known without error, as in a small world, but it can be inferior in a large world, where parameter values need to be estimated from limited samples of information. By analogy, if investment were a moral action, maximization would not necessarily lead to the best outcome. This is because of the error in the estimates of the probabilities and utilities that this method generates in an uncertain world.

The investment example also illustrates that the important question is an ecological one. In which environments does optimization lead to better outcomes than satisficing (answer for the investment problem: sample size is ≥ 500 years), and in which does it not (answer: sample size is < 500 years)? Contrary to the claim that heuristics are always second-best, there is now broad evidence that simple heuristics that ignore information can outperform strategies that use more information and computation (e.g., Brighton, 2006; Gigerenzer, 2008a; Makridakis & Hibon, 2000).

Heuristics perform well precisely because they ignore information. The take-the-best heuristic, which relies on one good reason alone and ignores the rest, has been shown in many situations to predict more accurately than a multiple regression that relies on all available reasons (Czerlinski, Gigerenzer, & Goldstein, 1999). The tit-for-tat heuristic memorizes only the last of the partner's actions and forgets the rest (a form of forgiving) but can lead to better cooperation and higher monetary gain than more complex strategies do, including the rational strategy of always defecting (e.g., in the prisoner's dilemma with a fixed number of trials). Similarly, $1/N$ ignores all previous information about the performance of investment funds. In each case the question is: In what environment does simplicity pay, and where would more information help?

As the Markowitz example illustrates, experts tend to rely on fast-and-frugal heuristics in order to make better decisions (Shanteau, 1992). Here is more evidence. To predict which customers are active and which are nonactive in a large database, experienced managers of airlines and apparel businesses rely on a simple *hiatus heuristic: Customers who have not made a purchase for 9 months are considered inactive.* This heuristic has been shown to be more accurate than sophisticated methods such as the Pareto/NBD (negative

binomial distribution) model, which uses more information and relies on complex computations (Wübben & von Wangenheim, 2008). British magistrates appear to base bail decisions on a fast-and-frugal decision tree (Dhami, 2003), most professional burglars' choice of target objects follow the take-the-best heuristic rather than the weighting and adding of all cues (Garcia-Retamero & Dhami, 2009), and baseball outfielders' intuitions about where to run to catch a fly ball are based on the gaze heuristic and its variants (Gigerenzer, 2007; Shaffer, Krauchunas, Eddy, & McBeath, 2004). Some of the heuristics used by people have also been reported in studies on birds, bats, rats, and other animals (Hutchinson & Gigerenzer, 2005).

In sum, there is evidence that people often rely on heuristics and, most important, that by ignoring part of the information, heuristics can lead to better decisions than more complex strategies do, including optimization methods. An important point is that optimizing and satisficing are defined by their process (optimizing strategies compute the maximum for a function using all information while heuristics employ limited search for a few important pieces of information and ignore the rest). The process should not be confused with the outcome. Whether optimizing or satisficing leads to better outcomes in the real, uncertain world is an empirical question. This result contradicts the widespread belief that complex calculation always leads to better decisions than are made using some simple heuristic. And, I believe, it provides a challenge to the related normative ideal that maximizing can define how people ought to behave in an uncertain world.

PRINCIPLE TWO: SIMON'S SCISSORS

Theories of unbounded rationality are typically based on logical principles, such as axioms of consistency and transitivity. Logic was also Piaget's metaphor for understanding thinking; when turning to moral judgment, he proposed that it follows the same development, with abstract logical thought as its final stage (Gruber & Vonèche, 1977). Similarly, Kohlberg (1968) entitled one of his essays "The Child as a Moral Philosopher," asserting that moral functioning involves systematic thinking, along with emotions. Bounded rationality, in contrast, is based on an ecological rather than a logical view of behavior, as articulated in Simon's scissors analogy:

> Human rational behavior (and the rational behavior of all physical symbol systems) is shaped by a scissors whose two blades are the structure of task environments and the computational capabilities of the actor (Simon, 1990, p. 7).

Behavior is a function of both mind and environment. By looking at only one blade, one will not understand how scissors cut. Likewise, by studying only the mind, be it by interview or brain imaging, one will only partially understand the causes of behavior. Similarly, the norm for evaluating a decision is not simply consistency, transitivity, or other logical principles, but success in the world, which results from the match between mind and environments. Consistency can still be relevant in a theory of bounded rationality if it fulfills a functional goal, such as in checking the validity of a mathematical proof. The study of *ecological rationality* asks in which world a given heuristic is better than another strategy, as measured by some currency.

By analogy, in this view of rationality, moral behavior is a function of mind and environments rather than the consequence of moral reasoning or character alone.

MORAL SATISFICING

Based on these two principles, I will attempt to sketch out the basis for a theory of moral satisficing. The theory has two goals:

1. *Explanation of moral behavior.* This goal is descriptive, that is, to explain how moral behavior results from the mind on the one hand and environmental structure on the other.
2. *Modification of moral behavior.* This goal is prescriptive, that is, to use the results under (1) to derive how a given moral goal can be realized. The solution can involve changing heuristics, designing environments, or both.

As mentioned before, moral satisficing is not a normative theory that tells us what one's moral goals should be—whether or not you should sign up as an organ donor, divorce your spouse, or stop wasting energy to protect the environment. But the theory can tell us how to help people reach a given goal more efficiently. Furthermore, a descriptive analysis can shed light on the plausibility of normative theories (Cokely & Feltz, 2009; Feltz & Cokely, 2009; Knobe & Nichols, 2008).

For illustration, let me begin with the organ donor problem (Johnson & Goldstein, 2003). It arises from a shortage of donors, contributes to the rise of black markets for selling organs, and sparks ongoing debates about government intervention and the rights of individuals.

> *The organ donor problem.* Every year, an estimated 5,000 Americans and 1,000 Germans die waiting in vain for a suitable organ donor. Although most citizens say that they approve of post mortem organ donation, relatively few sign a donor card: only about 28% in the United States and and 12% Germany. Why do so few sign up as potential donors? Various explanations have been proposed, such as that many people are selfish and have little empathy for the suffering of others, that people are hypersensitive to a post mortem opening of their bodies, and that people fear that doctors will not work as hard to save them in an emergency room situation. Yet why are 99.9% of the French and Austrians potential donors?

Normally, the striking difference in the rates of potential donors between countries (Figure 9-1) is likely to be explained by personality traits—selfishness or lack of empathy. But character is unlikely to explain the big picture. Consider next reasoning as an explanation. If moral behavior were the result of deliberative reasoning rather than personality traits such as selfishness, however, the problem might be that most Americans, Germans, or Dutch are not aware of the need for organs. This explanation would call for an information campaign. In the Netherlands, an exhaustive campaign was in fact conducted, with 12 million letters sent to a population of 16 million. As in similar attempts, the effect was practically nil. Nevertheless, in a

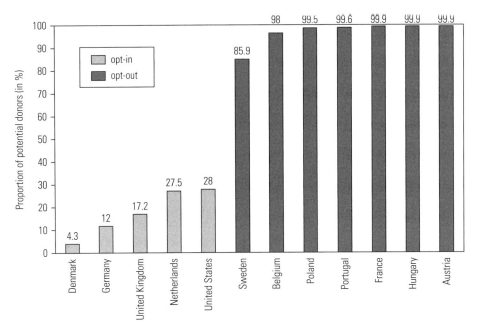

Figure 9-1. Why are so few citizens in Denmark, Germany, the United Kingdom, the Netherlands, and the United States potential organ donors, compared to in the other countries? The answer is not a difference in character or knowledge. Rather, most citizens in all 12 countries appear to rely on the same heuristic: *If there is a default, do nothing about it.* The outcome, however, depends on the default setting, and therefore varies strikingly between countries with opt-in policies and opt-out policies. There are nuances with which these systems function in practice that are not shown here. In the United States, some states have an opt-in policy, whereas others force citizens to make a choice (based on Johnson & Goldstein, 2003).

survey, 70% of the Dutch said they would like to receive an organ from someone who has died, should it be necessary, and only 16% said they were not willing to donate (Persijn, 1997). This natural experiment suggests that missing information is not the issue either. What then lies at the root of the organ donor problem?

Here is a possible answer. Despite the striking differences in Figure 9-1, most people seem to rely on the same heuristic:

If there is a default, do nothing about it.

The *default heuristic* leads to different outcomes because environments differ. In explicit-consent countries such as United States, Germany, and the Netherlands, the law is that nobody is a donor unless you *opt in*. In presumed-consent countries such as France and Austria, the default is the opposite: Everyone is a

donor, unless you *opt out*. From a rational choice perspective, however, this should have little effect because people are assumed to ignore a default if it is inconsistent with their preference. As Figure 9-1 also shows, a minority of citizens do not follow the default heuristic, and more of these opt in than out, consistent with the preference of the majority. These citizens might rely on some version of Pascal's moral calculus or on the golden rule. An online experiment found similar results (Johnson & Goldstein, 2003). Americans were asked to assume that they had just moved into a new state and were given the choice to confirm or change their donor status. In one group, being a donor was the default; in a second group, not being a donor was the default; and in a third group, there was no default. Even in this hypothetical situation where zero effort was necessary for overriding the default, more than 80% ended up as potential donors when the default was being a donor, compared to only half as many when the default was not being one. In the absence of a default, the far majority signed up as donors.

Why would so many people follow this heuristic? Johnson and Goldstein's experimental results indicate that it is not simply irresponsible laziness, because when participants could not avoid the effort of making a decision, the heuristic was still followed by many. Rather, the heuristic appears to serve a function that has been proposed as the original function of morality: the coordination of groups of individuals (Darwin, 1871/1981, pp. 161–167; Wilson, 2002). Relying on defaults, specifically legal defaults, creates homogeneity within a society and thus helps cement it together. In general, I think that heuristics that guide moral behavior might be those that help to coordinate behavior, feeling, motion, and emotion.

I will now use the case of organ donation to illustrate two hypotheses that follow from the analogy with bounded rationality.

Hypothesis 1: Moral behavior = f(mind, environment).

Several accounts, normative and descriptive, from virtue theories to Kohlberg's six stages of moral reasoning, assume that forces inside the mind—moral intuition or reasoning—are or should be the cause of moral behavior (unless someone actively prevents a person from executing it by threat or force). These theories provide a conceptual language for only one blade of Simon's scissors: the mind. As the organ donation problem illustrates, however, the second blade, the environment, contributes profoundly to the resulting outcome. Many who feel that donation is a good thing nevertheless do not opt in, and some of those who believe that donation is not a good thing do not opt out. Here, I would like to propose the notion of *ecological morality*, that is, that moral behavior results from an interaction between mind and environment. I think of ecological morality as a descriptive (how to explain moral behavior?) and prescriptive (how to improve moral behavior given a goal?) research program, but I can

imagine that it also has the potential for the basis of a normative theory. Here, one would expand questions such as "What is our duty?" and "What is a good character?" into interactive questions such as "What is a virtuous environment for humans?"

The main contribution of social psychology to the study of morality has been in demonstrating the power of social environments, including the power to make ordinary people exhibit morally questionable behavior. Milgram's (1974) obedience experiments and Zimbardo's (2007) prisoners' study are two classics. For instance, in one of Milgram's studies (Experiment 5), the experimenter instructed the participant to administer electric shocks of increasing intensity to a learner in a paired-associate learning task every time the learner gave an incorrect answer. The unsettling finding was that 83% of the participants continued to administer shocks beyond the 150-volt level, and 65% continued to administer shocks all the way to the end of the range—450 volts in 15-volt increments. Would people still obey today? Yes, the power of the environment is still remarkable. In a partial replication (with the 150-volt level), the obedience rate in 2006 was 70%, only slightly lower than what Milgram found 45 years earlier (Burger, 2009). This result was obtained despite participants having been told thrice that they could withdraw from the study at any time and still retain their $50 participation fee.

These studies document the strong influence of the situation on moral behavior, as opposed to internal accounts in terms of "personality types" and the like, as described in the literature on the authoritarian personality (Adorno, Frenkel-Brunswik, Levinson, & Sanford, 1950). When Milgram asked psychiatrists and Yale seniors to predict the outcome of the experiment, the predicted obedience rates were only 0.1% and 1.2%, respectively (Blass, 1991). Milgram (1974) himself said that his major motivation for conducting the studies was his own refusal to believe in the situation-based excuses made by concentration camp guards at the Nuremberg War Trials (e.g., "I was just following orders"). His experimental results changed his mind: "Often, it is not so much the kind of person a man is as the kind of situation in which he finds himself that determines how he will act" (p. 205). A situational understanding of behavior does not justify behavior, but it can help us to understand it and avoid what is known as the *fundamental attribution error*: to explain behavior by internal causes alone. To better understand why more than 100 million people died violently at the hands of others during the entire twentieth century (Doris, 2002), we need to analyze the environmental conditions that foster people's willingness to kill and inflict physical pain on others. This is not to say that character variables do not matter (Cokely & Feltz, 2009; Funder, 2001), but these express themselves in the interaction with specific environments.

Here I want to address two direct consequences of the ecological approach to moral behavior: inconsistency between moral intuition/reasoning and behavior, and moral luck.

Systematic Inconsistencies

Inconsistencies between moral intuition and behavior are to be expected from an ecological view of morality. Moreover, one can predict in what situation inconsistencies are more likely to arise, such as when there is no match between intuition and default. For instance, a survey asked citizens whether they would be willing to donate an organ after they have died; 69% and 81% of Danish and Swedish citizens, respectively, answered "yes," compared to about 4% and 86% (Figure 9-1) who are actually potential donors (Commission of the European Communities, 2007). The Danish appear to behave inconsistently; the Swedish do not. Inconsistencies or only moderate correlations between moral intuition and behavior have been reported in studies that both elicited people's moral intuitions and observed their behavior in the same situation (e.g., Gerson & Damon, 1978; Narvaez & Lapsley, 2005). Consider premarital sexual relations and American teenagers who publicly take a vow of abstinence. These teenagers typically come from religious backgrounds and have revived virginity as a moral value, as it had been up to the first half of the twentieth century. One would expect that their moral

intentions, particularly after having been declared in public, would guide their behavior. Yet teens who made a virginity pledge were just as likely to have premarital sex as their peers who did not (Rosenbaum, 2009). The difference was that when those who made the pledge had sex, they were less likely to use condoms or other forms of contraception. We know that teenagers' behavior is often guided by a coordination heuristic, called *imitate-your-peers*: Do what the majority of your peers do. If my friends make a virginity pledge, I will too; if my friends get drunk, I will too; if my friends already have sex at age 16, I will too; and so on. If behavior is guided by peer imitation, a pledge in itself makes little difference. Moreover, if the heuristic works unconsciously but teenagers nonetheless believe that their behavior is totally under their control, this would explain why they are not prepared for the event of acting against their stated moral values. The U.S. government spends about $200 million a year on abstinence-promotion programs, which seem to be as ineffective in preventing unwanted pregnancies as the Dutch mass mail campaign was in boosting organ donations.

Moral Luck

Matheson (2006) was troubled that bounded rationality implies a post-Enlightenment picture of "cognitive luck" because "in that case, there is little we can do to improve our cognitive abilities, for—so the worry continues—such improvement requires manipulation of what it is within our power to change, and these external, cognitively fortuitous features are outside that domain" (p. 143). I conjecture that cognitive luck is an inevitable consequence that one should not worry about or try to eliminate but instead use constructively for better theories. Similarly, moral philosophers have discussed the question of "moral luck." It arises from the fact that moral behavior is in part determined by our environment and thus not entirely controlled by the individual, and concerns the question whether behavior should be evaluated as right or wrong depending on its result shaped by situational circumstances (Statman, 1993; Williams, 1981). Nagel (1993,

p. 59) defines moral luck as follows: "Where a significant aspect of what someone does depends on factors beyond his control, yet we continue to treat him in that respect as an object of moral judgment, it can be called moral luck." Nagel claims that despite our intuition that people cannot be morally assessed for what is not their fault, we nevertheless frequently make moral judgments about people based on factors out of their control.

The worry about moral luck is based on the assumption that internal ways to improve cognition and morality are under our control, or should be, whereas the external ways are not. Changing environments, however, can sometimes be more efficient than changing minds, and creating environments that facilitate moral virtue is as important as improving inner values (Gigerenzer, 2006; Thaler & Sunstein, 2008). The donor problem illustrates this conjecture, where thousands of lives could be saved every year if governments introduced proper defaults rather than continuing to bet on the wrong "internal" psychology and send letters to their citizens. For instance, a 2008 European Union Bulletin (Bundesärztekammer, 2008) maintains the importance of increasing public awareness of the organ donation problem and urges the member states of the European Union to disseminate more information on it. This governmental policy is unwilling to grant citizens the benefit of a proper environment that respects human psychology and helps people to reach their own goals.

Hypothesis 2: The same social heuristics guide moral and nonmoral behavior.

You may have noticed that I avoided using the term *moral heuristics*. There is a reason for this. The term would imply that there are two different kinds of heuristics, those for moral decisions and those for self-regarding ones, that is, matters of personal taste. On the contrary, I believe that, as a rule, one and the same heuristic can solve both problems that we call moral and those we do not (Gigerenzer, 2008b). Let me explain why. The boundaries between what is deemed a moral issue shift over historical time and between cultures. Although contemporary

Western moral psychology and philosophy often center on the issues of harm and individual rights, such a constrained view of the domain of morality is unusual in history. There existed more important moral values than avoiding harm to individuals. Abraham was asked by the Lord to kill his son, and his unquestioning readiness to heed God's command signaled a higher moral value—faith. For the ancient world, where human sacrifice was prevalent, the surprising part of the story was that God stopped the sacrifice (Neiman, 2008). The story of the Sodomites who wanted to gang rape two strangers to whom Lot had offered shelter is another case in point. From a contemporary Western view, we might misleadingly believe that the major moral issue at stake here is rape or homosexuality, but hospitality was an essential moral duty at that time and remains so in many cultures. For Lot, this duty was so serious that he offered the raging mob his virgin daughters if they left his guests alone (Neiman, 2008). Similarly, in modern Europe, wasting energy, eating meat, or smoking in the presence of others were long seen as purely self-regarding decisions. However, environmental protection groups, vegetarians, and anti-smoking groups have reinterpreted these as moral infractions that cause environmental pollution, killing of animals, and lung cancer through second-hand smoking. I refer to the line that divides personal taste and moral concerns as the *moral rim*. The location of the moral rim describes whether a behavior is included in the moral domain. My hypothesis is that wherever the rim is drawn, the underlying heuristic is likely to remain the same.

As an example, consider renewable energy, environmental protection, and "green" electricity. For some, these are deeply moral issues that will determine the living conditions of our great-grand children; for others, these are merely matters of personal preference. Yet the default heuristic appears to guide behavior on both sides of the moral rim. A natural experiment in the German town Schönau showed that when green electricity was introduced as a default, almost all citizens went with the default, even though nearly half had strongly opposed its introduction. In contrast, in towns where "gray" energy was the default, only about 1% opted for green energy, a pattern replicated in laboratory experiments (Pichert & Katsikopoulos, 2008). As in the case of organ donation (Johnson & Goldstein, 2003), the willingness to go with the default was stronger in the natural world than in the hypothetical laboratory situation. The same heuristic also seems to be used when drivers decide on which insurance policy to buy, which is rarely considered a moral issue. The states of Pennsylvania and New Jersey offer drivers the choice between an insurance policy with unrestricted right to sue and a cheaper one with suit restrictions (Johnson, Hershey, Meszaros, & Kunreuther, 1993). The unrestricted policy is the default in Pennsylvania, whereas the restricted one is the default in New Jersey. If drivers based their decision on preferences concerning the right to sue, one would expect them to ignore the default settings. If many instead followed the default rule, one would expect more drivers to buy the expensive policy in Pennsylvania. Indeed, only 30% of the New Jersey drivers bought the expensive policy, whereas 79% of the Pennsylvania drivers did so. Many people avoid making a deviating decision, be it on money, life, or death. What we do not know is whether those who rely on the default heuristic for moral issues are the same persons who rely on it for other decisions.

The hypothesis that humans do not have a special moral grammar but that the same social strategies guide moral and nonmoral behavior is consistent with neuroscientific studies that failed to find a specific moral area in the brain or a specific moral activation pattern in several areas. Rather, the same network of activation that is discussed for moral decisions (e.g., Greene & Haidt, 2002) is also typical for social decisions without moral content (Amodio & Frith, 2006; Saxe, 2006).

In sum, I argue that the heuristics in the adaptive toolbox can be used for both moral and nonmoral behavior. This is why I do not attach the qualifier "moral" to heuristics (but see Sunstein, 2005). A behavior can be judged as moral or personal, depending on where a culture draws the moral rim. The underlying heuristics are likely the same.

THE STUDY OF MORAL SATISFICING

The interpretation of moral behavior as a form of bounded rationality leads to three research questions:

1. Which heuristics underlie moral behavior?
2. What are the social (including legal) environments that—together with the heuristics—produce moral behavior?
3. How can we design environments so that people can reach moral goals more quickly and easily?

I can only provide a sketch of an answer to each of these questions.

Which Heuristics Underlie Moral Behavior?

One obvious answer would be "don't kill," "don't lie," and so on. In my view, this is the wrong direction, as argued in Hypothesis 2. We should not confuse present-day Christian humanist values with heuristics that guide moral behavior. Certain forms of killing, for instance, are legal in countries with capital punishment, and morally acceptable in religious communities, for instance, when a father is expected to kill his daughter if her conduct is considered morally repulsive, such as having sex before marriage (Ali, 2002). We might get a pointer to a better answer when we first ask about the original function of morality (not necessarily the only one in modern societies). Darwin (1871/1981), who thought that a combination of social instincts plus sufficient intellectual powers leads to the evolution of moral sense, proposed the coherence or coordination of human groups:

> There can be no doubt that a tribe including many members who, from possessing in a high degree the spirit of patriotism, fidelity, obedience, courage, and sympathy, were always ready to give aid to each other and to sacrifice themselves for the common good, would be victorious over most other tribes; and this would be natural selection. At all times throughout the world tribes have supplanted other tribes; and as morality is one element in their success, the standard of morality and the number of

well-endowed men will thus everywhere tend to rise and increase (p. 166).

Selfish and contentious people will not cohere, and without coherence nothing can be effected (p. 162).

If Darwin's assumption that one original function of morality was the coherence of groups is correct, then the heuristics underlying moral behavior should include those that can provide this function. The default heuristic and imitate-your-peers are apt examples: They can foster social coherence, whatever the default is or whatever the majority does. Note that this opens up a different understanding of what might be the nature of potential universals underlying moral behavior. For instance, Hauser (2006) argued that there is a universal moral grammar with "hardwired" principles such as: do as you would be done by; don't kill; don't cheat, steal, or lie; avoid adultery and incest; and care for children and the weak. In his critique, Pippin (2009) responded that these values may be ours but not those of other cultures and times: children sold into slavery by parents who feel entitled to do so; guilt-free spousal abuse by men who see it as their right; moral sanctioning of pregnant unmarried women by humiliation or driving them into suicide; and so forth. A theory of moral behavior should avoid a Christian human- ist bias. Darwin (1871/1981, p. 73) captured this point long ago:

> If for instance, to take an extreme case, men were reared under precisely the same conditions as hive-bees, there can hardly be a doubt that our unmarried females would, like the worker-bees, think it a sacred duty to kill their brothers, and mothers would strive to kill their fertile daugh- ters; and no one would think of interfering.

Terrorists, the Mafia, and crack-dealing gangs run on moral principles (e.g., Gambetta, 1996). For his film *Suicide Killers*, filmmaker Pierre Rehow interviewed would-be terrorists who sur- vived because their bombs failed to explode. He relates: "Every single one of them tried to con- vince me that it was the right thing to do for moralistic reasons" (cited in Neiman, 2008, p. 87). Social psychologists have documented in our own cultures how a situation can stimulate evil behavior in ordinary people, and how easily physical abuse of others can be elicited (e.g., Burger, 2009; Zimbardo, 2007). I suggest that the heuristics underlying moral behavior are not the mirror images of the Ten Commandments and their modern equivalents, but embody more general principles that coordinate human groups.

Consider the following four heuristics as a starting point. Each guides both actions evalu- ated as moral or immoral and has the potential to coordinate groups; their success (the degree to which they reach a moral goal) depends on the structure of the environment.

1. *Imitate-your-peers:* Do what the majority of your peers do.

Unlike the default heuristic, which needs a default to be elicited, imitation can coordinate behavior in a wide range of situations. No spe- cies is known in which children and adults imi- tate the behavior of others as generally and precisely as *Homo sapiens*. Tomasello (2000) argued that the slavishness of imitation led to our remarkable culture. Imitation enables us to accumulate what our ancestors have learned, thus replacing slow Darwinian evolutionary learning by a Lamarckian form of cultural inheritance. Imitating the majority virtually guarantees social acceptance in one's peer group and fosters shared community values. For instance, the philosopher Otto Weininger (1903) argued that many men desire a woman not because of her features, but because their peers also desire her. Imitation can steer both good and bad moral action, from donating to charity to discriminating against minorities. Those who refuse to imitate the behavior and the values of their culture are likely to be called a coward or oddball if male, or a shame or dishonor to the family if female. A variant of this heuristic is *imitate the successful*, where the object is no longer the majority but an outstand- ing individual.

2. *Equality heuristic (1/N):* To distribute a resource, divide it equally.

The principle of allocating resources equally is used in self-regarding decisions, such as financial investment (as mentioned before), as well as in morally relevant decisions. For instance, parents try to divide their love, time, and attention among their children equally to generate a sense of fairness and justice. As a just, transparent distribution principle, it can foster the coherence of a family or a larger group. Similar to in the case of organ donation, the equality heuristic does not directly translate into a corresponding behavior; rather, the result depends on the environment and can even generate systematic inequality. For instance, parents that try to divide their time every day between their N children equally by $1/N$ will attain the long-term goal of providing each child with as much time as the other if they have only two children. But if there are three or more children (excepting multiple births), the goal will be missed, because the first-born and the last-born will end up receiving more time than the middle-borns (Hertwig, Davis, & Sulloway, 2002). This result illustrates again that a heuristic (divide equally) and its goal (all children should be given the same amount of time during childhood) is not the same—the environment has the last word.

3. *Tit-for-tat:* If *you* interact with another person and have the choice between being kind (cooperate) or nasty (defect), then: (1) be kind in the first encounter, thereafter (2) keep a memory of size one, and (3) imitate your partner's last behavior (kind or nasty).

"Keep a memory of size one" means that only the last behavior (kind or nasty) is imitated; all previous ones are ignored or forgotten, which can help to stabilize a relationship. Tit-for-tat can coordinate the behavior in a group in the sense that all actors will end up cooperating but are simultaneously protected against potential defectors. As with imitate-your-peers and the default heuristic, tit-for-tat illustrates that the same heuristic can lead to opposite behaviors, here kind or nasty, depending on the social environment. If a husband and wife both cooperate when engaging in their first interaction and subsequently always imitate the other's behavior, the result can be a long harmonious relationship. If, however, she relies on tit-for-tat but he on the maxim "always be nasty to your

wife, so that she knows who is the boss," her initially kind behavior will turn to being nasty to him as well. Behavior is not a mirror of a trait of being kind or nasty, but results from an interaction between mind and environment. An explanation of the tit-for-tat players' behavior in terms of traits or attitudes would miss this crucial difference between process (tit-for-tat) and resulting behavior (cooperate or not).

4. *Default heuristic:* If there is a default, do nothing about it (see above).

Whereas equality is a simple answer to the problem of allocating resources fairly among N alternatives, the default heuristic addresses the problem of which of N alternatives to pursue when one of these is marked as the default. It has the potential to create coherence in behavior even when no social obligation or prohibition exists.

These four heuristics are selected examples. Several others have been studied (see Cosmides & Tooby, 2008; Gigerenzer, 2007, 2008b; Haidt, 2001), but we do not have anything near a complete list. The general point is that moral satisficing assumes not one general calculus but several heuristics. This fact is reflected in the term "adaptive toolbox," where the qualifier *adaptive* refers to the evidence that heuristic tools tend to be selected, consciously or unconsciously, to match the task at hand (e.g., Bröder, 2003; Dieckmann & Rieskamp, 2007; Mata, Schooler, & Rieskamp, 2007). Acting in a morally responsible way can thus be reinterpreted as the ability to choose a proper heuristic for a given situation. The question whether there are one or several processes underlying morality is an old one. Adam Smith (1761), for instance, criticized Hutcheson's and Hume's theory of moral sense as a single feeling of moral approval. For him, the sense of virtue was distinct from the sense of propriety, of merit, or of duty, which is why Smith spoke of "moral sentiments" in the plural.

Building Blocks and Core Capacities. Heuristics can be composed from several building blocks, which enable new heuristics to be generated by recombination and modification. For instance, one weak point of tit-for-tat is that a single negative behavior (being nasty) can bring two people who play tit-for-tat into an endless cycle of violence or two social groups into a vendetta, each act of violence being justified as a fair response to the other's most recent attack. A modification of the second building block to a memory size of two can resolve this problem. This heuristic is called *tit-for-two tats*, where a person turns nasty only if the partner behaved nasty twice in a row. Heuristics and their building blocks are based on evolved and learned core capacities, such as recognition of individuals, inhibitory control, and the ability to imitate (Stevens & Hauser, 2004). Like the default heuristic and imitate-your-peers, tit-for-tat appears to be rare among other animals, unless they are genetically related (Hammerstein, 2003).

What Social Environments, Together with Heuristics, Guide Moral Behavior?

Structural features of the environment can interact with the mind in two ways. First, the presence or absence of a feature increases or limits the choice set of applicable heuristics. For instance, if no alternative is marked as the default, the default heuristic cannot be triggered; if there are no peers present whose behavior in a new task can be observed, the imitate-your-peers heuristic cannot be activated. Second, if more than one heuristic remains in the choice set, features of the environment can determine which heuristic is more likely to be relied on. Research on decision making has shown that people tend to select heuristics in an adaptive way (Payne, Bettman, & Johnson, 1993), and this selection process has been formalized as a reinforcement learning process in strategy selection theory (Rieskamp & Otto, 2006). Environmental features investigated in this research include time for decision, payoffs, and redundancy of cues.

One aspect of the environment is the structure of social relations that humans are born into or put into in an experimental situation. Fiske (1992) distinguished four kinds of relationships amongst which people move back and forth

during their daily activities. On the basis of these, we might ask what social environments are likely to trigger the equality heuristic. According to Fiske's classification, these environments consist of *equality matching relations*, where people keep track of the balance of favors and know what would be required to restore the balance. Examples are turn-taking in babysitting coops and voting systems in democracies that allocate each adult one vote. Equality is a simpler rule for fair division than equity; the latter divides a cake among N persons according to some measure of effort, time, or input of each individual (Deutsch, 1975; Messick, 1993). In Fiske's taxonomy, the environments in which distribution according to equity can be expected comprise *market pricing relations*, that is, social relations that are structured by some kind of cost–benefit analysis, as in business relations. Milgram's experiments implemented the third kind of relation, an *authority ranking relation*, where people have asymmetric relations in a hierarchy, subordinates react with respect and deference, and superiors take pastoral responsibility for them. Note that in this experimentally induced authority relation, the absence of monetary incentives—participants were paid independent of whether or not they applied shocks to a stranger—appeared to play little or no role (see above). Authority ranking relations tend to trigger heuristics of the kind: *if a person is an authority, follow requests*. It appears that not even a true authority relation is needed, but that mere signs of such a relation—for instance, a white coat—can trigger the heuristic and the resulting moral behavior (Brase & Richmond, 2004). The fourth relation in Fiske's taxonomy is *community sharing*, where people treat some group as equivalent or undifferentiated, as when sharing a commons.

That is not to say that triggering is a one-to-one process; conflicts can arise. For instance, in one condition of the obedience experiment, a confederate participant was introduced who sat next to the real participant and refused to continue the experiment after pressing the 90-volt switch and hearing the learner's groan (Burger, 2009). This situation might trigger both *imitate-your-peers* and *if a person is an authority, follow requests*, which are conflicting behaviors. The majority of participants (63%) followed the authority and went on to give shocks of higher intensity, compared to 70% of those who did so without seeing someone decline.

These are single examples, but not a systematic theory of the structure of social environments relevant to moral behavior. Such a theory could be constructed by combining the research on heuristics with that on social structures (e.g., Boyd & Richerson, 2005; Fiske, 1992; Haidt & Bjorklund 2008; Shweder, Much, Mahaptra, & Park, 1997).

The ecological view of morality has methodological consequences for the experimental study of morality.

1. *Study social groups in addition to isolated individuals.* If moral behavior is guided by social heuristics, these can hardly be detected in typical psychological experiments where individuals are studied in isolation. Heuristics such as imitate-your-peers and tit-for-tat can only unfold in the presence of peers.
2. *Study moral behavior in natural environments in addition to in hypothetical problems.* Hypothetical situations such as the trolley problems eliminate characteristic features of natural environments, such as the uncertainty about the full set of possible actions and their consequences. It needs to be addressed whether the results obtained from hypothetical small worlds and isolated individuals generalize to moral behavior outside the laboratory.
3. *Analyze moral behavior in addition to verbal reports.* Given that people are often unaware of the heuristics and environmental structures that guide their moral behavior, paper-and-pencil tasks and self-reports alone are insufficient research methods (Baumeister, Vohs, & Funder, 2007). This methodological point is consistent with the observation that people typically cannot explain why they feel that something is morally right or wrong, or why they did what they did (Haidt & Bjorklund, 2008).

These methodological consequences are exactly the same I recommend for studying decision making outside the moral domain, consistent with Hypothesis 2 above.

How can Environments Be Designed so that People Can Better Reach Moral Goals?

To begin with, we need public awareness that the causes of moral behavior are not simply inside the mind and that understanding the interplay between minds and environments is a useful starting point for moral policy. Note that this is not paternalistic as long as one helps, not forces, people to reach their own goals. Changing the law from opt-in to opt-out is an example of how to better reach the goal of increasing the number of potential organ donors and thus reducing the number of people who die for want of a donor. Abadie and Gay (2006) estimated that, once other factors influencing organ donation are taken into account (such as a country's rate of motor vehicle accidents involving fatalities, a main source of donors), actual donation rates are 25% to 30% higher on average in presumed-consent countries. However, as mentioned before, to this day many governmental agencies tend to bet on the internal causes and continue to proclaim the importance of raising public awareness and of disseminating more information. This program is based on an inadequate psychological theory and will likely fail in the future as it has in the past. Let me end with an illustration for the design of environments, crime in communities.

How should one deal with community crime, from littering to vandalism? Moral satisficing suggests considering potential candidate heuristics such as imitate-your-peers and then changing the environment to diminish the likelihood that it triggers the heuristic. In other words, as long as deviant behavior is publicly observed, this will trigger further deviant behavior. The program of "fixing broken windows" (Kelling & Coles, 1996) follows this line of thought, by repairing windows and fixing streetlights, cleaning sidewalks and subway stations, and so on. Supplemented by a zero tolerance program, this change in the environment substantially decreased petty crime and low-level antisocial behavior in New York City and other places, and may have even reduced major crime.

SATISFICING IN MORAL PHILOSOPHY

In this article, I invited you to consider the question: How can we understand moral behavior if we look at it from the perspective of bounded rationality? My answer is summarized in Propositions 1 to 5 at the beginning of the article. I will end by briefly comparing this perspective with the views of several moral philosophers in *Satisficing and Maximizing* (Byron, 2004). The key difference is that the two principles on which my essay is based, less-can-be-more and Simon's scissors, are absent in this interesting collection of essays. The common assumption is that an optimizing process leads to the optimal outcome and satisficing to a second-best outcome, because process and outcome are not distinguished (but see Proposition 2). Thus, less-can-be-more is not part of the picture. As a result, some philosophers make (misleading) normative statements such as: "satisficing may be a conceptual tool that fits the facts, but it is not good enough. We can do better" (Richardson, 2004, p. 127). The absence of the ecological dimension makes Propositions 2, 4, and 5 nonissues.

Although Herbert Simon is repeatedly invoked as the source of inspiration, some essays still define satisficing as a form of optimizing. As mentioned above, one common (mis)interpretation of Simon's concept of bounded rationality is that it is nothing other than optimization under constraints (e.g., Narveson, 2004, p. 62), overlooking the fact that optimization is typically impossible (e.g., computationally intractable) in large worlds (Proposition 1). A second more interesting interpretation starts from the observation that people have multiple goals. Here, satisficing means that people choose local optima for some goals (e.g., to spend less time than desired with family for one's career) but still seek the global optimum for their life as a whole (Schmidtz, 2004). This interpretation, in contradiction to Proposition 1, also assumes that optimization is always possible. An original

third interpretation (which does not reduce satisficing to optimizing) is that satisficing means pursuing moderate goals, and that moderation can be a virtue and maximization a vice, the latter leading to greed, perfectionism, and the decline of spontaneity (Slote, 2004; Swanton, 2004). There is a related claim in the psychological literature that satisficers are more optimistic and satisfied with life, while maximizers excel in depression, perfectionism, and regret (Schwartz et al., 2002).

A further proposal (not covered in this volume) is various forms of rule-consequentialism (Braybrooke, 2004). Because it is typically impossible to anticipate all consequences of each possible action and their probabilities in every single case, rule consequentialists emphasize the importance of rules, which do not maximize utility in every single case but—if they are followed—do so in the long run. Once again, the idea of maximization is retained, although the object of maximization is not directly the action but instead a rule that generally leads to the best actions. The similarity between moral satisficing and rule-consequentialism is in the focus on rules, whereas moral satisficing assumes that rules are typically unconscious social heuristics that are elicited by the structure of the environment (see also Haidt, 2001).

This broad range of interpretations can be taken to signal the multiple ways in which bounded rationality can inspire us to rethink morality. But it also indicates how deeply entrenched the notion of maximization is, and how alien Simon's scissors remain to many of us.

ECOLOGICAL MORALITY

Herbert Simon (1996, p. 110) once said, "Human beings, viewed as behaving systems, are quite simple. The apparent complexity of our behavior over time is largely a reflection of the complexity of the environment in which we find ourselves." An ecological view of moral behavior might be easier to accept for those who have experienced that their good and bad deeds are not always the product of deliberation but also of the social environment that puts pressure on them, for better or worse. Yet others will see too much "moral luck" in this vision, insisting that the individual alone is or should be responsible for what they do. Luck, I believe, is as real as virtue. It is the milieu in which we happen to grow up, but also the environment we actively create for our children and students.

ACKNOWLEDGMENTS

I am grateful to Will Bennis, Edward Cokely, Lorraine Daston, Adam Feltz, Nadine Fleischhut, Jonathan Haidt, Ralph Hertwig, Linnea Karlsson, Jonathan Nelson, Lael Schooler, Jeffrey R. Stevens, Rona Unrau, Kirsten Volz, and Tom Wells for their helpful comments.

Introduction to Chapter 10

Hindsight Bias: A By-Product of Knowledge Updating?

The great naturalist Louis Agassiz—who was a lifelong opponent of Darwin's theory of evolution—is said to have described scientific discovery as follows: "Every scientific truth goes through three stages: First, people say it conflicts with the Bible. Next they say it had been discovered before. Lastly, they say they always believed it." The last stage is known as *hindsight bias*. Many findings of the research program on simple heuristics have been subject to this hindsight bias, experienced by both the program's proponents and its critics. For instance, before the simulation results concerning the take-the-best heuristic (see Chapter 2) were published, it was almost impossible to meet a single researcher in judgment and decision making—including experts on regression analysis—who believed that heuristics such as take-the-best could be equally or more accurate than multiple regression. Today, the observation that less information and less computation can lead to higher accuracy is met with much less incredulity, and new demonstrations are sometimes received by a somewhat jaded, "Yes, we knew it all along." However, it should be said that numerous researchers, deep in their hearts, still believe that more information and more computation are always better.

Hindsight is a well-documented phenomenon across a wide range of domains. This article by Ulrich Hoffrage, Ralph Hertwig, and Gerd Gigerenzer was the first to offer a process model of the hindsight bias. The model, which includes the take-the-best heuristic and a knowledge-updating process, predicts for each person and each experimental stimulus whether hindsight bias, reversed hindsight bias, or no hindsight bias will occur. Moreover, it offers a new interpretation of the hindsight bias, according to which the bias is a by-product of an adaptive learning process. The learning process updates knowledge in a person's semantic memory in light of newly established facts in the world (e.g., outcome of political elections or sport events). However, as the old adage goes, "there ain't no such thing as a free lunch," and the process of knowledge updating exacts costs. The price is that as a result of updating, people are less likely able to accurately reconstruct their past states of knowledge. Yet, as the authors argue, this price may well be worth paying, given that knowledge updating increases the ability to make accurate inferences about the present and future. More generally, the model provides another demonstration that cognitive limits—for instance, not being able to store all knowledge states of the past—may enable memory and memory-based inferential strategies to work efficiently (see Chapter 4).

CHAPTER 10

Hindsight Bias: A By-Product of Knowledge Updating?

Ulrich Hoffrage, Ralph Hertwig, and Gerd Gigerenzer

Abstract: With the benefit of feedback about the outcome of an event, people's recalled judgments are typically closer to the outcome of the event than their original judgments were. It has been suggested that this *hindsight bias* may be due to a reconstruction process of the prior judgment. A model of such a process is proposed that assumes that knowledge is updated after feedback and that reconstruction is based on the updated knowledge. Consistent with the model's predictions, the results of 2 studies show that knowledge after feedback is systematically shifted toward feedback, and that assisting retrieval of the knowledge prior to feedback reduces hindsight bias. In addition, the model accounts for about 75% of cases in which either hindsight bias or reversed hindsight bias occurred. The authors conclude that hindsight bias can be understood as a by-product of an adaptive process, namely the updating of knowledge after feedback.

In attempting to understand the past, historians have to deal with a number of methodological problems. The problem that concerns us here stems from what Leo Tolstoy (1869/1982) described in *War and Peace* as the "law of retrospectiveness, which makes all the past appear a preparation for events that occur subsequently" (p. 843). Tolstoy speculated that this law explains why Russian historians, writing after Napoleon's defeat, believed that the Russian generals deliberately lured Napoleon to Moscow (and defeat), although the evidence points to luck rather than deliberate planning. What Tolstoy called the law of retrospectiveness may also have inspired experimental psychologists. In fact,

when Fischhoff (1975) began to study postevent memories, he referred to this methodological dilemma of historical research by quoting the historian Roberta Wohlstetter(1962):

> It is much easier after the event to sort the relevant from the irrelevant signals. After the event, of course, a signal is always crystal clear. We can now see what disaster it was signaling since the disaster has occurred, but before the event it is obscure and pregnant with conflicting meanings. (p. 387)

If this historian's intuition is true, *hindsight judgments*, that is, judgments made with benefit of feedback about the outcome of an event, should differ systematically from *foresight judgments*, that is, judgments made without knowledge of the outcome. Indeed, this is what Fischhoff (1975) found. He presented participants with historical scenarios, for instance, the 19th-century war between the British and the Gurkhas of Nepal. In the foresight condition, participants had to give confidence ratings for four possible outcomes, without knowing which of them had actually occurred. In the hindsight condition, participants were told the actual outcome and then asked to state their hypothetical confidence in all four possible outcomes, that is, the confidence they would have given had they not been told the actual outcome. Participants with hindsight were more confident about the actual outcome than those with foresight.

This phenomenon has been called *hindsight bias* or the "knew-it-all-along effect." It has been investigated in a number of studies, by using either a hypothetical or a memory design. With the hypothetical design (e.g., Fischhoff, 1975), two groups of participants are compared: One group has no outcome knowledge, and the other has outcome knowledge but is asked to ignore it. With the memory design, a comparison is made between the original and recalled answers of one group of participants. First, participants make a series of judgments about the outcome of certain events; second, they receive outcome information; and third, they have to recall their original answers. Note that the experimental condition of the hypothetical design approximates the situation of historians who normally write about an historical event without having given an assessment prior to its occurrence. In contrast, the experimental condition of the memory design approximates everyday situations in which individuals predict an event, receive feedback, and then eventually remember their judgment (e.g., elections, weather, etc.). Hertwig, Gigerenzer, and Hoffrage (1997) argued that the effects obtained in the two designs are systematically different, and they proposed reserving the term hindsight bias for an effect obtained in a memory design and the term knew-it-all-along effect for the hypothetical design. In this article, we adopt this distinction.

Hindsight bias and the knew-it-all-along effect have been identified in a wide range of task types, including confidence judgments in the outcome of events, choices between alternatives, and estimations of quantities as well as in a variety of domains, such as political events (Pennington, 1981), medical diagnosis (Arkes, Wortmann, Saville, & Harkness, 1981), outcomes of scientific experiments (Slovic & Fischhoff,

1977), economic decisions (Bukszar & Connolly, 1988), autobiographical memory (Neisser, 1981), and general knowledge (Hell, Gigerenzer, Gauggel, Mall, & Müller, 1988). Although the overall magnitude of the effects is small (according to a meta-analysis conducted by Christensen-Szalanski & Fobian Willham, 1991, $r = .17$, corrected for reliability, $r = .25$), the hindsight bias appears to be robust and difficult to eliminate (Fischhoff, 1982).

In their review, Hawkins and Hastie (1990) listed four general strategies for responding to the request for a hindsight judgment (for a discussion of these strategies, see Erdfelder & Buchner, 1998). Hawkins and Hastie concluded that the first two strategies—"direct recall of the original belief" and "anchor on the current belief and adjust to infer the original belief"—do not play an important role in explanations of results obtained in hindsight bias research. In contrast, the third and fourth strategy—"cognitive reconstruction" and "motivated self-presentation" (p. 320)—have been implicated in many of the findings they have reviewed.[1] Most promising, in Hawkins and Hastie's opinion, are those cognitive accounts where a hindsight judgment is seen as a "reconstruction of the prior judgment by 'rejudging' the outcome" (p. 321). In this view, hindsight bias emerges because of systematic differences between judging and rejudging the outcome. According to Stahlberg and Maass (1998), these differences are due to metacognitive processes; that is, participants who have forgotten their original estimates "are forced to guess and, in the presence of outcome information, are likely to utilize this information as an anchor, assuming that their estimates must have been somewhere in the proximity of the true outcome" (p. 110). However, it seems fair to say that neither this metacognition interpretation (inspired by McCloskey & Zaragoza, 1985) nor other interpretations of the cognitive reconstruction notion have specified a precise mechanism (for an exception, see Pohl & Eisenhauer, 1997). The model we propose offers such a mechanism: It allows us to explain at the level of individual responses (i.e., individual items for individual participants) why the effect occurred, did not occur, or even was reversed.

Previously (Hertwig et al., 1997), we proposed a model that assumed that observed hindsight bias results from the sum of true hindsight bias and the reiteration effect, that is, the phenomenon that mere repetition of an assertion increases confidence in the correctness of the assertion. This model accounts for the fact that observed hindsight bias is larger for assertions with "this assertion is true" feedback than for assertions with "this assertion is false" feedback, but it does not explain why there is true hindsight bias in the first place. The current model extends this previous work in two respects: It accounts for true hindsight bias, and it does so at the level of individual responses. In this article, we outline the model, derive three predictions from it, and report two studies that tested these predictions.

RECONSTRUCTION AFTER FEEDBACK WITH TAKE-THE-BEST (RAFT)

We explain and subsequently test the model with a task in which an original response is made at Time 1, feedback about the correct answer is given at Time 2, and the original response has to be recalled at Time 3 (recalled response). In developing the present model, we were inspired by the theory of probabilistic mental models (PMM; see Gigerenzer, Hoffrage, & Kleinbölting, 1991). The PMM theory models the cognitive processes in tasks in which a choice is made between two objects in terms of a quantitative criterion, and a confidence judgment is made that the chosen object is correct. Here, we apply the PMM framework to a context in which a previous response (i.e., choice and confidence judgment) needs to be reconstructed after receiving feedback on whether the choice was correct. We refer to this model as the RAFT model, where RAFT stands for Reconstruction After Feedback With Take-The-Best (take-the-best is a simple inferential heuristic that is described in the next section). The RAFT model makes three general assumptions. First, if (and only if) the original response cannot be retrieved from memory, it will be reconstructed by rejudging the problem. Second, the rejudgment involves a recall of the

cues and cue values underlying the original choice. Third, knowledge, in particular uncertain knowledge, is automatically updated by feedback. According to the RAFT model, feedback does not directly affect the memory trace for the original response but indirectly by changing (i.e., updating) the knowledge that is used as input for the reconstruction process. Although the process of knowledge updating is adaptive because it enables individuals to improve their inferences over time, it has a byproduct: the hindsight bias. We now specify the cognitive processes underlying the responses at Time 1 and Time 3.

Time 1: Original Response

Patricia, who is a visiting researcher from California, is concerned about eating a healthy diet. However, she has a sweet tooth, and at a restaurant she wants to order dessert. The menu provides her with the choice between chocolate fudge cake and pumpkin custard pie (Time 1). Because she wants to reduce her cholesterol consumption, she asks herself which of the two has more cholesterol (to choose the one having less). Not knowing the answer, she tries to infer it from what she knows about the two foods. According to PMM theory, she will construct a probabilistic mental model (PMM) to make this inference. Such a PMM consists of a reference class of foods, cues for cholesterol, and an inferential heuristic, as described below.

Knowledge about cues. In Patricia's case, the reference class might be foods in her local supermarket. According to PMM theory, knowledge about the objects in a reference class consists of probability cues and the values the objects have with respect to these cues. For example, saturated fat is such a cue: If one food item has more saturated fat than the other, then the one with more fat is also likely to have more cholesterol.

It is useful to think of knowledge stored in long-term memory as a matrix of Objects (e.g., food items) × Cues (e.g., saturated fat), in which one can search for information. Whereas all the examples in Gigerenzer et al. (1991) and Gigerenzer and Goldstein (1996) involve binary cues, we extend PMM theory to continuous cues. For cues with continuous values, there are four

Table 10-1. Hindsight Bias at the Level of Confidence

Knowledge and Choice	Time 1		Time 3
Saturated fat (80%)	cake ? pie	→	cake > pie
Calories (70%)	cake > pie		cake > pie
Protein (60%)	cake > pie		cake > pie
Choice	cake		cake
Confidence	70%		80%

Note. The probabilistic mental model contains three cues ranked according to their validity (specified in parentheses). The symbols > and ? denote the relations between objects on these cues. For example, in the Time 1 column, which describes the knowledge underlying the original response, the object relation on the saturated fat cue is unknown. As indicated by the arrow, this object relation changes after feedback that cake has more cholesterol than pie. The relation shifts toward feedback, that is, from ? to > in the updated mental model (Time 3 column). As a consequence, hindsight bias occurs. Note that take-the-best searches only for the object relations that appear in boldface.

possible relations among two objects with respect to any cue. The term *object relation* refers to the ordinal relation of objects with respect to a cue (rather than to the criterion). This relation can be larger (e.g., cake contains more saturated fat than pie), smaller, equal, or unknown (Table 10-1). The last is the case when entries are missing in the Object × Cue matrix because of limited knowledge. The relations (i.e., >, <, =, ?) can either be directly retrieved or deduced from knowledge about absolute cue values.

Some cues are better predictors than others. We call this predictive power *ecological validity*, which is defined as the relative frequency with which the cue correctly predicts which object scores higher on the criterion (in a defined reference class). Assume that Patricia's reference class consists of food items sampled from the local supermarket, with saturated fat, calories, and protein as quantitative cues for cholesterol. When we conducted a random sample in a Chicago supermarket, we found that in about 80% of the cases where one food item had more saturated fat (cue) than the other, it also had more cholesterol (criterion). This value is the ecological validity of the saturated fat cue. In this particular environment, saturated fat is the

"best" cue, that is, it has the highest ecological validity. It is followed by the calorie (about 70%) and protein (about 60%) cues.

Inferential heuristic. How can Patricia infer whether cake has more cholesterol than pie? We account for her inference with a heuristic called "take-the-best," which is the core heuristic of the PMM framework (Gigerenzer & Goldstein, 1996). This lexicographic heuristic starts with a subjective rank order of cues according to their validities and makes the inference on the basis of the highest ranking (best) cue that discriminates. The steps of take-the-best (excluding the recognition heuristic, which is not relevant here) are:

1. *Search rule*: Choose the cue with the highest validity and retrieve the objects' cue values from memory.
2. *Stopping rule*: If the best cue discriminates (object relation: > or <), stop searching. If the best cue does not discriminate (object relation: = or ?), continue with the next best cue until a cue that discriminates is found.
3. *Decision rule*: Choose the object to which the cue points, that is, the object with the higher cue value (if criterion and cues are negatively correlated, then choose the object with the lower cue value). If no cue discriminates, then make a random choice (guess).
4. *Confidence rule*: Use the cue validity of the cue that discriminates as the confidence in the choice. If the choice was made at random, confidence is 50%.

A seemingly irrational feature of the heuristic is that it does not integrate all the available information but uses what we call *one-reason decision making*, where a decision (e.g., a choice) is based on only one cue. To illustrate this, Table 10-1 shows take-the-best applied to Patricia's knowledge. At Time 1, her choice is based solely on the calorie cue. Because the cake has more calories than the pie, the heuristic chooses the cake as the alternative with more cholesterol; confidence in the correctness of the decision is 70% (the validity of the calorie cue).[2] Take-the-best is fast because it does not involve much computation, and it is frugal in the sense that it only searches for some of the available information.

The simplicity of take-the-best raises the suspicion that it might be highly inaccurate, compared with standard inferential algorithms that process and combine all available predictors. Yet in 20 real-world environments, it was able to compete well with other, more complex algorithms, such as multiple regression (Czerlinski, Gigerenzer, & Goldstein, 1999) or Bayesian networks (Martignon & Laskey, 1999). Because take-the-best is not only accurate but also both fast and frugal, it is particularly suitable for situations in which time and/or knowledge is limited. This heuristic has successfully explained a number of phenomena in memory-based inference in a single framework (see Gigerenzer et al., 1991). We now show how the RAFT model applies take-the-best to a situation in which a past choice and a confidence judgment have to be reconstructed.

Times 2 and 3: Feedback and Reconstruction

Some weeks after having dinner at the restaurant, Patricia remembers her dessert dilemma and decides to check the nutrition labels at her local supermarket. She finds out that chocolate cake has more cholesterol than pumpkin pie (Time 2) and then asks herself what she actually chose at the restaurant (Time 3).

How is the original response recalled? The cognitive processes as assumed by the RAFT model can be seen in Figure 10-1. First, an attempt is made to access the original response directly from memory. The chance of doing this successfully depends on factors such as length of time between original and recalled response (e.g., Fischhoff & Beyth, 1975) and depth of encoding of the original response (Hell et al., 1988).

If the original response cannot be retrieved, it will be reconstructed by repeating the steps taken at Time 1. A simple analogy may help to motivate this assumption: Imagine you are asked to multiply a two-digit by a three-digit number. A couple of days later you are asked to remember your result. If you cannot retrieve it from memory, you can compensate for this by performing the same calculation again; that is, lack of recall can be compensated for by recalculation.

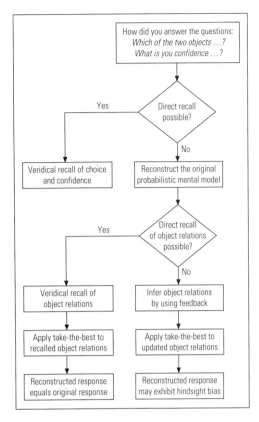

Figure 10-1. Cognitive processes at Time 3. The task is to remember the original response (choice and confidence) made at Time 1.

The same holds for a choice that has been made under uncertainty. To compensate for not being able to recall the choice, the probabilistic mental model used at Time 1 can be reconstructed at Time 3.

This process begins by retrieving the knowledge on which the choice at Time 1 was based, that is, by retrieving the original cues (in the original order) and the knowledge about those cues. In some cases, veridical retrieval may be possible; in others, memory of the cue values (object relations) may be vague or absent. RAFT's critical assumption is that feedback transforms some of the elusive relations into discriminating relations. This is due to the reversibility of the cue–criterion relationship: Because it is possible to draw inferences from a cue (e.g., saturated fat) to the criterion, the reverse is also possible—to draw inferences from the criterion to the cues. In other words, what used to be the distal variable (i.e., cholesterol) at Time 1 now turns into a proximal cue. This new proximal cue is used to infer what used to be a proximal cue at Time 1 (e.g., saturated fat) and what turns into a distal variable at Time 3, when an attempt is made to reconstruct the original PMM. Such a reversal between proximal cues and distal variables is possible because cues and criterion are correlated with each other.

We assume that the process of updating knowledge is not restricted to reconstructions made in hindsight. Rather, we think of this updating as a general and continuous process. When new knowledge is acquired, it does not remain isolated but is automatically integrated into existing knowledge, which might involve adapting this new knowledge to existing knowledge or vice versa. The RAFT model stresses an assimilation of old knowledge to new available knowledge. This updating of old knowledge serves an adaptive function: It results not only in a more coherent corpus of knowledge but, if the new knowledge is valid, a more accurate one, as well.

Illustrations of the RAFT Model

Consider Patricia's dilemma again. Her question was, which of the two food items, the cake or the pie, has more cholesterol. Saturated fat, calories, and protein were used as cues to infer the correct answer. As illustrated in Table 10-1, the most valid cue (saturated fat) did not discriminate at Time 1. Then at Time 2, she found out that the cake has more cholesterol than the pie. When she finally attempts, at Time 3, to reconstruct her original response, RAFT assumes that the new knowledge concerning cholesterol may be used to infer her (previous) cue values. As a result, the cue values (and their relations) are not veridically remembered but show systematic shifts toward feedback. For instance, the saturated fat cue discriminates now and points to the cake (Table 10-1, Time 3). If the same heuristic (here, take-the-best) is then applied to the updated knowledge base, the resulting choices and confidences will show systematic shifts toward feedback. In the example given, Patricia

infers at Time 3 that she chose the cake as the food with more cholesterol. She also infers that her confidence in this choice was 80% (the validity of the saturated fat cue). Thus, her reconstructed choice is identical to her original choice. However, her reconstructed confidence increased relative to her original confidence, thereby exhibiting hindsight bias. More generally, hindsight bias at the level of confidence occurs if recalled confidence increases after receiving feedback that the originally selected alternative was correct (or decreases after receiving feedback that it was wrong).

Not only confidence, but even choice may change from Time 1 to Time 3. Hindsight bias at the level of choice occurs if the original choice was wrong and the recalled choice was correct. The RAFT model can also explain hindsight bias at this level. For instance, in a variant of Table 10-1, neither the saturated fat nor the calorie cue but only the protein cue discriminated at Time 1 (Table 10-2). This cue points to the pie. At Time 3, the saturated fat cue discriminates, now pointing to the cake. The result is hindsight bias at the level of choice.

It is also conceivable that hindsight bias can be reversed. Reversed hindsight bias at the level of confidence occurs in cases where recalled confidence decreases although feedback indicates that the originally selected alternative was correct (e.g., original choice: cake has more cholesterol, 70%; feedback: cake; recalled choice: cake, 60%) or increases, although feedback indicates that the originally selected alternative was wrong. Reversed hindsight bias at the level of choice

Table 10-2. Hindsight Bias at the Level of Choice

Knowledge and Choice	Time 1		Time 3
Saturated fat (80%)	cake ? pie	→	cake > pie
Calories (70%)	cake = pie		cake = pie
Protein (60%)	cake < pie	→	cake ? pie
Choice	pie		cake
Confidence	60%		80%

Note. This table is a variant of Table 1, where the RAFT model predicts hindsight bias at the level of choice, not just confidence.

occurs when the original choice was correct and the recalled choice was wrong (e.g., original choice: cake; feedback: cake; recalled choice: pie). RAFT accounts for reversed hindsight bias by allowing for random shifts in the reconstructed object relations; that is, in addition to systematic shifts that are due to feedback, RAFT posits unsystematic shifts that are due to the imperfect reliability of one's memory of knowledge. Such random shifts are independent of feedback; this means they can either be manifested as hindsight bias (if they coincide with the direction of feedback) or as reversed hindsight bias (if they are counter to the direction of feedback).

Unless otherwise specified, we use the terms hindsight bias and reversed hindsight bias to refer to item-specific differences in original and recalled responses rather than to aggregated responses. Because RAFT specifies the conditions under which hindsight bias and reversed hindsight bias occur on an item-specific level, this theoretical precision allows us to apply the established terms to effects observed for individual items.

PREDICTIONS

Prediction 1 (Asymmetry in Shifts)

If feedback on the criterion is provided, then the object relations will shift asymmetrically, more often toward the correct alternative than away from it. If no feedback is provided, then both kinds of shift should be about equally prevalent.

This prediction is derived as follows. Feedback updates elusive or missing object relations. If, according to feedback, Object A scores higher (lower) on the criterion than Object B, it may be inferred that Object A probably also scores higher (lower) on the cue. In addition, there are random shifts, which will occur equally often toward and away from feedback. Across systematic and random shifts, more relations will change toward feedback than away from it.

Updating after feedback will be more likely when a cue did not discriminate at Time 1, compared with cases where it did discriminate. The rationale for this corollary of Prediction 1 is as follows. The fact that a cue discriminated at

Time 1 indicates that some knowledge was available. The mere existence of such knowledge increases the likelihood that it can be accessed again at Time 3 and that the relation will be veridically retrieved even after feedback. What if, by contrast, a cue did not discriminate at Time 1, either because a cue value for one or both objects was unknown or because the cue values were equal? If the relation was unknown at Time 1, then feedback does not need to overcome preexisting knowledge to become manifest. A similar implication holds for equal relations. If both cue values in a pair of objects are equal at Time 1, a shift in one cue value is sufficient to change the relation. For a discriminating relation, in contrast, a shift in one cue value may reduce the difference between the two values but not necessarily cause a shift in the relation.

Prediction 2 (Contingency of Hindsight Bias on Recalled Cue Values)

On the basis of a participant's recalled object relations for a particular item, RAFT is able to account for observed outcomes (hindsight bias, reversed hindsight bias, or veridical recall).

This prediction is derived as follows. In the RAFT model, feedback is not considered to have a direct impact on recalled choice and confidence but rather causes systematic shifts in the cue values (and, thus, in the object relations). These systematic shifts, in turn, can lead to biased recollections of choice and confidence: If the original response cannot directly be recalled from memory, it will be reconstructed by applying take-the-best to the (updated) object relations. By comparing the reconstructed response to the original response, RAFT is able to predict whether hindsight bias, reversed hindsight bias, or veridical "recall" occurs.

Prediction 3 (Reduction of Hindsight Bias)

If recall of the cue values is assisted, then hindsight bias will be reduced.

The rationale behind this prediction is as follows. Because hindsight bias is attributed to systematic changes between the cue values at Time 1 and at Time 3, experimental manipulations that reduce the likelihood of these changes should also reduce hindsight bias. This likelihood can be reduced by assisting the recall of cue values. In the studies reported herein, we used three ways of assisting the recall: (a) Participants' memory of cue values at Time 3 was refreshed by repeating the learning phase in which they were taught these cue values (Study 1); (b) the retention interval between Time 1 and 3 responses was shortened (Study 1); and (c) the cue values as recalled after the learning phase were presented to the participants before asking them to recall their original response (Study 2).

Note that to the extent that anything other than the modeled reconstruction process underlies hindsight bias (Erdfelder & Buchner, 1998; Hawkins & Hastie, 1990), assisting the recall of cue values should reduce but not eliminate hindsight bias. By providing one mechanism (in our view, a crucial one), RAFT does not invalidate other processes, such as metacognition or motivational response adjustments. There is one study that allowed us to derive a rough estimate of the size of reduction in hindsight bias that was due to assisting recall. In a hypothetical design, Davies (1987, Experiment 1) asked participants to read descriptions of four psychological experiments and to write down comments on the clarity of the instructions, appropriateness of the methods, and reasons why the experiment may turn out one way or the other. Two weeks later, they had to judge the likelihood of various experimental outcomes. Before participants made these judgments, researchers told one group the actual outcomes and asked them to ignore them; a control group did not receive this outcome information. In addition, half of the participants in each of these conditions were given the notes they had made in the first session. Among those participants who did not have the opportunity to look at their own notes, the mean likelihood ratings in the reported outcomes were 15.6 percentage points higher than those made by participants who had no outcome information, demonstrating the knew-it-all-along effect. Moreover, consistent with Prediction 3 of the RAFT model, among the participants who were shown their notes, this difference decreased to 7.5 percentage points; that is, the effect had been reduced by about half.

We conducted two studies. Study 1 was designed to test Predictions 1 through 3 for a two-alternative choice and confidence task with quantitative cues. Study 2 was designed to replicate the tests of Predictions 1 through 3 with binary cues.

STUDY 1

Method

Participants. Eighty students from the University of Chicago took part in the experiment. They were paid volunteers, recruited by advertisement from a broad spectrum of disciplines, and tested in groups of up to four people.

Design and procedure. A topic of significance for many people is nutrition: In the United States, cholesterol, in particular, has become a major concern. To provide participants with a context for the present study, we informed them of the physiological mechanism that explains why cholesterol is one of the main risk factors for heart disease. We then informed them that cholesterol tends to covary with three substances—saturated fat, calories, and protein—and that the amount of cholesterol can be inferred from the amounts of these substances.

Despite the potential significance of nutrition, most people do not have much specific knowledge about it. Therefore, the experiment started with a learning phase in which the participants learned the actual saturated fat, calorie, and protein values of 36 food items. They were instructed to read over the list several times and to learn the objects and cue values by heart. They were informed that this information would be instrumental in solving the task that followed. After each of three learning trials (10 min per trial), we checked whether the participants had actually acquired the information (5 min per test trial).

Immediately after the learning phase, participants were given a list of 18 food pairs (constructed from the pool of 36 items) and asked two questions about each pair: "Which food do you think has more cholesterol?" and "How confident are you that your choice is correct?" If the participants were absolutely certain, they were instructed to give 100% as their confidence. If their answer was simply a guess, they should give 50% as their confidence. In all other cases, they were asked to provide values between 50% and 100%, in 10-point increments. After they had given their choice and confidence rating, we instructed the participants to recall the amounts of saturated fat, calories, and protein they had learned for each food item in the learning phase or to indicate for each food pair the object relations with respect to each cue (knowledge before feedback).

After 1 day, 40 participants—and after 1 week, the other 40—attended the second session and were randomly assigned to one of three conditions. In the feedback condition, participants (n = 40; 20 after 1 day, 20 after 1 week) first received feedback for each of the 18 questions they had answered previously (e.g., "The cholesterol values for chocolate fudge cake and pumpkin custard pie are 44 mg and 31 mg per 100 g, respectively"). To ensure that they paid attention to the feedback given, the participants had to enter the cholesterol values for each food pair in a graph. Then they were asked to recall which food they had originally chosen as having more cholesterol and how confident they were that their choice was correct. Afterwards, in a new questionnaire, they were asked to recall the saturated fat, calorie, and protein values they had learned in the learning phase (knowledge after feedback). The recall of cue values was necessary to test Predictions 1 and 2. In the no-feedback condition, the procedure and tasks were identical to those in the feedback condition except that participants (n = 20; 10 after 1 day, 10 after 1 week) received no feedback. In the relearning condition, the procedure and tasks were identical to those in the feedback condition except that before receiving feedback, participants (n = 20) refreshed their memory of the cue values by studying the information they had originally learned for another 10 min (followed by a test of whether they had acquired the information).

Materials. We used a set of 36 food items selected from a supermarket near the University of Chicago. In the learning phase, participants learned 62 of the 108 cue values (36 food items ×

3 cues); the remaining 46 cue values were not specified. The cue validities that participants were taught (80%, 70%, and 60% for the saturated fat, calorie, and protein cues, respectively) corresponded closely to the actual validities (83%, 69%, and 62%) in the chosen set of food items. From the 36 food items, we constructed 18 pairs: In 9 pairs, the most valid cue that discriminated (on the basis of the information received in the learning phase) was saturated fat; in 6 pairs, it was the calorie cue; and in 3 pairs, it was the protein cue.

To control for possible sequencing effects, we used a different random order of food pairs in each session. In addition, for both sessions, we randomly determined the positions of food items for each food pair (i.e., which of the two objects was presented on the left and which on the right).

Results

Did we obtain aggregated hindsight bias? Following Winman, Juslin, and Björkman (1998), we mapped original and recalled confidence judgments to a full-range confidence scale, thereby recoding the confidence judgments for those food pairs where a wrong choice was made (e.g., a confidence judgment of 70% that the wrong alternative was the correct one was recoded as 30%). This way all confidence judgments were conditioned on the correct alternative, and hindsight bias should become manifest in an increase of confidence. We first computed the difference between the original and the recalled confidences for each participant separately by averaging across items. Figure 10-2 illustrates these differences, averaged across participants. Confidence increased in the feedback condition by an average of 3.7 percentage points (n = 39, SD = 9.4, SE = 1.5), whereas in the no-feedback condition it decreased by 1.1 percentage points (n = 19, SD = 5.4, SE = 1.2).[3] The effect size for the difference (Δ = 4.8), $t(56)$ = 2.04, p = .023, was d = 0.56 (see Cohen, 1988, p. 20, Formula 2.2.1). According to Cohen's (1988) classification, this hindsight bias is a medium effect and, thus, larger than the average effect size reported in Christensen-Szalanski and Fobian Willham's (1991) meta-analysis.

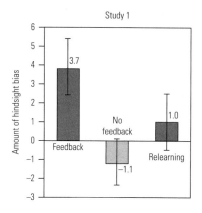
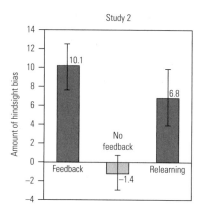

Figure 10-2. Amount of hindsight bias: (reflected) original confidence judgments minus (reflected) recalled confidence judgments. A positive difference indicates hindsight bias, and a negative difference indicates reversed hindsight bias. The bars denote standard errors.

We also determined the percentage of cases in which either the recalled choice or the recalled confidence differed from the original choice or confidence. We combined the two response modes (choice and confidence) as follows. First, we compared the original and recalled choices for each item. If they were different, we classified this item as showing either hindsight bias or reversed hindsight bias. If they were identical, we compared the original and recalled confidences and classified this item as showing hindsight bias, reversed hindsight bias, or veridical recollection. When averaged across all participants in the feedback condition, cases showing hindsight bias exceeded cases of reversed hindsight bias by 9.4 percentage points (34.5% vs. 25.1%). In the no-feedback condition, this difference was −7.9 percentage points (29.7% vs. 37.6%). If we considered only choices, the corresponding differences were 2.6 percentage points (11.0% vs. 8.4%) and −2.1 percentage points (8.0% vs. 10.1%) for the feedback and the no-feedback conditions, respectively.

The proportion of veridical recalled choices was almost identical in the feedback (80.6%) and in the no-feedback conditions (81.9%). Moreover, the proportion of cases in which both choice and confidence were veridically recalled was even slightly higher in the feedback than in the no-feedback condition. These findings are consistent with the biased reconstruction hypothesis (Stahlberg & Maass, 1998) but cannot be accounted for by the memory impairment hypothesis, which assumes that feedback changes existing memory traces. Likewise, Dehn and Erdfelder (1998), who used a multinomial model approach, concluded that they "failed to find any evidence for memory impairment hypotheses of the hindsight bias … in none of our experimental conditions does the probability of recollecting the original answer depend on whether feedback information is provided or not" (p. 144).

The fact that hindsight bias was reversed in the no-feedback condition can be attributed to a base rate effect:[4] Across all items and participants in the feedback (no-feedback) condition at Time 1, 67.3% (67.0%) of all the choices were correct. Thus, in about two thirds of the cases, feedback was supportive (i.e., initial choice was *a*, feedback was *a*) and, for those cases, only an identical recollection (recalled choice is *a*) or reversed hindsight bias (recalled choice is *b*) on the level of choice could occur. Accordingly, for the remaining 32.7% (33.0%) of cases where the initial choice was wrong, the only possible outcomes are a veridical recollection or hindsight bias. Thus, random guessing at Time 3 would lead not only to 50% veridical recollections but also to twice as many cases of reversed hindsight bias as cases of hindsight bias. Because the same percentage of cases was also correct at Time 1 in the feedback condition, such a base rate effect could be expected there as well. Thus, hindsight bias was not favored, but it nevertheless occurred (and it was even larger than the average bias observed by Christensen-Szalanski & Fobian Willham, 1991). In fact, 34% of the cases where feedback contradicted the original choice resulted in hindsight bias, whereas only 12% of the cases where feedback supported the original choice showed reversed hindsight bias. In the no-feedback condition, the corresponding percentages were 24% and 18%, respectively. We next turn to Prediction 1.

Is there an asymmetric shift in object relations? To reiterate, Prediction 1 states that if feedback on the criterion is provided, then the object relations will shift asymmetrically, more often toward the correct alternative than away from it. (If no feedback is provided, then both kinds of shift should be about equally prevalent.) For each item and cue, we determined whether the recollection of object relations was veridical or whether a shift toward or away from the correct alternative occurred. A shift toward the correct alternative included (a) relations that pointed to the smaller object at Time 1 but were recalled either as unknown or even reversed at Time 3 and (b) relations that were unknown at Time 1

but pointed to the larger object at Time 3. Shifts away from the correct alternative included all cases with shifts in the opposite direction, that is, where "smaller" and "larger" in (a) and (b) were exchanged. An object relation was classified as unknown if a participant did not specify the relation by entering either a relation symbol or the values for the two objects.

As can be seen in Figure 10-3, in the feedback condition, 20.8% of the cases shifted toward the correct alternative, and 13.2% shifted away from it ($n = 431$ and $n = 273$ of 2,076, respectively). In the no-feedback condition, the two kinds of shift occurred equally often (15.3%, or $n = 150$ of 981 for both kinds of shift), as predicted. The percentages of veridical recollections of the object relations were 66.1% (1,372 of 2,076) for the feedback condition and 69.4% (681 of 981) for the no-feedback condition.

A corollary of Prediction 1 is that cue validities that are based on participants' recollections of cue values after feedback should be higher than those before it. Cue validity is defined by the proportion of correct inferences that are based on a cue. If object relations systematically shift toward feedback, the proportion of correct inferences should increase. As depicted in Figure 10-4, across all cues and recalled cue values, the average validity indeed increased by 7.2 percentage

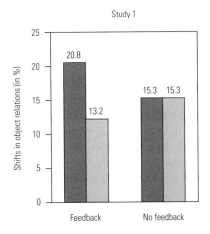
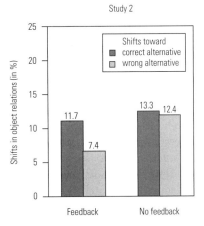

Figure 10-3. Percentages of shifts of object relations toward and away from the correct alternative in the feedback and no-feedback conditions. Veridical recollections are not included.

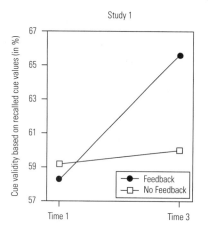
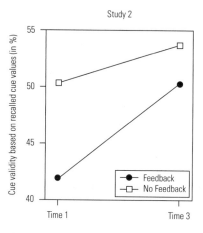

Figure 10-4. Cue validities based on participants' recollection of cue values before and after feedback (averaged across all cues and all recalled object relations).

points (from 58.3% to 65.5%) in the feedback condition, but only by 0.4 percentage points (from 59.2% to 59.6%) in the no-feedback condition.

Is the impact of feedback greater when a cue does not discriminate at Time 1 (either because a cue value for one or both objects is unknown, or because the values are equal)? In 710 of 2,076 responses in the feedback condition, a cue did not discriminate at Time 1. After feedback, 38.7% of these cases shifted to discriminating object relations, with 27.7% now pointing to the larger object and 11% to the smaller one ($\Delta = 16.7\%$). If, however, a cue did discriminate at Time 1, feedback had almost no impact: Here 32.4% of the object relations shifted (429 of 1,366), but shifts were almost symmetrical ($\Delta = 2.8\%$). Consistent with Prediction 1, in the no-feedback condition, there was symmetry, both when cues did not discriminate at Time 1 ($\Delta = 1.7\%$) and when they did ($\Delta = -1.5\%$).

To summarize, consistent with the RAFT mechanism of updating knowledge after feedback, more object relations shifted toward feedback than away from it. This difference was most pronounced when the original relations were nondiscriminating.

Is hindsight bias contingent on recalled object relations? To reiterate, Prediction 2 states that, on the basis of a participant's recalled object relations for a particular item, RAFT is able to

account for observed outcomes (hindsight bias, reversed hindsight bias, or veridical recall). We tested this prediction at the level of choices only and at the level of choice and confidence combined.

For the test on choices, we determined, for each participant and food pair, the observed outcome at the level of choice (hindsight bias, reversed hindsight bias, or veridical recall). Next, we applied take-the-best to the updated object relations at Time 3 and compared the choice (inferred by take-the-best) with the original choice given at Time 1. This comparison determined whether RAFT would lead us to predict hindsight bias, reversed hindsight bias, or no hindsight bias (if take-the-best was forced to guess, RAFT's possible predictions were treated as equally likely). If one defines hindsight bias as the percentage of choices exhibiting hindsight bias minus the percentage of choices exhibiting reversed hindsight bias across all responses, the observed difference in the resulting amount of hindsight bias between the feedback and the no-feedback condition was 4.7 percentage points. The predicted difference was 6.7 percentage points.

Thus, the predicted hindsight bias was of the same order of magnitude. However, these numbers do not provide a strict test of Prediction 2, because this prediction relates to the match between the observed and the predicted outcome at the level of individual responses. To determine this match, RAFT's predicted outcome was compared with the observed outcome, and, for each participant, we determined the percentage of correct predictions across all items. Across all participants in the feedback and no-feedback conditions, the averaged percentage of correct predictions was 83.5% (see Figure 10-5).

By what benchmark can this value be measured? Comparing the performance of the RAFT model with chance is especially important, because the two outcomes—observed and predicted—had the same reference point, namely, the original response. Thus, they are related, and chance performance might well be above 50%. Across all participants in the feedback and no-feedback conditions, RAFT's performance was 26.7 percentage points better than chance performance (56.8%, see Figure 10-5), $t(57) = 15.4$, $p = .001$.[5]

At Time 3, about 80% of the choice coincided with those of Time 1. Some of this high percentage of identical choices may be caused by direct recall rather than reconstruction (in which case RAFT is not applicable). For this reason, we conducted another test. In this test, we used a very strict operationalization of direct recall and excluded all cases in which the original and recalled choices were identical. Here RAFT's performance was still 19.1 percentage points better than that of chance (72.9% vs. 53.9%), $t(53) = 4.6$, $p = .001$.

How good is RAFT's predictive performance on the level of choices combined with confidence? Again, we excluded cases of direct recall (this time, those relatively rare cases in which both choice and confidence at Time 1 and 3 were identical). As Figure 10-6 shows, RAFT correctly predicted 76.2% of the observed outcomes. In contrast, the performance of the chance model (67.9%) was 8.4 percentage points worse, $t(57) = 5.0$, $p = .001$. The fact that RAFT fared better with predicting hindsight bias on the level of choices rather than hindsight bias on the level of choice and confidence is consistent with the common observation that it is more difficult to model confidences than choices (e.g., Hoffrage, 1995).

Could hindsight bias be reduced? To reiterate, Prediction 3 states that if recall of the cue values is assisted, then hindsight bias will be reduced. In the relearning condition, we tried to assist recall of the cue values by repeating the learning phase before giving feedback. The average increase in

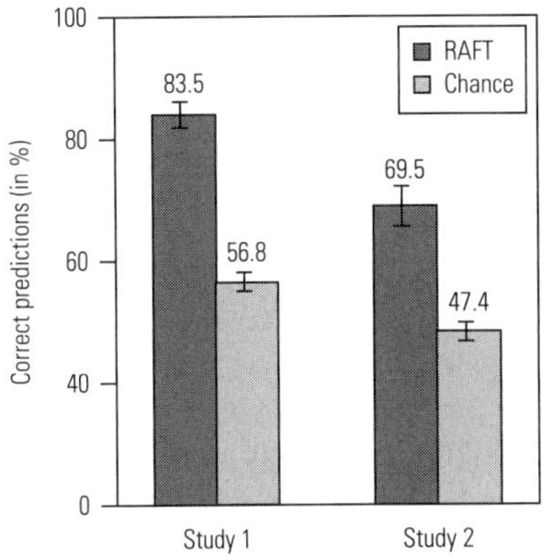

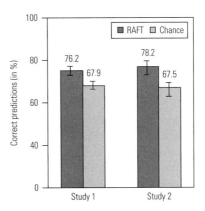

Figure 10-5. Match between observed outcomes at the level of choice (hindsight bias, reversed hindsight bias, or veridical recall) and outcomes as predicted by the RAFT model and by a chance model, respectively. Cases in which original choice and recalled choice were identical are included. The bars denote standard errors.

Figure 10-6. Match between observed outcomes at the level of choice and confidence (hindsight bias, reversed hindsight bias, or veridical recall) and outcomes as predicted by the RAFT model and by a chance model, respectively. Cases in which both choice and confidence were identical at Time 1 and Time 3 are excluded. The bars denote standard errors.

(reflected) original to recalled confidence in this condition was 1.0% ($n = 20$, $SD = 7.3$, $SE = 1.63$; see Figure 10-2), which is 2.7 percentage points less than in the standard feedback condition. If we set hindsight bias in the feedback condition (3.7%) at 100% and in the no-feedback condition (−1.1%) at 0%, then hindsight bias in the relearning condition amounted to 56%. In other words, relearning the cue values before giving feedback reduced the difference between the feedback and no-feedback conditions by about half (44%), which is consistent with Davies's (1987) finding.

We also manipulated the recall of the cue values indirectly by comparing a 1-day ("short") and 1-week ("long") interval between the original and recalled responses. On the basis of the plausible assumption (independent of the RAFT model) that memory traces become less accessible over time, we expected less hindsight bias for the short interval. The results were mixed: Consistent with this assumption, we found more veridical recollections of both choice and confidence after the short rather than the long interval (feedback condition: 46.2% and 34.7% for the short and long intervals, respectively; no-feedback condition: 33.3% and 32.0%). The same was true for choice only (feedback condition: 83.4% and 78.0%; no-feedback condition: 82.8% and 81.0%). Inconsistent with the assumption, hindsight bias was larger after the short interval than the long interval. Confidence in the correct alternative increased in the feedback condition by an average of 5.6 and 1.8 percentage points, whereas in the no-feedback condition, it decreased by 1.2 and 0.9 percentage points for the short and long intervals, respectively.

We can only offer a partial explanation for the unexpected result of the larger hindsight bias after the short rather than the long interval. Participants in the feedback condition, who came to their second session after 1 day, had in their first session 3.3 percentage points fewer correct choices than those after the 1-week condition (65.7% versus 69%). Because of fewer correct choices at Time 1, hindsight bias had a better chance to occur in the 1-day condition.

STUDY 2

RAFT can be applied to continuous and binary cues. In Study 1, we obtained evidence that the model performed well with continuous cues. In Study 2, we tested its performance with binary cues, using material unknown to our participants, which had the advantage of giving us better control over the participants' knowledge of cues. In Study 1, the participants might already have had some knowledge about the criterion (i.e., cholesterol) or might have used other information than the three cues we taught them. Another difference between the studies was the manipulation chosen to test Prediction 3. In Study 2, we adopted a method used by Davies (1987), who provided participants at the time of recall with the notes they had made in arriving at their original responses. Similarly, during the recollection phase (Time 3), we presented the participants with the cue values indicated by them at Time 1. Aside from these variations, in Study 2 we attempted to replicate the results obtained in Study 1.

Method

Participants. Fifty-five participants from the University of Salzburg (most of them psychology students) were paid for taking part in this experiment. They were divided into small groups, with a maximum of 5 members and a mean number of 2.3 members.

Design and procedure. The participants were asked to put themselves into the role of a health insurance company employee. The first task consisted of learning some facts about 12 fictional individuals: whether they "have (or had) parents with hypertension," "are overweight," and "are smokers." This learning phase lasted 18 min. The participants were then told that these people had submitted applications to purchase health insurance. We explained that the cost of health insurance depends on certain criteria, including risk factors such as high blood pressure, and that these 12 applicants for health insurance had not yet indicated their values for blood pressure.

For the following choice task, the applicants were paired (six pairs), and the participants were asked to decide for each pair, "Which of these two applicants has higher blood pressure?" and to express their confidence in having answered correctly on a scale of 50% to 100%, in 10-point increments. We told the participants that the three variables—parents' hypertension, over-weight, and smoking—were cues for high blood pressure. Then, after explaining the concept of cue validity to our participants, they learned that the validities were as follows: 80% for parents with hypertension, 70% for overweight, and 60% for smokers.

We tested participants' recall of the cue values in the following way. They were provided with four categories; "+" (cue value is positive), "–" (cue value is negative), "0" (no information was given about that person and that cue), and "?" (I have forgotten whether there was any informa-tion, or I have forgotten the information that was given about this applicant). Participants then had to (a) state a choice and a confidence and (b) recall the cue values. The sequence of tasks (a) and (b) was varied; one third of the partici-pants performed all the pair comparisons first for (a), another third started with (b), and the last third had to compare each pair for both tasks at the same time. This first session lasted about 1 hr altogether.

One week later, the participants were pre-sented with the same six pairs of applicants. As in Study 1, the participants had to carry out the tasks under one of three conditions: (a) the feed-back condition, where the participants were told which of the applicants had higher blood pres-sure; (b) the no-feedback condition; or (c) the relearning condition, where the participants not only received feedback but could also refresh their memories of their original knowledge base. Unlike in Study 1, we did not repeat the learning phase but showed each participant now he or she had previously (i.e., in the first session) recalled the cue values. The participants' task was to recall their original responses, as well as the cue values they had given in Session 1. (The partici-pants in the relearning condition did not have to recall the cue values.)

Materials. The names of the 12 applicants (6 women, 6 men) were randomly drawn from the local telephone book. In the learning phase,

the participants received information about the applicants on the three cues (i.e., parents with hypertension, overweight, smoking). We pro-vided 24 pieces of information; for three of the applicants we provided information on all three variables, for six on two variables, and for the last three on only one variable. For each of the six single-sex pairs, only one of the three cues discriminated—each cue discriminated twice, for one item followed by feedback that could have been predicted from the cue values, and for the other item with surprising feedback. For the second session, the left-right position of half the applicant pairs was reversed.

Results

Did we obtain aggregated hindsight bias? Confi-dence increased after feedback by an average of 10.1 percentage points ($n = 18$, $SD = 10.9$, $SE = 2.6$); in the no-feedback condition, confi-dence decreased by 1.4 percentage points ($n = 19$, $SD = 8.5$, $SE = 1.9$; the effect size for the differ-ence was $d = 1.15$; see also Figure 10-2). Across all responses in the feedback condition, the dif-ference between the percentage of cases with hindsight bias and reversed hindsight bias was 26.3 percentage points (48.5% vs. 22.3%; the remaining 29.1% were veridical recollections of both choice and confidence). For the no-feed-back condition, the difference was –5.3 percent-age points (34.5% vs. 39.8%). For choice only, the difference was 10.7 percentage points (19.4% vs. 8.7%) for the feedback condition and –2.7 percentage points (10.6% vs. 13.3%) for the no-feedback condition. Thus, in the feedback con-dition, cases of hindsight bias outnumbered cases of reversed hindsight bias, whereas in the no-feedback condition, we found the same small incidences of reversed hindsight bias as in Study 1. Study 2 also replicated the finding that only the difference between cases of hindsight bias and reversed hindsight bias was effected by feed-back, whereas the proportion of cases of veridi-cal recollections did not systematically differ (both choice and confidence: 29.1% and 25.7%; choice only: 71.9% and 76.1%, for feedback and no-feedback conditions, respectively).

Prediction I: Is there an asymmetric shift in object relations? As shown in Figure 10-3, in the feedback condition, 11.7% of the object relations shifted toward the correct alternative and 7.4% shifted away from it. (The remaining 80.9% were veridically recalled.) In the no-feedback condition, the corresponding percentages were 13.3, 12.4, and 74.3, respectively. The difference between the two conditions (4.3% vs. 0.9%) is not as large as in Study 1 but, again, points in the predicted direction.

Prediction 2: Is hindsight bias contingent on recalled object relations? As in Study 1, for each participant, we used the cue values recalled at Time 3 to predict choice and confidence for each item (a cue discriminated either if the value for one applicant was + and for the other it was –, or if it was + or – for one applicant and unknown for the other). The observed and predicted differences in hindsight bias— the difference between the feedback and the no-feedback conditions with respect to cases of hindsight bias minus cases of reversed hindsight bias—were 13.3 and 13.5 percentage points, respectively.

As argued earlier, the more interesting test is the match between observed and predicted outcomes on the level of individual responses as shown in Figure 10-5. RAFT's performance on the level of choice was again much higher than chance (69.5% vs. 47.4%), $t(36) = 5.3$, $p = .001$. As in Study 1, we tested RAFT's performance under more difficult conditions, that is, by also taking confidences into account and by excluding all cases in which the original and recalled response (both choice and confidence) were identical. Still, RAFT's performance (78.2%) was 10.7 percentage points better than that of the corresponding chance model (see Figure 10-6), $t(36) = 2.9$, $p = .003$.

Prediction 3: Could hindsight bias be reduced? In Study 1, we assisted the recall of cue values by repeating the learning phase in the relearning condition. In Study 2, we presented each participant with the cue values that he or she had indicated in the first session. When we compared the average original and recalled confidences in this condition, we obtained an increase of 6.8 percentage points ($n = 18$, $SD = 15.0$, $SE = 3.5$; Figure 10-2). As in Study 1, the extent of hindsight bias in Study 2 was between that of the

no-feedback condition (–1.4%) and the feedback condition (10.1%). If we give the no-feedback (feedback) conditions values of 0 (100) percent, then hindsight bias is reduced to 59%. This reduction is comparable with the one Davies (1987) observed in his Experiment 1 (48%).

Summary of Studies 1 and 2

RAFT specifies cognitive processes underlying hindsight bias: If people fail to recall their original response, this response will be reconstructed. Consistent with Prediction 1, we found in both studies that feedback on the criterion systematically influenced participants' recollections of their knowledge about cues. Updating of cue values toward feedback is an adaptive process and can lead to hindsight bias as a by-product. In fact, we were able to replicate the hindsight bias in both studies. Moreover, RAFT can explain why hindsight bias occurs, does not occur, or is reversed for individual responses. Consistent with Prediction 2, about 76% (Study 1) and 78% (Study 2) of all the cases in which either hindsight bias or reversed hindsight bias occurred were accurately predicted by RAFT. Consistent with Prediction 3, supporting the process of reconstruction by assisting the recall of cue values did reduce hindsight bias (as measured against the no-feedback condition)—in Study 1, during which the learning phase at the beginning of Session 2 was repeated, by 44% and in Study 2, during which each participant was presented with the cue values that he or she had indicated in the first session, by 41%. This reduction is particularly noteworthy when compared with the various attempts to reduce hindsight bias. In his review of debiasing strategies, Fischhoff (1982) concluded that "few of these techniques have successfully reduced the hindsight bias; none has eliminated it" (p. 428). The RAFT model provides a straightforward way to reduce hindsight bias by half.

GENERAL DISCUSSION

The RAFT model integrates theoretical concepts proposed by Frederic Bartlett, Egon Brunswik, and Herbert Simon. Remembering is seen as a process of reconstruction (Bartlett) that involves cue-based inferences (Brunswik) in a "satisficing" way (Simon). In his seminal book *Remembering*, Bartlett (1932/1995) concluded that

> remembering is not the re-excitation of innumerable fixed, lifeless and fragmentary traces. It is an imaginative reconstruction, or construction, built out of the relation of our attitude towards a whole active mass of organized past reactions or experience, and to a little outstanding detail which commonly appears in image or in language form. (p. 213)

However, Bartlett (1932/1995) did not specify how this (re)construction functions, that is, how exactly it is "built out of … our attitude towards a whole active mass." We suggest that, consistent with Brunswik's (1943, 1952) framework, this (re)construction is based on uncertain cues. Note that the framework of cue-based inferences inspired the RAFT model in a threefold way. First, cues in the original probabilistic mental model have been used to derive the original response; second, the reconstructed probabilistic mental model has been used to infer what this original response was; and third, feedback on the criterion served as a cue to update elusive cue values in the original probabilistic mental model. Rather than remaining vague as Bartlett did, or following the neo-Brunswikian idea that cues are weighted and integrated by multiple regression (Cooksey, 1996; Doherty, 1996; Hammond, 1955), we propose that the nature of the inferential mechanism is satisficing, following Simon (1982).

Fast and Frugal Inferences

How dependent is RAFT on the proposed inferential mechanism? To check the robustness of RAFT, we reanalyzed the data and tested Prediction 2 with several other heuristics, such as a unit-weight linear model, a linear model with cue validities as the weights, or naïve Bayes. None of the alternative heuristics modeled human judgment better than take-the-best; they all performed similarly well. The reason is that there were only three cues in our experiments; for most constellations of cue values, the various heuristics made the same inference (for the

problem of separability of heuristics, see also Hoffrage, Martignon, & Hertwig, 1997). Thus, the results reported here seem to be robust across various candidate heuristics.

Although the proportion of explained judgments does not allow us to discriminate between RAFT and other more complex strategies, we favor RAFT over other strategies. Why? The reason is that the processes underlying RAFT are psychologically more plausible. First, RAFT is more frugal than any of the other heuristics; that is, it requires less information to draw an inference. Second, by relying on only one cue, namely the one which discriminates between the two alternatives, it has a very simple stopping rule for search, does not integrate information, and is thus computationally simple. Third, there is now a growing number of studies—specifically designed to discriminate between various strategies—that show that people in fact use these simple heuristics.

Hindsight Bias as a By-Product of an Adaptive Process

We used the term hindsight bias because it is established in the literature. However, we do not view hindsight bias as a bias in the first place but as a consequence of learning by feedback (for a similar view, see Hoch & Loewenstein, 1989). Winman et al. (1998) recently proposed a model of the hindsight bias that is also based on the (helpful) role of feedback. Their "accuracy-assessment model" is formulated for tasks in which a "salient cognitive process" (p. 418) can be activated only to a low degree, such as for sensory discrimination tasks. Nevertheless, they arrive at a conclusion similar to ours, namely that the hindsight bias "is not an idiosyncratic and inexplicable information-processing bias but the consequence, or side-effect, of a perfectly reasonable consideration by the participants" (p. 429).

Whereas in the accuracy-assessment model, feedback affects the type of inference mechanism used, in the RAFT model it affects the input to the inference mechanism, which is the same prior to and after feedback. New incoming information, such as the feedback provided in our experiments, is evaluated against preexisting information; if the new information is more reliable, the preexisting information may be changed to obtain a more accurate corpus of knowledge. Such an automatic process of updating knowledge is consistent with Bartlett's (1932/1995) findings that schemata are constantly changing and being updated.

The adaptive function of this knowledge updating in our semantic memory is that it enables us to improve our inferences over time. In the case of hindsight bias, however, inferences about what we previously said may be in error, thus making it difficult for us to learn from our past. Nevertheless, hindsight bias may not be much of an adaptive disadvantage. Remembering the real state of affairs (e.g., whether something is true or really happened) is generally more important than remembering what one thought about it before learning the truth. As Bartlett (1932/1995) put it: "In a world of constantly changing environment, literal recall is extraordinarily unimportant" (p. 204). Moreover, the ability to access our previous knowledge states would require significant storage space and would lead to memory overload; forgetting may be necessary for memory to maintain its function (Hoffrage & Hertwig, 1999). Another advantage of forgetting is that it prevents one from using old information that may be outdated because of changes in the environment (Bjork & Bjork, 1988; Ginzburg, Janson, & Ferson, 1996). Taken together, the disadvantage of hindsight bias is a relatively cheap price to pay for making better inferences and maintaining a well-functioning memory.

ACKNOWLEDGMENTS

We are grateful to Hartmut Blank, Edgar Erdfelder, Klaus Fiedler, Reid Hastie, Peter Mueser, Rüdiger Pohl, members of the ABC Research Group, and two anonymous reviewers for helpful comments; to Heinz Mayringer for helping to collect the data; and to Anita Todd and Jill Vyse for editing the manuscript. We also thank the Deutsche Forschungsgemeinschaft (Grants Nos. 1847/1 and SFB 504) for their financial support.

NOTES

1. The simplest response strategy is to recall the old belief. It has been argued that outcome information could either destroy or disturb the memory trace of the original judgment (Fischhoff, 1975) or reduce its accessibility (Hell et al., 1988). This alone, however, cannot explain the occurrence of hindsight bias. The second strategy, anchoring and adjustment, would result in hindsight bias if the adjustment was not large enough. Although there is a large body of evidence suggesting that adjustment is usually insufficient (Tversky & Kahneman, 1974), Hawkins and Hastie (1990) and Hertwig et al. (1997) also pointed out problems with this explanation. For example, this explanation would lead us to predict the same effect for occurrences (anchor on 100%) and nonoccurrences (anchor on 0%), whereas occurrences actually do lead to larger effects. According to the motivational response-adjustment explanation, the bias is attributed to participants' motivation to appear intelligent, knowledgeable, or perspicacious. The empirical evidence supporting this view is scattered and weak. In line with most of the literature, Hawkins and Hastie concluded that motivational response adjustment appears to play either a minor role or no role in explaining hindsight bias.

2. Note that the term *choice* has two meanings here. The first refers to an inference, for example, "which of two foods has more cholesterol"; this is how we use the term throughout this article. The second meaning relates to an actual selection, for example, Patricia's order, at the restaurant, of the food with less cholesterol.

3. Two participants were excluded from the analysis because they apparently misunderstood the instructions: One was excluded in the feedback condition, because in the second session (after 1 day) he recalled exclusively 0% and 100% confidence judgments, whereas his original confidences were distributed across all confidence categories; the other was excluded in the no-feedback condition (after 1 week), because almost half of her confidence judgments were below 50%.

4. It is noteworthy that with numerical judgment tasks (e.g., "How high is the Eiffel Tower in Paris?") in the no-feedback conditions, the opposite result, namely hindsight bias, is usually obtained. This outcome has been explained as a

regression-toward-the-mean phenomenon (see Erdfelder & Buchner, 1998, Footnote 7).

5. Chance outcome was generated by using participants' actual knowledge distributions, rather than by assuming ignorance about cue values or a uniform probability distribution of cue values. To derive the prediction of chance for a specific item, we predicted, by using take-the-best, the outcome for this item on the basis of knowledge about the cue values for another item. Thus, for each participant in Study 1 and Study 2, we arrived at 17 and 5 predictions for each item, respectively. Then, we compared the original response for a specific item with each of the predicted responses and determined the percentages of correct predictions (first, within each participant and across all items and predictions, then averaged across participants). As can be seen in Figures 10-5 and 10-6, this procedure provided a benchmark that was much higher than the simple and unwarranted assumption that chance performance would be 50% (such a simple chance model ignores that, because of scale-end-effects, the probability of a match between observed and predicted outcome is larger than 50% for original responses with extreme confidence).

How are heuristics selected?

Introduction to Chapter 11

SSL: A Theory of How People Learn to Select Strategies

According to the adaptive toolbox view of cognition, people can avail themselves of a repertoire of strategies. Adaptive decision making arises from the ability to select a strategy that is appropriate for the current task environment. But how does the mind know which strategy to select? This is a difficult problem and has led some to argue that in order to solve it, the mind needs a Bayesian homunculus who determines each time whether it is better to use a heuristic rather than Bayes' rule. As described in Chapter 1, however, there are other solutions beyond optimization. The first is that memory restricts the set of heuristics that can be applied. When both options are recognized, for instance, the recognition heuristic cannot be applied, whereas the fluency heuristic can. Second, people may choose a strategy based on their knowledge about the structure of the environment. For instance, Dieckmann and Rieskamp (2007) showed that people can select an appropriate strategy after simply observing the structure of the environment (e.g., the degree to which cues were intercorrelated). No feedback about the accuracy of their inferences in the environment was necessary.

A third mechanism that can implement strategy selection is individual learning by feedback. Jörg Rieskamp and Philipp Otto propose a formal cognitive model of how learning by feedback leads to adaptive strategy selection. Their work also represents an example of theory integration, insofar as reinforcement theory is applied to the strategy selection problem. The innovative aspect of this application is that the unit being reinforced is a cognitive strategy, not behavior. According to their model, heuristics are not selected because of cognitive constraints, but because of their past success in particular environments.

One noteworthy observation by Rieskamp and Otto is that when confronted with an unknown environment, participants' early inferences were best predicted by a compensatory strategy that considers many cues (i.e., weighted additive; WADD). What does this result mean? Some authors have argued that people's apparent initial tendency to decide based on many cues shows that people only rarely rely on heuristics (e.g., Bröder & Newell, 2008). Alternatively, the result may simply reflect that when encountering a task with which they had previously had little experience, people began to explore cues and how to process them. As shown in Chapter 30, take-the-best is applied more frequently by people who have sufficient knowledge about a domain (e.g., burglary), which enables them to hit on the single best cue. People lacking this knowledge appear to prefer considering many cues.

CHAPTER 11

SSL: A Theory of How People Learn to Select Strategies

Jörg Rieskamp and Philipp E. Otto

Abstract: The assumption that people possess a repertoire of strategies to solve the inference problems they face has been raised repeatedly. However, a computational model specifying how people select strategies from their repertoire is still lacking. The proposed strategy selection learning (SSL) theory predicts a strategy selection process on the basis of reinforcement learning. The theory assumes that individuals develop subjective expectations for the strategies they have and select strategies proportional to their expectations, which are then updated on the basis of subsequent experience. The learning assumption was supported in four experimental studies. Participants substantially improved their inferences through feedback. In all four studies, the best-performing strategy from the participants' repertoires most accurately predicted the inferences after sufficient learning opportunities. When testing SSL against three models representing extensions of SSL and against an exemplar model assuming a memory-based inference process, the authors found that SSL predicted the inferences most accurately.

If one adopts the view that people are equipped with a strategy repertoire, the pressing question is how individuals select their strategies. We call this the *strategy selection problem*—the central focus of this article. As a solution to this problem, several authors have followed a cost-benefit approach (see Beach & Mitchell, 1978; Christensen-Szalanski, 1978; Payne, Bettman, & Johnson, 1988, 1993; Smith & Walker, 1993), according to which individuals trade a strategy's costs against its benefits in making their selections. The costs of a strategy are related to the cognitive effort required for processing it and the benefits are related to the

strategy's accuracy. People anticipate the "benefits and costs of the different strategies that are available and choose the strategy that is best for the problem" (Payne et al., 1993, p. 91). According to Payne et al. (1993), the selection process could be a conscious process of applying a metastrategy or an unconscious decision triggered by experience. The trade-off of costs and benefits is influenced by the characteristics of the task, the person, and the social context. However, applying a metastrategy to strategy selection could run into a recursive homunculi problem of deciding how to decide. Busemeyer (1993) has made the criticism that the trade-off process has not been explicated sufficiently. Therefore, it appears necessary to advance the theoretical approach by providing a computational model that describes the strategy selection process. In this article we argue that people select appropriate strategies on the basis of learning. From this learning perspective, we aim to answer three crucial questions: First, do people select different inference strategies in different environments? Second, do people learn to select the strategy of their strategy repertoire that performs best in a particular environment? Third, how can a learning process in the selection of strategies be described?

We first discuss the empirical evidence for the selection of different strategies. After that, we define the strategy selection learning (SSL) theory and describe competing alternative models, including three extensions of SSL and one exemplar model. We then report four experimental studies that (a) tested whether people learn to select the best-performing strategy from their repertoire for a particular environment and (b) tested the proposed learning theory.

DO PEOPLE SELECT DIFFERENT STRATEGIES FOR INFERENCES?

Consider the following problem: Of two companies, you have to choose the more creditworthy. For this inference, you could use the information garnered from different cues (e.g., the company's financial flexibility). But which and how many cues should be considered, and how should the information from the cues be used to make an inference? In this article, we focus on this type of probabilistic inference problem, which differs from the preferential choices that Payne et al. (1988) examined. Gigerenzer and Goldstein (1996) showed that a simple lexicographic heuristic, called "take-the-best" (TTB), can perform surprisingly well here: Assume each cue has either a positive or a negative cue value and that the cues can be ranked according to their validities. The cue validity is defined as the conditional probability of making a correct inference on the condition that the cue discriminates—in this example, that one company has a positive and the other a negative cue value. TTB searches for the cue with the highest validity and selects the company with the positive cue value. If the cue does not discriminate, then the second most valid cue is considered, and so on. If no cue discriminates, TTB selects randomly. This inference strategy is noncompensatory, because a cue cannot be outweighed by any combination of

less valid cues. In contrast with compensatory strategies, which integrate cue values. Gigerenzer and Goldstein (1996) showed that TTB outperforms many alternative strategies, including a linear weighted additive (WADD) strategy. For each alternative, the WADD strategy computes the sum of all cue values multiplied by the validity of the cue and then finally selects the alternative with the largest sum. Alternatively, the strategy can be implemented by computing a sum of the weighted differences of the alternatives' cue values (for details, see Tversky, 1969). Although TTB's simplicity and accuracy make it psychologically plausible, researchers have asked for (more) empirical support (e.g., Bröder, 2000; Chater, 2000; Lipshitz, 2000), to evaluate under which conditions people actually apply noncompensatory inference strategies.

Recent studies show that noncompensatory strategies, in particular TTB, were most suitable to predict people's inferences under time pressure (Rieskamp & Hoffrage, 1999, 2008), when there were relatively high explicit information acquisition costs (Bröder, 2000), when the cue information had to be retrieved from memory (Bröder & Schiffer, 2003), or when their application led to high payoffs (Bröder, 2003). Compensatory strategies, in particular WADD, were more suitable to predict participants' inferences in situations with low time pressure, low information acquisition costs, or when the information was simultaneously provided via a computer screen. Newell and Shanks (2003) and Newell, Weston, and Shanks (2003) showed that people search for cues as predicted by TTB under high information acquisition costs, whereas the search is consistent with compensatory strategies under low information costs. However, search behavior appears to be only loosely connected with the strategy's predicted information search, even if the strategy predicts the choices better than do alternative strategies. People, for instance, search for unnecessary information or look up information twice (Newell et al., 2003; Rakow, Newell, Fayers, & Hersby, 2005; Rieskamp & Hoffrage, 1999). Therefore, in this article, we assume that when people apply a strategy, they will search for the information required by the strategy, but they might also search for additional information (e.g., to consolidate their preliminary decision; Svenson, 1992). Likewise, Costa-Gomes, Crawford, and Broseta (2001) argued that it is reasonable to use a less strict criterion for classifying people's decision strategies, which still allows a high degree of flexibility in the search behavior. Accordingly, we identify selected strategies on the basis of individuals' choices and information search, with a stronger focus on their choices.

PREDICTING A STRATEGY SELECTION LEARNING PROCESS

Learning models have a long tradition in psychology, starting with the seminal work of Estes (1950), Bush and Mosteller (1955), and Luce (1959). More recent theories have proposed additional specific learning mechanisms (e.g., Börgers & Sarin, 1997; Busemeyer & Myung, 1992; Camerer & Ho, 1999a, 1999b; Erev, 1998; Erev & Roth, 1998; Rieskamp, Busemeyer, & Laine, 2003; Stahl, 1996, 2000; Sutton & Barto, 1998). Following this work, we propose a learning theory as an answer to how people select strategies for inferential choices.[1]

SSL Theory

According to SSL, people possess a repertoire of cognitive strategies to solve the inference problems they face. Through feedback, these unobservable cognitive strategies, instead of stimulus-response associations, are reinforced. From their strategy repertoire, people are most likely to select the strategy they expect to solve the problem well. These strategies' expectancies change through reinforcement learning depending on the strategies' past performances. For simplicity, we focus on a prototypical compensatory strategy—WADD—and a prototypical noncompensatory strategy—TTB—that were most suitable for predicting inferences under varying conditions as reported above.

SSL assumes that individuals have a set S of N cognitive strategies. For the following studies we assume that the strategy set of SSL consists of only two strategies, hence $N = 2$ and $S = \{WADD, TTB\}$. The individual's preference for a particular cognitive strategy is expressed by positive

expectancies $q(i)$, with i as an index for the cognitive strategies. Following Luce (1959, p. 25; cf. Thurstone, 1930) the probability that strategy i is selected at trial t is defined by

$$p_t(i) = \frac{q_t(i)}{\sum_{j=1}^{N} q_t(j)}. \qquad (11\text{-}1)$$

The strategies' expectancies in the first period of the task can differ, and are defined by

$$q_1(i) = r_{\max} w \beta_i, \qquad (11\text{-}2)$$

where $r_{\max}$ is the maximum payoff that can be obtained by a correct decision, w is the initial association parameter, and β is the initial preference parameter. The maximum payoff is defined as the maximum payoff received for a correct decision in the particular task; this component allows comparisons of SSL across tasks with different payoffs. The initial association parameter w is restricted to $w > 0$ and expresses an individual's initial association with the available strategies relative to later reinforcement; thus it essentially describes the learning rate. SSL assumes that individuals have initial preferences for selecting particular strategies at the beginning of a task. The initial preference parameter β_i for each strategy i is restricted to $0 < \beta < 1$ and $\sum_{i=1}^{N} \beta_i = 1$. The number of initial preference parameters equals the number of strategies minus 1; in the case of two strategies this implies one free parameter.[2] After a decision is made, the expectancies of the cognitive strategies are updated for the next trial t by

$$q_t(i) = q_{t-1}(i) + I_{t-1}(i) r_{t-1}(i), \qquad (11\text{-}3)$$

where $I_{t-1}(i)$ is an an indicator function and $r_{t-1}(i)$ is the reinforcement. The reinforcement of a cognitive strategy is defined as the payoff $r_{t-1}(i)$ that the strategy produced. The indicator function $I_{t-1}(i)$ equals 1 if strategy i was selected and equals 0 if the strategy was not selected. It is assumed that a strategy was selected if the necessary information for applying the strategy was acquired and the choice coincides with the strategy's prediction. Thus, contrary to previous research that has used either the choice or the information search to identify strategy selection, we combine both sources of data, a procedure often called for (Einhorn & Hogarth, 1981; Einhorn, Kleinmuntz, & Kleinmuntz, 1979; Pitz & Sachs, 1984) but rarely realized. The assumption that a strategy was selected when a choice coincides with the strategies' prediction becomes problematic if strategies make identical predictions and it is incorrectly inferred that both strategies were selected. Therefore, when two or more strategies make the same prediction that coincides with the individual's choice (and the necessary information for these strategies has been acquired), it is assumed that $I_{t-1}(i)$ equals the probability with which the model predicts the selection of these strategies. In this case, the strategies' expectancies increase, but the ratio of the strategies' expectancies does not change. By definition, if $q_t(i)$ falls below a minimum value ρ because of negative payoffs, $q_t(i)$ is set to ρ; for the following studies ρ = 0.0001 was used. We define the strategies' reinforcements explicitly in terms of the monetary gains and losses a strategy produces.

Finally, SSL assumes that people occasionally make errors when applying a strategy, so that, by mistake, they deviate from the strategy's prediction. Without an application error, the conditional probability $p(a|i)$ of choosing alternative a out of the set a and b when strategy i is selected is either $p(a|i) = 1$ or $p(a|i) = 0$ for deterministic strategies like TTB and WADD. In the case for which the cues do not allow discrimination between the alternatives, then the strategies choose randomly, so that $p(a|i) = 1/k$, with k as the number of available alternatives. Incorporating an application error ε into strategy application leads to the predicted probability of

$$p_t(a|i,\varepsilon) = (1-\varepsilon)\cdot p_t(a|i) + \frac{\varepsilon}{k-1}\cdot p_t(\overline{a}|i), \quad (11\text{-}4)$$

where $p_t(\overline{a}|i)$ denotes the probability of choosing any other alternative than a out of the available alternatives (i.e., alternative b in the case of two alternatives), given strategy i was selected. For simplicity, the application error is assumed to be the same across strategies. In sum, the probability of choosing alternative a depends on the probabilities of selecting the strategies and

the corresponding choice probabilities of the strategies, so that

$$p_t(a) = \sum_{i=1}^{N} p_t(i)\cdot p_t(a|i,\varepsilon). \quad (11\text{-}5)$$

Besides the psychological plausibility of a probabilistic character of choice (for a review, see Rieskamp, Busemeyer, & Mellers, 2006), the application error parameter allows an evaluation of whether a reasonable set of strategies was assumed. If people apply cognitive strategies that differ substantially from the assumed strategy set (i.e., strategies that make different predictions), then the result will be a relatively high application error.

When assuming that people possess a repertoire of cognitive strategies, SSL provides a computational description of how strategies are selected, thereby proposing how the strategy selection problem could be solved. SSL assumes that individuals have initial preferences for strategies that change because of feedback, so that after sufficient learning the selected strategy depends on the learning process described by SSL. The process that determines initial preferences for strategies is not specified by SSL, but it is reasonable to assume that these preferences rely on past experience, so that previously successful strategies will be preferred initially.

Here SSL connects to the cost-benefit approach of strategy selection, because initial strategy preference could also depend on the different costs and benefits of strategies. Strategies' benefits can include, among others, the strategy's accuracy (e.g., Payne et al., 1993), the social acceptability of applying a particular strategy (Lerner & Tetlock, 1999), or the monetary outcome produced by a strategy. Strategies' costs can include, among others, the cognitive effort to apply a strategy (e.g., Johnson & Payne, 1985), the negative consequences that result from wrong inferences, or the monetary search costs a strategy produces. Thus, strategies' costs and benefits are manifold and could affect individuals' initial preferences for strategies and could also represent strategies' reinforcements when applying the strategy. However, for simplicity's sake, SSL defines reinforcements solely in monetary terms. Because this is a simplification, future work will need to address how other forms of reinforcement could be included in the theory.

In sum, SSL is a simple learning model with three free parameters, implementing mechanisms that have been proposed in previous learning theories: the choice rule (e.g., Erev, 1998), expectancies for the objects (e.g., Camerer & Ho, 1999a; Erev & Roth, 1998), and conceptualizing strategies as the objects of reinforcement (e.g., Busemeyer & Myung, 1992; Erev & Roth, 2001; Stahl, 1996). SSL's prediction depends on its parameter values. Generally, however, when there is no extreme initial preference for one strategy, the initial attachment to the strategies is not too strong, and the application error rate is small, SSL predicts that the strategy of the repertoire that performs best will be selected after sufficient learning opportunity. We define the best performing strategy as the strategy that leads to the highest monetary outcome when applied consistently. In this case, "best" is only relative to the strategy repertoire considered, because there might always be alternative strategies that were not considered, yet perform better. We tested SSL against four alternative models: The first three represent more general learning models; the last represents an exemplar model.

Alternative Reinforcement Learning Theories

Three learning models were constructed by extending SSL, each incorporating one additional psychological mechanism.

Exponential strategy selection. SSL assumes that strategies are selected according to a proportional selection rule represented by Equation 11-1. This implies that when the decision maker detects a performance superiority of one strategy over the others, the best-performing strategy will not necessarily be selected exclusively. To allow for such more deterministic selections, many learning theories apply exponential selection rules (e.g., Camerer & Ho, 1999a, 1999b). Consistently, SSL can be extended by replacing Equation 11-1 with

$$p_t(i) = \frac{e^{\mu \ln q_t(i)}}{\sum_{j=1}^{N} e^{\mu \ln q_t(j)}}, \qquad (11\text{-}6)$$

where μ is a sensitivity parameter that in the case of a high value allows the model to predict relatively large selection probabilities, even for low-expectancy differences across strategies. However, in case of a low value for the sensitivity parameter (i.e., $\mu < 1$), the model predicts that a superior strategy is not learned, because it is selected too rarely. When $\mu = 1$, the exponential selection model is equivalent to SSL.

Forgetting. Many learning theories assume that recent reinforcement more strongly influences behavior than reinforcement that was received longer ago (e.g., Erev & Roth, 1998; Estes, 1976; Sutton & Barto, 1998). This implies that the strategies' expectancies decline over time and that a strategy becomes unlikely to be selected if it does not receive any reinforcement. Accordingly, a forgetting parameter, denoted ϕ and restricted to $0 \leq \phi \leq 1$, can be incorporated into SSL by modifying the updating rule (Equation 11-3) as

$$q_t(i) = (1 - \phi) q_{t-1}(i) + I_{t-1}(i) r_{t-1}(i). \qquad (11\text{-}7)$$

The forgetting parameter determines how strongly previous expectancies affect new expectancies. The forgetting model predicts an accelerated learning process compared with SSL, because the forgetting process quickly wipes out initial strategy preferences in favor of the best-performing strategy. In addition, because of forgetting, strategies' expectancies can converge to the minimum allowed value, so that the preferred strategy will be selected more or less exclusively. A value of zero for the forgetting parameter makes the model equivalent to SSL.

Imagination. The idea that people imagine strategies' performances goes back to theories of fictitious play (G. W. Brown, 1951). Through an imagination process, people can realize that alternative strategies could have solved a problem more adequately. Therefore, not only the selected strategy but unselected strategies as well receive reinforcement when people imagine their outcomes (cf. Camerer & Ho, 1999a, 1999b; Cheung & Friedman, 1997). To incorporate such an imagination process, the SSL updating rule (Equation 11-3) is modified to

$$q_t(i) = q_{t-1}(i) + [\delta + (1 - \delta) I_{t-1}(i)] \cdot r_{t-1}(i), \qquad (11\text{-}8)$$

With δ as an imagination parameter, restricted to $0 \leq \delta \leq 1$, Hence, the selected strategy receives a reinforcement of r, and unselected strategies receive a reinforcement of r multiplied by δ. If δ equals 1, all strategies receive reinforcement as if they had been selected; values between 0 and 1 allow lessened reinforcement for unselected strategies. The imagination model can predict particular learning effects: first, an accelerated learning process at the beginning of a learning situation, because the strategy that is not preferred by the decision maker will also be reinforced. Second, the strategies' expectancies will converge to a constant ratio so that, contrary to SSL, the model predicts that the learning process does not lead to an exclusive selection of the best-performing strategy even after sufficient learning but rather to a selection probability that depends on the ratio of the strategies' performances. If the imagination parameter equals zero (i.e., δ = 0), then the imagination model is equivalent to SSL.

EXEMPLAR-BASED INFERENCES

Our central aim in this article is to propose a computational theory for the strategy repertoire approach. However, there are alternative approaches that could describe people's inferences. Models that have been proposed for the domain of categorizations could also be applied to inferential choices. The models include, among others, neural network models (e.g., Gluck & Bower, 1988; Shanks, 1991; Sieck & Yates, 2001), exemplar models (Lamberts, 2000; Medin & Schaffer, 1978; Nosofsky, 1986; Nosofsky & Johansen, 2000), and combinations of both (Kruschke, 1992; Nosofsky, Kruschke, & McKinley, 1992). Exemplar models have been successfully applied in various domains, for example, memory (Hintzman, 1988), automatization (Logan, 1988), likelihood judgments (Dougherty, Gettys, & Ogden, 1999), and attention (Logan, 2002). Recently, Juslin and Persson (2002; see also Juslin, Jones, Olsson, & Winman, 2003; Juslin, Olsson, & Olsson, 2003) proposed an exemplar model for the inferential choice task that is the focus of this article. According to the exemplar-based approach,

inferences are made by comparing the present inference situation (probe) with similar inference situations (exemplars) in memory and making an inference according to the best responses to the memorized exemplars. Thus, people do not learn to select abstract strategies that they apply to an inference situation but instead learn stimulus-outcome associations. Because exemplar models have been applied successfully as an "all-purpose inference machine" (Juslin, Jones, et al., 2003, p. 925) and offer a fundamentally different explanation of inference processes, they are strong and interesting competitors for SSL.

In the following, we adapt the exemplar-based model (EBM) proposed by Juslin, Jones, et al. (2003). According to EBM, individuals compare the choice situation with previous choices. Contrary to Juslin, Jones, et al., we assume that during such a retrieval process the whole choice situation containing both alternatives is retrieved (as opposed to the retrieval of single alternatives). Each alternative is described by a vector of cue values that can be positive (+), negative (−), or unknown (?). The pairs of alternatives—representing an exemplar—can be described by a cue configuration. For each cue in this configuration, nine combinations of cue values are possible (i.e., +/+, +/−, +/?, −/+, etc.). When making inferences, the cue configuration of the current pair of alternatives (probe) is compared with the configuration of previous pairs (exemplars) by determining the similarity between the configurations, defined as

$$s(x, y) = \prod_{m=1}^{M} d_{xym}, \qquad (11\text{-}9)$$

where d_{xym} is an index that takes a value of 1 if the combination of cue values of the probe x corresponds with the combination of cue values of the exemplary for cue m; otherwise it takes the value s_m, which is an attention weight parameter varying between 0 and 1 (cf. Juslin, Jones, et al., 2003). The attention weights represent the subjective importance of cues; the smaller the value the greater the importance. The number of parameters equals the number M of cues. Finally, the probability that the first alternative a of the alternative pair $\{a, b\}$ will be chosen is determined by

$$p(a) = \frac{\Sigma_{j \in a} S(x, y_j)}{\Sigma_{j \in a} S(x, y_j) + \Sigma_{j \in b} S(x, y_j)} \qquad (11\text{-}10)$$

where the index $j \in a$ denotes that the sum is reached over all exemplars y_j, where the first alternative a was the correct choice, whereas the index $j \in b$ denotes that the sum is reached over all exemplars y_j where the second alternative b was the correct choice. Note that a particular exemplar for which alternative a was the correct choice could have cue values identical to another exemplar for which alternative b was the correct choice. Thus, with respect to categorization research, the choice situation is ill defined (Medin, Altom, & Murphy, 1984), because the correct responses can differ for a situation with identical available information. In Appendix A we provide a detailed description of how the exemplar model was implemented.

OVERVIEW OF THE EXPERIMENTAL STUDIES

In the following four studies, participants made repeated inferences in different environment conditions when provided with outcome feedback. The studies were designed to explore our three main questions: Do people select different strategies? Do they learn to select the strategy from their strategy repertoire that performs best in an environment? And, finally, can SSL predict the learning process? To evaluate this, we compared SSL pairwise with its competitors. In all four studies the participants were mainly students from various departments at the Free University of Berlin (i.e., 85%, 88%, 78%, and 88%, in Studies 1, 2, 3, and 4, respectively). The computerized tasks were conducted in individual sessions and lasted approximately 1 hr (with the exception of Study 2, which lasted 1.5 hr). In all studies, participants were paid according to their performance in the task (with €1 approximately corresponding to U.S. $1 at the time of the studies).

STUDY 1

In Study 1 we examined whether people improve their decisions when they repeatedly make inferences with feedback about their performance and how well TTB and WADD are able to predict the inferences. In Study 1 we also tested SSL's learning prediction that people learn to select the best-performing strategy out of their strategy repertoire and compared SSL to its competitors. For this test, participants made decisions in either a compensatory environment, in which the compensatory strategy WADD led to the highest performance, defined as the total received payoff, or in a noncompensatory environment, in which the noncompensatory strategy TTB led to the highest performance.

Method

Forty people (23 women and 17 men), whose average age was 25, participated in the experiment. Participants' average payment was approximately €14. Participants were instructed that, from two unnamed companies, they had to select the more creditworthy company (i.e., the company that would pay back a loan) and that only one company was the correct choice. For each decision made, the participants had to pay 15 cents, described as a "handling fee" and, for each correct decision, they earned a payoff of 30 cents (formally equivalent to receiving 15 cents for a correct decision and paying 15 cents for an incorrect decision). With this payoff structure, participants who randomly chose between the companies netted a payment of zero. Each company was described by six cues and their validities. The companies' cue values, which could be either positive or negative, were presented in a matrix form using a computerized information board (see Figure 11-1). The cue values were concealed in boxes that had to be opened by clicking on the box. Once a box was opened, the cue values remained visible until a choice was made. The importance of the six cues was explained by means of their validities, which were presented next to the names of the cues. The cues (with the cue validities shown to the participants) were efficiency (.90), financial resources (.85), financial flexibility (.78), capital

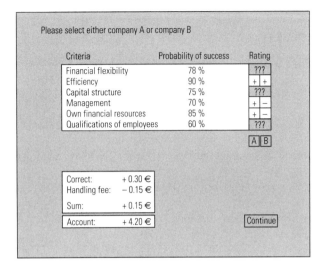

Figure 11-1. This information board was used in Study 1; similar ones were used in Studies 2 and 3. It showed the cue values for both alternatives, which could be acquired by clicking on the boxes. The boxes with three question marks could still be opened by the participants to view the cue values. The payoffs received were presented at the bottom of the screen.

structure (.75), management (.70), and qualifications of employees (.60). All these cues are common for assessing companies' creditworthiness (Rommelfanger & Unterharnscheid, 1985).

In both experimental conditions, participants made 171 choices under no time constraints. These 171 items consisted of 3 initial items to familiarize participants with the task, followed by seven trial blocks, each consisting of the same set of 24 items. The items within each trial block were randomly ordered, and the position of the two companies for each item (left or right on the screen) varied randomly. To examine participants' potential initial preferences for one of the two strategies for solving the task, we provided no feedback in the first trial block. In the trial blocks that followed, we provided outcome feedback on the decisions' correctness to allow for learning.

For all items, the strategies WADD and TTB always made an unambiguous prediction of which of the two companies to choose; therefore, their predictions never relied on random choice. In the compensatory environment, the item set was constructed such that WADD reached an accuracy of 92% (i.e., 22 correct of a possible 24 predictions) compared with TTB's accuracy of 58% (i.e., 14 correct of a possible 24). In the noncompensatory environment, the strategies' accuracies were reversed such that WADD reached an accuracy of 58% compared with TTB's accuracy of 92%. It is important that

the inferior strategy still leads to an accuracy above chance; otherwise an adaptive selection of a strategy would be to choose the opposite of the strategy's prediction.[3] To infer which strategy had been selected on the basis of the participant's choices, it was crucial for us to construct a decision problem for which strategies' predictions differed substantially. Therefore, in addition to the specific accuracy levels of the strategies, the items were constructed such that for both environment conditions, strategies' predictions differed for 12 of the 24 items. All items were created from a set of 50 companies, for which the validities of the cues were determined. However, because of the necessary properties of the item set, that is, the strategies' performances and the separability of the strategies' predictions, the validities of the selected item set in the experiment deviated from those told to the participants (the deviations ranged between 0.05 and 0.43). In sum, the experimental design has two factors: environment (between subjects; compensatory vs. noncompensatory environment) and trial block, with seven repetitions of the item set (within subject).

Results

Before evaluating the learning models, we first looked for learning effects.

Learning effects. Participants were able to increase their payoff substantially across the

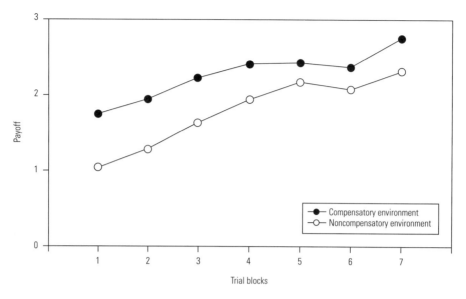

Figure 11-2. The average payoffs (in euros) received by the participants across the seven trial blocks in Study 1 in the compensatory and noncompensatory environment conditions.

seven trial blocks, illustrating a strong learning effect (see Figure 11-2). A repeated measurement analysis of variance (ANOVA) was conducted with the average obtained payoff as the dependent variable, the trial block as a within-subject factor, and the environment as a between-subjects factor. We used the average payoff as the dependent variable, because the reinforcement of the learning models has been defined by the received payoffs. Nevertheless, in Study 1 using the payoffs is identical with using the participants' accuracy, because the payoffs are a function of the proportion of correct and incorrect decisions. The average payoff of €1.36 ($SD = 0.78$; corresponding to an accuracy of 67% correct decisions) in the first trial block increased significantly to an average payoff of €2.50 ($SD = 0.67$; corresponding to an accuracy of 85%) in the last trial block, $F(4, 228) = 25.57$, $p < .01$, $\eta^2 = 0.41$. Additionally, there was an environment effect, because participants did better, with an average total payoff of €15.88 ($SD = 2.84$), in the compensatory environment compared with €12.41 ($SD = 3.94$) in the noncompensatory environment, $F(1, 38) = 10.18$, $p < .01$, $\eta^2 = 0.21$. We did not observe any interaction between trial block and environment.

But what strategy do people select for making their inferences? To answer this question, we determined the percentages of predicted choices by TTB and WADD for half of the items of each block for which the strategies made different predictions. Figure 11-3 shows the percentage of choices predicted by the better performing strategy for each environment condition.[4] At the beginning of the task, WADD was better at predicting participants' choices regardless of the environment condition. This indicated an initial preference for integrating all available information when making an inference. It also explained why participants received a higher payoff in the first trial block of the compensatory environment compared with the noncompensatory environment, because the initially preferred compensatory strategy led to a higher payoff in the compensatory environment. After the first trial block, this preference changed depending on the environment condition. For the compensatory environment, the fit of WADD increased over the trial blocks. In contrast, for the noncompensatory environment, TTB's fit increased, implying a decrease for WADD's fit. This result supports our hypothesis that people select different strategies for inferences and that they learn

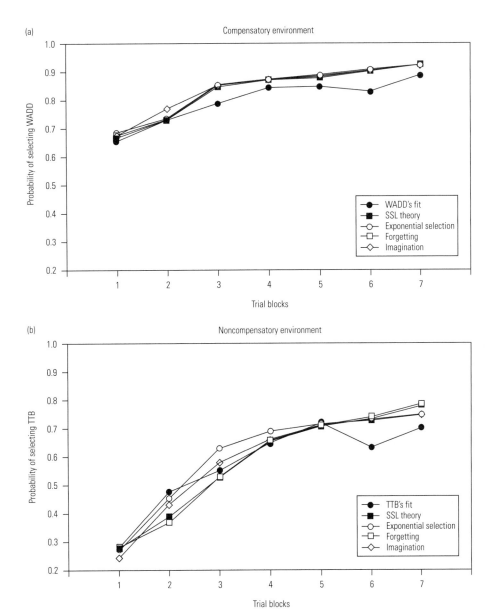

Figure 11-3. The percentage of choices predicted by the best-performing strategy in the compensatory (a) and the noncompensatory (b) environment conditions of Study 1 (only for those items for which the strategies made different predictions). Additionally, the figure shows the predicted probability by the different learning models with which the best-performing strategy is selected. SSL's prediction differed from the percentage of choices predicted by the best-performing strategy with a mean square error of 0.24%. The fit for the exponential selection model was $MSE = 0.20\%$, for the forgetting model was $MSE = 0.29\%$, and for the imagination model was $MSE = 0.18\%$. WADD = the weighted additive strategy; SSL = strategy selection learning; TTB = the take-the-best heuristic.

to select the best-performing strategy: In the last trial block, WADD predicted 88% of all choices in the compensatory environment, and TTB predicted 71% of all choices in the noncompensatory environment (for all items with differing predictions of the strategies).[5]

How did participants search for information? In 83% of all the choices they made, participants opened the information boxes in the order in which they were presented, starting with the cue at the top of the screen. On average, participants opened 98% of all information boxes. This search behavior was not surprising, because looking up information in the order presented was the quickest way of opening the boxes and because searching for all information did not incur any costs. Therefore, it appears reasonable to conjecture that most participants simply opened up all the boxes before they started to process the information.

Model comparison. How well did SSL predict the learning process we observed? For all four studies, each learning model was fitted separately to each individual's learning data as follows: The model predicts the probability with which a participant will choose each of the available alternatives for each trial conditioned on the past choices and payoffs received before that trial. It was operationally defined that a strategy was selected only if the necessary information for the strategy had been searched for and if the choice coincided with the strategy's prediction.[6] The accuracies of the models' predictions for each trial were evaluated by determining the likelihood of the observed choice, and a model's overall fit was assessed by determining the sum of the log likelihood for all choices across the 168 trials. As a goodness of fit, we used the G^2 measurement (Burnham & Anderson, 1998) defined in Equation 11-11, for which $f(y|\theta, t-1)$ is the likelihood function that denotes the probability of choice y given the model's parameter set θ and all information from the preceding trial $t-1$:

$$G^2 = -2 \sum_{i=1}^{168} \ln\left(f\left(y \mid \theta, t-1\right)\right). \qquad (11\text{-}11)$$

Reasonable parameter values were first selected by a grid search to minimize G^2; thereafter, the best-fitting grid values were used as a

starting point for subsequent optimization using the simplex method (Nelder & Mead, 1965) as implemented in MATLAB. For all models and all studies, the initial association parameter was restricted to $1 \leq w \leq 100$. Because our goal was to select the model that best captures the underlying cognitive process, we searched for the model with the highest generalizability (Pitt & Myung, 2002). Of the different model selection techniques (Pitt, Myung, & Zhang, 2002), we relied on the Akaike information criterion (AIC) that trades the model's fit against the model's complexity (see Akaike, 1973; Bozdogan, 2000; Burnham & Anderson, 1998) when estimating a model's generalizability (Browne, 2000). In particular for nested models, as SSL is a nested model of the three alternative learning models, AIC is an appropriate model selection criterion (Myung & Pitt, 1997). Because the models were fitted to the data, the model that predicts the data best is the model that is best at describing the results given the optimized parameters (see also Roberts & Pashler, 2000). Therefore, in the following we prefer the term *describing* whenever possible and use the term *predicting* in a broadly descriptive sense.

SSL predicted the choices with an average probability of .79: with an average probability of .82 (with $SD = .04$ across the seven blocks) for the compensatory environment and of .77 ($SD = .02$ across the seven blocks) for the noncompensatory environment. Ignoring the probability prediction and considering only whether the alternative SSL predicted as most likely was chosen by the participants, SSL could predict 85% of all choices. Thus, SSL obtained a good fit by taking the dynamics of the inference process into account. Consistent with the results shown in Figure 11-3, the obtained average initial preference parameter of $\beta_{TTB} = .30$ expressed a preference for WADD at the beginning of the task. In fact, only 6 of 40 participants obtained an optimized initial preference value for TTB above .50. The average value for the application error of $\varepsilon = .05$ demonstrates that the set of strategies assumed was reasonable. Only 1 participant obtained an error value above .20, indicating a relatively error-prone strategy application.

How well does SSL compete against the alternative learning models? We compared SSL pairwise with each alternative learning model by considering, for each participant, whether SSL or the alternative model had a better generalizability estimated by the AIC criterion (defined as AIC = $G^2 + 2k$, with k as the number of parameters). SSL reached a higher generalizability for the majority of participants when compared with the forgetting model and the imagination model. When compared with the exponential selection model, SSL reached a higher generalizability for only 52.5% of the participants (see Table 11-1). Thus, the more complex learning models do not provide better accounts of the learning process, which is adequately described by SSL.

Besides describing the choice behavior, can SSL also describe the adaptive selection of cognitive strategies? The percentage of choices predicted by the strategies TTB and WADD,

respectively, can be taken as an approximation of participants' strategy selections and can be compared to the probability with which SSL predicts this selection per trial block (see Figure 11-3). For both environments, the probability with which SSL predicted the selection of the best-performing strategy accurately matched the percentage of choices predicted by the best-performing strategy. The three alternative models did not obtain substantially better fits. This good match is surprising considering that the models' parameters were fitted with respect to participants' choices and not to the strategies' predictions.

Comparison of SSL against exemplar-based inferences. The exemplar model proposed by Juslin, Jones, et al. (2003) does not aim to describe the initial learning process. Instead, it focuses on how people make inferences after they have learned exemplars. Thus, to determine a fair, conservative test of SSL, we used EBM to predict

Table 11-1. The Optimized Parameter Values of SSL and the Alternative Learning Models for Study 1

Parameter	SSL	Exponential Selection Model	Forgetting Model	Imagination Model
		Learning Model		
Mean initial association w	40 ($SD = 39$)	20 ($SD = 29$)	57 ($SD = 41$)	44 ($SD = 38$)
Mean initial preference β_{TTB}	.30 ($SD = .16$)	.26 ($SD = .21$)	.31 ($SD = .15$)	.30 ($SD = .15$)
Mean application error ε	.05 ($SD = .07$)	.05 ($SD = .07$)	.05 ($SD = .07$)	.05 ($SD = .07$)
Additional parameter		$\mu = 1.4$ ($SD = 2.4$)	$\phi = 0.05$ ($SD = 0.11$)	$\delta = 0.04$ ($SD = 0.10$)
Predicted average probability of choices	.791	.796	.792	.793
Average G^2	111	109, $\chi^2(40) = 77$, $p < .01$[a]	111, $\chi^2(40) = 17$, $p = .99$[a]	110, $\chi^2(40) = 39$, $p = .45$[a]
Median AIC	107	106	107	107
Percentage of participants with AIC improvement for more general model[b]		47.5% ($p = .88$)	10% ($p < .01$)	25% ($p < .01$)

Note. SSL = strategy selection learning; TTB = take-the-best; AIC = Akaike information criterion.
[a] The fits of the models were also compared with a generalized likelihood ratio test (Wickens, 1989). For each model, the sum of the G^2 values for all 40 participants was determined (each participant's G^2 value was computed according to Equation 11-11). The difference of the sums is approximately chi-squared distributed with $df = 40$ (the degrees of freedom result from one additional free parameter for each of the 40 participants for the more general models).
[b] For the purpose of model selection, we compared SSL pairwise with the more general four-parameter models. The percentage of participants for which the more general model reached a lower (better) AIC value was determined: SSL obtained a better AIC value compared with all general models for the majority of participants (p according to a sign test).

the choices of the last two blocks only. For each of the 48 choices in the last two blocks, a prediction was made by comparing the cue configuration of the pair of alternatives to the cue configuration of the pairs in all subsequent trials excluding the first block of 24 trials, for which no feedback was provided. For instance, when making a prediction for the last trial, EBM determined the similarity of that pair of alternatives (probe) to the previous 143 pairs (exemplars) starting with the inference of the 25th trial and ending with the 167th trial. Because each block repeated the same 24 items, the similarity of a probe to identical exemplars was frequently determined. Therefore, in contrast to Juslin, Jones, et al. (2003), we used a frequency-sensitive form of EBM (cf. Nosofsky, 1988). Although the same items were presented repeatedly, the exemplars that were generated could, in principle, differ because of participants' information searches. (See Appendix A for an example of how the similarities for EBM were determined.)

The model predicts the probability with which a participant chooses either Company A or Company B. To assess the model's overall fit for a given individual and set of parameters, we determined the G^2 measurement for the last 48 choices. The six free attention-weight parameters, which were restricted for all studies to $0.001 \leq s_m \leq 0.999$, were fitted separately to each individual's data. Reasonable parameter values were first selected by a grid-search technique; thereafter, the best-fitting grid values were used as a starting point for subsequent optimization. The resulting parameter values are provided in Appendix B.

EBM predicted the choices with an average probability of .76 for the two environments. SSL reached a better fit, as it predicted the choices in the last two blocks with an average probability of .86 for the compensatory environment and .78 for the noncompensatory environment. When considering this advantage of SSL against EBM it should additionally be taken into account that SSL reached this good fit even though it was fitted to all choices, whereas EBM had the statistical advantage of being fitted only to the last two blocks of choices.

We compared SSL with EBM according to the AIC criterion for each participant. SSL was the preferred model for 87.5% of the participants ($p \leq .01$, according to a sign test). However, because the two models are not nested, this comparison should be interpreted with caution. In addition, we compared the two models simply by considering their fit according to the G^2 measurement, thereby ignoring the model's complexity. Again SSL was the preferred model for 72.5% of the participants ($p \leq .01$). Thus, even when ignoring the models' complexity, with EBM having six free parameters compared with three for SSL, SSL is the preferred model.

SSL allows an additional qualitative prediction. Following the strategy repertoire approach, it makes a difference whether strategies' predictions differ or coincide. If the strategies' predictions differ, the person's choice will depend on the strategy he or she selected. On the other hand, if the strategies' predictions coincide, the person will make the same choice regardless of the selected strategy. Thus, when TTB and WADD predict the same alternative, SSL's predicted choice probability of the most likely alternative will be relatively high. In contrast, when the two strategies predict different alternatives, the predicted choice probability of the most likely alternative could be moderate. When following the exemplar-based approach, the model's predictions depend only on the similarities of the inference situations to previous inference situations.

Therefore, as an additional model selection criterion, we determined, for all items in the last two blocks, the models' average predicted choice probabilities for the most likely alternative. This was done, first for incongruent items, defined as those items for which TTB and WADD made different predictions, and second for congruent items, defined as those items for which TTB and WADD made identical predictions. In fact, SSL's predictions differed as assumed, because the most likely alternative was predicted with an average probability of .82 for incongruent items compared with .95 for congruent items, $t(39) = 8.03$, $p < .01$, $d = 1.27$. EBM did not predict this difference, because the most likely alternative was predicted with an average probability of .82 for both types of items.

The results support SSL's prediction: Consistent with SSL, the participants chose the most likely alternative predicted by SSL in 79% of all cases for incongruent items compared with 96% for congruent items, $t(39) = 8.13$, $p < .01$, $d = 1.28$. For the exemplar model, a similar effect inconsistent with EBM's prediction was found, because the most likely alternative predicted by EBM was chosen in 74% of all cases for incongruent items compared with 92% for congruent items, $t(39) = 12.06$, $p < .01$, $d = 1.91$.

Discussion

Study 1 demonstrated that when people repeatedly make probabilistic inferences, their performance improves. In addition, it showed that people apparently select different inference strategies. In the first trial block with no feedback, WADD predicted more choices than did TTB, indicating that WADD is the strategy people initially prefer to select. This is what one would expect in an unfamiliar situation in which the information is provided without any costs and does not need to be retrieved from memory (for a discussion on the difference between inference from memory and inference from givens, see Bröder & Schiffer, 2003; Gigerenzer & Goldstein, 1996).

The standard cost-benefit approach (e.g., Payne et al., 1988) predicts that people select strategies depending on the experimental conditions, so that WADD should predict more choices in the compensatory environment and TTB should predict more choices in the noncompensatory environment. The results of Study 1 support this prediction. However, the cost-benefit approach does not specify how the strategy selection process changes over time. SSL fills this gap and describes how strategy selection changes adaptively. In particular, the shift from the selection of one strategy to another in the noncompensatory environment can be explained only by a learning approach. SSL is the best learning model when compared with the three competing learning models. Only when SSL is compared with the exponential selection model do both models perform equally well according to their generalizability. With the obtained average sensitivity parameter for the exponential selection model of $\mu = 1.4$, it is possible to predict a relatively high probability

with which a strategy is selected, even when the strategies do not differ much according to their expectancies. Thereby the exponential selection model is able to describe an accentuated learning rate at the beginning of the learning process, which gives the model—for some participants—a better fit compared with SSL. The robustness of this advantage was explored in Studies 2–4.

We derive the previous conclusions from a strategy repertoire perspective. Is this perspective justified on the basis of our comparison of it to the exemplar-based perspective? The results of the comparison of SSL to EBM suggest that the answer is yes. First, although SSL has only three free parameters compared with six in EBM, it still reached a better fit. Second, SSL makes a qualitative prediction: When the assumed strategies select the same alternative, then SSL predicts the choice of this alternative with a relatively high probability, compared with situations in which the strategies select different alternatives. Consistently, participants' choice proportions were in line with SSL's predictions but were inconsistent with EBM, which does not predict this difference. In sum, SSL provided the best account of people's inference processes. However, this conclusion needs to be restricted, because Study 1's inference situation might not have been advantageous to an exemplar-based inference process: The learning phase was relatively short given the large number of exemplars compared, for instance, to the study by Juslin, Jones, et al. (2003). Nevertheless, participants were still successful in making their choices, and we observed a strong learning effect. Thus, with the limited learning opportunity given in Study 1, individuals seemed to rely on an abstraction, that is, the application of a cognitive strategy, rather than on comparing inference situations to previously made inferences. Study 2 replicates results of Study 1 when cue validities had to be learned.

STUDY 3

The adaptive behavior in Studies 1 and 2 was observed under conditions of substantial accuracy differences of the strategies TTB and WADD. These large differences (about 30%) do not occur very often in real-world situations (Martignon & Laskey, 1999); instead, different strategies often reach very similar accuracies. The so-called flat maximum phenomenon states that the optimal set of weights in a linear model can often be replaced by many other sets of weights without losing much accuracy (Dawes & Corrigan, 1974; Wainer, 1976). This provides one explanation of why heuristics can work well. Generally, heuristics often have two advantages: Besides their robust accuracy levels, they possess low application costs, as they require only a small amount of information. In Study 3, strategies' costs were made salient by introducing explicit information acquisition costs.

According to SSL, strategies are selected proportional to their expectancies, and these depend on the gains and losses that the strategies produce. For the sake of simplicity, as described above, we have defined the strategies' reinforcement in SSL solely in monetary terms. Accordingly, in Studies 1 and 2, a strategy's reinforcement was exclusively a function of its accuracy, that is, whether it led to correct or incorrect decisions. Even with this simplification, SSL was able to predict the inference process adequately. In Study 3, we went a step further by introducing search costs, so that strategies' reinforcements in SSL became a mixture of their accuracy and their information costs, defined as the strategies' amount of required information. Thus, with Study 3 we tested SSL's prediction as to whether people are able to learn the best-performing strategy of their repertoire for an inference task for which the strategies' performances, defined by the strategies' payoffs, differ mainly because of different information acquisition costs. According to SSL, it is irrelevant whether a strategy receives reinforcement, because it is very accurate or because it produces very low search costs. It is of course an open question whether this simplified representation of strategies' reinforcements in an equal monetary currency is appropriate. Can the previous conclusions, that people adapt their strategy selection on the basis of strategies' performances, be generalized to yet another plausible inference situation?

Again we tested EBM against SSL. However, it could be argued that EBM is less well-suited to the inference situation of Study 3, because the model predicts that individuals memorize only the correct choice for an exemplar, and it does not predict how individuals evaluate and memorize an adequate amount of information to make an inference. However, in principle, this missing property does not restrict EBM's application. Individuals following an exemplar-based inference process might decide from the beginning to look up a constant subset of information to reduce costs. Then, they memorize exemplars on the basis of the acquired information and compare new instances with these stored exemplars. Thus, the way people search for information is not predicted by EBM, but this does not restrict its application.

Method

Forty people (23 women and 17 men), whose average age was 25, participated in the experiment. The average payment was €8. The instructions were similar to those in Study 1. Participants had to select the more creditworthy company of two unnamed companies, on the basis of six cues with given cue validities. The 171 items consisted of 3 initial items to familiarize participants with the task, followed by seven trial blocks, each consisting of the same set of 24 items, presented in random order. Feedback was provided after the first trial block to allow learning. The two strategies made unambiguous predictions for all items, and for 50% of the items, they made different predictions. The validities given to the participants were the same as in Study 1. Again, because of the necessary properties of the item set—the required performances and separability of the strategies—the validities of the selected item set in the experiment deviated from the ones given to the participants (with deviations varying between 0.14 and 0.38).

The experimental design had two factors: environment (between subjects) and trial block (within subject). In the first high search costs environment, WADD reached an accuracy of 79% (i.e., 19 correct predictions of 24) compared with TTB's accuracy of 71% (i.e., 17 correct predictions of 24). Participants earned 75 cents for a correct decision but paid 37.5 cents for each decision. For each acquired cue, an additional

3 cents had to be paid, so that the cost of acquiring one cue relative to the possible gain of a correct decision was 8%. With this payoff structure, the application of TTB led to a payoff of €15.50 compared with WADD with a payoff of €6.50 for all 168 items. In the second low search costs environment, the strategies' accuracies were reversed, with an accuracy of 71% for WADD compared with TTB's accuracy of 79%. Participants earned 35 cents for a correct decision and paid 17.5 cents for each decision. For each acquired cue, an additional 0.5 cents had to be paid, implying relative information costs to gains of 3%. The application of TTB led to a payoff of €15.40 compared with WADD's payoff of €7.20. Thus, in both environments, TTB's performance, defined as the overall payoff produced by a strategy, was higher than WADD's performance, because of lower information costs. Therefore, according to the strategies' performances, both environments can be classified as noncompensatory. Because of the strategies' performances, SSL predicts that people will learn to select TTB in both environment conditions. Because in both conditions the strategies' accuracy differences were relatively small, with only two additional correct decisions for the more

accurate strategy, SSL's predictions mainly originate from the strategies' different search costs.

Results

Before evaluating the learning models, we first looked for learning effects.

Learning effects. In Study 3, participants did not improve their payoffs across the seven trial blocks as much as observed in either Study 1 or Study 2 (see Figure 11-4). The repeated measurement ANOVA, with the average obtained payoff as the dependent variable, trial block as a within-subject factor, and environment as a between-subjects factor, showed only a weak learning effect: The average obtained payoff of €1.11 in the first block ($SD = 0.87$) increased to an average payoff of €1.55 ($SD = 0.91$) in the last block, $F(4,168) = 1.84$, $p = .12$, $\eta^2 = 0.05$. Participants' payoffs did not differ substantially between the two environments; participants received an average payoff of €6.80 ($SD = 5.80$) in the high search costs environment compared with an average payoff of €9.41 ($SD = 4.16$) in the low search costs environment, $F(1, 38) = 2.66$, $p = .11$, $\eta^2 = 0.07$. Participants searched on average for too much information, which explains why they received such a low payoff in

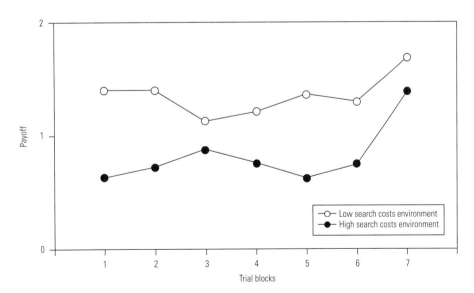

Figure 11-4. The average payoffs (in euros) received by the participants across the seven trial blocks in Study 3 in the high search costs and low search costs environment conditions.

the high search costs environment. No interaction between trial block and environment occurred.

Figure 11-5 shows the percentage of choices predicted by TTB, the best-performing strategy in both environments. At the beginning of the task with no feedback (first trial block), WADD predicted more choices compared with TTB, regardless of the environment, indicating an initial preference for WADD. After the first trial block, this weak initial preference changed: For both environments WADD's fit decreased in favor of an increasing fit of TTB, again supporting the prediction that the participants learned to select the best-performing strategy. In the last block, TTB predicted 68% of the choices in the high search costs environment and 66% of the choices in the low search costs environment when considering only items for which the two strategies make diverse predictions.[7]

How did subjects search for information? In contrast to Study 1, in only 5% of all choices did participants open up the information boxes in the order they were presented on the screen. Instead, in 60% of all choices, participants opened up the cues in the order of their validity. Compared with Studies 1 and 2, participants looked up much less information, because on average participants searched for only 65% of all information, which can be attributed to the monetary costs resulting from information search.

Model comparison. Analogously to Studies 1 and 2, each learning model was fitted separately to each individual's data (see Table 11-2). SSL predicted the individual choices with an average probability of .75 (.76 for the high search costs environment and .74 for the low search costs environment). When considering whether the alternative that was most likely predicted by SSL was chosen by the participants, SSL predicted 80% of all choices. Thus, SSL obtained a high fit by taking the dynamics of the decision process over time into account. The average initial preference parameter of $\beta_{TTB} = .43$ obtained for SSL reflected a slight preference for the selection of WADD at the beginning of the task. The application error parameter of $\varepsilon = .07$ is only slightly larger compared with that of Study 1 and identical to that of

Study 2, and for only 4 participants a value above .20 resulted. Thus, in general an adequate set of strategies was assumed.

How well did SSL compete against the alternative learning models? SSL's estimated generalizability was better for the majority of participants when compared with the alternative models, although SSL did not significantly outperform the exponential selection model, because SSL reached a better AIC value for 62.5% of the participants ($p = .15$, according to a sign test; see Table 11-2). Again, the percentages of predicted choices by TTB and WADD were taken as an approximation of strategy selection and were compared with the probability with which SSL predicted the selection (see Figure 11-5). For both environments, SSL's predicted probability of selecting the best-performing strategy accurately matched the percentage of choices predicted by this strategy. The three alternative models did not obtain substantially better fits.

Comparison of SSL against exemplar-based inferences. Identical with Studies 1 and 2, EBM was used to predict the inferences of the last two blocks on the basis of the preceding inferences excluding the first block. (The resulting optimized parameter values can be found in Appendix B.) EBM predicted the choices with an average probability of .64 for the high search costs environment and of .67 for the low search costs environment. In comparison, SSL predicted the choices of the last two blocks with an average probability of .79 for the high search costs environment and .75 for the low search costs environment. When comparing SSL with EBM according to the estimated generalizability, SSL is preferable for 80% of the participants. When comparing the models only with respect to their fit, disregarding the model's complexity, SSL had a better fit for 70% of the participants ($p = .02$). Thus, in Study 3, SSL clearly outperformed EBM in predicting participants' choices.

In addition, analogously to Studies 1 and 2, we determined the model's average predicted choice probability of the most likely alternative for all items in the last two blocks separately for incongruent and congruent items. SSL's prediction differed as assumed: SSL predicted the most likely alternative with an average probability of

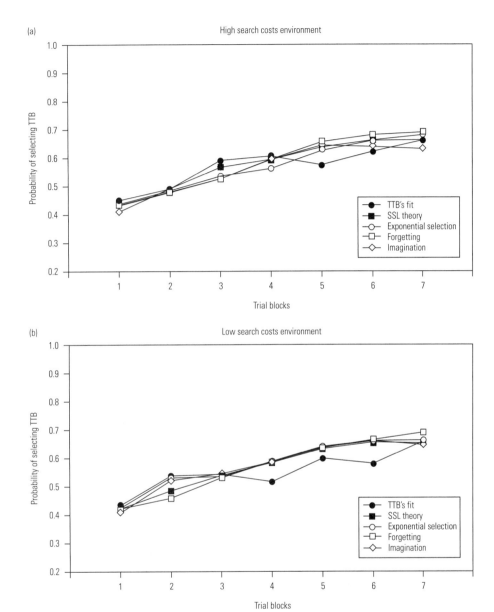

Figure 11-5. The percentage of choices predicted by the best-performing strategy in the high search costs (a) and the low search costs (b) environment conditions of Study 3 (only for those items for which the strategies made different predictions). Additionally, the figure shows the predicted probability by the different learning models with which the best-performing strategy is selected. SSL's prediction differed from the percentage of choices predicted by the best-performing strategy with a mean square error of 0.13%. The fit for the exponential selection model was $MSE = 0.13\%$, for the forgetting model was $MSE = 0.24\%$, and for the imagination model was $MSE = 0.13\%$. SSL = strategy selection learning; TTB = the take-the-best heuristic.

Table 11-2. The Optimized Parameter Values of SSL and the Alternative Learning Models for Study 3

Parameter	SSL	Learning Model		
		Exponential Selection Model	Forgetting Model	Imagination Model
Mean initial association w	49 (SD = 44)	34 (SD = 43)	63 (SD = 41)	44 (SD = 43)
Mean initial preference β_{TTB}	.43 (SD = .28)	.40 (SD = .32)	.42 (SD = .27)	.40 (SD = .30)
Mean application error ε	.07 (SD = .10)	.07 (SD = .10)	.07 (SD = .10)	.07 (SD = .10)
Additional parameter		μ = 2.14	ϕ = 0.02	δ = 0.46
		SD = 3.1	SD = 0.04	SD = 0.45
Predicted average probability of choices	.751	.755	.754	.753
Average G^2	127	125, $\chi^2(40)$ = 91, p < .01[a]	126, $\chi^2(40)$ = 46, p = .24[a]	126, $\chi^2(40)$ = 45 p = .28[a]
Median AIC	125	126	127	126
Percentage of participants with AIC improvement for more general model[b]		37.5% (p = .15)	5% (p < .01)	17.5% (p < .01)

Note. SSL = strategy selection learning; TTB = take-the-best; AIC = Akaike information criterion.
[a]The fits of the models were also compared with a generalized likelihood ratio test by comparing the difference of the sum of G^2 values, which are approximately chi-squared distributed with df = 40.
[b] For the purpose of model selection, SSL was compared pairwise with the more general four-parameter models. The percentage of participants for which the more general model reached a lower (better) AIC value was determined: SSL obtained a better AIC value compared with all general models for the majority of participants (p according to a sign test).

.70 for incongruent items compared with .93 for congruent items, $t(39)$ = 9.41, p < .01, d = 1.48. Contrary to Studies 1 and 2, EBM also predicted this difference but only to a small degree, because the most likely alternative was predicted with an average probability of .68 for incongruent items compared with .72 for congruent items, $t(39)$ = 3.84, p < .01, d = 0.61.

Consistent with SSL, the participants chose the most likely alternative predicted by SSL in 70% of all cases for incongruent items compared with 96% for congruent items, $t(39)$ = 8.42, p < .01, d = 1.33. For the exemplar model, a similar effect—much stronger than that predicted by EBM—was found, because the most likely alternative predicted by EBM was chosen in 71% of all cases for incongruent items compared with 84% for congruent items, $t(39)$ = 6.01, p < .01, d = 0.95.

Discussion

Study 3 provides further support for the adaptive view of strategy selection. As in Studies

1 and 2, participants in Study 3 apparently learned to select the best-performing strategy. In both environments, the strategy initially selected was discarded in favor of TTB. However, the learning effect we observed, measured by the obtained payoffs, was weaker compared with those in the previous studies. Apparently, the inference task is more difficult than those in the previous studies. In Studies 1 and 2, participants could focus solely on the strategies' accuracy, which determined the strategies' performance, ignoring the number of cues that they needed to look up. However, in Study 3, the strategies' performances depended on their accuracy and on their costs, namely, on the number of cues looked up. Thus, participants had to trade off strategies' accuracy against their information search costs, making learning more complicated. Additionally, this trade-off produced costs: When deciding which strategy to select, all information first needed to be acquired to compare TTB's and WADD's performances. Only after a preference in favor of TTB developed could

participants then search for a smaller amount of information, which would then no longer allow them to see whether WADD would perform better. In contrast, in Studies 1 and 2, participants always had the possibility of acquiring additional information to check WADD's performance. Obviously, these differences make Study 3's inference task more difficult and impede the learning process.

Nevertheless, SSL again represents a good account of the observed learning process of strategy selection. SSL not only predicts that TTB achieves a higher fit in predicting participants' choices compared with WADD but also predicts how the strategy selection process changes with learning. In this respect, it goes beyond a cost-benefit framework. As in the previous studies, SSL was preferable compared with the more general learning models in terms of the estimated generalizability, although the comparison to the exponential selection model was not significant. When comparing SSL to EBM, the former reached a better fit in predicting the inferences for the majority of participants. Moreover, SSL again made different predictions for incongruent and congruent items consistent with the results. EBM could predict these differences only to a small degree. In sum, in Study 3 EBM was less suitable for describing participants' inferences. Most exemplar models require feedback about whether a decision was correct or incorrect, thus representing forms of supervised learning (Sutton & Barto, 1998, p. 4). In contrast, SSL represents unsupervised reinforcement learning, because the theory requires only feedback about a decision's reward and no feedback as to whether a decision was correct or whether a better decision could have been made. The introduction of search costs in Study 3 emphasizes SSL's advantage as a model of unsupervised learning. Whereas in Studies 1 and 2, the feedback allowed the inference as to whether there could have been a better decision, this inference was not possible in Study 3. Here, the feedback regarding decisions' accuracy did not allow an inference as to whether the participants could have done better by searching for more cues. SSL is suitable for such a situation. Correct inferences based on less information simply provide greater reinforcement and can thus lead to a reduced information search. Although most exemplar models are based on supervised learning such as implemented in EBM, there have also been exemplar models that function with unsupervised learning and require only reinforcement as feedback (see Gonzales, Lerch, & Lebiere, 2003). In Study 4, we examined to what extent the SSL theory can be applied to multialternative inference tasks.

GENERAL DISCUSSION

How can the strategy selection problem be solved? According to the cost-benefit framework (e.g., Payne et al., 1993), people anticipate the accuracy and effort of a strategy in their strategy selection. SSL incorporates this initial selection process by assuming initial strategy preferences. However, initial strategy preferences are not sufficient, because learning can explain how individuals' strategy preferences change and thereby can lead to better predictions. We argue that learning is the key feature in solving the strategy selection problem. In all four reported studies, reinforcement feedback apparently led the participants to select the best-performing strategy of their strategy repertoire. In sum, according to SSL, people have an initial evaluation of strategies that changes continuously through feedback when making inferences, leading to a dynamic strategy selection process. In this way, unsuccessful strategies become less likely to be selected. Our learning approach supplements the cost-benefit frameworks with a computational theory of how the strategy selection process could be accomplished.

Is it possible to further simplify SSL? We constructed a two-parameter learning model by dropping SSL's application error parameter and for technical reasons (to apply maximum likelihood estimations), assuming a constant application error of $\varepsilon = .001$. When testing SSL against this simplified model, SSL reached a better generalizability for 77.5%, 82.5%, 70%, and 92% of all participants in Studies 1, 2, 3, and 4, respectively. In addition, we constructed a two-parameter model by dropping SSL's initial preference parameter, assuming that people have equal initial preferences for the two strategies. In fact, this simplification does not reduce SSL's generalizability: SSL reached a better generalizability for 60%, 57.5%, and 53% of all participants for Studies 1, 3, and 4, respectively. In Study 2, the simpler model with two parameters reached a better generalizability for 70% of all participants ($p = .02$), which is not surprising, as no initial preference for one of the two strategies was observed (see Figure 11-5). Should, then, the initial preference parameter be dropped in favor of a simplified SSL? Studies 1, 3, and 4 demonstrate initial preferences for strategies that can be captured only by the three-parameter SSL. Yet the initial preferences play an important role only at the beginning of the task (e.g., in the first two trial blocks). If one is interested in which strategies people select in the long run, the initial preferences could be neglected. However, when the interest is in how people begin to solve a problem, the initial preference parameter becomes an essential component of SSL.

Among others, Gigerenzer, Todd, & the ABC Research Group (1999) have argued that people possess a repertoire of strategies for the judgment and decision-making problems they face. On the basis of our findings, people's reasoning seems to be ruled by a flexible selection of cognitive strategies. Contrary to the single-purpose mechanism view, different strategies seem to be applied in different situations. People appear to select their strategies adaptively, such that strategies that perform well become more likely to be selected. SSL provides a computational theory that describes how this strategy selection process could take place. By following the traditional roots of psychology in learning, the strategy selection problem receives a promising solution.

ACKNOWLEDGMENTS

We gratefully acknowledge helpful comments on previous versions of this article by Guido Biele, Jerome R. Busemeyer, Nick Chater, Gerd Gigerenzer, Ralph Hertwig, Stefan Krauss, Thorsten Pachur, and Magnus Persson. We also thank Anita Todd for editing a draft of this article.

NOTES

1. This does not rule out strategies consisting of building blocks that might be learned and acquired separately. However, for simplicity's sake, we do not examine how specific building blocks are learned but rather focus on the selection process of complete strategies

2. We do not assume an initial expectancy parameter as a free parameter for each strategy, which would lead to an equivalent model compared with SSL. Instead, we follow our conceptualization for two reasons: First, both parameters should present two distinct psychological mechanisms. The initial preference parameter shows how participants evaluate strategies differently at the beginning of the task, whereas the initial association defines how strong and frequently new reinforcement has to be provided to change strategy selection. Second, our model simplifies generalizations to other tasks. When considering tasks in which it is reasonable to assume several strategies, one can keep the initial association parameter but may increase either the number of free initial preference parameters or group strategies according to their similarity, and one may use only one preference parameter for each group.

3. When analyzing participants' choices, such opposing applications of strategies need to be taken into consideration, making the data analysis complex. In addition, accuracies of strategies below chance are less realistic (Martignon & Laskey, 1999).

4. Because both strategies always make an unambiguous prediction and have no free parameters that are fitted to the data, their flexibility in predicting different choices is identical, so that using only their pure fit to evaluate them is appropriate.

5. Because the validities given to the participants differed from those of the item set used in the experiment, participants might have learned the validities of the item set for the strategies they used. However, a WADD strategy using the validities of the item set predicted only 64% of all choices in the compensatory environment compared with WADD's fit of 88% using the validities given to the participants. Likewise, a TTB strategy for the noncompensatory environment using the rank order of the validities of the item set predicted only 53% of all choices compared to TTB's fit of 76% using the rank order of the validities given to the participants.

Alternatively, a WADD strategy using the validities of the item set predicted only 56% of all choices in the noncompensatory environment.

6. Thus, if a participant, for instance, did not search for the most important cue, TTB could not have been selected, and if a single cue was acquired, WADD could not have been selected. However, we allowed a shortened information search for WADD: Given a subset of cues, it is often possible to infer WADD's prediction without searching for all cues (e.g., if the three most valid cues support one alternative). Therefore, if WADD's prediction could have been determined on the basis of information acquired, we allowed that WADD could have been selected.

7. Because the validities given to the participants differed from those of the item set used in the experiment, participants might have learned the validities of the item set for the strategies they used. However, a TTB strategy using the rank order of the validities of the item set predicted only 70% of all choices of the high search costs environment and only 67% of all choices of the low search costs environment. This is less compared with TTB using the rank order of the validities given to the participants, which predicted 75% of all choices for the high search costs environment and 74% of all choices for the low search costs environment. A WADD strategy using the validities of the item set predicted 65% of all choices for the high search costs environment and 66% of all choices for the low search costs environment, thus having a lower fit than did TTB.

APPENDIX A

Implementation of the EBM model

The exemplar model was used to predict the inferences for the last two blocks in all four studies. For illustration, we describe in the following how EBM's prediction is determined for the last inference made. Suppose for this last inference x, the first alternative a (second alternative b) had the following cue values for six cues: $+ (+), + (+), + (-), - (-), - (-),$ and $- (+)$, where the positive sign presents a positive and the negative sign represents a negative cue value. Now, the similarity of this inference x is determined with the first inference y_1 where feedback was provided

(in case of Study 1 this is the 25th inference). Suppose for this inference y_1, the first alternative a (the second alternative b) had the following cue values: $+ (+), + (+), + (+), + (+), - (-),$ and $- (+)$. Thus, the first, second, fifth, and sixth cue had the same combination of cue values, so that for these cues the index d equals the value 1, according to Equation 11-9 (i.e., $d_{xym} = 1$, for $m = 1, 2, 5,$ and 6). For the third and fourth cues, the combination of cue values of the inferences x and y are different, so that the index d takes a value according to the attention weights s_m, which, for example, could have values of $s_3 = 0.4$ and $s_4 = 0.5$. With these attention weights, the similarity between x and y is determined as

$$s(x, y) = \prod_{m=1}^{M} d_{xym} = 1 \cdot 1 \cdot 0.4 \cdot 0.5 \cdot 1 \cdot 1 = 0.2.$$

In the following steps, the similarity of the inference x with all past inferences y_t will be equivalently determined (i.e., starting with the second inference y_2 and stopping with the inference preceding the present inference x). To determine the choice probability of choosing the first alternative a from the two alternatives a and b for the present inference x, according to Equation 11-10, one determines the sum of the similarities of the present inference x with those past inferences y, where alternative a was the correct choice, and then divides this sum by the sum of the similarities of the present inference x to all past inferences.

APPENDIX B

EBM's Parameter Values

In the following, the resulting parameter values of the exemplar models are described for all four studies. In Study 1, the average optimized parameter values were, in decreasing order of the cues according to their validities, as follows: $s_1 = .10, s_2 = .40, s_3 = .50, s_4 = .09, s_5 = .32,$ and $s_6 = .66,$ for the compensatory environment, and $s_1 = .11, s_2 = .51, s_3 = .85, s_4 = .29, s_5 = .62,$ and $s_6 = .31,$ for the noncompensatory environment. Thus, the attention weights did not correlate substantially with cue validities; only the optimized attention weight of the most valid cue represents relatively high attention. However, one would not necessarily expect such a correlation because attention weights represent the importance of cues when determining the similarities between pairs of alternatives, whereas validities represent the importance of single cues for predicting a criterion in pair comparisons.

In Study 3, for the six attention weights, the optimized parameter values, in decreasing order of the cues according to their validity, were as follows: $s1 = .28$, $s_2 = .33$, $s_3 = .85$, $s_4 = .35$, $s_5 = .21$, and $s_6 = .52$, for the high search costs environment, and $s_1 = .07$, $s_2 = .12$, $s_3 = .65$, $s_4 = .65$, $s_5 = .53$, and $s_6 = .66$, for the low search costs environment. As in Studies 1 and 2, the attention weights did not correspond with the cue validities, and only to a small extent did cues with a higher validity have attention weights indicating greater importance.

PART II

Tests

When do heuristics work?

Introduction to Chapter 12

Fast, Frugal, and Fit: Simple Heuristics for Paired Comparison

From the beginning, our program has benefited from a healthy competition between the computer geeks and the mathematical nerds. First, using computer simulation, the counterintuitive result was discovered that the take-the-best heuristic could outperform multiple regression in prediction (see Chapter 2; Czerlinski, Gigerenzer, & Goldstein, 1999). But the geeks could not explain why. This challenged the nerds to prove that those who run simulations are simply too lazy to think. Ulrich Hoffrage spent a sleepless night working out a half-baked mathematical proof showing environmental conditions under which take-the-best excels. With the help of mathematician Laura Martignon and many days and nights of intense arguments, the first formal result on the ecological rationality of take-the-best emerged.

The result was this: The take-the-best heuristic is as accurate as any linear strategy in a noncompensatory environment (e.g., where the weights of binary cues are 1, 1/2, 1/4, 1/8, and so on), assuming that the order of cues is the same as that of the weights in the linear strategy. Loosely speaking, a heuristic that is noncompensatory works well in an environment that is noncompensatory. Back then, the nature of ecological rationality seemed to be best captured by the analogy of a "mirror": If the structure of the heuristic mirrors that of an environment, the heuristic will succeed. That conclusion fitted very well with the ecological theories of cognition by Roger Shepard (1990, p. 213), who assumed that cognition "looks very much like a reflection of the world."

But that was not the last word, and the geeks struck back. They showed, by means of computer simulations, the bounds of this and similar analytic results: The proofs hold when parameter estimation is error-free (e.g., the true order of cues according to their ecological validities is known, as in a "small world"). But as soon as parameters need to be estimated from samples, estimation error arises and the results can change considerably. For instance, the result that take-the-best works well in non-compensatory environments does not necessarily hold when a person needs to estimate the order (take-the-best) or weights (linear strategies) of cues based on a limited sample of information, as shown in detail in Chapter 1 (Figure 1-5). There is a fundamental difference between a certain world in which all parameters are known and an uncertain world in which the parameters have to be estimated from limited samples. In the first case, mathematical theorems can be deduced; in the latter, assessments have to be induced or conjectured. Thus, any analysis of ecological rationality needs to distinguish between what Savage (1954), the father of modern Bayesian decision theory, called "small worlds" and the large worlds in which uncertainty reigns. Unlike the case in large worlds, all alternatives, consequences, and probabilities are known in a small world, and nothing needs to be estimated from samples. What is true in a small world cannot necessarily be generalized to the large world, and vice versa.

The present article anticipates this important point when addressing the question of how to order cues. Theorem 1 says that ordering cues by conditional validity tends to lead to higher (or at least equal) accuracy compared to take-the-best's (unconditional) validity. This more-is-better result, however, holds only when all validities are perfectly known, not when these have to be estimated from samples (as later illustrated in Figure 12-3). Interestingly, the same applies to optimal ordering. The general lesson is that optimizing on known data (i.e., finding the parameters that result in the optimal fit) may be suboptimal in predicting new data. In prediction, a robust strategy rather than an optimal one is required, underlining again that robustness and optimality are two different things.

This insight has practical consequences. Harry Markowitz won a Nobel Prize for his mean-variance model that describes optimal asset allocations. Like the proofs in this article, this result only holds when parameter estimation is error-free. It does not mean that it is the best strategy in the real, uncertain world of financial investment. In fact, as Chapter 34 illustrates, a simple investment heuristic called $1/N$ led to better investments than the optimizing model for a window of 10 years of stock data. Only when the samples are large, such as 500 years of stock data for $N = 50$, could the optimization strategy outperform the simple heuristic.

CHAPTER 12

Fast, Frugal, and Fit: Simple Heuristics for Paired Comparison

Laura Martignon and Ulrich Hoffrage

Abstract: This article provides an overview of recent results on lexicographic, linear, and Bayesian models for paired comparison from a cognitive psychology perspective. Within each class, we distinguish subclasses according to the computational complexity required for parameter setting. We identify the optimal model in each class, where optimality is defined with respect to performance when fitting known data. Although not optimal when fitting data, simple models can be astonishingly accurate when generalizing to new data. A simple heuristic belonging to the class of lexicographic models is take-the-best (Gigerenzer & Goldstein, 1996, p. 684). It is more robust than other lexicographic strategies that use complex procedures to establish a cue hierarchy. In fact, it is robust due to its simplicity, not despite it. Similarly, take-the-best looks up only a fraction of the information that linear and Bayesian models require; yet it achieves performance comparable to that of models which integrate information. Due to its simplicity, frugality, and accuracy, take-the-best is a plausible candidate for a psychological model in the tradition of bounded rationality. We review empirical evidence showing the descriptive validity of fast-and-frugal heuristics.

1. INTRODUCTION

Heuristics have not only been studied in cognitive psychology. Other fields, such as artificial intelligence and machine learning, have sensed the necessity of investigating simple strategies for problem solving due to the intractability of normative solutions. One example is simple algorithms in machine learning, which can perform highly accurate classifications. For instance, Holte (1993) showed that very simple classification rules, based on the use of only one—namely the best—dimension, perform surprisingly well compared to neural networks for classification. Another class of simple heuristics in artificial intelligence are decision lists, introduced by Rivest (1987). These heuristics are simple both in their application and with respect to the procedure for constructing them. This is different for the classification and regression trees (CARTs) proposed by Breiman et al. (1984) which can be easily applied but may require enormous computational effort for their construction.

In the present paper we will focus on lexicographic strategies for paired comparison. For performing comparisons, speed can be achieved by searching for information with a simple search rule, stopping as early as possible, guaranteeing frugality, and making the inference with a simple decision rule. As we shall see, such fast-and-frugal heuristics can be astonishingly accurate and robust, and therefore, fit. They owe their fitness to their ecological rationality, that is, to the way in which they exploit the structure of their task environments.

2. APPROACHES TO THE COMPARISON TASK

In general terms, the task is to infer which object, A or B, has the higher value on a numerical criterion. This inference is to be made on the basis of cues. Here, for simplicity, we assume that all cue values are known for all objects and we restrict ourselves to binary cues, valued at either 1 or 0. From a formal point of view, the task is that of categorization: A pair (A, B) is to be categorized as $X_A > X_B$ or $X_B > X_A$ (where X denotes the criterion), based on cue information. Examples of such a task are "choose which of two German cities has the larger population," or "choose which of two stocks will yield a higher return."

The matrix of all objects of the reference class, from which A and B have been taken, and of the cue values which describe these objects constitute what we call an environment. A cue profile of an object is the vector formed by all the cue values of the object. Thus, an environment consists of a set of objects, where each object is characterized by a criterion value and a cue profile. As a concrete, real-world example we will consider the task originally investigated by Gigerenzer and Goldstein (1996), where pairs of German cities with more than 100,000 inhabitants were compared as to which one has a larger population. There were nine cues, such as whether the city is a state capital or whether it has a soccer team in the national league. Information on these cues is useful since cities which, for example, have a soccer team in the major league tend to have more inhabitants than those which do not. The performance of an inference mechanism is determined as the percentage of correct inferences in the complete paired comparison task, that is, across all possible combinations of objects of the environment.

How can one infer which of two objects, for example, city A with cue profile (100101010) and city B with cue profile (011000011), scores higher on the established criterion? Table 12-1 illustrates three traditional approaches to this task: lexicographic, linear, and Bayesian which are the focus of this paper (there are other possible approaches, e.g., neural nets and non-linear regression).

2.1. Lexicographic Strategies for Comparison

A comparison task we are all familiar with is looking up a word in the dictionary. We compare the entry we accidentally find with the target word and have to determine whether the target word is before or after. We do not have to read the whole word; rather, we compare corresponding characters with the target word from the beginning until we find a character that discriminates. The equivalent can be carried out when comparing the cue profiles of two objects: Compare cue values in a specified order and make an inference as soon as a discriminating cue is found. One essential feature of a lexicographic

Table 12-1. Three Approaches to the Task of Inferring which of the Two Alternatives Scores Higher on a Numerical Criterion

Complexity	Lexicographic Approach	Linear Approach	Bayesian Approach
Minimal	Minimalist*	Dawes' rule	Minimal Bayes
Simple	Take-the-best	Franklin's rule	Naïve Bayes (Idiot Bayes)
Sophisticated	Cue ordering based on conditional validity	Multiple regression at the object level	Friedman's network
Optimal	Optimal cue ordering	Logistic regression at the comparison level	Profile memorization

The variants within each of the three approaches vary with respect to their complexity in finding the parameters relevant to the model.

Note: *Although minimalist shares many features of lexicographic strategies, it does not belong to this class of strategies since it does not have a prespecified cue ordering.

strategy is its search rule, that is, the order in which the cues are checked. Methods to fix this order vary in complexity. We distinguish those that (1) require minimal effort, (2) are simple, or (3) sophisticated, and those that (4) strive for the optimum (Table 12-1). We will introduce and evaluate some of these methods in Section 3.

2.2. Linear Models for Comparison

Linear models are well established in decision theory (Cooksey, 1996; Kurz & Martignon, 1999). In contrast to lexicographic strategies, which may stop acquiring further information depending on the information already checked, linear models collect and process all information that is required. While a lexicographic strategy is characterized by its cue order, a linear model is characterized by its set of cue weights. Methods to set up these weights vary in complexity. There is a natural analogy between methods to set up weights for a linear model and search rules for lexicographic strategies (see Table 12-1). We will discuss the relation between lexicographic strategies and linear models in Section 4.

3. SEARCH RULES FOR LEXICOGRAPHIC STRATEGIES

Here, we introduce methods to set up the orderings for lexicographic comparison (Sections 3.1-3.5) and then evaluate them (Section 3.6–3.8).

3.1. A Simple Search Rule: Take-the-Best

An attractive way of searching for cue information is checking cue values along the order established by the cue validities (Gigerenzer et al., 1991). The validity of a cue is its predictive accuracy. This simple search rule defines a lexicographic strategy which has become known as the take-the-best heuristic (Gigerenzer & Goldstein, 1996). Take-the-best can be described as follows (excluding the recognition principle, which plays no role here, since we assume that all objects are recognized):

Pre-processing phase. Compute the validities defined by

$$v = \frac{R}{R+W} \tag{12-1}$$

for each cue, where R is the number of right (correct) inferences, and W the number of wrong (incorrect) inferences based on that cue alone, when one object has the value 1 and the other has the value 0. Cues with a validity of 0.5 are neutral and are, taken by themselves, of no assistance for the comparison task. Cues with a validity of more than 0.5 are beneficial, and so are cues with a validity of less than 0.5. For convenience, we will invert cues with validity less than 0.5, that is, change each 1 to a 0 and each 0 to a 1. After having inverted cues where necessary, we rank all cues according to their validity.

Step 1. Search rule: Pick the cue with the highest validity and look up the cue values of the two objects.

Step 2. Stopping rule: If one object has a cue value of one ("1") and the other has a value of zero ("0") then stop the search. Otherwise, pick the cue with the highest validity among the remaining ones and return to Step 1. (This simple stopping rule needs to be refined if binary cues can have unknown values (Lages et al., 1999), or if continuous cues are considered [Slegers et al., 2000].)

Step 3. Decision rule: If one object has a cue value of one ("1") and the other has a value of zero ("0") predict that the object with the cue value of one ("1") has the higher value on the criterion. If no cue discriminates, guess.

Thus, take-the-best simply looks up cues in the order of their validity. Note that to compute this validity all pairs of objects have to be considered. Another, quite different but practical way of computing the ecological validity is the following:

$$v = \frac{S_0 - \dfrac{N_0(N_0+1)}{2}}{N_0 N_1} \tag{12-2}$$

where S_0 denotes the sum of all ranks of objects (ordered according to decreasing criterion) with a 0 entry, N_0 is the number of 0 entries, and N_1 the number of 1 entries. The advantage of (12-2) is that cue validity can be computed without generating all pairs. Note that the numerator corresponds to the well-known *U*-value for the Mann–Whitney test and the denominator corresponds to $R + W$ (the equivalence between [12-1] and [12-2] is shown in the Appendix). Also note that the well-known Goodman–Kruskal rank correlation γ defined by

$$\gamma = \frac{R - W}{R + W} \tag{12-3}$$

is a positive rescaling of υ. In fact, a simple calculation shows that $\gamma = 2\upsilon - 1$. Thus, both notions of validity, υ and γ, establish the same hierarchy when used as a criterion to order cues, and both can be used as alternatives.

3.2. Other Simple Search Rules

The ecological validity υ is one possible criterion for ordering cues. Another approach to defining the validity of a cue is to view the performance of take-the-best when only the cue in question can be used. Each time the cue does not discriminate between two objects, we flip a coin. The performance of a take-the-best-type algorithm based only on this cue is what we call the *success* (*s*) of the cue.

$$s = \frac{R + 0.5(P - R - W)}{P} \tag{12-4}$$

where P is the total number of pairs. The ecological validity υ is related to success: It is the probability of the success of a cue, conditional on discrimination.

Another relevant candidate definition for validity is Kendall's τ, which is given by a slight modification of γ, namely,

$$\tau = \frac{R - W}{\sqrt{P(R + W)}} \tag{12-5}$$

where P again denotes the number of pairs, R the number of right inferences, and W the number of wrong inferences (for details on γ and τ, see Gigerenzer, 1981).

3.3. Random Search: Minimalist

Minimalist (Gigerenzer, Todd, & the ABC Research Group., 1999) is quite similar to take-the-best.

The only difference is in Step 1, which now reads: "Pick a cue randomly (without replacement) and look up the cue values of the two objects." Thus, minimalist does not have to know the validity of the cues, but only their direction (i.e., whether the validities are above or below 0.5, before the cue values are—eventually—inverted). Since the cues are not checked in a specified but in a random order, minimalist is—strictly speaking—not a lexicographic strategy. What is common for both heuristics is that search for information is stopped as soon as a cue is found on which the two alternatives differ. This simple stopping rule demands no cost–benefit considerations: Its motto is "Take the best reason and ignore the rest," in one case, and "Take any valid reason and ignore the rest," in the other.

3.4. A Sophisticated Search Rule: Conditional Validity

Take-the-best's rule for ranking cues is elementary: It inverts "bad" cues in its preprocessing phase and orders them according to their validities. This procedure is simple, but does it lead to the optimal ordering? There are reasons to be suspicious that other hierarchies may lead to better performance. Note that the hierarchy is determined by computing the validity for each cue in the complete set of all possible pairs, while each cue leads to inferences only on the subset of pairs left undiscriminated by preceding cues (i.e., pairs on which each of the preceding cues has coincident values). A sophisticated method to determine the cue hierarchy for a lexicographic strategy which eliminates this discrepancy is to turn to *conditional validity (cv)*, which is defined as follows. It is computed for each cue just on the set of pairs not discriminated by the cues already used. The first cue used by this type of search is the most valid, as for take-the-best. The second cue is the most valid on the set of pairs that the first cue did not discriminate, and so on; if the validity of a cue on the remaining pairs turns out to be below 0.5, the values of this cue are inverted by changing 1s into 0s and vice versa. Since the reference class, in which the conditional validity is determined, coincides with the set of pairs on which the cue with the highest conditional validity is checked, the following is a straightforward result.

THEOREM 1 (Conditional validity). *The accuracy of a lexicographic strategy with conditional validity is larger than (or equal to) that of take-the-best.*

A lexicographic strategy that uses conditional validity to establish the cue hierarchy is reminiscent of classification and regression trees (CARTs; Breiman, Friedman, Olshen, & Stone, 1993), which also determine their branches sequentially by optimizing performance at each step.

3.5. Optimal Ordering

Does using conditional validity already yield the optimal ordering for lexicographic comparison, that is, the ordering which achieves the highest performance? We ask the more general question: What is the optimal ordering and how can it be obtained? It can be obtained, for instance, by exhaustively searching through all possible permutations of the given cues (and their inverses) and by computing the performance obtained for each ranking. This is an extremely laborious task. Is there a simpler way to find the optimal ranking? By simpler we mean shorter, involving fewer steps (such as using conditional validity). To answer this question we first have to rigorously define simplicity/complexity of an algorithm. In theoretical computer science the complexity of a sequential algorithm can be defined in terms of the time required to perform all necessary operations.

One possibility is to count the number of operational steps in an algorithm, express this number as a function of the parameters involved in the algorithm, and determine the order of complexity of this function. The popular criterion for order of complexity is denoted by O() (usually called the Landau symbol) and is defined as follows: Given two functions $F(n)$ and $G(n)$ defined on the natural numbers, we state that F is—at most—of the order of G, and write $F = O(G)$, if a constant K exists such that

$$\frac{F(n)}{G(n)} < K \qquad (12\text{-}6)$$

for all natural numbers n. Thus, for instance, the function $F(n) = 3n + 1$ is of the order of $G(n) = n^2$, but not vice versa. Every polynomial in n, that is, every linear combination of powers of n, is of the order of its highest power of n. Since what is being counted is the number of steps in a sequential process, it is common to view the resulting O() criterion as the time complexity of the algorithm (more precisely, the amount of time needed by the algorithm to calculate the solutions), where n denotes the length of the given input.

A problem is said to be solvable in polynomial time if it is of the order of some polynomial in n. In contrast, if there is no machine, be it deterministic or nondeterministic (i.e., allowing for steps that involve stochastic decisions), which solves the problem in polynomial time, it is called NP (Garey & Johnson, 1979). In particular, if this process were to be simulated by a deterministic Turing machine it would require more than polynomial time. Informally, a computational problem is said to be NP-hard if its being in P implies that P = NP. NP-hardness results are in general obtained via so-called reductions. The reduction of a problem A to another problem B implies that any algorithm which solves B efficiently can be transformed into an efficient algorithm which solves A. A now widely used technique to prove NP-hardness of a problem works as follows: Choose a suitable problem in NP that is known to be NP-hard and find a reduction to the problem whose NP-hardness is to be established. This necessarily requires that the class NP contains NP-hard problems. By now, computer scientists have discovered a class of several hundred NP-hard problems in NP (Garey & Johnson, 1979). It has become a common trend in computer science to assume that P ≠ NP. Thus, although still standing on hypothetical grounds, the notion of NP-hardness has become an equivalent to intractability with relevant consequences for the use of algorithms in practical applications.

Now, let us return to the problem of finding an optimal ranking of cues. Given n cues, what is the complexity of finding an optimal ranking? Searching across all permutations of n objects requires $n!$ steps and is, hence, of an order larger than any fixed power of n. Recently it has been proven that there are no essentially simpler strategies to find the optimal ranking of n cues (Martignon & Schmitt, 1999).

THEOREM 2 (Intractability of optimal ordering search). *The problem of determining the optimal ordering of binary cues for lexicographic comparison is NP-hard.*

We sketch the concept of the proof without going into the formal details. It turns out that a famous problem called the vertex cover problem is suitable for proving the NP-hardness of the optimal ordering search of binary cues. The vertex cover problem stems from graph theory and consists of finding a set of nodes such that each edge is "covered," that is, touched by some node in the set, the cover and the cardinality of this set is minimal. The proof operates by displaying how to construct efficiently, from a given graph, a set of binary cues such that the cardinality of the smallest cover in the graph is a simple function of the number of correct inferences in the optimal cue ranking. Thus, a reduction is

established by showing that detecting the optimal ranking of binary cues is at least as difficult as finding a minimum cardinality vertex cover in a graph.

A consequence of Theorem 2 is that conditional validity does not necessarily yield the optimal ordering. The question whether in a *specific* environment conditional validity yields the optimal ordering can only be answered empirically, that is, by finding the optimal ordering through exhaustive search and comparing this ordering to the one implied by conditional validity.

3.6. Performance of Lexicographic Strategies in the Fitting Task

How does the performance of lexicographic strategies depend upon their search principles? We answer this question for the task of comparing German cities, using the environment shown in the Appendix of Gigerenzer and Goldstein (1996). Figure 12-1 shows the accuracy distribution of all possible orderings. The optimal ordering for this comparison task is, by definition, the one which achieves the highest performance

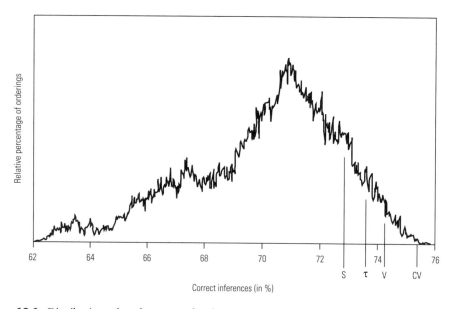

Figure 12-1. Distribution of performances for the 362,880 possible cue orderings in the German city environment. The mean of the distribution corresponds to the expected performance of minimalist (random ordering). The performance of lexicographic strategies, which search for cues according to ecological validity (i.e., take-the-best), success validity, Kendall's τ, and conditional validity are denoted by v, s, τ, and cv, respectively. (Reprinted with permission of Oxford University Press.)

(75.8%, the right extreme in this distribution). The mean of the distribution (70.0%) corresponds to the expected performance of minimalist. All other search principles have a performance between these two values: Conditional validity (*cv*) achieves 75.6%, ecological validity *v*, as used by take-the-best, achieves 74.2%; Kendall's *τ* achieves 73.5%; and Success (*s*) achieves 72.7%. Only 1.8% of the orderings allow a higher performance than the ordering of take-the-best. Thus, the search principle of take-the-best achieves a satisfying performance, in that improving this performance involves paying too high a price in terms of computational complexity; to determine the optimal ordering for the German city environment takes a UNIX machine two days!

3.7. Deviations from Take-the-Best's Cue Hierarchy

Take-the-best fixes its cue hierarchy by ranking cues according to their validities. Unlike a computer, humans may rank the cues in a given environment without *computing* their validities. Alternatively, they may *estimate* validities, that is, relative frequencies, to establish the order. Literature on automatic processing of frequencies (Hasher & Zacks, 1984) suggests that these estimates will be quite accurate. However, it is questionable whether a human's cue order perfectly matches take-the-best's order. The question is whether small violations of take-the-best's ordering cause dramatic changes in performance. We deal with this question in the specific case of the German city environment. First, as a measure of the distance from take-the-best's ordering to any other ordering, we use the minimal number of transpositions required to obtain this new ordering from take-the-best's original ordering. For instance, if take-the-best's ordering is 1, 2, 3, 4, 5, 6, 7, 8, 9, the distance to 2, 1, 3, 4, 5, 6, 9, 7, 8 is three, since we have to perform three transpositions. (one by changing the order of Cue_1 and Cue_2 and two others by moving Cue_9 from the end to its new position). The distances across all 362,880 possible orderings of the nine cues range from 0 to 36. Figure 12-2 displays the average performance—across all orderings with the same distance from take-the-best's ordering—as a function of this distance. Small

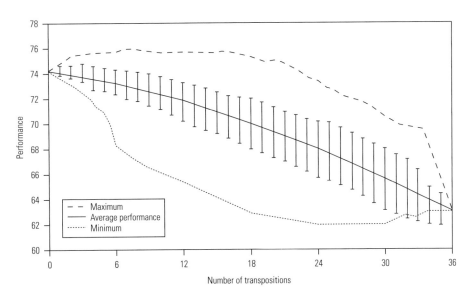

Figure 12-2. Performance of lexicographic strategies in the German city environment as a function of the minimal number of inversions which were necessary to match take-the-best's cue hierarchy. Dashed lines denote the maximum and minimum performance of all orderings for a given number of necessary inversions; bars denote the standard deviations.

violations against take-the-best's hierarchy have only negligible effects on performance. For instance, across the 628 orderings, with a distance of five to take-the-best's ordering, the average performance (73.6%) was only 0.6 percentage points below that of take-the-best. The expected distance from take-the-best's ordering to minimalist's ordering is 18, which corresponds to an average performance of 4.2 percentage points below take-the-best.

3.8. Performance of Lexicographic Strategies in a Generalization Task

It is one thing to fit known data, as we have done so far. It is another to train a model on a set of data and test it on another, unknown set. If both these sets are drawn from a larger, homogeneous one then the capacity of the model to generalize well depends on its ability to extract relevant structure without fitting noise. In cognitive psychology, models that generalize well from the training set to the test set are called robust (Dawes, 1979). The term "robust" has slightly different connotations in statistics and in mathematics (more precisely, in the theory of dynamical systems) but it always refers to stability of a model with respect to specific changes. A model is said to overfit the data if there is another model that performs less well on the training set but better on the test set.

How robust are the search rules introduced above? To answer this question, we need to compare the accuracy when fitting known data with the accuracy obtained when generalizing to unknown data within a homogeneous population—from a subset to either the whole population or to another subset. Here, we check the robustness of search principles by taking a random subset of half of the German cities, for which we determine the cue orderings, checking the performance first in the subset (i.e., the training set), and then in the other half of the cities (i.e., the test set). We repeated this procedure, known as cross-validation, 100 times for randomly chosen subsets. The results are shown in Figure 12-3. As expected, for all orderings, the performance in the test set is lower than that in the training set. Surprisingly, take-the-best uses the most robust search principle. The complex

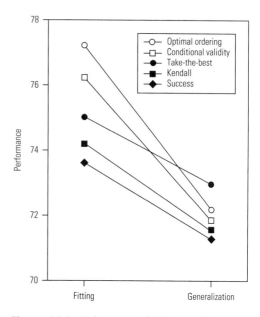

Figure 12-3. Robustness of lexicographic strategies with different principles of search in the German city environment. The training set consisted of half of the cities randomly drawn from the environment, the test set of the remaining half. Performance is averaged across 100 trials.

search principles (optimal ordering and *cv*) dropped the most, indicating that they fitted noise in the training set.

Let us briefly summarize this section. Take-the-best has been introduced as a fast-and-frugal lexicographic strategy. In its decision phase this strategy is fast since it does not involve any computation and can, thus, easily be applied. It is frugal since it uses only a fraction of the available information. Moreover, the computation necessary in the preprocessing phase is also fast-and-frugal. The cue validities, which determine take-the-best's cue hierarchy, can easily be calculated for each cue without considering relations between cues (as is the case, for instance, for conditional validity), and sorting the cues according to their validity is simple. The fact that its search rule is more robust than others that are more subtle leads us to the conclusion that take-the-best is the "best"—at least within the class of lexicographic strategies. We next turn to a comparison with linear models.

4. BENCHMARKS IN THE CLASS OF LINEAR MODELS

4.1. Variants of Linear Models

Assessing the performance of take-the-best requires a comparison with appropriate benchmarks. Such benchmarks can be found, for instance, in the class of linear models, which have a longstanding tradition in decision making. For the comparison task a linear model can be built on two levels, the object level and the comparison level. At the object level one computes a score for each object—by weighting the cue values and summing them in linear fashion—and inferring that the object with the larger score is also the one with the larger criterion value. This is the implementation used by Gigerenzer and Goldstein (1996), and Gigerenzer, Czerlinski, & Martignon (1999). At the comparison level, in contrast, one computes a score for a pair of objects and makes the inference based on a comparison between this score and a threshold value.

The most popular linear model is multiple linear regression, whose weights are calculated to minimize the average square distances between predictions and criterion values. Determining this vector of cue weights is simple for users of modern statistical packages; however, the underlying mathematics is sophisticated, involving the inversion of the cue intercorrelation matrix. Does this procedure yield the optimum in the linear world? When the task is to predict the criterion values of known objects, and when the optimum is defined as the minimum of the average square distances between predictions and criterion values, multiple regression is, by definition, the optimum. For the comparison task under common distributional assumptions, however, the optimum is logistic regression at the comparison level. From a psychological point of view, linear models at the object level are more plausible than those at the comparison level; therefore, the latter are not further pursued in the present paper.

Dawes and Corrigan (1974) have shown that using unit weights ("1" if the correlation between cue and criterion is positive; "–1" if it is negative), and even random weights (i.e., weights which are randomly chosen except for sign), yields astonishingly accurate results, in particular when generalizing to new data. Following Gigerenzer, Todd, and the ABC Research Group (1999), we call a simple linear model with *binary* unit weights *Dawes' rule*. Dawes' rule corresponds to minimalist (Table 12-1) in the sense that all it requires to know are the directions in which the cues point. Whereas Dawes and Corrigan (1974) used correlation coefficients to determine this direction, we use cue validities (which are simpler to calculate) to determine the sign of the unit weights ("1" if $v > 0.5$, "– 1" if $v < 0.5$). Thus, the scores for Dawes' rule are the number of 1s minus the number of 0s in the cue profile. If all cue values are known, as we assume in this paper, Dawes' rule is equivalent to comparing the scores obtained by counting the number of 1s in each profile. Twice the number of 1s minus the number of objects is equal to the number of 1s minus number of 0s. Therefore, the orderings defined by both scores coincide.

A slightly more complex linear model than Dawes' rule, yet simpler than regression, has been named *Franklin's rule* (Gigerenzer, Todd, et al., 1999). Franklin's rule uses the Goodman-Kruskal validities of the cues as their weights, and it is thus related with take-the-best, which uses validities to establish its cue ordering.

4.2. Performance of Linear Models

Figure 12-4 shows the performance of take-the-best, minimalist, and three linear models in 20 data sets collected from different real-world domains (Czerlinski, Gigerenzer, & Goldstein, 1999). As can be seen, take-the-best is well able to compete with these linear models, performing only four percentage points below multiple regression. The next step is to compare the algorithms in a generalization task. Czerlinski et al. (1999) also performed cross validation on these 20 data sets, by dividing the sets in half (determined at random), computing the required parameters (for the lexicographic strategies, cue direction and order; for the linear models, cue weights) on one half, and testing the algorithms with these parameters in the remaining half. The results, shown in Figure 12-4, are amazing!

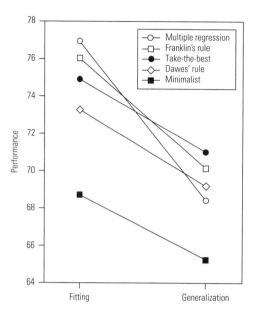

Figure 12-4. Performance of take-the-best, minimalist, and three linear models (Dawes' rule, Franklin's rule, multiple regression) averaged across 20 different data sets. In the generalization task, 50% of the objects in the data set were chosen, at random, 1,000 times and the model obtained on the training set was then tested on the remaining 50%. All results except for Franklin's rule were taken from Czerlinski et al. (1999).

When cross-validated, simple heuristics such as take-the-best even outperform sophisticated linear models. Take-the-best is robust due to its simplicity, not despite it. Its smart simplicity protects take-the-best from the danger of overfitting and "squeezing" spurious information out of the data.

4.3. Take-the-Best and Linear Models: The Case of Noncompensatory Information

Take-the-best is based on one-reason decision making: The decision which of two objects scores higher on the criterion is made solely on the basis of the most valid cue that discriminates between the two objects. The decision may be wrong, yet none of the remaining cues, nor any combination of them, will change it. In other words, take-the-best is a noncompensatory strategy. Such a strategy works best if the environment has a similar structure, where each cue is more important than any combination of less valid cues.

If cue weights are noncompensatory, then linearly combining cues yields the same performance as processing cues in lexicographic fashion, one cue at a time (see Theorem 3, below). This can be illustrated in the task of comparing two numbers written in the decimal system, that is, as linear combinations of powers of 10. For instance, to establish that 357 is larger than 318, we can check the value of the first digits on the left, and, since they coincide, move to the second digits, which differ. At this moment we make the decision that the number with 5 as second digit is larger than the number with 1. (Similar to the decimal system, any other base system has noncompensatory weights and would thus also allow for this type of strategy.)

We now define, in general terms, what a noncompensatory strategy is. Consider an ordered set of M binary cues, $C_1, \ldots, C_M$. Loosely speaking, these cues are noncompensatory for a given strategy if every cue C_j outweighs any possible combination of cues after C_j, that is, C_{j+1} to C_M. In the special case of a weighted linear model with a set of weights $W = \{w_1, w_2, \ldots, w_M\}$, a strategy is noncompensatory if for each $1 \le j \le M$ we have $w_j > \Sigma_{k>j} w_k$. In words, a linear model is noncompensatory if, for a given ordering of the weights, each weight is larger than the sum of all weights to come. A simple example is the set {1, 1/2, 1/4, 1/8, 1/16}.

A linear model with a noncompensatory set of weights results in making identical inferences as take-the-best. The converse is also true: The performance—but not the process!—of a lexicographic strategy is identical to that of a linear model with noncompensatory weights.

THEOREM 3 (Noncompensatory information). *The performance of take-the-best is equivalent to that of a linear model with a noncompensatory set of weights (decreasing in the same order of take-the-best's hierarchy). If an environment consists of cues, which for a specified order are noncompensatory for a given weighted linear model, this model cannot outperform the faster and more frugal take-the-best if that order coincides with the decreasing* *order of validities (an analytical proof is given in the Appendix).*

Liberally speaking, take-the-best embodies a noncompensatory structure and, if the environment has the same structure, then there is a fit. The degree to which this fit exists contributes to the ecological rationality of take-the-best. Three of the 20 data sets of Figure 12-4 have noncompensatory regression weights decreasing in the same order as do the validities of the cues; furthermore, as stated by Theorem 3, the performance of regression and that of take-the-best are identical. If the fit is not perfect, but approximate, then take-the-best will still be about as accurate as the corresponding linear model.

In a nutshell, take-the-best "bets" that the cues in the environment are noncompensatory, whereas Dawes' rule bets that they are equally important for making an inference. Multiple regression, in contrast, does not make blind bets, but computes its parameters to fit the structure. The price for this is more computation and, as could be seen in Figure 12-4, less robustness.

4.4. Scarce Information

If information is skewed, a lexicographic strategy can be used as a shortcut for a linear model, since both are equivalent in performance. The next two theorems specify conditions, under which take-the-best and Dawes' rule differ in performance (Martignon & Hoffrage, 1999). Theorem 4 considers the difference between these heuristics with respect to the (size of the) matrix of M binary cues and N objects. Environments are said to contain scarce information if $M \leq \log_2 N$. The rationale behind this definition is that one requires at most $\log_2 N$ yes-no questions to identify one out of N objects. More generally, according to information theory (Shannon, 1948), a class of N objects contains $\log_2 N$ bits of information. The following result has been shown to be true for small environments with up to 2^7 objects by exhaustive counting (with the help of a Cray computer; obtained by Michael Schmitt).

THEOREM 4 (Scarce information). *In the majority of small environments with scarce information, take-the-best is more accurate than Dawes' rule.*

Although we do not have a formal proof for environments with a larger numbers of objects, simulations suggest that Theorem 4 can be true for environments with more than 1024 objects. An intuitive explanation of this result is that when based on a large number of cues, Dawes' rule can compensate for possible errors in the first ones and has a high discrimination rate. With scarce information, these advantages are lost: Dawes' rule cannot really exploit compensation and is forced to make numerous guesses.

4.5. Abundant Information

The next theorem considers the opposite case, that is, environments with abundant rather than scarce information. In general, adding information to a scarce environment will do little for take-the-best, while it can compensate for mistakes Dawes' rule makes when based only on the first cues. Observe that Dawes' rule does not discriminate between profiles (110) and (011), whereas take-the-best does. What if more and more information, that is, more and more cues are added to a given number of objects? We state that an environment provides *abundant information* when all possible uncertain, yet valid, cues are present. In an environment with N objects and binary cues, the number of possible cues is the number of different 1–0 sequences of length N. Note that the expression "all possible uncertain, yet valid, cues" does not refer to all possible real-world cues but to the different 1–0 sequences. Whereas the number of real-world cues is infinite (since different real-world cues may have the same value for each object), the number of different 1–0 sequences is finite. The following result is true for environments with five or more objects (the analytical proof is given in the Appendix).

THEOREM 5 (Abundant information). *When information in an environment is abundant, Dawes' rule makes a correct inference for each possible pair of objects. The same is true of Franklin's rule.*

In contrast, the more frugal take-the-best cannot achieve perfection in such environments, because its errors cannot be compensated by later cues.

4.6. Cue Validities

In order to see how the performance of take-the-best (as compared to that of Dawes' rule and Franklin's rule with Goodman-Kruskal validities) depends on the validities, we artificially generated 10,000 environments, each with 16 objects and four binary cues. The cue values have been randomly generated. If the validity of a cue was below 0.5, the cue values were flipped, such that all validities were above 0.5 subsequent to this procedure. We subdivided these environments according to the average validity of their cues, taking the median of these averages as the split point. Across all 5,000 environments with mean validity above this split point, the performance of take-the-best, Franklin's rule, and Dawes' rule were 69.8, 70.0, and 66.9, respectively. Across those 5,000 environments with mean validity below the split point, the performance was 61.8, 62.0, and 59.7, respectively. Thus, the difference between the performance of take-the-best's and Franklin's rule (Dawes' rule) was mostly unaffected by mean validity: it was –0.2 (2.9) across all environments with higher mean validities and –0.1 (2.2) across all with lower mean validities. The correlation coefficients

between mean validity of an environment and the performance of the strategies in the particular environment was quite high (in each case at least 0.8), however, all strategies were effected in approximately the same manner. The correlation coefficients between the mean validity and the difference of take-the-best's performance minus Franklin's (Dawes') rule's performance was 0.03 (0.12). Thus, the average validity appears to play a negligible role in the comparison of take-the-best, Franklin's rule, and Dawes' rule with respect to their performance.

4.7. Cue Intercorrelations

For the same 10,000 environments we also computed how many of the six intercorrelations between the four cues turned out negative. Figure 12-5 displays the performance of take-the-best and the two linear models averaged across environments with the same number of negative intercorrelations (there were 663, 1726, 2759, 2909, 1534, 384, and 25 environments with 0, 1, 2, 3, 4, 5, and 6 negative intercorrelations, respectively). On average, take-the-best outperformed both Franklin's rule and Dawes' rule

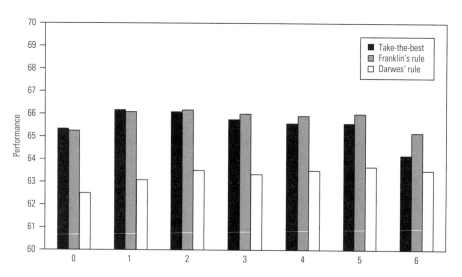

Figure 12-5. Performance of take-the-best, Franklin's rule, and Dawes' rule across all environments with the same number of positve cue intercorrelations. The environments consisted of 16 objects and four cues, for each environment (n = 10,000) cue values have been randomly generated - if the validity of a cue was below 0.5, the cue values have been flipped.

when there was no or only one negative inter-correlation between the four cues, whereas Franklin's rule could profit in environments with two or more negative intercorrelations. Note that although Dawes' rule showed, on average, the worst performance in each category, it was the only heuristic that showed a positive correlation between performance and number of negative cue-intercorrelations.

To summarize, we analyzed four information structures—skewness (noncompensatory versus compensatory), amount of information (scarce versus abundant), average validity (high versus low) and cue intercorrelations (ranging from all positive to all negative)—and examined how take-the-best performs in each context as compared with two linear models. Apart from average validity, each of these structures had an impact on the performance of take-the-best (as compared to that of Franklin's rule and Dawes' rule), demonstrating some aspects of take-the-best's ecological rationality. The fit between fast-and-frugal heuristics and the structure of environments explains why there need not always be a trade-off between simplicity and accuracy—a heuristic can have it both ways.

ACKNOWLEDGMENTS

Each of the authors made large substantial contributions to this article. We thank Nathan Berg, Valerie Chase, Gerd Gigerenzer, Elke Kurz, Peter Todd, and two anonymous reviewers for helpful comments on previous drafts; several members of the ABC Research Group for useful discussion; and Niko Kriegeskorte, Torsten Mohrbach, and Valentin Zacharias for programming the simulations. We also thank the German Research Foundation (Grant No. 1847/1) for financial support.

APPENDIX

Proof of Equation 12-2

We have to show that the following equation holds:

$$\frac{R}{R+W} = \frac{S_0 - \frac{N_0(N_0+1)}{2}}{N_0 N_1} \quad (12\text{-}A1)$$

where R and W denote the number of right and wrong inferences, respectively, in the complete paired comparison task, N_0 and N_1 are the numbers of 0 and 1 entries in the matrix that builds the environment, and S_0 denotes the sum of all ranks of 0 entries (the ranks are given to the objects ordered according to the criterion; the object with the highest criterion value has rank 1).

Let us begin by considering a cue with validity 1. There is a number K, satisfying $1 \le K < N$, such that the K objects with the largest criterion values have a value of 1 on the cue, while the remaining $(N-K)$ objects have a value of 0. Thus $N_0 = (N-K)$ and $N_1 = K$ (see Cue 1 in the following table).

Rank	Object	Cue 1	Cue 2
1	O_1	1	1
2	O_2	1	1
...	...	1	1
K	O_K	1	0
K+1	O_{K+1}	0	1
K+2	O_{K+2}	0	0
...	...	...	...
N–1	O_{N-1}	0	0
N	O_N	0	0

To compute S_0 we make use of the formula for the sum of an arithmetic progression, obtaining

$$S_0 = \frac{N(N+1) - K(K+1)}{2}$$

Replacing R (which for a cue with validity of 1 amounts to $K(N-K)$) and S_0 in (12-A1) and canceling the numerators of the two expressions in (12-A1) (which can be done because $R + W$, the total number of inferences performed by the cue, is equal to $N_0 N_1$) yields

$$K(N-K) = \frac{N(N+1) - (K(K+1)) - (N-K)(N-K+1)}{2}$$

which is easily obtained by multiplying out the terms on the right side and performing the necessary cancellations. Thus, we have shown that (12-A1) holds for a cue with validity 1.

The next step is to perform exactly one inversion in the cue values of Cue 1: For the two objects O_K and O_{K+1} we change the 1 into a 0 and the 0 into a 1, thereby obtaining Cue 2 (see Table). The number of 0s and the number of 1s for this cue are the same for Cue 1, and thus $R + W$ as well as $N_0 N_1$ are the same for both cues. However, Cue 2 makes exactly one less correct inference than Cue 1. Clearly for Cue 2 S_0 is also smaller than S_0 for Cue 1, and the difference is 1. Thus, the nominators of (1) and (2) (i.e., R and S_0, respectively) have both been diminished by 1, while their denominators remain the same. This proves our assertion for the cue obtained by performing one inversion in a cue of validity 1. Because any cue can be obtained by performing successive inversions on a cue of a validity 1, and because none of these inversions will change the identity between (1) and (2), as can be shown by complete induction, our assertion is true in general. ∎

Proof of Theorem 3. We now prove that take-the-best is equivalent—in performance—to a linear model with noncompensatory weights, where the highest weight corresponds to the cue with highest validity, the second highest weight to the cue with second highest validity, and so on. Consider an environment provided with a set of cues $Q = \{q_1, q_2, \ldots, q_M\}$, where $V(q_1) \geq V(q_2) \geq \ldots \geq V(q_i)$, and $V(q_i)$ is the validity of q_i. Define the score $s(O_j)$ of an object O_j by

$$s(O_j) = q_1(O_j)\frac{1}{2} + q_2(O_j)\frac{1}{2^2}$$
$$+ q_3(O_j)\frac{1}{2^3} + \ldots + q_M(O_j)\frac{1}{2^M}$$

We have to show that the lexicographic comparison of objects O_i and O_j implies that $O_i > O_j$ if and only if $s(O_i) > s(Oj)$.

Proof. Assume that the best cue q_1 in Q satisfies $q_1(O_i) > q_1(O_j)$. Because we only consider binary cues, this assumption implies that $q_1(O_i) = 1$ and $q_1(O_j) = 0$.

Since

$$\frac{1}{2} > \frac{1}{2^2} + \frac{1}{2^3} + \frac{1}{2^4} + \cdots + \frac{1}{2^M}$$

the score $s(O_i)$ is certainly larger than the score $s(O_j)$. For the reciprocal observe that it is impossible to have

$$\frac{1}{2}q_1(O_i) + \frac{1}{2^2}q_2(O_i) + \cdots + \frac{1}{2^M}q_M(O_i) >$$
$$\frac{1}{2}q_1(O_j) + \frac{1}{2^2}q(O_j) + \cdots + \frac{1}{2^M}q(O_j)$$

unless $q_1(O_i) = 1$ and $q_1(O_j) = 0$, based on the same argument that $1/2$ is larger than any sum of its lower powers. The same is valid if the first differing cue value occurs at some other column of the cue matrix. ∎

Proof of Theorem 4. Consider a reference class R of N objects $(O_1, \ldots, O_i, \ldots O_n)$. We define the score $s(O_i)$ of O_i as the sum of entries in its cue profile $Q(O_i)$. Theorem 4 holds if, in the cue matrix containing all favorable cues but not the secure cues, there are more ones in each row than in the following row (objects are rank ordered according to the criterion, with the object scoring highest in the first row). Consider the i-th row and its successor the $(i + 1)$-th row. Cues contained in the matrix that have the same values in the i-th and the $(i + 1)$-th entries are irrelevant to the theorem because they add equally to both sums.

The set of all cues in the matrix that have a 1 in the i-th entry and a 0 in the $(i + 1)$-th entry will be called M_i. The set of all cues in the matrix that have a 0 in the i-th entry and a 1 in the $(i + 1)$-th entry will be called M_{i+1}. It is sufficient to prove that the set M_i is larger than the set M_{i+1}.

For each element of M_{i+1} changing the 0 in the i-th entry into a 1 and the 1 in the $(i + 1)$-th entry into a 0 yields a cue of higher validity, because one inversion is transformed into an agreement. The resulting cue will be in the matrix (and thus an element of the set M_i) except when its validity becomes 1 after the transformation.

This can only happen for the cue that has all ones above the i-th entry and all zeros below the $(i + 1)$-th entry. It has thus been shown, that the set M_i is at least the size of the set M_{i+1} minus 1: inverting the i-th and $(i + 1)$-th entries maps all elements of M_{i+1} onto elements of M_i except for one element of M_{i+1}, which is mapped onto a cue of validity 1.

If there are two elements of M_i that are not elements of M_{i+1} with their i-th and $(i + 1)$-th entries inverted, then the set M_i is larger than the set M_{i+1}, and the theorem is proven. We will show that it is possible to construct two cues that:

- have a 0 in entry i and a 1 in entry $i + 1$
- are not in M_{i+1} because their validities are equal to or below 0.5
- can be transformed to elements of M_i by inverting their i-th and the $(i + 1)$-th entries (The inversion increases their validity so that it falls within $]0.5,1[$.)

The two cues resulting from the inversion are therefore in the set M_i without being elements of M_{i+1} with their i-th and $(i+1)$-th entries inverted. The two cues are therefore not within the subset of cues of M_i accounted for in the previous step. If the existence of two such cues can be shown then the set M_i is larger than the set M_{i+1} and the theorem is proven.

Case A: N Is Odd

If N is odd, then there is one central entry to the cue. In that case there are at least two ways to construct a symmetric cue that has a 0 in the i-th and a 1 in the $(i + 1)$-th entry: Entries i and $i + 1$ will be mirrored vertically around the cue's central entry. This will determine three or four entries of the cue: three if the i-th or the $(i + 1)$-th entry is the cue's central entry and four if it is not. The number of objects N is defined to be larger than 4, so there is at least one entry that can be set to 1 or 0 to obtain two symmetrical cues.

Since the obtained cues are symmetrical their validity is 0.5. Inverting the i-th and $(i + 1)$-th entries will increase their validities so that they will fall within $]0.5,1[$ and be elements of M_i. ∎

Case B: N Is Even

If N is even and $i \neq N/2$, two symmetrical cues that have a 0 in the i-th and a 1 in the $(i + 1)$-th entry can be constructed as explained above: by mirroring the i-th and $(i + 1)$-th entries around the cue's central axis and filling the remaining entries in two different ways to obtain two symmetrical cues. Inverting the i-th and $(i + 1)$-th entries, again, will increase the validities so that they will fall within $]0.5,1[$ and be elements of M_i.

If N is even and $i = N/2$, a slightly different approach must be taken: Whereas the i-th entry is set to 0 and the $(i + 1)$-th to 1 as before, the other entries are either all set to 1 or they are all set to zero. The resulting cues are symmetrical except for one central inversion. Their validities are thus below 0.5. Inverting the i-th and $(i + 1)$-th entries, will yield cues that are symmetrical except for one central agreement. Their validities will thus fall within $]0.5,1[$ and they will be elements of M_i. ∎

Introduction to Chapter 13

Heuristic and Linear Models of Judgment: Matching Rules and Environments

Together with Hillel Einhorn, Robin Hogarth published work on heuristics in the 1970s, specifically on models that use unit weights (rather than "optimal" beta weights). He has been critical of the view that complex problems always require complex solutions. One source of inspiration was an article by Dawes and Corrigan (1974) that showed that when the "optimal" weights in a linear model, determined by a least squares algorithm, were replaced by weights chosen at random (numbers between 0 and 1) with the appropriate sign, the result was very good and, in fact, for all four data sets considered, better than the predictions made by human judges with the same data. When Dawes and Corrigan's paper was first submitted to *Psychological Review*, the referees rejected it as "premature," and when Dawes presented the results at a professional conference, distinguished attendees called them "impossible" (Hogarth, in press). Two decades later, when Gigerenzer and Goldstein showed that relying on one good reason (take-the-best heuristic) could be equally or more accurate than linear models, the time was ripe, and the paper was accepted by the very same journal, although many researchers remained incredulous that less could be more.

Inspired by Dawes and Corrigan's results, Einhorn and Hogarth (1975) replaced random weights with unit weights (the expected values of random weights) and showed that there are conditions under which these simple heuristics predict more accurately than models that use optimal weights (based on ordinary least squares). Given these empirical and analytical results, one would expect diehard users of the regression technique to reconsider their assumption that derivation of best-fitting regression coefficients is the best approach for making predictions. Yet, with few exceptions, the evidence has had little impact.

In 2001, Robin Hogarth joined Chris Starmer and Gerd Gigerenzer as co-director of the Summer Institute for Bounded Rationality in Psychology and Economics, which is held annually in Berlin (now co-directed by Vernon L. Smith and Gerd Gigerenzer). Hogarth's interest in simplicity revived, he returned to his old topic. Together with his student Natalia Karelaia, he published a number of articles that investigated the ecological rationality of heuristics such as unit-weight linear strategies and take-the-best. Many of their joint ideas are synthesized in the article selected here. The approach taken is different from those in the previous two chapters, which used analysis and simulations with real-world data. Instead, it relies on normal distributions and assumptions about independent and identically distributed errors, and a neo-Brunswikian linear regression framework. Thus, in contrast to the analytical approach in Chapter 12, Hogarth and Karelaia's statistical analysis takes uncertainty into account. However, uncertainty is not captured by sampling of objects, but by introducing error terms into the system. A related test-theoretical approach to ecological rationality was taken by McGrath (2008), who confirmed the conclusion of this article that environments exist in which relying on the single best predictor leads to better performance than when integrating multiple predictors. These different frameworks illustrate that there is not one, but many methodological approaches to the study of ecological rationality.

CHAPTER 13

Heuristic and Linear Models of Judgment: Matching Rules and Environments

Robin M. Hogarth and Natalia Karelaia

Abstract: Much research has highlighted incoherent implications of judgmental heuristics, yet other findings have demonstrated high correspondence between predictions and outcomes. At the same time, judgment has been well modeled in the form of *as if* linear models. Accepting the probabilistic nature of the environment, the authors use statistical tools to model how the performance of heuristic rules varies as a function of environmental characteristics. They further characterize the human use of linear models by exploring effects of different levels of cognitive ability. They illustrate with both theoretical analyses and simulations. Results are linked to the empirical literature by a meta-analysis of lens model studies. Using the same tasks, the authors estimate the performance of both heuristics and humans where the latter are assumed to use linear models. Their results emphasize that judgmental accuracy depends on matching characteristics of rules and environments and highlight the trade-off between using linear models and heuristics. Whereas the former can be cognitively demanding, the latter are simple to implement. However, heuristics require knowledge to indicate when they should be used.

Two classes of models have dominated research on judgment and decision making over past decades. In one, explicit recognition is given to the limits of information processing, and people are modeled as using simplifying heuristics (Gigerenzer, Todd, & the ABC Research Group, 1999; Kahneman, Slovic, & Tversky, 1982). In the other, it is assumed that people can integrate all the information at hand and that this is combined and weighted as if using an

algebraic—typically linear—model (Anderson, 1981; Brehmer, 1994; Hammond, 1996).

The topic of heuristics has generated many interesting findings, as well as controversy (see, e.g., Gigerenzer, 1996; Kahneman & Tversky, 1996). However, whereas few scholars doubt that people make extensive use of heuristics (as variously defined), many questions are unresolved. One important issue—and key to the controversy—has been the failure to explicate the relative efficacy of heuristics and especially to define a priori the environmental conditions when these are differentially accurate.

At one level, this failure is surprising in that Herbert Simon—whose work is held in high esteem by researchers with opposing views about heuristics—specifically emphasized environmental factors. Indeed, some 50 years ago, Simon stated,

> if an organism is confronted with the problem of behaving approximately rationally, or adaptively, in a particular environment, the kinds of simplifications that are suitable may depend not only on the characteristics—sensory, neural, and other—of the organism, but equally on the nature of the environment. (Simon, 1956, p. 130)

At the same time that Simon was publishing his seminal work on bounded rationality, the use of linear models to represent psychological processes received considerable impetus from Hammond's (1955) formulation of clinical judgment and was subsequently bolstered by Hoffman's (1960) argument for "paramorphic" representation (see also Einhorn, Kleinmuntz, & Kleinmuntz, 1979). Contrary to work on heuristics, this research has shown concern for environmental factors.

Specifically—as illustrated in Figure 13-1—Hammond and his colleagues (Hammond,

Hursch, & Todd, 1964; Hursch, Hammond, & Hursch, 1964; Tucker, 1964) depicted Brunswik's (1952) lens model within a linear framework that defines both judgments and the criterion being judged as functions of cues in the environment. Thus, the accuracy of judgment (or psychological achievement) depends on both the inherent predictability of the environment and the extent to which the weights humans attach to different cues match those of the environment. In other words, accuracy depends on the characteristics of the cognitive strategies that people use and those of the environment. Moreover, this framework has been profitably used by many researchers (see, e.g., Brehmer & Joyce, 1988; Cooksey, 1996; Hastie & Kameda, 2005). Other techniques, such as conjoint analysis (cf. Louvière, 1988), also assume that people process information as though using linear models and, in so doing, seek to quantify the relative weights given to different variables affecting judgments and decisions (see also Anderson, 1981).

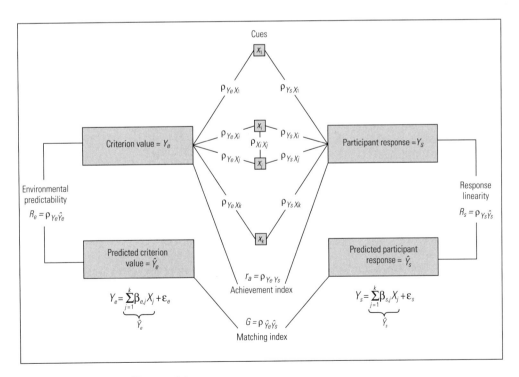

Figure 13-1. Diagram of lens model.

In many ways, the linear model has been the workhorse of judgment and decision-making research from both descriptive and prescriptive viewpoints. As to the latter, consider the influence of linear models on decision analysis (see, e.g., Keeney & Raiffa, 1976), prediction tasks (Camerer, 1981; Dawes, 1979; Dawes & Corrigan, 1974; Einhorn & Hogarth, 1975; Goldberg, 1970; Wainer, 1976), and the statistical-clinical debate (Dawes, Faust, & Meehl, 1989; Kleinmuntz, 1990; Meehl, 1954).

Despite the ubiquity of the linear model in representing human judgment, its psychological validity has been questioned for many decision-making tasks. First, when the amount of information increases (e.g., more than three cues in a multiple-cue prediction task), people have difficulty in executing linear rules and resort to simplifying heuristics. Second, the linear model implies trade-offs between cues or attributes, and because people find these difficult to execute—both cognitively and emotionally (Hogarth, 1987; Luce, Payne, & Bettman, 1999)—they often resort to trade-off avoiding heuristics (Montgomery, 1983; Payne, Bettman, & Johnson, 1993).

This discussion of heuristics and linear models raises many important psychological issues. Under what conditions do people use heuristics—and which heuristics—and how accurate are these relative to the linear model? Moreover, if heuristics neglect information and/ or avoid trade-offs, how do these features contribute to their success or failure, and when?

A further issue relates to how heuristic performance is evaluated. One approach is to identify instances in which heuristics violate coherence with the implications of statistical theory (see, e.g., Tversky & Kahneman, 1983). The other considers the extent to which predictions match empirical realizations (Gigerenzer et al., 1999). These two approaches, labeled coherence and correspondence, respectively (Hammond, 1996), may sometimes conflict in the impressions they imply of people's judgmental abilities. In this article, we follow the second because our goal is to understand how the performance of heuristic rules and linear models is

affected by the characteristics of the environments in which they are used. In other words, we speak directly to the need specified by Simon (1956) to develop a theory of how environmental characteristics affect judgment (see also Brunswik, 1952).

This article is organized as follows. We first outline the framework within which our analysis is conducted and specify the particular models used in our work. We then briefly review literature that has considered the accuracy of heuristic decision models. Our approach, developed in the subsequent section, explicitly recognizes the probabilistic nature of the environment and exploits appropriate statistical theory. This allows us to make theoretical predictions of model accuracy in terms of both percentage of correct predictions and expected losses. We emphasize here that these predictions are theoretical implications, as opposed to forecasts made by fitting models to data and extrapolating to new samples. Briefly, the rationale for this approach—discussed further below—is to capture the power of theory to make claims that can be generalized. To facilitate the exposition, we do not present the underlying rationales for all models in the main text but make use of appendices. We demonstrate the power of our equations with theoretical predictions of differential model performance over a wide range of environments, as well as using simulation. This is followed by our examination of empirical data using a meta-analysis of the lens model literature.

FRAMEWORK AND MODELS

We conduct our analyses within the context of predicting (choosing) the better of two alternatives on the basis of several cues (attributes). Moreover, we assume that the criterion is probabilistically related to the cues and that the optimal equation for predicting the criterion is a linear function of the cues.[1] Thus, if the decision maker weights the cues appropriately (using a linear model), he or she will achieve the maximum predictive performance. However, this could be an exacting standard to achieve. Thus, what are the consequences of abandoning the linear rule and using simpler heuristics? Moreover, when do different heuristics perform relatively well or badly?

Specifically, we consider five models and, to simplify the analysis, consider only three cues. Two of these models are linear, and three are heuristics. Whereas we could have chosen many variations of these models, they are sufficient to illustrate our approach.

First, we consider what happens when the decision maker can be modeled as if he or she were using a linear combination (LC) of the cues but is inconsistent (cf. Hoffman, 1960). Note carefully that we are not saying that the decision maker actually uses a linear formula but that this can be modeled *as if*. We justify this on the grounds that linear models can often provide higher-level representations of underlying processes (Einhorn et al., 1979). Moreover, when the information to be integrated is limited, the linear model can also provide a good process description (Payne et al., 1993).

Second, the decision maker uses a simplified version of the linear model that gives equal weight (EW) to all variables (Dawes & Corrigan, 1974; Einhorn & Hogarth, 1975).[2]

Third, the decision maker uses the take-the-best (TTB) heuristic proposed by Gigerenzer and Goldstein (1996). This model first assumes that the decision maker can order cues or attributes by their ability to predict the criterion. Choice is then made by the most predictive cue that can discriminate between options. If no cues discriminate, choice is made at random. This model is "fast and frugal" in that it typically decides on the basis of one or two cues (Gigerenzer et al., 1999).[3]

There is experimental evidence that people use TTB-like strategies, although not exclusively (Bröder, 2000, 2003; Bröder & Schiffer, 2003; Newell & Shanks, 2003; Newell, Weston, & Shanks, 2003; Rieskamp & Hoffrage, 1999). Descriptively, the two most important criticisms are, first, that the stopping rule is often violated in that people seek more information than the model specifies and, second, that people may not be able to rank-order the cues by predictive ability (Juslin & Persson, 2002).

The fourth model, CONF (Karelaia, 2006), was developed to overcome the descriptive shortcomings of TTB. Its spirit is to consult the cues in the order of their validity (like TTB) but not to stop the process once a discriminating cue has been identified. Instead, the process only stops once the discrimination has been confirmed by another cue.[4] With three cues, then, CONF requires only that two cues favor the chosen alternative. Moreover, CONF has the advantage that choice is insensitive to the order in which cues are consulted. The decision maker does not need to know the relative validities of the cues.[5]

Finally, our fifth model is based solely on the single variable (SV) that the decision maker believes to be most predictive. Thus, this differs from TTB in that, across a series of judgments, only one cue is consulted. Parenthetically, this could also be used to model any heuristic based on one variable, such as judgments by availability (Tversky & Kahneman, 1973), recognition (Goldstein & Gigerenzer, 2002), or affect (Slovic, Finucane, Peters, & MacGregor, 2002). In these cases, however, the variable would not be a cue that could be observed by a third party but would represent an intuitive feeling or judgment experienced by the decision maker (e.g., ease of recall, sensation of recognition, or a feeling of liking).

It is important to note that all these rules represent feasible psychological processes. Table 13-1 specifies and compares what needs to be known for each of the models to achieve its maximum performance. This can be decomposed between knowledge about the specific cue values (on the left) and what is needed to weight the variables (on the right). Two models require knowing all cue values (LC and EW), and one only needs to know one (SV). The number of cue values required by TTB and CONF depends on the characteristics of each choice faced. As to weights, maximum performance by LC requires precise, absolute knowledge; TTB requires the ability to rank-order cues by validity; and for SV, one needs to identify the cue with the greatest validity. Neither EW nor CONF requires knowledge about weights.

Table 13-1.   Knowledge Required to Achieve Upper Limits of Model Performance

Model	Values of Variables[a]			Weights Ordering			
	Cue 1	Cue 2	Cue 3	Exact[b]	First[c]	All[d]	None
Linear combination (LC)	Yes	Yes	Yes	Yes			
Equal weighting (EW)	Yes	Yes	Yes				Yes
Take-the-best (TTB)	Yes	Yes/no	Yes/no			Yes	
Single variable (SV)	Yes				Yes		
CONF	Yes	Yes	Yes/no				Yes

[a] Yes = value of cue required; Yes/no = value of cue may be required.
[b] Exact values of cue weights required.
[c] First = most important cue identified.
[d] All = rank order of all cues known a priori.

Whereas it is difficult to tell whether obtaining values of cue variables or knowing how cues vary in importance is more taxing cognitively, we have attempted an ordering of the models in Table 13-1 from most to least taxing. LC is the most taxing ceteris paribus. The important issue is to characterize its sensitivity to deviations from optimal specification of its parameters. CONF, at the other extreme, is not demanding, and the only uncertainty centers on how many variables need to be consulted for each decision.

In brief, our analytical results show that the performance of heuristic rules is affected by how the environment weights cues, cue redundancy, the predictability of the environment, and loss functions. Heuristics predict accurately when their characteristics match the demands of the environment; for example, EW is best when the environment also weights the cues equally. However, in the absence of a close match between characteristics of heuristics and the environment, the presence of redundancy can moderate the relative predictive ability of different heuristics. Both cue redundancy and noise (i.e., lack of predictability) also reduce differences between model performances, but these can be augmented or diminished according to the loss function. We also show that sensible models often make identical predictions. However, because they disagree across 8%–30% of the cases we examine, it pays to understand the differences.

We exploit the mathematics of the lens model (Tucker, 1964) to ask how well decision makers need to execute LC rule strategies to perform as well as or better than heuristics in binary choice using the criterion of predictive accuracy (i.e., correspondence). We find that performance using LC rules generally falls short of that of appropriate heuristics unless decision makers have high *linear cognitive ability*, or *ca* (which we quantify). This analysis is supported by a meta-analysis of lens model studies in which we estimate *ca* across 270 tasks and also demonstrate that, within the same tasks, individuals vary in their ability to outperform heuristics using LC models. Finally, we illustrate how errors in the application of both linear models and heuristics affect performance and thus the nature of potential trade-offs involved in using different models.

THEORETICAL DEVELOPMENT

Accepting the probabilistic nature of the environment (Brunswik, 1952), we use statistical theory to model both how people make judgments and the characteristics of the environments in which those judgments are made. To motivate the theoretical development, imagine a binary choice that involves selecting one of two job candidates, A and B, on the basis of several characteristics such as level of professional qualifications, years of experience, and so on. Further, imagine that a criterion can be observed at a later date and that a correct decision has been taken if the criterion is greater for the chosen candidate. Denote the criterion by the random variable Y_e

such that if A happened to be the correct choice, one would observe $y_{ea} > y_{eb}$.[6]

Within the lens model framework—see Figure 13-1—we can model assessments of candidates by two equations: one, the model of the environment; the other, the model of the judge (the person assessing the job candidates). That is,

$$Y_e = \sum_{j=1}^{k} \beta_{e,j} X_j + \varepsilon_e, \qquad (13\text{-}1)$$

and

$$Y_s = \sum_{j=1}^{k} \beta_{s,j} X_j + \varepsilon_s, \qquad (13\text{-}2)$$

where Y_e represents the criterion (subsequent job performance of candidates) and Y_s is the judgment made by the decision maker, the X_js are cues (here, characteristics of the candidates), and ε_e and ε_s are normally distributed error terms with means of zero and constant variances independent of the Xs.

The logic of the lens model is that the judge's decisions will match the environmental criterion to the extent that the weights the judge gives to the cues match those used by the model of the environment, that is, the matches between $\beta_{s,j}$ and $\beta_{e,j}$ for all $j = 1, \ldots, k$—see Figure 13-1.

Moreover, assuming that the error terms in Equations 13-1 and 13-2 are independent of each other, it can be shown that the achievement index—or correlation between Y_e and Y_s—can be expressed as a multiplicative function of three terms (Tucker, 1964). These are, first, the extent to which the environment is predictable as measured by R_e, the correlation between Y_e and $\sum_{j=1}^{k} \beta_{e,j} X_j$; second, the consistency with which the person uses the linear decision rule as measured by R_s, the correlation between Y_s and $\sum_{j=1}^{k} \beta_{s,j} X_j$; and third, the correlation between the predictions of both models, that is, between $\sum_{j=1}^{k} \beta_{e,j} X_j$ and $\sum_{j=1}^{k} \beta_{s,j} X_j$. This is also known as G, the *matching* index. (Note that $G = 1$ if $\beta_{e,j} = \beta_{s,j}$ for all $j = 1, \ldots, k$.)

This leads to the well-known lens model equation (Tucker, 1964) that expresses judgmental performance or achievement in the form

$$\rho_{Y_e Y_s} = G R_e R_s + \rho_{\varepsilon_e \varepsilon_s} \sqrt{\left(1 - R_e^2\right)\left(1 - R_s^2\right)} \qquad (13\text{-}3)$$

where, for completeness, we show the effect of possible nonzero correlation between the error terms of Equations 13-1 and 13-2.

Assuming that the correlation $\rho_{\varepsilon_e \varepsilon_s}$ is zero, we consider below two measures of judgmental performance. One is the traditional measure of achievement, $G R_e R_s$. The other is independent of the level of predictability of the environment and is captured by $G R_s$. Lindell (1976) referred to this as *performance*. However, we call it *linear cognitive ability*, or *ca*, to capture the notion that it measures how well someone is using the linear model in terms of both matching weights (G) and consistency of execution (R_s).

First, however, we develop the probabilities that our models make correct predictions within a given population or environment. As will be seen, these probabilities reflect the covariance structure of the cues as well as those between the criterion and the cues. It is these covariances that characterize the inferential environment in which judgments are made.

The SV Model

Imagine that the judge does not use a linear combination rule but instead simply chooses the candidate who is better on one variable, X_1 (e.g., years of experience). Thus, the decision rule is to choose the candidate for whom X_1 is larger, for example, choose A if $x_{1a} > x_{1b}$. Our question now becomes, what is the probability that A is better than B using this decision rule in a given environment, that is, what is

$$P\left\{\left(Y_{ea} > Y_{eb}\right) \cap \left(X_{1a} > X_{1b}\right)\right\}?$$

To calculate this probability, we follow the model presented in Hogarth and Karelaia (2005a). We first assume that Y_e and X_1 are both standardized normal variables (i.e., with means of 0 and variances of 1) and that the cue used is positively correlated with the criterion.[7] Denote the correlation by the parameter $\rho_{Y_e X_1}$ (>0).

Given these facts, it is possible to represent Y_{ea} and Y_{eb} by the equations

$$Y_{ea} = \rho_{Y_e X_1} X_{1a} + v_{ea} \tag{13-4}$$

and

$$Y_{eb} = \rho_{Y_e X_1} X_{1b} + v_{eb}, \tag{13-5}$$

where v_{ea} and v_{eb} are normally distributed error terms, each with mean of 0 and variance of $\left(1 - \rho_{Y_e X_1}^2\right)$, independent of each other and of X_{1a} and X_{1b}.

The question of determining $P\{(Y_{ea} > Y_{eb}) \cap (X_{1a} > X_{1b})\}$ can be reframed as determining $P\{(d_1 > 0) \cap (d_2 > 0)\}$ where $d_1 = Y_{ea} - Y_{eb} > 0$ and $d_2 = X_{1a} - X_{1b} > 0$. The variables d_1 and d_2 are bivariate normal with variance–covariance matrix

$$M_{f\_SV} = \begin{pmatrix} 2 & 2\rho_{Y_e X_1} \\ 2\rho_{Y_e X_1} & 2 \end{pmatrix}$$

and means of 0. Thus, the probability of correctly selecting A over B can be written as

$$\int_0^\infty \int_0^\infty f(\underline{d}) \, d\underline{d}, \tag{13-6}$$

where $f(\underline{d})$ is the normal bivariate probability density function with $\underline{d}' = (d_1, d_2)$.

To calculate the expected accuracy of the SV model in a given environment, it is necessary to consider the cases where both $X_{1a} > X_{1b}$ and $X_{1b} > X_{1a}$ such that the overall probability is given by $P\{((Y_{ea} > Y_{eb}) \cap (X_{1a} > X_{1b})) \cup ((Y_{eb} > Y_{ea}) \cap (X_{1b} > X_{1a}))\}$, which, because both its components are equal, can be simplified as

$$2P\{(Y_{ea} > Y_{eb}) \cap (X_{1a} > X_{1b})\}$$
$$= 2\int_0^\infty \int_0^\infty f(\underline{d}) \, d\underline{d}. \tag{13-7}$$

The analogous expressions for the LC, EW, CONF, and TTB models are presented in Appendix A, where the appropriate correlations for LC and EW are $\rho_{Y_t Y_1}$ and $\rho_{Y_e \bar{X}}$, respectively.

Loss Functions

Equation 13-7, as well as its analogues in Appendix A, can be used to estimate the probabilities that

the models will make the correct decisions. These probabilities can be thought of as the average percentage of correct scores that the models can be expected to achieve in choosing between two alternatives. As such, this measure is equivalent to a 0/1 loss function that does not distinguish between small and large errors. We therefore introduce the notion that losses from errors reflect the degree to which predictions are incorrect.

Specifically, to calculate the expected loss resulting from using SV across a given population, we need to consider the possible losses that can occur when the model does not select the best alternative. We model loss by a symmetric squared error loss function but allow this to vary in exactingness, or the extent to which the environment does or does not punish errors severely (Hogarth, Gibbs, McKenzie, & Marquis, 1991). We note that loss occurs when (a) $X_{1a} > X_{1b}$ but $Y_{ea} < Y_{eb}$ and (b) $X_{1a} < X_{1b}$ but $Y_{ea} > Y_{eb}$. Capitalizing on symmetry, the expected loss (EL) associated with the population can therefore be written as

$$EL_{sv} = 2P\{(Y_{ea} < Y_{eb}) \cap (X_{1a} > X_{1b})\} L, \tag{13-8}$$

where $L = \alpha (Y_{eb} - Y_{ea})^2$. The constant of proportionality, α (> 0), is the exactingness parameter that captures how heavily losses should be counted.

Substituting $\alpha (Y_{eb} - Y_{ea})^2$ for L and following the same rationale as when developing the expression for accuracy, the expected loss of the SV model can be expressed as

$$EL_{SV} = 2\alpha (Y_{eb} - Y_{ea})^2 P\{(Y_{ea} < Y_{eb}) \cap (X_{1a} > X_{1b})\} =$$
$$2\alpha \int_{-\infty}^0 \int_0^\infty d_1^2 f(\underline{d}) \, d\underline{d} \tag{13-9}$$

As in the expression for accuracy, the function $f(\underline{d})$ for SV involves the variance-covariance matrix M_{f-sv}. The expected losses of LC and EW are found analogically, using their appropriate variance-covariance matrices.

In Table 13-2, we summarize the expressions for accuracy and loss for SV, LC, and EW. In Appendix B, we present the formulas for the

Table 13-2.   Key Formulas for Three Models: SV, LC, and EW

Model	Variance–Covariance Matrix (M_f)
Single variable (SV)	$\begin{pmatrix} 2 & 2\rho_{Y_eX_i} \\ 2\rho_{Y_eX_i} & 2 \end{pmatrix}$
Linear combination (LC)	$\begin{pmatrix} 2 & 2\rho_{Y_sY_s} \\ 2\rho_{Y_sY_s} & 2 \end{pmatrix}$
Equal weights (EW)	$\begin{pmatrix} 2 & 2\rho_{Y_e\bar{X}}\sigma_{\bar{X}} \\ 2\rho_{Y_e\bar{X}}\sigma_{\bar{X}} & 2\sigma_{\bar{X}}^2 \end{pmatrix}$

Note: 1. The expected accuracy of models is estimated as the probability of correctly selecting A over B or B over A and is found as

$$2\int_0^\infty \int_0^\infty f(\underline{d})\,d\underline{d},$$

where $f(\underline{d})$ is the normal bivariate probability density function with $\underline{d}' = (d_1, d_2)$.
2. The expected loss of models is found as

$$2\alpha\int_{-\infty}^0 \int_0^\infty d_1^2 f(\underline{d})\,d\underline{d},$$

where α (>0) is the exactingness parameter.
3. The variance–covariance matrix M_f is specific for each model.

4. $\rho_{Y_e\bar{X}} = \bar{\rho}_{Y_eX}\sqrt{\dfrac{k}{\left(1+(k-1)\bar{\rho}_{X_iX_j}\right)}},$

where k = number of X variables, $\bar{\rho}_{Y_eX}$ = average correlation between Y and the Xs, and $\bar{\rho}_{X_iX_j}$ = average intercorrelations amongst the Xs.

5. $\sigma_{\bar{X}} = \sqrt{\dfrac{1}{k}\left(1+(k-1)\bar{\rho}_{X_iX_j}\right)}.$

loss functions of CONF and TTB. Finally, note that expected loss, as expressed by Equation 13-9, is proportional to the exactingness parameter, α, that models the extent to which particular environments punish errors.

EXPLORING EFFECTS OF DIFFERENT ENVIRONMENTS

We first construct and simulate several task environments and demonstrate how our theoretical analyses can be used to compare the

performance of the models in terms of both expected percentage correct and expected losses. We also show how errors in the application of both linear models and heuristics affect performance and thus illustrate potential trade-offs involved in using different models. We further note that, in many environments, heuristic models achieve similar levels of performance and explicitly explore this issue using simulation. To link theory with empirical phenomena, we use a meta-analysis of lens model studies to compare the judgmental performance of heuristics with that of people assumed to be using LC models.

Constructed and Simulated Environments: Methodology

To demonstrate our approach, we constructed several sets of different three-cue environments using the model implicit in Equation 13-1. Our approach was to vary systematically two factors: first, the weights given to the variables as captured by the distribution of cue validities, and second, the level of average intercue correlation. As a consequence, we obtained environments with different levels of predictability, as indicated by R_e (from low to high). We could not, of course, vary these factors in an orthogonal design (because of mathematical restrictions) and hence used several different sets of designs.

For each of these, it is straightforward to calculate expected correct predictions and losses for all our models[8] (see equations above), with one exception. This is the LC model, which requires specification of $\rho_{Y_sY_s}$, that is, the *achievement index*, or the correlation between the criterion and the person's responses (see Appendix A). However, given the lens model equation—see Equation 13-3 above—we know that

$$\rho_{Y_sY_s} = GR_eR_s, \tag{13-10}$$

where R_e is the predictability of the environment and GR_S or *ca* is the measure of linear cognitive ability that captures how well someone is using the linear model in terms of both matching weights and consistency of execution.[9]

In short, our strategy is to vary *ca* and observe how well the LC model performs. In other words, how accurate would people be in binary choice when modeled as if using LC with differing levels of knowledge (matching of weights) and consistency in execution of their knowledge?

For example, it is of psychological interest to ask when the validity of SV equals that of an LC strategy, that is, when $\rho_{Y_eX_1} = caR_e$ or $ca = \rho_{Y_eX_1}/R_e$. This is the point of indifference between making a judgment based on all the data (i.e., with LC) and relying on a single cue (SV), such as when using availability (Tversky & Kahneman, 1973) or affect (Slovic et al., 2002).

Relative Model Performance: Expected Percentage Correct and Expected Losses

We start by a systematic analysis of model performance in three sets of environments—A, B, and C—defined in Table 13-3. As noted above, we consider two main factors. First are distributions of cue validities. We distinguish three types: noncompensatory, compensatory, and equal weighting. Environments are classified as noncompensatory if, when cue validities are ordered in magnitude, the validity of each cue is greater than or equal to the sum of those smaller than it (cf. Martignon & Hoffrage, 1999, 2002). All other environments are compensatory. However, we distinguish between compensatory environments that do or do not involve equal weighting, treating the former as a special case. Case A in Table 13-3 involves equal weighting, whereas Case B is noncompensatory and

Case C is compensatory (but not with equal weighting).

Second, we use average intercue correlation to define redundancy. When positive, this can be large (.50) or small (.10). It can also be negative. Thus, the variants of all cases with indices 1 (i.e., A1, B1, C1) have small positive levels of redundancy, the variants with indices 2 (i.e., A2, B2, C2) have large positive levels, and the last variant of Case C (i.e., C3) involves a negative intercue correlation.[10]

Taken together, these parameters imply different levels of environmental predictability (or lack of noise), that is, R_e, which varies from .66 to .94. In the right-hand column, we show values of $\rho_{Y_eX_1}/R_e$. These indicate the benchmarks for determining when SV or LC performs better. Specifically, LC performs better than SV when *ca* exceeds $\rho_{Y_eX_1}/R_e$.

Figure 13-2 depicts expected percentages of correct predictions for the different models as a function of linear cognitive ability *ca*. We emphasize that our models' predictions are theoretical implications as opposed to estimates of predictability gained from fitting models to data and forecasting to new samples of data.

We show only the upper part of the scale of expected percentage correct because choosing at random would lead to a correct decision in 50% of choices. We stress that, in these figures, we report the performance of SV and TTB, assuming that the cues were ordered correctly before the models were applied. We relax this assumption further below to show the effect of human error in the use of heuristics.

Table 13-3. Environmental Parameters: Cases A, B, and C

Case	Cue Validities			Cue Intercorrelations			Re	$\rho_{Y_eX_1}/Re$
	ρ_{Y,X_1}	ρ_{Y,X_2}	ρ_{Y,X_3}	$\rho_{X_1X_2}$	$\rho_{X_1X_3}$	$\rho_{X_2X_3}$		
A1	.5	.5	.5	.1	.1	.1	.81	.62
A2	.5	.5	.5	.5	.5	.5	.66	.76
B1	.7	.4	.2	.1	.1	.1	.80	.88
B2	.7	.4	.2	.5	.5	.5	.76	.93
C1	.6	.4	.3	.1	.1	.1	.75	.80
C2	.6	.4	.3	.5	.5	.5	.66	.91
C3	.6	.4	.3	−.4	.1	.1	.94	.64

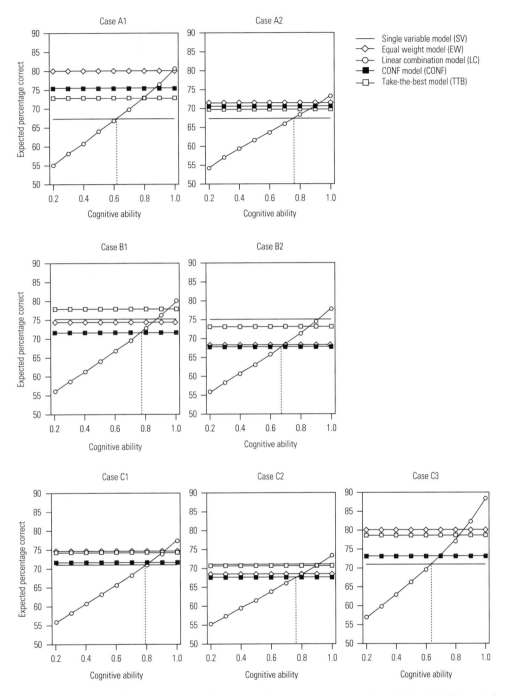

Figure 13-2. Model performance measured as expected percentage correct: Cases A, B, and C. SV = single variable model; EW = equal weight model; LC = linear combination model; CONF = CONF model; TTB = take-the-best model.

A first comment is that relative model performance varies by environments. In Case A1 (equal weighting and low redundancy), EW performs best (as it must). CONF is more accurate than TTB, and SV lags behind. In Case A2, where the redundancy becomes larger, the performance of all models except SV deteriorates. This is not surprising given that the increase in cue redundancy reduces the relative validity of information provided by each cue following the first one, and thus the overall predictability of the environment decreases (i.e., R_e in Case A1 equals .81, whereas, in A2, it decreases to .66). EW, of course, still performs best. However, the other heuristic models, in particular CONF and TTB, do not lag much behind.

This picture changes in the noncompensatory environment B. When redundancy is low (i.e., Case B1), TTB performs best, followed by SV and the other heuristics. When redundancy is greater (i.e., Case B2), the performance of TTB drops some 5%. This is enough for SV, which is insensitive to the changes in redundancy, to have the largest expected performance. EW and CONF lose in performance and remain the worst heuristic performers here.

The compensatory environment C shows different trends. With low positive redundancy (i.e., Case C1), EW and TTB share the best performance, and SV is the worst of the heuristics. Higher positive cue redundancy in Case C2 allows SV to become one of the best models, sharing this position with TTB. Finally, in the presence of negative intercue correlation (i.e., Case C3), EW does best, whereas TTB stays slightly behind it. SV is again the worst heuristic. Given the same cue validities across the C environments, negative intercue correlation increases the predictability of the environment to .94 (from .75 in C1 and .66 in C2). This change triggers improvements in the performance of all models and magnifies the differences between them (compare Case C3 with Cases C1 and C2).

Now consider the performance of LC as a function of ca. First, note that, in each environment, we illustrate (by dotted vertical lines) the level of ca at which LC starts to outperform the worst heuristic. When the latter is SV, this point

corresponds to the critical point of equality between LC and SV enumerated in the last column of Table 13-3. Thus, LC needs ca of from .62 to .80 (at least) to be competitive with the worst heuristic in these environments. The lowest demand is posed on LC in Cases A1 (minimum ca of .62) and C3 (.64). These cases are the most predictable of all examined in Figure 13-2 (R_es of .81 and .94, respectively). In the least predictable environments, A2, C1, and C2, the minimum ca needed to beat the worst heuristic is much larger: .76, .80, and .78, respectively.

Interestingly, in all the environments illustrated, ca has to be quite high before LC starts to be competitive with the better heuristics. In the most predictable environment, C3, LC has the best performance when ca starts to exceed .85. In the other environments, LC starts to have the best performance only when levels of ca are even higher.

The simple conclusion from this analysis—which we explore further below—is that unless ca is high, decision makers are better off using simple heuristics, provided that they are able to implement these correctly.

In Figure 13-3, we use the environment A1 to show differential performance in terms of expected loss where the exactingness parameter, α, is equal to 1.00 or .30. A comparison of expected loss with $\alpha = 1.00$ on the left panel of Figure 13-3 and expected accuracy in Case A1 in Figure 13-2 shows the same visual pattern of results in terms of relative model performance, a finding that was not obvious to us a priori. However, the differences between the models are magnified when the criterion of expected loss is used. To note this, compare the ranges of model performance at $ca = .20$ (extreme left point) in the two figures. When expected percentage correct is used as the decision criterion, the best model (EW in this case) is some .25 points (= 80%–55%) above the worst model (LC). When expected loss is used, the difference increases to about .70 points (= .80 of LC–.11 of SV).

The panel on the right of Figure 13-3 shows the effects of less exacting losses when $\alpha = .30$. Comparing it with the left panel of Figure 13-3,

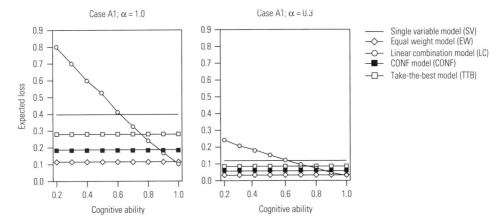

Figure 13-3. Model performance measured as expected loss (for α = 1.00 and α = .30): Case A1. SV = single variable model; EW = equal weight model; LC = linear combination model; CONF = CONF model; TTB = take-the-best model.

we find the same relative ordering between models but differences in expected loss are much smaller (as follows from Equation 13-9).

The Effect of Human Error in Heuristics

In Environments A, B, and C, we assume that the cues are ordered correctly before the heuristics are applied. However, this excludes the possibility of human error in executing the heuristics. To provide more insight, we relax this assumption in a further set of environments D. Similar to the environments described above, we consider two variants of D: D1, with low positive cue redundancy, and D2, with a higher level of redundancy (see Table 13-4). To show additionally the effect of predictability, R_e, within environments, we include eight subcases (i–viii) in both variants. The distribution of cue validities is noncompensatory in Subcases i, ii, and iii; compensatory in Subcases iv, v, and vi; and equal weighting in the last two subcases, vii and viii. A consequence of these specifications is a range of environmental predictabilities, R_e, from .37/.39 to .85/.88 across all eight sets of subcases.

In Table 13-4, we report both expected percentage correct and losses (for α = 1.00) for all models. To illustrate effects of human error, we present heuristic performance under the assumption that the decision maker fails to order the cues according to their validities and thus uses them in random order. This error affects the results of SV and TTB. EW and CONF, however, are immune to this lack of knowledge of the environmental structure. For SV and TTB, we present in addition results achieved with correct knowledge about cue ordering. To illustrate the effect of knowledge on the performance of LC in the same environments, we show results using three values for *ca*: *ca* = .50 for LC1, *ca* = .70 for LC2, and *ca* = .90 for LC3.

The trends in Table 13-4 are illustrated in Figures 13-4 and 13-5, which document percentage correct and expected loss, respectively, of the different models as a function of the validity of the most valid cue, $\rho_{Y_e X_1}$. Because, here, $\rho_{Y_e X_1}$ is highly correlated with environmental predictability R_e, the horizontal axis of the graphs can also be thought of as capturing noise (more, on the left, to less, on the right).

In the upper (lower) panel of the figures, we show the effect of error on the performance of SV (TTB). The performances of SV and TTB under random cue ordering are illustrated with the corresponding lines. The range of possible performance levels of the models from best (i.e., achieved under the correct cue ordering) to worst (i.e., achieved when the least valid cue is examined first, the second least valid second, etc.) is illustrated with the shaded areas.

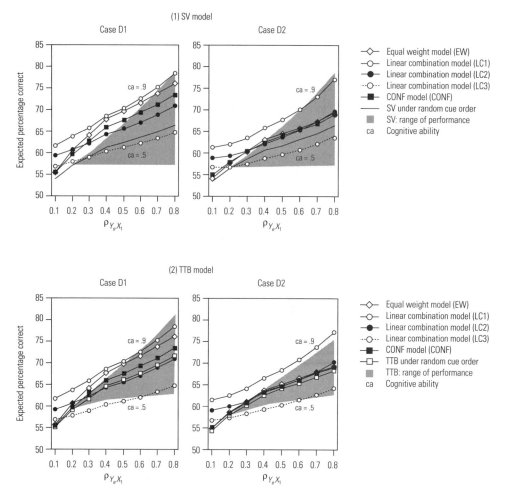

Figure 13-4. The effect of human errors on expected percentage correct: Case D. SV = single variable model; EW = equal weight model; LC = linear combination model; CONF = CONF model; TTB = take-the-best model.

First, we compare performance among the heuristic models. Note that, as noise in the environment decreases, there is a general trend for differences in heuristic model performance to increase, in addition to a tendency for performance to improve (see Figure 13-4). Second, relative model performance is affected by distributions of cue validities and redundancy (see Table 13-4). In noncompensatory environments with low redundancy (Subcases i-iii), TTB performs best, provided that the cues are ordered correctly (Figure 13-4, lower panel, the right-hand part of Case D1, the upper limit of the range of TTB). However, as these environments

become more redundant, the advantage goes to SV (Figure 13-4, upper panel, the right-hand side of Case D2, the upper limit of the range of SV). When environments involve equal weighting (Subcases vii and viii), EW is the most accurate, followed by CONF. In the compensatory environments (Subcases iv-vi), EW does best when redundancy is low, but this advantage switches to TTB (provided that the cues are ordered correctly) when redundancy is higher. We discuss these trends again below.

Second, comparing Figures 13-4 and 13-5, we note again that expected loss rank-orders the models similarly to expected percentage correct.

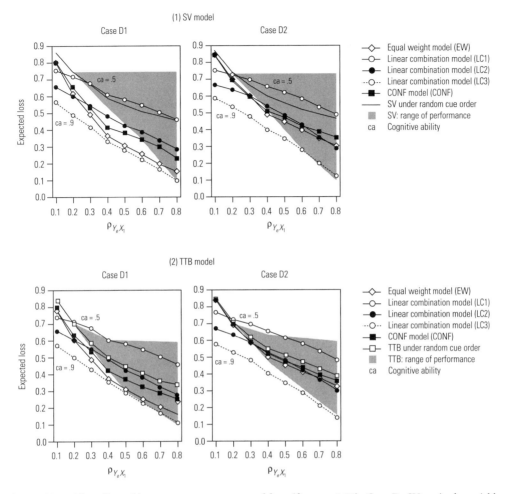

Figure 13-5. The effect of human errors on expected loss (for α = 1.00): Case D. SV = single variable model; EW = equal weight model; LC = linear combination model; CONF = CONF model; TTB = take-the-best model.

The differences among the models are more pronounced and evident, however, when expected loss is used.

Third, extreme errors in ordering the cues according to their validities decrease the performance of SV and TTB so much that even in the most predictable environments (observe the lower bounds of SV and TTB at the right-hand side of illustrations in Figures 13-4 and 13-5), this can fall almost to the levels of performance corresponding to the most noisy environments (same bounds at the left-hand side of the illustrations). In addition, SV is punished relatively more than TTB by ordering the cues incorrectly (compare the vertical

widths of the SV and TTB shaded ranges in both Figures 13-4 and 13-5). When knowledge about the structure of the environment is lacking, more extensive cue processing under EW and CONF hedges the decision maker irrespective of the type of environment (i.e., compensatory or not).

Note that, in equal-weighting environments (i.e., Subcases vii and viii, $\rho_{Y_e X_1}$ = .10 and .20), it does not matter whether SV and TTB identify the correct ordering of cues because each has the same validity. In these environments, the ranges of performance of SV and TTB coincide with the model performance under random cue ordering.

Table 13-4. The Effect of Human Error on Model Performance: Case D

Environmental Parameters										Percentage Correct	
										SV	
	Cue Validities									Cue Order	
Case and Subcase	1	2	3	Cue Redundancy	R_e	$\rho_{Y,X_i}/R_e$	LC1	LC2	LC3	Correct	Random
D1				0.1							
i	0.8	0.4	0.2		0.88	0.91	64	71	79	**80**	66
ii	0.7	0.4	0.2		0.80	0.88	63	69	76	**75**	65
iii	0.6	0.4	0.2		0.73	0.83	62	67	<u>73</u>	**70**	63
iv	0.5	0.4	0.2		0.66	0.75	61	65	<u>70</u>	**67**	62
v	0.4	0.4	0.2		0.61	0.65	60	64	<u>69</u>	**63**	61
vi	0.3	0.3	0.2		0.52	0.57	58	62	<u>66</u>	**60**	59
vii	0.2	0.2	0.2		0.45	0.44	57	<u>60</u>	<u>63</u>	**56**	56
viii	0.1	0.1	0.1		0.39	0.26	<u>56</u>	59	<u>61</u>	**53**	53
D2				0.5							
i	0.8	0.4	0.2		0.85	0.94	64	70	78	**80**	66
ii	0.7	0.4	0.2		0.76	0.93	62	68	74	**75**	65
iii	0.6	0.4	0.2		0.67	0.89	61	66	<u>71</u>	**70**	63
iv	0.5	0.4	0.2		0.60	0.83	60	64	<u>68</u>	**67**	62
v	0.4	0.4	0.2		0.54	0.74	59	62	<u>66</u>	**63**	61
vi	0.3	0.3	0.2		0.47	0.64	58	<u>61</u>	<u>64</u>	**60**	59
vii	0.2	0.2	0.2		0.41	0.48	57	<u>59</u>	<u>62</u>	**56**	56
viii	0.1	0.1	0.1		0.37	0.27	<u>56</u>	<u>58</u>	<u>61</u>	**53**	53

Note: For LC1, *ca* = 0.5; for LC2, *ca* = 0.7; for LC3, *ca* = 0.9. The performance of the best heuristic in each environment is highlighted with boldface characters. The performance of LC is underlined when it is superior or equal to that of the best performer among heuristics. LC = linear combination model; SV = single variable model; TTB = take-the-best model; EW = equal weight model; CONF = CONF model; *ca* = linear cognitive ability.

Fourth, when expected loss is used instead of expected percentage correct, the decrease in performance due to incorrect cue ordering is more pronounced. This is true for both SV and TTB. (Compare the vertical width of the shaded ranges between Figures 13-4 and 13-5, within the models. Note that the scales used in Figures 13-4 and 13-5 are different and that using equivalent scales would mean decreasing all the vertical differences in Figure 13-4).

Fifth, for the LC model, it is clear (and unsurprising) that more *ca* is better than less. Interestingly, as the environment becomes more predictable, the accuracy of the LC models drops off relative to the simpler heuristics. In the environments examined here, the best LC model (with *ca* = .90) is always outperformed by one of the other heuristics when $\rho_{Y_r X_i} > .60$ (see Table 13-4). Error in the application of heuristics, however, can swing the advantage back to LC

models even in the most predictable environments (the right-hand side of illustrations in Figure 13-4, below the upper bounds of SV and TTB). In addition, errors in the application of heuristic models mean that LC can be relatively more accurate at the lower levels of *ca*.

Agreement Between Models

In many instances, strategies other than LC have quite similar performance. This raises the question of knowing how often they make identical predictions. To assess this, we calculated the probability that all pairs of strategies formed by SV, EW, TTB, and CONF would make the same choices across several environments. In fact, because calculating this joint probability is complicated, we simulated results on the basis of 5,000 trials for each environment.

Table 13-5 specifies the parameters of the E environments, the percentage of correct

Table 13-4. (continued)

Percentage Correct				Loss ($\alpha = 1.00$)								
TTB		EW	CONF	LC1	LC2	LC3	SV		TTB		EW	CONF
Cue Order							Cue Order		Cue Order			
Correct	Random	EW	CONF	LC1	LC2	LC3	Correct	Random	Correct	Random	EW	CONF
82	72	76	74	0.5	0.3	0.1	0.1	0.5	0.1	0.3	0.2	0.2
78	69	74	71	0.5	0.3	0.2	0.2	0.5	0.1	0.4	0.2	0.3
73	67	72	69	0.6	0.4	0.2	0.3	0.5	0.2	0.4	0.3	0.3
70	66	70	67	0.6	0.4	0.3	0.4	0.5	0.3	0.4	0.3	0.4
66	64	68	66	0.6	0.5	0.3	0.5	0.6	0.4	0.5	0.4	0.4
62	61	64	62	0.7	0.5	0.4	0.6	0.7	0.6	0.6	0.5	0.5
58	58	60	59	0.7	0.6	0.5	0.8	0.7	0.7	0.7	0.6	0.6
54	54	55	55	0.8	0.7	0.6	0.9	0.9	0.8	0.8	0.8	0.8
76	68	69	69	0.5	0.3	0.1	0.1	0.5	0.2	0.4	0.3	0.4
73	67	68	67	0.5	0.4	0.2	0.2	0.5	0.2	0.4	0.4	0.4
70	65	66	66	0.6	0.4	0.3	0.3	0.5	0.3	0.5	0.4	0.4
67	64	65	64	0.6	0.5	0.3	0.4	0.5	0.4	0.5	0.5	0.5
64	62	63	63	0.7	0.5	0.4	0.5	0.6	0.5	0.5	0.5	0.5
61	60	61	60	0.7	0.6	0.5	0.6	0.7	0.6	0.6	0.6	0.6
57	57	58	58	0.7	0.6	0.5	0.8	0.7	0.7	0.7	0.7	0.7
54	54	54	54	0.8	0.7	0.6	0.9	0.9	0.9	0.9	0.8	0.9

predictions for each model in each environment,[11] and the probabilities that models would make the same decisions. There are two variants, E1 and E2 (with low and higher redundancy), each with eight subcases (i–viii). For both cases, the environments of Subcases i–v are noncompensatory, Subcase vi is compensatory, and Subcases vii and viii involve equal weighting. Across each case, predictability (R_e) varies from high to low.

We make three remarks. First, there is considerable variation in percentage-correct predictions across different levels of predictability that are consistent with the results reported in Table 13-4. However, agreement between pairs of models hardly varies as a function of R_e and is uniformly high. In particular, the rate of agreement lies between .70 and .92 across all comparisons and is probably higher than one might have imagined a priori.[12] At the same time, this means that differences between the models occur in 8%–30% of choices, and from a practical perspective, it is important to know when this happens and which model is more likely to be correct. Second, as would be expected, the effect of increasing redundancy is to increase the level of agreement between models. Third, for the environments illustrated here, CONF and EW have the highest level of agreement whereas SV-EW and SV-TTB have the lowest. The latter result is surprising in that both SV and TTB are so dependent on the most valid cue.

Relative Model Performance: A Summary

Synthesizing the results of the 39 environments specified in Tables 13-3, 13-4, and 13-5, we can identify several trends in the relative performance of the models.

First, the models all perform better as the environment becomes more predictable. At the same time, differences in model performance grow larger.

Table 13-5. Rates of Agreement between Heuristic Strategies for Different Environments

Case and Subcase	Cue Validities			Cue redundancy	R_e	Percentage Correct				Rates of Agreement					
	1	2	3			SV	EW	TTB	CONF	SV-EW	SV-CONF	SV-TTB	CONF-EW	TTB-EW	CONF-TTB
E1				0.1											
i	0.8	0.6	0.2		0.96	80	82	86	79	0.72	0.77	0.72	0.87	0.80	0.77
ii	0.7	0.5	0.2		0.84	75	77	79	74	0.73	0.77	0.73	0.86	0.80	0.77
iii	0.6	0.4	0.2		0.73	71	72	73	69	0.72	0.77	0.72	0.86	0.80	0.77
iv	0.5	0.3	0.2		0.63	66	67	67	66	0.71	0.76	0.71	0.85	0.78	0.76
v	0.4	0.2	0.2		0.54	62	63	63	61	0.73	0.77	0.73	0.86	0.80	0.78
vi	0.3	0.2	0.2		0.49	59	61	61	61	0.70	0.76	0.70	0.85	0.78	0.76
vii	0.2	0.2	0.2		0.45	57	59	58	58	0.72	0.78	0.72	0.86	0.79	0.76
viii	0.1	0.1	0.1		0.38	53	54	53	53	0.71	0.77	0.71	0.85	0.79	0.76
					Mean	65	67	68	65	0.72	0.77	0.72	0.86	0.79	0.77
E2				0.5											
i	0.8	0.6	0.2		0.90	80	73	79	71	0.81	0.83	0.81	0.91	0.88	0.85
ii	0.7	0.5	0.2		0.78	74	70	74	68	0.81	0.84	0.81	0.91	0.88	0.85
iii	0.6	0.4	0.2		0.67	71	67	70	65	0.81	0.83	0.81	0.91	0.88	0.84
iv	0.5	0.3	0.2		0.58	67	64	66	63	0.80	0.83	0.80	0.91	0.88	0.85
v	0.4	0.2	0.2		0.50	64	61	63	60	0.80	0.83	0.80	0.91	0.87	0.84
vi	0.3	0.2	0.2		0.44	59	59	60	59	0.81	0.84	0.81	0.91	0.87	0.84
vii	0.2	0.2	0.2		0.42	58	59	58	59	0.80	0.83	0.80	0.91	0.88	0.85
viii	0.1	0.1	0.1		0.38	53	54	53	53	0.80	0.83	0.80	0.92	0.88	0.84
					Mean	66	63	65	62	0.81	0.83	0.81	0.91	0.88	0.85
					Overall Mean	66	65	66	64	0.76	0.80	0.76	0.88	0.84	0.81

Note: Results are from simulations with 5,000 trials for each environment. SV = single variable model; EW = equal weight model; TTB = take-the-best model; CONF = CONF model.

Second, relative model performance depends on both how the environment weights cues (noncompensatory, compensatory, or equal weighting) and redundancy. We find that when cues are ordered correctly, (a) TTB performs best in noncompensatory environments when redundancy is low; (b) SV performs best in non-compensatory environments when redundancy is high; (c) irrespective of redundancy, EW performs best in equal-weighting environments in which CONF also performs well; (d) EW (and sometimes TTB) performs best in compensatory environments when redundancy is low; and (e) TTB (and sometimes SV) performs best in compensatory environments when redundancy is high.

Third, subject to the differential predictive abilities noted, the heuristic models exhibit high rates of agreement.

Fourth, any advantage of LC models falls sharply as environments become more predictable. Thus, a high level of *ca* is required to outpredict the best heuristics. On the other hand, error in the execution of heuristics can result in more accurate performance by LC models.

Fifth, when the decision maker does not know the structure of the environment and therefore cannot order the cues according to their validity, the more extensive EW and CONF models are the best heuristics, irrespective of how the environment weights cues and redundancy. This is an important result in that it justifies use of these heuristics when decision makers lack knowledge of the environment, that is, these are good heuristics for states of comparative ignorance (see also Karelaia, 2006).

We discuss this summary again below.

Comparisons with Experimental Data

The above analysis has been at a theoretical level and raises the issue of how good people are at making decisions with linear models as opposed to using heuristics. To answer this question, we undertook a meta-analysis of lens model studies to estimate *ca*. This involved attempting to locate all lens model studies reported in the literature that provided estimates of the elements of Equation 13-3. Studies therefore had to have a criterion variable and involve the judgments of individuals (as opposed to groups of people).[13] Moreover, we considered only cases in which there was more than one cue (with one cue, $G = 1.00$ necessarily). We located 84 (mainly) published studies that allowed us to examine judgmental performance across 270 different task environments (i.e., environments that vary by statistical parameters and/or substantive conditions).[14]

In Table 13-6, we summarize statistics from the meta-analysis (for full details, see Karelaia & Hogarth, 2007). First, we note that these studies represent much data. They are the result of approximately 5,000 participants providing a total of some 320,000 judgments. In fact, many of these studies involved learning, and because we characterize judgmental performance by that achieved in the last block of experimental trials reported, the participants actually made many more judgments. Second, we provide several breakdowns of different lens model and performance statistics that are the means across studies of individual data that have been averaged within studies (i.e., the units of analysis are the mean data of particular studies). We distinguish between expert and novice participants, laboratory and field studies, environments that involved different numbers of cues, different weighting functions, and different levels of redundancy (or cue intercorrelation).

Briefly, we find no differences in performance between participants who are experts or novices (the latter, however, are assessed after learning). Holding the predictability of the environment constant (i.e., R_e), performance is somewhat better with fewer cues and when the environment involves equal weighting as opposed to being compensatory or noncompensatory. Controlling for the number of the cues, there is no difference in performance between laboratory and field studies.

Overall, the LC accuracy reported in the right-hand column of Table 13-6 is about 70%. This represents the percentage correct in binary choice of a person whose estimated linear cognitive ability (*ca* or GR_s) is .66. Moreover, this figure is a mean estimate across individual studies, each of which is described by the mean of

Table 13-6. Description of Studies in Lens Model Meta-Analysis

Characteristics of Tasks	Number of Studies	Average Number		Mean Lens Model Statistics						LC Accuracy (%)
		Judges	Judgments	r_a^a	G^a	R_e	R_s	C^a	GR_s	
All studies	270	20	86	0.56	0.80	0.79	0.80	0.05	0.66	70
Participants										
Experts	61	15	153	0.53	0.74	0.72	0.83	0.12	0.62	69
Novices	206	20	66	0.57	0.83	0.82	0.80	0.03	0.67	71
Unclassified	3	53	66	0.24	0.45	0.72	0.74	0.00	0.24	58
Type of study										
Laboratory	214	20	86	0.57	0.83	0.80	0.80	0.04	0.68	71
Field	53	16	87	0.50	0.72	0.75	0.83	0.08	0.60	68
Unclassified	3	22	96	0.41	0.52	0.81	0.88	0.00	0.44	65
Number of cues										
2	69	26	48	0.63	0.88	0.79	0.79	0.07	0.71	73
3	90	19	93	0.55	0.88	0.00	0.81	0.00	0.72	70
>3	108	16	105	0.52	0.71	0.79	0.81	0.07	0.58	69
Unclassified	3	21	56	0.17	0.32	0.74	0.86	−0.01	0.02	56
Type of weighting function										
Equal weighting	42	29	65	0.66	0.91	0.82	0.81	0.02	0.75	75
Compensatory	91	16	97	0.56	0.83	0.79	0.82	0.04	0.68	70
Noncompensatory	60	22	40	0.56	0.81	0.85	0.75	0.04	0.64	70
Unclassified	77	16	120	0.49	0.72	0.74	0.82	0.08	0.60	68
Cue redundancy[b]										
None	106	20	50	0.61	0.89	0.82	0.81	0.03	0.73	72
Low-medium	89	19	91	0.55	0.78	0.79	0.83	0.03	0.65	70
High	25	26	101	0.54	0.76	0.76	0.80	0.10	0.64	69
Unclassified	50	15	150	0.48	0.72	0.76	0.74	0.10	0.53	67

Note: LC = linear combination model.

[a] These statistics correspond to the sample estimates of the elements of the lens model equation presented in the text—Equation 13-3 (r_a is the estimate of the "achievement" index, ρ_{Y,Y_s}; G is the estimate of the matching index; and C is the estimate of the correlation between residuals of the models of the person and the environment, $\rho_{e_s e_t}$).

[b] We define redundancy level by the average intercue correlation: None denotes 0.0; low–medium denotes absolute value ≤ 0.4; and high otherwise.

individual data. Table 13-6 obscures individual variation, which we discuss further below.

To capture the differences in performance between LC and the heuristic models, one needs to have specific information on the statistical properties of tasks (essentially the covariation matrix used to generate the environmental criterion) and to make predictions for each environment. Recall also that, in the lens model paradigm, performance—or achievement—is measured in terms of correlation. We therefore transformed this measure into one of performance in binary choice using the methods described above. Thus, to estimate the accuracy of LC relative to any heuristic in a particular environment, we considered the difference in expected predictive accuracies between LC based on the mean *ca* observed in the environment and that of the heuristic. In other words, we asked how well the average performance levels of humans using LC compare with those of heuristics.

In Table 13-7, we summarize this information for environments involving three and two cues (details are provided in Appendices C and D). Unfortunately, not all studies in our meta-analysis provided the information needed, and thus, our data are limited to approximately two thirds of tasks involving three cues and one half of tasks involving two cues. We also note, parenthetically, that although some environments had identical statistical properties, they can be considered different because they involved different treatments (e.g., how participants had been trained, different feedback conditions, presentation of information, etc.).

The upper panel of Table 13-7 summarizes the data from Appendix C. The first column (on the left) shows the maximum performance that could be achieved in environments characterized by equal-weighting, compensatory, and noncompensatory functions, respectively. This captures the predictability of the environments—81% for equal-weighting and noncompensatory and 79% for compensatory environments. These environments are also marked by little redundancy. About 77% have mean intercue correlations of 0.00. In the body of the table, we present performance in terms of percentage correct for LC—based on mean *ca* observed in each of the experimental studies—as well as the performance that would have been achieved by the different heuristics in those same environments.

As would be expected, the EW strategy performs best in equal-weighting environments (80%) and the TTB strategy best in the noncompensatory environments (78%). Interestingly, in the compensatory environments here, it is the EW model that performs best (76%). The mean LC model never has the best performance. Compared with the heuristic models, its performance is relatively better in the equal-weighting as opposed to the other environments.

In the discussion so far, we have concentrated on effects of error in using LC (by focusing on *ca*). However, the columns headed SVr and TTBr illustrate the effects of making errors when using heuristics (the suffix *–r* indicating models with random cue orderings).[15] This shows that the performance of LC (at mean *ca* level) is as good as or better than SVr and TTBr across all three types of environments.

In the lower panel of Table 13-7, we present the data based on analyzing studies with two cues, where, once again, most environments involve orthogonal cues (76%)—details are provided in Appendix D. Conclusions are similar to the three-cue case. EW is necessarily best when the environment involves an equal-weighting function, and TTB performs well in the noncompensatory environments, although it is bettered here by the SV model (just).[16]

Because most published studies do not report individual data, it is difficult to assess the importance of individual variation in performance and, specifically, how individual LC performance compares with heuristics. Two studies involving two cues did report the necessary data (Steinmann & Doherty, 1972; York, Doherty, & Kamouri, 1987). Table 13-8 summarizes the comparisons. This shows (reading from left to right) the number of participants in each task, statistical properties of the tasks, percentage performance correct by the LC model (mean and range), and the percentages of participants who have better performance with LC than with particular heuristics.

Clearly, one cannot generalize from the four environments presented in Table 13-8.

Table 13-7. Performance of Heuristics and Mean LC in Three-Cue and Two-Cue Environments

Weighting Function	Maximum Possible Percentage Correct	Performance—Percentage Correct							Numbers of Environments
		LC[a]	SV	SVr	EW	CONF	TTB	TTBr	
Three-cue environments[b]									
Equal weighting	81	72	65	65	**80**	74	71	70	9
Compensatory	79	69	69	64	**76**	71	73	67	25
Noncompensatory	81	68	74	64	75	71	**78**	68	30
								Subtotal	64
Two-cue environments[c]									
Equal weighting	88	77	71	71	**87**	71	78	78	17
Noncompensatory	84	69	**76**	67	73	67	75	70	21
								Subtotal	38
								Total	102

Note: Boldface indicates largest percentage correct in each row. LC = linear combination model; SV = single variable model; SVr = SV executed under random cue order; EW = equal weight model; CONF = CONF model; TTB = take-the-best model; TTBr = TTB executed under random cue order.
[a] Based on empirically observed mean linear cognitive ability (*ca*).
[b] Averages calculated on the 64 environments detailed in Appendix C.
[c] Averages calculated on the 38 environments detailed in Appendix D.

Table 13-8. Levels of Individual Performance Relative to Heuristics

Study	Number of Participants	Statistical Properties of Tasks				LC Performance (% correct)			Percentage of Participants with Better LC Performance than:					
		R_e	$\rho_{Y_eX_i}$	$\rho_{Y_eX_r}$	$\rho_{X_iX_r}$	Mean	Maximum	Minimum	SV	SVr	TTB	TTBr	EW	CONF
Steinmann and Doherty (1972)	22	0.95	0.69	0.65	0.00	73	85	58	45	50	18	18	0	50
York, Doherty, and Kamouri (1987)														
Group 1	15	0.86	0.78	0.37	0.00	70	84	53	7	57	7	36	7	57
Group 2	15	0.86	0.78	0.37	0.00	67	78	54	0	29	0	21	0	29
Group 3	15	0.86	0.78	0.37	0.00	72	80	54	14	71	0	57	0	71

Note: LC = linear combination model; SV = single variable model; SVr = SV executed under random cue order; TTB = take-the-best model; TTBr = TTB executed under random cue order; EW = equal weight model; CONF = CONF model.

However, it is of interest to note, first, that there is a large range of individual LC performances and, second, that for a minority of participants, LC performance is better than that of heuristics.

SUMMARY

At a theoretical level, we have shown that the performance of heuristic rules is affected by several factors: how the environment weights cues, that is, noncompensatory, compensatory, or equal weighting; cue redundancy; the predictability of the environment; and loss functions. Heuristics work better when their characteristics match those of the environment. Thus, EW predicts best in equal-weighting situations and TTB in noncompensatory environments. However, redundancy allows SV to perform better than TTB in noncompensatory environments. When environments are compensatory, redundancy further mediates the relative performances of TTB, SV, and EW (TTB and SV are better with redundancy). As environments become more predictable, all models perform better, but

differences between models also increase. However, when the environmental structure is unknown, the heuristics involving more extensive information processing, EW and CONF, dominate the lexicographic-type simple models, that is, SV and TTB, irrespective of cue redundancy and of how environments weight cues. Finally, the effect of loss functions is to accentuate or dampen differences between evaluations of model predictions.

We have also used simulation to investigate the extent to which models agree with each other. At one level, all the models we investigated are sensible and use valid information. As such, they exhibit much agreement. The extent of the agreement, however, is surprising. Even when the predictability of the environment varies greatly, the level of agreement between particular models hardly changes (see Table 13-5). From a predictive viewpoint, this might be thought comforting. However, it also accentuates the need to know which heuristic is more likely to be correct in the 8%–30% of cases in which they disagree. In addition, whereas some differences between models may seem small on

Table 13-9. Regression of Model Performance (Percentage Correct) on Environmental Characteristics for Populations in Tables 13-3, 13-4, and 13-5

Independent Variable	SV Regression Coefficient	t	SVr Regression Coefficient	t	TTB Regression Coefficient	t	TTBr Regression Coefficient
Intercept	34.3	30.7	43.9	50.9	36.6	37.6	41.7
Dummy: compensatory	2.2*	3.1					
Dummy: noncompensatory	4.9	6.1					−1.7*
Redundancy	6.7	5.4	4.1	4.3			
Predictability (R_e)	39.2	20.0	25.7	22.2	49.1	33.2	35.8
Linear cognitive ability (GR_s)	—	—	—		—		—
Adjusted R^2	0.97		0.93		0.97		0.94

Note: The regressions are based on 39 observations, except for the regression explaining LC, which is based on 127 observations. The dummy variables for compensatory and noncompensatory weighting functions are expressed relative to equal weighting, the effect of which is captured within the intercept term. There are only three levels of redundancy: mean intercue correlation of –0.07, 0.1, and 0.5. Only statistically significant coefficients are shown ($p < .001$; except where marked with an asterisk). SV = single variable model; SVr = SV executed under random cue order; TTB = take-the-best model; TTBr = TTB executed under random cue order; EW = equal weight model; CONF = CONF model; LC = linear combination model.
* $p < .05$.

single occasions, cumulative effects could be large if people were to persist in using inappropriate heuristics across many decisions.

The differential impact of environmental factors is illustrated quantitatively in Table 13-9, which reports the results of regressing performance of the heuristics (percentage correct) on environmental factors: type of weighting function, redundancy (cue intercorrelation), and predictability (R_e). This is done for the 39 populations specified in Tables 13-3, 13-4, and 13-5. Results show the importance of noncompensatory and compensatory environments (vs. equal weighting) as well as of redundancy on SV (positive). Both EW and CONF depend (negatively) on whether environments are noncompensatory, EW being affected additionally by redundancy (negatively). Interestingly, for the conditions examined here, the performance of TTB is not affected by these factors (it is fully explained by predictability R_e), thereby suggesting a heuristic that is robust to environmental variations (as has also been demonstrated theoretically by Hogarth & Karelaia, 2005b, 2006b; and Baucells, Carrasco, & Hogarth, 2008).

Finally, all these models benefit from greater predictability.

When cues are ordered at random, the SV and TTB models (denoted by SVr and TTBr, respectively) become less dependent on predictability R_e (compare also the intercepts for SV and SVr and for TTB and TTBr). The LC model is explained almost equally by environmental predictability, R_e, and linear cognitive ability, ca or GR_s—see regression LC(a). On the other hand, when purposely omitting predictability, R_e, from the LC regression, compensatory and noncompensatory characteristics (vs. equal weighting) become significant (positive), as well as redundancy (negative)—see regression LC(b). Moreover, the value of the intercept increases (from 29.4 to 48.2).

An important conclusion from our theoretical analysis is that unless ca is high, people are better off relying on trade-off-avoiding heuristics as opposed to linear models. At the same time, however, the application of heuristic rules can involve error (i.e., variables not used in the appropriate order in SV and TTB). This therefore raises the issue of estimating ca from

Table 13-9. (continued)

EW		CONF		LC(a)		LC(b)	
t	Regression Coefficient	t	Regression Coefficient	t	Regression Coefficient	Regression Coefficient	t
44.2	41.7	38.6	41.6	34.5 / 36.8	29.4	48.2	40.7
						2.3*	2.9
−3.0	−2.0*	−2.6	−1.5*	−2.1		4.6	5.7
	−4.8*	−7.9				−7.0	−4.7
21.8	43.0	38.4	38.1	18.2 / 28.9	25.9	—	—
—	—	—	—	45.2	27.3	24.6	17.8
	0.94		0.92		0.95		0.73

empirical data and noting when this is large enough to do without heuristics.

Our theoretical analyses suggest that *ca* needs to be larger than about .70 for LC models to perform better than heuristics. Across the 270 task environments of the meta-analysis, we estimate *ca* to be .66. However, this is a mean and does not take account of differences in task environments. For those environments in which precise predictions could be made, LC models based on mean *ca* estimates perform at a level inferior to the best heuristics but equal to or better than heuristics executed with error. Unfortunately, the data do not allow us to make a thorough investigation of individual variation in *ca* values.

GENERAL DISCUSSION

An important contribution of our analysis is to highlight the role of error in the use of different models—as opposed to error or noise in the environment. Within LC, error is measured by the extent to which linear cognitive ability (*ca* or GR_s) falls short of 1.00. Here, error can have two sources: incorrect weighting of variables and inconsistency in execution. With the TTB model, the analogous error results from using variables in an inappropriate order (and, in SV, from using less valid cues). Thus, the errors in the two types of models involve both knowledge and execution, although, in the latter, execution errors are less likely given the simpler processes involved.

Our work has many normative implications in that it spells out the conditions under which different heuristics are accurate. Moreover, the fact that this is achieved analytically—instead of through simulation—represents an advance over current practice (see also Hogarth & Karelaia, 2005a, 2006a). The analytical methods have more potential to develop results that can be generalized.

An interesting normative implication relates to the trade-offs in different types of error when using heuristics or linear models. As noted above, one way of characterizing our empirical analysis is to say that judgmental performance using the LC models is roughly equal to that of using heuristics with error, that is, of SV and TTB under random cue ordering

(SVr and TTBr). However, is there a relation between *ca* and the knowledge necessary to know when and how to apply heuristic rules?

Given our results, how should a decision maker approach a predictive task? Much depends on prior knowledge of task characteristics and thus on how the individual acquired the necessary knowledge. Basically—at one extreme—if either all cues are approximately equally valid or one does not know how to weight them, EW should be used explicitly. Indeed, our results specifically demonstrate the validity of using the EW or CONF heuristics in the absence of knowledge about the structure of the environment. Similarly—at the other extreme—when facing a noncompensatory weighting function, TTB or SV would be hard to beat with LC.

ACKNOWLEDGMENTS

This research has been funded within the EUROCORES European Collaborative Research Project (ECRP) Scheme jointly provided by ECRP funding agencies and the European Science Foundation. A list of ECRP funding agencies can be consulted at http://www.esf.org/ecrp_countries. It was specifically supported by Spanish Ministerio de Educación y Ciencia Grant SEC2005-25690 (Hogarth) and Swiss National Science Foundation Grant 105511-111621 (Karelaia). We have greatly benefited from the comments of Michael Doherty, Joshua Klayman, and Chris White, as well as from presentations at the annual meeting of the Brunswik Society, Toronto, Ontario, Canada, November 2005; FUR XII, Rome, Italy, June 2006; the University of Basel, Basel, Switzerland; INSEAD, Fontainebleu, France; and the Max Planck Institute, Berlin, Germany. We are particularly indebted to Thomas Stewart, Michael Doherty, and the library at Universitat Pompeu Fabra for helping us locate many lens model studies, as well as to Marcus O'Connor for providing data.

NOTES

1. Whereas the linear assumption is a limitation, we note that many studies have shown that linear functions can approximate nonlinear functions well provided the relations between the cues and criterion are conditionally monotonic (see, e.g., Dawes & Corrigan, 1974).

2. In all of the models investigated, we assume that if the decision maker uses a variable, he or she knows its zero-order correlation with the criterion.

3. In Gigerenzer and Goldstein's (1996) formulation, TTB operates only on cues that can take binary values (i.e., 0/1). We analyze a version of this model based on continuous cues where discrimination is determined by a threshold, that is, a cue discriminates between two alternatives only if the difference between the values of the cues exceeds a specified value t (> 0).

4. In our subsequent modeling of CONF, we assume that any difference between cue values is sufficient to indicate discrimination or confirmation. In principle, one could also assume a threshold in the same way that we model TTB.

5. Parenthetically, with $k > 3$ cues, CONF is also insensitive to cue ordering as long as the model requires at least $k/2$ confirming cues when k is even and at least $(k - 1)/2$ confirming cues when k is odd (Karelaia, 2006).

6. We use uppercase letters to denote random variables, for example, Y_e, and lowercase letters to designate specific values, for example, y_e. As exceptions to this practice, we use lowercase Greek letters to denote random error variables, for example, ε_e, as well as parameters, for example, $\beta_{e,j}$.

7. We consider the implications of our normality assumption in the General Discussion.

8. For the TTB model, we defined a threshold of .50 (with standardized variables) to decide whether a variable discriminated between two alternatives. Whereas the choice of .50 was subjective, investigation shows quite similar results if this threshold is varied between .25 and .75. We use the threshold of .50 in all further calculations and illustrations.

9. The assumption made here is that $P_{\varepsilon_e \varepsilon_s} = 0$; see Equation 13-3. Recall also that *using* is employed here in an *as if* manner.

10. Defining redundancy by average cue intercorrelation could, of course, be misleading by hiding dispersion among correlations. In fact, with the exception of Case C3, the intercorrelations of the variables within cases were equal— see Table 13-3.

11. We also calculated the theoretical probabilities of the simulated percentage of correct predictions. Given the large sample sizes (5,000), theoretical and simulated results are almost identical.

12. In the populations A–C, the analogous rates of agreement were .64 to .92. Interestingly, it was the environment with negative intercue correlation that had the lowest rates of agreement (mean agreement between models .70).

13. We also excluded studies from the interpersonal conflict paradigm in which the criterion for one's person's judgments is the judgment of another person (see, e.g., Hammond, Wilkins, & Todd, 1966).

14. It is important to bear in mind that, although investigators in the lens model paradigm model judgments as though people are using linear models, judges may, in fact, be using quite different processes (Michael E. Doherty, personal communication, July 2006).

15. The TTBr model is identical to what Gigerenzer et al. (1999) referred to as MINIMALIST.

16. The following rule was used to adapt the CONF model for two cues: If both cues suggest the same alternative, choose it. Otherwise, choose at random.

APPENDIX A

The Expected Accuracies of LC, EW, CONF, and TTB

The LC Model

Following the same rationale as the single variable (SV) model, we can also determine the probability that using a linear combination (LC) of cues will result in a correct choice. That is, expressing Y_{ea} and Y_{eb} as functions of Y_{sa} and Y_{sb}, define appropriate error terms, ω_a and ω_b, and substitute $\rho_{Y_e Y_s}$ for $\rho_{Y_e X_1}$, and Y_{sa} and Y_{sb} for X_{1a} and X_{1b}, respectively. Thus, $2P\{(Y_{ea} > Y_{eb}) \cap (Y_{sa} > Y_{sb})\}$ can also be found through Equation 13-7, with $f(\underline{d})$ defined as in SV. The only difference between SV and LC lies in the variance-covariance matrix, M_f, that, for the LC model, is

$$M_{f\_LC} = \begin{pmatrix} 2 & 2\rho_{Y_e Y_s} \\ 2\rho_{Y_e Y_s} & 2 \end{pmatrix}.$$

The EW Model

Equal weighting (EW) is, of course, a special case of LC. Define $d_2 = \overline{X}_a - \overline{X}_b$, where $\overline{X}_a = \dfrac{1}{k}\sum_{j=1}^{k} X_{ja}$

and $\overline{X}_b = \frac{1}{k} \sum_{j=1}^{k} X_{jb}$, and note that d_2 is a normal variable with a mean of 0. (The variable d_1 for EW is the same as for LC: $d_1 = Y_{ea} - Y_{eb}$.) Thus, the expected accuracy of EW can be defined by Equation 13-7, taking into consideration that the appropriate variance–covariance matrix is

$$M_{f\_EW} = \begin{pmatrix} 2 & 2\rho_{Y_e\overline{X}}\sigma_{\overline{X}} \\ 2\rho_{Y_e\overline{X}}\sigma_{\overline{X}} & 2\sigma_{\overline{X}}^2 \end{pmatrix}$$

(Note that from Equation 13-3, it follows that $\rho_{Y_e\overline{X}} = \rho_{\hat{Y}_e\overline{X}}R_e$, assuming $\rho_{\varepsilon_e\varepsilon_s} = 0$.)

The CONF Model

CONF examines cues sequentially and makes a choice when two cues favoring one alternative are encountered. Therefore, this model selects the better alternative out of two with the probability given by

$$2\begin{bmatrix} P\{(Y_{ea} > Y_{eb}) \cap (X_{1a} > X_{1b}) \cap (X_{2a} > X_{2b})\} + \\ P\{(Y_{ea} > Y_{eb}) \cap (X_{1a} > X_{1b}) \cap (X_{2a} < X_{2b}) \\ \cap (X_{3a} > X_{3b})\} + \\ P\{(Y_{ea} < Y_{eb}) \cap (X_{1a} > X_{1b}) \cap (X_{2a} < X_{2b}) \\ \cap (X_{3a} < X_{3b})\} \end{bmatrix}$$

$$= 2\left[\int_0^\infty \int_0^\infty \int_0^\infty f_1(\underline{d})d\underline{d} + \int_0^\infty \int_0^\infty \int_{-\infty}^0 \int_0^\infty f_2(\underline{d})d\underline{d} \right.$$

$$\left. + \int_{-\infty}^0 \int_0^\infty \int_{-\infty}^0 \int_{-\infty}^0 f_2(\underline{d})d\underline{d} \right],$$

(13-A1)

where both $f_1(\underline{d}) = f_1(d_1, d_2, d_3)$ and $f_2(\underline{d}) = f_2(d_1, d_2, d_3, d_4)$ are the normal multivariate probability density functions, the variance-covariance matrix specific to each being

$$M_{f_1} = \begin{pmatrix} 2 & 2\rho_{Y_eX_1} & 2\rho_{Y_eX_2} \\ 2\rho_{Y_eX_1} & 2 & 2\rho_{X_1X_2} \\ 2\rho_{Y_eX_2} & 2\rho_{X_1X_2} & 2 \end{pmatrix}$$

and

$$M_{f_2} = \begin{pmatrix} 2 & 2\rho_{Y_eX_1} & 2\rho_{Y_eX_2} & 2\rho_{Y_eX_3} \\ 2\rho_{Y_eX_1} & 2 & 2\rho_{X_1X_2} & 2\rho_{X_1X_3} \\ 2\rho_{Y_eX_2} & 2\rho_{X_1X_2} & 2 & 2\rho_{X_2X_3} \\ 2\rho_{Y_eX_3} & 2\rho_{X_1X_3} & 2\rho_{X_2X_3} & 2 \end{pmatrix}.$$

The TTB Model

The take-the-best (TTB) model also assesses cues sequentially. It makes a choice when a discriminating cue is found. In this article, we consider TTB with a fixed threshold t (>0). Thus, the model stops consulting cues and makes a decision when $|x_{ia} - x_{ib}| > t$. This involves both cases when $x_{ia} - x_{ib} > t$ and cases when $x_{ib} - x_{ia} > t$. Because the two cases are symmetric, the probability that TTB selects the better alternative is

$$2\begin{bmatrix} P\{(Y_{ea} > Y_{eb}) \cap (X_{1a} - X_{1b} \geq t)\} + \\ P\{(Y_{ea} > Y_{eb}) \cap (|X_{1a} - X_{1b}| < t) \cap (X_{2a} - X_{2b} \geq t)\} + \\ P\{(Y_{ea} > Y_{eb}) \cap (|X_{1a} - X_{1b}| < t) \cap (|X_{2a} - X_{2b}| < t) \\ \cap (X_{3a} - X_{3b} \geq t)\} \end{bmatrix}$$

$$+ P\{(Y_{ea} > Y_{eb}) \cap (|X_{1a} - X_{1b}| < t) \cap (|X_{2a} - X_{2b}| < t) \\ \cap (|X_{3a} - X_{3b}| < t)\}$$

$$= 2\left[\int_0^\infty \int_t^\infty f_3(\underline{d})d\underline{d} + \int_0^\infty \int_{-t}^t \int_t^\infty f_1(\underline{d})d\underline{d} \right.$$

$$\left. + \int_0^\infty \int_{-t}^t \int_{-t}^t \int_t^\infty f_2(\underline{d})d\underline{d} \right]$$

$$+ \int_0^\infty \int_{-t}^t \int_{-t}^t \int_{-t}^t f_2(\underline{d})d\underline{d},$$

(13-A2)

where both $f_1(\underline{d}) = f_1(d_1, d_2, d_3)$ and $f_2(\underline{d}) = f_2(d_1, d_2, d_3, d_4)$ are the same as in CONF and $f_3(\underline{d}) = f_3(d_1, d_2)$ is defined similarly, using the appropriate variance–covariance matrix:

$$M_{f_3} = \begin{pmatrix} 2 & 2\rho_{Y_eX_1} \\ 2\rho_{Y_eX_1} & 2 \end{pmatrix}.$$

APPENDIX B

The Expected Loss of the CONF and Take-the-Best (TTB) Models

The expected loss of CONF is

$$2L\begin{bmatrix} P\{(Y_{ea} < Y_{eb}) \cap (X_{1a} > X_{1b}) \cap (X_{2a} > X_{2b})\} + \\ P\{(Y_{ea} < Y_{eb}) \cap (X_{1a} > X_{1b}) \cap (X_{2a} < X_{2b}) \\ \cap (X_{3a} > X_{3b})\} + \\ P\{(Y_{ea} > Y_{eb}) \cap (X_{1a} > X_{1b}) \cap (X_{2a} < X_{2b}) \\ \cap (X_{3a} < X_{3b}) \end{bmatrix}$$

$$= 2\alpha \left[\int_{-\infty}^{0} \int_{0}^{\infty} \int_{0}^{\infty} d_1^2 f_1(\underline{d}) d\underline{d} + \int_{-\infty}^{0} \int_{0}^{\infty} \int_{0}^{\infty} d_1^2 f_2(\underline{d}) d\underline{d} \right.$$
$$\left. + \int_{0}^{\infty} \int_{0}^{\infty} \int_{-\infty}^{0} \int_{-\infty}^{0} d_1^2 f_2(\underline{d}) d\underline{d} \right],$$

(13-B1)

where $f_1(\underline{d})$ and $f_2(\underline{d})$ are as defined in Appendix 13-A.

The expected loss of TTB is

$$2L \begin{bmatrix} P\{(Y_{ea} < Y_{eb}) \cap (X_{1a} - X_{1b} \geq t)\} + \\ P\{(Y_{ea} < Y_{eb}) \cap (|X_{1a} - X_{1b}| < t) \cap (X_{2a} - X_{2b} \geq t)\} + \\ P\{(Y_{ea} < Y_{eb}) \cap (|X_{1a} - X_{1b}| < t) \cap (|X_{2a} - X_{2b}| < t) \\ \cap (X_{3a} - X_{3b} \geq t)\} \end{bmatrix}$$

$$+ LP\{(Y_{ea} < Y_{eb}) \cap (|X_{1a} - X_{1b}| < t) \cap (|X_{2a} - X_{2b}| < t)$$
$$\cap (|X_{3a} - X_{3b}| < t)\}$$

$$\alpha \left(2 \left[\int_{-\infty}^{0} \int_{t}^{\infty} d_1^2 f_3(\underline{d}) \, d\underline{d} + \int_{-\infty}^{0} \int_{-t}^{t} \int_{t}^{\infty} d_1^2 f_1(\underline{d}) \, d\underline{d} \right. \right.$$
$$\left. + \int_{-\infty}^{0} \int_{-t}^{t} \int_{-t}^{t} \int_{t}^{\infty} d_1^2 f_2(\underline{d}) \, d\underline{d} \right] + \int_{-\infty}^{0} \int_{-t}^{t} \int_{-t}^{t} \int_{-t}^{t} d_1^2 f_2(\underline{d}) \, d\underline{d} \left. \right)$$

(13-B2)

where $f_1(\underline{d})$ and $f_2(\underline{d})$ are as defined in Appendix A.

APPENDIX C

Selected Three-Cue Studies

APPENDIX D

Selected Two-Cue Studies

Appendix C   Selected Three-Cue Studies

Environment and Study	Task	Number of Conditions/ Tasks	Total Number of Participants	Stimuli per Participant	R_e across Conditions (Range)	Mean Human Performance across Conditions (Range)	
						r_a	GR_s
Equal weighting environments							
1. Ashton (1981)	Predicting prices	3	138	30	0.01–0.98	-0.17–0.19	0.01–0.87
2a. Brehmer and Hagafors (1986)	Artificial prediction task	1	10	15	1.00	0.97	0.95
3. Chasseigne, Grau, Mullet, and Cama (1999)	Artificial prediction task	5	220	120	0.57–0.98	0.37–0.78	0.67–0.82
Compensatory environments							
4. Holzworth and Doherty (1976)	Artificial prediction task	6	58	25	0.71	0.54–0.64	0.76–0.91
5. Chasseigne, Mullet, and Stewart (1997)–Experiment 1	Artificial prediction task	6	96	26	0.96	0.34–0.70	0.35–0.73
6. Kessler and Ashton (1981)	Prediction of corporate bond ratings	4	69	34	0.74	0.52–0.64	0.71–0.88
7a. Steinmann (1974)	Artificial prediction task	9	11	300	0.63–0.78	0.45–0.57	0.68–0.84
Noncompensatory environments							
2b. Brehmer and Hagafors (1986)	Artificial prediction task	2	20	15	0.77–1.00	0.74–0.78	0.71–0.75
8. Deane, Hammond, and Summers (1972)–Experiment 2	Artificial prediction task	2	40	20	0.94	0.59–0.84	0.65–0.89
9. Hammond, Summers, and Deane (1973)	Artificial prediction task	3	30	20	0.92	0.05–0.78	0.14–0.83
10. Hoffman, Earle, and Slovic (1981)	Artificial prediction task	9	182	25	0.94	0.09–0.71	0.15–0.78
7b. Steinmann (1974)	Artificial prediction task	6	11	100	0.63–0.74	0.44–0.65	0.70–0.85
11. O'Connor, Remus, and Lim (2005)	Artificial prediction task	4	77	20	0.81–0.84	0.59–0.72	0.71–0.87
12. Youmans and Stone (2005)	Prediction of income levels	4	117	50	0.44	0.35–0.42	0.88–0.97
Total		64	1,079				

Note: All studies reported involved between-subject designs except for Studies 7a and 7b. Three studies—8, 9, and 10—were said to have identical parameters. However, there must have been some rounding differences because of marginally different values reported for R_e.

Appendix D   Selected Two-Cue Studies

Environment and Study	Task	Number of Conditions/ Tasks	Total Number of Participants	Stimuli per Participant	R_e across Conditions (Range)	Mean Human Performance across Conditions (Range)	
						r_a	GR_s
Equal weighting environments							
1. Jarnecke and Rudestam (1976)	Predict academic achievement	1	15	50	0.42	0.28	0.71
2. Lafon, Chasseigne, and Mullet (2004)	Artificial prediction task	4	439	30	0.96	0.00–0.90	0.00–0.94
3. Rothstein (1986)	Artificial prediction task	6	72	100	1.00	0.81–1.00	0.80–1.00
4. Summers, Summers, and Karkau (1969)	Judging the age of blood cells	1	16	64	0.99	0.73	0.73
5. Brehmer and Kuylenstierna (1980)	Artificial prediction task	5	40	15	0.57–0.81	0.38–0.76	0.67–0.90
Noncompensatory environments							
6. Armelius and Armelius (1974)	Artificial prediction task	3	63	25	0.99–1.00	0.32–0.96	0.32–0.95
7. Doherty, Tweney, O'Connor, and Walker (1988)							
Experiment 2	Artificial prediction task	3	45	25	0.79–1.00	0.70–0.73	0.74–0.92
Experiment 6	Artificial prediction task	2	30	50	0.87–1.00	0.53–0.66	0.58–0.73
8. Hammond and Summers (1965)	Artificial prediction task	3	30	20	0.71	0.49–0.85	0.48–0.59
9. Lee and Yates (1992)	Postdicting student success	2	40	NA	0.38	0.24–0.29	0.51–0.59
10. Muchinsky and Dudycha (1975)							
Experiment 1	Artificial prediction task	2	160	150	0.72	0.04–0.30	0.11–0.54
Experiment 2	Artificial prediction task	2	160	150	0.96	0.03–0.45	0.01–0.32
11. Steinmann and Doherty (1972)	Assessing subjective probabilities in a bookbag and poker chip task	1	22	192	0.95	0.67	0.70
12. York, Doherty, and Kamouri (1987)	Artificial prediction task	3	45	25	0.86	0.53–0.64	0.62–0.74
Total		38	1,177				

Note: The numbers of participants in Studies 3 and 9 are approximations because this information is not available. In Study 11, human performance was measured through medians

Introduction to Chapter 14

Categorization with Limited Resources:
A Family of Simple Heuristics

This article by Laura Martignon, Konstantinos Katsikopoulos, and Jan Woike builds on Chapter 6, which introduced a family of heuristics called *fast-and-frugal decision trees*. Fast-and-frugal trees are simple rules for categorization; they are called fast and frugal because they permit a classification decision at each level of the tree. Fast-and-frugal trees are descriptive insofar as they have been shown to describe processes underlying expert decisions, such as magistrates' bail decisions (see Chapter 28). Because fast-and-frugal trees are transparent, users can immediately understand the policy that they embody. Consequently, as argued by Katsikopoulos, Pachur, Machery, and Wallin (2008), professionals such as doctors may be much more likely to employ them than complex and opaque expert systems in their daily routines.

Of course, the psychological appeal of these trees can only justify their prescriptive use if this leads to accurate decisions, especially in domains in which stakes are high (e.g., the decision of whether or not to allocate a patient to the coronary care unit; see Chapter 6). Yet how accurate are they? To answer this, the authors investigated the accuracy of two fast-and-frugal trees by using cross-validation and by comparing their accuracy with that of two sophisticated benchmark models, logistic regression and another type of classification and decision tree studied in the machine-learning literature. In a computer simulation, the four classification models were tested against 30 real-world data sets drawn from a wide range of domains including medicine, sports, and economics. The main result echoes a distinction often observed in contests between complex and simple strategies. In fitting, in which strategies know all information, the benchmark strategies clearly outperform the simple trees. However, in prediction, in which strategies are applied to new cases, the accuracy of the fast-and-frugal trees is close or identical to that of the sophisticated benchmark models. This result underlines the prescriptive potential of fast-and-frugal trees.

CHAPTER 14

Categorization with Limited Resources: A Family of Simple Heuristics

Laura Martignon, Konstantinos V. Katsikopoulos, and Jan K. Woike

Abstract: In categorization tasks where resources such as time, information, and computation are limited, there is pressure to be accurate, and stakes are high, as when deciding if a patient is under high risk of having a disease or if a worker should undergo retraining, and it has been proposed that people use, or should use, simple adaptive heuristics. We introduce a family of deterministic, noncompensatory heuristics, called fast-and-frugal trees, and study them formally. We show that the heuristics require few resources and are also relatively accurate. First, we characterize fast-and-frugal trees mathematically as lexicographic heuristics and as noncompensatory linear models, and also show that they exploit cumulative dominance (the results are interpreted in the language of the paired comparison literature). Second, we show, by computer simulation, that the predictive accuracy of fast-and-frugal trees compares well with that of logistic regression (proposed as a descriptive model for categorization tasks performed by professionals) and of classification and regression trees (used, outside psychology, as prescriptive models).

1. INTRODUCTION

In a categorization task, the participant has to assign objects x, y, ... to one of the mutually exclusive categories C_0, C_1, ... , C_k based on the values of the objects on *cues* (also called aspects, dimensions, or features) c_1, c_2, ... , c_n. Understanding categorization is not only of intrinsic interest but may also be useful for understanding other cognitive functions such as attention, recognition, and memory (Lamberts, 2000).

A lot of work in psychology has focused on what can be called *perceptual* categorization. Lamberts (2000) defines it as "assigning a visually presented object to a category," noting that it" should be distinguished from categorization

of other types of stimuli such as verbal descriptions of people or situations." Experimental stimuli used in this research are, for example, colors or geometric shapes.

Behavior in perceptual categorization tasks is often captured well by models that aim at computing the probabilities $p_i(x)$ that x belongs to C_i (to do this it is often assumed that categories can be represented by probability distributions [Rosseel, 2002; see also Ashby, 1992; Ashby & Alfonso-Reese, 1995; for a review of other models, see Ashby & Maddox, 2005]). Furthermore, the $p_i(x)$ are often determined by the similarities between objects. For instance, exemplar models (Medin & Schaffer, 1978; Nosofsky, 1984) compute $p_i(x)$ as the ratio of the total similarity of x to the objects that belong to C_i over the total similarity of x to all objects. Similarity is usually computed by taking into account all cue values. In exemplar models, for instance, the similarity between two objects is computed by a transformation of all differences between the cue values of the objects (Nosofsky, 1984; for other approaches, see Juslin & Persson, 2002; Rosseel, 2002). More recently, there have also been models that attempt to describe response times in addition to categorization probabilities (Lamberts, 2000).

A possible complaint about such models of categorization is that they describe the outcome but not the underlying cognitive processes. Exemplar models, for instance, specify a set of equations for computing similarities but do not typically propose an order in which the computations are done (for an exception, see, for example, Lamberts, 2000). In terms of Marr's (1982) three levels of analysis of the cognitive system, it seems that there is something left unspecified about the time, or process, aspects of the algorithm that takes the cue values of an object as input and returns its category as an output. We appreciate, however, that there are many views of what constitutes a process model, so we do not press this point further and move on to other motivations for considering the class of models we will study.

It may be argued that it is not so clear if exemplar-based and other current models apply to categorization tasks where the stimuli to be categorized are not relatively simple laboratory constructions such as colors or shapes (Berretty, Todd, & Martignon, 1999). Consider the categorizations that need to be made by professionals—how do, for example, doctors categorize patients as healthy or sick? In such tasks, which are typically studied outside the psychological laboratory, it has been claimed that people engage in more heuristic processing.

For example, take the decision of whether a patient is at a high risk, or not, of having ischemic heart disease, based on cues such as the indications of an electrocardiogram, an important decision that has to be made quickly and accurately (Green & Mehr, 1997). Medical doctors do not seem willing to assume that patients belong to categories with some probability or, if they do, they could not compute these probabilities. When a decision aid for computing probabilities according to logistic regression was provided, the doctors still did not use it, but according to Green and Mehr, acted as if they searched for cues and based their decision on a subset of the cues available, by using a simple heuristic rule (described in the next section). Green and Mehr (1997) also claim that doctors are wise to use this heuristic.

More generally, methods for categorization abound in the biochemical, epidemiological, and medical literature. It is important to note that instruments such as classification and regression trees, and networks (neural or probabilistic) have been met with a lack of enthusiasm by doctors and, even more so, by patients; they do not want to work with methods they do not fully grasp. An influential paper by Pozen, D'Agostino, and Mitchell (1980) spawned many years of a somewhat artificial effort to convince doctors to use an instrument for reducing inappropriate admissions to the coronary care unit. The decay in the use of expert systems as methods for diagnosis in the nineties was followed by a decay in their use for medical decision making. The lack of enthusiasm from doctors and patients motivated studies such as that by Green and Mehr (1997) and other studies on simple heuristics.

Other researchers have investigated the categorization processes of medical doctors (Dhami & Harries, 2001; Kee, Jenkins, McIllwaine, Patterson, Harper, & Shields, 2003; Smith & Gilhooly, 2006). It was found that logistic regression and heuristics described behavior about equally well. It should be noted, however, that models were evaluated according to mere fit to the data, without adjusting, for example, for the number of parameters used which is higher in regression. All in all, Dhami and Harries (2001, p. 5) argue that the heuristic is "easier to convey to physicians and is also more psychologically plausible." When a more rigorous method (cross-validation; more details later) was used to evaluate models, a simple heuristic was found to describe how mock jurors decide whether to grant bail or not better than a linear model (Dhami, 2003).

Overall, categorization tasks with limits in time, information, and computation, and also with pressure to perform accurately because there are real and high stakes, have been studied in a number of fields such as biology (Payne & Preece, 1980), training (Wottawa, 1987), engineering

(Katsikopoulos & Fasolo, 2006), law (Dhami, 2003), and medicine (Dhami & Harries, 2001; Fischer, Steiner, Zucol, Berger, Martignon, & Bossart, 2002; Green & Mehr, 1997). In that work, it has been proposed that people use—or should use—simple adaptive heuristics. The aim of our paper is to formalize this family of models and study it mathematically and by means of simulation. We show that the heuristics require little time, information, and computation, and are also relatively accurate.

The heuristics use cues sequentially and with no integration. Heuristics of that type have been applied successfully to study other kinds of inference such as paired comparisons (Bröder, 2000, 2003; Gigerenzer & Goldstein, 1996; Newell & Shanks, 2003; Newell, Weston, & Shanks, 2003; Payne, Bettman, & Johnson, 1993). To paraphrase Gigerenzer and Selten's (2001) program on modeling preferences, we model categorization "without probabilities and similarities."

We want to emphasize that our approach is not necessarily meant to apply to perceptual categorization tasks that have been successfully tackled by other models. The heuristics we will present are, rather, aimed at those real-world categorization tasks, often performed by professionals, where objects are described verbally and there are limits in time, information, and computation, as well as high stakes and demands for accuracy. We acknowledge that it is not yet completely clear why and in which aspects categorizing a shape is fundamentally different for the cognitive system than categorizing a patient (and also current models have been applied to some conditions that appear in the real world such as time pressure, as in Lamberts, 1995; Nosofsky & Palmeri, 1997). We chose to contribute by focusing on heuristics for categorization that have been suggested by researchers of professional decision making (such as in medicine or law), but have not been studied mathematically. Our study of these categorization heuristics is in the same spirit as the mathematical study of other heuristics (e.g., Martignon & Hoffrage, 2002; Lee & Corlett, 2003; Lee & Cummins, 2004; Hogarth & Karelaia, 2005a, 2005b, 2006, 2007; Katsikopoulos & Martignon, 2006). Finally, the heuristics are not meant to answer questions

that other adaptive approaches to categorization have been concerned with, such as predicting the probabilities of unseen cue values of objects (Anderson, 1991).

In the next section, we define a family of simple heuristics, called fast-and-frugal trees. Then we characterize them as lexicographic heuristics. In the next two sections, we show that fast-and-frugal trees can be characterized as linear models and that they exploit a property called cumulative dominance. We finally compare their predictive accuracy to that of logistic regression and of trees used in statistics and machine learning.

2. FAST-AND-FRUGAL TREES

We first introduce informally some elements from the general theory of trees (for more details, see Breiman, Friedman, Olshen, & Stone, 1984). A categorization tree can be graphically represented by the root node, on the tree's first *level*, and subsequent levels with one cue processed at each level (Figure 14-1). There are two types of nodes. First, a node may specify a question about the value of the object on a cue; the answer then leads to another node at the next level, and the process continues in this way. The root node is of that type. For nodes of the other type there is an *exit*; the object is categorized and the process stops. In sum, starting from the root node and

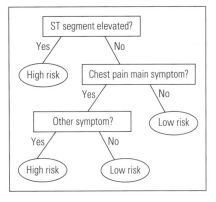

Figure 14-1. A fast-and-frugal tree for categorizing patients as having a high or low risk of ischemic heart disease (for more details, see Green & Mehr, 1997).

answering a sequence of questions, an exit is reached and the object is categorized.

Trees have been studied in statistics and machine learning (Breiman et al., 1984). This research is prescriptive, focused on constructing trees that avoid fitting noise and are more accurate in *predicting*, i.e., in categorizing previously unseen objects (Myung, Forster, & Browne, 2000). Increased predictive accuracy is sometimes achieved by not necessarily using all cues to categorize an object but, for some objects, using a subset of cues. For example, Figure 14-1 shows such a tree, constructed by two physicians, that categorizes patients as having a high or a low risk of ischemic heart disease (Green & Mehr, 1997).

Definition 1 (Martignon, Vitouch, Takezawa, & Forster, 2003). A categorization tree is *fast and frugal* if and only if it has at least one exit at each level.

Example 1. The tree of Figure 14-1 is fast and frugal. If a second question were asked for all patients with elevated ST-segment, the tree would not have been fast and frugal.

Fast-and-frugal trees are "minimal" in the sense of using the fewest number of question nodes and still involving all available cues, one at a time. Fast-and-frugal trees specify a number of cognitive processes. They specify how information is searched for, how is search stopped, and how a decision is taken based on the obtained information. For example, a physician using the tree of Figure 14-1 first looks up the ST-segment, then the chest pain, and finally other symptoms (later in the paper we model the ordering of cues).

The labels "fast" and "frugal" have precise meanings: The frugality of a tree for a set of objects is the mean number of cues, across these objects, it uses for making a categorization. The speed of a tree, also for a set of objects, is the mean number of basic operations—arithmetic and logical—used for making a categorization. It is clear that, by these definitions, changing question nodes into exits makes a tree faster and more frugal.

A tree that uses fewer than all of the n available cues is called *truncated*. A fast-and-frugal tree that is not truncated is called *complete*.

We assume that an object x is completely characterized by a vector $[x_1, x_2, \ldots, x_n]$ where x_i is the value of object x on cue c_i. We call these vectors *cue profiles*.

We also assume that cues are binary-valued ($x_i = 1$ or $x_i = 0$). Some cues are naturally binary (in the heart disease problem, whether chest pain is the main symptom) and others may be assumed to be binary because it is more psychologically plausible (for example, it is not easy to know how elevated the ST-segment is, but one can know if it is elevated a lot or not). When drawing fast-and-frugal trees we make the following conventions. An exit node reached by a "yes" answer hangs to the left side of the question node above it and a "yes" answer for cue c_i is denoted by $x_i = 1$ (for "no" answers the exit hangs to the right and $x_i = 0$). We also assume two categories, C_0 and C_1. Cues are coded so that if an object x exits at the ith level, it is assigned to category C_1 if $x_i = 1$ and to C_0 if $x_i = 0$.

Fast-and-frugal trees differ from many other categorization models in three respects: First, the trees are deterministic, that is, they predict $p_i(x) = 0$ or $p_i(x) = 1$. The motivation for this is that under conditions of limited time, information, and computation, people might not attempt or be able to compute probabilities. There are, of course, arguments against deterministic models, such as the inherent variability of human behavior or the presence of individual differences. On the other hand, one may worry how reliably the parameters of probabilistic models can be estimated or argue that deterministic models make stronger predictions and are easier to falsify. This is a difficult debate to settle and here we take the easy way out by acknowledging the issue and choosing to study a deterministic model.

Second, fast-and-frugal trees can make only qualitative predictions about response times. For example, according to the tree of Figure 14-1, a patient with an elevated ST-segment would be categorized faster than a patient without an elevated ST-segment. But, with no additional assumptions, it cannot be predicted how long these categorizations will take. This may be viewed as an incompleteness of the model but note that the model can still be falsified based on ordinal data (assuming that it is possible to measure response times reliably).

Finally, cues are not combined and are considered one at a time. Specifically, in the next section, we will show that fast-and-frugal trees implement a particular type of one-reason decision making.

3. FAST-AND-FRUGAL TREES AND LEXICOGRAPHIC HEURISTICS

It is possible to characterize fast-and-frugal trees without referring to exits, but as heuristics that categorize *lexicographically*. We start with a definition of a lexicographic order.

Definition 2. A cue profile x is lexicographically larger than a cue profile y ($x >_l y$) if and only if there exists $1 \leq i \leq n$ such that $x_i = 1$ and $y_i = 0$ and $x_j = y_j$ for all $j < i$ (equivalently y is lexicographically smaller than x, or $y <_l x$). If neither $x >_l y$ nor $x <_l y$, it holds that $x = y$.

Example 2. To get familiar with lexicographic orders and get a glimpse of their connection to fast-and-frugal trees, consider the Green and Mehr tree (see Figure 14-1). Let $x_1 = 1$ if and only if the ST-segment is elevated, $x_2 = 1$ if and only if chest pain is the main symptom, and $x_3 = 1$ if and only if there are other symptoms. Also let C_1 represent high risk and C_0 low risk. Now take two objects, $x_1 = [0, 1, 1]$ and $x_0 = [0, 0, 1]$. Verify that x_1 belongs to C_1 and x_0 belongs to C_0. Additionally, note that $x_1 >_l [0, 1, 0]$ and $[0, 1, 0] >_l x_0$. In fact, it holds that only those objects x such that $x >_l [0, 1, 0]$ belong to C_1.

In the remainder, without loss of generality, we assume that, in a fast-and-frugal tree, cues are inspected in the order $c_1, c_2, ..., c_n$. The following result formalizes the connection between fast-and-frugal trees and lexicographic orders. It does so by establishing a one-to-one correspondence between fast-and-frugal trees and cue profiles. The proof of this and the other three results of the paper are in the Appendix.

Result 1 (*Splitting Profile*). (i) For every fast-and-frugal tree f there exists a unique cue profile $S(f)$ so that f assigns x to C_1 if and only if $x >_l S(f)$. (ii) For every cue profile S there exists a unique

fast-and-frugal tree f such that $S(f) = S$ where f is truncated if and only if $S_n = 1$.

Example 2 (*Continued*). The splitting profile of the Green and Mehr tree is $[0, 1, 0]$. The cue profile $[0, 1, 1]$ is the splitting profile of a truncated tree, where, in Figure 14-1, the "yes" answer to the question "Chest pain main symptom?" would have led to an exit.

Remark 1. Result 1 says that, formally, fast-and-frugal trees implement one-reason categorization in the same way with fast-and-frugal heuristics for paired comparison (in this task, the goal is to infer which one of two objects has the higher value on a criterion; see Gigerenzer, Todd, and the ABC research group (1999) and Todd, Gigerenzer, and the ABC Research Group (in press): Categorizing an object x by using a fast-and-frugal tree reduces to comparing x with a dummy object d that has a cue profile identical to the tree's splitting profile. This paired comparison is done lexicographically as in heuristics that consider one cue at a time (Martignon & Hoffrage, 2002) such as take-the-best (Gigerenzer & Goldstein, 1996). All objects x such that $x >_l d$ are assigned to C_1 and all other objects are assigned to C_0.

Remark 2. Other models of categorization can be linked to one-reason heuristics too: First, Nosofsky and Palmeri (1998, p. 366) write: "We find the parallels between RULEX and these one reason decision-making algorithms to be striking. Both models suggest that human observers may place primary reliance on information from single dimensions." Second, fast-and-frugal trees are similar to another family of sequential heuristics, those for *categorization by elimination* (Berretty et al., 1999), although in categorization by elimination it may not be possible for an exit to lead to only one category.

Remark 3. Finally, Result 1 suggests a graphical interpretation of fast-and-frugal trees that may also be used to illustrate their connection to Bayesian models. In Figure 14-2, we graph the *natural frequency* tree (see also Gigerenzer & Hoffrage, 1995; Martignon et al., 2003) of the Green and Mehr study. Each one of the 89 patients was checked on the three cues

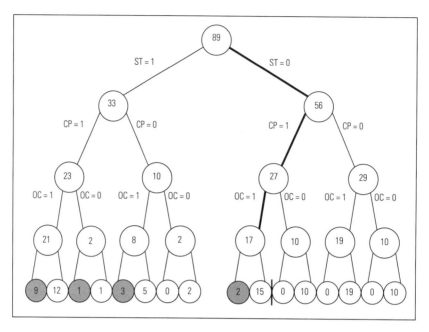

Figure 14-2. The natural frequency tree of the Green and Mehr study; shaded nodes correspond to people with infarctions (and nonshaded nodes to people without). Bold branches outline the fast-and-frugal tree of Figure 14-1 and the bold vertical bar denotes the position of its splitting profile.

(ST-segment elevation or *ST*; chest pain or *CP*; and other symptoms or *OC*). The fourth level of the tree shows how many patients share each one of the eight possible cue profiles (e.g., there are 17 patients that have the cue profile [0, 1, 1]). Note that the cue profiles are arranged in their lexicographic order, getting smaller from left to right.

The fifth level of the tree shows how many patients, in each cue profile, did turn out to be sick (shaded nodes) and how many turned out to be healthy (nonshaded nodes) as measured by a subsequent infarction. Based on this information one could assess the prior probability of an infarction for a given cue profile (e.g., it is .12 for the cue profile [0, 1, 1]). A simple Bayesian threshold model would assign a cue profile to a category according to whether the probability of infarction for the profile exceeds a threshold or not.

With this model, it may happen that a cue profile that is lexicographically larger (i.e., more towards the left in Figure 14-2) than another profile is assigned to the "healthy" category while

the lexicographically smaller profile is assigned to the "sick" category. For example, if the threshold for "sick" is .1, all patients with profile [1, 1, 0] will be categorized as "healthy" while all patients with profile [0, 1, 1] will be categorized as "sick."

Fast-and-frugal trees do not attempt to match the statistical structure of the problem in as much detail as Bayesian models do. They bet that the lexicographic structure approximates the statistical structure well: a cue profile is picked—the splitting profile—that is taken to (lexicographically) split the world into the two categories according to items having larger or smaller profiles. In Figure 14-2, the position of the splitting profile for the Green and Mehr tree is denoted by a bold vertical line bar (the branches, starting from the root node, that lead to this position are also marked in bold font). Here, the fast-and-frugal tree is not taking an unreasonable bet; for example, all patients with an infarction have a "large" profile (i.e., lexico-graphically larger than the splitting profile). How successful this bet is overall will be addressed in the section on predictive accuracy.

3.1. Types of Fast-and-Frugal Trees

Without loss of generality, we consider complete fast-and-frugal trees with $S_n = 0$. For any splitting profile S, one of the following holds: $\{S_i = 1$ for all $i < n\}$, $\{S_i = 0$ for all $i < n\}$, or $\{S_i \neq S_j$ for some $i,j < n\}$. Trees with a splitting profile of the first two types are used in biology for plant identification (Payne & Preece, 1980) and are called *pectinates*. These trees have been applied to other fields as well. Fischer et al. (2002) proposed a pectinate for deciding to prescribe macrolide to children who may suffer from community-acquired pneumonia. Dhami (2003) argued that the decision of mock juries to grant, or not, bail can be described by pectinates.

Pectinates have simple visual representations. In Figure 14-3, *strict* pectinates that have a splitting profile of the form $[1, \dots, 1, 0]$, are drawn in the upper panel. *Lenient* pectinates that have a splitting profile of the form $[0, \dots, 0, 0]$ are drawn in the lower panel. Strict pectinates assign only the cue profile $[1, \dots, 1, 1]$ to C_1. Lenient pectinates assign only $[0, \dots, 0, 0]$ to C_0. Thus, an interpretation of pectinates is that they require,

for one of the two possible categorizations, the maximum possible amount of evidence.

In the third type of fast-and-frugal trees, the values of the components of the splitting profile (excluding the last one) alternate between 1 and 0. We call such trees *zig-zag*. The simplest zig-zag trees (with just one alternation) are *L-shaped*. Wottawa (1987) used an L-shaped tree to model how employment agencies decide whether unemployed people should be assigned to vocational retraining programs.

There are two types of L-shaped trees, with splitting profiles $[1, \dots, 1, 0, \dots, 0, 0]$ and $[0, \dots, 0, 1, \dots, 1, 0]$. To visualize the first type of L-shaped trees, imagine that the two trees of Figure 14-3 are connected by replacing the C_1 node of the upper panel tree with the root node of the lower panel tree. The Green and Mehr (1997) tree is of the second type.

4. FAST-AND-FRUGAL TREES AND LINEAR MODELS

The analogy between the tasks of categorization and paired comparison suggests the following class of categorization models. In *linear* models, each cue c_i has a *weight* $w_i > 0$ and for $x = [x_1, x_2, \dots, x_n]$ the score $R(x) = \Sigma_i x_i w_i$ is computed. The *threshold* $h > 0$ transforms scores into categories: x is assigned to C_1 if and only if $R(x) > h$. As in the literature in paired comparison (Dawes, 1979; Einhorn, 1970; Martignon & Hoffrage, 2002), we focus on some interesting types of linear models.

Definition 3. A linear model is *noncompensatory* if and only if $w_i > \Sigma_{k > i} w_k$ for all $i = 1, 2, \dots, n - 1$.

It is known that, in paired comparison, lexicographic heuristics make the same predictions as noncompensatory linear models (Katsikopoulos & Fasolo, 2006; Martignon & Hoffrage, 1999, 2002). The following example illustrates that this also holds in categorization.

Example 3. The Green and Mehr tree makes identical categorizations with the linear model with $R(x) = 4x_1 + 2x_2 + x_3$ and $h = 2$ (they both assign $[0, 0, 0]$, $[0, 0, 1]$ and $[0, 1, 0]$ to C_0 and all other cue profiles to C_1). This linear model is

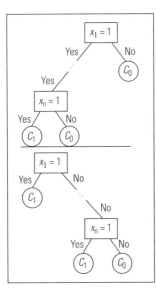

Figure 14-3. The two types of pectinates: Strict pectinates (upper panel) have splitting profile $[1, \dots, 1, 0]$. Lenient pectinates (lower panel) have splitting profile $[0, \dots, 0, 0]$.

compensatory because $4 > 2 + 1$. Note also that the value of the threshold equals the score of the model for the tree's splitting profile $R([0, 1, 0])$. Additionally, the linear model with $R(x) = 4x_1 + 2x_2 + x_3$ and $h = 1.5$ makes identical categorizations with a truncation of the Green and Mehr tree where the "yes" answer to the question "Chest pain main symptom?" leads to an exit node (they both assign $[0, 0, 0]$ and $[0, 0, 1]$ to C_0 and all other cue profiles to C_1).

Result 2 *(Noncompensatory Models)*. (i) For every fast-and-frugal tree f there exist $h > 0$ and $w_i > 0$ with $w_i > \Sigma_{k>i} w_k$ for $i = 1, 2, \ldots, n-1$, so that f makes identical categorizations as the linear model with weights w_i and threshold h. (ii) For every linear model with weights $w_i > 0$ so that $w_i > \Sigma_{k>i} w_k$ for $i = 1, 2, \ldots, n-1$ and a threshold $h > 0$, there exists a fast-and-frugal tree f (complete or truncated) that makes identical categorizations.

Remark 4. Fast-and-frugal trees are noncompensatory in the sense that the categorization such a tree makes will not change if more cues were looked up after the first cue that led to an exit (see also Einhorn, 1970; Martignon et al., 2003). Note, however, that Result 2 does not imply that it is impossible to empirically distinguish between fast-and-frugal trees and noncompensatory linear models. The process predictions of fast-and-frugal trees—for example, that information search is limited—can distinguish between the two.

Noncompensatory models are at one extreme of the spectrum of linear models (Hogarth & Karelaia, 2005b, 2006). At the other extreme we have tallying models.

Definition 4. A *tallying* model is a linear model with $w_i = 1$ for all $i = 1, 2, \ldots, n$.

Our next result relates fast-and-frugal trees to tallying models. The following example illustrates that fast-and-frugal trees make the same predictions with tallying models.

Example 4. Consider first a lenient fast-and-frugal tree (Figure 14-3). It is clear that it makes the same predictions with a tallying model with threshold $h = 1$. Analogously, a strict fast-and-frugal tree makes the same predictions with a tallying model with $h = n$.

For Result 3, we use the following terminology. As in the case of fast-and-frugal trees, a tallying model is truncated if and only if it uses k cues where $k < n$. Also, a tallying model is lenient if and only if $h = 1$ and it is strict if and only if $h = n$ (or $h = k$ if it is truncated). A tallying model is moderate if and only if it is neither lenient nor strict. Finally, a *Boolean combination* of two or more categorization models (trees or tallying models) is interpreted in the usual sense, after treating the assignment of an object to category C_1 as the assignment of the truth value "true" and the assignment of an object to category C_0 as the assignment of the truth value "false." For example, if model m_1 assigns x to C_1 and model m_2 assigns x to C_0, then the conjunction $m_1 \wedge m_2$ assigns x to C_0 and the disjunction $m_1 \vee m_2$ assigns x to C_1.

Result 3 *(Tallying Models)*. (i) Any lenient pectinate makes identical categorizations with a lenient tallying model and vice versa. (ii) Any strict pectinate makes identical categorizations with a strict tallying model and vice versa. (iii) Any zig-zag makes identical categorizations with a Boolean combination, involving only disjunctions and conjunctions, of truncated lenient and strict tallying models. (iv) Any moderate tallying model makes identical categorizations with a disjunction of truncated strict pectinates.

Remark 5. In the language of adaptive heuristics (Gigerenzer et al., 1999), Result 3 says that fast-and-frugal trees and tallying models can be used as building blocks for each other. Furthermore, the building processes are simple. It is known that categorization trees can be expressed as Boolean combinations of constraints involving cues (Mitchell, 1997), but, in general, the formulas are cumbersome. The contribution of Result 3 is to show how more simple are exactly the formulas for fast-and-frugal trees.

5. FAST-AND-FRUGAL TREES AND CUMULATIVE DOMINANCE

To begin, we state the definition of *cumulative dominance* (see also Baucells, Carrasco, & Hogarth, 2008).

Definition 5. A cue profile $y = [y_1, y_2, \ldots, y_n]$ is cumulatively dominated by a cue profile

$x = [x_1, x_2, \ldots, x_n]$ ($y <_c x$) if and only if $\Sigma_{k=1}, \ldots,$ $_i y_k \leq \Sigma_{k=1}, \ldots, _i x_k$ for all $i = 1, 2, \ldots, n$ (where strict inequality holds for at least one i).

Note that the concept of cumulative dominance assumes a cue order. For our purposes, we assume that this is the order by which a fast-and-frugal tree searches cues.

Cumulative dominance is important for the study of paired comparisons. In the language of our paper, Baucells et al. (2008, Proposition 4), showed that if the criterion value of each object is (the same) linear function of the object's cue values, it is not possible that an object has a higher criterion value than a second object by which it is cumulatively dominated. It is thus a desirable property for a model of paired comparison—lexicographic, linear, or anything else—that if it picks an object, this object is *not* cumulatively dominated. It is easy to see that lexicographic heuristics for paired comparison, such as take-the-best (Gigerenzer & Goldstein, 1996), satisfy this property.

What is the role of cumulative dominance in categorization? To begin, in analogy to Baucells et al. (2008), we assume the following *cues-to-categories* linear model. For every object x, first compute the score $R(x) = \Sigma_i x_i w_i$ (with $w_i > 0$) and second use the score to assign x to C_1 if and only if $R(x) > h$ (with $h > 0$). Note that this is a model of how cues are related to categories in the environment, not of how people use cues to infer categories.

Given this model, we can ask: (i) what property holds about the category of an object cumulatively dominated by another object? And (ii) do fast-and-frugal trees satisfy this property? Our final result answers these questions. We first use the following example to illustrate the answers.

Example 5. Assume that the category of an object $x = [x_1, x_2, x_3]$ is determined by whether its score $R(x) = x_1 + x_2 + x_3$ exceeds the threshold $h = 1.5$ or not. Take $x = [0, 1, 0]$ and $y = [0, 0, 1]$. Verify that $y <_c x$ and that both x and y belong to C_0. Note that it is not possible to find a fast-and-frugal tree that assigns x to C_0 and y to C_1. Recall also similar comments in Remark 3.

Result 4 (*Cumulative Dominance*). Assume the cues-to-categories linear model. (i) For every cue profiles x and y such that $y <_c x$ it holds that if x belongs to C_0 then y belongs to C_0. (ii) For every fast-and-frugal tree f and cue profiles x and y such that f assigns x to C_0 and y to C_1 it cannot hold that $y <_c x$.

Remark 6. Result 4 says that, as a consequence of cumulative dominance, a desirable property of a categorization model is that it does not assign to the "big" category an object that is cumulatively dominated by a second object, when the second object belongs to the "small" category. Fast-and-frugal trees satisfy this property. In analogy to Baucells et al. (2008) we say that fast-and-frugal trees exploit cumulative dominance.

To sum our results so far, fast-and-frugal trees are a simple heuristic way of implementing one-reason categorization, without computing probabilities and similarities. They can be represented as lexicographic heuristics for paired comparison or as noncompensatory linear models for categorization, and they also exploit cumulative dominance. Fast-and-frugal trees seem to fit our goal of providing a family of models for categorization under limited information, time, and computation. Recall, however, that we also wanted our models to be relatively accurate as professionals are pressured to be in many real-world categorization tasks. The next section addresses this issue.

6. PREDICTIVE ACCURACY

Like all models of inference, a categorization model may be accurate in two ways: First, by setting its parameters to *fit* the known assignment of some objects to their categories. Second, by using parameters that have been independently set to *predict* the categories of not yet encountered objects (as, e.g., in cross-validation). It is recognized that prediction is a more meaningful test (Myung, Forster, & Browne, 2000), both for describing and improving human performance.

There are a number of measures of predictive accuracy. Perhaps the most commonly used in psychology is cross-validation (Browne, 2000). Briefly, in cross-validation a fixed number of objects in the population are used as the fitting sample where parameters are set and the remaining objects in the population are used as the prediction sample on which to measure accuracy. To average out random variation, the objects in the fitting sample are resampled. Simulations are used to repeat the process many times.

The size of the fitting sample is often fixed at 50% of the population. The problem with fixing the size of the fitting sample is that this essentially corresponds to fixing the relative importance ascribed to goodness-of-fit and to model complexity (as measured, e.g., by the number of parameters in the model or by the functional form of the model's equation). In our study, we used, in addition to 50% of the population, two more sizes of the fitting sample: a small one (15%) and a large one (90%).

In the concluding section, we discuss another approach to measuring predictive accuracy by simulation, as well as the possibility of deriving analytical results for the predictive accuracy of fast-and-frugal trees. Here we present the results of cross-validation that compare fast-and-frugal trees against two benchmarks. We first outline the basics of the four models we compared.

6.1. Models

A benchmark that comes to mind from statistics is logistic regression *(LR)*. Long, Grith, Selker, and D'Agostino (1993) applied LR with success to the problem of ischemic heart disease. In fact, Green and Mehr (1997) compared LR with the fast-and-frugal tree of Figure 14-1 (their results seemed to favor the fast-and-frugal tree, but see Martignon, Vitouch, Takezawa, & Forster, 2003, for a critique of their method and note that there were only 89 data points). LR is the first benchmark we tested. In the medical decision making literature, LR is considered a psychologically plausible model of categorization (e.g., Dhami & Harries, 2001).

The machine learning community has also contributed models for categorization. Prominent among them are types of trees called classification and regression trees *(CART;* Breiman et al., 1984). These are not constrained to be fast-and-frugal (though they may be in a particular

application). As far as we know, it has not been claimed that such trees are psychologically plausible. We test them because they are, among machine learning methods, relatively simple and still quite accurate. Cues are looked up sequentially but not necessarily one at a time. For example, if cue c_1 is continuous with values between 0 and 100, and cue c_2 is binary, a question that may be asked at one level of the tree is "Does it hold that $x_1 > 50$ and $x_2 = 1$?" Deciding which cues to use in each question and how to order the questions is done by statistical tests that determine how informative different cues are. CART is the second benchmark we tested.

Now we describe the two kinds of fast-and-frugal trees we tested. The construction of a fast-and-frugal tree requires that two problems be solved: (i) how are the *n* cues ordered and (ii) whether, for each one of the first *n* - 1 cues, the exit is located to the left or to the right. We consider two approaches to solving (i) and (ii). Other approaches are also possible (Dhami & Harries, 2001; Martignon et al., 2003) but we implemented two that we judged to be more psychologically plausible in the sense of requiring fewer computations and being in the spirit of other lexicographic heuristics such as take-the-best (see below).

Table 14-1 lists the kind of information available for each one of the *n* binary cues (it is a contingency table). Note that the benchmarks use more information than what is in the table: LR and CART use continuous cue values and an unpacked version of the data in Table 14-1 where it is known which object had which cue values and to which category it belonged.

The two approaches that we consider differ in the following sense: One approach first tries to solve the problem of (i) cue order and the other approach first tries to solve the problem of

Table 14-1. The Information for Each Cue c_i, $i = 1, 2, ..., n$, that Is Available for Constructing Fast-and-Frugal Trees

	$x \in C_1$	$x \in C_0$
$x_i = 1$	a_i	b_i
$x_i = 0$	c_i	d_i

(ii) exit location. We will see how heuristically solving one problem immediately suggests a solution to the other.

Consider first the problem of cue order. A reasonable heuristic solution is to order the cues according to some measure of goodness. Each cue c_i can be correct or, as we will say, *valid* in two ways, when $\{x_i = 1$ and $x \in C_1\}$ and when $\{x_i = 0$ and $x \in C_0\}$. Using the notation of Table 14-1, these two validities are computed as follows.

$$v_i^1 = a_i/(a_i+b_i),$$
$$v_i^0 = d_i/(c_i+d_i).$$

Our first approach for constructing fast-and-frugal trees, called *Max*, uses the following cue order rule (ties are broken randomly):

"Order cues by decreasing value of max $\{v_i^1, v_i^0\}$."

Remark 7. Heuristics for paired comparison such as take-the-best (Gigerenzer & Goldstein, 1996) also order cues by a measure of goodness. In paired comparison, a cue c_i is correct not in two, but in one way: if $x_i = 1$ for the object with the larger criterion and $x_i = 0$ for the other object. There is one validity, the conditional probability that the cue is correct given that $x_i = 1$ on one object and $x_i = 0$ on the other. To obtain the fast-and-frugal-tree analogue of take-the-best (see also Martignon et al., 2003) we can lump together the two kinds of correct categorizations with the measure $v_i^p = (a_i + d_i)/(a_i + b_i + c_i + d_i)$. Analytical results on take-the-best, which involve cue validities (Katsikopoulos & Martignon, 2006) apply to a fast-and-frugal tree that orders cues according to v_i^p.

Remark 8. We have claimed that fast-and-frugal trees do not compute probabilities. But v_i^1 and v_i^0 are, at least from the frequentist point of view, probabilities. We do not, however, see this as a contradiction for two reasons. The first is that it may be claimed that these v_i^1 and v_i^0 are relative frequencies that are automatically available in memory (see also Gigerenzer & Goldstein, 1996; Martignon & Hoffrage, 2002). Second, fast-and-frugal trees avoid the computation of

the more basic, for categorization, probabilities $p_i(x)$.

Using the cue order rule of Max, each cue is put in one of the levels of the fast-and-frugal tree. The cue may then lead to a right or to a left exit. A way of solving the exit location problem is to use which of the two validities was the reason for the cue to be put in that level. In Max, the following exit location rule is used (ties are broken randomly):

"If max $\{v_i^1, v_i^0\} = v_i^1, c_i$ leads to a left exit.

If max $\{v_i^1, v_i^0\} = v_i^0, c_i$ leads to a right exit."

If $v_i^1 > v_i^0$ or $v_i^0 > v_i^1$ for all cues, Max will construct a pectinate.

Pectinates may be reasonable in applications with a few cues (as in the studies of Dhami, 2003; Fischer et al., 2002). But if the number of cues is large, nearly all objects will be classified as belonging to one category. In the dataset we used for testing the models, the average number of cues is 10.9. We therefore decided to test another approach for constructing fast-and-frugal trees where trees will almost certainly not be pectinates (unless almost all objects do belong to the same category).

The second approach, called *Zig*, is, in a way, the dual of Max. Zig starts with an exit location rule and uses its output to determine cue order. The rule guarantees that zig-zag trees are constructed:

Alternate between right and left exits until the $(n - 1)$st level, after determining if the exits in the first k levels, with $k \geq 1$, are left or right ones. To find k, first compute the ratio, r, of number of objects in the category with the most objects to the number of objects in the other category. Then k is the unique integer solution of $2^{k-1} \leq r \leq 2^k$. If more objects belong to category C_1, the exits in the first k levels are left ones. If more objects belong to category C_0, the exits in the first k levels are right ones.

Given that it is determined whether the exits at the first $n-1$ levels are left or right, the cue order rule of Zig has as follows:

If the exit in the first level is left, put the cue with the maximum v_i^1 first. If the exit in the first level is right, put the cue with the maximum v_i^0 first. Repeat this step with the exit in the next level until the $(n-1)$st level.

Example 6. Assume 20 objects, of which 11 belong to category C_1, with values on 3 cues such that $a_1 = 7$, $b_1 = 3$, $c_1 = 4$, $d_1 = 6$; $a_2 = 5$, $b_2 = 5$, $c_2 = 6$, $d_2 = 4$ and $a_3 = 3$, $b_3 = 7$, $c_3 = 8$, $d_3 = 2$. Thus, $v_1^1 = .7$, $v_1^0 = .6$, $v_2^1 = .5$, $v_2^0 = .4$ and $v_3^1 = .3$, $v_3^0 = .2$. Max constructs a lenient pectinate. Zig constructs an L-shaped tree that has the same visual representation as the Green and Mehr tree in Figure 14-1.

6.2. Results

We tested LR, CART, Max, and Zig in 30 datasets, mostly from the UC Irvine Machine Learning Repository. We included very different problems (from medicine to sports to economics) with widely varying number of objects (from 50 to 4052) and cues (from 4 to 69). Because this study is not focused on predictive accuracy, we do not analyze the statistical characteristics of the datasets (but they are available from the third author).

The accuracy of each model (for the two categories together) was evaluated in four cases: fitting and prediction based on 15%, 50%, and 90% of all objects. In two problems, 15% of objects were too few for the parameters of the models to be estimated reliably (for example, the regression weights could not be estimated). The results are in Figure 14-4.

As is often the case, the more complex models (LR and CART) did much better in fitting. For example, CART achieved .93 while Max scored 19 points fewer. What about robustness? Take first the 90% prediction case. Now LR is the most accurate model but the difference from Max is smaller (.82 vs. .73). And the other fast-and-frugal tree, Zig, almost catches up with CART (.78 vs. .80). The situation is almost identical in the 50% case with the only differences being that CART and LR each lost one point.

The 15% case represents a situation where novel categorizations have to be made with little learning. The performance of all four models is now very close, with a range of just four percentage points, from .72 (Max) to .76 (CART). Just below the top (.75), Zig achieves the same accuracy with LR. Overall, fast-and-frugal trees are almost as robust as two benchmarks from statistics and machine learning, especially as the learning sample decreases.

As often done for paired comparison tasks, we discuss the relative performance of regression

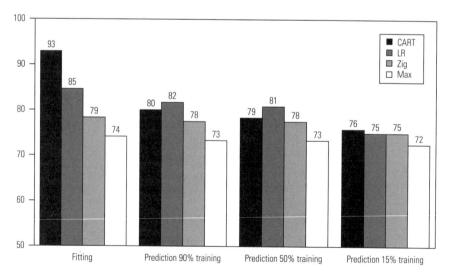

Figure 14-4. Results of computer simulations for the accuracy of LR, CART, Max, and Zig in 30 real-world datasets. The accuracy of each model was evaluated in four cases: fitting and three kinds of prediction (with access to 15%, 50%, and 90% of all objects for estimating parameters and contingency tables).

and fast-and-frugal heuristics. In fitting, we found a six-point difference between LR and Zig. Across the three prediction conditions, the difference in favor of LR shrunk to two points. How does this result compare to the results of studies of predictive accuracy in paired comparison tasks? In a study with 20 datasets, take-the-best came ahead of linear regression by three points (Gigerenzer et al., 1999). But to be consistent with take-the-best using binary cues, that version of linear regression used binary cues, while the logistic regression in our study used continuous cues. When linear regression used continuous cues, it outperformed binary take-the-best by five points in 50% prediction, which is similar to our result. (Note that a yet unpublished study found that take-the-best with continuous cues outperformed regression with continuous cues (Katsikopoulos, Schooler, & Hertwig, 2008)).

Finally, let us mention something particular about Zig. In all four conditions, Zig had the smallest standard deviation among the four models. We point this out because it is related to a recent observation by Brighton (2007). Note first that it is known that the performance of an algorithm can be broken down into three components: bias, variance, and irreducible error. Brighton conjectures that the good performance of fast-and-frugal heuristics can be largely attributed to low variance, just as we found here.

7. CONCLUSIONS

Categorization tasks with limits in time, information, and computation, high stakes, and with pressure to perform accurately have been studied in a number of fields concerned with professional decision making such as biology, education, engineering, law, and medicine. In that work, it has been proposed that people use—or should use—simple adaptive heuristics. These heuristics do not compute similarities or probabilities but use cues sequentially and with no integration.

The aim of our paper was to introduce that family of heuristics, which we call fast-and-frugal trees, and study it formally. We characterized fast-and-frugal trees mathematically as lexicographic heuristics for paired comparison and as

noncompensatory linear models for categorization, and also showed that they exploit cumulative dominance. We also showed, by computer simulations, that fast-and-frugal trees have good predictive accuracy compared to benchmarks from statistics and machine learning, especially when there is little learning.

APPENDIX

Proof of Result 1 (*Splitting Profile*). (i) For a fast-and-frugal tree f, define its splitting profile $S(f)$ as follows.

$S(f)_n = 0$, and for all $i = 1, 2,..., n - 1$:

$S(f)_i = 0$ if the exit of f at the ith level leads to C_1

$S(f)_i = 1$ if the exit of f at the ith level leads to C_0. (*)

Based on (*), $S(f)$ is uniquely defined by f. We show that f assigns x to C_1 if and only if $x >_l S(f)$.

Consider first an object x such that $x = S(f)$. It is clear that x will not exit before the nth level of f where it will be assigned to C_0.

If it does not hold that $x = S(f)$, then either $S(f) >_l x$ or $x >_l S(f)$. If $S(f) >_l x$, there is $1 \leq i \leq n$ such that $x_i = 0$ and $S(f)_i = 1$ as well as $x_j = S(f)_j$ for all $j < i$, and x will exit at the ith level of f and will be assigned to C_0.

If $x >_l S(f)$, there is $1 \leq i \leq n$ such that $x_i = 1$ and $S(f)_i = 0$ as well as $x_j = S(f)_j$ for all $j < i$. Thus, x will exit at the ith level of f and will be assigned to C_1.

(ii) We first show existence. Let S be a cue profile with $S_n = 0$. Define f as a tree with n levels so that for $i = 1, 2, \ldots, n - 1$, if $S_i = 0$, f has exactly one exit at the ith level leading to C_1 and if $S_i = 1$, f has exactly one exit at the ith level leading to C_0. At the nth level f has two exits. It is clear that f is a fast-and-frugal tree and, using the arguments of (i), $S(f) = S$.

If S is a cue profile with $S_n = 1$, define $k < n$ such that $S_k = 0$ and $S_i = 1$ for all $i > k$. Define f as a tree with k levels so that for $i = 1, 2, \ldots, k - 1$, if $S_i = 0$, f has exactly one exit at the ith level leading to C_1 and if $S_i = 1$, f has exactly one exit at the ith level leading to C_0. At the kth level f has two exits. It is clear that f is a truncated fast-and-frugal tree and, using the arguments of (i), $S(f) = S$.

To show uniqueness, we show that a cue profile S cannot be the splitting profile of two fast-and-frugal trees, f_1 and f_2, that are different (meaning that the trees do not use the same cues or, if they do, they assign at least one possible cue profile to different categories). If S were the splitting profile of both f_1 and f_2, $S(f_1) = S$ and $S(f_2) = S$, and thus also $S(f_1) = S(f_2)$. But, by (i), this means that f_1 and f_2 make identical categorizations and thus they cannot be different.

Proof of Result 2 *(Noncompensatory Models)*. (i) Let $S(f)$ be the splitting profile of f. Also, let $w_i > 0$ be weights such that (a) for $i = 1, 2, \ldots,$ $n - 1$, $w_i > \Sigma_{k > i} w_k$ and $h > 0$ be such that (b) $R(S(f)) = h$.

It suffices to show that, for any object x, it holds that

$$x >_l S(f) \text{ if and only if } R(x) > h. \quad (*)$$

It is known (Martignon & Hoffrage, 1999, 2002) that (a) implies that for any two objects x and y, $x >_l y$ if and only if $R(x) > R(y)$. So, $x >_l S(f)$ if and only if $R(x) > R(S(f))$.

Then, $(*)$ follows from combining $\{x >_l S(f)$ if and only if $R(x) > R(S(f))\}$ with (b).

(ii) Let $S^1 = (1,1, \ldots, 1)$, $S^2 = (1, 1, \ldots, 0)$, $\ldots,$ $S^m = (0, 0, \ldots, 0)$, with $m = 2^n$, be all possible cue profiles with n components, ordered lexicographically.

As in (i), from (a) it holds that $R(S^1) > R(S^2) > \ldots > R(S^m)$.

In both cases when $h > R(S^1)$ or $h < R(S^m)$, all objects belong to the same one category.

Otherwise, let l be such that $h \geq R(S^l)$ and $h < R(S^{l-1})$. It is clear that the fast-and-frugal tree f with splitting profile S^k makes identical categorizations with the linear model with weights w_i and threshold h. More specifically, based on the proof of Result 1(ii), f is truncated if and only if $S^l_n = 1$, in which case it has k levels for $k < n$ with $S^l_k = 0$ and $S^l_i = 1$ for all $i > k$.

Proof of Result 3 *(Tallying Models)*. (i) and (ii) follow directly from the definitions.

(iii) We show this for the simplest zig-zag trees, the L-shaped trees (it will be clear below how the argument extends). If f is L-shaped, then its splitting profile $S(f)$ equals $[1, \ldots, 1, 0, \ldots, 0]$ or $[0, \ldots, 0, 1, \ldots, 1, 0]$. Let $m + 1$ be the number of zeros in $S(f)$.

Take first $S(f) = [0, \ldots, 0, 1, \ldots, 1, 0]$. It is easy to verify that f makes identical categorizations with the model $t_0 \vee [t_1 \wedge \ldots \wedge t_m \wedge t_{m+1}]$ where t_i are truncated tallying models that use cue set S_i and have threshold h_i, given as follows:

$S_0 = \{c_1, \ldots, c_m\}; h_0 = 1,$
$S_i = \{1 - c_i\}; h_i = 1,$ for $i = 1, 2, \ldots, m,$
$S_{m+1} = \{c_{m+1}, \ldots, c_n\}; h_m = n - m.$

Similarly, if $S(f) = [1, \ldots, 1, 0, \ldots, 0, 0]$, f makes identical categorizations with the model $t_1 \wedge \cdots \wedge t_m \wedge t_{m+1}$ where t_i are truncated tallying models with $h_i = 1$ for all i, $S_i = \{c_i\}$ for $i = 1, 2, \ldots, m$ and $S_{m+1} = \{c_{m+1}, \ldots, c_n\}$.

(iv) Let t be a moderate tallying model that uses $k \leq n$ cues and has threshold h. It is easy to see that t makes identical categorizations with the disjunction of a total of $\sum_{l \geq h} c(k, l)$ strict pectinates, each using one of the possible cue subsets with l out of the k cues, where $l \geq h$.

Proof of Result 4 *(Cumulative Dominance)*. (i) From Baucells et al. (2008, Proposition 4), $y <_c x$ together with the cues-to-categories linear model implies $R(y) < R(x)$. Again from the model, x belonging to C_0 implies $R(x) \leq h$. It thus also holds that $R(y) < h$ which means that y belongs to C_0.

(ii) From Result 1, it holds that $S(f) >_l x$ or $x = S(f)$ because f assigns x to C_0. Again from this result, because f assigns y to C_1, it also holds that $y >_l S(f)$. Thus it cannot hold that $y <_l x$ which means that it cannot hold that $y <_c x$.

Introduction to Chapter 15

A Signal Detection Analysis of the Recognition Heuristic

A belief that one has previously heard the name of a company, a city, a country, or a river may be right or wrong. The recognition heuristic, as suggested by Goldstein and Gigerenzer (see Chapter 3), is agnostic regarding the veridicality of a person's recognition judgment. It takes these judgments at face value and infers that the recognized object scores higher than the nonrecognized object on the quantitative criterion. When Timothy Pleskac joined Ralph Hertwig's lab at the University of Basel as a postdoctoral researcher, he began to think about the recognition heuristic. His important insight was that the signal detection framework, often used by theories of recognition memory, is the perfect tool for analyzing the extent to which a fallible recognition memory affects the performance of the recognition heuristic. Pleskac's investigation is thus another instance of theory integration, combining a signal detection model of recognition memory with the recognition heuristic.

When recognizing an object, people can go wrong by erroneously recognizing something that they have never encountered before ("false alarms") and by not recognizing something that they had previously encountered ("misses"). It is not immediately clear how these mistakes affect the average accuracy of the inferences that people make. Pleskac's article cites the example of a German professor using recognition to pick teams in the 2006 NCAA Division I basketball tournament. The professor thought that he had heard of Northwestern State, when, in fact, he mistook it for Northwestern University. To Pleskac's chagrin, Hertwig (the unnamed German professor and basketball ignoramus) predicted the outcomes of the tournament better than Pleskac, the basketball buff. Hertwig was lucky. As Pleskac's analysis shows, as the error rate of recognition increases, the accuracy of the recognition heuristic declines. His analysis also shows that when people who are cognizant of their level of recognition knowledge make judgments, they could increase their inferential accuracy by adjusting their decision criterion accordingly. When their knowledge is very low, they should be most conservative in calling something "old"; with increasing knowledge, however, it is best for them to become more liberal and call something "old," even if they are not absolutely certain.

CHAPTER 15

A Signal Detection Analysis of the Recognition Heuristic

Timothy J. Pleskac

Abstract: The recognition heuristic uses a recognition decision to make an inference about an unknown variable in the world. Theories of recognition memory typically use a signal detection framework to predict this binary recognition decision. In this article, I integrate the recognition heuristic with signal detection theory to formally investigate how judges use their recognition memory to make inferences. The analysis reveals that false alarms and misses systematically influence the performance of the recognition heuristic. Furthermore, judges should adjust their recognition response criterion according to their experience with the environment to exploit the structure of information in it. Finally, the less-is-more effect is found to depend on the distribution of cue knowledge and judges' sensitivity to the difference between experienced and novel items. Theoretical implications of this bridge between the recognition heuristic and models of recognition memory are discussed.

Simon (1990) observed that recognition is a natural mechanism for helping people to solve problems, such as those found in chess, medical diagnosis, or reading. Similarly, Axelrod (1984) postulated that recognition may be necessary for cooperation to be sustained in social interactions. The recent development of the recognition heuristic has added inferences to this list of indirect applications of recognition memory (Goldstein & Gigerenzer, 1999, 2002). According to the heuristic, recognition serves as a cue for making inferences about pairs of objects. The recognition heuristic can be quite accurate. These areas include, among others, making population inferences about German, U.S., and Swiss cities (Gigerenzer & Goldstein, 1996; Goldstein & Gigerenzer, 2002; Pohl, 2006),

selecting stocks during a bull market (Borges, Goldstein, Ortmann, & Gigerenzer, 1999), and identifying National Hockey League players who have a high number of career points (Snook & Cullen, 2006).

Heuristics that use recognition as a predictor variable, such as the recognition heuristic, typically start with a judge's binary recognition decision (Gigerenzer & Goldstein, 1996, 1999; Goldstein & Gigerenzer, 1999, 2002). In contrast, memory research often focuses on the process that leads up to the recognition decision (Raaijmakers & Shiffrin, 2002). Research examining these memorial processes relies on laboratory experiments that have a defined learning phase in which participants study a list of items—sometimes novel, sometimes common—followed by a test phase in which their recognition memory is tested on the items that they learned. The results from the laboratory typically reveal that signal detection theory is useful for understanding why correct and incorrect recognition decisions are observed during memory experiments

(Banks, 1970). In particular, two factors give rise to both decisions during memory experiments: (1) the ability to detect the difference between the familiarity of learned and unlearned items (sensitivity); and (2) various response factors (criterion location). Correct and incorrect recognition decisions, however, are more difficult to examine within the ecological framework of the recognition heuristic and the broader class of fast-and-frugal heuristics. The difficulty arises because their ecological framework requires heuristics to be examined with a representative sample of stimuli drawn from an environment or reference class experienced outside of the laboratory (see Gigerenzer, Todd, & the ABC Research Group, 1999). Furthermore, the environment should be selected in such a way that the heuristic could sensibly be used in the environment to make inferences (see Gigerenzer et al., 1999). Consequently, the researcher does not typically know the items a respondent has or has not experienced, making it difficult—if not impossible—to identify correct and incorrect recognition decisions.

The different methodology needed to study the recognition heuristic does not imply, however, that judges use a functionally different recognition process for items drawn from ecologically defined reference classes than for items learned in a laboratory setting. In fact, a recent fMRI study demonstrated a link between the recognition heuristic and recognition memory when areas of the medial parietal cortex—areas typically associated with recognition memory—were activated during the use of the recognition heuristic (Volz et al., 2006). A natural question is: How do these recognition processes affect the accuracy of recognition as a predictor variable? In this article, I formally address this question by integrating signal detection theory with the recognition heuristic to show the effect that correct and incorrect recognition decisions have when recognition is used as a predictor cue. In doing so, I rely on the generalizability of signal detection theory as a model of recognition memory examined in the laboratory (see, e.g., Banks, 1970; Ratcliff, Clark, & Shiffrin, 1990; Shiffrin, Huber, & Marinelli, 1995) to the inferential paradigm of the fast-and-frugal program of research

(Gigerenzer et al., 1999). Next, to facilitate the integration, I introduce the recognition heuristic, the empirical evidence that supports its use, and the less-is-more effect that the recognition heuristic produces.

THE RECOGNITION HEURISTIC

The recognition heuristic is a single-variable decision rule that relies on recognition alone to make a judgment about an unknown target variable. When judges are confronted with a two-alternative, forced-choice question, such as choosing whether San Antonio or San Diego is more populous, the recognition heuristic states: If one of two objects is recognized and the other is not, then infer that the recognized object has the higher value with respect to the target variable.

In some domains, people who use this heuristic have a good chance of being correct. For example, Goldstein and Gigerenzer (2002) reported that the average Spearman correlation between American students' recognition of German cities with a population over 100,000 and their respective population size is .60 (the *recognition correlation*). This correlation occurs because people learn city names from mediators in the environment, such as the news media. The *surrogate correlation* between American students' recognition of German city names and the number of mentions of those cities in the *Chicago Tribune* was .79. The mediators, in turn, can reflect other statistical relationships. The citation rates of the city names have an *ecological correlation* of .70 with the populations of German cities (Goldstein & Gigerenzer, 2002).[1] The recognition heuristic, by exploiting the structure of information diagrammed in Figure 15-1, is ecologically rational when inferring city populations or for any domain with the same information structure (Goldstein & Gigerenzer, 2002).

Judges with partial ignorance—those who have experience with some but not all of the objects in a specified reference class—benefit most from the recognition heuristic. For example, Goldstein and Gigerenzer (1999) reported that the recognition heuristic can explain why Germans answered the San Diego/

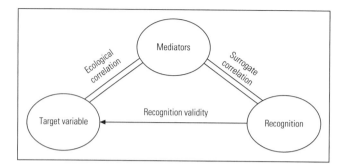

Figure 15-1. The ecological rationality of the recognition heuristic. In some domains, recognition of objects can be correlated with an unknown target variable (e.g., city population). This is because judges experience objects via mediators in the environment (e.g., newspapers), and the mediators reflect the target variable (e.g., more populous cities tend to be in the news more often). (From "Models of Ecological Rationality: The Recognition Heuristic," by D. G. Goldstein and G. Gigerenzer, 2002, *Psychological Review, 109*, p. 78. Copyright 2002 by the American Psychological Association. Adapted with permission.)

San Antonio question quite accurately—100% in their sample—whereas only 62% of Americans answered the question correctly. This is because the recognition heuristic can be used only when just one of the items is recognized. American students recognized both cities and therefore resorted to other, less accurate cues to make an inference. When given a larger test bank of questions, partially ignorant judges can capitalize on their ignorance when the recognition heuristic is paired with a knowledge heuristic that follows the process diagrammed in Figure 15-2. Possible heuristics that follow this procedure include "take-the-best," "take-the-last," and "minimalist" (Gigerenzer & Goldstein, 1996). Together, these heuristics give rise to a less-is-more effect, in which less knowledge or experience can be beneficial (see Gigerenzer, 2004; Gigerenzer & Goldstein, 1996, 1999; Goldstein & Gigerenzer, 1999, 2002).[2]

To explain how and why the less-is-more effect can emerge, Goldstein and Gigerenzer (1999, 2002) derived the expected accuracy of judges who used the recognition heuristic when given an inferential test on pairs of objects. During the test, judges had to identify which object had a larger value on a target variable, such as population. The pairs were formed in such a way that the individual objects were a representative sample of a well-defined population

of objects or reference class with N objects (e.g., German cities with over 100,000 inhabitants). A representative sample has the property that individual stimuli are equally likely to be selected (with replacement) from the reference class (Brunswik, 1955; Dhami, Hertwig, & Hoffrage, 2004; Gigerenzer, Hoffrage, & Kleinbölting, 1991).[3]

The recognition heuristic divides the N objects into two groups: n recognized objects and $N - n$ novel objects. If a person is confronted with a randomly drawn pair of items from $N(N - 1)/2$ of the possible pairs, then the recognition heuristic can be expected to be used for $2n(N - n)/[N(N - 1)]$ proportion of the pairs, where one item is recognized and the other is not.[4]

The *recognition validity* reflects the recognition correlation (see Figure 15-1) and is the proportion of times that the recognized object has a higher value on the target variable:

$$\alpha = \frac{R}{R + W}. \tag{15-1}$$

The variable R is the number of pairs that would lead to the correct inference, and W is the number of pairs that would lead to the incorrect inference, given a set of recognized and novel items. Goldstein and Gigerenzer (2002) suggested

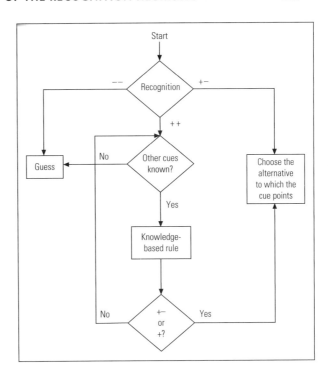

Figure 15-2. A flow diagram of knowledge heuristics that use the recognition heuristic in the first step. Typically, these algorithms include "take-the-best," "take-the-last," and "minimalist." The discrimination rule for these knowledge heuristics specifies that the judge choose the object with a "+" cue value when it is paired with an object whose cue value is "−" or "?". (From "Reasoning the Fast and Frugal Way: Models of Bounded Rationality," by G. Gigerenzer and D. G. Goldstein, 1996, *Psychological Review, 103*, p. 653. Copyright 1996 by the American Psychological Association. Adapted with permission.)

that this validity corresponds to Brunswik's (1955) *ecological validity*, in which the ecological cue validity is the true relative frequency of any object, p, having a larger value on the target variable than any other object, q, in a reference class in which p has a positive cue value on the particular cue and q does not (Gigerenzer et al., 1991). Typically, the ecological cue validity should be defined independently of any particular person (see Goldstein & Gigerenzer, 1999, note 1). Goldstein and Gigerenzer (2002) argued that recognition validity is different from other ecological validities in that the relationship between the target variable and the cue is mediated by the structure of the environment. A second difference that I will return to is that recognition validity is not defined independently of a person's psychological or memorial processes.

For the set in which neither object will be recognized, the judge must guess (see Figure 15-2). This is expected to happen for $[(N - n) \times (N - n - 1)]/[N(N - 1)]$ proportion of the pair with an expected accuracy of ½. Finally, a

knowledge-based rule can be used for the remaining pairs in which both items are recognized $[n(n - 1)]/[N(N - 1)]$ proportion of the time. This collapses across the subset of objects that the knowledge heuristic does and does not discriminate among (see Goldstein & Gigerenzer, 1999, note 1). According to Figure 15-2, the knowledge heuristic discriminates between objects when one has a positive cue and the other does not; otherwise, it does not discriminate, and judges must guess. The expected accuracy for the pairs of items sent to the knowledge heuristic reflects this concept. It is the probability of a correct inference given that both items are recognized, β. Only in the limit when the knowledge heuristic has perfect discrimination is β the cue validity as defined in Equation 15-1. In all other cases, β is a weighted average between the cue validity and ½ in which the weights are determined by the discrimination rate of the knowledge heuristic.[5]

Summing the proportion of correct inferences for the recognition heuristic, guessing, and the knowledge heuristic produces the expected proportion of correct inferences, *P*, for the given reference class,

$$P = \frac{2n(N-n)}{N(N-1)}\alpha$$
$$+ \frac{(N-n)(N-n-1)}{N(N-1)} \cdot \frac{1}{2} + \frac{n(n-1)}{N(N-1)}\beta. \quad (15\text{-}2)$$

Using Equation 15-2, *P* can be plotted as a function of *n*, the number of items a judge has recognized. Setting *N* = 100 and α = .8, the curves in Figure 15-3 show this for four different levels of β. Goldstein and Gigerenzer (1999) illustrated the predictions with a story about three brothers with different levels of experience who take this inferential test. The youngest brother, who had no experience, recognized none of the objects (*n* = 0), had to guess on all the inferences, and was correct 50% of the time (see the dot on the left side of Figure 15-3). The middle brother had some experience and recognized half of the objects (*n* = 50). He also had extra cue knowledge so that when he recognized both cities, he was correct 60% of the time

(β = .6). In this case, using Equation 15-2, the middle brother would score 68% on the test (see the middle dot in Figure 15-3). The oldest brother had extensive experience with the reference class (*n* = 100). Consequently, he could not use recognition and instead relied on cue knowledge. His cue knowledge was similar to that of the middle brother, so he would be correct 60% of the time and his score of 60% on his test reflected this (see the rightmost dot in Figure 15-3). Hence, the scores of the middle and oldest brothers exhibit the less-is-more effect: The middle brother benefited from partial ignorance and scored 8% better than the more knowledgeable brother. In general, to find the less-is-more effect, the recognition validity must be greater than the accuracy of the knowledge heuristics (α > β); otherwise, the maximal performance will always be at *n* = *N* (see Goldstein & Gigerenzer, 2002).

To use recognition as a binary predictor, whether in a single- or multiple-variable heuristic, judges must first generate a recognition decision. These decisions do not map directly

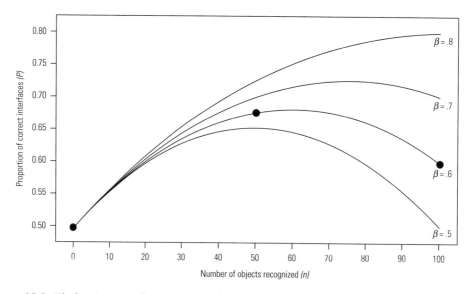

Figure 15-3. The less-is-more effect. The graph displays the proportion of correct inferences in solid lines when α = .8 at four levels of β. When the knowledge validity β is .5, .6, or .7, a less-is-more effect occurs. The performance of the three brothers is indicated by the three points on the curve for β = .6. (From "Models of Ecological Rationality: The Recognition Heuristic," by D. G. Goldstein and G. Gigerenzer, 2002, *Psychological Review, 109*, p. 79. Copyright 2002 by the American Psychological Association. Adapted with permission.)

onto past experience. Instead, they depend on judges' sensitivity to the difference between the familiarity of experienced versus novel items and their goals at the time of making their inference. Referring to Figure 15-1, these dependencies imply that memorial explanations other than an imperfect assessment of all possible mediators may explain why the surrogate correlation is not perfect. Integrating the recognition heuristic with signal detection theory reveals one possible explanation for the imperfect surrogate correlation and can explain how recognition memory processes affect inferential performance.

INTEGRATING THE RECOGNITION HEURISTIC AND SIGNAL DETECTION THEORY

The recognition heuristic makes an implicit assumption that recognition decisions perfectly reflect the split between experienced and novel items. Goldstein and Gigerenzer (2002) stated "Thus, with the term recognition, we divide the world into the novel and the previously experienced" (p. 77). However, judges are unlikely to both recognize all experienced objects and not recognize (reject) all novel objects.

In fact, the research Goldstein and Gigerenzer (1999, 2002) cited as evidence for the remarkable ability and accuracy of recognition memory also directly acknowledges that recognition is fallible (see Craik & McDowd, 1987; Jacoby, Woloshyn, & Kelley, 1989; Shepard, 1967; Standing, 1973). For example, Craik and McDowd and Jacoby et al. reported nonzero miss and false alarm rates for their respective recognition experiments. Shepard found that when respondents learned words and were later tested in his forced-choice paradigm on what they had learned, they responded correctly 88.4% of the time; with sentences, they were correct 89% of the time; and with pictures, they were correct 99.7% of the time.

Shepard (1967) showed that two classes of models might account for the observed data: (1) a signal detection framework where recognition is a function of a continuous construct and judges use an optimal criterion; and (2) a two-state threshold model where recognition is a function of a binary all-or-none process. Assuming no response bias, both models can account for the errors and the differences among stimuli as a function of the judges' sensitivity. Both models can be incorporated into the recognition heuristic.

Schooler and Hertwig (2005) have developed one possible high-threshold account with ACT–R. Global memory models, in comparison, embody the signal detection framework and have been successful in accounting for a range of different phenomena (Raaijmakers & Shiffrin, 2002). Examples include MINERVA-2 and MINERVA-DM (Dougherty, Gettys, & Ogden, 1999; Hintzman, 1988), REM (Shiffrin & Steyvers, 1997), SAM (Gillund & Shiffrin, 1984), and TODAM (Murdock, 1997). In general, these models presume that when a judge is shown a stimulus, a representation of the stimulus is formed in a memory probe. The probe is then compared with each item in memory, giving rise to a continuous level of activation or familiarity.[6] If the familiarity is above a criterion value, the judge decides the stimulus is old (he has recognized the item). If the familiarity is below the criterion, the judge decides the stimulus is new (he has not recognized the item).

From this perspective, the judge's familiarity with items from a reference class is correlated by means of the environmental mediators of the target variable (e.g., population size). During the inferential test, the judge must transform his familiarity into a binary decision in order to use recognition as a predictor variable. To make the model as general as possible, I do not use any specific global memory model but instead use the more basic Gaussian signal detection model. Furthermore, to keep as much of the recognition heuristic intact as possible, I assume that the use of memory is comparable to a detection task. Specifically, when judges are presented with two stimuli (e.g., San Antonio and San Diego) and want to make an inference about some target variable (e.g., city size) based on recognition, they first look at one stimulus (San Antonio), decide whether it is old or new, and then turn to the remaining stimulus and decide whether it is old or new.[7] Each experienced item can be either correctly identified as old (hit) or incorrectly identified as new (miss). If the item is novel, then it can be either incorrectly identified as old (false alarm) or correctly identified as new (correct rejection).

These distribution-free, detection-based assumptions elicit novel predictions. When judges do not make recognition mistakes, there are three possible pair types. The recognition heuristic operates on the (hit, correct rejection) pairs. The guessing component is used on the (correct rejection, correct rejection) pairs, and the knowledge-based rules are used on the (hit, hit) pairs. As the rate of mistakes increases, the number of possible pair types increases from 3 to 10, and the distribution of pairs among these pair types changes.[8] The first column of Table 15-1 illustrates the 10 different possible pair types.

The specific component—recognition heuristic, guessing, or knowledge heuristic—that handles each of the 10 pair types is identified in the second column. To calculate the proportion

Table 15-1. The 10 Possible Pair Types That Judges' Recognition Decisions Can Produce

Pairs	Heuristic	Proportion of Pairs	Expected Proportion Correct
Hit, correct rejection	Recognition	$\dfrac{2hn_e(1-f)(N-n_e)}{N(N-1)}$	A
Miss, false alarm	Recognition	$\dfrac{2(1-h)n_e f(N-n_e)}{N(N-1)}$	$1-A$
Hit, miss	Recognition	$\dfrac{2(h-h^2)n_e^2}{N(N-1)}$	½
False alarm, correct rejection	Recognition	$\dfrac{2(f-f^2)(N-n_e)^2}{N(N-1)}$	½
Correct rejection, correct rejection	Guess	$\dfrac{(1-f)(N-n_e)\left[(1-f)(N-n_e)-1\right]}{N(N-1)}$	½
Miss, miss	Guess	$\dfrac{(1-h)n_e\left[(1-h)n_e-1\right]}{N(N-1)}$	½
Miss, correct rejection	Guess	$\dfrac{2(1-h)n_e(1-f)(N-n_e)}{N(N-1)}$	½
Hit, hit	Knowledge	$\dfrac{hn_e(hn_e-1)}{N(N-1)}$	B
Hit, false alarm	Knowledge	$\dfrac{2hn_e f(N-n_e)}{N(N-1)}$	$zA+(1-z)\cdot½$
False alarm, false alarm	Knowledge	$\dfrac{f(N-n_e)\left[f(N-n_e)-1\right]}{N(N-1)}$	½

Note: The second column identifies which heuristic judges would use to arrive at an answer for each pair. The third column gives the proportion of pairs of each type for a given reference class with N objects, n_e objects experienced by a judge, and hit and false alarm rates h and f, respectively. The fourth column gives the expected accuracy of each pair type.

of pairs for each of the 10 pair types using the signal detection model, the number of objects experienced, n_e, will be used, where the subscript "e" indicates the change from number recognized to number experienced. This is because the framework now predicts the recognition of objects on the basis of experience. The variables h and f represent the hit and false alarm rates, respectively. To illustrate the calculations, consider the pairing when both items are hits. There are hn_e items that are expected to be a hit for the first item and, once one item is removed from this set, $hn_e - 1$ items are left for the second item.[9] The expected number of pairs in which both items are hits, therefore, is $hn_e(hn_e - 1)$. Dividing that expression by the total number of possible pairs, $N(N-1)/2$, produces the expected proportion of (hit, hit) pairs. The remaining expressions are found in a similar manner. The equations are shown in the third column of Table 15-1.

The expected accuracy associated with each pairing can also be derived. The accuracy of the recognition heuristic depends on which of the four pair types it is fed. However, the recognition validity, α, cannot be used; the cue validity must be independent of the judge's recognition ability. Consequently, I used the cue validity of the previously experienced and novel items, A. The value of A is the ecological validity of experience independent of any psychological or memorial process within the judge. It reflects the true environmental correlation between environmental mediators and the target variable (see Figure 15-1). Hypothetically, we could arrive at A if we could generate a list of German cities with more than 100,000 citizens that a typical judge might have encountered by reading the *Chicago Tribune*. More than likely, this list would not be a comprehensive list of cities from the reference class, and, according to past analyses, it would probably tend to include more of the larger cities (see Goldstein & Gigerenzer, 2002). Using this list, the number of pairs that would lead to a correct inference, R, and an incorrect inference, W, could be found. Like the cue validity of cues in the environment (e.g., whether a city has a soccer team or not), this cue validity is derived directly from the structure of the environment using Equation 15-1.

Of the four pairings that enter the recognition heuristic, only (hit, correct rejection) retains the expected accuracy of A. The second pairing, (false alarm, miss), has a different expected accuracy. If a judge accurately recognized both items, then this pair would also have gone into the recognition heuristic and retained A as the expected accuracy. However, now the novel item, false alarm, has been identified as recognized and the experienced item, miss, has been identified as not recognized, and the recognition heuristic would therefore pick the false alarm as the item with a higher target variable. Thus, referring to Equation 15-1, the W pairs used to calculate A would now lead to the correct inference, whereas the R pairs would lead to the incorrect inference. This results in an expected accuracy for (false alarm, miss) of $1 - A$.

The remaining two pairs, (hit, miss) and (false alarm, correct rejection), also have an expected accuracy different from A. Each of these two pairs comprises a correct and an incorrect detection. Consider first the (hit, miss) pair. A particular item is correctly recognized as old with a probability of h and is incorrectly identified as new with a probability $1 - h$. The recognition heuristic will produce the correct response for a (hit, miss) pairing only when the higher valued item is a hit and the lower valued item is a miss. This happens with a probability of $h(1 - h)$. The opposite can also happen. The higher valued item can be missed and the lower valued item can be correctly recognized, producing an incorrect inference. This particular pairing of a (hit, miss) also occurs with probability $(1 - h)h$. Thus, a (hit, miss) pairing produces a correct inference half of the time and an incorrect inference half of the time. Similar logic holds for the (false alarm, correct rejection) pair.

For the next three pairs (correct rejection, correct rejection), (correct rejection, miss), and (miss, miss), the guessing rule would be employed. For all three of these pair types, the judge is expected to be correct half of the time.

Judges would use a knowledge-based heuristic for the remaining pairs when both items in a pair were recognized (see bottom three rows of Table 15-1). Although the cue validity of the knowledge cues—such as whether a city has a soccer team—is defined independently of the recognition ability of a judge, the probability of a correct inference given that both items are recognized (β), is not. To derive the expected accuracy of these items, I instead use B, the probability of a correct inference given that both items are experienced. In this case, only the original pairing (hit, hit) would retain the expected accuracy of B. The items in the pair with two false alarms are actually novel, so this pair has the lowest accuracy, ½.

Interestingly, the remaining pair type, (hit, false alarm), can benefit indirectly from experience. It can have an expected accuracy as high as A or as low as ½. To see why, consider Table 15-2, which models a hypothetical judge's experience with 20 items ($a - t$), recognition of the same 20 items, and knowledge of five cues for 20 items. The objects are displayed in descending order in terms of rank on the basis of a hypothetical target variable. For example,

object a might be the city in a country with the largest population, and object t might be the city with the 20th largest population. The person has experienced 10 of the objects, as indicated by a "+" in the experience column. The "−" in the experience column indicates that the objects were novel. For these novel objects, the judge also has no binary cue knowledge. This is indicated by a "?" in the cue columns. The recognition column identifies the classification of the person's recognition decision at the time of the inferential test. As Table 15-2 shows, there are two types of (hit, false alarm) pairs. Pair (a, i) is one. For this pair, the knowledge heuristic would infer item a as the larger item and be correct on the basis of the discrimination rule detailed in Figure 15-2, in which judges choose the positive cue over negative and unknown cue values. In fact, the hit item will always be chosen in a pair of this type whenever at least one positive cue value is associated with it in memory. Table 15-2

Table 15-2. A Hypothetical Person's Experience and Recognition of a Reference Class of 20 Objects ($a - t$) and Level of Knowledge of Five Knowledge Cues

Rank	Object	Experience	Recognition	Cue 1	2	3	4	5
1	a	+	Hit	+	−	−	+	−
2	b	+	Hit	−	−	−	−	−
3	c	+	Miss	−	+	+	−	−
4	d	−	CR	?	?	?	?	?
5	e	+	Hit	−	+	−	−	−
6	f	+	Hit	−	−	−	−	−
7	g	−	CR	?	?	?	?	?
8	h	+	Hit	−	−	−	−	−
9	i	−	FA	?	?	?	?	?
10	j	+	Miss	−	−	+	−	−
11	k	+	Hit	−	+	−	−	−
12	l	−	CR	?	?	?	?	?
13	m	−	CR	?	?	?	?	?
14	n	+	Miss	−	−	−	+	−
15	o	+	Hit	−	−	−	−	−
16	p	−	CR	?	?	?	?	?
17	q	−	FA	?	?	?	?	?
18	r	−	CR	?	?	?	?	?
19	s	−	CR	?	?	?	?	?
20	t	−	FA	?	?	?	?	?

Note: The objects are ordered according to a hypothetical target variable. A "+" or "−" in the experience column indicates whether the object is experienced or novel, respectively. The Recognition column identifies the recognition decision at the time of the inferential test. CR, correction recognition; FA, false alarm. A "+," "−," or "?" in the cue columns indicates a positive, negative, or unknown cue value, respectively.

reveals that these (hit, false alarm) pairs are sampled from pairs that the experience cue would have differentiated among (i.e., one item has a "+" and the other a "−" in the experience column) and that the hit choices are consistent with the choices that the experience cue would have led to. As a result, this subset has an expected accuracy of A. However, some of the hit items (such as b and f) have no positive cue values. This can occur because of the structure of the environment or the limited cue knowledge of the judge. Either way, the discrimination rule (i.e., when both objects lack a positive cue value, guess) dictates that the judge would have to guess on this subset of (hit, false alarm) pairs. Thus, the expected accuracy for the (hit, false alarm) pair is a weighted average between A and ½, with the weight determined by z, the proportion of experienced items with at least one positive cue value.

To find the expected proportion of correct inferences for each pair type, multiply the expected proportion of pairs (column 3 of Table 15-1) by the accuracy rate (column 4 of Table 15-1). Table 15-3 provides a summary of the variables introduced for this derivation. To produce more precise predictions, I assume that novel and experienced stimuli give rise to a familiarity, t, that is normally distributed. For scaling purposes, the novel stimuli have a mean of 0, and experienced stimuli have a mean of d'. The parameter d' indexes the level of sensitivity to the difference between the familiarity of experienced versus novel items. As d' increases, judges become more sensitive to the difference between the two types of stimuli. Shepard's (1967) set of recognition experiments—using pictures, statements, and words—provides a convenient example of how sensitivity can vary according to item type. Interesting or important items can also induce higher levels of sensitivity within a domain (see, e.g., Gronlund, Ohrt, Dougherty, Perry, & Manning, 1998). Additionally, sensitivity can vary among domains on the basis of meaningfulness, similarity, and pleasantness of the objects, among other things (see also Glanzer & Adams, 1985). Finally, sensitivity can vary among people for a given domain. For example, repetitions and study time can improve

Table 15-3. Parameters and Variables Used for the Signal Detection Analysis

Variable	Description
N	Number of objects in a specified reference class
n	Number of objects recognized in the reference class
α	Validity of recognition in the reference class
β	Probability of a correct inference in the reference class, given that both items have been recognized
n_e	Number of objects experienced in the reference class
A	Ecological validity of experience in the reference class
B	Probability of a correct inference in the reference class given that both items have been experienced
h	Hit rate
m	Miss rate
f	False alarm rate
c	Correct rejection rate
t	Familiarity of an item
d'	Sensitivity to the difference between the familiarity of experienced and that of novel items

discrimination. Consider two geography students, one diligent and one lackluster. The diligent student will study her list of cities more frequently and for longer periods of time, becoming more sensitive to differences between experienced and novel items, whereas the lackluster student will study the same list once and again only briefly the morning before the exam and would thus be less sensitive.

I also make a simplifying assumption that both distributions of familiarity have an equal variance, σ^2, set at 1.[10] At test, judges have a criterion, k, set at one point along the possible values that the familiarity could take. The rule for deciding whether a given item is old or new can now be formally stated as: Respond "old" if and only if $t > k$; if not, respond "new."

With the distributions specified, the probability of a hit for a given value of d' and k can be calculated as $h = 1 - \Phi(k - d')$, where the function $\Phi(\bullet)$ represents the standardized normal cumulative distribution function. The miss rate, m, is $m = (1 - h)$. The false alarm rate is $f = 1 - \Phi(k)$, and the correct rejection rate is $c = 1 - f$. The expected proportion of each type of pairings can now be calculated given a value for k and d'.

Besides changing the applicability of the recognition heuristic, experience can also change the recognition response process.[11] Prior experience with the reference class increases the number of items the judge has experienced (n_e) prior to the test, thus making it a priori more likely during a representative test that the judge will be shown a previously experienced item. Within signal detection theory, a judge should capitalize on this by picking whichever decision (old or new) has the greater likelihood given his familiarity $p(\text{old} \mid \text{familiarity})$ or $p(\text{new} \mid \text{familiarity})$ and adjust his response criterion according to his level of prior experience. Thus, a judge with little to no experience would be fairly conservative in deciding whether he recognizes an item, but as his experience increased, his criterion would become more liberal.

To see this formally, the comparison can be stated in terms of the posterior odds,

$$\Omega = \frac{p(\text{old} \mid \text{familiarity})}{p(\text{new} \mid \text{familiarity})}$$
$$= \frac{p(\text{familiarity} \mid \text{old})}{p(\text{familiarity} \mid \text{new})} \frac{p(\text{old})}{p(\text{new})}, \quad (15\text{-}3)$$

where the first component on the far right side is the likelihood ratio, $p(\text{familiarity} \mid \text{old})/p(\text{familiarity} \mid \text{new})$, and the second component is the prior odds, $p(\text{old})/p(\text{new})$. The likelihood ratio of the data is found using the distributions specified for the experienced and novel items. The representative sampling of the stimuli in the inferential test—where all objects are equally likely to occur in a pair (see Gigerenzer et al., 1991)—specifies the prior odds for the judge. For example, if an observer has experienced only 40 of 100 items in a reference class, the prior odds of an old item's appearing on the inferential test are .4/.6. More generally,

$$\frac{p(\text{old})}{p(\text{new})} = \frac{n_e}{N - n_e}.^{11} \quad (15\text{-}4)$$

To maximize the probability of a correct detection, a judge's decision rule for recognition must be

$$\begin{cases} \text{If } \Omega \geq 1 \text{ or } n_e = N, \text{then select old.} \\ \text{If } \Omega < 1 \text{ or } n_e = 0, \text{then select new.} \end{cases}$$

Substituting Equation 15-4 into Equation 15-3 and taking the logarithm, the response can be reformulated in terms of a likelihood ratio observer who adopts a criterion with

$$k = -\log\left(\frac{n_e}{N - n_e}\right),$$

with the constraint that $0 < n_e < N$. The same decision rule can now be stated in terms of the likelihood ratio

$$\begin{cases} \text{If } R(\text{old:new}) \geq k \text{ or } n_e = N, \text{then select old.} \\ \text{If } R(\text{old:new}) < k \text{ or } n_e = 0, \text{then select new.} \end{cases}$$

The likelihood-ratio observer is consistent with recent empirical evidence from recognition experiments (see Glanzer, Adams, Iverson, & Kim, 1993; Shiffrin & Steyvers, 1997). This strategy can also be understood as adaptive. It maximizes the probability of correctly detecting whether an item is old or new and minimizes the interference that imperfect recognition memory would have on the recognition heuristic. To illustrate this, Figure 15-4 shows that the recognition error rate follows an inverted U centered around $n_e = 50$ for three different levels of d'.

An alternative strategy is to keep the criterion fixed. The dashed lines in Figure 15-4 show the effects this strategy would have on the error rate for three levels of a centered criterion (−1, 0, and 1) holding d' constant at 0.5.[12] The error rate for these strategies is a linear function of experience whose slope depends on how liberal the judge is in making a positive recognition decision. These error rates reveal that this decision rule is maladaptive and would lead to more recognition errors across all levels of experience, resulting in decreased inferential accuracy. A third class of criterion strategies, not shown in Figure 15-4, would be that of a respondent who grows more conservative with experience. This in effect would

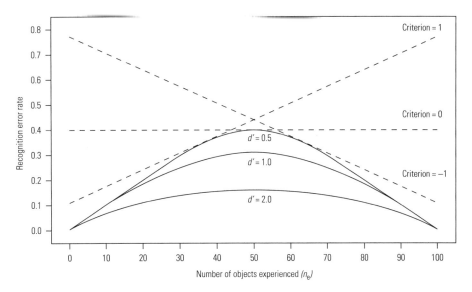

Figure 15-4. Hypothetical error rates for judges who adopt two different response strategies. The first strategy is to adjust the response criterion according to the level of experience, a Bayesian observer. The inverse U curves in the figure illustrate this strategy. At low levels of experience, judges are most conservative in deciding that they recognize an object; they grow more liberal with experience. This strategy minimizes the number of recognition errors. With increases in d', the error rate decreases. The second strategy is to fix the response criterion. The dashed lines show the predicted error rate for three different levels of criteria when $d' = 0.5$. The criterion values shown are centered so that a criterion of 0 indicates a criterion exactly between the two distributions. All possible fixed criterion strategies can be derived from the figure using the tangent of the inverted U of a given Bayesian observer. These fixed-criterion judges commit a large number of errors regardless of experience.

minimize the probability of a correct detection and would produce an upright U in Figure 15-4 (not shown). This does not seem very adaptive or plausible given the stated goal of inferential accuracy in the task.[13] Furthermore, the strategy would lead to odd predictions regarding the procedures outlined in Figure 15-2. For example, a complete expert $(n_e = N)$ would completely neglect his knowledge and guess on 100% of the pairs. Taken together, this implies that the ecologically based response rule consistent with a Bayesian observer would allow a judge to fully exploit the ecological correlation in the environment and be ecologically rational (Gigerenzer, 2001).

THE IMPACT OF RECOGNITION SENSITIVITY ON INFERENTIAL ACCURACY

With this level of specification, the impact of d' on the judge's inferential accuracy can be assessed. Besides an imperfect assessment of all possible mediators that control a judge's experience in the environment, the model attributes sensitivity as a second psychological source for the imperfect surrogate correlation. To demonstrate this, I calculated the average predicted recognition validity, α, from the model using the four pairs that the judge would answer using the recognition heuristic (see Table 15-1). Specifically, I set $N = 100$ and calculated α for each level of n_e as a function of d' for four different levels of A (.6, .7, .8, and .9) when there was a nonzero probability of employing the recognition heuristic. Figure 15-5 shows the average α averaged across n_e. Lower levels of sensitivity can bring about substantial decrements to the accuracy of recognition-based inferences. For example, a d' with a value of 0.5 decreases an experience validity from $A = .8$ to a recognition validity of $\alpha = .59$; a d' of 1.0 decreases it to $\alpha = .63$; and a d' of 2.0 decreases it to $\alpha = .70$.

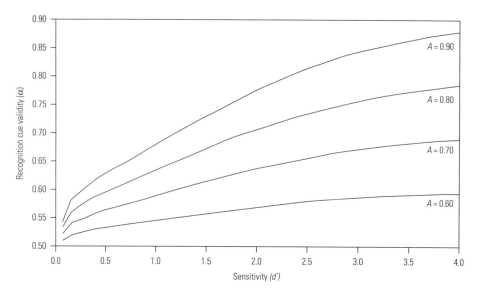

Figure 15-5. The average α as a function of d' averaged across all levels of experience for four different levels of A (.6, .7, .8, and .9). Lower levels of sensitivity can bring about substantial decrements to the accuracy of their inferences.

With its impact on both the recognition and knowledge heuristics, the recognition process also influences the less-is-more effect. With $N = 100$ and $A = .8$, the panels in Figure 15-6 plot the predicted proportion of correct inferences as a function of experience, n_e, when judges take the same inferential test described earlier. Three values of d' (0.5, 1.0, and 2.0) are varied across the columns, and three values of z (1/3, 2/3, or 1) are represented in the rows. Within each panel, there are four different levels of B, which is the probability of a correct inference when both items are experienced. Recall that judges are making recognition decisions to maximize the probability of a correct detection; therefore, the criterion, k, changes with each level of experience. As a result of this response rule, the oldest and youngest brothers for all levels of d' and z have the same scores as their counterparts in Figure 15-3. The bottom two rows of Figure 15-6 illustrate that decreasing sensitivity (from right to left) can mitigate the less-is-more effect and give way to the less counterintuitive more-is-more effect. The less-is-more effect is not existent for $B = .7$ for all six panels in the bottom two rows. Even for $B = .6$, where the less-is-more effect tends to persist, the

magnitude of the effect is diminished. Consider, for example, the middle brother when $d' = 2.0$ and $z = 2/3$. He is predicted to score 63%, a mere three-point advantage over his more experienced brother. Recall that, originally, partial ignorance gave the middle brother an eight-point advantage.

The signal detection model also reveals that the influence of sensitivity depends on the distribution of positive cue values across items. The top row of Figure 15-6 shows that when $z = 1$, the less-is-more effect is robust against lower levels of sensitivity. However, even here the range of experience for which the less-is-more effect is predicted to occur is reduced. In the figure, when $d' = 2.0$, the middle brother outscores his brother with an expected score of 64%. When $d' = 0.5$, he would get 58% correct, and when $d' = 1.0$ he would get 60% correct. In comparison, a person who has experienced $n_e = 75$ of the objects is predicted to score 66%, 65%, and 65% correct for d' values of 0.5, 1.0, and 2.0, respectively.

Why is the less-is-more effect predicted regardless of sensitivity and why does the range of experience where it is predicted become restricted when $z = 1$? The answer is that judges

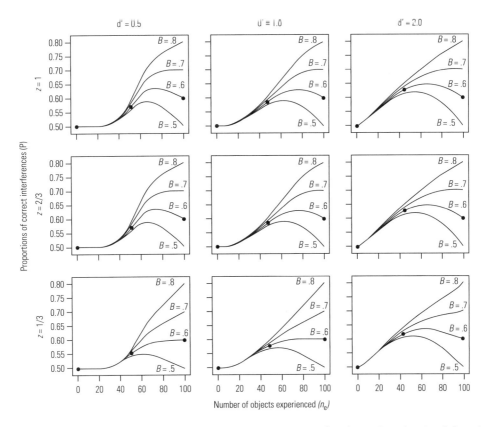

Figure 15-6. A reanalysis of the less-is-more effect assuming an equal-variance Gaussian signal detection model of the recognition process. The plots show different levels of sensitivity, d' and the proportion of experienced items with at least one positive cue, z. Three values of d' are varied across the columns and three values of z are varied up the rows. Within each panel, there are four different levels of B. Judges are making recognition decisions so as to maximize the probability of a correct detection; therefore, the criterion, k, changes with each level of experience. The bottom two rows of the figure illustrate that decreasing sensitivity (from right to left) can mitigate the less-is-more effect and give way to the less counterintuitive more-is-more effect. In the top row, the knowledge heuristics benefit indirectly from the judges' false alarms and help to maintain the less-is-more effect.

with intermediate levels of experience ($50 < n_e < 100$) have more false alarms and consequently more (hit, false alarm) pairs. When $z = 1$, the accuracy for these pairs is A, which protects judges from their mistaken recognition decisions. However, z and B are correlated. As the proportion of items with positive cue knowledge, z, decreases, the probability of a correct inference when both items are experienced, B, will also decrease. This is because the discrimination rule for the knowledge heuristic specifies that the judge guess when neither item has a positive cue value. Consequently, the very thing

that can make the less-is-more effect more probable—less cue knowledge and therefore lower knowledge heuristic accuracy—also counteracts it to make it more susceptible to a judge's recognition sensitivity.

DISCUSSION

When presented with a two-alternative forced choice task, judges who employ the recognition heuristic first look at one item in a pair, decide whether they recognize it or not, and then look at the other item in the pair and decide whether they recognize it or not (Goldstein & Gigerenzer, 2002). If one item is recognized and the other is not, then judges can use the recognition heuristic. Integrating a signal detection model of recognition memory with the recognition heuristic is a first step in understanding how recognition memory contributes to the recognition heuristic. Moreover, the integrated model makes it possible to assess how experience in the world translates to recognition serving as an accurate inferential predictor. To do so, the implicit assumption that recognition perfectly reflects experience was relaxed. That is, when recognizing objects, people make false alarms and misses, and these errors impact the inferences people make. For example, a German professor using recognition to pick teams in the 2006 NCAA Division I basketball tournament might think that he recognizes Northwestern State—a fourteenth seed in the tournament—and pick it to win a game or two. Chances are, however, that this school, located in Natchitoches, Louisiana, has been mistaken for a school with a similar name located in Evanston, IL: Northwestern University.[14]

Expanding the analysis to an inferential test showed that as the error rate of recognition increased, the accuracy of the recognition heuristic fell. The errors also changed what tool or heuristic was used to answer the test questions. Furthermore, the ecologically rational goal for judges was shown to be one in which they adjusted their recognition response criteria according to their experience with the reference class. Finally, the less-is-more effect was shown to depend on judges' sensitivity to the difference between the familiarity of experienced versus novel items as well as the distribution of cue knowledge.

In the discussion that follows, I summarize how the signal detection framework makes it possible to assess how recognition sensitivity and response rules give rise to these errors and interact with the recognition heuristic to produce the observed inferential performance of the judge. I also discuss how the model can be used as a bridge between the recognition heuristic and other theories of recognition and how it can be informative for evaluating other knowledge heuristics. Finally, I will return to Simon's (1956) principle of bounded rationality and address

how the signal detection framework can move the recognition heuristic closer to this principle.

Recognition sensitivity and response rules. From the perspective of theories of recognition memory, when there is an ecological correlation in the environment, the covert familiarity with objects from the environment can be correlated with the target variable of the inferential task. If judges want to exploit this correlation with the recognition heuristic, they have to transform their familiarity into a binary recognition decision (see Slegers, Brake, & Doherty, 2000, for an alternative framework to transform continuous knowledge cues into binary cues). The response rule that judges use to make this transformation depends on their goals and expectations during the task.

The ecologically rational goal in fast-and-frugal heuristics is "to exploit the structure of the information in the natural environment" (Goldstein & Gigerenzer, 2002, p. 76). Accordingly, to fully exploit the environmental correlation, judges need to adjust their criteria according to their level of experience with the reference class: When they have little to no experience, judges should be the most conservative in recognizing objects; as their experience increases, they should become more liberal. This Bayesian-observer response strategy (see Wickens, 2002) minimizes the error rate and allows judges to fully exploit the association between their familiarity and the inference's target variable (e.g., city population).

Given this response rule, a judge's sensitivity to the difference between experienced and novel items also influences his ability to exploit this correlation. With perfect sensitivity, the recognition validity reflects the validity of the judge's experience, and with lower sensitivity, the recognition validity systematically decreases away from the validity of experience (A). As a result of this systematic change in the recognition validity, the original condition of the less-is-more effect still holds, $\alpha > \beta$ (Goldstein & Gigerenzer, 2002). Instead of changing this condition, the signal detection model parses this single condition into conditions related to structures of the environment and conditions related to the cognitive processes of judges. In the environment, the accuracy of experience has to be greater than the accuracy achievable when comparing objects that have both been experienced, $A > B$. At the same time, a judge's sensitivity needs to be high enough that recognition based on experience is still more accurate than the knowledge heuristics. For example, in this model, when $A \geq .8$ and $B \leq .6$, the less-is-more effect tends to persist when $d' > 1$, regardless of the distribution of positive cue knowledge, z. A final condition depends on both the environment and the judge: The more positive cue knowledge distributed among the objects in a reference class, the more robust the less-is-more effect against a judge's recognition errors. Recall, this can occur because of the distribution of positive cue values in the environment or because of the lack of cue knowledge on the part of the judge. In this model, values of z greater than approximately .8 tend to counteract lower values of sensitivity and maintain the less-is-more effect.

Admittedly, these are less precise criteria than the original derivation of $\alpha > \beta$. More precise conditions depend on the distributional assumptions of the models. However, disentangling the psychological and environmental contributions to the less-is-more effect continues to move questions about the recognition heuristic from empirical *what* questions (e.g., "What happens when the recognition heuristic … ?") toward more theoretically framed *why* questions (e.g., "Why can recognition make accurate inferences?"). See Wallsten (1996) and Wallsten, Erev, and Budescu (2000) for a similar argument about investigating the cognitive processes involved in confidence judgments.

A bridge to theories of recognition memory. The framework can also serve as a bridge to larger and more expanded theories of recognition memory, like global memory models (Raaijmakers & Shiffrin, 2002). The REM global memory model (Shiffrin & Steyvers, 1997) has the most features in common with the signal detection framework that I have developed in this article. According to REM, an error-prone image or vector of feature values is stored in memory after an item has been studied. At retrieval, a probe is generated containing the features of the to-be-recognized test item, and this probe is matched with all images stored in

episodic memory to produce a determination of the likelihood that the test item has been previously learned. In a manner similar to how this article describes the response strategy of ecologically rational judges, REM then calculates the posterior odds that the test item is old and makes a decision on the basis of this estimate, just like the response strategy of ecologically rational judges using the recognition heuristic.

Besides offering a competing recognition model for Schooler and Hertwig's (2005) ACT–R model of the recognition heuristic, an REM implementation of the recognition heuristic has potential benefits for both the fast-and-frugal heuristics as well as REM. Although respondents can move the criterion to other values, the REM framework usually deals only with a default criterion set at equal odds (Shiffrin & Steyvers, 1997). Extending REM to encompass the ecological framework provides a natural prediction that judges adjust their criterion according to their prior experience with a reference class. In turn, REM can bring a more precise understanding to how judges learn sequentially about objects in the environment, develop a familiarity with items via encoding processes, and subsequently produce an estimate of an item's familiarity via retrieval processes.

CONCLUSION

Using signal detection theory, this article has modeled judges' recognition of objects when they use the recognition heuristic to make an inference about the objects. The model shows that recognition ability plays a crucial role in the performance of the recognition heuristic and the subsequent heuristics that use it. This is an important extension, because the recognition heuristic specifically, and fast-and-frugal heuristics in general, are supposed to be constructed according to Simon's principle of bounded rationality, which states: "To describe, predict, and explain the behavior of a system of bounded rationality we must both construct a theory of the system's processes and describe the environments to which it is adapting" (Simon, 1990, p. 6). This principle was developed in response to theories of economics being independent of the actor and solely a function of the environment. That is, theories such as expected utility assume that people make choices to maximize their own utility in a given environment, but ignore the cognitive abilities of the actor. The development of the recognition heuristic to date puts a great deal of emphasis on the characteristics of the environment that make it adaptive. Accounting for the recognition process within the heuristic better heeds the cognitive abilities of judges and moves the model closer to the principle of bounded rationality.

NOTES

1. Spearman correlations are reported for continuity. A more appropriate and meaningful measure of association, given the structure of the data, may be Kendall's τ (see Gonzalez & Nelson, 1996). According to Kendall's τ, the recognition correlation is .43, the ecological correlation is .63, and the surrogate correlation is .53.

2. Other integration algorithms do not capitalize on the recognition heuristic per se but can use recognition as a cue within their frameworks. See Gigerenzer and Goldstein (1996) for more details.

3. An alternative sampling method would be proportional sampling, in which stimuli are sampled from a reference class on the basis of their relative frequency of occurrence in the environment (Dhami et al., 2004).

4. A necessary assumption for these calculations is that each object in the reference class has a unique value on a target variable.

5. The discrimination rate of a heuristic is the relative frequency with which the heuristic discriminates between any two objects from the reference class; it is directly related to the discrimination rate of a cue (see Gigerenzer & Goldstein, 1996).

6. This activation level can go under the guise of many labels, such as familiarity, strength, confidence, and activation.

7. An alternative use of memory would be consistent with a two-alternative forced-choice task (see Wickens, 2002) in which the inference problem involves determining which of two stimuli (San Antonio or San Diego) is more familiar. However, under these forced choice assumptions, the recognition heuristic, along with the entire flow of processes shown in Figure 15-1, breaks down. This is because familiarity, as a continuous predictor, would always discriminate between the two alternatives, and a judge would never guess or resort to a knowledge heuristic. As a result, a judge's expected accuracy would only be a function of the correlation between familiarity and the target variable, and the less-is-more effect would never be predicted (see Dougherty, Franco-Watkins, & Thomas, 2008, for such an implementation).

8. More than 10 are possible if more than one distribution characterizes the familiarity of experienced objects.

9. An alternative and perhaps more appropriate way to make these derivations is in terms of relative experience, n/N. To be consistent with past work however, I will continue to make derivations in terms of absolute experience, n.

10. Memory researchers typically find that the distributions tend to have unequal variances (see Nelson, 2003; Ratcliff, Gronlund, & Sheu, 1992). This has no substantial effect on the conclusions reached here.

11. In environments in which each item is not equally likely to occur (e.g., in a study using proportional sampling; see note 3), this expression would change to reflect the nonuniform nature of the distribution. Regardless, the general behavior of the response criterion developed here would still remain; that is, with increasing experience, a judge would adjust the response criterion to be more liberal in recognizing items. The adjustment of the criterion, however, would not move in equal intervals and would depend on the distribution of objects in the particular environment.

12. The criterion values are centered so that a criterion of 0 lies exactly between the two distributions.

13. Other goals are entirely possible and can give rise to different predictions. For instance, more conservative responding could go hand in hand with more experience if judges were increasingly punished for false alarms. Another instance that can lead to conservative responding occurs when the response criterion is set fixed but relative to the signal distribution, and the signal distribution shifts up in familiarity (see Hirshman, 1995).

14. Unfortunately for this article and this author, the German professor's error was a benefit. Northwestern State upset the third-seeded University of Iowa in their first-round game of the 2006 tournament.

Introduction to Chapter 16

The Relative Success of Recognition-Based Inference in Multichoice Decisions

The recognition heuristic turns ignorance into an asset. If familiar with all the objects in an environment, one cannot exploit recognition's predictive power. But if there are some objects that one has not heard of, this partial ignorance can be highly informative. As analyzed in Chapter 3, reliance on the recognition heuristic can lead to a counterintuitive phenomenon. Under certain circumstances, people who recognize many objects can end up making less accurate inferences than people who recognize fewer objects (see also Pachur, 2010). Less can be more. The recognition heuristic has often been studied using almanac questions such as which of two companies has a higher revenue or which of two billionaires has a larger fortune. Almanac questions usually consist of two objects, one of which is correct. The world, however, does not always present itself in terms of two options. When employees have to pick a 401(k) retirement plan, for instance, they often face many options. Does the less-is-more effect also hold in choices involving more objects? Rachel McCloy, Philip Beaman, and Philip Smith extend the less-is-more analyses to choices between three and more objects and find that the size of the effect was even larger than when only two objects were involved. Moreover, they show analytically that with more than two objects, the framing of the question impacts the magnitude of the less-is-more effect. For instance, for the question "Which of the persons is richest?" the less-is-more effect is more pronounced than for the question "Which of the persons is poorest?" In a wealth judgment task, Frosch, Beaman, and McCloy (2007) found evidence for the predicted framing effect when participants had to choose among four of the richest individuals in the UK (see also McCloy, Beaman, Frosch, & Goddard, 2010). The work by McCloy, Beaman, and Smith thus shows once again the importance of analytical investigations for understanding empirical results, which would otherwise only be explained *post hoc.*

CHAPTER 16

The Relative Success of Recognition-Based Inference in Multichoice Decisions

Rachel McCloy, C. Philip Beaman, and Philip T. Smith

Abstract: The utility of an "ecologically rational" recognition-based decision rule in multichoice decision problems is analyzed, varying the type of judgment required (greater or lesser). The maximum size and range of a counterintuitive advantage associated with recognition-based judgment (the "less-is-more effect") are identified for a range of cue validity values. Greater ranges of the less-is-more effect occur when participants are asked which is the greatest of m choices ($m > 2$) than when asked which is the least. Less-is-more effects also have greater range for larger values of m. This implies that the classic two-alternative forced-choice task, as studied by Goldstein and Gigerenzer (2002), may not be the most appropriate test case for less-is-more effects.

Simply stated, the recognition heuristic provides the following rule of thumb: "If one of two objects is recognized and the other is not, then infer that the recognized object has the higher value" (Goldstein & Gigerenzer, 1999, p. 41). For example, an individual may be asked to judge which of two cities has the larger population. If they recognize only one of the cities, they can use the recognition heuristic to choose the recognized city. A counterintuitive finding of great interest is the "less-is-more effect" whereby the judgments of participants who recognize only one of the cities are more accurate than those of participants who recognize both cities (Goldstein & Gigerenzer, 1999, 2002). The reason for this is the positive correlation between the likelihood of recognizing the city and the size

of the city. In this task, recognition works because the probability of recognition is influenced by a mediator variable that itself reflects the "real" but inaccessible criterion. The simple recognition heuristic makes use of this information, latent in the structure of the environment, to inform judgments on the city size task—to the extent that the heuristic can outperform judgments based on city knowledge.

As a practical example, a mediating variable for magnitude-related choices, such as the cities task, might be the number of times the city has appeared in newspaper reports. This correlates with city size and influences the probability that the city name is recognized. Larger cities are more likely to be encountered (e.g., mentioned in a newspaper) and are more likely to be recognized. Smaller cities may either not have been encountered or may have been forgotten in the time since they were last encountered. Recognition, therefore, provides a cue to size. Ironically, more knowledgeable participants who recognize both cities cannot make use of this cue and must rely on other, possibly less reliable, knowledge to inform their judgments. These individuals perform poorly when, in two-alternative forced-choice (2-AFC) decisions, *recognition validity* (the extent to which a correct choice can be made by recognition alone) exceeds *knowledge validity* (the probability of making the correct choice when both objects are recognized). This counterintuitive less-is-more effect has been reported in the literature (Goldstein & Gigerenzer, 1999, 2002; Reimer & Katsikopoulos, 2004; Snook & Cullen, 2006), although not all empirical studies have observed the effect (Pachur & Biele, 2007; Pohl, 2006; but see Frosch, Beaman, & McCloy, 2007).

A 2-AFC task is often used as a test-bed for magnitude judgment (or "which is best") studies such as these because it is considered representative of the set of decisions that involve selecting a subset of objects from a larger set (Goldstein & Gigerenzer, 1999, p. 41). However, ecologically rational heuristics rely for their success on the informational structure of the environment; and when the structure of information within the environment changes (e.g., as when the information given within the choice options varies), the relative usefulness of a simple heuristic also varies (cf. Hogarth & Karelia, 2006). The appearance of counterintuitive effects, such as less-is-more, can be tracked across different task demands; and this article develops equations that describe the behavior of an idealized individual, who consistently uses the recognition heuristic. These equations are applied to a wide range of experimental situations, enabling us to identify situations where less-is-more effects are most likely to occur.

To begin with, a situation where one is required to judge, from m alternatives, which item has the greater magnitude along some dimension (e.g., which city has the highest population, which sporting team has the greatest ability) is a more generally applicable version of the 2-AFC choice task. The general model for an m-AFC situation is as follows: Let N be the population of objects from which objects on a given trial are selected; let n be the number of objects out of the total population that a participant is able to recognize; then $p(n)$,

the probability of success on a given trial, is given by

$$p(n) = \Sigma_i \alpha_i b(i, m, n/N), \qquad (16\text{-}1)$$

where α_i is the probability of the participant making the correct decision if exactly i out of the m objects presented on a given trial are recognized, and $b(i, m, n/N)$ is the familiar binomial probability of recognizing exactly i out of the m objects presented on a given trial, when the probability of recognizing an individual object is n/N; i in the summation ranges from 0 to m. If the participant is to choose the greatest object, on a given trial the recognition heuristic operates as follows:

G1: Consider the set of recognized objects.
G2: If the set contains 1 object, select it.
G3: If this set contains no objects, guess among the non-recognized objects.
G4: If the set contains i objects, $1 < i \leq m$, use any available knowledge to choose between the recognized objects.

However, if, conversely, the participant is asked to choose the least object, then the recognition heuristic operates as follows:

L1: Consider the set of recognized objects.
L2: If the set contains $m - 1$ objects, choose the non-recognized object.
L3: If the set contains i objects, $0 \leq i < m - 1$, guess among the non-recognized objects.
L4: If the set contains all m objects, use any available knowledge to choose between them.

The two algorithms operate on similar principles. In both cases, choice is based on which objects are recognized, and both algorithms assume that additional knowledge is available only for recognized objects and employed only if recognition fails to produce an unambiguous choice. The two procedures differ in that, given the *greatest* question, the assumption is that the correct choice lies among the recognized objects; whereas when asked to choose the *least*, the assumption is that the answer lies among the non-recognized objects.

For the case of $m = 2$ (as studied by Goldstein & Gigerenzer, 2002), the greatest and the least tasks are equivalent. Making the binomial probabilities explicit, Equation 16-1 can be written as follows:

$$p(n) = \alpha_0[(N-n)(N-n-1)]/[(N(N-1)]$$
$$+ \alpha_1[2n(N-n)]/[N(N-1)]$$
$$+ \alpha_2[n(n-1)]/[N(N-1)], \qquad (16\text{-}2)$$

where α_0, the probability of making the correct decision when no objects are recognized, is chance ($\frac{1}{2}$); α_1, the probability of being correct when one object is recognized reflects recognition validity; and α_2, the probability of making the correct choice when both objects are recognized, reflects knowledge validity. A less-is-more effect is predicted by Equation 16-2 when the plot of $p(n)$ against n forms an inverted U—that is, $p(n)$ has a maximum in the range $0 < n < N$ (see Figure 16-1). This amounts to the condition that $p(n)$ is decreasing when $n = N$—that is, that $dp/dn < 0$ when $n = N$. Differentiating Equation 16-2 with respect to n, and setting $n = N$, gives

$$N(N-1)dp/dn = 2(\alpha_2 - \alpha_1)N + \frac{1}{2} - \alpha_2. \qquad (16\text{-}3)$$

For large N, we need consider only terms of order N on the right-hand side of this equation, so we can say that dp/dn will be negative when $\alpha_1 > \alpha_2$. In other words, using Goldstein and Gigerenzer's (2002) terminology, the potential for a less-is-more effect exists when recognition validity exceeds knowledge validity. Figure 16-1, redrawn from Goldstein and Gigerenzer (2002), shows the success rate $p(n)$ derived from Equation 16-2 when recognition validity, α_1, is held constant at .8 and knowledge validity, α_2, is varied. This figure shows many curves indicating superior performance for intermediate n (number of objects recognized) than for large n—that is, a less-is-more effect.

The next question to be addressed is how this effect fares when the nature of the question is varied. As previously intimated, for 2-AFC asking which of the two objects is smaller or worse (the least question) is equivalent to asking which of the two objects is larger or best (the greatest question) because identifying which object is the greatest of two choices effectively labels the other object as the least. Thus, the information required to make the choice, and the information within the environment, are

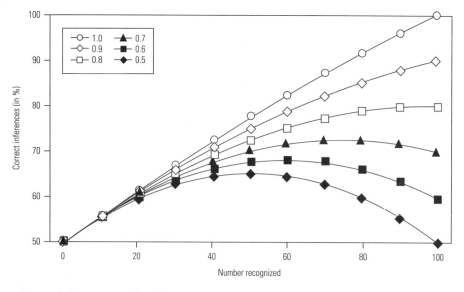

Figure 16-1. The less-is-more effect for two-alternative forced choice situations. *Note:* Recognition validity is set to 0.8, and knowledge validity varies between 0.5 and 1.0 as indicated by the legend.

identical for both questions, and the pattern shown in Figure 16-1 will also be shown in the least task. However, the distinction between *which-is-greatest* and *which-is-least* tasks becomes crucial in m-AFC problems where $m > 2$. Consider the 3-AFC task. For this task, there are four possible states of affairs: The individual might recognize three, two, one, or none of the objects. Writing out Equation 16-1 fully when $m = 3$ leads to the following:

$$p(n) = \alpha_0[(N-n)(N-n-1)(N-n-2)]/$$
$$[N(N-1)(N-2)]$$
$$+ \alpha_1[3n(N-n)(N-n-1)]/$$
$$[N(N-1)(N-2)]$$
$$+ \alpha_2[3n(n-1)(N-n)]/$$
$$[N(N-1)(N-2)]$$
$$+ \alpha_3[n(n-1)(n-2)]/$$
$$[N(N-1)(N-2)]. \quad (16\text{-}4)$$

Not all the parameters can be directly associated with recognition and knowledge validity when $m > 2$, and identifying less-is-more effects is accordingly more problematic. In particular, the association of α with either recognition or knowledge validity varies according to task. In both greatest and least tasks, α_3, the probability of making the correct choice among all recognized objects, is a measure of knowledge validity; but α_2 in the greatest task and α_1 in the least task depend partly on recognition and partly on knowledge. Our strategy is first to understand the properties of $m = 3$ performance, as characterized by Equation 16-4, and then consider plausible ranges of values for each of the parameters in the greatest and least tasks.

First, an obvious point: Because the less-is-more effect in Figure 16-1 derives from an inverted-U relationship between performance and recognition, there will inevitably be portions of any such performance-recognition curve where the curve goes up and performance increases above chance level. The definition of a less-is-more effect as given by Goldstein and Gigerenzer (2002) is any point at which imperfect recognition of the items produces superior performance to recognizing all the items. Under these circumstances, it is trivial to demonstrate a less-is-more effect somewhere on the graph simply by assuming a level of knowledge validity (for full recognition) little better than chance. To overcome this, we focus on areas of the graph where adding to the number recognized (additional learning) reduces rather than enhances the level of performance and henceforth reserve the term *less-is-more* for these situations. A situation where recognizing more items improves performance arguably represents a trend toward "more-is-more" even if, at any given point along the curve, performance associated with incomplete recognition is superior to that obtained with full recognition. By contrast, the identification of areas where broader knowledge (higher recognition rates) actively and systematically impairs performance maps out regions where paradoxically counterproductive, and actively harmful, effects of further learning are to be found (cf. Hogarth & Karelia, 2006).

Under our definition, less-is-more effects should be associated with materials that already give rise to fairly high levels of recognition. Low levels of recognition are associated with the upward-sloping portion of the performance-recognition curve, a situation in which additional numbers of items recognized improves performance. A less-is-more effect thus defined occurs when $p(n_1) > p(n_2)$ for some n_1, n_2, such that $0 < n_1 < n_2 < N$. This will be achieved either (a) if $p(n)$ is an inverted-U shape (as in Figure 16-1 and the upper portion of Figure 16-2) or (b) if $p(n)$ contains both a maximum and a minimum in the range $n = 0$ to N (the lower portion of Figure 16-2). Condition (a) can be approached by differentiating $p(n)$: It is straightforward to show that when $n = N$

$$N(N-1)(N-2)dp/dn = 3N^2(\alpha_3 - \alpha_2)$$
$$+ \text{terms of order N or less.} \quad (16\text{-}5)$$

Therefore, for large N, an inverted U will appear when $\alpha_2 > \alpha_3$. Condition (b) does not lend itself to simple analytic expressions; but $\alpha_2 < \alpha_3 < \alpha_1$, with α_1 quite large, often satisfies these conditions.

In order to delineate conditions where the use of the recognition heuristic might have real value, and additional learning be actively

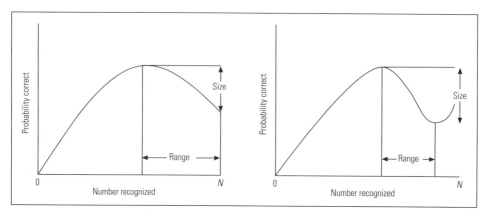

Figure 16-2. Diagram demonstrating the measurement of the less-is-more effect in terms of size and range where $p(n)$ is an inverted-U function (left-hand panel) or an s-shaped function (right-hand panel).

harmful, we set out to identify values of the parameters in Equation 16-4, where less-is-more effects are pronounced. The magnitude of less-is-more effects can be defined in two ways. The first is the *range of n* for which less-is-more effects prevail (i.e., the values of n for which $p(n)$, the probability of making a correct judgment, is a decreasing function of n, the total number of recognizable items). The greater the range of values that show less-is-more effects, the greater the chance of observing such effects across multiple judgments where n may vary (or across multiple participants whose n may vary). The second way of measuring the magnitude of the less-is-more effect is by comparing the peak of the probability correct function $p(n)$ with an appropriate minimum, which will be the value of $p(n)$ when $n = N$ if $p(n)$ is an inverted-U function and the actual minimum if $p(n)$ is an s-shaped function (see Figure 16-2). This difference between the peak and the appropriate minimum we call the *size* of the less-is-more effect.

Figures 16-3 and 16-4 show the range and size of less-is-more effects for the 3-AFC task, for two values of α_1 (0.8 and 0.4). Less-is-more effects are more widespread, and have larger ranges, with the larger estimate of α_1. The calculations are based on setting N, the population of potential objects, to be 100; but similar patterns appear for any other large values of N.

We now consider how this analysis can illuminate specific tasks. When $m = 3$, the steps in

the *which-is-greatest* task are outlined as (G1) through (G4) above. α_0, chance guessing, is 1/3. In tasks where a recognition heuristic is likely to work, it makes sense that $\alpha_1 > \alpha_2 > \alpha_3$ because the probability of making a correct decision based on recognizing only 1 item (α_1) should reflect recognition validity, and the probability of making a correct decision among 3 recognized items (α_3) reflects knowledge validity; α_2 should be larger than α_3 because it should be easier to choose between 2 recognized items than 3 recognized items. The set of parameters $\alpha_1 = 0.72$, $\alpha_2 = 0.54$, and $\alpha_3 = 0.36$ provided a reasonable fit to human performance in an experimental study of 3-AFC judgments by Frosch et al. (2007). In their study, Frosch et al. observed superior performance for less than total name recognition on a task where participants were asked to judge either the wealthiest or the least wealthy of three celebrities. Table 16-1(a) shows that these parameters produce a less-is-more effect of moderate size and quite substantial range but, crucially, it is clear from Figures 16-3 and 16-4 that similar conclusions can be reached with several sets of values satisfying α_1 large and $\alpha_1 > \alpha_2 > \alpha_3$.

For the *which-is-least* task, using the algorithm outlined in L1 through L4. α_0 is again chance and α_1, the probability of success when one object is recognized, must be less than ½ because the participant is guessing between two non-recognized objects. Thus, for any plausible

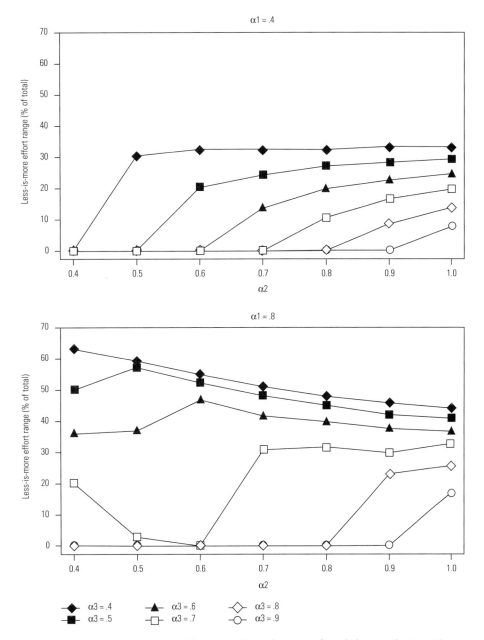

Figure 16-3. Range of the less-is-more effect in the three-alternative forced choice task. *Note*: The range of values of n ($0 \leq n \leq 100$) for which dp/dn is negative (a less-is-more effect) is graphed for $\alpha_1 = .4$ (appropriate for the least task) and .8 (appropriate for the greatest task). A range value of 0 implies $p(n)$ is monotonically increasing. A less-is-more effect with range $\geq 30\%$ might be considered large.

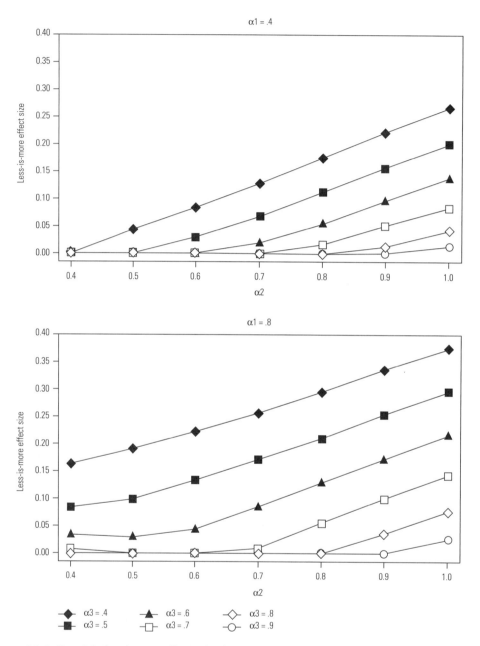

Figure 16-4. Size of the less-is-more effect in the three-alternative forced choice task for $\alpha_1 = .4$ (appropriate for the least task) and .8 (appropriate for the greatest task). *Note:* Suppose, for $0 \leq n \leq 100$, the largest value of $p(n)$ occurs at $n = n_{max}$, then the size of the less-is-more effect is defined as the difference between $p(n_{max})$ and the smallest value of $p(n)$ for $n_{max} \leq n \leq 100$. A less-is-more effect of size ≥ 0.1 might be considered large.

Table 16-1. Parameter Values and Magnitude of the Less-Is-More Effect in the m-Alternative Forced-Choice Task

(a) $m = 3$ Plausible Values

Task	α_1	α_2	α_3		Less-Is-More Effect Size	Range
Greatest	0.72	0.54	0.36		0.205	54%
Least	0.36	0.72	0.36		0.162	30%

(b) Extreme Values

m	Task	α_1	α_2	α_3	α_4	α_5	Less-Is-More Effect Size	Range
2	Greatest	1	0.5				0.253	50
	Least	0.5	1				0.253	50
3	Greatest	1	0.5	0.33			0.341	62
	Least	0.5	1	0.33			0.341	38
4	Greatest	1	0.5	0.33	0.25		0.388	70
	Least	0.33	0.5	1	0.25		0.388	30
5	Greatest	1	0.5	0.33	0.25	0.2	0.416	75
	Least	0.25	0.33	0.5	1	0.2	0.416	25

scenario, α_1 for the least task $< \alpha_1$ for the greatest task; α_2, the probability of success when two objects are recognized, should be quite large if recognition validity is high because the algorithm requires selection of the non-recognized object. Frosch et al. (2007) estimated $\alpha_1 = 0.36$, $\alpha_2 = 0.72$, and $\alpha_3 = 0.36$. Table 16-1a shows that with these parameters a less-is-more-effect size of 0.162 and range of 30% are predicted. The size is comparable to that in the which-is-greatest task (0.205), but with the range much diminished (from 54%). This suggests that the less-is-more effect is less widespread and more difficult to detect in which-is-least judgments. Figure 16-5 shows performance in the two tasks using the parameters suggested by Frosch et al. Again, Figures 16-3 and 16-4 show the same conclusion holds for other parameter choices.

To summarize the mathematics for "which is greatest" questions, recognition is helpful when few objects are recognized. For "which is least" questions, (lack of) recognition is only helpful if many objects are recognized. "Greatest" questions will, therefore, have larger ranges because

the peak always comes earlier (i.e., at lower recognition rates) than for "least" questions. This means that further learning (higher recognition rates) is actively harmful for more of the time. There is no asymmetry of size of effect when alphas take complementary values for the two questions, as in Frosch et al. (2007).[1] These results are not restricted to 3-AFC but can be extended to larger values of m (the number of objects the participant must choose between). For tractability, attention is confined to extreme cases where the recognition heuristic works perfectly. This is unrealistic, but the general shapes of the $p(n)$ should be similar in situations where use of the recognition heuristic is plausible (high recognition validity, little knowledge). For the which-is-greatest task, $\alpha_0 = 1/m$ and $\alpha_i = 1/i$, $0 < i \le m$. For the which-is-least task, $\alpha_i = 1/(m-i)$, $0 \le i < m$ and $\alpha_m = 1/m$. These results follow directly from the participant needing to guess among either i recognized or $m-i$ non-recognized objects. Table 16-1(b) shows the size and range of the less-is-more effect for these extreme cases, for m from 2 through 5. The curves become more skewed as m increases,

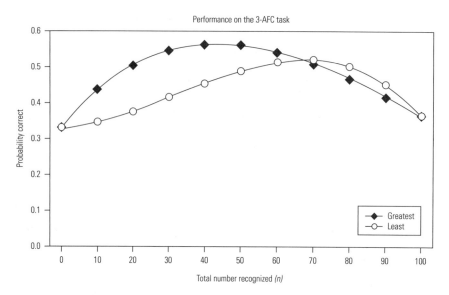

Figure 16-5. Graph of three-alternative forced choice (3-AFC) probability correct for plausible parameters of the least and greatest tasks.

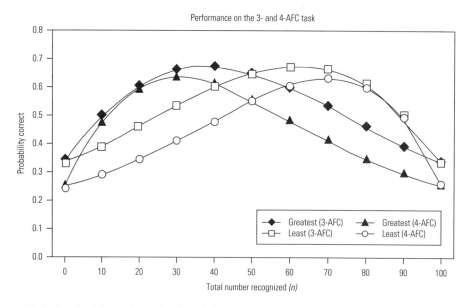

Figure 16-6. Graph of three-alternative forced choice (3-AFC) and four-alternative forced choice (4-AFC) probability correct for the lesser and greater tasks with extreme parameters (perfect recognition validity, zero knowledge validity).

with the positively skewed curves for the greatest task showing a greater range for the less-is-more effect than the negatively skewed curves for the least task. Figure 16-6 shows this for $m = 3$ and 4.

In sum, greater ranges of the less-is-more effect will occur with the which-is-greatest than the which-is-least task, rendering recognition more effective relative to knowledge on this task because recognition is more helpful for lower recognition rates. This is not obvious on the basis of 2-AFC studies alone. The range of the less-is-more effect for the which-is-greatest task also increases the greater the value of m (the number of objects the participant has to choose between), indicating that the relative utility of incomplete knowledge increases alongside the number of choices available. This again follows from the observation that recognizing few of the available choices produces a level of success that further learning erodes. This result formally expands the applicability of recognition-based inference but implies that the classic 2-AFC task developed by Goldstein and Gigerenzer (2002) may not be the most sensitive paradigm for studying less-is-more effects (and, by extension, the recognition heuristic).

ACKNOWLEDGMENTS

This research was supported in part by the Leverhulme Trust, Grant No. F/00 239 U, awarded to Rachel McCloy and C. Philip Beaman. Thanks are extended to Caren Frosch for a critical reading of earlier versions of this manuscript and to Kate Goddard for spotting the potential asymmetry between greatest and least questions. An Excel worksheet for calculating $p(n)$ as a function of varying alpha on multi-alternative forced choice (where $2 \leq m \leq 5$) is available from Philip Beaman on request.

NOTES

1. Where complementary refers to the following equalities between greatest and least: α_0 greatest = α_0 least, α_1 greatest = α_2 least, α_1 least = $.5 \times \alpha_2$ least, α_3 greatest = α_3 least. Thanks to David Danks for this elegant formulation.

When do people rely on one good reason?

Introduction to Chapter 17

The Quest for Take-the-Best: Insights and Outlooks from Experimental Research

The early stage of the simple heuristics program centered on the questions of whether and under which conditions simplicity can compete with or even outperform complexity. The focus was on pursuing existence proofs, which were crucial to liberating heuristics from the dominant view that they, at best, are second-rate and, at worst, are harbingers of cognitive fallacies. Because of this focus, investigations into the heuristics' descriptive validity were rare at that stage, but by no means ignored, as testified to by Rieskamp and Hoffrage's (1999) process-tracing study of heuristics; Hoffrage, Hertwig, and Gigerenzer's (see Chapter 10) empirical investigations of the hindsight bias; and Goldstein and Gigerenzer's (see Chapter 3) empirical investigations of the recognition heuristic.

Understandably, various commentators criticized the rarity of empirical tests of the heuristics' value as descriptive models. In hindsight, however, one benefit of this transitional phase was that experimentalists outside of the ABC Research Group, their curiosity piqued by these strange new animals, began to study fast-and-frugal heuristics. Such a division of labor could be considered as ideal: The progenitors themselves do not conduct experimental tests on their brainchild, but this is done by others devoid of any parental affection. Arndt Bröder was one of these emotionally distant experimentalists. Since 2000, he has contributed a large number of experimental articles to the ever-growing body of empirical evidence concerning fast-and-frugal heuristics in general and take-the-best and tallying in particular. Rather than presenting a sample of these investigations, this article summarizes Bröder's "quest for take-the-best," as he calls it. The products of Bröder's experimental and methodological efforts are impressive and have inspired numerous new questions and investigations. He has developed a methodology for distinguishing between different models of heuristics and has championed the study of inferences from memory, which early on had been designated as the proper domain of take-the-best (see Chapter 2).

One potential risk of having distant observers do the experimental work is that they sometimes misinterpret the theory, which admittedly may occur because its authors did not spell out everything that they took for granted. Bröder began his investigation before the concept of the adaptive toolbox was spelled out in *Simple Heuristics that Make Us Smart* (Gigerenzer, Todd, & the ABC Research Group, 1999). Hence, he first tested the hypothesis that take-the-best is a general theory of inference under uncertainty. When this overly simplistic hypothesis was refuted, however, he refined his research questions by taking into account the match between heuristics and environments. The chapter provides a summary of his experimental work and the gradual change in direction of his research questions.

CHAPTER 17

The Quest for Take-the-Best: Insights and Outlooks from Experimental Research

Arndt Bröder

Abstract: The chapter summarizes empirical work of the author by employing a historical perspective. This view of experimental research on take-the-best nicely shows that accumulating knowledge about a phenomenon may dynamically change the relevant research questions themselves. The summary shows that take-the-best is no general theory of decision making, but that people adaptively use it when appropriate. This adaptivity has limits, however, if behavior becomes routinized. Memory-based decisions appear to differ from those based on given information. The search for personality variables explaining strategy selection has been elusive. A particularly important finding is that the cognitive costs of strategy execution may have been overstated in contingency models and the toolbox metaphor.

What is sometimes required is not more data or more refined data but a different conception of the problem.

Roger N. Shepard

Roger Shepard's (1987) insight into new questions versus new data is an important reminder for all of us concerned with scientific research, but it is frequently overlooked in the busy rush of "normal" science. Rather than filling journals and textbooks with new experiments apparently corroborating old claims or piling up data in support of minuscule theories, it can be fruitful (and may turn out to be crucial) to question the very assumptions behind existing paradigms and to reconceptualize the problems being studied. This may either help to shatter old beliefs or lead to a more coherent view of seemingly separate fields. The ecological rationality perspective developed in this book is a new look at the apparent "rationality paradox" typified by the

observation that "we can put a man on the moon, so why can't we solve those logical-reasoning problems?" (O'Brien, 1993, p. 110). Instead of taking the pessimistic view that empirical results imply errors in reasoning, this perspective suggests the optimistic view that errors may instead lie in posing the wrong research questions (McClelland & Bolger, 1994). We should not ask why people make so many mistakes but rather what environments and tasks our minds are particularly suited to. The study of ecological rationality does just this, seeking to identify the cognitive mechanisms in the mind's adaptive toolbox, which are effective in defined ecological settings, precisely specified in an algorithmic manner, and computationally tractable (the latter being a precondition for psychological plausibility).

What must be added to Shepard's statement, though, is the obvious fact that inventing new conceptions is not enough—it is only a starting point for new empirical investigations. Hence, however pretty it might be, any new conception is "only" a new theory, and it has to pass rigorous empirical tests like any other. As a consequence,

The chapter is a shortened version of: Bröder, A. (in press). The quest for take-the-best. In P. M. Todd, G. Gigerenzer & the ABC Reseach Group (Eds.), *Ecological rationality*. New York: Oxford University Press.

it will be pulled onto the dissection table by merciless experimentalists (like myself), at least if such curious people find it interesting in the first place. This has certainly been the case for the new conception of ecological rationality. In the beginning, many scholars bemoaned the limited empirical evidence for the adaptive toolbox concept and one of its first-studied tools, the take-the-best heuristic (see Allen, 2000; Bröder, 2000b; Chater, 2000; Cooper, 2000; Lipshitz, 2000; Luce, 2000; Newell & Shanks, 2003; Newstead, 2000; Oaksford, 2000; Shanks & Lagnado, 2000), or they criticized the existing evidence for take-the-best (e.g., Gigerenzer, Hoffrage, & Kleinbölting, 1991; Hoffrage, Hertwig, & Gigerenzer, 2000) as too weak to be convincing (Bröder, 2000b). Since that time, however, a few dozen experiments have been conducted that have increased our understanding of why, when, and how people use simple heuristics such as take-the-best in making inferences. This chapter will present some of that empirical work—that is, my own efforts to

dissect the adaptive toolbox and take-the-best to see if they really have anything of substance inside.

Although a number of researchers who have experimentally investigated take-the-best and similar heuristics have significantly influenced my thinking through a direct or indirect exchange of ideas (Hausmann, 2004; Lee & Cummins, 2004; Newell & Shanks, 2003; Newell, Weston, & Shanks, 2003; Newell, Rakow, Weston, & Shanks, 2004; Rieskamp & Hoffrage, 1999; Rieskamp & Otto, 2006), here I will mainly focus on work from my own lab. I will provide a synopsis of our results in an effort to bring together the scattered messages of separate journal articles. Table 17-1 gives an overview of the questions addressed and the experiments and results reported in this chapter (which will be numbered consecutively in the text and do not necessarily match the experiment numbers in the original papers), together with the published sources that provide more detailed information about procedures and data. Altogether, the work reported here

Table 17-1. Overview of the Experiments Mentioned in This Chapter

No.	Source	Main Research Question	Tentative Answer
1	Bröder (2000c), Exp. 1	Do all people use take-the-best in all decisions?	No
2	Bröder (2000b), Exp. 1	Do all people use take-the-best, but possibly with errors?	No
3	Bröder (2000c), Exp. 2		No
4	Bröder (2000b), Exp. 2	Are people adaptive take-the-best users?	Probably
5	Bröder (2000b), Exp. 3		Probably
6	Bröder (2000b), Exp. 4		Probably
7	Bröder (2003), Exp. 1	Are people adaptive take-the-best users?	Yes
8	Bröder (2003), Exp. 2		Yes
9	Bröder and Schiffer (2006a), Exp. 1	Do routines hinder adaptivity?	Yes
10	Bröder and Schiffer (2006a), Exp. 2		Yes
11	Bröder and Eichler (2001)	Do take-the-best users have a particular personality?	Probably not
12	Bröder and Schiffer (2003a)	Does lowering cognitive capacity promote take-the-best?	No
13	Bröder (2005), Exp. 4a	Do take-the-best users have a particular personality?	No
14	Bröder (2005), Exp. 4c		No
15	Bröder and Schiffer (2003b), Exp. 1	Does memory retrieval induce cognitive costs?	Yes
16	Bröder and Schiffer (2003b), Exp. 2		Yes
17	Bröder and Schiffer (2003b), Exp. 3		Yes
18	Bröder and Schiffer (2003b), Exp. 4		Yes
19	Bröder and Schiffer (2006b)	Does stimulus format influence strategy selection?	Yes
20	Bröder and Gaissmaier (2007)	Does take-the-best predict decision times?	Probably yes

sheds some light on the following questions: *Is take-the-best a universal theory of probabilistic inferences? Are people adaptive decision makers? What personality factors influence strategy use? And what is the role of cognitive and memory limitations and capabilities in selecting strategies?* One main feature of my work has been that the research questions themselves changed dynamically with new insights. My hope is to communicate the spirit of this development and to distill some general conclusions about principles governing adaptive strategy selection and use. I will start with a few fundamental methodological remarks.

THE MAN WHO MISTOOK TAKE-THE-BEST FOR A THEORY

Take-the-best can match the fitting accuracy of a wide range of linear models, such as multiple linear regression, Franklin's rule (weighting cues by their importance and then summing them all), and Dawes' rule (tallying positive and negative cues and comparing them), all of which involve combining cue values (Czerlinski, Gigerenzer, & Goldstein, 1999). However, its virtue of accuracy compared to linear models turns out to be a curse for the experimenter, because the enormous overlap between take-the-best's predictions and those of linear models makes empirical distinctions between the mechanisms difficult to achieve (Bröder, 2000c; Rieskamp & Hoffrage, 1999). Hence, one has to rely either on process tracing techniques, which monitor information acquisition patterns that may distinguish between strategies (e.g., Payne, 1976; van Raaij, 1983), or on formalized methods for classifying choice outcome patterns by strategy (e.g., Bröder, 2002; Bröder & Schiffer, 2003a). Because process tracing only allows very limited conclusions concerning heuristic decision rules (see the critiques of Abelson & Levi, 1985; Bröder, 2000a), I prefer outcome-based assessments, but I use both techniques. Whether the search patterns identified by process tracing and the decision strategies specified by the formal methods fit together as coherent mechanisms is then treated as an *empirical* question rather than an a priori assumption. Box 17-1 contains a description of our experimental method and the logic of our strategy classification.

Our first attempts to put take-the-best (as it was introduced in the theory of *probabilistic mental models* by Gigerenzer et al., 1991) to an empirical test were somewhat plagued by an incomplete understanding of its theoretical status. Take-the-best is a hypothesized cognitive mechanism and a component in the theory of the adaptive toolbox. But I mistook it for a whole theory and set out to destroy it because it seemed too simplistic, and empirical arguments to date were not convincing. A theory must have what Popper (1959) called "empirical content" and make falsifiable predictions. Whereas the falsifiability of take-the-best as a mechanism is rather high because of its precise predictions, it is rather low when viewed as a whole theory because Gigerenzer et al. (1991) and Gigerenzer and Goldstein (1996) originally only broadly specified its domain of application, namely, memory-based probabilistic inferences, and did not specify how generally they thought it would apply: Did they expect all people to use take-the-best whenever possible, or all people to use it sometimes, or some people to use it always, or even only some to use it sometimes? (At the time that I conducted my first experiments, the notion that take-the-best is only one tool in the mind's adaptive toolbox had not been spelled out.) Hence, our initial research question in approaching take-the-best empirically was, "*Is take-the-best a universal theory of inductive inferences, that is, always used by everyone?*"

In the first three experiments I conducted with 130 participants in total, I assumed either that all people use take-the-best all the time (i.e., deterministic use with no errors, Experiment 1) or that all people use it, but they occasionally make errors (Experiments 2 and 3). Both versions of the hypothesis were clearly rejected: First, only 5 of the 130 participants used take-the-best all the time (in 15 or 24 trials; see Lee & Cummins, 2004, for a comparable result). Second, for the other participants, choices were clearly influenced by other cues than just the most valid discriminating one that take-the-best would use; this systematic influence clearly showed that the deviations from take-the-best's

---

Box 17-1 How We Conducted Experiments and Why We Did It This Way

Deciding About Decision Strategies

If we want to know the manner in which people integrate cue information for inductive inferences (i.e., their decision strategies), we must first know which cues people use. One way to be sure of this in an experiment is to give people the cues to use explicitly. We provided our participants with four (or five) binary cues (either seen on a computer screen or learned in training for later recall and use in the experiment) and cue validities (either by telling them directly or letting them acquire the knowledge indirectly via frequency learning) and then had them make inferences by choosing between two or three objects. The pattern of decisions allowed us to draw conclusions about the strategy probably employed by each participant, using a maximum likelihood classification principle (see Bröder & Schiffer, 2003a, for details). We used domains without much preexisting knowledge to prevent participants from relying on cues they might bring in from outside the experiment.

The Tasks

- *Extraterrestrial ethnology.* Participants were scientists judging the population sizes of beings on another planet by considering the existence or nonexistence of different cultural achievements (Experiments 1—4).
- *Stockbroker game.* Participants inferred which one of multiple shares had the best prospects for profit by considering different cues about the associated firms, such as turnover growth (Experiments 5—13).
- *Criminal case.* Participants were detectives judging which of two suspects was more likely to have committed a murder, based on evidence found at the scene of the crime. The features (cues) of the suspects had to be retrieved from memory (Experiments 14—20).

---

predictions could not be explained away as random response errors.

We could have stopped here and declared the heuristic a dead end (some authors with similar critical results came close to this conclusion, e.g., Lee & Cummins, 2004; Newell & Shanks, 2003; Newell, Weston, & Shanks, 2003). However, we felt that this would be a premature burial, since no theory of decision making predicts behavior correctly 100% of the time. A more realistic version of the theory would probably allow for both (unsystematic) response errors *and* a heterogeneous population of decision makers. For instance, a small minority of people relying on other heuristics, averaged together with a group of predominantly take-the-best users, could have led to my results, as we will see in the next section.

Obvious conclusions of these first experiments were that (1) not everybody uses take-the-best in every probabilistic inference task and

(2) if some people do use take-the-best, one has to allow for unsystematic response errors as psychologists routinely do in other areas. Thus, I had a definitive—and negative—answer to my initial research question about take-the-best's universality, but I began to doubt that it had been a good question in the first place! Before claiming that take-the-best was not a reasonable cognitive model, I thought it worthwhile to confront a more realistic version of the hypothesis instead of a universal, deterministic straw man.

THE TOOLBOX ASSUMPTION—ARE PEOPLE ADAPTIVE DECISION MAKERS?

I next asked, therefore, if a significant proportion of people use take-the-best. This, as we will soon see, was again not the best question to ask. Nonetheless, to answer it, I had to develop methods to assess individual decision strategies, which is challenging if one wants to avoid arbitrary criteria (see Bröder, 2002). First, the unit of analysis must be the individual rather than a group mean, because the latter would obscure potential individual differences. Second, one has to compare different strategies (or, technically, models) rather than just assess the fit of one strategy of interest to each individual's choice data. A good model fit per se is not very informative (Roberts & Pashler, 2000). Third, I preferred modeling based on decision outcomes rather than process-tracing measures because the latter rely on some questionable assumptions (see Abelson & Levi, 1985; Bröder, 2000a) and focus on information search rules instead of the decision rules in which I was primarily interested (Bröder & Schiffer, 2003a). In a nutshell, the methods I and my colleagues developed assess which strategy (take-the-best, Franklin's rule, Dawes' rule, guessing) best fits an observed pattern of choices of a participant in an experiment. Experiment 4 was our first to assess the number of participants whose best-fitting strategy was take-the-best. In this experiment, participants were sent to a distant planet as extraterrestrial scientists who had to judge the level of development of different cultures (the same task as in the first three experiments). For 11 of 40 participants (28%), their choices could best be described by take-the-best's decision rule. Is that a lot or a little? To decide, we need to compare with the other possible strategies we had tested. The number of participants whose choices could be best described by Dawes' rule was 0%, but presumed users of Franklin's rule (72%) were more prevalent than those of take-the-best. While the proportion of presumed take-the-best users is not overwhelming, it is still comparatively large enough that it should not be entirely ignored. So now what?

As we did not get a satisfying answer, we reexamined our question. Rather than asking if there is a sufficient proportion of take-the-best users to take the heuristic seriously, we turned to the question of whether there are conditions under which take-the-best use is boosted and whether these conditions fit the model of contingent decision making or the concept of ecological rationality (i.e., that there are environment

structures that take-the-best can exploit to do well). Hence, we changed our research question by asking now, *"Are people adaptive take-the-best users?"* To elaborate on the second point, the ecological rationality of heuristics lies in their match with a certain environment structure (Czerlinski et al., 1999; Johnson & Payne, 1985; Martignon & Hoffrage, 2002) and according to the adaptive toolbox assumption, people should use take-the-best when it is appropriate. Hence, we began to examine environment and task variables that could be expected to influence take-the-best deployment. If the proportion of take-the-best users was unaffected by such variables and continued to hover around the 28% level found in Experiment 4, this would render the adaptive use of take-the-best questionable.

One potential criticism of Experiments 1 to 4 is that they all involved the simultaneous presentation of cue values on a computer screen during decision making. In contrast, Gigerenzer and Goldstein (1996, p. 651) had explicitly defined the task of take-the-best as one involving search for information, and specifically search in memory. In my first experiments, there were no costs of searching for or retrieving information, which if included would probably shift the balance of ecological rationality in take-the-best's favor (see Gigerenzer & Todd, 1999). In addition, the experiments involved neither feedback on successful choices nor incentives for good decisions, possibly hindering the ability and desire of participants to behave adaptively. We therefore changed the experimental setting to a hypothetical stock broker game on a computer screen in which participants could acquire cue information about stocks before choosing one of two or three alternatives to invest in (an idea modified after Rieskamp, 1998). The binary cues included information about the firms (e.g., whether there was turnover growth during the last year), and participants acquired this information by clicking appropriate fields on the screen. This paradigm allows for monitoring information search and manipulating the (relative) costs of information acquisition. Furthermore, the success of the chosen stock provides feedback that allows the participant to adjust strategy choice accordingly. In the first experiment using this paradigm

(Experiment 5, $n = 40$) we used a crude manipulation of information costs: To see a cue value in each trial, participants had to pay either 1% or 10% of the maximum amount they could win in this trial.[1] This measure boosted the percentage of probable take-the-best users to 40% in the low-cost condition and to 65% in the high-cost condition. In Experiment 6 ($n = 80$), we replicated the result of the 65% who were take-the-best users when the information costs were high, and by isolating these variables we found that neither outcome feedback nor the successive cue retrieval per se was responsible for the rise in take-the-best use. The message so far was plain and simple: If you raise information costs, people become reluctant to use all of the information and instead adhere to a frugal lexicographic strategy like take-the-best, using just the first cue that allows a decision to be made.

This conclusion may not sound too surprising, and it is also compatible with the assumption that people are miserly rather than smart. But are monetary costs the only environmental factor to which people adapt their strategy use? Earlier studies of the ecological rationality of take-the-best showed other forms of environment structure that the heuristic could exploit, including high variance of cue validities, high redundancy between cues, and scarce information (Martignon & Hoffrage, 1999, 2002). We next investigated an important instance of the first form, namely *noncompensatory* versus *compensatory* environments. In noncompensatory environments, when cues are ranked according to their importance (e.g., their weight in a linear combination), each cue cannot be outweighed by any combination of the lower-ranked cues. In compensatory environments, some cues can be outweighed—or compensated for—by a combination of other lesser cues. This has implications for the performance of different strategies, in that noncompensatory decision mechanisms that do not combine cues work better in noncompensatory environments than in compensatory environments where cue combinations cannot beat individual cues. In particular, take-the-best, as a non-compensatory strategy, cannot be outperformed in terms of decision accuracy by a linear combination rule in a noncompensatory environment (if the

order of the cues corresponds to that of the linear weights—see Martignon & Hoffrage, 1999, 2002).

To find out whether people are sensitive to the difference between noncompensatory and compensatory environments, we ran four further experiments (Experiments 7–10 with $N =$ 100, 120, 121, and 120, respectively), in which we kept the nominal prices for acquiring cue information constant but varied the importance distribution of the cues as defined by their weights in the payoff function. This meant that in the noncompensatory environments, the expected payoff of consistently using take-the-best was greater than the expected payoff of Franklin's rule, a compensatory strategy, because the former paid for fewer cues than the latter; or in other words, the cost of checking all the cues exceeded the expected return of the information they provided. In contrast, in the compensatory environments, the acquisition of more than one cue value was profitable in the long run, and it was detrimental to ignore information. What we found in all four experiments was that the majority of participants used the strategy appropriate for the given environment: adaptive strategy use. However, more people used compensatory strategies overall, which points to a slight preference for compensatory strategies, at least in this stock broker task. Hence, while many people were quite efficient at figuring out appropriate strategies based on feedback (payments) they received, others seemed to rely on an apparently "safe" compensatory strategy.

We see these patterns in Figure 17-1. The clear adaptive trend appears across the experiments for greater use of the take-the-best heuristic the more appropriate it is: The higher the ratio of expected gains in favor of take-the-best, the more people employ this strategy. At the same time, looking only at the circles (experimental conditions without further significant manipulations), one can see that in all three compensatory environments (payoff ratio < 1), compensatory strategies were most prevalent, while take-the-best was the most prevalent strategy in only five of the nine conditions with a noncompensatory environment. This points to a conservative bias in favor of compensatory

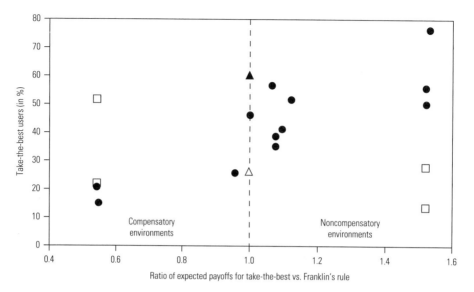

Figure 17-1. Percentages of take-the-best users in various settings of the stock market game with environment structure that is characterized by different expected payoff ratios for take-the-best versus Franklin's rule. Ratios less than 1 denote "compensatory" environments; ratios greater than 1 denote "noncompensatory" environments. The circles depict 12 conditions in Experiments 7—10; there is a clear adaptive trend ($r = .87$) as environment structure changes. Squares show the maladaptive tendency to maintain a routine that was established before a change of the environment's payoff structure (Experiments 9 and 10). The open and filled triangles depict the "high cognitive load" and the control condition, respectively, from Experiment 12. (Adapted from Bröder & Newell, 2008.)

decision making (see Rieskamp & Otto, 2006, for comparable results).

Three of the four squares in Figure 17-1 are a profound exception to the adaptive strategy use trend. They all represent conditions from Experiments 9 and 10 in the *second* half of each experiment after the payoff structure of the environment had changed from compensatory to noncompensatory or vice versa. Although these payoff changes were rather extreme, participants obviously did not react adequately—the level of take-the-best use mostly remained appropriate to the previous environment structure. Neither receiving a hint (Experiment 9) nor a change to a related but different task along with an additional monetary incentive (Experiment 10) helped greatly to overcome this maladaptive reliance on a previously established routine. Hence, we concluded that most people readily and quickly adapt to the payoff structure of a new task (with a slight compensatory bias), but they have difficulties in overcoming a routine that

they had established in the same or a similar task before. These routine-retaining tendencies were particularly extreme for the information acquisition behavior (e.g., number of cues looked up, time spent on info search, or Payne's, 1976, strategy index). Maladaptive routine effects have been known in cognitive psychology for a long time (see Luchins & Luchins, 1959) and have also been demonstrated in the domain of decision making (see Betsch & Haberstroh, 2005, for an overview). Nevertheless, we were quite surprised to find their massive impact in our studies, contrasting with the participants' general ability to adapt.

To summarize, the evidence so far looked fairly supportive of the idea of the adaptive decision maker (e.g., the contingency model of Payne, Bettman, & Johnson, 1993) in general and the adaptive toolbox in particular. Take-the-best seems to be a part of the mind's toolbox, and under appropriate circumstances, many people will employ this tool. However, the routine effects suggest that people are reluctant to change a tool they have just gotten used to using. Obviously, other cognitive processes play a role when an apparently known situation changes. One may speculate that strategy selection is more deliberate and effortful when people are first confronted with a new situation, such as when entering a new experiment session. They may switch to simpler and slower learning processes (e.g., reinforcement learning, see Rieskamp & Otto, 2006) when the situation is well known, such as after the session has been underway for a while.

WHO ARE THE PEOPLE WHO USE TAKE-THE-BEST?

Although the payoff structure of the environment was a major determinant of take-the-best use (see Figure 17-1), there were obviously individual differences—not everyone employed the same strategy. In noncompensatory environments, a proportion of participants continued to use Franklin's rule or Dawes' rule, whereas others still used take-the-best if a compensatory strategy was more favorable. Individual differences in decision making strategies have been widely reported (e.g., Brehmer, 1994; Einhorn, 1970; Lee & Cummins, 2004; Newell & Shanks, 2003; Slovic & Lichtenstein, 1971). Zakay (1990) emphasized this individual variation and hypothesized that "strategy selection in decision making is dependent both on a basic tendency toward using a specific strategy and a cost benefit analysis" (p. 207). Subsequently, Shiloh, Koren, and Zakay (2001) bemoaned a surprising lack of systematic studies concerning these hypothesized "basic tendencies," which they conceptualized as presumably stable personality traits. Thus, in addition to investigating "adaptivity," as discussed above, we had to think about the causes of individual differences: In other words, *do take-the-best users have a particular personality?*

The way in which psychologists assess individual differences is simple in principle: They administer well-validated personality tests and correlate them with the behavior of interest. In our case, the behavior of interest was the decision strategy people use. To look for correlations with this behavior, we had our participants play the stock market game in four experiments (11–14) and additionally fill out self-descriptive questionnaires intended to measure different fundamental personality traits that we thought could be plausible determinants of noncompensatory decision behavior. In Experiment 11 ($N = 61$), the traits measured were action orientation, achievement motive, self efficacy, need for cognition, impulsivity, and rigidity (see Table 17-2 for a list of traits tested and references). Although we had no strong a priori hypotheses, our intuition was that achievement motive, self efficacy, need for cognition, and rigidity would be associated with more elaborative compensatory decision making, whereas take-the-best users might show higher action orientation and impulsivity. (We also measured rigidity and action orientation in Experiment 7, $N = 100$.) Next, in the two similar Experiments 12 and 13 ($N = 60$ for each, analyzed here together) we assessed the impact of the so-called "Big Five" traits nowadays considered to be fundamental personality dimensions (emotional stability, extraversion, openness, agreeableness, and conscientiousness; see Costa & McCrae, 1992). In addition, we assessed both facets of socially desirable responding, namely, impression management and self-deception (Paulhus, 1984). In each of the experiments we computed the multiple correlation between the personality construct and the decision strategy used, shown in Table 17-2. To make a long story short, *none* of the personality measures showed a substantial correlation with selected strategies.[2]

Thus, we did not find any evidence for a basic personality trait that might be associated with the default tendency to use lexicographic rather than compensatory decision strategies. Furthermore, an experimental manipulation of achievement motivation did not have any impact on strategy use (Experiment 14, $N = 60$): In one group, we told participants that performance in the stock market game is highly correlated with intelligence, whereas the control group was told only that they were involved in a preliminary study of a new experimental task. Of course, we cannot exclude the possibility that we were looking at the wrong personality traits the whole

Table 17-2. Multiple Correlations (Adjusted R^2) between Decision Rules and "Big Five" Personality Traits in Several Experiments

Study	Scale	Source	Adjusted R^2	P
Experiment 11 ($N = 61$)	Achievement motive (12 items)	Fahrenberg et al. (1994)	.03	.14
	Action orientation (24 items)	Kuhl (1994)	.02	.25
	Self-efficacy (10 items)	Schwarzer and Jerusalem (1999)	.01	.30
	Need for cognition (16 items)	Bless et. al. (1994)	.01	.31
	Impulsivity (16 items)	Stumpf et al. (1984)	.08	.04
	Rigidity (8 items)	Zerssen (1994)	.00	.42
Experiment 7 ($N = 100$)	Achievement motive (12 items)	Fahrenberg et al. (1994)	−.02	.79
	Action orientation (24 items)	Kuhl (1994)	.00	.36
	Impulsivity (16 items)	Stumpf et al. (1984)	−.01	.51
Experiments 12 and 13 ($N = 120$)	Emotional stability (12 items)	Borkenau and Ostendorf (1993)	−.02	.84
	Extraversion (12 items)		−.01	.55
	Openness (12 items)		.00	.38
	Agreeableness (12 items)		.00	.40
	Conscientiousness (12 items)		.02	.19
	Impression management	Musch et al. (2002)	.01	.24
	Self-deception		−.00	.27

Note: The strategy classification is a nominal variable that was dummy coded for these analyses. Adjusted R^2 estimates the proportion of shared variance of the dummy-coded strategy variables and the personality trait.

time, while ignoring more important ones. However, given the broad class of cognitive and motivational variables we examined, we consider this possibility unlikely. We tend to conclude that the individual differences observed may be dependent on participants' transient states rather than stable traits. This possibility should be examined in further studies investigating the stability of strategy preferences.

So we still do not know who these take-the-best users are! One somewhat comforting fact is that other areas such as personality-oriented consumer research have been no more successful in answering this question (Foxall & Goldsmith, 1988). The inability to find good predictors of individual decision-making strategies seems to be widespread. But there may be a reason for this, namely, that we again asked the wrong question. Rather than asking about the relation between personality and default strategy use, the adaptive question would be whether there is a correlation between individual capacities and

the ability to choose an appropriate strategy in different environments.

One result of Experiment 11 left us somewhat puzzled and helped us aim our individual differences question in a new direction: In addition to the personality measures, participants completed several scales of an intelligence test (Berliner Intelligenz-Struktur-Test, Jäger, Süß, & Beauducel, 1997; see Bröder (2005) for details of the subscales used), and the intelligence score was slightly, but significantly, correlated with selected strategies ($R^2 = .10$). However, contrary to our expectation, it was the *clever* ones who used take-the-best!

INDIVIDUAL DIFFERENCES IN COGNITIVE CAPACITY AND STRATEGY USE

So our next question became, *do differences in intelligence help explain strategy use in different environments?* Experiment 11 had only one environment structure: a 10% expected payoff advantage for using take-the-best compared with using Franklin's rule, which we thought would be negligible. But what we found was that take-the-best use was positively correlated with intelligence: The take-the-best users had an intelligence score on average about 0.3 standard deviations above Franklin's rule users and about 1.0 standard deviation above Dawes' rule users. The more intelligent participants seemed to be better at figuring out the subtle payoff difference between strategies and consequently using the more frugal take-the-best strategy. We replicated this trend in two other experiments (Experiments 7 and 8) with different environmental payoff structures. In both experiments, there was a significant correlation between selected strategies and intelligence for *noncompensatory* environments ($R^2 = .20$ and $R^2 = .14$, respectively), whereas a correlation was absent in environments with a *compensatory* payoff structure ($R^2 = .05$ and $R^2 = .00$). Apparently, the smartest people used take-the-best in noncompensatory environments, while in compensatory environments, there was no strategy difference between participants with different intelligence scores. So the answer to the question of a particular take-the-best personality was surprising: Concerning motivational variables and cognitive style, we did not find a specific take-the-best user profile. On the other hand, cognitive ability was related to strategy used, but in an unexpected way— higher intelligence scores were related to greater use of an *appropriate* strategy, not to greater use of a particular strategy.

How can the consistent pattern of strategy use that we found be explained? Our proposal is that most participants entered the experiments with an initial "conservative" preference for compensatory decision making because they considered it risky to ignore information. The feedback during the first decision trials would in principle have enabled them to figure out the appropriate strategy, but only the clever ones effectively used this information. In noncompensatory environments, these participants adjusted their strategy (and used take-the-best), whereas in compensatory environments they stuck to the compensatory strategy almost everybody used anyhow.

(This explanation holds in situations such as ours where people already know the order of cue importance or validity; when this order must be learned, noncompensatory heuristic users may take a long time to find the order which could make it adaptive to start with a compensatory strategy and greater cue exploration in those situations as well.)

DOES LOWERING COGNITIVE CAPACITY PROMOTE SIMPLER STRATEGIES?

According to the common reasoning about contingency models of strategy selection, compensatory strategies are much more costly than noncompensatory strategies to perform, but they are on average more accurate (Beach & Mitchell, 1978; Christensen-Szalanski, 1978; Chu & Spires, 2003; Payne et al., 1993). This traditional view of decision making postulates an accuracy–effort trade-off, in which to make better decisions, people have to use more information and processing—more is better. In this view, the reason why people use simple heuristics is that we have limited cognitive capacities.

The accuracy–effort trade-off implies that people will have to sacrifice some decision accuracy if their processing costs increase. Typically, this will mean using simpler—for example, noncompensatory—strategies. Since lowering cognitive capacity raises relative processing costs, simpler strategies such as take-the-best should prevail when people are put under cognitive load. This kind of accuracy–effort trade-off does not follow from the ecological rationality perspective, focusing as it does on environment-driven strategy selection, and furthermore seems to be at odds with our results on individual differences in intelligence and strategy use. This makes it interesting to test a more experimental manipulation of capacity, allowing us to answer a new research question: "*Does lowering a person's cognitive capacity promote simpler strategy use?*"

Experiment 12 ($N = 60$) was designed to test this implication of contingency models, and it yielded another unexpected result. In this experiment, the environment was set up to give a slight advantage to take-the-best users. We had a control group of participants play the stock market game and make decisions while hearing a series of digits they were instructed to ignore. The experimental group, in contrast, was put under heavy attentional demands: They had to attend to the digit string (while investing in stocks!) and count the occurrences of the digit "nine." Occasionally, they were prompted to type in the number of nines presented since the last prompt, and wrong answers were punished with charges subtracted from their virtual bank account. This secondary task massively decreased the cognitive resources available for the primary decision task. What did we expect to happen in terms of people's decision strategies? In accordance with the beliefs of researchers who favor contingency models of decision making (Beach & Mitchell, 1978; Christensen-Szalanski, 1978; Payne et al., 1993) and of laypeople (Chu & Spires, 2003), we expected that a decreased cognitive capacity would *increase* the relative processing costs of elaborate (i.e., compensatory) strategies and therefore shift the balance toward more take-the-best use.

Exactly the opposite happened: Only 27% of the people with lowered cognitive capacity (high cognitive load) employed take-the-best while 60% employed take-the-best in the low-load control condition (depicted by the triangles in Figure 17-1). As with our IQ results, greater cognitive capacity did *not* generally lead to more "elaborated" compensatory decision making but rather, we believe, to a more efficient detection of the tiny payoff advantage (less than 1%) of take-the-best in this environment (or to realizing that using the less-effortful take-the-best would at least not harm their performance). Correspondingly, limited cognitive capacity seems to have hindered the detection of take-the-best's advantage and so prevented deviation from the default compensatory strategy. We therefore conclude that higher as opposed to lower cognitive capacity (intelligence or working memory load) does not *directly* determine the type of strategy used. Rather, cognitive capacity is helpful in executing the *metaprocess* of strategy selection in an efficient and adaptive manner (see Bröder & Newell, 2008, for a more extensive discussion). To put it bluntly: If you have sufficient cognitive resources, you do

not always use more complex strategies. Rather, you are better able to find out which information can safely be ignored. Without sufficient resources, you may stick to an apparently safe compensatory strategy. This interpretation implies that the cognitive costs that matter most are those caused not by strategy execution (as implied by Beach & Mitchell, 1978), but rather by adaptive strategy selection. Hence, a high cognitive capacity does not foster more "elaborate" strategies per se, but it enables people to figure out appropriate strategies.

UNEXPECTED COGNITIVE COSTS: MEMORY RETRIEVAL

The experiments reported so far followed a research tradition that Gigerenzer and Todd (1999) termed "inferences from givens." The reason for the popularity of this approach is mentioned in Box 17-1: Researchers who study information integration have to know what information participants use in their judgments. Hence, they provide participants with that information rather than not knowing what participants might happen to pull from the environment or from memory. Gigerenzer and Todd criticized this approach for studying fast-and-frugal heuristics because it did not involve the cue search common to much of daily decision making, as, for instance, in "inferences from memory" where each cue value must be recalled. Although our results reported above clearly showed that high information costs promoted the use of take-the-best, we did not know whether cue retrieval from memory would itself induce sufficient cognitive costs to influence people's inference strategies. After all, retrieving information from memory usually seems like one of our most effortless everyday activities, and hence Gigerenzer and Todd's criticism seemed at least bold (if not implausible). This time, our skeptical research question was this: "*Does memory retrieval really induce cognitive costs that impact strategy selection?*"

Gigerenzer and Todd (1999) forgot to provide suggestions for how their hypothesis could be tested. As just mentioned, there are good methodological reasons for using an "inference from givens" approach—but can we gain similar control over the information that people use in an "inferences from memory" task? Our simple solution to this methodological challenge was to let people learn a set of objects and their respective features by heart (following a related idea of Hoffrage et al., 2000). After that, they would make decisions based on the cues they had to retrieve from memory. There were two consequences of this method: First, we could only rely on outcome-based strategy classifications because process-tracing data would not be available. Second, we had to choose a domain in which the cues themselves did not suggest a to-be-judged target variable during learning, because that would probably lead to inferences being made already in the learning phase rather than in the decision phase where we wanted to observe them. After several pilot experiment attempts that tortured innocent participants with bizarre stimuli such as Pokémon creatures and geometric shapes, some students of mine came up with the ingenious idea of using an invented criminal case. This had the invaluable advantages of much higher participant motivation and relatively easy-to-learn material, namely, potential murder suspects and their characteristics (such as clothes, perfume, cigarette brand, vehicle, accompanying dog, etc.).

In a pilot experiment (Experiment 15, $N = 50$), my colleague Stefanie Schiffer and I wanted merely to test the suitability of the material—but we were very much surprised to find 74% of our participants classified as take-the-best users! Because of the general tendency to use compensatory strategies that we had observed before and our disbelief in Gigerenzer and Todd's claim of costly memory retrieval (as also earlier expressed in Gigerenzer & Goldstein, 1996), we had expected a low percentage of take-the-best users. Before we accepted this perplexing result as a confirmation of the memory-search hypothesis, though, we had to test the possibility that this take-the-best upsurge was caused by some peculiarity of the material we had used. In Experiment 16 ($N = 50$) we directly compared two groups with identical material solving the same criminal case after learning all suspects by heart. The experimental group had to retrieve the cue information

from memory whereas the control group saw all the information on the screen during decision making. Although the percentage of take-the-best users in the experimental group was less than in Experiment 15 (44%), it was significantly higher than in the control condition (20%) in which Franklin's rule (60%) and Dawes' rule (20%) together were clearly dominant. Again, we were surprised because the screen versus memory difference remained even when the materials were made identical. In Experiment 17 ($N = 50$) we presented cue information either verbally or pictorially and expected consequent processing differences, which we did not find (64% take-the-best users in both conditions).

A more effective manipulation of the two presentation formats as depicted in Figure 17-2 (Experiment 18, $N = 114$) had a dramatic effect: 47% of participants appeared to use take-the-best in the verbal condition, whereas only 21% used it when processing the holistic pictorial stimuli. Recently, we found this format effect even more strongly (Experiment 19, $N = 151$, 70 vs. 36% take-the-best use—see Bröder & Schiffer, 2006b). At first, we interpreted this as evidence for simultaneous parallel processing of feature matching for holistically retrieved pictorial stimuli (Bröder & Schiffer, 2003b), but one piece of evidence does not readily fit this interpretation: The decision time patterns for verbal and pictorial stimuli are virtually identical, which may indicate equally costly memory retrieval in the two cases. In summary, the results of our memory-based inference studies corroborate Gigerenzer and Todd's (1999) memory search hypothesis claiming appreciable cognitive costs of information retrieval.

Outcome-based strategy classification allows for an assessment of whether people are using the decision rule postulated by take-the-best. But what about their search and stopping rules? The results reported can also be accounted for by assuming people used a weighted additive strategy (e.g., Franklin's rule) that mimics take-the-best performance when the cue weights are noncompensatory (see Martignon & Hoffrage, 2002). How do we know that people did not just use a compensatory strategy with different cue weights when deciding from memory? Although

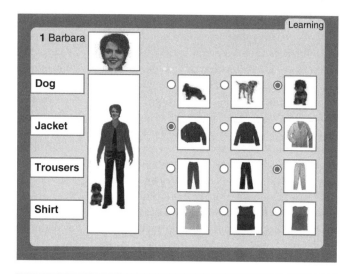

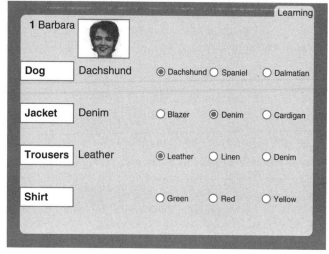

Figure 17-2. Stimuli presented during the learning trials for the criminal case game to investigate memory-based decisions in the pictorial (top) and verbal (bottom) conditions of Experiments 18 and 19. (Adapted from Bröder & Schiffer, 2006b; originals were in color, with labels in German.)

genuine process tracing data are not available with memory-based decisions, one can analyze the time used for each decision. We classified the decision trials in our experiments into different sets: The first set contained choice pairs in which the most valid cue differentiated between objects—that is, one suspect possessed the critical feature and the other did not. The second set contained those decision trials in which only the second most valid cue differentiated between the suspects, while the most valid one did not. We proceeded similarly with the third and fourth cues to construct four different decision type sets. Figure 17-3 shows the mean decision times

of the 415 participants from Experiments 15 to 19, split into their different outcome-based strategy classifications and further divided by the four decision types. The time patterns observed fit the processing assumptions of the four strategies reasonably well: Those participants classified as take-the-best users show a marked increase in decision time the more cues they have to retrieve to make a decision (about one additional second per cue on average). This fits the assumption that take-the-best users stop their information search when they find the first discriminating cue (Bröder & Gaissmaier, 2007).

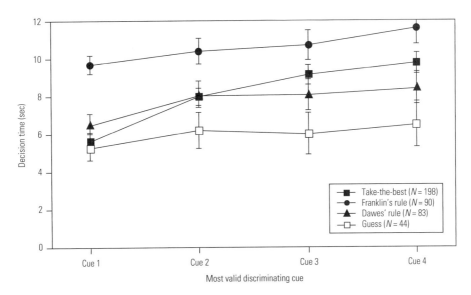

Figure 17-3. Mean decision times (and SE) of participants with different outcome-based strategy classifications aggregated across Experiments 15 to 19. The x-axis denotes different classes of decision trials in which the most valid cue discriminates (labeled Cue 1), the second most valid cue (but not the first) discriminates (Cue 2), and so forth. The decision time patterns roughly fit the process descriptions of take-the-best (TTB), Franklin's rule (FR), Dawes' rule (DR), and guessing (Guess; see text).

Participants classified as guessing were the quickest decision makers and did not show a significant increase in time depending on the pattern of cue information, consistent with not systematically searching for information but deciding randomly. Franklin's rule users showed a smaller decision time increase than take-the-best users as the most valid cue changed and needed much more time for their decisions. This is compatible with the assumption that these participants always retrieve more information than just the most important cue[3] and integrate it in an effortful manner. The time increment of Dawes' rule users was also small, as they must usually also retrieve most available cues, and they were much quicker than Franklin's rule users overall, reflecting their much simpler and faster integration rule. Hence, the decision times are an "indirect" process indicator that corroborates the sequential retrieval assumptions of take-the-best.

Skeptics may worry that in all our experiments validity and retrieval ease were confounded: Participants learned the cues in a specific order, which was in terms of decreasing validities. Therefore, we ran one more study (Experiment 20) to disentangle cue validity and learning-order-based ease of retrieval by making the cue-learning sequence differ from the validity order. Specifically, the learning order of the cues was now Cue 3–Cue 1–Cue 4–Cue 2, where the numbers denote the validity ranks. Because the two orders no longer matched, this would make a validity-based retrieval sequence cognitively harder to perform than in Experiments 15–19. Nonetheless, the outcome-based strategy assessment suggested that only 5 of 82 participants in this new experiment followed a take-the-first decision rule ordering cues by learning order (and hence retrieval ease), while 32 participants appeared to use take-the-best and ordered cue retrieval by validity. Figure 17-4 shows the mean decision times of both sets of participants. The order of decision time means for take-the-first users exactly follows the expected 3–1–4–2 cue sequence, indicating that these people retrieved cues in the order of retrieval ease and stopped search when a discriminating cue was found.

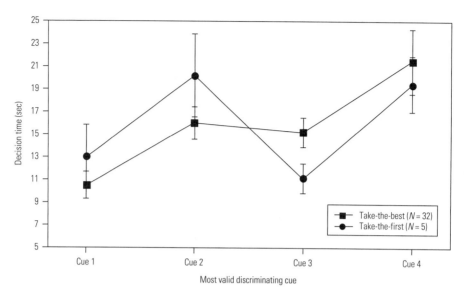

Figure 17-4. Mean decision times (and SE) of participants classified as using take-the-best (TTB) or take-the-first (TTF) in Experiment 20. The latter ad hoc strategy was apparently used by five participants who ordered cues according to retrieval ease rather than validity. The sequence of decision time means follows cue validity order for take-the-best users and the sequence of cues during learning (3–1–4–2) for take-the-first users.

This hardly seems like a coincidence—we believe it is evidence that the decision times reflect part of the learning process, particularly showing its sequential nature. The important insight is that this reaction time evidence indicates that both take-the-first users and take-the-best users process cues sequentially and ignore further information in a lexicographic fashion.

PUTTING THINGS TOGETHER: INSIGHTS AND OUTLOOKS

The research program summarized here pursued an experimental approach in order to put claims about the adaptive toolbox in general and take-the-best in particular to a strict test. So now what do we know, 20 experiments and 1,491 participants later? I started out motivated to smash what I took to be an all-too-simple theory, and my very first attempts did not look too promising for take-the-best. But upon relaxing the unrealistic assumption that take-the-best is used universally, I found that under certain conditions, the behavior of a considerable proportion of people can best be described by this simple heuristic. Hence, take-the-best definitely seems to be a part of the mind's toolbox. However, as Lee and Cummins (2004, p. 344) have criticized, "although there is no inherent contradiction in arguing that different people make decisions in different ways under different conditions, it is a less than completely satisfying conclusion." But there are two ways to be unsatisfied with this state of affairs: If it is because not everyone is behaving the same way (e.g., using take-the-best), then we are back to the position of expecting universal behavior, which we already abandoned. (There are other good arguments for expecting variation in behavior, such as adaptive coin-flipping in which genetic "coins" are "flipped" in individuals to get varied phenotypic traits—see Gigerenzer, 2000, pp. 207–209.) On the other hand, we can be dissatisfied because the picture is incomplete: We want to know *when* and *why* people behave differently, choosing different strategies. This is the path that the rest of our studies pursued, and it led to a variety of important new questions and insights.

One of these new findings is that people do not seem to always have a default preference for fast-and-frugal decision making. Rather, with inferences from givens people show a small initial bias for compensatory decision making. At least in our experimental settings, participants' general a priori belief seems to be that all information could be relevant and needs to be explored, and they must actively *learn* to ignore information. A second insight is that people are generally able to adapt to payoff structures of environments and use appropriate strategies, whether frugal or greedy concerning information. Thus, our results regarding adaptive strategy selection for probabilistic inference tasks are in line with those of Payne, Bettman, and Johnson (1988, 1993) for preferential choices. Inference strategy selection is influenced not only by obvious task variables such as time pressure (Payne et al., 1988; Rieskamp & Hoffrage, 1999) and information costs (Bröder, 2000b), but also by subtle payoff differences. However, not everyone is sensitive to these differences—adaptivity requires cognitive processes that different people can deploy to varying degrees. Our results regarding intelligence as well as the effects of the secondary task in Experiment 12 clearly show that available cognitive capacity fosters adaptivity of decision making.

The next insight is that even if this capacity is available in principle, it is not always used. This conclusion is suggested by the massive routine effects observed in Experiments 9 and 10. In these experiments, most participants stuck to the strategy they had learned in the first half of the experiment, regardless of whether they were given a hint about an environmental change, an additional monetary incentive, or a switch to a different but similar task. Why are people so reluctant to change a once-successful strategy when it becomes suboptimal? This question can be investigated at two levels. At the environmental level, one can look at different task domains and assess whether abrupt changes are common. If they are, the routine effects observed here are potentially a threat to adaptivity, because people would benefit from being sensitive to such recurring changes (Todd & Goodie, 2002). If abrupt payoff changes turn out to be rare, though, then routines may be viewed as a successful adaptation to avoid switching strategies in response to false alarms. At the psychological level, a model would have to explain why people are quick adaptors in a brand-new task but adjust slowly to payoff changes or task switches. One preliminary speculation is that after quick but effortful strategy selection, people adopt a routine mode in which adjustment can better be described by a slow incremental reinforcement learning process (e.g., Rieskamp & Otto, 2006). Furthermore, if one accepts the notion that our collection of personality traits investigated as potential moderators of strategy preference was not completely out of place, another finding is that there are probably no stable strategy preferences related to fundamental personality characteristics.

An additional insight is that memory retrieval of cue information is indeed a crucial variable that can trigger the use of take-the-best. For me, this was a most unexpected result. Given the default preference for compensatory decision making in low-cost screen-based experiments, one can hardly escape the conclusion that memory retrieval appears to incur at least subjective cognitive costs.

With all this in mind, a major implication of the results as a whole concerns the presumed cognitive costs of decision strategies. All contingency models of decision making (especially Beach & Mitchell, 1978; Payne et al., 1993) assume that compensatory strategies are more effortful than noncompensatory strategies (see also Christensen-Szalanski, 1978; Chu & Spires, 2003). According to our results, though, it is not the *integration* of cue information as done in compensatory strategies that is costly. Rather, it is the *retrieval* of cue information from memory if necessary and the operation of the *meta-decision rule* to select a strategy in the first place that together induce cognitive costs. Note that even under heavy cognitive load, 73% of the participants in Experiment 12 were well able to apply compensatory strategies (53% Franklin's rule, 20% Dawes' rule). Hence, accuracy–effort tradeoffs probably concern the strategy selection process more than the use of the strategy itself.

The data and conclusions we have amassed naturally lead, as Shepard's quote intimated at the beginning of this chapter, to a revised conception of the central questions to study within the framework of the adaptive toolbox: How exactly do participants figure out the heuristic–environment match that enables choosing one appropriate tool from the adaptive toolbox? And when and how is this apparently effortful process initiated? These questions of strategy selection are at the heart of all contingency model frameworks in decision making as well as the adaptive toolbox, but the topic has hitherto largely been a blind spot in empirical research except for some speculations (see Payne et al., 1993).

The adaptive toolbox metaphor of the mind as incorporating a collection of discrete heuristics is attractive on theoretical grounds, and our experiments have further given it empirical support. Other metaphors for how we make adaptive inferences have also been proposed, for instance, a single adjustable power tool with changeable thresholds for controlling information accumulation (Hausmann, 2004; Lee & Cummins, 2004; Newell, 2005). But models derived from such metaphors also face challenges, such as the question of how their thresholds are adjusted. Hermann Ebbinghaus (1885/1966) formulated a simple but important truth about metaphors: The only thing we definitely know about our metaphors is that they are wrong. Metaphors have limits, and it makes no sense to ask whether they are true or false. Rather, we should ask whether they are *fruitful* for

describing phenomena and for stimulating new research. The results presented in this chapter indicate that the adaptive toolbox has hitherto been a very fruitful metaphor.

NOTES

1. The "amounts" were hypothetical, not real. In most experiments involving the stock market paradigm we had monetary prizes for the best brokers to increase motivation.
2. The small but significant correlation with impulsivity ($R2 = .08$) in Experiment 11 was not replicated in Experiment 7 despite substantially higher statistical power.
3. Critics may complain that there should not be an increase in decision times with Franklin's rule and Dawes' rule because these strategies always use all information. But even if one follows a perfect compensatory decision rule (e.g., Franklin's rule with four cues), one does not always have to retrieve the third and fourth cue. For instance, if the first two cues (when presented in validity order) favor one option and speak against the other, this impact cannot be overruled by *two* less valid cues. Hence, retrieving them is pointless. This argument is valid, however, only for a fixed number of cues as in our experiments. Another interpretation of the slight increase is that participants classified as using Franklin's rule or Dawes' rule did this in the majority of trials, but they used take-the-best in some of the trials. The outcome-based classification assumes constant strategies as a simplification.

Introduction to Chapter 18

Empirical Tests of a Fast-and-Frugal Heuristic: Not Everyone "Takes-the-Best"

After Arndt Bröder set off on his quest for take-the-best (see Chapter 17), Ben Newell, David Shanks, and their collaborators independently published a series of experimental articles on this heuristic. Although openly critical of the proposition that people rely on heuristics, in our view, these authors have contributed considerably to the evidence for take-the-best. The methodological differences are instructive. Bröder developed a number of classification methods, for instance, a regression-based classification method in which take-the-best is represented as a linear model with noncompensatory weights, such as weights of 8, 4, 2, and 1 in the case of four binary cues, whereas tallying is represented by equal weights. Newell and colleagues instead relied on a version of the Mouselab technology that Rieskamp and Hoffrage (1999) had used for investigating how people make inferences. The important difference, however, lies in the competitive testing of strategies. Unlike Bröder, who tested take-the-best against Dawes' rule and weighted linear strategies and Rieskamp and Hoffrage (1999; 2008), who compared eight strategies, Ben Newell, Nicola Weston, and David Shanks did not conduct competitive tests. They tested only take-the-best. Why do competitive tests matter?

No model in psychology can come even close to correctly predicting behavior 100% of the time. Therefore, a model's performance needs to be evaluated against the performance of its best competitors. For instance, Bröder (2000, Experiment 3) reported that for low and high information costs, 40% and 65% of participants were classified as take-the-best users, respectively, compared with 0% and 0% as users of an equal-weight strategy. If there is no competitor, however, one can evaluate a 65% rate of correct predictions as impressive or unimpressive, depending on one's priors. In the general discussion of the present article, the authors report that the predictions of the search, stopping, and decision rules of take-the-best were correct in 75%, 80%, 89%, 89%, 89%, and 92% of all cases. But in the abstract they report that only 33% of participants behaved in a manner "completely consistent" with take-the-best. This discrepancy results from the authors' decision to classify only those individuals as "completely consistent" who followed each rule—the search, stopping, and decision rules—at least 90% of the time. If reliability on just one of these rules was below 90%, a value rarely reached in psychological experiments, few would be classified as relying on take-the-best. For instance, one participant in Experiment 1 (No. 20 in Table 18-2) followed the stopping rule of take-the-best in 88% of the 60 trials. She was nevertheless classified as evidence against this strategy and in favor of an unspecified "weight of evidence" strategy, disregarding the fact that she followed the latter at most in only 12% of the trials. In Experiment 2, a participant who followed the stopping rule in 89% of the trials ended up being interpreted as support for the opposite strategy (No. 18 in Table 18-4). Testing strategies needs to be competitive. Two or more models need to be specified and evaluated in the same way, as shown in Chapter 19, where Bergert and Nosofsky conducted competitive tests between take-the-best and a specified "weight of evidence" strategy.

To avoid misunderstandings: We completely agree with Newell and colleagues that "not everyone 'takes-the-best.'" The existence of individual differences in judgment tasks is ubiquitous, and the real challenge is to identify the key heuristics or other strategies beyond take-the-best. Heterogeneity is inherent to the concept of an adaptive toolbox, and the question of how to account for the striking individual differences is waiting to be answered (see Chapters 17 and 22).

CHAPTER 18

Empirical Tests of a Fast-and-Frugal Heuristic: Not Everyone "Takes-the-Best"

Ben R. Newell, Nicola J. Weston, and David R. Shanks

Abstract: The fast-and-frugal heuristics approach to decision making under uncertainty advocated by Gigerenzer and colleagues (e.g., Gigerenzer & Goldstein, 1996) has achieved great popularity despite a relative lack of empirical validation. We report two experiments that examine the use of one particular heuristic—"take-the-best" (TTB). In both experiments the majority of participants adopted frugal strategies, but only one-third (33%) behaved in a manner completely consistent with TTB's search, stopping and decision rules. Furthermore, a significant proportion of participants in both experiments adopted a nonfrugal strategy in which they accumulated more information than was predicted by TTB's stopping rule. The results provide an insight into the conditions under which different heuristics are used, and question the predictive power of the fast-and-frugal approach.

1. INTRODUCTION

The "fast-and-frugal" approach to judgment and decision making has achieved recent wide popularity (Gigerenzer, 2000; Gigerenzer & Goldstein, 1996; Gigerenzer & Selten, 2001; Gigerenzer & Todd, 1999). The approach has been applied to many areas including legal decision making (Dhami & Ayton, 2001), decision analysis in patient care (Elwyn, Edwards, Eccles, & Rovner, 2001), decision making in colonies of social insects (Seeley, 2001), and has also been tested in a number of studies employing more traditional cognitive psychological paradigms (Bröder, 2000; Jones, Juslin, Olsson, & Winman, 2000; Newell & Shanks, 2003).

This seductive appeal of heuristics that are both simple and plausible has undoubtedly contributed to their popularity. For example, Elwyn et al. (2001) have argued that there needs to be a paradigm shift in the way decisions are managed that reflects the importance of analyzing the trade-off between accuracy and frugality in the practice of evidence-based medicine. They argue that although methods of decision making based on classical approaches embodied by Bayesian reasoning and expected utility theory (e.g., decision analysis) might improve patient autonomy by involving patients in the decision process, their use by health professionals with limited time is wholly unrealistic. Elwyn et al. (2001) propose that the "new frontier" will involve the development of fast-and-frugal heuristics for both clinicians and patients to enhance the transparency of diagnosis and decision making.

Is this talk of "new frontiers" and paradigm shifts warranted? In this paper we are interested not so much in whether fast-and-frugal heuristics are *plausible* but rather in whether they are accurate in describing *actual* human behavior. There is now a growing body of evidence that documents the formal properties and efficiency of a number of fast-and-frugal heuristics (Czerlinski, Gigerenzer, & Goldstein, 1999; Goldstein et al., 2001; Martignon & Hoffrage, 1999) but this work needs to be complemented by empirical validation demonstrating that people do indeed use these heuristics in the environments in which they are claimed to operate. Without such empirical validation it seems that talk of a paradigm shift is premature.

"Take-the-best" (TTB) is frugal because it bases its decision on a single feature, and fast because it does not bother searching through and integrating information about other alternatives (i.e., it is noncompensatory). Thus the TTB strategy can be thought of as comprising three basic building blocks: the search rule (search cues in order of descending validity), the stopping rule (stop after the first discriminating cue is discovered), and the decision rule (choose the outcome pointed to by the first cue that discriminates).

The few studies that have sought empirical validation of TTB have found some evidence for its use (up to 65% of participants under conditions that favor the heuristic, e.g., Bröder, 2000, Experiment 4). In a previous set of experiments (Newell & Shanks, 2003) we used a share prediction task and created an experimental environment that we argued would promote adoption of the TTB strategy. The basic task required participants to predict which of two shares from two fictional companies was the more profitable. To help them make their predictions, participants were able to buy information relating to the companies' financial status. This information took the form of binary cues (e.g., Is it an established company?—YES/NO). On each trial participants were able to buy up to four pieces of information prior to making their prediction. This sequential buying of pieces of information—rather than the simultaneous and automatic provision of information used in some other tests of TTB (Bröder, 2000, Experiments 1 and 2; Jones et al., 2000)—allowed us to analyze participants' information search and buying behavior. The aspect of participants' behavior in which we were most interested was whether or not they continued to buy information *after*

discovering a cue that discriminated between the two companies. We reasoned that seeking such "unnecessary" information (i.e., information bought after the discovery of a discriminating cue) constituted a clear violation of TTB's stopping rule. The stopping rule seems to us to be the most important of TTB's components as it is the one that best distinguishes between the noncompensatory nature of the fast-and-frugal approach and the compensatory character of the more classic approaches to decision making such as linear regression or Bayesian calculation.

The experimental environments employed by Newell and Shanks (2003) were designed to promote the use of TTB. Participants were given a hint telling them the validities of the cues to encourage them to buy information in the order of the validities. The relative cost of information was high to discourage buying of unnecessary information. Furthermore, in one experiment a deterministic rather than a probabilistic environment was used to make it easier for participants to learn the relationships between the cues and the outcome. Despite these conditions contrived to promote the use of TTB, there was a high proportion of behavior that was inconsistent with the heuristic, particularly its stopping rule. In all the experiments a significant number of participants bought unnecessary information on some of the trials and in one experiment unnecessary information was bought on an average of 44% of the 120 test trials. We described this tendency to buy unnecessary information as a "weight of evidence" strategy. Such behavior is consistent with many other examples in the literature in which people are not always satisfied to make a decision on the basis of one piece of discriminating information but instead seek additional evidence to increase their confidence in their choice (Harvey & Bolger, 2001; Svenson, 1992, 1996).

It is worth noting that the experimental environments used by us and others to test fast-and-frugal heuristics (e.g., Bröder, 2000; Jones et al., 2000; Newell & Shanks, 2003) can be described as "menu-based" inference tasks, because all the cue information required to make a decision is available (usually at some cost) on a "menu" (i.e., on the computer screen or a piece of paper) in front of participants. These menu-based tasks contrast with "memory-based" inference tasks in which cue information has to be retrieved from memory (Hastie & Park, 1986 have drawn a similar distinction between "online" and "memory-based" judgment tasks). Slegers, Brake, and Doherty (2000) have argued that fast-and-frugal heuristics are only applicable to memory-based inference tasks and therefore cannot be tested using menu-based tasks. Although the heuristics were designed for memory-based problems (such as the city population task, Gigerenzer & Goldstein, 1996) we argue that the explicit and precise descriptions of the heuristics lend themselves to being tested in experimental environments using a "menu" of cues. Furthermore, proponents of the fast-and-frugal approach have used menu-based tasks to test its assumptions (e.g., Rieskamp & Hoffrage, 1999, see below).

Our results in conjunction with other empirical investigations of TTB (e.g., Bröder, 2000; Jones et al., 2000) demonstrate that TTB is clearly not universally adopted by participants—even under conditions strongly constrained to promote its use. We acknowledge that Gigerenzer and his colleagues do not assume that TTB is universal in the sense that it will be used by everyone regardless of the environment; in fact Gigerenzer is at pains to stress that the notion of an adaptive toolbox implies that the use of *different* heuristics is determined by the nature of the environment. Nevertheless, the failure to find any circumstances, however restricted, in which a particular heuristic (such as TTB) is almost universally employed seems to us to be problematic for the fast-and-frugal approach. It is problematic simply because if one cannot predict which heuristics will be used in which environments then determining the heuristic that will be selected from the toolbox for a particular environment becomes necessarily post hoc and thus the fast-and-frugal approach looks dangerously like becoming unfalsifiable. In this paper we ask whether an experimental environment can be constructed in which we might observe a higher proportion of participants adhering to the strategy, and thus provide further insight into the conditions under which particular heuristics are used.

One candidate task characteristic for promoting the use of TTB-consistent behavior was proposed by Rieskamp and Hoffrage (1999). They speculated that an increase in the complexity of a task would lead more participants to adopt simple noncompensatory strategies like TTB. Their speculation is based on the finding in a number of process-tracing studies that increasing the number of alternatives in a given decision domain and the number of dimensions or cues on which the alternatives are evaluated generally leads to the use of simplifying, noncompensatory strategies (e.g., Ford, Schmitt, Schechtman, Hults, & Doherty, 1989; Payne, 1976; Timmermans, 1993). In a review of 45 process-tracing studies, Ford et al. (1989) concluded, "Compensatory strategies were typically only used when the number of alternatives and dimensions were small" (p. 75). A clear prediction that follows from this conclusion is that increasing the complexity of the share task used by Newell and Shanks (2003) should provide an environment in which more people adopt noncompensatory strategies like TTB.

Our previous experiments and others that have employed similar tasks (e.g., Bröder, 2000; Jones et al., 2000) all used environments with four binary cues. In Experiment 1 we increased the number of cues to six. We reasoned that the addition of two cues should create an environment in which we were less likely to observe violations of the stopping rule of TTB. The key indicator of stopping rule violations was whether or not participants continued to buy information *after* discovering a discriminating cue. The experimental environment also allowed us to monitor participants' adherence to TTB's other two building blocks—the search rule (searching cues in order of descending validity) and the decision rule (choose the outcome pointed to by the first cue that discriminates).

2. EXPERIMENT 1

2.1. Participants

Twenty-four members of the University College London community took part in the experiment. Eleven were male and 13 were female. They had a mean age of 23.8 years (range 19–44, $SD = 5.5$). Most of the participants were undergraduate or graduate students at UCL.

2.2. Stimuli and Design

The experiment was programmed in Microsoft Visual Basic 6 and run on an IBM compatible PC. Participants were presented with a series of two-alternative forced-choice decisions between the shares of two fictional companies (Share A and Share B). The shares were described by six binary cues with semantic labels concerning aspects of the company's financial status. The cues had validities .90, .85, .80, .75, .70, and .65, where validity is defined as the probability that the cue will identify the correct alternative on a random selection of alternatives that differ on this cue. The assignment of the validities to the six nominal cues was counterbalanced across participants, but the screen position of the cues was constant. For each share there were 64 distinct cue patterns, and thus 2016 possible paired comparisons. A subset of 180 of these comparisons was randomly selected for each participant. For each comparison there was an associated probability of Share A being the more profitable. After each choice the probability that the chosen share was more profitable was computed according to Bayes' rule, assuming conditional independence of the cues. It is true, of course, that conditional independence will not hold in some environments, but making the cues in our task conditionally independent facilitates testing the heuristic and interpreting the data, and for at least some real-world environments is probably a reasonable approximation. Appendix A provides details of the experimental environment and the calculations. A random number generator then determined which share was more profitable according to this probability.

2.3. Procedure

Participants were told that on each trial they would be asked to choose a share (one of two alternatives) that they thought would turn out to be the more profitable. To help them make this choice participants were able to buy up to six pieces of information about the two companies

that the shares were from. The six pieces of information were: *Was the share trend positive over the last few months? Does the company have financial reserves? Does the company invest in new projects? Is it an established company? Is the company listed on the FTSE?* and *Is the employee turnover low?* Each piece of information cost 1p and was bought by clicking on a screen-button which revealed the value (YES or NO) of the piece of information for each share. Participants bought as much information as they desired and then selected either Share A or Share B. They were then told which share was most profitable for that trial and if they had made the correct prediction their account was incremented by 7p minus any money they had invested in buying information.[1]

Participants were told that in making their predictions they should try to work out which pieces of information were most useful as not all the pieces were equally informative. To assist participants in learning the relative usefulness of the cues a hint was provided after the first 60 trials and then again after 120 trials. This hint provided participants with the order of the usefulness of the six cues as determined by their actual validities (e.g., "'Share Trend' is the most useful piece of information followed by 'Financial reserves,' then 'Invest in new projects,'" etc.). We note that "useful" is a somewhat ambiguous term as it could apply either to the validity of a cue, the discrimination rate or a function of these two properties, namely "success" (Martignon & Hoffrage, 1999).[2] However, the hint simply told participants that it would be more useful to them in terms of increasing their number of correct predictions to know the answer to the question, for example, "Is it an established company?" than "Is it listed on the FTSE?" The hint was given twice at 60 trial intervals to encourage participants to follow the search rule by buying information in order of descending validity of the cues. There were 180 trials in total.

On completion of the 180 trials participants were asked to record their ratings (a number between 1 and 100) of the usefulness of each piece of information for helping them make their predictions. Finally, participants were given a post-test questionnaire asking them about the strategy they had used in making their predictions.

2.4. Results

2.4.1. Proportion correct

Figure 18-1 shows the proportion of times the share chosen was the most profitable across the three 60 trial blocks. The overall mean proportion correct across the 180 trials was 70%, and above the chance level of 50% ($t(23) = 12.68$, $p < .001$). An analysis of variance revealed a significant linear trend across blocks of 60 trials ($F(1, 23) = 16.68$, $p < .001$).

2.4.2. Online ranking and estimated usefulness of information

The computer recorded the order in which participants bought information. Each time information about the most valid cue was bought a "1" was recorded, when information about the second most valid cue was bought a "2" was recorded, and so on. This "online" ranking of information buying behavior served as a

manipulation check to establish whether participants bought information in the order of usefulness dictated by the hint, and thus followed TTB's search rule. The top row of Table 18-1 displays the mean online rankings derived from this measure collapsed across all 180 trials. To analyze this pattern we used a nonparametric Page Trend test for ordered alternatives (Siegel & Castellan, 1988). The Page Trend test evaluates the hypothesis that the means are ordered in a specific sequence versus the null hypothesis that the means are the same. The test indicated a significant trend ($z_L = 8.32$, $p < .0001$)[3] across the six rankings in the predicted ascending order from the most valid to the least valid cue. A clearer picture of buying behavior was obtained by looking at rankings over the final 60 trials (after two hints had been provided) which are displayed in the second row of Table 18-1. As expected, the Page Trend test indicated a significant trend for the rankings on the final 60 trials ($z_L = 9.28$, $p < .0001$).

The estimated usefulness ratings of the six pieces of information were normalized by summing the ratings given to each cue and dividing each rating by this total for each participant. The mean, normalized, usefulness ratings for the six pieces of information are displayed in the third row of Table 18-1. A Page Trend test for ordered alternatives indicated a significant trend ($z_L = 8.51$, $p < .0001$) across the six ratings in the predicted descending order from the objectively most useful to the objectively least useful piece of information.

2.4.3. Analysis of TTB's three components

Previous research indicates that large individual differences in strategy use exist for these types of task (Bröder, 2000; Newell & Shanks, 2003) and thus we examined group and individual data patterns for the three components of TTB— search, stopping, and decision. Participants needed to learn about the structure of the environment prior to receiving any hints about the validities of cues. This learning may have led to fluctuations in behavior that are not accurate representations of participants' strategies. For this reason we analyzed behavior during only the final 60 trials. In this final stage after 120 trials

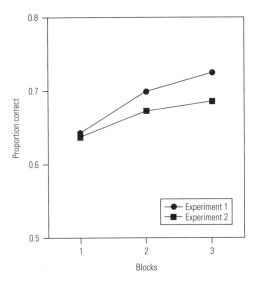

Figure 18-1. Mean proportion of trials on which the "correct" share was chosen in Experiments 1 and 2. *Note.* For Experiment 1 each block represents 60 trials, for Experiment 2 each block represents 40 trials.

Table 18-1.   Experiment 1

Cue Validity	Most			Least		
Online ranking (*SD*)—all trials	2.08 (1.0)	2.67 (.49)	3.16 (.49)	3.98 (.71)	4.33 (.66)	4.49 (1.1)
Online ranking (*SD*)—last 60 trials	1.29 (.68)	2.18 (.51)	2.94 (.40)	4.32 (.81)	4.78 (.66)	5.16 (1.1)
Estimated usefulness (*SD*)	.30 (.15)	.22 (.07)	.18 (.08)	.12 (.08)	.09 (.06)	.09 (.08)

Top row: online ranking of the six cues over all 180 trials. Second row: online ranking of the six cues over the last 60 trials. Third row: normalized estimated usefulness ratings of the six cues.

and two hints we reasoned that any violations of the heuristic's components were less likely to be attributable to exploration of the experimental environment. Table 18-2 displays individual data for Experiment 1 for these final 60 trials.

2.4.4. Search rule

The online ranking and estimated usefulness measures illustrate that at a group level participants behaved in a way that is consistent with the underlying assumptions of the search rule of TTB—namely that they had access to a hierarchy of cues that they subjectively ordered correctly and that they searched through in order of descending validity. The second column of Table 18-2 indicates that this search behavior was fairly consistent across participants. Recall that the computer recorded a "1" every time the most valid piece of information was bought, a "2" for the second most valid and so on. Thus the values in the second column of Table 18-2 are the mean rankings for the piece of information bought first, second, third, fourth, etc., across the final 60 training trials. Only two participants (p4 and p10) failed to buy the most valid piece of information first, and 18 participants (75%) correctly bought the most valid first followed by the second most valid piece of information.

2.4.5. Stopping rule

For the stopping rule we wanted to test whether search was terminated after a participant found a cue that discriminated between the alternatives. In order to test whether participants adopted this strategy the computer recorded the number of trials on which information was bought after a discriminating cue was identified. This allowed us to identify trials on which a

participant bought a discriminating cue (e.g., "YES" for Share A and "NO" for Share B) and then went on to buy "unnecessary" information about another cue.

The mean proportion of unnecessary information bought was .20 (*SE* = .05). Thus at a group level, participants' behavior was inconsistent with the stopping rule, because strict adherence to the strategy would predict a value of 0 for the unnecessary information measure. However, the third column of Table 18-2 indicates that in fact eight participants (p7, p10, p12, p13, p15, p18, p23, and p24) out of 24 (33%) did not buy any unnecessary information. These participants thus completely adhered to the stopping rule. In contrast, five participants bought unnecessary information on over 50% of trials.

2.4.6. Decision rule

For testing the decision rule we were interested in the proportion of trials on which unnecessary information was bought, and participants' decisions were *not* in the direction pointed to by the first discriminating cue that they purchased. For example, if a participant bought the most valid cue and it discriminated (e.g., "YES" for Share A and "NO" for Share B) but then went on to buy further cues, and finally chose Share B this constituted a violation of the decision rule (and the stopping rule). Note that this measure does not distinguish between trials on which the cues acquired after the first discriminating cue point in the opposite direction, the same direction, or are tied (i.e., both "YES" or both "NO").

The mean proportion of trials on which there were decision rule violations was .11. Thus at a group level, participants' behavior was somewhat inconsistent with the decision rule, because

Table 18-2.   Individual Participant Data for Experiment 1 (Last 60 Trials)

Participant No.	Online Ranking	Unnecessary Information	Decision Rule Violations	No Information (Guessing)
1	1–2–3–6–5–4	.23	.07	0
2	1–2–3–5–•–•	.65	.31	0
3	1–2–3–4–5–6	.03	0	0
4	2–3–4–1–5–6	.75	.27	0
5	1–2–3–5–4–•	.71	.06	.25
6	1–3–2–6–4–5	0	0	0
7	1–2–3–•–•–•	0	0	0
8	1–2–3–4–5–6	.02	0	0
9	1–2–3–4–5–6	.56	.12	0
10	3–1–2–5–4–6	0	0	0
11	1–2–3–•–•–•	.33	.50	.90
12	1–2–3–4–5–6	0	0	.02
13	1–2–•–•–•–•	0	0	0
14	1–2–3–•–•–•	.10	.17	0
15	1–2–3–4–5–6	0	0	0
16	1–2–3–4–5–6	.36	.30	.07
17	1–2–3–4–5–6	.52	.13	0
18	1–2–3–•–•–•	0	0	.65
19	1–2–6–3–4–5	.02	0	0
20	1–3–2–4–•–•	.12	.29	0
21	1–3–5–6–2–4	.16	.29	.28
22	1–2–6–3–4–5	.30	.06	0
23	•–•–•–•–•–•	0	0	1.0
24	1–2–3–4–•–•	0	0	0

Note: Online ranking is derived from the order in which participants bought information and thus provides an indication of whether participants followed the search rule. A • indicates that no further pieces of information were bought. Unnecessary Information refers to the proportion of trials on which information was bought after discovering a discriminating cue (violating the stopping rule). This measure is conditionalized on whether any information was bought at all. For example p5 guessed on 25% of trials (15 out of 60); on the remaining 75% of trials (45 out of 60) she bought unnecessary information on 71% of trials (32 out of 45). Decision rule violations refer to the proportion of trials on which unnecessary information was bought and participants' choices were *not* in the direction pointed to by the first discriminating cue that they purchased. No information or "guessing" refers to the proportion of trials on which participants did not purchase any information prior to making their decision.

strict adherence to the strategy would predict a value of 0 for this measure. However, at an individual level, the fourth column of Table 18-2 shows that 12 (p3, p6, p7, p8, p10, p12, p13, p15, p18, p19, p23, and p24) out of 24 participants (50%) never violated the decision rule.

2.4.7. Classification of participants' strategies

We have argued that the measure which distinguishes best between fast-and-frugal behavior and a more compensatory mechanism, is the acquisition of "unnecessary" information. For this reason, we decided to classify participants' strategies on the basis of this measure. This

resulted in the identification of three separate strategies: a "frugal" strategy in which a decision was made after discovering one discriminating cue, a "weight of evidence" strategy in which participants continued to buy "unnecessary" information after discovering a discriminating cue, and "guessing" in which no information was bought at all.

2.4.8. Frugal strategy

Table 18-2 indicates that 11 (p3, p6, p7, p8, p10, p12, p13, p14, p15, p19, and p24) out of 24 participants (46%; 95% $CI = \pm 20\%$) appear to have adopted a frugal stopping rule. Some of these participants did still buy some unnecessary information, but the small amounts (a maximum of 10% by p14) could arguably be attributed to response error or attention lapses.[4] Participants in this behavioral category bought an average of 1.77 pieces of information per trial (out of a maximum of 4) and earned an average of £5.92, in addition to their participation fee, and their mean proportion correct across all 180 trials was 73%.

2.4.9. Weight of evidence

Table 18-2 shows that nine (p1, p2, p4, p5, p9, p16, p17, p20, and p22), out of the 24 participants (38%; 95% $CI = \pm19\%$) adopted what we have termed a weight of evidence strategy. On a significant proportion of trials (mean 44%, minimum 12%, and maximum 75%) these participants bought more information after discovering a discriminating cue. For these participants, presumably basing their decisions on what for certain trials was only one sixth of the available information was perceived as too risky. However, it is not the case that these participants bought all available information on each trial. The mean amount of information bought per trial was 2.55, and the mean amount of unnecessary information was 1.26. The average amount earned by participants in this category was £4.36 and their mean proportion correct across all 180 trials was 71%.

2.4.10. Guessing

Four participants, (p11, p18, p21, and p23), (16%; 95% $CI = \pm15\%$) guessed on a considerable proportion of trials. Three other participants guessed on some trials, notably p5, but in each case it was not their dominant strategy. These participants earned an average of £6.07 and their mean proportion correct across all 180 trials was 58%.

2.4.11. Post-test questionnaires

In addition to behavioral data we collected participants' reports of the strategy they thought they had used. In general, self-reports matched behavior, but a number of inconsistencies were apparent. Therefore, we grouped participants solely on their behavior as this provided a less ambiguous classification of the actual strategy adopted.

2.5. Discussion

We examined the possibility that increasing the number of cues in the share prediction task would create an experimental environment in which violations of the TTB strategy were minimized. The results of Experiment 1 clearly demonstrate that using an environment with six cues did not eliminate violations of TTB. If adherence to each rule (i.e., validity ordered search for the first two cues, and values for the stopping, decision and guessing measures within the 10% margin for attention lapses, see Footnote 4) is demanded then eight participants (p3, p7, p8, p12, p13, p15, p19, and p24) (33%) can be classified as displaying behavior consistent with TTB.

Although the TTB strategy may not have fared too well in our environment, the fast-and-frugal approach in general did well. The majority of participants displayed validity ordered search, at least for the first two or three cues. Furthermore, the largest proportion of participants were those adopting a frugal stopping rule, who in addition to stopping search after acquiring only one piece of discriminating information, conformed to the decision rule by always choosing the alternative pointed to by the discriminating cue (with the exception of p14 who chose in the opposite direction on 17% of trials).

However, almost 40% of participants tended to buy more information than was necessary— even when it was cognitively (in terms of effort) and financially disadvantageous to do so, thus violating the stopping rule. These participants all violated the decision rule too, on at least some of the trials (minimum .06, maximum .30, and mean .18). We classified these participants as adopting a weight of evidence strategy. This strategy appears not to be compensatory in the sense that a classical weighted additive rule is because participants did not buy *all* the information available on each trial. It seems rather that these participants wanted to accumulate one extra piece of information per trial on average, *after* discovering a discriminating cue, perhaps in order to reduce their uncertainty about the outcome of, or the risk associated with, their choice.

Finally, a small proportion of participants chose to guess on a large proportion of trials. Although this guessing strategy was perhaps economically adaptive in this environment (this group had marginally higher earnings than the frugal strategists) it was not a successful strategy for learning about the usefulness of the cues or increasing the number of correct predictions made. Note that both these objectives were explicitly stated in the instructions, and this is probably why only a minority of participants chose to adopt a guessing strategy. It is also of course possible that for these few participants the pay-off structure of the environment was not sufficient to engage their critical thinking.

The pattern of results leaves open the question whether any environment would favor the TTB strategy to the extent that all, or almost all of the participants would conform to each of its components. In Experiment 2 we approached this question by designing what we considered to be the simplest possible situation in which TTB might operate.

3. EXPERIMENT 2

TTB is a decision heuristic used to make choices between two alternatives. When information about the two alternatives is known, a decision is made on the basis of the most valid piece of information that discriminates between the alternatives—without seeking any further information. Thus, the simplest situation in which TTB can be tested is one in which there are two alternatives and two cues that differ in validity. TTB predicts that the less valid cue should *only* be examined when the most valid cue does not discriminate. This prediction would be especially strong in a situation in which participants know the validities of the cues and where the relative cost of information is high. Experiment 2 used such an environment. We reasoned that the simplicity and the transparency of the environment in terms of the relationship between the cues and the outcome would reduce the temptation for participants to seek further evidence after discovering a discriminating cue.

Of course, one could argue on the basis of the evidence from the process-tracing literature that the reduction to two cues should favor nonfrugal strategies and that TTB use will be low in such environments. However, Experiment 1 illustrated that behavior in the share prediction task was not congruent with the findings in the process-tracing literature—we found that a significant proportion of participants used nonfrugal strategies when the environment was relatively complex. Given this incongruence, we felt confident that the two cue environment would promote rather than discourage TTB use. Furthermore, we speculated that some participants in Experiment 1 might have been reluctant to make their decisions on the basis of one piece of discriminatory information because of the potential impact on the outcome of up to five remaining pieces of information. With only one extra piece of information to buy, would participants still be tempted to seek further evidence after discovering a discriminating cue?

3.1. Participants

Twenty-four members of the University College London community took part in the experiment. Nineteen were female and five were male. They had a mean age of 22.5 years (range 18–38, $SD = 4.7$). The majority were undergraduate or graduate students at UCL.

3.2. Stimuli, Design, and Procedure

Experiment 2 used the same share prediction task as Experiment 1 with some modifications. Information concerning aspects of the company's financial status was described by only two, rather than six, binary cues, which had validities of .80 and .60. For each share there were 4 distinct cue patterns and thus 12 possible paired comparisons. Each comparison was shown ten times in a different random order for each participant for a total of 120 trials. The two pieces of information were: *Does the company invest in new projects?* and *Is it an established company?* A hint telling participants the order of usefulness of the two pieces of information was provided after 30 trials. If the correct share was chosen the private account was incremented by 5p minus any money that had been invested to buy information. As in

Experiment 1 each piece of information cost 1p. Thus there was a slight increase in the relative cost of information from a seventh of the potential profit in Experiment 1 to a fifth in this experiment.

3.3. Results

3.3.1. Proportion correct

Figure 18-1 shows the proportion of times the share chosen was the more profitable one over the 120 trials. The mean was 66%. This proportion was well above the chance level of 50% ($t(23) = 11.17$, $p < .001$). However, an analysis of variance did not reveal a significant linear trend across the three blocks ($F(1, 23) = 2.31$, $p = .14$).

3.3.2. Online ranking and estimated usefulness of information

Table 18-3 displays the mean online rankings over the total 120 trials and the last 30 trials and the estimated usefulness of each piece of information. A Wilcoxon test revealed a significant difference between the two rankings ($z = 2.86$, $p < .01$) and between the usefulness ratings of the two cues, ($z = 3.67$, $p < .001$). The pattern for these measures indicates that participants both subjectively rated and searched through cues in the correct order. This behavior is even more apparent for the rankings of the final 30 trials (second row of Table 18-3), and as expected the Wilcoxon test revealed a significant difference between the rankings ($z = 3.28$, $p < .002$).

Table 18-3. Experiment 2

Cue Validity	Most	Least
Online ranking (SD)—all trials	1.19 (.25)	1.76 (.33)
Online ranking (SD)—last 30 trials	1.13 (.31)	1.86 (.33)
Estimated usefulness (SD)	.71 (.19)	.29 (.19)

Top row: online ranking of the six cues over all 120 trials. Second row: online ranking of the six cues over the last 30 trials. Third row: normalized estimated usefulness ratings of the two cues.

3.3.3. Analysis of TTB's three components

We examined trials from the latter stages of the experiment, concentrating on the last block of 30 trials after participants had received a hint and had had 90 trials to learn about the experimental environment.

3.3.4. Search rule

The second column of Table 18-4 displays individual participant data for online ranking—our indicator of search rule adherence. As the group analysis suggested, all but two participants (p7 and p10) followed the search rule by buying the most valid piece of information first.

3.3.5. Stopping rule

The mean proportion of unnecessary information bought was .11. Thus again at a group level performance did not strictly adhere to the stopping rule. However, the third column of Table 18-4 indicates that an impressive 15 participants (p1, p2, p3, p4, p7, p8, p12, p13, p14, p15, p16, p20, p21, p22, and p23) out of 24 (62%) never violated the stopping rule.

3.3.6. Decision rule

The mean proportion of trials on which the decision rule was violated was .11. Thus again at a group level performance did not strictly adhere to the rule. However, the fourth column of Table 18-4 shows that a very high number of participants, 17 (p1, p2, p3, p4, p5, p7, p8, p12, p13, p14, p15, p16, p19, p20, p21, p22, and p23) out of 24 (71%) never violated the decision rule.

3.3.7. Classification of participants' strategies

Consistent with the analysis of Experiment 1 we focused on participants' patterns of information acquisition as a key indicator of the type of strategy being used. Participants were classified as adopting a frugal, a weight of evidence, or a guessing strategy with regard to information acquisition.

3.3.8. Frugal strategy

As the stopping rule analysis above indicated, 62% (95% $CI = \pm19\%$) of participants appear to

Table 18-4. Individual Participant Data for Experiment 2 (last 30 trials)

Participant No.	Online Ranking	Unnecessary Information	Decision Rule Violations	No Information (Guessing)
1	1–2	0	0	.50
2	1–•	0	0	0
3	1–2	0	0	0
4	1–•	0	0	0
5	1–2	.07	0	0
6	1–2	.07	.50	0
7	2–•	0	0	0
8	1–2	0	0	0
9	1–2	.20	.67	0
10	2–1	.70	.48	0
11	1–2	.67	.05	0
12	1–2	0	0	0
13	1–•	0	0	.53
14	1–2	0	0	.03
15	1–2	0	0	0
16	1–•	0	0	0
17	1–2	.26	.25	0
18	1–2	.11	.67	.10
19	1–2	.10	0	0
20	1–•	0	0	.01
21	1–•	0	0	.23
22	1–2	0	0	0
23	1–•	0	0	0
24	1–2	.48	.14	.03

Note: See note accompanying Table 18-2 for a description of each measure.

have used a frugal stopping rule. Consistent with Experiment 1 some participants (p5 and p6) did buy some unnecessary information on some trials (7%) but at levels arguably low enough to be attributed to response error or attention fluctuations (see Footnote 4). Participants who adopted a frugal strategy bought an average of 1.15 pieces of information per trial, earned on average £2.59 in addition to their participation fee and their mean proportion correct across all 120 trials was 67%.

3.3.9. Weight of evidence

Table 18-4 shows that six (p9, p10, p11, p17, p18, and p24) out of 24 participants (25%; 95% CI = ±17%) adopted a weight of evidence strategy seeking further information after discovering a discriminating cue. Participants 10 and 11 did in fact, buy the unnecessary information on every trial in which it was possible to do so. Note

that out of the 12 possible comparisons in our experimental environment, on four there was no unnecessary information to buy as the most valid cue did not discriminate; thus the maximum value for our measure across all 120 trials was .66. In the final 30 trials the mean amount of unnecessary information bought by these participants was 40% (maximum 70%, minimum 10%). (Note that the maximum was 70 and not 66% due to sampling from the final 30 trials). Participants who adopted the weight of evidence strategy bought 1.62 pieces of information per trial, and 1.0 pieces of unnecessary information, on average. They earned an average of £2.19 and their mean proportion correct across the 120 trials was 68%.

3.3.10. Guessing

Three participants (p1, p13, and p21), (13%; 95% CI = ±13%) chose not to buy any information on a significant proportion of trials. These participants earned an average of £2.59 and their mean proportion correct across the 120 trials was 58%.

From this simplified, two-cue version of the task, we were able to identify a further group of participants who guessed in a slightly different manner. In addition to guessing on the basis of no information, participants could guess after buying a nondiscriminatory piece of information, rather than going on to buy another piece of information as TTB predicts. Out of the 12 possible paired comparisons, there were four on which the first cue did not discriminate. An examination of individual data over the last 30 trials revealed that seven participants (p2, p3, p4, p12, p20, p21, and p23) simply guessed whenever the more valid piece of information did not discriminate. They did this on 100% of trials that it was possible to do so (in the last 30 trials, there were on average 9 trials where the first cue did not discriminate). Therefore, these participants were not strictly adhering to the particular type of "frugal" strategy to which they had previously been classified (see above). They made a decision to only buy one piece of information on every trial, and made their choice regardless of whether this piece of information was discriminatory.

Due to the large number of cues in Experiment 1, and hence a more complex environment, this behavior could not be clearly identified. When presented with six cues it would be possible for participants to both buy unnecessary information and make their choice after buying a nondiscriminatory cue on the same trial, thus making it very difficult to classify behavior.

3.3.11. Post-test questionnaires

Consistent with Experiment 1, verbal report data indicated some discrepancies between behavior and reported strategies. For this reason we again based strategy classifications purely on the behavioral data.

3.4. Discussion

We suggested that a simple and transparent environment in which there were only two cues would favor a fast-and-frugal strategy like TTB. Eight participants (p3, p5, p8, p12, p14, p15, p19, and p22) (33%) behaved in a manner consistent with all of TTB's building blocks (validity ordered search, and violations of the stopping, decision and guessing measures within a 10% margin). This is the same proportion as observed in Experiment 1. Consistent with Experiment 1, the remaining two thirds of participants displayed behavior that violated at least one of TTB's rules, including a sizable proportion that used a weight of evidence strategy.

It was the case, however, that the majority of participants used a frugal stopping rule. This frugal rule either ended search after discovering a discriminating cue, as predicted by the TTB heuristic, or terminated search after just looking at the most valid cue—regardless of whether it discriminated. This second strategy could be described as the "take-one" heuristic (Gigerenzer, personal communication), in which the stopping rule states "stop after the most valid cue is bought—regardless of whether it discriminates." We acknowledge that guessing—either on the basis of no information or nondiscriminatory information—is both fast-and-frugal and therefore consistent with the framework.

4. GENERAL DISCUSSION

The aim of this research was to create an environment in which violations of the TTB strategy that we had observed previously (Newell & Shanks, 2003) were eliminated or reduced. We attempted to achieve this aim by manipulating the number of cues or pieces of information in the experimental environment. In Experiment 1 we increased the number of cues to six (from four that we and others had used previously) in the hope that increasing the complexity of the task would promote the adoption of noncompensatory strategies like TTB (cf. Ford et al., 1989; Payne, 1976; Rieskamp & Hoffrage, 1999). Despite using a six-cue environment, only eight participants out of 24 were classified as adhering to each of TTB's rules (search, stopping, and decision). Furthermore, although a fairly large proportion of participants adopted frugal strategies (46%) a similar number (38%) adopted a nonfrugal weight-of-evidence strategy.

In Experiment 2 we tried to design the simplest situation in which TTB can operate—a two-alternative, two-cue environment. We reasoned that the simplicity and transparency of the environment would promote TTB use to the point that violations might be eliminated. In this environment, again only eight out of 24 participants behaved in a manner completely consistent with each of TTB's rules, but overall the adoption of frugal strategies clearly outnumbered the use of nonfrugal strategies (62 and 25% of participants, respectively).

We noted in Section 1 that the fast-and-frugal approach has become increasingly popular in recent years and has been applied to a variety of domains (e.g., Dhami & Ayton, 2001; Elwyn et al., 2001; Seeley, 2001). It is important to emphasize that our results do not challenge this popularity in terms of the applicability of the approach. The results do not undermine the power of the TTB heuristic. Indeed those participants who did adopt the heuristic or components of it earned more money than those who used a less frugal strategy. Our results simply help us to understand the type of conditions under which we might expect people to adopt particular heuristics—this we believe is the most important challenge facing the fast-and-frugal approach. There is a strong need to complement research showing how effective heuristics can be with research showing that they provide an accurate description of *actual* human behavior.

4.1. Violations of TTB's "Building Blocks"

A conservative estimate of TTB-consistent behavior across both experiments suggests that 16 participants out of 48 (33%) conformed to all three of TTB's explicitly defined building blocks, even allowing for a degree of lapses in attention (see Footnote 4). The presence of a high proportion of deviations from TTB (be they frugal or nonfrugal) suggests that either the heuristic is only adopted by a minority of the population and thus that its psychological reality is doubtful, or that we are still just "looking in the wrong place" for the conditions that promote its use. Obviously no test of a theory can be exhaustive and we stress that we are only testing the assumptions of the fast- and-frugal approach for this particular type of decision task, but at the very least our results suggest that the description

of TTB as it stands is too restrictive to encompass the wide variability in the behavior we observed.

For example, the description of the heuristic only permits guessing when there are either no cues available in the environment or when all the cues present are nondiscriminatory. In contrast to these situations we observed participants who chose to guess rather than purchase remaining discriminating cue information (the take-one heuristic). It is relatively easy to think of other situations in which the current description of TTB is rather restrictive. Consider an experimental environment identical to the one employed here, but in which making the correct choice on the final trial determines whether or not the participant receives all the money accumulated throughout the experiment. It seems likely (although we acknowledge that it is an empirical speculation) that the participant would want to be as sure as possible about being correct and would therefore buy all the information available and not just one discriminating piece.

This issue of the severity of the outcome of decisions is one that needs to be addressed within the fast-and-frugal framework. It may be that when an outcome is severe a different heuristic or a combination of heuristics are selected from the "toolbox" but at this stage it is not clear how the environment and/or a homunculus predicts or controls this selection process—a point that has not passed unnoticed (Goldstein et al., 2001). As we emphasized in the introduction, unless one can a priori specify the conditions under which certain heuristics will be selected over others—*and provide human data consistent with these predictions*—the predictive and explanatory power of the fast-and-frugal approach remains questionable.

4.2. Ecological Analysis of Environments

One method for predicting when particular heuristics might be used is to analyze a task environment from an ecological perspective. One potential criticism of the experiments reported here is that we relied on the findings from other process-tracing studies to inform our predictions about whether or not we would observe TTB-consistent behavior. Although this seems to us to be a legitimate way to conduct research, another approach is to create an environment and then to determine the ecologically rational heuristics for that environment.[5] For the sake of simplicity we will consider the environment used in Experiment 2, though the same rationale holds for Experiment 1.

The two cues in Experiment 2 had validities of .80 and .60; one cue had a discrimination rate of .66 and the other a discrimination rate of .33. Each cue cost 1p, which was deducted from the maximum winnings of 5p. Therefore the maximum expected winnings for a TTB strategy can be calculated as follows:

$$E(\text{TTB}) = .80 \times .66 \times (5-1)p + .60 \times .33 \times (5-2)p$$
$$= £2.73p.$$

A similar analysis for the take-one (TO) heuristic demonstrates that the expected winnings through using this heuristic is the sum of two terms, the expected winnings from buying the most valid cue and the expected winnings from guessing:

$$E(\text{TO}) = .80 \times .66 \times (5-1)p + .50 \times .33 \times (5-1)p$$
$$= £2.80p.$$

Finally, a simple guessing strategy in which no information is bought at all has expected winnings of:

$$E(\text{guess}) = .50 \times 5p = £2.50p.$$

This kind of ecological analysis suggests that TTB is not the only heuristic that we should observe in the environment used in Experiment 2. Indeed the closeness of the expected winnings for the three strategies suggests that we should observe all the heuristics with guessing being the least frequent—which is the pattern we found.

However, what such an ecological analysis does not predict—and can never predict in the noncompensatory environments used in the current experiments and previously (Newell & Shanks, 2003)—is the existence of a weight of evidence strategy of the kind adopted by a significant proportion of participants. An ecological analysis is undoubtedly a useful tool in helping to establish when particular heuristics

might be used, but the presence of the weight of evidence strategists highlights that such an analysis is unable to predict the full variability present in actual human behavior.

It is worth clarifying here that by using the label "weight of evidence" we are *not* implying an analytic strategy in which each piece of information is obtained and given a relative weight (e.g., a type of weighted additive rule). The strategy we observed was not one in which a participant bought every available piece of information, it was simply one that involved obtaining, on average, one extra "unnecessary" piece of information before making a decision. Note also that obtaining this unnecessary information did not necessarily imply that the final decision rule of TTB was violated. As indicated in Tables 18-2 and 18-4, many participants in both experiments bought information after discovering a discriminating cue but ultimately chose the option pointed to by the *first* discriminating cue that they had discovered (as predicted by the decision rule). Although behavior of this kind is not a violation of the decision rule, accumulating *more* than one piece of discriminating information before making a decision does not seem, to our minds at least, to be synonymous with *one-reason* decision making.

We speculate that the extra piece of information served to reduce participants' uncertainty about an outcome or the risk associated with a choice. Evidently this element of risk assessment or uncertainty reduction is an important factor for a significant proportion of participants. Another possible reason for the accumulation of extra information is to increase the amount of differentiation between the two alternatives. Svenson (1992, 1996) cites evidence in support of a "differentiation and consolidation" theory, which proposes that people continue to acquire information until a particular candidate is "sufficiently superior for a decision" (Svenson, 1992, p. 143). Montgomery and colleagues (e.g., Montgomery, 1983; Montgomery & Willén, 1999) propose a similar idea in the "search for dominance structure" theory in which information is structured and restructured "in such a way that one alternative becomes the self-evident choice" (Montgomery & Willén,

1999, p. 148). Although these theories are typically applied to situations involving a greater number of alternatives and attributes (e.g., Harvey & Bolger, 2001) than in the experiments presented here, it is clear that they support the conjecture that people are not always satisfied to make a decision on the basis of one piece of discriminating information.

4.3. Half Full versus Half Empty, or a Fundamental Problem?

Throughout this article and previously (Newell & Shanks, 2003), we have tended to highlight participants' violations of the component rules of particular heuristics rather than adherence to those rules. This focus lays us open to the criticism that we are being too negative in our assessment of the fast-and-frugal approach. It could be said that we are taking "the glass is half empty" view rather than emphasizing that it is "half full." However, we argue that our position does not reflect a simplistic negative bias, but rather that the violations of the heuristics are more "newsworthy" because they represent a fundamental problem for the fast-and-frugal approach.

In Experiment 1, at a group level, participants adhered to the search, stopping and decision rules in 75, 80, and 89% of all possible cases respectively. For Experiment 2 the figures are even more impressive: 92% for the search rule and 89% for the stopping and decision rules. Despite the fact that these group means belie wide individual variability (see Tables 18-2 and 18-4) these results appear extremely good for the fast-and-frugal approach—especially as they were achieved in an environment with no adjustable parameters or error terms.

However, this latter point is perhaps both the most appealing and yet potentially the most problematic aspect of the fast-and-frugal approach. The determinism of the rules is appealing because it makes them simple and thus supposedly more psychologically plausible than more computationally complex decision models (though see Chater, Oaksford, Nakisa, & Redington, 2003). But because the heuristics are described deterministically there is no room for error and therefore any deviations from the predicted behavior are necessarily problematic and can only be explained by the introduction of another heuristic or building block (and another, and another—potentially). At this point the division between the simple, transparent heuristic, and a complex, opaque model—a division much championed by Gigerenzer and colleagues—becomes rather muddied. If the "free parameters" are the invention of additional heuristics, why is this preferable to a model that incorporates free parameters and by doing so achieves wider predictive ability—e.g., PROBEX (Juslin & Persson, 2002)?

5. CONCLUSION

In his paper "Rational choice and the structure of the environment," Simon (1956) concluded that his approach to the description of rational behavior was in "closer agreement with the facts of behavior as observed in laboratory and field" (p. 138) than that of more traditional economic and statistical theories. Before the current extensions of Simon's ideas as expounded by Gigerenzer and colleagues (e.g., Gigerenzer & Todd, 1999) induce any paradigm shifts in judgment and decision making, empirical validation of the fast-and-frugal heuristics is highly necessary. Our results suggest that the approach is yet to achieve "close agreement" with behavior observed in the laboratory.

NOTES

1. Note that UK1p = UK£.01 = US$.02 = Eur.02 approximately.
2. Our recent investigations suggest that search in a similar task environment where no hint is provided is more closely associated with the order predicted by the success of the cues rather than their objective validity (Newell, Rakow, Weston, & Shanks, 2004).
3. We report the z_L value for the Page Trend tests following the conversion formula for an N exceeding 12 (Siegel & Castellan, 1988).
4. It is unrealistic to assume that the rule is completely error-free and therefore unnecessary information will sometimes be bought by mistake. To estimate the frequency of such occasions we calculated the proportion of trials on which

unnecessary information was bought by those participants in the two experiments whose individual online ranking, estimation and self-report data were completely consistent with the systematic use of a frugal stopping rule. These eight participants bought unnecessary information on an average of 1% of trials ($SD = 2\%$). Thus the upper limit of 10% that we used as a "cut-off" point is a generous estimate.

5. We thank Gerd Gigerenzer for suggesting this analysis.

APPENDIX A

Probabilities that Share A or B Is More Profitable for the Different Cue Patterns, and the Likelihood Ratio (LR) Favoring A over B in Experiment 1

Cue	Pattern	$P(A = 1/C_i)$	$P(B = 1/C_i)$	LR (A:B)
C_1	10	.90	.10	9/1
	01	.10	.90	1/9
C_2	10	.85	.15	85/15
	01	.15	.85	15/85
C_3	10	.80	.20	4/1
	01	.20	.80	1/4
C_4	10	.75	.25	3/1
	01	.25	.75	1/3
C_5	10	.70	.30	7/3
	01	.30	.70	3/7
C_6	10	.65	.35	65/35
	01	.35	.65	35/65

Note: C_1–C_6 refer to the individual cues (e.g., Established company?). A cue is diagnostic only when there is a YES for one share and a NO for the other share. The Pattern column displays the two diagnostic patterns for each of the four cues (1 = YES, 0 = NO). $P(A = 1/C_i)$ refers to the probability that Share A is more profitable (i.e., A = 1) for a given cue pattern; $P(B = 1/C_i)$ refers to the probability that Share B is more profitable (i.e., B = 1) for a given cue pattern.

To calculate the likelihood of a share from company A being more profitable than one from company B, the likelihood ratios corresponding to the particular patterns are multiplied. For example, if the pattern for company A was 111111 and for company B was 000000, then all six cues would be diagnostic and the share from company A would be $(9/1 \times 85/15 \times 4/1 \times 3/1 \times 7/3 \times 65/35) = 2638$ times more likely to be more profitable. In contrast, if the patterns were 000001 for company A and 000000 for company B only C_6 would be diagnostic and the share from company A would be 65/35 or approximately twice as likely to be the more profitable. The method for calculating share profitability was the same for Experiment 2.

Introduction to Chapter 19

A Response-Time Approach to Comparing Generalized Rational and Take-the-Best Models of Decision Making

Transparency is an important value in cognitive modeling. Simple heuristics such as take-the-best are highly transparent. Based on two objects' values on a set of cues and their ecological validities, one can easily derive take-the-best's predictions. Although it fosters transparency, take-the-best's simplicity also makes very strong assumptions. For instance, the heuristic does not consider possible errors in search or errors in decision. Bryan Bergert and Robert Nosofsky argue that in comparative empirical tests, these strong assumptions might put take-the-best at a disadvantage with other models. Their first major contribution is to propose generalized forms of take-the-best and a weighted additive model, RAT, which can capture errors and individual differences in cue importance and decision.

Testing these generalized versions against their strict counterparts, Bergert and Nosofsky find not only that take-the-best performed better in explaining people's inferences (even accounting for the generalized models' larger number of adjustable parameters) but also that using the generalized models could lead to drastically different conclusions. Whereas in the study of Lee and Cummins (2004), participants' inferences were better predicted by the strict version of RAT than by the strict version of take-the-best, Bergert and Nosofsky find the opposite result for the generalized versions. This suggests that transparency can exact a price. Even if correct in spirit, the strict version of take-the-best seems to sacrifice competitiveness in empirical tests. The fitted parameters of the generalized take-the-best indicate that the superiority of the generalized over the strict version is due to its ability to capture individual variability in cue hierarchy. Once participants had figured out a particular cue hierarchy, they seemed to follow take-the-best's search, stopping, and decision rules consistently.

Bergert and Nosofsky's second major contribution is their systematic comparison of take-the-best and RAT based on process—rather than only outcome—predictions. This is an important test (see also Chapter 7, where reaction times were used to test process predictions of the priority heuristic), and Bergert and Nosofsky found that when take-the-best predicts less extensive information search, people's inferences are indeed faster. Conversely, they found no evidence for RAT's prediction that inferences are faster when the accumulated evidence for one alternative is considerably larger than for the other (compared to when the difference in accumulated evidence is small). The process analyses thus corroborate those on the outcome level. Note that these results were obtained for inferences from givens, whereas Gigerenzer and Goldstein (1996) originally envisioned take-the-best as a tool primarily for inferences from memory (where search costs are high).

Bergert and Nosofsky's work is remarkable for another reason as well. Robert Nosofsky's home turf is the psychology of classification, not inference. With his generalized context model, Nosofsky contributed greatly to the development of one of the major modeling approaches in classification, exemplar models. Although there is usually very little crosstalk between the classification and inference literatures, Nosofsky saw the similarities between classification and inference (see also Juslin, Olsson, & Olsson, 2003). In another article, Nosofsky and Bergert (2007) put exemplar models to the test against take-the-best in inference. The result amazed Nosofsky: Take-the-best seemed to capture the results better than the exemplar model. We applaud Nosofsky for publishing results even when they contradict his own favorite model.

CHAPTER 19

A Response-Time Approach to Comparing Generalized Rational and Take-the-Best Models of Decision Making

F. Bryan Bergert and Robert M. Nosofsky

Abstract: The authors develop and test generalized versions of take-the-best (TTB) and rational (RAT) models of multiattribute paired-comparison inference. The generalized models make allowances for subjective attribute weighting, probabilistic orders of attribute inspection, and noisy decision making. A key new test involves a response-time (RT) approach. TTB predicts that RT is determined solely by the expected time required to locate the 1st discriminating attribute, whereas RAT predicts that RT is determined by the difference in summed evidence between the 2 alternatives. Critical test pairs are used that partially decouple these two factors. Under conditions in which ideal observer TTB and RAT strategies yield equivalent decisions, both the RT results and the estimated attribute weights suggest that the vast majority of subjects adopted the generalized TTB strategy. The RT approach is also validated in an experimental condition in which use of a RAT strategy is essentially forced upon subjects.

Recent research in decision making has introduced heuristics that dramatically simplify processing while maintaining a high level of accuracy. Gigerenzer and Todd (1999) and Gigerenzer and Selten (2001) refer to these heuristics as "the adaptive toolbox." They theorize that much decision making results from an application of one or more of these simple heuristics, instead of from an application of the classically "rational" strategies that make exhaustive use of all available information. Such heuristics as *recognition* and *take-the-best*

(TTB) are thought to be adaptations to natural information environments, and they constitute an alternative vision of rationality, called *ecological rationality* or *bounded rationality* (Gigerenzer & Goldstein, 1996; Gigerenzer & Selten, 2001; Goldstein & Gigerenzer, 2002; Simon, 1956).

A great deal of research has been devoted to comparing the predictions from the TTB model and classically rational models of decision making. In this article, however, we suggest that the compared models make quite strong assumptions. For example, within the framework of the compared models, it is often assumed that subjects attach certain ideal observer weights to the multiple attributes that compose the alternatives and also that the underlying choice mechanisms are fully deterministic in nature. The main purpose of the present research was to consider generalized versions of the models that relax these assumptions, leading to what we view as more psychologically plausible models. Furthermore, we introduce a new response-time method for distinguishing between the predictions from the generalized models.

THE TAKE-THE-BEST MODEL

In making a decision about which of two alternatives is higher on some variable of interest, TTB considers the features of the alternatives in order of diagnosticity and makes a decision according to the first feature found that distinguishes between the alternatives. For example, suppose first that the presence of a professional basketball team provides a good indication of the size of a city, and then imagine that one city has a team and another does not. On the basis of this cue, in a pairwise comparison, TTB could make a decision immediately. If both cities have a team, or if both cities do not—that is, if they match on this cue—then TTB would consider the next cue in order of diagnosticity, and so on until a decision is made.

Researchers have argued that in numerous natural-world environments, TTB strikes an adaptive balance between the quality of an agent's final decision and the efficiency with which that decision is made (Gigerenzer & Todd, 1999; Simon, 1956, 1976). TTB maximizes speed by making its decision on the basis of a single discriminating cue, but, of course, the order of consideration of cues is important. TTB would make fast decisions if uninformative cues were examined first, but those decisions would be of poor quality. Therefore, to strike a balance between speed and decision quality, TTB inspects cues from the best predictor of the variable of interest to the worst.

The predictor value of a feature for a certain variable, also known as its *cue validity*, is defined as the proportion of distinctions a feature makes that are correct. For example, to determine the validity of having a professional basketball team for predicting city size, one would consider all pairs of cities and count the number of pairs in which one city has a team and the other does not. The cue validity would be the proportion of these pairs in which the city with a team is actually larger than the city without

a team. In general, the validity of cue $i (v_i)$ is defined as

$$v_i = \frac{correct\_distinctions_i}{total\_distinctions_i}. \qquad (19\text{-}1)$$

One consequence of the definition given in Equation 19-1 is that a cue that makes 1 out of 1 distinction correctly will have a cue validity identical to a cue that makes 100 out of 100 distinctions correctly. In fact, a cue that makes 1 out of 1 distinction correctly will have a higher cue validity than one that makes 999 out of 1,000 distinctions correctly. The Bayesian modification (Lee, Chandrasena, & Navarro, 2002; Lee & Cummins, 2004) given in Equation 19-2 has been used to address this counterintuitive result:

$$v_i = \frac{1 + correct\_distinctions_i}{2 + total\_distinctions_i}. \qquad (19\text{-}2)$$

Thus, cues that make a small number of distinctions have a low Bayesian cue validity. Following Lee and Cummins (2004), we adopt the Equation 19-2 definition of cue validity in the present article.

Once cue validities have been calculated, TTB begins by inspecting cues in order of validity, from most valid cue to least valid cue, until a feature is found for which the alternatives have different feature levels. TTB then uses this feature to make a decision.[1]

A RATIONAL (RAT) MODEL

A weighted additive model (Payne & Bettman, 2001; Rieskamp & Otto, 2006)—which we will call *RAT*, after Lee and Cummins's (2004) "rational" model—is often chosen as the embodiment of rational decision making, for purposes of comparison with the heuristic approaches. RAT assigns to each feature a weight (w_i), calculates the summed total evidence in favor of each alternative, and chooses the alternative with more total evidence. The evidence in favor of each alternative is calculated only over those features that mismatch and therefore discriminate between the alternatives. Thus, the decision rule in RAT is to "choose A" if

$$\sum_{a \in FA} w_a > \sum_{b \in FB} w_b, \qquad (19\text{-}3)$$

where FA and FB denote the sets of all discriminating features that favor alternatives A and B, respectively. Thus defined, RAT assumes that each feature makes an independent contribution to the evidence in favor of an alternative. Given this assumption, it turns out that the optimal value to use for w_i is the log odds of the cue validity, v_i, given in Equation 19-4:

$$w_i = \log\left(\frac{v_i}{1 - v_i}\right). \qquad (19\text{-}4)$$

Lee and Cummins (2004) give a conceptual explanation of Equation 19-4, and Katsikopoulos and Martignon (2006) provide a proof.

EXPERIMENTS ON THE USE OF TTB AND RAT

The existence and relative efficiency of the heuristics in the adaptive toolbox have naturally led to experiments to determine whether people actually use them in making decisions (for a review, see Payne & Bettman, 2001). A combination of process tracing and outcome approaches has been used (Rieskamp & Hoffrage, 1999; Rieskamp & Otto, 2006). In a typical process-tracing experiment, a person must actively uncover each cue to see its value, so the experimenter can observe the order, extent, and time course of information search (e.g., Bröder, 2000; Johnson, Payne, Schkade, & Bettman, 1991; Newell, Rakow, Weston, & Shanks, 2004; Newell & Shanks, 2004; Rieskamp & Hoffrage, 1999; Rieskamp & Otto, 2006). In contrast, in an outcome-oriented experiment, certain decisions are predicted by certain models, so researchers can infer which strategy was used from the final decision made (Juslin, Jones, Olsson, & Winman, 2003; Lee & Cummins, 2004; Rieskamp & Hoffrage, 1999).

Numerous experiments have shown that people's choice of strategy is contingent upon the characteristics of the task and stimuli. If a decision task (Rieskamp & Otto, 2006) or a categorization task (Juslin et al., 2003) affords different strategies different levels of accuracy, people tend to adopt the most accurate strategy. Conversely, if strategies produce the same level of performance, people tend to adopt the simplest strategy (Juslin et al., 2003). However, increases in time pressure and information-acquisition costs, as well as presentation formats involving separate attribute listings as opposed to holistic images, lead to increased use of TTB-like strategies (Bröder & Schiffer, 2003; Gigerenzer & Todd, 1999; Martignon & Hoffrage, 1999; Payne, Bettman, & Johnson, 1988, 1993).

The current research is most directly motivated by an experiment conducted by Lee and Cummins (2004), who used an outcome analysis to determine whether subjects would tend to adopt RAT or TTB in a domain for which either strategy would work equally well. The task for subjects in Lee and Cummins (2004) was to look at the molecular makeup of two gases, presented simultaneously and in their entirety, and to decide which one of them was more poisonous. To avoid biasing subjects toward the use of one strategy or the other, Lee and Cummins specifically chose stimuli so that, for every pair, the same choice was made by RAT and by TTB.[2] An illustration is provided in Figure 19-1A.

In the figure, we assume that the presence of a cue (represented by a value of 1) is diagnostic of poison and that cues are arranged from left to right in decreasing order of validity. RAT chooses the item with more total evidence, so it chooses the left item because most of the evidence is in that alternative's favor; TTB chooses the same item because it bases its decision on the single most valid discriminating cue. Exposure to 119 different stimulus pairs with the property illustrated in Figure 19-1A constituted the training phase. The point of this training was to familiarize subjects with the decision task and to give subjects the opportunity to infer the validities of the various cues that made up the stimuli. After training, new pairs of stimuli were introduced for which RAT and TTB make opposite choices. As illustrated in Figure 19-1B, RAT chooses one item because it has a greater total amount

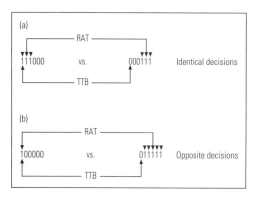

Figure 19-1. (a) The rational model (RAT) and the take-the-best (TTB) heuristic yield identical decisions on training pairs. Cues are arranged from left to right in decreasing order of validity. RAT chooses the alternative with more total evidence; TTB chooses the same item because it has the most valid discriminating cue. (b) In contrast, RAT and TTB yield opposite decisions on test pairs. RAT chooses the alternative to the right because it has more total evidence; TTB chooses the left item because it has the most valid discriminating cue.

of evidence, whereas TTB chooses the opposite item because it is favored by the single most valid cue.

Because the two strategies predict opposite choices on these stimulus pairs, one can use them to determine which strategy a subject adopted as a result of training. The results from these test pairs indicate that some subjects (35%) consistently made RAT decisions, others (13%) consistently made TTB decisions, and still others (52%) were inconsistent in their choice of strategy. In addition to analyzing subjects' performance on these test pairs, Lee and Cummins (2004) fit versions of the RAT and TTB models to subjects' choice data with a model fit criterion known as minimum description length (MDL; Rissanen, 1978). The average fits for RAT (MDL = 130.7) and TTB (MDL = 138.6) were similar, so neither model was conclusively favored.

GENERALIZING THE TTB AND RAT MODELS

As we describe in our General Discussion, Lee and Cummins's (2004) central motivation was

to move toward the development of a unified approach to decision making that combines TTB and RAT within a common framework. To provide faithful tests, Lee and Cummins followed numerous other researchers by considering the TTB and RAT models in their strong forms. Our own view, however, is that the strong forms of TTB and RAT are based on assumptions that are psychologically implausible. A central purpose of the present work, therefore, is to consider generalizations of these models that relax these assumptions while preserving important component themes of the original models. By considering these generalized models, we investigated whether certain processing strategies embodied in the original models might indeed govern human performance, even if the strong special cases of the models are ruled out.

The first assumption that we find implausible is that all subjects learn and use the optimal feature weights. In RAT, it is assumed that the weight that is attached to each cue is the log odds of its objective cue validity, given by Equation 19-4. In TTB, the cues are examined in order of objective cue validity until a discriminating cue is found.

In our view, it is implausible that every subject learns and uses the objective cue validities from experience with the decision domain. We think it is more likely that subjects occasionally make mistakes in their assignment of weights to cues (e.g., see Newell & Shanks, 2003). Calculating cue validity for each dimension requires a great deal of memory capacity and experience with the domain (for similar arguments, see, e.g., Newell, 2005). For this reason, we consider natural generalizations of both RAT and TTB that relax the assumption that optimal feature weights are always learned and used. In these generalized models, the feature weights are simply free parameters; for each subject, the weights that yield the best fit to the subject's data are found, and the models' predictions depend on these weights. The original, strong versions of the models are special cases of these general models with weights set to cue validities or log odds of cue validities.

The second assumption we find implausible is that subjects respond deterministically. The original RAT model makes a deterministic decision in favor of the alternative with more evidence. Similarly, in TTB, cues arc always inspected in a deterministic, fixed order, and once a discriminating cue is found, the alternative with the correct discriminating cue value is chosen. Thus, there is no error theory associated with the models.

A simple generalization involves making allowance for probabilistic decision making. Our generalized versions of RAT and TTB make responding probabilistic in several ways. First, we introduce a guessing parameter to all models under consideration, such that a subject is assumed to guess with probability g ($0 < g < 1$) on any trial and to use the model of interest (RAT or TTB) otherwise, with probability $1 - g$.

The guessing mechanism provides a rudimentary form of error theory,[3] but there is good reason to believe that it will be insufficient. Consider, for example, an observer who uses a RAT strategy. In one case, the summed evidence for alternative A may be dramatically greater than the summed evidence for alternative B, whereas in a second case the difference in evidence may be minuscule. Extending the deterministic decision rule of the RAT model with an all-or-none guessing parameter would still lead the model to predict identical choice probabilities in these two cases. Clearly, however, an observer is more likely to choose an alternative when the evidence that favors the alternative is dramatic than when it is minuscule.

Thus, in our generalization of RAT, we assume that the probability that alternative A is chosen from pair AB is given by

$$P(\text{"}A\text{"} \mid AB) = \frac{\left[\sum_{a \in FA} w_a\right]^{\gamma}}{\left[\sum_{a \in FA} w_a\right]^{\gamma} + \left[\sum_{b \in FB} w_b\right]^{\gamma}},$$ (19-5)

where γ is a response-scaling parameter. First, note that this response rule allows the model to predict increases in choice probability as the degree of evidence in favor of alternative A increases. Second, note that the response rule incorporates the original, deterministic RAT model as a special case: If $\gamma = \infty$, the decision is deterministic in favor of the alternative with more evidence (compare with Equation 19-3).

Another important special case arises when $\gamma = 1$. In this case, the decision is probabilistic and matches the theoretic response probability $P(\text{"}A\text{"}|AB)$ to alternative A's proportion of the total evidence.

Likewise, the strong version of TTB considered by Lee and Cummins (2004) also assumed a form of strict deterministic behavior having to do with the order in which cues are inspected. Specifically, the original TTB model automatically inspected features in order of validity, from most valid to least valid cue. Our initial generalization, allowing for subjective feature weights, would allow for the cues to be inspected in an order other than that prescribed by cue validity. For example, if a subject assigned the highest weight to feature i, then the subject would inspect feature i first. However, even with free feature weights, the original assumption that features would always be inspected in some fixed order would remain.

We thought a reasonable further generalization of the TTB model would be to make allowances for a probabilistic order of inspection. Thus, for each step of the process, we assumed that the probability of inspecting a feature was simply proportional to its weight,

$$P(\text{inspect feature}_i) = \frac{w_i}{\sum w}.$$ (19-6)

Because features that have already been inspected are eliminated from further consideration, the total weight in the denominator is calculated only over features that have not yet been inspected.

The probability of a particular order being used is the product of the individual probabilities of feature inspections. For example, the probability of order (1, 2, 3, 4, 5, 6) would be given by

$$P(order = (1,2,3,4,5,6)) = \frac{w_1}{w_1 + \ldots + w_6}$$

$$\times \frac{w_2}{w_2 + \ldots + w_6} \times \frac{w_3}{w_3 + \ldots + w_6}$$

$$\times \frac{w_4}{w_4 + \ldots + w_6} \times \frac{w_5}{w_5 + w_6} \times \frac{w_6}{w_6}.$$ (19-7)

To find the overall probability of an "A" response for a given stimulus pair AB, one finds the probability of choosing an order that favors A, which is just the sum of the probabilities of all orders that favor A:

$$P("A" \mid AB) = \sum_{order \in O_A} P(order), \qquad (19\text{-}8)$$

where O_A is the set of orders of cue inspection that lead the TTB model to choose alternative A from pair AB.

This generalized, probabilistic choice of orders of cue inspection contains as a special case the original, deterministic inspection of cues in

order of validity. We can visualize this relation by creating weights that are in the same rank order as cue validity and are as different in magnitude from each other as possible. As the weights get further apart in magnitude, the probability of inspecting the features in order of cue validity approaches 1, as is illustrated in Figure 19-2.

It is interesting that the straightforward generalizations of TTB described here—making feature weights free parameters and allowing for probabilistic orders of cue inspection—transform TTB into exactly Tversky's (1972) elimination by aspects (EBA) choice model. In EBA, a cue is chosen for inspection with probability equal to its proportion of the total weight (Equation 19-6).

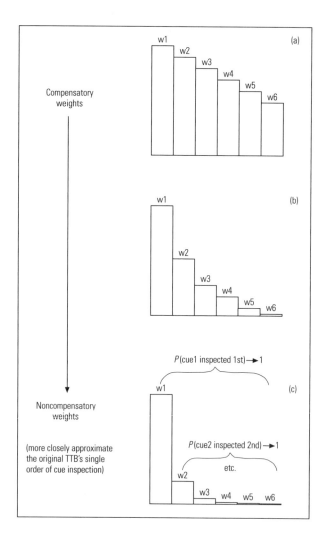

Figure 19-2. In the general version of take-the-best (TTB) with free weights and probabilistic choice of cue inspection order, the order of cue inspection can be made deterministic by making the weights sufficiently noncompensatory. As the weights become more and more dissimilar, the probability of choosing the highest one first increases to 1; if it fails to discriminate, the probability of choosing the second highest one next increases to 1; et cetera.

Any alternatives without this feature are eliminated from further consideration, and a second feature is chosen for inspection from among the remaining uninspected cues. Elimination continues until there is only one alternative left, or until all features have been inspected, whereupon a choice is made randomly.

A point of great importance is the relation between the generalized version of TTB, which we will call gTTB, and the generalized version of RAT, which we will call gRAT. Clearly, the underlying processes that are represented by the models are dramatically different. Remarkably, however, gTTB's prediction of the probability of choosing item A from among A and B (i.e., Equations 6–8) yields an expression that is formally identical to gRAT's prediction (Equation 19-5) when gRAT's response-scaling parameter γ is set equal to 1 (see Tversky, 1972, p. 287, Equation 19-6). We illustrate the reason for the formal identity in Appendix A for a simple case in which the two alternatives contain no matching features.

One important implication of this identity between the generalized models is that the test pairs used by Lee and Cummins (2004) to distinguish between the original RAT and TTB models do not, of course, distinguish between the general versions. Thus, for example, consider again the stimulus pair in Figure 19-1B, in which the difference between a TTB choice and a RAT choice is dramatic. The original strong version of TTB chooses the left item because it possesses the most valid cue, and the original strong version of RAT chooses the right item because it contains the greatest amount of summed evidence. Suppose, however, that a gTTB subject gave greatest weight to the second attribute instead of to the first. Then, such a subject would tend to choose the right item rather than the left. Thus, considering the predictions of only the strong versions of TTB and RAT could lead to potential misinterpretations of the subject's decision-making behavior.

Because the gTTB and gRAT ($\gamma = 1$) models are formally identical, we cannot tell them apart on the basis of fits to choice-probability data. Nevertheless, as we argue later in this article, certain types of parameter estimates derived from

fits of the models are far more in the spirit of a TTB-like process than a RAT-like process. The main purpose of Experiment 1 is to test the utility of the generalized models and to use the best-fitting parameter estimates to reach interpretations about subjects' behavior. Then, in Experiments 2 and 3 we move to the central goal of our research, which involves the introduction of a new response-time (RT) method for distinguishing between the predictions from the generalized models.

EXPERIMENT 1

The main initial goal of Experiment 1 is to address the question of whether the generalizations of RAT and TTB we have outlined offer an improvement over the original strong versions. We evaluate this question by conducting quantitative fit comparisons among the models, where the measure of fit penalizes the generalized models for their increase in the number of free parameters. Once we establish the usefulness of the generalizations, we then interpret the nature of subjects' decision strategies in terms of the best-fitting parameter estimates from the generalized models.

To test whether the generalizations of RAT and TTB were necessary, our first experiment replicated Lee and Cummins's (2004) experiment, with a few modifications. First, Lee and Cummins used the presence and absence of individual colored dots (representing "molecules") to instantiate their abstract stimulus structure. Thus, their physical stimuli were composed from a set of relatively homogeneous, present–absent features. In our experiments, we instead used pictures of insects that varied along six heterogeneous, binary-valued "substitutive" dimensions. (For binary-valued substitutive dimensions, one of two feature values is always present.) As discussed by Lee and Cummins, the use of present–absent features might bias subjects toward counting strategies involving the total number of features that are present on a stimulus. Thus, during the test phase, these researchers used stimulus pairs in which each member always had the same number of present features. By using substitutive dimensions, we avoided the need to impose this constraint because six heterogeneous features were always present on each stimulus. In addition, we were interested in testing the models in a domain involving integrated perceptual displays.

As in Lee and Cummins (2004), subjects were first trained on pairs for which both RAT and TTB made identical decisions. Then, to examine which strategy they had adopted during training, subjects were tested on new pairs for which the original strong versions of RAT and TTB made opposite decisions. A second difference between our experiment and the earlier study conducted by Lee and Cummins (2004) is that our transfer phase included a large number of test pair trials in order to obtain a data set suitable for quantitative fitting.

Method

Subjects. The subjects were 61 undergraduate students at Indiana University Bloomington who participated as part of a course requirement. Subjects were told at the beginning of the experiment that if they performed well on the test phase they would be paid a $3 bonus; those who achieved 80% correct or better were paid the bonus.

Stimuli. Table 19-1 contains the 16 abstract stimulus patterns used in the training phase and their corresponding poison levels. These abstract stimulus patterns were mapped onto pictures of poisonous insects, with six features corresponding to body parts: body, eyes, legs, antennae, fangs, and tail. The binary values of these features were different appearances of the same feature (e.g., long or short legs). The $2^6 = 64$ possible insects were created by separating the body, eyes, legs, antennae, fangs, and tail from two drawings of beetles and then recombining them in all possible combinations. Figure 19-3 provides examples of the stimuli used in the experiments. The mapping of the six physical features onto the six abstract features was randomized across subjects, so that, for example, Feature 1 corresponded to the eyes for one subject and the legs for another subject. Similarly, the level of each feature that was diagnostic of poison was randomized across subjects, so that long legs indicated poison for some subjects, whereas short legs indicated poison for other subjects.

Table 19-1. Training Stimulus Patterns Used in Lee and Cummins (2004) and in Experiments 1 and 2.

Stimulus Number	Stimulus Pattern	Decision Variable (Poison)
1	0 0 0 1 0 0	16
2	0 1 0 0 1 0	18
3	0 0 1 0 0 1	21
4	0 0 0 1 1 0	25
5	0 0 0 0 1 0	31
6	1 0 0 0 1 1	40
7	0 0 1 1 1 1	44
8	1 1 0 1 0 0	51
9	1 1 1 0 0 1	62
10	1 1 0 0 1 0	70
11	1 1 0 1 1 1	97
12	1 1 1 1 0 0	104
13	1 1 1 1 1 1	280
14	1 1 1 1 0 1	285
15	1 1 1 0 1 0	347
16	1 1 1 1 1 0	444

As in Lee and Cummins (2004), all possible pairs of stimuli were shown except pair (2, 7), which was the only pair for which RAT and TTB made opposite choices. As described earlier, the point of the training phase was to train subjects on the stimulus domain without biasing them toward one model or the other by having one model make more accurate decisions. Therefore, pair (2, 7) was eliminated so that both models would make identical choices for every training pair. Table 19-2 shows the calculation of Bayesian cue validity for each cue (from Equation 19-2), along with the optimal feature weight (from Equation 19-4). (The calculations are slightly different for Lee & Cummins [2004] and the present experiments because we used twice as many training trials—see the present *Procedure* section.)

Table 19-3 contains the five pairs used in the test phase to distinguish RAT from TTB choices, by virtue of the fact that the original strong versions of RAT and TTB make opposite decisions for these pairs.

Procedure. The experimental design was a training phase followed by a testing phase, with

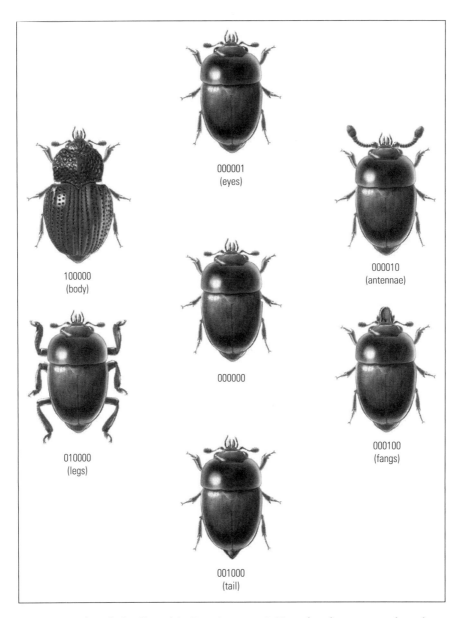

Figure 19-3. Examples of stimuli used in Experiments 1–3. Note that the correspondence between the underlying stimulus pattern (e.g., 001000) and a particular appearance was completely randomized for each subject. To see the six features, notice that each stimulus in the outer ring differs from the central stimulus by one feature. (Eye color = blue or green on color monitor.)

each phase consisting of a number of decision trials. During each trial of the training phase, a subject was shown a pair of insects, one to the left and one to the right, on a computer screen and was asked to decide which of the two was more poisonous. A subject gave his or her response by pressing the *F* key (labeled *Left*) or the *J* key (labeled *Right*). After responding, the subject was given feedback about which response was correct in the form of a red rectangular border appearing around the more poisonous insect. The word *Correct* or *Incorrect* also

Table 19-2. Calculation of Cue Validities (v) and Optimal Feature Weights (w) for Lee and Cummins (2004) and Experiments 1 and 2

Feature$_i$	Dcorrect$_i$	Dtotal$_i$	v_i	$w_i = \ln (v_i/[1 - v_i])$
		Lee and Cummins (2004)		
1	59	60	60/62 = .968	3.40
2	55	59	56/61 = .918	2.42
3	52	63	53/65 = .815	1.49
4	40	62	41/64 = .641	0.578
5	34	60	35/62 = .565	0.260
6	34	62	35/64 = .547	0.188
		Experiments 1 and 2		
1	118	120	119/122 = .975	3.68
2	110	118	111/120 = .925	2.51
3	104	126	105/128 = .820	1.52
4	80	124	81/126 = .643	0.588
5	68	120	69/122 = .566	0.264
6	68	124	69/126 = .548	0.191

Note: Dcorrect$_i$ reports how many correct discriminations Feature i makes out of all 119 (Lee & Cummins, 2004) or 238 (Experiments 1 and 2) training trials; Dtotal$_i$ reports the total number of discriminations, correct and incorrect; and v_i is the Bayesian validity, calculated by using Equation 19-2. The optimal weights, which are the log of the odds of the Bayesian validities, are shown in the last column.

appeared below the pair of insects during this feedback. The subject was allowed to study the feedback and the pair of insects for as long as he or she wished. To move on to the next trial, the subject pressed the space bar, making each trial self-paced.

Training was designed to familiarize subjects with the cue validities and with the decision task. Our training phase differed from Lee and Cummins's (2004) design in that stimulus pairs were shown twice each, instead of once, for a total of 238 training trials. The increased training was intended to improve the chances that observers would learn the correct cue-validity ordering of the attribute values.

The test phase included presentations of each of the original training pairs and each of the critical transfer pairs (see Table 19-3) from Lee and Cummins (2004). The test phase also differed from the training phase in that no feedback was provided; instead, following Lee and Cummins (2004), subjects were asked to rate how confident they were about every decision. As was the case in training, subjects initiated the next trial by pressing the space bar. We showed the five critical transfer pairs eight times each, instead of

Table 19-3. Transfer Stimulus Pairs Used by Lee and Cummins (2004)

Transfer Stimulus Pair	TTB Item	RAT Item
1	100001	011000
2	100010	011000
3	100011	011100
4	100110	011100
5	100111	011110

Note: The classic rational (RAT) and take-the-best (TTB) models make opposite predictions for these pairs. In each pair, TTB chooses the left item because it has the most valid cue, and RAT chooses the right item because it has more total evidence (assuming the use of optimal feature weights).

once each as in Lee and Cummins. The main reason we increased the number of test pairs is because we wished to create a rich data set suitable for quantitative model fitting at the individual subject level. For the same reason, we showed the 119 training pairs once each during testing (whereas Lee & Cummins, 2004, did not show the training pairs). We also showed the excluded pair (2, 7) once during testing, for a total of 160 test trials. Lee and Cummins's test phase consisted of only the five test pairs, shown once each.

Results

We start by describing the general pattern of results in the data. Table 19-4 shows the individual subjects' choices on the critical test pairs

designed to distinguish strong RAT from strong TTB behavior. Each data column shows how many times the TTB item was chosen for the test pairs, each of which was shown eight times. Most subjects were extremely consistent in their patterns of choices, both within each test pair and across test pairs.

Table 19-4. Response Patterns for Consistent Take-the-Best (TTB) Subjects, Inconsistent Subjects, and Consistent Classic Rational (RAT) Model Subjects from Experiment 1

	Test Pair						Test Pair				
Subject Number	1	2	3	4	5	Subject Number	1	2	3	4	5
TTB Subjects						**Inconsistent Subjects**					
1	8	8	8	8	8	24	7	8	8	8	6
3	8	8	8	8	8	19	7	8	8	7	7
6	8	8	8	8	8	55	7	8	8	7	6
13	8	8	8	8	8	7	7	8	7	7	8
14	8	8	8	8	8	61	7	8	7	7	5
17	8	8	8	8	8	22	7	7	8	8	8
25	8	8	8	8	8	9	7	6	5	7	6
28	8	8	8	8	8	35	5	5	5	7	3
31	8	8	8	8	8	27	3	3	5	1	3
33	8	8	8	8	8	57	3	3	3	3	2
34	8	8	8	8	8	45	2	7	4	7	7
38	8	8	8	8	8	15	2	5	4	4	0
39	8	8	8	8	8	56	2	3	0	0	0
40	8	8	8	8	8	50	2	2	6	5	4
41	8	8	8	8	8	2	2	1	0	0	0
52	8	8	8	8	8	49	1	4	5	1	2
54	8	8	8	8	8	42	1	2	3	0	0
58	8	8	8	8	8	47	1	2	0	1	1
59	8	8	8	8	8	12	1	1	2	1	6
60	8	8	8	8	8	46	1	0	0	1	1
						53	0	6	2	6	0
						48	0	2	5	6	1
						5	0	0	1	2	1
Inconsistent Subjects						**RAT Subjects**					
51	8	8	8	8	7	4	0	0	0	0	0
18	8	8	8	7	8	8	0	0	0	0	0
44	8	8	8	7	7	11	0	0	0	0	0
23	8	8	8	6	8	16	0	0	0	0	0
10	8	8	7	8	8	20	0	0	0	0	0
37	8	8	7	7	8	29	0	0	0	0	0
21	8	7	8	8	8	36	0	0	0	0	0
26	8	7	8	8	8						
32	8	7	8	8	8						
43	8	7	8	8	8						
30	8	7	7	7	7						

Note: Each data column indicates the number of trials, out of eight, on which the subject chose the TTB item from test pair.

Among both consistent and inconsistent subjects, TTB choices dominate. This result contrasts with Lee and Cummins's (2004) finding of more RAT choices than TTB choices. Although not the focus of the present research, we should note several possible reasons for this contrasting result. First, one possibility is that Lee and Cummins's use of stimuli composed of a set of homogeneous present–absent features may have promoted more use of "summing" strategies than is the case when heterogeneous, substitutive dimensions are involved. A second possibility is that, because Lee and Cummins's design used fewer training trials, perhaps fewer subjects in their study learned that the first attribute had the greatest cue validity. As explained previously in our article, even if subjects had adopted a TTB-like strategy, they might still make a RAT choice if they failed to inspect the most diagnostic dimension first. Still another possibility involves the differing nature of the transfer tasks used in the two studies. Whereas Lee and Cummins's design used only a single presentation of each of the five critical test pairs, in our design there were 160 test pair presentations. Thus, in Lee and Cummins's design, subjects may have been more inclined to consider more of the evidence in making their decisions. A TTB procedure would provide a reasonable shortcut in our much longer and more demanding transfer task. We consider this possibility in greater depth later in our article.

Next, we address the main initial question of Experiment 1: Were our generalizations of RAT and TTB necessary? That is, do gRAT and gTTB provide better explanations of subjects' choice probabilities than do RAT and TTB? The original versions of RAT and TTB are parameter-free and predict completely deterministic responding. Recall that to provide a rudimentary form of error theory, we allow each model a guessing parameter g ($0 < g < 1$). Thus, for example, the probability that TTB chooses "A" given pair AB is given by $P(\text{"A"}|AB) = g/2 + (1 - g)\text{TTB}_A$, where $\text{TTB}_A = 1$ if the original version of TTB chooses A, and $\text{TTB}_A = 0$ otherwise.

For purposes of comparability, we add the guessing parameter g to the generalized versions of the models as well. In addition, gRAT and

gTTB have free parameters for feature weights and, in the case of gRAT, for γ, which determines how deterministic the response rule is. Because only the relative magnitudes of the weights are relevant, the weights can be normalized to sum to 1 without changing the models' predictions. Thus, the full version of gRAT has seven free parameters (guessing, five free weights, and γ), and gTTB has six (guessing and weights).

To evaluate the utility of the generalized models, we used the Bayesian information criterion (BIC; Schwarz, 1978) as a measure of fit. As described in Appendix B, the BIC includes a term that penalizes a model for its number of free parameters. The BIC gets smaller as the probability of observing the data given the model increases; however, the BIC gets larger as the number of free parameters increases. The model that yields a smaller BIC is considered to provide a more likely account of the data. We used a computer-search algorithm (Hooke & Jeeves, 1961) to locate the values of the free parameters that minimized the BIC for each individual subject.

Table 19-5 shows the fits of the strong and general versions of the models, averaged across subjects. Rows 1 and 2 of Table 19-5 show that RAT and TTB achieve average BIC fits of 181 and 140, respectively. (Not surprisingly, TTB better fit the subjects who made TTB choices on the critical test pairs, whereas RAT better fit the subjects who made RAT choices.) More important, Rows 3 and 4 show that gRAT (with $\gamma = 1$) and gTTB, which are equivalent in terms of choice predictions, achieve average fits of 111. Thus the generalizations led to a marked improvement in fit. Row 5 shows that allowing γ to vary freely in the gRAT model yielded a slightly worse average BIC of 113. Thus, in general, the extra free parameter, γ, did not yield a sufficient improvement in fit to offset its increase in model complexity.

A comparison of fits at the individual subject level further supports the conclusion that the generalized models provided an improvement. The leftmost column of Table 19-6 shows the fit of the equivalent gRAT and gTTB, the middle column shows the fit of RAT, and the rightmost column shows the fit of TTB. The generalized

Table 19-5. Average Bayesian Information Criterion (BIC) Fits of the Strong and General Versions of RAT and TTB in Experiment 1, Along With the Assumptions Made in Each Model

Model	Guess	Weights	Gamma	Inspection Order	Parameters	BIC
RAT	Free	Optimal	∞		1	181
TTB	Free	Optimal		Fixed	1	140
gRAT	Free	Free	1		6	111
gTTB	Free	Free		Probabilistic	6	111
gRAT	Free	Free	Free		7	113

Note: RAT, classic rational model; TTB, take-the-best model; gRAT, general version RAT; gTTB, general version TTB.

Table 19-6. Comparison of Individual Subjects' Model Fits for Experiment 1

Table 19-6. (continued)

Subject	gRAT/gTTB + Guess	RAT + Guess	TTB + Guess
1	65.2	201.5	95.2
2	189.2	188.2	216.0
3	82.4	189.7	62.6
4	155.3	165.7	224.4
5	191.0	185.5	211.8
6	135.9	210.8	121.7
7	77.3	180.1	87.4
8	145.8	143.9	219.6
9	133.7	164.2	117.3
10	94.6	200.7	109.2
11	106.4	126.0	216.7
12	173.3	160.1	189.9
13	77.6	197.8	85.2
14	88.1	197.8	85.2
15	125.3	157.9	177.9
16	112.8	136.8	217.7
17	42.9	193.9	74.2
18	82.0	197.7	100.4
19	107.2	189.7	109.2
20	80.4	77.7	200.4
21	78.1	197.7	100.4
22	110.4	202.9	128.5
23	102.4	186.2	83.6
24	97.8	198.9	129.5
25	60.3	213.4	129.5
26	67.0	196.0	95.8
27	199.6	182.9	189.3
28	67.9	191.8	68.6
29	66.9	98.8	206.8
30	135.0	193.5	130.4
31	52.0	193.9	74.3
32	112.6	197.5	91.1
33	70.6	203.2	100.0
34	102.7	204.8	104.6
35	160.8	177.5	164.2
36	149.2	150.6	221.2
37	95.3	204.1	132.0
38	72.9	213.4	129.5
39	97.0	222.9	162.4
40	74.1	195.9	79.8
41	57.7	201.5	95.2
42	148.3	147.9	196.8
43	151.1	220.5	171.5
44	92.0	195.4	109.3
45	141.2	175.6	155.1
46	136.9	160.2	210.1
47	117.9	120.8	189.1
48	152.2	183.9	197.1
49	169.8	180.0	192.8
50	212.1	190.3	190.3
51	75.1	200.8	109.2
52	77.9	213.4	129.5
53	133.6	142.5	177.0
54	86.6	201.5	95.2
55	99.5	177.6	85.0
56	97.7	101.2	184.0
57	189.1	167.9	182.3
58	113.1	212.1	125.7
59	60.3	197.8	85.1
60	115.7	217.8	136.8
61	104.0	170.4	101.1
Average	111.0	181.5	140.4

Note: Column 2 contains the fit for the general version of the rational model (gRAT) and the general version of the take-the-best model (gTTB), which are formally identical in predicting choice probabilities and therefore achieve the same fit. Column 3 contains each subject's fit of the original RAT with optimal weights and deterministic responding. Column 4 contains the fit of the original TTB model with inspection of cues in order of cue validity.

model fit better than RAT for 85% of the subjects, better than TTB for 80% of the subjects, and simultaneously better than both RAT and TTB for 70% of the subjects.

Next, we turn from the overall fits of the models to an analysis of the best-fitting feature weights from gRAT/gTTB, which are shown in Table 19-7 for each subject. One way to describe the pattern of results is to note that 57 (93%) of the 61 subjects gave over half the total weight to some single feature. This pattern of weighting is noncompensatory in the sense that, if the single feature discriminated between the alternatives, then it would dictate the direction of choice, regardless of the values on the remaining five features. In other words, if the single feature pointed to alternative A, and the remaining five features pointed to alternative B, then the subject would still tend to choose A with probability greater than one half.

Table 19-7. Individual Subjects' Best-Fitting Weights for the Equivalent gRAT and gTTB Models, Fit to Experiment 1's Test Phase Choice Probabilities

Subject	w_1	w_2	w_3	w_4	w_5	w_6
1	1.00E+00	3.43E−13	4.91E−07	1.04E−10	1.57E−07	1.00E−15
2	1.35E−13	7.20E−01	2.80E−01	1.35E−13	1.87E−09	3.07E−08
3	1.00E+00	6.44E−09	2.08E−08	1.86E−09	1.00E−12	1.00E−15
4	1.00E−15	1.00E+00	4.69E−07	7.56E−07	1.00E−15	3.46E−07
5	1.00E−15	1.00E+00	5.75E−08	1.00E−15	3.07E−08	1.00E−15
6	1.00E+00	1.00E−15	1.76E−08	1.00E−15	1.00E−15	1.00E−15
7	8.66E−01	5.12E−02	4.25E−02	1.50E−02	2.51E−02	1.76E−10
8	7.23E−05	1.00E+00	4.29E−08	4.29E−08	1.00E−15	4.91E−12
9	9.17E−01	1.26E−05	8.31E−02	2.05E−09	7.59E−11	7.59E−11
10	1.00E+00	1.00E−15	7.52E−08	2.75E−08	2.39E−08	2.74E−12
11	2.50E−11	7.75E−01	4.76E−02	1.41E−01	3.67E−02	2.50E−11
12	9.66E−02	1.87E−01	3.98E−01	2.23E−01	6.01E−12	9.57E−02
13	1.00E+00	1.49E−05	1.49E−05	1.00E−15	2.00E−09	7.29E−13
14	1.00E+00	3.31E−09	9.42E−05	6.75E−09	8.36E−09	2.10E−09
15	9.72E−02	4.55E−11	5.43E−01	3.25E−02	3.28E−01	7.11E−07
16	1.00E−15	1.00E+00	1.37E−06	6.40E−14	1.33E−12	1.25E−13
17	1.00E+00	1.00E−12	1.18E−07	1.69E−09	9.66E−09	1.00E−15
18	1.00E+00	7.29E−13	1.41E−07	1.00E−09	6.64E−09	1.00E−15
19	1.00E+00	3.66E−08	5.15E−08	6.94E−08	2.41E−08	1.00E−15
20	1.13E−07	1.00E+00	2.16E−13	8.00E−15	8.00E−15	1.00E−15
21	1.00E+00	6.86E−09	1.00E−15	1.00E−15	1.00E−15	9.41E−10
22	1.00E+00	1.00E−15	4.43E−05	1.76E−10	9.41E−10	4.74E−09
23	1.00E+00	6.99E−08	1.41E−07	2.75E−08	3.65E−09	1.00E−15
24	9.85E−01	1.48E−02	6.95E−10	1.54E−09	7.52E−06	9.85E−16
25	1.00E+00	1.25E−10	4.44E−08	1.00E−15	1.82E−04	3.43E−13
26	9.99E−01	1.29E−15	8.35E−04	1.29E−15	1.03E−14	3.49E−14
27	1.09E−07	2.28E−04	1.00E+00	1.00E−15	5.06E−11	5.06E−11
28	1.00E+00	2.20E−12	3.32E−05	8.74E−09	1.73E−12	1.00E−15
29	1.23E−09	1.00E+00	9.97E−07	1.00E−12	4.89E−07	1.00E−15
30	1.00E+00	8.62E−07	4.97E−04	1.00E−15	1.00E−09	1.00E−09
31	1.00E+00	9.73E−11	8.10E−05	3.43E−13	2.62E−08	1.00E−15
32	1.00E+00	1.03E−09	1.03E−09	1.00E−15	1.00E−15	1.00E−15
33	1.00E+00	1.00E−15	2.16E−07	3.28E−11	3.90E−08	2.16E−13
34	1.00E+00	6.59E−10	2.07E−05	1.23E−09	7.05E−10	5.51E−10
35	3.29E−01	1.60E−01	1.03E−01	7.15E−11	4.07E−01	2.34E−06
36	2.32E−11	9.96E−01	3.32E−03	2.21E−04	2.32E−11	2.32E−11
37	9.61E−01	6.56E−07	4.91E−03	5.40E−03	2.86E−02	1.60E−10

Table 19-7. (continued)

Subject	w_1	w_2	w_3	w_4	w_5	w_6
38	1.00E+00	2.00E–09	1.30E–09	2.05E–09	5.84E–08	1.00E–15
39	5.16E–01	4.58E–11	4.58E–11	7.20E–02	2.20E–01	1.91E–01
40	1.00E+00	2.98E–11	4.57E–06	9.26E–12	7.41E–11	1.00E–15
41	1.00E+00	1.00E–15	2.31E–07	3.43E–13	1.15E–07	7.41E–11
42	1.88E–03	9.98E–01	5.71E–05	8.07E–08	6.06E–05	6.06E–11
43	1.00E+00	4.74E–09	2.20E–12	7.79E–08	1.00E–15	3.34E–08
44	1.00E+00	1.00E–15	3.39E–07	3.43E–13	9.80E–08	6.89E–11
45	2.20E–01	3.74E–06	1.28E–01	3.92E–01	2.60E–01	5.84E–11
46	9.23E–08	1.00E+00	1.00E–15	2.70E–08	3.59E–07	8.46E–08
47	6.42E–02	7.80E–01	2.65E–02	9.73E–02	3.24E–02	4.10E–11
48	4.97E–08	1.86E–01	1.80E–01	6.81E–11	6.34E–01	1.20E–06
49	3.80E–11	5.93E–05	5.97E–01	3.80E–11	4.03E–01	2.25E–06
50	9.96E–16	3.68E–03	1.94E–07	1.38E–11	9.96E–01	9.96E–16
51	1.00E+00	1.00E–15	8.62E–09	2.08E–08	1.19E–08	1.00E–12
52	9.75E–01	3.48E–11	3.22E–07	1.63E–02	3.48E–11	8.99E–03
53	1.32E–01	8.23E–02	4.50E–01	7.48E–02	2.61E–01	6.51E–11
54	1.00E+00	2.74E–12	5.67E–05	1.91E–09	1.19E–08	1.00E–15
55	9.59E–01	8.48E–03	3.08E–02	2.87E–04	1.14E–03	4.34E–04
56	9.25E–02	8.09E–01	6.70E–02	6.27E–03	2.57E–02	6.74E–11
57	1.01E–01	5.77E–01	9.90E–02	2.77E–06	4.27E–07	2.23E–01
58	1.00E+00	6.86E–12	4.47E–05	6.86E–12	1.00E–15	1.60E–08
59	1.00E+00	2.16E–13	1.06E–04	3.93E–11	4.51E–08	1.00E–15
60	1.00E+00	1.26E–04	1.00E–15	2.18E–07	3.43E–13	2.27E–10
61	9.26E–01	4.59E–04	7.29E–02	1.31E–04	7.12E–04	4.19E–05
Average	6.27E–01	2.19E–01	6.82E–02	1.76E–02	6.00E–02	8.52E–03

Note: In comparison, optimal normalized weights (*w*) are .4204, .2870, .1735, .0671, .0301, and .0218. Parameter values are represented in scientific notation, such that $1.57E-07$ represents 1.57×10^{-7} or .000000157. This level of precision is required to determine the extent to which noncompensatory weighting strategies were used by subjects.

Furthermore, 50 (82%) of the 61 subjects gave noncompensatory weights to both of their two most highly weighted cues; for these subjects, the highest weight was greater than all other weights combined, and the second highest weight was greater than all remaining weights combined. This pattern implies that if a pair of alternatives mismatched on either the most highly weighted feature or the second most highly weighted feature, the direction of choice was determined by the value of a single cue.

Perhaps more indicative of the noncompensatory nature of most subjects' responding was that 41 (67%) of the 61 subjects gave over 99% of their weight to some single feature. In this case, not only was the direction of responding dictated by the single feature, it was essentially completely determined by that single feature.

Table 19-8 lists the proportions of subjects weighting each feature most highly, with the features listed in decreasing order of objective

TABLE 19-8. Proportion of Subjects Weighting Each Feature Most Highly in Experiment 1

Feature	Proportion of Subjects
1	.62
2	.23
3	.08
4	.02
5	.05
6	.00

Note: Features are listed in decreasing order of cue validity.

validity. There were 38 subjects (62%) who assigned the highest weight to the most valid cue, leaving 23 subjects (38%) who made a mistake in ordering the most diagnostic cue's validity. Inspection of Table 19-7 reveals that the vast majority of subjects ordered the remaining cues suboptimally as well.

Discussion

In summary, the generalized versions of RAT and TTB provided a substantially better fit to subjects' choice data than did the original strong versions of these models, even when the generalized models were penalized for their extra parameters by BIC. The improvements in fits are due, at least in part, to the generalized models' allowance of subjective feature weights. The strong version of RAT assumes that subjects use a compensatory set of decision weights (see Table 19-2); however, 93% of subjects used their most highly weighted feature in a noncompensatory manner (see Table 19-7). Furthermore, virtually all subjects assigned weights to the dimensions in a manner that departed from their rank order of objective cue validity. This result poses a challenge to the strong version of TTB.

Because gRAT and gTTB are formally identical in their predictions of choice probabilities, we cannot tell them apart on the basis of goodness-of-fit to subjects' choice data. However, in our view, the pattern of estimated feature weightings is far more in the spirit of the TTB process than the RAT process. To elaborate, because the feature weightings tended to be noncompensatory, the value of the single most highly weighted feature dictated the direction of choice between alternatives, regardless of the values on the remaining features. Indeed, for two-thirds of subjects, the single most highly weighted feature received over 99% of the total weight, meaning that their choices were essentially determined by that feature value alone, at least for trials on which that feature discriminated between the alternatives. This type of process is as envisioned by the TTB model and can be viewed as only a rather degenerate case of RAT. In this degenerate case, the observer is presumed to evaluate and integrate all cues, but the choice is determined by the value of just a single cue. Martignon (2001)

echoes this view: "A linear model with a non-compensatory set of weights ends up making exactly the same inferences as TTB" (p. 156).

Recall also that, in terms of the gTTB model, the finding of highly noncompensatory weights implies that most subjects followed an essentially fixed order in inspecting the cues that composed the stimulus pairs (see Figure 19-2C). Thus, although the particular order that most individual subjects used did not conform precisely to the cue-validity ordering, it nevertheless tended to be fixed.

For a much smaller subset of subjects, the feature weights showed a compensatory pattern. Although this result may point to subjects who adopted a RAT-like strategy, it is also consistent with another possibility. In particular, such subjects might have inspected the cues in a probabilistic order but still might have responded on the basis of the first single cue that discriminated between the alternatives, as envisioned in the gTTB model. This possibility can be examined with the RT method that we introduce in Experiment 2.

Although noncompensatory weights provided the best fits to the vast majority of subjects' data, it is possible that comparable fits could be achieved with compensatory weights. A computer-based parameter-search algorithm follows any improvement in fit through the parameter space, however small. It is possible that less extreme weights could yield similar fits and that these less extreme weights would be compensatory. Therefore, though the finding of noncompensatory weights seems to point toward a process in the spirit of the gTTB model, it is important to seek converging evidence for this finding. In Experiments 2 and 3, we use an RT approach to seeking such evidence.

EXPERIMENT 2

Although gTTB and gRAT yield formally identical predictions of choice probabilities, they embody dramatically different decision-making processes. One approach to distinguishing between the models would be to use the process-tracing techniques that have proved valuable in past work, in which subjects uncover cues one by one to inspect their values. As acknowledged by other investigators, however, the decision-making behavior of subjects under such overt monitoring conditions may not conform to their strategies under more natural, covert conditions. The central theme of the present research was to pursue an alternative, complementary avenue to contrasting the models that relies on their RT predictions.

Consider stimulus pairs such as those shown in Figure 19-4, in which the two stimuli to be compared differ on every feature. All such pairs yield an equally efficient decision process for gTTB. An observer might inspect the cues in any order, depending on the feature weights, but regardless of which order is used the first cue examined would discriminate between the alternatives and therefore allow gTTB to make a decision. Pairs like those shown in Figure 19-4 guarantee gTTB an identical, maximally fast decision after only one inspection, regardless of the order of cue inspection.

In contrast, gRAT will have a much easier time with pair AB than with pair CD. The gRAT decision is based solely on the total evidence in favor of each alternative. The top pair in Figure 19-4, AB, is a "RAT-easy" pair, in that the difference in evidence between the alternatives is large: All of the evidence points to A being more poisonous. In contrast, the bottom pair, CD, is a "RAT-hard" pair, in that the difference in evidence between the alternatives is small: Half of the features favor C, whereas the other half

favor D. Thus, assuming that responding is faster for easy decisions than for hard decisions, gRAT would predict fast RTs for RAT-easy pairs and slow RTs for RAT-hard pairs.

This definition of RAT-hard and RAT-easy pairs assumes that gRAT is using compensatory weights. With extremely noncompensatory weights, a single feature would dominate the contribution to each item's evidence, so the same evidence difference would exist for every pair of stimuli with completely mismatching features. Thus, the goal here is to distinguish gTTB from compensatory versions of gRAT.[4]

In addition to the types of RAT-easy/RAT-hard pairs illustrated in Figure 19-4, we also tested RAT-easy/RAT-hard pairs of the form shown in Figure 19-5. In this case, the two alternatives match on the first cue but mismatch on all other cues. Once again, gTTB predicts no difference in RTs for RAT-easy versus RAT-hard pairs. With some probability, the observer might first check Cue 1 and find that it fails to discriminate between the two alternatives. Thus, the decision will be made upon checking the next cue. However, the probability of first checking Cue 1 is identical for RAT-easy and RAT-hard pairs, so gTTB predicts identical RTs for such pairs. By contrast, gRAT (with compensatory weights) again predicts faster RTs for RAT-easy pairs than for RAT-hard pairs.

Finally, although gTTB predicts no difference in RTs between RAT-easy and RAT-hard pairs, note that it does predict a difference between the

	w						Evidence	
	3.68	2.51	1.52	0.59	0.26	0.19		
A	1	1	1	1	1	1	8.75	RAT-easy
B	0	0	0	0	0	0	0.00	
C	1	0	0	1	0	1	4.46	RAT-hard
D	0	1	1	0	1	0	4.29	

Figure 19-4. Two pairs of alternatives (AB and CD) that differ (mismatch) on every feature, along with the optimal feature weights and the total objective evidence for each alternative. Pair AB has a large difference in total evidence ($8.75 - 0.00 = 8.75$), whereas pair CD has a small difference ($4.46 - 4.29 = 0.17$). The general version of take-the-best predicts identical response times (RTs) for pairs AB and CD because the expected number of cue inspections is the same for both pairs. In contrast, the general version of the rational (RAT) model predicts a faster RT for pair AB because of its larger difference in evidence.

			w				
	3.68	2.51	1.52	0.59	0.26	0.19	Evidence
A	1	1	1	1	1	1	5.07	RAT-easy
B	1	0	0	0	0	0	0.00	
C	1	1	0	0	0	0	2.51	RAT-hard
D	1	0	1	1	1	1	2.56	

Figure 19-5. Two pairs of alternatives (AB and CD) that differ (mismatch) on every feature except the first, along with the optimal feature weights and the total objective evidence for each alternative. Pair AB has a large difference in total evidence (5.07 − 0.00 = 5.07), whereas pair CD has a small difference (2.56 − 2.51 = 0.05). The general version of take-the-best predicts identical response times (RTs) for pairs AB and CD because the expected number of cue inspections is the same for both pairs. In contrast, the general version of the rational model (RAT) predicts a faster RT for pair AB because of its larger difference in evidence.

six mismatch pairs (see Figure 19-4) and the five mismatch pairs (see Figure 19-5), particularly for subjects who give high weight to Cue 1. Such subjects will tend to inspect Cue 1 first, thereby making an immediate decision for the six mismatch pairs. However, because Cue 1 fails to discriminate between the alternatives for the five mismatch pairs, gTTB predicts that decision making will be delayed for those pairs.

Method

Subjects. The subjects were 114 undergraduates at Indiana University Bloomington who participated as part of a course requirement. Subjects were told at the beginning of the experiment that if they performed well on the test phase of the experiment they would be paid a $3 bonus; those who achieved 80% correct or better were paid the bonus.

Stimuli. The stimuli used in the training phase were the same 119 training stimulus pairs (each presented twice) that were used in Experiment 1. Testing introduced two new types of stimulus pairs: some with all six features mismatching and some with five out of six features mismatching. In the latter case, the most diagnostic feature, Cue 1, always matched. The six-mismatch pairs all have the property, described above, of identical gTTB-predicted RTs but different gRAT-predicted RTs, assuming that gRAT uses compensatory weights. The same is true of the five-mismatch pairs. Stimulus pairs of these

types were ranked in order of difference in total evidence, assuming optimal weights. From the six-mismatch pairs, the 10 pairs with the largest difference in total evidence (RAT-easy), and the 10 pairs with the smallest difference in total evidence (RAT-hard), were included in the experiment. We used the same procedure to choose the five-mismatch pairs. This procedure yielded 20 six-mismatch pairs and 20 five-mismatch pairs with the most diagnostic feature matching. The complete list of these critical RT test pairs is presented in Table 19-9. The test phase also included the various pairs used in Experiment 1.

Procedure. The training phase was identical to the one described in Experiment 1.

The test phase included one presentation of each of the 119 training pairs, plus one trial of the untrained pair (2, 7), plus eight presentations of each of the five diagnostic test pairs used by Lee and Cummins (2004), plus three presentations of each of the 40 RAT-easy and RAT-hard RT pairs, for a total of 280 test trials. The order of presentation of pairs was randomized for each subject.

The procedure for the test phase was identical to the one used in Experiment 1, except that subjects were instructed that they should try to answer as quickly as possible without making mistakes. Furthermore, we imposed a 15-s time limit per response. If a subject took longer than 15 s to respond, a message would appear on the

Table 19-9. RAT-Easy and RAT-Hard Test Pairs Used in Experiment 2

A1	A2	A3	A4	A5	A6	EvA	B1	B2	B3	B4	B5	B6	EvB	EvDIFF
						Six-Mismatch Pairs: RAT-Easy								
0	0	0	0	0	0	0.00	1	1	1	1	1	1	8.75	8.75
0	0	0	0	0	1	0.19	1	1	1	1	1	0	8.56	8.37
0	0	0	0	1	0	0.26	1	1	1	1	0	1	8.49	8.23
0	0	0	0	1	1	0.45	1	1	1	1	0	0	8.30	7.84
0	0	0	1	0	0	0.59	1	1	1	0	1	1	8.17	7.58
0	0	0	1	0	1	0.78	1	1	1	0	1	0	7.98	7.20
0	0	0	1	1	0	0.85	1	1	1	0	0	1	7.90	7.05
0	0	0	1	1	1	1.04	1	1	1	0	0	0	7.71	6.67
0	0	1	0	0	0	1.52	1	1	0	1	1	1	7.24	5.72
0	0	1	0	0	1	1.71	1	1	0	1	1	0	7.04	5.33
						Six-Mismatch Pairs: RAT-Hard								
0	1	0	1	1	0	3.36	1	0	1	0	0	1	5.39	2.03
0	1	1	1	1	1	5.07	1	0	0	0	0	0	3.68	1.39
0	1	0	1	1	1	3.55	1	0	1	0	0	0	5.20	1.64
0	1	1	1	1	0	4.88	1	0	0	0	0	1	3.87	1.01
0	1	1	1	0	1	4.81	1	0	0	0	1	0	3.94	0.87
0	1	1	1	0	0	4.62	1	0	0	0	1	1	4.14	0.48
0	1	1	0	0	0	4.03	1	0	0	1	1	1	4.72	0.69
0	1	1	0	1	1	4.49	1	0	0	1	0	0	4.27	0.22
0	1	1	0	0	1	4.22	1	0	0	1	1	0	4.53	0.31
0	1	1	0	1	0	4.29	1	0	0	1	0	1	4.46	0.16
						Five-Mismatch Pairs: RAT-Easy								
1	0	0	0	0	0	0.00	1	1	1	1	1	1	5.07	5.07
0	0	0	0	0	0	0.00	0	1	1	1	1	1	5.07	5.07
0	0	0	0	0	1	0.19	0	1	1	1	1	0	4.88	4.69
1	0	0	0	0	1	0.19	1	1	1	1	1	0	4.88	4.69
1	0	0	0	1	0	0.26	1	1	1	1	0	1	4.81	4.55
0	0	0	0	1	0	0.26	0	1	1	1	0	1	4.81	4.55
0	0	0	0	1	1	0.45	0	1	1	1	0	0	4.62	4.16
1	0	0	0	1	1	0.45	1	1	1	1	0	0	4.62	4.16
1	0	0	1	0	0	0.59	1	1	1	0	1	1	4.49	3.90
0	0	0	1	0	0	0.59	0	1	1	0	1	1	4.49	3.90
						Five-Mismatch Pairs: RAT-Hard								
1	0	1	0	1	1	1.97	1	1	0	1	0	0	3.10	1.13
0	0	1	0	1	1	1.97	0	1	0	1	0	0	3.10	1.13
0	0	1	1	0	0	2.11	0	1	0	0	1	1	2.97	0.86
1	0	1	1	0	0	2.11	1	1	0	0	1	1	2.97	0.86
1	0	1	1	0	1	2.30	1	1	0	0	1	0	2.78	0.48
0	0	1	1	0	1	2.30	0	1	0	0	1	0	2.78	0.48
0	0	1	1	1	0	2.37	0	1	0	0	0	1	2.70	0.33
1	0	1	1	1	0	2.37	1	1	0	0	0	1	2.70	0.33
0	0	1	1	1	1	2.56	0	1	0	0	0	0	2.51	0.05
1	0	1	1	1	1	2.56	1	1	0	0	0	0	2.51	0.05

Note: RAT, classic rational model; EvA, total evidence for A; EvB, total evidence for B; EvDIFF, |EvA − EvB|. The average difference in total evidence is 7.27 for six-mismatch, RAT-Easy pairs; 0.88 for six-mismatch, RAT-hard pairs; 4.47 for five-mismatch, RAT-easy pairs; and 0.57 for five-mismatch, RAT-hard pairs.

screen reminding the subject of the time limit. We felt that this time limit was sufficiently long to allow subjects to inspect all cues, yet it also established the RT context of the experiment. Trials in which subjects exceeded the 15-s deadline (less than 1% of the trials) were excluded from the analyses. RT was measured to the nearest millisecond from the time that the test pair first appeared on the screen to the time that the subject completed his or her button press.

Results

Using the methods described previously, we fitted gRAT/gTTB to the choice-probability data of each individual subject. The best-fitting feature weights are reported in Table 19-10.

The general pattern of estimated weights was the same as observed in Experiment 1. Of the 114 subjects, 103 (90%) gave over half their weight to a single feature. In addition, of these 103 subjects, 92 (89%) gave over half their remaining weight to the next most highly weighted feature. Thus, once again, an analysis of the best-fitting parameters points to a highly noncompensatory pattern of weighting. Nevertheless, only 65 (57%) of the subjects assigned the highest weight to the most valid cue, leaving 43% of the subjects who made a mistake in ordering the cues' validities. Once again, the pattern of feature weighting challenges the strong versions of both RAT and TTB.

We turn now to the central question of interest, namely the RT contrast for the RAT-easy

Table 19-10. Individual Subjects' Best-Fitting Weights for the Equivalent gRAT and gTTB, Fit to Choice Probabilities in Experiment 2

Subject	BIC	w_1	w_2	w_3	w_4	w_5	w_6
1	215	4.94E−01	2.15E−01	9.18E−03	7.12E−03	2.74E−01	5.88E−05
2	176	9.86E−06	9.86E−01	3.90E−03	3.18E−03	4.04E−03	2.80E−03
3	412	9.36E−01	5.96E−02	9.36E−06	9.26E−04	8.42E−05	3.72E−03
4	228	9.90E−01	2.03E−03	3.37E−03	1.35E−03	1.35E−03	1.81E−03
5	113	7.92E−01	1.07E−03	1.21E−02	9.50E−05	1.95E−01	7.92E−06
6	284	9.93E−01	1.38E−03	1.11E−03	1.61E−03	1.62E−03	1.36E−03
7	252	2.23E−02	4.70E−01	3.18E−01	2.23E−03	1.87E−01	2.23E−04
8	267	1.70E−04	2.34E−01	5.09E−01	1.70E−04	2.56E−01	1.70E−04
9	145	9.55E−01	3.04E−03	4.16E−02	5.73E−05	5.16E−04	9.55E−06
10	333	1.46E−01	4.92E−03	5.42E−01	3.02E−01	5.08E−03	1.69E−04
11	312	2.55E−03	9.94E−06	9.94E−01	1.22E−03	1.12E−03	1.10E−03
12	146	9.93E−06	9.93E−01	2.82E−03	1.76E−03	2.20E−03	9.93E−06
13	267	5.57E−01	1.14E−01	8.60E−02	1.62E−01	8.05E−02	5.51E−04
14	113	9.91E−01	1.29E−04	4.45E−03	2.14E−03	2.01E−03	9.91E−06
15	242	9.52E−02	1.55E−04	3.16E−01	2.63E−01	3.22E−01	3.56E−03
16	212	4.55E−01	1.04E−01	2.55E−01	6.95E−02	5.62E−02	6.00E−02
17	196	5.78E−01	4.07E−03	3.02E−01	6.49E−02	5.08E−02	2.72E−04
18	159	2.25E−02	5.16E−01	1.85E−01	2.44E−03	2.74E−01	2.44E−04
19	233	1.78E−01	2.66E−01	2.74E−01	1.51E−01	1.31E−01	1.47E−04
20	118	6.64E−01	1.13E−01	2.22E−01	2.71E−04	5.42E−04	2.71E−04
21	248	3.06E−01	1.35E−01	1.82E−01	1.57E−01	1.58E−01	6.20E−02
22	410	9.89E−01	9.89E−06	9.89E−06	1.68E−04	5.69E−03	5.19E−03
23	200	2.36E−01	3.48E−01	3.92E−01	1.66E−03	2.26E−02	2.07E−04
24	108	9.97E−01	7.98E−05	1.14E−03	8.57E−04	9.97E−04	9.97E−06
25	208	2.02E−01	2.48E−01	1.89E−01	2.05E−01	1.55E−01	1.20E−04
26	140	9.88E−01	9.88E−06	3.84E−03	2.24E−03	3.66E−03	2.04E−03
27	202	9.93E−01	9.93E−06	1.89E−03	9.93E−05	3.07E−03	2.14E−03
28	291	1.80E−04	2.63E−01	1.82E−01	1.55E−01	2.18E−01	1.83E−01
29	140	9.94E−01	5.96E−05	3.84E−03	2.98E−04	2.29E−03	9.94E−06

Table 19-10.   (continued)

Subject	BIC	w_1	w_2	w_3	w_4	w_5	w_6
30	111	3.01E–02	6.59E–01	2.99E–01	3.04E–04	4.56E–03	6.39E–03
31	415	1.65E–04	8.43E–03	3.49E–01	3.59E–01	2.83E–01	1.65E–04
32	174	5.96E–01	1.81E–01	1.14E–01	4.08E–03	1.04E–01	2.92E–04
33	203	2.72E–02	3.95E–01	5.48E–01	2.75E–02	2.36E–03	2.62E–04
34	259	6.03E–01	2.64E–04	2.64E–04	3.96E–01	2.64E–04	2.64E–04
35	109	9.97E–06	9.97E–01	7.98E–05	9.97E–06	1.84E–03	1.13E–03
36	137	9.93E–01	9.93E–06	1.43E–03	9.93E–06	5.76E–03	9.93E–06
37	268	9.87E–01	4.05E–03	2.45E–03	2.64E–03	9.87E–06	4.10E–03
38	420	9.65E–06	1.85E–03	1.35E–04	9.65E–06	9.65E–01	3.30E–02
39	417	6.40E–06	2.56E–04	8.19E–03	6.40E–01	6.40E–06	3.52E–01
40	297	3.11E–01	2.36E–01	8.25E–02	2.19E–01	1.19E–01	3.32E–02
41	265	3.86E–01	1.99E–01	6.35E–03	4.05E–01	3.98E–03	8.47E–05
42	144	9.54E–01	9.54E–06	3.34E–02	7.35E–04	1.18E–02	8.59E–05
43	286	4.62E–01	2.26E–04	2.44E–01	9.00E–02	2.00E–01	3.84E–03
44	211	1.90E–04	5.08E–01	3.01E–01	8.13E–02	5.75E–02	5.20E–02
45	251	2.33E–01	5.00E–03	3.03E–01	1.61E–04	2.33E–01	2.26E–01
46	166	2.07E–01	7.91E–01	9.36E–04	7.20E–05	1.14E–03	8.00E–06
47	218	5.78E–01	2.62E–04	2.03E–01	3.14E–03	3.40E–03	2.13E–01
48	223	9.91E–01	9.91E–06	1.98E–03	1.96E–03	3.61E–03	1.31E–03
49	156	9.41E–01	9.41E–06	1.43E–02	9.41E–05	4.39E–02	9.59E–04
50	273	9.90E–01	9.90E–06	2.32E–03	2.97E–03	2.99E–03	1.95E–03
51	215	4.11E–01	2.29E–04	5.08E–01	3.14E–02	2.93E–02	2.04E–02
52	82	2.72E–04	5.87E–01	1.85E–01	8.52E–02	1.43E–01	2.72E–04
53	239	9.93E–01	2.15E–03	9.93E–06	1.97E–03	1.88E–03	1.25E–03
54	412	1.74E–04	2.93E–01	4.36E–01	9.23E–03	1.74E–04	2.61E–01
55	108	6.27E–01	2.33E–04	1.39E–01	1.63E–03	2.20E–01	1.14E–02
56	96	9.85E–01	9.85E–06	9.81E–03	1.76E–03	3.28E–03	1.18E–04
57	162	8.38E–01	8.05E–03	1.53E–01	8.30E–04	8.38E–06	8.38E–05
58	177	9.89E–01	9.89E–06	3.93E–03	2.76E–03	2.33E–03	2.11E–03
59	162	9.97E–01	1.79E–04	1.90E–03	3.99E–05	1.01E–03	9.97E–06
60	419	2.96E–01	6.74E–06	1.99E–03	2.84E–02	6.74E–01	1.01E–04
61	121	9.58E–01	9.58E–06	3.73E–02	2.16E–03	2.16E–03	1.15E–04
62	238	9.83E–01	3.60E–03	3.34E–03	3.06E–03	3.18E–03	3.91E–03
63	202	9.88E–01	9.88E–06	4.17E–03	3.22E–03	2.70E–03	1.85E–03
64	289	2.09E–01	1.91E–01	2.01E–01	2.24E–01	1.48E–04	1.75E–01
65	262	5.37E–01	1.84E–04	3.11E–01	1.01E–02	1.40E–01	1.29E–03
66	248	4.92E–01	3.87E–01	3.28E–02	1.87E–02	4.48E–02	2.49E–02
67	376	1.77E–04	3.07E–01	2.41E–01	1.97E–01	2.54E–01	1.77E–04
68	390	9.84E–01	2.36E–04	9.84E–06	7.85E–03	7.55E–03	2.36E–04
69	358	2.56E–01	2.38E–01	2.94E–01	5.66E–03	8.40E–03	1.98E–01
70	214	1.84E–04	3.43E–01	2.94E–01	1.41E–01	2.21E–01	1.84E–04
71	341	4.43E–01	5.01E–03	1.16E–01	2.30E–01	2.06E–01	2.09E–04
72	406	3.13E–01	4.29E–01	1.57E–04	1.32E–02	2.43E–01	1.89E–03
73	150	9.89E–01	1.38E–04	5.05E–03	1.96E–03	4.14E–03	9.89E–06
74	146	1.00E+00	1.00E–05	4.00E–05	1.00E–05	1.00E–05	1.00E–05
75	121	2.26E–02	9.75E–01	8.97E–04	1.14E–03	9.75E–06	8.78E–05
76	367	3.15E–01	1.45E–02	3.45E–01	1.52E–03	3.23E–01	1.90E–04
77	266	9.94E–01	1.22E–03	1.85E–03	1.27E–03	1.16E–03	9.94E–06
78	419	5.99E–06	2.40E–04	5.99E–01	3.91E–01	5.99E–06	1.02E–02
79	416	9.43E–06	1.60E–04	5.48E–02	9.43E–01	1.98E–03	9.43E–06

Continued

Table 19-10. (continued)

Subject	BIC	w_1	w_2	w_3	w_4	w_5	w_6
80	109	3.71E−02	9.56E−01	2.89E−03	9.56E−06	3.45E−03	1.43E−04
81	261	4.90E−01	2.69E−03	4.80E−01	1.32E−02	1.32E−02	2.24E−04
82	208	3.35E−01	4.23E−01	1.22E−01	2.33E−04	1.16E−01	3.72E−03
83	185	9.92E−01	9.92E−06	4.73E−03	9.92E−06	3.09E−03	9.92E−06
84	103	9.96E−01	9.96E−06	1.69E−03	4.68E−04	1.17E−03	6.37E−04
85	222	9.88E−01	1.88E−04	2.16E−03	9.88E−06	4.09E−03	5.82E−03
86	130	9.96E−01	1.28E−03	3.12E−03	1.99E−05	1.99E−05	9.96E−06
87	419	5.60E−06	4.28E−01	5.60E−01	5.60E−06	2.74E−04	1.20E−02
88	145	9.94E−01	8.95E−05	3.38E−03	1.23E−03	9.15E−04	9.94E−06
89	214	9.91E−01	1.59E−04	4.70E−03	9.91E−06	2.09E−03	1.98E−03
90	198	1.74E−03	9.92E−01	1.91E−03	1.10E−03	2.90E−03	9.92E−06
91	185	9.88E−06	9.88E−01	5.12E−03	2.06E−03	2.75E−03	2.24E−03
92	417	2.14E−04	2.11E−01	2.52E−01	2.14E−04	2.59E−01	2.77E−01
93	219	5.62E−01	1.24E−02	3.94E−01	1.19E−02	1.36E−02	6.89E−03
94	184	3.29E−03	9.90E−01	1.57E−03	2.00E−03	1.98E−03	1.41E−03
95	168	2.94E−03	5.10E−01	3.54E−01	2.10E−04	1.28E−01	4.20E−03
96	229	9.89E−01	2.52E−03	2.77E−03	3.30E−03	2.20E−03	9.89E−06
97	176	9.93E−01	1.83E−03	3.07E−03	9.93E−05	2.02E−03	9.93E−06
98	84	9.53E−01	5.72E−05	4.36E−02	2.77E−04	2.58E−03	9.53E−06
99	158	6.83E−01	4.54E−03	1.68E−01	4.58E−02	9.80E−02	2.06E−04
100	175	9.89E−01	5.94E−05	5.81E−03	3.36E−04	4.48E−03	9.89E−06
101	245	6.43E−06	4.82E−01	5.15E−01	1.18E−03	1.31E−03	6.56E−04
102	318	5.80E−01	2.74E−04	2.10E−01	4.11E−03	1.39E−01	6.66E−02
103	114	3.48E−04	9.93E−01	3.50E−03	5.96E−05	2.73E−03	9.93E−06
104	144	6.68E−01	1.10E−01	6.40E−02	4.72E−02	6.83E−02	4.29E−02
105	186	9.85E−01	3.34E−03	5.11E−03	3.67E−03	9.85E−06	2.85E−03
106	324	9.82E−01	9.82E−06	5.37E−03	4.33E−03	4.04E−03	3.79E−03
107	416	3.50E−05	4.17E−01	2.50E−01	3.50E−03	3.26E−01	3.50E−03
108	235	5.41E−01	1.76E−04	1.12E−01	7.09E−02	1.92E−01	8.43E−02
109	260	2.89E−05	9.63E−01	1.88E−03	9.63E−06	3.52E−02	1.35E−04
110	119	9.89E−01	2.48E−03	6.76E−03	1.09E−04	2.02E−03	9.89E−06
111	191	1.38E−02	8.39E−01	1.44E−01	1.17E−03	1.04E−03	7.64E−04
112	143	2.16E−04	5.61E−01	4.17E−01	1.73E−03	2.03E−02	2.16E−04
113	134	9.93E−01	9.93E−06	1.24E−03	3.83E−03	2.01E−03	8.94E−05
114	166	9.91E−01	9.91E−06	4.71E−03	4.33E−03	9.91E−06	9.91E−06
Average	228	6.35E−01	1.99E−01	7.29E−02	4.23E−02	4.06E−02	1.10E−02

Note: Optimal normalized weights (w) are .4204, .2870, .1735, .0671, .0301, and .0218. Parameter values are represented in scientific notation, such that 1.57E − 07 represents 1.57×10^{-7}, or .000000157. BIC = Bayesian information criterion.

and RAT-hard pairs. First, we constructed a histogram of subjects' proportions correct on the test phase in order to discard subjects who performed at a very low level due to lack of motivation or inability to learn the task. The histogram showed what appeared to be a boundary at 65% correct between a distribution of high-performing subjects and a distribution of low-performing subjects. We therefore

excluded from analysis subjects with less than 65% correct on trained pairs during the test phase. Out of 114 total subjects, this left 98 (86%) good performers.

In one approach to analyzing the RT data, we conducted independent samples t tests for each individual subject comparing log RTs for all RAT-easy and RAT-hard trials. For the five-mismatch pairs, only 16 (16%) of the 98 high-performing subjects showed a significant difference ($p < .05$) in the expected direction (RAT-easy trials faster than RAT-hard trials); for the six-mismatch pairs, only 21 (21%) showed a significant difference; and for the five-and six-mismatch pairs taken together, only 21 (21%) showed a significant difference. Thus, less than one-quarter of subjects showed a pattern of RTs indicative of gRAT with compensatory weights. Instead, the vast majority of subjects had an RT signature that points toward gTTB behavior.

In a second method, we used a Bayesian modeling approach to analyze the RT results. In this Bayesian hypothesis test, we treated the null hypothesis of "no difference" between RAT-easy and RAT-hard trials as a model to be fit to a subject's data and the alternative hypothesis of "difference" as another model. The no-difference model assumes that the RTs for both easy and hard trials come from a single distribution. In contrast, the difference model assumes that easy and hard trials' RTs come from two separate distributions. The Bayesian approach then determines which hypothesis is more likely. The details of the analysis are reported in Appendix C. We conducted the analysis separately for the five-mismatch pairs, the six-mismatch pairs, and the five- and six-mismatch pairs taken together. The two-distribution model was favored for the five-mismatch pairs by only 8% of the subjects, for the six-mismatch pairs by only 9% of the subjects, and for the five-and six-mismatch pairs taken together by only 10% of the subjects. Thus, the results of the Bayesian analysis point even more strongly to the gTTB interpretation of the data.

Another RT test of the models concerns the five- versus six-mismatch pairs. The five-mismatch pairs contain one matching feature (Feature 1, the most diagnostic feature), so gTTB predicts a total of two feature inspections whenever Feature 1 is inspected first. By contrast, according to gTTB, only one feature will ever be inspected for the six-mismatch pairs, so the six-mismatch pairs should tend to be faster than the five-mismatch pairs. Furthermore, subjects who attach a large weight to Feature 1 will inspect Feature 1 first very often. Therefore, we would expect these subjects to almost always make

two feature inspections when confronted with five-mismatch pairs and therefore to show a pronounced difference in average RT between five- and six-mismatch pairs. In contrast, subjects who attach a small weight to Feature 1 should rarely inspect Feature 1 first and therefore show little or no difference between five-and six-mismatch pairs.

Note that an RT difference between the five-and six-mismatch pairs is also predicted by the gRAT model because of the greater average evidence difference for the six-mismatch pairs compared with the five-mismatch pairs (see Table 19-9). However, although the finding of such a difference would not distinguish between gTTB and gRAT, it would still be important for two reasons. First, it would provide clear evidence of the ability of the RT measure to reveal such predicted differences. Thus, it would suggest that the null results involving the earlier RAT-easy versus RAT-hard comparisons were not due to a noisy performance measure. Second, if the RT difference held primarily for subjects giving high weight to Feature 1, it would provide evidence of the "psychological reality" of the estimated feature weights. That is, the weights estimated by fitting the models to the choice-probability data would be making correct independent predictions of the pattern of RTs.

In accordance with these predictions, among the 43 subjects with over .99 of the total weight assigned to Feature 1, 41 (95%) showed a significant difference in RT between the five- and six-mismatch pairs. By contrast, among the 35 subjects with less than .50 of the total weight assigned to Feature 1, only 3 (9%) showed a significant difference between the five- and six-mismatch pairs. Thus, the pattern of results comparing the five- and six-mismatch pairs is as predicted by gTTB.

One concern that may be raised is that, because of the extended number of trials in the test phase, subjects who initially adopted a RAT strategy may have eventually shifted to a TTB strategy to ease their processing burden. To address this concern, we also conducted all of the aforementioned analyses on just the first 70 trials of the test phase (i.e., the first quarter of test phase data). The results were essentially identical to those that we have already reported for the complete set of 280 test trials. For example, among the full set of 98 learners, only 9 (9%) showed a significant difference in RT between the RAT-easy and the RAT-hard pairs. By contrast, among the 43 learners who gave highly noncompensatory weight to Cue 1, 41 (95%) showed significantly faster RTs to the six-mismatch pairs than to the five-mismatch pairs. Thus, the main pattern of results appears to have arisen fairly early during the testing sequence.

Discussion

As in Experiment 1, the best-fitting weight patterns indicate that about 80% of subjects adopted a noncompensatory strategy. Again, the decision making of a vast majority of subjects seems to have been based on single discriminating features, a finding which seems to rule out the classic conception of a rational strategy and points instead toward the use of gTTB.

Turning to the RT data, we see as well that the results follow the predictions of gTTB. That is, the model predicted no difference in RT on RAT-hard versus RAT-easy pairs that differed on every feature or that matched on one particular feature and mismatched on all others. Compensatory versions of gRAT, on the other hand, predicted differences in RT on the basis of differences in total evidence, a result not supported by our data. Moreover, we corroborated gTTB's prediction that, for those subjects giving noncompensatory weight to Feature 1, decision making would be faster for the six-mismatch pairs than for the five-mismatch pairs. Experiment 3 shows that RT measures can detect RAT-compensating behavior.

GENERAL DISCUSSION

One of the main issues in the field of multiattribute probabilistic inference has involved a contrast between models derived from the "fast-and-frugal heuristics" framework and models that embody classical rationality. A major representative of the former is TTB, and a major representative of the latter is RAT.

Numerous experiments have been conducted to determine the conditions in which each processing strategy tends to be used. However, in most cases, quite strong versions of each model have been compared and contrasted with one another. For example, it is usually assumed that subjects use attribute weights based on the objective cue validities of the attribute values. In addition, deterministic versions of the models are generally applied, with no allowance for any noise in the decision process.

Although this research strategy allows one to develop elegant qualitative contrasts between the predictions of competing models, our view is that such strong models are not psychologically plausible. Furthermore, a class of models may be correct in spirit, even if the results of certain qualitative tests falsify a strong special case. For example, observers may indeed follow a TTB-like process in making their decisions, even if they make errors in precisely estimating the cue validities of the attributes in the experienced environment.

For this reason, an initial purpose of the present research was to consider generalized versions of the TTB and RAT models with greater psychological plausibility and to study performance from the perspective of these generalized models. The generalizations that we considered made allowances for the attribute weights to be free parameters and for probabilistic mechanisms to enter into the decision process. Although this research strategy has the obvious disadvantage of requiring quantitative parameter estimation, our view is that, at least in the present situation, some reasonably clear-cut insights were achieved.

First, despite penalizing the generalized models for their increase in the number of free parameters, the quantitative fit indices provided clear evidence that the generalizations were needed. Furthermore, the fits to the choice probability data yielded parameter estimates of the attribute weights that departed markedly from those prescribed for an ideal observer. Subjective feature weights differed from the ideal-observer weights not only in their magnitudes, but also in their ordering. Thus, the results challenge the very strong assumptions made by TTB and RAT. In these respects, there is a considerable difference between the generalized models and the original formulations of both the TTB and RAT models of decision making.

Nevertheless, a second clear-cut result was that, for the vast majority of subjects, the estimated weight parameters followed a noncompensatory pattern (at least for the two most highly weighted dimensions). We argue that such a pattern is far more in the spirit of a TTB-like decision process than a RAT-like process. It implies that the most highly weighted discriminating attribute decides the direction of choice, regardless of the values of the remaining attributes. Indeed, for the majority of subjects, the magnitudes of the weight estimates implied an essentially fixed order of inspection of the cues and a deterministic choice based on the value of a single attribute.

Consider a subject who compared alternatives on an attribute by attribute basis, stopped when a single discriminating cue was located, and then chose the alternative with the positive cue value but that had attribute weight values that did not conform precisely to the cue-validity ordering. Whereas previous research approaches, such as the one adopted by Lee and Cummins (2004), would likely have classified such an observer as a non-TTB decision maker, the present strategy would indicate that there are strong elements of TTB-like decision making in operation. Thus, consideration of the generalized versions of these models can provide insights that would be missed by consideration of the strong versions alone.

A second major contribution of this work was the introduction of an RT method for discriminating between the predictions from the generalized models. In our view, this RT method provides an important form of evidence that complements alternative process-tracing techniques. In the process-tracing techniques, observers are generally required to uncover attribute information one attribute at a time until a decision is made, and the subjects' overt attribute inspections are monitored. Although such methods provide important

insights about behavior, investigators have acknowledged potential limitations of the methods as well. In particular, the process-tracing techniques provide an example in which a measurement method can possibly influence the very behavior it is intended to measure. For example, on the one hand, requiring subjects to inspect alternatives one attribute at a time might promote strategies such as TTB. On the other hand, in these situations, subjects have knowledge that their attribute-inspecting behavior is being monitored. Perhaps such knowledge gives rise to demand characteristics, leading subjects to inspect attributes that they might not inspect otherwise.

The RT method therefore provides a potentially useful complement to the process-tracing techniques because it provides a window into the underlying cognitive processes without altering the nature of the testing situation. In the present case, the method provided strong converging evidence that the vast majority of subjects in our experiments adopted a TTB-like decision-making process. Observers' RTs were well predicted by the expected number of inspections required to find a single discriminating cue. Furthermore, the RTs were not influenced by whether a decision was "hard" or "easy" from a classic rationality perspective. On the other hand, in an environment in which the summing strategy of classic rationality was essentially forced upon subjects, the RT predictions from the gRAT model were finally observed. Thus, the method appears to provide an important source of converging evidence bearing on the nature of people's decision-making strategies.

ACKNOWLEDGMENTS

This work was supported by National Institute of Mental Health Grant R01 MH48494. We thank Frances Fawcett of Cornell University for allowing us to use her drawings of beetles as stimuli in these experiments. We also thank Ben Newell for his helpful criticisms of an earlier version of this article and Peter Todd for numerous helpful discussions.

NOTES

1. Martignon and Hoffrage (1999) have pointed out that this order of inspection of cues is not necessarily optimal but that to find the optimal ordering "there is no simpler procedure than testing all possible permutations of cues and comparing the performance of a lexicographic strategy [TTB] for each of these orderings" (p. 132). Inspecting cues in order of validity is a highly efficient, "approximately rational" compromise.

2. By contrast, in previous related experiments, use of a TTB strategy would lead to markedly worse performance than use of a weighted additive strategy (e.g., Juslin et al., 2003). It is interesting that the stimulus structure that Lee and Cummins (2004) used was adapted from a real-world environment, previously considered by Czerlinski, Gigerenzer, and Goldstein (1999), that relates certain geographic features of the Galapagos Islands to a count of the number of species on each island. It is precisely for such real-world environments that Gigerenzer and colleagues have argued that fast-and-frugal heuristics, such as TTB, have been adapted.

3. As discussed in detail in the *Results* sections of our article, we use likelihood-based methods of evaluating the fits of the alternative models. If a subject makes a single response that is not in accord with the deterministic versions of TTB or RAT, then these likelihood-based methods would evaluate the models as being infinitely wrong. A rudimentary error theory is needed to avoid this difficulty.

4. Note that even if the weights are compensatory (in the sense described earlier in this article), gTTB still predicts no difference in RT between RAT-easy and RAT-hard pairs. If the weights are compensatory, then the order in which gTTB inspects the cues will be probabilistic and will vary across trials. Regardless of the order in which the cues are inspected, however, the model predicts identical RTs because the first cue that is inspected will lead to a decision. Furthermore, even if the time to make a decision varies as a function of which particular cue is inspected (e.g., due to encoding-time differences), the predicted RTs are still identical because the probability of inspecting any given cue is identical for RAT-easy and RAT-hard pairs.

APPENDIX A

Proof of Formal Equivalence of gRAT ($\gamma = 1$) and gTTB's Predictions of Response Probabilities

Because the pair of stimuli contains no matching features, the first cue that is inspected will lead gTTB to make a decision. The probability that gTTB chooses alternative A is therefore found by computing the probability that the first cue inspected favors alternative A—that is, that the first cue inspected is one in which alternative A has a positive cue value. Letting cue_1 denote the first cue inspected, FA the set of cues favoring alternative A, FA_i the ith cue favoring alternative A, and N_{FA} the number of cues favoring alternative A, then

$$
\begin{aligned}
P("A"\mid AB) &= P(cue_1\ favors A) \\
&= P(cue_1 \in FA) \\
&= P[(cue_1 = FA_1)P\vee(cue_1 = FA_2)\vee\cdots \\
&\qquad \vee(cue_1 = FA_{N_{FA}})] \\
&= P(cue_1 = FA_1) + P(cue_1 = FA_2) + \cdots \\
&\qquad + (cue_1 = FA_{N_{FA}}) \\
&= \frac{w_{FA_1}}{\sum w} + \frac{w_{FA_2}}{\sum w} + \frac{w_{FA_{N_{FA}}}}{\sum w} \\
&= \frac{w_{FA_1} + w_{FA_2} + \cdots + w_{FA_{N_{FA}}}}{\sum w} \\
&= \frac{\displaystyle\sum_{i\in FA} w_i}{\displaystyle\sum_{i\in FA} w_i + \sum_{i\in FB} w_i},
\end{aligned}
$$

which is the predicted probability of $P(A\mid AB)$ from gRAT when $\gamma = 1$ (compare with Equation 19-5).

APPENDIX B

Method of Model Evaluation

The BIC fit for a model is given by

$$
\text{BIC} = -2\ln(L) + N_{par}\ln(N_{obs}), \qquad (19\text{-}B1)
$$

where $\ln(L)$ is the log-likelihood of the data given the model, N_{par} is the number of free parameters in the model, and N_{obs} is the number of data observations on which the fit is based.

In the present case, the likelihood of the data set is given by

$$L = \prod_{m=1}^{M} \binom{N_m}{f_m} p_m^{fm} (1 - p_m)^{(N_m - f_m)}, \qquad (19\text{-}B2)$$

where M = total number of stimulus pairs being modeled, N_m = number of observations for pair m, f_m = frequency of observing an "A" response for pair m, and p_m = predicted probability of an "A" response for pair m. This likelihood function assumes that the response choices are binomially distributed and that the observations are independent. The best-fitting parameters for a model are the ones that maximize the Equation 19-B2 likelihood function and that thereby minimize the BIC expressed in Equation 19-B1.

APPENDIX C

Bayesian Hypothesis Testing

In the Bayesian t test, we treat the null hypothesis of no difference between RAT-easy and RAT-hard trials as a model to be fit to a subject's data and the alternative hypothesis of difference as another model. The no-difference model assumes that the RTs for both easy and hard trials' RTs come from a single distribution. In contrast, the difference model assumes that easy and hard trials' RTs come from two separate distributions.

As in the classical t tests we conducted, we make the standard assumption that log(RT) follows a normal distribution. Fitting the single-distribution model involves the estimation of two free parameters, the mean (μ) and the standard deviation (σ) of the normal distribution. To evaluate its fit, one calculates the probability density of observing a subject's entire data set of easy and hard trial RTs from a normal distribution with the given μ and σ. The probability density of a single observed $\ln(RT_i)$ with value x is therefore given by

$$P(x \mid \mu, \sigma) = \frac{1}{\sigma \sqrt{2\pi}} e^{-\frac{(x-\mu)^2}{2\sigma^2}}. \qquad (19\text{-}C1)$$

The probability density of observing a subject's entire data set $\bar{x}$ of RTs is then simply the product of the individual probability densities:

$$P(\bar{x} \mid \mu, \sigma) = \prod_i P(x_i \mid \mu, \sigma). \qquad (19\text{-}C2)$$

For the two-distribution model, the procedure is very similar, except that the probability density of observing an individual RT depends on whether that RT was for an easy or a hard pair. If it was for an easy pair, its probability is calculated by using Equation 19-C1, but with $\mu = \mu_{easy}$ and $\sigma = \sigma_{easy}$; if it was for a hard pair, its probability is calculated by using $\mu = \mu_{hard}$ and $\sigma = \sigma_{hard}$. Once the individual RTs' probability densities have been calculated, the probability density of the entire data set of all easy and hard trials is calculated as the product of the individual trials' probability densities. Finally, one uses a computer search method to find the values of the free parameters that maximize the likelihood for each model, and one compares the fits by using the BIC statistic described in Appendix B.

Introduction to Chapter 20

Sequential Processing of Cues in Memory-Based Multiattribute Decisions

One of the tenets of the ABC Research Group at the Max Planck Institute is to bring together research-ers from different disciplines to study decision making. This has led to new discoveries and intense criticism. A second tenet is to invite its critics to spend a period of time at the Institute, enabling them to learn from each other. Arndt Bröder is one critic who accepted the invitation and who stayed for 7 months. In his previous research, he had collected both choice and response time data on take-the-best but never analyzed the latter. Because take-the-best predicts how long search in memory lasts for each task, reaction times provide a window for analyzing the process of judgment, just as in Berger and Nosofsky's work (see Chapter 19). After Arndt's arrival, Wolfgang Gaissmaier, then a graduate student, therefore began nagging him to jointly analyze the response time data; his perseverance eventually led to a successful collaboration.

Models of heuristics are typically intended to model both the outcome (e.g., choice, inference clas-sification) and the process of decision making. That is, the models predict not only the final decision but also specific steps of information processing, such as the order in which information is searched, how search for information is terminated, and how information is used to arrive at a decision. As a consequence, models of heuristics—unlike as-if models of cognition—can be tested on two levels. Even if a heuristic predicts outcomes well, it may still fail in describing the process. There are different methods to put process predictions to test. One is response times. In contrast to Bergert and Nosofsky, who openly presented information to the participants, Bröder and Gaissmaier focused on inference from memory, in which people have to recall information.

Bröder and Gaissmaier reanalyzed the response times of five of Bröder's previously published experiments and one new experiment. Importantly, their analysis was based on a combination of outcome-based and process-based tests. Users of take-the-best or compensatory strategies (e.g., Dawes' rule) were identified using an outcome-based classification method, and their response time patterns were then compared. The main result is that the response times provided process evidence for take-the-best and other strategies. The earlier that take-the-best predicted search to be stopped, the faster its users responded. In contrast, the responses of users of compensatory strategies were generally slower.

CHAPTER 20

Sequential Processing of Cues in Memory-Based Multiattribute Decisions

Arndt Bröder and Wolfgang Gaissmaier

Abstract: When probabilistic inferences have to be made from cue values stored in long-term memory, many participants appear to use fast-and-frugal heuristics, such as "take-the-best" (TTB), that assume sequential search of cues. A simultaneous global matching process with cue weights that are appropriately chosen would mimic the decision outcomes, albeit assuming different cognitive processes. We present a reanalysis of response times (RTs) from five published experiments ($n = 415$) and one new experiment ($n = 82$) that support the assumption of sequential search. In all instances in which decision outcomes indicated the use of TTB's decision rule, decision times increased monotonically with the number of cues that had to be searched in memory. Furthermore, RT patterns fitted the outcome-based strategy classifications, which further validates both measures.

Recently, Bergert and Nosofsky (2007) analyzed response times (RTs) as convergent evidence for an outcome-based strategy classification in a decision-making task from givens. We suggest that RT analyses could similarly be applied to investigate different strategies in memory-based decisions. We hypothesize that RTs increase with the number of information pieces that have to be retrieved to make a decision, which differs for different items and/or strategies.

We will report RT analyses of five published experiments and of one new experiment.

EXPERIMENTS 1–5

Method

All experiments reported subsequently differed in minor procedural details, which are fully

reported in Bröder and Schiffer (2003b, 2006). All studies employed a hypothetical criminal case involving 10 suspects of a murder: A famous singer was murdered near the pool, presumably by one of his former girlfriends. The participants were asked to help find the murderer. The basic idea of all the studies was to separate the acquisition of knowledge about the suspects from making decisions about them, so that knowledge had to be retrieved from memory when making decisions.

Each experiment consisted of four phases: First, in an anticipation learning paradigm, participants acquired knowledge about the individual cue patterns of 10 suspects, which differed on four cues (e.g., dog breed). Each of the cues could have three different values (e.g., spaniel, Dalmatian, or dachshund). A portrait and a name of a suspect appeared on the screen, and participants had to reproduce the cue values with appropriate feedback. All 10 patterns were repeated until 90% of the responses were correct, indicating a sufficiently reliable knowledge base in memory.

To avoid the participants' making inferences during learning, a cue hierarchy was established only in a second phase by informing them about the evidence (cues) witnessed at the site of the crime and its relative importance. The relative importance of the four cues (predictive cue validity) was established by telling participants how many witnesses agreed on them. For example, they were told that four witnesses agreed that the suspect had a spaniel dog, whereas only two witnesses agreed that the suspect was wearing leather trousers.

The third phase consisted of complete paired comparisons of all suspects in which participants had to decide which suspect was more likely to be the murderer. Importantly, only the names of the suspects and their portraits were displayed. The cues that allowed deciding between the two suspects had to be retrieved from memory.

After this decision phase, a final memory test assessed the stability of cue memory as a manipulation check.

Description of the Strategies and RT Predictions

The strategies we considered to potentially underlie the participants' decisions are "take-the-best" (TTB), Dawes' rule (DR), Franklin's rule (FR), and guessing. When comparing two suspects, the lexicographic TTB heuristic assumes that participants sequentially retrieve cues describing the suspects in the order of their validity. A person using TTB searches the most valid cue for both suspects first. If this cue discriminates, the person does not search further and makes a decision. Otherwise, searching for cues (in order of validity) continues until a discriminating cue is found. Therefore, the best (i.e., most valid) discriminating cue determines when TTB stops searching and decides, so that we predict a monotonic increase in RTs, depending on the number of cues that have to be retrieved until this best discriminating cue is found.

Going back to Robyn Dawes' (1979) work on unit-weight models, DR is a rule that takes all cues into account, but does not consider their validity. A DR user tries to retrieve all cues and decides for the suspect who is "favored" by more cues. In the case of a tie, the person has to guess.

FR—similar to DR—takes all the information into account, but weighs it according to cue validity. Since less valid cues can overrule more highly valid cues, DR and FR are compensatory strategies. Both DR and FR, at least in a strict sense, require searching all cues in an unspecified order. RTs should therefore not depend on the best discriminating cue. Since DR and FR do not specify a search order, it is more difficult to distinguish between sequential search and global matching for users of these strategies. One prediction that in our view follows from the sequential search assumption, but not from the global matching assumption, is that people classified as using FR should be slower on average than DR users, since FR (in addition to DR) requires weighing cues according to their validity and is thus cognitively more complex.

The last strategy, guessing, consists of retrieving no cues at all and just randomly decides for one of the suspects. Therefore, the RTs of guessers should not vary with the position of best discriminating cue, and they should be the quickest overall.

Results and Discussion

To decide which of the strategies was being used, the choice vector produced by each participant was classified by a maximum-likelihood procedure, details of which are provided in Bröder and Schiffer (2003a). The method assumes a uniform response error probability and stable strategy use across trials and determines the strategy for which the data are most likely.

Table 20-1 contains an overview of the experiments reported previously. In sum, the results show that the need to retrieve cue information from memory induced fast-and-frugal decision making, especially when cues were represented verbally and when working memory load was high.

To analyze RTs, we combined participants from all five experiments and split them into four groups with identical strategy classifications. There were 198 TTB users, 90 FR users, 83 DR users, and 44 participants who appeared to guess. Nine unclassified patterns (with identical likelihoods for more than one strategy) were excluded. For each participant, we computed the

Table 20-1. Overview of Studies

Source	Experiment	% TTB Users	× Condition	N	Cue Descriptions
Bröder and Schiffer (2003b)	1	Load[a]	No Load[a]	50	Blood type, cigarette brand, perfume, vehicle
		72.0%	56.0%		
	2	Memory	Screen	50	Jacket, shoes, bag, vehicle
		44.0%	20.0%		
	3	Verbal	Pictorial	50	Jacket, shoes, bag, vehicle
		64.0%	64.0%		
	4	Verbal	Pictorial	114	Dog breed, jacket, trousers, shirt color
		47.4%	26.4%		
Bröder and Schiffer (2006)	5	Verbal	Pictorial	151	Dog breed, jacket, trousers, shirt color
		69.7%	36.0%		
		Load[a]	No Load[a]		
		53.0%	34.2%		
Present article	6	Match[b]	Mismatch[b]	82	Dog breed, jacket, trousers, shirt color
		51.2%	26.8%		

Note: TTB, "take-the-best."
[a] Working memory load.
[b] Between validity and ease of retrieval.

outlier robust median RT for each of the four item types, depending on the position of the best discriminating cue. These individual RT medians were entered in the subsequent ANOVA.[1]

The mean RTs for each strategy group are depicted in Figure 20-1. There was a main effect of the position of the best discriminating cue, Greenhouse-Geisser corrected [$F(2.53, 1041.48) = 20.63, p < .001$], showing increasing decision times in general. There was also a main effect of strategy [$F(3, 411) = 6.92, p < .001$] and, much more important, a significant interaction [$F(2.53, 1041.84) = 3.41, p = .001$]. For all strategies, the decision times increased with the position of the best discriminating cue, but this increase was most pronounced for TTB users. To substantiate this claim, regression slopes were computed for each individual and compared across strategy groups, showing an overall difference [$F(3, 411) = 9.52, p < .001$]. According to Scheffé post hoc tests, TTB slopes ($B = 1.31$) differed significantly from all others, whereas DR, FR, and guess slopes did not significantly differ (*Bs* = 0.49, 0.24, and 0.26, respectively). FR and guess slopes did not significantly differ from zero [both *ts*(>42) < 1.30, both *ps* > .20], whereas TTB slopes did

[$t(197) = 8.49, p < .001$], as did DR slopes [$t(82) = 3.27, p < .01$].

The RTs thus followed the predicted pattern and supported the assumption of sequential search: The increase was much less pronounced for FR, DR, and guessing than for TTB, which would be expected if people generally search more cues than the best discriminating one, or no cues at all (when guessing). Still, there is a slight descriptive increase in RTs also for FR and DR users, which we will discuss in the General Discussion. FR users needed generally more time than DR users (which we expected, given that DR users only have to count evidence), whereas FR users also have to weigh it. Participants with predominantly nonsystematic guessing behavior generally needed less time than all others.

An alternative interpretation is that the results are not due to sequential search, but to option similarity and, hence, item difficulty. The more nondiscriminating cues TTB has to retrieve, the more similar on average the options must be. Hence, both variables are confounded. If the sequentiality assumption is correct for TTB users, their decision times should be related more strongly to the position of the best differentiating

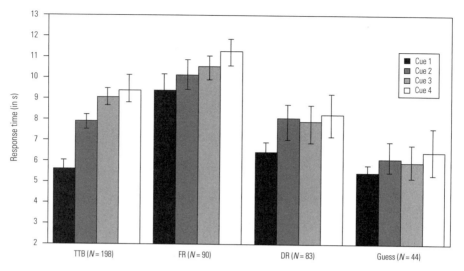

Figure 20-1. Mean decision times in seconds (and standard errors) as a function of best discriminating cue and outcome-based strategy classification in the combined Experiments 1–5. TTB, "take-the-best"; FR, Franklin's rule; DR, Dawes' rule.

cue than to the number of identical cue values indicating similarity or difficulty. Since position and similarity are correlated, we computed individual multiple regressions of RTs on both predictors. As expected, people classified as using TTB showed a steeper increase with position (mean $B = 1.08$) than with similarity ($B = 0.37$) [$t(197) = 2.76$, $p < .01$], whereas there was the opposite tendency for DR users (0.14 vs. 0.57) [$t(82) = -1.69$, $p = .09$]. There was no difference in slopes for FR users (0.26 vs. -0.02) [$t(89) = 0.89$, $p = .37$]. The same pattern of results emerges when raw rather than partial correlations are analyzed by Wilcoxon tests or t tests on the Fisher z-transformed values. Hence, we find no support for the alternative explanation that the TTB RT results were caused by item difficulty rather than sequential search, whereas the opposite is true for DR users.

However, a second criticism could argue that the results reported here are an artifact of a procedural peculiarity used in Experiments 1–5. In all cases, the cue validity hierarchy was equivalent to the order in which the cue values were learned. Hence, the sequential search for cues in the order of their validities could potentially reflect a search in order of learning. To rule out

this interpretation, we conducted an experiment in which we disentangled both factors.

EXPERIMENT 6

Method

Design. Experiment 6 also used the paradigm of the invented murder case. A two-group design was used to disentangle the two possible search orders—search by learning and search by validity. In the *match* condition, the cue validities matched the order in which the cues were learned. In the *mismatch* condition, cue order and validity order were different. For instance, the learning order was *dog breed, jacket, trousers, shirt color,* whereas the scrambled validity order of cues was *trousers, dog breed, shirt color, jacket.* Hence, if the cues are numbered according to the learning sequence, the validity order in the mismatch condition was 3–1–4–2. The labels of the cues were counterbalanced by reversing the validity and learning order for half of the participants (i.e., *dog* was now the most valid cue, and *trousers* was the topmost cue in the learning order). Both of those cue orders were also used in two counterbalanced match conditions in which learning and validity order coincided. Since there was no difference between the counterbalancing conditions, we merged them and subsequently only refer to cues in order of validity or in order of learning, irrespective of the actual content of the cue.

Participants. Ninety-four participants attended the study; almost 90% of them were students. Twelve participants were excluded because they did not reach the learning criterion in Phase 1 within 1 hour. The remaining 82 participants (50 female, age 25.6 years, $SD = 3.25$, range = 20–36) were randomly assigned to the match or the mismatch condition, resulting in 41 participants each. Participants received €15 for their participation with an additional chance to win €10, which was granted to the 5 participants with the best performance in the final memory task.

Procedure. Participants first had to learn cue profiles of 10 potential suspects before a cue validity order was established. After that, participants had to compare pairs of suspects and decide which of the two was more likely to be the murderer. After the test phase, participants were asked again to indicate all cue values for all suspects in a final memory test.

Results and Discussion

Learning phase. There was no difference between the conditions with regard to learning. People needed on average 85 trials to finish the learning phase $(SD = 20.43;$ range = 65–142), and they remembered 86% of cue values in the final test, showing that cue knowledge was reliable.

Strategy classification. People were classified as users of one of the different strategies following the outcome-based strategy classification after Bröder and Schiffer (2003a). In the match condition, cue validity order and learning order were identical. In the mismatch condition, however, participants could either use the validity order as a search sequence (according to TTB) or search cues in the order of learning, which we will refer to as a "take-the-first" (TTF) heuristic. Consequently, we included TTF in the set of possible strategies for the mismatch condition.

In the match condition, there were 21 TTB users, 9 FR users, 8 DR users, and 3 people who

were guessing. Thus, like in the comparable Bröder and Schiffer (2003b) experiments, there was a majority of people whose decisions can best be described with TTB. In the mismatch condition, there were only 11 TTB users, 8 FR users, 12 DR users, and 5 people who appeared to guess. In addition, 5 of the 41 participants were classified as using TTF. The strategy distributions across conditions differed significantly $[\chi^2(4, N= 82) = 9.48, p = .05]$. However, if TTF and TTB participants are combined into one class, the difference between the conditions disappears $[\chi^2(3, N = 82) = 2.04, p = .56]$. Hence, the data support the interpretation that the proportion of TTB users that is found when validity and learning order are confounded may be a composite of "real" TTB users and others using TTF.

Decision times. There was no difference between the match and the mismatch condition regarding group decision times $[F(1, 80) = 0.06]$, and no interaction between cue and condition $[F(2.17, 173.7) = 0.14]$. Therefore, decision times for people classified as using the same strategy were pooled across the conditions. The mean decision times for each outcome-based strategy are presented in Figure 20-2. The pattern is very similar to the one we obtained when combining Experiments 1–5, although it is somewhat noisier, since the sample size is only one fifth of the combined sample size of Experiments 1–5.

The main effect of cue is significant $[F(2.08, 160.19) = 6.55, p = .002]$. Decision times increased with the position of the best discriminating cue. There was also a trend for a main effect of strategy $[F(4, 77) = 2.07, p = .09]$, and an interaction between cue and strategy $[F(8.32, 160.19) = 2.40, p = .02]$. Again, TTB users show the largest increase in RTs, followed by FR, DR, and guessing. RTs are again generally higher for FR than for DR. A striking pattern can be seen for the five TTF users: They show the shortest response if Cue 3 discriminates, followed by Cue 1, Cue 4, and Cue 2. This pattern of RTs exactly matches the learning order of the cues. Note that this result is far from trivial: The strategy classifications were exclusively based on choices. Hence, this congruence of classification and RTs

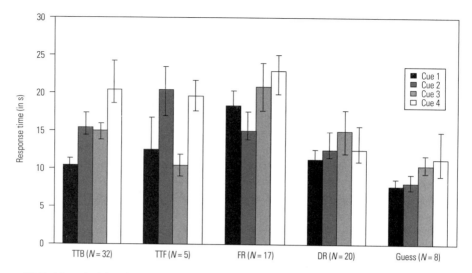

Figure 20-2. Mean decision times in seconds (and standard errors) as a function of best discriminating cue and outcome-based strategy classification in Experiment 6, including five participants who apparently searched in the order of cue retrievability ("take-the-first" [TTF]) in the mismatch condition; TTB, "take-the-best"; FR, Franklin's rule; DR, Dawes' rule.

constitutes true converging evidence for this strategy and the notion of sequential cue search.

GENERAL DISCUSSION

The goal of this article was to find converging evidence for processes that we assumed to underlie memory-based multiattribute decisions. Direct process tracing is not possible for memory-based decisions. Therefore, we analyzed RTs to validate the idea of sequential cue search in multiattribute decisions from memory and as an independent source of support for the outcome-based strategy classification method.

Both the reanalysis of the five published experiments and the results of the new experiment support the idea of sequential cue search. For users of TTB, this support is clearest, since their RTs increased with the number of cues that need to be looked up until the best discriminating cue was found. This result seems better explained by sequential search than by global matching, because regression analyses revealed only a weak relation between RT and item difficulty that was based on feature similarity. For users of DR and FR, the increase that was based

on the position of the best discriminating cue was much weaker and, contrary to TTB users, depended more on item difficulty that was based on similarity (at least for DR). In principle, this result could be explained by both sequential search and global matching. However, we think that the additional finding that DR users are generally quicker than FR users is more supportive of sequential search—assuming that DR users only add up information—whereas FR users additionally weigh it. At least, it is not clear to us how a global matching model could explain this difference. Finally, for TTF users, RT patterns fitted the presumed search order and stopping rule, which also favors sequential search.

A slight increase in RTs for users of compensatory strategies, as was observed, is likely to occur nevertheless, because it is possible that someone classified as using FR sometimes applies TTB. Moreover, retrieving information in order of validity also makes sense for compensatory strategies. For example, an FR user who knows that the two most valid cues point toward one suspect does not need to look up further information, because the less valid cues could never overrule this judgment.

The strength of these sequential search effects surprised us. In none of the experiments were people instructed to decide quickly, which is usually a prerequisite to obtain interpretable RT data. Large interindividual and intraindividual differences normally inflate noise and demand for large effects.

After demonstrating the usefulness of RT data in addition to outcome-based strategy classifications, the next step in evaluating the sequential search hypothesis should strive at reaching more precision in RTs and classifications by moving from the group level to the individual level, which is the final appropriate benchmark for testing cognitive models.

ACKNOWLEDGEMENTS

This research was supported by Deutsche Forschungsgemeinschaft Grant No. BR-2130/1-2 and by the Max Planck Institute for Human Development. We thank Thorsten Pachur and Lael J. Schooler for comments on an earlier draft of this article.

NOTES

1. Individual z scores of RTs or log-transformed response yielded the same patterns of significant results in all analyses.

Introduction to Chapter 21

Does Imitation Benefit Cue Order Learning?

How should individuals order cues to make good decisions? One answer is that they should try to learn the optimal order, that is, the one that leads to the highest accuracy. Perhaps feasible in the small world of a laboratory task, learning optimal orders quickly becomes impossible in the real world for several reasons. First, finding the optimal order is NP-hard, that is, computationally intractable for large numbers of cues (Theorem 2 in Chapter 12). Second, even if cues are relatively few and it is possible to determine the optimal order for a sample of objects, using this optimal order is likely to be a bad move in an uncertain world. When inferences have to be made from samples, the optimal order in the sample is unlikely to be the best in the future. As Figure 12-3 illustrates, the optimal order leads to the highest accuracy in hindsight (data fitting) but is second-best in prediction (generalization). Unless sample sizes are very large and the future is highly predictable, the optimal order is not robust; the challenge is to find not an optimal order, but a robust one. Ordering cues by validity is one learning principle that leads to a robust cue order (see Figure 12-3). Which ordering principle succeeds, however, systematically depends on the structure of the environment (see Figure 1-5).

How can an organism learn to order cues by validity or by some other robust principle? One way is evolutionary learning. For instance, female sage grouses first screen males on the basis of the quality of their songs and then visit only those who pass this test for a closer inspection of display rate (see Chapter 5). A second way is individual reinforcement learning, as used in experiments reported in previous chapters. In individual learning, orders are estimated from samples, not from full knowledge about the entire population, and therefore do not require computing the perfect ecological validities—in contrast to Juslin and Persson's (2002) and Dougherty, Franco-Watkins, and Thomas's (2008) conclusions. Because ordering by validity ignores dependencies between cues, it involves less computation than when estimating beta weights or conditional probabilities, as assumed in psychological theories proposing cognitive processes that optimize. All principles based on individual learning, however, share a common problem: Individual learning requires large numbers of reinforcement trials, and the larger the number of cues and the closer the validities or weights of the cues are, the slower is reinforcement learning of cue orders. A third route toward learning, namely, social learning, such as teaching and imitation, sidesteps this problem. For instance, young doctors are taught what diagnostic cues to look up first when a patient is suspected of ischemic heart disease. Their patients cannot afford doctors who learn by trial and error (Green & Mehr, 1997). More generally, in situations outside the psychological laboratory in which health, money, or other precious things are at stake, individual learning is often simply too dangerous and social learning is used instead.

The article by Rocio Garcia-Retamero, Masanori Takezawa, and Gerd Gigerenzer addresses the issue of slow individual learning, using computer simulations combined with subsequent experimental tests. One result is that learning good cue orders can be sped up considerably by interspersing it with social exchanges—even a single exchange can help—in which people obtain information about the cue order (and their accuracy) used by others. This information is integrated based on social rules. Yet not every social rule proves successful. Imitate-the-best and imitate-the-majority succeed, whereas the Borda rule does not. The article also shows that imitate-the-best is even better at finding cue orders than take-the-best with the exact ecological validities, that is, with full knowledge of the environment. This result is remarkable, because Chapter 12 (see Figure 12-1) indicates that there is not much room for improvement beyond using ecological validities. Last but not least, this article indicates that people do not learn by updating orders through feedback, but by first figuring out what the best cue might be, then the second-best, and so on. Thus, rather than being a simultaneous process of updating, learning cue orders may itself be sequential.

CHAPTER 21

Does Imitation Benefit Cue Order Learning?

Rocio Garcia-Retamero, Masanori Takezawa, and Gerd Gigerenzer

Abstract: Inferences are often based on uncertain cues, and the accuracy of such inferences depends on the order in which the cues are searched. Previous research has shown that people and computers progress only slowly in individual learning of cue orderings through feedback. A clue to how people (as opposed to computers) solve this problem is social learning: By exchanging information with others, people can learn which cues are relevant and the order in which they should be considered. By means of simulation, we demonstrate that *imitate-the-best* and *imitate-the-majority* speed up individual learning, whereas a third social rule, the *Borda rule*, does not. Imitate-the-best also leads to a steep increase in learning after a single social exchange, to cue orders that are more accurate than ecological validity, and to faster learning than when individuals gain the learning experience of all other group members but learn without social exchange. In two experiments, we find that people speed up cue learning in a similar way when provided with social information, both when they obtain the information from the experimenter or in free discussions with others.

In daily life, we frequently make inferences about current and future states of the world. For instance, when New York City taxi drivers pick up customers in the Bronx, Brooklyn, or other dangerous neighborhoods, they need to screen potential passengers to decide whether they are trustworthy. Taxi drivers have to make up their minds quickly. Many report that in cases of doubt, they drive past people to assess them before pickup. An error in judgment means losing a fare, being robbed, or even murdered. Refusing a harmless client, however, means losing money. Inferences concerning trustworthiness are based on uncertain cues, and there are some cues for trust that are shared by virtually all drivers, including older over younger, and female over male (Gambetta & Hamill, 2005).

In this article, we consider the problem of which of two alternatives, varying on several dichotomous cues, has a higher value on a quantitative criterion (i.e., a two-alternative forced-choice task), such as which of two passengers is the more trustworthy one based on cues like age or sex. Research indicates that people often base such inferences on a sequential analysis of a few cues, rather than weighting and adding several of them (e.g., Bröder & Gaissmaier, 2007; Garcia-Retamero, Hoffrage, & Dieckmann, 2007; Lee & Cummins, 2004; Rieskamp & Hoffrage, 2008; Rieskamp & Otto, 2006). Sequential processing is effective if cues are ordered according to their usefulness rather than randomly. One formal model for such a process is take-the-best (Gigerenzer & Goldstein, 1996), which orders cues according to validity, that is, the relative frequency of making a correct inference given that the cue discriminates between the two alternatives. For instance, Bergert and Nosofsky (2007) compared a generalized version of take-the-best with a "rational" weighted additive model, and concluded that the vast majority of participants adopted take-the-best. Nosofsky and Bergert (2007) found similar results when comparing take-the-best with exemplar models.

THE PROBLEM OF LEARNING GOOD CUE ORDERINGS

Laboratory experiments using two-alternative forced-choice tasks showed that without explicit knowledge about cue validities, people seem to be rather slow in learning which cues are good and producing orderings that approximate ecological validity, even within the confined range of the four to six cues usually available in these experiments (Rakow, Hinvest, Jackson, & Palmer, 2004). Yet the reason for this is not necessarily to be found in people's minds alone but also in the task. For instance, Newell and Shanks (2003) had four cues with ecological validities .80, .75, .70, and .69, and gave participants 60 trials to learn a cue ordering. To learn the order of the validities of the last two cues, however, one would need 100 trials in which the third cue discriminates and another 100 trials for the fourth cue in order to experience that one results in 70 and the other in 69 correct inferences, assuming perfect memory. The same problem holds for Newell, Rakow, Weston, and Shanks' (2004) experiment. Thus, learning of ecological cue orderings can be a lengthy process, depending on the number of cues and the differences between cue validities. Moreover, research in multiple cue probability learning suggests that interference effects exist when multiple cues are available and their validities have to be learned concurrently. For instance, if irrelevant cues are present, the utilization of valid cues is reduced and the accuracy of judgments is lower than in a condition in which the irrelevant cues are not included (Brehmer, 1973; Edgell & Hennessey, 1980; see Newell, Lagnado, & Shanks, 2007, for a review). How can individuals learn efficient cue orderings if cue validities are not available beforehand?

One could assume that people can use take-the-best and update a cue ordering by using only the cues they searched. That is, a cue ordering could be acquired by learning-while-doing. Note that learning while one makes inferences with take-the-best or another lexicographic heuristic (exploitation) demands even more trials than when all cue values for the two objects in each trial are provided, as in Newell and Shanks' exploration phase (see above). The reason it requires more trials is that in each trial, the validity of only one cue can be updated, since the heuristic stops search immediately. This "worst-case" scenario is what is addressed in the present article. We first analyze by means of computer simulation which social exchange rules can speed up learning. Then in two experiments we test whether humans take advantage of social learning in ways similar to the simulation.

The question of how a cue ordering is learned has been considered only recently by Todd and Dieckmann (in press; see also Todd & Dieckmann, 2005). In a series of computer simulations, the authors evaluated the performance of the *validity algorithm*, a simple learning rule for forced-choice paired comparison tasks that updates cue orderings by validity on a trial-by-trial basis. The accuracy of the cue orderings resulting from the application of the validity algorithm was tested using the German cities data set, which consists of the 83 German cities having more than 100,000 inhabitants at the time (Fischer Welt Almanach, 1993). These cities were described by nine cues, such as whether a city has a university (see Table 21-1).

The validity algorithm starts with a random cue ordering and searches one cue at a time until it finds a cue that discriminates between the alternatives, which is used to make the decision (i.e., the algorithm chooses the alternative favored by the first discriminating cue). After each decision, feedback is provided, and the cue ordering is updated. The validity algorithm retains two pieces of information for each cue: how often a cue stopped search (and led to a decision), and a count of the correct decisions. The validity of each cue is computed by dividing the number of current correct decisions by the number of current discriminations.[1]

Todd and Dieckmann (in press) tested the performance of the validity algorithm in 100

Table 21-1. Description of the Eight Inference Problems Used in the Simulation

Description of the Real-World Problems	Average VAL (DR)	Standard deviation of VAL (DR)	Range of VAL (DR)	Skewness of VAL (DR)	Kurtosis of VAL (DR)
Rainfall. Predicting the amount of rainfall after cloud seeding for 24 weather observations (Woodley, Simpson, Biondini, & Berkeley, 1977), described by 6 cues (e.g., suitability for seeding or percent cloud cover)	.62 (.49)	.08 (.07)	.76–51 (.52–.34)	.80 (−2.40)	2.38 (6.00)
Homelessness. Predicting the rate of homelessness of 50 U.S. cities (Tucker, 1987), described by 6 cues (e.g., unemployment rate or public housing)	.58 (.51)	.06 (.00)	.68–52 (.51–51)	1.60 (−2.40)	3.05 (6.00)
Lifespan. Predicting the lifespan of 58 mammals (Allison & Cicchetti, 1976), described by 8 cues (e.g., brain weight or gestation time)	.74 (.51)	.12 (.00)	.93–53 (.51–50)	−.20 (−2.41)	−.15 (4.50)
Population. Predicting the population of the 83 German cities with at least 100,000 inhabitants (Fischer Welt Almanach, 1993), described by 9 cues (e.g., whether the city has a soccer team or university)	.76 (.30)	.16 (.13)	1.00–51 (.51–.02)	−.30 (−.80)	−.39 (3.1)
Obesity. Predicting obesity at age 18 of 58 children (Weisberg, 1985), described by 11 cues (e.g., height at age 9 or leg circumference at age 9)	.67 (.51)	.10 (.01)	.87–56 (.51–49)	.80 (−3.00)	.18 (9.1)
Fuel consumption. Predicting the average motor fuel consumption per person for each of the 48 contiguous United States (Weisberg, 1985), described by 7 cues (e.g., population of the state or number of licensed drivers)	.73 (.51)	.09 (.00)	.82–57 (.51–51)	−1.40 (−2.60)	1.28 (7.0)
Car accidents. Predicting the accident rate per million vehicle miles for 39 segments of highway (Weisberg, 1985), described on 13 cues (e.g., segment's length and average traffic count)	.65 (.48)	.07 (.08)	.76–52 (.51–23)	−.10 (−2.90)	−.97 (8.9)
Mortality. Predicting the mortality rate in 60 U.S. cities (McDonald & Schwing, 1973), described by 15 cues (e.g., average January temperature and percentage of population aged 65 or older)	.67 (.51)	.09 (.00)	.81–54 (.51–51)	.02 (−3.20)	−.64 (11.1)

Note: VAL = validity, DR = Discrimination rate.

trials, that is, in 100 paired comparisons that were randomly selected from the set of German cities. There were nine cues. The differences between their validities ranged between .01 and .15. The authors tested predictive accuracy, that is, how well the cue ordering learned in each trial would do if it were applied to the entire set of paired comparisons (i.e., 3,403 pairs of 83 cities). The simulation results showed that the validity algorithm performance soon rose above that achieved by a random ordering. Simulated individuals, however, made slow progress in learning efficient cue orderings: Even after updating cue validities through feedback for 100 trials, accuracy remained well behind that when the ecological cue validities were used. This is not just a problem for the validity algorithm, but also applies to other ordering principles that require learning conditional weights such as β weights. The delta rule (used in neural networks) and the validity algorithm were the fastest learning rules, but both needed more than 2,900 trials to match the ecological validity ordering.

In a corresponding experimental setting, Todd and Dieckmann (in press) also showed that, just like computers, after 100 trials, participants were slow in learning cue orderings by validity when they could update such orderings through feedback. This result is in line with previous findings from two-alternative forced-choice tasks and multiple cue probability learning mentioned above, and shows that learning good cue orderings can take a long time.

DOES SOCIAL LEARNING IMPROVE THE PERFORMANCE OF CUE ORDER LEARNING? A SIMULATION STUDY

In contrast to many laboratory tasks, in real-world environments people often exchange information with other individuals before making a judgment. Consider once again the question of which passenger might be more trustworthy. Rather than collecting information only individually, taxi drivers might also discuss with other drivers which cues are more useful. Thus, people could learn to order cues both individually and socially by exchanging information.

In group decision making, several authors have analyzed whether individuals are able to gain valuable knowledge from other group members to improve inferential accuracy. Empirical results show that groups are often more accurate than average individuals (Hastie & Kameda, 2005; Hill, 1982; Kameda & Nakanishi, 2002; Kerr & Tindale, 2004). For instance, even when individuals' quantitative judgments are systematically biased, the performance of the average estimates comes close to models that weigh and add cues (see Einhorn, Hogarth, & Klempner, 1977; Hogarth, 1978). Hastie and Kameda (2005) theoretically demonstrated that following the decision of the majority has the same error-reduction function in discrete decision-making tasks. In a series of computer simulations, they also showed that decisions supported by the majority or by the most capable person in the group achieve higher accuracy than those made by average individuals.

All in all, research in group decision making has identified situations in which group-based judgments are superior to individual judgments. Although previous research has focused on group consensus processes, the findings may be relevant to our research question. Our hypothesis is that the exchange of information can help individuals to solve the problem of learning good cue orderings in less time. To test this hypothesis, we conducted a series of computer simulations in which we evaluated the success of several *social rules* when they were implemented in the validity algorithm for ordering cues. In two subsequent experiments, we analyze whether people's behavior conforms to the results of the simulations.

METHOD

In our simulations, we used data for a variety of inference problems that have been studied in different disciplines, including psychology, economics, and computer science. The task was to infer, on the basis of several cues, which of two objects had a higher criterion value. Altogether we considered 8 inference problems (see Table 21-1). The problems differed by the number of objects considered and the number of cues provided for making a decision.

In the simulations, we included three conditions of social learning and two of individual learning. In the three social learning conditions, a group of 5 simulated individuals went through a trial block of five paired comparisons. In these trials, the simulants individually updated a cue ordering with feedback by applying the validity algorithm while making inferences with take-the-best. In the first trial, simulants started with random cue orderings. For each trial, the corresponding cue ordering was used to look up cues until a discriminating cue was found, which was in turn used to make the decision. After each decision, feedback was provided, and the cue ordering was updated. The group as a whole received the same set of paired comparisons, whereas different simulated individuals within a group received different paired comparisons. Therefore, groups in the three social conditions came up with the same cue orderings after the first trial block, whereas each simulant within a group typically came up with a different cue ordering.

After the trial block, simulants exchanged information about the cue orderings that they learned individually with the other group members. All simulants within the group used a social rule, which differed among the three conditions, to arrive at a single *social cue ordering* (Hastie & Kameda, 2005). The first social rule was *imitate-the-majority*: Individuals vote for the cue with the highest validity, and the one with the most votes becomes the top cue in the social cue ordering. Everyone then votes for the next best cue, and this process is repeated for all the cues. In cases of ties, one cue is randomly selected. The second social rule was *imitate-the-best*: Individuals imitate the cue ordering of the most successful group member. Unlike imitate-the-majority, imitate-the-best requires ordinal information about success. Finally, according to the *Borda rule* (named after the French mathematician Jean-Charles de Borda, who designed a voting system for the French Academy of Science to elect its members), voters rank all cues, and the sum of ranks is taken as the social ordering. Among all three social rules, imitate-the-best involves the least computation.

After exchanging information socially, simulants worked individually on the next block of five trials, in which they looked cues up using the social cue ordering instead of the cue orderings that they had learned on their own. The social cue ordering was then updated with feedback by using the validity algorithm on an individual basis. The process of exchanging social information, computing a social cue ordering, and updating the social cue ordering individually was repeated for each of the 20 trial blocks (or 100 trials in total).

For control, we introduced two individual learning conditions. In the individual-1 condition, each simulant received the same set of paired comparisons as those in the corresponding social learning conditions but did not exchange any information socially. In the individual-5 condition, each simulant within the group went through the entire set of paired comparisons that the 5 simulants in the social learning conditions received (i.e., 25 trials in total). The individual-1 condition is the baseline for evaluating the benefits of the three social learning rules, and the individual-5 condition enables evaluating whether gains by social rules can be explained solely by the larger number of paired comparisons that a group experiences over an individual.

Predictive accuracy of the validity algorithm was examined for each of the 8 inference problems (see Table 21-1) in the 5 learning conditions (i.e., imitate-the-majority, imitate-the-best, Borda, individual-1, and individual-5), providing 40 conditions altogether. For each of these conditions, we simulated 1,000 groups of 5 simulants, who made 100 decisions between randomly selected paired comparisons (i.e., 20,000,000 observations in total).

RESULTS AND DISCUSSION

Figure 21-1 shows the performance of imitate-the-majority, imitate-the-best, and the Borda rule when learning cue orderings compared to that of individual-1 (thin solid jagged line) and the more competitive version of individual learning (i.e., individual-5; thick solid jagged line). The performance of the rules was averaged across the 1,000 groups and the 8 inference problems. As benchmarks, the performance of a

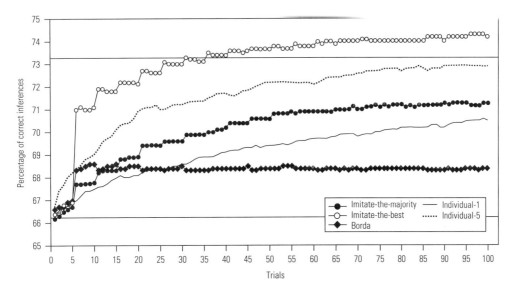

Figure 21-1. Predictive accuracy of imitate-the-majority, imitate-the-best, and Borda rule when implemented in the validity algorithm for 100 trials between randomly selected paired comparisons. For comparison, the performance of individual learning according to validity (individual-1; thin solid jagged line), a more competitive version of individual learning (individual-5; thick solid jagged line), ecological ordering (upper straight line), and random ordering (i.e., lower straight line) were added.

random ordering of cues (lower straight line) and the ecological ordering (upper straight line) are shown.

Both imitate-the-majority and imitate-the-best improved the performance of individual cue order learning substantially, with a particular boost by imitate-the-best after the first social exchange. The Borda rule, however, was less successful and did not even reach the performance level of individual learning. Imitate-the-best led to a steep increase in accuracy after the first exchange and eventually made even more correct decisions than can be obtained with the exact ecological cue validities. Most important, imitate-the-best alone led to more accurate decisions than the individual-5 benchmark did. Since individual-5 had exactly the same information as the groups who used imitate-the-best, the performance of imitate-the-best cannot be reduced to that of individual learning.

As a second performance measure, we also computed the tau correlation between the subjective cue orderings and the ecological cue validities for each condition. Consistent with previous analyses, the correlation increased from .25 to .65 and from .23 to .47 when using imitate-the-best or imitate-the-majority, respectively, whereas increments were barely visible when using the Borda rule or the less competitive version of individual learning (i.e., individual-1). In such cases, correlations only increased from .24 to .27 and from .25 to .30, respectively. When using the more competitive version of individual learning (i.e., individual-5), the correlation increased from .23 to .55. These results, therefore, are consistent with those presented above and suggest that imitate-the-best is an efficient strategy for improving individual cue order learning, whereas the Borda rule that adds individuals' ranks fails.

Note that the combination between individual learning and imitate-the-best generated cue orderings with higher accuracy than that achieved by ecological validity (Figure 21-1). An individual analysis shows that at trial 100, 45% of the cue ordering led to more accurate inferences, whereas 34% arrived at orderings that matched ecological validity, and only the other cue orderings performed below. Note that ordering cues by validity is a heuristic rather than an optimizing principle; for instance, ordering by validity ignores the dependencies between cues (Brighton & Gigerenzer, 2008; Martignon and Hoffrage, 2002). The results in Figure 21-1 show that imitate-the-best can perform not only better than the validity orderings computed from the sample an individual has experienced so far, but also better than the ecological validity ordering (which no individual can know unless she has complete information about the entire environment). This suggests that the effect of imitate-the-best cannot be reduced to a convenient speeding up of learning the validity order by indirectly increasing the sample size (see the individual-5 learning condition), but actually results, on average, in cue orders that outperform subjective (sample-based) validity and even ecological validity.

How robust are the results of this simulation? First, the average result shown in Figure 21-1 holds for each of the 8 inference problems in Table 21-1. Second, we modified two parameters of the basic simulation: the group size (2, 10, 25, and 100 individuals), and the number of trials after which social information is exchanged (5, 25, and 50 trials). The results showed that the higher the group size, the higher the group's accuracy, regardless of the social rule they used. Group size showed diminishing returns; for instance, the increase in accuracy from 5 to 25 individuals was larger than from 25 to 100. Furthermore, the higher the frequency of exchanging social information, the higher the performance was in the long run. Again, imitate-the-best proved to be the most effective way of resolving the problem of slow individual learning. For instance, when 10 simulants exchanged information on just one occasion (after 50 trials), this single social exchange was sufficient to achieve the accuracy of the ecological validity ordering. In summary, the superiority of imitate-the-best, as observed in the basic simulation, remained stable with an increasing number of simulants in the group, even when the number of social exchange opportunities was reduced.

DOES SOCIAL LEARNING SOLVE THE LIMITATIONS OF INDIVIDUAL LEARNING? EMPIRICAL STUDIES

The simulation results provide a theoretical context for empirical studies. Would real people profit from social exchange like the simulated ones did? To our knowledge, there is no experimental research that tests whether social learning improves individual cue order learning. It is also unclear which strategy people use to process social information in cue order learning. To answer these questions, we conducted two experiments using a similar procedure to that in the simulation study. On the basis of several cues, participants had to infer which of two objects had a higher criterion value. In both experiments, one group in which individuals learned cue orderings by feedback was compared with groups where individuals received information after each trial block about the cue orderings of all group members. In Experiment 1, the social information was provided by the experimenter, whereas in Experiment 2, no such information was given, but participants were allowed to talk to each other without any constraints.

If people's behavior conforms to the results of the simulations, those who can exchange information will learn more efficient cue orderings than those who only learn individually if they use imitate-the-majority or imitate-the-best. As a consequence, they will make more correct inferences and focus on high validity cues more often.

EXPERIMENT 1

Method

Participants. A total of 240 students (131 women and 109 men, average age 24 years, range 18–35) at the Free University of Berlin participated in the experiment. Participants were randomly assigned to one of four equally sized learning conditions ($n = 60$). The computerized task was conducted on groups of 5 individuals and lasted approximately 1 hour. Participants received a show-up fee of €8 plus half of the amount they earned in the task, with an average payment of €11 (ranging from €8 to €17).

Stimuli and design. Participants had to infer which of two job candidates (displayed column-wise) for an open position would be more productive in the future. To make these inferences, they could search for information about six cues describing the candidates (i.e., whether they had organizational skills, social skills, positive letters of recommendation, computer skills, whether they spoke foreign languages, or were reliable). These cues are common for assessing job candidates (see Garcia-Retamero & Rieskamp, 2008). The cues had a positive or negative value for each candidate, represented as "+" and "−," respectively. The order in which the cues were presented on the screen was fixed for each group of participants but varied randomly between groups of participants. Likewise, the position of the two candidates (left or right on the screen) varied randomly.

We created an inference problem that consisted of 30 pairs of candidates described by six cues with the cue validities .83, .75, .69, .64, .58, and .50, and cue discrimination rates .40, .40, .43, .37, .40, and .40. The discrimination rate of a cue is the number of pairs in which cue values differ between alternatives. Neither cue validities nor cue discrimination rates were given to the participants. For each group of participants, cue labels were randomly assigned to the different cues. Participants made 210 inferences, broken down into seven trial blocks comprising 30 paired comparisons each. The same set of paired comparisons was presented within each block but in random order. After each trial block, participants ranked cues according to the subjective cue validities. Specifically, participants were told: "In the following you should rank the cues in the order of their validity. What does validity mean? Suppose one candidate has a positive evaluation and the other candidate has a negative evaluation. The validity tells you how probable it is that the candidate with the positive evaluation is also the candidate who will be more productive."

The experiment included four conditions. In the *social-information condition*, after ranking cues according to the subjective cue validities, each participant received information about the cue orderings of all the members of his/her group

in that trial block. The *imitate-the-majority condition* was identical to the previous condition, except that participants were also informed about the cue ordering computed according to the majority rule. In the *imitate-the-best condition*, participants received information about the final payoff of all group members in the trial block in addition to information about their cue orderings. In short, we refer to these three conditions as "social learners." Finally, in the *individual condition*, participants did not receive any information after ordering cues according to the subjective validities.

In sum, the experimental design had two factors: the learning condition (social-information, imitate-the-majority, imitate-the-best, and individual; between-subjects), and trial block, with seven repetitions of the 30 pairs of objects (within-subjects).

Procedure. The experimental instructions told participants to imagine that they worked for a company that had grown substantially. It was their job to make recommendations for new personnel. They had to make choices between pairs of candidates and select the one that would be most productive on the basis of six descriptive cues. Participants could search for information about these cues by clicking boxes on the computer screen. Once a box with information on a cue for both candidates was opened, the cue values remained visible until a decision was made. For each cue looked up, 1 cent was deducted from a participant's overall payoff. After a decision was made by clicking on a button, outcome feedback was displayed. For each correct decision, participants earned 7 cents; for incorrect decisions, no money was deducted. The current balance of their account was always visible on the computer screen.

Five dependent variables were recorded in each trial: (1) the number of cues searched for, (2) which cues were searched for, (3) the order in which cues were searched for, (4) whether the decision was correct, and (5) the time participants invested in searching for cues.[2] Additionally, after each trial block, participants' cue orderings were recorded according to the subjective validity of the cues.

Results

Do social learners learn more efficient cue orderings than individual learners do? Figure 21-2 shows that in all three social conditions, the tau correlation between participants' subjective cue orderings and the ecological validity ordering increased much faster than in the individual learning condition. In fact, individual learning was quite slow and barely visible, and from the second to the last trial block, social learners achieved higher correlations than individual learners did. Can the benefit of social exchange be explained solely by the larger number of paired comparisons a group indirectly experiences over an individual? To answer this question, participants in the individual learning conditions were randomly assigned to groups of five individuals, and social cue orderings in the artificially generated groups were computed by using imitate-the-best or imitate-the-majority. These groups received the same amount of information than those in the social conditions but did not have the opportunity for social exchange. The correlation between these cue orderings and the ecological validity ordering was computed.

As Figure 21-2 shows, in the artificially generated individual conditions, correlations do not reach the social learning groups. For imitate-the-majority the results are even indistinguishable from individual learning. Overall, these results show that people—like simulants—do indeed learn more efficient cue ordering through social exchange.

Do social learners search for the most valid cue more often than individual learners do? Figure 21-3 shows the percentage of trials in which each cue was looked up for each trial block. For instance, the most valid cue was looked up by the participants in all four conditions about half of the time before the first social exchange (i.e., after the first block of 30 trials). For each of the social conditions, this percentage increased to about 71 to 82 after the first social exchange, and continued to increase but at a less accelerated pace up to 80 to 90 percent. Individual learners, in contrast, learned to look up the best cue more often over trials, but their average did not reach 70%. A similar but less pronounced effect can be seen for the second-best cue, except for the social-information condition, which had the least social information. On the other end, the

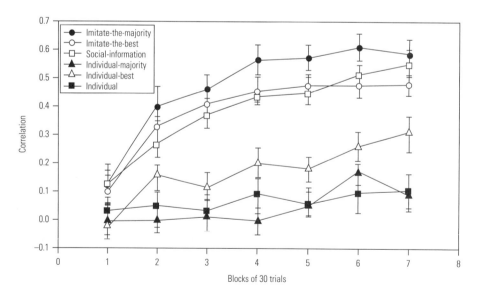

Figure 21-2. Correlation between participants' subjective cue rankings (after each trial block) and the ranking according to ecological validity across the seven trial blocks in Experiment 1. Error bars represent one standard error.

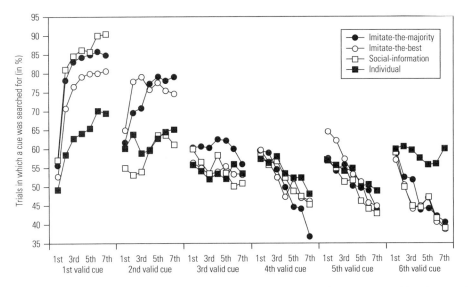

Figure 21-3. Percentage of trials in which a cue was searched for depending on cue ranking (most to less valid cue) and the trial block in Experiment 1.

least valid cue was looked up before the first social exchange about as often as or more than the most valid one, but this frequency decreased from trial block to trial block in the three social conditions, not in the individual one. The intermediate cues showed no difference. Figure 21-4 shows a similar pattern for the reaction times, that is, the time between trial onset and the mouse click on the cue. Participants in the social conditions were faster than individual learners at learning to look for the most valid cue and did not look up the least valid cue as quickly. An analysis of variance is consistent with both of these results, showing an interaction between learning condition, the cue ranking, and the trial block, $F(46.7, 3676.2) = 1.52$, $p = .013$, $\eta_p^2 = .10$, and $F(46.7, 3676.2) = 2.54$, $p = .001$, $\eta_p^2 = .10$, for frequency and response time, respectively.[3]

Do social learners learn to make correct inferences more often than those who just learn individually? Inferential accuracy increased from 65% ($SEM = .25$) to 74% ($SEM = .25$) in the social-information condition; from 65% ($SEM = .28$) to 74% ($SEM = .25$) in the imitate-the-majority condition, and from 66% ($SEM = .25$) to 73% ($SEM = .31$) in the imitate-the-best condition. In contrast, inferential accuracy only

increased from 64% ($SEM = .26$) to 67% ($SEM = .30$) in the individual condition. From the third to the last trial block, social learners achieved higher accuracy than individual learners did. Consistent with these results, an analysis of variance with percentage correct as the dependent variable shows an interaction between the learning conditions and the trial block, $F(15, 1144) = 1.97$, $p = .015$, $\eta_p^2 = .10$.

DISCUSSION

Experiment 1 showed that social exchange during individual learning speeds up the learning of efficient cue orderings and increases the frequency of looking up the most valid cues as well as the accuracy of inferences. This effect is not due to differences in the amount of information that participants in different conditions searched for, as both social and individual learners searched for the same number of cues (i.e., about 3.5 of the 6 cues per trial). Experiment 1 could not, however, answer the question of which strategy social learners use, because the social information was provided by the experimenter rather than searched for by the participants. In the real world, we rarely receive a

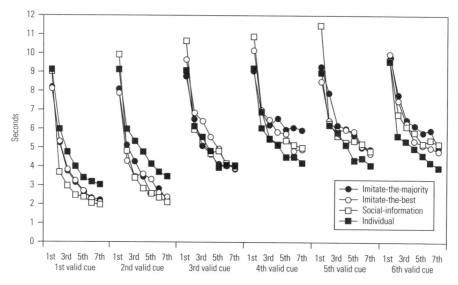

Figure 21-4. Time between trial onset and the mouse click on the cue depending on cue ranking (most to less valid cue) and the trial block in Experiment 1.

summary of other individuals' cue orderings but would have to approach people to obtain information. To test whether the results generalize to situations in which people can freely communicate, we used a group discussion setting in Experiment 2.

EXPERIMENT 2

In this experiment, participants had no constraints on the information they could talk about. Would participants naturally engage in exchanging information about relevant cues in this situation? If so, would social learners prefer to imitate the most competent group member or to aggregate social information by using the majority rule?

Method

Participants. A total of 120 students (55 men and 65 women), whose average age was 26 (range 19–39), participated in the experiment. Participants were randomly assigned to one of two equally sized learning conditions ($n = 60$). The computerized task was conducted in groups of 5 individuals and lasted approximately 1 hour. Participants received a show-up fee of €8 plus

half of the amount they earned in the task, with an average payment of €10.40 (ranging from €8 to €15).

Design and procedure. The instructions and the procedure of Experiment 2 were identical to those of Experiment 1, except that the three social conditions were replaced by a *discussion condition.* Specifically, after each trial block, individuals ranked cues according to subjective cue validity and then met in groups of 5 individuals to converse freely for 10 minutes. Participants were not instructed what to discuss. Afterwards, the group members had to agree on a cue ranking according to cue validities. In contrast, in the *individual condition,* participants did not meet or exchange any information with other individuals. In sum, the experimental design had two factors: the learning condition (discussion and individual; between-subjects) and trial block, with seven repetitions of the 30 pairs of objects (within-subjects).

Results

Do participants in the discussion condition learn more efficient cue orderings than those who learn individually? Figure 21-5 shows that all conditions (including the artificially generated ones)

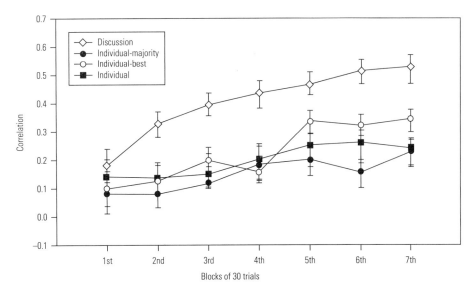

Figure 21-5. Correlation between participants' subjective cue rankings (after each block) and the ranking according to ecological validity across the seven trial blocks in Experiment 2. Error bars represent one standard error.

started out with about the same tau correlation between participants' subjective cue orderings and the ecological validity ordering, but thereafter, the correlation increased much faster in the discussion condition than in the rest. As in Experiment 1 (Figure 21-2), individual learning was quite slow, and from the second to the last trial block, social learners achieved higher correlations than individual learners did. This result, which cannot be explained solely by the larger number of paired comparisons a group indirectly experiences over an individual, shows that participants can learn by means of free discussion as efficiently as simulated individuals or real individuals who receive the relevant information prepackaged by the experimenter.

Which strategy did participants use when they exchanged information? Results showed that the correlation between subjective cue orderings and the cue ordering of the most competent group member increased from .26 (*SEM* = .07) to .58 (*SEM* = .07) from the first to the last trial block. In contrast, the correlation with the cue ordering of the majority only increased from .26 (*SEM* = .06) to .35 (*SEM* = .06). Furthermore, the analyses of the recorded conversations that

participants had in the discussion sessions showed that in 65.7% of the sessions, at least one participant mentioned information about payoffs. These results are consistent with the hypothesis that participants exchanged information about their payoffs in the group discussion sessions and imitated the cue ordering of the best group member.

Do people in the discussion condition search for the most valid cue more often than individual learners? Figure 21-6 shows, for each trial block, the percentage of trials in which each cue was looked up. The most valid cue was looked up by the participants in both conditions equally often before the first social exchange (i.e., after the first block of 30 trials with feedback). For the discussion condition, this percentage increased to about 80, whereas this number remained around 65% for individual learners. For the less valid cues, participants in the discussion condition learned to avoid these faster than those in Experiment 1 (Figure 21-3). Figure 21-7 shows a similar pattern for the reaction times, that is, the time between trial onset and the mouse click on the cue. Participants in the discussion condition were faster than individual learners in learning

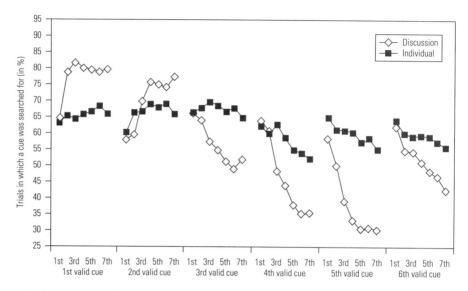

Figure 21-6. Percentage of trials in which a cue was searched for depending on cue ranking (most to less valid cue) and the trial block in Experiment 2.

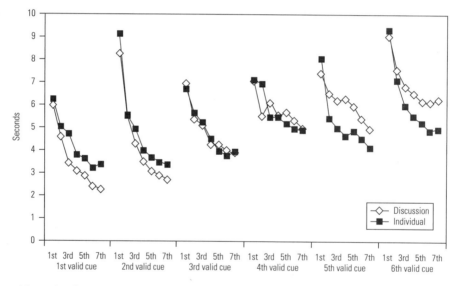

Figure 21-7. Time between trial onset and the mouse click on the cue depending on cue ranking (most to less valid cue) and the trial block in Experiment 2.

to look for the most valid cue and did not look up the least valid cue as quickly, replicating the corresponding result in Experiment 1. An analysis of variance is consistent with both of these results, showing an interaction between learning condition, the cue ranking, and the trial block, $F(13, 1575) = 3.98$, $p = .001$, $\eta_p^2 = .10$, and $F(13, 1575) = 1.55$, $p = .04$, $\eta_p^2 = .04$, for frequency and response time, respectively. These results replicate those in Experiment 1 in a situation where participants could gather information by talking freely with other group members.

Do people who exchange information about the task make correct inferences more often than those who learn individually? Inferential accuracy increased from 64% (*SEM* = .20) to 73% (*SEM* = .31) correct inferences in the discussion condition. In contrast, inferential accuracy only increased from 65% (*SEM* = .20) to 67% (*SEM* = .35) in the individual condition. From the third to the last trial block, participants in the discussion condition achieved greater accuracy than participants in the individual condition. Consistent with these results, an analysis of variance with percentage correct as the dependent variable showed an interaction between the learning conditions and the trial block, $F(5, 544) = 3.27$, $p = .008$, $\eta_p^2 = .05$.

When social learners were able to discuss the task freely with other group members, they also became more frugal (i.e., they searched for less of the available information) than individual learners in making inferences. This result, along with the increase in inferential accuracy, explains why participants who exchanged information obtained a higher overall payoff than those who learned individually (€9.50 vs. €8.90).

GENERAL DISCUSSION

In this paper we addressed the problem that individual learning to order cues by feedback is relatively slow, as demonstrated by previous experiments and computer simulations. By means of simulation, we showed that individual learning can be expedited by two social rules, imitate-the-majority and imitate-the-best, but not with the Borda rule. Moreover, imitate-the-best, unlike imitate-the-majority, was more accurate than ecological validity and was also better than individual-5 is, that is, than an individual with all the learning experience to which all group members are exposed. In two experiments, the improvement observed in the simulations was replicated for real participants, both when the relevant social information was provided by the experimenter and when it was not but the participants were able to engage

in free discussion. Overall, these findings suggest that imitate-the-best and imitate-the-majority, but not the Borda rule, are efficient strategies for improving individual cue order learning. Results in the group experiments further indicate that imitate-the-best is a prime strategy when people exchange information about cue orderings.

Social and Individual Learning

Figure 21-6 provides a hypothesis about a key difference between social and individual learning of cue orderings. Previous theories on individual learning assumed a simultaneous updating of the entire order of N cues, either by updating validity or by other means such as tally and swap (e.g., Todd & Dieckmann, 2005). That would suggest that the speed of learning is about equal for all cues, regardless of whether the cues are relevant. However, Figure 21-6 shows that when people can freely exchange information, they learn to search for the best cue more frequently after the first exchange, and there is little further learning. In contrast, learning for the second cue occurs mainly after the second social exchange. In the course of learning, all the cues with lower validity are searched for less often, apparently in keeping with a more continuous decrease in the percentage of trials that are searched. The pattern suggests that in situations with unconstrained social exchange, people try to determine the best cue first and the second-best only later, and so on.

This observation provides a different view on cue learning than does the picture of simultaneous updating of validities, or more generally, weights, as in Bayesian probability updating. Learning cue ordering is assumed to be sequential: First, try to establish what the best cue out of *N* cues is. Then, using the remaining *N*-1 cues, determine what the second-best cue might be. Such a sequential procedure reduces the problem space quickly, and allows for a stable ordering that does not require constant updating. This corresponds well with the observation that in laboratory tasks, participants tend to settle into a routine at some point, that is, move from an exploration-oriented phase to an exploitation phase (Bröder & Schiffer,

2006; see also Betsch & Haberstroh, 2005, for a summary).

Open Questions

To the best of our knowledge, the present paper is the first to propose that social learning can help individual cue order learning. At the same time, it leaves several questions open for future research. Although our results were robust across the inference problems in Table 21-1 and are also applicable to various learning algorithms reported by Todd and Dieckmann (in press), they may depend on the nature of the task. Other authors (e.g., Hastie & Kameda, 2005) investigated how the members of a group who made decisions individually arrived at a collective decision. That is, they focused on social learning of decisions. In contrast, our focus was on social learning of the information that individuals use to make decisions. Despite these differences, we all found that cognitively simple social rules perform better than individual learning. Which social rules improve individual learning in other tasks, where learning is slow, still needs to be studied. Other open questions relate to the fact that our experiments embodied an ideal situation where feedback was given after each individual trial and was always correct, and external search rather than internal search in memory was used. If feedback is scarce and partly erroneous, as in many aspects of our lives, or if inferences are made from memory, individual learning can be expected to slow down even further than shown in Figures 21-2 and 21-4. Is the benefit of social learning here comparable to what we found, or is it equally slowed down? In situations where feedback is scarce or when inferences are made from memory, will people still tend to imitate the successful member, or rather the majority? Furthermore, participants in the experiments had to learn about an environment in which the cue validities varied, but not the discrimination rates. If discrimination rates also vary, then a combination between validity and discrimination rate, such as success (Martignon & Hoffrage, 2002; Newell et al., 2004), is a viable alternative principle for cue ordering. In this case, one could learn through social exchange about which cues allow decision

making more often, that is, have higher discrimination rates, or greater success. We do not know of any research that addresses these questions.

We began this research with the question: *What social learning rules can speed up individual learning so that cue orders approximating the ecological validity order can be found faster?* The results indicate that there is an interesting follow-up question: *Which social rules can improve orders beyond ecological validity, and why?*

Social Learning as Part of the Study of Bounded Rationality

According to Gigerenzer and Selten (2001), bounded rationality asks two questions: What are the heuristics in the adaptive toolbox? And, in which environments is a given heuristic ecologically rational? The study of heuristics, both for preferences (Payne, Bettman, & Johnson, 1993) and for inferences (Gigerenzer, 2008), has focused to a large degree on individual decision making, and initially paid little attention to the question of how heuristics and their building blocks, such as cue orderings, are learned. Recently, the question of learning has been addressed by a number of researchers (e.g., Brighton & Gigerenzer, 2008; Rieskamp & Otto, 2006), but predominantly in the form of individual reinforcement learning. Yet increasingly evident are the limitations of mere individual learning, including the lack of reliable feedback in many situations, the potential dangerousness of individual learning by feedback in matters of food and health, and the relative slowness of individual learning even if feedback is ideal and safe. These environmental factors that limit the efficacy of individual learning call for special attention to forms of social learning in the study of bounded rationality. The research presented in this article does not abandon individual learning, but tries to open up a perspective on how people rely on both individual and social learning to improve their heuristics over time. It also shows an area of intersection between the research on group decisions and the human tendency to conform to the majority's behavior. By integrating these various theoretical strands, we might eventually better understand how people mix social with individual learning, and how this mix depends on the structure of the social environment.

NOTES

1. The resulting (sample-based) cue ordering when using the validity algorithm should not be confused with the ecological validity ordering, as Dougherty, Franco-Watkins, and Thomas (2008) did. The latter is based on complete knowledge of the environment, whereas the former models people's subjective updating of the ordering of validities based on samples (Gigerenzer, Hoffrage, & Goldstein, 2008). It is this subjective, sample-based ordering that is the input to take-the-best or to other cognitive strategies.

2. Time measures were corrected excluding observations outside the ±2SD interval around the individual mean.

3. Degrees of freedom for the analyses containing repeated-measures factors were corrected by using the Greenhouse–Geisser (1959) technique.

Introduction to Chapter 22

The Aging Decision Maker: Cognitive Aging and the Adaptive Selection of Decision Strategies

This article by Rui Mata, Lael Schooler, and Jörg Rieskamp owes its existence to the unique set-up of the Max Planck Institute for Human Development in Berlin, where much of the work on heuristics was initiated. The institute's vision is to bring together under one roof research groups that share an interest in understanding human development but differ in research focus or even disciplinary background. For example, the institute has accommodated both Paul Baltes' group studying cognitive aging and Gerd Gigerenzer's ABC Research Group studying models of bounded and ecological rationality. Ideally, the interaction of the different groups will spark new ideas only possible within such an interdisciplinary environment. In this case the spark flew. Rui Mata, while working as a doctoral student with the ABC Research Group, also participated in the International Max Planck Research School LIFE, founded by Paul Baltes and others to promote interdisciplinary life span research. This combination exposed him to two very strong research programs—Baltes' theory of selection, optimization, and compensation (SOC) and the ABC program. Mata became intrigued by the idea of connecting them. Although both programs share an interest in adaptive behavior, SOC focuses primarily on adaptation across the life span. What role might heuristics play in adapting to age-related change in decision making?

Mata, Schooler, and Rieskamp found that both young and older adults were able to select simple and complex strategies adaptively (i.e., choose the strategy that matches the task environment). Nevertheless, older adults showed a stronger tendency to use simple strategies, even in an environment in which a more complex one would be more appropriate. These age differences in strategy use were mediated by age difference in fluid intelligence, namely, cognitive speed. Mata et al.'s results suggest that the aging decision maker adapts to losses in cognitive functioning by relying increasingly on simple strategies. Pachur, Mata, and Schooler (2009) later extended this line of research to the recognition heuristic, comparing young and older adults' adaptive use of the recognition heuristic in different environments. These authors found that young and older adults relied more on recognition when the recognition validity was high (compared to when it was low), but also that older adults showed a stronger tendency to use the recognition heuristic, even when this led to a (slightly) reduced inference accuracy. Both studies illustrate how changes over the life course can be investigated in terms of changes in the use of heuristics in the adaptive toolbox.

CHAPTER 22

The Aging Decision Maker: Cognitive Aging and the Adaptive Selection of Decision Strategies

Rui Mata, Lael J. Schooler, and Jörg Rieskamp

Abstract: Are older adults' decision abilities fundamentally compromised by age-related cognitive decline? Or can they adaptively select decision strategies? One study (*N* = 163) investigated the impact of cognitive aging on the ability to select decision strategies as a function of environment structure. Participants made decisions in either an environment that favored the use of information-intensive strategies or one favoring the use of simple, information-frugal strategies. Older adults tended to (a) look up less information and take longer to process it and (b) use simpler, less cognitively demanding strategies. In accordance with the idea that age-related cognitive decline leads to reliance on simpler strategies, measures of fluid intelligence explained age-related differences in information search and strategy selection. Nevertheless, both young and older adults seem to be equally adaptive decision makers in that they adjust their information search and strategy selection as a function of environment structure, suggesting that the aging decision maker is an adaptive one.

A common concern of both research on decision making and research on aging is how individuals balance their personal resources and the demands of a task to behave adaptively. Researchers in decision making have argued that people are equipped with a repertoire of strategies to solve the decision problems they face, and they select strategies as a function of both cognitive constraints and characteristics of the decision situation (e.g., Gigerenzer, Todd, & the ABC Research Group, 1999; Payne, 1976; Payne, Bettman, & Johnson, 1988, 1993; Simon, 1956; Svenson, 1979). Research on aging has examined

loss of cognitive capacity with age and has investigated how individuals compensate for these losses, for example, by relying on knowledge originating from years of experience (e.g., Baltes & Baltes, 1990; Baltes, Staudinger, & Lindenberger, 1999). The goal of the present article was to bring these two areas together. More specifically, we examined how the strategies people select depend on the nature of the information available in the environment[1] and on the individual's cognitive resources, which change across the life span.

In the remainder of this introduction, we first summarize the strategy approach to decision making, which sees decision behavior as the result of the selection of specific strategies. Second, we provide an overview of previous work on cognitive aging and strategy selection. Finally, we hypothesize how age-related cognitive change may impact adaptive strategy selection and describe the experimental study.

THE STRATEGY APPROACH TO DECISION MAKING

The assumption that there are multiple strategies to solve the problems we face is common to various research domains, including preferential choice (Einhorn, 1970; Payne et al., 1988), mathematical skills (Lemaire & Siegler, 1995), and memory (Coyle, Read, Gaultney, & Bjorklund, 1998). The strategy approach assumes that people select a strategy that is successful in a specific situation—that is, they adapt their strategy use to the structure of the task (Gigerenzer & Selten, 2001; Gigerenzer et al., 1999; Rieskamp & Otto, 2006; Simon, 1956). For example, in the inference domain, in which people can make use of several cues to infer objects' criterion values, an environment can be statistically characterized by low or high correlations between cues. When cues are only moderately correlated with each other, high inference accuracy often results from integrating all available information, whereas with strong correlations between cues a heuristic that focuses on a single cue is often sufficient for making accurate inferences (cf. Dieckmann & Rieskamp, 2007). Moreover, in many cases, such simple strategies can outperform strategies that integrate information, particularly when it comes to making predictions (Gigerenzer et al., 1999). Accordingly, it is assumed that cognition and environment are deeply intertwined: Having a repertoire of strategies allows people to choose those that fit specific environments and therefore perform adaptively.

When assuming that people have a repertoire of strategies for solving different problems, the pressing question of how people select strategies from their repertoire arises. Cost–benefit approaches to strategy selection propose that decision makers establish a balance between their personal resources and the expected benefits of selecting a particular strategy (Beach & Mitchell, 1978; Christensen-Szalanski, 1978; Payne et al., 1993). According to these theories, each strategy can be evaluated on two dimensions, costs and benefits. The costs are related to the cognitive effort necessary to apply a strategy, whereas the benefits are related to the accuracy of the strategy. The decision maker anticipates, although not necessarily deliberately, the effort required to apply and the accuracy obtained from applying the strategies, selecting the most appropriate for the problem at hand. Empirical evidence for these cost-benefit models lies in people's apparent skill at selecting strategies appropriate for the task. For example, people rely on simpler decision strategies when the task involves choosing from a large number of alternatives (e.g., Ford, Schmitt, Schechtman, Hults, & Doherty, 1989; Payne, 1976; Payne et al., 1993), when they are under time pressure (Payne, 1976; Payne et al., 1993; Rieskamp & Hoffrage, 2008; see Svenson & Maule, 1993, for a review), or when there are high costs associated with searching for information (Bröder, 2000; Newell & Shanks, 2003).

AGE-RELATED CHANGES IN STRATEGY SELECTION

Research on aging and strategy selection suggests that young and older adults may select different cognitive strategies. For example, older adults tend to select less cognitively demanding strategies compared with young adults in the arithmetic computation and memory domains (Dunlosky & Hertzog, 1998, 2000; Geary, Frensch, & Wiley, 1993), and they may have difficulties selecting appropriate strategies for a particular problem than young adults (e.g., Lemaire, Arnaud, & Lecacheur, 2004). Overall, these findings suggest that age-related cognitive decline may lead to deficits in adaptive strategy selection. Yet age-related differences in strategy selection are not always observed (cf. Salthouse, 1991); research on aging has found sustained or improved strategy use in old age in some domains, such as spatial cognition and arithmetic division (e.g., Cohen & Faulkner, 1983; Geary & Wiley, 1991).

Research on decision making and aging (for reviews, see Mather, 2006; Peters, Finucane, MacGregor, & Slovic, 2000; Sanfey & Hastie, 1999) suggests that older adults use less information and view it longer when making a decision (Johnson, 1990, 1993; Johnson & Drungle, 2000; Riggle & Johnson, 1996), have problems with more complex relations between criterion and cues (e.g., Chasseigne et al., 2004), have greater difficulties in understanding information concerning available options (Finucane, Mertz, Slovic, & Schmidt, 2005; Finucane et al., 2002), show rapid forgetting of the options' values (Wood, Busemeyer, Koling, Cox, & Davis, 2005; but see Kovalchik, Camerer, Grether, Plott, & Allman, 2005), and are less consistent in their decisions (Finucane et al., 2002, 2005; but see Kim & Hasher, 2005). These findings correspond well with research in everyday problem solving, suggesting decline in performance associated with increased age (Thornton & Dumke, 2005).

Most of the previous work has focused on showing age differences in various preferential choice and comprehension tasks "rather than examining specific mechanisms underlying the differences" (Finucane et al., 2002, p. 159). Consequently, little is known about age-related differences in the selection of decision strategies. Moreover, the existing evidence is inconclusive; some work suggests that older adults tend to use less information-intensive strategies compared with young adults (Chen & Sun, 2003; Johnson, 1990), whereas other work does not (Johnson, 1993; Riggle & Johnson, 1996). More important, past research has neglected the question of to what extent the ability to choose appropriate strategies for a particular environment is age related. In the present work, we evaluate whether young and older adults differ in the adaptive selection of strategies for an inference problem and look for the potential underlying causes.

INTELLECTUAL FUNCTIONING AND ADAPTIVE STRATEGY SELECTION

Crystallized intelligence and fluid intelligence, two main components of intellectual functioning, undergo different change trajectories across the life-span (Horn & Cattell, 1967). How do these components relate to decision behavior? Fluid intelligence declines with age (Baltes et al., 1999), and age-related decline in its components (e.g., working memory, speed, inhibitory function) may impact adaptive strategy selection. In fact, decline in fluid abilities has been related to age-related differences in decision-making

behavior (e.g., Finucane et al., 2005). Bröder (2003) also showed that individual differences in fluid abilities are associated with the adaptive selection of decision strategies (for an example in another domain, see Schunn & Reder, 2001).

We assume that deficits in fluid intelligence impact strategy selection by setting an upper limit on the cognitive effort that can be expended, constraining the range of possible strategies that can be used in a particular situation. For instance, information-intensive strategies are likely to be out of reach of individuals with severe memory limitations. Of course, selecting simpler strategies also affects basic levels of the decision process, such as the search for information: Simpler strategies tend to require less information than more complex ones (e.g., Rieskamp & Otto, 2006). This perspective is in line with evidence that suggests older adults look up less information before making a decision (Johnson, 1990, 1993) and the hypothesis that older adults may rely more on strategies that require fewer cognitive resources (Gigerenzer, 2003; Sanfey & Hastie, 1999). This view leads to the expectation that older adults select strategies less adaptively compared with young adults: Older adults might have to rely on simpler strategies, regardless of environment structure.

Crystallized intelligence usually increases over the life span and can be seen as a reflection of experience. Previous work on decision making suggests that crystallized intelligence may not be a major determinant of age differences in information search (Johnson, 1990). However, the relation between crystallized intelligence and adaptive strategy selection has not been investigated. Theories of successful aging suggest that increases in experience may compensate for age-related cognitive decline and lead to a "higher level of adaptive capacity" (Baltes et al., 1999, p. 478). Crystallized intelligence or knowledge could be associated with a better understanding of the fit between the statistical structure of environments and particular cognitive strategies, leading to increased adaptivity in decision making. If knowledge is a good predictor of success in selecting the appropriate strategy for a task environment, one could expect older adults to outperform young adults in selecting adaptive strategies for a particular task or environment, at least to the extent that their strategy repertoire is not constrained by age-related cognitive decline.

Summing up, considering the role of both fluid and crystallized intelligence provides two possible views of the impact of aging on decision making. First, a "negative" view suggests that age-related cognitive decline constrains the repertoire of strategies potentially applicable in an inference situation. This could lead older adults to rely on simpler strategies regardless of environment structure. A second, more "positive" view suggests that older adults' experience may have equipped them with knowledge concerning the correspondence between strategies and environments, that is, knowledge about what is the right tool for a particular job. In this case, older adults may be as adaptive as young adults in their strategy selection, at least to the extent allowed by their cognitive abilities. Our study aimed to increase our understanding of how these two processes play out in determining adaptive strategy selection.

OVERVIEW AND LOGIC OF THE PRESENT STUDY

Our study investigated the impact of cognitive aging on the adaptive selection of strategies in an inference situation. The participants had to infer which of two diamonds was more expensive, on the basis of sequential acquisition of cues concerning, for example, the diamonds' size, cut, and clarity. Participants were explicitly instructed about one of two environmental structures: an equal validities environment (i.e., an environment in which all cues shared the same predictive power) or an unequal validities environment (i.e., an environment in which all cues differed in predictive power and were ordered in descending order as a function of predictive power). Participants were then asked to make a number of decisions in one of these environments and were given feedback about their performance only at the end of the inference task.

Participants' decisions were compared with the predictions of decision strategies to determine whether young and older adults selected

appropriate strategies as a function of environmental structure. We chose three strategies to represent a wide spectrum of cognitive demands: take-the-best (TTB; Gigerenzer & Goldstein, 1996), Take Two (Dieckmann & Rieskamp, 2007), and a weighted additive rule (WADD; e.g., Payne et al., 1988; see Payne et al., 1988, for additional strategies). TTB is the least effortful, followed by Take Two, and finally WADD.[2] This set allowed us to construct a reasonable number of discriminating trials in which the strategies led to different decisions, and thus we could meaningfully perform comparative model testing. TTB is a noncompensatory strategy, in which the decision is based solely on one piece of discriminating information. In our task, someone using TTB would first look up the information for the most predictive cue with which to compare the two diamonds (e.g., size of diamond) and select the diamond for which the cue speaks. If the first cue failed to discriminate between the diamonds (e.g., both diamonds were large), the second most predictive cue would be acquired, and so on, until a discriminating piece of evidence was found (e.g., one diamond was clear and the other cloudy). WADD is an information-intensive, fully compensatory strategy, in which the sum of all cue values (i.e., a large diamond would be coded as a 1 and a small one as a 0) is computed for each alternative and is multiplied by the cues' validities; the alternative with the largest sum is then selected. In Take Two, the alternatives are compared on successive cues and the information search is ended when two cues that favor one alternative are found; that alternative is then selected. Thus, in Take Two, as in TTB, the alternatives are evaluated in a cue-wise fashion and the focus is on little information, but as in WADD, Take Two allows for compensation, so that two cues that favor one alternative can compensate for another cue that favors the other alternative.

Which strategies should people apply in the equal validities versus unequal validities environments? A cost-benefit analysis (Beach & Mitchell, 1978; Christensen-Szalanski, 1978; Payne et al., 1993) allows us to make specific predictions given some assumptions concerning participants' perceived accuracy and costs of decision strategies. Concerning perceived accuracy, in the equal validities environment, the different cues have the same validity, so that evidence provided by a single cue can be compensated for (overruled) by the evidence from other cues. Consequently, in the equal validities environment, individuals reasonably expect information-intensive strategies to have a higher expected accuracy than a noncompensatory strategy that relies on less information. In contrast, in the unequal validities environment, the cues have varying validities and thus the evidence of a high validity cue is less frequently overruled by the sum of the evidence of lower validity cues. As a consequence, participants may expect that in the unequal validities environment, an information-intensive strategy, such as WADD, does not have much of an advantage over a less information-intensive strategy. In this case, search costs may become a crucial factor in determining which strategy people select. Because TTB and Take Two require much less information than WADD to arrive at a decision, they should be selected more frequently in the unequal validities environment compared with the equal validities environment. In sum, people are more likely to select the cognitively demanding WADD strategy when faced with the equal validities environment, whereas the simpler strategies, TTB and Take Two, are more likely to be selected when people are confronted with an unequal validities environment.

How does cognitive aging play out in our task? The idea that decision-making behavior may be determined by both age-related cognitive decline and an increase in knowledge generates two sets of predictions.

1. The assumption that older adults' cognitive deficits constrain their repertoire of employable inference strategies suggests the following: (a) Older adults may be unable to select the more cognitively demanding WADD strategy and have to rely on simpler strategies, such as TTB or Take Two, regardless of the environment, and (b) older adults should be constrained to search for less information and take longer to process acquired information compared with young adults. One further

consequence of the assumption that cognitive capacity constrains the repertoire of employable strategies is that a significant proportion of age-related differences in strategy selection and information search behavior can be explained by individual differences in cognitive abilities (e.g., memory abilities).

2. An alternative view of cognitive aging that considers older adults' increase in knowledge leads to the following suggestions: (a) Older adults may better understand strategy-environment correspondence and thus be more adaptive than young adults, at least in those cases in which older adults are not constrained by capacity limitations. For example, older adults could be more apt to rely on simpler strategies such as TTB and Take Two in the appropriate unequal validities environment compared with young adults. (b) If this were the case, a measure of crystallized intelligence, such as verbal knowledge (Lindenberger, Mayr, & Kliegl, 1993), should account for a significant proportion of the age-related differences in strategy selection.

To test these predictions, we used two different environments and conducted a comprehensive assessment of intellectual abilities, which included measures of both fluid and crystallized intelligence. We thus aimed to contribute to the understanding of young and older adults' strategy selection as a function of both environment structure and individual characteristics.

METHOD

Participants

A total of 169 adults (83 young adults, 86 older adults) participated in the experiment. Most (85%) of the young adults were students at the Free University of Berlin and were on average 24 years old ($SD = 3.3$). The older adults were healthy members of the community with an average age of 71 ($SD = 4.9$). Most of the older adults were retired. Overall, the young adults took about 2.5 hr and older adults 3.5 hr to complete all tasks. Participants received a fixed hourly payment of 10 euros for taking part in the experiment. In addition, they received an extra bonus payment dependent on their performance. Specifically, they received an extra 10 euro cents for each correct choice. We had to exclude 6 participants from our final sample: One participant stuttered, making it difficult to test him in tasks demanding oral responses; 1 tried to tamper with the experimental program while performing the decision task; and 4 participants faced technical problems with the experimental program implementing the decision task. The final sample comprised 80 young participants (41 female, 39 male), and 83 older participants (49 female, 34 male).

Design

The study had two between-subject conditions varying the environments the participants encountered, in particular, the distribution of cue validities. The validity of a cue is defined as the conditional probability of making a correct inference with the cue on the condition that the cue discriminates. For example, a validity of 71% means that out of 100 paired comparisons in which a cue discriminates between two diamonds, the diamond with a positive cue value will be the most expensive in 71 of the cases. Participants in the condition with the equal validities environment were informed that all cues had a validity of 71%. In the second, unequal validities environment, the validities of the cues varied substantially. In this condition, the first presented cue had the highest validity, the second cue had the second highest validity, and so on. The validities presented were 81%, 71%, 69%, 66%, 63%, 60%, 57%, and 54%. The average discrimination rate, that is, the proportion of times a cue discriminated between the two objects, was 70% for all cues. We chose this medium-size discrimination rate, first, because it provided a large number of discriminating cues, which increased memory demands. Second, it prevented the possibility that after observing a cue value on one alternative, one could infer the cue value of the other alternative without acquiring this information: As the discrimination rate of a cue approaches unity, the incentive to look up the value for a second alternative decreases if one has seen the value on the first alternative.

All participants had access to the following cues: size, overall proportions of the diamond, crown proportions, pavilion proportions, size of table, color, clarity, and certification laboratory. All cues had binary values (e.g., big vs. small diamond, colored vs. uncolored diamond). The assignment of labels to cues was randomized across participants. Each participant observed a different set of 50 pair comparisons randomly generated with the constraints of having the previously specified cue validities and discrimination rate and an adequate number of discriminating trials for each pair of the three strategies (TTB, Take Two, WADD), in which each strategy in the pair would lead to different predictions in order to allow comparative model testing (at least 10 discriminating trials for each pair). The participants were paid 10 euro cents whenever they chose the more expensive diamond. However, note that no outcome feedback was given during the experiment, and payments were made after the experiment so they could not influence participants' inferences.

To examine the fit between the three inference strategies and the two task environments that we constructed, we examined the payoffs the participants could expect to receive, if they consistently used one of the inference strategies. WADD performed best in the equal validities environment with a mean expected payoff of 4.20 euros, followed by Take Two and TTB with a mean expected payoff of 3.90 euros and 3.60 euros, respectively. In contrast, in the unequal validities environment, TTB provided the highest expected payoff of 4.00 euros, followed by Take Two and WADD with an expected payoff of 3.90 euros and 3.60 euros, respectively. Thus, the participants would on average receive a higher payoff by applying WADD in the equal validities condition and TTB in the unequal validities condition.

We tested our young sample before testing our older sample. For the young adults, the experimenter used the first trial as a practice trial, and we consequently analyzed only the remaining 49 choices; thus the actual proportion of discriminating items varied slightly across participants. When we later tested older adults, we gave them 5 additional practice trials to make sure they understood the task and were familiarized with the computerized display and apparatus before performing the 50 experimental trials.

Measures

A battery of 11 psychometric tests was administered to all participants. The tests assessed various intellectual abilities including verbal knowledge (spot-a-word, vocabulary; Lindenberger et al., 1993), processing speed (boxes, digit symbol substitution, identical pictures; Lindenberger et al., 1993), reasoning (figural analogies, letter series, practical problems; Lindenberger et al., 1993), and memory (operation span, Hamm, 2002; Brown-Peterson test, Kane & Engle, 2000; forward digit span, Wechsler, 1981).

Procedure

The participants first performed the inference task. On each trial, they had to infer which of two diamonds was more expensive. Participants were first familiarized with the task and the concept of cue validity. They were then informed about the structure of the environment in which they would make their inferences by receiving a listing of cues, their validities, and direction (i.e., which cue values were associated with more expensive diamonds). Participants performed 50 inferences on the basis of an information search with a computerized display. They were able to search up to eight cue values per diamond, and each cue value was briefly presented (2 s before disappearing) individually and only once. Participants had to touch appropriate buttons on a touch screen to obtain cue values and to make a decision (see Figure 22-1). Participants could make their decision at any point during each trial. The order of information acquisition was partially constrained, with participants having to follow a predetermined cue order, from the most valid to the least valid cue in the unequal validities environment. Participants were otherwise unconstrained in their information search, being able

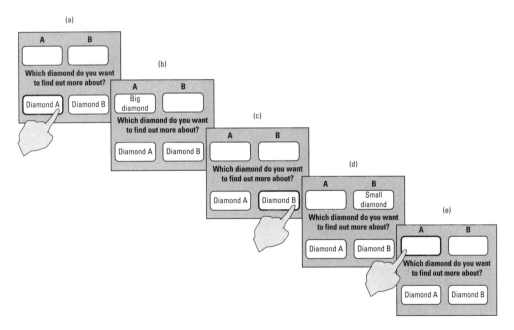

Figure 22-1. Experimental display and example of applying the take-the-best strategy: (**a**) The participant presses a button to see information concerning Diamond A and (**b**) observes the cue value for 2 s; (**c**) the participant presses a button to see information concerning Diamond B and (**d**) observes the cue value for 2 s; (e) the participant chooses Diamond A by pressing the appropriate button.

to search both values on one cue for the two diamonds before considering another cue (cue-wise search) or, alternatively, to search for all the cues on a single diamond before the second diamond was considered (alternative-wise search). Mixed strategies were possible as well in which participants could search, say, half the cues in an alternative-wise fashion and the remainder in a cue-wise search. Thus, participants were not overly constrained in terms of the strategies that they could employ. After participants performed the decision task, we assessed their cognitive capacity using the comprehensive battery of tests mentioned above.

RESULTS

The Results section is structured as follows: First, we give an overview of participants' payoffs and information search in the inference task. Second, we report what proportions of their choices were predicted by the different strategies. How well participants conformed to the various strategies gives an indication of how well they were able to exploit the statistical structure of the conditions. We also classify participants as users of particular decision strategies on the basis of their decisions and information search. Third, we provide a description of participants' intellectual abilities. Finally, we assess the relation between individuals' information search and strategy use and their cognitive capacity.

Payoffs

How well did young and older adults perform in the two environments? To answer this question, we considered participants' monetary payoff in the inference task. A higher payoff resulted when participants made inferences in line with WADD in the equal validities condition and in line with TTB in the unequal validities condition. Consequently, participants' payoffs reflect their ability to select the appropriate strategy for an environment on the basis of their understanding of environment-strategy fit. In addition, to examine possible effects of practice, we considered participants' performance in the first half and second half of the sequence of inference trials. More specifically, we conducted a repeated

measures analysis of variance with participants' payoff (first half vs. second half) as the dependent variable and with environment, age group, and their interaction as independent factors. The analysis revealed an effect of environment, which matches the strategies' differences in expected payoff between the environments (see Method section). Participants in the equal validities environment received a lower payoff ($M = 3.75$, $SD = .45$) than those in the unequal validities environment ($M = 3.95$, $SD = .4$), $F(1, 159) = 11.22$, $p = .001$, partial $\eta^2 = .07$. Older adults earned slightly less ($M = 3.7$, $SD = .5$) than young adults ($M = 4$, $SD = .35$), $F(1, 159) = 21.92$, $p < .001$, partial $\eta^2 = .12$. Although the difference between older and young adults' payoffs was slightly larger in the equal validities environment than in the unequal validities environment ($-.35$ vs. $-.20$), this interaction was not significant (partial $\eta^2 = .01$). The analysis did not detect significant changes in payoff across the two halves or an interaction with age (partial $\eta^2 < .025$), suggesting that young and older adults' performance was fairly constant across the series of trials.

Information Search

Participants' information search behavior was characterized by three measures (e.g., Bröder, 2003; Payne et al., 1993; Rieskamp & Hoffrage, 1999): *Number of acquisitions* (ACQ) concerns the depth of search and is defined as the total number of cue values looked up. *Search index* (INDEX; Payne, 1976) reflects the general pattern of information search. This variable aggregates two types of search transitions. Starting from the first cue on one of the diamonds, for example, size, another cue for the same diamond can be viewed, such as clarity (alternative-wise transition) or the size of the second diamond can be looked up (cue-wise transition). The index is determined by the number of alternative-wise transitions minus the number of cue-wise transitions, divided by the sum of these two types of transitions, yielding values from -1 to 1. Positive values indicate a more alternative-wise search, and negative values indicate a more cue-wise search. An alternative-wise search is inconsistent with TTB and Take Two, strategies in which a cue-wise search is expected. In contrast, for

WADD, an alternative-wise search is more natural, but a cue-wise search that considers at least a majority of the cues is also possible. Finally, *look-up time* (TIME) refers to a person's median look-up time, that is, the median time each person took to process each cue value.

The values for the three search variables by age and environment are summarized in Table 22-1. The three measures are conceptually independent; for example, whether a participant searched for information in a cue-wise manner does not, in principle, determine the total number of cues for which he or she searched. Empirically, there is no relation between ACQ or TIME and INDEX ($r = -.10$, $r = .08$, respectively; $ps > .10$). However, the data suggest that those participants who could or were willing to search for more information also took less time to process it: There was negative correlation between amount of information searched for and time taken to process each cue value ($r = -.39$, $p = .04$).

We assessed whether there was an effect of environment structure as well as age on the search measures. We conducted a multivariate analysis of variance (MANOVA) with environment (equal validities vs. unequal validities) and age (young vs. older) as independent variables, and the three search measures described above as the dependent variables. Table 22-1 shows that both young and older participants searched for less information (ACQ), did so in a more cue-wise fashion (INDEX), and took longer to process each cue (TIME) in the unequal validities environment than in the equal validities environment, $F(3, 157) = 14.42$, $p < .01$, partial $\eta^2 = .22$. (Univariate tests showed that the effect held for all three variables.) Older adults searched for less information ($M = 9.62$, $SD = 4.52$) and took longer to process each cue value ($M = 1.48$, $SD = .60$) compared with young adults ($M = 12.07$, $SD = 3.10$; $M = .67$, $SD = .23$), $F(3, 157) = 44.85$, $p < .01$, partial $\eta^2 = .46$. Univariate tests showed that this effect held for ACQ and TIME but not for INDEX, in which the age groups did not differ substantially ($M = -.28$, $SD = .65$; $M = -.36$, $SD = .63$, older and young adults, respectively). Finally, there was no interaction between environment and age, $F(3, 157) = .84$, $p = .48$, partial $\eta^2 = .02$. For comparison, we computed the effect size of environment on the search variables for the two age groups independently. Both groups showed a small effect of environment (partial $\eta^2 = .20$, partial $\eta^2 = .26$, older and young adults, respectively), suggesting the two age groups were equally sensitive to the distribution of cue validities when searching for information.

One might wonder whether participants' inference process changed during the experiment, considering the relatively large number of inferences. To examine potential changes, we compared participants' search behavior in the first half of the experiment with their search in the second half. More specifically, we conducted repeated measures ANOVAs with the different

Table 22-1. Means and Standard Deviations (SDs) for the Search Variables by Age Group and Environment

Search Variables	Young Adults				Older Adults			
	Equal Validities		Unequal Validities		Equal Validities		Unequal Validities	
	M	SD	M	SD	M	SD	M	SD
Acquisitions	13.00	2.00	11.00	3.00	11.00	4.00	8.00	4.00
Search index	−.12	.74	−.61	.33	−.16	.75	−.40	.51
Look-up time	610.00	210.00	710.00	250.00	1,350.00	350.00	1,600.00	630.00

Note: Acquisitions represents the number of cue values searched for. Search index characterizes the type of information search: Positive values indicate a more alternative-wise search and negative values indicate a more cue-wise search. Look-up time represents the median time required to process a cue value (in milliseconds).

search measures as the dependent variables and the two halves of the experiment as a within-subject factor. Our results suggest that participants did not change how much information they considered over time (ACQ), $F(1, 160) = .02$, $p = .90$, partial $\eta^2 < .001$, the general pattern of information search (INDEX), $F(1, 160) = .001$, $p = .97$, partial $\eta^2 < .001$, or the time to process each cue (TIME), $F(1, 160) = 2.6$, $p = .11$, partial $\eta^2 = .02$.

Overall, the differences in participants' search behavior between the two environments are compatible with the adaptivity hypothesis (Gigerenzer et al., 1999; Payne et al., 1988), that is, the idea that people adjust their decision behavior according to the characteristics of the decision environment: Both older and young adults looked up less information in the unequal validities compared with the equal validities environment. Nevertheless, there were considerable age-related differences in search behavior, with older adults searching for less information overall and taking longer to do so compared with young adults.

Strategy Classification

To provide another measure of participants' performance, we determined the proportion of inferences that were correctly predicted by the three strategies we considered, TTB, Take Two, and WADD. As described earlier, if participants adapt to the environment they face, their choices should be more consistent with the WADD strategy in the equal validities environment and with the TTB and Take Two strategies in the unequal validities environment. In fact, WADD predicted 80% ($SEM = .01\%$) of the inferences in the equal validities environment compared with TTB with 67% ($SEM = .01\%$) and Take Two with 73% ($SEM = .01\%$). In contrast, in the unequal validities environment, TTB was best, predicting 76% of the inferences ($SEM = .01\%$) compared with Take Two with 73% ($SEM = .01\%$) and WADD with 70% ($SEM = .01\%$). These results suggest that the participants selected their inference strategies appropriately in the different environments.

To get a more detailed picture of participants' inference strategies, we classified participants as predominantly using specific strategies. A classification technique using participants' inferences and search behavior for classification is superior to a classification technique using only one type of information.[3] More specifically, we relied on a procedure that counts for each participant the number of inferences for which the information search *and* the final choice corresponded to the predicted search and choice by the particular strategy (see Appendix). The strategy that predicted the most inferences correctly for a participant was assigned to the participant. Recall that TTB predicts that the information search stops after one discriminating cue has been encountered. In Take Two, the information search stops after seeing two discriminating cues favoring the same alternative. Finally, for WADD, we assumed that all cue values had to be searched on both alternatives. Participants were assigned to the strategy with the highest fit and those participants for which the fit of two or more strategies coincided were left unclassified.

The results of the classification are presented in Table 22-2. WADD was overall the preferred strategy, which replicates previous findings in the literature suggesting that compensatory strategies are preferred over noncompensatory strategies for unfamiliar tasks with low information search costs (e.g., Bröder, 2000; Rieskamp, 2006; Rieskamp & Otto, 2006). TTB was preferred by only a few participants. Due to the small number of participants assigned to TTB and to our desire to increase the reliability of our analysis, we grouped TTB users with the participants assigned to Take Two. The participants classified as using TTB or Take Two were then compared with those participants classified as using the information-intense WADD strategy. The rationale for this grouping is that WADD is an information-greedy strategy, which uses all available information, whereas TTB and Take Two stop the information search and therefore frequently only use a small proportion of the available information. Moreover, in contrast to WADD, both TTB and Take Two do not weigh cues according to their validities to arrive at a decision.

On the whole, the results concerning strategy selection behavior suggest that a large proportion

Table 22-2. Strategy Classification by Age Group and Environment

	Young Adults				Older Adults			
	Equal Validities		Unequal Validities		Equal Validities		Unequal Validities	
Strategy	No.	%	No.	%	No.	%	No.	%
TTB	1	2	1	3	3	8	14	33
Take Two	5	12	13	33	10	24	10	24
WADD	35	86	24	61	27	66	17	41
Unclassified	0	0	1	3	1	2	1	2
Total	41	100	39	100	41	100	42	100

Note: TTB = take-the-best; WADD = weighted additive rule.

of both young and older participants selected strategies as a function of environment structure. As can be observed in Table 22-2, a larger proportion of participants selected the simpler TTB or Take Two strategies in the unequal validities environment compared with the equal validities environment, whereas the opposite is true for the information-intensive WADD strategy, $\chi^2(1, N = 160) = 10.59$, $p < .01$, $w = .26$. Moreover, the effect of environment was evident in both the young, $\chi^2(1, N = 79) = 5.14$, $p = .02$, $w = .25$, and older sample, $\chi^2(1, N = 81) = 5.53$, $p = .02$, $w = .26$. Nonetheless, there was an age-related effect on strategy distributions. Older adults selected the simpler TTB or Take Two more often than did their young counterparts, $\chi^2(1, N = 160) = 7.23$, $p < .01$, $w = .21$. This result suggests that older adults may have a stronger initial preference for simpler, less cognitively demanding strategies than young adults.

Individual Difference Measures

Table 22-3 lists the 11 cognitive function tests in our battery. To construct composite measures from the individual tests, we hypothesized two ways of grouping tests into domains (see Wilson et al., 2002, for a similar procedure). In one grouping, we simply distinguished between measures of fluid and crystallized intelligence. In the second grouping, we looked at the functional domains of the different types of intelligence: the verbal knowledge component of crystallized intelligence and the components of reasoning, speed, and memory of fluid intelligence. We next

developed an empirical grouping of the tests on the basis of the outcome of a principal components factor analysis (with varimax rotation) on the 11 tests. The analysis identified three factors and is summarized on the right side of Table 22-3. We grouped the tests that loaded higher than .50 on a common factor. As can be seen in Table 22-3, the empirical solution shows some resemblance to both theoretical groupings although it seems not to distinguish between the reasoning and speed subdomains. To quantify the agreement of each conceptual grouping with the empirical one, we used Kendall's tau, a measure that calculates the proportion of concordant pairs of tests (agreements between groupings) minus the discordant proportion (disagreements between groupings). When both young and older adults' scores were considered, the overall agreement between the factor analytic and the theoretical groupings was similar for both the two-factor and four-domain groupings: Agreement with the two-factor theoretical grouping was .42 ($p = .17$); agreement with the four-domain grouping was .37 ($p = .18$). However, when the factor analysis was performed separately for young and older adults, the four-domain grouping was better (.67 and .82, both $ps < .01$, young and older adults, respectively) compared with the two-factor grouping (.0 and −.14, both $ps > .6$, young and older adults, respectively). We chose the four-domain grouping because it fit better and allowed us to examine the impact of the different subdivisions of fluid intelligence on decision behavior.

Table 22-3. Psychometric Information on the 11 Cognitive Tests

Test	Grouping 1	Grouping 2	Factor Loading		
			1	2	3
Spot-a-word	Crystallized	Verbal knowledge	−.23	**.86**	−.04
Vocabulary	Crystallized	Verbal knowledge	.37	**.69**	.10
Digit symbol	Fluid	Speed	**.82**	−.07	.10
Identical pictures	Fluid	Speed	**.82**	−.27	.06
Boxes	Fluid	Speed	**−.79**	.13	.03
Figural analogies	Fluid	Reasoning	**.83**	.08	−.05
Letter series	Fluid	Reasoning	**.78**	.12	.04
Practical problems	Fluid	Reasoning	**.64**	.25	−.03
Operation span	Fluid	Memory	**.69**	.21	.20
Brown-Peterson	Fluid	Memory	.21	−.04	**−.81**
Forward digit span	Fluid	Memory	.37	−.01	**.64**

Note: We distinguished between a general grouping of tests into those measuring fluid vs. crystallized intelligence (Grouping 1) and a more detailed one distinguishing between four functional domains (Grouping 2). Factor loadings are from principal components analysis with varimax rotation: Loadings of .50 or higher are in boldface.

Table 22-4. Participants' Characteristics and Individual Difference Measures by Age Group

Measure	Young Adults		Older Adults		Statistical Test	
	M	SD	M	SD	F	p
Knowledge	47.7	9.2	52.2	10.3	56.71	<.01
Speed	58.2	5.5	42.1	6.4	105.83	<.01
Reasoning	56.4	6.7	43.8	8.8	300.52	<.01
Memory	55.2	8.4	45.0	8.9	8.62	<.01

Summary measures of the different domains were obtained by computing unit-weighted composites of the individual tests and scaling them (T metric, $M = 50$, $SD = 10$). Table 22-4 shows the average values for the different domains by age group. Average results seem to match earlier findings with similar populations (cf. Baltes & Lindenberger, 1997; Li et al., 2004). We also computed the correlations between the different factors. As can be seen in Table 22-5, the correlations among abilities are mostly positive, which replicates the positive manifold reported in the literature (e.g., Ackerman, Beier, & Boyle, 2002; Lindenberger et al., 1993). All variables correlate negatively with age with the exception of knowledge. These results reflect the known pattern of decline in fluid intelligence and sustained or increased knowledge with increasing age (Baltes

et al., 1999). Also, as expected, participants in the two experimental conditions did not differ with respect to their abilities, $F(4, 158) = 1.39, p = .24$, partial $\eta^2 = .03$.

Cognitive Capacity and Information Search

Can the individual differences in cognitive capacity explain the observed age-related differences in number of cues looked up and look-up time? To answer this question, we performed an analysis consisting of the following steps: First, we estimated a set of regression models using the search variable as the dependent variable and age or each cognitive capacity measure as a predictor. Second, age and each capacity measure were used as predictors to test whether age substantially increased the fit (R^2) of the regression over each cognitive capacity variable. The first

Table 22-5. Intercorrelations Among Abilities and Age

Measure	1	2	3	4	5
1 Knowledge	—	−.09	.06	.12	.23
2 Speed		—	.67	.55	−.82
3 Reasoning			—	.57	−.65
4 Memory				—	−.53
5 Age					—

Note: Significance levels: $r = .15$, $p < .05$.

"restricted" regression including the cognitive capacity predictor was compared with the "complete" regression with both age and the particular cognitive capacity variable (cf. Cohen, Cohen, West, & Aiken, 2003, p. 465). This procedure allows one to test whether age adds to the explained variance when each individual difference measure has been considered, thus answering whether individual difference measures account for age-related variance in information search.

Table 22-6 summarizes the results of the regression analysis for the different cognitive measures. Age is negatively correlated with number of cue values acquired (ACQ) and positively correlated with the time participants took to look up a cue value (TIME), which

reflects older participants' tendency to search for fewer cue values and to take longer to process information compared with young adults. Concerning the relation between individual difference measures and information search, the crystallized intelligence factor—verbal knowledge—was not associated with any of the information search variables. In contrast, the fluid intelligence factors—speed, reasoning, and memory—were related to both ACQ and TIME.

Do individual difference measures of fluid intelligence account for age-related variance in information search variables? As indicated in Step 2 of Table 22-6, when age was added as a predictor to the model with ACQ as a dependent variable, we detected a significant increment in explained variance beyond that provided by each cognitive capacity variable except when speed and reasoning were considered. Thus, speed and reasoning accounted for all the age-related variance in ACQ. Concerning the regression models with TIME as a dependent variable, age produced increments in explained variance beyond the effects of all individual difference factors. Speed and reasoning factors correlated strongly (see Table 22-5). To understand the contribution of speed and reasoning factors to the number of acquisitions, we considered a regression model using both as predictors. The results

Table 22-6. Hierarchical Linear Regressions with Search Measures as the Dependent Variables

Variable	Acquisitions				Look-up Time			
	R^2	F	p	B	R^2	F	p	B
Step 1								
Age	0.12	21.61	<.01	−0.35	0.21	40.72	<.01	0.45
Knowledge	0.00	0.01	.92	0.01	0.00	0.57	.45	0.06
Speed	0.13	23.65	<.01	0.36	0.18	33.54	<.01	−0.42
Reasoning	0.20	39.30	<.01	0.45	0.13	24.12	<.01	−0.36
Memory	0.09	14.87	<.01	0.29	0.07	12.66	<.01	−0.27
Step 2								
Knowledge + age	0.13	23.28	<.01	0.10	0.20	40.36	<.01	−0.05
Speed + age	0.01	1.52	.22	0.23	0.04	7.40	<.01	−0.15
Reasoning + age	0.01	1.14	.32	0.38	0.08	16.20	<.01	−0.12
Memory + age	0.05	9.30	<.01	0.15	0.13	26.17	<.01	−0.05

Note: In Step 1, B corresponds to the age coefficient or to the cognitive abilities coefficients. In Step 2, R^2 represents the difference between R^2 of the model with age and each capacity as predictors and that of a model with only the cognitive capacity measure as a predictor.

suggest that reasoning ($\beta = .34$, $p < .01$) but not speed ($\beta = .12$, $p = .20$) accounted for variance in ACQ. In sum, the results show that individual difference measures could account for considerable variance in search behavior: Individual differences in reasoning were able to explain all age-related variance in number of cues searched.[4] However, there were age-related differences in TIME not accounted for by individual difference measures.

To ensure our results were not influenced by differences in years of education between our young and older samples, we conducted the same set of analyses with education as a predictor of information search. The relation between education and information search was very small ($R^2 = .02$ for both ACQ and TIME), and the pattern of effects remained the same when education was included as a predictor in the regression models for the two age groups. Likewise, the pattern of results remains unchanged when environment was added as a predictor.

Cognitive Capacity and Strategy Selection

We were interested in determining whether age-related differences in strategy selection behavior could be explained by cognitive capacity measures. Because strategy classification was a dichotomous variable, we performed a series of logistic regressions to investigate the relation between strategy selection and cognitive capacity. First, we estimated a set of logistic regression models using the strategy selected by the participants as the dependent variable (with the TTB/Take Two group as a base) and age or each cognitive capacity measure as a predictor. Second, the combined effect of age and cognitive capacity was considered. Improvements in prediction were tested by comparing "restricted" and "complete" logistic regressions using a log-likelihood ratio test (Cohen et al., 2003, p. 504). The fit of each logistic regression model is defined by the G^2 measurement (e.g., Burnham & Anderson, 1998), defined as -2 times the sum of the log likelihoods of the model. When two logistic regression models are nested, they can be compared via a log-likelihood ratio test, so that the G^2 of the simpler, restricted model is subtracted from the G^2 of the more complex,

unrestricted model. The resulting difference is approximately chi-square distributed with the difference in number of free parameters as the degrees of freedom.

Results of the logistic regression analysis are summarized in Table 22-7. Overall, individual difference measures seem to account for age-related differences in strategy selection. The odds ratio concerning the effect of age is below 1 ($p < .01$), which reflects older adults' greater tendency to rely on the simpler TTB and Take Two strategies (vs. WADD) compared with young adults. Concerning the effect of cognitive capacity, the odds ratios above 1 ($p < .01$) concerning speed, reasoning, and memory factors indicate that higher scores on these were associated with using the more cognitively demanding WADD strategy compared with the TTB and Take Two strategies. Finally, Step 2 in Table 22-7 shows that adding age to a model including speed, reasoning, or memory factors as predictors did not improve the fit significantly. Including years of education or environment as predictors in the

Table 22-7. Hierarchical Logistic Regressions with Strategy Classification as the Dependent Variable

Variable	Model Deviance	G^2	p	Exp(B) Odds Ratio
Step 1				
Age	199.2	9.20	<.01	0.98
Knowledge	208.3	0.09	.76	1.01
Speed	198.5	9.86	<.01	1.06
Reasoning	188.1	20.25	<.01	1.08
Memory	199.1	9.31	<.01	1.06
Step 2				
Knowledge + age	198.1	10.23	<.01	1.02
Speed + age	197.9	0.68	.41	1.03
Reasoning + age	188.1	0.05	.83	1.08
Memory + age	196.3	2.83	.09	1.04

Note: In Step 1, *Exp(B)* corresponds to the age coefficient or the cognitive capacity coefficients. In Step 2, G^2 represents the difference between the G^2 of the model with age and each capacity as predictors and that of the model with only capacity as predictor.

logistic regression models did not change the general pattern of results. In an additional regression model in which speed, reasoning, and memory factors were included as predictors, only reasoning proved to be a predictive factor: $\exp(B) = 1.00$, $p = .97$, speed; $\exp(B) = 1.07$, $p < .01$, reasoning; $\exp(B) = 1.02$, $p = .52$, memory. In sum, individual differences in reasoning, a measure of fluid intelligence, account for all age-related differences in strategy selection, suggesting that older adults' increased reliance on simpler strategies is due to age-related decline in fluid intelligence.

DISCUSSION

What is the impact of cognitive aging on the selection of decision strategies? To help answer this question, we examined how young and older adults inferred which of two alternatives had a higher criterion value on the basis of several cues. Our study varied the structure of the decision environment, such that in one condition, all cues had equal predictive power, and in the other, the cues' predictive power differed substantially. This manipulation created one environment that would favor the selection of a cognitively demanding compensatory strategy and a second environment in which simpler strategies would do well. Participants' decisions were compared with the predictions of three strategies— the compensatory strategy WADD, and two simpler strategies, TTB and Take Two— to determine whether young and older adults chose appropriate strategies as a function of environmental structure when they did not have the opportunity to learn from outcome feedback. We examined how age-related differences were associated with differences in information search and strategy selection, and, in turn, how these were related to individual differences in cognitive functioning, such as fluid and crystallized abilities.

Overall, strategy selection was moderated by the environmental structure that the participants encountered: Both young and older adults appropriately selected the simpler strategies more often in the unequal validities environment compared with the equal validities environment.

Thus, older adults did not always rely on simpler strategies but were adaptive in their strategy selection. This finding is compatible with the idea that young and older adults have an equally good understanding of strategy-environment correspondence. One possibility that we raised on the basis of reports in the aging literature (Baltes et al., 1999) was that older adults could have an advantage in adaptive strategy selection because of their richer knowledge of the strategy–environment correspondence. We reasoned that such an advantage would imply that crystallized intelligence should be a good predictor of adaptive strategy selection. However, our results show virtually no relation between measures of crystallized intelligence and decision behavior. One possibility is that our measures of crystallized intelligence do not tap into the relevant knowledge. Baltes et al. (1999) distinguished between normative knowledge, associated with formal schooling and more idiosyncratic person/domain-specific knowledge. Arguably, we have measured only normative knowledge, which may not be indicative of a person's understanding of strategy-environment correspondence. However, the pattern of results we observed is more in line with the view that older adults selected the simpler strategies more frequently out of necessity; they simply did not have the cognitive resources to use the more cognitively intensive WADD: Measures of fluid intelligence (i.e., reasoning) could account for the age-related differences in both information search and strategy selection, suggesting that older adults relied on simpler strategies due to age-related decline in fluid abilities.

Relation to Previous Findings

Past research in decision making has investigated which task characteristics, such as number of alternatives and attributes, influence strategy selection (Ford et al., 1989), the dispersion of the winning probabilities in gambles (Payne et al., 1993), time pressure (Svenson & Maule, 1993), and environment structure (Bröder, 2003; Rieskamp & Otto, 2006). Overall, the work suggests that people do behave adaptively; that is, they are able to select appropriate strategies as a function of task characteristics. Hence, people are usually described as adaptive decision makers (Beach & Mitchell, 1978; Payne et al., 1993). The results of our study add to the existing body of research in that they show that adaptivity can be observed even in the absence of extensive performance feedback and for both young and older adults.

Previous research on the impact of aging on decision-making abilities has provided a good description of age-related differences in comprehension of decision problems and has showed that these are related to individual differences in fluid intelligence (e.g., Finucane et al., 2002, 2005). Our study explored the impact of aging on information integration. In particular, we investigated the strategies used to integrate cue values and arrive at an inference. We found that older adults relied on less information, which is consistent with previous results found in preferential choice (e.g., Johnson, 1990, 1993). Moreover, in the present work, we conducted a comprehensive assessment of cognitive ability and assessed the relation between ability and strategy selection. A major finding is that fluid intelligence—in particular, reasoning abilities—but not crystallized intelligence accounted for the age-related variance in strategy selection: Older adults' age-related decline in fluid intelligence seems to be related to their increased reliance on simpler strategies.

Our results are seemingly at odds with Bröder's (2003) findings on the relation between cognitive ability and strategy selection in young adults, which suggests that higher scores on fluid intelligence measures may be related to increased reliance on simpler strategies: Young adults with higher scores on a reasoning measure were more likely to select simpler strategies in the appropriate environment. However, Bröder observed this relation in inference situations in which participants learned the structure of the environment through extensive outcome feedback, suggesting that the effect of reasoning in Bröder's work may be associated with the ability to learn the structure of the environment and strategy-environment contingencies. In contrast, in our study, which did not involve learning through outcome feedback, the effect of reasoning seems to be related to people's abilities to use cognitively demanding strategies. Support for this interpretation is that other measures of fluid intelligence (e.g., memory) were also negatively correlated with the use of simpler strategies in our study but unrelated to strategy selection in Bröder (2003).

There is a close connection between our effort to understand how cognitive aging impacts adaptive selection of decision strategies and research in the arithmetic domain. For example, Lemaire et al. (2004) investigated the ability of young and older adults to select strategies as a function of arithmetic problem type and found that older adults were able to adapt to task characteristics but were in general worse in their strategy selection and application. Likewise, in our study, older adults were adaptive, adjusting their strategy selection as a function of task characteristics, but they tended to rely more often on simpler strategies than did the young adults. Overall, these results provide a picture of the aging decision maker as adaptive yet challenged by cognitive limitations.

CONCLUSION

Researchers in decision making (Gigerenzer et al., 1999; Payne et al., 1993) and aging (Baltes & Baltes, 1990) conceptualize adaptive behavior as the result of a balance between individual potential and the demands and resources provided by the environment. Our work reflects this position by characterizing aging decision makers as adaptively selecting strategies as a function of their cognitive resources and task characteristics, such as the statistical structure of environments. The focus on environmental structure delivers another important insight: Older adults' increased reliance on less cognitively demanding strategies may not always be a drawback, as these simpler strategies may fit particular environments. We hope this thought will encourage researchers in cognitive aging to study the potential of simple heuristics in decision making as well as other domains.

ACKNOWLEDGMENTS

This work was supported by the Max Planck Society and a fellowship to Rui Mata from the German

Academic Exchange Service (DAAD). The authors thank the fellows and faculty of the International Max Planck Research School "Life Course: Evolutionary and Ontogenetic Dynamics" (LIFE) and the members of the Center for Adaptive Behavior and Cognition for many helpful comments and discussions.

NOTES

1. We use environment to refer to the objects or conditions by which one is surrounded, more specifically, the statistical structure of the relevant set of objects or conditions.
2. To quantify the cognitive effort associated with the strategies TTB, Take Two, and WADD, we computed the number of elementary information processes (see Huber, 1980; Payne et al., 1988) each decision strategy required.
3. To evaluate this classification method in comparison to a classification method based on participants' inferences alone, we performed a model recovery analysis. In a model recovery analysis, different models generate data; then whether a specific method identifies the data-generating model correctly is assessed. We examined classification methods that rely only on inferences, only on search behavior, or both. The analysis showed the superiority of the classification methods that consider search (for details, see Appendix).
4. Lindenberger and Pötter (1998) have pointed out the limitations of hierarchical linear regression in providing an adequate account of variance explained due to the existing inter-correlations between predictor variables. Consequently, our findings concerning the role of fluid intelligence should receive further scrutiny in future studies which manipulate aspects of the decision task to specifically test the impact of different cognitive components (e.g., speed, reasoning, memory) on decision-making abilities.

APPENDIX

Model Recovery Analysis of the Accuracy of Classification Methods

We used model recovery techniques to test the adequacy of different classification procedures. Model recovery techniques involve (a) generating data on the basis of a known process or distribution, usually adding some variance to its outcome and (b) using some method of interest to identify the underlying structure of the data and comparing it to the known distribution underlying the data to obtain an estimate of the accuracy of the recovery process. The general strategy adopted was to determine how successful outcome-only, search-only, and outcome-and-search classification methods are at uncovering the strategies used by simulated participants. By using simulated participants, one is able to control the underlying distribution of strategy users and thus quantify the success of different methods in recovering the true state of events. Naturally, if participants perfectly apply a particular strategy throughout all trials all classification methods should be equivalent. However, people make errors when applying decision strategies and thus one should ask whether the different classification methods are equally reliable when considering different distributions and types of errors, such as errors in reading and comparing information, or in making a decision.

Data Generation

We first generated data for a number of simulated participants using one of three strategies: TTB, Take Two, and WADD. We incorporated strategy application errors by assuming that with a specific probability, the necessary elementary information processes (EIPs) of a strategy were performed incorrectly. The following EIPs were performed: (a) a storing process (READ), responsible for storing cue values in working memory, (b) a retrieval process (COMPARE), responsible for the retrieval and comparison of values in working memory, and (c) a decision process (DECIDE), responsible for the choice of a particular option. The probability with which an EIP was performed incorrectly at each time step was varied from .05 to .25. An error in the storing process led to storing a cue value as 1 when it was in fact 0, and vice versa. An error in the retrieval process consisted of not being able to see a difference between options: This led TTB and Take Two either to look up another cue if one was available or to guess if it was not; for WADD, which compares the values of the tallies of the two options after looking up all information, such a mistake always led to guessing. Finally, an error in the decision process led to the opposite choice as predicted by the strategy. For simplicity, errors in different components occurred with equal probability. The simulated participants' responses corresponded to the algorithms' responses to data from randomly selected input samples from our study.

Data Recovery

Following the data generation, we used an outcome-only, a search-only, and an outcome-and-search classification method to classify

participants as users of a particular strategy. The outcome-only classification procedure involved counting for each participant the number of inferences for which the final choice corresponded to the one predicted by the different strategies. The search-only classification procedure involved counting for each participant the number of inferences for which the information search (i.e., number of cues searched) corresponded to that predicted by the different strategies. The outcome-and-search classification involved counting for each participant the number of inferences for which the information search *and* the final choice corresponded to the

Table 22-A.   Percentage of Classifications as a Function of Generating Strategy and Error Rate

Generating strategy	Error Rate	Classification			
		TTB	Take Two	WADD	Unclassified
		Outcome-only classification			
TTB	.05	**100**	—	—	—
	.10	**87**	7	5	1
	.25	**58**	21	15	6
Take Two	.05	1	**94**	1	4
	.10	12	**40**	30	18
	.25	22	**26**	37	15
WADD	.05	—	—	**99**	1
	.10	10	8	**71**	11
	.25	25	18	**44**	13
		Search-only classification			
TTB	.05	**100**	—	—	—
	.10	**100**	—	—	—
	.25	**100**	—	—	—
Take Two	.05	—	**100**	—	—
	.10	—	**100**	—	—
	.25	—	**87**	8	5
WADD	.05	—	—	**100**	—
	.10	—	—	**100**	—
	.25	—	—	**100**	—
		Outcome-and-search classification			
TTB	.05	**100**	—	—	—
	.10	**100**	—	—	—
	.25	**100**	—	—	—
Take Two	.05	—	**100**	—	—
	.10	—	**100**	—	—
	.25	—	**87**	7	6
WADD	.05	—	—	**100**	—
	.10	—	—	**100**	—
	.25	—	—	**100**	—

Note: Percentages of accurate classifications are presented in bold. TTB = take-the-best; WADD = weighted additive rule.

predicted search and choice of the different strategies. In all methods, the strategy that predicted the most inferences correctly for a simulated participant was assigned to it.

Table 22-A1 shows the proportion of classified simulated participants as a function of the generating strategy and error rate. Each row is based on 10,000 simulated patterns. The results can be summarized as follows: The accuracy of the outcome-only classification method is sensitive to application errors; percentage of correct classifications drops substantially with increasing error rate regardless of whether the generating strategy is TTB, Take Two, or WADD. In contrast, the two classifications that consider search do not seem to be affected with increased probability of application errors regardless of error rate and strategy (with the exception of Take Two). In sum, classifications that take search into account seem to be superior to outcome-only classifications.

When do people rely on name recognition?

Introduction to Chapter 23

On the Psychology of the Recognition Heuristic: Retrieval Primacy as a Key Determinant of Its Use

For Herbert Simon, thought consists of, first, a great capacity for recognition, and second, a capability for limited search. Although recognition has played no role in classical theories of rationality and limited search only in the form of optimal stopping rules, both are key principles of bounded rationality. The recognition heuristic (Chapter 3) combines these two principles: When only one of two objects is recognized and recognition validity is substantial, search is stopped and the inference is made that the recognized object has the higher value on a criterion.

The beauty of the recognition heuristic is that it can exploit missing information, that is, the lack of recognition, to make better inferences. A famous example of the diagnostic relevance of a missing cue is provided in Arthur Conan Doyle's *The Hound of the Baskervilles*. Noting that the family dog did not bark when a murder was committed, Sherlock Holmes inferred that the dog knew the criminal and the murder was an inside job. Lack of recognition, like lack of barking, can be informative.

If a person relies on the recognition heuristic, this means that recognition trumps other cues about the recognized object, if they can be retrieved. Note that for the unrecognized object, no direct cue information can be retrieved *from memory*; otherwise the object would, of course, be recognized. It is only possible to recall something about Arthur Conan Doyle if one has heard his name or recognizes his face. Thus, there is a logical connection between recognition and further recall of cue values: Recognition is first, and recall is second. This logical relation holds for inferences from memory, but not for inferences from givens, that is, in experiments where information about the features of unknown or hypothetical companies or other objects is presented to participants who have never heard of them. This logical relation is one reason why Gigerenzer and Goldstein (Chapter 2) emphasize the difference in cognitive processes for inferences from memory and inferences from givens. The assumption that recognition has such a privileged power to terminate search for cues was consequently challenged when researchers began to test the recognition heuristic for inferences from givens (e.g., Newell & Shanks 2004).

This article by Thorsten Pachur and Ralph Hertwig deals with the primary role of recognition compared to recall. According to the authors, recognition is provided more or less automatically by the cognitive system, whereas retrieving additional cues takes longer and demands more effort. Consistent with this hypothesis, they show that response times were considerably faster when participants' inferences followed the recognition heuristic than when they did not (see also Pachur, Mata, & Schooler, 2008). In addition, participants' inference followed the recognition heuristics more often when they were put under time pressure.

The article also addresses demonstrations, for instance, by Oppenheimer (2003), that people do not always blindly follow the recognition heuristic, and asks: In what situations is recognition likely to be overruled? Connecting the recognition heuristic to Gigerenzer, Hoffrage, and Kleinbölting's (1991) theory of probabilistic mental models, Pachur and Hertwig emphasize that the heuristic is a mental tool for inference problems, as opposed to situations where no uncertain inferences need to be made and where the solution can be logically derived by constructing a "local mental model." Accordingly, the authors demonstrate that the recognition heuristic is not used when people already have conclusive criterion knowledge.

Recognition's retrieval primacy shows how characteristics of the cognitive system can constrain strategy selection. Because recognition is provided faster than further cues, memory provides the recognition heuristic with an edge on other heuristics that rely on cues whose retrieval is effortful.

CHAPTER 23

On the Psychology of the Recognition Heuristic: Retrieval Primacy as a Key Determinant of Its Use

Thorsten Pachur and Ralph Hertwig

Abstract: The recognition heuristic is a prime example of a boundedly rational mind tool that rests on an evolved capacity, recognition, and exploits environmental structures. When originally proposed, it was conjectured that no other probabilistic cue reverses the recognition-based inference (Goldstein & Gigerenzer, 2002). More recent studies challenged this view and gave rise to the argument that recognition enters inferences just like any other probabilistic cue. By linking research on the heuristic with research on recognition memory, the authors argue that the retrieval of recognition information is not tantamount to the retrieval of other probabilistic cues. Specifically, the retrieval of subjective recognition precedes that of an objective probabilistic cue and occurs at little to no cognitive cost. This retrieval primacy gives rise to 2 predictions, both of which have been empirically supported: Inferences in line with the recognition heuristic (a) are made faster than inferences inconsistent with it and (b) are more prevalent under time pressure. Suspension of the heuristic, in contrast, requires additional time, and direct knowledge of the criterion variable, if available, can trigger such suspension.

You are a contestant on the ABC show *Who Wants to Be a Millionaire.* As your final $1 million question, Regis Philbin asks you: "Which of the following two musicians has as of today sold more albums in the U.S.A.: George Strait or Billy Joel?" What is your answer? If you are American, the question may strike you as quite problematic. You may, for instance, remember that pop legend Billy Joel has won numerous Grammy Awards, was inducted into the Rock and Roll Hall of Fame, and has released several Top 10

albums. At the same time, you may also think of the many platinum albums that country music legend George Strait has earned, not to mention his many American Music Awards and Academy of Country Music honors. If the choice were tough for an American who happens to know all these facts, how difficult would it be for a European, say, a Swiss, who in all likelihood has never heard of George Strait (93% of students at the University of Basel did not recognize his name; Herzog, 2005), let alone his many achievements?

Yet, could it be that the clueless Swiss contestant would be, paradoxically, more likely to hit on the right answer than the clued-up American counterpart? More generally, is it possible that people who know less about a subject nevertheless make more correct inferences than their better-informed counterparts? Indeed, it is possible. If the less-informed person—for instance, the Swiss facing the Billy Joel versus George Strait question—exploited his or her ignorance by using the recognition heuristic, he or she would answer the question correctly (for further details on such a less-is-more effect, see Goldstein & Gigerenzer, 2002). For a two-alternative choice task, such as choosing between Billy Joel and George Strait, the recognition heuristic can be stated as follows:

If one of two objects is recognized and the other is not, then infer that the recognized object has the higher value with respect to the criterion.

Accordingly, the Swiss contestant would infer that the recognized artist has sold more albums. Having heard of both artists, the savvy American contender, ironically, knows too much to be able to take advantage of the recognition heuristic.

As with other strategies from the mental toolbox, the recognition heuristic can afford to be a simple, one-reason decision-making strategy (Gigerenzer, Todd, & the ABC Research Group, 1999) because it feeds on the outcome of an evolved (and automatized) capacity. In this case, it is the capacity for recognition that enables processes such as face, voice, and name recognition. By co-opting this capacity—that in itself is likely to be a complex ability (e.g., Wallis & Bülthoff, 1999)—the recognition heuristic taxes the cognitive resources only modestly. In addition, the recognition heuristic exploits a frequent informational regularity in the environment: Whether we recognize something is often not random but systematic. Therefore, the recognition heuristic promises to be useful, as Goldstein and Gigerenzer (2002) pointed out, whenever there is a strong correlation—in either direction—between recognition and the criterion (for simplicity, we assume henceforth that the correlation is positive). As the mind-as-an-adaptive-toolbox metaphor implies, people should resort to using other tools if this correlation is weak or even nonexistent (see also Gigerenzer & Goldstein, 1996, p. 653). Before we turn to what we know about how people appear to use recognition knowledge, we first describe how Goldstein and Gigerenzer envisioned its use.[1]

THE NONCOMPENSATORY STATUS OF RECOGNITION INFORMATION: MIXED EVIDENCE

The capacity for recognition is often assumed to have played a pivotal role in a number of adaptive problems, ranging from avoidance of strangers (Scarr & Salapatek, 1970) to avoidance of poisonous food. In these evolutionarily important domains, recognition is typically observed to be used in a noncompensatory way (e.g., Galef, McQuoid, & Whiskin, 1990). In light of its evolutionary history, Goldstein and Gigerenzer (2002, p. 77) referred to recognition as a "primordial psychological mechanism" and proposed that the capacity for recognition is being co-opted for drawing probabilistic inferences in the here and now. The recognition heuristic embodies one mind tool through which this co-optation occurs. Moreover, the same authors assumed that the typically noncompensatory status of recognition information observed in evolutionarily important domains generalizes to probabilistic inferences: "The recognition heuristic is a noncompensatory strategy: If one object is recognized and the other is not, then the inference is determined" (Goldstein & Gigerenzer, 2002, p. 82)

The term *noncompensatory* means that for a decision task that is solved using probabilistic information—cues or attributes—a choice for an object based on one attribute "cannot be reversed by other attributes of the object," that is, the attributes are not integrated into a single judgment (Elrod, Johnson, & White, 2005, p. 2; see also Payne et al., 1993, p. 29). Relatedly, the recognition heuristic is noncompensatory in that it does not allow room for the integration of recognition knowledge with other probabilistic cues: It "relies only on subjective recognition and not on objective cues" (Goldstein & Gigerenzer, 2002, p. 82). This does not mean, however, that no other knowledge—such as direct knowledge of the object's criterion value—can override the verdict of the recognition heuristic.

In an inventive set of studies, Newell and Shanks (2004) extended the test of the recognition heuristic to a situation in which participants learned to "recognize" fictional company names (consisting of nonwords—i.e., none of the names were recognized before the experiment), which were presented repeatedly to them (Bröder & Eichler, 2006, used a similar methodology). Moreover, the validity of the induced recognition was manipulated. In a subsequent judgment task the participants were to infer which of two companies—one recognized, one unrecognized—had the more profitable stock. To aid their decision, people could purchase additional cues in the form of experts' advice. The validity of the cues (i.e., recognition and the recommendations of three advisors) was learned through feedback over the course of the experiment. Consistent with the recognition heuristic, in the majority of choices the recognized company was chosen to be more profitable (88%; see Newell & Shanks, 2004, Table 2). In addition, recognition was frequently (68% of all cases) the only cue used (i.e., no further information was purchased). However, this was only so when recognition was the most valid cue. When it was the cue with the lowest validity, most participants (64%) purchased additional information and, based on the experts' advice, a substantial proportion picked the stock they did not recognize (in 38% of cases). Newell and Shanks (2004) concluded: "We found little evidence suggesting that recognition is treated any differently from other cues in the environment" (p. 932). In their view, recognition is usually integrated with other available cue knowledge (see also Richter & Späth, 2006). On the basis of the observation that knowledge of additional probabilistic cues—participants learned them during the experiment—affected the use of (induced) recognition, Bröder and Eichler (2006) arrived at the same conclusion.

Thus, Newell and Shanks's (2004) findings appear to suggest that people stray from the use of recognition as described in the model of the recognition heuristic. How representative, however, is the context in which their participants found themselves in these studies? They knew that recognition was inferior to all other accessible cues. They knew the context in which they learned to recognize an object. Outside the laboratory one is rarely so clairvoyant. For instance, one is typically not able to pin down and discern between the various contexts in which one may have previously encountered the names of cities, Goldstein and Gigerenzer's (2002) domain of inference. Thus, Newell and Shanks's (and Bröder & Eichler's, 2006) results may in fact demonstrate that an induced sense of recognition—which can be unmistakably traced to one source, the experiment—may not give rise to the same use of recognition as would a naturally evolved sense of recognition. The latter typically cannot be traced exclusively to one specific source. Such an interpretation of their results also conforms with evidence indicating that in making inferences people appear to rely less on subjective assessments of memory (e.g., processing fluency) when they can attribute this memory to the experiment than when such an explicit attribution is impossible (e.g., Jacoby, Kelley, Brown, & Jasechko, 1989; Oppenheimer, 2004; Schwarz et al., 1991).

The relation of recognition and other knowledge was also the subject of Oppenheimer's (2003) investigation. Unlike Newell and Shanks's (2004) studies, his involved recognition that partly evolved outside the laboratory. Specifically, he presented Stanford University students with pairs of well-known and fictitious cities. Their task was to choose the larger one. The well-known cities were carefully selected such that participants either knew that the city they recognized was relatively small (e.g., Sausalito in his Experiment 1) or they knew that their ability to recognize a city was due to factors other than its size (e.g., Chernobyl in his Experiment 2). In both contexts, Oppenheimer found that recognition information was overruled. The unrecognized fictitious cities were systematically inferred to be *larger* than the recognized cities (i.e., > 50% of the time).

Suspending the recognition heuristic when one explicitly knows that a city is very small, however, does not conflict with the model of the heuristic. In answering questions such as which of two cities is larger, it is plausible to assume that the mind attempts a direct solution by retrieving definitive knowledge about the criterion that gives rise to a *local mental model* (LMM; Gigerenzer, Hoffrage, & Kleinbölting, 1991). In general, an LMM can be successfully constructed if (a) precise figures can be retrieved from memory for both alternatives (e.g., cities), (b) nonoverlapping intervals of possible criterion values can be retrieved, or (c) elementary logical operations can compensate for missing knowledge (e.g., if one city is the largest or the smallest in the set, then any other will by definition be smaller or larger, respectively). An LMM represents a local and direct solution. No use of the probabilistic cue-environment structure is made, and merely the presented alternatives and their criterion values are taken into account.[2] According to Gigerenzer et al., only if no LMM can be constructed will inductive inferences involving probabilistic cues need to compensate for missing direct knowledge. The recognition heuristic is meant to be one model for such an inductive inference, in which "the criterion is not immediately accessible to the organism" (Goldstein & Gigerenzer, 2002, p. 78; see also Gigerenzer & Goldstein, 1996). Returning to Oppenheimer's (2003) results, one interpretation is that his students did not use the recognition heuristic because they succeeded in constructing an LMM, for instance, by assuming that Sausalito is so small that one can safely deduce that the other city, even if not recognized, is larger. Pohl's (2006) results can be interpreted similarly. Across four studies, he found that the choice of a recognized object depends, sometimes to a great extent, on whether this choice proves to be correct or incorrect. This contingency would arise if direct (valid) criterion knowledge were available. Finally, Richter and Späth's (2006, Experiment 1) findings are also consistent with the view that criterion knowledge mediates the use of the recognition heuristic.[3]

In our view, Newell and Shanks's (2004) and Oppenheimer's (2003) studies identified two important situations in which people clearly do not use the recognition heuristic. First, the heuristic appears not to be triggered or is overruled when recognition knowledge did not evolve naturally or when recognition can be traced to one source that is dissociated from the criterion variable. Second, the heuristic, as an inductive device, will only be used if a direct solution fails. Under these conditions, the evidence suggests

that people's inferences are not determined by recognition but by information beyond recognition. But these boundary conditions, in our view, do not warrant the conclusion that recognition information is treated on a par with any other probabilistic information. We submit the thesis that recognition information—independent of its precise confluence with direct and probabilistic knowledge—is not just like "any other" probabilistic cue (Newell & Shanks, 2004, p. 928). Because of its mnemonic properties, recognition has an exceptional status. To appreciate this thesis, let us turn next to research on recognition memory.

RECOGNITION INFORMATION: FIRST ON THE MENTAL STAGE

For more than 30 years, memory researchers have attempted to identify the processes underlying recognition judgments (see Yonelinas, 2002, for an overview). Although there is ongoing debate as to whether recognition is based on a single, global matching process (see Clark & Gronlund, 1996, for a review) or can better be described in terms of a dual-process account (e.g., Jacoby, 1991), there is consensus that two different kinds of information contribute to recognition.[4] One is a global sense of familiarity, which is "generally thought to reflect an assessment of the global similarity between studied and tested items." The other is recollection, entailing "the retrieval of specific information about studied items, such as physical attributes … , associative/ contextual information … , or other source-specifying information" (both quotes are from Curran, 2000, p. 923).

To illustrate, for the task of discriminating between a studied word and a dissimilar nonstudied word, one can often rely primarily on a global sense of familiarity. This global information, however, will not suffice to reject a word, for example, *house,* that was received aurally when the word *house* was initially studied as a written item. To reject the heard word *house,* one has to recollect associative knowledge, namely the modality in which the word was studied. Similarly, in a memory game, it does not suffice to recognize that a currently turned-over card is the counterpart of a card turned over previously. One also has to recollect the position of the previously revealed card.

A key difference between familiarity and recollection is that familiarity enters the mental stage earlier than information accrued by recollection (Gronlund & Ratcliff, 1989; Hintzman & Curran, 1994; McElree, Dolan, & Jacoby, 1999; Ratcliff & McKoon, 1989). This retrieval advantage is taken to indicate that familiarity represents an automatic form of memory, whereas recollection involves an intentional, slow, and effortful retrieval process (Atkinson & Juola, 1974; Jacoby, 1991; Mandler, 1980).

Using the distinction between familiarity and recollection, Payne, Richardson, and Howes (2000) examined the role of recognition in problem solving. Similarly, we ask whether the same distinction, and in particular, the temporal dissociation between familiarity and recollection, can also be relevant for the recognition heuristic. We believe so. First, recall that Goldstein and Gigerenzer (2002) used the term *recognition* to refer to the discrimination "between the truly novel and the previously experienced" (p. 77). To render this discrimination possible, familiarity information often suffices, and no associative information (episodic or other knowledge associated with the objects) needs to be recollected (as, for instance, in many lexical decision tasks).

Second, and more important, we suggest that the dissociation between familiarity and recollection observed in recognition tasks extends to recognition and other cue knowledge in inference tasks. Specifically, information about an object—including probabilistic cues such as whether a given German city has a soccer team or whether Billy Joel has won numerous Grammy Awards—requires effortful retrieval, just as does recollection of knowledge about the modality in which an item was studied. Recognition knowledge, by contrast and in analogy to familiarity, is provided automatically. As a consequence, recognition is first on the mental stage and ready to enter inferential processes when other probabilistic cues still await retrieval. Henceforth, we refer to these properties as the *retrieval primacy* of recognition information.

PREDICTIONS

The notion that recognition has a retrieval primacy has testable implications. In what follows, we elaborate these implications in terms of three predictions.

Prediction 1. Shorter response times are needed for recognition-based inferences. Inferences that agree with the recognition heuristic require less response time than choices that are inconsistent with the recognition heuristic.

This prediction is derived as follows: Information about a global sense of familiarity, which suffices to make a recognition judgment, is available almost immediately. Therefore inferences based on recognition will be made expeditiously. In contrast, inferences inconsistent with the recognition heuristic need to rely on information beyond recognition (unless they are produced by mere guessing), such as associative information (e.g., source information), probabilistic cues, or knowledge of the criterion variable. As the latter typically require effort and time for retrieval, such inferences will, on average, require more time than inferences consistent with the recognition heuristic.

Prediction 1 has an interesting corollary: The longer it takes to arrive at a response, the more likely the response will disagree with the recognition heuristic (provided that the additionally retrieved information contradicts the choice determined by recognition). In other words, with increasing response time there will be a monotonic drop in the proportion of inferences consistent with the recognition heuristic. This regularity follows from the fact that the more time elapses, the more knowledge beyond recognition (if available) can be retrieved. Consequently, the longer the response time, the weaker the impact of recognition on the final judgment.

Prediction 2. Time pressure fosters recognition-based inferences. Limited time to make inferences will lead to greater use of the recognition heuristic, and consequently to more inferences consistent with the heuristic.

Prediction 2 is derived as follows: Recognition is assumed to precede the retrieval of other knowledge such as probabilistic cues. Because recognition is available when other knowledge could not yet be accessed, it will have more impact on the inferences when this process is subject to time pressure.

The final set of predictions concerns the notion of the adaptive use of the recognition heuristic. Recognition information is generated automatically and thus cannot be suppressed. Arguably, this retrieval primacy, being a result of our cognitive architecture, holds irrespective of how well recognition tracks the criterion. This raises the question of how people take account of recognition when it poorly predicts the criterion. Will they then resort to other knowledge and other strategies? We conjecture that the notion of the adaptive toolbox strongly implies that people can and will resort to other strategies if reliance on recognition is anticipated to be futile. To render precise predictions possible, we exploit another key property of the recognition heuristic. The recognition heuristic is domain specific; that is, its use will only be successful if recognition is correlated with the criterion. The heuristic's attainable accuracy (i.e., the percentage of correct inferences) in an environment is indexed by the *recognition validity* α, which can be calculated as $\alpha = R / (R + W)$, where R and W equal the number of correct and incorrect inferences, respectively (across all inferences in which one object is recognized and the other is not). Typically, the recognition validity α is calculated for each participant, and the average of these "personal" αs (across participants) is then taken as an indicator of the recognition validity in a domain (see Goldstein & Gigerenzer, 2002, p. 87).

How is the heuristic used in environments in which recognition is but a poor predictor of the criterion? Gigerenzer and Goldstein (1996) acknowledged this situation and argued that "in cases where recognition does not predict the target, [the inference is performed] without the recognition principle" (p. 663). Goldstein and Gigerenzer (2002), however, did not specify any specific threshold of α for the use of the heuristic. Instead, they suggested that as long as α surpasses .5, the heuristic is used, even if conflicting and markedly more valid cues could be retrieved (given the purported noncompensatory use of

recognition). In our view, the notion of a match between environments and heuristics implies that people should resort to other knowledge if in a given domain recognition knowledge proves a poor predictor. But how would such an adaptive use be achieved? In particular, given that recognition is likely to precede the retrieval of other knowledge and is impossible to hold back, how can one adjust the heuristic's use? In what follows, we propose three hypotheses (Predictions 3a–3c) for a restrained use of the recognition heuristic in environments with low α.

Prediction 3a: Threshold hypothesis. Users of the heuristic rely invariably on recognition as long as α exceeds a threshold. If a given environment's α is below this threshold, users will not employ the heuristic.

Such a threshold hypothesis is consistent with the observation in previous studies that the mean rates of adherence to the recognition heuristic were consistently high (i.e., around 90%) in spite of highly variable αs (see, e.g., Pachur & Biele, 2007; Pohl, 2006; Reimer & Katsikopoulos, 2004; Serwe & Frings, 2006).

The threshold hypothesis suggests three testable regularities. First, although (given the currently limited knowledge) we cannot precisely pin down the numerical value of such a threshold, it should be located between .5 and the lowest α observed to date in association with a high adherence rate, namely .7 (Pachur & Biele, 2007). Second, the hypothesis predicts two distinguishable clusters of adherence rates: one encompassing high adherence rates (users whose α exceeds the threshold) and another including low adherence rates (users whose α is below the threshold). Third, there should be a strong positive correlation between individuals' αs and their adherence rates (under the assumption that people have some ability to correctly assess the validity of their recognition knowledge for a given inference task).

Prediction 3b: Matching hypothesis. Users of the heuristic follow it with a probability that matches their individual α, the recognition validity.

This hypothesis is inspired by the frequent observation of people choosing the more likely of two events with a probability matching that event's probability of success. Specifically, when people have to choose between two options A and B, and A leads to a success with probability p and B leads to a success with probability $q = 1 - p$, people respond as if they were probability matching. That is, if $p > q$, rather than always choosing A (i.e., probability maximization), they distribute their responses such that A is chosen with a probability of p and B is chosen with a probability of $1 - p$ (e.g., Gallistel, 1990; Vulkan, 2000).

In the context of the recognition heuristic, this hypothesis predicts that people match their use of the heuristic to their individual α. Consequently, the recognized object is chosen to be the larger one with a probability of $p = \alpha$, whereas the unrecognized object is chosen to be the larger one with a probability of $q = 1 - \alpha$. From this, it follows that the proportion of inferences consistent with the recognition heuristic should equal α. That is, like the threshold hypothesis, the matching hypothesis implies a strong correlation between adherence rates and individuals' αs (again assuming some correspondence between people's perceived and actual recognition validity). Pohl (2006) obtained some evidence for such a correlation. In contrast to the threshold hypothesis, the matching hypothesis does not imply two clearly distinguishable clusters of adherence rates but a graded variation in adherence rates as a function of people's α.

Prediction 3c: Suspension hypothesis. The nonuse of the recognition heuristic does not hinge on recognition validity α but on object-specific knowledge that is at odds with recognition.

Such object-specific contradictory knowledge can come in different forms, including (a) source knowledge (i.e., if a person realizes that her recognition of an object is clearly due to a factor other than the object's criterion value, for instance, the presentation of an object within an experiment) and (b) direct conflicting knowledge of an object's criterion value (see Oppenheimer, 2003), which, as pointed out above, allows for the construction of an LMM. Here we focus on the latter. If, for instance, a Stanford University student is asked to judge which city has more inhabitants, Sausalito or Gelsenkirchen, the student might zero in on Gelsenkirchen even though he

or she does not recognize this German city. The reason is that the student knows that Sausalito, with around 7,500 residents, is a very small city and therefore he or she suspends the recognition heuristic for this specific inference.

Unlike the first two hypotheses, the suspension hypothesis implies marked variability in the use of the recognition heuristic across objects and across participants. This is because some objects are more likely to be associated with direct knowledge than others (e.g., students of Stanford University are likely to know that Sausalito is comparatively small and may put the recognition heuristic aside in all pairs that involve Sausalito), and some people have direct knowledge where others lack it. By probing for the individual availability of LMMs, we will be able to investigate whether they are likely to co-occur with the nonuse of the heuristic. If they do, there will likely not be a strong link between people's αs and their recognition heuristic adherence, a link obligatory for the other two hypotheses.

Predictions 3a–3c represent three different hypotheses of how users of the recognition heuristic restrain the use of the recognition heuristic. Such restrained use may be particularly apt when α is low. Before we turn to an empirical test of Predictions 1–3, let us address an important objection. Does the notion of the recognition heuristic's adaptive use render it too flexible and, perhaps, unfalsifiable? For two reasons, we do not think so. First, the adaptive use of the heuristic implies that environments with low α are less likely to give rise to its use than environments with medium or high α. Adaptive use is thus tantamount to a robust and systematic pattern of both use and nonuse. Similarly, the specific hypotheses underlying the nonuse of the recognition heuristic define testable constraints. Nonuse is not thought to be random but to manifest itself in predictable and testable ways. By testing such constraints, we follow Newell's (2005) call to further elucidate the boundary conditions of the adaptive toolbox.

THE ENVIRONMENT

Two studies tested Predictions 1, 2, and 3. Both studies used variants of the same experimental procedure. Participants were given pairs of infectious diseases, and their task was to choose the more prevalent in each pair. We chose this domain primarily because it requires the retrieval of knowledge acquired outside the laboratory, thus liberating us from using experimentally induced recognition or artificially created environments. Equally important, Prediction 3 requires the study of an environment in which recognition is of comparatively low validity. Conveniently, such an environment is also appropriate to test Predictions 1 and 2. Both necessitate an environment in which at least some of the knowledge people have conflicts with the recognition heuristic. This is likely to happen in an environment with low recognition validity. The domain of infectious diseases represents such an environment (see Hertwig, Pachur, & Kurzenhäuser, 2005).[5]

Figure 23-1 depicts the relationships between annual incidence rates of 24 notifiable infectious diseases in Germany, the frequency with which the names of the diseases were mentioned in the media, and *collective recognition* (i.e., the proportion of participants recognizing each infection in Study 1; see Goldstein & Gigerenzer, 2002).[6] The frequencies of mentions in the media, assumed to operate as the mediator between the criterion and recognition, were determined using COSMAS (Corpus Search, Management and Analysis System) I, an extensive data archive of German daily and weekly newspaper articles.[7] We determined the number of times the names of the 24 infections were mentioned and rank correlated these numbers with collective recognition. As Figure 23-1 shows, media coverage was highly correlated with collective recognition *(surrogate correlation: $r_s = .84$, $p = .001$)*, in line with the assumption that recognition is determined by how often the names of infections occur in the environment (for which mention frequency in the media is assumed to be a proxy; Goldstein & Gigerenzer, 2002). In contrast, the correlation between the

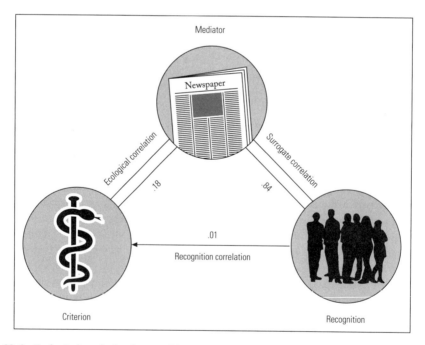

Figure 23-1. Ecological analysis of recognition. Recognition is highly correlated with media coverage, whereas both media coverage and recognition are uncorrelated with incidence rates of the infectious diseases. Recognition is a very poor indicator of incidence rates of the diseases, because media coverage, acting as mediator, does not (only) reflect the incidence rates (but possibly also the severity of the disease).

criterion and the mediator, the *ecological correlation*, was weak ($r_s = .18$, $p = .39$). It is notable that the correlation between collective recognition and the infections' incidence rates turned out to be nil ($r_s = .01$, $p = .95$). That is, the proportion of participants who recognized the infections did not reflect the actual incidence rates of the diseases. Undeniably, recognition is a poor predictor of the criterion in this environment *hostile* to the recognition heuristic.

STUDY 1: DOES THE RECOGNITION HEURISTIC GIVE WAY TO FASTER CHOICES?

If one object is recognized and the other is not, the recognition heuristic can determine the choice without searching and retrieving other probabilistic cues about the recognized object. The reversal of a choice determined by recognition, in contrast, requires retrieval of further information (unless the reversal reflects mere guessing). Hinging on this difference, Prediction 1 states that inferences agreeing with the recognition heuristic require less response time than choices that are inconsistent with the recognition heuristic. Study 1 tests this prediction as well as the predictions following from the three candidate hypotheses of how a restrained use of the recognition heuristic in environments with a low α is implemented (Prediction 3).

Method

Participants and design. Forty students from Free University (Berlin, Germany) participated in the study (27 women and 13 men, mean age = 24.2 years), which was conducted at the Max Planck Institute for Human Development in Berlin. They were presented with pairs of names of infectious diseases and asked to choose the infection with the higher annual incidence rate in a typical year in Germany (henceforth *choice task*). They also indicated which of the infections they recognized (henceforth *recognition task*). All were paid for participating. Half of the participants received a flat fee of 9 Euros ($11.80 U.S.) and monetary incentive in the form of a performance-contingent payment. Specifically, they earned 4 cents (5 cents U.S.) for each correct choice and lost 4 cents for each wrong one. The other half of participants received a flat fee of 10 Euros ($13.10 U.S.). Participants were randomly assigned to one of the four conditions of a 2 (recognition test before/after the choice task) × 2 (monetary incentive/no incentive) design, with 10 participants in each condition.

Materials. For the choice task, we used all 24 infectious diseases (see Table 23-1) and generated all 276 possible pairs, which were presented in 12 blocks (each containing 23 pairs). Both the order in which the 276 pairs of infections appeared and the order of the infections within each pair were determined at random for each participant. The recognition task comprised all 24 infections.

Procedure. After reading an introductory text explaining the relevance of accurate judgments of the frequency of dangerous infectious diseases, participants read the following instructions:

We ask you to judge the annual frequency of occurrence of different types of infections in Germany.... Each item consists of two different types of infections. The question you are to answer is: For which of the two infections is the number of new incidents per year larger?

Pairs of the names of infections were displayed on a computer screen. Participants were asked to indicate their choice by pressing one of two keys. In addition, they were instructed to keep the index fingers of the right and left hands positioned on the keys representing the right and left elements in the pair of infections, respectively, for the entire duration of one block. They were encouraged to respond as quickly and accurately as possible (although they were not told that their response times were being recorded). The time that elapsed between the presentation of the infections and participants' keystrokes was measured. Each choice began with the presentation of a fixation point (a cross in the center of the screen), followed after 1,000 ms by the infections. The names appeared simultaneously (left and right from the fixation point) and remained on the screen until a response was given. Participants were informed that once the response key was pressed, their choice could not be reversed. After each response, the screen remained blank for 1,000 ms. To accustom participants to the procedure, we asked them

Table 23-1. The 24 Infectious Diseases Used as Target Events in Studies 1 and 2

Target Event	Annual Incidence Rate	Study 1 (N = 40)			Study 2 (N = 60)				
		Recognized by % of Participants	Proportion of Choices in line with RH (M)	n	Recognized by % of Participants	Proportion of Choices in Line with RH (M)	n	Estimated Incidence (Mdn)	% of Participants with Direct Knowledge
Polionyelitis	0.25	100.0	.57	40	100.0	.70	59	50	30.0
Diphtheria	1	97.5	.66	39	98.3	.70	58	500	18.3
Trachoma	1.75	7.5	.76	3	13.3	.49	7	50	5.0
Tularemia	2	2.5	1.00	1	3.3	.57	1	50	1.7
Cholera	3	100.0	.30	40	100.0	.47	59	5	31.7
Leprosy	5	100.0	.15	40	100.0	.37	59	5	30.0
Tetanus	9	100.0	.66	40	100.0	.69	59	500	23.3
Hemorrhagic fever	10	20.0	.76	8	33.3	.82	19	500	6.7
Botulism	15	22.5	.63	8	18.3	.70	10	50	8.3
Trichinosis	22	20.0	.60	9	23.3	.67	13	50	5.0
Brucellosis	23	12.5	.66	5	15.0	.83	8	50	5.0
Leptospirosis	39	7.5	.42	3	25.0	.68	14	50	5.0
Gas gangrene	98	27.5	.38	11	28.3	.65	16	50	11.7
Ornithosis	119	7.5	.54	3	10.0	.79	5	50	5.0
Typhoid and paratyphoid	152	87.5	.46	35	90.0	.77	53	50	16.7
Q fever	179	12.5	.37	5	16.7	.56	9	50	5.0
Malaria	936	100.0	.63	40	100.0	.59	59	500	26.7
Syphilis	1,514	95.0	.59	38	100.0	.76	59	500	21.7
Shigellosis	1,627	5.0	.90	2	20.0	.64	11	50	5.0
Gonorrhea	2,926	95.0	.74	38	96.7	.72	57	5,000	18.3
Meningitis and encephalitis	4,019	97.5	.79	39	91.7	.88	54	5,000	20.0
Tuberculosis	12,619	100.0	.67	40	98.3	.69	58	500	26.7
Viral hepatitis	14,889	90.0	.91	36	86.7	.84	51	5,000	18.3
Gastroenteritis	203,864	85.0	.97	34	96.7	.92	57	200,000	26.7

Note: RH = recognition heuristic.

to respond to 10 practice trials. The practice trials consisted of 10 pairs randomly drawn from the 276 pairs of infections, which were used again in the main task.

After conclusion of the choice task, half of the participants took the recognition task. In this task, the 24 infections were presented in alphabetical order on a questionnaire, and participants indicated whether they had heard of the infection before the experiment. Half of participants took the recognition test prior to the choice task. On average, the complete session lasted around 60 min.

Results

First, we describe the obtained inferences in more detail. On average, participants scored 60.9% ($SD = 5.6\%$) correct. Neither incentives, $F(2, 35) = 0.43$, $p = .66$, nor the order of the recognition task, $F(2, 35) = 1.24$, $p = .30$, had a significant effect on the level of accuracy or the proportion of choices in line with the recognition heuristic. Therefore, we pooled the data for the following analyses. On average, participants recognized 58% (range = 37.5%–95.8%) of the 24 infections. Recognition rates are listed in Table 23-1. The frequency of recognized infections did not increase significantly when the recognition task succeeded the choice task, $t(38) = 1.31$, $p = .20$. Across all participants and items, the recognition heuristic was applicable in almost half of all pairs ($M = 48.5\%$, $SD = 8.0\%$). Finally, the average recognition validity α was .60 ($SD = .07$); thus recognition knowledge (measured in terms of α) proved, on average, modestly helpful in inferring disease incidence rates. The average knowledge validity β—expressing the accuracy in cases when both diseases were recognized—was .66 ($SD = .08$).

Did the recognition heuristic predict people's inferences? For each participant, we computed the percentage of inferences that were in line with the recognition heuristic among all cases in which it could be applied (i.e., where one infection was recognized and the other not). The mean percentage of inferences in line with the recognition heuristic was 62.1% ($Mdn = 62.7\%$). The present adherence rate is markedly lower than in Goldstein and Gigerenzer (2002), who

found proportions of 90% and higher (in a task involving choosing the larger of two cities). Hence, we succeeded in investigating an environment in which people did not obey the recognition heuristic in a substantial portion of their judgments, thus creating a test bed for Prediction 1.

Were inferences in accordance with the recognition heuristic made faster (Prediction 1)? We analyzed the response times by taking choices rather than participants as the unit of analysis. Figure 23-2 shows the 25th, 50th, and 75th percentiles of the response-time distribution, separately for inferences consistent and inconsistent with the recognition heuristic. In line with Prediction 1, we found that response times for inferences that agreed with the heuristic were substantially shorter at each of the three percentiles than choices conflicting with the heuristic.

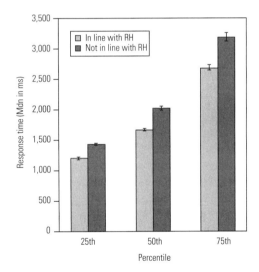

Figure 23-2. Distribution of the response times of choices where the recognition heuristic (RH) was applicable. The 25th, 50th, and 75th percentiles of response times are shown as a function of whether or not the choice was in line with the recognition heuristic. The error bars indicate standard errors. Because standard errors are not defined for percentiles, we used the standard deviations of the sampling distribution of the 25th, 50th, and 75th percentiles (Howell, 2002). These standard deviations were obtained using a bootstrapping procedure based on 10,000 draws with replacement.

For instance, the response times for the 50th percentile were 1,668 ms and 2,022.5 ms, respectively. Inferences in line with the recognition heuristic also took less time than inferences in which the recognition heuristic was not applicable, with medians of 2,032 ms and 1,953.5 ms when both diseases were unrecognized and recognized, respectively.

Prediction 1 was also confirmed by a second analysis, in which response times were natural log-transformed to reduce the skewness of the data. Figure 23-3 compares the average response times for inferences consistent and inconsistent with the recognition heuristic. Inferences that conflicted with the recognition heuristic took longer ($M = 7.7$, $SD = 0.6$) than those consistent with the recognition heuristic ($M = 7.5$, $SD = 0.6$), $t(5,353) = 10.8$, $p = .001$, Cohen's $d = 0.30$. As Figure 23-3 also shows, the response times for incorrect inferences were markedly longer than for correct inferences, irrespective of whether they agreed with the recognition heuristic. This pattern reflects a typical finding in the memory literature, especially in tasks in which the overall accuracy is low (e.g., Ratcliff & Smith, 2004).

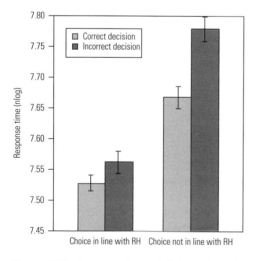

Figure 23-3. Response times of choices where the recognition heuristic (RH) was applicable as a function of whether or not the choice was in line with the recognition heuristic, and of the accuracy of the choice. Error bars indicate standard errors.

Thus, in support of Prediction 1, inferences that agreed with the recognition heuristic were made faster than those that went against it. This observation supports the notion that recognition information outruns other inferential information. The decision not to use the recognition heuristic appears to exact the cost of longer response times.

Which hypothesis captures the restricted use of the recognition heuristic best (Predictions 3a–3c)? As observed earlier, the recognition heuristic accordance is markedly lower in the infectious diseases environment than in other environments previously studied. At the same time, we have obtained support that recognition is the first cue on the mental stage, so people somehow managed to escape from relying too much on this instantaneous information. Thus, we now have an opportunity to investigate which of the proposed hypotheses—the threshold, the matching, or the suspension hypothesis—best captures people's restrained use of the recognition heuristic in this environment. We begin with the threshold hypothesis, according to which the average recognition heuristic accordance represents the combination of two clusters of adherence rates: first, the high rates of participants who invariably rely on the heuristic because their individual recognition validity α exceeds the critical threshold, and second, the low rates of those who never use the heuristic because their α is below threshold. Figure 23-4 plots each participant's adherence rate (i.e., the percentage of inferences that agreed with the recognition heuristic among all cases in which it could be applied) as a function of that participant's recognition validity α. Each point in Figure 23-4 represents 1 participant. As can be seen, the distribution of adherence rates does not resemble that implied by the threshold hypothesis. Rather than showing two clusters of adherence rates— one cluster of high rates and one of low rates— the actual rates varied continuously between 35.8% and 95.1%.

Looking at the data in Figure 23-4 also renders possible a test of the matching hypothesis. According to this hypothesis, the user of the recognition heuristic uses it with a probability corresponding to his or her recognition validity α. On an aggregate level, the proportion of choices following the recognition heuristic indeed closely matched the average α: .62 versus .60. As Figure 23-4 shows, however, when individual adherence rates and αs are considered, this match proves spurious. Rather than being lined up along the diagonal (which would indicate a strong relationship), the adherence rates vary freely at different levels of α. That is, the recognition validity is not indicative of how often the participants followed the heuristic. The correlation between participants' αs and their adherence rate is small $(r = -.19, p = .24)$, a result that disagrees with both the threshold and the matching hypotheses.[8]

Finally, according to the suspension hypothesis, object-specific knowledge in conflict with the recognition heuristic can prompt the user to suspend its use temporarily. Assuming that objects differ in the degree to which they are associated with such knowledge, the hypothesis implies varied adherence rates across objects. To investigate this possibility, we calculated for each infection (averaged across participants) the proportion of cases in which the infection was inferred to be the more frequent one, provided that it was recognized and paired with an unrecognized infection. Figure 23-5 plots

these proportions, separately for each infection (averaged across participants). Indeed, there were large differences between the infections. Some, such as gastroenteritis (.97) and viral hepatitis (.91), were almost invariably chosen over unrecognized ones (when the former were recognized). In contrast, infections such as cholera (.30) and leprosy (.15) were mostly inferred to be the less frequent ones. As Table 23-1 and Figure 23-5 show, adherence rates are by no means closely lined up with recognition rates $(r = -.10, p = .98)$: Commonly recognized infections such as cholera, leprosy, malaria, and diphtheria are not necessarily those that command high adherence rate to the recognition heuristic. What drives people's decisions to distrust recognition? We suspect it is the direct and conclusive knowledge that infections such as cholera and leprosy are virtually extinct in Germany, a possibility that we further explore in Study 2.

To summarize, we investigated three candidate hypotheses underlying the restrained use of the recognition heuristic in an environment in which the heuristic does not promise to be highly successful. Two of the three hypotheses—the threshold and the matching hypotheses—received little support: People did not invariably draw on the heuristic as a function of whether their recognition validities a surpassed a threshold (threshold hypothesis). Similarly, users of the recognition heuristic did not use it with a probability corresponding to their αs. Instead, we observed (a) only a small correlation between individuals' αs and their heuristic adherence rates and (b) enormous variability across infections in terms of participants' reliance on the recognition heuristic. The latter finding suggests that it is object-specific conflicting knowledge that prompts users not to use the heuristic. This finding raises the question of whether relying on this knowledge helped people to boost their inferential accuracy.

Could participants boost their inferential accuracy by temporarily suspending the recognition heuristic? Suspending the recognition heuristic temporarily can improve a person's accuracy (compared with the person's individual α, representing the proportion of correct choices he or she would achieve by invariably using the

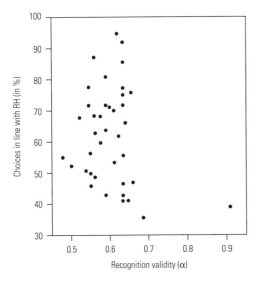

Figure 23-4. Adherence to the recognition heuristic (RH) as a function of recognition validity.

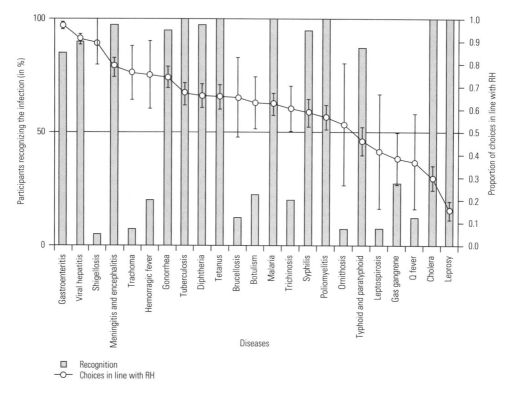

Figure 23-5. Object-specific recognition and adherence to the recognition heuristic (RH). For each disease, the average (across participants) proportion of choices in line with the predictions of the recognition heuristic (when the disease was recognized and paired with an unrecognized one) is shown. Because only one person recognized it, tularemia is not shown. Error bars indicate standard errors. The columns represent the percentage of participants who recognized the disease.

recognition heuristic whenever applicable). This boost in accuracy, however, will occur only if a person's additional knowledge exceeds the accuracy of his or her recognition knowledge. Did such a boost occur?

We tested this possibility as follows: We first turned to the general question of whether people can discriminate at all between cases in which the heuristic arrives at correct inferences and cases in which the inferences are incorrect. An analysis based on *signal detection theory* (see Appendix for the rationale and details of the analysis) yielded that participants were indeed able to distinguish—although not perfectly—between cases in which recognition would have been an invalid piece of information and those in which it would prove valid. But did this ability actually translate into a higher accuracy?

For each participant, we calculated the actual accuracy among all items in which the heuristic was applicable. Then, we compared this value with the participant's α (the level of accuracy if he or she had invariably applied the heuristic). Compared with their αs, 24 of 40 participants (60%) managed to boost their accuracy (among the cases in which the recognition heuristic was applicable) by occasionally suspending the recognition heuristic. The accuracy of 16 participants worsened. On average, there was no increase in accuracy: Across all participants, the recognition heuristic would have scored 60.3% ($SD = 6.7$) correct. In comparison, the empirical percentage correct was 60.9% ($SD = 7.4$), a nonsignificant difference: paired-samples t test, $t(39) = 0.39$, $p = .70$. In other words, by temporarily suspending the recognition heuristic, people did not succeed in increasing their inferential accuracy beyond the level attainable if they had invariably used the heuristic.

Summary

In the first study, we tested Predictions 1 and 3. Consistent with Prediction 1, we observed markedly shorter response times for recognition-based inferences: Inferences that were in line with the recognition heuristic proved to require substantially less response time than those conflicting with it (see Volz et al., 2006, for similar results). This finding is consistent with the notion of recognition's retrieval primacy. In contrast with other knowledge, recognition information arrives first on the mental stage and thus has a competitive edge over other pieces of information. Yet, people appear to frequently overrule recognition information in an environment in which there is little to no relationship between recognition and the criterion. Indeed, we found that in such an environment, the use of the recognition heuristic was restrained. Compared with the typically very high adherence rates for the recognition heuristic, we observed an average rate of about 62%. Of three candidate hypotheses concerning how a restrained use of the recognition heuristic is implemented, the suspension hypothesis obtained the strongest support (Prediction 3c). Specifically, people appear to decide case by case whether they will obey the recognition heuristic. Moreover, these decisions are not made arbitrarily but demonstrate some ability to discriminate between cases in which the recognition heuristic would have yielded correct judgments and cases in which the recognition heuristic would have led astray. This ability, however, does not result in a performance boost because the level of accuracy in cases in which the heuristic was set aside does not exceed α.

STUDY 2: DOES TIME PRESSURE INCREASE ADHERENCE TO THE RECOGNITION HEURISTIC?

In Study 1, we found evidence supportive of the notion that recognition has a retrieval primacy and that the decision to set aside recognition information requires extra time. On the basis of this evidence, we now turn to Prediction 2: Bounds on the available response time will increase reliance on the recognition heuristic and will result in a higher rate of inferences consistent with it. Study 2 tests this prediction. In addition, by manipulating the time available for an inference, we address a potential objection to our conclusions in the previous study. In Study 1, participants decided whether to respond swiftly or slowly. Response times, however, can be fast or slow for a number of reasons, including the frequency of the item words in natural language (e.g., Balota & Chumbley, 1984; Scarborough, Cortese, & Scarborough, 1977) or the sheer length of the words. As a consequence, the observed differences in response time in Study 1 could be due to factors other than use of the recognition heuristic. To address this objection, in Study 2, we forced participants to respond swiftly, thus reducing the possible impact of the type of infection (i.e., the characteristics of the infection's name). In addition, we controlled in the analysis for the possible impact of infection type on response time.

Finally, Study 2 further investigates the restrained use of the recognition heuristic in a "hostile" environment. In Study 1, we observed that participants temporarily set aside reliance on recognition. Across infections, such suspension was not distributed evenly but was more pronounced for some infections than for others (see Figure 23-5). We now explore what kind of knowledge triggers the suspension of the recognition heuristic. Consistent with the results of Oppenheimer (2003), one possibility is the presence of *direct* and *conclusive* knowledge of the incidence rate of a recognized infection that conflicts with recognition information. For instance, a person may remember that cholera has been virtually eliminated (in Germany). This knowledge suffices for the person to conclude that cholera cannot be more frequent and is likely to be less frequent than any other infection, irrespective of whether it is recognized. In general, we suggest that direct knowledge on the criterion variable will overrule recognition information if an LMM can be constructed (see Gigerenzer et al., 1991). An LMM can rest on (a) nonoverlapping criterion intervals and (b) precise figures (ranks) that in combination with elementary logical operations can compensate for missing knowledge (e.g., a particular infection is known to be the rarest infection, thus by extension any other infection is more frequent). It is worth pointing out that by measuring the availability of an LMM independently of the use or nonuse of the recognition heuristic, we can empirically test this view and either refute the suspension hypothesis or accumulate more converging evidence.

Method

Participants and design. Sixty students (none of whom had taken part in Study 1) from Free University (Berlin) participated in the study (41 women and 19 men; mean age = 24.6 years), which was conducted at the Max Planck Institute for Human Development. As in Study 1, the participants were presented with 276 pairs of infectious diseases and were asked to choose the one with the higher annual incidence rate. Furthermore, each participant indicated which infections he or she recognized. Half of the participants took this recognition test before the choice task and half after. They received an initial fee of 9 Euros ($11.80 U.S.) and earned

4 cents (5 cents U.S.) for each correct answer and lost 4 cents for each wrong answer.

Material. Participants responded to the same 276 infection pairs used in Study 1. In addition, they classified each infection in one of the following six frequency categories: < 1–9, 10–99, 100–999, 1,000–9,999, 10,000–99,999, and > 100,000.

Procedure. Participants read the same introductory text as in Study 1 (see previous Method section), after which they were presented with pairs of infections. Time pressure in this choice task was realized as follows (Figure 23-6): The pairs of infections were presented sequentially on a computer screen in 12 blocks. Each presentation was preceded by an acoustic signal (Tone 1, 10 ms in length), followed by a second signal (900 ms later) that coincided with the presentation of a small fixation cross in the middle of the screen. Again 900 ms later, the cross disappeared, and a third signal followed, accompanied by a pair of infections (left and right from the location of the fixation cross). The pair remained on the screen for 700 ms before disappearing. Participants indicated their response by pressing one of two keys on the keyboard. They were instructed to respond as quickly and as accurately as possible, but not later than a fourth

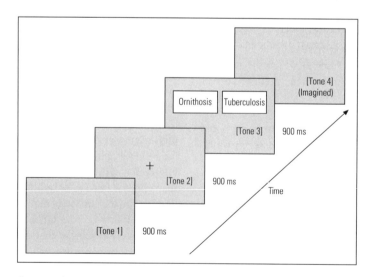

Figure 23-6. Induction of time pressure in Study 2.

imaginary signal, 900 ms after the third tone and the onset of the stimulus presentation (i.e., the signals followed each other in equally spaced intervals; see Figure 23-6). The reason for using an imaginary signal was to avoid interference of the signal indicating the response deadline with the processing of the stimulus pair (this is a procedure used in research on the lexical decision task; see, e.g., Wagenmakers, Zeelenberg, Steyvers, Shiffrin, & Raaijmakers, 2004). If a response was markedly delayed (i.e., > 1,200 ms after the presentation of the stimulus pair), the message "too late" would appear on the screen, accompanied by an aversive tone. A delayed response reduced the participant's income by 4 cents (5 cents U.S.). In the recognition task, participants saw the names of the 24 infections one at a time (in random order) on the computer screen. They were asked to decide whether they had heard of the infection and to express their positive or negative answer by pressing one of two keys. At the close of the experiment, every participant was asked to classify each infection in one of six frequency categories and to determine whether this judgment was made on the basis of certain knowledge of the criterion variable.

To acquaint participants with the procedure in the choice task, we gave them 10 practice trials. Each practice trial consisted of a pair of arrows (">" and "<", randomly ordered). The task was to indicate within the time limit whether the ">" arrow was shown on the left or right side of the screen. In a second block of 10 practice trials, arrows were replaced by the names of infections, randomly drawn from the pool of infections (and used again in the main choice task).

Results

We first describe the obtained inferences and recognition judgments in more detail. On average, participants scored 58.8% correct ($SD = 4.9$). The cap on response time resulted in somewhat fewer accurate choices, as a comparison with the average score in Study 1 shows, $t(98) = 1.99$, $p = .049$, $d = .41$. On average, participants recognized 61.0% ($SD = 12.6$, range = 41.6%–100%) of the infections (see Table 23-1). As in Study 1, the frequency of recognized infections was not affected

significantly when the recognition task succeeded the choice task (in fact, it was even slightly lower), $t(58) = -1.07$, $p = .29$. The recognition heuristic was applicable in 46.4% ($SD = 11.8$) of the pairs. A student of veterinary medicine recognized all 24 infections, thus rendering the application of the heuristic impossible. Therefore, the recognition validity α was calculated for only 59 participants. The average α was .62 ($SD = .10$), echoing the value obtained in Study 1 (.60). The knowledge validity β, however, was substantially lower than in Study 1: $Ms = .62$ versus .66, $t(98) = -3.18$, $p = .002$. It appears that, under time pressure, participants' ability to retrieve additional knowledge was compromised, thus giving way to more guessing responses when both infections were recognized.

Did time pressure increase adherence to the recognition heuristic (Prediction 2)? Consistent with Prediction 2, the proportion of choices in accordance with the recognition heuristic rose under time pressure. Bearing in mind the potential problems with cross-experimental comparisons, the mean proportion of inferences agreeing with the heuristic was 69.2% ($SD = 10.7$, range = 41.4%–90.0%), compared with 62.1% in Study 1, $t(63.5) = 2.5$, $p = .02$, $d = 0.55$. Moreover, the variance in adherence rate (across participants) was smaller in Study 2 than in Study 1, $F(1, 97) = 10.6$, $p = .02$. Note that this increase in the use of the recognition heuristic is not trivial. Time pressure could simply have provoked more guessing. In that case, the proportion of inferences agreeing with the heuristic would have dropped rather than risen. Instead it appears as if time pressure both fostered the use of the recognition heuristic and preempted the retrieval of more knowledge (thus attenuating β).

As Figure 23-7 shows, the increase in adherence to the recognition heuristic was also manifest on the level of individual infections. For 16 of the 23 infections (70%; as in Study 1, tularemia was not included), more choices agreed with the recognition heuristic than in Study 1 (see also Table 23-1). In addition, five of the six diseases for which the adherence rate dropped were among the seven diseases with the highest adherence rate in Study 1, thus suggesting a regression effect.

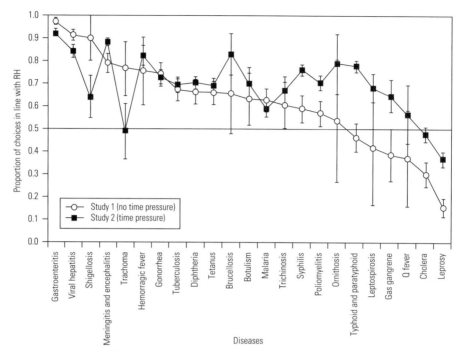

Figure 23-7. Object-specific adherence to the recognition heuristic (RH) for Studies 1 and 2 (cf. Figure 5). Tularemia, recognized by only one participant each in the two studies, is not shown. Error bars indicate standard errors.

Were inferences in accordance with the recognition heuristic made faster (Prediction 1)? Study 2 also provides another test of Prediction 1. Specifically, we can examine whether within the limited response-time window the inferences agreeing with the recognition heuristic declined as a function of time. Such an outcome would support Prediction 1, according to which inferences in line with the recognition heuristic are made faster than those that conflict with it. We divided the response-time window into eight bins, starting with 400–499 ms and ending with responses that lasted longer than 1,100 ms. (Because few responses took less than 400 ms, we omitted them from the analysis.) We then analyzed, for each bin and each infection (for the 15 infections for which there were at least 100 choices within each bin; note that again the choices rather than the participants were taken as the unit of analysis), the proportion of choices in accordance with the recognition heuristic. Figure 23-8 shows the mean proportions (across

infections, thus giving each infection the same weight) in line with the recognition heuristic as a function of response time. Note that as the proportions were calculated across infections, we control for the possibility that the different time bins contained different amounts of choices for the different infections, which could confound the influence of type of infection and response time. Proportions were above 70% for the early bins (i.e., 400–700 ms bins). For later bins, however, the mean proportion dropped rapidly. Consistent with Prediction 1, the more time a response took, the less likely it was to be consistent with the recognition heuristic.

Did conclusive and conflicting criterion knowledge trigger the heuristic's suspension? As Figure 23-7 shows, choices involving leprosy and cholera (when recognized and paired with an unrecognized disease) resulted in the lowest proportion of recognition adherence in Studies 1 and 2. Why was that? One possibility is that people assumed the diseases to be the least frequent

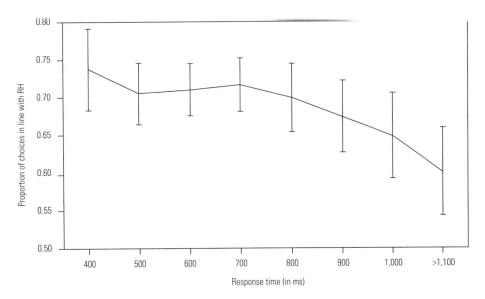

Figure 23-8. Proportion of choices following the recognition heuristic (RH) as a function of processing time. Over time, there is a decrease in the proportion of choices following the heuristic. The 15 diseases included were gastroenteritis, viral hepatitis, tuberculosis, meningitis and encephalitis, gonorrhea, syphilis, malaria, typhoid and paratyphoid, gas gangrene, hemorrhagic fever, tetanus, leprosy, cholera, diphtheria, and poliomyelitis. The number of choices in the eight bins (400–>1,100) was 141; 747; 1,639; 2,076; 1,354; 752; 260; and 267, respectively.

ones. If so, any other disease (even if not recognized) can be inferred to be more frequent than either of the two. Consistent with this view, we found that both infections produced lower frequency estimates than any other infection (see Table 23-1): The median estimate of their annual incidences was 5.[9] In addition, both infections were those for which the highest proportions of participants (30% and 31.7%, respectively; see Table 23-1) indicated that they had direct knowledge of incidence rates. These findings suggest that direct and conclusive criterion knowledge for the recognized infection—for instance, knowing that it is virtually extinct—appears to trigger the suspension of the recognition heuristic.

To assess more generally how criterion knowledge impinges on the likelihood of a recognized object being chosen, we reanalyzed people's choices when one infection was recognized but not the other. We focused on those cases in which recognition and criterion knowledge conflicted, specifically those in which the frequency estimate

for the recognized infection was *conclusively* lower than that for the unrecognized infection. Criterion knowledge was treated as conclusively lower if (a) the estimate for the recognized infection in a pair was lower than the estimate for the unrecognized one by at least two category bins (e.g., the recognized infection was assigned to frequency category "2," the unrecognized one to "4," corresponding to the frequency ranges "10–99" and "1,000–9,999," respectively),[10] and (b) the recognized infection for which a person indicated having direct criterion knowledge was assigned the lowest possible frequency category (i.e., "1") by that person. As pointed out above, both conditions may give rise to an LMM (Gigerenzer et al., 1991), thus rendering reliance on probabilistic cues such as recognition unnecessary. Collapsing across participants, 866 cases (out of 16,560, or 5.2%) met one of the two criteria. The proportion of choices of the recognized infection, averaged across participants for whom there was at least one such case, was below chance level, namely, 45.7%. In addition, the mean proportion of choices of the recognized infection when recognition and criterion knowledge converged was considerably higher, 86.4%, $t(47) = 9.9$, $p = .001$. (Criterion knowledge converging with recognition was defined as cases in which the frequency estimate for a recognized disease was higher than the frequency estimate for the unrecognized infection by at least two category bins; for instance, the recognized infection was assigned to frequency category "4," the unrecognized one to "2," etc.). These results suggest that if an LMM can be constructed, it, rather than the recognition heuristic, guides people's choices.

This conclusion was also corroborated in a reanalysis of participants' choices in Study 1. For this analysis, we took advantage of the median estimates of the diseases' incidence rates obtained in Study 2. Specifically, we focused on those 167 critical pairs (of 11,040, or 1.5%) in Study 1 that contained one unrecognized and one recognized infection, and in which the frequency estimate (from Study 2) for the recognized infection was lower than for the unrecognized one by at least two category bins. The proportion of choices of the recognized infection was 19.1% (again, across all participants where there was at least one critical pair), around 67 percentage points lower than the proportion (of the same participants) in the cases in which recognition and criterion knowledge converged (86.6%), $t(31) = -11.6$, $p = .001$.

Summary

Consistent with Prediction 2, the mean proportion of inferences in accordance with the recognition heuristic increased under time pressure. That is, the competitive edge that recognition information enjoys over other knowledge—its retrieval primacy—translates into more judgments in accordance with the heuristic when people are pressed for time. We also found additional evidence in support of Prediction 1: The longer participants took to make an inference, the lower the proportion of choices in line with the recognition heuristic. Finally, we observed that conclusive and conflicting criterion knowledge appears to be a key condition for the suspension of the recognition heuristic.

GENERAL DISCUSSION

When Goldstein and Gigerenzer (2002) proposed the recognition heuristic, they treated recognition as the ability to discriminate between the "novel and the previously experienced" (p. 77). Their intuition was that in many situations an initial sense of recognition (or lack thereof) suffices to make this discrimination. The frugal recognition heuristic does not require additional information such as in which context one encountered the object or what other knowledge about the recognized object one can marshal. Moreover, Goldstein and Gigerenzer assumed that recognition gives rise to noncompensatory inferences: If one object is recognized and the other is not, then the inference can be locked in. Because search for information is then terminated, no other—conflicting—cue information about the recognized object can reverse the judgment suggested by recognition, simply because it is not retrieved. However, this thesis of the recognition heuristic as a strictly noncompensatory strategy has been challenged. Newell and Shanks's (2004) results clearly demonstrate that judgments based on *induced* recognition are reversed when other cues are available that conflict with recognition and when their validity is known to exceed that of recognition. In their view, recognition is a cue as any other.

We aimed to demonstrate that recognition is not like any other cue. To this end, we linked research on the heuristic with research on recognition memory. On the basis of the distinction between a global sense of familiarity and recollection, we proposed that mere recognition is already available while other probabilistic cues are still waiting in the wings. It is retrieved with little to no cognitive effort, whereas other knowledge needs to be searched for. These properties represent what we have termed recognition's retrieval primacy. Based on this notion, we have derived three predictions, and the evidence we have obtained supports them.

Specifically, we found in Studies 1 and 2 that inferences in accordance with the recognition heuristic were made faster than inferences inconsistent with it. In addition, reliance on the recognition heuristic increased when inferences had to be made under time pressure. Finally, we observed that in an environment in which recognition and criterion were not strongly correlated, the recognition heuristic was not as frequently used as had been observed in environments in which there is a strong correlation. Although there are likely to be others (see below), one key factor that triggers the temporary suspension of the use of the heuristic, all other things being equal, seems to be the presence of certain and conclusive knowledge that the recognized object has a low criterion value. In what follows, we discuss the implications of our results.

Is Subjective Recognition a Compensatory or a Noncompensatory Cue: A False Dichotomy?

Goldstein and Gigerenzer (2002) depicted the recognition heuristic as noncompensatory, thus entailing inferences that cannot be reversed by additional *probabilistic cues*. In addition, they showed that treating recognition as a noncompensatory piece of information pays: Specifically, they demonstrated that the performance of compensatory models such as unit-weight or weighted-additive strategies can suffer if recognition is treated like any other cue (Gigerenzer & Goldstein, 1996, p. 660). Challenging the assumed noncompensatory status, Newell and Shanks (2004; see also Bröder & Eichler, 2006) demonstrated that when recognition validity is low, recognition information no longer dominates people's inferences.

One possible way to reconcile these conflicting views is to elaborate the circumstances under which they have been shown to hold. Take, for example, Newell and Shanks's (2004) studies: Recognition information was overruled when participants knew that recognition was an inferior cue—in fact, the worst of all available cues—when they could attribute their sense of recognition unambiguously to one source (the experiment), and when they were cognizant of the presence of superior cues. It seems fair to conclude that people outside of the psychological laboratory may rarely find themselves in such a state of omniscience. How often do we remember the exact source of our recognition knowledge? How often do we know that recognition

knowledge is inferior to any other probabilistic cue? Studies investigating processing fluency suggest that its use in inferential tasks is moderated by whether or not it can be attributed to the experiment. By extension, one may expect that recognition is less likely to be overruled in situations in which source knowledge of recognition is nonexistent or diffuse (Johnson, Hastroudi, & Lindsay, 1993), thus suggesting an unspecific, unbiased source of recognition as well as the natural mediation of the criterion variable (see Figure 23-1).

In contrast to Newell and Shanks (2004), Goldstein and Gigerenzer (2002) investigated the recognition heuristic using naturally evolved recognition. In testing its noncompensatory status, however, they pitted recognition information against a cue that was not consistently superior to α (the validity of the soccer team cue was 78%, whereas Gigerenzer and Goldstein [1996] estimated the recognition validity to be 80%). Thus, unlike in Newell and Shanks's study, and ignoring all other differences, in Goldstein and Gigerenzer's study, recognition information was not ostensibly inferior to that of objective cue knowledge. Thanks to Goldstein and Gigerenzer's and Newell and Shanks's studies and results, one can now ask: Will naturally evolved recognition be overturned by conflicting probabilistic cues with ostensibly higher validity?

Recent studies by Richter and Späth (2006, Experiments 2 and 3) addressed this question, at least partially. As in Goldstein and Gigerenzer (2002), participants were taught additional relevant cue knowledge about objects that they had learned to recognize outside the experimental setting. In contrast to Goldstein and Gigerenzer, Richter and Späth found that the frequency with which a recognized object was chosen to be the larger one in a subsequent inference task was mediated by additional cues. Specifically, recognized objects were less likely judged to be larger when cue knowledge conflicted with recognition knowledge (compared with when recognition and cue knowledge converged). Further investigation is needed, however, of the extent to which and under which conditions probabilistic cues can overturn recognition. For instance, it is still unclear how naturally evolved cue knowledge (rather than induced cue knowledge) interacts with naturally evolved recognition. Moreover, does the relative standing of recognition knowledge and cue knowledge depend on their respective validities?

Regardless of how these questions will be answered, it is important to keep in mind that, for a couple of reasons, recognition is not like any other cue. First, because of its mnemonic properties, recognition represents immediate, insuppressible, and inexpensive information. Studies 1 and 2 demonstrate the implications of these properties for inferences based on recognition. Second, recognition, if applicable, gives rise to an information asymmetry: Because a person typically has no further knowledge about a non-recognized object, further search *in memory* would typically yield additional information (if any) only about the recognized object. This information asymmetry, in turn, renders the use of information difficult. Hsee (1996; Hsee, Loewenstein, Blount, & Bazerman, 1999) showed that cue values—in particular, continuous cue values—are often ignored when they prove difficult to evaluate. Lack of a reference point (naturally provided by the other object's value), for instance, renders evaluation tricky. Consider, for example, an American student who is asked to infer which of two German cities, Augsburg or Munich, has more inhabitants. She has never heard of Augsburg but has heard of Munich. She also happens to know that Munich has, say, 500 beer gardens—a quantity that she expects to be positively related to city size. However, how big a number is 500? Lacking a standard of comparison (as the corresponding figure for Augsburg is unknown), the student may ignore this cue altogether and rely on recognition only.

Last but not least, with the ongoing debate over the noncompensatory versus compensatory use of the recognition heuristic, it is worth remembering that one of the most robust observations in the evolving science of heuristics is that different people use different heuristics. In other words, there is no single mental strategy that is consistently used by everyone. As has been shown for other fast-and-frugal heuristics (e.g., Bröder, 2000, 2003; Newell & Shanks, 2003),

there may be differences between how people exploit recognition and lack thereof. The recognition heuristic is one model of this exploitation. Some people may only rely on recognition, regardless of whether other cue knowledge is available. Others may use recognition noncompensatorily if its validity exceeds that of other cues. Still others may combine recognition with other cues into a single judgment. The task ahead is to model such individual differences and their link to the probabilistic structure of the environment (e.g., the validity of recognition and other cues).

How is the Recognition Heuristic Suspended, and is Suspension Successful?

We intentionally investigated the recognition heuristic in a real-world domain in which recognition was only weakly correlated with the criterion (see Figure 23-1). We turned to this "hostile" environment to increase the likelihood of inferences that differ from those determined by recognition and thus to be able to test Predictions 1–3. We found that people relied less on recognition, compared with a domain with a strong correlation between recognition and criterion. Although we do not yet have a solid understanding of how suspension of the heuristic is implemented, we can exclude some candidate mechanisms. First, users do not appear to employ a threshold strategy that demands suspension if α is below a specific threshold (Prediction 3a). Second, users also do not seem to adjust their reliance on recognition to α directly, as described by the matching hypothesis (Prediction 3b).

At this point, the most promising candidate is the suspension hypothesis (Prediction 3c). When time and cognitive resources are available, recognition is followed by an evaluative step in which people assess such aspects as the availability of conclusive criterion knowledge and, perhaps, the availability of source information. From this view, the use of the recognition heuristic could be understood to be akin to a two-stage process proposed in recent memory models. Such models involve a production stage followed by an evaluation stage in which aspects of the production, such as production efficacy, are interpreted and their relevance for a given cognitive task assessed (e.g., Whittlesea, 1997). Indeed, some recent results of a functional magnetic resonance imaging study of the recognition heuristic suggest that recognition knowledge fed into the heuristic might be subjected to such an evaluative filter (Volz et al., 2006).

An evaluative stage that precedes the use of recognition does not contradict the notion that recognition is immediate, insuppressible, and inexpensive. Our thesis of recognition's retrieval primacy only refers to the production of the recognition judgment. It does not refer to the evaluative filter whose activation is likely to require additional cognitive resources (and about whose precise functions one can presently only speculate). It is also unclear whether the evaluative step is a necessary condition for the use of recognition information. This seems to be Newell and Shanks's (2004) view:

> It is not that an object is recognized and chosen without justification, but that the decision-maker has a reasonable idea of why he or she recognizes the object and makes an inference based on this secondary knowledge. Under such an interpretation it is this secondary knowledge that is the driving force behind the inference, not recognition per se. (p. 933)

If, however, secondary knowledge were indeed necessary to clear recognition, the proportion of guesses would be expected to be larger under time pressure (or cognitive load) than under no time pressure, thus causing a decrease in the proportion of choices in line with recognition. We observed the opposite (Study 2).

How successful is the evaluation of recognition information prior to its use? We found that the decision to temporarily suspend the recognition heuristic may not necessarily increase inferential accuracy. To do so, the validity of the knowledge that comes into play when recognition is dismissed[11] must exceed the recognition validity (for this selected set of items). Only then does the user of the heuristic benefit from thinking twice. This raises two interesting issues. First, in environments with a strong correlation between recognition and criterion, it is plainly difficult to top the recognition validity. Thus, high rs in combination with unfavorable odds of finding even more valid information may foster the noncompensatory use of the recognition strategy in such domains. Second and conversely, a low recognition validity in combination with the better odds of finding more valid information may foster the temporary suspension of the recognition heuristic, a speculation consistent with our results.

Conclusions

The recognition heuristic piggybacks on the complex capacity for recognizing objects for making inferences. It bets on a probabilistic link between recognition and environmental quantities, thus turning partial but systematic ignorance into inferential potency. In addition, recognition precedes the arrival of any other probabilistic cue and exacts little to no cognitive cost. Notwithstanding its exceptional properties, the recognition heuristic is only one player in an ensemble of heuristics residing in the mental toolbox. Therefore, there should be limits to its use and boundary conditions that trigger other tools. In this article, we aimed to describe and model some of these conditions. Doing so is key to understanding a heuristic's psychology. In this sense, the cumulative research on the recognition heuristic—despite its currently conflicting conclusions—promises to turn into an exemplary case study in an evolving science of heuristics.

ACKNOWLEDGMENTS

This work was supported by Swiss National Science Foundation Grant 100013-107741/1 to Ralph Hertwig. Our thanks go to Gerd Gigerenzer, Ben Newell, Tim Pleskac, Caren Rotello, and Lael Schooler for many constructive comments. We also thank Laura Wiles and Anita Todd for editing the manuscript.

NOTES

1. Recognition information has been shown to be used across a range of inferential tasks such as the prediction of outcomes at sports events

(Pachur & Biele, 2007; Serwe & Frings, 2006), political elections (Marewski, Gaissmaier, Dieckmann, Schooler, & Gigerenzer, 2005), and the judgment of demographic, geographic, and biological quantities (Pohl, 2006; Reimer & Katsikopoulos, 2004; Richter & Späth, 2006).

2. Because people's knowledge is imperfect, it is not guaranteed that LMMs yield accurate solutions. Moreover, factors such as forgetting and fluctuations in retrieval performance can result in intervals of criterion values rather than precise point estimates.

3. In the decision task of Richter and Späth's (2006) Experiment 1, participants judged which of two animal species has a larger population. Additional knowledge was assessed by asking participants to indicate whether a species is an endangered one. As endangered species have by definition a small population size, this knowledge represents criterion knowledge.

4. See Gronlund and Ratcliff (1989) and Clark and Gronlund (1996) for accounts of the possible contribution of these two kinds of information to recognition judgments in (modified) global matching models.

5. Hertwig et al. (2005) did not investigate the recognition heuristic directly. However, they found only a modest correlation ($rs = .23$) between the incidence rates of the diseases and the frequency with which the infections were mentioned in the media, the latter being a strong predictor of recognition (according to Goldstein & Gigerenzer, 2002).

6. Classified as particularly dangerous, occurrences of these diseases have to be registered. To determine the correct answers, we used statistics prepared by the Federal Statistical Office of Germany and the Robert Koch Institute (e.g., Robert Koch Institute, 2001). To reduce year-to-year fluctuations, we averaged the data across 4 consecutive years (1997–2000).

7. COSMAS is the largest online archive of German literature (e.g., encyclopedias, books, and newspaper articles; http://corpora.ids-mannheim.de/~cosmas/). Our analysis was based on a total of 1,211 million words.

8. As inspection of Figure 23-4 reveals, the negative correlation is mainly due to a single participant. When this outlier is excluded, the correlation is $r = .02$ ($p = .91$).

9. We computed these values by replacing each of the six frequency categories (see *Method* section) with the midpoints of each category. For instance,

the first category ranging from 1 to 9 was replaced by the value 5. The last category "> 100,000" was replaced by the value 200,000.

10. It is noteworthy that participants did not consistently give extremely low-frequency estimates for unrecognized diseases. The mean estimated frequency (based on the midpoints of each category) for unrecognized infections was 2,378.0 ($SD = 5,771.4$), which was significantly different from the lowest frequency category, $t(57) = 3.13$, $p = .003$.

11. Note that this knowledge is not necessarily equivalent to the knowledge captured by the β parameter. It can also encompass knowledge regarding the source of one's recognition and direct criterion knowledge.

APPENDIX

To address the question of whether people are able to discriminate between cases in which the heuristic arrives at correct inferences and those for which the inferences are incorrect, we used signal detection theory (Green & Swets, 1966). This theory describes a decision maker who must choose between two (or more) alternatives on the basis of ambiguous evidence. This uncertain evidence is summarized by a random variable that has a different distribution under each of the alternatives, here correct versus incorrect inferences when the recognition heuristic is used. The evidence distributions typically overlap, thus sometimes evidence is consistent with both alternatives. To render a discrimination between the alternatives possible, the person establishes a decision criterion c that divides the continuous strength of evidence axis into regions associated with each alternative. Applied to the question examined here, if the evidence value associated with the event in question exceeds c, the person will conclude, "Following the recognition heuristic leads to a correct inference." Otherwise he or she will conclude, "Following the recognition heuristic leads to an incorrect inference." The person's conclusions can result in four types of outcomes: hits (use of the recognition heuristic yields a correct inference), correct rejections (suspending it yields a correct inference), misses (suspending it yields an incorrect inference), and false alarms (use of the recognition heuristic yields an incorrect inference).

One measure of a person's ability to distinguish between cases in which the recognition heuristic ought and ought not to be used is the distance between the means of the distributions under the two alternatives. If this sensitivity index, d', is small (i.e., the two distributions overlap considerably), a person's decision to temporarily suspend the recognition heuristic is not likely to be more accurate than chance. Across all participants, the observed mean d' differed significantly from zero ($M = .56$, $SD = .43$), $t(38) = 8.11$, $p = .001$. Because 1 participant had a false-alarm rate of zero, the sensitivity measure d' could be calculated for only 39 participants. The d' measure was highly correlated with the sensitivity measure A' ($M = .67$, $SD = .11$), $r = .98$. The mean hit and false-alarm rates were .70 ($SD = .16$) and .50 ($SD = .21$), respectively. Participants thus exhibited some ability to distinguish between cases in which recognition would have been an invalid piece of information and those in which it would prove valid.

Introduction to Chapter 24

The Recognition Heuristic in Memory-Based Inference: Is Recognition a Non-compensatory Cue?

Many heuristics process information without making trade-offs, that is, in a noncompensatory way. For instance, the "availability heuristic" predicts that judgments are based on the ease with which things come to mind. The "affect heuristic" captures the notion that judgments are based on the affective tag associated with an object. Both heuristics suggest that people make judgments based on only a single piece of information—ease of retrieval and affect, respectively—and ignore all further information. Being described phenomenologically rather than in a precise process model, the assumption of noncompensatory processing is usually not spelled out in these heuristics. Perhaps this explains why one-reason decision making embodied in the heuristics of the heuristics-and-biases program has sparked so little debate.

Not so with the recognition heuristic. When Goldstein and Gigerenzer (2002) spelled out that recognition overrides further probabilistic cues, their assumption of noncompensatory processing drew heavy fire. In their article, Thorsten Pachur, Arndt Bröder, and Julian Marewski address those critics, many of whom tested the heuristic in situations that deviated substantially from what Goldstein and Gigerenzer had in mind. Pachur and colleagues show that in a domain where the recognition validity is high, inferences from memory frequently follow recognition, irrespective of the number of cues contradicting it. Individual analyses revealed strong individual differences. Nevertheless, an amazing 50% of the participants in their study chose the recognized object in every single trial, even when they had knowledge of three cues indicating that the recognized object had a small criterion value. As predicted by the recognition heuristic, cue knowledge beyond recognition often seemed to be ignored.

The authors' investigations were prompted by Bröder and Eichler's (2006) study, in which recognition and additional cue knowledge were induced experimentally. Bröder and Eichler argued that—contrary to the predictions of the recognition heuristic—the amount of knowledge beyond recognition had a strong impact on the degree to which people judged a recognized city to be larger than an unrecognized one. Pachur and Marewski, however, wondered about the appropriateness of this test, in which recognition and its validity were not acquired in natural environments. When Bröder spent 7 months with the ABC Research Group, they therefore seized the opportunity to jointly investigate whether the use of recognition depends on its being merely experimentally induced or naturally acquired. Indeed, it seems as if the psychological power of recognition cannot be easily captured with experiments in which recognition is induced rather than learned in people's natural environments.

CHAPTER 24

The Recognition Heuristic in Memory-Based Inference: Is Recognition a Non-compensatory Cue?

Thorsten Pachur, Arndt Bröder, and Julian N. Marewski

Abstract: The recognition heuristic makes the strong claim that probabilistic inferences in which a recognized object is compared to an unrecognized one are made solely on the basis of whether the objects are recognized or not, ignoring all other available cues. This claim has been seriously challenged by a number of studies that have shown a clear effect of additional cue knowledge. In most of these studies, either recognition knowledge was acquired during the experiment, and/or additional cues were provided to participants. However, the recognition heuristic is more likely to be a tool for exploiting natural (rather than induced) recognition when inferences have to be made from memory. In our study on natural recognition and inferences from memory, around 85% of the inferences followed recognition information even when participants had learned three cues that contradicted recognition and when some of the contradictory cues were deemed more valid than recognition. Nevertheless, there were strong individual differences in the use of recognition. Whereas about half of the participants chose the recognized object regardless of the number of conflicting cues— suggestive of the hypothesized noncompensatory processing of recognition—the remaining participants were influenced by the additional knowledge. In addition, we found that the use of recognition for an inference may be affected by whether additional cue knowledge has been learned outside or within the experimental setting.

One important insight into how boundedly rational agents simplify a decision task is the notion that they use noncompensatory strategies (Einhorn, 1970; Keeney & Raiffa, 1993; Simon, 1955; Tversky, 1972). Rather than integrating all the available cue information—and thus

* This article presents collaborative work of proponents (T.P., J.N.M.) and a skeptic (A.B.) of the recognition heuristic. Although minor disagreements remain on aspects of interpretation and emphasis, the text represents compromise statements that are acceptable to all authors.

allowing a low value on one cue to be compensated for by a high value on another—noncompensatory strategies ignore some of the information. From a review of 45 process-tracing studies, Ford, Schmitt, Schechtman, Hults, and Doherty (1989) concluded that noncompensatory strategies actually represent the dominant mode used by decision makers.[1]

Goldstein and Gigerenzer (2002) proposed a particularly simple noncompensatory strategy: the *recognition heuristic.* This *fast-and-frugal* decision rule is assumed to be part of an "adaptive toolbox," from which decision strategies are selected according to the current task environment (Gigerenzer, Todd, & the ABC Research Group, 1999). The recognition heuristic was proposed for the task of inferring—based on probabilistic cues (i.e., known features of the objects that are correlated with the objects' criterion values)—which of two objects has a higher value on a quantitative criterion. The heuristic is an elaboration of an idea developed earlier by Gigerenzer and Goldstein (1996); they proposed that when recognition is a valid cue in the reference class and when cues are not provided by the experimenter (i.e., which would be an *inference from givens*) but have to be retrieved from memory (i.e., *inference from memory*), inferences are often based exclusively on recognition.[2] To illustrate: suppose you are asked which of two German cities has a higher population, Frankfurt or Koblenz. If you have never heard of Koblenz but are familiar with the city name Frankfurt (and do not know its population size), the recognition heuristic predicts that you will judge Frankfurt to have a larger population. This choice would be rather smart because recognition is often correlated with quantity in the environment, in this case, city size. Indeed recognition has been shown to be a valid predictor in many domains, such as geographical quantities (Goldstein & Gigerenzer, 2002; Pohl, 2006), quality of American colleges (Hertwig & Todd, 2003), success in sports (Pachur & Biele, 2007; Scheibehenne & Bröder, 2007; Serwe & Frings, 2006; Snook & Cullen, 2006), political elections (Marewski, Gaissmaier, Dieckmann, Schooler, & Gigerenzer, 2005), and, to some extent, disease incidence rates (Pachur & Hertwig, 2006).

The important point is that Goldstein and Gigerenzer (2002) proposed the recognition heuristic as a noncompensatory strategy: "No other information about the unrecognized object is searched for and, therefore, no other information can reverse the choice determined by recognition" (p. 82). In other words, even when people have access to additional relevant cue knowledge—by which we mean knowledge about an object's value on a probabilistic cue that indicates its criterion value—search is stopped after assessing recognition of the two objects, and the recognized object is chosen. For instance, in the German cities example, other characteristics of the cities that are correlated with their size (e.g., whether they have an international airport) are ignored. The recognition heuristic thus predicts that the recognized object is chosen even when other cue knowledge is known that suggests that the recognized object has a small criterion value.

The thesis that recognition gives rise to noncompensatory processing when it is a valid cue was tested empirically (and, as the authors claimed, corroborated) in Goldstein and Gigerenzer's (2002) second study, but it has been challenged by a number of other studies since then. In this paper, we first briefly review Goldstein and Gigerenzer's (2002) empirical evidence and then offer an overview of other findings conflicting with the claim that recognition gives rise to noncompensatory processing. Second, we discuss possible objections to the conclusions drawn from these challenging results. Third, we present three experimental studies in which we address two major objections: (a) that experimentally induced (rather than natural) recognition might affect the way it is used as a probabilistic cue and (b) that teaching participants cue knowledge during an experiment might (artificially) enhance its use.[3] Moreover, in contrast to most previous studies on the recognition heuristic (e.g., Bröder & Eichler, 2006; Richter & Späth, 2006; but see Newell & Shanks, 2004), we not only examine participants' choice behavior on the aggregate level but also look at possible individual differences in how recognition information is used.

PREVIOUS TESTS OF THE NONCOMPENSATORY STATUS OF RECOGNITION

In Goldstein and Gigerenzer (2002; Study 2), U.S. participants were informed that in about 78% of cases German cities that have a soccer team in the premier league are larger than cities that do not. In addition, participants learned whether certain recognized cities had a soccer team or not (nothing was learned about unrecognized cities). In a subsequent inference task in which they were asked to pick the larger of two cities, participants chose a recognized city over an unrecognized one in 92% of all cases even when they had learned that the recognized city had no soccer team (and thus recognition information was contradicted by additional cue knowledge). According to Goldstein and Gigerenzer, this "supports the hypothesis that the recognition heuristic was applied in a non-compensatory fashion" (p. 83). This conclusion has been questioned for a number of methodological reasons (summarized in Bröder & Eichler, 2006; Newell & Fernandez, 2006; Richter & Späth, 2006). The main counterargument is that one additional cue that is less valid than recognition would not suffice to reverse a recognition-based judgment. Even if people integrate recognition with this cue, their judgments could be indistinguishable from judgments based exclusively on recognition.

A first set of empirical studies challenging the claim that recognition is used in a noncompensatory fashion was presented by Oppenheimer (2003). In Experiment 1, Stanford University students were presented with pairs consisting of small nearby cities, which were highly recognized (e.g., Sausalito), and fictitious cities (a diverse set of made-up foreign-sounding names, such as Heinjing) about which no further knowledge was available.[4] The task was to decide which city is larger, and here participants' choices often did not conform to the recognition heuristic. In Experiment 2, participants compared the artificial stimuli to cities that were well-known for reasons other than their size (e.g., Chernobyl). Again, the recognized cities were not chosen very often. In both studies participants clearly based their judgments not just on the recognition cue, but also considered additional knowledge (although this knowledge was probably not cue knowledge, but criterion and source knowledge; we will turn to this issue shortly).

Newell and Shanks (2004) attempted to achieve more experimental control over the cue and recognition knowledge that people could use for a probabilistic inference. In two experiments they set up a hypothetical stock market in which some artificial company names were presented repeatedly—participants thus learned to recognize these names during the experiment. Participants also learned that this induced recognition was a valid cue to predict the success of stocks. To judge which of two stocks is more profitable, participants were able to acquire—at some cost—advice from three experts, so the experiments involved inferences from givens (rather than inferences from memory). As it turned out, participants often purchased additional information (48% of the time), even when they had seen one company name before but not the other. Moreover, when the purchased advice was favorable to the unrecognized stock, the unrecognized stock was chosen almost 60% of the time, so this additional information was clearly incorporated into the decision.

Using a methodology similar to that of Newell and Shanks (2004), Bröder and Eichler (2006) repeatedly presented unknown city names to participants. In addition, participants had to memorize further cue knowledge about the cities they learned to recognize. Subsequently, they had to decide which of two cities was larger, which, in contrast to Newell and Shanks' experiments, thus represented inferences from memory. The judgments about pairs in which one city was recognized but the other was not showed that the additional cue knowledge had a large impact on the proportion of judgments that followed recognition (see Figure 24-1a). This finding is inconsistent with the claim that recognition is used in a noncompensatory fashion.

A series of experiments that involved both natural recognition and a memory-based design was reported by Richter and Späth (2006). Participants had to judge the population sizes of animal species (Experiment 1), airline safety (Experiment 2), and city sizes (Experiment 3). Well-recognized and unrecognized names had been identified in pre-studies. Moreover, in all experiments additional knowledge was available (for some recognized objects), and in Experiments 2 and 3 participants acquired cue knowledge in a learning phase. All three experiments showed that the knowledge that participants had in addition to name recognition exerted an influence on their judgments. Figure 24-1b shows the impact of additional cue knowledge in Experiment 2. As in Bröder and Eichler (2006), the proportion of choices of the recognized object increased monotonically with the number of positive cues; again this challenges the claim that recognition is used in a noncompensatory way.

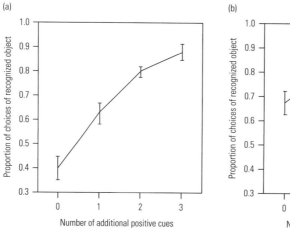 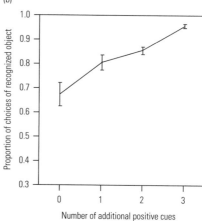

Figure 24-1. Proportion of choices of recognized object in (**a**) Bröder and Eichler (2006) and (**b**) Richter and Späth (2006; Experiment 2). Error bars show ±1 standard error.

Newell and Fernandez (2006; Experiment 1) replicated Goldstein and Gigerenzer's Study 2 but added a second condition in which the soccer team cue was a more useful indicator of a city's size (specifically, the probability that an unrecognized city had a soccer team was increased). In this second condition, only 55.5% of the judgments were consistent with recognition, whereas this was the case for 72.6% of the judgments in the replication of the original study. Hence, the additional cue clearly influenced the judgments.

Last but not least, Pohl (2006) presented four experiments in which Swiss, German, Italian, and Belgian cities, as well as mountains, rivers, and islands, had to be judged on various quantitative target variables. Based on the objects' recognition ratings and their values on the target variables, Pohl divided the items in the judgment task into two sets: In one set the recognition heuristic led to a correct decision, and in the other set, to an incorrect decision. Comparing these two sets, Pohl found significant differences in the proportion of judgments that followed recognition. This implies that additional knowledge *must* have been used, because otherwise, ceteris paribus, the proportions of judgments following recognition would not differ between the two sets of items.

HOW CAN THE RECOGNITION HEURISTIC BE TESTED?

Note that *none* of the experiments reviewed denies that recognition (be it binary or continuous; see Newell & Fernandez, 2006; but see Schooler & Hertwig, 2005) plays a major role in decision-making. For example, Bröder and Eichler (2006) demonstrated that the recognition cue entailed a large additional effect (partial $\eta^2 = .52$). This effect was obtained when trials where recognized cities for which people had additional cue knowledge were paired with unrecognized cities were contrasted with trials where these recognized cities were paired with merely recognized ones (for which no further cue knowledge was available). However, all experiments (except Goldstein & Gigerenzer, 2002) claim to show that recognition is not used exclusively and thus that the recognition heuristic is not descriptive of how people make judgments. At the same time, most of these studies tested the recognition heuristic in experimental situations that differed in potentially critical ways from the situations for which Goldstein and Gigerenzer formulated the heuristic. An overview of the methodological differences between previous tests of the noncompensatory use of recognition is shown in Table 24-1. In the

Table 24-1. Methodological Differences in Previous Experiments Testing the Noncompensatory Use of Recognition

	Oppenheimer (2003, Exp. 1)	Oppenheimer (2003, Exp. 2)	Newell and Shanks (2004, Exp. 1)	Newell and Shanks (2004, Exp. 2)	Bröder and Eichler (2006)	Richter and Späth (2006, Exp. 1)	Richter and Späth (2006, Exp. 2)	Richter and Späth (2006, Exp. 3)	Pohl (2006, Exps. 1–4)	Newell and Fernandez (2006, Exp. 1)
Induced (rather than natural) recognition			X	X	X					X
Induced (rather than natural) cue knowledge			X	X	X		X	X		
Criterion (instead of cue) knowledge		X				X				
Menu-based (rather than memory-based) inference			X	X						
Domain with low recognition validity			(X)[a]			X	X			
Unknown nature of additional cue knowledge									X	
Artificial stimuli		(X)[b]	X	X	(X)[c]					
Cue knowledge available about unrecognized object			X							(X)[d]

Notes:
[a] Newell and Shanks (2004) manipulated the recognition validity experimentally and used both a high validity and a low validity condition.
[b] Oppenheimer (2003) used a mixture of artificial and real stimuli.
[c] The stimuli used by Bröder and Eichler (2006) were real cities, but were selected for being unrecognized by most participants.
[d] Newell and Fernandez (2006) provided information about the unrecognized object only indirectly, as they manipulated the probability that the unrecognized object has a particular cue value.

following, we focus on four central issues: the availability of conclusive criterion knowledge, the use of induced recognition, the use of induced cue knowledge, and low recognition validity.

Conclusive Criterion Knowledge

Goldstein and Gigerenzer (2002) formulated the recognition heuristic for "cases of inference, [where] the criterion is not immediately accessible to the organism" (p. 78) and where an inference has to be made based on probabilistic cues. In Oppenheimer (2003; Experiment 1), however, it is likely that participants knew the sizes of the recognized nearby cities and that the sizes were very small (e.g., Sausalito has around 7,000 inhabitants). If one makes the—not completely implausible—assumption that participants believed that the typical city size in the countries alluded to by the fictitious names (e.g., China) was rather large, this knowledge could be used to deduce that the recognized city is the smaller one. From the perspective of Gigerenzer, Hoffrage, and Kleinbölting's (1991) theory of probabilistic mental models (PMM), one could thus argue that participants might have solved the task based on a local mental model (LMM). In contrast to a PMM, an LMM does not exploit the probability structure of the environment (e.g., the recognition cue; see Gigerenzer et al., 1991, for further details). In other words, in a situation where an inference can be deduced the use of a tool for probabilistic inductive inference is unnecessary (although the decision might still involve some uncertainty). Similarly, in Richter and Späth's (2006) Experiment 1, additional knowledge was defined as knowing whether a species is endangered, which is equivalent to knowing whether a population is very small. Both of these experiments thus might have involved *conclusive criterion knowledge* (rather than cue knowledge; Pachur & Hertwig, 2006), defined as direct knowledge of an object's criterion value that locates the object on an extreme (either very high or very low) position on the criterion dimension; conclusive criterion knowledge allows a decision maker to deduce a judgment without engaging in processes of inductive inference. For instance, if one knows that a disease is practically extinct, one can deduce that it is less frequent

than any other disease. Conclusive criterion knowledge could also—at least partially—have driven the results reported by Pohl (2006), where the nature of the knowledge that was available in addition to recognition information was unclear: Participants merely indicated whether they also had further knowledge about an object, but not whether it was cue or criterion knowledge.

Use of Induced Recognition

In both Newell and Shanks (2004) and Bröder and Eichler (2006), recognition was induced during the experiment rather than having been established outside the experimental setting, and participants were able to clearly attribute their recognition knowledge to this manipulation (in Newell and Shanks' experiments, participants were even explicitly reminded that their recognition was restricted to the experimental context; see p. 926). As the ecological rationality of the recognition heuristic lies in its "ability to exploit the structure of the information in *natural* environments" (Goldstein & Gigerenzer, 2002, p. 76, emphasis added), experimenter-induced recognition may not be the appropriate test-bed for the heuristic (although it is of course possible that a heuristic evolved in natural environments is also applied in artificial ones). As is well-known for other assessments of memory (such as fluency or the number of recalled instances), people use such assessments considerably less to infer quantities outside the laboratory situation when they believe that memory has been manipulated experimentally (e.g., Jacoby, Kelley, Brown, & Jasechko, 1989; Oppenheimer, 2004; Schwarz, Bless, Strack, Klumpp, Rittenauer-Schatka, & Simons, 1991)—or, more generally, when they can pin down the source of the memory to one specific factor. It is thus conceivable that, analogously, people rely less on recognition that was induced in the laboratory than on recognition that evolved outside the experimental setting (where one's recognition typically cannot be attributed exclusively to a specific source). As a consequence, in tests of the recognition heuristic using induced (rather than natural) recognition, recognition information could be underweighted. Consistent with this hypothesis, Marewski, Gaissmaier, Schooler, Goldstein, and Gigerenzer (2010) observed that experimentally induced recognition was followed less in inferential judgments when participants knew that it was induced compared to when they falsely believed that they had acquired it outside the laboratory.

Note, however, that the fact that natural and induced forms of recognition seem to be treated differently for inferences implies that people do indeed take the source of recognition (if a specific one sticks out) into account—a process that Goldstein and Gigerenzer did not consider in their original model. Such attribution or evaluation processes are also apparent in Oppenheimer (2003; Experiment 2), where people only rarely relied on recognition of cities they knew because of a factor that was clearly unrelated to the city's size. Evidence for the involvement of evaluation processes was also provided by a functional magnetic resonance imaging (fMRI) study by Volz, Schooler, Schubotz, Raab, Gigerenzer, and von Cramon (2006), who observed neural activity that is usually associated with metacognitive evaluation processes in situations in which the recognition heuristic could be applied.

Use of Induced Cue Knowledge

All the above reviewed experiments in which additional knowledge was controlled involved induced cue knowledge. That is, participants were instructed to memorize cue knowledge immediately before making their inferences (Newell & Fernandez, 2006; Bröder & Eichler, 2006; Goldstein & Gigerenzer, 2002; Richter & Späth, 2006, Experiments 2 and 3) or the cues were provided to them on a computer screen (Newell & Shanks, 2004). To be sure, this procedure allowed the experimenter to control which information participants could use for an inference. Nevertheless, inducing cue knowledge can potentially increase participants' tendency to search and use additional cue knowledge due a demand effect. Specifically, the participant might ask: "Why would the experimenter provide a cue if I am not supposed to use it?" (e.g., Grice, 1975; Hilton, 1995); teaching the cue values might thus make participants pay more attention to additional cue knowledge than they usually would. As regards the menu-based procedure

used by Newell and Shanks (2004), where cue knowledge does not have to be retrieved from memory but is presented on the computer screen, it has been shown that the use of noncompensatory decision strategies such as take-the-best (TTB) is much more prevalent in memory-based than in menu-based decisions (Bröder & Schiffer, 2003, 2006). Taken together, inducing cue knowledge in the experiment might lead to an overweighting of this knowledge.

Low Recognition Validity

According to the notion of an adaptive toolbox, whether the recognition heuristic is selected depends on the current task environment. One central aspect of the task environment is the validity of the recognition cue in the reference class from which the items are drawn (see Gigerenzer et al., 1991). Accordingly, one should assume that the heuristic is used in particular when recognition is a good predictor of the criterion, but considerably less when recognition is only slightly better than chance. (In fact, recognition might be used in more complex ways when its validity is low. For a test of possible mechanisms for suspending the use of recognition, see Pachur & Hertwig, 2006.) Pohl (2006) provides some evidence in support of this assumption. One can thus argue that in Richter and Späth's (2006) Experiments 1 and 2, the recognition heuristic (i.e., using recognition as the sole basis for a judgment) was not an adaptive strategy. In Experiment 1, where participants judged the population size of animal species, the recognition validity was probably low since both very common *and* endangered (and thus very rare) species are well-known. In Experiment 2, the correlation between recognition rates and airline casualties per person miles was −.28 only *after* controlling for the year in which the airline was established. First, this correlation is rather low, and second, controlling for the year in which the airline was established seems unwarranted, since this information is usually unavailable to participants.

In our view, those studies that might have involved conclusive criterion knowledge (rather than cue knowledge) and those that used a low-validity domain are the least critical tests of the recognition heuristic (Oppenheimer, 2003, Experiment 1; Richter & Späth, 2006, Experiments 1 and 2). When conclusive criterion knowledge is available, no probabilistic inference is required. In domains with low recognition validity, the use of the heuristic is not adaptive—although we agree that studying people's use of the recognition heuristic in such environments is important for testing the notion of adaptive decision-making. Two further studies involved experimentally induced rather than naturally acquired recognition (Bröder & Eichler, 2006; Newell & Shanks, 2004). Finally, all studies that pitted recognition against contradictory cue knowledge involved induced rather than natural cue knowledge (Bröder & Eichler, 2006; Goldstein & Gigerenzer, 2002; Newell & Fernandez, 2006; Newell & Shanks, 2004; Richter & Späth, 2006, Experiments 2 and 3). We submit that teaching cue knowledge to participants in the context of the experimental setting might create a demand effect and thus artificially enhance the use of additional cues. Of the previous experiments, Richter and Späth's (2006) Experiment 3 represents, in our view, the best test hitherto conducted of the claim that recognition is used in a noncompensatory way. This experiment involved the task of judging city sizes, a domain where a high recognition validity has been established (see Goldstein & Gigerenzer, 2002), along with natural recognition and a memory-based procedure. The only critical point concerns the teaching of cue knowledge, which could create a demand effect. We will address this objection in our Experiment 3.

Before we go on, two comments are in order. First, even if we argue that some of the criticism of the recognition heuristic may be unwarranted, we do not wish to devalue the studies that fuelled the criticism. Rather, we see them as important tests of how far the idea of noncompensatory processing of recognition can be taken; these tests identified a number of important moderating factors, some of which had been anticipated by Goldstein and Gigerenzer (2002). Second, despite our reservations concerning some of the evidence against the recognition heuristic, we still think it is necessary to revise the original model. We see increasing evidence that people

do evaluate the validity of recognition for a specific decision situation (e.g., Oppenheimer, 2003, Experiment 2; Volz et al., 2006). Goldstein and Gigerenzer's original version of the model, however, is mute in this regard, or assumes that the source of one's recognition is disregarded (cf. Goldstein & Gigerenzer, 2002, p. 76). For a more veridical description of how recognition is used for inferences, a revision of the recognition heuristic should make these processes more explicit. In this paper, however, we focus on testing the heuristic under the circumstances that fit the purposes of the heuristic as it was originally formulated. Under these circumstances, do people follow recognition even when substantive evidence points against it?

OVERVIEW OF THE EXPERIMENTS

Our general approach to testing the noncompensatory use of recognition was as follows: We contrasted the situation in which an unrecognized city was compared with a recognized city and the participants had cue knowledge indicating that the recognized city was small with the situation in which participants had cue knowledge indicating that the recognized city was large. To avoid the potential limitations of earlier studies outlined in the previous section, in our experiments we used naturally acquired recognition about real objects in a high-validity domain (cities) and assessed the impact of cue knowledge in a memory-based setting. Experiments 1 and 2 assessed participants' use of additional cue knowledge taught in the laboratory, whereas Experiment 3 assessed the impact of *natural* (rather than induced) cue knowledge, which participants had acquired outside the experimental situation. The relevant cues were determined in a pre-study with a different sample of participants. In our view, this constitutes a fair and strict test of the hypothesis that recognition is used in a noncompensatory fashion. We thus strove (a) to examine whether additional cue knowledge affects the proportion of cases where a recognized city is chosen over an unrecognized one in a situation in which recognition is natural (while, in Experiments 1–2, manipulating the additional cue knowledge) and

(b) to assess the effect of inducing cue knowledge by comparing results to a situation where cue knowledge is not manipulated. Although most previous studies only looked at choices on an aggregate level, we also analysed participants individually. An analysis on the individual level may be important as even when only a minority of participants use recognition in a compensatory way (whereas all others use it in a noncompensatory fashion), on the aggregate level it may look as if recognition is generally used in a compensatory way.

In Experiment 1, participants learned additional cue knowledge about cities that—as shown in a pre-study with German participants—were highly recognized and for which relatively little cue knowledge was available. In Experiment 2, the amount of cue knowledge contradicting recognition was increased. Importantly, at no point during the learning or the judgment phases of Experiments 1 and 2 was the potential usefulness of the cues for making inferences about the cities mentioned; rather, we relied on participants' subjective assessment of the relevance of these cues. Participants' subsequent estimates of the cue validities confirmed that the selected cues were indeed perceived to be valid indicators of the size of British cities. Nevertheless, teaching cue knowledge might still artificially enhance the use of additional cue knowledge. Therefore, in Experiment 3, rather than teaching cue knowledge to participants, we examined the impact of pre-existing cue knowledge. In all three experiments, we obtained participants' subjective validity ratings for the cues involved, allowing, to the best of our knowledge for the first time, the comparison of the perceived validities of natural recognition and other cues.

EXPERIMENT 1: DOES INDUCED CUE KNOWLEDGE OVERRIDE NATURAL RECOGNITION?

The first experiment had the goal of replicating the results found by Bröder and Eichler (2006) using natural rather than induced recognition. We thus addressed the possibility that induced recognition is treated differently from natural recognition (i.e., recognition knowledge that

arises through the natural process of encountering objects in the real world). We predicted that if participants trust their natural recognition knowledge more than experimentally induced recognition, additional cue knowledge should be less likely to overturn recognition in people's inferences.

Method

Participants. Forty students (19 females; mean age = 24.6 years) participated in the experiment, which was conducted at the Max Planck Institute for Human Development in Berlin. They received a flat fee of €9 ($11.50 U.S.) and an extra payment depending on their performance in the inference and memory tasks (see below).

Materials. Two pre-studies were conducted to create appropriate materials. In the first pre-study ($N = 100$ participants), we assessed the recognition rates of the 50 largest cities of each of four European countries (France, United Kingdom, Italy, Spain; 25 participants for each country). In addition, to identify cues with a high subjective validity for inferring the population size of European cities, participants were asked to provide, in a free-answer format, cues they would consider ("Which characteristics might be useful to distinguish between large and small cities?"). Based on participants' recognition ratings, we calculated the recognition validity for the four reference classes. In line with previous results, the city domain turned out to have a high recognition validity (.78, .74, .76, and .72 for France, United Kingdom, Italy, and Spain, respectively). Because the recognition rates varied most markedly among the British and Italian cities, we retained these two city sets for the second pre-study. The cues mentioned most often as useful for inferring city size were the existence of an international airport (mentioned by 43% of the participants), the existence of significant industry (42%), a university (37%), a world-famous tourist site (34%), and a team in the major national soccer league (30%).

In the second pre-study (with $N = 60$ participants), we assessed cue knowledge and subjective validity ratings for the cities and 11 cues identified in the first pre-study respectively. The 15 most and 15 least recognized cities (as identified in Pre-study 1) from the United Kingdom and Italy were used. The cities of London and Rome were excluded as they are probably known to be the largest British and Italian cities, respectively (which would represent conclusive criterion knowledge and thus allow participants to solve an inference based on an LMM). Participants indicated whether a city possessed a particular feature (e.g., international airport, responses "yes," "no," or "don't know"). Later, the concept of cue validity was explained and participants estimated the validities of the five cues on a scale ranging from 50% to 100%. The three cues deemed as most valid turned out to be industry ($M = 81.1\%$), airport ($M = 80.3\%$) and soccer team ($M = 71.9\%$). These cues were chosen for the experiments.

The cities that were selected as critical stimuli for the experiments had to meet two criteria: In order to create many pairs comparing recognized with unrecognized cities, we chose homogeneous subsets of cities that were recognized either most of the time (>75%) or very rarely (<15%). In addition, we aimed for the additional cue knowledge for a given recognized city being homogeneous, too. To achieve this, the cue value assigned to a city on a given cue most frequently had to be assigned (to that city) at least 20 percentage points more frequently than the cue value assigned second-most frequently. Since the latter criterion was met by merely four Italian cities, we decided to use the British cities only. Altogether eight highly recognized (i.e., recognized by >75% of the participants; "R" cities) British cities were chosen, as well as 10 unknown (i.e., recognized by <15% of the participants; "U" cities; British cities. These two types of cities were used to create the critical (i.e., RU) city pairs, for which we expected that participants would recognize one, but not the other (in the analysis of the experiments we took participants' actual recognition responses into account). In addition, a separate set of five highly recognized cities was used to create filler items. For two of the R cities (Manchester and Liverpool), the most frequently assigned cue value was "yes" for all three cues. For the other six R cities (Aberdeen, Bristol, Brighton, Nottingham, Sheffield, York), the most common value for all cues was "don't

know". Given that for these six cities pre-existing cue knowledge (which could interfere with learned cue knowledge) was relatively rare, in Experiments 1 and 2 cue values were learned for them. The cue values that the participants learned were those that were indicated most frequently (after "don't know") in the second pre-study (in Experiment 2 these cue patterns were slightly modified). To increase the likelihood that participants would have knowledge of the relevant cue dimensions, Aberdeen and Bristol were replaced by Manchester and Liverpool in Experiment 3, which examined how natural cue knowledge influences the use of recognition in inference.

Importantly, although not specifically selected for this purpose, the cities of York and Brighton had the desirable property of being rather small. In fact, they were the 46th and 50th largest cities (of the 50 largest cities), and thus *smaller* than most of the unrecognized cities. It is thus not the case simply that the R cities were large and the U cities were small, which could confound recognition with knowledge of a city's size (but note that this "confound" is what makes recognition a powerful cue in many domains).

Design and procedure. The experiment started with a *learning task*, in which participants acquired cue knowledge about six cities. The task was described as involving the learning of geographical facts about British cities. The cue knowledge consisted of the cue values (either "yes" or "no") that were indicated most frequently in Pre-study 2 (see Table 24-2). A positive cue value (= "yes") suggests that the city is large, and a negative cue value (= "no") that the city is small. Note that no city had negative cue values on all three cues. We used an anticipation learning paradigm, which proceeded as follows (cf. Bröder & Eichler, 2006; Bröder & Schiffer, 2003). At every learning trial, participants were presented with a city and a cue on a computer screen and instructed to find out the correct cue value by clicking on either "yes" or "no," in the beginning often by simply guessing. Immediately after a response, they received feedback and were asked to memorize the correct value (they were informed that they would be tested again later). Then the next cue followed (for the same city;

Table 24-2. Cue Profiles of the Cities Used in Experiments 1–3 (the Proportion of Responses for These Cue Values in Experiment 3 Are Given in Parentheses)

	City							
Cue	Aberdeen[a]	Bristol[a]	Manchester[b]	Liverpool[b]	Nottingham	Sheffield	Brighton	York
Industry	Yes	Yes	Yes (0.97)	Yes (1)	Yes (0.50)	Yes (0.67)	Yes[c] (0.64)	Yes[c] (0.69)
Airport	Yes	Yes	Yes (0.91)	Yes (0.83)	No (0.80)	No (0.91)	No (0.66)	No (0.80)
Soccer	Yes	Yes	Yes (0.97)	Yes (0.97)	Yes (0.57)	Yes (0.56)	No (0.69)	No (0.55)
Number of positive cues	3	3	3	3	2	2	1	1

Note. In Experiments 1 and 2, the cues values were learned during the experiment.
[a]Only used in Experiments 1–2.
[b]Only used in Experiment 3.
[c]In Experiment 2, the values of Brighton and York on the industry cue were replaced by "No."

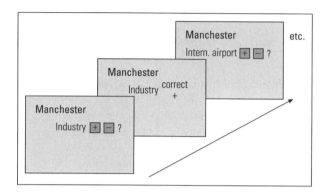

Figure 24-2. Procedure used in the cue-learning task.

see Figure 24-2). In contrast to previous studies (e.g., Bröder & Eichler, 2006; Richter & Späth, 2006) the sequence of cues was determined at random and changed with every learning cycle. By this procedure, we wanted to reduce the possibility that after learning, the cue profiles would be represented as chunks rather than as individual cue values. After the third cue, the procedure was repeated (with the cues presented in a new sequence) until all cue values for the city had been correctly reproduced twice in a row. Then the next city followed. After the last city, the procedure was repeated (in a new random order) until the participants had reproduced all cue values for all cities without error twice in a row. The potential usefulness of the cues for inferring the size of British cities was mentioned at no point during the learning task.

After having learned the cue values perfectly, participants performed an *inference task* in which they were presented with a total of 120 pairs of British cities (in blocks of 20 pairs, after each of which participants could take a short break) and instructed to choose the one with more inhabitants (no feedback was given). For each trial, a pair was drawn at random from one of three item types. First, the six recognized cities were combined with all 10 unrecognized cities, yielding 60 RU pairs. These 60 pairs were critical for our purposes. Second, there were 30 pairs consisting of two unrecognized cities (UU pairs), drawn at random from all possible pairings of the 10 unrecognized cities. Third, to equalize the presentation frequency of the R and U cities as

much as possible, there were 30 pairs with two recognized cities, drawn at random from a pool consisting of the six R cities and the five filler cities. As a result, each of the R cities was presented, on average, 11.5 times, the U cities 12 times, and the filler cities 5.5 times. For each correct inference (according to the official statistics[5]), participants earned an additional 4¢ (5¢ U.S.), and the same amount was subtracted for every incorrect inference.

The inference task was followed by a *recognition task*. Participants were presented with the 21 cities (6 R, 10 U, and 5 filler cities) in a random order and asked to indicate whether they had heard of them before participating in the experiment. After the recognition task, participants performed a *memory task* in which they had to reproduce the cue values ("yes" or "no") they had learned for the six R cities in the learning task. If they could not recall the correct values, they were allowed to respond don't know." A "no" response thus did not simply mean that the participants could not remember the city having a positive cue value. Every correctly recalled cue value earned them 10¢ (13¢ U.S.), and 10¢ was subtracted for every incorrect answer and "don't know" response. Finally, in a *cue validity estimation task*, participants judged the validities of the four cues (the three cues identified in the pre-study and recognition, presented in a random order) for the task of inferring the population of British cities (using a frequentistic format, ranging from 50% to 100%).

Results and Discussion

Cue knowledge, recognition, and cue validity estimates

On average, participants took 12.4 minutes ($SD = 7.1$) to learn the 18 (3 cues × 6 cities) cue values perfectly. The mean accuracy in the subsequent memory task (after the inference task) was 95% ($SD = 7$; range 72–100%). Twenty of the 40 participants recalled the cue values perfectly. The option "don't know" was chosen in 1% of the responses. Of the 60 critical pairs (i.e., the RU pairs), the mean proportion of comparisons where one city was recognized and the other not was .82 ($SD = 0.16$). To address the possible objection that the repeated presentation of previously unrecognized cities during the learning and inference tasks might distort the responses in the recognition task, in Figure 24-A1 in the Appendix the recognition rates obtained in Experiments 1–3 for the individual cities are compared with the respective rates obtained in Pre-study 1 (where participants saw the cities only once). As can be seen, if there are any differences at all, they are very small, suggesting that participants are very capable of disregarding their experimental familiarity with the city names. Concerning the estimated cue validities, Table 24-3 shows that all four cues were estimated to be relevant, with the international airport cue deemed to be the most valid one (replicating Richter & Späth, 2006), followed by the industry site cue, recognition, and the soccer team cue.[6] Importantly, the airport cue was estimated to be significantly more valid than recognition, $t(39) = 4.18$, $p = .001$. We thus had the opportunity to submit the recognition heuristic

to a tough test, since according to the cue patterns that the participants learned, the airport cue contradicted recognition. Would participants follow recognition even when it was contradicted by a cue deemed as more valid than recognition?

Effect of additional cue knowledge on choice of recognized city

Overall, participants' judgments followed recognition in, on average, 95.6% ($SD = 0.08$) of the critical RU pairs where one city was recognized but the other was not. Did this figure vary as a function of the number of additional positive and negative cue values known? Depending on the responses in the memory task, each item was categorized according to the number of cue values—positive or negative—known about the R city. There were three categories: 1, 2, or 3 cues.

To test for an effect of additional cue knowledge, we collapsed the choices of all participants and compared the proportion of choices of the recognized city across the three different categories. Recall that the recognition heuristic predicts that further cue knowledge does not affect the choice of the recognized object. In line with this prediction, we did not find the proportion of choices of the recognized city to differ across the varying levels of additional cue knowledge, and this was true for both positive [$\chi^2(2, N = 1,947) = 2.61$, $p = .27$; two-tailed; $w = .04$] and negative cue knowledge [$\chi^2(2, N = 1,958) = 0.55$, $p = .76$; two-tailed; $w = .02$]. Figure 24-3a shows the proportion of choices of the recognized city across the different levels of additional cue knowledge (1, 2, or 3 positive and 1, 2, or 3 negative cues, respectively). The results for positive and

Table 24-3. Estimated Validities (expressed as the Percentage of Correct Inferences when the Cue Value Is Positive) of Recognition and the Three Cues Deemed Most Valid in the Pre-Studies

		Industry	Airport	Soccer	Recognition
Experiment 1	M	75.0	82.1	63.5	70.2
	SD	14.7	11.4	11.1	13.4
Experiment 2	M	77.7	83.3	63.4	72.2
	SD	15.5	11.1	11.7	12.6
Experiment 3	M	78.5	83.3	61.5	71.3
	SD	12.8	8.4	9.9	13.6

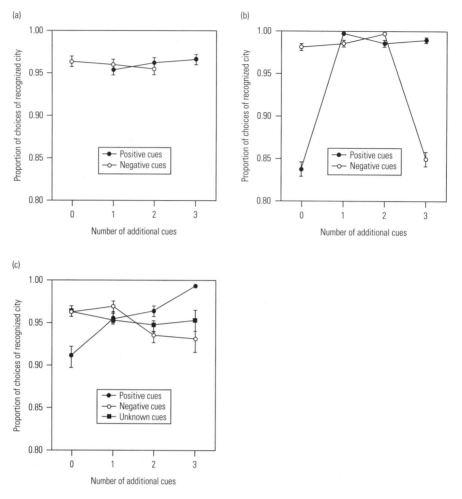

Figure 24-3. (a–c). Proportion of choices of the recognized city as a function of the number of additional cues in Experiment 1 (a), Experiment 2 (b), and Experiment 3 (c). Error bars show ±1 standard error.

negative cue values are shown separately because, due to "don't know" responses, the two could potentially diverge (see Experiment 3). As, however, unknown cue values were very rare in this experiment, the results for positive and negative cues are practically symmetrical. To test for a monotonic trend across the different levels of additional cue knowledge, we conducted a trend test developed by Pfanzagl (1974, p. 193). For this test, α was set at .05, with a corresponding critical threshold of 1.65. The observed test value T did not reach this critical threshold for positive ($T = 1.62$) or negative ($T = 0.65$) cue values. In an analysis on the individual level we considered only those participants with at least one case

where the recognized city had only one additional positive cue (where the influence of the recognition cue could potentially be equalized; the median number of such cases was 16). Of these participants, 60% (22 of 37) *always* chose the recognized city.

In sum, in contrast to Bröder and Eichler (2006) and Richter and Späth (2006), we did not find additional cue knowledge to affect the proportion of choices of a recognized object over an unrecognized one. Although one might be quick to attribute the discrepancy between these previous and present findings to methodological differences (in particular, to the fact that we prevented cue values from being learned as chunks), note that the proportion of choices of the recognized city was generally very high, and thus the lack of impact of additional cue knowledge could be due to a ceiling effect. In addition, the test of a monotonic trend failed to reach the critical threshold only by a little ($Ts = 1.62$ vs. 1.65, for positive cue values). Finally, one could object that the additional cue knowledge contradicting recognition was too weak to show an effect. Recall that, due to the cue profiles used, the recognized city always had an additional cue supporting recognition (although in both Bröder and Eichler and Richter and Späth, the proportion of choices of the recognized object differed also between 1 and 3 positive cues; see Figure 24-1). In other words, it is possible that the amount of cue knowledge indicating that the recognized city might be small was not sufficient to overturn recognition. (But note that this result was in no way obvious before the experiment, as recognition was still contradicted by the most valid cue.) We addressed this possibility in Experiment 2.

EXPERIMENT 2: REPLICATION WITH INCREASED AMOUNT OF EVIDENCE CONTRADICTING RECOGNITION

Experiment 2 constituted an even tougher challenge for the recognition heuristic and tested it in the situation in which recognition was contradicted by three cues that participants in the pre-studies had mentioned as reliable indicators of city size. To carry out such a test, we changed the cue profiles that participants learned about recognized cities in Experiment 1 such that they now involved two cities that had negative values on all three cues. In all other respects, Experiment 2 was identical to Experiment 1.

Method

Participants and procedure. Forty students (25 females; mean age = 25.2 years) took part in this experiment, which was conducted at the Max Planck Institute for Human Development in Berlin. Payment, design, and procedure were identical to those in Experiment 1.

Material. The only difference between Experiments 1 and 2 was that for the cities of Brighton and York the positive values on the industry cue were replaced by negative ones (see Table 24-2).

Results and Discussion

Cue knowledge, recognition, and cue validity estimates

The mean proportion of critical pairs where one city was recognized was .84 ($SD = 0.19$). On average, participants took 9.8 minutes ($SD = 4.6$) to learn the cue values perfectly and achieved, on average, an accuracy of 96% ($SD = 9$; range 67–100%) in the subsequent memory task. Thirty of the 40 participants recalled the cue values perfectly. The response "don't know" was chosen in 0.8% of the responses.

Effect of additional cue knowledge on choice of recognized city

Overall, participants' judgments followed recognition in, on average, 94% ($SD = 0.12$) of the critical RU pairs where one city was recognized but the other was not. As shown in Figure 24-3b, the introduction of a cue pattern with exclusively negative cues had a large effect (though the same cities were used as in Experiment 1. Note that due to the modified cue patterns, there were now 4 categories for the amount of cue knowledge: 0, 1, 2, or 3 cues). Replicating the result of previous studies, but contrasting with Experiment 1, the proportion of choices of the recognized city was now strongly affected by the amount of additional cue knowledge, for both positive [$\chi^2(3, N = 2,020) = 188.1, p = .001$; two-tailed; $w = 0.31$] and negative [$\chi^2(3, N = 2,020) = 153.9, p = .001$; two-tailed; $w = 0.28$] cue knowledge. A trend test (again using the critical threshold of 1.65 for $\alpha = .05$) indicated a significant monotonic trend for both positive ($T = 12.82$) and negative ($T = 11.41$) cue knowledge.

To illustrate the effect of additional cue knowledge, take the cities of Brighton and York, for which the cue patterns learned in Experiments 1 and 2 differed. Whereas in Experiment 1, where participants had learned one positive cue value and two negative cue values in addition to recognition,

95.5% of the choices involving the two cities followed recognition, this percentage dropped to 85.9% in Experiment 2, where all three cues that participants learned about the cities contradicted recognition. Yet, the high proportion of choices of the recognized city indicates that the choices were still heavily influenced by recognition, given that all three additional cues contradicted recognition. Note that this figure is considerably higher than the 66% of choices following recognition reported for Richter and Späth's (2006) Experiment 2 in the same situation (but different domain) of recognition being contradicted by three additionally learned cues. Nevertheless, one might object that our results are still marred by ceiling effects. We would like to emphasize, however, that the high proportions of choices of the recognized city— close to 100%—are in themselves an important result, if one recalls that in two of the conditions recognition is contradicted by one and two cues, respectively, that were judged by the participants as more valid than recognition. Even in this critical situation, recognition seemed to dominate the judgment.

As in Experiment 1 there were substantial individual differences. Forty-six percent (18 of 39) of the participants with at least one case where a recognized city had no additional positive cue (but mostly negative cues, contradicting recognition; *Mdn* = 18 cases) *always* chose the recognized city. In other words, although on the aggregate level it looks as if participants' behavior is at odds with the recognition heuristic, an individual analysis reveals that almost half of our participants made inferences in a way consistent with the heuristic. Experiment 3 replicates the results of Experiment 2 using natural rather than induced cue knowledge.

ADDITIONAL ANALYSES

Additional cue knowledge had an effect in Experiments 2 and 3; yet in all experiments, we observed that a substantial number of participants always chose the recognized city and thus did not seem to be affected by additional cue knowledge. For illustration, the upper row of Figure 24-4 shows for individual participants in

Experiments 2 and 3 the proportions of choices of the recognized city when no additional positive cue knowledge was known (and where most additional cues suggested that the recognized city is small). As can be seen, in both experiments, half of the participants always chose the recognized city. At the same time, there was a (small) group of participants who seemed to decide systematically *against* the recognized city: In Experiment 2, there were four participants who chose the recognized city only 17%, 10%, 20%, and 29% of the time, and in Experiment 3, two participants *never* chose the recognized city. One way to interpret the consistency of the participants who always chose the recognized city is that these participants used the recognition heuristic. That is, although the participants reported after the inference task to have additional relevant cue knowledge about a recognized city that contradicted recognition, they appeared to have stopped information search after assessing recognition for the two objects; other participants, by contrast, integrated that other knowledge into their inferences.

Importantly, the existence of large and sometimes dramatic individual differences in the use of recognition does not seem restricted to our experiments: the lower row of Figure 24-4 shows the data of two other experiments with natural recognition and inferences from memory that found additional cue knowledge to have an effect on the aggregate level (Newell & Fernandez, 2006; Richter & Späth, 2006). Depicted are the individual participants' proportions of choices of the recognized object when recognition was contradicted by three (out of three) and one (out of one) additional cues, respectively. As can be seen, there are large individual differences as well, and a substantial number of participants who chose the recognized object irrespective of conflicting cue knowledge.

GENERAL DISCUSSION

We found evidence suggesting that recognition operates as a highly dominant cue in probabilistic inferences: Even when the recognition cue is not perceived as most valid and in addition

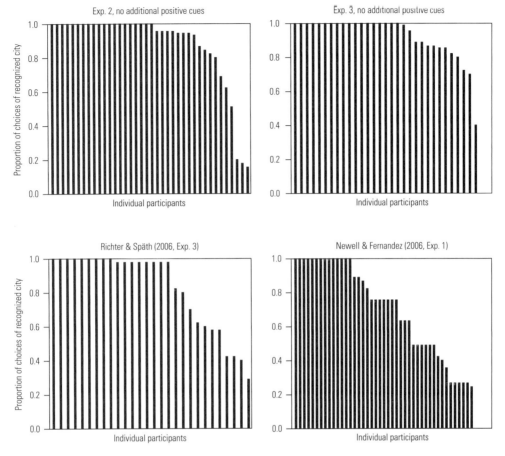

Figure 24-4. Distribution of individual proportions of choices of the recognized city when no additional positive cue knowledge was available in Experiments 2 and 3, shown in the upper row, and in a reanalysis of Richter and Späth (2006, Exp. 2; 28 participants) and Newell and Fernandez (2006, Exp. 1; 48 participants), shown in the lower row.

is contradicted by a substantial amount of additional and relevant cue knowledge, there seems to be strong reliance on recognition. As the difference between Experiments 1 and 2 suggests, a comparatively large amount of negative evidence is necessary to override its impact. Importantly, this does not seem to be the case with induced recognition, which was used in earlier experiments (e.g., Bröder & Eichler, 2006; Newell & Shanks, 2004). An interesting result is that the dominating effect of recognition does not seem to depend on recognition being perceived as the most valid cue; in fact, participants estimated the cue validity of recognition to be lower than

the validity of two of the three cues that they were taught in addition to recognition (although, at over .70, the absolute value of recognition's validity was still rather high).

Although cross-experiment comparisons have to be treated with caution, a direct comparison of our results with those, for instance, of Bröder and Eichler (2006) suggests that additional knowledge has stronger effects in tests involving both induced recognition and additional cue knowledge taught in the experiment than in tests involving naturally evolved recognition and knowledge that people have acquired outside the laboratory. Hence, previous experiments that used induced recognition and/or induced cue knowledge may have overstated the impact of additional cue information on probabilistic inferences. The same holds true for studies testing the recognition heuristic in domains with a low recognition validity.

The need to make explicit individual differences in decision behaviour has been emphasized repeatedly (e.g., Brehmer, 1994; Bröder, 2000b; Einhorn, 1970). And individual differences in strategy use have also been observed in experimental research on other noncompensatory inference heuristics, such as "TTB" (Gigerenzer & Goldstein, 1996). For example, Bröder (2000b, Experiment 1) showed that not all people use TTB in probabilistic inferences. But hypothesis rejections at the group level may throw out the baby with the bath water if individual strategy differences are not taken into account. Almost all experimental studies on TTB have shown that varying proportions of participants do adhere to this heuristic, depending on task demands and classification criteria (Bergert & Nosofsky, 2007; Bröder, 2000b, 2003; Lee & Cummins, 2004; Newell & Shanks, 2003; Newell, Rakow, Weston, & Shanks, 2004; Newell, Weston, & Shanks, 2003; Rieskamp & Hoffrage, 1999; Rieskamp & Otto, 2006). Conversely, whereas the proportion of TTB users varies—often in an adaptive fashion—there are always at least some participants who seem to prefer other—compensatory or noncompensatory—strategies.

In light of these findings, the focus of research on TTB has shifted away from initial attempts to refute the notion that the heuristic is always used towards systematic explorations of factors that affect noncompensatory strategy use (such as information costs and cognitive capacity; Bröder, 2003; Bröder & Schiffer, 2003, 2006). Richter and Späth (2006) proposed a similar shift for research on the recognition heuristic, summarizing: "The conclusion that the recognition heuristic is not universally applied leaves us with the question of whether there are situations in which people use recognition in a noncompensatory way and, if so, which factors yield a noncompensatory use of recognition" (p. 160).

In research on TTB, a more refined approach that examines strategy use at the individual level has proven to be fruitful, as the boundary conditions of the theory continue to be refined. Likewise with the recognition heuristic, recent work has begun to systematically flesh out the boundary conditions of its use (e.g., Newell & Shanks, 2004; Pachur & Hertwig, 2006). In our view, it is now clear that the recognition heuristic—in particular in terms of the hypothesized noncompensatory use of recognition—is not used by all people all the time and under all circumstances, so we think it is time to reformulate the research question accordingly. For instance, one important task would be to identify factors driving individual differences in the use of the recognition heuristic. In the context of TTB, such an approach has led to promising results in the quest to better understand adaptive decision-making (Bröder, 2003; Mata, Schooler, & Rieskamp, 2007), and some encouraging insights are emerging for the recognition heuristic as well (Pachur, Mata, & Schooler, 2009).

Individual differences pose a problem for theorizing and empirical studies. Theorizing has been largely "nomothetic" in the decision-making domain, in the sense that the focus was on identifying general laws of information processing. On the other hand, some researchers have tried to identify personal preferences for processing styles in an "idiographic" fashion, that is, they tried to explain strategy selection based on individual traits (e.g., Schunk & Betsch, 2006; Zakay, 1990). If, however, personality differences consistently moderate the general laws, one is probably forced to model situation × person interaction in full-fledged theories of decision-making (Mischel & Shoda, 1995). This is also a challenge for empirical research because viable methods for assessing strategy use have to be developed. We feel that such a research agenda is overdue since strategy differences between people appear to be the rule rather than marginal exceptions.

ACKNOWLEDGMENTS

Our thanks go to Bryan Bergert, Wolfgang Gaissmaier, Gerd Gigerenzer, Daniel Goldstein, and Lael Schooler for many constructive comments. In addition, we are grateful to Tobias Richter and Ben Newell for making available the raw data of their experiments.

NOTES

1. Note, however, that conclusions based on process-tracing studies have been criticized (Bröder, 2000a).
2. We use the term "recognition" here to refer to what can be called *semantic* recognition, in contrast to *episodic* recognition, which is often studied in the recognition memory literature. Episodic recognition refers to the ability to discriminate known objects (i.e., objects one has encountered outside the experimental context, usually words such as HOUSE or GARDEN) that had been previously presented in the experimental context, from other known words that had not been previously presented in the experimental context; semantic recognition refers to the ability to discriminate known objects from (subjectively) *novel* objects.
3. We are aware that the term "natural" used here repeatedly is a rather fuzzy one since there are no clear defining boundaries between natural and artificial environments (such as the laboratory). Here we use the term for a task that (a) uses real world stimuli and (b) for which the crucial recognition knowledge must have been acquired before the experiment and outside the laboratory.
4. Note that the names of the fictitious cities were chosen such that they allowed for an informed guess about their country of origin.
5. Relevant statistics were obtained from: http://www.citypopulation.de/UK.html (retrieved on April 15, 2005).
6. An analysis of the cues' actual, that is, their *ecological* validities (cf. Gigerenzer et al., 1991) indicated that these estimates were very accurate: for the reference class of the 50 largest British cities the ecological validities for the industry, airport and soccer cues were .78, .85, and .69,

respectively. The average recognition validity in Pre-study 1 was .74.

APPENDIX

Were Participants' Recognition Rates Affected by Experimental Familiarity to the City Names?

Recall that we had participants indicate whether or not they have heard of a city name before participating in the experiment *after* the experiment. By using these recognition assessments as a basis for testing the recognition heuristic, we assumed that participants were able to disregard the familiarity with the city names produced by the exposures during the experiment. How reasonable is this assumption? Evidence that people are indeed capable of screening out experimental familiarity comes from at least two sources: First, none of the studies that controlled for the order of recognition and judgment tasks found a significant effect of task order (Pohl, 2006; Pachur & Hertwig, 2006). Second, Figure A1 compares (for the cities used in Experiments 1–3) the recognition rates obtained in Pre-study 1—where participants saw the city names only once—with the recognition rates obtained in Experiments 1–3—where each unrecognized city was presented in total around 12 times before a recognition judgment was made. Although the recognition rates for the very unfamiliar cities obtained in Experiments 1–3 are slightly higher than in the pre-study (interestingly, in particular in Experiment 3), the difference is rather small. Moreover, note that in spite of having been presented a dozen times, the highly recognized cities seemed to be slightly *less* recognized in Experiments 1–3 than in Pre-Study 1, suggesting that the differences are also due to a normal regression effect.

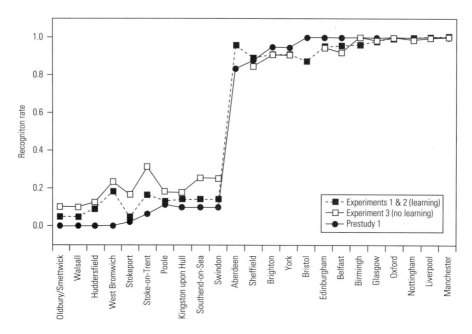

Figure 24-A1. Recognition rates for the cities used in the experiments.

Introduction to Chapter 25

Why You Think Milan Is Larger than Modena: Neural Correlates of the Recognition Heuristic

The recognition heuristic is a prime example of a simple heuristic that exploits an evolved capacity (recognition) to make inferences about the world. There are two interpretations in the literature of how the heuristic is used: an "automatic" and an "adaptive" view. The automatic interpretation assumes that if one object is recognized and the other is not, the mind blindly relies on the recognition heuristic. In one study, Oppenheimer (2003) asked students at Stanford University which of two cities is more populous: Sausalito (a well-known nearby city with only 7,500 inhabitants) or Heingjing (a nonexistent city, but which was implied to be real). The majority, 80%, picked Heingjing and thus did not rely on the recognition heuristic. Oppenheimer took this as evidence against the very concept of the recognition heuristic. Yet blindly relying on the heuristic and thus picking Sausolito was not what Goldstein and Gigerenzer (2002) had in mind. They specified a recognition validity "higher than chance ($\alpha > .5$)" (p. 87) as one necessary condition (it is impossible to determine this validity for made-up cities). Moreover, if students already knew that Sausalito is as small as a city can get, there was no need to make an inference at all.

The ecological view assumes that people try to use the heuristic in an adaptive way (Gigerenzer & Selten, 2001). This assumption is supported by a positive correlation of $r = .64$ between the recognition validity and the proportion of judgments consistent with the recognition heuristic across a set of 11 studies (Pachur, Todd, Schooler, Gigerenzer, & Goldstein, in press). If people rely on the recognition heuristic in an adaptive way, this implies an evaluation process in addition to the recognition process.

Written by a team of neuroscientists and psychologists, namely, Kirsten Volz, Lael Schooler, Ricarda Schubotz, Markus Raab, Gerd Gigerenzer, and Yves von Cramon, the present article tests the hypothesis of a separate evaluation and recognition process by asking whether the neural correlates are the same when mere recognition judgment is involved ("have you ever heard of Modena? of Milan?") or when people make an inference based on recognition that involves the recognition heuristic ("which city has the larger population: Milan or Modena?"). The results indicate that the two situations are not identical, as the automatic interpretation would imply, but suggest a separate evaluation process that determines whether it makes sense to follow the recognition heuristic in a given situation. The evaluation process corresponds to a judgment about the ecological rationality of the heuristic in the task at hand. This judgment appears to be specific to the anterior frontomedian cortex, which has been linked in earlier studies to evaluative judgments and self-referential evaluations.

CHAPTER 25

Why You Think Milan Is Larger than Modena: Neural Correlates of the Recognition Heuristic

*Kirsten G. Volz, Lael J. Schooler, Ricarda I. Schubotz, Markus Raab,
Gerd Gigerenzer, and D. Yves von Cramon*

Abstract: When ranking two alternatives by some criteria and only one of the alternatives is recognized, participants overwhelmingly adopt the strategy, termed the *recognition heuristic* (RH), of choosing the recognized alternative. Understanding the neural correlates underlying decisions that follow the RH could help determine whether people make judgments about the RH's applicability or simply choose the recognized alternative. We measured brain activity by using functional magnetic resonance imaging while participants indicated which of two cities they thought was larger (Experiment 1) or which city they recognized (Experiment 2). In Experiment 1, increased activation was observed within the anterior frontomedian cortex (aFMC), precuneus, and retrosplenial cortex when participants followed the RH compared to when they did not. Experiment 2 revealed that RH decisional processes cannot be reduced to recognition memory processes. As the aFMC has previously been associated with self-referential judgments, we conclude that RH decisional processes involve an assessment about the applicability of the RH.

We often need to rank two alternatives by some criterion, for example, which road to a city is faster. In one experiment done to explore how people do such rankings, Goldstein and Gigerenzer (2002) presented U.S. students with pairs of large U.S. cities and with pairs of large German cities. The task was to infer which city in each pair had the larger population. The students performed equally well on the German and U.S. city pairs. How can this be that the students performed as well with German cities as with the American cities, when they knew almost nothing about the German cities? Goldstein and

Gigerenzer found that people reliably employ a remarkably effective decision strategy they dubbed the *recognition heuristic* (RH), which can be stated as follows: "If one of two objects is recognized and the other is not, then infer that the recognized object has the higher value with respect to the criterion" (p. 76). According to Goldstein and Gigerenzer, the students' imperfect recognition of the German cities allowed them to frequently apply the RH, which led them to pick the recognized German cities, which tend to be larger than those that are unrecognized. The students could not use this heuristic when comparing U.S. cities, though, because they recognized all of them.

The RH works only in domains, or environments, in which recognition is correlated—in either direction—with the inaccessible criterion being predicted, for example, between city name recognition and population size. To the extent that the RH functions well by exploiting characteristics

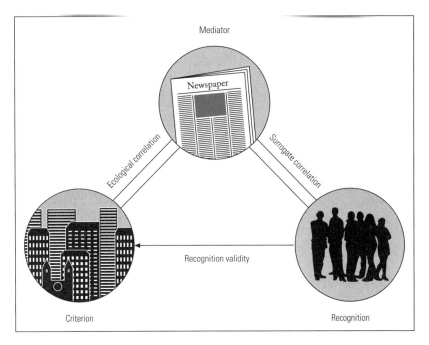

Figure 25-1. The ecological rationality of the recognition heuristic (RH), that is, the ability to exploit the structure of the information in the environment: An inaccessible criterion (e.g., the population size of a certain city) is reflected but not revealed by a mediator variable (e.g., the number of times a city is mentioned in the media), and the mediator influences the probability of recognition. The recognition information is then used to infer the criterion. This inference is successful only if recognition is correlated with the criterion. Adapted from Goldstein and Gigerenzer (2002).

of an environment, it is ecologically rational with respect to that particular environment. Goldstein and Gigerenzer (2002) argue the effectiveness of the RH in the city judgment task depends on three correlations: Population size is reflected by how often a city is mentioned in the media, which in turn influences the probability of recognition (Figure 25-1). Thus, recognition information correlates with and can be used to infer the inaccessible criterion. Accordingly, the effective use of the RH depends on the outcome of two processes. The first yields whether the alternatives are recognized and so whether the RH can be applied. The second process assesses whether the RH should be applied, and so is essentially a judgment about its ecological rationality. The judgment of ecological rationality could, for example, depend on an assessment of whether the chain of correlations linking the criterion to recognition through the mediator (e.g., the frequency of city name in the media) justifies following the RH.

Yet, it is not necessarily the case that subjects have to judge the ecological rationality of the RH before applying it. Instead, subjects could simply choose the recognized alternative without considering why recognition should be predictive of population size. Such a strategy would be successful here because recognition is so highly correlated with how often a stimulus occurs in the environment.

Understanding the neural correlates underlying the use of the RH could help determine whether RH-based decisional processes depend on additional judgments of ecological rationality. Such judgments of ecological rationality should draw on brain areas beyond those known to reflect recognition memory processes.

Some have concluded from behavioral studies that declarative memory (episodic memory [events] and semantic memory [facts]; cf. Squire, 1994) is supported by at least two distinct processes: The assessment of what has been termed item familiarity and the recollection of the context in which an item was encountered before (Yonelinas et al., 2002). Neuropsychological as well as neuroscientific evidence supports the proposed dual-process framework in that recollection and familiarity draw on distinct neural mechanisms: Whereas the hippocampus is considered to play a crucial role in recollection (e.g., Aggleton et al., 2005; Ranganath et al., 2003; Yonelinas et al., 2002; Aggleton & Shaw, 1996; for an overview, see Rugg & Yonelinas, 2003), adjacent medial temporal lobe (MTL) regions (perirhinal cortex) are hypothesized to reflect familiarity-based recognition (Yonelinas et al., 2002). Yet, a recent review on the MTL outlines that the available data may not support such a simple dichotomy (Squire, Stark, & Clark, 2004). Rather, the authors suggest that the various anatomical components of the MTL all signal information that is significant to successful recognition memory performance: The hippocampal formation provides a conjunctive recognition signal, whereas adjacent cortices provide stimulus-specific (recognition) signals. Both components are considered necessary for intact recognition memory performance and hence may account for why there is only little support of a sharp distinction of labor within the MTL. Besides these cortices, parietal areas have consistently been shown to be crucial for remembering, particularly for episodic retrieval processes (Wagner, Shannon, Kahn, & Buckner, 2005). For example (lateral and medial) parietal areas have been shown to increase their activity to recognized old items as well as to erroneously recognized new items and to correlate with the subjective experience of remembering. Accordingly, if RH-based decisional processes in the present study were not only premised on recognition information but rather depend on additional judgments of ecological rationality, we expected regions beyond MTL regions and parietal areas to be activated when participants decided according to the RH.

Thus, by using functional magnetic resonance imaging (fMRI) and an adapted version of the two-alternative forced-choice task used by Goldstein and Gigerenzer (2002), we contrasted the neural correlates of decisions based on the RH to those in which the heuristic was not

applied. Yet, finding activation in areas besides those regions known to reflect recognition memory processes would not definitively rule out an alternative interpretation, namely, that those areas reflect decisional processes that simply opt for recognized alternatives. For this reason, we ran the same experiment again with a different group of participants and with the instruction to simply choose the recognized city in each pair (Experiment 2). The test of city recognition and the paired comparison test were run as a between-subjects design to avoid potential carryover effects. In Experiment 2, participants were asked to execute the task "Which city do you know?" instead of "Which city is larger?" By contrasting trials in which participants were instructed to choose the recognized city with trials in which they were instructed to choose the unrecognized city, we built a contrast parallel to the RH contrast from Experiment 1. In doing so, we could compare the activation patterns of both experiments. To the extent that the RH-based decisional processes (1) can be adequately explained by participants simply choosing the recognized alternative and (2) do not depend on a judgment of the ecological rationality, the activation patterns of the two contrasts should not differ with respect to the critical activations.

METHODS

Experiment 1

Participants

Eighteen (10 women, mean age 25.6 years, *SD* 3.4, range 20–32 years) right-handed, healthy volunteers participated in the fMRI experiment. Informed consent was obtained prior to the experiment from each participant according to the Declaration of Helsinki. Experimental standards were approved by the local ethics committee of the University of Leipzig. Data were handled anonymously.

Stimuli, Task, and Experimental Session

Stimuli consisted of two concurrently presented words, one on the right and one on the left side of the screen (horizontal visual angle, 11°;

vertical visual angle, 1.7°). Participants had their index fingers on a left and a right response button, spatially corresponding to the stimulus locations on the screen. Within each trial a cue was presented for 500 msec signaling that the next trial was about to start, followed by a fixation cross presented for 500 msec. Subsequently, word pairs were presented for a maximum of 4 sec during which participants' response was recorded. As soon as participants indicated their choice by a button press, the stimuli disappeared and were replaced by a fixation cross. No performance feedback was delivered whatsoever. The participants' task was to indicate which city in each pair had the larger population.

An experimental session consisted of 140 experimental trials and 30 null events, in which no stimulus was presented and so the blood oxygenation level dependent (BOLD) response was allowed to return to a baseline state. All trials lasted for 8 sec each (i.e., four scans of repetition time [TR] 2 sec). To allow for measurements to be taken at numerous time points along the BOLD signal curve, the onset of each stimulus presentation relative to the beginning of the first of the four scans was varied randomly in four time steps (0, 500, 1000, and 1500 msec). The purpose of this procedure was to enhance the temporal resolution of the image acquisition (Birn, Cox, & Bandettini, 2002; Miezin, Maccotta, Ollinger, Petersen, & Buckner, 2000).

After the fMRI session, a recognition test was administered in which participants had to indicate whether or not they knew each city from *before* the experimental session. It was emphasized to the participants that they should declare as recognized only those cities that they had heard of before the functional session. These data were used to determine individual trial types, that is, whether both, none, or only one of the cities were recognized. Accordingly, we could individually determine RR (recognized–recognized), RU (recognized–unrecognized), and UU (unrecognized–unrecognized) trials. Furthermore, the data of the recognition test were also used to assess in which RU trials participants decided in favor of the recognized city, that is, the application of the RH. After the recognition test, participants were asked to fill out a questionnaire asking

wherefrom they knew most of the cities; subsequently, they were debriefed and thanked.

Our experimental design called for the city comparison task to always come first, followed by the recognition test, rather than counterbalancing the task order. Having the recognition test before the city task could have biased participants towards using the RH by making salient to the participants that we (the experimenters) were interested in whether or not they recognized the stimuli. In addition, by keeping a fixed task order, we were able to reliably measure the hemodynamic response elicited by recognition judgments that are presumed to underlie the RH. That is, judgments about whether the city can be recognized from their daily life, and so can be used to make inferences about the cities. Had the recognition task come first, the participants would have had to judge not only whether they recognized the city, but also whether the source of the recognition was just from the experiment or possibly from elsewhere. The additional demands of this discrimination task means that the recognition judgments from the two task orders could draw on somewhat different brain structures and so involve brain structures that would not otherwise be involved in the application of the RH. Nevertheless, we expect that in the recognition task, participants could reliably report whether they saw the city from the experiment or from elsewhere. That is, they would rarely miscategorize as recognized a city that they had only encountered in the experiment. Support for this comes from the studies of Pohl (2006) and Goldstein and Gigerenzer (2002). Neither study found any difference in the recognition rates that depended on the order of the two tasks.

Pilot Study for Stimulus Material Preparation

A key design goal of the present study was that each city in the experiment should only be seen once, so that participant's recognition judgments would not be contaminated by their experience within the experiment. For this reason, the city task always preceded the recognition test. To construct the trials so that subjects would be faced with approximately equal proportions of RR, RU, and UU trials, we ran a behavioral pilot study to obtain average recognition rates for 400 cities necessary to make 140 experimental trials. In this pilot study, administered as a paper-and-pencil task, 60 students from Berlin and Flensburg were asked to answer the following question: Please indicate if you have heard the name of this city before. Students answered this question for 400 cities from following countries: Argentina, Brazil, Canada, China, France, Great Britain, Holland, India, Iraq, Italy, Japan, Poland, Portugal, Russia, Spain, South Africa, Sweden, Switzerland, and the United States. The cities were blocked by country and both the order of the country blocks and the cities within each country block were randomized. As a complete counterbalancing of the country blocks would result in 20! (= 2.4329^{E+18}) different orders, to keep things simple, one ordering of stimuli was used for all participants. Countries with a larger number of cities potentially known by a German population had a higher proportion of cities on the list than countries that we expected to be less familiar (e.g., United States vs. China). Based on the pilot study England, France, Holland, Italy, Canada, Spain, and the United States were the only countries with approximately equal proportions of recognized and unrecognized cities.

For the paired comparison task a new set of stimuli was generated for each subject as follows. Pairs were generated for each country separately. From those cities that had yet to be included in the experiment, all possible pairs of cities from the same country were generated. For each pair, the expected proportion of participants who would recognize both, just one, or neither city was estimated based on the recognition rates of the Flensburg and Berlin participants. Take, for example, the English cities of Sheffield and Poole, with respective recognition rates of .95 and .1, which we refer to, respectively, as a and b. By making the strong assumption that these recognition judgments are independent, we can estimate that the probability that the average participant will recognize both cites is .095 ($= a \times b$), that the probability that only one alternative will be recognized is .86 ($= a[1 - b] + [1 - a]\, b$), and that the probability that neither city will be recognized is .045 ($= [1 - a][1 - b]$). Next, the city pair that

would do the most to equalize the proportion of RR, RU, and UU trials was selected. The process was repeated for the remaining cities.

After the functional session, we compared the recognition rates of all 280 cities between the Berlin and Flensburg participants (60) on the one hand and the Leipzig participants (18) on the other and found recognition values were highly correlated ($r = .91$; $p < .0001$). Furthermore, the distribution of RR, RU, and UU trials was not significantly different from an equal distribution (Kolmogorov–Smirnov test: $Z = 1.10$; $p = .18$), as was intended.

Experiment 2

Participants

Fourteen (8 women, mean age 25.8 years, SD 2.5, range 22–30 years) right-handed, healthy volunteers participated in the fMRI experiment. Informed consent was obtained prior to the experiment from each participant according to the Declaration of Helsinki. Experimental standards were approved by the local ethics committee of the University of Leipzig. Data were handled anonymously.

Stimuli, Task, and Experimental Session

Experiment 2 differed from Experiment 1 in the following points: In the functional session, participants had to perform two tasks that were indicated by different color cues; in addition, the city pairs were also presented in the color corresponding to the indicated task. In one task (respond–recognize), participants had to indicate which city they recognized by pressing with their index finger that key spatially corresponding to the stimulus locations on the screen. In those cases when participants recognized both cities, they were instructed to indicate this with their right middle finger, whereas in cases when they recognized none of the cities, they were instructed to indicate this with their left middle finger. The mappings for the middle fingers were counterbalanced between participants. In another task (respond–unrecognized) that was signaled by a color cue, participants were required, in case they recognized only one city, to indicate which one they did *not* recognize. The response had to be made with the index fingers spatially correspond-ing to the stimulus locations on the screen of the unrecognized city. In case both or none of the cities were recognized, the assignment for the keys stayed the same as in the respond–recognize task, that is, right and left middle fingers. Across the entire experiment, the two tasks were never performed on the same stimuli. Respond–recognize and respond–unrecognized trials were intermixed and presented in random order. One quarter of the trials assigned as RU trials were categorized as such. As in Experiment 1, the actual number of RU trials was individually dif-ferent depending on the knowledge of the par-ticipants. Parallel to Experiment 1, one functional session consisted of 140 experimental trials and 30 null events lasting for 8 sec each. In addition, the procedure of the oversampling was kept iden-tical to that of Experiment 1.

MRI Scanning Procedure

Imaging

Imaging was performed on a 3T scanner (Siemens TRIO, Erlangen, Germany). Twenty-two axial slices (4 mm thickness, 20% spacing, field of view [FOV] 19.2 cm, data matrix of 64×64 voxels, and in-plane resolution of 3 mm $\times$ 3 mm) parallel to the bicommissural plane (AC–PC) covering the whole brain were acquired using a single-shot echo-planar imaging (EPI) sequence (TR 2 sec, echo time [TE] 30 msec, flip angle 90°). One functional run with 872 time points was run with each time point sampling over the 22 slices. Prior to functional runs, 22 anatomical T1-weighted modified driven equi-librium Fourier transform (MDEFT; Norris, 2000; Ugurbil et al., 1993) images (data matrix 256×256, TR 1.3 sec, TE 10 msec) were acquired as well as 22 T1-weighted EPI images with the same spatial orientation as the functional data. The latter were used to co-register the functional scans with previously acquired high-resolution full-brain 3-D brain scans.

Data Analysis

The MRI data were processed by using the software package LIPSIA (Lohmann et al., 2001). Functional data were motion-corrected off-line

with the Siemens motion-correction protocol. To correct for the temporal offset between the slices acquired in one scan, a cubic spline interpolation was applied. A temporal high-pass filter with a cutoff frequency of 1/160 Hz was used for baseline correction of the signal and a spatial Gaussian filter with 5.65-mm full width half maximum (FWHM) was applied. The anatomical slices were coregistered with the high-resolution full-brain scan that resided in the stereotactic coordinate system and then transformed by linear scaling to a standard size (Talairach & Tournoux, 1988). The transforma-tion parameters obtained from this step were subsequently applied to the preprocessed func-tional slices so that the functional slices were also registered into the stereotactic space. This linear normalization process was improved by a subsequent processing step that performed an additional nonlinear normalization known as "demon matching." In this type of nonlinear normalization, an anatomical 3-D data set (i.e., the model) is deformed such that it matches another 3-D anatomical data set (i.e., the source) that serves as a fixed reference image (Thirion, 1998). The voxel size was interpolated during the coregistration from $3 \times 3 \times 4$ mm to $3 \times 3 \times 3$ mm. The statistical evaluation was based on a least-squares estimation using the general linear model for serially autocorrelated observations (random effects model; Friston, Frith, Turner, & Frackowiak, 1995; Worsely & Friston, 1995). The general linear regression performs a "precolor-ing" of the data; that is, it applies a temporal Gaussian smoothing with a user-specified kernel width given by the parameter FWHM. The smoothing imposes a temporal autocorrelation that determines the degrees of freedom. An event-related design was implemented; that is, the hemodynamic response function was mod-eled by means of the experimental conditions for each stimulus (event = onset of stimulus presen-tation). The design matrix was generated using a synthetic hemodynamic response function and its first and second derivative (Friston et al., 1998) and a response delay of 6 sec. The model equa-tion, including the observation data, the design matrix, and the error term, was convolved with a Gaussian kernel of dispersion of 4 sec FWHM to deal with the temporal autocorrelation (Worsley & Friston, 1995). Contrast images, that is, estimates of the raw score differences between specified conditions, were generated for each subject. The single-subject contrast images entered into a second-level random effects analysis for each of the contrasts. The group analysis consisted of a one-sample t test across the contrast images of all subjects that indicated whether observed differences between conditions were significantly different from zero. Subsequently, t values were transformed into Z scores. Group statistical parametric maps were thresholded at $Z > 3.09$ ($p = .001$, uncorrected). Only clusters of at least six connected voxels (i.e., 162 mm³) were reported to ensure an overall imagewise false-positive rate of 5% (Forman et al., 1995). This nonarbitrary voxel cluster size was determined by using the program AlphaSim (afni. nimh.nih.gov/afni/doc/manual/AlphaSim by Ward, 2000).

RESULTS

Experiment 1

Behavioral Results

Reaction times (RTs) of all RR, RU, and UU trials as well as of correctly answered trials are shown in Table 25-1. On average, participants were faced with 55 (±13) RR, 46 (±5) RU, and 39 (±15) UU trials during an experimental session. A repeated measures analysis of variance of all trials as well as of correctly answered trials revealed the three experimental conditions to differ significantly with regard to RT: [all

trials: $F(2, 16) = 21.93$; $p = .001$; correctly answered trials: $F(2, 16) = 23.76$; $p = .001$]. Likewise, the three experimental conditions differed significantly with regard to the rate of correct responses, $F(2, 16) = 15.83$; $p = .001$. Kolmogorov–Smirnov tests indicate that the means of the subjects' RTs as well as the rate of correct responses were normally distributed (all Z values > .478). As the standard errors for all conditions were less 2.7%, it is apparent that performance in the RR and RU condition differed significantly from chance level of 50%, whereas performance in the UU condition was at 50.1%. Regarding the use of the RH, participants applied the heuristic in 84% of the cases. Whether reliance on the RH pays is indicated by the strength of the relationship between recognition and criterion, which is referred to as recognition validity in a specific environment or data set. In the present experiment, the recognition validity averaged .63, which is calculated as the proportion of times a recognized city was indeed larger than an unrecognized city. Yet, as no performance feedback was given, participants could not determine the recognition validity. Taken together, the present results are consistent with previous results (Goldstein & Gigerenzer, 2002).

After the experimental session, participants were asked wherefrom they knew most of the cities. It was revealed that more than half of the recognized cities were known from the media, such as newspapers, news on television or the Internet, and novels (63%). As other important sources, participants indicated schooling (17%) and holiday (10%).

Table 25-1. Behavioral Results of Experiment 1

Condition	RT$_{all}$	SE$_{(RTall)}$	RT$_{corr}$	SE$_{(RTcorr)}$	% Correct	SE$_{(\%corr)}$
RR	2818	92	2815	92	63.2	1.9
UU	3024	108	3074	116	50.1	1.9
RU	2804	89	2767	84	69.2	1.5
RU$_{(R)}$	2781	90	2735	80	73.5	1.5
RU$_{(U)}$	3042	116	3064	159	44.2	3.8

Reaction times (RTs) of all experimental trials as well as for correctly answered trials and the rates of correct responses (each with standard error [SE]) are shown for condition RR (both cities recognized), RU (one city recognized), and UU (no city recognized). The last two rows show RTs and rates of correct responses for RU trials in which participants decided in favor of the recognized alternative (RU$_{(R)}$) and in favor of the unrecognized alternative (RU$_{(U)}$).

MRI Results

Generally, to control for the RT differences between the conditions (cf. Behavioral Results), we included RT parameters for each condition as covariates. This covariation analysis is capable of removing extraneous variability that derives from RT differences between conditions. To test for the specific neural correlates of RH-based decisions we investigated the hemodynamic response elicited by all RU trials in which the RH was applied as in contrast to all those (RU) trials in which this was not the case (all trials of each condition were included regardless of correctness so as to reliably estimate the beta values). The analysis revealed a significantly higher hemodynamic activity for decisions based on the RH within the anterior frontomedian cortex (aFMC) and the precuneus bilaterally extending into the retrosplenial cortex (Figure 25-2, Table 25-2). No brain region showed significant activation for the inverse contrast. Results remained even if the number of RH trials was randomly and individually adjusted to match the number of non-RH trials (Figure 25-2, Table 25-2). For example, if a participant chose in a specific number of RU trials, say 20 trials, the unrecognized alternative, we would have included in the model 20 randomly chosen RU trials in which the participant selected the recognized alternative.

To investigate which brain areas were involved with successful recognition, RR trials were contrasted with UU trials. Significant activation was revealed bilaterally within the midportion of the parahippocampal gyrus, the ventral striatum extending into the caudate nucleus, the retrosplenial cortex extending into the medial parietal cortex, the intraparietal sulcus, within the posterior frontomedian cortex (pFMC), ventromedial prefrontal cortex (VMPFC), and left inferior prefrontal cortex (LIPFC; Figure 25-2, Table 25-2).

To identify regions commonly activated by RH-based decisional processes and recognition memory processes, we calculated a conjunction analysis, that is, a test for a logical AND (Nichols, Brett, Andersson, Wager, & Poline, 2005). A positive conjunction test implies those regions that are commonly activated across the two kinds of cognitive processes. According to Nichols et al. (2005), a correct test for a logical AND requires that all the comparisons in the conjunction are individually significant at a specified alpha rate. Accordingly, if a voxel showed a Z score less than the critical Z value of 3.09 then the associated voxel in the other Z map was set to zero. That is, if either the map of the RH contrast or the map of the recognition–memory contrast contained a zero, then the conjunction was false. The resulting conjunction map reveals the intersection of the two statistical maps thresholded at a specific alpha rate and hence reliably displays those regions where there is an effect in both maps. In the present study, results of the conjunction analysis revealed significant activation only within two areas: within the retrosplenial cortex and precuneus (Figure 25-2, Table 25-2). This finding suggests the retrosplenial cortex activation and precuneus activation but not aFMC activation during RH-based decisions to reflect recognition and retrieval processes.

To test whether medial parietal cortex activation can indeed be considered as an index of the strength of the recognition signal, we calculated a parametric analysis (post hoc) by including a covariate reflecting the average recognition signal per trial, that is, the mean recognition value of the two presented cities. The recognition value for each city in turn was calculated as the percentage of participants in Experiment 1 that recognized it. When testing for the effect of an increasing recognition strength, the same activation pattern as for the recognition memory contrast was revealed: activation revealed bilaterally within the midportion of the parahippocampal gyrus, ventral striatum, retrosplenial cortex extending into the medial parietal cortex, intraparietal sulcus bilaterally, within the pFMC, VMPFC, and LIPFC. Accordingly, medial parietal cortex activation that was revealed when participants applied the RH as compared when they did not is taken to reflect the strength of the recognition signal.

Experiment 2

Behavioral Results

Behavioral results of Experiment 2 are shown in Table 25-3: RT of the four experimental

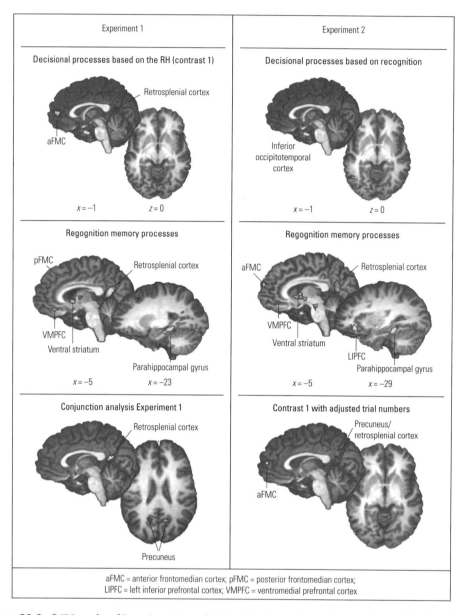

Figure 25-2. fMRI results of Experiments 1 and 2. Top: Results are shown for the effects of decisional processes based on the RH in Experiment 1 (contrast: RU trials in which the RH was applied > RU trials in which the RH was not applied) and effects of decisional processes solely based on recognition in Experiment 2 (contrast: RU trials in which the recognized alternative was chosen > RU trials in which the unrecognized alternative was chosen). Middle: The effects of recognition memory processes are shown for both experiments (contrasts: RR trials > UU trials). Bottom: left, results of the conjunction analysis of the two pictured contrasts in Experiment 1; right, result of Contrast 1 when trial numbers were adjusted.

Table 25-2. Experiment 1

Area	x	y	z	Z
RH-based decisional processes				
aFMC	−5	54	6	4.6
Retrosplenial cortex	4	−48	15	3.8
Medial parietal cortex	−17	−62	24	3.9
	10	−62	27	4.1
Recognition memory processes				
Midportion of the parahippocampal gyrus	−23	−36	−6	4.4
	28	−35	−6	4.4
Precuneus extending into retrosplenial cortex	−11	−54	15	4.4
	4	−53	12	4.7
VMPFC	−5	36	−9	4.2
Ventral striatum extending into the caudate nucleus	−11	6	9	4.7
	7	3	9	4.1
pFMC	−2	30	39	3.8
Intraparietal sulcus	−29	−65	42	4.8
Posterior parietal cortex	40	−68	39	4.0
LIPFC	−29	36	−3	4.7
Conjunction analysis of the contrasts RH-based decisional				
processes and recognition memory processes				
Retrosplenial cortex	7	−53	15	4.2
Precuneus	10	−60	24	4.0
	−20	−57	24	3.6
Parametric analysis of increasing recognition strength				
Midportion of the parahippocampal gyrus	−20	−33	−6	4.4
	28	−36	−6	4.5
Retrosplenial cortex extending into precuneus	−5	−54	21	4.7
	7	−53	12	4.9
VMPFC	−5	34	−9	4.4
Caudate nucleus	−11	6	9	4.5
	7	4	3	4.0
pFMC	−2	30	39	3.9
Posterior parietal cortex/intraparietal sulcus	−29	−65	42	4.7
	37	−66	39	4.4
LIPFC	−29	39	−6	4.7
Cerebellum	10	−86	−18	4.2

aFMC = anterior frontomedian cortex; VMPFC = ventromedial pre-frontal cortex; pFMC = posterior frontomedian cortex; LIPFC = left inferior prefrontal cortex.
Anatomical specification, Talairach coordinates (x, y, z) and maximal Z scores of significantly activated voxels are shown for each contrast calculated in Experiment 1.

conditions (trials in which participants recognized both cities, neither, or one city and had to choose the recognized city or the unrecognized city) differed significantly in that participants were faster on trials in which they recognized neither of the two presented cities, $F(3,11) = 2.98$; $p = .04$ (Table 3); a Kolmogorov–Smirnov test indicates that the means of the subjects RTs were normally distributed (all Z values $> .527$). Regarding the RU trials, participants were only 156 msec faster when choosing the recognized alternative as compared to choosing the unrecognized alternative, $t(13) = − 1.94$; $p = .08$.

MRI Results

Generally, to control for the RT differences between the conditions, we included RT parameters for each condition as in Experiment 1. Parallel to the heuristic contrast in Experiment 1, we compared trials in which participants

Table 25-3. Behavioral Results of Experiment 2

Condition	RT	SE (RT)
RR	3114	69
UU	3015	86
RU$_R$	3121	111
RU$_U$	3277	70

Reaction times (RTs) of the following conditions are shown: participants recognized both cities (RR), no city (UU), participants recognized one city and had to choose the recognized alternative (RU$_R$) or had to choose the unrecognized alternative (RU$_U$).

recognized one alternative and chose the recognized one with trials in which they recognized one alternative and chose the unrecognized one. A significantly higher hemodynamic activity was elicited within the left inferior occipitotemporal cortex and inferior frontal sulcus when participants chose the recognized city (Figure 25-2, Table 25-4).

To investigate which brain areas were involved with successful recognition, we contrasted RR trials with UU trials parallel to Experiment 1. Significant activation was observed bilaterally within the midportion of the parahippocampal gyrus, right precuneus extending into retrosplenial cortex, bilaterally within the ventral striatum extending into caudate nucleus, LIPFC, aFMC

(Brodmann's area 9), and VMPFC (Figure 25-2, Table 25-4). A conjunction analysis between these two contrasts revealed no area to be commonly activated.

To identify overlap in activation patterns for successful recognition memory processes in Experiments 1 and 2, we calculated a test for the logical AND (Nichols et al., 2005). Regions that revealed to be commonly activated by recognition memory processes in both experiments were bilaterally the midportion of the parahippocampal gyrus, precuneus extending into the retrosplenial cortex, ventral striatum bilaterally, and LIPFC. Activation within the MTL and medial parietal cortex have repeatedly been associated with recognition memory processes (e.g., Henson, 2005; Wagner et al., 2005), and LIPFC activation with controlled semantic processing (e.g., Gold, Balota, Kirchhoff, & Buckner, 2005). Thus, the activation obtained in these experiments suggests that recognition memory processes were engaged both when assessing which city was larger (Experiment 1) and when assessing which city was recognized (Experiment 2).

DISCUSSION

The present study investigated the neural correlates of decisional processes that are based on the RH. Simply stated, the RH claims that when

Table 25-4. Experiment 2

Area	X	y	z	Z
Decisional processes based on recognition only				
Inferior occipitotemporal cortex	−44	−59	0	3.8
Inferior frontal sulcus	−44	36	9	3.6
Recognition memory processes				
Midportion of the parahippocampal gyrus	−29	−38	−6	4.4
	25	−36	−11	3.6
Precuneus extending into retrosplenial cortex	−11	−59	15	4.0
VMPFC	−8	39	−9	4.0
Ventral striatum extending into the caudate nucleus	−2	7	3	4.7
aFMC (Brodmann's area 9)	−11	60	24	4.2
LIPFC	−29	28	−8	4.4

VMPFC = ventromedial prefrontal cortex; aFMC = anterior frontomedian cortex; LIPFC = left inferior prefrontal cortex.
Anatomical specification, Talairach coordinates (x, y, z), and maximal Z scores of significantly activated voxels are shown for each contrast calculated in Experiment 2.

making a judgment about two items, a person recognizing only one of the alternatives will infer the recognized one has the higher criterion value. The effective use of the RH depends on the outcome of two processes: whether the alternatives are recognized and a judgment about the ecological rationality of the RH, that is, whether the chain of correlations linking the (inaccessible) criterion to recognition through a mediator variable justifies following the RH. Accordingly, RH-based decisional processes are special in that they feature a judgment of ecological rationality compared to decisional processes that solely rely on recognition information.

In the following we will discuss the medial parietal activation and the frontomedian activation that was found to be specific to the application of the RH. Subsequently, we will discuss why there was no frontomedian activation when the RH was not applied.

Activation within Medial Parietal Areas Reflect Recognition Processes When Decisions Follow the RH

Generalizing from anatomical studies in monkeys, the precuneus and retrosplenial cortex are upstream to the medial temporal memory system (Kobayashi & Amaral, 2003). Thus, medial parietal areas are directly or indirectly connected to the MTL. The retrosplenial cortex is special in that its afferent connections are dominated by MTL projections. Based on this finding, Kobayashi and Amaral (2003) suggested parietal midline structures as the major pathways through which the MTL influences cortical information processing in the service of declarative memory. This assumption is further supported by a phenomenon referred to as "retrosplenial amnesia." Damage to the retrosplenial cortex has been associated with the loss of verbal episodic memory as well as with a loss for spatial relations (Maeshima et al., 2001; Valenstein et al., 1987). Imaging studies repeatedly reported activation within parietal midline structures that extend from the retrosplenial cortex and posterior cingulate to the precuneus for episodic memory retrieval processes (Krause et al., 1999; Maguire, Frith, & Morris, 1999; Squire et al., 1992): Activation within medial parietal areas, specifically within

the precuneus, has been shown to be sensitive to successful retrieval (old/new effects; Henson, Rugg, Shallice, Josephs, & Dolan, 1999; Fletcher et al., 1995), autobiographical memory retrieval (Addis, McIntosh, Moscovitch, Crawley, & McAndrews, 2004; Gilboa, Winocur, Grady, Hevenor, & Moscovitch, 2004), retrieval orientation (Dobbins, Rice, Wagner, & Schacter, 2003), and for the subjective perception that information is old (perceived recognition; Kahn, Davachi, & Wagner, 2004; Wheeler & Buckner, 2003). Yet, at the same time, precuneus activation has also been found in studies of visuospatial imagery, self-processing operations, and consciousness (for an overview, see Cavanna & Trimble, 2006; Naghavi & Nyberg, 2005). Given the involvement of the precuneus in such a wide spectrum of higher order cognitive functions, the exact nature of the precuneus function has long been considered elusive, and domain-specific interpretations dominated. By reviewing current knowledge about the anatomical and cytoarchitectonic structure of the precuneus as well as functional imaging data, Cavanna and Trimble (2006) have suggested a functional subdivision within the precuneus: an anterior region that is especially involved in self-centered mental imagery strategies, and a posterior region mainly subserving successful episodic memory retrieval, irrespective of the imagery content of the retrieved information.

The precuneus activation in the present study for RH-based decisional processes occurred in the posterior part of the precuneus, specifically anterior to the parieto-occipital sulcus, and thus is suggested to be associated with successful retrieval attempts. This interpretation is in line with the assumption that the precuneus particularly responds to familiarity confidence (Yonelinas, Otten, Shaw, & Rugg, 2005). Yonelinas et al. (2005) reported a positive correlation between posterior precuneus activation and recognition confidence, suggesting that activation within the posterior precuneus can be used as proxy for the overall strength of the recognition signal. Additional support for this comes from our parametric analysis linking medial posterior parietal cortex with how likely a city was recognized by our participants. Experiment 1 revealed higher activation within the aFMC and precuneus extending into the retrosplenial cortex when participants responded according to the RH (i.e., choosing the recognized city as larger) as compared to when they did not. The activation foci that were elicited by RH-based decisional processes (i.e., aFMC, precuneus, and retrosplenial cortex) could be dissociated with respect to their involvement in recognition memory processes: The medial parietal areas alone were found to be activated both by the application of the RH and recognition. Accordingly, we suggest medial parietal cortex activation to mainly reflect recognition memory processes during RH-based decisions, whereas aFMC activation could be specific to judgmental processes about the RH's ecological rationality.

Activation within the aFMC Reflects Judgments of Ecological Rationality When Decisions Follow the RH

Based on Experiment 1, one could entertain the hypothesis that aFMC is doing nothing more than accumulating a recognition signal from medial parietal areas, implying that decisions are made strictly on the basis of recognition. This suggests that to the extent that RH-based decisional processes can adequately be explained by participants simply choosing the recognized alternative, aFMC activation should also be elicited by decisional processes based solely on recognition information. To test this hypothesis, we ran Experiment 2, but instead asked participants to choose the recognized alternative in each trial. Contrasting trials (in Experiment 2) in which participants chose the recognized alternative with trials in which they did the opposite revealed no significant aFMC activation, but instead activation within the left inferior occipitotemporal cortex. This area has repeatedly been found for lexical decisions in the visual domain (e.g., for word–pseudoword discrimination; Fiebach, Friederici, Müller, & von Cramon, 2002). This finding led to the assumption that occipitotemporal brain areas could be conceived of as a functionally specialized word recognition region within the ventral visual pathway. Fiebach and Friederici (2002) replicated the lexical decision task in the auditory domain and again found activation within the occipitotemporal cortex

for real words as compared to pseudowords, which led the authors to suggest this area to be related to modality-independent aspects of word recognition. Accordingly, when participants (in Experiment 2) chose the recognized city, they simply opted for that word whose word representation form was stored in their lexicon.

These results further bolster the claim that the aFMC activation observed in Experiment 1 is specific to judgments of ecological rationality and not merely for the strength of the recognition signal. Recently, the aFMC has been proposed to reflect self-related processes or social–cognitive judgments (Northoff & Bempohl, 2004; Ochsner et al., 2004; Gusnard, Akbudak, Shulman, & Raichle, 2001). Generally, such processes can be characterized by the requirement to relate an aspect of the external world to oneself involving the ranking, scaling, and evaluating of one's own priorities and notions in relation to parameters of the external situation (Goldberg & Podell, 1999). A feature of paradigms investigating the cerebral correlates of self-related processes is that responses cannot be scored against an absolute standard; rather, correct responses are relative and actor centered, such as what is conceived of as moral (Heekeren, Wartenburger, Schmidt, Schwintowski, & Villringer, 2003; Moll et al., 2002; Greene, Sommerville, Nystrom, Darley, & Cohen, 2001) or as coherent (Ferstl & von Cramon, 2002) or as beautiful (Jacobsen, Schubotz, Hofel, & von Cramon, 2006). In the city judgment task in Experiment 1, participants had to evaluate the applicability of the RH, which could be done by inferring a rough correlation between the (strength of) recognition and city population. Hence, judgments of the RH's ecological rationality are largely self-referential, as they depend on assessing one's own sense of recognition.

Why Wasn't There aFMC Activation When the RH Was Not Followed?

One might expect judgments of ecological rationality should be required in those trials in which the RH was not applied. Yet, these trials did not elicit aFMC activation. To investigate whether aFMC activation results from a relative difference in signal strength between the two sorts of

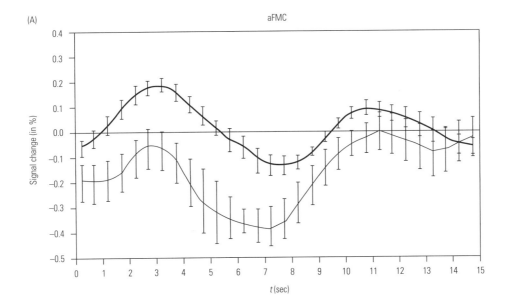

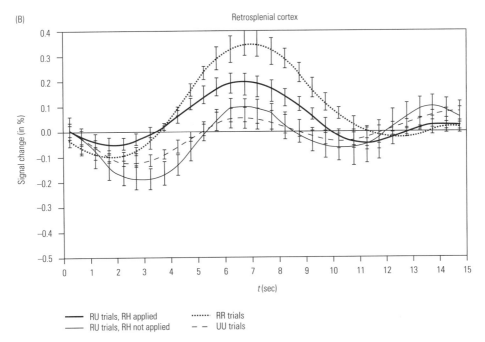

Figure 25-3. Mean percentage signal changes (MPSCs, i.e., event-related averages) with error bars for the aFMC, retrosplenial cortex, and (right) precuneus in Experiment 1: (A) MPSCs are shown for the aFMC for trials in which the RH was applied (bold line) and was not applied (thin line). (B) MPSCs in the retrosplenial cortex for all conditions (see legend for details). (C) MPSCs for the (right) precuneus for all conditions (see legend for details). The stimulus presentation of the two city names, lasting for 4 sec, started at time point zero.

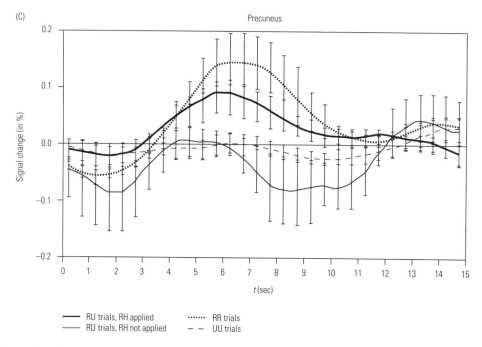

Figure 25-3. (continued).

trials or rather because trials in which the RH was not applied did not activate the aFMC at all, we plotted the time course of the mean percentage signal change in the aFMC. Results revealed less deactivation for trials in which the RH was applied as compared to those trials in which the RH was not applied (Figure 25-3). The time course of the aFMC supports the default-mode hypothesis ascribed to the medial prefrontal cortex that was put forward by Gusnard et al. (2001). The finding that the aFMC is among those brain regions showing the highest baseline metabolic activity and task-related activation reductions during goal-directed cognitive processing led to the assumption that the medial prefrontal cortex subserves functions that are essential to the self-concept: During attention-demanding tasks the self-referential activity of the aFMC is reduced. In the present study, activation in the aFMC was reduced more when participants failed to apply the RH, suggesting that the suspension of the RH required more cognitive effort than judgments in line with the heuristic, suggesting participants follow the RH

by default. This conclusion is consistent with the RT data: Participants in Experiment 1 took significantly longer to decide against the RH, that is, when assessing the unrecognized alternative as the larger city ($F(1, 17) = 30.2$; $p = .0001$). The finding that it takes additional time to suspend the RH has also been reported by Pachur and Hertwig (2006).

There could be multiple reasons that would lead participants to go against the RH. For instance, a person could discount their recognition because they know that the city is small (Oppenheimer, 2003). For example, the city of Pisa in Italy is probably known by its leaning tower, so participants may infer that the recognition of Pisa is not directly indicative of a large population size (about 86,000 inhabitants). Another possibility is that they are not only taking into account whether they recognize the city or not, but how confident they are that they recognize it. Evidence for this comes from the time course for activation in the precuneus and retrosplenial cortex when the RH was followed and when it was not. Figure 25-3 shows activation in the precuneus and retrosplenial areas for the four kinds of trials of interest in Experiment 1. Notice that the UU, $RU_{(R)}$, and RR trials are ordered in terms of the number of alternatives recognized, in line with the suggestion of Yonelinas et al. (2005) that the precuneus reflects recognition confidence and with our parametric analysis of recognition rates and activation in these regions. The surprising result is the paltry activation in medial parietal areas for the $RU_{(U)}$ trials where the activation is not significantly different from the signal of UU trials, that is, when neither item was recognized [precuneus: $t(17) = -0.42$; $p = .68$; retrosplenial cortex: $t(17) = -1.5$; $p = .17$] (Figure 25-3), consistent with the hypothesis that they failed to follow the RH when recognition confidence is low.

Taken together, the present fMRI studies converge on the following conclusions: (1) Whereas RH-based decisions do depend on the strength of the recognition signal, as measured by activation in medial parietal areas (2) the processes underlying RH-based decisions go beyond simply choosing the recognized alternative. (3) Specifically, RH-based decisional processes are distinguished by judgments about the ecological rationality of the RH that are specific to the aFMC.

ACKNOWLEDGMENTS

The authors thank Jennifer Kittel for assistance in data collection, Ralph Hertwig for valuable considerations and productive discussions, and two anonymous reviewers for their very constructive and helpful comments on a prior version of the manuscript.

Introduction to Chapter 26

Fluency Heuristic: A Model of How the Mind Exploits a By-Product of Information Retrieval

When Hertwig and Schooler (see Chapter 4) implemented the recognition heuristic within the ACT-cognitive architecture, they "discovered" the fluency heuristic. The fluency heuristic works when both objects are recognized and the recognition heuristic can no longer be applied (see Chapter 3). It is also a potential alternative to the take-the-best heuristic (see Chapter 2), especially if a person has no cue knowledge about the objects beyond recognition. Of course, fluency and the fluency heuristic had been widely established and frequently studied concepts long before Hertwig and Schooler. Yet, by implementing the fluency heuristic within ACT-R, Schooler and Hertwig were able to precisely define the somewhat vague concept of fluency in terms of a memory record's activation, which tracks environmental regularities (i.e., frequency of occurrences and recency), and in terms of a phenomenological response that is correlated with activation in ACT-R, namely, how quickly a record can be retrieved.

In this article, Ralph Hertwig, Stefan Herzog, Lael Schooler, and Torsten Reimer pursue both a prescriptive and a descriptive goal. The prescriptive one entails an ecological analysis of fluency across several domains. Adopting the ecological analysis of recognition conducted by Goldstein and Gigerenzer (see Chapter 3), the authors examined the validity of fluency across five different environments featuring criterion variables such as number of residents, revenue, sales figures, and wealth. Consistent with the analyses within the ACT-R framework, fluency validity was always lower than recognition validity. Yet across all domains, the validity was above chance and sometimes as high as 66%. In other words, by relying on recognition latency and nothing else, people could to some extent infer properties of the world that were unknown to them. But is that what they actually do?

Answering this descriptive question is the other goal of the article. The authors approached it in two ways. First, they analyzed whether people can accurately tell the difference between two recognition latencies. People proved to be quite good at discriminating between recognition latencies whose difference exceeded 100 ms [we have omitted this study from the present article]. Second, they tested whether people's actual inferences conformed to those predicted by the fluency heuristic. Across three environments, the mean proportions of inferences consistent with the fluency heuristic were 74%, 63%, and 68%, respectively. Moreover, these accordance rates were as high as 82% when differences in recognition latency were large. Deriving the fluency heuristic's prediction for individual people and individual items is a strong test. Yet it is not how the impact of fluency is commonly tested in social and cognitive psychology, where researchers tend to manipulate fluency experimentally and observe the consequences. The authors hence conducted a study honoring this methodological approach as well and found that experimentally manipulated fluency indeed shapes inferences.

CHAPTER 26

Fluency Heuristic: A Model of How the Mind Exploits a By-Product of Information Retrieval

Ralph Hertwig, Stefan M. Herzog, Lael J. Schooler, and Torsten Reimer

Abstract: Boundedly rational heuristics for inference can be surprisingly accurate and frugal for several reasons. They can exploit environmental structures, co-opt complex capacities, and elude effortful search by exploiting information that automatically arrives on the mental stage. The fluency heuristic is a prime example of a heuristic that makes the most of an automatic by-product of retrieval from memory, namely, retrieval fluency. In four experiments, the authors show that retrieval fluency can be a proxy for real-world quantities, that people can discriminate between two objects' retrieval fluencies, and that people's inferences are in line with the fluency heuristic (in particular, fast inferences) and with experimentally manipulated fluency. The authors conclude that the fluency heuristic may be one tool in the mind's repertoire of strategies that artfully probes memory for encapsulated frequency information that can veridically reflect statistical regularities in the world.

The human mind has long been regarded as tailored to register and to exploit frequencies of occurrence. Take, for instance, David Hume's (1740/1978) view, expressed in *A Treatise of Human Nature*:

As the habit, which produces the association, arises from the frequent conjunction of objects, it must arrive at its perfection by degrees, and must acquire new force from each instance, that falls under our observation. The first instance has little or no force: The second makes some addition to it: The third becomes still more

sensible; and 'tis by these slow steps, that our judgment arrives at a full assurance (p. 130).

Hume (1740/1978) believed that the mind unconsciously tallies frequencies and apportions degrees of belief (for Hume, the *vivacity* of an idea). He held that the mechanism for converting observed frequency into belief was finely tuned: "When the chances or experiments on one side amount to ten thousand, and on the other to ten thousand and one, the judgment gives the preference to the latter, upon account of that superiority" (p. 141). Today, we know that Hume endowed the human mind with too exquisite a sensitivity to frequencies and that there is typically no direct mapping of environmental frequencies onto degrees of beliefs. Yet, numerous treatments of human cognition and memory center on the effects of environmental frequencies and repetition on memory and judgment (e.g., Dougherty, Gettys, & Ogden, 1999). Various mental tools exploit the "force" of these repetitions on memory. One of these

541

mental tools is the *ACT-R fluency heuristic* that cashes in on *retrieval fluency* (Schooler & Hertwig, 2005). In what follows, we describe the fluency heuristic, and its close relative the recognition heuristic, before discussing their intellectual antecedents.

THE FLUENCY HEURISTIC AND THE RECOGNITION HEURISTIC

The research program on fast-and-frugal heuristics (Gigerenzer, Todd, & the ABC Research Group, 1999) has demonstrated that a user of heuristics who invested modest amounts of cognitive effort—for instance, in terms of searching for information and integrating it—could nevertheless achieve high levels of performance. Arguably the simplest of these heuristics, the *recognition heuristic* is a key example of just how far a little cognitive effort can go. It predicts which of two objects, *a* or *b*, has the higher value on a quantitative criterion. The heuristic's policy states:

> If one of two objects, *a* or *b*, is recognized and the other is not, then infer that the recognized object has the higher value with respect to the criterion.

Recognition knowledge (i.e., knowledge of the previously experienced or believed to be previously experienced) is cognitively inexpensive. In the process of retrieving a memory record, it arrives automatically and instantaneously on the mental stage, thus ready to enter inferential processes when other knowledge still awaits retrieval (Pachur & Hertwig, 2006). Low-cost recognition information, of course, will not inevitably result in high levels of accuracy. For good performance, recognition needs to be correlated with the criterion to be inferred, an issue to which we return shortly. Since Goldstein and Gigerenzer (2002) proposed the recognition heuristic, numerous studies have demonstrated that recognition is an important piece of information across various inferential tasks such as the prediction of outcomes at sport events (e.g., Pachur & Biele, 2007; Serwe & Frings, 2006) and the judgment of demographic, geographic, and biological quantities (e.g., Pohl, 2006; Reimer & Katsikopoulos, 2004; Richter & Späth, 2006).[1]

Heuristics are not all-purpose inferential tools. Rather, they are applicable under limited circumstance that, ideally, can be defined. This is the case for the recognition heuristic: It cannot be applied when both objects are either recognized or unrecognized. If both objects are recognized, one applicable strategy is the fluency heuristic (Schooler & Hertwig, 2005; see Gigerenzer & Goldstein, 1996, for other heuristics) that exploits ease of retrieval and can be expressed as follows:

> If two objects, *a* and *b*, are recognized, and one of two objects is more fluently retrieved, then infer that this object has the higher value with respect to the criterion.

Like the recognition heuristic, the fluency heuristic is useful whenever there is a substantial correlation—in either direction—between a criterion and recognition and/or retrieval fluency. For simplicity, we assume that the correlation is positive. The fluency heuristic relies on one inexpensive piece of mnemonic information to make an inference, namely, the fluency with which memory records (of the objects' names) are retrieved from long-term memory. That is, even if two objects are recognized, the fluency with which the names are retrieved may be different. Such differences can be exploited to make inferences about other properties of the objects.

Schooler and Hertwig (2005) implemented the fluency heuristic and the recognition heuristic within the ACT-R cognitive architecture (Anderson et al., 2004; Anderson & Lebiere, 1998), thereby being able to precisely define fluency in terms of the time it takes to retrieve memories (or chunks, to use the ACT-R terminology). ACT-R makes the assumption that information in long-term memory is stored in discrete chunks and that retrieval entails search through these to find the one that achieves some processing goal of the system. The explanatory power of the approach depends on the system's estimates of the probability that each record in long-term memory is the one sought. These probabilities are encoded in a record's *activation*. Activation tracks environmental regularities, such as an object's frequency and recency of occurrence (and is also a function of parameters such as decay of activation over time). Therefore, activation differences partly reflect frequency differences, which, in turn, may be correlated with differences in objective properties of objects. A cognitive system may be able to capitalize on differences in activation associated with various objects by gauging how it responds to them. Two phenomenological responses that are correlated with activation in ACT-R are (a) whether a record associated with a specific object can be retrieved and (b) how quickly the record can be retrieved (henceforth, *retrieval fluency*). The first binary response was the basis for Schooler and Hertwig's implementation of the recognition heuristic. The second continuous response provided the basis for their implementation of the fluency heuristic and the existence proof that a cognitive system that relies on fluency can make moderately accurate inferences about real-world quantities. It does so by tapping indirectly— via retrieval fluency—into the environmental frequency information locked in the chunks' activation values.

Here are the goals of the current article: Schooler and Hertwig's (2005) ACT-R analysis of the fluency heuristic was theoretical in nature. From their analysis, however, follow four empirical questions that we aim to answer: First, does retrieval fluency correlate at all with objective properties of the world (Study 1)? Second, how accurately can people discriminate between often-minute differences in retrieval fluency (Study 2)? Third, to what extent do individuals' inferences actually agree with the fluency heuristic (Study 3)? Fourth, is there direct experimental evidence that fluency guides inferences about real-world quantities (Study 4)? Before we turn to these studies, we review some intellectual roots of the fluency heuristic.

FLUENCY, THE FLUENCY HEURISTIC, AND THE AVAILABILITY HEURISTIC

There are many different variants of fluency, including processing fluency and the distinctions between absolute and relative fluency, conceptual and perceptual fluency (see Alter & Oppenheimer, 2007; Reber, Schwarz, &

Winkielman, 2004; Winkielman, Schwarz, Fazendeiro, & Reber, 2003). The fluency heuristic as investigated here focuses on retrieval fluency, a proximal cue that can inform and influence human inference across a wide range of target criteria. It has been demonstrated to underlie, for instance, a person's memory of the past and prediction of future memory recall performance (Benjamin, Bjork, & Hirshman, 1998; Benjamin, Bjork, & Schwartz, 1998); an eyewitness's confidence in her or his memory (Shaw, 1996; Shaw, McClure, & Wilkens, 2001); assessments of one's ability to learn (e.g., Koriat & Ma'ayan, 2005); and people's confidence in their general knowledge (e.g., Kelley & Lindsay, 1993; Unkelbach, 2007). It has also been invoked in explaining consumer decisions (e.g., Schwarz, 2004).

Schooler and Hertwig's (2005) use of the term *fluency heuristic* hearkens back to a long research tradition on fluency, in particular the work by Jacoby and Dallas (1981); Kelley and Jacoby (1998); Kelley and Lindsay (1993); Whittlesea (1993); and Whittlesea and Leboe (2003). Abstracting from the different meanings of the term *fluency heuristic* across these articles, the gist involves three properties: (a) the attribution of "fluent" processing to prior experience, (b) the resulting conscious experience of familiarity, and (c) the assumption that relative fluency can be used as a basis for recognition memory.[2]

A second intellectual root of the fluency heuristic, as studied here, is the availability heuristic, one of the key heuristics proposed and investigated in the heuristics-and-biases research program (Tversky & Kahneman, 1974). Two interpretations of this heuristic have emerged, one of which includes the notion of retrieval fluency (Tversky & Kahneman, 1973, pp. 208, 210; see also Schwarz et al., 1991; Schwarz & Wänke, 2002). In one version, the availability heuristic rests on the *actual frequencies* of instances or occurrences retrieved, for instance, the occurrences of heart attack among one's acquaintances to assess the risk of heart attack among middle-aged people. Another rests on the ease, that is, *fluency* with which the operation of retrieval of these instances and occurrences can be performed (for more on the distinction between these two notions of availability, see Hertwig, Pachur, & Kurzenhäuser, 2005; Sedlmeier, Hertwig, & Gigerenzer, 1998).

Although there are similarities between the fluency heuristic and the latter version of the availability heuristic, fluency researchers have conceptualized them as two distinct heuristics (Jacoby & Dallas, 1981, p. 701; Jacoby & Whitehouse 1989, p. 127). One difference concerns the entities that are being retrieved. The availability heuristic derives its assessment of the frequency (probability) of the target event, say, risk of heart attack among middle-aged people, from the effortlessness (or lack thereof) with which prior instances of the target event could be retrieved (Tversky & Kahneman, 1974). The fluency heuristic, as defined by Schooler and Hertwig (2005), by contrast, bases its inferences simply on the speed with which the event category itself (e.g., myocardial infarction) is recognized. We realize, however, that the extent to which this property renders the fluency and the availability heuristics distinct depends on one's definition of availability. If availability extends to the retrieval of the event category itself, the fluency heuristic and the availability heuristic will be indistinguishable. Let us therefore reiterate the view we expressed in Schooler and Hertwig (2005, p. 626):

> We would have no objection to the idea that the fluency heuristic falls under the broad rubric of availability. In fact, we believe that our implementation of the fluency heuristic offers a definition of availability that interprets the heuristic as an ecologically rational strategy by rooting fluency in the informational structure of the environment.

Moreover, we believe that researchers in both the availability heuristic and the fluency heuristic traditions will find the present set of studies relevant. If one interprets the heuristics as distinct, our studies will foster the understanding of the predictive power of the fluency heuristic. Researchers interpreting availability and fluency as two sides of the same coin may find the present studies enriching to the extent that they provide one precise definition of availability and investigate its predictive power in making inferences about the world. That predictive power or lack thereof is, in fact, the focus of Study 1.

STUDY 1: IS IT WORTH EXPLOITING RETRIEVAL FLUENCY?

How can one learn the association between retrieval fluency and a criterion when the criterion is not accessible? In the context of the recognition heuristic, Goldstein and Gigerenzer (2002) proposed that there are "mediators" in the environment that both reflect (but do not reveal) the criterion and are accessible to decision makers' senses. For example, one may have no direct information about the ability of a tennis player, say, Roger Federer. Yet, his strength as a player may be reflected by how often his name is mentioned in the newspaper (*ecological correlation*). Because the newspaper is accessible, it can operate as a mediator. The frequency of mentions in the newspaper, in turn, is correlated with how likely someone is to recognize the player's name (*surrogate correlation*). Finally, how good or poor a proxy a person's recognition knowledge is of the criterion is captured in the *recognition validity*. Based on this chain of correlations between the criterion, the mediator, and the mind, a person would be able to make inferences about a player's strength depending on whether he or she recognized his name.

The same ecological analysis can also be conducted for the fluency heuristic, except that retrieval fluency replaces recognition. Frequency of mentions in the newspaper may be correlated not only with recognition but also with how quickly a person can retrieve the memory record representing the name Roger Federer. That is, the mediator can influence the recognition latency (thus giving rise to varying degrees of fluency) and the probability of recognition. Fluency, however, can be high for the wrong reasons and need not reflect environmentally valid variations in exposure. It may be sensitive to recent exposures, thus compromising the link between fluency and the criterion.

So, what is the ecological validity of retrieval fluency? Investigations of the chain of correlations between the criterion, frequency of mentions, and retrieval fluency in a clearly defined reference class of objects do not exist.[3] One rare exception is the investigation by Alter and Oppenheimer (2006). They found that the complexity of a share's name and the pronounceability of companies' three-letter stock ticker codes—both variables are indicators of the verbal fluency of a share's name—are predictive of the actual performance of those shares in the stock market immediately after their release onto the stock exchange. This analysis is particularly interesting insofar as fluency in their investigation is not just an indicator of the criterion, the share's performance on the stock market, but appears to causally determine stock performance in the short term.

In Study 1, we investigated whether retrieval fluency, like recognition, is a proxy for real-world quantities across five different reference classes in which we expected retrieval fluency to be effective. In this and the subsequent studies, we could not directly measure retrieval fluency, so instead we collected recognition latencies, that is, how long it took participants to judge an object as recognized or not. Of course, recognition latency is not a perfect proxy for retrieval fluency. Recognition latency includes other systematic and unsystematic components such as the time it takes to read a word, to decide whether it is recognized, and to output a motor response. It may well be that these factors drown out the contribution that retrieval latency makes to the overall recognition time.

Method

Participants. One hundred and sixty students from the University of Basel participated in the study (98 women and 62 men, mean age = 24.9 years), which was conducted at the Department of Psychology. Participants received either money (7.50 Swiss francs = US$6.10) or a course credit for their participation.

Material. To study the predictive power of fluency across different domains, we compiled five different environments: (a) the cities environment comprising all 118 U.S. cities with more than 100,000 inhabitants (Butler, 2003); (b) the companies environment containing all 100 German companies with the highest revenue in 2003 ("Die 100 grössten deutschen Unternehmen," n.d.); (c) the music artists environment including all 106 most successful artists in the U.S., in terms of the cumulative sales of recordings in the U.S. from 1958 to 2003 ("Top artists," 2003); (d) the athletes environment including the 50 richest athletes in 2004 ("The Best-Paid Athletes", 2004); and (e) the billionaires environment including the 100 wealthiest people in 2004 ("The World's Richest People", 2004). For each environment, we first determined the frequencies of mentions in the media (the mediator), by using COSMAS, the largest online archive of German print media (e.g., encyclopedias, books, and daily and weekly newspaper articles).[4]

Procedure. We recorded people's recognition latencies for each of the total of 474 objects. To avoid exhaustion, each participant saw a subset of the 474 objects. Forty participants were presented with the names of 100 German companies, 106 music artists, 50 sportspeople, and 100 billionaires, one at a time on the computer screen.[5] The order of objects within each environment was randomized across participants, as was the order of environments. A second group of 120 participants saw approximately a third of a pool of 525 cities drawn from different regions of the world, including 118 U.S. cities with more than 100,000 inhabitants (see the material used in Volz et al., 2006). Because the set of U.S. cities is the largest and the only one that encompasses all objects within a defined size range, we focus on the U.S. set in the following analysis. The names of the objects were presented one at a time (in random order), and respondents were asked to decide whether they had heard of the object. Both groups of participants indicated their decisions by pressing one of two keys, with the assignment of keys to responses counterbalanced across participants. In addition, respondents were instructed to make their decisions as quickly and as accurately as possible. The time that elapsed between the presentation of the object's name and the participant's keystroke was measured. After each response, the screen remained blank for 1,000 ms. Participants responded to 10 practice trials.

Results

How ecologically valid is retrieval fluency? To quantify the strength of the relationship between the environmental criteria, the frequency with which the names of the objects were mentioned in the media, and retrieval fluency (measured in terms of recognition latency), we calculated three measures: the fluency validity, the ecological validity, and the surrogate validity. The strength of the relationship between retrieval fluency and the criterion is defined as the proportion of times a faster recognized object has a higher criterion value than an object requiring more time to be recognized (in a given reference class). The fluency validity v_f is thus:

$$\dot{v}_f = R_f / (R_f + W_f),$$

where R_f is the number of correct (right) inferences made by the fluency heuristic computed across all pairs in which the difference in recognition latencies between two recognized objects equals or exceeds a just noticeable difference (JND), and W_f is the number of incorrect (wrong) inferences under the same circumstances. Note that validity is linearly related to Goodman-Kruskal's γ, an ordinal measure of association. Concerning the JND, Schooler and Hertwig (2005) assumed that there are limits to people's ability to discriminate between retrieval times. They assumed that the difference needs to be as large or larger than a JND of 100 ms, otherwise people resort to guessing. This value of 100 ms was based on Fraisse's (1984) extensive review of the timing literature—on his conclusion that durations of less than 100 ms are perceived as instantaneous—and is consistent with our findings in Study 2. Although all analyses reported in this article assume a JND of 100 ms, results do not depend on this specific value.

Ecological validity describes the relation between the criterion to be inferred and how often an object was mentioned in the media (its environmental frequency, measured with COSMAS). Ecological validity is defined as the proportion of times an object with the higher number of mentions in the media has a higher criterion value than does an object with a lower number of mentions. The *ecological validity* v_e is thus:

$$v_e = R_e / (R_e + W_e),$$

where R_e is the number of correct cases and W_e the number of incorrect cases computed across all pairs where one object occurs more frequently in the media than does the other.

Finally, the surrogate validity describes the relation between the mediator and recognition latencies. It is defined as the proportion of times an object with a higher number of mentions in the media is retrieved faster than an object with a lower number of mentions. The *surrogate validity* v_s is thus:

$$v_s = R_s / (R_s + W_s),$$

where R_s is the number of correct cases and W_s the number of incorrect cases computed across all pairs where one object occurs more frequently in the media than does the other (this calculation also assumes a JND of 100 ms). Goldstein and Gigerenzer (2002) and Schooler and Hertwig (2005) described the relations between criterion, mediator, and mind in terms of one validity measure and two correlation measures (ecological correlation and surrogate correlation). To simplify comparisons between these correlations, we consistently quantify them in terms of one currency, validity. All three validities can be interpreted as the conditional probability that object *a* scores higher (or lower) on one dimension than does object *b*, given that object *a* scores higher (or lower) on a second dimension than does object *b*.

Table 26-1 shows, separately for each environment, the median response time, the average and median number of occurrences in COSMAS per object, and the recognition rates. Across environments, the capacity to recognize objects varied widely, ranging from 68% (music artists) to merely 11% (billionaires) recognized objects (Table 26-1). Mirroring their low recognition rates, the median environmental frequencies of the names of the billionaires and athletes, respectively, is a magnitude smaller than that in the

Table 26-1. Response Time, Recognition Rates, and Environmental Frequencies Obtained Across the Five Environments Investigated in Study 1

Environment	Median Response Time per Object (ms)				Recognition Rate		Environmental Frequencies[a]	
	Recognized		Unrecognized					
	M	Mdn	M	Mdn	M	Mdn	M	Mdn
Cities	887	835	1129	1013	.53	.51	741	85
Companies	890	871	1045	999	.47	.48	671	142
Music artists	737	699	1045	1043	.68	.71	240	55
Athletes	948	920	1027	963	.26	.22	218	7
Billionaires	1591	1460	1176	1040	.11	.09	22	1

[a] Measured in terms of hits in COSMAS (see Footnotes 4 and 5).

other domains. Finally, except in the billionaires environment, the median time for recognized objects was markedly shorter than the response time for unrecognized objects.

To what extent is retrieval fluency a proxy for inferring real-world quantities? Figure 26-1 depicts the relations between the criterion, the frequency with which the names of the objects occurred in the media, and recognition latency and recognition, respectively. In all five environments, fluency validity exceeded chance level (.50), ranging from .66 in the cities environment to .58 in the music artists and companies environments, respectively. Figure 26-1 also shows that recognition validity consistently exceeds fluency validity—an observation to which we return in the final discussion.

Figure 26-2 plots fluency validity as a function of the magnitude of the objective differences in latencies (summarized for four bins: 0–99 ms, 100–399 ms, 400–699 ms, > 700 ms), separately for the five environments. There is a clear tendency that the larger the objective difference, the higher the validity of fluency. This tendency follows from the ACT-R framework, in which the activation of a memory record tracks environmental frequencies. Objects with larger criterion values tend to occur more frequently in the environment, and thus their memory records tend to be more quickly retrieved. Consequently, large differences in latencies are likely to represent a pair of objects in which one object has a

large criterion value and one has a small value. For such pairs, fluency can be expected to be quite valid.

To conclude, we found that differences in recognition latencies are indicative of criteria across five different environments. The strength of the relationship varies across environments. In the cities environment, for which we recorded the strongest relationship between the mediator and the criterion, we also observed the highest fluency validity. Similarly, environments with low ecological validity such as the companies and the music artists environments also yielded relatively low levels of fluency validity. Based on this ecological analysis of fluency across five environments, we can now conclude that, based on retrieval fluency, one can at least theoretically infer distal properties of the world. Study 2 shows that people can reliably discriminate between retrieval times of two recognized objects.

STUDY 3: ARE PEOPLE'S INFERENCES IN LINE WITH THE FLUENCY HEURISTIC?

The next study addresses three issues: First, we investigated the extent to which people's inferences are in line with the fluency heuristic and the recognition heuristic. Second, we examined the extent to which differences in retrieval fluency affect people's accordance to the fluency

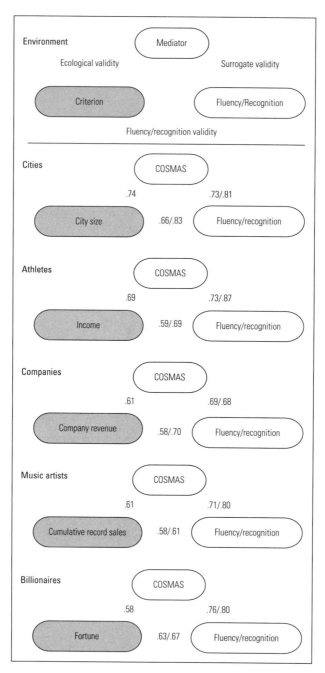

Figure 26-1. Ecological analysis of fluency validity and recognition validity across five environments. The triangles, adapted from Goldstein and Gigerenzer (2002; Figure 7), show the relationship between criterion, mediator, and the mind, measured in terms of validity. The inaccessible criterion is reflected but not revealed by the mediator variable (ecological validity). The mediator (environmental frequencies as measured by frequency of occurrences in COSMAS) influences retrieval speed (and probability of recognition); this link is expressed in terms of the surrogate validity. The mind in turn may use recognition speed or recognition to infer the criterion (the accuracy of this inference is captured in terms of fluency or recognition validity). Note that the ecological validity (the relationship between mediator and criterion) is independent of whether the mind uses retrieval speed or recognition.

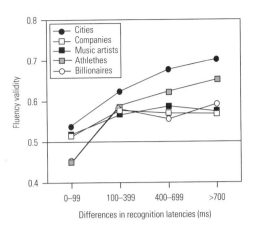

Figure 26-2. Increasing fluency validity accuracy as a function of increasing differences in recognition latencies. Differences in objects *a* and *b*'s recognition latencies were classified into four bins. Then, we calculated the fluency validity per bin. We chose to create bins such that each bin included judgments of nearly all participants. Other ways of creating the bins, however, result in the same general trend. The horizontal line at 0.5 represents chance level validity.

heuristic. Third, we tested the prediction that inferences agreeing with the fluency heuristic require less time, relative to inferences conflicting with the fluency heuristic. Let us briefly develop the latter two issues.

Does Accordance to the Fluency Heuristic Increase as a Function of the Difference in Recognition Latencies?

In Studies 1 and 2, we found that the larger the differences between the two objects' recognition latencies, the more likely that the exploitation of fluency leads to a correct inference (Figure 26-2) and the more accurate the discrimination between them. Rather than assuming that differences beyond 100 ms give rise to the same degree of fluency heuristic accordance, adherence may depend on the magnitude of the difference.

Do Inferences that Agree With the Fluency Heuristic Require Less Time?

Pachur and Hertwig (2006) predicted and found evidence that inferences consistent with the

recognition heuristic require less time than do inconsistent inferences. This prediction can also be extended to fluency information. Recognizing an object requires the memory record of the object to be retrieved, and the speed with which this process unfolds can be used as a proxy for people's senses of fluency. Therefore, fluency information is essentially produced at first sight of the names of the objects. It is available and ready to enter the inferential process while other information has yet to be retrieved. In contrast, inferences inconsistent with the fluency heuristic need to rely on information beyond recognition and recognition speed. Unless the result of mere guessing, such inferences rely on the retrieval of probabilistic cues or explicit knowledge about the criterion. This logic suggests that inferences based on fluency information may be made faster than inferences inconsistent with the fluency heuristic. Yet, if reliance on fluency requires additional checks such as whether the difference in latencies is "good enough," then fluency-based inference may turn out not to be made faster.

Method

Participants and design. Eighty students from the Free University (Berlin) participated in the study (42 women and 37 men; 1 participant failed to indicate gender information; mean age = 25.3 years). As in Study 2, participants were presented with 156 pairs of U.S. cities (*n* = 59), German companies (*n* = 46), and music artists (*n* = 51), and within each pair were asked to choose the object with the higher value on the criterion (*inference task*). Furthermore, each participant indicated which objects he or she recognized (*recognition task*). Half of participants took this recognition test before the inference task and half after. They received a flat fee of €10 (US$12.50).

Material. For the inference task, items were constructed in a similar way as in Study 2. For each environment, we randomly created 40 lists of pairs of objects (with the constraint that each object could occur only once in a list). Each of these lists was then presented to 2 participants; 1 received the recognition test before and the other after the inference task. Pairs of objects were presented in three blocks (representing the three environments). Once all inferences were made, the individual objects were again presented in three environmental blocks (in the same order as in the inference task). Participants were asked to report whether they recognized the name. The order of the blocks, the order of objects within each block, and the location of objects within each pair (left side vs. right side of the screen) were determined at random for each participant.

Procedure. After an introductory text explaining the inference task, pairs of objects were displayed on a computer screen. Participants indicated their inferences by pressing one of two keys. They were encouraged to respond as quickly and accurately as possible. The time that elapsed between the presentation of the objects and participants' keystroke was measured. Each inference trial began with the presentation of a fixation point (a cross in the center of the screen), followed after 500 ms by the respective pair. The names appeared simultaneously (left and right of the fixation point) and remained on the screen until a response was given. After each response, the screen remained blank for 1,100 ms. Participants first responded to six practice trials. The group of participants that had completed the inference task first then immediately took the recognition task, in which they indicated whether or not they had ever heard the name of the respective object.

Results

Recognition rates and latencies mimicked those observed in Studies 1 and 2, except in the companies environment, in which participants recognized more objects than in the previous studies. This boost in recognition, however, is consistent with the fact that Study 3 recruited only German students (and no Swiss students).

To what degree do people's inferences agree with the fluency heuristic? For each participant, we computed the percentage of inferences that were in line with the fluency heuristic among all cases in which it could be applied (i.e., pairs in which both objects were recognized), excluding pairs with differences in recognition latencies

smaller than 100 ms. Table 26-2 shows fluency applicability and fluency validity across environments. The values track those obtained in Study 2. The fluency heuristic applicability ranged between about a fourth and a third of all inferences. The mean fluency heuristic accordances (i.e., proportion of inferences consistent with the fluency heuristic) were .74, .63, and .68 in the cities, the companies, and the music artists environments, respectively.[6] As Figure 26-3a shows, in all environments there was substantial interindividual variation in the proportion of judgments that agreed with the heuristic. The rate of an individual's fluency heuristic accordance ranged between 1.00 and .30 across environments. Only a few participants appear to have systematically decided against fluency: Across environments, merely 12% of participants' accordance rates were below .50. Finally, Table 26-2 also shows participants' average score of correct inferences (in pairs in which both objects were recognized), which ranged between .58 (companies environment) and .71 (cities environment).

Next to comparing fluency accordance with a 50% baseline, one can also test whether observed fluency accordance is higher than that expected by chance: Let us assume that a person does not make use of the fluency heuristic. By mere chance one would expect that his or her inferences and those predicted by the heuristic coincide in more than 50% of the cases (assuming the person's accuracy and fluency validity are better than chance). There are two ways in which the person's and the heuristic's inferences can coincide: (a) both choose a (the larger object) or (b) both choose b (the smaller object). The probability that both choose a equals the person's level of accuracy (acc) times the fluency validity: $acc \times v_f$. The probability that both choose b is the product of the complementary probabilities: $(1 - acc) \times (1 - v_f)$. Consequently, the overall probability of the person and heuristic choosing the same object by chance (henceforth, baseline accordance) equals the sum of both products. Averaged across individuals, the rates of baseline accordance were 59%, 53%, and 52% in the cities, the companies, and the music artists environments, respectively.

Table 26-2 Applicability, Accordance, and Validity Rates for the Recognition and Fluency Heuristics, Respectively, Across Three Environments Investigated in Study 3

| Environment | Fluency Heuristic | | | | | | | | Recognition Heuristic | | | | | | | |
| | Fluency Applicability | | Fluency Accordance | | Fluency Validity | | Participant Accuracy | | Recognition Applicability | | Recognition Accordance | | Recognition Validity | | Participant Accuracy | |
	M	CI	M	CI	M	CI	M	CI	M	CI	M	CI	M	CI	M	CI
Cities	.23	.21, .26	.74	.71, .78	.67	.64, .70	.71	.67, .74	.47	.45, .49	.91	.89, .93	.84	.83, .86	.80	.77, .83
Companies	.30	.27, .32	.63	.60, .66	.60	.57, .63	.58	.55, .61	.45	.42, .47	.90	.87, .93	.74	.72, .76	.70	.67, .73
Music artists	.33	.31, .35	.68	.65, .70	.56	.53, .59	.59	.56, .62	.39	.37, .41	.93	.91, .96	.57	.55, .60	.59	.56, .61

Note: Participant accuracy denotes the level of inferential accuracy that respondents reached. CI = 95% confidence interval.

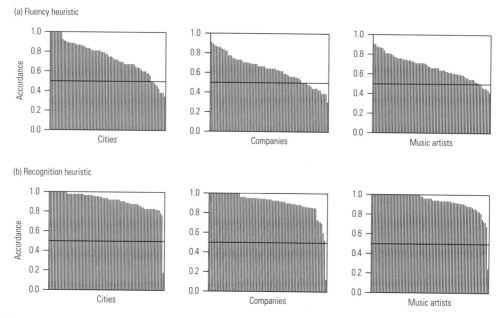

Figure 26-3. Accordance to the fluency and recognition heuristic. Percentage of inferences consistent with the fluency heuristic (Panel a) and recognition heuristic (Panel b) for participants in the cities, companies, and music artists environments, respectively. The individuals are ordered from left to right according to how often their judgments agreed with the respective heuristic. The horizontal line at 0.5 represents chance level accordance.

For each person, we then calculated the difference between his or her baseline accordance and his or her observed fluency accordance. In the cities environment, the observed accordance was 16 percentage points ($SD = 15\%$; CI = 12%, 19%; $Mdn = 16\%$; $d = 1.03$) higher than the individual-specific baseline accordance. In the companies environment, the respective difference was 11 percentage points ($SD = 13\%$; CI = 8%, 13%; $Mdn = 12\%$; $d = 0.83$); finally, in the music artists environment the difference was 15 percentage points ($SD = 11\%$; CI = 13%, 18%; $Mdn = 15\%$; $d = 1.38$). That is, when comparing the empirically found fluency accordance against a benchmark that takes the occurrence of coincidental accordance into account, the predictive power of the fluency heuristic remains sizeable.

To what degree do people's inferences agree with the recognition heuristic? Figure 26-3b shows individuals' accordance rates across environments. A vast majority of inferences can be captured by the recognition heuristic, when it can

be applied (see Table 26-2 for applicability rates). The mean proportion of recognition heuristic accordance was .91, .90, and .93 in the cities, companies, and music artists environments, respectively. Averaged across environments, 27% of respondents conformed to the recognition heuristic every time. Participants' average score of correct inferences (in pairs in which one object was recognized and the other was not) ranged between .59 (music artists environment) and .80 (cities environment).

Challenging Goldstein and Gigerenzer's (2002) assumption that the recognition heuristic takes into account only whether an object is recognized or not, Newell and Fernandez (2006, p. 333) found a negative correlation between the proportion of times a city was chosen over unrecognized cities and the speed with which participants correctly categorized the name of this city ($r = -.382$). Consistent with Newell and Fernandez and across all environments, we also found that a recognized object was more often inferred to be the larger one (relative to the unrecognized object), the faster it was recognized: cities (Spearman $r = -.343$, $p = .001$), companies ($r = -.268$, $p = .01$), and music artists ($r = -.325$, $p = .001$), respectively. Convergent evidence that recognition strength correlates with following the recognition heuristic comes from an fMRI study by Volz et al. (2006). They found that decisions in accordance with the heuristic correlate with higher activation in areas of the brain that have previously been associated with greater recognition confidence.

Is accordance to fluency a function of the difference in recognition latencies? Study 2 showed that the larger the differences between the objects' recognition speed, the more accurately people can discriminate between the two objects' recognition latencies. Does the regularity also relate to the likelihood with which people accord to the fluency heuristic? Figure 26-4 plots fluency heuristic accordance as a function of differences in recognition latencies. Accordance rates, indeed, do increase with larger differences.[7]

Do inferences that agree with the fluency heuristic and the recognition heuristic require less response time? To answer this question, for each participant we calculated the median response time—separately for each of the three environments—for inferences consistent and inconsistent with both the recognition and the fluency

heuristics. Figure 26-5 shows the mean of the differences between these two values. Across all environments, inferences conflicting with the fluency heuristic take markedly longer than do inferences consistent with it. The same regularity also holds for the recognition heuristic, replicating Pachur and Hertwig's (2006) finding. As the confidence intervals indicate, the mean of each of the six differences is significantly greater than zero. Moreover, the effect sizes (Cohen's *d*; Cohen, 1988) for the differences in response times are greater for the recognition heuristic than for the fluency heuristic across all three environments (cities: $d = 0.74$ vs. $d = 0.54$; companies: $d = 0.62$ vs. $d = 0.48$; and music artists: $d = 0.85$ vs. $d = 0.53$).

To summarize, in about two thirds to three fourths of inferences in which the fluency heuristic was applicable, people's actual choices conformed to those predicted by the heuristic. We also found that the larger the difference between recognition latencies (for two objects), the greater the likelihood that the actual inference adheres to that predicted by the fluency heuristic. Moreover, consistent with the notion of recognition and fluency's retrieval primacy, we found that inferences that agree with both heuristics take less time than do those that conflict with the heuristics (see Pachur & Hertwig, 2006). Last but not least, it is worth pointing out that the fluency

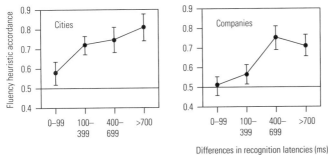

Differences in recognition latencies (ms)

Figure 26-4. Increasing fluency heuristic accordance as a function of increasing differences in recognition latencies. Differences in objects *a* and *b*'s recognition latencies were classified into four bins. Then, we calculated the mean fluency accordance per bin (across participants). Error bars indicate 95% confidence intervals. The analyses reported in Footnote 7 show a significant linear trend across bins. The horizontal line at 0.5 represents chance level accordance.

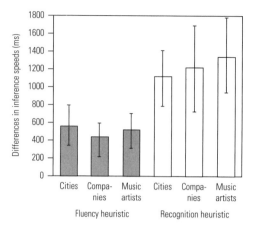

Figure 26-5. Inferences consistent with the fluency and recognition heuristics require less time. Bars represent the differences between median response times for inferences inconsistent and consistent with the fluency (left) and recognition heuristic (right), respectively. Positive differences indicate that inconsistent inferences took longer than consistent inferences. Error bars indicate 95% confidence intervals.

heuristic was applicable in 23% to 33% of inferences, depending on the environment (Table 26-2). These rates appear modest. The rate of applicability, however, is a function of both the heuristic and the environment in which it is used. If we had chosen, for instance, German or Swiss cities with more than 100,000 inhabitants, rather than U.S. cities, the rate of fluency applicability would have skyrocketed (given our German and Swiss respondents). Even when applicable, however, people would likely have not relied on any inferential tool because of their direct knowledge of the criterion variable (Pachur & Hertwig, 2006), thus rendering tests of strategies such as the fluency heuristic mute.

STUDY 4: ARE PEOPLE'S INFERENCES IN LINE WITH THE FLUENCY HEURISTIC: EXPERIMENTAL EVIDENCE?

The goal of the final study is to provide evidence whether or not fluency itself, rather than other factors possibly associated with fluency (e.g., the

amount of knowledge about the objects, ease of retrieving this information, etc.), can guide inferences. Specifically, in Study 3, what made respondents choose the more fluently retrieved object need not have been fluency per se, but may have been, for example, the mere amount of knowledge associated with it. Reliance on fluency would then just be a spurious phenomenon. To find out whether fluency per se can drive inferences about environmental variables, we experimentally manipulated fluency rather than measuring naturally existing fluency.

Method

Participants and design. Fifty students from the University of Basel participated in the study (36 women and 14 men; mean age = 24.1 years). Participants were presented with 49 pairs of cities. For each pair, participants were asked to infer which of the two cities has more residents (*inference task*). This task was identical to that in Study 3. Furthermore, each participant indicated which objects he or she recognized (*recognition task*). Students received a flat fee of 15 Swiss francs (US$13) or course credit.

Material. For experimentally induced fluency to have a reasonable chance of overcoming people's naturally existing retrieval fluency, we selected items that had similar degrees of preexisting, relatively low levels of fluency. Specifically, we took advantage of Volz et al.'s (2006) pool of 525 cities drawn from different regions of the world. From this pool we first removed 10% of cities with the longest names (thus reducing uncontrolled variance in recognition time due to vastly different reading times). Then, we removed all cities that were not recognized by at least two thirds of those participants in a previous study, to increase the chance of obtaining pairs of cities in which both cities are recognized and the fluency heuristic is thus applicable. Finally, we winnowed down the pool further by splitting it into two halves according to recognition latency; the subset of the fastest recognized items was excluded to avoid ceiling effects in recognition latency. By using this procedure, we arrived at 68 cities (*target items*), with about equally long names and substantially reduced variance in preexisting fluency (i.e., recognition latency). In addition, we randomly sampled from the set of excluded items 15 of the quickly recognized cities and 15 rarely recognized cities to form 15 filler pairs as well as 100 cities to serve as fillers in the fluency manipulation task (see below).

We assigned the 68 target items to two sets. They had comparable (a) recognition rates, (b) average median recognition speeds, (c) average number of letters in the names, and (d) average population sizes. Finally, we constructed pairs of cities by randomly selecting one city from each of the two sets of target items, thus arriving at 34 pairs. This whole procedure was implemented 25 times, thus creating 25 different lists of 34 pairs. Each of the 25 lists was administered in two versions. In one version, city X in each pair was selected for the fluency manipulation; in the other version, city Y was selected. That is, in each pair, one item was the experimental, the other the control item. By thus counterbalancing the manipulated city within each pair, the fluency manipulation was not confounded with any idiosyncrasy of the constructed pairs.

Our fluency manipulation was a syllable counting task. Participants saw a sequence of 134 names of cities in a random order (the 34 target cities for which we intended to boost fluency, and the 100 filler city items) and were asked to judge whether each name had an even or uneven number of syllables. This fluency manipulation task was adapted from Yonelinas (2001, Experiment 3).

Procedure. After an introductory text explaining the syllable task, participants were presented with a sequence of 134 names of cities. By pressing one of two keys, people indicated whether the city name consisted of an even or uneven number of syllables. Following the syllable task, there was a 1-min break after which people worked on the inference task (as implemented in Study 3), involving 34 pairs of target items and 15 filler pairs. Once the inference task was completed, participants took the recognition task (as implemented in Study 3). The recognition judgments were used to identify those pairs in which a respondent recognized both items, a precondition for the fluency heuristic. Finally,

participants' memories of the experimental manipulation were probed. Specifically, they indicated for each of the 68 target cities whether they thought that it was included in the syllable task at the outset of the study. To avoid invalid assumptions about the base rates, they were informed that 34 of the 68 cities were indeed included. After indicating whether a city was or was not included, they were asked to indicate on a 3-point scale how confident they were in their assessments. The rationale for monitoring memory of the experimental manipulation was that if people attributed their senses of fluency to the experiment rather than to their naturally acquired senses of fluency, they would be less likely to base their inferences on fluency (e.g., Jacoby & Whitehouse, 1989; Lombardi, Higgins, & Bargh, 1987).

Results

How did the fluency manipulation affect people's inferences of city size? To answer this question, we computed people's tendency to select the "manipulated" city (e.g., the city processed in the syllable task) over the nonmanipulated one. Across all respondents, in .55 of all inferences, the manipulated city was chosen over the nonmanipulated one ($SD = .13$; CI = .52, .59), one-sample t test against .5: $t(49) = 2.94$, $p = .005$. According to Cohen's (1988) classification, this effect of the fluency manipulation amounts to a small to medium size ($d = .37$). In addition, double as many people had a fluency adherence rate above .5 than below .5 (28 vs. 14; binomial test: $p = .02$).

The effect of fluency is moderated by people's memory of the experimental manipulation. Based on each individual's 68 signal detection judgments and his or her confidence ratings (see above), we calculated A_z, fitting a parametric smooth receiver operating characteristics (ROC) curve (ROCFIT; see Metz, Shen, Wang, & Kronman, 1994; using JROCFIT; Eng, n.d.). A_z is a measure of how well people can discriminate between signal and noise (technically speaking, it is the area under the ROC curve). The average A_z value was .66 ($SD = .08$; CI = .64, .68.), suggesting that the ability to discriminate is better than chance (.5) but also far from perfect (1.0).

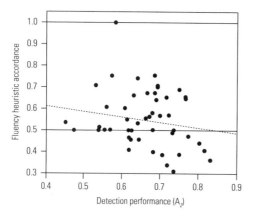

Figure 26-6. Fluency heuristic accordance as a function of the ability to remember correctly which items were subjected to the experimental manipulation of fluency. A_z is the area under the ROC curve and can be interpreted as the probability of a correct response. The line represents the robust regression of the fluency heuristic accordance as a function of the ability to correctly remember which items were included in the syllable task. The horizontal lines at 0.5 and 1.0 represent chance level and maximum accordance, respectively.

Figure 26-6 plots people's fluency adherence as a function of A_z. The slope of the robust regression line suggests that those who were poorer at remembering which items had been part of the syllable task had a higher adherence rate than did those who remembered better (slope = −0.31; SE = 0.19, p = .06, one-tailed).

A final analysis concerns the combined effect of experimental and pre-experimental fluency. By using recognition speed data from a previous study, we determined that the faster recognized cites were chosen in Study 4 to be larger, on average, in 55% of cases. How did the experimentally induced fluency change this proportion? If the manipulated city was indeed the one recognized faster than the nonmanipulated one (based on the previous results), fluency adherence grew from .55 to .60 (SD = .12; CI = .57, .63). In contrast, if the manipulated city was the one recognized slower than the nonmanipulated one (based on the previous results), fluency adherence grew from .45 to .49 (SD = 13; CI = .45, .52).

To conclude, Study 4 shows that experimentally manipulated fluency shapes inferences. This result is compatible with the vast literature on the influence of fluency on preferences (see, e.g., Alter & Oppenheimer, 2007, for a review) and with previous results reported by, for instance, Kelley and Lindsay (1993), who demonstrated experimentally the impact of fluency of confidence in the domain of general knowledge questions. The effects in Study 4 are small to medium in size, but it is worth keeping in mind that our experimental manipulation of fluency consisted of merely the judgment of whether or not a city name has an even or uneven number of syllables. Thus it was just the proverbial drop in the ocean compared to the lifetime of exposure to these city names.

GENERAL DISCUSSION

Automatically generated in the process of retrieval from memory, recognition and retrieval fluency are two pieces of information that are likely to precede the arrival of many other probabilistic cues retrieved from memory. The recognition heuristic and the fluency heuristic are two mind tools that have been proposed to exploit both pieces of mnemonic information. In several studies, we have investigated the fluency heuristic side by side with the recognition heuristic. In Study 1, we found that retrieval fluency can be a valid predictor of objective properties of the world, but the degree to which it is indicative of the criterion varies across environments. To the best of our knowledge, this is one of the first systematic demonstrations of the ecological validity of fluency information, based on the chain of correlations between criterion, mediators, and retrieval fluency within precisely defined reference classes. In Study 2, we examined whether people can reliably discriminate differences in retrieval fluency, a prerequisite for employing the fluency heuristic. Indeed, latencies that differ by more than 100 ms can be distinguished. The larger the differences, the better people can discriminate and the larger fluency validity proved to be. In Study 3, we found that between about three fourths and two thirds of the inferences in which the fluency heuristic could be applied conformed to the heuristic. Furthermore, accordance with the fluency heuristic increased with larger differences in recognition latencies—a manifestation of ecological rationality insofar as retrieval fluency is more likely to yield accurate inferences with larger differences (given an ecological correlation). Finally, in Study 4, we experimentally manipulated fluency and found that it had a direct impact on inferences.

In what follows, we turn to a possible explanation of the robust observation that recognition validity surpasses fluency validity, and we discuss what people can gain from the fluency heuristic and under what circumstances it may be used.

Why Is Recognition More Valid than Fluency Information?

In our studies, recognition validity consistently exceeded fluency validity. Why is that? Recognition and retrieval fluency both depend on activation, which encodes environmental frequencies, which, in turn, can be associated with the criterion (ecological validity). Within ACT-R, the difference between recognized and unrecognized objects maps onto the difference between items that exceed a retrieval threshold and those that fall below. For a moment, let us treat the threshold as the median value of a predictor variable that splits the criterion distribution into two parts. On average, recognized objects will score higher on the criterion than will unrecognized ones, just as items above the median will, on average, have a higher criterion value than those below. The fluency heuristic is akin to restricting the calculation of a correlation between predictor and criterion to those items that score above the median of the predictor variable. In all likelihood, the correlation and, by extension, the fluency validity will be lower relative to calculating the correlation across the whole range of the criterion value. Because the fluency heuristic requires both objects to be recognized, the relevant range of objects' activations is restricted, and, consequently, the link between activation and criterion is less pronounced. In contrast, the recognition heuristic requires one object to be recognized and the other not.

Consequently, the range of activations exceeds that for the fluency heuristic, and therefore the link between activation and criterion will be more pronounced, relative to the fluency heuristic. On this view, recognition validities exceed fluency validities, because the fluency heuristic, unlike the recognition heuristic, applies to objects whose activations exceed the retrieval threshold. Metaphorically speaking, the fluency heuristic deals with a world full of shades of white, whereas the recognition heuristic faces a black-and-white world.

What Do People Gain from Relying on Fluency?

When this question is interpreted simply with respect to accuracy, the answer depends on which of two benchmarks is used. If the alternative to the fluency heuristic is guessing (for example, in cases in which no further knowledge is available), the heuristic clearly tops chance performance. As Study 1 demonstrated, fluency validity surpasses chance performance, ranging from .58 to .66 (Figure 26-1). Although one would hesitate to go mushroom picking with such accuracy, one could make a comfortable living picking stocks. If the alternative to relying on fluency is mustering additional cue knowledge, however, the performance of the fluency heuristic depends on the accuracy of other decision strategies that depend on this knowledge (see Gigerenzer & Goldstein, 1996, for candidate strategies). Should the validity of these knowledge-based strategies exceed that of fluency, by using fluency a person sacrifices some accuracy.

We have no direct measure of the validity of these knowledge-based strategies but we can use a proxy to extrapolate it, namely, the level of accuracy in those cases in which inferences are inconsistent with the fluency heuristic. In all three environments in Study 3, the average fluency validity was as high as or higher than the average accuracy of additional knowledge: .66 vs. .59 ($Mdn = .67$, $SD = .34$), .58 vs. .47 ($Mdn = .5$, $SD = .26$), and .58 vs. .52 ($Mdn = .5$, $SD = .25$) in the cities, companies, and music artists environments, respectively. These numbers stem from a selective set of items and thus need to be interpreted with care. Yet, they provide a first indication that even when compared with the accuracy of knowledge-based strategies, the fluency heuristic stands its ground in the environments investigated. At the same time, let us emphasize that there are domains in which reliance on fluency can undoubtedly result in disadvantageous decisions. Companies, for instance, pay great sums to influence the public's recognition and fluency of product names (Goldstein, 2007). No doubt, the more fluent product name need not always signal the better product.

In any consideration of what the fluency heuristic has to offer, two of its properties deserve attention. First, the heuristic is least likely to be used in cases in which its validity hits bottom, that is, when people find it difficult to tell the recognition latencies apart (see Figure 26-2). In the cities environment, for instance, the adherence rate in the 50% of inferences with the smallest differences in recognition latencies is .62, relative to .77 in the 50% of inferences with the largest differences. The corresponding fluency validities for the smaller and larger differences are .56 and .69, respectively. In other words, the heuristic's requirement that the recognition latencies be discernible inures the user from using fluency when it is least beneficial. Second, the wisdom of the fluency heuristic should be evaluated in light of the fact that the retrieval of other cue knowledge is effortful and time consuming. In other words, the decision maker faces an accuracy–effort tradeoff (Payne, Bettman, & Johnson, 1993). Using the fluency heuristic may not be the best people can do, but it enables them to arrive at inferences swiftly and to surpass chance performance if they have no other cue knowledge; in addition, they are protected from using it when it is least appropriate.

When Do People Resort to the Fluency Heuristic?

In light of the fluency heuristic's competitors (Gigerenzer & Goldstein, 1996), what are the circumstances under which people use it? Some critics of the adaptive toolbox metaphor suggest that the issue of strategy selection runs the risk of making the dubious assumption of some kind of omniscient homunculus or überheuristic that selects from the toolbox (e.g., Newell, 2005). However, possible solutions to the thorny issue of strategy selection have been proposed that make do without a mysterious homunculus. One solution is that people learn to match specific heuristics to specific statistical structures in the world through feedback (Rieskamp & Otto, 2006). Alternatively, the various mind tools in the toolbox may be arranged according to the same criteria that the ACT-R framework (Anderson et al., 2004; Anderson & Lebiere, 1998) uses in order to determine the activation strength of a memory record, namely, recency and frequency of occurrence. That is, the various tools may be ordered such that the most frequently and most recently used tool is examined first; if it does not enable an inference, the next tool in the hierarchy will be examined, and so on.

There is still another, albeit not exclusive, route to strategy selection. Knowledge and time, or lack thereof, may also guide the selection process. Recently, Marewski and Schooler (2010) found that the fluency heuristic appears most likely to be used when both objects are recognized and no other probabilistic cue knowledge is available. When knowledge was available, a knowledge-based strategy described people's inferences better than the fluency heuristic. This result suggests the possibility that people may be inclined (a) to use the recognition heuristic if one object is recognized and the other is not (see Figure 26-3b) and if people have no definite and conclusive knowledge of the target variable that renders use of cues unnecessary (Pachur & Hertwig, 2006); (b) to use the fluency heuristic if both objects are recognized and no other knowledge (e.g., in terms of probabilistic cues) is available; and (c) to use knowledge-based strategies when both objects are recognized and additional knowledge (e.g., in terms of probabilistic cues) is available.

Let us end with a clarification. We have specified the fluency heuristic in terms of a condition–action production ("If–then") rule, so that it can be instantiated as a computer program.

This specification, however, does not mean that we have already completely understood which antecedence conditions need to be met for the action to be executed. Our studies have confirmed that the difference between recognition latencies needs to be at least 100 ms, otherwise the action cannot not be executed (e.g., Figure 26-4). Future investigations will help to clarify which additional conditions need to be met. Such other conditions may relate, for instance, to the presence or absence of other probabilistic cue knowledge, or to the validity of present cue knowledge.

CONCLUSION

David Hume (1740/1978) believed that the mind meticulously tallies frequencies and apportions degrees of belief accordingly. Today, we know that Hume endowed the human mind with too exquisite a sensitivity to frequencies. Yet, as various memory models assume, there is a mapping between environmental frequencies and mnemonic information such as activation strengths. The fluency heuristic is one mind tool that artfully and swiftly probes memory for the encapsulated frequency information that can veridically reflect statistical regularities in the world.

ACKNOWLEDGMENTS

Ralph Hertwig was supported by Swiss National Science Foundation Grants 100013-107741/1 and 100014-118283/1. Our thanks go to Julian Marewski, Thorsten Pachur, and Tim Pleskac for many constructive comments. We also thank Laura Wiles for editing the manuscript and Gregor Caregnato, Arne Fesche, and Renato Frey for conducting the experiments.

NOTES

1. At the same time, the assumption that no other probabilistic information beyond recognition will be used if the recognition heuristic is applicable has been vigorously challenged (e.g., Bröder & Eichler, 2006; Newell & Fernandez, 2006; Oppenheimer, 2003; Pohl, 2006; Richter & Späth, 2006; but see also Pachur, Bröder, & Marewski, 2008; Pachur & Hertwig, 2006).

2. Whittlesea and Leboe (2003; Whittlesea, 1993) make an important distinction between two kinds of fluency heuristics. In their view, a person's feeling of fluency can either be a reflection of enhanced processing, or, alternatively, a person's perception of fluency can be relative to his or her "fluency" expectations. We focus on the first notion of fluency. Moreover, we also do not address the role of naïve theories that may trigger the use or disuse of the fluency heuristic (see Schwarz, 2004).

3. Two experts on fluency, P. Winkielman (personal communication, October 13, 2007) and C. Unkelbach (personal communication, October 12, 2007) confirmed our impression that there are hardly any systematic analyses of the ecological validity of fluency in general and retrieval fluency in particular. Ecological analyses remain rare, however, even if one equates availability and fluency. Although Tversky and Kahneman (1973) stressed that "availability is an ecologically valid clue for the judgment of frequency because, in general, frequent events are easier to recall or imagine than infrequent ones" (p. 209), many subsequent studies have focused on circumstances under which reliance on availability leads astray (for a systematic analysis of the validity of availability in a classic task, see Sedlmeier et al., 1998).

4. We used print material published between 2000 and 2004. COSMAS can be accessed on the Internet: http://corpora.ids-mannheim.de/~cosmas/

5. For the analyses of Studies 1–3, we excluded the names of eight companies and four musicians because of their lengths (e.g., "Bob Seger and the Silver Bullet Band"), that is, the risk of measuring reading times rather than recognition latencies. We also checked whether there is a correlation between the lengths of names (i.e., number of letters) and the criterion in question; we found none. For 23 of the 92 German companies, the official company name is different from the colloquial name. For these companies, the media mentions were substantially higher for the colloquial names than for the official names. Therefore, the ecological analyses rest on the former.

6. The order of the recognition and inference tasks had no statistically significant effect on

the accordance to the fluency and recognition heuristics in the cities, companies, and music artists' environments, respectively. None of the implications of the reported analysis changed when analyzing the two task orders separately.

7. Repeated measures analyses of variance showed linear trends in accordance rates over the four bins: cities environment, $F(1, 65) = 26.66$, $MSE = 0.079$, partial $\eta^2 = .29$; companies environment, $F(1, 61) = 24.15$, $MSE = 0.080$, partial $\eta^2 = .28$; and music artists, $F(1, 61) = 25.55$, $MSE = 0.066$, partial $\eta^2 = .30$.

Introduction to Chapter 27

The Use of Recognition in Group Decision-Making

Unlike general-purpose models of cognition, heuristics are domain-specific mental tools. However, their adaptation to specific environments does not mean that a heuristic cannot be co-opted across more than one domain. For instance, heuristics that are used in nonsocial environments can also guide decisions in social contexts. Fast-and-frugal trees, for instance, can guide the diagnosis of an individual emergency physician (see Chapter 6) as well as the bail decisions of a bench of three magistrates (see Chapter 28). Similarly, the equality heuristic can guide not only individual investments in funds (see Chapter 34) but also parents' investment in their children (see Chapter 35). This article by Torsten Reimer, a social psychologist, and Konstantinos Katsikopoulos, a systems engineer, extends the role of name recognition from individual to collective decision making. In this interdisciplinary collaboration, the consequences that follow from relying on recognition in group decisions were first derived analytically and then tested experimentally. Assuming that group members rely on the recognition heuristic, how accurate will their decisions be? When are less-is-more effects implied? And to what degree do real groups rely on recognition, and do they exhibit less-is-more effects when predicted?

The analytical results show that less-is-more effects can emerge in a group context, where they are even stronger in magnitude than in individual decisions. The conditions are similar to those for individual decisions: If the recognition validity is higher than the knowledge validity, both are independent of the number of objects recognized, and some further assumptions concerning the homogenity of the groups hold, then the relationship between accuracy and n is inversely U-shaped. This less-is-more effect is also demonstrated empirically in an experiment, in which a fascinating phenomenon emerged: When, in a group of three, one member recognized only one object and the other two recognized both objects, the individual who knew less and could rely on the recognition heuristic often seemed to determine the group's final decision. This result suggests that recognition has a special status not only in individual decisions, as proposed by Goldstein and Gigerenzer (see Chapter 3), but in group decisions as well.

CHAPTER 27

The Use of Recognition in Group Decision-Making

Torsten Reimer and Konstantinos V. Katsikopoulos

Abstract: Goldstein and Gigerenzer (2002) [Models of ecological rationality: The recognition heuristic. *Psychological Review, 109* (1), 75–90] found evidence for the use of the recognition heuristic. For example, if an individual recognizes only one of two cities, they tend to infer that the recognized city has a larger population. A prediction that follows is that of the less-is-more effect: Recognizing fewer cities leads, under certain conditions, to more accurate inferences than recognizing more cities. We extend the recognition heuristic to group decision making by developing majority and lexicographic models of how recognition information is used by groups. We formally show when the less-is-more effect is predicted in groups and we present a study where three-member groups performed the population comparison task. Several aspects of our data indicate that members who can use the recognition heuristic are, not in all but in most cases, more influential in the group decision process than members who cannot use the heuristic. We also observed the less-is-more effect and found that models assuming that members who can use the recognition heuristic are more influential better predict when the effect occurs.

Goldstein and Gigerenzer (2002) considered the task of an individual wanting to infer which one of two objects has a larger value on a quantitative dimension of interest, or *criterion*. A popular example is when one wants to infer which one of two cities, say San Diego or San Antonio, has a larger population. How can group members integrate their individual decisions to form a joint group decision on the population comparison task? Dichotomous choice tasks have been extensively studied in psychological research on group decision-making (Hinsz, Tindale, & Vollrath, 1997). This research has revealed that the rule for combining individual inferences that groups prefer depends on task characteristics (Davis, 1992). For example, if a task is *intellective*, that is, if it has a correct solution, which can

be demonstrated like in a mathematical task, group behavior often follows a truth-wins scheme, which predicts that the group is correct if one member is correct. In contrast, if a task is *judgmental*, that is, it has no correct solution like when choosing a place to live, or if the correctness can not be demonstrated, groups are more likely to apply some type of a majority rule (Gigone & Hastie, 1997; Laughlin & Ellis, 1986; Sorkin, West, & Robinson, 1998). Because it can hardly be "proven" by any group member what the solution of the population comparison task is, it is reasonable to assume that, in this task, groups integrate individual decisions through a majority rule.

The most common majority rule is a democratic principle that weights individual votes equally and infers that the object with the most overall votes has the highest criterion. According to this simple majority rule, a group combines all individual decisions on the city comparison task irrespective of whether individuals make a recognition-based or a knowledge-based inference. We additionally consider two oligarchic majority rules that model the idea that some members are more influential. Specifically, we also test models which assume that only those individuals contribute to the group decision who (a) can use the recognition heuristic—*recognition-based* majority rule, or who (b) can use knowledge—*knowledge-based* majority rule.

Note that models that use these rules make predictions only when there is no tie among the voters. That is, a group may not always be able to apply these rules. This is a common problem in evaluating psychological models. A model may predict decisions well but may be only applicable to a small number of cases, whereas another model may predict decisions less well but be applicable to more cases. Then, it lies in the eyes of the beholder, which model explains behavior better. In group research, an often used method is to extend models by assuming that groups resolve ties by a proportionality rule (Davis, 1973). In the case of a dichotomous inference task the proportionality rule then reduces to guessing.

When presenting the empirical study, we will report the predictive accuracy of models both with and without guessing. When analytically deriving the models' predictions and relating them to the less-is-more effect, however, we use guessing like in the Goldstein and Gigerenzer (2002) model of individual inferences. We do so because the number of inferences for which a decision maker has to guess can strongly affect the predictions for the less-is-more effect. In what follows, we refer to the object inferred to have the larger criterion value by the group as the *group choice*.

> *Simple majority rule*: "The group choice is the object inferred to have the larger criterion value by the majority of group members."

The majority of m members, which we symbolize by majority(m) equals $(m + 1)/2$ if m is odd, and $(m/2 + 1)$ if m is even. For example, in a group composed of three sisters where the youngest and middle sisters have inferred that San Diego is larger than San Antonio, while the eldest sister has inferred that San Antonio is larger than San Diego, the group choice is San Diego. Thus, a three-member group is correct if two or three members are correct. And a two-member group is correct if both members are correct or one member is

correct and the guess that resolves the tie is correct. We assume that a guess is correct with probability 1/2. It follows that a single individual is equally accurate when deciding alone and when forming a group with an individual with equal accuracy. This is so because, if q is the common accuracy, the accuracy of the group of two members also equals $q^2 + 2q(1 - q)(1/2) = q$. For more than two equally accurate members, however, the accuracy of the simple majority rule increases as the number of group members increases (Condorcet, 1785; Groffman & Owen, 1986, p. 94).

The simple majority rule assumes that all group members, those that are able to use the recognition heuristic *and* those that are not, have the same impact on the group choice. A sister who recognizes both San Diego and San Antonio and somehow infers that San Diego is larger has equal influence with a sister who infers that San Diego is larger because she does not recognize San Antonio. But if, as Goldstein and Gigerenzer (2002) propose, recognition information has a special role in making inferences, it may be that the second sister has more of a say in the combination of individual inferences. On the other hand, it can also be claimed that members who can use knowledge are more influential because they probably have access to more cues in favor of their position and are judged higher in expertise. Thus, data are needed to evaluate these claims.

MODELING THE IMPACT OF MEMBERS WHO CAN USE THE RECOGNITION HEURISTIC

The first model we discuss is a variant of the simple majority rule. In this restricted majority rule, individuals who recognize both or neither object are ignored.

> *Recognition-based majority rule*: "The group choice is determined by the simple majority rule applied to these group members who can use the recognition heuristic."

Consider that two sisters recognize both San Antonio and San Diego, and based on their knowledge infer that San Antonio is larger. The third sister recognizes only San Diego. According to the simple majority rule, the group choice is San Antonio. The prediction, however, of the recognition-based majority rule is that the group choice is San Diego. Thus, according to the recognition-based majority rule, just one individual, who can use the recognition heuristic, can overturn a majority.

The implicit assumption of guessing when no member can use the recognition heuristic may be too strong. For this reason, we also tested the following *lexicographic* model, where the group first attempts to combine the inferences of those members that can use the recognition heuristic, and then to combine the inferences of those members that can use knowledge.

> *Recognition-first lexicographic model:* "If there are members who can use the recognition heuristic, the group uses the recognition-based majority rule. If no members can use the recognition heuristic, but there are members who can use knowledge, the group choice is determined by the simple majority rule applied to these group members who can use knowledge."

MODELING THE IMPACT OF MEMBERS WHO CAN USE KNOWLEDGE

We also construct two models that assume that members who can use knowledge are more influential in the combination of inferences than members who can use the recognition heuristic. The first model assumes that only members who recognize both objects have a say in the combination process. The second model assumes that the members who recognize one object enter the combination process if there are no members who recognize both objects.

> *Knowledge-based majority rule:* "The group choice is determined by the simple majority rule applied to these group members who can use knowledge."

> *Knowledge-first lexicographic model:* "If there are members who can use knowledge, the group uses the knowledge-based majority rule. If no members can use knowledge, but there are members who can use the recognition heuristic, the group choice is determined by the simple majority rule applied to these group members who can use the recognition heuristic."

In sum, in addition to a simple majority rule, we developed two restricted majority models and two lexicographic models. None of the models has any free parameters. All models, except the simple majority model, are noncompensatory and predict that just one individual can overturn a majority. Models, however, differ in which individuals are assumed to have a larger influence in the combination process. Before we test the models empirically, we derive their predictions for the less-is-more effect.

WHEN IS THE LESS-IS-MORE EFFECT PREDICTED?

We first define the less-is-more effect—Table 27-1 lists all relevant symbols. Let α be the *recognition validity*, that is, the probability of a correct inference given that an individual uses the recognition heuristic, and β be the *knowledge validity*, that is, the probability of a correct inference given that the individual uses knowledge. Let $f(n)$ be the accuracy as a function of the number of objects recognized, n, out of the total number of objects N, when α and β are fixed—an equation that specifies $f(n)$ is provided in the Appendix. The less-is-more effect is defined as the situation in which there exist n_1 and n_2 so that $n_1 < n_2$ but $f(n_1) > f(n_2)$. That is, less information (n_1) leads to higher accuracy than more information (n_2). We call

Table 27-1. Interpretations of Symbols

Symbol	Interpretation
N	Number of objects in population
n	Number of objects recognized by a fixed group member
α	Recognition validity of fixed group member
β	Knowledge validity of fixed group member
$f(n)$	Accuracy of fixed group member recognizing n objects, using α and β
m	Number of group members
p	Prevalence of less-is-more effect
$g(n)$ (only in Appendix)	Accuracy of group where each member recognizes n objects and has same α and β

prevalence, p, of the less-is-more effect the proportion of pairs (n_1, n_2) with $n_1 \neq n_2$ for which the less-is-more effect occurs. The prevalence of the less-is-more effect varies between zero for increasing $f(n)$ and unity for strictly decreasing $f(n)$.

Goldstein and Gigerenzer (2002) discuss the special case of $n_2 = N$, which we call the *strong less-is-more effect*. In the strong less-is-more effect, full recognition information (N) is less accurate than partial recognition information ($n_1 < N$). Goldstein and Gigerenzer showed that a necessary and sufficient condition for the strong less-is-more effect for individuals is that the recognition validity is larger than knowledge validity. As an example, they discuss three Parisian sisters that have to compare the population of $N = 100$ German cities. All sisters have $\alpha = .8$ and $\beta = .6$, but they vary on the number of recognized objects: The youngest sister has $n = 0$, the middle sister has $n = 50$, and the eldest sister has $n = 100$. Because $\alpha > \beta$ the strong less-is-more effect is predicted: for the middle sister, $f(50) = .68$, while for the eldest sister $f(100) = .60$. Accuracy for $\alpha = .8$ and $\beta = .6$, interpolated for all n, is graphed on Figure 27-1.

The prevalence of the less-is-more effect for individuals depends on both α and β. For $\alpha = .8$ and $\beta = .6$, enumeration of all possible cases yields $p = 1/3$. In the Appendix, we formally show that p increases as α increases or β decreases and that $p = 0$ if $\alpha \leq \beta$ as long as it is assumed that α and β are larger than 1/2.

Figure 27-1 also includes the curve of accuracy for *triplets* of girls when their inferences are combined according to the simple majority rule. All three girls in a triplet have $\alpha = .8$ and $\beta = .6$ and equal n, that is, triplets are *homogeneous*. On the other hand, n varies from 0 to 100 across triplets. It is also assumed that the recognition and inference processes of any girl are *independent* of these processes for her sisters. That is, whether one girl recognizes a city or not does not influence whether her sisters recognize this city, and which one of two cities one girl infers to be larger does not influence which one of the cities her sisters infer to be larger. Assume that $n = 0$ for the triplet of the three youngest girls, $n = 50$ for the triplet of the three middle girls, and $n = 100$ for the triplet of the three eldest girls. The middle triplet again outperforms the eldest triplet. The effect is also more pronounced

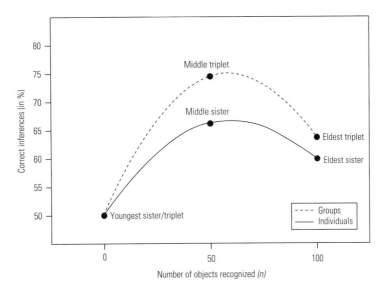

Figure 27-1. Predicted accuracy of Parisian sisters and of Parisian triplets that use the simple majority rule, as a function of the number of cities recognized, n. All sisters have $\alpha = .8$ and $\beta = .6$ and all sisters in a triplet have the same n.

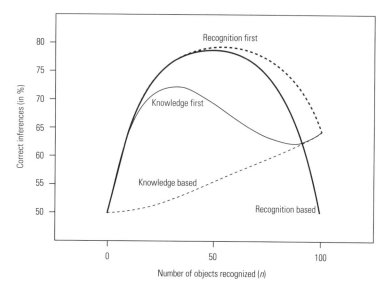

Figure 27-2. Predicted accuracy of Parisian triplets that use the recognition-based and knowledge-based majority rules, as well as the recognition-first and knowledge-first lexicographic models, as a function of the number of cities recognized, n. All sisters have $\alpha = .8$ and $\beta = .6$ and all sisters in a triplet have the same n.

compared to the individual case in the sense that the difference in accuracy is larger, 10 percentage points versus 8 percentage points. The prevalence of the less-is-more effect again equals 1/3.

Figure 27-2 shows the curves of accuracy for the same triplets of girls when their inferences are combined according to the restricted majority and to the lexicographic models. Note that for $n = 0$ the predictions of all models coincide because no city is recognized by any sister and the group guesses. For $n = 100$, the predictions of the two lexicographic models and the knowledge-based majority rule coincide because all cities are recognized by all sisters and the group uses the simple majority rule.

The curve of the recognition-based majority rule is concave and symmetric around $N = 50$ and thus the strong less-is-more effect is predicted. The prevalence of the less-is-more effect equals 50/101. If the triplet uses the knowledge-based majority rule, the situation is different. The curve of the knowledge-based majority rule is increasing and thus the strong less-is-more effect is not predicted and the less-is-more effect has zero prevalence. More generally, we prove the following in the Appendix.

Result: Assume a homogeneous group where the recognition and inference processes of members are independent given criterion. The following statements hold.

(i) If the group uses the simple majority rule, the strong less-is-more effect is predicted if and only if $\alpha > \beta$, and p equals the prevalence of the effect for one member.

(ii) If the group uses the recognition-based majority rule, the strong less-is-more effect is predicted, and $p = N/[2(N+1)]$ for even N and $p = (N-1)/(2N)$ for odd N.

(iii) If the group uses the knowledge-based majority rule, the strong less-is-more effect is not predicted, and $p = 0$.

The homogeneity and independence assumptions are not necessary for all parts of this result. For example, the simple majority model can predict the strong less-is-more effect for heterogeneous groups as long as recognition validity is greater than knowledge validity for all members. This prediction can also be derived if independence is replaced with the weaker assumption that all members contribute positively to group accuracy. Note that as N increases, $N/[2(N+1)]$

and $(N-1)/(2N)$ tend to 1/2. That is, when there is a large enough number of objects and the group uses the recognition-based majority rule, the less-is-more effect is predicted half of the time—in practice, $p > .45$ for $N > 10$, and $p \approx 1/2$ for $N = 100$.

The accuracy curves of the lexicographic models in Figure 27-2 have more complicated shapes and we do not have general results. We do know, however, that both models predict less-is-more effects, as for example the strong less-is-more effect. For the recognition-first lexicographic model, accuracy is maximized at $n = 53$ and exceeds accuracy at $n = 100$ by 14 percentage points. For the knowledge-first lexicographic model, accuracy is maximized at $n = 33$ and exceeds accuracy at $n = 100$ by 7 percentage points.

Surprisingly, the effect is *more* prevalent when members who can use knowledge are more influential (.64) than when members who can use recognition are more influential (.32). This is driven by the curve of the knowledge-first model decreasing for n between 33 and 53 and the curve for the recognition-first model increasing in this range. This happens because, in that range of n, it becomes increasingly more likely that a member recognizes only one rather than two objects; see the Appendix for the relevant formulas. It thus becomes more likely that the group forms a larger recognition-based majority, and this decreases the accuracy of the knowledge-first model and increases the accuracy of the recognition-first model.

METHOD

Since Goldstein and Gigerenzer (2002) found that the recognition heuristic described individual inferences well in the population comparison task, we also used this task so that we could study how individual recognition processes interact with group decision processes. The details are as follows.

Participants and Compensation

Ninety participants (46 female and 44 male, mean age of 23.2 years) were recruited from the Free University of Berlin, Germany. Each participant attended two approximately hour-long sessions, 1 week apart. A fixed amount of 18 euros was received for participation in both sessions, plus 3 euro-cents per correct inference made on the second session, with a maximum compensation of 21.15 euros.

Design and Procedure

In the first session, participants were first individually asked which of 40 American cities they recognized. These cities are provided in Table 27-2. The responses allowed us to determine the parameters n and α for each individual. Specifically, α was estimated as the proportion of correct inferences each individual would make if they used the recognition heuristic for all these pairs of cities where only one city was recognized. For example, for an individual who recognized San Diego but not San Antonio, the inference made for this pair of cities would count

Table 27-2. The Forty Cities Used in the First Session

Cities			
1. New York	11. San Jose	21. Portland	31. Oakland
2. Los Angeles	12. *Indianapolis*	22. *Oklahoma City*	32. *Omaha*
3. Chicago	13. *San Francisco*	23. Tucson	33. Minneapolis
4. Houston	14. *Jacksonville*	24. Las Vegas	34. *Miami*
5. *Philadelphia*	15. Columbus	25. Long Beach	35. *Wichita*
6. Phoenix	16. Austin	26. Albuquerque	36. Pittsburgh
7. San Diego	17. Milwaukee	27. *Kansas City*	37. Arlington
8. *Dallas*	18. *Washington*	28. *Fresno*	38. Cincinnati
9. *San Antonio*	19. *El Paso*	29. Atlanta	39. Toledo
10. Detroit	20. Charlotte	30. Sacramento	40. *Raleigh*

Italicized are the fifteen cities used in the second session.

as correct. Then, participants were asked to perform the population comparison task for all pairs of cities that were both recognized. The parameter β was estimated as the proportion of correct responses for these pairs.

The averages of the individual parameter estimates of the first session were α = .72 and β = .65. It is not trivial that we came up with such values for there is no a-priori reason to suppose that the situation α > β ever occurs in the real world—only Goldstein and Gigerenzer (2002) have observed this before. We then chose 15 cities, which are italicized in Table 27-2, so that the average α (.81) and β (.58) of the individuals were as close as possible to .8 and .6, respectively. We chose 15 cities so that it would be possible to perform the population comparison task on all possible 105 pairs, in 1 hour.

A test of the less-is-more effect in groups requires groups with approximately equal average α and β but different average n. For this reason, the 84 participants who returned for the second session were grouped into 28 groups of three so that the variability of the average n across groups was reasonably high, SD = 9.5, while the variability in the average α and β across groups was reasonably low, SD = 5.9. This procedure allowed us to identify seven pairs of groups that had approximately equal average α and β but different average n. Two groups were considered having equal average α and β if these averages differed by at most .03. This threshold was chosen as the smallest one for which slightly higher averages did not increase the number of pairs.

Groups performed the population comparison task as follows. Members sat around a table so that everybody could see the computer screen where all pairs of cities were presented randomly. Groups discussed and after coming to a joint decision, one group member had to mark the decision on a paper—all members took turns at doing this in a clockwise fashion. Then, the experimenter pressed the corresponding key and the next pair appeared on the screen. There was no opportunity to correct answers afterwards. There was no feedback during this session—or after the first session—but groups were told that 3 euro-cents would be paid to each group member per correct group choice after the session was over.

EVALUATING THE MODELS

How well do the models predict the group choices? Unless stated otherwise, for each model, we averaged, across groups, the number of cases to which the model can be applied. All groups together made a total of 28 × 105 = 2,940 inferences. The simple majority rule can be applied to 2,798 inferences and 84% of its predictions agree with the group choices. Figure 27-3 graphs the predictive accuracy of the two restricted majority rules. Groups are ordered according to the predictive accuracy of the recognition-based rule and the bars indicate the percentage of cases in which the group choice matched the prediction of the models when these were applicable. Overall, the knowledge-based majority rule can be applied to 2,091 inferences and 78% of its predictions agree with the group choices. The recognition-based majority rule can be applied to somewhat less choices, 1,775, but its predictions agree with the observations in an impressive 90% of these cases. Recall that Goldstein and Gigerenzer (2002) found that the recognition heuristic accurately predicted individual choices in 90% of cases as well.

By construction, the lexicographic models can be applied to more choices than the restricted majority rules—the recognition-first model can be applied to 2,796 choices and the knowledge-first model can be applied to 2,709 choices. Predictive accuracy does not change much with the order by which the group attempts to form a majority. If it is first attempted to form a recognition-based majority, the predictions agree with observations in 84% and this drops to 82% if it is first attempted to form a knowledge-based majority. There were no strong differences in the ease of the items to which the five models could be applied. The average absolute differences in population rank between the two cities of a pair ranged from 5.1 to 5.7 and did not strongly deviate from the average difference of 5.3 for all possible pairs.

If the models are applied to all choices, that is, if guessing is included, choices are described best

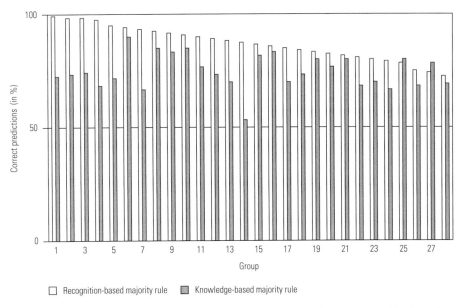

Figure 27-3. Match between observed and predicted group choices for the recognition-based and the knowledge-based rules, for each individual group, without guessing. Groups are ordered according to the match of the recognition-based rule.

by the simple majority model (82%) and by the recognition-first (83%) and the knowledge-first (81%) models, followed by the recognition-based (74%) and the knowledge-based rules (70%), which have to guess more often. These predictions overall suggest that some type of majority rule describes well how groups combine individual inferences. The question then becomes *which* members participate in the formation of the majority: those that use the recognition heuristic, those that use knowledge, or both?

Overall, the data were described well by the simple majority rule which resolves ties by guessing and assumes that the group members form their individual inferences as described by Goldstein and Gigerenzer (2002). But, more specifically, the predictive accuracy of the simple majority model is better when majority consists of members that can use the recognition heuristic rather than knowledge. Group choices deviated much more often from the simple majority rule when the majority consisted of members who could use knowledge than when the majority consisted of members who could use the recognition heuristic. Note that these cases are

exclusive. Agreement with the majority rule was in 77% of the 1,051 choices in which the majority was formed by members who could use their knowledge, and in 96% of the 1,379 choices in which the majority was formed by members who could use the recognition heuristic. This behavior is functional since groups were more accurate when the majority consisted of members that could use the recognition heuristic (.85) than when the majority had to base their inference on knowledge (.63).

The above constitute indirect evidence for the following claim: *It is the members that use the recognition heuristic that are more influential in the process of combining judgments.* By analyzing some special cases, we found more direct evidence for this claim—in most of the cases where recognition-based criteria are in conflict with knowledge-based criteria, the recognition-based criteria seem to be preferred by groups.

Do Members Who Can Use Recognition Heuristic Have More Impact?

In order to evaluate this claim more directly, we additionally analyzed those cases in which *both* the recognition-based and the knowledge-based models could be applied. For example, both models are applicable when there is one member recognizing both, one member recognizing one, and one member recognizing zero cities. Overall, there are 1,023 such cases. In 85% of those cases the two models made identical predictions—this happens, for example, when member(s) who can use knowledge and member(s) who can use the recognition heuristic make the same inference. In these cases the percentage of correct predictions is very high, 94% on the average.

What happens in the 15% of cases for which the two models make contrasting predictions? These 154 cases may be of one of three different types: (a) two members can use their knowledge and one member can use the recognition heuristic—34 cases; (b) one member can use knowledge and two members can use the recognition heuristic—75 cases; and (c) one member can use knowledge, one member can use recognition, and one member has to guess—45 cases. We had a closer look on each of these three types of situations.

Two Members Can Use Knowledge

Consider the situation where two members recognize both cities and infer that a certain city is larger while the third member recognizes the other city. Surprisingly, the single individual seems to *trump* the majority more often than not: In 59% of these cases, the group choice matches the inference suggested by the recognition heuristic. Note that the knowledge-based majority rule and the knowledge-first lexicographic model, as well as the simple majority model, predict 0%. A probability-matching scheme like the proportionality rule would predict 33%. These data are more consistent with the recognition-based majority rule and the recognition-first lexicographic model.

We did, however, also look at these inferences that cannot be predicted by the recognition-based majority rule and the recognition-first lexicographic model. These comparisons do not seem to be more difficult than those that could be accounted by the models: the difference in population rank between the two cities is practically the same—on the average 4.3 for correct

predictions and 4.2 for incorrect predictions. Rather, the models fail when one of three particular cities—Jacksonville, San Antonio, El Paso—was an alternative. Some of these cases might mostly reflect an inconsistency with the recognition heuristic as a description of individual inferences, as opposed to an inconsistency with the assumptions on combining those inferences: The city of El Paso was recognized by the single individual but not chosen by the group in six cases. It is plausible that El Paso is recognized as a relatively small city and thus the individual choice is also that El Paso is the smaller city, contrary to the prediction of the recognition heuristic.

Two Members Can Use Recognition Heuristic

What happens when two members recognize only one city while the third member recognizes both cities and infers that the city that is not recognized by the other two members is larger? In 76% of these cases the group choice matched the suggestion of the recognition heuristic.

Thus, in agreement with the assumption that members who can use the recognition heuristic are more influential in the combination process, it is not so likely that an individual who can use knowledge overturns a majority of two group members who can apply the recognition heuristic. We, however, also took a closer look at the eighteen cases where this happened. Many of these cases are due to two particular groups making inferences in which two particular cities are involved. Overall, these cases involved only five cities whereas the cases in which the group choice was in accordance with the recognition heuristic referred to eleven cities. Furthermore, just two cities—Fresno and Raleigh—were involved in five cases each. Consistently, nine cases referred to just two groups and one of these groups contributed three Fresno cases and the other group contributed four Raleigh cases.

Inspecting the group discussions suggests that the Fresno and Raleigh cases were extraordinary. For example, when two members recognized Indianapolis but not Fresno, the third member stated that "he was 99% sure that Fresno was more populous." In other cases, arguments were used instead of confidence: An individual who recognized both Raleigh and Oklahoma City managed to convince two members who only recognized Oklahoma City by arguing that Raleigh is a state capital and that it is in the East Coast which is densely populated. Thus, we observed cases, in which recognition was used in a compensatory manner, that is, in which one group member who could use knowledge overturned a majority of two group members who could use the recognition heuristic. However, these cases were rare and restricted to few groups that made inferences on particular cities.

One Member Can Use Knowledge and/or One Member Can Use Recognition

In the third type of situation where the recognition-based and knowledge-based models make contradictory predictions, one member recognizes both cities and makes the opposite inference from a second member who can use the recognition heuristic. Also, the third member does not recognize any city. Here, groups chose in accordance with the recognition heuristic in 61% of the cases. We also looked for patterns underlying the 39% of cases in which the group choice agreed with the members who could use their knowledge. However, in contrast to the two situations described before, we did not find any systematic patterns.

What happens if two members recognize zero cities? In a similar vein, if two members did not recognize either city while the third member recognized only one city, the group choice matched the suggestion of the recognition heuristic in 78% of 106 cases. In 27 cases where two members did not recognize any city and the third member recognized both cities, the match between group choice and the choice of the third member dropped to 58%.

In sum, we found that members who can use the recognition heuristic are usually more influential in the process of combining inferences than members who can use their knowledge. First, when guessing was ignored, the predictive accuracy was 90% for the recognition-based rule and 78% for the knowledge-based rule. When guessing was included, these percentages were 74% and 70%, respectively. The differences were smaller for the lexicographic models, but again in favor of the recognition-first as opposed to the knowledge-first model. Note also that the simple majority model described the data better when the majority consisted of members who could use the recognition heuristic than when the majority consisted of members who could use knowledge.

Second, more direct evidence comes from the finding that in the cases in which both the recognition-based and the knowledge-based models can be applied, but make contradictory predictions, the recognition-based model described the data better. Across 154 discriminating cases, the group choices matched the predictions of the recognition-based majority rule almost twice as often as those of the knowledge-based majority rule—65% versus 35%. More specifically, one member who could use recognition heuristic more often than not seemed to win over one member (61%) as well as two members (59%) who could use knowledge, while the reverse pattern occurred less often—39% and 24%, respectively. The final piece of evidence comes from the predictions of the less-is-more effect.

Did the Less-Is-More Effect Occur and Which Models Capture It?

The less-is-more effect can be investigated by looking at group accuracies rather than at group choices. Note that these two measures do not necessarily correlate perfectly. For example, assume that there are two choices to be made and the group makes one correct and one incorrect choice. A model that says that the group choice is the opposite from what it actually is has 0% match rate but predicts perfectly the group accuracy of 50%.

On Figure 27-4, we graph the observed group accuracies—groups are ordered in decreasing order of these observations. In addition, the figure shows the predictions of group accuracies according to the restricted majority rules—for the formal details of the derivations see the Appendix. On average, the groups made accurate decisions in 71% of all choices. The average of the predictions of the recognition-based models matched this well, from 74% to 77%,

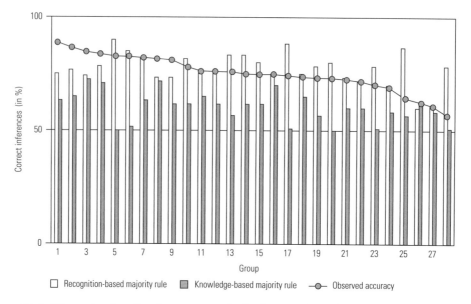

Figure 27-4. Observed and predicted group accuracies for the recognition-based and the knowledge-based rules, for each individual group, with guessing. Groups are ordered according to observed accuracy.

while the average of the predictions of the knowledge-based models was lower than observed, from 60% to 64%.

We have seven pairs of groups with approximately equal average α and β but different average *n*. As is indicated by the observed accuracies in Table 27-3, in five pairs the group with smaller average *n* had higher accuracy. This is the first empirical demonstration that the less-is-more effect occurs in groups.

How well can the models predict when the effect occurs and when it does not? Note that the formal result we stated above does not apply because it assumes homogeneous groups. For example, note that because homogeneity is violated, the knowledge-based rule can also predict less-is-more effects. Thus, we use the predictions graphed in Figure 27-4. The recognition-first lexicographic model and the recognition-based majority rule correctly predict whether the effect occurs or not in all seven cases. On the other hand, the knowledge-based majority rule and the simple majority rule make six correct predictions, and the knowledge-first lexicographic model makes five correct predictions.

We also considered how well the models capture the magnitude of the effect or its inversion. This is indexed by the sum of absolute values of the differences between observed and predicted accuracies in the two groups. The recognition-first lexicographic model again outperformed the other models, with the index equaling 12 percentage points. The index equaled 15, 19, 24, and 36 percentage points for the simple majority, recognition-based majority, knowledge-first lexicographic, and knowledge-based majority rule, respectively.

CONCLUSIONS

Goldstein and Gigerenzer (2002) investigated how individuals can use the recognition heuristic and exploit the structure of the environment in order to make inferences with limited time and information. We pushed this approach to a more complex paradigm, that of a group of people making a joint inference. In doing so, we developed models of how individual inferences are combined, derived and tested their predictions, and predicted and tested when the less-is-more effect occurs in groups.

Table 27-3. Seven Pairs of Groups with Approximately Equal Average α and β

	Pair						
	1	**2**	**3**	**4**	**5**	**6**	**7**
Average n							
Smaller n	9.0	10.3	11.3	11.3	9.3	10.7	8.0
Larger n	12.0	12.0	13.0	12.3	12.3	12.0	9.7
Average α							
Smaller n	.79	.78	.88	.72	.68	.79	.77
Larger n	.79	.81	.87	.70	.66	.81	.79
Average β							
Smaller n	.60	.64	.64	.61	.62	.58	.53
Larger n	.58	.62	.66	.60	.64	.60	.54
Observed accuracy							
Smaller n	.83	.73	.78	.67	.66	.67	.56
Larger n	.75	.69	.75	.63	.64	.73	.66
Simple majority rule							
Smaller n	.78	.78	.81	.71	.69	.72	.71
Larger n	.73	.75	.78	.68	.71	.74	.79
Recognition based							
Smaller n	.75	.73	.76	.67	.67	.70	.75
Larger n	.70	.71	.69	.63	.61	.72	.83
Recognition first							
Smaller n	.77	.77	.81	.71	.68	.72	.76
Larger n	.74	.76	.78	.67	.66	.76	.84
Knowledge based							
Smaller n	.64	.65	.68	.61	.59	.60	.51
Larger n	.61	.64	.68	.60	.66	.61	.55
Knowledge first							
Smaller n	.70	.70	.70	.63	.64	.64	.63
Larger n	.62	.65	.68	.61	.67	.63	.65

Average n, α, β, observed accuracy, and predicted accuracies are reported for both groups and all models.

What did we learn from this work? First, in analogy to Goldstein and Gigerenzer showing that recognition is applied in a noncompensatory fashion with respect to other cues, we showed that—in most of the cases—recognition was applied in a noncompensatory fashion with respect to other individuals: When both recognition-based and knowledge-based models could be applied but made different predictions, recognition-based criteria captured the group choice in 65% of cases. This behavior was also functional because the groups performed better when their choices matched the prediction of the recognition heuristic. Second, we provided theoretical analyses and empirical data that contradict the established claim in group decision making that groups always make better decisions when they have more information—see Reimer and Hoffrage (2003) for a discussion. Overall, it appears that the recognition heuristic interacts with group decision-making processes in a way that can again lead to the less-is-more effect, and that this interaction can be modeled in a simple fashion, for example, by the recognition-based majority rule and the recognition-first lexicographic model.

Future directions of this research could investigate the processes by which a group manages to exploit the recognition information. For example, it may be that group members who can use the recognition heuristic when forming an individual decision are more influential in the group decision process because they make their decision faster and are more confident. Moreover, those group members may be at an advantage because they can justify their decision by using a simple but strong argument—one city must be smaller because they do not even recognize the name of this city.

Another future direction could be to investigate tasks other than simple magnitude estimations. The recognition heuristic is a recent model, but there has already been research in domains like sport (Andersson, Ekman, & Edman, 2003) or election forecasting (Zdrahal-Urbanek & Vitouch, 2004).

ACKNOWLEDGMENTS

We would like to thank Anja Dieckmann, Gerd Gigerenzer, Peter Todd, and several other members of the ABC Group for their helpful comments.

APPENDIX

Goldstein and Gigerenzer (2002) have shown that an individual who recognizes n out of N objects can use the recognition heuristic with probability $r(n) = 2n(N - n)/[N(N - 1)]$, knowledge with probability $k(n) = n(n - 1)/[N(N - 1)]$, and has to guess with probability $u(n) = (N - n)(N - n - 1)/[N(N - 1)]$. Thus, the following holds for individual accuracy.

$$f(n) = r(n)\alpha + k(n)\beta + u(n)\left(\frac{1}{2}\right). \qquad (27\text{-A1})$$

Prevalence of less-is-more effect for individuals: Assuming $\alpha, \beta > 1/2$, we show that p increases in α and decreases in β if $\alpha > \beta$ and that $p = 0$ if $\alpha \leq \beta$.

If we let n vary continuously, $f(n) = [(-4\alpha + 1 + 2\beta)n + (2\alpha - 1)N + 1/2 - \beta]/[N(N - 1)]$, and $f''(n) = (-4\alpha + 1 + 2\beta)/[N(N - 1)]$. The second derivative is negative for $\alpha > \beta$ and $\alpha > 1/2$ because $-4\alpha + 1 + 2\beta = (1 - 2\alpha) + 2(\beta - \alpha)$. Thus, $f(n)$ is concave with the maximum being achieved at $n^* = -[(2\alpha - 1)N + 1/2 - \beta]/(-4\alpha + 1 + 2\beta)$. Because $f(n)$ is concave,

p decreases in n^*. Also, n^* decreases in α and decreases in β, and thus p increases in α and decreases in β.

If $\alpha = \beta$, the first derivative reduces to $(N - n - 1/2)(2\beta - 1)/[N(N - 1)]$, which, if $\beta > 1/2$, is positive for $n < N$, and thus $f(n)$ is increasing and $p = 0$. Increasing β also increases $f(n)$ for $n > 0$, and thus again $p = 0$.

In what follows, assume a homogeneous group with $m \geq 2$ members, each with accuracy $f = f(n)$, where members recognize objects and make inferences independently of each other.

Proof of main result.

(i) Let X be the number of individuals that make a correct inference. X is a binomial random variable with parameters m and f. For the simple majority model, group accuracy, $g = g(n)$, is increasing in X. Thus, for fixed m, g increases as f increases because it is more likely that X increases as f increases. It follows that the results for the strong less-is-more effect and the prevalence of less-is-more effects for a single individual also hold for the group.

(ii) Let R be the number of individuals that can use the recognition heuristic, and X_R the number of these individuals that make a correct inference. R is a binomial random variable with parameters m and $r(n)$, and X_R is a binomial random variable with parameters R and α.

For the recognition-based majority model, when m is fixed, g is increasing in $r(n)$ since it is more likely that there are more voters when $r(n)$ is larger and the *Condorcet jury theorem* (Condorcet, 1785; Groffman & Owen, 1986, p. 94) states that the accuracy of a majority increases with the number of voters. Note that it is assumed that $\alpha > 1/2$. Furthermore, the strong less-is-more effect is predicted for $r(n) = 2n(N - n)/N(N - 1)$ because it is concave and symmetric in n. Thus, the strong less-is-more effect is predicted. This prediction does not require $\alpha > \beta$.

Thus, group accuracy $g(n)$ is concave and symmetric in n and, for discrete n, achieves its maximum at $N/2$ when N is even and at $(N-1)/2$ and $(N+1)/2$ when N is odd. It follows that, for even N, the number of pairs (n_1, n_2) with $n_1 \neq n_2$ for which the less-is-more effect is predicted equals $(N/2) + 2[1 + \cdots + (N/2 - 1)]$. This is so because the number of n_2 for which the less-is-more effect is predicted when $n_1 = N/2$, equals $N/2$, and this number decreases by one as n_1 increases or decreases by one. Computing this sum, dividing with the total number of (n_1, n_2) pairs, $N(N+1)/2$, and simplifying yields $p = N/[2(N+1)]$. The derivation is similar for odd N.

(iii) Similar arguments hold for the knowledge-based majority model. The difference is that group accuracy is now increasing in the probability $k(n)$ that a member can use knowledge, and $k(n) = n(n-1)/[N(N-1)]$ which is increasing in n.

In what follows, $c(m, i)$ symbolizes the number of ways in which i objects can be chosen, without replacement, out of m objects, $(m!)/(m-i)!\,(i!)$

Group accuracy predictions: Let $F(i)$ be the probability of exactly i members being accurate *and* the group, using the simple majority model, being accurate. Based on the arguments in the proof of (i), $F(i) = c(m, i)f(n)^i (1-f(n))^{m-i}$ for $i \geq \text{majority}(m)$, except for $i = \text{majority}(m)$ when m is even, in which case $F(i) = c(m, i) f(n)^i (1-f(n))^{m-i}(1/2)$. Then the following holds for the group accuracy of the simple majority model.

$$g(n) = \sum_{i=\text{majority}(m),\ldots,m} F(i). \tag{27-A2}$$

Group accuracy for the recognition-based majority model is derived similarly. The difference is that first we need to determine the probability that r out of the m members can use the recognition heuristic and then the probability that the majority of these r members make the correct inference. If $A(i)$ is the probability of exactly i members, using the recognition heuristic, being accurate *and* the group, using the recognition-based majority model, being

accurate, then $A(i) = c(r, i)\alpha^i(1 - \alpha)^{r-i}$ for $i \geq \text{majority}(m)$, except for $i = \text{majority}(r)$ when r is even, in which case $A(i) = c(r, i)\alpha^i (1-\alpha)^{r-i}(1/2)$. Thus, the group accuracy of the recognition-based majority model is given by the following.

$$g(n) = \sum_{r=1,\ldots,m} \left[c(m,r)r(n)^r \left(1-r(n)\right)^{m-r} \right]$$
$$\sum_{i=\text{majority}(r),\ldots,r} A(i) + \left(1-r(n)\right)^m \left(\frac{1}{2}\right) \tag{27-A3}$$

The same reasoning applies to the knowledge-based majority rule with $k(n)$ playing the role of $r(n)$ and β playing the role of α. If $B(i) = c(k, i)\beta^i(1 - \beta)^{k-i}$, except for $i = \text{majority}(k)$ when k is even, in which case $B(i) = c(k, i)\beta^i(1 - \beta)^{k-i}(1/2)$, the following holds:

$$g(n) = \sum_{k=1,\ldots,m} \left[c(m,k)k(n)^k \left(1-k(n)\right)^{m-k} \right]$$
$$\sum_{i=\text{majority}(k),\ldots,k} B(i) + \left(1-k(n)\right)^m \left(\frac{1}{2}\right). \tag{27-A4}$$

The equations for the lexicographic models are derived by combining the logic of (27-A3) and (27-A4). For the recognition-first model, there are two events to be considered: first, there are members who can use the recognition heuristic—then, (27-A3) without the guessing term applies—second, there are no such members—then, a version of (27-A4) applies which takes into account that members who cannot use knowledge have to be guessing. The guessing terms for the whole group is adjusted as well since guessing now occurs only if all members guess. Thus, we have the following:

$$g(n) = \sum_{r=1,\ldots,m} \left[c(m,r)r(n)^r \left(1-r(n)\right)^{m-r} \right]$$
$$\sum_{i=\text{majority}(r),\ldots,r} A(i)$$
$$+ \left(1-r(n)\right)^m \sum_{k=1,\ldots,m} \left[c(m,k)k(n)^k u(n)^{m-k} \right]$$
$$\sum_{i=\text{majority}(k),\ldots,k} \left[B(i) + u(n)^m \left(\frac{1}{2}\right) \right]. \tag{27-A5}$$

The same reasoning applies to the knowledge-first model with $k(n)$ playing the role of $r(n)$ and β playing the role of α.

$$g(n) = \sum_{k=1,\dots,m} \left[c(m,k)k(n)^k \left(1-k(n)\right)^{m-k} \right]$$
$$\sum_{i=\text{majority}(k),\dots,k} B(i)$$
$$+ \left(1-k(n)\right)^m \sum_{r=1,\dots,m} \left[c(m,r)r(n)^r u(n)^{m-r} \right]$$
$$\sum_{i=\text{majority}(r),\dots,r} A(i) + u(n)^m \left(\frac{1}{2}\right).$$

(27-A6)

Equations 27-A2 to 27-A6 were used to generate the idealized curves in Figure 27-2. The predictions of the models for the empirical data were generated by similar equations with the observed α, β, and n for each group member—the only differences were due to the parameters varying across members.

PART III

Heuristics in the Wild

Crime

Introduction to Chapter 28

Psychological Models of Professional Decision Making

How do British magistrates decide whether a defendant is trustworthy and can be granted bail, or might commit another crime or leave the country before the trial and thus should be denied bail? How can such a consequential decision be made in 5 to 10 minutes? There is a long tradition in which experts' judgments have been modeled by weighting-and-adding-of-all-evidence strategies. If Mandeep Dhami had followed this tradition, her conclusion would have been that some weighting-and-adding models provided a good fit, apparently implying that magistrates integrate all information into their decisions. But in addition to a weighting-and-adding model, she tested a fast-and-frugal tree (see Chapters 6 and 14), the *matching heuristic*, which relies on only a few pieces of evidence. As it turned out, the heuristic predicted magistrates' bail decisions in two London courts consistently better than a weighting-and-adding model named after Benjamin Franklin, who promoted such a strategy.

The fast-and-frugal trees for the magistrates in both courts had the same specific structure (a "rake" or Type 1 in Chapter 6), suggesting defensive decision making. A defensive decision is one that is less concerned with finding the best solution than with protecting the decision maker should something go wrong. A magistrate can make two errors—to imprison a defendant who would have done nothing wrong while on bail or to grant bail to a defendant who then violates the law or obstructs justice. Only the second error, however, can be detected. In the event that it occurs, magistrates are protected by the structure and content of the fast-and-frugal trees. For instance, the magistrates in Court A could argue that neither the prosecution nor a previous court nor the police had requested or imposed a punitive action, so how could the magistrates themselves have foreseen it?

However, this defensive heuristic violates what the law calls *due process*. The magistrates appeared to "pass the buck" rather than use the information that the Bail Act asks them to consider. In a study with hypothetical cases, Dhami and Ayton (2001) also found that although magistrates relied on only a few cues, they claimed to use several to make a decision. The magistrates seemed oblivious of their actual behavior and told a different story when interviewed. None of the magistrates said that they used the cues as specified in the matching heuristic. Consistent with the fact that the two fast-and-frugal trees ignore information about the defendant, British bail information schemes for gathering and providing information about defendants' community ties had no effect on decisions (Dhami, 2002).

This article caused some turmoil in the legal community. If the analysis held true for other courts as well, what needed to be changed? One solution would be to replace magistrates' decisions with a simple algorithm. In England and Wales alone, that would avoid court hearings of some 2 million defendants every year. A second solution would be to give the magistrates feedback, train them in decision making that observes due process, and change the legal institutions so that they no longer feel obliged to make defensive decisions. A conference volume on heuristics and the law (Gigerenzer & Engel, 2006) discusses in detail the uses and abuses of heuristic decisions in the making of the law and in litigation. Some legal scholars at this conference objected to Dhami's analysis of the London Court A because the model predicted "only" 92% of the bail decisions (and fitted 95%). That was too low a percentage, they argued; only 100% would be good enough for the law.

CHAPTER 28

Psychological Models of Professional Decision Making

Mandeep K. Dhami

Abstract: People are often expected to make decisions based on all of the relevant information, weighted and combined appropriately. Under many conditions, however, people use heuristic strategies that depart from this ideal. I tested the ability of two models to predict bail decisions made by judges in two courts. In both courts, a simple heuristic proved to be a better predictor of judicial decisions than a more complex model that instantiated the principles of due process. Specifically, judges were "passing the buck" because they relied on decisions made by the police, prosecution, and previous bench. Problematically, these earlier decisions were not significantly related to case characteristics. These findings have implications for the types of models researchers use to capture professional decision-making policies.

Ideally, we expect decision makers to use all of the relevant information, and weight and combine it appropriately. Moreover, we expect them to behave like this when their decisions have significant consequences. For more than 50 years, researchers have captured judgment policies in domains such as medicine (see Wigton, 1996), education (see Heald, 1991), and accounting (see Waller, 1988) using multiple linear regression. This model depicts professionals as behaving in an ideal way. It is reported that people combine multiple differentially weighted cues in a compensatory way, so, for example, a low weight attached to one cue is compensated by a high weight attached to another cue. However, the regression approach assumes large attentional, memory, and processing abilities, and ignores the impact of sequential processing (e.g., Dhami & Harries, 2001; Gigerenzer, Todd,

& the ABC Research Group, 1999). This approach is also inflexible because it assumes the same cues are used to make decisions on different cases. Furthermore, policy-capturing researchers have overlooked the fact that decision strategies are adapted to the demands of the task. For instance, under conditions of time pressure, people tend to use fewer cues and simple noncompensatory strategies, so, for example, an initial leaning toward a decision based on a cue with a high weight will not be altered by cues with lower weights (e.g., Payne, Bettman, & Johnson, 1993; Rieskamp & Hoffrage, 1999).[1]

There are several nonstatistical and cognitively simpler strategies that represent viable alternatives to the regression model. Two such models are Franklin's rule and the matching heuristic. The processes by which these models predict whether a judge makes a punitive bail decision[2] are described in the appendices. Like the regression model, Franklin's rule (originally described by Benjamin Franklin) involves the compensatory combination of multiple differentially weighted cues, and is limited in its inflexible cue use. However, it differs from the regression model in that it does not compute optimal weights as in the least squares regression, nor does it take into account the interdependencies among cues. By contrast, the matching heuristic (Dhami & Ayton, 1998, 2001) uses an even simpler cue-weighting method, searches through a small subset of the cues, and bases its predictions on one cue alone. It is noncompensatory because a decision is based on the value of one cue, and so is not altered by values of other cues. It is also flexible because different cues can be used to make decisions on different cases. The matching heuristic is therefore a "simple" or "fast-and-frugal" heuristic (see Gigerenzer et al., 1999).

To date, most research comparing the predictive validity of the regression model and these simple heuristics has been based on simulations in which models predict a criterion. Studies show that whereas the regression model is the best predictor of a criterion at the model-fitting stage, simple heuristics tend to outperform the regression model at the cross-validation stage (see Gigerenzer & Goldstein, 1996; Gigerenzer et al., 1999).[3] In behavioral studies, the matching heuristic performed as well as the regression model when predicting doctors' prescription decisions (Dhami & Harries, 2001), and outperformed Franklin's rule when predicting judges' bail decisions (Dhami & Ayton, 2001). In both studies, however, participants made decisions on systematically designed hypothetical cases (in which cues are independent), which are common in policy-capturing research. The validity of the captured policies is thus questionable (e.g., Ebbesen & Konecni, 1975; Phelps & Shanteau, 1978). Furthermore, critics argue that support for simple heuristics is needed from behavioral data gathered under naturalistic conditions (e.g., Lipshitz, 2000). Indeed, some may consider that a strong test of these heuristics would involve participants, such as judges, who are explicitly guided and motivated to reason in a manner that is neither fast nor frugal.

THE PRESENT STUDY

Like most professional decisions, judicial decisions are guided by formal rules. In Anglo-American jurisdictions, judicial decisions must comply with the principles of due process. In theory, when deciding to convict, judges or jurors should search through all information pertaining to guilt and innocence, weight it according to its reliability and validity, and combine it, so that, for example, an initial leaning toward a verdict of guilt can be altered by evidence indicating innocence (Packer, 1968). A similar process is advocated for making bail decisions. Like most judicial decisions, bail decisions have huge ramifications for defendants and the public. The bail decision is one of the most frequent decisions made by judges, and may influence later decisions to convict and sentence (Davies, 1971). The present study compared the ability of Franklin's rule and the matching heuristic to predict the bail decisions made by judges on real cases appearing in real time. On the basis of past psychological research, I hypothesized that the matching heuristic would be the better predictor of judges' decisions. By contrast, a hypothesis derived from legal theory (that judges would observe the principles of due process) suggests that Franklin's rule will outperform the simple heuristic in predicting judicial decisions. This study pitted these two hypotheses against one another.

METHOD

Observers and Observed Judges

The decisions made by benches of judges in two London, United Kingdom, courts were observed over a 4-month period. Observer 1 recorded 159 decisions made by 25 benches in Court A, and Observer 2 recorded 183 decisions made by 32 benches in Court B. The benches comprised different combinations of 55 judges in Court A and 56 judges in Court B. There was no significant difference between the average years of experience of judges sitting in Court A ($M = 10.1$, $SD = 7.8$) and Court B ($M = 9.5$, $SD = 7.3$), $t(108) = 0.59$.[4]

Observational Coding Scheme

Details of the cases presented and the decisions made were recorded using a structured coding scheme. Construction of the scheme was informed by a task analysis, and the scheme was pilot-tested on 15 bail hearings observed in 1 week in a third court. Data were recorded on 25 verbal, nonverbal, and written cues that the task analysis indicated may be available to judges during bail hearings. The cues are shown in Table 28-1. They can be divided into those referring to (a) the personal characteristics of the defendant, (b) the offense with which the defendant is charged, (c) the defendant's previous record, and (d) the bail hearing. In addition to recording details of each case and the decision, observers measured the duration of bail hearings using a stopwatch.

Interobserver Reliability

Interobserver reliability was assessed in the middle of the observation period, when both observers recorded data on 26 hearings in 1 week in the two courts (i.e., 8 in Court A and 18 in Court B). Calculation of Cohen's kappa indicated that agreement ranged from perfect (i.e., 1.0) to excellent (i.e., $\geq$.75) on most variables. The recorded duration of bail hearings was also highly consistent between the two observers, $r = .98$, $p < .001$.

Observed Cases: Availability and Intercorrelations of Cues

Information was often unavailable to judges for the following 4 of the 25 cues: defendant's previous convictions, defendant's bail record, defendant's community ties, and bail decision by the police. Chi-square analyses revealed that compared with Court A, in Court B, a greater

Table 28-1. Observed Cues and Their Values

Cue	Values
Defendant's characteristics	
Age	18–20/21 +
Gender	Male/female
Race	White/visible ethnic group
Strength of community ties	Has job or child or partner or home/has none of these
Current offense	
Seriousness of offense	Trial in lower courts/trial by jury in higher court
Category of offense	Against person/against property or other
Number of offenses	1/2+
Victim	Known or unknown person(s)/consensual crime or business victim
Is defendant solely involved?	Yes/no
Plea	Guilty/not guilty/no plea
Strength of prosecution case	Has physical evidence or witness/has none of these
Maximum penalty if convicted	Custodial/noncustodial
Defendant's previous record	
Previous convictions	None/yes-similar/yes-dissimilar
Bail record	None or good/breached bail
Bail hearing	
Is defendant in court?	Yes/no
Is defendant legally represented?	No/yes by own or court-appointed solicitor
Who is the prosecutor?	Crown prosecution service/other
Circumstances of adjournment	For trial/for sentence or appeal or other reason
Who requested the adjournment?	Defense/prosecution/court
Length of adjournment	1 week/2 weeks/3 weeks/4 weeks/5 weeks/6 weeks
Number of previous adjournments	0–1/2+
Prosecution request	Do not oppose bail/ask for conditions or oppose bail
Defense request	Unconditional bail/conditional bail/no application for bail
Previous court bail decision	None/unconditional bail/conditional bail or remand in custody
Police bail decision	Unconditional bail/conditional bail or remand in custody

Note: Values separated by "or" were observed separately, but were combined for analysis.

percentage of defendants were present in the courtroom during the hearing, were of ethnic origin, were legally represented, and had been charged with crimes against a person, and a smaller percentage had pleaded guilty and had previous adjournments ($p < .05$). First-order intercorrelations among the 25 cues were computed for each court. Seventy-three of the coefficients in Court A and 58 in Court B were statistically significant ($p < .05$), although none would be if a Bonferroni correction were applied. The mean cue intercorrelation was .2 ($SD = .3$) in Court A and .1 ($SD = .3$) in Court B.

RESULTS

Bail Hearings: Decisions and Duration

There was a significant difference between the proportion of punitive decisions made in Court A (i.e., 40.9%) and Court B (i.e., 54.1%), $\chi^2(2, N = 342) = 7.76$, $p < .05$. Furthermore, the duration of bail hearings in Court A ($M = 6.7$ min, $SD = 6.0$) was significantly different from the duration in Court B ($M = 9.5$ min, $SD = 8.4$), $t(312) = 3.54$, $p < .05$.

Bail Decision-Making Policies

Franklin's rule and the matching heuristic were used to capture the policies of each court separately because the courts differed in the cases presented, the decisions made, and the duration of hearings. Policies were not captured for individual benches because benches are not stable groups—judges are constantly rotated, and individual benches make too few decisions for meaningful analysis. The 25 cues were simplified (most converted to binary cues) for ease of analysis (see Table 28- 1). This process was informed by the task analysis and was compatible with past research (Dhami & Ayton, 2001). As in past research, both models were constructed so that they aimed to predict a punitive decision and made nonpunitive decisions only by default. The models were formed so that they treated unavailable cue information in a similar way, and the two models computed the same number of parameters. Each court's decisions were randomly divided into a modeling set and a cross-validation set (i.e., 80 modeling and 79 cross-validation cases in Court A, and 92 modeling and 91 cross-validation cases in Court B). So that an idiosyncratic division would be avoided, this process was repeated 10 times, yielding 10 different modeling and cross-validation sets for each court. Each time the model was constructed on the modeling set, and predicted decisions first for this set and then for the cross-validation set.

Whereas Franklin's rule searched through all 25 cues, the maximum number of cues searched (K) by the matching heuristic was on average 3.0 ($SD = 0.7$) for Court A and 2.8 ($SD = 0.4$) for Court B. As Table 28- 2 shows, despite this large difference in cue use between the models, for both courts, the matching heuristic outperformed Franklin's rule when predicting decisions at the model-fitting stage. Although the predictive power of both models was reduced at the cross-validation stage, the matching heuristic remained the better predictor of judges' decisions for both courts. A similar pattern of results emerged in a comparison of the ability of the models to predict the nonpunitive and punitive decisions separately (with the exception that Franklin's rule outperformed the matching heuristic in predicting Court B's nonpunitive decisions).

The maximum number of cues searched (K) by the matching heuristic and the rank order of cues differed slightly across the 10 tests because the properties of the modeling set changed from test to test. For illustrative purposes, Figure 28-1 shows the matching heuristic for each court, where K and the percentage of correct predictions was close to the mean found at the model-fitting stage. The model in Figure 28-1a correctly predicted 96.3% of decisions in Court A. The model in Figure 28-1b correctly predicted 94.6% of decisions in Court B.

DISCUSSION

In the present study, judicial decisions made in two courts were better predicted by the matching heuristic than by Franklin's rule. The matching heuristic depicts judges as basing decisions on one cue. Judges' reliance on the decisions made by the police, previous bench, and prosecutor

Table 28-2. Mean Percentage of Court Decisions Predicted Correctly by the Models

Test Stage and Decisions	Model			
	Franklin's Rule		Matching Heuristic	
	M	SD	M	SD
Court A				
Model-fitting				
Overall	89.1	3.2	95.4	1.6
Nonpunitive	86.4	5.2	92.5	2.2
Punitive	93.5	4.3	99.5	1.7
Cross-validation				
Overall	86.3	2.7	91.8	3.6
Nonpunitive	81.1	6.4	89.0	5.1
Punitive	93.3	3.3	95.2	8.2
Court B				
Model-fitting				
Overall	82.3	3.8	91.6	2.8
Nonpunitive	87.3	2.2	86.8	28.9
Punitive	78.3	6.7	95.5	1.5
Cross-validation				
Overall	73.4	4.9	85.4	22.1
Nonpunitive	78.7	9.6	77.9	37.1
Punitive	68.8	6.8	92.9	8.8

Note: Means and standard deviations are calculated over 10 tests.

(see Figures 28-1a and 28-1b) suggests that they were either intentionally or unintentionally "passing the buck." (Note that these cues were not significantly correlated with other cues such as the nature and seriousness of the offense.) Although this study does not bear upon the accuracy of the decisions, judges behaved contrary to the ideals of due process, according to which the number of innocent defendants who are treated punitively should be minimized. Converging evidence for the fast and frugal nature of judicial decisions derives from the observed brevity of the bail hearings and the consequent rapidity with which decisions must have been made.

The present findings support the validity of simple heuristics in capturing decision policies under naturalistic conditions and in the group context. In fact, the predictive validity of the matching heuristic was greater than that reported in the past (Dhami & Ayton, 2001; Dhami & Harries, 2001), and greater than the predictive validity of other simple heuristics (see Gigerenzer et al., 1999) and the regression model (see Brehmer & Brehmer, 1988).

Several conditions may have enabled the heuristic strategy to prevail in the present study. First, judges were presented with numerous cues and were often faced with a heavy caseload. There is evidence that people switch to simple noncompensatory strategies that use few cues as the number of cues increases and as time pressure increases (e.g., Payne et al., 1993; Rieskamp & Hoffrage, 1999). Second, judges made decisions as a bench. Groups making decisions involving shared responsibility tend to use few cues (Weldon & Gargano, 1985). Finally, the law affords judges considerable discretion concerning the cues they use to make their decisions. Notably, however, these conditions are not very dissimilar from those faced by professionals making decisions in other domains.

The present findings have implications for policy-capturing research. One explanation for the popularity of the regression model in policy-capturing research relates to the efficacy of alternative models available in the past. For instance, the conjunctive and disjunctive models (Einhorn, 1970) have performed poorly relative

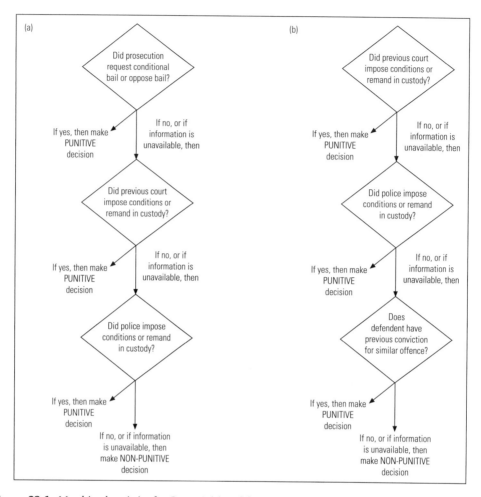

Figure 28-1. Matching heuristics for Court A (a) and for Court B (b).

to the regression model (Ogilvie & Schmitt, 1979), and the predictive validity of models developed via process tracing is difficult to test (see Juslin & Montgomery, 1999). Predictive validity has been the main reason for employing the regression model (Hoffman, 1960; Stewart, 1988). As the present study demonstrates, non-compensatory simple heuristics can be excellent predictors of decisions—even outperforming compensatory models that share key features with the regression model.

Clearly, another criterion for choosing models should be their psychological plausibility (Gigerenzer et al., 1999). Simple heuristics are grounded in research on human cognitive capacities. For example, the matching heuristic uses

frequencies when determining the critical value on a cue. It is claimed that this is a natural form of processing (e.g., Cosmides & Tooby, 1996). Definition of the critical value and utilization validity is supported by evidence that people use a subset of the available information when learning about the relations between cues and an outcome (Nisbett & Ross, 1980). The critical value embodies a type of positive-test bias in which only the information that indicates a focal (in this case punitive) decision is searched and used. There is general evidence for such strategies in other domains (e.g., Klayman & Ha, 1987). Finally, the heuristic embodies the idea of matching characteristics of individual cases with those of a prototype and is thus consistent with exemplar models in categorization, although they tend to be more complex (see Estes, 1994). Therefore, simple heuristics also meet the criterion of psychological plausibility.

A sound psychological theory of human decision making is possible only if we test the relative predictive validity of cognitively plausible models. Future research should involve models that have been constructed so that individual decision processes (e.g., compensation, linearity, cue weighting) are systematically manipulated, and tested under different task conditions (e.g., time pressure, number of available cues, cue redundancy). A full understanding of decision processes is essential as practitioners and policy makers often rely on our help in developing appropriate tools for training, evaluating, and aiding professional decision making.

ACKNOWLEDGMENTS

I am grateful to Michelle Gates for her assistance in conducting the observations and Torsten Mohrbach for programming the models. I also thank Laura Martignon for her helpful comments on the models, David Mandel and Peter Ayton for their comments, and Barbara Spellman and three anonymous reviewers.

NOTES

1. Indirect support for the use of simple strategies is obtained from studies reporting only one statistically significant beta weight in the regression model (e.g., Deshpande & Schoderbek, 1993; Gonzalez-Vallejo, Sorum, Stewart, Chessare, & Mumpower, 1998).
2. In the United Kingdom, remanding a defendant into custody or granting bail subject to conditions is referred to as a punitive decision, and releasing a defendant on unconditional bail is a nonpunitive decision.
3. At the model-fitting stage, the model is used to make predictions on the cases that were used to construct the model. At the cross-validation stage, the model is used to make predictions on a new, equally sized sample of cases.
4. All tests are two-tailed.
5. For ease of exposition, Appendices A and B refer to constructing models for predicting punitive and nonpunitive decisions, but the procedures described would be the same for whatever decision is of interest (e.g., to prescribe or not prescribe a particular medication).

APPENDIX A

Franklin's Rule

In this model, cues are differentially weighted. For each case, cue values are multiplied by their weights and then summed. If the sum is equal to or greater than a threshold value, then a punitive decision is predicted.[5] If not, a nonpunitive decision is predicted.

Construction of the Model

Cue values are coded. For example, in the present study, females were coded as 0 and males as 1 for the gender cue. A threshold value for predicting a punitive decision is established by taking the sum of each case in the modeling set, totaling these sums, and dividing this total by the number of cases in the modeling set. The weight for each cue is determined from the modeling set by calculating for each cue value the proportion of cases treated punitively, comparing the proportions for the different cue values, and then taking the greatest proportion as the weight for the cue. For example, if the proportion of males treated punitively is .78 (i.e., 14 treated punitively out of 18) and the proportion of females treated punitively is .33 (i.e., 3 treated punitively out of 9), the weight for the gender cue is .78.

Example: Decision of Judge 1 on Case 3 (taken from Dhami & Ayton, 2001)

The threshold value for this judge was 3.52. Based on this judge's cue weights, consideration of Case 3 was as follows: gender$(0)(0.72)$ + race$(1)(0.67)$ + age$(0)(0.67)$ + seriousness of the offense$(1)(0.78)$ + prosecution request$(1)(0.72)$ + past criminal record$(0)(0.73)$ + strength of prosecution case$(0)(0.78)$ + defendant's community ties$(0)(0.67)$ + police bail decision$(1)(0.67)$ = 2.84. The case sum was below the threshold; thus, Franklin's rule predicted a nonpunitive decision. In fact, the judge made a punitive decision on this case.

APPENDIX B

Matching Heuristic

In this model, cues are rank-ordered by their utilization validities. For each case, K cues are searched in order, for a critical value that indicates a punitive decision. If a critical value on a cue is found, search is terminated and a punitive decision is predicted. Otherwise, search continues until K cues have been searched, and if by this time no critical value has been found, a nonpunitive decision is predicted.

Construction of the Model

For each cue, the critical value indicating a punitive decision is the value of that cue that was most frequently treated punitively in the cases in the modeling set. For example, the critical value for the gender cue is male if more males than females were treated punitively (i.e., 14 males treated punitively compared with 3 females). (If these absolute frequencies are equal, the cue value with the lowest absolute frequency of cases treated nonpunitively is selected as the critical value; if the frequencies treated nonpunitively are also equal, a critical value is selected randomly.)

Cues are rank-ordered according to their utilization validity, which is defined as the proportion of cases with the critical value that were treated punitively in the modeling set. To continue the example, the validity of the gender cue would be the proportion of males treated punitively, or .78 (14 males treated punitively out of 18). A rank of 1 is assigned to the cue with the largest validity. (Cues with tied ranks are placed in order of their presentation to the judges.)

The maximum number of cues the heuristic searches (i.e., K) is determined by systematically testing the heuristic's ability to correctly predict decisions in the modeling set where $K = N$ cues, $K = N - 1$ cues, $K = N - 2$ cues, and so forth. The value of K that yields the greatest percentage of correct predictions is selected.

Example: Decision of Judge 1 on Case 3 (taken from Dhami & Ayton, 2001)

For this judge, the heuristic would search for information on only one cue—the seriousness of the alleged offense. It would predict a punitive decision if the offense was indictable (serious). In Case 3, the offense was serious, so the heuristic predicted a punitive decision. In fact, the judge did make a punitive decision.

Introduction to Chapter 29

Geographic Profiling: The Fast, Frugal, and Accurate Way

One of the scariest movies of all time is Jonathan Demme's *The Silence of the Lambs*. Many of us will never forget the strangely fascinating but creepy moments when the promising FBI student Clarice Starling interviews the notorious Hannibal Lecter. Her hope is that the brilliant psychiatrist and incarcerated cannibalistic serial killer will allow her to pick his brain, thus helping her to profile the vicious serial killer Buffalo Bill. Psychological profiling involves studying the behavioral characteristics of the offender (e.g., serial killer, arsonist, rapist) to thus establish a composite "profile," which, in turn, provides the police with helpful clues about the kind of person they are looking for. A complementary approach is geographic profiling; that is, using the sites of a perpetrator's crimes to predict where the person is most likely to live. Simply put, psychological profiling tells the police "who," whereas geographic profile tells the police "where." Typically, geographical profiling is performed by sophisticated statistical software that calculates a probability distribution across possible locations, taking the crime sites into account and assuming that the probability of locating an offender's residence decreases with increasing distances from any given crime site.

Brent Snook, Paul Taylor, and Craig Bennell's article, which is one in a series (e.g., Snook, Zito, Bennell, & Taylor, 2005), investigates whether geographic profiling could also be successfully carried out without using complex algorithms. Snook, Taylor, and Bennell taught laypeople in criminology—prospective undergraduate students and their accompanying guardians—two simple heuristics to identify the likely location of the offenders. One heuristic bets on the fact that the majority of offenders' homes can be located within a circle, with its diameter defined by the distance between the offender's two farthermost crimes. The other heuristic assumes that the majority of offenders commit offenses close to home. After being trained to use both heuristics, participants' performance in predicting the likely residence was about as good as one leading implementation of the complex algorithmic approach to geographical profiling. The demonstration that simple heuristics can match the predictive power of complex actuarial methods has stimulated a controversy in research on geographic profiling (Rossmo, 2005; Taylor, Bennell, & Snook, 2008).

The professional prediction of events, from where offenders live to the commercial success of a movie plot or a particular stock, is a huge business. Some estimate it to be a $200 billion-per-year industry (Sherden, 1998). With so much money at stake, tensions come as no surprise. Some experts, for instance, oppose actuarial techniques such as complex algorithms for geographical profiling. Typically, their criticism is not that the complexity of these techniques is beyond their grasp.

Rather, they argue that their own expertise is superior because it can take additional idiosyncratic variables (the proverbial "broken leg cues") into account that the inflexible actuarial techniques will ignore. As the current article shows, there is a third alternative to complex actuarial techniques and experts' supposedly complex clinical approach, namely, simple heuristics that can be easily taught to nonexperts and can match the performance of complex prediction software.

CHAPTER 29

Geographic Profiling: The Fast, Frugal, and Accurate Way

Brent Snook, Paul J. Taylor, and Craig Bennell

Abstract: The current article addresses the ongoing debate about whether individuals can perform as well as actuarial techniques when confronted with real world, consequential decisions. A single experiment tested the ability of participants ($N = 215$) and an actuarial technique to accurately predict the residential locations of serial offenders based on information about where their crimes were committed. Results indicated that participants introduced to a "circle" or "decay" heuristic showed a significant improvement in the accuracy of predictions, and that their post-training performance did not differ significantly from the predictions of one leading actuarial technique. Further analysis of individual performances indicated that approximately 50% of participants used appropriate heuristics that typically led to accurate predictions even before they received training, while nearly 75% improved their predictive accuracy once introduced to either of the two heuristics. Several possible explanations for participants' accurate performances are discussed and the practical implications for police investigations are highlighted.

A more efficient use of resources and an increase in offender apprehension are the rewards for the police decision-maker who is able to predict accurately the location of an offender's residence from information about where his or her crimes were committed. Although most researchers accept that individuals can address such prediction tasks by using cognitive heuristics, many view heuristic-led judgments as vulnerable to cognitive errors and significantly less accurate than predictions obtained through actuarial techniques (Arkes & Hammond, 1986; Kahneman & Tversky, 1973). However, several recent findings have questioned this assumption, suggesting instead that individuals use fast-and-frugal heuristics that yield predictions that are as accurate as actuarial techniques (Gigerenzer, Todd, & the ABC Research Group, 1999; Snook, Canter, & Bennell, 2002). The current paper reports a replication of an earlier comparison of human and actuarial performance on a real-world "geographic profiling" task (Snook et al., 2002), and extends the previous work by examining both individual differences in the availability of appropriate heuristics and the possibilities of reaching effective performance through explicit heuristic training.

THE ACTUARIAL APPROACH TO GEOGRAPHIC PROFILING

Although actuarial techniques are not likely to guarantee perfect decisions, it is often argued that they will yield better decisions on average than human judges (Hogarth, 1987; Meehl &

Rosen, 1955; Swets, Dawes, & Monahan, 2000). In contrast to human decision-makers, actuarial techniques are able to avoid the problems associated with prior expectations, overconfidence, information retrieval, and information processing (Jacob, Gaultney, & Salvendy, 1986; Kahneman, Slovic, & Tversky, 1982; Kleinmuntz, 1990). The demonstration of human judgmental deficiencies has been seen by many as justification for the development of actuarial techniques (Edwards, 1972; Hastie & Dawes, 200l; Meehl, 1954). Such techniques have now been developed and implemented in a variety of contexts, which range from diagnosing and treating infectious diseases (Shortliffe, 1976) to developing win-win agreements in conflict resolution (Sainfort, Gustafson, Bosworth, & Hawkins, 1990).

One quickly developing area of application for actuarial techniques is police investigations, where the outcome of predictions can often have significant consequences for both public safety and human rights (Adhami & Browne, 1996; Rossmo, 2000; Taylor, Bennell, & Snook, 2002). The problem of predicting an offender's home location from crime scene information has received particular attention, with actuarial systems being developed and implemented in both Europe and North America (Rossmo, 2000; Shapiro, 2000). In its most basic form, this geographic profiling task involves using knowledge about the relative locations of an offender's crime sites to predict the highest probable location of his or her residence. By far the most common approach to this task uses mathematical functions to produce a probability surface that shows the likelihood of an offender residing at various locations around the area where their crimes were committed (Canter, Coffey, Huntley, & Missen, 2000; Rossmo, 1993; Taylor et al., 2002). Based on decades of offender spatial behavior research (Brantingham & Brantingham, 1981; Rengert, Piquero, & Jones, 1999; Turner, 1969), the mathematical functions are typically computed from large data sets to reflect the distribution of distances between offender home and crime locations. Research has demonstrated the accuracy of these geographic profiling systems, with serial offenders' residences typically falling in the top 10% of the prioritized area (Canter et al., 2000; Rossmo, 1993).

AN ALTERNATIVE APPROACH TO ACTUARIAL PREDICTIONS

Recent work has questioned the assumption that actuarial techniques always outperform human judges (Gigerenzer et al., 1999). Studies exploring a number of different prediction tasks have shown that the heuristics, or cognitive shortcuts, used by individuals to reduce complex problems into simpler judgmental ones can perform as accurately as actuarial techniques (Gigerenzer, 2000). This occurs when the heuristic is ecologically rational; that is, when it matches the structure of the environment such that it exploits the general patterns and tendencies in behavior (Martignon & Hoffrage, 1999; Simon, 1956). The structure of the environment refers to "… information that a person, animal or institution knows about a physical or social environment" (Gigerenzer & Selten, 2001, p. 187). According to recent work, then, individuals would be expected to have heuristics available to make predictions on the geographic profiling task, where some of these heuristics will be ecologically rational and yield performances that are as accurate as predictions from an actuarial technique.

Although the research on heuristics indicates that they may offer a powerful solution to real-world prediction tasks, the applicability of heuristics to complex and consequential decision tasks, such as geographic profiling, has received little attention (Shanteau & Thomas, 2000; Sternberg, 2000). In an effort to address this lack of research, Snook et al. (2002) compared the performance of participants and an actuarial technique on a geographic profiling task that required predictions of offenders' home locations based on the distribution of five crime locations. Participants were introduced to a "decay" heuristic, which states that many offenders live near their crime locations, and a "circle" heuristic, which states that many violent serial offenders live within a circle with the diameter defined by the distance between the offender's two farthermost crime locations.

The decay heuristic is based on the long-established finding that offenders do not travel far from their home to offend (for an extensive review, see Rossmo, 2000) and that the frequency of offending decreases with increased distance from an offender's home location; a concept known as "distance-decay" (Capone & Nichols, 1975; Turner, 1969). The circle heuristic originated from evidence showing that the majority of violent serial offenders' homes are located within an area demarcated by their two most distant crimes; a concept known as the "circle hypothesis" (e.g., Canter & Larkin, 1993; Kocsis & Irwin, 1997; Tamura & Suzuki, 1997). These two heuristics were taught because they mirror those rules that are fundamental to existing actuarial techniques (Canter et al., 2000; Rossmo, 2000). By comparing the accuracy of predictions before and after being provided with these heuristics, Snook et al. demonstrated that groups of participants were able to use these heuristics to improve the accuracy of their predictions. More importantly, the average predictions of participants using these heuristics were found to be as accurate as one popular actuarial technique.

THE CURRENT STUDY

The previous study by Snook et al. (2002) raises the possibility that, in their enthusiasm to develop geographic profiling systems, some researchers have neglected to test the basic question of whether decision-makers can perform accurately given ecologically rational heuristics (Canter et al., 2000; Rossmo, 2000). However, as Snook et al. acknowledge, their study involved only a small number of participants and should be viewed as pilot work whose findings suggest the need for replication and expansion. One area for development is to explore the different types of heuristics that participants use to make predictions and the accuracy produced by those heuristics. Snook et al. did not attempt to determine whether participants inherently used appropriate heuristics (i.e., before training) to complete the task and so were unable to test for individual differences in their strategies. Moreover, the original study design presented

the decay and circle heuristics simultaneously, leaving open questions of whether these heuristics have independent effects on predictive accuracy and, more importantly, whether the improvement in performance following training was actually the result of the decay or circle heuristic being implemented. Thus, the original study was unable to argue conclusively that teaching heuristics led to participants adopting strategies that improved predictive accuracy.

Given the importance of these questions for understanding the limits and characteristics of heuristics, the current paper replicates and extends the Snook et al. (2002) study. The current experiment tests four hypotheses concerning the ability of participants and an actuarial technique to predict the likely residences of serial offenders based on their crime scene locations. Figure 29-1 is a schematic overview of the experiment, in which the boxes depict the stages of the experiment and the arrows running between the boxes indicate the order in which the stages were presented. Annotations H_1 through to H_4 indicate the stages of the procedure relevant for testing the following four hypotheses:

H_1: Participants will improve the accuracy of their predictions when provided with ecologically rational heuristics.

H_2: Participants introduced to an ecologically rational heuristic will make predictions that are as accurate as an actuarial technique.

H_3: Some individuals will use ecologically rational heuristics to make predictions prior to training and these predictions will be more accurate than those who do not use ecologically rational heuristics.

H_4: Participants who initially do not use ecologically rational heuristics will adopt those that are provided during training.

Stages in the top half of Figure 29-1 combine to allow aggregate performance to be compared before and after training (H_1) and post-training performance to be compared to predictions made by an actuarial technique (H_2). Stages in the bottom half of Figure 29-1 focus on individual differences in performance and examine the type of heuristics used to complete the prediction task before (H_3) and after training (H_4).

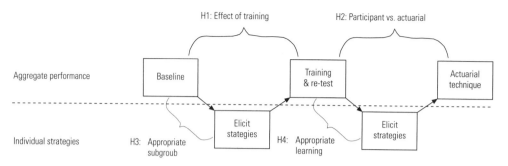

Figure 29-1. Schematic overview of the experiment.

METHOD

Participants

Participants were 215 prospective undergraduate participants and their accompanying guardians attending a recruitment day at The University of Liverpool, UK. Participants were randomly assigned to a control ($N = 73$), circle ($N = 68$) or decay ($N = 74$) group, where the difference in N across the three groups resulted from true random assignment.

Materials

A set of 10 maps, each depicting the first three murder locations of a different offense series, were randomly generated from a larger database of geographic information for solved serial murder cases in Germany (for more details of the database see Harbort & Mokros, 2001). The maps were scaled from actual maps to fit onto a sheet of A4 paper (map size = 235 mm × 163 mm). The maps were presented in black and white and without topographical features in order to remain consistent with the information used by current actuarial techniques. The maps were integrated into an experimental booklet that contained, in order, on separate pages: (a) a blank cover sheet, (b) instructions to indicate (by marking an "X") on each of the 10 maps a place where they thought the offender's home was most likely to be located, (c) the 10 maps, (d) instructions to record the strategies they used to reach their decisions, (e) instructions to place the completed maps out of their reach,

(f) heuristic training material, (g) the same 10 maps, and (h) instructions to record the strategies they used to reach their decisions. Blank sheets of paper were interleaved between each of the sections of the booklet to ensure that participants could not see the upcoming pages.

The heuristic training section of the booklet (section f) differed according to participants' group assignment. Participants in the control group were not given any heuristic. Participants in the decay group received written instructions describing the decay heuristic, which read, "The majority of offenders commit offenses close to home." Participants in the circle group were given written instructions on the circle heuristic, which read, "The majority of offenders' homes can be located within a circle with its diameter defined by the distance between the offender's two farthermost crimes."

Procedure

The three groups of participants completed all phases of the experiment in a single session while seated within a large lecture theater. Participants were informed that they would be making predictions about the likely home location of 10 serial murderers and that the experiment was not concerned with memory performance. Each participant was asked to work individually through the booklet at his or her own pace and specifically told to refrain from turning over pages until the booklet instructed them to do so. Two experimenters remained in the theater throughout the experiment to answer any questions and to ensure that the task was completed individually. Completion of all tasks in the booklet took approximately 20 min, after which participants were debriefed through a 15-min presentation on geographic profiling.

Attaining actuarial predictions

Actuarial predictions for each of the 10 presented maps were derived using a negative exponential function (Canter et al., 2000). This function assumes that the probability of locating an offender's residence decreases with increasing distance from an offense, and takes the general form:

$$f\left(d_{ij}\right) = a^* e^{-c^* d_{ij}}$$

where $f(d_{ij})$ is the likelihood that an offender's residence will be located at a particular location, d_{ij} is the distance from the center of the grid cell (i) to an offense (j), a is an arbitrary coefficient used to provide an indication of the likelihood of finding a home, e is the base of the natural logarithm, and c is an exponent that determines the gradient of the function (Levine & Associates, 2000; Taylor et al., 2002). In the current study, the constant a and exponent c were given values of 1, since this is consistent with the base algorithm implemented in a popular actuarial technique (Canter et al., 2000).

Predictions from the negative exponential function were obtained by inputting x and y coordinates of each crime location into *CrimeStat* (Levine & Associates, 2000). *CrimeStat* is a spatial statistics program for the analysis of crime incident locations. Based on the exact measurement sizes of the standardized maps provided to participants, the total area under consideration in *CrimeStat* was 235 mm × 163 mm. Therefore, each of the 7,000 cells that made up the superimposed grid was 2.35 mm × 2.33 mm in size. The negative exponential function was then applied around each of the crime locations in order to assign a probability value to each of the grid cells. The probability scores assigned to each grid cell were then summed to produce an overall probability value for each grid cell. The resulting output provides the x and y coordinates of the cell with the highest probability, which was

chosen as the predicted home location for the actuarial technique and used in all further analyses.

Measuring predictive accuracy

For both the participant and the actuarial technique, the predictive accuracy was measured in millimeters as the straight-line distance between the predicted and actual home location (henceforth referred to as the "error distance"). A larger error distance indicates a less accurate prediction of the offender's residence.

Analyzing written responses

The strategies participants used to make their predictions were content analyzed by the first author. Categories were derived through a typical grounded approach to categorizing written text, which entailed an iterative refinement and modification of the content dictionary until it clearly reflected the content of descriptions across all participants' data (Glaser & Strauss, 1967; Holsti, 1969; Krippendorff, 1980). The coding scheme was applied by the first author to the responses of each participant, both after the baseline (section d) and after the re-test (section h). Reliability of the coding was assessed by having the second author independently code each response provided by participants after the baseline and having the third author code the responses provided after the re-test. The reliability of coding, measured using Cohen's Kappa (Cohen, 1960), was 0.89 in relation to the heuristics used in the baseline and 0.90 in relation to the heuristics used in the re-test. Both values suggest a high level of agreement between the coders (Fleiss, 1981). Disagreements between the coders were resolved through discussion and mutual agreement prior to analysis.

RESULTS

Hypothesis 1: The effect of teaching ecologically rational heuristics

Figure 29-2 shows the mean error distances of predictions made across all 10 maps as a function of training. A 2 (pre test × post test) by 3 (Control × Circle × Decay) by 10 (across maps)

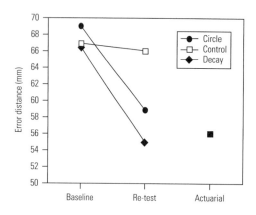

Figure 29-2. The mean error distances for predictions made in the baseline and the re-test for the three groups and the actuarial technique.

analysis of variance was computed on participants' error distances with training submitted as a within-subjects variable. The within-subjects comparisons showed a significant main effect of training, $F(1, 2108) = 131.13, p < 0.05, \eta^2 = 0.05$, and a significant two-way interaction of training with group, $F(2, 2108) = 22.26, p < 0.05, \eta^2 = 0.02$. These were subsumed by a significant three-way interaction, $F(18, 2108) = 6.30, p < 0.05, \eta^2 = 0.05$.

Simple main effects were calculated across training for each of the three groups to examine the effectiveness of teaching the heuristics on aggregate performance. There was no significant difference in mean error distance observed for the control group across baseline (67.3 mm, $SD = 19.0$ mm) and re-test (65.8 mm,

$SD = 19.9$ mm), $F(1, 72) = 2.10$, *ns.* This contrasts with the circle group, whose performance showed a significant decrease in mean error distance from baseline ($M = 69.3$ mm, $SD = 22.3$ mm) to re-test ($M = 59.0$ mm, $SD = 13.3$ mm), $F(1, 67) = 21.90, p < 0.05, \eta^2 = 0.25$. Similarly, for the decay group, there was a significant decrease in mean error distance from the baseline ($M = 67.3$ mm, $SD = 19.9$ mm) to re-test ($M = 55.4$ mm, $SD = 6.6$ mm), $F(1, 73) = 26.70, p < 0.05, \eta^2 = 0.27$.

The between-subject comparisons showed a significant difference in performance across the maps, $F(9, 2108) = 199.86, p < 0.05, \eta^2 = 0.45$. In order to explore the variations in performance among the maps, participants' performance on each map was examined separately. Table 29-1 contains the results of repeated-measure t-tests calculated on the mean group accuracy of predictions across baseline and re-test for each map. A Bonferroni correction was implemented to control the Type-I error rate associated with conducting 10 tests on the data from each group ($\alpha = 0.005$). We adopted a correction for 10 tests because the comparisons intended for each group are independent of the comparisons intended for the other groups, both in terms of involving different participants and different data. The symbol "+" in Table 29-1 indicates a significant improvement in accuracy from the baseline to the re-test, "−" indicates a significant decrease in accuracy, and "±" indicates that there was no significant change. As can be seen in Table 29-1, the control group showed no significant change in predictive accuracy from

Table 29-1. Test of change in accuracy from the baseline to the re-test for each of the groups across the 10 maps

Group	Map									
	1	2	3	4	5	6	7	8	9	10
Control	±	±	±	±	±	±	±	±	±	±
Circle	+	+	±	±	+	+	+	±	+	+
Decay	+	+	+	+	+	+	+	±	+	−

+ Significant improvement in accuracy from the baseline to the re-test; − significant decrease in accuracy from the baseline to the re-test; ± no significant change from the baseline to the re-test.

the baseline to the re-test for any of the maps. In contrast, the circle group showed significant improvement in accuracy for seven of the 10 maps, while the decay group showed a significant improvement in accuracy for eight of the 10 maps.

Hypothesis 2: Comparison between cognitive heuristics and an actuarial technique

Figure 29-2 also shows the mean error distance for the negative exponential function ($M = 55.9$ mm) across the 10 maps. Since the mean predictive accuracy of the negative exponential function is a constant value, one-sample t-tests were used to compare the performance of the function against participants' performances following training. Specifically, the mean error distance of the negative exponential function (i.e., 55.9 mm) was used as the test-value and this was separately compared against post-training mean error distances for the control, circle, and decay groups. As predicted, the control group's performance at re-test was significantly worse than the mean predictive accuracy for the negative exponential function ($t = 4.24$, $df = 72$, $p < 0.05$). However, there were no statistically significant differences between the predictive accuracy achieved by participants in both the circle ($t = 1.92$, $df = 67$, ns) and decay ($t = -0.67$, $df = 73$, ns) groups at re-test and the mean predictive accuracy for the negative exponential function.

As in the previous analysis, the mean error distance for each map was examined separately to determine whether these findings were dependent on the differences among maps. For each map, a one-sample t-test was conducted to determine if the known predictive accuracy of the actuarial technique was significantly better than the mean of re-test performance scores for the control, circle, and decay groups (see Table 29-2). Since each of these comparisons will draw on the actuarial data, this approach requires 30 tests to be computed on related aspects of the data. Consequently, a Bonferroni correction was implemented to limit the potential Type-I errors associated with conducting 30 tests ($\alpha = 0.0016$). The "+" symbol in Table 29-2 indicates that the heuristic was significantly more accurate than the actuarial technique, the "−" indicates that the heuristic was significantly less accurate than the actuarial technique, and the "±" indicates no significant difference in accuracy between the heuristic and actuarial technique. As can be seen in Table 29-2, predictions of the control group were significantly more accurate than the actuarial technique for one map, significantly worse for seven maps, but not significantly different from the actuarial technique for the other two maps. In contrast, the predictions of the circle group were significantly more accurate than the actuarial technique for one map, significantly worse for five maps, but not significantly different from the actuarial technique for the other four maps. Predictions of the decay group were significantly more accurate than the actuarial technique for three maps, significantly worse for three maps, but not significantly different from the actuarial technique for the other four maps.

Table 29-2. Test between the Control, Circle, and Decay Group Accuracy in Re-test and the Actuarial Technique in Relation to Each Map

Group	Map									
	1	2	3	4	5	6	7	8	9	10
Control	−	−	−	−	−	±	−	−	±	+
Circle	±	−	−	−	−	±	±	−	±	+
Decay	±	−	±	−	−	±	±	+	+	+

+ Heuristic significantly more accurate than the actuarial technique; − heuristic significantly less accurate than the actuarial technique; ± no significant difference in accuracy.

Hypothesis 3: Do participants implicitly use ecologically rational heuristics?

The content analysis identified a comprehensive set of 12 strategies that were used by participants before training, five of which were combinations of six core heuristics. Combination categories were retained to ensure that participants' responses could be assigned to a single category, thereby eliminating the double-counting that would occur if participants were allowed to be assigned to multiple categories. Table 29-3 shows each of the 12 strategies together with a coding definition and their percentage of occurrence in the baseline. As can be seen from Table 29-3, a total of 49% of participants reported using either the equidistant heuristic (36.3%), cluster heuristic (4.2%), or a combination of equidistant and cluster heuristics (i.e., Combo 1, 8.4%) prior to instruction.

The three graphs on the left hand-side of Figure 29-3 represent participants' mean error distances as numbers on a stacked bar graph for each of the experimental groups. The numbers denote the heuristic reported by the participant before training, as coded using the heuristics listed in Table 29-3. For instance, the number "7" represents a participant who reported making predictions based on the heuristic that the offender should live far away from his crimes (i.e., commuter). Since the graphs on the left side of Figure 29-3 show participants' performance at baseline they can be used to determine whether relatively accurate participants also report using a different type of heuristic.

As can be seen from the three left hand graphs in Figure 29-3, participants reporting the use of the equidistant, cluster, or Combo 1 (i.e., equidistant and cluster) heuristics tended to have smaller error distances than those using alternative strategies. Specifically, 35% of participants who reported using the equidistant heuristic, 33% of participants who reported using the cluster heuristic, and 33% of participants who reported using Combo 1, fell in the lowest quartile of all error distances. In contrast, participants using heuristics that previous research has shown to be ineffective performed particularly poorly (Canter et al., 2000; Rossmo, 2000). For instance, eight of the 10 participants using the commuter heuristic typically made predictions that were in excess of 100 mm from the offender's actual home location (falling in the largest 7% of all error distances).

Table 29-3. Descriptions of the Strategies Used to Make Geographic Predictions Reported by Participants in the Baseline (percentage of occurrence is in brackets)

Heuristic	Definition
1. Guess (26%)	No strategy indicated or a guess was made
2. Equidistant (36.3%)	Prediction that the offender's residence should be located in the center of the crimes' locations or equidistant from crime locations
3. Cluster (4.2%)	Prediction that the offender's residence should be located near two crimes clustered together
4. Combo 1 (8.4%)	Equidistant and cluster heuristic
5. Outlier (1.9%)	Prediction that the offender's residence should be located near an outlier crime location
6. Proximity (10.7%)	Prediction that the offender's residence should be located "near" the crimes
7. Commuter (4.7%)	Prediction that the offender's residence should be located "away" from the crimes
8. Combo 2 (0.5%)	Equidistant, commuter, and proximity heuristic
9. Combo 3 (2.8%)	Equidistant and commuter heuristic
10. Combo 4 (1.9%)	Proximity and commuter heuristic
11. Combo 5 (0.9%)	Cluster and commuter heuristic
12. Combo 6 (1.9%)	Equidistant and proximity heuristic

Hypothesis 4: Can individuals quickly adopt ecologically rational heuristics?

Graphs on the right hand-side of Figure 29-3 summarize performance after training and so can be used to identify whether participants adopted the heuristics we introduced and whether these were responsible for the observed improvement in performance. A comparison of the left and right graphs in the top panel of Figure 29-3 suggests that participants in the control group made no changes to the heuristics they used to make predictions across the two

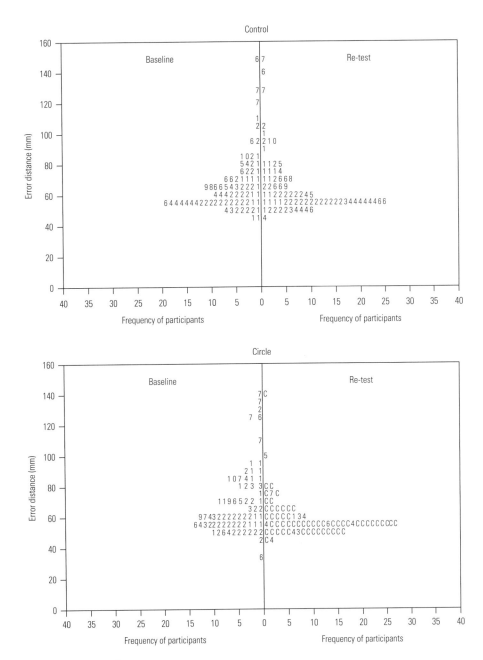

Figure 29-3. (continued).

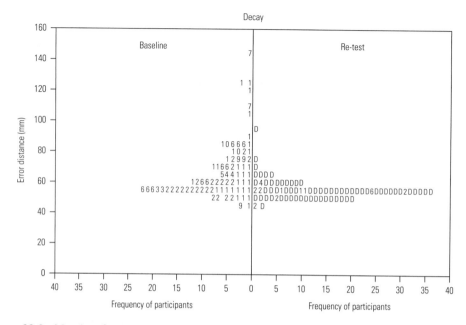

Figure 29-3. (*Continued*)Average error distance for each participant in the baseline and the re-test for each of the three groups. The numbers on the graphs represent the heuristic used by the participant.

phases, and, consequently, there is little change in the distribution. Indeed, in the absence of an intervention, 93% of participants in the control group used the same heuristic in both phases. A comparison of the left and right hand-side graphs in the middle panel of Figure 29-3 indicates that 85% of the participants introduced to the circle heuristic during training report using the circle heuristic during re-test (indicated by the letter "C" in the right graph). Similarly, a comparison of graphs in the bottom panel of Figure 29-3 indicates that 88% of the participants introduced to the decay heuristic during training report using the decay heuristic at re-test (indicated by the letter "D" in the right graph). For both experimental groups, this change in strategy is accompanied by a downward shift in the distribution of predictions compared to baseline, with those adopting the heuristics falling toward the bottom of the distribution (compare the left and right graphs of the middle and bottom panels of Figure 29-3). Specifically, 69% of the participants who reported using the circle heuristic after training showed some improvement in their mean predictive accuracy. Similarly, 78% participants who reported using

the decay heuristic after training showed some improvement in their accuracy across the maps. These findings suggest that participants adopted the introduced heuristics and that adopting the heuristics is associated with an improvement in average predictive accuracy for approximately 75% of participants.

DISCUSSION

Although recent research has indicated that individuals may be able to draw on cognitive heuristics to make accurate predictions, a debate continues as to whether these predictions can reach the levels of accuracy reported for actuarial systems. The current findings shed light on this debate, showing that participants trained in simple cognitive heuristics can perform as accurately as a leading actuarial technique when predicting the location of an offender's residence based on the locations of their crimes.

Results from the aggregate level analysis showed that participants informed about the circle or decay heuristic improved their predictions of offenders' residences to a level of accuracy that was not significantly different from the actuarial technique. Consistent with the findings of Snook et al. (2002), these results indicate that certain cognitive heuristics are effective for this particular real-world prediction task. Interestingly, the findings indicate that teaching one heuristic is sufficient to improve performance, suggesting that there is a considerable degree of overlap between the circle and decay heuristics.

Despite this similarity in performance, the circle and decay heuristics are not qualitatively identical since predictive accuracy in each of the experimental groups was not consistent across the 10 maps. Specifically, the results showed that participants in the circle group were, on average, equal to or better than the actuarial technique for five of 10 maps, while the decay group showed marginally better performance with equal or improved prediction occurring on seven of the 10 maps. Determining why the decay heuristic led to superior performance is an avenue for further exploration, but it is likely to be the result of a combination of factors including the degree of applicability, the clarity of definition, and the degree of match to the structure of offender spatial behavior. A detailed comparison of the effectiveness of different heuristics is likely to require more precise definitions of the cognitive heuristics, as has been achieved by using mathematical definitions in other areas (Gigerenzer et al., 1999).

A second implication of the aggregate level results is to question why, on some of the maps, the heuristics had very little impact on participants' predictive accuracy. One important explanation relates to the different types of offender spatial behavior that characterize this group of serial offenders. For example, a number of studies have shown that a minority of serial offenders do not live near their crimes and that the spatial behavior of these "commuter" offenders is not effectively predicted by the circle or decay heuristic. For instance, Lundrigan and Canter (2001) found that 11% of US and 14% of UK serial murders were commuters (they lived outside a circle defined by their crime site locations).

Since the heuristics we presented were based on the concepts of distance-decay and the circle hypothesis, the lack of improvement on some maps may reflect instances of commuter offenders. If the different behavioral pattern of commuters is the cause of poor performance, neither current actuarial strategies nor the heuristics taught in the current study can claim to be useful (i.e., ecologically rational) in solving the profiling task for all serial offenses.

Lastly, the findings reported in this study clearly open up the question about the ability to use simple cognitive heuristics to make other sorts of predictions in the forensic context. The use of heuristics is likely to branch across many police prediction tasks such as comparative case analysis (Bennell & Canter, 2002) and anticipating the likelihood of negotiation success in hostage crises (Taylor, 2002). By taking a step back to basics, it may become clear that prescriptions for actuarial techniques may be unwarranted and that individuals' heuristic-led judgments may suffice without significant loss in accuracy or effectiveness.

The findings presented in this paper might surprise those researchers and software developers who have assumed that human decision-making is limited and that accurate geographic predictions require actuarial support, extensive training, or both (Canter et al., 2000; Rossmo, 2000). In terms of actuarial support, the present findings suggest that individuals using simple heuristics can make accurate predictions. Indeed, the present findings suggest that technological advances in the field of geographic profiling over the last 10 years may have overcomplicated what may, in reality, be a relatively simple task.

ACKNOWLEDGMENTS

We thank Oliver Eastman and Brenda Colbourne for assisting with data collection and preparation. This research was supported by Overseas Research Scholarships awarded to B.S. and C.B. by the Overseas Research Student Award Scheme.

Introduction to Chapter 30

Take-the-Best in Expert–Novice Decision Strategies for Residential Burglary

The FBI's Uniform Crime Reporting Program defines *burglary* as the unlawful entry of a structure to commit a felony or theft. It is a frequent occurrence. In 2007, there were an estimated 2,179,140 burglaries in the United States; 68% of these targeted residential properties, and the total cost to victims was an estimated $4.3 billion in lost property (http://www.fbi.gov/). In light of these numbers, insurance companies urge owners to "case" their homes before someone else does it for them. Allstate, the second largest home insurer in the United States, provides four tips for throwing off potential thieves. One is to "think like a thief: "case" the outside of your house or apartment the way a burglar would look for easy ways to enter" (*The New York Times*, February 19, 2009).

This is well-meant advice, but how do thieves think? Rocio Garcia-Retamero and Mandeep Dhami's fascinating article affords us a good glimpse into the mindset of expert burglars. By studying burglars directly, the authors investigated both the cues that burglars use to infer which of two residential properties is more likely to be burgled and the strategies they use to process the cues. Their burglars were no greenhorns; they had reportedly done their job an average of 57 times each. The authors link this first study of expert burglars and simple heuristics to previous research on what are considered more socially desirable kinds of expertise. One consistent finding from the study of expertise is that experts have mastered the art of ignoring information. They tend to focus on a few valid and predictive pieces of information that are processed in a simple way. Consistent with this nature of expertise, the authors found that the expert burglars' decisions on which of two residential properties is most likely to be burgled can be better described in terms of the take-the-best heuristic (see Chapter 2) than in terms of strategies that combine all cues. The same was true for police officers experienced in investigating residential burglaries. Novices' decisions—made by graduate students who had not learned to discern the important from the unimportant—were best described in terms of the combination strategy.

Think like a thief, so goes the home insurer's advice to the homeowners. One important finding of the current investigation is that even longtime police officers who had worked cases of residential burglary failed to completely trace a burglar's thoughts. For expert burglars, the most important cue is the presence of an alarm system. For the police officers, in contrast, access to the property, that is, doors and windows on the ground floor, tops all other cues. Based on Garcia-Retamero and Dhami's investigation, police officers could fine-tune their mental models of the criminal mind's adaptive toolbox.

CHAPTER 30

Take-the-Best in Expert–Novice Decision Strategies for Residential Burglary

Rocio Garcia-Retamero and Mandeep K. Dhami

Abstract: We examined the decision strategies and cue use of experts and novices in a consequential domain: crime. Three participant groups decided which of two residential properties was more likely to be burgled, on the basis of eight cues such as location of the property. The two expert groups were experienced burglars and police officers, and the novice group was composed of graduate students. We found that experts' choices were best predicted by a lexicographic heuristic strategy called take-the-best that implies noncompensatory information processing, whereas novices' choices were best predicted by a weighted additive linear strategy that implies compensatory processing. The two expert groups, however, differed in the cues they considered important in making their choices, and the police officers were actually more similar to novices in this regard. These findings extend the literature on judgment, decision making, and expertise, and have implications for criminal justice policy.

Evidence reveals that experts and novices differ in their decision making (Shanteau, 1992a, 1992b). For instance, experts use less, but more relevant, information than do novices (e.g., Shanteau, Grier, Johnson, & Berner, 1991), who are influenced by irrelevant information. Experts appear to rely on implicit, automatic, and fast processes, whereas novices rely on explicit, controlled, and slower processes (e.g., Shanteau, 1988). Experts may employ noncompensatory strategies, whereas novices may rely on more cognitively complex strategies (Johnson & Payne, 1986; although there are claims that clinicians use nonlinear strategies). *Cognitive continuum theory* (see Hammond, 2000) proposes that familiar tasks are more likely to induce intuitive

processing, which has been associated with use of heuristics (Gigerenzer, 2007). To date, no one has examined the decision strategies of experts and novices in terms of whether they are more likely to employ heuristics such as take-the-best (TTB) or more complex strategies such as a weighted-additive linear model (WADD). Furthermore, no one has compared the strategies of experts who approach a task from different perspectives. They may be similar in their strategy (e.g., employing heuristics) but different in their cue use (i.e., relying on different cues), or vice versa. Indeed, one expert's perspective may be closer to that of a novice than to another expert's.

These questions are pertinent where crime is concerned. Novices (citizens) and expert police officers must predict the behavior of expert offenders. In residential burglary, for example, researchers have found that experienced burglars exhibit characteristics associated with expertise (e.g., Wright, Logie, & Decker, 1995). Burglars are more likely than residents to distinguish between cues that are incentives or deterrents for burglary (Nee & Taylor, 2000). Recently, Nee and Meenaghan (2006) found that burglars use sequential search, focus on relevant cues, and employ automatic and speedy strategies. Furthermore, experienced burglars differ from nonoffenders or residents and police officers in the cues they use to select targets (e.g., Shaw & Gifford, 1994; Wright et al., 1995). However, it is unknown whether burglars differ from police officers and residents in the decision strategy they employ (rather than in the cues they use).

We examined the strategies and cue use of experts with different perspectives (i.e., experienced burglars and police officers) and novices (i.e., graduate students) when predicting residential burglary. Are experts' choices more likely to be predicted by TTB and novices' choices more likely to be predicted by WADD? Is one expert perspective more similar to novices' in terms of cue use? How is the degree of expertise related to strategy? Answers to these questions have implications for theories of decision making and expertise, as well as for criminal justice policy and practice.

METHOD

Participants

One hundred and twenty individuals volunteered to participate in the study, without financial incentive. They formed three equally sized groups: burglars, police officers, and graduate students. Forty burglars were recruited from one English prison for men. Their mean age was 33.20 years (SD = 6.26), and the majority (69.23%) had at most a secondary school education (i.e., up to age 16). Burglars had reportedly committed burglary on an average of 57.18 occasions (SD = 39.82). Forty police officers were recruited from a professional graduate program at a British university. They were mostly male (33), with a mean age of 41.28 years (SD = 6.03); the majority (82.50%) had a university education. Police officers had worked for an average of 19.39 years (SD = 6.63) and had investigated residential burglaries. Finally, 40 students were recruited from the regular graduate program at the same university. Thirteen were male; the

sample had a mean age of 26.13 years (SD = 5.97). Students reported being a victim of burglary on an average of 0.58 occasions (SD = 1.01).

Design and Stimuli

Participants completed a three-part survey that allowed comparison of experts and novices in terms of the cues they considered to be important for choosing which of a pair of residential properties was more likely to be burgled, and in terms of the strategy that best predicted their choices in such a task. The study focused on decision making with already acquired strategies. Issues of information search and choice accuracy were not within the scope of the study.

In the first part of the survey, participants were provided with information, such as whether there was a burglar alarm system (see Figure 30-1), on eight cues describing each of 40 pairs of properties. These cues were selected after a review of the literature on residential burglary (e.g., Buck, Hakim, & Rengert, 1993; Ham-Rowbottom, Gifford, & Shaw, 1999; Shaw & Gifford, 1994). The cue values for both properties were coded as either positive or negative, and, according to the literature, positive values put the property at greater risk of burglary (see Table 30-1). For each pair, participants chose which property was more likely to be burgled.

The 40 pairs of properties were created to test which strategy, TTB or WADD, better predicted participants' choices (see Rieskamp & Otto, 2006, for a similar procedure). Cue values for each property were generated randomly under the following constraints: For each cue, half the properties had a positive value and half a negative value. Therefore, the discrimination rate (i.e., the number of paired comparisons in which cue values differed between properties) of all the cues was 50%. The intercorrelations among the cues ranged from –.10 to .10. At least one cue discriminated between each pair of properties. Therefore, for each paired comparison, the strategies made unambiguous predictions, and participants made unambiguous choices.

In the second part of the survey, participants ranked the cues according to how useful they would be in predicting the likelihood of a

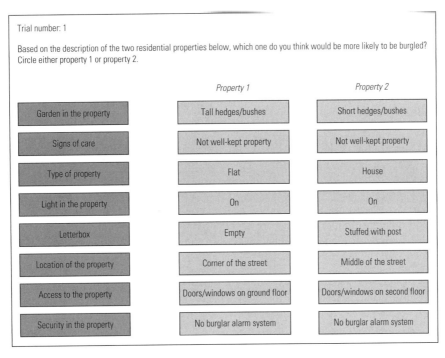

Figure 30-1. Screenshot depicting the task.

Table 30-1 Positive and Negative Values for the Eight Cues

Cue	Positive Value	Negative Value
Garden in the property	Tall hedges/bushes	Short hedges/bushes
Signs of care	Not well-kept property	Well-kept property
Type of property	Flat	House
Light in the property	Off	On
Letterbox	Stuffed with post	Empty
Location of the property	Corner of the street	Middle of the street
Access to the property	Doors/windows on ground floor	Doors/windows on second floor
Security in the property	No burglar alarm system	Burglar alarm system

property's being burgled, where the first rank was assigned to the most useful cue.

Finally, in the third part, participants estimated the weight of each cue (see Garcia-Retamero, Takezawa, & Gigerenzer, 2008). For instance, for the security in the property cue, they were asked,

> Imagine two residential properties. One of the properties has no burglar alarm system. The other has a burglar alarm system. In how many cases like this would the property with no burglar alarm system be more likely to be burgled than the property with a burglar alarm system?

Participants responded on scales from 50 to 100, marked with 10-point intervals.

Procedure

The paper-and-pencil survey was individually self-administered. Participants also provided their own demographic details. There were no time constraints, but the survey took approximately 45 min to complete. The order of the 40 pairs of properties was randomized across participants. The order of cues was fixed for each participant but varied randomly across participants.

RESULTS

Do Experts Differ from Novices in Their Cue Weights?

A mixed ANOVA with participants' cue weight estimations as the dependent variable, and group and cue as between- and within-subjects factors, respectively, was computed. There was only a significant main effect of group [F(5.55, 655.01) = 21.99, $p < .01$], and a significant group × cue interaction effect [F(11.11, 655.01) = 3.63, $p < .01$]. As can be seen in Figure 30-2, police officers' mean cue weight estimations were similar to those of students, but significantly different from those of burglars ($p < .05$ for both comparisons, using Tukey's HSD test). Burglars' mean cue weight estimations for security in the property, location of the property, and type of property were significantly higher than those of police officers and students. In contrast, police officers' and students' mean cue weight estimations for access to the property were significantly greater than those of burglars ($p < .05$ for all comparisons).

Do Experts Differ from Novices in the Decision Strategies that Predict Their Choices?

Participants' cue weight estimations were used as the cue weights for WADD and to imply cue rankings for TTB (see, e.g., Garcia-Retamero et al., 2008).[1] For each participant, the predictions of TTB and WADD were compared with his/her choices, and the percentage of choices predicted correctly by each strategy was computed (i.e., strategy fit).[2]

We computed the fit of TTB and WADD over all 40 paired comparisons by determining the proportion of participants' choices accurately predicted by each strategy. The percentage fits for WADD and TTB were 63.00% and 71.66%, respectively, for burglars [t(39) = −8.25, $p < .001$]; 66.98% and 73.65%, respectively, for police officers [t(39) = −4.47, $p < .001$]; and 77.00% and 65.05%, respectively, for students [t(39) = 11.45, $p < .001$]. Thus, experts' choices are more likely to be predicted by TTB, and novices' choices are more likely to be predicted by WADD.

We further analyzed the fit of the two strategies on the paired comparisons in which the strategies made opposite predictions (i.e.,

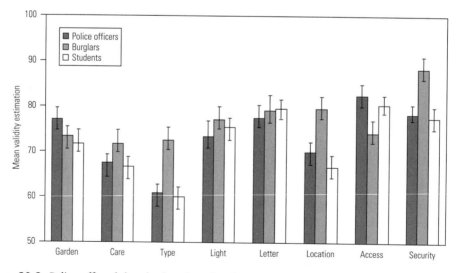

Figure 30-2. Police officers', burglars', and students' cue weight estimations. Error bars represent one standard error.

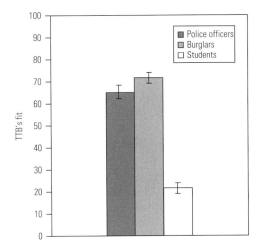

Figure 30-3. Percentage of choices predicted by TTB for police officers, burglars, and students in the discriminating trials where TTB and WADD made opposite predictions. Predictions for the two strategies sum up to 100%; a low fit for TTB implies a high fit for WADD and vice versa. Error bars represent one standard error.

discriminating trials; see, e.g., Rieskamp & Otto, 2006).[3] A mixed ANOVA was computed on these trials with participants' choices as the dependent variable.[4] Group and strategy were the between- and within-subjects factors, respectively. There was only a significant group × strategy interaction effect [$F(2,117) = 100.64$, $p < .001$] (see Figure 30-3). Using Tukey's HSD test for post hoc comparisons, we found that WADD had a significantly higher fit for students than TTB did, with an average of 77.94% correct predictions as opposed to 22.06%, respectively ($ps < .01$). By contrast, TTB had a significantly

greater fit on average for burglars and police officers than WADD did, with TTB correctly predicting 71.39% and 65.36% of burglars' and police officers' choices, respectively, as opposed to WADD's 28.61% and 34.64%, respectively ($ps < .01$).

To further explore the strategies that best predicted participants' choices on the discriminating trials, we classified participants as using either TTB or WADD, according to the strategy that achieved the highest fit, if the fit of the two strategies differed by at least 10%. This was based on the distribution of the fitting scores (see Mata, Schooler, & Rieskamp, 2007). Those participants ($n = 5$) for whom the fit of the two strategies coincided or differed by less than 10% were unclassified. As Table 30-2 shows, most police officers' and burglars' choices were classified as being better fit by TTB than by WADD [$\chi^2(1) = 39.00$, $p < .001$, for police officers, and $\chi^2(1) = 37.00$, $p < .001$, for burglars]. In contrast, most students' choices were better fit by WADD than by TTB [$\chi^2(1) = 39.00$, $p < .001$].

How Is Degree of Expertise Related to Decision Strategy?

We correlated the fit of TTB over the discriminating trials with the degree of expertise of participants in each group.[5] Degree of expertise was measured in terms of the number of years the police officers had worked for the force, the number of occasions on which burglars reported having committed burglary, and the number of occasions on which students had reported being victims of burglary. The correlation was .36 for police officers, .37 for burglars ($ps = .05$), and −.10 for students ($p > .50$).

Table 30-2. Strategy Classification by Group

	Police Officers		Burglars		Students	
	N	%	N	%	N	%
WADD	8	20.00	3	7.50	38	95.00
TTB	31	77.50	34	85.00	1	2.50
Unclassified	1	2.50	3	7.50	1	2.50

Note: $N = 40$ for all three groups.

DISCUSSION

We examined the decision strategies that best predicted the choices made by two expert groups with different perspectives (i.e., experienced burglars and police officers) and one novice group (i.e., graduate students). Burglars' and police officers' choices of residential properties likely to be burgled were better predicted by TTB, a noncompensatory, lexicographic heuristic. By contrast, students' choices on the same task were better predicted by WADD, a compensatory strategy. This conclusion was consistent across analyses over all 40 paired comparisons, over only the discriminating trials, and via classification of participants to their best fit strategy using a stringent criterion (i.e., 10% point difference between fit of strategies). Moreover, this conclusion was not tempered by group differences in age, gender, and education. In fact, the fit of TTB was positively associated with degree of expertise within the burglar and police groups, but was not associated with expertise in the student group. These results support the idea that task familiarity and experience or training are more likely to result in use of heuristics because they induce intuition.

Although it could be argued that participants' choices might have been even better predicted by variants of TTB and WADD, it is unlikely that our main conclusion—namely, that experts' choices are better predicted by a noncompensatory strategy and novices' choices are better predicted by a compensatory strategy—would change. Johnson and Payne (1986) noted that, as people become more experienced in a task, they are more likely to employ noncompensatory strategies. In fact, the present findings are consistent with previous research showing that the decisions of experienced professionals are more likely to be predicted by simple heuristics than by WADD (Dhami & Ayton, 2001; Dhami & Harries, 2001), whereas naive participants' choices are better predicted by WADD than by TTB (Rieskamp & Otto, 2006).

Our findings on cue use are compatible with evidence that experts may rely on one cue, whereas students may use multiple cues (Ettenson, Shanteau, & Krogstad, 1987). Interestingly, the two expert groups differed in the specific cues they considered, and one expert group was more similar to the novices in this regard. Specifically, for burglars, security in the property (i.e., the absence of a burglar alarm system) was the most important cue for determining burglary, whereas for police officers and students, the most important cue was access to the property (i.e., doors and windows on the ground floor). Others have similarly shown that burglars considered target hardening via alarm systems to be important (e.g., Buck et al., 1993). Furthermore, Ham-Rowbottom et al. (1999) found that access to the property was important to police officers, and there was more concordance between police officers and residents, but less between these two groups and burglars. Finally, the finding that novices used several less relevant cues is consistent with past research on expert–novice differences (Shanteau, 1992b).

The differences we observed between burglars and police officers in cue use may have arisen from the fact that their different perspectives are also associated with different types of learning experiences (i.e., direct learning for the former vs. indirect learning via observation, interview, and education and training for the latter). Typically, through direct learning with more-or-less immediate feedback, burglars would have learned the best cues for selecting a property to be burgled. By contrast, police officers may be missing information about a property that was burgled or even have misinformation. They also only receive information about burglaries that are reported. Furthermore, typically they are not given immediate feedback about the outcomes of their predictions (i.e., investigations and charges). Such conditions make learning difficult (Bolger & Wright, 1994), and so may lead to poor performance (Shanteau, 1992a). Residents (students, in this case) may share the views of police officers, because they may acquire their knowledge from police messages.

From a practical standpoint, the present findings raise some concerns. First, there are concerns over the ability of the police to detect and investigate residential burglary, and to advise on its prevention. Second, there are concerns over the ability of citizens (in this case, students who have a high rate of burglary; see Nicholas, Kershaw, & Walker, 2007) to effectively protect themselves against becoming victims of burglary. Fortunately, the fact that burglars may be using a heuristic implies that it may be easy for the police and citizens to adjust their thinking about burglary to concord with burglars'. This concordance is crucial, since residential burglary is a frequent crime. In the meantime, our findings underscore the problem that although police officers have learned to think like a criminal in terms of the decision strategy used, they have yet to know what the criminal is thinking in terms of the cues used.

ACKNOWLEDGMENTS

We thank Karen Souza for her assistance with the literature review of burglary and Bettina von Helversen for her useful comments.

NOTES

1. Cue rankings were used to break ties between cues when generating the predictions of TTB when cues had the same weight. This occurred in 1.34% (police officers), 3.13% (students), and 5.45% (burglars) of cases. Alternatively, breaking ties randomly did not affect our conclusions.

2. Evaluating the two strategies on the basis of this fit measure is appropriate, because the two strategies make unambiguous predictions in all trials, and they have no free parameters fitted to the data. This means that their flexibility in prediction is identical.

3. For example, imagine that the cue values for Properties A and B are 10000000 and 01111111, respectively, where 1 represents the presence of a cue value, and cues are arranged from left to right in decreasing order of weight. Here, TTB would predict the choice of Property A, because the first ranked cue discriminates between the two properties and the property with the cue value present (i.e., A) is chosen. By contrast, WADD would predict the choice of Property B, because it has more cue values, and so has the greater sum. This trial therefore discriminates between TTB and WADD, and participants using one of the two strategies would make opposite choices to those who employed the other strategy.

4. Because subjective cue weights were used to generate the strategies' predictions, the proportion of discriminating trials varied slightly across participants. The average percentage of discriminating trials was 22.88% (SD = 2.23), 21.31% (SD = 1.95), and 21.44% (SD = 2.18) for police officers, burglars, and students, respectively.

5. Computing the correlation on the basis of the strategy fit over the discriminating trials means that the correlation for WADD would be the same size as that for TTB, but in the reverse direction.

Sports

Introduction to Chapter 31

Predicting Wimbledon 2005 Tennis Results by Mere Player Name Recognition

A frequent complaint about experimental research in the social and natural sciences is that researchers' data collection is steered to support their hypotheses. Even Michael Faraday, famous for his pioneering experiments in electricity and magnetism and referred to by some historians of science as the best experimentalist in the history of science, was not free of this tendency. According to Tweney and Doherty's (1983) analysis of his diaries, he was likely to seek confirming evidence and ignore disconforming evidence in the initial phase of experimentation.

The work that inspired this chapter by Benjamin Scheibehenne and Arndt Bröder is a counterexample to the strategy of seeking confirming evidence. Extremely skeptical of the power of the recognition heuristic to yield good decisions, Serwe and Frings (2006) set out to test the heuristic in a task in which they were confident that it would fail: predicting the winners of Wimbledon. First, tennis heroes often rise and fall quickly; by the time their names have finally found a place in collective recognition memory, their star may already be fading. Second, athletes are best known within their home country, even if they do not perform particularly well in the international arena. Recognition of an athlete should thus be a poor guide to predicting whether he or she will win an international match. To demonstrate this suspected Achilles' heels of the recognition heuristic, Serwe and Frings needed semi-ignorant people who could use the recognition heuristic. They asked German amateur tennis players which players they had heard of in the 2004 Wimbledon Gentlemen's Singles tennis tournament. (The amateurs recognized on average only about half of the contestants.) All Wimbledon players were ranked according to the number of participants who had heard of them. How well would this collective recognition predict the winners of the matches? Recognition turned out to be a better predictor than both ATP rankings (ATP Champions Race and ATP Entry Ranking), the official worldwide rankings of tennis players, and the seeding of the Wimbledon experts. These unexpected results took the authors by surprise.

When the two authors presented their results to the ABC Research Group, the surprise was on both sides. Could it have been a lucky strike, ripe for publication in the *Journal of Irreproducible Results*? Scheibehenne and Bröder (2007) set out to test whether the findings would replicate for Wimbledon 2005—and found the same result. In addition, when asked to predict the match winners, in around 90% of the cases where recognition could be used, their participants predicted that the recognized player would win. We chose their replication study for this volume because it uses a similar method, but included the complete set of Wimbledon players.

The power of recognition to predict winners in sport and its actual use by people to make predictions is not limited to tennis. Pachur and Biele (2007), for instance, found that lay people predicting the match winners at the European soccer championships followed the recognition heuristic in 91% of the cases; Snook and Cullen (2006) observed that participants relied 95% of the time on the recognition heuristic when predicting which of two Canadian National Hockey League players had achieved more career points. Moreover, in the latter study, participants were accurate in 81% of these trials. If these results are combined with the role of systematic forgetting, as investigated by Schooler and Hertwig (see Chapter 4), it appears that systematic forgetting can increase the accuracy of predictions not only in static environments involving population sizes, but also in dynamic environments such as sports, where rankings can change quickly.

CHAPTER 31

Predicting Wimbledon 2005 Tennis Results by Mere Player Name Recognition

Benjamin Scheibehenne and Arndt Bröder

Abstract: The outcomes of matches in the 2005 Wimbledon Gentlemen's tennis competition were predicted by mere player name recognition. In a field study, amateur tennis players ($n = 79$) and laypeople ($n = 105$) indicated players' names they recognized, and predicted match outcomes. Predictions based on recognition rankings aggregated over all participants correctly predicted 70% of all matches. These recognition predictions were equal to or better than predictions based on official ATP rankings and the seedings of Wimbledon experts, while online betting odds led to more accurate forecasts. When applicable, individual amateurs and laypeople made accurate predictions by relying on individual name recognition. However, for cases in which individuals did not recognize either of the two players, their average prediction accuracy across all matches was low. The study shows that simple heuristics that rely on a few valid cues can lead to highly accurate forecasts.

Common sense suggests that the prediction of event outcomes and other probabilistic inferences improve when more information is integrated. In contrast to statistical approaches, which try to integrate all potentially relevant information, a recent study by Andersson, Edman, and Ekman (2005) reports that American and Swedish students with little knowledge about soccer were nevertheless more successful in predicting the results of the Soccer World Cup 2002 than were soccer experts (sport journalists, soccer fans, and soccer coaches). Andersson et al.'s results are in line with a growing body of evidence showing that simple models, which only use minimal amounts of information, are often as accurate as complex statistical models that integrate many pieces of information

(Gigerenzer, Todd, & the ABC Research Group, 1999). Along the same lines, Spyros Makridakis and his colleagues (Fildes & Makridakis, 1995; Makridakis & Hibon, 1979, 2000; Makridakis et al., 1982, 1993) showed in a series of studies (the so-called M-competitions) that for predicting real-life time series, simple models lead to more accurate forecasts than statistically sophisticated methods. The same case was argued by Robyn Dawes (1979), who showed that in many situations an "improper" linear model that uses equal weights leads to better predictions than a model based on presumably "optimal" or fitted weights.

In this paper, we investigate the success of a specific decision rule, the fast-and-frugal recognition heuristic (Goldstein & Gigerenzer, 2002), in predicting the 2005 Wimbledon tennis tournaments. In doing so, we also provide a potential explanation as to why and how the recognition heuristic works in predicting the outcomes of sport events. Our work confirms and extends the results of Serwe and Frings (2006), who used a similar approach to study the 2003 Wimbledon tournaments.

The recognition heuristic works as follows: If you have to judge which one of two objects scores higher on a criterion, and you recognize one of them but not the other, then choose the recognized object (Gigerenzer & Goldstein, 1996). Although it is extremely simple, this strategy can be very successful if the probability of recognition is highly correlated with the criterion to be judged. Hence, there are many domains in which mere recognition has been shown to be a valid predictor: for example, in judging city sizes (Goldstein & Gigerenzer, 2002), predicting stock performance in a bull market (Borges, Goldstein, Ortmann, & Gigerenzer, 1999; but see Boyd, 2001, for a bear market), predicting record sales of pop stars (Herzog, 2005), the quality of American colleges (Hertwig & Todd, 2003), and the results of political elections (Marewski, Gaissmaier, Dieckmann, Schooler, & Gigerenzer, 2005). It has also been shown to predict sports success. In a study on predicting the outcome of the F.A. Cup, a major knockout tournament for English football clubs, Ayton and Önkal (2006) found that by relying on name recognition, Turkish students who knew little about the English league were almost as successful as British students in predicting the outcome of the games. Similar results were found by Pachur and Biele (2007) in predicting the 2004 European Soccer Championships, by Serwe and Frings (2006) in predicting the outcome of the 2003 Wimbledon tennis competition, and by Snook and Cullen (2006) in predicting which of two Canadian hockey players has more career points.

Although there is debate about the claim that recognition is the *only* cue used in probabilistic inferences when applicable (Bröder & Eichler, 2006; Newell & Fernandez, 2006; Newell & Shanks, 2004; Pohl, 2006; Richter & Späth, 2006), all these studies show that people's inferences are heavily influenced by recognition information. Thus, people apparently use the recognition cue in forecasts.

However, in a dynamic setting such as sports predictions, the success of the recognition heuristic might be impaired, because sporting

excellence is relatively short-lived while name recognition remains relatively stable over time. For example, Björn Borg is still a well known player even though his professional career is long over. In their study on the prediction of the men's Wimbledon tournament 2003, Serwe and Frings asked laypeople and tennis amateurs which of the player names they knew. Based on this name recognition data, they predicted that each match would be won by the player whose name was recognized by more participants. What they found was that, despite the dynamic change in the criterion, recognition still served as a valid predictor in predicting the results of the Wimbledon tournament.

At the same time, if the tennis environment is indeed "dynamic," the positive results for the recognition heuristic in 2003 might have been a coincidence. For example, recognition of company names was a good predictor of stock performance in the study of Borges et al. (1999), but it completely failed in a different market situation (Boyd, 2001). Hence, before praising partial ignorance as the silver bullet in tennis prediction, one has to show that Serwe and Fring's results are systematic. Also, there is a need to better understand the underlying reason for why, and in which domains, recognition serves as a valid predictor. The present study aims to further explore these issues by testing the recognition heuristic in predicting the 2005 Wimbledon Gentlemen's singles competition.

METHOD

To test the success of the recognition heuristic in predicting the outcome of the 2005 Wimbledon competition, we asked laypersons, as well as amateur tennis players, to indicate which of the names of the 128 Wimbledon contestants (112 regular players plus 16 qualifiers) they recognized. From these judgments, predictions were generated for all 127 matches of the tournament, from the first round of 64 to the final. Predictions were generated in two ways: first, across all participants in our study, each Wimbledon player was assigned a rank indicating how many participants recognized him, and for each match, the winner was predicted by that ranking. Second, for each individual participant in our study, predictions were generated for the matches in which the recognition heuristic could be applied. This is the case when one of the players is recognized and the other is not. The former ranking method may be more effective, because partial ignorance is aggregated across participants. The latter individual method is psychologically more plausible because every participant, of course, has access only to his or her own partial knowledge.

Both prediction methods were compared to predictions based on the official ATP Champions Race ranking (ATP-CR) and the ATP Entry ranking (ATP-ER). The ATP-CR ranks players according to their performance during the calendar year. In January, each player starts with zero points, and the performance at major tournaments is summed up over the course of the year. Although this rarely happens, ties between two or more players may occur. At the end of the year, the ATP-CR determines the year-end world Number 1 player. The ATP-ER, commonly referred to as the 'world ranking', reflects players' performance at major tournaments during the immediate past 52 weeks at any point. A player who ranks first on this list is said to be the Number 1 player in the world. In the domain of sports forecasting, models that rely on publicly listed data such as past performance and team rankings have proven to be valid predictors that outperform newspaper tipsters (Forrest & Simmons, 2000). The predictive power of player rankings and expert seedings has also been shown for other sports like basketball, tennis, and (American) football (Boulier & Stekler 1999, 2003).

As additional standards of comparison, we also included betting odds taken from several international online betting sites and the Wimbledon seedings (SEED). The 32 seeded players are determined by an official committee of experts that evaluates players' ability to perform on the rye grass of the Wimbledon tennis courts. Players who are seeded do not play against each other until late in the tournament and the two players seeded first and second will not play against each other until the final.

While the committee uses the official ATP rankings as an orientation, it maintains the prerogative to deviate from it. Accordingly, in the year of our study (2005), 4 of the top 32 ATP-ER were not seeded, and 7 of the top 32 ATP-CR were not seeded. In addition to the recognition data, we also asked our participants to predict the results of the individual matches in the Wimbledon competition.

Materials and Procedure

As the pairings unfolded during the course of the tournament, we collected data at two points in time. Data on the prediction of the first round (64 games) were collected between the end of the qualifying round and the start of the first round. Data on the prediction of the fourth round (8 games) and the quarterfinals (4 games) were collected after the end of the third round and before the start of the fourth round. In both sampling waves, data were collected using a questionnaire that consisted of a recognition section and a prediction section. The recognition section of the questionnaire listed the full names of all 128 male players who qualified for the 2005 Wimbledon Gentlemen's singles competition. For each player, participants were asked whether they knew the name or not. Note that for both rounds this left only a narrow window of little more than 24 h to prepare the questionnaires and collect the data.

The prediction section that followed differed in the two sampling waves. For the first wave, the questionnaire listed the 64 fixtures of the first round. For the second wave, the 8 fixtures of the fourth round and the 4 fixtures of the quarterfinals were listed. Since the opponents of the quarterfinals were not determined at that point in time, all 16 possible combinations for the quarterfinal encounters were listed. For the analysis we only used the combinations that were actually played. In each case, participants had to tick the name of the player they predicted to win the game.

To distinguish laypersons from amateur players, participants were asked whether they were a member of a tennis club and whether they were active tennis players. To increase the chances of finding amateurs, half of the questionnaires were administered on the sites of several tennis clubs in Berlin, while the other half were administered in several public parks within Berlin. To control for order effects, two different questionnaire versions were used, with the players' names in randomized orders. Participants received €2.00 for filling out a questionnaire. In addition, participants earned a lottery ticket for each correct prediction. The number of correct predictions determined their chances of winning €50.00 at the end of the study.

In each sampling wave, the recognition section of the questionnaire preceded the prediction section. As one reviewer noted, this might have primed participants to make use of recognition in their predictions. While we cannot fully rule out this possibility, we believe that we counteracted this by setting a monetary incentive for making correct predictions. More importantly, we were concerned that by doing it the other way round (first prediction, then recognition) we might have induced recognition because the participants would have already had seen the names before, a problem that researchers have faced in the past (Marewski et al., 2005). As having reliable recognition data was paramount for our analyses, we decided to ask for it first.

Since the data were collected in the field, some questionnaires were not fully completed. We excluded every participant with 10 or more missing values in either the recognition or the prediction segment.

Differences and Extensions to Previous Work by Serwe and Frings

Our methodology is similar to the one used by Serwe and Frings (2006), but it extends their approach in several important ways. For the first round of 64, Serwe and Frings asked their participants about name recognition, but did not ask them to make predictions. In our study, we elicited recognition and prediction judgments from the same participants for the first round, which allowed us to more reliably assess the prescriptive, as well as the descriptive, value of the recognition heuristic. Moreover, Serwe and Frings did not include the 16 players that qualified for the competition in the week prior to the start of the tournament, while our study included

all 128 Wimbledon players (rather than only 112 as in their study). Serwe and Frings sampled amateurs from one specific tennis club and recruited university students as laypeople. To rule out the possibility that their results were due to special properties of this sample (e.g., members of one single tennis club might recognize the same player names) we used a sample of amateur tennis players from 9 different tennis clubs. We also used a more heterogeneous sample of laypeople by recruiting participants "on the street". To further analyze when and why the recognition heuristic works, we also collected data on the public media coverage of the players.

Participants

From the initial sample, 26 participants were excluded due to missing values, which resulted in a total of 184 remaining participants for both weeks; 105 of them were laypeople and 79 were members of a tennis club, henceforth called *amateurs*. 24% of the amateurs were male and 50% of the laypeople were male. The average age of the amateurs was 37 years (SD = 14.9), and that of the laypeople was 30 years (SD = 11.0).

RESULTS

Prediction of Recognition Ranking

On average, laypeople recognized 11.1 of the 128 players, or 9%. Two thirds of the laypeople recognized between 2% and 11% of the players, and there were 0.2 missing values on average. Amateurs recognized 49.9 players, or 39%. Two thirds of the amateurs recognized between 13% and 53%, and on average there were 0.9 missing values. From these data, a ranking was calculated based on how often each of the 128 players was recognized by our participants. Under the assumption that recognition is not random, but is related to the criterion of interest (here, the tennis players' success), the recognition heuristic predicts that the player that is recognized by more participants is more likely to win a match. The rule derived for predicting the outcomes of the Wimbledon matches is straightforward: if one player is recognized by more people, predict that this player will win the game. If both players are recognized by the same number of people, guess. In total, 127 matches were played during the tournament that could be used to test this prediction. We calculated three recognition rankings, one for the laypersons (RR-Lay), one for the amateurs (RR-Amateurs), and one for all participants (RR-All). The amateur ranking and the laypeople ranking are highly correlated ($\varphi = .87$), and therefore the predictions based on the rankings are quite similar. RR-Lay led to correct predictions in 84 of the 127 games, and it had to guess the outcome of two matches; thus, it successfully predicted 67% of all of the games. RR-Amateurs and RR-All both had to guess in one case. RR-Amateurs successfully predicted 86 matches (68%), and RR-All predicted 89 matches (70%). But how good is it to get 70% correct predictions?

Comparison of the Recognition Ranking with Other Rankings

In order to assess the predictive power of our recognition rankings, we compared them to ATP-ER, ATP-CR, and SEED. Both ATP rankings were collected one day before the official start of the tournament. As the Wimbledon tournament takes place in the middle of the year, the ATP-CR and ATP-ER are highly correlated, and therefore often lead to similar predictions. Table 31-1 gives an overview of the correlations among all of the rankings.

The rule for predicting the matches from the ATP rankings and the seedings worked like the

rule used for the recognition rankings: predict that the player with the higher ranking will win the game; if two players have the same ranking, guess.[1] Based on this rule, ATP-ER never had to guess, and correctly predicted 88 of the 127 games (69%). ATP-CR had to guess once and correctly predicted 89 games (70%). As only 32 players were seeded, SEED had to guess in 42 cases, and correctly predicted 68 games (54%). An analysis of variance reveals no difference between the ranking predictions ($F[5, 756] = 0.13$). Thus, even though most participants in our study were far from being tennis experts, the predictions based on recognition rankings were as good as the predictions from both ATP rankings, and the predictions of the Wimbledon expert committee.

Predictions of Betting Odds

We also compared the predictions of the recognition rankings to the betting odds for each individual game from five different online bookmakers.[2] For all five online bookmakers, the predictions based on betting odds for all matches are correct 79% of the time. However, these predictions cannot be compared to the rankings directly, because the betting odds change dynamically during the course of the tournament, and therefore contain a lot of information that is not accessible prior to the start of the tournament. Table 31-2 provides an overview of the prediction accuracies of the different rankings and the betting odds, separated for each round of the tournament.

Table 31-1. Spearman Correlation between the Rankings ($N = 127$)

	Recognition Ranking — Laypeople	Recognition Ranking — All Participants	ATP Champions Race	ATP Entry Ranking	Wimbledon Seedings
Recognition ranking — amateurs	.87	.98	.68	.69	.73
Recognition ranking — amateurs		.94	.58	.52	.68
Recognition ranking — all participants			.67	.64	.73
ATP champions race				.87	.88
ATP entry ranking					.86

TABLE 31-2. Percentage of Correct Predictions of the Different Rankings, and the Betting Odds for Each Round

	ATP		Recognition Ranking			Wimbledon Seedings	Betting Odds*
	Entry Ranking	Champions Race	Lay People	Amateurs	All Participants		
1st round (64 matches)	.66	.65	.63	.69	.71	.63	.78–.80
2nd round (32 matches)	.69	.66	.63	.61	.59	.69	.72–.75
3rd round (16 matches)	.75	.94	.63	.63	.63	.78	.81
4th round (8 matches)	.75	.75	1.00	.88	1.00	.88	.75
Quarterfinals (4 matches)	.75	.75	1.00	.75	1.00	1.00	.75
Semifinals (2 matches)	1.00	1.00	1.00	1.00	1.00	1.00	1.00
Final (1 match)	1.00	1.00	1.00	1.00	1.00	1.00	1.00
Total (all 127 matches)	.69	.70	.67	.68	.70	.70	.79

*As the number of correct predictions within the first two rounds differ slightly between the 5 online bookmakers, we report the range of correct predictions.

Individual Recognition Validities

Thus far we have analyzed rankings based on aggregated recognition, and we have shown that these rankings serve as useful predictors. However, in its original formulation, the recognition heuristic was introduced as a psychological model that describes a cognitive process (Goldstein & Gigerenzer, 2002), and as such, it applies to individual human beings making predictions based on their individual recognitions. Since the individuals in our study did not have access to aggregated recognition rankings, it remains unclear whether people can make accurate predictions based solely on their individual recognition knowledge.

To answer this question we first calculated the number of matches that each individual participant could have predicted using the recognition heuristic. The recognition heuristic can only be applied to pairs where the name of one player was recognized but not the other. If both or neither of the players are known, the recognition heuristic does not allow for a prediction. As the range of use depends on the percentage of recognized players, it differs among participants. For all of the decisions that each participant could make based on his or her recognition of the names, we then calculated the conditional probability of them making correct predictions, given that participants always used the recognition heuristic. This probability is commonly referred to as the recognition validity α.

On average, laypersons could have used the recognition heuristic to predict 21 of the 127 matches (17%), and out of these 21 games, using the recognition heuristic would have resulted in correct predictions for 15 matches ($\alpha = 69\%$, $SD = 17\%$).[3] The average amateur could have used the heuristic to predict 50 matches (40%). Of these matches, 35 could have been predicted correctly based on the recognition heuristic ($\alpha = 71\%$, $SD = 7\%$). Thus, even though laypeople knew far fewer players than amateurs, they were about equally successful in predicting the outcomes of matches for which the heuristic was applicable.

To make a fair comparison between predictions made using the individual's recognition and its competitors ATP-CR, ATP-ER, and SEED, we calculated the percentage of correct predictions based on each of the competitors separately for those matches where the recognition heuristic could have been used by each participant. By doing this, we know, for each participant, whether he or she would have been better off deciding based on recognition, or based on the information from the competitors. For amateurs, the average percentage of correct predictions based on both ATP rankings is 70% ($SD = 6\%$) in these cases, which is slightly lower than the recognition validity. SEED makes 71% ($SD = 5\%$) and BET 79% ($SD=4\%$) correct predictions. Stated differently, from the 79 amateurs in our sample, 47 or 59% would have been equally well or better off deciding based on their recognition than based on ATP-CR. When compared with SEED, 40 amateurs (51%) would have been better off using their own recognition. Thus, for the matches for which the heuristic can be applied, most individual amateurs can be as accurate as, or even more accurate than, the Wimbledon experts and the predictions based on ATP rankings. For laypeople, individual recognition is not as accurate. Five laypeople could not use recognition at all, and for the remaining 100 laypeople, 80 would have been better off relying on ATP-CR, and 75 would have been better off relying on SEED. Table 31-3 gives an overview of the individual comparisons.

Accordance to the Recognition Heuristic

Given the relatively high recognition validity for both laypersons and amateurs, the question arises whether our participants actually made predictions in accordance with the heuristic.

For the 64 matches predicted in the first round, the average amateur could have used the recognition heuristic in 23.5 cases. Of these 23.5 cases, 20.9 decisions were in accordance with the prediction of the heuristic (89%). The average layperson could have used it in 10.3 cases, and 8.1 cases were in accordance (79%). For the 12 matches predicted in the 4th round and the quarterfinals, amateurs (on average) could have used the heuristic in 3.6 cases. Of these cases, 3.2 decisions (92%) turned out as the heuristic

Table 31-3. Percentage of Correct Predictions Based on Individual Recognition and Other Predictors for All Tennis Matches for which the Recognition Heuristic Was Applicable

	Individual Recognition Validity A	Betting Odds	ATP Champions Race	ATP Entry Ranking	Wimbledon Seedings
Amateurs	.71 (SD = .07)	.79 (SD = .04)	.70 (SD = .06)	.70 (SD = .06)	.71 (SD = .06)
Laypeople	.69 (SD = .17)	.82 (SD = .11)	.78 (SD = .13)	.75 (SD = .14)	.75 (SD = .12)

would have predicted. Laypersons could have used the heuristic in 2.7 cases, and on average 2 decisions were in accordance (76%). Even though other researchers report even higher accordance rates (e.g., Serwe & Frings, 2006, report accordance rates of 88 to 93% and Ayton & Önkal, 2006, report accordance rates of 95%), in the present study concordances of amateurs and laypersons for both weeks were still quite high. Given that the recognition heuristic proved to be a valid predictor, this result is in line with the idea that our participants adaptively used a prediction strategy that worked well for the task they were facing. In the cases in which people decided against the recognition cue, and thus predicted that an unknown player would win over a known player, they were correct in 34% (average layperson) and 28% (average amateur) of the predicted matches respectively. As this is well below chance, whatever information this decision was based on had a lower validity than the recognition cue.

Actual Performance of Laypersons and Amateurs

It does not necessarily follow from a high validity that the participants in our study made accurate predictions across all matches. As mentioned above, the recognition heuristic can only be applied to cases in which one of the players is known and the other is not. If both players are known, participants might be able to use additional knowledge to make a prediction, but in cases in which neither of the players is recognized, participants can only make a guess. As a consequence, the actual accuracy may be very different from the recognition validity.

In the first round, amateurs on average recognized both players (and thus might have utilized additional knowledge) in 10 of the 64 matches. They did not recognize either of the players (and thus had to guess) for 29 matches. In the 4th round and the quarterfinals, amateurs on average recognized both players in 7 of the 12 matches and had to guess for 1 match. When the names of both players were known, amateurs made correct predictions in 75% (first round) and 79% (4th round and quarterfinals) of the matches. When the names of both players were unknown, amateurs were correct in 51% (first round) and 49% (4th round and quarterfinals) of the matches respectively.

Laypeople recognized far fewer players than amateurs, and thus had to guess more often. In the first round, laypeople on average only recognized both players in 1 of the 64 matches, and they had to guess the outcomes of 52 matches. In the 4th round and the quarterfinals, the average layperson recognized both players in 1 of the 12 matches, and had to guess in 8 cases. When the names of both players were known, the average layperson made correct predictions in 83% (first round) and 78% (4th round and quarterfinal) of the matches. When both player names were unknown, laypeople were correct in 49% (first round) and 60% (4th round and quarterfinals) of the matches. The 60% accuracy in the last case is significantly different from the 50% that would be expected for random guessing ($t[57] = 3.6$; $p = .001$), which might be due to sloppy or incomplete completion of the recognition questionnaire in the field.

In summary, for the first 64 matches predicted in the first round, the average amateur predicted 61% correctly. For the 12 matches predicted in the 4th round and the quarterfinals, amateurs predicted 75% correctly. Laypeople predicted 52% (first round) and 61% (4th round and quarterfinals) of all matches correctly.

DISCUSSION

Our results show that a ranking of tennis players based on aggregated name recognition by laypeople and amateurs was as effective in predicting match outcomes as official ATP rankings and Wimbledon experts' seedings. Also, for cases in which the recognition heuristic can be applied, individual decisions made based on mere name recognition are as accurate as predictions made by ATP rankings or Wimbledon experts. Our results are in line with those of Andersson et al. (2005), who showed that non-expert predictions of soccer games can be as successful as those of experts.

The idea that aggregating independent sources of information leads to better forecasts, even if the individual sources are not very accurate by themselves, has been raised by other researchers. Makridakis and Winkler (1983), as well as Winkler and Makridakis (1983), increased the accuracy of time series predictions by averaging across different forecasting models. In a study on medical decision making, Poses, Bekes, Winkler, Scott, and Copare (1990) found that when predicting patients' mortality risk, averaging across the opinions of rather inexperienced physicians (junior house officers in British hospitals) led to better estimates than the assessments of individual experienced physicians, even though the individual predictions of the inexperienced physicians were worse than those of the experienced ones. When forecasting the number of advertising pages sold by a news magazine, Hubbard Ashton and Ashton (1985) found that most of the improvement in accuracy is achieved by a simple average across three opinions. The influence of group size, individual accuracy, and the correlation between individuals on aggregated accuracy was explored in detail by Hogarth (1978). A comprehensive overview of the literature on combining forecasts was published by Clemen (1989).

Despite our use of larger samples, the inclusion of the names of all tennis players, and the prediction of more matches in two rounds, our results closely resemble the findings reported by Serwe and Frings (2006), who report an average accuracy of 72% for the aggregated amateur recognition and 66% for the aggregated recognition of laypeople in the 2003 tournament. For individual predictions, Serwe and Frings report a mean recognition validity of 73% for individual amateurs and 67% for individual laypeople respectively, which also matches the recognition validities in our study.

Although it is still possible that this match is a coincidence, the fact that two studies in different years and with different samples substantiate it, renders this unlikely. Hence, we conjecture that the relationship between recognition and success in sports might be more systematic than, for example, that between stock performance and recognition. But why might this be the case?

Ecological Rationality of the Recognition Heuristic

In the present case, recognition is clearly not random, but rather is systematic, as it makes correct predictions in about 70% of the cases in which it can be applied. The fact that most decisions in our study are made in accordance with the recognition heuristic suggests that the participants implicitly understood that it is a useful strategy, and thus well adapted to the task they were facing. But why is there a relationship between name recognition and tennis performance at all? One explanation could be that the recognition validity is mediated by a third variable that relates to both individual recognition and the criterion to be predicted. If the criterion is a success in an international tennis tournament like Wimbledon, a potential mediator is mass media coverage. If the media report more on successful tennis players, there will be a correlation between the ability of a player and the number of times his name is mentioned. As this correlation between the criterion and a mediator is a property of the environment, it has been called an ecological correlation (Goldstein & Gigerenzer, 2002). If at the same time people recognize the players' names through the media, there will be a correlation between the mediator and recognition memory, the so-called surrogate correlation. To test whether media coverage really links the criterion to recognition, we counted how often the names of the 128 players were mentioned in both the sport section of a local newspaper (*Tagesspiegel*) and a national newspaper (*Süddeutsche Zeitung*) during the 12 months prior to the start of the competition. We then calculated the surrogate correlation between the newspaper coverage and the recognition ranking (RR-All), based on Goodman and Kruskal's γ-coefficients[4] (Gonzalez & Nelson, 1996). The surrogate correlation between RR-All and *Tagesspiegel* is $\gamma = .58$; between RR-All and *Süddeutsche Zeitung*, the γ-coefficient equals .59 (Figure 31-1). We calculated the ecological correlation between the newspaper coverage and the success in the tournament based on a rule that was similar to the one used for the recognition rankings: predict that the player who is mentioned in the news more often will win the game, and do not count the cases in which the two players are mentioned equally often.

The resulting proportion of correct predictions can be linearly transformed into a γ-coefficient. For the two newspapers, the ecological correlation, as expressed in the γ-coefficients, equals .33 ($\alpha = .67$). These results are not trivial, as players could be in the news, and thus recognized, for reasons unrelated to their ability on the tennis court, such as private matters or injuries.

In order to make accurate predictions based on few pieces of information, a heuristic must be ecologically rational. That is to say, it needs to be suited to the structure of the environment in which it operates. In the domain of professional tennis, media coverage—and through this, also recognition—is correlated with success. This could explain why the recognition heuristic performs well, even though it makes predictions based on partial ignorance.

Betting Odds

Among the competitors, the information contained in the betting market is the best predictor of success. This result is in line with Boulier and Stekler (2003), who found the same for the

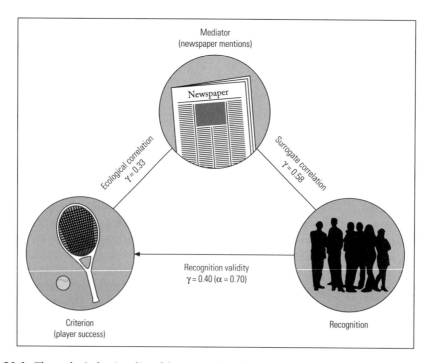

Figure 31-1. The ecological rationality of the recognition heuristic.

outcomes of NFL games. Similar results were also reported by Forrest, Goddard, and Simmons (2005), who showed that by the end of the soccer season, odds setters' forecasts were superior to tipsters', as well as to those of sophisticated statistical benchmark models. However, as mentioned above, betting odds change dynamically, and thus are not directly comparable to either the Wimbledon seedings or the recognition data.

SUMMARY

Our results show that, when predicting the outcome of a sport event like the 2005 Wimbledon tennis tournament, relying on the mere recognition of player names by non-experts can be as accurate as forecasts based on expert ratings and on official ATP rankings. The systematic relationship between recognition and player success is presumably mediated by mass media coverage. Thus, by relying on their partial ignorance, non-experts are able to make accurate predictions by exploiting an environmental structure that contains relevant information and that is available at almost no cost.

NOTES

1. Guessing occurs mainly for the SEED ranking because the Wimbledon committee only seeds 32 players. To make use of the SEED ranking, we assigned a dummy-seed of 33 to all unseeded players.
2. The data stems from 5 international online betting sites, namely Bet365.com, Centrebet.com, Expekt.com, Interwetten.com, and Pinnacle Sports. We thank Joseph Buchdahl from tennis-data.co.uk for providing us with the data.
3. The slight differences in the percentage figures from the absolute values are due to rounding.
4. Because the calculation of Goodman and Kruskal's γ-coefficient is very similar to the calculation of the recognition validity α, one can easily be transformed into the other based on the following linear equation: $\gamma = 2\alpha - 1$.

Introduction to Chapter 32

Simple Heuristics that Help Us Win

According to Gary Klein (1998), fireground commanders make around 80% of their decisions in less than 1 minute. Severe time constraints prevent them from implementing anything like a complete search for all possible alternatives and complex weighting and integrating information into one verdict. They cannot help but rely on principles of bounded rationality such as sequential search, one-reason decision making, and aspiration levels. Many real-world contexts require professionals to make split-second decisions, some of which involve human lives; in others, such as sports, fame and success are at stake. In fact, there are few domains where speed and frugality matter more than in sports. For instance, shots are often as fast as 100 miles per hour in professional soccer, leaving the goalkeeper and defense players barely any time to decide where to move. In team sports, an individual player usually has only a very limited perspective on the playing field, in which players move around quickly and in complex patterns. At the same time, the massive amount of practice involved in many sports gives rise to automatic processes that can be exploited by simple heuristics. Altogether, these conditions may make sports one of the quintessential domains for studying fast-and-frugal heuristics. Yet relatively few such investigations exist (see Chapter 31 for an illustration of how the recognition heuristic can be used to study sports forecasting). This chapter by Will Bennis and Thorsten Pachur (a revised version of Bennis & Pachur, 2006) summarizes existing research on heuristics in sports and illustrates the potential of this approach to provide further insights into how athletes, coaches, and fans make decisions. For instance, how could the well-known "belief in the hot hand" arise from the use of a fast-and-frugal heuristic? How does the performance of such a heuristic depend on the structure of the environment, and when would such a heuristic be adaptive?

CHAPTER 32

Simple Heuristics that Help Us Win

Will M. Bennis and Thorsten Pachur

Abstract: This chapter summarizes the fast-and-frugal-heuristics (FFH) approach to judgment and decision making, particularly as it applies to sports. The aim is to provide a framework through which current sports psychologists may apply this approach to better understand sports decision making. FFH are studied using a variety of methods, including (1) computer simulations and mathematical analysis of heuristic performance as it depends on environmental structure (what we call the ecological rationality of heuristics); (2) empirical analysis of the heuristics' performance in naturally occurring environments; and (3) experimental research examining whether people actually use the identified heuristics. Simulations and analysis have shown that FFH can perform as well as complicated optimizing models while using less information and without integrating this information. Furthermore, in many cases FFH are more robust than optimizing models, outperforming these models when generalizing to new cases. FFH depart from many models of human decision making in that they set a reasonable standard of rationality based on real-world constraints such as limited time, information, and cognitive capacity; decision tasks that may have no calculable optimal solution; and the structured environments within which humans have learned and evolved. These simple heuristics are particularly appropriate in the sports domain, in which athletes often have to make rapid, high-stakes decisions with limited information and divided attention.

How can we model experienced baseball or cricket players catching a fly ball? For simplification, imagine that the ball is already on its descent and that its trajectory is in line with the ball-catcher. At first glance the task still seems an extraordinarily complex one, as a multitude of factors—such as the ball's distance, angle, velocity, and acceleration of descent, as well as the wind speed and direction—influence where the ball will land. Nevertheless, experienced baseball players—but also fish, flies, and bats—accomplish the feat of catching fly balls or intercepting other flying objects with apparent ease. But does this mean that they consider all these variables

and can perform the necessary calculations? Optimizing approaches to cognition often assume (at least implicitly) that organisms are equipped with tremendous computational capabilities (e.g., Bayesian cognitive models; Oaksford & Chater, 2007). Given the constraints of time, information, and processing capacity that baseball players (and other boundedly rational agents) have to deal with, this assumption seems highly unrealistic. An alternative approach to model how players catch a fly ball would be in terms of heuristics, which neither require all relevant information nor integrate the information that is used.

In the case of the outfielder catching the ball, one heuristic that players rely on has been called the *gaze heuristic* (Gigerenzer, 2004). The gaze heuristic involves three steps: (1) Fixate one's gaze on the ball, (2) start running, and (3) adjust one's speed so that the angle of gaze remains constant. The gaze heuristic does not require estimating any of the variables necessary to compute the ball's trajectory, yet it enables outfielders to catch successfully. Empirical evidence shows that experienced ball-catchers use the gaze heuristic and similar heuristics, as do dogs when trying to catch Frisbees (McLeod & Dienes, 1996; Shaffer, Krauchunas, Eddy, & McBeath, 2004).

The gaze heuristic exemplifies what Gigerenzer and Goldstein have called a "fast-and-frugal heuristic" (1996b, Chapter 2, this volume; Gigerenzer, Todd, & the ABC Research Group, 1999). "Frugal" refers to the fact that these heuristics use little information and require few cognitive steps. "Fast" refers to the speed with which decisions can be made: the outfielder does not wait and calculate the trajectory before he runs toward the point where he predicts the ball to hit the ground. Note that much of the power of the gaze heuristic stems from our evolved capacity to track objects. This highlights the fact that although heuristics themselves are fast, simple, and effective, they often exploit evolved capacities that, though requiring little cognitive effort, may not be simple at all. To illustrate, we cannot design a robot able to catch fly balls as well as a skilled child can. The purpose of this chapter is to describe and discuss how fast-and-frugal heuristics have been and can be used to understand decision-making in the sports domain.

EXISTING RESEARCH ON FAST-AND-FRUGAL HEURISTICS IN SPORTS

This section will review some existing research on heuristics in sports. These include take-the-first (TTF), a heuristic that can be used by players to choose from among practical options; the recognition heuristic, which relies on partial ignorance to make powerful inferences; and take-the-best (TTB), which allows for inferences about known options based on limited search. The latter two heuristics have been primarily tested with sports forecasting (i.e., predicting which teams or athletes will win) rather than with decisions by athletes or coaches.

Take-the-First (TTF)

How do athletes generate different options and subsequently choose among them given the limited time they often have to make decisions? Consider the constellation of players in a handball match depicted in Figure 32-1a. What options does the center back (CB) have?[1] One option would be to attempt a shot on the goal. Alternatively, he might prefer to pass the ball to one of his teammates, the left wing (WL), left half-back (HL), center front (CF), right half-back (HR), or right wing (WR). But to whom and how?

Investigating such a situation, Johnson and Raab (2003) found that experienced players do not try to exhaustively generate all possible options. Instead they seem to rely on the order in which options are spontaneously generated in a particular situation and choose the first option that comes to mind. Johnson and Raab called this strategy take-the-first (TTF; see Table 32-1).

Why should options generated quickly be more useful than those generated more slowly? Taking an associative network perspective, Johnson and Raab (2003) argue that better options are more likely to be activated first in a particular situation due to their stronger connections in the network. This, however, requires that the player has experience with the task and has learned how suitable possible options are in different situations. In other words, once a player has some expertise with the task, he can rely on the quality of spontaneously generated options and "take the first." Work by Gary Klein provides empirical evidence for a positive correlation between generation order and quality of an option (Klein, 1998; Klein, Wolf, Militello, & Zsambok, 1995).

TTF shares some properties with other fast-and-frugal heuristics. For instance, like the fluency heuristic (Schooler & Hertwig, 2005, Chapter 4, this volume) it exploits the fluency with which memory traces are made available by the cognitive system. Moreover, it is based on sequential information search and uses simple search and stopping rules. It also "bets" on a particular pattern in the task environment, namely that there is a correlation between the position

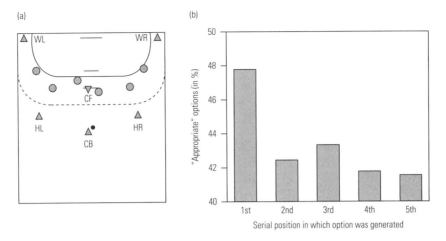

Figure 32-1. (a) Typical position of the offensive players in the handball scene, at the point where it was "frozen" to begin each trial. Triangles represent offensive (attack) players, circles represent defensive players. CB, center back; WR, wing player on the right; WL, wing player on the left; HL, half-back player on the left; HR, half-back player on the right; CF, center-front (pivot) player at the 6-meter line; long solid line, goal; short solid line, 6-meter line (defense zone); dotted line, 9-meter line (from Johnson & Raab, 2003). (b) Mean percentage of "appropriate" decisions per participant, as rated by experts, summed over trials, for the generated options in each serial position.

Table 32-1. Overview of Efficient Heuristics for Decision Making in Sports

Heuristic	Rule	Function	Bets on
Gaze heuristic	"(1) Fixate one's gaze on the ball, (2) start running, (3) adjust one's speed so that the angle of gaze remains constant."	Catching a fly ball	Ball is on descent and trajectory is in line with the catcher
Take-the-first	"Choose the first option that comes to mind"	Making allocation decisions	Good options are generated faster than bad ones
Recognition heuristic	"Choose the recognized option"	Forecasting the winner in a competition	More successful athletes or teams are more likely to be recognized
Take-the-best	"(1) Search through cues in order of their validity, (2) stop search if a cue discriminates between the objects, (3) predict that the object with a positive cue value has the higher criterion value."	Forecasting the winner in a competition	Skewed distribution of cue weights
Hot-hand heuristic	"If an athlete has scored two or more times in a row, predict she will score on her next attempt."	Making allocation decisions	Good players show streaks more frequently than bad players

of an option in the generation process and the option's quality. Finally, TTF relies on evolved capacities which allow it to accomplish a computationally difficult task. In this case, the evolved capacity is the ability to match the current situation with previously experienced ones and to retrieve successful solutions to these previous constellations efficiently.

Investigating teenage handball players from area handball clubs in an empirical study,

Johnson and Raab (2003) indeed found support for some of the predictions of TTF. They presented the players with situations from a handball match on a video screen, froze the picture after 10 seconds, and asked the players which option first came to mind for that specific situation. Participants were then allowed to inspect the still-frozen video picture for another 45 seconds, generated further options, and finally picked from the generated options (including the first) the one they considered best overall. The quality of the generated options was subsequently rated by four coaches from professional-level handball teams.

Supporting the assumption that options most likely to be activated quickly are successful ones, the percentage of options judged by the coaches as appropriate decreased markedly after the first position (see Figure 32-1b). Did participants also "take the first"? As it turned out, they chose the first option that came to their mind in around 60% of the cases. Although this result provides support for TTF, it is not immediately obvious how strong that support is. In 40% of the cases, participants' final choice differed from their first choice. Note, however, that in Johnson and Raab's (2003) experiment participants had 45 seconds after making their immediate choice during which they were explicitly instructed to generate additional options. In a real handball game, of course, players would make their choices in seconds or fractions of a second with little if any consideration of subsequent options, in which case all or nearly all of their choices would correspond to TTF. As Johnson and Raab's analyses show, these choices would often be good ones.

As such, a more telling question than whether players stuck to their first choice after deliberation may be which of the two choices would have in fact contributed to a better outcome: (a) the *first* choice, corresponding to TTF and the choice players would likely make during actual handball matches, or (b) the *final* choice, involving 45 additional seconds of deliberation and option generation. As it turned out, extended option generation did not improve the quality of participants' final choices. If participants had not generated any further options after the first,

their choices would have been better than the options that they finally picked. Less time would have been more, which is exactly what might be expected of a heuristic adapted to the competitive sports environments, where "taking the first" may be all that time allows.

Recognition Heuristic

Less can be more not only with respect to the time available to make a decision. It can also be more with respect to knowledge of a domain. The *recognition heuristic* (Goldstein & Gigerenzer, 2002, Chapter 3, this volume) is a strategy to predict which of a set of objects has a higher value on some criterion (e.g., which team or athlete will win a competition). In binary choice, the heuristic can be used when out of two opponents (players, teams), one is recognized but the other is not. The recognition heuristic predicts that the recognized opponent will win the competition (see Table 32-1). The heuristic is ecologically valid if the recognition validity (defined as the proportion of cases where a recognized object has a higher criterion value than an unrecognized one) is substantially higher than chance.

Note that in order to apply the recognition heuristic, partial ignorance is required. When both opponents are recognized the recognition heuristic cannot be applied. Note also that, as with take-the-first, the recognition heuristic relies on a particular pattern in the environment: it "bets" that successful athletes or teams are also more frequently mentioned in the media, and thus are more likely to be recognized (Pachur & Biele, 2007, obtained evidence for this pattern).

Goldstein and Gigerenzer (2002) analytically showed that the recognition heuristic can lead to a counterintuitive *less-is-more effect*. This effect concerns the relationship between the number of objects recognized (from among a set of objects)—for instance, the number of teams or athletes—and the overall accuracy achieved when all objects are compared. One condition for the effect to occur is that the recognition validity is higher than the validity of further knowledge about the objects. Assuming that both validities are independent from the number of objects recognized, they showed that full knowledge can be associated with fewer successful predictions than when fewer objects are recognized. Recent work by McCloy, Beaman, and Smith (2008, Chapter 18, this volume) has examined the recognition heuristic when an inference has to be made among more than two objects. The authors find that a less-is-more effect also occurs in this situation.

Several studies have examined the recognition heuristic in the context of sports. Three questions have been of primary interest. First, can the recognition heuristic predict people's forecasts? Second, how well does recognition predict outcomes in sports compared to other predictors? And, third, is there evidence for the less-is-more effect?

Concerning its descriptive accuracy (i.e., whether or not it predicts people's judgments), there is consistent support for the recognition heuristic in situations where the recognition validity is substantial (Ayton & Önkal, 2004; Pachur & Biele, 2007; Scheibehenne & Bröder, 2007, Chapter 33, this volume; Serwe & Frings, 2006; Snook & Cullen, 2006). For instance, Serwe and Frings asked tennis amateurs to make forecasts of matches at the 2003 Wimbledon tennis tournament and used the recognition heuristic to model the forecasts. It was found that more than 90% of the time when a recognized player played against an unrecognized player, the tennis amateurs predicted the recognized player to win (similar results were found for soccer matches by Ayton & Önkal and Pachur & Biele and for hockey players by Snook & Cullen).

The second question is prescriptive. Can recognition help to make correct forecasts? In other words, is reliance on recognition an ecologically rational strategy in the sports domain? Snook and Cullen (2006) found that when a recognized National Hockey League (NHL) player was judged to have achieved more career points than an unrecognized one, this inference was correct more than 86% of the time. Pachur and Biele (2007), studying the recognition heuristic in predicting the winners at the 2004 European Football Championship, found that recognition was considerably better than chance—although

it was not able to reach the predictive accuracy of "expert" indicators such as rankings, previous performance, or betting odds.

Serwe and Frings (2006) examined how well recognition was able to predict the actual winner of tennis matches at Wimbledon (see also Scheibehenne & Bröder, 2008, Chapter 33, this volume). They compared recognition to three alternative prediction benchmarks: betting odds from an online bookmaker and two types of official world-wide rankings from the Association of Tennis Professionals (ATP): the Champions Race (ATP-CR), which ranks male tennis players based on their performance over the current calendar year; and the Entry Ranking (ATP-ER), which ranks them over the preceding 52 weeks. Among laypeople, the recognition heuristic performed significantly better than chance (making correct predictions 67% of the time), although it did not outperform ATP rankings (70-72% correct predictions) or the betting market (79% correct predictions). Among amateurs, however, recognition performed markedly better, correctly predicting 73% of the winners and outperforming the rankings, which correctly predicted the winner 68–69% of the time. The betting market still performed best, predicting the winner in 78% of comparisons.[2]

Finally, what of the less-is-more effect? When Ayton and Önkal (2004) studied forecasts for matches in the English FA Cup by both British and Turkish participants, it was observed that in spite of their greater knowledge about English soccer teams, the British participants were on about the same performance level as their Turkish counterparts. A similar result was reported by Snook and Cullen (2006) in their study where participants had to judge which of two NHL players had achieved more career points. Comparing participants with different levels of knowledge (in terms of the number of teams that they recognized), the authors found that judgmental accuracy increased as the number of recognized players increased until about half of the players were recognized. Beyond this point accuracy leveled off, akin to the less-is-more effect.

Pachur and Biele (2007) highlighted an important boundary condition of the less-is-more effect. In their study on lay forecasts of soccer matches at the 2004 European Football Championship, although the average recognition validity was higher than the validity of knowledge beyond recognition—fulfilling the condition for a less-is-more effect specified by Goldstein and Gigerenzer (2002)—there was no less-is-more effect. Pachur and Biele proposed that this failure of the effect to manifest itself was due to the positive correlation between the number of recognized objects and the recognition validity that they observed (i.e., participants who recognized more teams tended to have a higher recognition validity). In Goldstein and Gigerenzer's analytical investigation of the less-is-more effect, these two variables were uncorrelated. (For a systematic analysis of the impact of validity dependencies on the less-is-more effect, see Pachur, 2010).

Take-The-Best (TTB)

The recognition heuristic requires ignorance. Often, however, sports forecasters have a considerable knowledge base, barring them from using the heuristic. To illustrate, most of the soccer experts studied by Pachur and Biele (2007) had heard of all the teams participating in the European Football Championship and thus were never able to exploit ignorance. In such cases, other strategies must be used to make an inference. Take-the-best (TTB; Gigerenzer & Goldstein, 1996) is one candidate. As with the recognition heuristic, this heuristic relies on limited search. TTB searches cues in order of their validity, beginning with the most valid. If this cue discriminates between the two objects being compared (i.e., two athletes have different values on the cue), the information search is ended and the object with the higher value on this cue is inferred to have a higher criterion value. If the cue does not discriminate between the objects (i.e., if two athletes both have the same value for that cue), TTB moves on to the next most valid cue, continuing down the line of cues in order of validity until it comes upon a cue that does discriminate.

As with other heuristics, environmental structure is critical to TTB's performance. For example, TTB's performance is influenced by whether or not the environment is *noncompensatory*. A noncompensatory environment is one in which the weight for each binary cue is greater than the sum of all subsequent cues, assuming the cues are ordered by weight. Within such environments, when cue validities are known, TTB matches the performance of optimizing models (in this case, multiple regression; Martignon & Hoffrage, 2002, Chapter 12, this volume). For further investigations of the conditions under which TTB outperforms complex models, and vice versa, see Hogarth and Karelaia (2007, Chapter 14, this volume) and Gigerenzer and Brighton (2009, Chapter 1, this volume).

Analytical tests of how TTB's performance depends on environmental structure address just one aspect of its ecological rationality; another aspect is how it performs in natural environments. For instance, how well does TTB perform in sports forecasting environments? Furthermore, in addition to examining a heuristic's ecological rationality, it is important to assess whether people actually use the heuristic. Do sports forecasters use TTB?

Todorov (2001) compared TTB to Bayes' rule with respect to its ability to predict the results of 1,187 games in one season of the National Basketball Association (NBA). Bayes' rule is an example of an optimizing model of rational choice that starts with an initial estimation of a team's probability to win, and updates this probability based on the outcome of subsequent matches. As it turned out, TTB performed as well as Bayes' rule (for similar results, see Gröschner & Raab, 2006). In a second study, this time examining whether or not people actually use the heuristic when predicting sports outcomes, Todorov found that participants ordered cues based on their validity, just as take-the-best would predict. Moreover, the heuristic predicted participants' forecasts very well.

In sum, simple models that rely on limited search, such as take-the-first, the recognition heuristic or take-the-best offer efficient and robust decision tools in the sports domain. Moreover, both sports athletes and forecasters seem to rely on ordered and limited search, as exemplified by these heuristics. Fast-and-frugal heuristics thus offer a powerful framework for understanding decision making in sports.

THE BELIEF IN THE HOT HAND: REFLECTION OF AN ADAPTIVE HEURISTIC?

Studying the psychology of sports using a heuristics framework is a relatively new endeavor and few heuristics have been well specified for this domain. Indeed, of the four heuristics discussed above, only two (the gaze heuristic and take-the-first) are about making decisions in the heat of competition (the other two are about forecasting winners). At the same time, because decisions by athletes, coaches, and referees usually must be made quickly based on limited information, fast-and-frugal heuristics likely play a dominant role in sports decision making. As such, the sports domain is particularly promising area for applying this approach. Using the phenomenon of a "belief in the hot hand" (Gilovich, Vallone, & Tversky, 1985), in this section we illustrate how established phenomena in sports decision making can be studied from the perspective of fast-and-frugal heuristics.

Gilovich, Vallone, and Tversky (1985; Tversky & Gilovich, 1989) found that although many people (including players and coaches) believe that a basketball player's chance of making a basket are greater following a success (and streak of successes), there was no empirical evidence for such a "hot hand". Although the existence of a hot hand in sports continues to be debated (Bar-Eli, Avugos, & Raab, 2006; Frame, Hughson, & Leach, 2006; Oskarsson, Van Boven, McClelland, & Hastie, 2009), the psychological phenomenon seems to be established: people, including the athletes themselves, think that athletes who succeeded on their previous attempt—or streak of attempts—are more likely to succeed on the subsequent attempt, and allocation decisions in a game are based on this belief. How would this phenomenon be studied from a fast-and-frugal-heuristics perspective?

Three questions are central: (1) What simple heuristic might give rise to a belief in a hot hand? (2) How does such a heuristic perform in actual basketball games or in other sports to which it is applied and what is the range of environments across which it is successful? In short, what is the ecological rationality of the heuristic?

(3) What evolved capacities might such a heuristic exploit?

For instance, consider the following *hot-hand heuristic*: "If an athlete has scored two or more times in a row, predict she will score on her next attempt" (see Table 32-1). Bruce Burns (2004) suggested that an important consideration regarding heuristics in general, and ball allocation decisions in particular, is whether they help decision makers achieve their goals rather than whether they rely on correct beliefs. Burns pointed out that even if there is no such thing as a hot hand in basketball, using streak information to decide where to pass the ball can help get the ball to better shooters. Because streaks occur more often and over longer duration among players with higher overall shooting percentages, the occurrence of a streak is an indicator of the player's overall shooting percentage.

Admittedly, there are some complicating factors with this example. Professional basketball players and coaches know their teammates' shooting percentages, and so it is unclear how they would benefit from such a heuristic unless players really do get "hot". Nevertheless, there may be sports in which players are more likely to have teammates or face opponents who are still on a strong learning curve, in which case a hot-hand heuristic would likely be more effective than longer-term shooting percentage information (indeed, this might be the case in high-school or college basketball, where most NBA players developed their skills and may have developed their belief in the hot hand). Moreover, in some sports, or at non-professional levels, base-rate information may be unavailable and a hot-hand heuristic may be a useful tool for inferring it. Finally, as noted earlier, there remains controversy as to whether the original finding that players do not sometimes get "hot" is accurate. Perhaps basketball players get "hot" in ways not apparent from statistical measures simply because the opponents are aware of the hot hand and compensate with stronger defense on the hot player. If athletes truly get hot hands, then allocation decisions based on immediately preceding streaks may be adaptive above and beyond their cue validity for determining the longer-term base-rate performance levels of the athlete.

One way to examine these issues would be by studying the belief in a hot hand in a sport for which the opposition cannot selectively increase defensive pressure. Raab, Gula, and Gigerenzer (2009) conducted such a study, examining the hot hand among twenty-six of the top players in German first-division volleyball players. In volleyball, a net separates the teams, and the possibility of increasing defensive pressure against a particular "hot" player is limited. The authors found that not only did players believe in the hot hand and used it to make allocation decisions, but also that players did get "hot" beyond expectations of chance. In other words, these allocation decisions were adaptive.

A final step in investigating the hot-hand heuristic from a fast-and-frugal-heuristics perspective would be to specify the evolved capacities that the heuristic recruits. For instance, certain regions of the brain seem to be particularly sensitive to patterns in sequences of events (even if these patterns occur randomly; Huettel, Mack, & McCarthy, 2002). This ability to detect patterns in the environment is a prerequisite for, and is thus exploited by the hot-hand heuristic.

CONCLUSION

How does and how should a football (soccer) player decide where to kick the ball when making a corner kick, when to shoot for a goal, or to whom to pass the ball? How do basketball coaches decide whether and which players to substitute for another? How do players decide when it is best to foul members of the opposing team, or whether to try for a three-point basket? How does a snooker player decide between playing offensively or defensively, a tennis player decide when to go to the net, or a Nascar racer decide whether to try to pass another driver? What cues can a referee or judge use to assess a performance or identify an illegal play given that their view is sometimes from an unreliable perspective? And in all these cases, how does the choice and performance of the strategy adopted depend on the structure of the environment? Rather than assuming an optimizing rational demon equipped with omniscience and unlimited computational power, the fast-and-frugal-heuristics approach acknowledges that such decisions often have to be made quickly and based on little information. Therefore, this approach promises to be particularly relevant to the study of decision making in the sports domain, where speed is of the essence and multiple tasks and goals limit cognitive capacity, but where the decision makers are often experts.

NOTES

1. The center back (CB) is depicted by the triangle with a small circle, representing the ball, next to it.
2. Note that the performance of the betting market and the two ATP rankings differed for laypeople and amateurs. This was because comparisons were limited to cases when the recognition heuristic could be applied, which differed between the two groups.

Introduction to Chapter 33

How Dogs Navigate to Catch Frisbees

The evolution of species has been investigated at the level of morphology, nervous systems, or communication abilities, but relatively little is known about the evolution of cognitive strategies, or heuristics. Heuristics are simple only because they exploit evolved or learned capacities. One important capacity is tracking—that is, the ability to trace moving objects against a noisy background. The gaze heuristic (see Chapter 32), and the related *LOT* heuristic described in the article by Dennis Shaffer, Scott Krauchunas, Marianne Eddy, and Michael McBeath exploit this cognitive ability. The gaze heuristic can be relied on unconsciously, as with outfielders who cannot explain what they do automatically, or consciously. In sailing, for instance, beginners are taught to use it to avoid collisions. When fixing their gaze on the other boat, sailors determine whether the angle of gaze remains constant over time: If so, a collision is doomed to occur, unless the boat's course is changed. The same heuristic was also consciously relied upon in the "miracle of the Hudson river" on January 15, 2009. With both engines out after the plane struck a flock of birds during takeoff, the pilots of US Airways Flight 1549 had to decide whether they could make it to LaGuardia Airport. Copilot Jeffrey Skiles explained how they made this decision using the gaze heuristic (Charlie Rose, *The Charlie Rose Show*, February 11, 2009):

> "It's not so much a mathematical calculation as visual, in that when you are flying in an airplane, a point that you can't reach will actually rise in your windshield. A point that you are going to overfly will descent in your windshield."

For an outfielder, the gaze heuristic works only when the object is already high in the air. Otherwise, it needs to be modified to the LOT heuristic described in this article, by exchanging a building block. The evidence that dogs, bats, flies, and other animals also rely on these heuristics implies two possible interpretations. First, *homology*, which is a similarity of structures (here: heuristics) between different species based upon their descent from a common evolutionary ancestor. This is to be contrasted with, second, *analogy*, which is a functional similarity based upon something other than a common ancestor. We do not know which interpretation is correct. But we can safely assume that the original goal of the tracking heuristics was to intercept prey or mates, as well as the opposite, to avoid being caught. Humans appear to recruit these heuristics beyond the initial purposes such as for performing in competitive sports.

Catching a Frisbee is a more challenging task than catching a ball because the Frisbee can change direction and speed in dramatic ways. One fascinating result of the article by Shaffer and colleagues is that their dogs nevertheless managed to solve the task relying on the same simple heuristic.

CHAPTER 33

How Dogs Navigate to Catch Frisbees

Dennis M. Shaffer, Scott M. Krauchunas, Marianna Eddy,
and Michael K. McBeath

Abstract: Using micro-video cameras attached to the heads of 2 dogs, we examined their optical behavior while catching Frisbees. Our findings reveal that dogs use the same viewer-based navigational heuristics previously found with baseball players (i.e., maintaining the target along a linear optical trajectory, LOT, with optical speed constancy). On trials in which the Frisbee dramatically changed direction, the dog maintained an LOT with speed constancy until it apparently could no longer do so and then simply established a new LOT and optical speed until interception. This work demonstrates the use of simple control mechanisms that utilize invariant geometric properties to accomplish interceptive tasks. It confirms a common interception strategy that extends both across species and to complex target trajectories.

With little training, dogs can be remarkably good at chasing and catching airborne objects like Frisbees, even when the objects travel through complex trajectories that may dramatically change directions. In the present study, we tested whether dogs utilize the same simple viewer-based navigational heuristics that have been established for human baseball fielders catching fly balls (McBeath, Shaffer, & Kaiser, 1995a, 1996; McLeod & Dienes, 1993, 1996; McLeod, Reed, & Dienes, 2001; Michaels & Oudejans, 1992; Shaffer & McBeath, 2002). Using these heuristics, a pursuer controls the geometric relationship between him- or herself and the target, maintaining an optical image of the target that travels along a straight-line, constant-speed trajectory. We refer to these geometric relationships as optical linearity and

optical speed constancy, respectively. Behavior consistent with the maintenance of optical linearity and speed constancy has been found in a variety of navigation-related domains (Adams, 1961; Bruce, Green, & Georgeson, 1996, pp. 267–285; Roscoe, 1968; Toates, 1975, pp. 151–257; Vishton & Cutting, 1995; Wickens, 1992, pp. 466–481). In the experiment reported here, we investigated whether nonhuman species intercepting targets use the same simple control mechanisms that baseball outfielders use to catch fly balls.

When baseball outfielders run to catch fly balls, they use natural, geometrically invariant properties to optically maintain control over the balls. When balls are headed off to the side, fielders select a running path that maintains a linear optical trajectory (LOT) for the ball relative to home plate and the background scenery. In our previous work, we found evidence indicating that the optical information available to the outfielder can be simply analyzed by examining it as a unified two-dimensional (2D) optical image. The geometry of the unified 2D optical image is shown in the top left panel of Figure 33-1, where α and β specify the vertical and lateral optical angles, respectively, between the ball and its initial optical location (home plate); ψ specifies the optical trajectory projection angle, or the observed angle of ball movement in the picture plane relative to the background horizon. In short, an LOT results when the fielder's running speed and direction maintain a rate of change in the horizontal optical angle, β, that matches the rate of change in the vertical optical angle, α.

This is equivalent to maintaining a constant angle of the ball in the picture plane, ψ, as shown in the top right panel of Figure 33-1. To maintain a constant rate of lateral change, the outfielder remains fixated on the image of the ball while running along a path so as to actively rotate his or her vantage at a constant rate. This typically results in the fielder running fastest laterally at the start, getting a little ahead of the ball, and then easing up somewhat at the end.

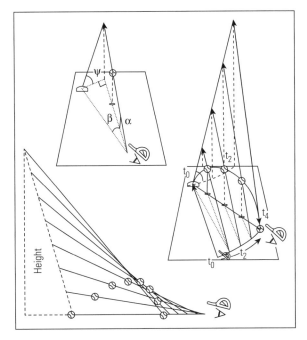

Figure 33-1. The linear-optical-trajectory (LOT) model. The top illustrations show the view from a center-field bleacher as a fielder converges on a ball headed to his or her right. The trapezoidal box represents the perspective projection of the ground plane. The optical trajectory is shown with vectors from the fielder's position through the ball. The LOT model specifies that outfielders catch fly balls by running along a path that maintains a monotonically increasing linear optical trajectory of the ball. The illustration at the top left shows how the vertical optical angle (α), lateral optical angle (β), and projection plane optical angle (ψ) are defined. Operationally, α and β, respectively, are defined as the ongoing sums of all instantaneous vertical and lateral angular changes in the position of the target image. The illustration at the top right shows how the LOT heuristic maintains a constant projection angle across time (t_0–t_4). The fielder selects a running path such that the lateral optical ball movement remains proportional to the vertical optical ball movement. Because equal lateral optical angles span smaller distances for nearer than farther objects, the fielder ends up slowing down laterally as the ball approaches. The resultant running path curves slightly and circles under the ball. The bottom illustration is a side view of a fielder intercepting a fly ball in equal temporal intervals. This view shows a ball trajectory (with air resistance) and the fielder approaching from the right while maintaining optical acceleration cancellation. Mathematically, the fielder keeps the tangent of the vertical optical angle increasing at a constant rate.

A number of researchers have noted that when fielders run off to the side to catch fly balls, they simultaneously maintain a constant increase in the tangent of the vertical optical angle, tan α, which serves as a complementary cue to optical linearity (McBeath, Shaffer, & Kaiser, 1995b; McLeod et al., 2001). As the ball rises, tan α increases at a rate that is a function of the running path selected by the fielder. The fielder arrives at the correct destination by selecting a running path that keeps optical ball speed constant, achieving optical acceleration cancellation (OAC) in the vertical direction. This is shown in the bottom panel of Figure 33-1, where the optical ball trajectory is like that of an imaginary elevator rising from home plate at constant velocity.

We have shown previously that for balls headed to the side, the LOT is the dominant strategy, and OAC serves as a complementary cue for movement of the ball in the vertical direction (Shaffer & McBeath, 2002). In that work, we confirmed that for missed balls, both the LOT and the OAC strategies must eventually break down as the image of the ball curves toward the horizon. Yet even in those degenerative cases, fielders select a lateral path that continues to keep the image moving along a linear trajectory well after speed constancy is abandoned.

Recently, McLeod et al. (2001) questioned the LOT strategy, noting that there appears to be systematic optical curvature of the ball image near the end of trajectories, particularly in the extreme case of infield pop-ups. In a reanalysis of their pop-up data, we explained that the LOT model still provides an excellent fit, accounting for a median of more than 97% of the variance (McBeath, Shaffer, & Sugar, 2002; McBeath, Shaffer, Sugar, & Roy, 2002). We also replicated the conditions of McLeod et al. and confirmed that the terminal optical curvature is consistent with threshold-level errors expected for LOT control theory with nonideal, real-world participants. The optical curvature is attributable to the increase in optical ball size near terminus, coupled with a combination of individual differences in aggressiveness and handedness. Some fielders systematically err in the laggardly direction, whereas others favor running ahead,

and balls exhibit more terminal optical curvature as the destination point of the fielder's hand is extended away from his or her eyes.

McLeod et al. (2001) also observed that fielders often initiate lateral movement within the 220 ms before the optical trajectory appears to curve, in seeming contradiction to LOT theory. We noted that this supposition is a misinterpretation of control theory, an interpretation that a control mechanism can respond to errors only reactively (McBeath, Shaffer, Sugar, & Roy, 2002). Using robotic modeling, we confirmed that anticipatory movement to the side is easily accounted for by the parameter-level setting of an active feed-forward mechanism, and that the inclusion of such a mechanism leads to behavior that matches that of humans (Sugar & McBeath, 2001; Suluh, Sugar, & McBeath, 2001). In short, there has been some debate concerning the range of generality of the LOT mechanism for interception, and this has led to insights regarding realistic thresholds, systematic individual differences, and parameter settings of control variables.

Use of the LOT and simultaneous maintenance of OAC in the vertical direction have been proposed as generic strategies that are geometrically constrained to ensure collision between a pursuer and its target. If so, then these strategies may be used to intercept any of a variety of types of moving targets both in domains outside of baseball and by other species. In the present study, we tested whether dogs use similar optical tracking strategies when trying to catch a Frisbee. This task provided a method of testing two different aspects of the generality of the LOT and OAC strategies. First, it allowed us to test whether these two strategies are used across species. Second, it allowed us to test whether these strategies are used irrespective of the flight complexity of the target being pursued. Baseball trajectories are somewhat predictable once initiated, even though aerodynamic drag and ball spin cause them to deviate from perfect parabolic motion (Brancazio, 1985; Watts & Bahill, 1990, pp. 133–149). However, Frisbees can dramatically change direction and speed depending on factors such as how they are thrown, gusts of wind, and the Frisbee angle during flight (Bloomfield, 1999). Thus, it is possible that a strategy like the LOT coupled with OAC may be used only until the occurrence of an unpredictable perturbation in the trajectory of the Frisbee, and then a separate strategy or set of strategies may be initiated.

METHOD

Participants

One Springer Spaniel, Romeo, and one Border Collie, Lilly, participated in the experiment. Both were experienced in catching Frisbees.

Procedure

We mounted a Supercircuits in-line weather-resistant micro-video camera (Model PC75WR) on each dog's head with ace bandages in order to obtain the optical trajectories of Frisbees as the dogs navigated toward them. Each camera was wired to a battery pack and to a transmitter that the dog wore on its back. The equipment setup on Lilly is shown in Figure 33-2. The signal from the camera was transmitted to a receiver attached to a remote VCR, so that the VCR recorded the image from the micro-video camera.

Frisbees were launched at a variety of angles, all off to the side of the dog's initial position, at varying force from a distance of between 9 and 19 m. The dogs ran between 2 and 14 m to catch the Frisbees. We coded 63 trials in which the dog

Figure 33-2. Lilly the dog with the camera attached to her head and battery packs and transmitter located in a "doggie backpack" on her back. This picture was taken during a training trial in which Lilly was getting accustomed to the equipment.

kept the Frisbee within the field of view of the camera and eventually caught the Frisbee. For these trials, we separately analyzed the Frisbee trajectory for an LOT and vertical OAC.

On five additional trials, we deliberately threw the Frisbee to one side at an angle such that it began moving in the opposite direction at greater speed in midflight. These trials on which the Frisbee changed direction and speed dramatically were analyzed separately to test the fit of a pair of LOTs and pair of OAC rates (i.e., a double LOT and OAC).

For each trial, we measured the trajectory of the Frisbee from the perspective of the moving dog. We recorded the ongoing instantaneous optical position of the center of the Frisbee relative to distant background markers each 1/30 of a second. We defined α and β, respectively, as the ongoing sums of all instantaneous vertical and lateral changes in the position of the Frisbee image. We also recorded the vertical speed pattern of the optical trajectory (plotted as tan α by time).

RESULTS AND DISCUSSION

For each of the first 63 trials, we plotted the ongoing optical position of the Frisbee in terms of α (the vertical visual angle) by β (the lateral visual angle) and determined the best-fit linear function to assess the variance accounted for by a straight-line optical trajectory (i.e., an LOT). A linear function accounted for a median of 93% of the variance in the optical movement of the Frisbee (*Mdn* = 89% for Romeo and 97% for Lilly). This provided significant support for the use of the LOT strategy as measured by a sign test, $z = 10.55$, $p < .001$.

Figure 33-3 shows sample optical trajectories while the dogs chased and caught Frisbees. The lines over the trajectories are estimates of the best-fit lines used to compute the R^2 values and help illustrate that the trajectories remained close to straight lines. Each optical trajectory, or path of the Frisbee from the perspective of the camera positioned on the dog's head, was maintained along a straight line that continued to rise throughout the Frisbee trajectory. The sample trajectories in this figure are remarkably similar

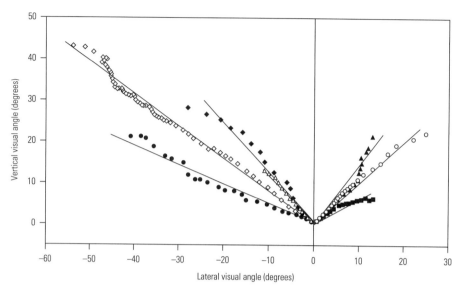

Figure 33-3. The optical trajectories of Frisbees on seven representative trials. Frisbee position is plotted as the lateral visual angle, β (in degrees), by the vertical visual angle, α (in degrees), at each 1/30-s video frame. The line over each of the trajectories is the estimate of the best-fit line used to compute the R^2 value. Open symbols are optical trajectories for Lilly, and filled symbols are optical trajectories for Romeo.

to ones showing the LOTs maintained by outfielders running to catch fly balls and support the premise that dogs utilize the same strategy to catch Frisbees as baseball outfielders use to catch fly balls (McBeath et al., 1995a). The findings for the optical trajectories support the notion that the LOT is a generic tracking strategy used not only by humans pursuing ballistic objects, such as in baseball, but also by dogs chasing Frisbees.

We also analyzed the same 63 trials to test whether the dog simultaneously kept the Frisbee moving at a constant optical speed in the vertical direction. To test this, we plotted the acceleration of the vertical optical angle (i.e., tan α) by time and found that a linear function accounted for a median of 94.12% of the variance in the vertical tangent, tan α (*Mdn* = 94.18% for Romeo and 93.87% for Lilly). This result supports the hypothesis that the dogs were keeping the image of the Frisbee moving at a constant rate in the vertical direction. Thus, dogs catching Frisbees appear to maintain a path that nulls acceleration of the vertical optical angle α (i.e., OAC) and use the OAC as a complement to the LOT. These results replicate our previous

findings with outfielders catching fly balls headed off to the side.

We analyzed separately the optical paths from the five trials in which the Frisbee began moving in a new direction and at a new speed during midflight. Figure 33-4 shows sample optical trajectories from these trials. In these cases, the optical path of the Frisbee was moving in one direction and then suddenly began moving in a dramatically different direction. As Figure 33-4 shows, the dogs did not appear to abandon the LOT strategy, but simply chose one LOT strategy before the large perturbation and then a new LOT strategy after the perturbation. For these five trials, we found that two lines (i.e., a double LOT) accounted for a median of 91% of the variance in optical movement. The data provided significant support for the use of the LOT strategy, as indicated by a sign test, $z = 4.35$, $p < .001$.

As Figure 33-4 shows, not only did these optical trajectories appear to fall along two separate straight lines, but they also displayed two characteristic optical speeds along the two lines. We found that two rates of optical speed

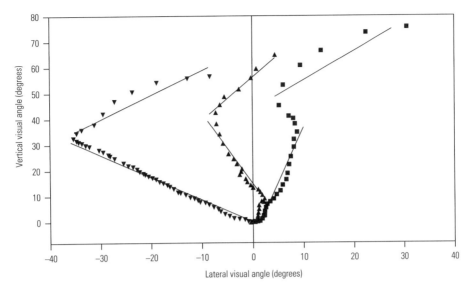

Figure 33-4. The optical trajectories of Frisbees on three representative trials in which the Frisbee was deliberately thrown to make a large perturbation in its trajectory. Frisbee position is plotted as the lateral visual angle, β (in degrees), by the vertical visual angle, α (in degrees), at each 1/30-s frame. The line over each of the trajectories is the estimate of the best-fit line used to compute the R^2 value.

constancy accounted for a median of 92.36% of the variance in the rate of change of the vertical tangent. Thus, both before and after the Frisbee made its shift, the dogs maintained temporal constancy to a large degree, at the same time that they maintained an LOT. This result supports our previous findings showing that for aerial targets headed off to the sides of pursuers, temporal constancy in the vertical direction is maintained as a secondary cue complementary to spatial linearity.

GENERAL DISCUSSION

Our findings with dogs catching Frisbees further support the generality of viewer-based navigational strategies and control heuristics (Cutting, Springer, Braren, & Johnson, 1992; Cutting & Wang, 2000; Royden & Hildreth, 1996). Behavior consistent with maintaining spatiotemporal constancy between a pursuer and a moving target is found in many domains. For example, airplane pilots are very accurate at spatial tasks of error nulling and pursuit tracking that allows them to maintain constant angle position

relative to a target. They also appear to use a strategy of maintaining constant angular changes to guide their turning radius when approaching a runway from an oblique angle (Beall & Loomis, 1997). In general, both aircraft and boat pilots can produce a collision course with another moving craft by maintaining an angle of heading or bearing angle that remains constant relative to the image of the other craft (Pollack, 1995).

Further evidence of the generality of viewer-based interception strategies comes from research with predators tracking prey, and with organisms tracking potential mates, which has shown that adjustments in position are made to maintain control of relative angle of motion between the pair. Tracking research with hoverflies and teleost fish (*Acanthaluteres spilomelanurus*) indicates that they "lock on" to the motion of their target in a manner that maintains optical angle constancy to guide their pursuit (Collett & Land, 1978; Lanchester & Mark, 1975). Maintenance of optical angle constancy to guide pursuit has also been found in tethered flies and free-flying houseflies (Collett & Land, 1975; Reichardt & Poggio, 1976). Research investigating the predator-prey characteristics of bats, birds, and dragonflies has found that they maintain a constant optical angle between themselves and their prey (Jablonski, 1999; Olberg, Worthington, & Venator, 2000; Simmons, Fenton, & O'Farrell, 1979). Finally, our work with automated mobile robots confirms the viability of viewer-based strategies like the LOT and OAC for interception of moving projectiles.

The LOT with concomitant use of OAC appears to be a generic tracking strategy that can be used by a pursuer to navigate toward a moving target in the environment. Additionally, neither the LOT nor the OAC strategy needs to be constrained to the domain of relatively simple, predictable target trajectories, such as in baseball. The current study supports the generality of the use of viewer-based spatiotemporal constancy cues in navigation both across species and across targets varying in flight-path complexity. The present work indicates that when the path of a moving target is sufficiently altered, maintenance of linearity is momentarily disrupted, and then the pursuer adopts a second LOT and OAC that are maintained until interception (i.e., a double LOT). Thus, an LOT-with-OAC strategy can be generalized to situations with complex target movement. In general, pursuers try to maintain a single LOT and OAC, and when the behavior of the target is sufficiently altered, they appear to simply adopt a newer, updated LOT and OAC. In short, the LOT and OAC strategies appear to be widely used viewer-based navigational heuristics for pursuing and intercepting moving targets in three-dimensional space.

ACKNOWLEDGMENTS

We would like to thank Romeo and Lilly for their participation and Barbara Bartlett for helping code data. We would also like to thank Lisa Lavalley and Candice Langenfeld for training the dogs and Karen McBeath and Jeffrey Anastasi for editorial assistance. This work was supported in part by a grant from the Interval Research Corporation, Palo Alto, CA.

Investment

Introduction to Chapter 34

Optimal versus Naive Diversification: How Inefficient Is the 1/N Portfolio Strategy?

You have just inherited a chunk of money and want to invest it without putting all your eggs into one basket. You want to diversify—but how? Harry Markowitz received his Nobel Prize in economics for finding the optimal solution to this question, the mean-variance portfolio. In plain terms, it maximizes the gain (mean) and minimizes the risk (variance). In recent years, many banks worldwide have sent letters to customers informing them that they rely on Markowitz's or similar optimization methods, with a warning against laypeople relying on naïve intuition. Complex problems require complex solutions, so the story goes. Yet, as mentioned in Chapter 1, Markowitz himself did not use his optimization model when making his own retirement investments. He relied on a simple heuristic, 1/N: Invest equally in the N alternatives.

Was that a foolish idea? If relying on a heuristic implies trading off accuracy against effort, one should not expect 1/N to even approximate the performance of an optimizing model. The study by Victor DeMiguel, Lorenzo Garlappi, and Raman Uppal analyzed the ecological rationality of 1/N, compared to the mean-variance model and a dozen Bayesian and non-Bayesian optimization models. They found that with 10 years of investment data, none of the optimization models could consistently beat the simple 1/N rule on various financial measures. If N = 50, the mean-variance portfolio would need some 500 years of stock data to surpass 1/N. That is, in the year 2500, it will pay to rely on the optimizing model—assuming that the same funds and the stock market are still around. The banks that inform their customers of Markowitz's optimization method do not seem to have noticed that they are sending their letters out 500 years too soon.

The general theoretical issue that this article helps clarify is the difference between the ecological rationality of a strategy (heuristic or optimizing) in situations where the parameter values are known and in situations where these have to be estimated from samples. Markowitz proved that the mean-variance portfolio is optimal, assuming that the parameter values are known or can be estimated without error (a so-called small world). Yet when one has to estimate the parameter values from samples (a large world), as firms and individual investors have to do, the gain from optimization can be more than offset by estimation error. Similarly, whatever error is introduced by the bias inherent in 1/N, it is more than offset by the heuristic's robustness against estimation errors. Because 1/N uses no free parameters, it has zero error due to variance (the trade-off between bias and variance is described in Chapter 1). The same distinction is important for the study of the ecological rationality of heuristics in general. For instance, the analytic results concerning the ecological rationality of heuristics in Chapter 12 concern situations where the parameter values are known. Just as Markowitz's proof of the optimality of the mean-variance portfolio does not necessarily hold when parameters need to be estimated from small samples, the proof that take-the-best results in the same accuracy as a linear strategy in a noncompensatory environment also does not necessarily generalize when parameters need to be estimated (see Chapter 1).

One last, practical observation. Inspired by the analysis of DeMiguel and colleagues, one of us (Gigerenzer) worked with the head of the investment department of a major international insurance company, reanalyzing their data from 1969 onwards and testing various rebalancing methods for $1/N$. The insurance officials were surprised to find that they would have done better using $1/N$ over the last 40 years. The particular rebalancing method did not make a systematic difference, if one did any rebalancing at all. After they had convinced themselves through extensive analyses that a simple heuristic can make more money than their previous complex allocation strategies, the head of department asked: "But how can we sell a $1/N$ portfolio to our customers? They might say, we can do that ourselves!"

CHAPTER 34

Optimal versus Naive Diversification: How Inefficient Is the 1/N Portfolio Strategy?

Victor DeMiguel, Lorenzo Garlappi, and Raman Uppal

Abstract: We evaluate the out-of-sample performance of the sample-based mean-variance model, and its extensions designed to reduce estimation error, relative to the naive 1/N portfolio. Of the 14 models we evaluate across seven empirical datasets, none is consistently better than the 1/N rule in terms of Sharpe ratio, certainty-equivalent return, or turnover, which indicates that, out of sample, the gain from optimal diversification is more than offset by estimation error. Based on parameters calibrated to the US equity market, our analytical results and simulations show that the estimation window needed for the sample-based mean-variance strategy and its extensions to outperform the 1/N benchmark is around 3000 months for a portfolio with 25 assets and about 6000 months for a portfolio with 50 assets. This suggests that there are still many "miles to go" before the gains promised by optimal portfolio choice can actually be realized out of sample.

In about the fourth century, Rabbi Issac bar Aha proposed the following rule for asset allocation: "One should always divide his wealth into three parts: a third in land, a third in merchandise, and a third ready to hand."[1] After a "brief" lull in the literature on asset allocation, there have been considerable advances starting with the pathbreaking work of Markowitz (1952),[2] who derived the *optimal* rule for allocating wealth across risky assets in a static setting when investors care only about the mean and variance of a portfolio's return. Because the implementation of these portfolios with moments estimated via their sample analogues is notorious for producing extreme weights that fluctuate substantially over

time and perform poorly out of sample, considerable effort has been devoted to the issue of handling estimation error with the goal of improving the performance of the Markowitz model.[3]

A prominent role in this vast literature is played by the *Bayesian approach* to estimation error, with its multiple implementations ranging from the purely statistical approach relying on diffuse-priors (Barry, 1974; Bawa, Brown, & Klein, 1979), to "shrinkage estimators" (Jobson, Korkie, & Ratti, 1979; Jobson & Korkie, 1980; Jorion, 1985, 1986), to the more recent approaches that rely on an asset-pricing model for establishing a prior (Pástor, 2000; Pástor & Stambaugh, 2000).[4] Equally rich is the set of *non-Bayesian* approaches to estimation error, which include "robust" portfolio allocation rules (Goldfarb & Iyengar, 2003; Garlappi, Uppal, & Wang, 2007); portfolio rules designed to optimally diversify across market *and* estimation risk (Kan & Zhou, 2007); portfolios that exploit the moment restrictions imposed by the factor structure of returns (MacKinlay & Pástor, 2000); methods that focus on reducing the error in estimating the covariance matrix (Best & Grauer, 1992; Chan, Karceski, & Lakonishok, 1999; Ledoit & Wolf, 2004a, 2004b); and, finally, portfolio rules that impose shortselling constraints (Frost & Savarino, 1988; Chopra, 1993; Jagannathan & Ma, 2003).[5]

Our objective in this paper is to understand the conditions under which mean-variance optimal portfolio models can be expected to perform well even in the presence of estimation risk. To do this, we evaluate the *out-of-sample* performance of the sample-based mean-variance portfolio rule—and its various extensions designed to reduce the effect of estimation error—relative to the performance of the *naive* portfolio diversification rule. We define the naive rule to be one in which a fraction $1/N$ of wealth is allocated to each of the N assets available for investment at each rebalancing date. There are two reasons for using the naive rule as a benchmark. First, it is easy to implement because it does not rely either on estimation of the moments of asset returns or on optimization. Second, despite the sophisticated theoretical models developed in the last 50 years and the advances in methods for estimating the parameters of these models, investors continue to use such simple allocation rules for allocating their wealth across assets.[6] We wish to emphasize, however, that the purpose of this study is *not* to advocate the use of the $1/N$ heuristic as an asset-allocation strategy, but merely to use it as a benchmark to assess the performance of various portfolio rules proposed in the literature.

We compare the out-of-sample performance of 14 different portfolio models relative to that of the $1/N$ policy across seven empirical datasets of monthly returns, using the following three performance criteria: (i) the out-of-sample Sharpe ratio; (ii) the certainty-equivalent (CEQ) return for the expected utility of a mean-variance investor; and (iii) the turnover (trading volume) for each portfolio strategy. The 14 models are listed in Table 34-1 and discussed in Section 1. The seven empirical datasets are listed in Table 34-2 and described in Appendix A.

Our first contribution is to show that of the 14 models evaluated, none is consistently better than the naive $1/N$ benchmark in terms of Sharpe ratio, certainty-equivalent return, or turnover. Although this was shown in the literature with regard to some of the earlier models,[7] we demonstrate that this is true: (i) for a wide range of models that include several developed more recently; (ii) using three performance metrics; and (iii) across several datasets. In general, the *unconstrained* policies that try to incorporate estimation error perform much worse than any of the strategies that constrain shortsales, and also perform much worse than the $1/N$ strategy. *Imposing constraints* on the sample-based mean-variance and Bayesian portfolio strategies leads to only a modest improvement in Sharpe ratios and CEQ returns, although it shows a substantial reduction in turnover. Of all the optimizing models studied here, the minimum-variance portfolio with constraints studied in Jagannathan and Ma (2003) performs best in terms of Sharpe ratio. But even this model delivers a Sharpe ratio that is statistically superior to that of the $1/N$ strategy in only one of the seven empirical datasets, a CEQ return that is not statistically superior to that of the $1/N$ strategy in any of these datasets, and a turnover that is always higher than that of the $1/N$ policy.

To understand better the reasons for the poor performance of the optimal portfolio strategies relative to the $1/N$ benchmark, our second contribution is to derive an *analytical* expression for the *critical length* of the estimation window that is needed for the sample-based mean-variance strategy to achieve a higher CEQ return than that of the $1/N$ strategy. This critical estimation-window length is a function of the number of assets, the *ex ante* Sharpe ratio of the mean-variance portfolio, and the Sharpe ratio of the $1/N$ policy. Based on parameters calibrated to US stock-market data, we find that the critical length of the estimation window is 3000 months for a portfolio with only 25 assets, and more than 6000 months for a portfolio with 50 assets. The severity of estimation error is startling if we consider that, in practice, these portfolio models are typically estimated using only 60 or 120 months of data.

Because the above analytical results are available only for the sample-based mean-variance

Table 34-1. List of Various Asset-Allocation Models Considered

#	Model	Abbreviation
Naïve		
0.	1/N with rebalancing (*benchmark strategy*)	ew or 1/N
Classical approach that ignores estimation error		
1.	Sample-based mean-variance	mv
Bayesian approach to estimation error		
2.	Bayesian diffuse-prior	Not reported
3.	Bayes-Stein	bs
4.	Bayesian Data-and-Model	dm
Moment restrictions		
5.	Minimum-variance	min
6.	Value-weighted market portfolio	vw
7.	MacKinlay and Pástor's (2000) missing-factor model	mp
Portfolio constraints		
8.	Sample-based mean-variance with shortsale constraints	mv-c
9.	Bayes-Stein with shortsale constraints	bs-c
10.	Minimum-variance with shortsale constraints	min-c
11.	Minimum-variance with generalized constraints	g-min-c
Optimal combinations of portfolios		
12.	Kan and Zhou's (2007) "three-fund" model	mv-min
13.	Mixture of minimum-variance and 1/N	ew-min
14.	Garlappi, Uppal, and Wang's (2007) multi-prior model	Not reported

This table lists the various asset-allocation models we consider. The last column of the table gives the abbreviation used to refer to the strategy in the tables where we compare the performance of the optimal portfolio strategies to that of the 1/N strategy. The results for two strategies are not reported. The reason for not reporting the results for the Bayesian diffuse-prior strategy is that for an estimation period that is of the length that we are considering (60 or 120 months), the Bayesian diffuse-prior portfolio is very similar to the sample-based mean-variance portfolio. The reason for not reporting the results for the multi-prior robust portfolio described in Garlappi, Uppal, and Wang (2007) is that they show that the optimal robust portfolio is a weighted average of the mean-variance and minimum-variance portfolios, the results for both of which are already being reported.

strategy, we use simulated data to examine its various extensions that have been developed explicitly to deal with estimation error. Our third contribution is to show that these models too need very long estimation windows before they can be expected to outperform the 1/N policy. From our simulation results, we conclude that portfolio strategies from the optimizing models are expected to outperform the 1/N benchmark if: (i) the estimation window is long; (ii) the *ex ante* (true) Sharpe ratio of the mean-variance efficient portfolio is substantially higher than that of the 1/N portfolio; and (iii) the number of assets is small. The first two conditions are intuitive. The reason for the last condition is that a smaller number of assets implies fewer parameters to be estimated and, therefore, less room for

estimation error. Moreover, other things being equal, a smaller number of assets makes naive diversification less effective relative to optimal diversification.

The intuition for our findings is that to implement the mean-variance model, both the vector of expected excess returns over the risk-free rate and the variance-covariance matrix of returns have to be estimated. It is well known (Merton, 1980) that a very long time series of data is required in order to estimate expected returns precisely; similarly, the estimate of the variance-covariance matrix is poorly behaved (Green & Hollifield, 1992; Jagannathan & Ma, 2003). The portfolio weights based on the sample estimates of these moments result in extreme positive and negative weights that are far from optimal.[8] As a result,

Table 34-2. List of Datasets Considered

#	Dataset and Source	N	Time Period	Abbreviation
1	Ten sector portfolios of the S&P 500 and the US equity market portfolio Source: Roberto Wessels	10 + 1	01/1981–12/2002	S&P Sectors
2	Ten industry portfolios and the US equity market portfolio Source: Ken French's Web site	10 + 1	07/1963–11/2004	Industry
3	Eight country indexes and the World Index Source: MSCI	8 + 1	01/1970–07/2001	International
4	SMB and HML portfolios and the US equity market portfolio Source: Ken French's Web site	2 + 1	07/1963–11/2004	MKT/SMB/HML
5	Twenty size- and book-to-market portfolios and the US equity MKT Source: Ken French's Web site	20 + 1	07/1963–11/2004	FF-1-factor
6	Twenty size- and book-to-market portfolios and the MKT, SMB, and HML portfolios Source: Ken French's Web site	20 + 3	07/1963–11/2004	FF-3-factor
7	Twenty size- and book-to-market portfolios and the MKT, SMB, HML, and UMD portfolios Source: Ken French's Web site	20 + 4	07/1963–11/2004	FF-4-factor
8	Simulated data Source: Market model	{10, 25, 50}	2000 years	—

This table lists the various datasets analyzed; the number of risky assets N in each dataset, where the number after the "+" indicates the number of factor portfolios available; and the time period spanned. Each dataset contains monthly excess returns over the 90-day nominal US T-bill (from Ken French's Web site). In the last column is the abbreviation used to refer to the dataset in the tables evaluating the performance of the various portfolio strategies. Note that as in Wang (2005), of the 25 size- and book-to-market-sorted portfolios, we exclude the five portfolios containing the largest firms, because the market, SMB, and HML are almost a linear combination of the 25 Fama-French portfolios. Note also that in Datasets 5, 6, and 7, the only difference is in the factor portfolios that are available: in Dataset #5, it is the US equity MKT; in Dataset #6, they are the MKT, SMB, and HML portfolios; and in Dataset #7, they are the MKT, SMB, HML, and UMD portfolios. Because the results for the "FF-3-factor" dataset are almost identical to those for "FF-1-factor," only the results for "FF-1-factor" are reported.

"allocation mistakes" caused by using the $1/N$ weights can turn out to be *smaller* than the error caused by using the weights from an optimizing model with inputs that have been estimated with error. Although the "error-maximizing" property of the mean-variance portfolio has been described in the literature (Michaud, 1989; Best & Grauer, 1991), our contribution is to show that because the effect of estimation error on the weights is so large, even the models designed explicitly to reduce the effect of estimation error achieve only modest success.

A second reason why the $1/N$ rule performs well in the datasets we consider is that we are using it to allocate wealth across portfolios of stocks rather than individual stocks. Because diversified portfolios have lower idiosyncratic volatility than individual assets, the loss from naive as opposed to optimal diversification is much smaller when allocating wealth across portfolios. Our simulations show that optimal diversification policies will dominate the $1/N$ rule only for very high levels of idiosyncratic volatility. Another advantage of the $1/N$ rule is that it is straightforward to apply to a large number of assets, in contrast to optimizing models, which typically require additional parameters to be estimated as the number of assets increases.

In all our experiments, the choice of N has been dictated by the dataset. A natural question that arises then is: What is N? That is, for what number and kind of assets does the $1/N$ strategy outperform other optimizing portfolio models? The results show that the naive $1/N$ strategy is more likely to outperform the strategies from the optimizing models when: (i) N is large, because this improves the potential for diversification, even if it is naive, while at the same time increasing the number of parameters to be estimated by an optimizing model; (ii) the assets do not have a sufficiently long data history to allow for a precise estimation of the moments. In the empirical analysis, we consider datasets with $N = \{3, 9, 11, 21, 24\}$ and assets from equity portfolios that are based on industry classification, equity portfolios constructed on the basis of firm characteristics, and also international equity indices. In the simulations, $N = \{10, 25, 50\}$ and the asset returns are calibrated to match returns on portfolios of US stocks. The empirical and simulation-based results show that for an estimation window of $M = 120$ months, our main finding is not sensitive to the type of assets we considered or to the choice of the number of assets, N.

We draw two conclusions from the results. First, our study suggests that although there has been considerable progress in the design of optimal portfolios, more effort needs to be devoted to improving the estimation of the moments, and especially expected returns. For this, methods that complement traditional classical and Bayesian statistical techniques by exploiting empirical regularities that are present for a particular set of assets (Brandt, Santa-Clara, & Valkanov, 2007) can represent a promising direction to pursue. Second, given the inherent simplicity and the relatively low cost of implementing the $1/N$ naive-diversification rule, such a strategy should serve as a natural benchmark to assess the performance of more sophisticated asset-allocation rules. This is an important hurdle both for academic research proposing new asset-allocation models and for "active" portfolio-management strategies offered by the investment industry.

The rest of the paper is organized as follows. In Section 1, we describe the various models of optimal asset allocation and evaluate their performance. In Section 2, we explain our methodology for comparing the performance of these models to that of $1/N$; the results of this comparison for seven empirical datasets are given in Section 3. Section 4 contains the analytical results on the critical length of the estimation window needed for the sample-based mean-variance policy to outperform the $1/N$ benchmark; and in Section 5 we present a similar analysis for other models of portfolio choice using simulated data. The various experiments that we undertake to verify the robustness of the findings are described briefly in Section 6, with the details reported in a separate appendix titled "Implementation Details and Robustness Checks," which is available from the authors. Our conclusions are presented in Section 7. The empirical datasets we use are described in Appendix A.

1. DESCRIPTION OF THE ASSET-ALLOCATION MODELS CONSIDERED

In this section, we discuss the various models from the portfolio-choice literature that we consider. Because these models are familiar to most readers, we provide only a brief description of each, and instead focus on explaining how the different models are related to each other. The list of models we analyze is summarized in Table 34-1, and the details on how to implement these models are given in the separate appendix to this paper.

We use R_t to denote the N-vector of *excess* returns (over the risk-free asset) on the N risky assets available for investment at date t. The N-dimensional vector μ_t is used to denote the *expected* returns on the risky asset in excess of the risk-free rate, and Σ_t to denote the corresponding $N \times N$ variance-covariance matrix of returns, with their sample counterparts given by $\hat{\mu}_t$ and $\hat{\Sigma}_t$, respectively. Let M denote the length over which these moments are estimated, and T the total length of the data series. We use 1_N to define an N-dimensional vector of ones, and I_N to indicate the $N \times N$ identity matrix. Finally, x_t is the vector of portfolio weights invested in the N risky assets, with $1 - 1_N^T x_t$ invested in the risk-free asset. The vector of *relative* weights in the portfolio with only-risky assets is

$$w_t \frac{x_t}{\left| 1_N^T x_t \right|}, \qquad (34\text{-}1)$$

where the normalization by the absolute value of the sum of the portfolio weights, $\left| 1_N^T x_t \right|$, guarantees that the direction of the portfolio position is preserved in the few cases where the sum of the weights on the risky assets is negative.

To facilitate the comparison across different strategies, we consider an investor whose preferences are fully described by the mean and variance of a chosen portfolio, x_t. At each time t, the decision-maker selects x_t to maximize expected utility[9]:

$$\max_{x_t} x_t^T \mu_t - \frac{\gamma}{2} x_t^T \Sigma_t x_t, \qquad (34\text{-}2)$$

in which γ can be interpreted as the investor's risk aversion. The solution of the above optimization is $x_t = (1/\gamma)\Sigma_t^{-1}\mu$. The vector of *relative* portfolio weights invested in the N risky assets at time t is

$$w_t = \frac{\Sigma_t^{-1}\mu_t}{1_N \Sigma_t^{-1}\mu_t}. \qquad (34\text{-}3)$$

Almost all the models that we consider deliver portfolio weights that can be expressed as in Equation 34-3, with the main difference being in how one estimates μ_t and Σ_t.

1.1 Naive Portfolio

The naive ("ew" or "1/N") strategy that we consider involves holding a portfolio weight $w_t^{ew} = 1/N$ in each of the N risky assets. This strategy does not involve any optimization or estimation and completely ignores the data. For comparison with the weights in Equation 34-3, one can also think of the 1/N portfolio as a strategy that does estimate the moments μ_t and Σ_t, but imposes the restriction that $\mu_t \propto \Sigma_t 1_N$ for all t, which implies that expected returns are proportional to total risk rather than systematic risk.

1.2 Sample-Based Mean-Variance Portfolio

In the mean-variance ("mv") model of Markowitz (1952), the investor optimizes the tradeoff between the mean and variance of portfolio returns. To implement this model, we follow the classic "plug-in" approach; that is, we solve the problem in Equation 34-2 with the mean and covariance matrix of asset returns replaced by their sample counterparts $\hat{\mu}$ and $\hat{\Sigma}$, respectively. We shall refer to this strategy as the "sample-based mean-variance portfolio." Note that this portfolio strategy completely ignores the possibility of estimation error.

1.3 Bayesian Approach to Estimation Error

Under the Bayesian approach, the estimates of μ and Σ are computed using the *predictive distribution* of asset returns. This distribution is obtained by integrating the *conditional likelihood*, $f(R|\mu, \Sigma)$, over μ and Σ with respect to a certain *subjective prior*, $p(\mu, \Sigma)$. In the literature, the Bayesian approach to estimation error has been implemented in different ways. In the following sections, we describe three common implementations we consider.

1.3.1 Bayesian diffuse-prior portfolio

Barry (1974), Klein and Bawa (1976), and Brown (1979) show that if the prior is chosen to be diffuse, that is, $p(\mu, \Sigma) \propto |\Sigma|^{-(N+1)/2}$, and the conditional likelihood is normal, then the predictive distribution is a student-t with mean $\hat{\mu}$ and variance $\hat{\Sigma}(1+1/M)$. Hence, while still using the historical mean to estimate expected returns, this approach inflates the covariance matrix by a factor of $(1 + 1/M)$. For a sufficiently long estimation window M (as in our study, where $M = 120$ months), the effect of this correction is negligible, and the performance of the Bayesian diffuse-prior portfolio is virtually indistinguishable from that of the sample-based mean-variance portfolio. For this reason, we do not report the results for this Bayesian strategy.

1.3.2 Bayes-Stein shrinkage portfolio

The Bayes-Stein ("bs") portfolio is an application of the idea of shrinkage estimation pioneered by Stein (1955) and James and Stein (1961), and is designed to handle the error in estimating expected returns by using estimators of the form

$$\hat{\mu}_t^{bs} = (1 - \hat{\phi}_t)\hat{\mu}_t + \hat{\phi}_t\hat{\mu}_t^{min}, \qquad (34\text{-}4)$$

$$\hat{\phi}_t = \frac{N+2}{(N+2) + M(\hat{\mu}_t - \mu_t^{min})^T \hat{\Sigma}_t^{-1}(\hat{\mu}_t - \mu_t^{min})}, \qquad (34\text{-}5)$$

in which $0 < \hat{\phi}_t < 1$, $\hat{\Sigma}_t = \dfrac{1}{M - N - 2}$ $\sum_{s=t-M+1}^{t}(R_s - \hat{\mu}_t)(R_s - \hat{\mu}_t)^T$ and $\hat{\mu}_t^{min} \equiv \hat{\mu}_t^T \hat{w}_t^{min}$ is the average excess return on the sample global minimum-variance portfolio, $\hat{w}_t^{min}$. These estimators "shrink" the sample mean toward a common "grand mean," $\bar{\mu}$. In our analysis, we use the estimator proposed by Jorion (1985, 1986), who takes the grand mean, $\bar{\mu}$, to be the mean of the minimum-variance portfolio, μ^{min}. In addition to shrinking the estimate of the mean, Jorion also accounts for estimation error in the covariance matrix via traditional Bayesian-estimation methods.[10]

1.3.3 Bayesian portfolio based on belief in an asset-pricing model

Under the Bayesian "Data-and-Model" ("dm") approach developed in Pástor (2000) and Pástor and Stambaugh (2000), the shrinkage target depends on the investor's prior belief in a particular asset-pricing model, and the degree of shrinkage is determined by the variability of the prior belief relative to the information contained in the data. These portfolios are a further refinement of shrinkage portfolios because they address the arbitrariness of the choice of a shrinkage target, $\bar{\mu}$, and of the shrinkage factor, ϕ, by using the investor's belief about the validity of an asset-pricing model. We implement the Data-and-Model approach using three different asset-pricing models: the Capital Asset Pricing Model (CAPM), the Fama and French (1993) three-factor model, and the Carhart (1997) four-factor model. In our empirical analysis, we consider a Bayesian investor whose belief in the asset-pricing model is captured by a prior about the extent of mispricing. Let the variable α reflect

this mispricing. We assume the prior to be normally distributed around $\alpha = 0$, and with the benchmark value of its tightness being $\sigma\alpha = 1\%$ per annum. Intuitively, this implies that the investor believes that with 95% probability the mispricing is approximately between -2% and $+2\%$ on an annual basis.

1.4 Portfolios with Moment Restrictions

In this section, we describe portfolio strategies that impose restrictions on the estimation of the moments of asset returns.

1.4.1 Minimum-variance portfolio

Under the minimum-variance ("min") strategy, we choose the portfolio of risky assets that minimizes the variance of returns; that is,

$$\min_{w_t} w_t^T \Sigma_t w_t, \quad \text{s.t. } 1_N^T w_t = 1 \qquad (34\text{-}6)$$

To implement this policy, we use only the estimate of the covariance matrix of asset returns (the sample covariance matrix) and completely ignore the estimates of the expected returns.[11] Also, although this strategy does not fall into the general structure of mean-variance expected utility, its weights can be thought of as a limiting case of Equation 34-3, if a mean-variance investor either ignores expected returns or, equivalently, restricts expected returns so that they are identical across all assets; that is, $\mu_t \propto 1_N$.

1.4.2 Value-weighted portfolio implied by the market model

The optimal strategy in a CAPM world is the value-weighted ("vw") market portfolio. So, for each of the datasets we identify a benchmark "market" portfolio and report the Sharpe ratio and CEQ for holding this portfolio. The turnover of this strategy is zero.

1.4.3 Portfolio implied by asset-pricing models with unobservable factors

MacKinlay and Pástor (2000) show that if returns have an exact factor structure but some factors are not observed, then the resulting mispricing is contained in the covariance matrix of the residuals. They use this insight to construct an estimator of expected returns that is more stable and reliable than estimators obtained using traditional methods. MacKinlay and Pástor show that, in this case, the covariance matrix of returns takes the following form[12]:

$$\sum = v\mu\mu^T + \sigma^2 I_N$$ (34-7)

in which v and σ^2 are positive scalars. They use the maximum-likelihood estimates of v, σ^2, and μ to derive the corresponding estimates of the mean and covariance matrix of asset returns. The optimal portfolio weights are obtained by substituting these estimates into Equation 34-2. We denote this portfolio strategy by "mp."

1.5 Shortsale-Constrained Portfolios

We also consider a number of strategies that constrain shortselling. The sample-based mean-variance-constrained (mv-c), Bayes-Stein-constrained (bs-c), and minimum-variance-constrained (min-c) policies are obtained by imposing an additional nonnegativity constraint on the portfolio weights in the corresponding optimization problems.

To interpret the effect of shortsale constraints, observe that imposing the constraint $x_i \geq 0$, $i = 1,\ldots, N$ in the basic mean-variance optimization, Equation 34-2 yields the following Lagrangian,

$$L = x_t^T \mu_t - \frac{\gamma}{2} x_t^T \Sigma_t x_t + x_t^T \lambda_t,$$ (34-8)

in which λ_t is the $N \times 1$ vector of Lagrange multipliers for the constraints on shortselling. Rearranging Equation 34-8, we can see that the constrained mean-variance portfolio weights are equivalent to the unconstrained weights but with the adjusted mean vector: $\tilde{\mu}_t = \mu_t + \lambda_t$. To see why this is a form of shrinkage on the expected returns, note that the shortselling constraint on asset i is likely to be binding when its expected return is low. When the constraint for asset i binds, $\lambda_{p,i} > 0$ and the expected return is increased from $\mu_{t,i}$ to $\tilde{\mu}_{t,i} = \mu_{t,i} + \lambda_{t,i}$. Hence, imposing a shortsale constraint on the sample-based mean-variance problem is equivalent to "shrinking" the expected return toward the average.

Similarly, Jagannathan and Ma (2003) show that imposing a shortsale constraint on the minimum-variance portfolio is equivalent to shrinking the elements of the variance-covariance matrix. Jagannathan and Ma (2003, p. 1654) find that, with a constraint on shortsales, "the sample covariance matrix performs almost as well as those constructed using factor models, shrinkage estimators or daily returns." Because of this finding, we do not evaluate the performance of other models—such as Best and Grauer (1992); Chan, Karceski, and Lakonishok (1999); and Ledoit and Wolf (2004a, 2004b)—that have been developed to deal with the problems associated with estimating the covariance matrix.[13]

Motivated by the desire to examine whether the out-of-sample portfolio performance can be improved by ignoring expected returns (which are difficult to estimate) but still taking into account the correlations between returns, we also consider a new strategy that has not been considered in the existing literature. This strategy, denoted by "g-min-c," is a combination of the $1/N$ policy and the constrained-minimum-variance strategy, and it can be interpreted as a simple generalization of the shortsale-constrained minimum-variance portfolio. It is obtained by imposing an additional constraint on the minimum-variance problem (6): $w \geq a1_N$, with $a \in [0, 1/N]$. Observe that the shortsale-constrained minimum-variance portfolio corresponds to the case in which $a = 0$, while setting $a = 1/N$ yields the $1/N$ portfolio. In the empirical section, we study the case in which $a = \frac{1}{2}\frac{1}{N}$, arbitrarily chosen as the middle ground between the constrained-minimum-variance portfolio and the $1/N$ portfolio.

1.6 Optimal Combination of Portfolios

We also consider portfolios that are themselves combinations of other portfolios, such as the mean-variance portfolio, the minimum-variance portfolio, and the equally weighted portfolio. The mixture portfolios are constructed by applying the idea of shrinkage *directly* to the portfolio weights. That is, instead of first estimating the moments and then constructing portfolios with these moments, one can directly construct (nonnormalized) portfolios of the form

$$x^S = cx^c + dx^d, \quad \text{s.t. } 1_N^T x^S = 1, \qquad (34\text{-}9)$$

in which x^c and x^d are two reference portfolios chosen by the investor. Working directly with portfolio weights is intuitively appealing because it makes it easier to select a specific target toward which one is shrinking a given portfolio. The two mixture portfolios that we consider are described as follows.

1.6.1 The Kan and Zhou (2007) three-fund portfolio

In order to improve on the models that use Bayes-Stein shrinkage estimators, Kan and Zhou (2007) propose a "three-fund" ("mv-min") portfolio rule, in which the role of the third fund is to minimize "estimation risk." The intuition underlying their model is that because estimation risk cannot be diversified away by holding only a combination of the tangency portfolio and the risk-free asset, an investor will also benefit from holding some other risky-asset portfolio; that is, a third fund. Kan and Zhou search for this optimal three-fund portfolio rule in the class of portfolios that can be expressed as a combination of the sample-based mean-variance portfolio and the minimum-variance portfolio. The nonnormalized weights of this mixture portfolio are

$$\hat{x}_t^{\text{mv-min}} = \frac{1}{\gamma}\left(c\,\hat{\Sigma}_t^{-1}\hat{\mu}_t + d\,\hat{\Sigma}_t^{-1}1_N\right), \qquad (34\text{-}10)$$

in which c and d are chosen optimally to maximize the expected utility of a mean-variance investor. The weights in the risky assets used in our implementation are given by normalizing the expression in Equation 34-10; that is,

$$\hat{w}_t^{\text{mv-min}} = \hat{x}_t^{\text{mv-min}}/|1_N^T\,\hat{x}_t^{\text{mv-min}}|.$$

1.6.2 Mixture of equally weighted and minimum-variance portfolios

Finally, we consider a new portfolio strategy denoted "ew-min" that has not been studied in the existing literature. This strategy is a combination of the naive $1/N$ portfolio and the

minimum-variance portfolio, rather than the mean-variance portfolio and the minimum-variance portfolio considered in Kan and Zhou (2007) and Garlappi, Uppal, and Wang (2007).[14] Again, our motivation for considering this portfolio is that because expected returns are more difficult to estimate than covariances, one may want to ignore the estimates of mean returns but not the estimates of covariances. And so, one may wish to combine the $1/N$ portfolio with the minimum-variance portfolio. Specifically, the portfolio we consider is

$$\hat{w}^{ew\text{-}min} = c\,\frac{1}{N}1_N + d\hat{\Sigma}^{-1}1_N, \quad \text{s.t. } 1_N^T\,\hat{w}^{ew\text{-}min} = 1, \qquad (34\text{-}11)$$

in which c and d are chosen to maximize the expected utility of a mean-variance investor.

2. METHODOLOGY FOR EVALUATING PERFORMANCE

Our goal is to study the performance of each of the aforementioned models across a variety of datasets that have been considered in the literature on asset allocation. The datasets considered are summarized in Table 34-2 and described in Appendix A.

Our analysis relies on a "rolling-sample" approach. Specifically, given a T-month-long dataset of asset returns, we choose an estimation window of length $M = 60$ or $M = 120$ months.[15] In each month t, starting from $t = M + 1$, we use the data in the previous M months to estimate the parameters needed to implement a particular strategy. These estimated parameters are then used to determine the relative portfolio weights in the portfolio of only-risky assets. We then use these weights to compute the return in month $t + 1$. This process is continued by adding the return for the next period in the dataset and dropping the earliest return, until the end of the dataset is reached. The outcome of this rolling-window approach is a series of $T - M$ monthly *out-of-sample* returns generated by each of the portfolio strategies listed in Table 34-1, for each of the empirical datasets in Table 34-2.

Given the time series of monthly out-of-sample returns generated by each strategy and in each dataset, we compute three quantities. One, we measure the *out-of-sample Sharpe ratio* of strategy k, defined as the sample mean of out-of-sample excess returns (over the risk-free asset), $\hat{\mu}_k$, divided by their sample standard deviation, $\hat{\sigma}_k$:

$$\widehat{SR}_k = \frac{\hat{\mu}_k}{\hat{\sigma}_k}. \qquad (34\text{-}12)$$

To test whether the Sharpe ratios of two strategies are statistically distinguishable, we also compute the p-value of the difference, using the approach suggested by Jobson and Korkie (1981) after making the correction pointed out in Memmel (2003).[16]

In order to assess the effect of estimation error on performance, we also compute the *in-sample Sharpe ratio* for each strategy. This is computed by using the *entire* time series of excess returns; that is, with the estimation window $M = T$. Formally, the in-sample Sharpe ratio of strategy k is

$$\widehat{SR}_k^{IS} = \frac{Mean_k}{Std_k} = \frac{\hat{\mu}_k^{IS^T} \hat{w}_k}{\sqrt{\hat{w}_k^T \hat{\Sigma}_k^{IS} \hat{w}_k}}, \qquad (34\text{-}13)$$

in which $\hat{\mu}_k^{IS}$ and $\hat{\Sigma}_k^{IS}$ are the in-sample mean and variance estimates, and w_k is the portfolio obtained with these estimates.

Two, we calculate the *certainty-equivalent (CEQ) return*, defined as the risk-free rate that an investor is willing to accept rather than adopting a particular risky portfolio strategy. Formally, we compute the CEQ return of strategy k as

$$\widehat{CEQ}_k = \hat{\mu}_k - \frac{\gamma}{2} \hat{\sigma}_k^2, \qquad (34\text{-}14)$$

in which $\hat{\mu}_k$ and $\hat{\sigma}_k^2$ are the mean and variance of out-of-sample excess returns for strategy k, and γ is the risk aversion.[17] The results we report are for the case of $\gamma = 1$; results for other values of γ are discussed in the separate appendix with robustness checks. To test whether the CEQ returns from two strategies are statistically different, we also compute the p-value of the difference, relying on the asymptotic properties of functional forms of the estimators for means and variance.[18]

Three, to get a sense of the amount of trading required to implement each portfolio strategy, we compute the portfolio *turnover*, defined as the average sum of the absolute value of the trades across the N available assets:

$$\text{Turnover} = \frac{1}{T-M} \sum_{t=1}^{T-M} \sum_{j=1}^{N} \left(\left| \hat{w}_{k,j,t+1} - \hat{w}_{k,j,t^+} \right| \right), \qquad (34\text{-}15)$$

in which $\hat{w}_{k,j,t}$ is the portfolio weight in asset j at time t under strategy k; $\hat{w}_{j,t^+}$ is the portfolio weight *before* rebalancing at $t + 1$; and $\hat{w}_{k,j,t+1}$ is the desired portfolio weight at time $t + 1$, after rebalancing. For example, in the case of the $1/N$ strategy, $w_{k,j,t} = w_{k,j,t+1} = 1/N$, but w_{k,j,t^+} may be different due to changes in asset prices between t and $t + 1$. The turnover quantity defined above can be interpreted as the average percentage of wealth traded in each period. For the $1/N$ benchmark strategy we report its absolute turnover, and for all the other strategies their turnover relative to that of the benchmark strategy.

In addition to reporting the raw turnover for each strategy, we also report an economic measure of this by reporting how proportional transactions costs generated by this turnover affect the returns from a particular strategy.[19] We set the proportional transactions cost equal to 50 basis points per transaction as assumed in Balduzzi and Lynch (1999), based on the studies of the cost per transaction for individual stocks on the NYSE by Stoll and Whaley (1983), Bhardwaj and Brooks (1992), and Lesmond, Ogden, and Trzcinka (1999).

Let $R_{k,p}$ be the return from strategy k on the portfolio of N assets before rebalancing; that is, $R_{k,p} = \sum_{j=1}^{N} R_{j,t+1} \hat{w}_{k,j,t}$. When the portfolio is rebalanced at time $t + 1$, it gives rise to a trade in each asset of magnitude $|\hat{w}_{k,j,t+1} - \hat{w}_{k,j,t^+}|$. Denoting by c the proportional transaction cost, the cost of such a trade over all assets is $c \times \Sigma_{j=1}^{N} |\hat{w}_{k,j,t+1} - \hat{w}_{k,j,t^+}|$. Therefore, we can write the evolution of wealth for strategy k as follows:

$$W_{k,t+1} = W_{k,t}(1 + R_{k,p})$$
$$\left(1 - c \times \sum_{j=1}^{N} \left| \hat{w}_{k,j,t+1} - \hat{w}_{k,j,t^+} \right| \right) \qquad (34\text{-}16)$$

with the return *net* of transactions costs given by $\frac{W_{k,t+1}}{W_{k,t}} - 1$.

For each strategy, we compute the *return-loss* with respect to the $1/N$ strategy. The return-loss is defined as the additional return needed for strategy k to perform as well as the $1/N$ strategy in terms of the Sharpe ratio. To compute the return-loss per month, suppose μ_{ew} and σ_{ew} are the monthly out-of-sample mean and volatility of the net returns from the $1/N$ strategy, and μ_k and σ_k are the corresponding quantities for strategy k. Then, the return-loss from strategy k is

$$return-loss_k = \frac{\mu_{ew}}{\sigma_{ew}} \times \sigma_k - \mu_k. \qquad (34\text{-}17)$$

3. RESULTS FROM THE SEVEN EMPIRICAL DATASETS CONSIDERED

In this section, we compare empirically the performances of the optimal asset-allocation strategies listed in Table 34-1 to the benchmark $1/N$ strategy. For each strategy, we compute across all the datasets listed in Table 34-2, the in-sample and out-of-sample Sharpe ratios (Table 34-3), the CEQ return (Table 34-4), and the turnover (Table 34-5). In each of these tables, the various strategies being examined are listed in rows, while the columns refer to the different datasets.

Table 34-3. Sharpe Ratios for Empirical Data

Strategy	S&P sectors $N = 11$	Industry portfolios $N = 11$	Inter'l portfolios $N = 9$	Mkt/SMB/ HML $N = 3$	FF 1-factor $N = 21$	FF 4-factor $N = 24$
$1/N$	0.1876	0.1353	0.1277	0.2240	0.1623	0.1753
mv (in sample)	0.3848	0.2124	0.2090	0.2851	0.5098	0.5364
Mv	0.0794	0.0679	−0.0332	0.2186	0.0128	0.1841
	(0.12)	(0.17)	(0.03)	(0.46)	(0.02)	(0.45)
Bs	0.0811	0.0719	−0.0297	0.2536	0.0138	0.1791
	(0.09)	(0.19)	(0.03)	(0.25)	(0.02)	(0.48)
dm ($\sigma_\alpha = 1.0\%$)	0.1410	0.0581	0.0707	0.0016	0.0004	0.2355
	(0.08)	(0.14)	(0.08)	(0.00)	(0.01)	(0.17)
Min	0.0820	0.1554	0.1490	0.2493	0.2778	−0.0183
	(0.05)	(0.30)	(0.21)	(0.23)	(0.01)	(0.01)
Vw	0.1444	0.1138	0.1239	0.1138	0.1138	0.1138
	(0.09)	(0.01)	(0.43)	(0.00)	(0.01)	(0.00)
Mp	0.1863	0.0533	0.0984	−0.0002	0.1238	0.1230
	(0.44)	(0.04)	(0.15)	(0.00)	(0.08)	(0.03)
mv-c	0.0892	0.0678	0.0848	0.1084	0.1977	0.2024
	(0.09)	(0.03)	(0.17)	(0.02)	(0.02)	(0.27)
bs-c	0.1075	0.0819	0.0848	0.1514	0.1955	0.2062
	(0.14)	(0.06)	(0.15)	(0.09)	(0.03)	(0.25)
min-c	0.0834	0.1425	0.1501	0.2493	0.1546	0.3580
	(0.01)	(0.41)	(0.16)	(0.23)	(0.35)	(0.00)
g-min-c	0.1371	0.1451	0.1429	0.2467	0.1615	0.3028
	(0.08)	(0.31)	(0.19)	(0.25)	(0.47)	(0.00)
mv-min	0.0683	0.0772	−0.0353	0.2546	−0.0079	0.1757
	(0.05)	(0.21)	(0.01)	(0.22)	(0.01)	(0.50)
ew-min	0.1208	0.1576	0.1407	0.2503	0.2608	−0.0161
	(0.07)	(0.21)	(0.18)	(0.17)	(0.00)	(0.01)

For each of the empirical datasets listed in Table 2, this table reports the monthly Sharpe ratio for the $1/N$ strategy, the in-sample Sharpe ratio of the mean-variance strategy, and the out-of-sample Sharpe ratios for the strategies from the models of optimal asset allocation listed in Table 1. In parentheses is the *p*-value of the difference between the Sharpe ratio of each strategy from that of the $1/N$ benchmark, which is computed using the Jobson and Korkie (1981) methodology described in Section 2. The results for the "FF-3-factor" dataset are not reported because they are very similar to those for the "FF-1-factor" dataset.

Table 34-4. Certainty-Equivalent Returns for Empirical Data

Strategy	S&P Sectors $N = 11$	Industry Portfolios $N = 11$	International Portfolios $N = 9$	Mkt/SMB/ HML $N = 3$	FF 1-Factor $N = 21$	FF 4-Factor $N = 24$
1/N	0.0069	0.0050	0.0046	0.0039	0.0073	0.0072
mv (in sample)	0.0478	0.0106	0.0096	0.0047	0.0300	0.0304
Mv	0.0031	−0.7816	−0.1365	0.0045	−2.7142	−0.0829
	(0.28)	(0.00)	(0.00)	(0.31)	(0.00)	(0.01)
Bs	0.0030	−0.3157	−0.0312	0.0043	−0.6504	−0.0362
	(0.16)	(0.00)	(0.00)	(0.32)	(0.00)	(0.06)
dm ($\sigma_\alpha = 1.0\%$)	0.0052	−0.0319	0.0021	−0.0084	−0.0296	0.0110
	(0.11)	(0.01)	(0.08)	(0.04)	(0.00)	(0.11)
Min	0.0024	0.0052	0.0054	0.0039	0.0100	−0.0002
	(0.03)	(0.45)	(0.23)	(0.45)	(0.12)	(0.00)
Vw	0.0053	0.0042	0.0044	0.0042	0.0042	0.0042
	(0.12)	(0.04)	(0.39)	(0.44)	(0.00)	(0.00)
Mp	0.0073	0.0014	0.0034	−0.0026	0.0054	0.0053
	(0.19)	(0.05)	(0.17)	(0.04)	(0.09)	(0.10)
mv-c	0.0040	0.0023	0.0032	0.0030	0.0090	0.0075
	(0.29)	(0.10)	(0.29)	(0.28)	(0.03)	(0.42)
bs-c	0.0052	0.0031	0.0031	0.0038	0.0088	0.0074
	(0.36)	(0.15)	(0.23)	(0.46)	(0.05)	(0.44)
min-c	0.0024	0.0047	0.0054	0.0039	0.0060	0.0051
	(0.01)	(0.40)	(0.21)	(0.45)	(0.12)	(0.17)
g-min-c	0.0044	0.0048	0.0051	0.0038	0.0067	0.0070
	(0.04)	(0.41)	(0.28)	(0.40)	(0.17)	(0.45)
mv-min	0.0021	−0.2337	−0.0066	0.0044	−0.0875	−0.0318
	(0.07)	(0.00)	(0.01)	(0.28)	(0.00)	(0.07)
ew-min	0.0037	0.0052	0.0050	0.0039	0.0093	−0.0002
	(0.04)	(0.42)	(0.24)	(0.43)	(0.12)	(0.00)

For each of the empirical datasets listed in Table 2, this table reports the monthly CEQ return for the 1/N strategy, the in-sample CEQ return of the mean-variance strategy, and the out-of-sample CEQ returns for the strategies from the models of optimal asset allocation listed in Table 1. In parentheses is the *p*-value of the difference between the Sharpe ratio of each strategy from that of the 1/N benchmark, which is computed using the Jobson and Korkie (1981) methodology described in Section 2. The results for the "FF-3-factor" dataset are not reported because these are very similar to those for the "FF-1-factor" dataset.

3.1 Sharpe Ratios

The first row of Table 34-3 gives the Sharpe ratio of the naive 1/N benchmark strategy for the various datasets being considered.[20] The second row of the table, "mv (in-sample)," gives the Sharpe ratio of the Markowitz mean-variance strategy *in-sample*, that is, when there is no estimation error; by construction, this is the highest Sharpe ratio of all the strategies considered. Note that the magnitude of the difference between the in-sample Sharpe ratio for the mean-variance strategy and the 1/N strategy gives a measure of the loss from naive rather than optimal diversification when

there is no estimation error. For the datasets we are considering, this difference is substantial. For example, for the first dataset considered in Table 34-3 ("S&P Sectors"), the in-sample mean-variance portfolio has a monthly Sharpe ratio of 0.3848, while the Sharpe ratio of the 1/N strategy is less than half, only 0.1876. Similarly, in the last column of this table (for the "FF-4-factor" dataset), the in-sample Sharpe ratio for the mean-variance strategy is 0.5364, while that for the 1/N strategy is only 0.1753.

To assess the magnitude of the potential gains that can actually be realized by an investor, it is necessary to analyze the *out-of-sample*

Table 34-5. Portfolio Turnovers for Empirical Data

Strategy	S&P Sectors N = 11	Industry Portfolios N = 11	Inter'l Portfolios N = 9	Mkt/SMB/ HML N = 3	FF-1-Factor N = 21	FF-4-Factor N = 24
1/N	0.0305	0.0216	0.0293	0.0237	0.0162	0.0198
Panel A: Relative turnover of each strategy						
mv (in sample)	–	–	–	–	–	–
Mv	38.99	606594.36	4475.81	2.83	10466.10	3553.03
Bs	22.41	10621.23	1777.22	1.85	11796.47	3417.81
dm (σα = 1.0%)	1.72	21744.35	60.97	76.30	918.40	32.46
Min	6.54	21.65	7.30	1.11	45.47	6.83
Vw	0	0	0	0	0	0
Mp	1.10	11.98	6.29	59.41	2.39	2.07
mv-c	4.53	7.17	7.23	4.12	17.53	13.82
bs-c	3.64	7.22	6.10	3.65	17.32	13.07
min-c	2.47	2.58	2.27	1.11	3.93	1.76
g-min-c	1.30	1.52	1.47	1.09	1.78	1.70
mv-min	19.82	9927.09	760.57	2.61	4292.16	4857.19
ew-min	4.82	15.66	4.24	1.11	34.10	6.80
Panel B: Return-loss relative to 1/N (per month)						
mv (in sample)	–	–	–	–	–	–
Mv	0.0145	231.8504	1.1689	0.0003	7.4030	1.5740
Bs	0.0092	9.4602	0.3798	−0.0004	2.0858	1.1876
dm (σα = 1.0%)	0.0021	8.9987	0.0130	0.0393	0.1302	−0.0007
Min	0.0048	0.0015	0.0000	−0.0004	−0.0008	0.0024
Vw	−0.0001	0.0037	0.0012	0.0157	0.0021	0.0028
Mp	0.0001	0.0050	0.0021	0.0227	0.0023	0.0030
mv-c	0.0085	0.0048	0.0034	0.0041	−0.0005	0.0002
bs-c	0.0061	0.0038	0.0030	0.0023	−0.0004	−0.0000
min-c	0.0042	−0.0001	−0.0007	−0.0004	0.0006	−0.0025
g-min-c	0.0019	−0.0003	−0.0006	−0.0003	0.0001	−0.0029
mv-min	0.0085	6.8115	0.1706	−0.0003	0.9306	1.8979
ew-min	0.0030	0.0008	−0.0001	−0.0004	−0.0011	0.0024

For each of the empirical datasets listed in Table 2, the first line of this table reports the monthly turnover for the 1/N strategy, panel A reports the turnover for the strategies from each optimizing model *relative* to the turnover of the 1/N model, and panel B reports the return-loss, which is the extra return a strategy needs to provide in order that its Sharpe ratio equal that of the 1/N strategy in the presence of proportional transactions costs of 50 basis points. The results for the "FF-3-factor" dataset are not reported because these are very similar to those for the "FF-1-factor" dataset.

performance of the strategies from the optimizing models. The difference between the mean-variance strategy's in-sample and out-of-sample Sharpe ratios allows us to gauge the severity of the estimation error. This comparison delivers striking results. From the out-of-sample Sharpe ratio reported in the row titled "mv" in Table 34-3, we see that for *all* the datasets, the sample-based mean-variance strategy has a substantially lower Sharpe ratio out of sample than in-sample. Moreover, the out-of-sample Sharpe ratio for the sample-based mean-variance strategy is less than that for the 1/N strategy for all but one of the datasets, with the exception being the "FF-4-factor" dataset (though the difference is statistically insignificant). That is, the effect of estimation error is so large that it erodes completely the gains from optimal diversification. For instance, for the dataset "S&P Sectors," the sample-based mean-variance portfolio has a Sharpe ratio of only 0.0794 compared to its in-sample value of 0.3848, and 0.1876 for the 1/N strategy. Similarly, for the "International" dataset, the in-sample Sharpe ratio for the mean-variance strategy is 0.2090, which drops to −0.0332 out of sample, while the Sharpe ratio of the $1/N$ strategy is 0.1277.

The comparisons of Sharpe ratios confirm the well-known perils of using classical sample-based estimates of the moments of asset returns to implement Markowitz's mean-variance portfolios. Thus, our first observation is that *out of sample*, the $1/N$ strategy typically outperforms the sample-based mean-variance strategy if one were to make no adjustment at all for the presence of estimation error.

But what about the out-of-sample performance of optimal-allocation strategies that explicitly account for estimation error? Our second observation is that, in general, Bayesian strategies do not seem to be very effective at dealing with estimation error. In Table 34-3, the Bayes-Stein strategy, "bs," has a lower out-of-sample Sharpe ratio than the $1/N$ strategy for all the datasets except "MKT/SMB/HML" and "FF-4-factor," and even in these cases the difference is not statistically significant at conventional levels (the p-values are 0.25 and 0.48, respectively). In fact, the Sharpe ratios for the Bayes-Stein portfolios are only slightly better than that for the sample-based mean-variance portfolio. The reason why in our datasets the Bayes-Stein strategy yields only a small improvement over the out-of-sample mean-variance strategy can be traced back to the fact that while the Bayes-Stein approach does shrink the portfolio weights, the resulting weights are still much closer to the out-of-sample mean-variance weights than to the in-sample optimal weights.[21] The Data-and-Model strategy, "dm," in which the investor's prior on the mispricing α of the model (CAPM; Fama and French, 1993; or Carhart, 1997) has a tightness of 1% per annum ($\sigma_\alpha = 1.0\%$), improves over the Bayes-Stein approach for three datasets—"S&P Sectors," "International," and "FF-4-factor." However, the "dm" strategy outperforms the $1/N$ strategy only for the "FF-4-factor" dataset, in which the "dm" strategy with $\sigma_\alpha = 1\%$ achieves a Sharpe ratio of 0.2355, which is larger than the Sharpe ratio of 0.1753 for the $1/N$ strategy, but the difference is statistically insignificant (the p-value is 0.17). As we document in the appendix

"Implementation Details and Robustness Checks" that is available from the authors, the improved performance of the "dm" strategy for the "FF-4-factor" dataset is because the Carhart (1997) model provides a good description of the cross-sectional returns for the size- and book-to-market portfolios.

Our third observation is about the portfolios that are based on restrictions on the moments of returns. From the row in Table 34-3 for the minimum-variance strategy titled "min," we see that ignoring the estimates of expected returns altogether but exploiting the information about correlations does lead to better performance, relative to the out-of-sample mean-variance strategy "mv" in all datasets but "FF-4-factor." Ignoring mean returns is very successful in reducing the extreme portfolio weights: the out-of-sample portfolio weights under the minimum-variance strategy are much more reasonable than under the sample-based mean-variance strategy. For example, in the "International" dataset, the minimum-variance portfolio weight on the World index ranges from −140% to + 124% rather than ranging from −148195% to + 116828% as it did for the mean-variance strategy. Although the $1/N$ strategy has a higher Sharpe ratio than the minimum-variance strategy for the datasets "S&P Sectors," and "FF-4-factor," for the "Industry," "International," and "MKT/SMB/HML" datasets, the minimum-variance strategy has a higher Sharpe ratio, but the difference is not statistically significant (the p-values are greater than 0.20); only for the "FF-1-factor" dataset is the difference in Sharpe ratios statistically significant. Similarly, the value-weighted market portfolio has a lower Sharpe ratio than the $1/N$ benchmark in all the datasets, which is partly because of the small-firm effect. The out-of-sample Sharpe ratio for the "mp" approach proposed by MacKinlay and Pástor (2000) is also less than that of the $1/N$ strategy for all the datasets we consider.

Our fourth observation is that contrary to the view commonly held among practitioners, constraints alone do not improve performance sufficiently; that is, the Sharpe ratio of the sample-based mean-variance-*constrained* strategy, "mv-c," is less than that of the benchmark

$1/N$ strategy for the "S&P Sectors," "Industry," "International," and "MKT/SMB/HML" datasets (with p-values of 0.09, 0.03, 0.17, and 0.02, respectively), while the opposite is true for the "FF-1-factor" and "FF-4-factor" datasets, with the difference being statistically significant only for the "FF-1-factor" dataset. Similarly, the Bayes-Stein strategy with shortsale constraints, "bs-c," has a lower Sharpe ratio than the $1/N$ strategy for the first four datasets, and outperforms the naive strategy only for the "FF-1-factor" and "FF-4-factor" datasets, but again with the p-value significant only for the "FF-1-factor" dataset.

Our fifth observation is that strategies that *combine* portfolio constraints with some form of shrinkage of expected returns are usually much more effective in reducing the effect of estimation error. This can be seen, for example, by examining the *constrained*-minimum-variance strategy, "min-c," which shrinks completely (by ignoring them) the estimate of expected returns, while at the same time shrinking the extreme values of the covariance matrix by imposing shortsale constraints. The results indicate that while the $1/N$ strategy has a higher Sharpe ratio than the "min-c" strategy for the "S&P Sectors" and "FF-1-factor" datasets, the reverse is true for the "Industry," "International," "MKT/SMB/HML," and "FF-4-factor" datasets, although the differences are statistically significant only for the "FF-4-factor" dataset. This finding suggests that it may be best to ignore the data on expected returns, but still exploit the correlation structure between assets to reduce risk, with the constraints helping to reduce the effect of the error in estimating the covariance matrix. The benefit from combining constraints and shrinkage is also evident for the generalized minimum-variance policy, "g-min-c," which has a higher Sharpe ratio than $1/N$ in all but two datasets, "S&P Sectors" and "FF-1-factor," although the superior performance is statistically significant for only the "FF-4-factor" dataset.[22]

Finally, the two mixture portfolios, "mv-min" and "ew-min," described in Sections 1.6.1 and 1.6.2, do not outperform $1/N$ in a statistically significant way.

3.2 Certainty Equivalent Returns

The comparison of CEQ returns in Table 34-4 confirms the conclusions from the analysis of Sharpe ratios: the in-sample mean-variance strategy has the highest CEQ return, but out of sample none of the strategies from the optimizing models can consistently earn a CEQ return that is statistically superior to that of the $1/N$ strategy. In fact, in only two cases are the CEQ returns from optimizing models statistically superior to the CEQ return from the $1/N$ model. This happens in the "FF-1-factor" dataset, in which the constrained-mean-variance portfolio "mv-c" has a CEQ return of 0.0090 and the "bs-c" strategy has a CEQ return of 0.0088, while the $1/N$ strategy has a CEQ of 0.0073, with the p-values of the differences being 0.03 and 0.05, respectively.

3.3 Portfolio Turnover

Table 34-5 contains the results for portfolio turnover, our third metric of performance. The first line reports the actual turnover of the $1/N$ strategy. Panel A reports the turnover of all the strategies relative to that of the $1/N$ strategy, and in panel B we report the return-loss, as defined in Equation 34-17.

From panel A of Table 34-5, we see that in all cases the turnover for the portfolios from the optimizing models is much higher than for the benchmark $1/N$ strategy. Comparing the turnover across the various datasets, it is evident that the turnover of the strategies from the optimizing models is smaller, relative to the $1/N$ policy in the "MKT/SMB/HML" dataset than in the other datasets. This is not surprising given the fact that two of the three assets in this dataset, HML and SMB, are already actively managed portfolios and, as explained above, because the number of assets in this dataset is small ($N = 3$), the estimation problem is less severe. This is also confirmed by panel B of the table, where for the "MKT/SMB/HML" dataset several strategies have a return-loss that is slightly negative, implying that even in the presence of proportional transactions costs, these strategies attain a higher Sharpe ratio than that of the $1/N$ strategy.

Comparing the portfolio turnover for the different optimizing models, we see that the turnover for the sample-based mean-variance portfolio, "mv," is substantially greater than that for the 1/N strategy. The Bayes-Stein portfolio, "bs," has less turnover than the sample-based mean-variance portfolio, and the Data-and-Model Bayesian approach, "dm," is also usually successful in reducing turnover, relative to the mean-variance portfolio. The minimum-variance portfolio, "min," is even more successful in reducing turnover, and the MacKinlay and Pástor (2000) strategy is yet more successful. Also, as one would expect, the strategies with shortsale constraints have much lower turnover than their unconstrained counterparts. From panel B of Table 34-5, we see that for some of the datasets the "min-c" and "g-min-c" strategies have a slightly negative return-loss, implying that in these cases these strategies achieve a higher Sharpe ratio than that of the 1/N strategy even in the presence of proportional transactions costs.

3.4 Summary of Findings from the Empirical Datasets

From the above discussion, we conclude that of the strategies from the optimizing models, there is no single strategy that always dominates the 1/N strategy in terms of Sharpe ratio. In general, the 1/N strategy has Sharpe ratios that are higher (or statistically indistinguishable) relative to the constrained policies, which, in turn, have Sharpe ratios that are higher than those for the unconstrained policies. In terms of CEQ, no strategy from the optimal models is consistently better than the benchmark 1/N strategy. And in terms of turnover, only the "vw" strategy, in which the investor holds the market portfolio and does not trade at all, is better than the 1/N strategy.

4. RESULTS FROM STUDYING ANALYTICALLY THE ESTIMATION ERROR

This section examines analytically some of the determinants of the empirical results identified previously. Our objective is to understand why the strategies from the various optimizing models do not perform better relative to the 1/N strategy. Our focus is on identifying the relation between the expected performance (measured in terms of the CEQ of returns) of the strategies from the various optimizing models and that of the 1/N strategy, as a function of: (i) the number of assets, N; (ii) the length of the estimation window, M; (iii) the ex ante Sharpe ratio of the mean-variance strategy; and (iv) the Sharpe ratio of the 1/N strategy.

As in Kan and Zhou (2007), we treat the portfolio weights as an estimator, that is, as a function of the data. The optimal portfolio can therefore be determined by directly solving the problem of finding the weights that maximize expected utility, instead of first estimating the moments on which these weights depend, and then constructing the corresponding portfolio rules. Applying this insight, we derive a measure of the expected loss incurred in using a particular portfolio strategy that is based on estimated rather than true moments.

Let us consider an investor who chooses a vector of portfolio weights, x, to maximize the following mean-variance utility [see Equation 34-2]:

$$U(x) = x^T \mu - \frac{\gamma}{2} x^T \Sigma x \qquad (34\text{-}18)$$

The optimal weight is $x^* = \frac{1}{\gamma} \Sigma^{-1} \mu$, and the corresponding optimized utility is

$$U(x^*) = \frac{1}{2\gamma} \mu \Sigma^{-1} \mu \equiv \frac{1}{2\gamma} S_*^2, \qquad (34\text{-}19)$$

in which $S_*^2 = \mu \Sigma^{-1} \mu$ is the squared Sharpe ratio of the ex ante tangency portfolio of risky assets. Because μ and Σ are not known, the optimal portfolio weight is also unknown, and is estimated as a function of the available data:

$$\hat{x} = f(R_1, R_2, \ldots, R_M). \qquad (34\text{-}20)$$

We define the expected loss from using a particular estimator of the weight $\hat{x}$ as

$$L(x^*, \hat{x}) = U(x^*) - E[U(\hat{x})], \qquad (34\text{-}21)$$

in which the expectation $E[U(x)]$ represents the average utility realized by an investor who "plays" the strategy $\hat{x}$ infinitely many times.

When using the sample-based mean-variance portfolio policy, $\hat{x}^{mv}$, μ and Σ are estimated from their sample counterparts, $\hat{\mu} = \frac{1}{M}\Sigma_{t=1}^{M} R_t$ and $\hat{\Sigma} = \frac{1}{M}\Sigma_{t=1}^{M}\left(R_t - \hat{\mu}\right)\left(R_t - \hat{\mu}\right)^T$, and the expression for the optimal portfolio weight is $\hat{x} = \frac{1}{\gamma}\hat{\Sigma}^{-1}\hat{\mu}$. Under the assumption that the distribution of returns is jointly normal, $\hat{\mu}$ and $\hat{\Sigma}$ are independent and are distributed as follows: $\hat{\mu} \sim N(\mu, \Sigma/M)$ and $M\hat{\Sigma} \sim W_N(M-1, \Sigma)$, in which $W_N(M-1, \Sigma)$ denotes a Wishart distribution with $M-1$ degrees of freedom and covariance matrix Σ.

Following an approach similar to that in Kan and Zhou (2007), we derive the expected loss from using the 1/N rule. By comparing the expected loss, L_{mv}, from using the sample-based mean-variance policy to the expected loss, L_{ew}, from using the 1/N strategy, we can analyze the conditions under which the 1/N rule is expected to deliver a lower/higher expected loss than the mean-variance policy. To facilitate the comparison between these policies, we define the *critical value* M^*_{mv} of the sample-based mean-variance strategy as the smallest number of estimation periods necessary for the mean-variance portfolio to outperform, on average, the 1/N rule. Formally,

$$M^*_{mv} \equiv \inf\{M : L_{mv}(x^*, \hat{x}) < L_{ew}(x^*, w^{ew})\}. \quad (34\text{-}22)$$

Just as in Kan and Zhou, we consider three cases: (1) the vector of expected returns is not known, but the covariance matrix of returns is known; (2) the vector of expected returns is known, but the covariance matrix of returns is not; and (3) both the vector of expected returns and the covariance matrix are unknown and need to be estimated. The following proposition derives the conditions for the sample-based mean-variance rule to outperform the 1/N rule for these three cases.

Proposition 1. Let $S^2_* = \mu\Sigma^{-1}\mu$ be the squared Sharpe ratio of the tangency (mean-variance)

portfolio of risky assets and $S^2_{ew} = \left(1_N^T\mu\right)^2/1_N^T\Sigma1_N$ the squared Sharpe ratio of the 1/N portfolio. Then:

1. If μ is unknown and Σ is known, the sample-based mean-variance strategy has a lower expected loss than the 1/N strategy if:

$$S^2_* - S^2_{ew} - \frac{N}{M} > 0. \quad (34\text{-}23)$$

2. If μ is known and Σ is unknown, the sample-based mean-variance strategy has a lower expected loss than the 1/N strategy if:

$$kS^2_* - S^2_{ew} > 0, \quad (34\text{-}24)$$

where $k = \left(\dfrac{M}{M-N-2}\right)$

$$\left(2 - \frac{M(M-2)}{(M-N-1)(M-N-4)}\right) < 1. \quad (34\text{-}25)$$

3. If both μ and Σ are unknown, the sample-based mean-variance strategy has a lower expected loss than the 1/N strategy if:

$$kS^2_* - S^2_{ew} - h > 0, \quad (34\text{-}26)$$

where $h = \dfrac{N\,M(M-2)}{(M-N-1)(M-N-2)(M-N-4)} > 0.$

$$(34\text{-}27)$$

From the inequality (34-23), we see that if μ is unknown but Σ is known, then the sample-based mean-variance strategy is more likely to outperform the 1/N strategy if the number of periods over which the parameters are estimated, M, is high and if the number of available assets, N, is low. Because k in Equation 34-25 is increasing in M and decreasing in N, the inequality (24) shows that also for the case where μ is known but Σ is unknown, the sample-based mean-variance policy is more likely to outperform the 1/N strategy as M increases and N decreases. Finally, for the case in which both parameters are unknown, we note that because $h > 0$, the left-hand side of Equation 34-26 is always smaller than the left-hand side of Equation 34-24.

To illustrate the implications of Proposition 1 above, we compute the critical value M^*_{mv}, as defined in Equation 34-22, for the three cases considered in the proposition. In Figure 34-1, we plot the critical length of the estimation period for these three cases, as a function of the number of assets, for different values of the *ex ante* Sharpe ratios of the tangency portfolio, S^*, and of the $1/N$ portfolio, S_{ew} We calibrate our choice of S^* and S_{ew} to the Sharpe ratios reported in Table 34-3 for empirical data. From Table 34-3, we see that the in-sample Sharpe ratio for the mean-variance strategy is about 40% for the S&P Sectors dataset, about 20% for the Industry and International datasets, and about 15% for the value-weighted market portfolio; so we consider these as the three representative values of the Sharpe ratio of the tangency portfolio: $S^* = 0.40$ (panels A and B), $S^* = 0.20$ (panels C and D), and $S^* = 0.15$ (panels E and F). From Table 34-3, we also see that the Sharpe ratio for the $1/N$ strategy is about half of that for the in-sample mean-variance strategy. So, in panel A, we set the Sharpe ratio of the $1/N$ strategy to be $S_{ew} = 0.20$, and in panel C we set this to be 0.10. We also wish to consider a more extreme setting in which the *ex ante* Sharpe ratio of the $1/N$ portfolio is much smaller than that for the mean-variance portfolio—only a quarter rather than a half of the Sharpe ratio of the in-sample mean-variance portfolio, S^*; so, in panel B we set $S_{ew} = 0.10$, and in panel D we set it to 0.05. Similarly, for panels E and F, which are calibrated to data for the US stock market, we set $S_{ew} = 0.12$ and $S_{ew} = 0.08$, respectively.

There are two interesting observations from Figure 34-1. First, as expected, a large part of the effect of estimation error is attributable to estimation of the mean. We can see this by noticing that the critical value for a given number of assets N increases going from the case in which the mean is known (dash-dotted line) to the case in which it is not known. Second, and more importantly, the magnitude of the critical number of estimation periods is striking. In panel A, in which the *ex ante* Sharpe ratio for the mean-variance policy is 0.40 and that for the $1/N$ policy is 0.20, we see that with 25 assets, the estimation window required for the mean-variance policy to outperform the $1/N$ strategy is more than 200

months; with 50 assets, this increases to about 600 months; and, with 100 assets, it is more than 1200 months. Even for the more extreme case considered in panel B, in which the Sharpe ratio of the $1/N$ portfolio is only one-fourth that of the mean-variance portfolio, the critical length of the estimation period does not decrease substantially—it is 270 months for 25 assets, 530 months for 50 assets, and 1060 months for 100 assets.

Reducing the *ex ante* Sharpe ratio of the mean-variance portfolio increases the critical length of the estimation window required for it to outperform the $1/N$ benchmark; this explains, at least partly, the relatively good performance of the optimal strategies for the "FF-1-factor" and "FF-4-factor" datasets, for which the Sharpe ratio of the in-sample mean-variance policy is around 0.50, which is much higher than in the other datasets. From panel C of Figure 34-1, in which the Sharpe ratio of the mean-variance portfolio is 0.20 and that for the $1/N$ portfolio is 0.10, we see that if there are 25 assets over which wealth is to be allocated, then for the mean-variance strategy that relies on estimation of both mean and covariances to outperform the $1/N$ rule on average, about 1000 months of data are needed. If the number of assets is 50, the length of the estimation window increases to about 2000 months. Even in the more extreme case considered in panel D, in which the $1/N$ rule has a Sharpe ratio that is only one-quarter that of the mean-variance portfolio, with 50 assets the number of estimation periods required for the sample-based mean-variance model to outperform the $1/N$ policy is over 1500 months. This is even more striking in panels E and F, which are calibrated to data for the U.S. stock market. In panel E, we find that for a portfolio with 25 assets, the estimation window needed for the sample-based mean-variance policy to outperform the $1/N$ policy is more than 3000 months, and for a portfolio with 50 assets, it is more than 6000 months. Even in panel F, in which the Sharpe ratio for the $1/N$ portfolio is only 0.08, for a portfolio with 25 assets, the estimation window needed is more than 1600 months, and for a portfolio with 50 assets, it is more than 3200 months.

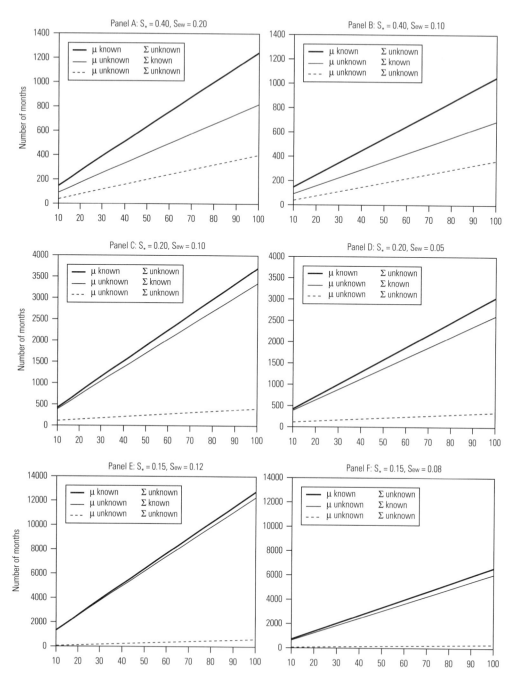

Figure 34-1. Number of estimation months for mean-variance portfolio to outperform the 1/N benchmark. The six panels in this figure show the critical number of estimation months required for the sample-based mean-variance strategy to outperform the 1/N rule on average, as a function of the number of assets, N. Each panel is drawn for different levels of the Sharpe ratios for the *ex ante* mean-variance portfolio, S^*, and the equally weighted portfolio, S_{ew}. Critical values are computed using the definition in Equation 34-22. The dashed-dotted line reports the critical value of the estimation window for the case in which the means are known, but the covariances are not. The dashed line refers to the case in which the covariances are known, but the means are not. And the solid line refers to the case in which neither the means nor the covariances are known.

5. RESULTS FOR OTHER SPECIFICATIONS: ROBUSTNESS CHECKS

In the benchmark case reported in Tables 3–5, we have assumed that: (i) the length of the estimation window is $M = 120$ months rather than $M = 60$; (ii) the estimation window is rolling, rather than increasing with time; (iii) the holding period is one month rather than one year; (iv) the portfolio evaluated is that consisting of only-risky assets rather than one that also includes the risk-free asset; (v) one can invest also in the factor portfolios; (vi) the performance is measured relative to the $1/N$-with-rebalancing strategy, rather than the $1/N$-buy-and-hold strategy; (vii) the investor has a risk aversion of $\gamma = 1$, rather than some other value of risk aversion, say $\gamma = \{2, 3, 4, 5, 10\}$; and (viii) the investor's level of confidence in the asset-pricing model is $\sigma_\alpha = 1\%$ per annum, rather than 2% or 0.5%. To check whether our results are sensitive to these assumptions, we generate tables for the Sharpe ratio, CEQ returns, and turnover for all policies and empirical datasets considered after relaxing each of the assumptions aforementioned. In addition, based on each of these three measures, we also report the rankings of the various strategies. Because of the large number of tables for these robustness experiments, we have collected the results for these experiments in a separate appendix titled "Implementation Details and Robustness Checks," which is available from the authors. The main insight from these robustness checks is that the relative performance reported in the paper for the various strategies is not very sensitive to any of these assumptions.

6. CONCLUSIONS

We have compared the performance of 14 models of optimal asset allocation, relative to that of the benchmark $1/N$ policy. This comparison is undertaken using seven different empirical datasets as well as simulated data. We find that the *out-of-sample* Sharpe ratio of the sample-based mean-variance strategy is much lower than that of the $1/N$ strategy, indicating

that the errors in estimating means and covariances erode all the gains from optimal, relative to naive, diversification. We also find that the various extensions to the sample-based mean-variance model that have been proposed in the literature to deal with the problem of estimation error typically do not outperform the $1/N$ benchmark for the seven empirical datasets. In summary, we find that of the various optimizing models in the literature, there is no single model that consistently delivers a Sharpe ratio or a CEQ return that is higher than that of the $1/N$ portfolio, which also has a very low turnover.

To understand the poor performance of the optimizing models, we derive analytically the length of the estimation period needed before the sample-based mean-variance strategy can be expected to achieve a higher certainty-equivalent return than the $1/N$ benchmark. For parameters calibrated to US stock-market data, we find that for a portfolio with only 25 assets, the estimation window needed is more than 3000 months, and for a portfolio with 50 assets, it is more than 6000 months, while typically these parameters are estimated using 60–120 months of data. Using simulated data, we show that the various extensions to the sample-based mean-variance model that have been designed to deal with estimation error reduce only moderately the estimation window needed for these models to outperform the naive $1/N$ benchmark.

These findings have two important implications. First, while there has been considerable progress in the design of optimal portfolios, more energy needs to be devoted to improving the estimation of the moments of asset returns and to using not just statistical but also other available information about stock returns. As our evaluation of the approach proposed in Brandt, Santa-Clara, and Valkanov (2007) shows, exploiting information about the cross-sectional characteristics of assets may be a promising direction to pursue. Second, in order to evaluate the performance of a particular strategy for optimal asset allocation, proposed either by academic research or by the investment-management industry, the $1/N$ naive-diversification rule should serve at least as a first obvious benchmark.

ACKNOWLEDGMENTS

We wish to thank Matt Spiegel (the editor), two anonymous referees, and Lubos Pástor for extensive comments; John Campbell and Luis Viceira for their suggestions and for making available their data and computer codes; and Robert Wessels for making available data on the ten sector portfolios of the S & P 500 Index. We also gratefully acknowledge the comments from Pierluigi Balduzzi, John Birge, Michael Brennan, Ian Cooper, Bernard Dumas, Bruno Gerard, Francisco Gomes, Eric Jacquier, Chris Malloy, Francisco Nogales, Anna Pavlova, Lorianna Pelizzon, Nizar Touzi, Sheridan Titman, Rossan Valisanov, Yihong Xia, Tan Wang, Zhenyu Wang, and seminar participants at BI Norwegian School of Management, HEC Lausanne, HEC Montreal, London Business School, Manchester Business School, Stockholm School of Economics, University of Mannheim, University of Texas at Austin, University of Venice, University of Vienna, the Second McGill Conference on Global Asset Management, the 2004 International Symposium on Asset Allocation and Pension Management at Copenhagen Business School, the 2005 Conference on Developments in Quantitative Finance at the Isaac Newton Institute for Mathematical Sciences at Cambridge University, the 2009 Workshop on Optimization in Finance at the University of Coimbra, the 2005 meeting of the Western Financial Association, the 2005 annual meeting of INFORMS, the 2005 Conference of the Institute for Quantitative Investment Research (Inquire UK), the 2006 NBER Summer Institute, the 2006 meeting of the European Finance Association, and the First Annual Meeting of the Swiss Finance Institute.

NOTES

1. Babylonian Talmud: Tractate Baba Mezi'a, folio 42a.
2. Some of the results on mean-variance portfolio choice in Markowitz (1952, 1956, 1959) and Roy (1952) had already been anticipated in 1940 by de Finetti, an English translation of which is now available in Barone (2006).
3. For a discussion of the problems in implementing mean-variance optimal portfolios, see Hodges and Brealey (1978), Michaud (1989), Best and Grauer (1991), and Litterman (2003). For a general survey of the literature on portfolio selection, see Campbell and Viceira (2002) and Brandt (2007).
4. Another approach, proposed by Black and Litterman (1990, 1992), combines two sets of priors—one based on an equilibrium asset-pricing model and the other on the subjective views of the investor—which is not strictly Bayesian, because a Bayesian approach combines a prior with the data.
5. Michaud (1998) has advocated the use of resampling methods; Scherer (2002) and Harvey et al. (2003) discuss the various limitations of this approach.
6. For instance, Benartzi and Thaler (2001) document that investors allocate their wealth across assets using the naive $1/N$ rule. Huberman and Jiang (2006) find that participants tend to invest in only a small number of the funds offered to them, and that they tend to allocate their contributions evenly across the funds that they use, with this tendency weakening with the number of funds used.
7. Bloomfield, Leftwich, and Long (1977) show that sample-based mean-variance optimal portfolios do not outperform an equally-weighted portfolio, and Jorion (1991) finds that the equally weighted and value-weighted indices have an out-of-sample performance similar to that of the minimum-variance portfolio and the tangency portfolio obtained with Bayesian shrinkage methods.
8. Consider the following extreme two-asset example. Suppose that the true per annum mean and volatility of returns for both assets are the same, 8% and 20%, respectively, and that the correlation is 0.99. In this case, because the two assets are identical, the optimal mean-variance weights for the two assets would be 50%. If, on the other hand, the mean return on the first asset is not known and is estimated to be 9% instead of 8%, then the mean-variance model would recommend a weight of 635% in the first asset and −535% in the second. That is, the *optimization* tries to exploit even the smallest difference in the two assets by taking extreme long and short positions *without* taking into account that these differences in returns may be the result of estimation error. As we describe in Section 3, the weights from mean-variance optimization when using actual data and more than just two assets are

even more extreme than the weights in the given example.

9. The constraint that the weights sum to 1 is incorporated implicitly by expressing the optimization problem in terms of returns in excess of the risk-free rate.

10. See also Jobson and Korkie (1980), Frost and Savarino (1986), and Dumas and Jacquillat (1990) for other applications of shrinkage estimation in the context of portfolio selection.

11. Note that expected returns, μt, *do* appear in the likelihood function needed to estimate Σt. However, under the assumption of normally distributed asset returns, it is possible to show (Morrison, 1990) that for any estimator of the covariance matrix, the MLE estimator of the mean is always the sample mean. This allows one to remove the dependence on expected returns for constructing the MLE estimator of Σt.

12. MacKinlay and Pástor (2000) express the restriction in terms of the covariance matrix of *residuals* instead of returns. However, this does not affect the determination of the optimal portfolios.

13. See Sections III.B and III.C of Jagannathan and Ma (2003) for an extensive discussion of the performance of other models used for estimating the sample covariance matrix.

14. Garlappi, Uppal, and Wang (2007) consider an investor who is averse not just to risk but also to uncertainty, in the sense of Knight (1921). They show that if returns on the N assets are estimated jointly, then the "robust" portfolio is equivalent to a weighted average of the mean-variance portfolio and the minimum-variance portfolio, where the weights depend on the amount of parameter uncertainty and the investor's aversion to uncertainty. By construction, therefore, the performance of such a portfolio lies between the performances of the sample-based mean-variance portfolio and the minimum-variance portfolio. Because we report the performance for these two extreme portfolios, we do not report separately the performance of robust portfolio strategies.

15. The insights from the results for the case of $M = 60$ are not very different from those for the case of $M = 120$, and hence, in the interest of conserving space, are reported only in the separate appendix.

16. Specifically, given two portfolios i and n, with $\hat{\mu}_i, \hat{\mu}_n, \hat{\sigma}_i, \hat{\sigma}_n, \hat{\sigma}_{i,n}$ as their estimated means,

variances, and covariances over a sample of size $T - M$, the test of the hypothesis $H_0 : \mu_i / \sigma_i - \mu_n / \sigma_n = 0$ is obtained via the test statistic $\hat{z}_{JK}$, which is asymptotically distributed as a standard normal:

$$\hat{z}_{JK} = \frac{\hat{\sigma}_n \hat{\mu}_i - \hat{\sigma}_i \hat{\mu}_n}{\sqrt{\hat{\vartheta}}}, \text{ with}$$

$$\vartheta = \frac{1}{T-M} \left(2\hat{\sigma}_i^2 \hat{\sigma}_n^2 - 2\hat{\sigma}_i \hat{\sigma}_n \hat{\sigma}_{i,n} + \frac{1}{2} \hat{\mu}_i^2 \hat{\sigma}_n^2 \right.$$
$$\left. + \frac{1}{2} \hat{\mu}_n^2 \hat{\sigma}_i^2 - \frac{\hat{\mu}_i \hat{\mu}_n}{\hat{\sigma}_i \hat{\sigma}_n} \hat{\sigma}_{i,n}^2 \right).$$

Note that this statistic holds asymptotically under the assumption that returns are distributed independently and identically (IID) over time with a normal distribution. This assumption is typically violated in the data. We address this in Section 5, where we simulate a dataset with T = 24,000 monthly returns that are IID normal.

17. To be precise, the definition in Equation 34-14 refers to the level of expected utility of a mean-variance investor, and it can be shown that this is approximately the CEQ of an investor with quadratic utility. Notwithstanding this caveat, and following common practice, we interpret it as the certainty equivalent for strategy k.

18. If v denotes the vector of moments $v = (\mu_i, \mu_n, \sigma_i^2, \sigma_n^2)$, $\hat{v}$ its empirical counterpart obtained from a sample of size $T - M$, and

$$f(v) = \left(\mu_i - \frac{\gamma}{2} \sigma_i^2 \right) - \left(\mu_n - \frac{\gamma}{2} \sigma_n^2 \right) \text{ the difference}$$

in the certainty equivalent of two strategies i and n, then the asymptotic distribution of $f(v)$ (Greene, 2002) is $\sqrt{T} \left(f(\hat{v}) - f(v) \right) \rightarrow$

$$N \left(0, \frac{\partial f}{\partial v}^T \Theta \frac{\partial f}{\partial v} \right) \text{ in which}$$

$$\Theta = \begin{pmatrix} \sigma_i^2 & \sigma_{i,n} & 0 & 0 \\ \sigma_{in} & \sigma_n^2 & 0 & 0 \\ 0 & 0 & 2\sigma_i^4 & 2\sigma_{i,n}^2 \\ 0 & 0 & 2\sigma_{i,n}^2 & 2\sigma_n^4 \end{pmatrix}.$$

19. Note that while the turnover of each strategy is related to the transactions costs incurred in implementing that strategy, it is important to realize that in the presence of transactions costs, it would not be optimal to implement the same portfolio strategy.

20. Because the 1/N strategy does not rely on data, its in-sample and out-of-sample Sharpe ratios are the same.
21. The factor that determines the shrinkage of expected returns toward the mean return on the minimum-variance portfolio is $\hat{\phi}$ [see Equation 34-4]. For the datasets we are considering, $\hat{\phi}$ ranges from a low of 0.32 for the "FF-4-factor" dataset to a high of 0.66 for the "MKT/SMB/HML" dataset; thus, the Bayes-Stein strategy is still relying too much on the estimated means, $\hat{\mu}$.
22. The benefit from combining constraints and shrinkage is also present, albeit to a lesser degree, for the constrained Bayes-Stein strategy ("bs-c"), which improves upon the performance of its unconstrained counterpart in all cases except for the "MKT/SMB/HML" dataset, in which the effect of constraints is to generate corner solutions with all wealth invested in a single asset at a particular time.
23. In the interest of space, the table with the results for the case with idiosyncratic volatility of 75% is not reported in the paper.
24. As in Wang (2005), we exclude the five portfolios containing the largest firms because the market, SMB, and HML are almost a linear combination of the 25 Fama-French portfolios.

APPENDIX A

Description of the Seven Empirical Datasets

This appendix describes the seven empirical datasets considered in our study. Each dataset contains excess monthly returns over the 90-day T-bill (from Ken French's Web site). A list of the datasets considered is given in Table 2.

A.1 Sector portfolios

The "S&P Sectors" dataset consists of monthly excess returns on 10 value-weighted industry portfolios formed by using the Global Industry Classification Standard (GICS) developed by Standard & Poor's (S&P) and Morgan Stanley Capital International (MSCI). The dataset has been created by Roberto Wessels, and we are grateful to him for making it available to us. The 10 industries considered are Energy, Material,

Industrials, Consumer-Discretionary, Consumer-Staples, Healthcare, Financials, Information-Technology, Telecommunications, and Utilities. The data span from January 1981 to December 2002. We augment the dataset by adding as a factor the excess return on the US equity market portfolio, MKT, defined as the value-weighted return on all NYSE, AMEX, and NASDAQ stocks (from CRSP) minus the one-month treasury-bill rate.

A.2 Industry portfolios

The "Industry" dataset consists of monthly excess returns on 10 industry portfolios in the United States. The 10 industries considered are Consumer-Discretionary, Consumer-Staples, Manufacturing, Energy, High-Tech, Telecommunication, Wholesale and Retail, Health, Utilities, and Others. The monthly returns range from July 1963 to November 2004 and were obtained from Kenneth French's Web site. We augment the dataset by adding as a factor the excess return on the US equity market portfolio, MKT.

A.3 International equity indexes

The "International" dataset includes eight international equity indices: Canada, France, Germany, Italy, Japan, Switzerland, the UK, and the US. In addition to these country indexes, the World index is used as the factor portfolio. Returns are computed based on the month-end US-dollar value of the country equity index for the period January 1970 to July 2001. Data are from MSCI (Morgan Stanley Capital International).

A.4 MKT, SMB, and HML portfolios

The "MKT/SMB/HML" dataset is an updated version of the one used by Pástor (2000) for evaluating the Bayesian "Data-and-Model" approach to asset allocation. The assets are represented by three broad portfolios: (i) MKT, that is, the excess return on the US equity market; (ii) HML, a zero-cost portfolio that is long in high book-to-market stocks and short in low book-to-market stocks; and (iii) SMB, a zero-cost portfolio that is long in small-cap stocks and short in large-cap stocks. The data consist of monthly returns from July 1963 to November 2004. The data are taken from Kenneth French's Web site. The Data-and-Model approach is implemented by assuming that the investor takes into account his beliefs in an asset-pricing model (CAPM; Fama and French, 1993; or Carhart, 1997) when constructing the expected asset returns.

A.5 Size- and book-to-market-sorted portfolios

The data consist of monthly returns on the 20 portfolios sorted by size and book-to-market.[23] The data are obtained from Kenneth French's Web site and span from July 1963 to December 2004. This dataset is the one used by Wang (2005) to analyze the shrinkage properties of the Data-and-Model approach.[24] We use this dataset for three different experiments. In the first, denoted by "FF-1-factor," we augment the dataset by adding the MKT. We then impose that a Bayesian investor takes into account his beliefs in the CAPM to construct estimates of expected returns. In the second, denoted by "FF-3-factor," we augment the dataset by adding the MKT, and the zero-cost portfolios HML and SMB. We now assume that a Bayesian investor uses the Fama-French three-factor model to construct estimates of expected returns. In the third experiment, denoted by "FF-4-factor," we augment the size- and book-to-market-sorted portfolios with four-factor portfolios: MKT, HML, SMB, and the momentum portfolio, UMD, which is also obtained from Kenneth French's Web site. For this dataset, the investor is assumed to estimate expected returns using a four-factor model.

Introduction to Chapter 35

Parental Investment: How an Equity Motive Can Produce Inequality

Many social scientists have bought into the idea that complex problems require complex strategies to master them. This belief looms large, for instance, when researchers argue that human social environments are more complex, unpredictable, or challenging than nonsocial ones. From this assumption, some have concluded that social environments require intellectual faculties of the highest order. Only thus can we get right those decisions that require us to put ourselves in someone else's shoes and guess what they are thinking, knowing that the other person will be going through exactly the same process. The view that complexity necessitates complex strategies implies that simple heuristics are out of their league in social environments.

Challenging this implication, Hertwig and Herzog (2009) and Hertwig, Hoffrage, and the ABC Research Group (in press) have argued that human social intelligence is not qualitatively different from nonsocial intelligence, and that important parts of social intelligence can be modeled in terms of simple heuristics. The reason is that, like its nonsocial counterpart, the social world often requires people to make fast decisions based on limited and uncertain information. Under these bounds, robustness is the key concern, and robustness is, in turn, exactly what fast-and-frugal heuristics promise.

One simple heuristic that illustrates that the cognitive processes of social intelligence may not be qualitatively different from the processes of nonsocial intelligence is the $1/N$ rule or the equity heuristic. This rule has been proposed to describe how people invest their resources in N options, with the options referring to both nonsocial entities (e.g., saving options for retirement) and, as the current article argues, social entities such as children. Although derided as being naïve by behavioral economists such as Benartzi and Thaler (2001), the $1/N$ rule may outperform optimizing strategies in matters of asset allocation, especially in environments with a large degree of uncertainty, a large number of assets, and small learning samples (see Chapter 34).

Written by a psychologist (Ralph Hertwig), an evolutionary psychologist (Jennifer Davis), and a historian of science (Frank Sulloway), this article proposes and provides evidence that the $1/N$ heuristic also captures how many contemporary parents invest their resources in their offspring. Parental resources such as affection, time, and money (e.g., for education) are notoriously limited, and parents with more than one child cannot help but choose how to allocate their resources among their N children. In egalitarian societies, parents endorse the ideal of trying to treat their children equally. A heuristic that seemingly embodies and executes this ideal is the equity heuristic. It specifies that parents attempt to split resources equally among all N children at any given investment period. This simple heuristic has several interesting properties. One is its social sensitivity, which eases tensions between parents and children: By implementing an equal ("fair") allocation of resources, this heuristic takes into account people's assumed inequity aversion (e.g., Bolton & Ockenfels, 2000; Fehr & Schmidt, 1999), and allows parents to easily justify their allocation decisions to both quarreling children and observant family members (e.g., grandparents).

A counterintuitive property of the equity heuristic is that it produces different outcomes, depending on the level of aggregation. Notwithstanding parental egalitarianism at any given point in time, the cumulative resources still end up being distributed unequally, thus causing middleborns to receive fewer total resources than earlierborns or laterborns. Moreover, laterborns are predicted to receive fewer resources than earlierborns in the first period of their lives, and earlierborns fare worse than laterborns in the last period of their development. These resource inequalities, for which the authors found evidence, arise on account of the presence or absence of resource-depleting siblings at different time periods in the development of the children.

The present article also offers two interesting methodological insights. First, like economists, psychologists can test heuristics against data sets collected in the real world, here parental resource allocations. It took economists a long time to discover the powerful potential of experiments. Hopefully, it will not take psychologists equally long to discover that their theories can be tested against large-scale data collected in the wild (for an example, see Chapter 40). Another insight is that a simple heuristic—whose policy here of giving each child an equal share of the resources at any given time appears utterly transparent—can produce unexpected outcomes, dependent on the properties of the environment. Properties of the environment in the present case are, for instance, birth order, number of other children, and interbirth intervals. In interaction with these properties, the equity heuristic produces a complex and counterintuitive distribution of allocations. To come full circle: Complexity does not require complex solutions; rather, complexity can be produced by simple mechanisms. To understand such a counterintuitive phenomenon, it is not enough to grasp a heuristic's formal structure; one also needs to understand how it interacts with the structure of the environment, which can produce unintended results.

CHAPTER 35

Parental Investment: How an Equity Motive Can Produce Inequality

Ralph Hertwig, Jennifer Nerissa Davis, and Frank J. Sulloway

Abstract: The equity heuristic is a decision rule specifying that parents should attempt to subdivide resources more or less equally among their children. This investment rule coincides with the prescription from optimality models in economics and biology in cases in which expected future return for each offspring is equal. In this article, the authors present a counterintuitive implication of the equity heuristic: Whereas an equity motive produces a fair distribution at any given point in time, it yields a cumulative distribution of investments that is unequal. The authors test this analytical observation against evidence reported in studies exploring parental investment and show how the equity heuristic can provide an explanation of why the literature reports a diversity of birth order effects with respect to parental resource allocation.

Israel loved Joseph more than all his children, because he was the son of his old age: and he made him a coat of many colours. And when his brethren saw that their father loved him more than his brethren, they hated him, and they could not speak peaceably unto him.

—Book of Genesis, King James Bible

The belief that one's brother or sister is favored by one's parents has been portrayed as the key cause of antagonistic sibling relationships throughout history, not just in the story of Joseph, but in numerous other places in the Bible (e.g., in the stories of Cain and Abel and Jacob and Esau). Similar stories about parental favoritism and sibling jealousy are found in Shakespeare's plays (e.g., in *Richard III* and *King Lear*) and in the writings of John Steinbeck (e.g., *East of Eden*), to name just a few other literary instances. The consequences of this belief,

whether mistaken or correct, have often been destructive and tragic. Is this theme so pervasive throughout human history because parental favoritism is pervasive too, or is such favoritism merely a misperception on the part of jealous siblings? Or, paradoxically, could such inequality actually be the inevitable consequence of parental attempts to treat their children equally?

This last, counterintuitive possibility is the focus of this article. Leaving aside the issue of sibling rivalry (and siblings' perception of parental behavior), we direct our attention to the major factor thought to cause it: parental favoritism, or the unequal distribution of parental investment. On the basis of simple arithmetic computations, we argue that even if a parent's investment heuristic is guided by a motive of equity, such a motive could still produce inequality in the cumulative distribution of resources among children of different birth ranks.[1] In other words, we argue that even if parents attempt to invest equally, the amount of resources each child receives may still, as a consequence of birth order, be unequal.

Before we explicate this argument, let us address one likely misconception. In analyzing the consequences of equal resource allocation, we do not mean to suggest that factors that have been found to affect the allocation of parental resources are irrelevant (such as paternity uncertainty, children's temperament, or parenting experience; see e.g., Geary, 2000; Neiderhiser, Reiss, Hetherington, & Plomin, 1999). Moreover, we also do not intend to imply that parents are truly and strictly egalitarian no matter what their children's needs, abilities, social, and economic prospects are. Such claims would be naive. The aim of our analysis is, instead, to highlight an overlooked possibility—namely, that those parents who cherish a motive of equity may, all things being equal, still end up biasing investment for reasons due to the counterintuitive consequences of the equity heuristic.

This article consists of four sections: a brief exploration of how parents ought to invest in their offspring according to evolutionary biologists and economists, an exposition and analysis of the equity heuristic, a test of predictions of the equity heuristic against available evidence in the literature, and a general discussion of alternative explanations for birth order effects and the developmental implications of the equity heuristic.

HOW TO DIVIDE PARENTAL RESOURCES?

Answers from Evolutionary Biology

According to Trivers (1972), parental investment is any investment by the parent in an individual offspring that increases the offspring's chance of survival (and the offspring's reproductive potential) at the cost of the parent's ability to invest in other offspring. The most important aspects of parental investment for our purposes are that (a) it is something that parents have in only a limited supply and that (b) when faced with the task of raising offspring born at different times, investment in one offspring generally detracts from resources available for other offspring that are still under parental care. How, then, should parents distribute their limited

resources among their offspring? This is not only a very difficult but also a very important evolutionary problem for parents to solve, and we expect that natural selection has endowed them with decision-making mechanisms that provide them with good solutions. But what constitutes a good solution?

According to evolutionary theory, in particular the work of Trivers (1974), parents and children often disagree about what is a good solution for the distribution of parental resources. Such disagreement hinges on the joint influence of two factors: the *marginal value* of each unit of resource to each child and the *degree of relatedness*. According to this logic, reasoned by Trivers from Hamilton's (1964a, 1964b) inclusive fitness principle, children favor an unequal distribution of parental investment. The key to their bias is the notion of relatedness: A child shares a given gene with itself with a probability of 1.0, but it shares the same gene with a probability of only .5 with a sibling. For this reason, a child is expected to strive to monopolize a unit of resource unless the marginal value of consuming an extra unit of resource is less than the benefit, scaled by degree of relatedness, of donating the resource to its relative.[2] Parents, in contrast, share a given gene with each of their offspring with a probability of .5. Thus, they strive to divide a unit of resource equally unless the marginal benefit resulting for this unit is larger for one child compared with another.

Daly and Wilson (1988) have provided the following illustration of children and parents' conflicting interests. Suppose a mother comes home from a day of gathering with two food items to give her children, A and B. Both children have equal survival prospects and reproductive potential. With food and many other resources, there are diminishing returns associated with increased consumption. That is, the first unit of food, for example, may prevent the child from starving, whereas the second unit of food may just make the child a little bit more full. Assume that both siblings' consumption of the two food items follow the same marginal utility curve—that is, the first item would raise their survival prospects (and thus potentially add to their reproductive potential) by four units, and the second item of food would raise it an additional three units. Parent–offspring conflict arises because, from the mother's perspective, the ideal allocation would be to give one unit of food to Sibling A and one to Sibling B, thus reaping a net benefit of eight units of increase. By contrast, if one sibling monopolized all the food, the gain would only be seven units (four for the first food item plus three for the second food item). Thus, from the mother's perspective an equal allocation between her children would yield the best outcome, whereas from each sibling's perspective the ideal allocation is to monopolize all the food (the boundary condition being specified by Hamilton's 1964a, 1964b, rule; see Note 2).

Evolutionary biologists typically answer the question of what constitutes a good solution to the problem of how to allocate parental resources not by designing specific mechanisms (e.g., decision heuristics) but by identifying and modeling the selection pressures that are expected to have shaped them. Following this approach, any kind of decision heuristic that satisfies the constraints of, for instance, Hamilton's (1964a, 1964b) rule can be selected for, and decision rules that, on average, do a better job of satisfying this rule would benefit from a selective advantage.

Answers from Economics

In an economic analysis of how rational parents should optimally distribute investment among their children, Becker (1991) assumed that parents try to maximize total child quality as defined by the sum of their children's adult wealth. The quality of a child—that is, the parental payoff—is assumed to be a function of the resources invested in the child, the child's own skills and abilities, and any extra income the child might earn as an adult through sheer luck. Becker's analysis suggests that, as long as the payoff curve is the same for all children, parents should distribute investment equally among them. If, however, the abilities of some children are such that increasing the amount of investment in them relative to their siblings leads to greater payoff to parents in overall child quality, they should bias investment in favor of those children (Becker & Tomes, 1976, 1986).

Although Becker's (1991) analysis is a celebrated case of extending economic theory beyond its usual domain of application, it has the character of an "as if" approach (Elster, 1997) insofar as it validates the utility-maximizing model by the accuracy of outcome predictions rather than by the psychological plausibility of the implied processes. In fact, if one were to try to use these prescribed investment policies as decision mechanisms, their intractability would quickly become apparent. To use them as such, one has to assume that parents have some means of calculating the effects of each individual unit of investment on the future payoff they expect to gain from each child, compounded over time for every discrete investment and maximized across all children. To be able to do this, parents not only need to keep track of the effect of every act of current and potential future investment on the eventual outcome of each child (a problem of combinatorial explosion) but they also need to convert the effects of such varied types of investment as piano lessons, doctors appointments, and meals prepared into a common currency.

The problem of how actual parents make investment decisions cannot easily be solved by optimization. The range of possibilities that must be taken into account is far too vast and the number of required calculations too high. Nevertheless, the fact that it is impossible for parents to calculate the optimal investment strategy directly does not mean that parents are not using very good, albeit much simpler, decision strategies (see Chase, Hertwig, & Gigerenzer, 1998; Gigerenzer, Todd, & the ABC Research Group, 1999). What sort of decision rules could parents use? At an abstract level, the problem faced by human parents trying to figure out how to divide investment among multiple children is identical to the problem faced by any species in which multiple dependent offspring of differing ages are raised simultaneously. Such circumstances are relatively common in birds. Davis and colleagues (Davis & Todd, 1999; Davis, Todd, & Bullock, 1999) modeled the success of a variety of potential parental investment decision rules in one species, the Western bluebird. These rules specify moment-to-moment parental decisions about which chick in the nest to feed (the main currency of divisible parental investment in birds). The authors found that the success of different rules is highly dependent on the amount of resources available to parents. Specifically, the less parents have, the more biased they ought to be in their distribution of investment. Parents faced with extremely poor resources ought to invest heavily, or even exclusively, in a single chick, ignoring the others. As resources become more plentiful, parents do best by becoming gradually more egalitarian. Parents with plentiful resources, defined in this case as enough resources to successfully raise all of the chicks in the nest to adulthood, do best by using decision rules that divide these resources equally among all chicks. At a more general level, one can conclude that the degree to which parents divide current investment unequally among offspring is a function of the amount of resources available to them.

It is important to note that in this avian model, and in evolutionary biology in general, divisible parental investment is primarily understood in terms of provisioning (Clutton-Brock, 1991). Whereas this assumption is true of humans as well, it does not capture the full extent of human parental care. In particular, this assumption misses all the things that parents provide, such as education, sporting activities, or music lessons, that are seen, from an economic perspective, as investment in children's economic capital. From an evolutionary perspective, such behavior has no obvious, direct effects on survivorship, and thereby requires additional explanation. Why would parental motivation to invest include such considerations? One likely answer is that such motivation reflects an evolved disposition to invest in children's later social competitiveness, something that could evolve if social competitiveness covaried with reproductive outcomes and inversely with mortality risks, which it seems to (Boone & Kessler, 1999; for additional discussion of this and related issues, see Geary, 2000; Geary & Flinn, 2001).

Another important point is that the parent birds in the previous model faced extreme resource shortages, which were so dire that it was impossible for all of the chicks to survive. As soon as there were enough resources to keep them all alive, egalitarian division rules did the best. If one assumes that human parents typically do have enough resources available to them to raise all of their children to adulthood, especially in modern Western societies, then this assumption leads to the expectation that human parents may use a decision rule that divides investment equally among all of their children.[3]

THE EQUITY HEURISTIC

This decision rule is what we call the *equity heuristic*. The rule specifies that parents attempt to split resources equally among all children. Is there any evidence that parents use the equity heuristic? Historically, there is. In the Italian city-states of medieval Europe, wealth was mostly based on financial speculation and could be won or lost in a single generation. In this situation, "given the role that chance plays in the survival of any lineage, an equal distribution of parental investment reduces the risk that family lineage will go extinct" (Sulloway, 1996, p. 65). In fact, parents wisely hedged their genetic bets, distributing their assets equally among their children (Herlihy, 1973). But what about contemporary parents?

If parents are using the equity heuristic, this should be reflected both in parental self-reports and behavior. There is a body of evidence that suggests they do. For instance, Schooler (1972) discussed several studies from the 1960s that examine parents' reports of their treatment of children of different birth ranks and concluded that there were no differences in treatment by birth rank in the mid-1960s. According to Daniels, Dunn, Furstenberg, and Plomin (1985), this conclusion still held true in the 1980s. Zervas and Sherman (1994) argued that "as members of an egalitarian society, Americans typically espouse equal treatment of children by parents" (p. 31). Others have shown that children themselves also believe that they receive equal treatment (e.g., Plomin & Daniels, 1987). Measurement of actual parental behavior seems to validate these perceptions, as parents have been observed to be relatively egalitarian (Caldwell & Bradley, 1984; Vandell & Beckwith, 1989).

The observation of egalitarian treatment has not remained unchallenged. For instance, one study by Dunn and McGuire (1994) reported that only one mother in three says that she gives similar attention to each child. In other studies, children themselves have reported perceived differences in the treatment they and their sibling receive from parents (e.g., Daniels & Plomin, 1985; Koch, 1960), and still other researchers have demonstrated that parents consistently direct more behaviors toward younger rather than older siblings (Brody & Stoneman, 1994; Maccoby & Martin, 1983).

Although this mixed evidence suggests that at least some parents under some circumstances appear to split the resources equally among all children, there is one key finding that seems to challenge even this cautious conclusion. Does the very existence of widely documented birth order effects not exclude the equity heuristic as a plausible decision rule for how real parents make their decisions? Our answer is no, for at least two reasons.

How the Equity Heuristic Creates Inequality

One reason is that even in the face of actual equality, treatment is still perceived as unequal. Vandell and Beckwith (1989) made this observation in their study of mothers' behavior toward twins. Each twin was randomly assigned to an observer who rated the treatment received by that twin. Although there was remarkable consistency in both observers' reports of maternal behavior, during the course of the study each observer came to identify with "their" twin and reported thinking that the mothers preferred the other twin. Siblings' perception of unequal treatment might similarly be driven by sibling and parents' disparate understanding of equality. As described earlier, offspring, unlike parents, generally prefer to acquire more of any scarce resource than a sibling receives (Daly & Wilson, 1988; Hamilton, 1964a, 1964b). If birth order effects are more a function of the perceived than the actual resource distribution, then siblings may see themselves as being treated unfairly even when there is an equitable distribution.

Perhaps the most interesting reason why birth order effects may not be contrary to the application of the equity heuristic is that birth order effects can actually be a consequence of parental egalitarianism. That is, even if at any given point in time parental investment is distributed according to the equity heuristic, cumulative investment may still end up being unequal. How can this occur? Let us assume that a family has n children, all of whom are born at equal time intervals. In addition, we assume that the entire growth period can be divided into a number of time periods of equal length and that parents invest in a child during a finite number of periods. We assume that the parents' resources are limited, that is, increasing the number of children does not increase the total amount of investment they can provide. We also assume that parents use the equity heuristic, splitting resources equally among children (i.e., for n children, a proportional split means that each offspring receives $1/n$ of the total resources). As a consequence, the amount of resources obtained by a child in any given period is a function of the number of siblings it has during this same time period.

In the upper part of Figure 35-1, we present the proportion of resources obtained for a child in each of several birth ranks, in sibship sizes ranging from one to three, and across four periods of growth ("years"). The bars in the lower part of Figure 35-1 show the cumulative resource distribution for children in an only-child, a two-child, and a three-child family. Several patterns emerge from this figure. Not surprisingly, the larger the family size, the smaller the amount of received resources per child. An only child receives the most resources, followed by children in a two-child family, whereas children in a three-child family receive the least. In terms of cumulative investment (expressed as a percentage of the total resources the only child receives) children in a two-child family receive 62.5% each, and children in a three-child family receive 54%, 41.5%, and 54% respectively. There are two surprising patterns in Figure 35-1. First, despite the application of the equity heuristic, a birth order effect emerges in the three-child family (and not in the two-child family) with

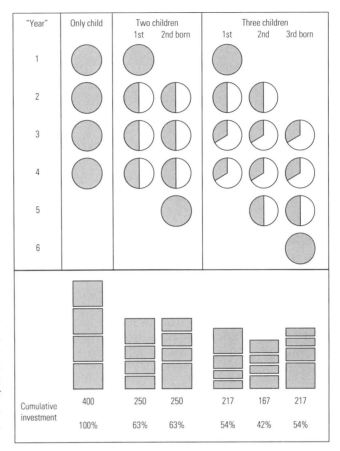

Figure 35-1. Spheres in the upper part of the figure represent resource allocation according to the equity heuristic as a function of birth rank in families with one, two, and three children. The bars in the lower part show the absolute and relative (i.e., calculated as a proportion of that for an only child) cumulative investments across four growth periods ("years").

respect to the cumulative resource distribution. Second, in this scenario one can actually observe three seemingly contradictory birth order effects, namely, a middleborn, a laterborn, and an earlierborn resource handicap. We describe each handicap in more detail.

Middleborn resource handicap. Despite the fact that resources are equally distributed among children in each year, the cumulative resources (i.e., the total amount of resources received over four periods relative to the amount received by an only child) are not the same for each child in the three-child family. Compared with the middleborn, the firstborn and the lastborn children have an advantage. The reason is simple: Unlike these other siblings, the middle child never has the opportunity to be the only child in the household at any point in its life.

The middleborn resource handicap, however, is only one of three handicaps; to understand the other two, one must first challenge a common assumption in utility-maximization models (Becker & Tomes, 1976; Taubman & Behrman, 1986), namely, that different resources can be translated into one subdividable commodity. Contrary to this assumption, various authors have argued that real organisms allocate qualitatively different types of parental resources (e.g., Borgerhoff Mulder, 1998; Frank, 1990; McGinley & Charnov, 1988; Rosenheim, Nonacs, & Mangel, 1996). Acknowledging the multidimensional nature of parental resources allows one to consider an interesting possibility. Assume that the utility function of a resource (e.g., time) is not constant across a child's growth period but rather that some resources may be more important at an earlier than at a later developmental stage. If this assumption were true, how would it affect the relative advantages or disadvantages of a specific birth rank?

Laterborn resource handicap. Assume that the presence of some resources is most critical when a child is most helpless, that is, at the very beginning of his or her life. One crucial parental currency at this stage may be time spent on child care. If this assumption is true, then the resource environment puts laterborn children at a disadvantage. In their first year, newborns (in both two-child and three-child families) receive different amounts of resources contingent on birth rank: For instance, the firstborn child in a three-child family receives 100% of these resources, whereas the middle and lastborn child only receive 50% and 33% of the resources, respectively (see upper part of Figure 35-1).

Earlierborn resource handicap. Figure 35-1 reveals still another potential birth order effect. There may be resources such as an allowance or privileges such as borrowing the car or staying out late that are exclusive to the last years of a child's development. For these resources, the earlierborn children (in both two-child and three-child families) are at disadvantage compared with the last-born, assuming that such parental resources have some critical value for development.

In sum, despite parental attempts at equality, the equity heuristic shows how three seemingly contradictory birth order effects in the distribution of parental resources can emerge. We suggest that these theoretically predicted birth order effects may help to integrate some of the diverse findings regarding parental resource allocation that exist in the birth order literature. Before we turn to this possibility, however, we ought to clarify the assumptions that underlie our analysis of the equity heuristic.

Underlying Assumptions

The simple analysis of the equity heuristic depicted in Figure 35-1 rests on several assumptions. First, we assume that the entire growth period can be divided into a number of intervals of equal length. For simplicity, we label those intervals *years.* This label is not meant to imply that parents conceive of allocation schedules based on a yearly basis. Rather, the equity heuristic assumes that parents try to distribute their resources fairly among their children during a

given arbitrary unit of time. Second, we assume that the parents' resource budget is limited and stable, a reasonable assumption for currencies such as time, attention, and emotional energy. In these cases, new demands, such as the addition of a newborn infant to the family, must be met at the cost of old demands—for example, the time devoted to the newborn's older siblings. In contrast, financial resources are limited but also likely to increase as a function of increasing age of parents. Thus, a new child does not necessarily force parents to decrease their monetary investment in older offspring if the new demand can be compensated by a larger budget or by reallocating resources.

Finally, in Figure 35-1 we assume that resources are split equally among children. How plausible is this assumption? Although we have described several studies that are consistent with it, we do not mean to suggest that equal splitting of resources is ubiquitously applied regardless of important circumstances such as the family's economic condition or children's age-specific needs (an important issue to which we return in the General Discussion section). Rather, the aim of our analysis is to highlight the possibility that birth order effects can at least in principle arise from parental attempts at equal treatment. In other words, unequal output (i.e., birth order effects) does not require unequal input (e.g., discriminatory parental behavior).

Moderating Circumstances

Research on the potential effects of birth order has often been criticized for its lack of control of confounding variables (e.g., Ernst & Angst, 1983). Note the words of Lindert (1977), for instance:

> [The] entire literature remains vulnerable to a single line of attack: other important variables have not been held constant, and any correlation between these omitted variables and sibling position ... can yield misleading estimates of the impact of the latter (p. 199).

The simple analysis displayed in Figure 35-1 affords us the opportunity to describe how other variables affect the distribution of resources, assuming that parents use the equity heuristic.

We focus on three variables frequently mentioned, length of growth period, interbirth interval, and sibship size, and discuss how each variable interacts with the resource handicaps we have identified.

Length of growth period. As shown earlier, the cumulative resources of a middle child are smaller than those of its elder and younger siblings because the middle child lacks the opportunity to be the only child in the household at any time in its life. This handicap, however, is moderated by the length of the growth period. For the sake of argument, assume that a child is mature after eight periods rather than after four periods, as we posit in Figure 35-1. How does the size of the mature middleborn handicap change? Some simple arithmetic calculations show that in this case the cumulative resources for a three-child family would be 44%, 37%, and 44% for the firstborn, secondborn, and thirdborn child, respectively (expressed as a percentage of the total resources the only child receives). Thus, compared with the size of the difference between the middle child and its younger and older siblings in Figure 35-1, the handicap decreases, becoming 7 as opposed to 12 percentage points. The longer the time of parental care, all things being equal, the smaller the middleborn handicap. The reason is that the proportion of the total child-care time, in which the younger and elder siblings benefit by having some period of exclusive attention, becomes smaller.

Interbirth interval. Although dependency may be slightly reduced when compared with that of infants, children's reliance on their parents is certainly not over after the first 3 or 4 years. One way to mitigate a resource allocation dilemma is to avoid or reduce the overlap of sequential offspring. The Ache, hunter–gatherers of eastern Paraguay, are reported to use infanticide as a mechanism to increase child spacing (e.g., K. Hill & Hurtado, 1996). In hunter–gatherer societies more generally, it has also been suggested that prolonged lactation produces contraceptive amenorrhea for the mother for up to 4 years after the birth of a child (Lee, 1979). In modern society, average interbirth intervals are slightly smaller (3.83 years in a recent survey of 28,562 individuals living

predominantly in the United States, Canada, and Europe; Sulloway, 2001b).

How does the amount of overlap affect resource allocation for the middle child? In Figure 35-2, we plot the cumulative investment for the middle child and the resource handicap as a function of interbirth intervals. Here, we assume a three-child family in which a child is mature after 18 years. (In fact, in hunter–gatherer populations, children are net calorie consumers until they reach their mid- to late teens, Kaplan, Hill, Lancaster, & Hurtado, 2000.) In addition, we assume that all children are born at equal time intervals and that the intervals can range between 1 and 18 years.

Consistent with Kidwell's (1981) suggestion about the benefits of more "breathing room" (p. 317), middle children (as well as their siblings) receive more resources with longer interbirth intervals. The reason is that, with more spacing between children, the proportion of the total growth period in which each child benefits by having no sibling or only one sibling becomes larger. However—and this is another surprising observation—more resources do not necessarily mean that the middle child is not subject to an increasing resource handicap. In fact, as Figure 35-2 also shows, the larger the interbirth interval, the bigger the middleborn resource handicap. With larger child spacing, the proportion of the total growth period in which the elder and younger siblings benefit by having some period of exclusive attention becomes larger, and the middle child is increasingly at a disadvantage. However, if the interval exceeds half of the total growth period (here, 9 years), this trend reverses and the handicap becomes increasingly smaller. This is because when the interbirth interval is larger than half the total growth period, the firstborn child matures before the youngest child is born, giving the middle child a period of exclusive attention.

Sibship size. How do resource handicaps change as a function of increasing family size? As Figure 35-3 shows, the middleborn resource handicap increases as a function of increasing family size (here, assuming a 18-year growth period). This happens because an increased number of children entails fewer resources for

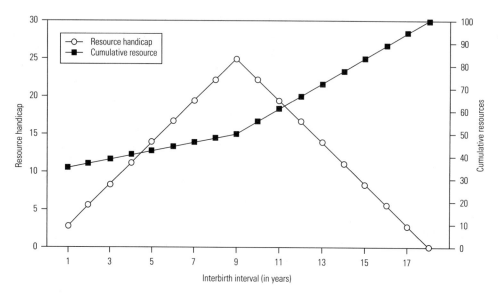

Figure 35-2. Middleborn resource handicap and amount of cumulative resources as a function of length of interbirth interval (assuming a family of three children and a 18-year growth period). Cumulative investment equals the total amount of investments expressed as a percentage of the total resources the only child receives, and the resource handicap is the difference in cumulative investments for the middle child and the first and lastborn child, respectively.

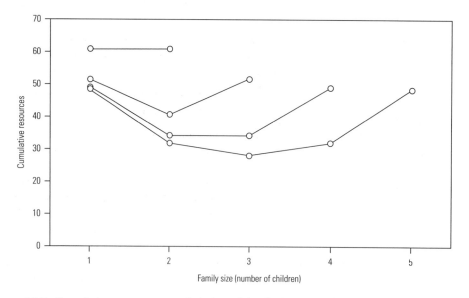

Figure 35-3. Cumulative resources as a function of family size (assuming a 18-year growth period). Cumulative investment equals the total amount of investments expressed as a percentage of the total resources the only child receives. The number of children is represented by the number of dots on a line.

each individual child. Firstborns and laterborns are less strongly affected by this resource depletion because they still benefit from having some period of exclusive attention in which resources are not shared. Sibship size also affects the size of the laterborn and earlierborn resource handicaps; both effects become more extreme as the size of the family increases. Technically, the sibship size effect should eventually dissipate with increasing family size if families become so large that older siblings leave home before the younger ones are born, but in practice we expect this situation to be exceedingly rare.

TESTS OF THE THREE HANDICAP PREDICTIONS

Up to this point in our argument, all observations have been purely theoretical. Is there any evidence for these analytical expectations of a cumulative inequality effect? To answer this question, we now turn to the published literature. Parental investment studies have been carried out across several disparate disciplines. To identify studies that empirically measure parental investment, we conducted a literature search through four different databases: *SocioFile* (sociology), *EconLit* (economics), *Biosis Preview* (biology), and PsycINFO (psychology). In all four data bases, we searched for the key words *birth order* in combination with *parental* (we used *parental* rather than the technical term *parental investment*, for which various other terms such as *parental behavior*, or *parental treatment* are also used).[4] To further extend the sample of studies appropriate to test the handicap predictions, we also combined *birth order* with three specific parental resource terms, namely, *time* (in *EconLit*), *vaccination* (in *Biosis*), and *college expenses* (in *EconLit* and *SocioFile*). All four searches yielded a combined total of 379 articles.

We read the title and abstract of each article to identify those that could possibly be relevant for testing the predictions of the equity heuristic. If there was any indication that the amount of parental investment (in terms of time, money, vaccination records, nutrition, etc.) was empirically studied as a function of birth order, we read

the complete article. We then culled this group, keeping only those articles that (a) provided direct measures of parental investment, (b) distinguished between birth ranks (rather than between firstborn and laterborns), and (c) reported birth ranks in combination with family size (if cumulative investment was measured).[5] If one of the articles referenced a study that appeared relevant, we also looked it up and included it if the study met the described criteria. We found a total of nine studies: all the studies listed in Table 35-1 as well as Lindert (1977), Taubman and Behrman (1986), and Steelman and Powell (1989).

Two features of the parental investment literature may account for why this sample is relatively small. The first is that, as Borgerhoff Mulder (1998) pointed out, "most studies of parental investment in humans ... rely on *outcomes* (such as survival probabilities, educational attainment, or marital placements) as proxies for parental investment" (p. 136). In contrast, to test the equity heuristic we focus on direct measures of parental investment. The second feature is that different studies tend to include different moderating variables, and by no means do all studies include the variables that are necessary to test the handicap predictions (e.g., birth order and family size). In the following sections, we test the handicap predictions against the evidence reported in the set of nine studies.

Is There Evidence for a Middleborn Resource Handicap?

We found only one study (Lindert, 1977) that analyzed cumulative resource allocation as a function of birth rank and family size.[6] This study used time-use surveys of 1,296 Syracuse families in 1967–1968 to infer how much childcare time each child in the family received (each child had completed schooling). Lindert used regression analysis to derive the relationship between time spent in child care by all people in the household and the ages and number of children living in the household. He then used this regression model to estimate the total care time received by each child (corrected for the number and ages of the siblings) over the 18 years that he or she spent in the household (for details, see

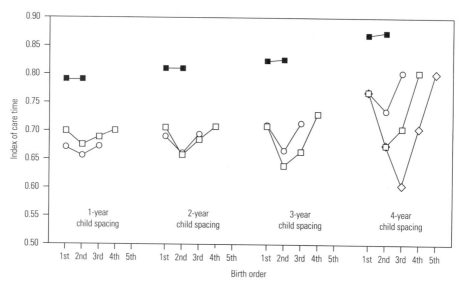

Figure 35-4. Distribution of total child care as a function of birth rank, family size (two, three, four, or five children; the number of children is represented by the number of symbols), and average interbirth interval. Data are from Table 4 of "Sibling position and achievement," by P. H. Lindert, 1977, *The Journal of Human Resources, 12*, p. 212. Copyright 1977 by The University of Wisconsin Press. Adapted with permission. The figure represents child-care time as a fraction of that predicted for an only child (1.0 = 8,227 hr). Interbirth interval was coded such that, for instance, 2-year average spacing covered periods including 1.5 to 2.5 years (see Lindert, 1977, p. 207).

Lindert, 1977, p. 213). Figure 35-4 shows the distribution of child-care time as a function of birth order, family size, and (average) child spacing; child-care time is expressed relative to the child-care time for an only child.

Time is a limited resource that parents divide among offspring. Thus, according to the equity heuristic, its cumulative distribution should reveal a middleborn handicap in families of three or more, and it does in each case. Also consistent with this heuristic is the lack of a birth order effect in two-child families. In five out of the nine test cases (all families with more than two children), the resources received for the first and last birth rank are (almost) identical, and in four cases the lastborn child receives slightly more than the firstborn child. However, this advantage is relatively minor compared with the middleborn resource handicap. As predicted by the equity heuristic, the size of the middleborn resource handicap increases with increasing sibship size (see, e.g., the three-child, four-child,

and five-child families in the 4-year child-spacing chart in Figure 35-4), and the middleborn resource handicap also increases as a function of interbirth interval (although we urge caution in evaluating the latter result because Lindert, 1977, reported the average interbirth intervals).[7] One finding is inconsistent with the middleborn handicap prediction of the equity heuristic: In each of the four-child families in Figure 35-4, the secondborn child received less of the cumulative resources than the thirdborn child, but this birth rank is still at a disadvantage compared with the first and fourth birth rank, which is consistent with the overall prediction.

Since the early 1980s, an increasing number of studies have observed that middleborns appear to be different from firstborns and lastborns on various dimensions of well-being (e.g., Griffore & Bianchi, 1984; Richter, Richter, Eisemann, & Mau, 1997). Unfortunately, these studies do not include direct measures of parental investment, and thus do not enable us to strictly test the predictions of the equity heuristic. Nevertheless, this emerging picture of middleborn effects on well-being is certainly not inconsistent with the middleborn resource handicap predicted by the heuristic. We briefly describe one piece of this picture: Salmon's work on family sentiments. In a series of studies, Salmon (1998, 1999; Salmon & Daly, 1998) uncovered large and consistent middleborn effects when she asked college students (19- to 22-year-olds) about kinship and family ties. For instance, when asked to whom they would turn for emotional or financial support, first and lastborns were significantly more likely than middleborns to nominate a parent in both scenarios (by an overall factor of 1.5). First and lastborns were also significantly more likely to nominate their mothers as the person to whom they felt the closest, a pattern that was replicated in three separate studies (Salmon & Daly, 1998, see also Kennedy, 1989; Rohde et al., 2002). Middleborns' family sentiments are also associated with less frequent contact with parents and grandparents.

If one assumed that cumulative parental investment shapes children's sentiments toward their family, then the equity heuristic could account for some of the above findings. For instance, the equity heuristic suggests that middleborns' more negative family sentiments and less close ties to their families may be related to lower cumulative parental investment and that firstborns' and lastborns' closer relationship to their families may stem from higher cumulative parental investment. However, we urge caution in drawing such conclusions. Ideally, to predict how (in)equality in parental investment affects various dimensions of children's well-being, one needs an understanding of the mechanism through which the type of invested resource influences the dimension of well-being being analyzed. We do not know of any studies that present such causal analyses.

Is There Evidence for a Laterborn Resource Handicap?

B. A. Kaplan, Mascie-Taylor, and Boldsen (1992) analyzed the relationship between birth order and health status in a British national sample. This study used the National Child Development

Study, a British national survey sampling more than 18,500 children born in Great Britain during the first week of March 1958, to examine the relationship between birth order and a variety of health-related and medical experiences in young children. The survey measured such variables as immunization records and attendance at infant and toddler welfare clinics. These are measures of parental investment primarily from early childhood, during the time period when, according to the equity heuristic, each additional child in the family is expected to suffer a decrease in the total amount of parental investment received. We therefore expect to see a laterborn resource handicap in these data. This linear effect is exactly what B. A. Kaplan et al. found. Table 35-1 shows the percentage of children who attended toddlers' clinics and who were immunized against childhood diseases (diphtheria, small pox, and polio) as a function of birth order. Fewer laterborns attended toddler clinics, and laterborns were less likely to be immunized than firstborns. We agree with B. A. Kaplan et al. (1992), and similarly with Li and Taylor (1993), that this effect may be the result of competition for parental time: Parents with older children have less time available to take their younger children to the clinic.

In addition to the B.A. Kaplan et al. (1992) study, we found five other studies that can be used to evaluate the laterborn handicap prediction. Table 35-1 summarizes the results obtained in those studies. Most studies in Table 35-1 analyzed vaccination adherence during early childhood (e.g., measles, polio, mumps, and rubella) as a function of birth order. Consistent with B. A. Kaplan et al.'s (1992) findings, four large-scale surveys (see Angelillo et al., 1999; Barreto & Rodriguez, 1992; Li & Taylor, 1993; Lewis & Britton, 1998) consistently observed that the percentage of children who received vaccination declines as a function of birth order; that is, younger children are less likely to receive complete vaccinations or to be vaccinated at all.

We also found one study that examined the effect of birth order on child nutritional status as measured by children's height for their age. Horton (1988) used a within-family sample in addition to a pooled sample. One of the dependent variables

Table 35-1. Studies that Provide a Test of the Laterborn Resource Handicap

Authors	Research Question	Sample	General Results
Horton (1988)	What is the effect of birth order on child nutritional status, as measured by children's height and weight for their age?	1,903 households in the Bicol region of the Philippines (children age 15 or younger)	In the within-family sample (but much less so in the pooled data—for possible reasons see Horton, 1988, p. 350), the higher the birth order, the more nutritionally disadvantaged children are ($r = 17$). For example, "the last-born child in a family of seven has a height for age (long-run nutritional status) which is .5 SD–2.5 SD below that of the firstborn" (p. 350).
Barreto and Rodrigues (1992)	Which factors affect vaccination adherence for measles, polio, and other diseases?	455 children in an urban area in Sao Paulo, Brazil (all children born from 1971 to 1981 who were registered at a public health system)	Next to year of birth, "birth order was also strongly associated with vaccination completeness" (p. 360). Calculated in terms of odds ratios, laterborns were less likely to receive vaccination than firstborns. Specifically, secondborns, third-and fourthborns, and fifthborns (and still laterborn children) were only 0.71, 0.63, and 0.42 as likely.[a]
B. A. Kaplan et al. (1992)	What is the relationship between birth order and a variety of health-related and medical experiences (e.g., immunization records, attendance at infant and toddler welfare clinics) in young children?	National Child Development Study, a British national survey sampling more than 18,500 children born in Great Britain during the first week of March, 1958	Fewer laterborns attended toddler clinics and laterborns were less likely to be immunized (for diphtheria, small pox, polio) than firstborns (based on 1965 immunization records). The percentage of firstborn, secondborn, thirdborn, and fourthborn (and higher birth orders) children who attended toddler clinics was 63, 56, 49, and 44, respectively. The percentage of children who were immunized against childhood diseases (diphtheria, small pox, polio) was 93, 90, 86, and 79, respectively.[b]

Li and Taylor (1993)	Which factors affect vaccination adherence (measles, mumps, and rubella)?	7,841 children born in January to March 1990 in the northeast and northwest Thames regions (aged 19 to 21 months at the time of data collection)	Among other indicators of parental attention, percentage of children receiving vaccination is affected by birth order: Firstborns (43), secondborns (32), thirdborns (15), fourthborns (6), fifth- and laterborns (4). Li and Taylor concluded that each "unit" of increase in birth order was responsible for a decrease in the odds of being vaccinated by about 20%. They speculated that parents with other children to take care of "may find it difficult to get around to having their children immunized" (p. 170).
Lewis and Britton (1998)	What is the relationship between birth order and measles vaccination?	6,350 children born in one week of April 1970 in England, Scotland, and Wales (immunization was recorded at age 5)	The percentage of children receiving vaccination was 68, 58, 50, 39, and 34 for firstborns, secondborns, thirdborns, fourthborns, fifthborns (and higher birth orders), respectively.
Angelillo et al. (1999)	Which factors affect mandatory vaccination adherence (poliomyelitis, tetanus, diphtheria, hepatitis B)?	841 infants who attended public kindergarten in Cassino and Crotone, Italy	Among various mother and child attributes, only birth order "significantly predicted vaccination nonadherence" (p. 226). Calculated in terms of odds ratios, laterborns were only 0.73 as likely as firstborns to receive vaccination (95% confidence interval: 0.57–0.95).

[a] In their Table III, Barreto and Rodrigues (1992) reported the odds ratio for lack of vaccination (compared with a firstborn). Here we reversed their odds ratios. [b] The results are calculated from the frequency data reported in Kaplan et al.'s (1992) Tables 1 and 2 (we pooled across socioeconomic status).

used was the deviation of the individual child's long-run nutritional status from the household mean (expressed in terms of z scores above or below the U.S. reference population). In the within-family sample, Horton found the effect of birth order to be significant, with children from higher birth ranks being more poorly nourished (see Table 1).[8] One observation relevant for our discussion of the equity heuristic is that Horton did not observe an effect of birth order on *current* nutritional status (as measured by children's weight for height). In her view, this finding

> suggests that parents at a single point in time seem to allocate resources relatively equitably among children of different birth orders. However, the long-run outcome is far from equitable, since later-born children are born when per capita resources are smaller (p. 349).

Increased malnourishment and lack of vaccination may also contribute to why laterborn children tend to be shorter than earlierborn children (see Davie, Butler, & Goldstein, 1972; Goldstein, 1971) and why they suffer higher mortality rates in developing countries (e.g., Brittain, 1992; Hrdy, 1999; Scheper-Hughes, 1992; Scrimshaw, 1978, 1984; for conflicting evidence, see Lynch & Greenhouse, 1994, who found that the probability of dying as an infant in 19th-century Sweden, according to birth order, is U-shaped). For instance, in her analysis of 4,275 births that took place on the island of St. Barthélemy (French West Indies) between 1878 and 1970, Brittain (1992) found that children (ages > 2 weeks but < 1 year) of maternal and paternal higher birth order are more likely to die than children of lower birth order ($eta = .05$ and .06, respectively). Brittain suggested that the higher mortality rates in early childhood were not due to endogenous or gestational factors but probably due to "exogenous or social factors such as the availability of maternal time or family resources" (p. 1266).

In addition, Ballweg and Pagtolun-An (1992) reported that in their sample of 986 women from the Northern Mindanao region of the Philippines "the higher is the birth order of a child, the greater is the chance that the child will die before reaching age five" (p. 85; birth order, independent of other factors, explained more than 30% of the variation in infant and child mortality). According to their regression and structural equation analyses, less parental investment (e.g., as measured by the frequency of parental care and the quality and quantity of nutrition) "represents a significant link in the association between birth order and infant and child mortality" (p. 85). Finally, in a study of 14,192 children born in Sweden between 1915 and 1929, Modin (2002) observed that laterborn children generally have higher mortality than firstborn children. For instance, the odds ratio of dying before age 10 among third- and fourthborns relative to firstborns was 2.65 for girls and 1.54 for boys (Table 5 in Modin, 2002). In middle and old age, however, mortality varied little with birth rank, suggesting that the long-term influence of birth rank on mortality is "partly mediated by adult social class, education and income" (Modin, 2002, p. 1051).

Some of the studies included in Table 35-1 afford us the opportunity to examine whether the size of the laterborn resource handicap depends on the families' socioeconomic status (SES). On average, the results suggest that it does not. In the context of children's nutritional status, Horton (1988) observed that "higher asset ownership is apparently not particularly important in reducing inequality among siblings" (p. 351), and Barreto and Rodrigues (1992) reported that "family income per capita did not influence vaccination uptake" (p. 359; for a similar conclusion, see Lewis & Britton, 1998). Only B. A. Kaplan et al.'s (1992) data suggest that the laterborn resource handicap tends to be more pronounced for families of lower SES (represented by fathers in less skilled occupations): Specifically, the percentage of firstborns who were immunized against childhood diseases (diphtheria, small pox, polio) was four percentage points lower for families of lower SES compared with firstborns from families of higher SES, whereas for thirdborns and fourthborns (and higher birth orders), this difference amounted to eight and seven percentage points (calculated from B. A. Kaplan et al.'s, 1992, Table 2). In the General Discussion section, we return to the question of why the laterborn resource handicap, on average, appears to be largely independent of a family's SES.

Is There Evidence for an Earlierborn Resource Handicap?

The earlierborn resource handicap suggests that there may be resources, such as an allowance, or privileges that are exclusive to the last years of a child's development. For these resources, the earlierborn children are at disadvantage compared with the laterborn children. One of these resources is the ability of parents to cover the expenses of a postsecondary education for their children. The American system of higher education assumes contributions from the family toward meeting college expenses. Although we found numerous studies that were concerned with the relationship between economic support and higher educational outcomes, many could not be used here because they either did not empirically test the relationship or they did not include birth order and sibship size information (see the references in Steelman & Powell, 1989).[9]

We found two studies that pertain to the earlierborn resource handicap. Taubman and Behrman (1986) analyzed 1-year college room and board expenses and found that "the larger one's family, the more heavily one relies on scholarships and loans and the less heavily on parental contributions" (p. 33). In contrast to the prediction derived from the equity heuristic, they did not find birth order effects in the sources of funding for college (e.g., monetary resources available from parents or from working)—a finding they speculated could be due to the small sample size.

In their study of 3,279 college students who entered college in the fall of 1972 (data stemmed from the National Longitudinal Survey of high school seniors from both public and private schools in the United States), Steelman and Powell (1989) also investigated the influence of number of siblings and birth order on financial arrangements for college. Using regression models, the authors estimated both the likelihood of parental assistance and the extent of parental contribution. For this sample, they found that "sibship size has a very strong negative influence on the amount of parental aid, whether the amount is measured in absolute dollars or as a proportion of total college costs" (p. 850). This result is consistent with the equity heuristic, which predicts a reduction of resources per child (at any given time) with increasing sibship size. The authors also reported that the number of younger siblings is associated with a larger reduction in parental support than the number of older siblings, "suggesting an advantage to laterborn children" (pp. 849–850). Specifically, the "effect of the number of younger siblings is over twice that of the number of older siblings" (p. 850). This finding also conforms to the equity heuristic if one assumes that, by the time a child requires resources that are exclusive to the last years of a child's development, the older—but not the younger—siblings are less likely to still rely on parental resources.

GENERAL DISCUSSION

Although we urge caution in evaluating the results from the relatively small sample of studies that we were able to identify from our review of the existing literature, it seems fair to conclude that the equity heuristic provides a parsimonious explanation for the diverse findings obtained. This heuristic explains why Lindert (1977) found a middleborn resource handicap in the cumulative distribution of invested time in the three-child, four-child, and five-child families. It suggests that fewer cumulative resources may be one reason why middleborns appear to be different from firstborns and lastborns on diverse measures of well-being. Furthermore, the equity heuristic also explains why for medical and nutritional resources that are most important in the early years, multiple large-scale studies have consistently found a laterborn handicap. Finally, the equity heuristic provides an explanation for why Steelman and Powell (1989) reported that earlierborns have a disadvantage in expenses for postsecondary education.

In the following discussion, we distinguish between different classes of parental resources. We then review various alternative explanations for birth order effects and put forth the idea of parental resource allocation as an example of adaptive decision making. We conclude with a discussion of the developmental implications of the equity heuristic.

Parental Investments: Some Steps Toward a Taxonomy

In his classic work, Trivers (1972) defined parental investment as any cost associated with raising offspring that reduces the parent's ability to produce or invest in other offspring. In recent years, there has been an increasing recognition among behavioral ecologists of the multidimensional nature of parental investments (see Borgerhoff Mulder, 1998, p. 147). In accordance with this recognition, we propose that at least three general classes of parental resources can be distinguished: (1) *material resources* such as food, health care, and money for higher education; (2) *cognitive resources* such as intellectual stimulation as well as other forms of time spent training and instructing children; and (3) *interpersonal resources* such as attention, time, love, affection, and general encouragement by parents.

In theory, it appears important to distinguish between these resource dimensions because the transmission mechanisms between the type of invested resource and outcome (in terms of the child's health, education, or psychological well-being) are not likely to be the same across the resources. Pragmatically, it is worth distinguishing between these resources because each class is tied to a different research literature, set of models, and associated tests and controversies. Cognitive resources, for instance, are most closely associated with the debate over whether birth order differences in IQ really exist (as proponents of the confluence theory argue) or whether family-size effects alone exist (as proponents of dilution theories insist). We return to this debate below. Clearly, the above dimensions are not exhaustive, and a comprehensive classification of parental resources may also include distinctions based on the following properties.

Resource limits. Some resources are naturally limited and thus will, all else being equal, not significantly vary as a function of a family's SES. Let us take interpersonal resources such as attention as an example. A parent has only a limited amount of attention available and thus needs to divide it among offspring. Material resources, in contrast, hinge on a family's SES. Thus, all else being constant, one may speculate that material resources vary more across families (as a function of their SES), whereas the pool of interpersonal resources may tend to be more constant across families.

"Gatekeeper" resources. When testing the handicap predictions of the equity heuristic against the available evidence, we consistently observed that the percentage of children who receive vaccination declines as a function of birth order. B. A. Kaplan et al. (1992) suggested that this tendency is the result of competition for parental time, whereby parents with older children have less time available to take their younger children to a clinic (see also Horton, 1988, p. 351, for discussion of the constraining role of parental time in the context of children's nutritional status). If so, this finding suggests that certain parental investments such as vaccination are withheld, not because financial resources available for health care are depleted—in fact, vaccination is typically provided for by health care systems—but because another resource, parental time, is available to a lesser degree. That is, some key resources serve as a gatekeeper for other resources, enabling or disabling other investments, thus providing one candidate explanation for why the laterborn resource handicap for health care seems to be independent of a family's SES.

Surrogate resources. Parents are not the only ones to invest in children. Older siblings, grandparents, and sometimes even unrelated individuals can also provide resources. More generally, in kin-based societies such as the pastoralist peoples of Africa, families are embedded in a wider kin network in which reciprocal investment in the children of kin is common (Ivey, 2000). The availability of such surrogate resources has implications for the equity heuristic's predictions. In its present formulation, the predictions of this heuristic are relevant only in domains in which the majority of investment comes from parents, and for this reason, we must caution that an analysis based on the equity heuristic should apply only to situations in which a child's kin (e.g., grandparents) do not provide substantial surrogate resources that compensate for parental ones. We should also note, however, that surrogate resources may well be invested in offspring according to the equity heuristic, in which case their effect would be fully consistent with the expectations derived from this heuristic. For instance, grandparents who often have more grandchildren than children may choose to divide their resources equally, thus benefiting from a distribution principle which is easily defensible (to parents and grandchildren) in that it does not differentiate between the recipients.

Alternative Explanations for Birth Order Effects

In what follows, we briefly describe four other accounts proposed to explain birth order effects, namely, the resource dilution hypothesis, the confluence model, the admixture hypothesis, and the family dynamics model. Each of these models—which are not mutually exclusive—has received considerable, if still hotly debated, empirical support.

The resource dilution hypothesis. One domain that consistently shows effects of birth order, family size, and birth spacing is academic achievement. This form of achievement is typically measured through standardized test scores or number of years of education. The standard finding is that laterborn children, children in larger families, and children with siblings who are close to them in age perform worse on these measures (Heer, 1985, 1986; Powell & Steelman, 1993; Taubman & Behrman, 1986). Some of these effects persist even when academic ability is held constant (Powell & Steelman, 1993). Birth order is also negatively correlated with children's educational aspirations and continues to affect occupational status into young adulthood (Marjoribanks, 1988, 1989).

Perhaps the most popular explanation that has been advanced for these findings is the resource dilution hypothesis (Blake, 1981, 1989; Downey, 1995, 2001; Lindert, 1977; Powell & Steelman, 1989). Like the equity heuristic, this hypothesis takes as its basic assumption the fact that parental resources are limited. This hypothesis also postulates that children provided with greater intellectual, social, and economic resources will excel in academic and intellectual arenas. Therefore, as family size increases or birth spacing decreases, children are predicted to suffer from the depletion of resources. Reduced investment is in turn expected to translate into reduced achievement (Heer, 1985; Powell & Steelman, 1993; but see Marjoribanks, 1991). Because their elder siblings reach each new academic stage before them, laterborn children may suffer from reduced investment as financial resources available for further education are used up. This effect appears to be stronger in middle-class families than in families with either abundant or scarce resources, and it may be compensated for in lastborn children if they are reared at more prosperous economic periods of their parents' life cycle (Travis & Kohli, 1995).

The equity heuristic is itself a variant of the resource dilution hypothesis. In the form of its three resource handicaps, the equity heuristic postulates three alternative developmental outcomes that are dependent on the availability and importance of key parental resources at different periods in the life course. Like the equity heuristic, all resource dilution models assume the equitable distribution of parental resources, and some of these other models also consider the developmental consequences of life course timing in specific parental investments, such as education (Downey, 2001). Only the equity heuristic, however, formally highlights the unexpected consequences of parental investment in creating cumulative inequality from equality, and only the equity heuristic systematically applies this principle to an explication of diverse patterns of birth order effects.

The confluence model. First proposed by Zajonc and Markus (1975; see also Zajonc, Markus, & Markus, 1979), this model attempts to specify how parental resources—conceived in terms of the intellectual environment that parents provide—translate into children's intellectual attainment. Like other resource dilution models, the confluence model posits that parental resources are finite and become depleted by the addition of offspring to the family. Unlike other resource dilution models, the confluence model includes a role for offspring themselves. Also unlike other resource dilution models, which have been applied to varied consequences of parental investment, the confluence model addresses itself only to intellectual ability.

One of the major insights deriving from the confluence model is that children can be treated as part of their own dynamically changing environments. Thus, the intellectual environment is defined as a function of the absolute intellectual levels of all family members, including the intellectual level of the person whose development is being analyzed. The confluence model assumes that the greater the intellectual maturity of people who interact with the growing child, the more mature the child's verbal, analytical, and conceptual experiences will be. Because children must share their parents' intellectual resources, each successive sibling is born into a more depleted intellectual environment. In larger sibships, however, elder siblings tend to enrich the family's intellectual environment as they approach adulthood, so lastborns may experience a more favorable environment in such families compared with middleborns. Various predictions based on the confluence model are supported by evidence from more than 50 different studies of birth order and intelligence (Zajonc, 2001).

Although application of the confluence model has previously been limited to trends in intellectual ability, this model could also be applied to behavioral domains, such as attachment behavior and psychological well-being, in which offspring are capable of providing surrogate resources. In general, such models would predict that initially linear trends by birth order become transformed into quadratic trends as laterborns (and particularly lastborns) benefit from an increased presence of surrogate resources within the family system.

The admixture hypothesis. Some critics of birth order research maintain that reported effects are mostly or entirely artifactual (Ernst & Angst, 1983; Page & Grandon, 1979; Rodgers, 2001). According to these theorists, birth order effects are generally spurious consequences of the failure of researchers to control for important background influences, especially sibship size and social class. Lower class families, for example, tend to be larger than upper class families and are therefore biased for an overrepresentation of

laterborns. In uncontrolled studies, artifactual birth order effects can arise owing to between-family differences in sibship size, which are often mediated by associated differences in social class and other background variables. Some advocates of the admixture hypothesis insist that the only trustworthy studies are those that examine siblings who have grown up in the same family. Unfortunately, there are relatively few such within-in-family studies, and sample sizes in these studies tend to be small, giving them relatively modest statistical power compared with well-controlled, between-family studies.

To date, within-family studies of intelligence have generally yielded null results, in accordance with the predictions of admixture theorists (Rodgers, Cleveland, van den Oord, & Rowe, 2000; but see Zajonc, 2001). By contrast, within-family studies of personality have consistently produced significant birth order differences (Chao, 2001; Paulhus, Trapnell, & Chen, 1999; Price, 1969; Sulloway, 1999, 2001a). It is nevertheless possible that personality assessments by siblings and other family members are affected by stereotypes or by sibling contrast effects (a process whereby siblings magnify small differences in personality into larger ones). It is just as plausible, however, that birth order stereotypes reflect real differences in within-family roles and behavior, which siblings perceive and report as differences in personality.

Sulloway's family dynamics model. Sulloway (1996, 2001a) has discussed four different causes of birth order effects in personality and behavior as part of a family dynamics model of human development. The first causal mechanism is associated with differing levels of parental investment and is therefore a variant of other resource dilution models. When reproductive success is linked to scarce resources, such as land in agrarian societies, parents may invest more heavily in one offspring than another (typically firstborns and, to a lesser extent, lastborns). Sulloway's second causal mechanism builds on the observation that siblings tend to occupy differing niches within the family system. For example, firstborns often cultivate the niche of a surrogate parent. The third causal component of Sulloway's family dynamics model invokes the supposition that firstborns are bigger, stronger, and smarter than their younger siblings, and that they are therefore better able to use competitive strategies that take advantage of these traits. A fourth causal mechanism involves sibling *deidentification*, or the fact that adjacent siblings, in an effort to minimize direct competition, seek to differentiate themselves by becoming different in their interests, social attitudes, and personalities (Davis, 1997; Schachter, Gilutz, Shore, & Adler, 1978; Skinner, 1992).

Sulloway (1996, 2001a) has linked the first three of these four causal mechanisms to specific attributes within the Five Factor Model of personality (Costa & McCrae, 1992; McCrae & Costa, 1987). In addition, he predicts that most birth order effects involving personality should exhibit both linear and quadratic (U-shaped) trends. Linear trends are implicit in birth order's status as a proxy for differences in age, size, and strength, as well as in the potential for surrogate parenting. Quadratic trends are implicit in the tendency for parents to invest more in firstborns and lastborns relative to middleborns. Sulloway's family dynamics model also allows for the possibility that parental favoritism and sibling strategies will elicit counterstrategies. Some of these sibling counterstrategies are anticipated to entail quadratic birth order trends. For example, middle children, who are expected to receive less parental investment than other offspring, are also expected to be less conscientious than their siblings, when controlled for the linear effects expected in this personality dimension. In a study involving more than 4,000 subjects, Sulloway (2001a) found that the expected linear and quadratic trends associated with birth order and personality do exist in within-family data. Moreover, for each dimension of the Five Factor Model of personality, these various birth order trends (mean $r = .11$) agree closely with the predictions of his family dynamics model. The same general pattern of birth order effects has been found in studies of nonfamily members, although effect sizes are typically smaller than those obtained in within-family studies.

Although Sulloway's (1996, 2001a) family dynamics model and the equity heuristic both predict that parental investment will create quadratic trends in birth order effects, the two theories differ regarding how these effects will emerge on a developmental basis. In particular, the advantage to lastborns that is posited to occur under the equity heuristic can only emerge after other siblings have left the home, whereas the advantage for earlierborns should be present from early childhood. In contrast, the family dynamics model predicts that both effects should be present throughout childhood. We do not know of any study that uses direct measures of parental investment to test such age-contingent effects; however, there are studies that use indirect measures. For instance, Kidwell (1982; see also 1981) analyzed the self-esteem of a sample of young American males (15 to 16 years old) as a function of their birth order. She found that "middleborns have a significantly lower self-esteem than both firstborns and lastborns" (p. 225). Assuming the typical age spacing between children, the lastborns in Kidwell's study—being only 15 to 16—should not have exhibited more self-esteem than middleborns because they had yet to be alone in the family or had not been alone for more than a year or two. If one posits a direct link between the total amount of parental investment and self-esteem, Kidwell's finding would contradict the prediction of the equity heuristic and support that of the family dynamics model. Future work can provide strict tests of age-contingent birth order effects.

Strengths and limitations of the equity heuristic. In our view, what the equity heuristic contributes to an understanding of birth order effects, beyond these existing models, is the realization that a simple parental decision rule can, in principle at least, induce both linear birth order effects (by means of the laterborn and earlierborn resource handicaps) and quadratic birth order effects (by means of the middleborn resource handicap). This heuristic is thus more parsimonious than the family dynamics model, which postulates several different causal mechanisms to predict both linear and quadratic components. The equity heuristic also suggests ways to make predictions from the other models more specific. For instance, both the laterborn resource handicap and the resource dilution hypothesis share the notion of resource depletion with increasing family size. The equity heuristic, however, suggests resource dilution to be of particular relevance for resources that are critical for the earlier stages in life. Generally, it treats parental investment as multifaceted, thus acknowledging that parental resources are not just a single kind of resource.

The equity heuristic also has significant limitations. For instance, unlike the other approaches we have reviewed, it is more cautious in predicting how parental resources translate into behavior, intellect, or personality. We also think that (in its present formulation) the predictions of the equity heuristic are relevant only in domains in which the majority of investment comes from parents, and for this reason, we must caution that an analysis based on the equity heuristic should apply only to situations in which a child's siblings, or a child itself, do not provide substantial surrogate resources that compensate for parental ones.

Parental Resource Allocation: An Instance of Adaptive Decision Making?

As we pointed out in the beginning of this article, the aim of our analysis is not to argue that parents necessarily follow the equity heuristic. Our point is much more modest—namely, to draw attention to the counterintuitive consequences that eventuate if they do so. Nevertheless, we must ask the question: How plausible is the equity heuristic as a decision strategy for parental resource allocation? We answer this question by way of a small detour to the related (yet unfortunately insufficiently connected) research field of behavioral decision making. In their work on the "adaptive decision maker," Payne, Bettman, and Johnson (1993) emphasized that a decision maker typically has a multitude of strategies available and chooses among them depending on their costs and accuracy, given circumstances such as time pressure or accountability.

Inspired by this view, we propose that parental resource allocation may be an instance of adaptive decision making. That is, parents are likely to have multiple investment strategies available, and the strategy selection would depend on circumstances such as time pressure, parental

goals (e.g., conflict avoidance), social norms (e.g., egalitarian values), and the nature and extent of the resource involved. Thus, one may suggest that conditions such as time pressure and goals such as conflict avoidance favor—but do not necessitate—the use of the equity heuristic. This suggestion is consistent with the claim that dividing equally requires less information processing and calculation effort than other distribution principles (e.g., Messick, 1993; Ohtsubo & Kameda, 1998, p. 91) and also has the benefit of being easily defensible in that it does not differentiate between the recipients (Messick & Schell, 1992).[10]

There is, however, at least one important argument why the equity heuristic may not always be a plausible model for parental resource allocations: It allocates resources regardless of the recipients' situational and age-specific needs. An ill or a very young child, for instance, draws more care from parents than a healthy or an older child. Moreover, it seems likely that the effective allocation of resources, which are dedicated to the children's future social competitiveness (Geary, 2000; H. Kaplan et al., 1998), are influenced by feedback provided by children, for instance, in terms of their educational achievements. Because children's ability to benefit from investment in "embodied capital" is likely to be more variable then their ability to benefit from, for instance, nutrition, such feedback may override the equity heuristic. But do investments in children's future social competitiveness rule out the equity heuristic? Not necessarily. Although it may turn out that the equity heuristic is an inappropriate model for resources that target children's later social competitiveness, it may still be an appropriate model for the early stages of their allocation (i.e., prior to feedback about how effectively children use the investment).

Do age-specific needs rule out the equity heuristic? There exists a body of research that suggests that parents may treat each successive child equally at the same age rather than treating children equally at any given point in time. Dunn, Plomin, and colleagues (Dunn & Plomin, 1986; Dunn, Plomin, & Daniels, 1986; Dunn, Plomin, & Nettles, 1985) have concluded that mothers are quite consistent in their treatment of each successive child when children are at the same age, and change their maternal behavior as the child ages. If each child is, in fact, treated strictly equally at the same age, this form of implementation of the equity heuristic will not yield the kind of resource handicaps we identified. However, it is important to point out that dilution of parental resources (such as time and attention) makes truly equal treatment at the same ages unlikely if not impossible. This is likely to be true even when age-specific needs are most pronounced: A newborn of a mother having two children is not likely to receive the same amount of attention (or probably health care) as a newborn who is an only child. Hence, age-specific parental investments will almost always be diluted by increases in family size.

In addition, to respond appropriately to age-specific needs, parents might reasonably attempt to find a compromise between equity and age-specific needs. Under this circumstance, the equity heuristic would provide a weight, pulling the allocated resources toward an equal split, which is then modified by parents' attempts to meet each child's age-specific needs. Such a compromise can still produce resource handicaps. To illustrate, let us assume the same distribution of resources as depicted in Figure 35-1, but that in addition, the secondborn and thirdborn in their first period of growth receive an additional one-tenth of the total resources. Even then, the various resource handicaps still continue to exist. For example, the middleborn resource handicap (calculated as a proportion of the total investment in an only child, see Figure 35-1) changes as follows: for firstborns, from 54% to 51%; for middleborns, from 42% to 43%; and for lastborns, from 54% to 57%. In addition, there are certain limited resources that would be difficult to equalize as a function of children's ages and as the number of children in a family increases. Of course, there may be other resources, such as the nature of the attention a child receives, that are equalizable. Thus, the equity heuristic and an age-specific decision rule can both be plausible and independent candidates for parents' adaptive investment strategies, and they may operate simultaneously depending on the resource, or they may serve as interdependent motives between which parents attempt to find a satisfactory compromise.

Parental Investment and Children's Well-Being: Two Sides of the Same Coin?

Although we have speculated about how a particular resource might impinge on children's development (e.g., malnourishment and size), our analysis has focused primarily on the resources (and their distributions) rather than on their consequences. Despite this limited focus, our analysis seems to imply that more parental investment is invariably good for children. Is it actually true that more investment is always better? We do not believe so. Whereas there may be linear relationships between resources and children's well-being (e.g., in the context of health care), assuming such linear relationships across all stages of children's development and across resources would be naive and would contradict findings and theories from developmental psychology.

By way of illustration, consider a classic study in the framework of life course theory. In *Children of the Great Depression*, Elder (1974) showed that parents and children often worked out successful adaptations to drastic reductions in family's resources resulting from the economic depression of the 1930s. As Elder (1998) has noted about potentially positive outcomes of resource exhaustion, "the developmental impact of a succession of life transitions or events is contingent on when they occur in a person's life" (p. 3). In the context of parental investment, this observation implies that the (possibly cumulative) consequences that a resource advantage or disadvantage has depends on when it occurs in a child's life. Take as an example the time of exclusive parental care. As Figure 35-1 illustrates, firstborns enjoy exclusive care at an early stage of their lives, whereas lastborns experience such exclusive care at a late stage in their development (during adolescence). Will this different timing yield differential effects? Some attachment theorists would strongly suggest so. *Attachment* is typically defined as a close emotional bond between the infant and caregiver, and it is assumed that this bond, among others, rests on the availability of parental care and attention.

For example, securely attached babies have care-givers who are consistently available to respond to their infants' needs (Santrock, 2002, p. 189). In particular, the early attachment theorists such as Erikson (1968) and Bowlby (1988) empha-sized the first year of life as the key period for the development of attachment (see Kagan, 1987, for a different view). If this were true, and if early attachment to a caregiver were crucial and foreshadowed later functioning (Schneider, Atkinson, & Tardif, 2001), then firstborns would profit much more from the period of exclusive care than lastborns. Such a prediction could be tested both in terms of children's attachments (and adolescents' family sentiments, Salmon, 1998) and their cognitive and emotional func-tioning. What these considerations also suggest is that one has to be cautious in drawing conclu-sions from, for instance, the distribution of child-care time reported in Figure 35-4. Although the first and last birth ranks receive (almost) identical child-care time, lastborns might not profit from the availability of resources to the same degree as the firstborns because the period of exclusive care may come too late to have a sig-nificant impact on the person's development.

In addition to the insight that parental invest-ment and children's well-being are often not lin-early related, developmentalists have also, more fundamentally, highlighted the importance of parental treatment for children's development. They stress, for instance, how different two chil-dren growing up in the same household can become. Although there is not yet a comprehen-sive causal model explaining such differences (Mekos, Hetherington, & Reiss, 1996), work in behavior genetics suggests that within-family variations are not due to genotypic differences alone but also to differences in family environ-ment (e.g., Plomin & Daniels, 1987). In other words, children reared in the same family can receive different parental treatment (e.g., Brody, Stoneman, & Burke, 1987; Daniels & Plomin, 1985).[11] Differential parental treatment in turn has been consistently demonstrated to be associ-ated with adolescent adjustment (e.g., McHale & Pawletko, 1992). Reiss et al. (1995), for example, showed that lower levels of parental support and monitoring and higher levels of parental

negativity directed uniquely to one sibling pre-dicted higher levels of depressive symptoms and antisocial behavior in that adolescent. Similarly, Mekos et al. (1996) demonstrated that differen-tial treatment was more strongly related to prob-lem behavior in remarried families where siblings did not share the same biological parent (for an evolutionary psychology perspective on steppar-enthood, see Daly & Wilson, 1996).

To conclude, any comprehensive theory of parental investment and its impact on children's development ultimately rests on insights from multiple disciplines.[12] Such a theory should take into account crucial developmental insights and model the complex nature of parental invest-ment that is likely to be shaped by a myriad of factors such as paternal uncertainty, parents' experience and values, and children's tempera-ment. The modest contribution of our own analysis to such an integrative view is the obser-vation that differential parental treatment and its effects on the children's development is a suf-ficient, but by no means a necessary, condition for differential outcomes: The very attempt by parents to treat children equally may, counterin-tuitively, lead to differential treatment, and ulti-mately to differential development.

ACKNOWLEDGMENTS

We thank the Deutsche Forschungsgemeinschaft for its financial support of Ralph Hertwig with Grant He 2768/6-1 and Clark H. Barrett, Harald Euler, Alexandra M. Freund, Monique Borgerhoff Mulder, Andreas Ortmann, and Eckert Voland for many helpful comments.

NOTES

1. In research on distributional justice, the terms *equity* and *equality* describe two distinct allocation principles (Deutsch, 1975). In contrast, we use the terms *equity* and *equality* interchangeably, which accords with the most general definition of *equity* in the English language (namely, the quality of being equal or fair), a meaning that is derived ety-mologically from the Latin *æquus*, meaning "equal, fair" (Simpson & Weiner, 1989, p. 358).
2. According to Hamilton's rule, a gene (e.g., for altruism) can evolve and remain stable in a

population if $rB > C$. In this formulation, B is the benefit to the recipient (e.g., a sibling) of an altruistic act (e.g., food sharing), r is the coefficient of relatedness between the altruist and the recipient (i.e., the probability of sharing a given gene by descent), and C is the cost to the altruist.

3. One objection that has been raised to this conclusion is that Davis et al.'s (1999) analysis of birds cannot easily be extended to humans for two reasons: Birds are born in clutches of approximately the same age and secondly, they have a far more limited period of parental investment than humans. It is important to realize that in species with asynchronous hatching, the chicks in the nest are not the same age, albeit age differences are small and measured in days. Baby songbirds grow very fast, going from newly hatched to fledged in a matter of 2 to 3 weeks, and an age difference of as little as a day does make a significant difference in the size and developmental stage of a chick. For this reason, one may reasonably argue that bird parents do, in fact, face an ecological situation similar to that of human parents. This situation is unlike that faced by most other mammals, among whom young are typically born and raised simultaneously rather than at intervals. Finally, that the period of investment is short simply makes birds an easier model for study than humans.

4. The four databases covered the following time range: *EconLit* (1969–December 1999), *SocioFile* (1974–1999), *Biosis Preview* (1985–1999), and PsycINFO (1887–1999). For the *EconLit* search we also used the key word *birth order* only because the combination of *birth order* and *parental* only yielded three hits; using *birth order* only yielded 23 more hits. In all four databases, we limited the search to English language journal articles.

5. For analyses of the distribution of cumulative resources, family size is an important moderating variable. To see this, consider the birth rank *secondborn* as an example. Dependent on the size of the family, secondborns can functionally be lastborns (in two-child families), middleborns (in three-child and four-child families), or earlierborns (in families of five or more children). If one averages the cumulative resources for second-borns—regardless of family size and their actual functional role—then the resource distribution can become distorted. Take the resource allocation depicted in Figure 35-1.

If one collapses the resources for each birth rank across family sizes (only child, two-child, and three-child families), the U-shaped (or quadratic) effect in the three-child family would disappear: Expressed as a percentage of the total resources the only child receives, the firstborns then receive 72% of the resources, the secondborns 65%, and the thirdborns 58%. Thus, the cumulative resource allocation seemingly follows a linear rather than a quadratic trend. This problem does not arise for those resources that are most critical at the beginning of a child's life. Here only the presence of older children is crucial (because younger children join the family when those resources are no longer critical or are less critical). Thus, we can also use studies that report birth ranks only to test for the laterborn resource handicap.

6. We found several studies that analyzed allocation of parental time to children (e.g., C. R. Hill & Stafford, 1974, 1980; Leibowitz, 1974a, 1974b, 1977). Unfortunately, those studies did not provide information about either birth order or family size—both of the variables necessary to test the middleborn resource handicap. Other studies reported birth order and family size information but did not observe actual parental time allocation. Instead they used, for instance, children's achievement patterns as a function of the cumulative parental input (e.g., Hanushek, 1992).

7. Lindert's index of child-care time also includes the time older siblings spent taking care of younger kids. This fact may account for some patterns in the data that are also not predicted by the equity heuristic. For instance, with longer interbirth interval (3 and 4 years) the firstborn may take care of laterborns, thus explaining why the youngest child appears to receive slightly more resources than the firstborn child.

8. Horton (1988) did not report the children's average age as a function of birth order. However, because she restricted her analysis to children age 15 years or less, and the average number of children per family was 6.8, one can infer that the laterborn children were relatively young. This is important. If degrees of malnutrition coincide with critical developments such as the rapid brain growth in early years of life, it is likely to have cumulative consequences (by age 2, the brain already weighs 75% of its eventual adult weight and by age 5, it has grown to 90%; Berger, 2000; see also Huttenlocher, 1994).

9. In addition to the key words *college expenses* and *birth order*, we also used the key word *education*. Although we found numerous studies that explored the relationship between birth order and schooling or educational attainment (e.g., Behrman & Taubman, 1986; Kuo & Hauser, 1996; Steelman, 1985; Travis & Kohli, 1995), we did not uncover any additional studies that explored how many financial resources parents invest in their children's education as a function of their birth order.

10. In the context of parenting, an equity motive may not always be easy to realize, nor may equity always be easy to assess. For example, does getting up three times in the middle of night to feed an infant for a total of 2 hr really equate chaperoning the infant's older sibling to a 2-hr movie?

11. As Neiderhiser et al. (1999) have stressed, the family ecology variable *parental treatment* may itself be driven by genetically influenced characteristics of the child. Thus, an irritable and difficult-to-soothe child may elicit a more withdrawn and negative parenting style. Such a parenting style, if continued, may in turn contribute to adolescent maladjustment.

12. We regret that we seem to be remote from such a comprehensive perspective as is, for instance, illustrated by the observations that textbooks in developmental psychology provide little to no reference to the existing parental investment literature. We searched the subject index of several recent textbooks of developmental psychology (Berger, 2000; Berk, 2000; Cole & Cole, 1993; Santrock, 2002) and did not find a single mentioning of key words such as *parental investment* or *parental resources*. Similarly, we found only one reference to Trivers (1972); Hamilton was not mentioned at all.

Introduction to Chapter 36

Instant Customer Base Analysis: Managerial Heuristics Often "Get It Right"

We are all familiar with the experience of mailboxes overflowing with flyers, brochures, credit card mailing offers, and sales catalogs. For customers—in particular, those who have no intention of making further purchases from a company that keeps flooding them with their materials—these marketing activities are often a nuisance. For companies, however, such investments can be effective ways of targeting past and possibly new customers. Nevertheless, gun-shot advertising campaigns are expensive. In light of scarce marketing resources, every company aims to spend them on valuable customers loyal to the company rather than on less valuable customers who may have already switched to a competitor. But how does one distinguish active from inactive customers?

Complex statistical models have been proposed for this task. A downside of these models is that customer managers appear to resist using them—a phenomenon well known from other domains such as medical decision making, in which complex expert systems have not found their way into the daily practice of physicians. In reality, customer managers appear to follow simple heuristics to distinguish active from inactive customers. One heuristic is the recency-of-last-purchase or hiatus heuristic. It assumes a time window of, say, nine months. If a customer did not purchase from the company for more than nine months, he or she would be categorized as inactive.

Markus Wübben and Florian von Wangenheim observed that experienced managers rely on the hiatus heuristic, rather than the Pareto/NBD (negative binomial distribution) model or similar state-of-the-art approaches in marketing. Intending to demonstrate the superiority of complex statistical models to managers (personal communication), they compared the predictive performance of complex forecast models with that of simple heuristics. The result came as a surprise. Across three different companies, the hiatus heuristic, for instance, performed at least as well as or even better than the complex models. The authors' finding is another illustration that the assumption of an accuracy–effort trade-off (according to which the rationale for heuristics is a trade-off between accuracy and effort) is not generally true. Some heuristics can have it both ways. Moreover, the results also suggested that one important difference between experts and nonexperts in a particular domain is the ability of the former to ignore noise and extract the few robust predictors (see Chapter 30).

CHAPTER 36

Instant Customer Base Analysis: Managerial Heuristics Often "Get It Right"

Markus Wübben and Florian von Wangenheim

Abstract: Recently, academics have shown interest and enthusiasm in the development and implementation of stochastic customer base analysis models, such as the Pareto/NBD model and the BG/NBD model. Using the information these models provide, customer managers should be able to (1) distinguish active customers from inactive customers, (2) generate transaction forecasts for individual customers and determine future best customers, and (3) predict the purchase volume of the entire customer base. However, there is also a growing frustration among academics insofar as these models have not found their way into wide managerial application. To present arguments in favor of or against the use of these models in practice, the authors compare the quality of these models when applied to managerial decision making with the simple heuristics that firms typically use. The authors find that the simple heuristics perform at least as well as the stochastic models with regard to all managerially relevant areas, except for predictions regarding future purchases at the overall customer base level. The authors conclude that in their current state, stochastic customer base analysis models should be implemented in managerial practice with much care. Furthermore, they identify areas for improvement to make these models managerially more useful.

Consider a marketing executive at a catalog retailer who faces the following challenges: First, she wants to distinguish customers in the customer base who are likely to continue buying from the firm (active customers) from those who are likely to defect or from those who have already defected (inactive customers). This information should help (1) identify profitable, inactive customers who should be reactivated; (2) remove inactive, unprofitable customers from the customer base; and (3) determine active customers who should be targeted with regular marketing activities, such as new catalogs or mailings. Second, she wants to

generate transaction forecasts for individual customers to identify the company's future 10% best customers, or to compute customer lifetime value (CLV). Such information should help her target those groups with perks, differential mailing frequencies, and loyalty program offerings. Third, she wants to predict the purchase volume of the entire customer base to make provisions for capacity planning, to compute the firm's customer equity, and to know when customer acquisition efforts need to be strengthened.

For the executive, the central problem in successfully coping with these tasks is that the time at which a customer defects from the firm is unobservable. The customer may have been disenchanted with the purchased product or the provider and now buys at a different supplier, the customer may have moved to another city, or the customer may have even passed away.

This phenomenon exists for most service providers that operate in noncontractual settings: For example, when a customer purchases from a catalog retailer, walks off an aircraft, checks out of a hotel, or leaves a retail outlet, the firm has no way of knowing whether and how often the customer will conduct business in the future (Reinartz & Kumar, 2000).

In contrast, in a contractual setting, the buyer–seller relationship is governed by a contract, which often predetermines not only the length but also the usage pattern of the relationship (e.g., telephone and Internet "flat-rate" services, magazine subscriptions). In this context, hazard regression or logistic regression models (Bolton, 1998; Li, 1995) provide promising approaches in determining the probability that a customer will still be with the firm at a particular future time. In the noncontractual setting, the state-of-the-art approach in determining the activity and future purchase levels of a customer is the Pareto/NBD model (Schmittlein, Morrison, & Colombo, 1987; Schmittlein & Peterson, 1994). The Pareto/NBD model has recently been employed in several studies (Fader, Hardie, & Lee, 2005a, 2005b; Ho, Park, & Zhou, 2006; Krafft, 2002; Reinartz & Kumar, 2000, 2003), and its implementation has been recommended on an even larger scale (Balasubramanian et al., 1998; Jain & Singh, 2002; Kamakura et al., 2005; Rust & Chung, 2006). Recently, Fader, Hardie, and Lee (2005a) introduced the BG/NBD model, which is a variant of the Pareto/NBD model but is much easier to implement and estimate. Both models are attractive because they (1) make forecasts of individuals' future purchase levels and (2) operate on past transaction behavior. More precisely, they operate solely on the frequency and recency information of a customer's past purchase behavior. The Pareto/NBD model has an additional feature; for each customer, it yields the probability that he or she is still active.

In light of increased calls for closer cooperation between marketing academics and practitioners, it must be of concern for academics that these models have not found their way into managerial practice. Instead, a survey by Verhoef and colleagues (2002) shows that simple heuristics are still commonly applied.

Given the time and money costs associated with implementing complex stochastic models in managerial practice, the marketing executive will be convinced to make use of the academic methods only when their superiority is clearly demonstrated on the aggregate level and, even more important, on the individual customer level. However, practitioners are not the only ones who would benefit from such insights. For research, it is important to know the circumstances under which the predictions of these models can be trusted to produce accurate forecasts for future implementation of these models in, for example, CLV research (e.g., Reinartz & Kumar, 2000, 2003).

Few studies have compared the performance of complex versus noncomplex models for customer purchase behavior and lifetime value prediction. Donkers, Verhoef, and De Jong (2007) find that using complex methods instead of simple models for CLV prediction in a contractual setting (insurance company) does not substantially improve predictive accuracy. In a semicontractual context, Borle, Singh, and Jain (2008) find that a simple RFM (recency, frequency, and monetary value) model performs as well as the Pareto/NBD model that includes monetary value (Schmittlein & Peterson, 1994) in predicting CLV. They also propose a hierarchical Bayesian model that works better than both the Pareto/NBD and the RFM models in the semicontractual setting. However, none of the studies on the stochastic models (Fader, Hardie, & Lee, 2005a; Schmittlein, Morrison, & Colombo, 1987; Schmittlein & Peterson, 1994) have validated their predictions on the individual customer level in a noncontractual setting using multiple data sets from different industries. The current research aims to fill this gap.

In what follows, we briefly cover heuristics in managerial practice and provide an introduction to the Pareto/NBD and BG/NBD models. We then describe the data sets from three different industries on which we performed our validation. Next, we present the results of the predictive performance of the models versus the simple management heuristics. Finally, we discuss our findings and offer recommendations for using customer base analysis models in academic research and managerial practice.

HEURISTICS IN MANAGERIAL PRACTICE

There are reasons to believe that simple heuristics may work better than more complex strategies for various types of tasks, even though they often require less information and computation (Gigerenzer, Todd, & The ABC Research Group 1999). Support for Gigerenzer's work is manifold (Bröder, 2000, 2003; Bröder & Schiffer, 2003; Lee & Cummins, 2004; Newell et al., 2004; Newell & Shanks, 2003; Newell, Weston, & Shanks, 2003; Rieskamp, 2006; Rieskamp & Hoffrage, 1999; Rieskamp & Otto, 2006). A survey conducted by Jagdish Parikh (discussed in Buchanan & O'Connell, 2006, p. 40) shows that executives "used their intuitive skills as much as they used their analytical abilities, but they credited 80% of their successes to instinct." Especially in direct marketing, experienced managers are likely to be accurate (Morwitz & Schmittlein, 1998) because this environment is characterized by two properties that are essential for learning to occur: repetition and feedback (Camerer & Johnson, 1991; Goldberg, 1968). "Repetition" refers to the repeated occurrence of the task, and "feedback" means that the outcome of the manager's decision is easily observed and evaluated. The previously described decisions to distinguish between active and inactive customers and between high- and low-value customers both are highly repetitive and offer feedback.

A survey conducted in May 2002 by executive search firm Christian and Timbers reveals that 45% of corporate executives now rely more on instinct than on facts and figures in running their businesses (Bonabeau, 2003). Nevertheless, even if facts and figures are used, managers still rely on intuition and long-standing methods. A survey by Verhoef and colleagues (2002) on 228 database marketing companies shows that cross-tabulation and RFM analysis are the most popular methods for response modeling. In the context of the current study, at least two of the three companies (airline and apparel retailer) whose customer bases are analyzed apply simple recency-of-last-purchase (hiatus) analysis to distinguish active from inactive customers. For example, the managers of the airline who have "expert" knowledge of their customer base informed us that the cutoff time was nine months. This finding is in line with an article in the *New York Times* (Wade, 1988) that illustrates the use of the hiatus heuristic in frequent-flier programs. For future purchase–level determination, average past purchase behavior is often employed as a simple predictor for future behavior. The managers of focal firms also confirmed this. A series of short telephone interviews with eight people responsible for customer management within their firms revealed that the hiatus heuristics was applied in all companies to determine active and inactive customers. For determining future best customers, somewhat varying approaches were applied, but number of past purchases was always a central variable (e.g., in an RFM-type approach).

STOCHASTIC CUSTOMER BASE ANALYSIS MODELS

Both the Pareto/NBD and the BG/NBD models were developed to model repeat-buying behavior in a setting in which customers buy at a steady (albeit stochastic) rate and eventually become inactive at some unobserved time. The information they operate on consists solely of customers' past purchase behavior. More precisely, for each customer, the models operate on three values (X = x, t, T), where X = x is the number of purchases made in time frame (0, T], with the last purchase occurring at time t, where $0 < t \leq T$. In addition, the models must be calibrated on the customer base to which they are applied. This calibration process yields several model parameters that describe the purchase and dropout process of the analyzed customer base.

Pareto/NBD

The Pareto/NBD model builds on the assumption that purchases follow Ehrenberg's (1988) NBD model, whereas dropout events follow a Pareto distribution of the second kind.

More precisely, the Pareto/NBD model assumptions are as follows:

1. Individual Customer
   - Poisson purchases: While active, each customer makes purchases according to a Poisson process with purchase rate λ.
   - Exponential lifetime: Each customer remains active for a lifetime, which has an exponentially distributed duration with dropout rate μ.
2. Heterogeneity Across Customers
   - Individuals' purchase rates distributed gamma: The purchasing rate λ for the different customers is distributed according to a gamma distribution across the population of customers.
   - Individuals' dropout rates distributed gamma: The customers' dropout rates μ are distributed according to a gamma distribution across the population of customers.
   - Rates λ and μ are independent: The purchasing rates λ and the dropout rates μ are distributed independently of each other.

Among other things, the Pareto/NBD model yields the following information:

- $P(\text{Active}|X = x, t, T)$ is the probability that a random customer with purchase pattern $(X = x, t, T)$ (whose individual purchase rate and dropout rate may be unknown) is active at some time T (see Schmittlein, Morrison, & Colombo, 1987, Equations 11, 12, and 13).
- $E(X^*|X = x, t, T, T^*)$ is the expected number of transactions X^* of a random customer with purchase pattern $(X = x, t, T)$ (and unknown individual purchase rate and dropout rate) in time $(T, T + T^*]$ (see Schmittlein et al., 1987, Equation 22).

BG/NBD

There is only one assumption in the BG/NBD model that differs from the assumptions of the Pareto/NBD model. Whereas the Pareto timing model assumes that dropout of a customer can occur anytime, the BG/NBD model assumes that dropout occurs only directly after purchases. This slight change greatly reduces the complexity of the model because a beta-geometric (BG) model can be used to represent the dropout phenomena instead of the exponential gamma (Pareto) model. More precisely, the BG/NBD model assumptions are as follows:

1. Individual Customer
   - Poisson purchases: While active, each customer makes purchases according to a Poisson process with purchase rate λ.
   - Geometric lifetime: Each customer remains active for a lifetime, which is distributed over the number of transactions according to a (shifted) geometric distribution with dropout probability p.
2. Heterogeneity Across Customers
   - Individuals' purchase rates distributed gamma: The purchase rate λ for the different customers is distributed according to a gamma distribution across the population of customers.
   - Individuals' dropout probabilities distributed beta: The customers' dropout probabilities p for different customers is distributed according to a beta distribution across the population of customers.
   - Rates λ and p are independent: The purchase rates λ and dropout probabilities p are distributed independently of each other.

Among other things, the BG/NBD model yields the following information:

- $E(X^*|X = x, t, T, T^*)$ is the expected number of transactions X^* of a random customer with purchase pattern $(X = x, t, T)$ (and unknown individual purchase rate and dropout rate) in time $(T, T + T^*]$ (see Fader, Hardie, & Lee, 2005a, Equation 10).

The BG/NBD model also includes the expression $P(\text{Active}| X = x, t, T)$ to compute the probability that a customer is active at some time T, but the application of this expression is limited to customers whose individual purchase rate λ and dropout probability p is known. However, determining the dropout probability p for an individual is virtually impossible.

DATA

We conducted our study on three different data sets from three different industries. The first data set comes from an apparel retailer and covers 46,793 customers and their purchases from January 2003 through August 2004. We based our analysis on a cohort of 2,330 customers who began their buyer–seller relationship with the apparel retailer in the last week of January 2003. Thus, for this cohort, the available data cover the initial and repeat purchases for each customer over a period of 80 weeks. To calibrate the models, we used repeat-purchase data for the 2,330 customers over the first 40 weeks of the 80-week period, leaving a 40-week holdout period to validate the models.

The second data set comes from a major global airline and covers 146,961 customers and their purchases from January 1999 through December 2002. The available data only provided aggregated quarterly transactions for each customer and did not include the exact purchase dates. Our analysis of this data set focused on a cohort of 2,891 customers who conducted their initial purchase from the airline in the first quarter of 1999. For this cohort, we chose a calibration period of eight quarters

(January 1999–December 2000), leaving eight quarters for the holdout period (January 2001– December 2002).

The third data set covers customers of the online CD retailer CDNOW. The data track 23,570 customers and their purchases from January 1997 through June 1998 (78 weeks), all of whom initiated their first purchase at CDNOW in the first quarter of 1997. Fader and Hardie (2001) already used this data in multiple studies. More precisely, we used the 2,357 customer cohort available on Bruce Hardie's Web site (see Fader, Hardie, & Lee, 2005a). The calibration and holdout periods are 39 weeks each. Detailed descriptive statistics of all three data sets appear in Table 36-1.

ANALYSIS

Given the lack of empirical analysis for the superiority of the considered academic methods in determining active customers and forecasting future purchase levels, the following analyses try to shed light on this open question. First, we analyze how well the hiatus heuristic, which is used by the managers of the firms whose customer bases we analyze in this article, performs in comparison with the Pareto/NBD P(Active)

Table 36-1. Descriptive Statistics

	Airline	Apparel	CDNOW
Sample size (n)	2891	2330	2357
Available time frame	16 quarters	80 weeks	78 weeks
Time split (estimation/holdout[a])	8/8	40/40	39/39
Available time units	Quarters	Weeks/months/ quarters	Weeks
Zero repeaters in estimation periods	193	371	1411
Zero repeaters in holdout periods	1376	395	1673
Zero repeaters in estimation and holdout periods	163	184	1218
Number of purchases in estimation periods	31,479	10,855	2457
Number of purchases in holdout periods	23,033	11,351	1882
Average number of purchases per customer in estimation periods (SD)	10.88/customer (15.988)	4.658/customer (5.412)	1.04/customer (2.190)
Average number of purchases per customer in holdout periods (SD)	7.967/customer (16.810)	4.871/customer (5.598)	.798/customer (2.057)
Average T (SD)	4.393 quarters (3.006)	25.15 weeks (14.21)	6.845 weeks (10.731)

[a]Holdout period length was varied from 1 to max(holdout periods) in the analyses.

facility. Second, we analyze how well the Pareto/ NBD and BG/NBD models forecast future purchase behavior for both the individual customer and the customer base as a whole. Although aggregated sales forecasts are important statistics in terms of, for example, capacity planning or customer equity computation, we specifically focus on the forecast performance for the individual customer. This stems from the notion that there must be a decent individual customer purchase–level forecast for proper computation of metrics, such as CLV (Reinartz & Kumar, 2000, 2003) or customer value segment classification (e.g., gold, silver, and bronze segments). Picking up on this idea, not only do we present mere performance measures for individuals' forecasts, but in a third analysis, we also show how well the models perform in identifying a company's future 10% (20%) best customers.

Parameter Estimation

Both the Pareto/NBD and the BG/NBD models need to be calibrated on the customer base to which they are applied. The Pareto/NBD model has four parameters (r, α, s, β), where (r, α) represent the shape and scale parameters of the gamma distribution that determines the distribution of the purchase rates across individuals of the customer base and (s, β) represent the scale and shape parameters of the gamma distribution that determines the distribution of the dropout rates across individuals. The BG/NBD model

holds four model parameters (r, α, a, b) as well, where (r, α) (as in the NBD/Pareto model) determine the shape and scale of the purchase rate gamma distribution and (a, b) represent the shape parameters of a beta distribution that determines the distribution of the dropout probabilities across individuals of the customer base. For both models, we used a maximum likelihood approach under MATLAB to estimate the model parameters. Tables 36-2 and 36-3 report each cohort's parameters for the Pareto/NBD and BG/NBD models.

The Pareto/NBD and BG/NBD model parameters computed for the airline and CDNOW data sets are reasonable. According to the Pareto/ NBD model, an average airline customer initiates 1.9877 transactions per quarter and remains active for 7.83 quarters.[1] An average CDNOW customer initiates .0523 transactions per week (one purchase every 19.12 weeks) and remains active for 19.26 weeks. According to the BG/ NBD model, an average airline customer initiates 2.110 transactions per quarter and remains active for 4.34 quarters.[2] An average CDNOW customer initiates .0549 transactions per week (one purchase each 18.21 weeks) and purchases from the company for 73.95 weeks.

For the apparel data set, both the Pareto/ NBD and the BG/NBD models compute notable results. Although the purchasing rate of an average customer (.1190 purchases per week [one purchase every 8.40 weeks] for the Pareto/NBD

Table 36-2. Results of the Pareto/NBD Maximum Likelihood Estimation

	r	α	r/α	s	β	s/β	Log-Likelihood
Apparel	1.0954	9.2029	.1190	1.0885	973.7829	.0011	− 31338.7
Airline	1.4304	.7196	1.9877	2.5086	19.6408	.1277	− 2150.2
CDNOW	.5533	10.5776	.0523	.6061	11.6650	.0519	− 9595.0

Table 36-3. Results of the BG/NBD Maximum Likelihood Estimation

	r	α	r/α	a	b	$a/(a+b)$	Log-Likelihood
Apparel	1.0592	8.8371	.1198	.0324	2.6243	.0122	− 31336.6
Airline	1.15186	.545781	2.11048	.456637	3.73439	.108956	− 2238.34
CDNOW	.2426	4.4135	.0549	.7931	2.426	.2463	− 9582.43

model and .1198 purchases per week or one purchase every 8.34 weeks for the BG/NBD model) is reasonable, the lifetime of an average customer is exceptionally long. According to the Pareto/NBD model, an average customer remains active for 909.09 weeks (~17.48 years). According to the BG/NBD model, an average customer remains active for 684.2 weeks (~13.15 years). In other words, the models predict an average apparel customer to be ultimately loyal. This effect will be reflected in very high P(Active) values of the apparel customers.

Determining Active and Inactive Customers

If the Pareto/NBD model is used for customer activity determination, each customer's P(Active) value is computed on the basis of the customer's purchase pattern in the observation period (i.e., estimation period). However, for the continuous P(Active) values to be useful in managerial application, a cutoff threshold $c_{P(Active)}$ (decision boundary) must be determined. Customers whose P(Active) value is greater than or equal to $c_{P(Active)}$ are classified as active, and customers whose P(Active) value is less than $c_{P(Active)}$ are classified as inactive. More precisely, for the Pareto/NBD model, given a cutoff threshold $c_{P(Active)}$ and a customer with purchase pattern $(X = x, t, T)$, the customer is classified according to the following:

- $P(Active)_T \geq c_{P(Active)} \Rightarrow$ Customer is classified as active, and
- $P(Active)_T < c_{P(Active)} \Rightarrow$ Customer is classified as inactive.

To validate the classifications, we use the holdout period according to the following scheme: If a customer has made at least one purchase in the holdout period, he or she is considered "active"; if the customer has not purchased in the holdout period, he or she is considered "inactive." This scheme induces four possible classification outcomes based on whether a customer has or has not been correctly classified as active or inactive.

Likewise, for the hiatus heuristic, there needs to be a cutoff threshold c_{hiatus} below which customers are classified as active and above which customers are classified as inactive. In other

words, if a customer has not purchased for more than a time span of length c_{hiatus}, he or she is considered inactive; otherwise, he or she is considered active. More precisely, let $(X = x, t, T)$ be a customer's purchase pattern and c_{hiatus} be a cutoff threshold. Then,

- $T - t < c_{hiatus} \Rightarrow$ Customer is classified as active, and
- $T - t \geq c_{hiatus} \Rightarrow$ Customer is classified as inactive.

We obtain the same four possible classification outcomes as in the P(Active) case.

For the Pareto/NBD model, a "natural" choice for the cutoff threshold $c_{P(Active)}$ could be .5, which is in line with the work of Reinartz and Kumar (2000) on the Pareto/NBD model and the classification literature (Sharma, 1996). Helsen and Schmittlein (1993) also use .5 in the prediction of purchase events in survival analysis.

For the hiatus heuristic, airline and apparel firm mangers informed us that customers were considered inactive if they had not purchased from the firm for more than nine months. For the CDNOW data set, we did not have access to this information. Furthermore, we do not know whether CDNOW uses the hiatus heuristic at all. Given that online firms operate in fast-moving markets, we decided to use a hiatus length of six months, which should match the circumstances of an online retailer.

However, neither the managers' chosen hiatus nor a P(Active) threshold of .5 may necessarily be optimal thresholds in terms of overall correctly classified customers. We observe how far the managers' chosen hiatus and the P(Active) threshold of .5 deviate from their "optimal" values and the effect of this difference in terms of the classification performance. First, we show how well the hiatus heuristic with the threshold determined by managers' expert knowledge distinguishes the active from the inactive customers in comparison with a P(Active) analysis with a natural cutoff threshold of .5. Second, we show how sensitive the classification performance is to the choice of the thresholds.

Table 36-4 shows the results of the first analysis. The hiatus heuristic performs better

Table 36-4. P(Active) Versus Hiatus Heuristic

	Airline		Apparel		CDNOW	
	Three Quarters Hiatus	P(Active).5	Nine Months Hiatus	P(Active).5	Six Months Hiatus	P(Active).5
Inactive, correctly classified (%)	84.1569	84.6656	47.8478	.0000	82.6659	87.3881
Active, correctly classified (%)	69.9667	64.3564	89.8708	100.0000	63.5965	53.0703
Overall correctly classified (%)	76.7208	74.0228	82.7467	74.8972	77.1319	77.4289
Inactive but classified active (%)	15.8430	15.3343	52.1521	100.0000	17.3340	12.6120
Active but classified inactive (%)	30.0332	35.6435	10.1291	.0000	36.4034	46.9300
Overall incorrectly classified (%)	23.2791	25.9771	17.2532	25.1072	22.8680	22.5710

Notes: Numbers represent percentage hit rate of the active/inactive class. Overall hit rate percentages are weighted according to the distribution of active/inactive customers in the data set.

(in terms of overall correctly classified customers) than the P(Active) facility in two of the three cases; the P(Active) facility performs only slightly better on the CDNOW data set. Even more notable, the P(Active) facility fails to classify any of the inactive customers in the apparel data set correctly, whereas the hiatus heuristic classifies 47.84% of the inactive customers in the cohort correctly. This suggests that the optimal cutoff threshold $c_{P(Active)}$ for this cohort may deviate considerably from .5. What about the other P(Active) cutoff thresholds $c_{P(Active)}$ and hiatus heuristic cutoff thresholds c_{hiatus}? Are these optimal? If not, what are the optimal values? This is the subject of our next analysis.

As we mentioned previously, we consider a cutoff threshold of $c_{P(Active)}$ or c_{hiatus} optimal if it maximizes the percentage of overall correctly classified active and inactive customers of a cohort using our classification procedure.[3] Our algorithm for finding the optimal cutoff thresholds simply iterates over the domain of valid cutoff thresholds. More precisely, for the Pareto/NBD model, the algorithm is as follows:

- For $c_{P(Active)} \in \{0, \dots, 1\}$, choose $c_{P(Active)}$ so that the sum of correctly classified active and inactive customers is maximized.

For the hiatus heuristic, the algorithm is as follows:

- For $c_{hiatus} \in \{0, \dots, \infty\}$, choose c_{hiatus} so that the sum of correctly classified active and inactive customers is maximized.

Table 36-5 presents an overview of the analysis results. Surprisingly, for all three cohorts, the hiatus heuristic performs slightly better than the more complex Pareto/NBD model. Indeed, the optimal cutoff thresholds for the hiatus heuristic (4 quarters, 40 weeks, and 23 weeks) are close to the managers' and our chosen threshold (3 quarters, 39 weeks, and 26 weeks). If the optimal cutoff thresholds were used instead of expert knowledge, it would result in a marginal gain of only .8302% (airline), .1713% (apparel), and 1.0607% (CDNOW) in terms of overall correctly classified customers.

With respect to the optimal P(Active) thresholds, only for the CDNOW cohort, the optimal value of .44 is close to the natural cutoff value of .5, and its use improves performance by only .17% in terms of overall correctly classified customers. For both the apparel and the airline cohorts, the optimal P(Active) thresholds of .67 and .21, respectively, deviate substantially from the natural cutoff threshold of .5, and the gain

Table 36-5. P(Active) Versus Hiatus Heuristic Using Optimal Thresholds

	Airline		Apparel		CDNOW	
	Hiatus Heuristic	P(Active)	Hiatus Heuristic	P(Active)	Hiatus Heuristic	P(Active)
Optimal cutoff threshold	4 quarters	.21	40 weeks	.67	23 weeks	.44
Inactive, correctly classified (%)	77.109	78.489	46.581	1.009	85.4752	86.3120
Active, correctly classified (%)	77.954	72.343	90.337	99.535	60.3800	56.2863
Overall correctly classified (%)	77.551	75.268	82.918	82.832	78.1926	77.5986
Inactive but classified active (%)	22.891	21.511	53.419	98.991	14.5247	13.6879
Active but classified inactive (%)	22.046	27.657	9.663	.465	39.6199	43.7133
Overall incorrectly classified (%)	22.448	24.731	17.082	17.167	21.8074	22.4014

Notes: Numbers represent percentage hit rate of the active/inactive class. Overall hit rate percentages are weighted according to the distribution of active/inactive customers in the data set.

from using the optimal threshold rather than the natural cutoff threshold is a considerable 7.9848% and 1.2452%, respectively, in terms of overall correctly classified customers. However, if we carefully examine the analysis results for the apparel cohort, we observe that when the optimal P(Active) of .67 is used, virtually none of the inactive customers are correctly classified (1.009%). The reason is the (estimated) exceptionally long lifetime of an average apparel customer that we already briefly covered in the parameter estimation section. This property causes P(Active) values to be close to 1 for almost all apparel customers and purchase patterns; few customers had P(Active) values in the range of .67–.9. Because we optimized for maximizing the overall correctly classified statistic and given the high percentage of apparel retailer repurchasers, it is more favorable for the optimization algorithm to classify as many active customers correctly as possible. We explore the reasons for these unrealistically high P(Active) values in the "Discussion" section. Nevertheless, the natural cutoff value of .5 may not necessarily be close to its optimal value, as the apparel and airline data sets show. This makes the interpretation of the

P(Active) values counterintuitive if a P(Active) value is considered a customer's propensity to repurchase.

Predicting Future Purchase Levels

In this analysis, we focus on the Pareto/NBD and BG/NBD models' capability to predict future purchase levels cumulative for the cohort as a whole and on an individual customer basis.[4] More precisely, we benchmarked both models' predicated number of transactions against a simple management heuristic: Every customer continues to buy at his or her past mean purchase frequency.

We compare the performance of the Pareto/NBD model, the BG/NBD model, and the simple heuristic in predicting cumulated purchases on the basis of the mean absolute percentage error (MAPE) (Leeflang et al., 2000). To measure the performance on the individual customer level, we computed the (root) mean square errors ([R]MSE) for each customer over the predicted and actual transactions in the holdout period (Leeflang et al., 2000). We also computed the mean (R)MSE (median [R]MSE), which represents the mean (median) of all individual customer (R)MSE. Table 36-6 presents the results of the analysis.

On all three cohorts, the stochastic models outperform the simple heuristic on both the individual and the aggregate levels, and the Pareto/NBD and BG/NBD models perform almost identically. Although the stochastic models deliver decent results on the aggregated level, as the MAPE statistic shows, the results are split on the individual level. The models show poor performance in terms of the mean (R)MSE over all customers, but at least for 50% of the cohorts, the stochastic models predict future purchases precisely, as the median (R)MSE statistics show.

Identifying Future Best Customers

The previous analysis shows that the stochastic models under consideration precisely predict future purchases for 50% of the individuals in a cohort. Nevertheless, this figure tells us little about the applicability of individuals' transaction forecasts in a managerial context. Often, companies implement disproportionate marketing investment strategies on the basis of a customer value rating because it is common for a small percentage of customers to account for a large percentage of revenues and profits (Mulhern, 1999). For example, an airline might want to prioritize high-value customers in an overbooking occasion and deny boarding to lower-value customers. Likewise, apparel retailers may want to invite their best customers to special events (i.e., fashion shows), and an online CD store might be interested in sending sample CDs of new albums and/or artists to its best customers.

In this analysis, we assume that a company offers two levels of treatment: "best-customer" treatment and "normal-customer" treatment (Malthouse & Blattberg, 2005). Optimally, a customer should receive the best-customer treatment if he or she belongs to the future best customers. Past best customers may not necessarily belong to the group of future best customers (Wangenheim & Lentz, 2005). Under the assumption that a customer's future value cannot be estimated perfectly, a company can make two types of classification errors. First, a

future best customer may be classified as a future normal customer and thus may be denied the treatment he or she "deserves." This misclassified and, therefore, mistreated customer may spread negative word of mouth or even switch the provider completely. Second, a future normal customer may be misclassified as a future best customer, leading to extra and unjustified spending of scarce marketing resources.

If the complex models under consideration are used to identify future best customers, they need to perform better than a simple management heuristic. This is the subject of our next analysis. More precisely, we try to identify the future 10% (20%, respectively) best customers in the customer bases (in terms of future number of transactions) on the basis of the Pareto/NBD and BG/NBD models' individual customer purchase–level prediction. This classification is benchmarked against yet another simple management judgment rule: The past 10% (20%, respectively) best customers in a customer base will also be the future 10% (20%) best customers.

The results of the analysis appear in Tables 36-7 and 36-8. In line with the intention to identify a company's future best customers, the "correctly-classified-as-high" statistic is the one of interest. This statistic represents the fraction of the future best customers who actually have been classified as future best customers by the models. The complementary figure is the "incorrectly-classified-as-low" statistic. It represents the fraction of the future best customers who have falsely been classified as future low customers. In four of the six cases, the heuristic performs better that the stochastic models in terms of correctly-classified-as-high customers. Only for the airline data set do the stochastic models outperform the heuristic. We also report the Gini coefficients in Table 36-9. Instead of focusing only on the 10% and 20% best customers, this measure also includes the models' performance in classifying less valuable customers. The 10% and 20% best-customers statistic and the Gini coefficient provide complementary information; a model can be good at classifying only the 10% or 20% best customers but may be less effective at recognizing the less valuable customers. However, for both the airline and the apparel data sets, the

Table 36-6. Summary Statistics for Purchase-Level Prediction

Statistic	Airline			Apparel			CDNOW		
	BG/NBD	Pareto/NBD	Heuristic	BG/NBD	Pareto/NBD	Heuristic	BG/NBD	Pareto/NBD	Heuristic
MAPE	14.582	25.049	28.187	11.3486	12.1242	9.54866	12.15	11.49	55.69
Mean MSE	79.2123	78.2362	95.8921	4.8598	4.8857	5.02916	2.59	2.57	4.89
Median MSE	2.79177	2.3345	7.15625	1.32253	1.3309	1.38375	.061	.027	0
Mean RMSE	4.16536	4.04075	5.24889	1.6338	1.63334	1.63818	.785	.754	1.02
Median RMSE	1.67086	1.5279	2.67512	1.15001	1.15365	1.17633	.248	.166	0

Table 36-7. The 10% Best Future Customers

Statistic	Airline		Apparel			CDNOW		
	BG/NBD	Pareto/ NBD	Heuristic	BG/NBD	Pareto/ NBD	Heuristic	BG/NBD	Pareto/ NBD	Heuristic
High, correctly classified (%)	61.09	61.09	57.84	63.15	63.15	70.15	53.92	54.18	61.51
Low, correctly classified (%)	95.22	95.22	94.85	95.63	95.63	94.49	91.08	91.13	86.22
Overall correctly classified (%)	91.76	91.76	90.93	92.18	92.18	91.80	85.06	85.15	82.22
Incorrectly classified high (%)	38.90	38.90	42.15	36.84	36.84	29.84	8.91	8.86	13.77
Incorrectly classified low (%)	4.77	4.77	5.14	4.36	4.36	5.50	46.07	45.81	38.48
Overall incorrectly classified (%)	8.23	8.23	9.06	7.81	7.81	8.19	14.93	14.84	17.77

Table 36-8. The 20% Best Future Customers

Statistic	Airline			Apparel			CDNOW		
	BG/NBD	Pareto/NBD	Heuristic	BG/NBD	Pareto/NBD	Heuristic	BG/NBD	Pareto/NBD	Heuristic
High, correctly classified (%)	64.26	63.40	63.60	67.13	67.13	73.72	61.25	61.69	71.78
Low, correctly classified (%)	89.99	90.60	89.27	91.18	91.18	89.11	84.16	84.33	72.80
Overall correctly classified (%)	84.81	85.12	84.05	86.09	86.09	85.49	77.51	77.76	72.50
Incorrectly classified high (%)	35.73	36.59	36.39	32.86	32.86	26.27	15.83	15.66	27.19
Incorrectly classified low (%)	10.01	9.39	10.72	8.81	8.81	10.88	38.74	38.30	28.21
Overall incorrectly classified (%)	15.18	14.87	15.94	14.37	14.42	15.49	22.48	22.23	27.49

Table 36-9. Gini Coefficients: Best Customer Classification

Data Set	Pareto/ NBD	BG/NBD	Heuristic
Airline	.043330	.042874	.041942
Apparel	.071798	.071764	.053581

Notes: The CDNOW data set does not provide enough information to compute Gini coefficients.

simple heuristic has smaller Gini coefficients than the stochastic models (i.e., it performs better overall customer groups). Because of data constraints, we could not compute the Gini coefficient for the CDNOW data set.

DISCUSSION

The finding that P(Active) classifications do not outperform the simple hiatus heuristic in determining active and inactive customers is a devastating result for what has been called the "key result of the NBD/Pareto model" (Reinartz & Kumar, 2000, p. 21). As we already mentioned, in at least two cases (the apparel retailer and airline), managers are using the simple hiatus heuristic to determine customer (in)activity in their companies. Their expert assessment coincides almost perfectly with the optimal hiatus length that we determined in our analysis. This is an indication that managerial judgment may well act as a decent estimate of customer (in)activity. Consequently, researchers need to stop recommending the Pareto/NBD model to managers and fellow researchers for this purpose.

For identifying future best customers, the admittedly simple approach of assuming that past best customers are future best customers and the stochastic models deliver unconvincing results, even though we can correct Malthouse and Blattberg's (2005) 20–55 rule to a more positive figure. If we use the Pareto/NBD model or the BG/NBD model, approximately 33% (or less) of the top 20% customers are misclassified, making it a 20–33 rule.[5] Nevertheless, if disproportionate marketing investment decisions are made on the basis of the focal models (i.e., valuable customers receive better service, more perks,

and so on, than less valuable customers), these are likely to be inefficient. Scarce marketing resources would be spent on less valuable customers whose behavior does not justify this best-customer treatment. However, many valuable customers who are falsely classified as less valuable customers would not receive the treatment they deserve. Being disenchanted, these customers could switch to a competitor or spread negative word of mouth (Malthouse & Blattberg, 2005; Mitchell, 2005).

It appears that the managerial applicability of the Pareto/NBD and BG/NBD models is limited to customer equity computation. For this purpose, to both managers and academics, we recommend using the BG/NBD model because of its relatively easier implementation, faster computation, and superior performance compared with the Pareto/NBD model and the simple heuristic. Given the increasing interest in valuing firms on the basis of customer equity (Gupta, Lehman, & Stuart, 2004), the stochastic models are good candidates for valuing customer bases in noncontractual settings. Thus, it would be worthwhile to benchmark these models against the approach that Gupta et al. (2004) use.

CONCLUSION

This article examines the performance of what have frequently been called state-of-the-art models in customer activity determination and purchase-level prediction in noncontractual settings. To validate these models, we not only used metrics and methods recommended in the statistical literature but also simulated the implementation of those models in managerial practice. However, we find no clear evidence for the superiority of these models for managerially relevant decisions in customer management compared with simple methods that our industry partners used.

ACKNOWLEDGMENTS

The authors thank Katherine N. Lemon, Bruce Hardie, Pete Fader, Dan Goldstein, and the anonymous *JM* reviewers for their valuable comments during the preparation of this manuscript.

This work was supported by the German Research Foundation (DFG).

NOTES

1. Within the Pareto/NBD model, r/α represents the number of purchases of an average customer in one time unit, and s/β represents the dropout rate of an average customer per time unit. The lifetime of an average customer is exponentially distributed with parameter s/β and has an expected value of $1/(s/\beta)$. Therefore, according to the estimated parameters, an average CDNOW customer remains active for $1/(.0519) = 19.26$ weeks.

2. Within the BG/NBD model, r/α represents the number of purchases of an average customer in one time unit, and an average customer remains active until time τ, which is exponentially distributed with parameter $p\lambda$, and has an expected value of $1/(p\lambda,)$, given that $\lambda = r/\alpha$ and $p = a/(a + b)$. Therefore, according to the estimated parameters, an average CDNOW customer remains active for $1/(.0549 \times .2463) = 73.95$ weeks.

3. Although it is also possible to optimize for a maximum of correctly classified active or inactive customers depending on the purchase of the marketing action (i.e., reactivation or elimination), we believe that our approach to maximize for the sum of correctly classified active and inactive customers is reasonable because it combines both approaches.

4. See Schmittlein, Morrison, and Colombo (1987, Equation 22) and Fader, Hardie, and Lee (2005a, Equation 10).

5. Our analysis confirms Malthouse and Blattberg's (2005) 80–15 rule.

Everyday things

Introduction to Chapter 37

Green Defaults: Information Presentation and Pro-environmental Behaviour

The clichéd opening sentence in books on decision making asserts that every one of us has to make thousands of decisions a day. Yet we do not. We often avoid making them by letting others decide, or by simply doing nothing. But what situations are likely to encourage our passivity? Default represents such a situation. Legal defaults, for instance, keep many people from making an active decision about organ donation; even in an experimental study where no costs occurred for an active decision, the majority still went with the default option (Johnson & Goldstein, 2003). The default heuristic "if there is a default, do nothing" illustrates that behavior is jointly determined by mind and environment—Simon's scissors principle. In the case of organ donation, the same heuristic can lead to opposite outcomes, depending on the environment; that is, whether a country has an opt-in or opt-out policy. Similarly, the tit-for-tat heuristic ("cooperate first, then imitate what your partner did") can lead to opposite behaviors, being nice or nasty, cooperative or otherwise, depending on the partner's behavior (Gigerenzer, 2007). Behavior is often not a mirror of an underlying trait or preference but rather an adaptive response to one's environment.

The article by Daniel Pichert and Konstantinos Katsikopoulos applies this analysis to the choice of renewable energy sources and "green energy." It combines "natural" experiments with laboratory experiments. To the degree that choice of energy is a consequence of social preference, environmental attitude, or political motivation, defaults should not matter. One should buy the energy that fits one's preferences, be it gray or green, everything else being equal. But is that so? Are our preferences stronger than defaults when they are in conflict? The results reported in this article suggest that defaults tend to dominate preferences, and even more so in natural situations than in laboratory experiments.

CHAPTER 37

Green Defaults: Information Presentation and Pro-environmental Behaviour

Daniel Pichert and Konstantinos V. Katsikopoulos

Abstract: There is inconsistency in many people's choice of electricity. When asked, they say they prefer a 'green' (i.e., environmentally friendly) source for this energy. Yet, although green electricity is available in many markets, people do not generally buy it. Why not? Motivated by behavioral decision research, we argue that the format of information presentation drastically affects the choice of electricity. Specifically, we hypothesize that people use the kind of electricity that is offered to them as the default. We present two natural studies and two experiments in the laboratory that support this hypothesis. In the two real-world situations, there was a green default, and most people used it. In the first laboratory experiment, more participants chose the green utility when it was the default than when 'gray' electricity was the default. In the second laboratory experiment, participants asked for more money to give up green electricity than they were willing to pay for it. We argue that changing defaults can be used to promote pro-environmental behavior. Potential policymaking applications of this work are discussed.

1. INTRODUCTION

The way we currently use energy is not sustainable. First, we are heavily reliant on fossil fuels—such as oil, coal, and gas—that will one day be depleted (Roberts, 2005). Second, and perhaps even more importantly, the burning of fossil fuels is the biggest source of emissions of carbon dioxide, one of the greenhouse gases that contribute to global warming. Already fuel prices and temperature have been rising. Furthermore, the International Energy Agency (IEA) predicts that the global hunger for energy is likely to grow in the future (Organisation for Economic Cooperation and Development/International

Energy Agency, 2006). The goal of reducing greenhouse gas emissions, as formulated in the 1997 Kyoto Protocol, seems hard to meet: Developing countries are rapidly approaching the levels of consumption found in Western countries and emissions are still growing (albeit at a slower rate) in the more industrialized nations. The IEA has called for strong and coordinated government action (Organisation for Economic Co-operation and Development/International Energy Agency, 2006).

The goal of those policies would presumably be to facilitate the switch to using renewable energy sources such as water, wind, biomass, and the sun. The European Commission, for example, is promoting renewable energy with a broad mix of measures ranging from tax policy to research and development.[1] The objective is to induce changes in human behavior (Gardner & Stern, 2002; Nickerson, 2003). Since the start of the liberalization of European energy markets several years ago, most European consumers of electricity now have the "power to choose." This is the title of the official European Union information brochure,[2] which tells consumers that " ... because your supplier now has to indicate the source of their bills, you can choose the most environmentally friendly supplier."

Consumers can purchase this so-called 'green' electricity by choosing a green tariff, participating in a green electricity program, or contracting with a utility specialized in trading green electricity (Bird, Wüstenhagen, & Aabakken, 2002). Choice of carrier, including the possibility to buy green electricity, has been established in the United Kingdom, a number of US states, Germany (where this study takes place), and a number of other countries (Bird et al., 2002; Clark, Kotchen, & Moore, 2003). By means of labeling and information disclosure, consumers are now able to know how the electricity they use is produced (Roe, Teisl, Rong, & Levy, 2001; Truffer, Markard, & Wüstenhagen, 2001). Note that buying green electricity does not make a difference in the actual household electricity supply, but rather in investment flows. The idea is that increasing demand for green power will result in fewer conventional fuels and more environmentally benign energy sources being used.

Have these efforts brought results? In theory, yes: Opinion polls and market analyses in the United States, the United Kingdom, and other European countries show strong public support for green energy (Farhar, 1999; Laboratory for Energy and the Environment, 2005; MORI, 1996; Roe, Teisl, Levy, & Russell, 2001). Typically 50–90% of those asked say that they favor renewable energy and are willing to pay at least a small premium to have it. But, unfortunately, these statements do not reflect behavior. The percentage of people who consume green electricity is marginal in nearly all countries, for example, 1% in Ireland, .4% in Finland, 1% in Germany, 2% in Switzerland, and .5% in the United Kingdom (Bird et al., 2002).

In short, when asked, people prefer green electricity. This kind of electricity is available in the market, but people do not buy it. Instead, most of us rely on 'gray' electricity, that is, electricity generated from detrimental or at least controversial energy sources such as coal or atomic power. Why is this?

2. DEFAULTS

A default is the condition that is imposed when an individual fails to make a decision (Johnson & Goldstein, 2003) or the option that consumers receive if they do not explicitly request something different (Brown & Krishna, 2004). Many decision-making studies have shown that defaults tend to 'stick', that is, people do not switch to another alternative (e.g. Anderson, 2003; Sunstein & Thaler, 2003). Johnson and Goldstein (2003) provided a striking illustration of the power of defaults. They showed that consent rates for organ donation in different European countries are largely the product of national defaults. Some countries have an opt-in policy (one has to register to become an organ donor) and others use an opt-out policy (one is a donor unless one registers not to be a donor). The two policies result in large differences in consent rates. In Austria, for example, 99% of the people are organ donors whereas in Germany the consent rate is 12%. Johnson and Goldstein (2003) argued that such differences could not be explained by socio-economic variables. Generally, although they are free to do so at any time, most people simply do not change the default.

Default effects have also been found in the participation in 401(k) retirement plans (Choi, Laibson, Madrian, & Metrick, 2002; Madrian & Shea, 2001), in insurance choices (Johnson, Hershey, Meszaros, & Kunreuther, 1993), in consumer research (Brown & Krishna, 2004; Park, Youl Jun, & MacInnis, 2000; Puto, 1987), and in Internet privacy policies (Johnson, Bellman, & Lohse, 2002). Camerer (2000, p. 295) writes: "Making one option the status quo or default or endowing a person with a good (even hypothetically) seems to establish a reference point people move away from only reluctantly, or if they are paid a large sum."

The influence of the default seems to be even stronger when consumers are not so familiar with a product and have little knowledge about it (Sunstein & Thaler, 2003). This describes the commodity of electricity, which is an intangible product (it is, in a real sense, difficult to grasp). Moreover, Western citizens have been described as 'energy illiterates' (Roberts, 2005). Thus, one might expect that consumers' preferences are constructed in the sense that they are developed on the spot and are highly contingent upon context and information presentation factors (Payne, Bettmann, & Johnson, 1992; Slovic, 1995).

Why do defaults work? Explanations in the literature often involve biases, that is, departures from what is considered rational according to standard norms of logic and probability (Kahneman & Tversky, 1979; Samuelson & Zeckhauser, 1988). This kind of explanation has been criticized because such norms can be argued to be irrelevant to successful behavior in the real world (Fasolo, McClelland, & Todd, 2007; Gigerenzer, Todd, & the ABC Research Group, 1999). Sticking to defaults can be considered rational because it can save time, effort, and money. Whereas accepting the default is effortless and requires no time commitment, people intending to switch have to search for information (e.g. on the Internet or by asking others), choose from the possible options, and finally act. In addition, the default may be cheaper as is the case with gray electricity, or transaction costs might be charged: In an early stage of the market liberalization, Norwegian customers had to pay a fee in order to switch (Nordic Energy Regulators, 2005).

There are also good reasons for sticking with the default that do not have to do with rationality (at least in a strict sense). For one, it does not seem unreasonable to interpret the default as a recommendation from the policymaker, indicating the socially desired behavior (Johnson & Goldstein, 2003; McKenzie, Liersch, & Finkelstein, 2006). Similarly, when a company offers a 'standard product' (Brown & Krishna, 2004) as a default option, the customer might interpret this product as the one that is known to the company to fit most of its customers. Second, it is generally difficult for people to perform trade-offs (Irwin & Baron, 2001) and reconcile conflicting objectives such as saving money and preserving the environment. This becomes even harder when some of the objectives have a moral connotation, as does preserving the environment. Sticking with the default seems to allow one to bypass a stressful and awkward decision (even though doing nothing is also a decision). Finally, people are creatures of habit—interestingly, the word 'customer' historically derives from 'custom', meaning 'habit'. In a way, being a customer already refers to the psychological attachment to a vendor or a service.

In summary, the decision-making literature shows that defaults have a strong influence on behavior. There are a number of reasons for this effect and they seem applicable to the choice of an electricity utility. Therefore we formulate the following hypothesis:

Hypothesis. Defaults affect the choice of electricity. Thus, currently, most people use gray electricity because gray electricity is usually the default. In those cases where green electricity is the default, most people will use green electricity.

In the next section, we present two natural experiments and two laboratory experiments that we used to put our hypothesis to the test.

3. STUDIES

The most critical test of our hypothesis is whether people who are subject to a green default also use green electricity. It is difficult to find such a naturally occurring situation. We contacted a number of power suppliers but could not obtain relevant data. In the end, however, we succeeded in finding two cases where a group of consumers had a green default. In the first case, a green default was established in a small town. In the second case, a supplier used green electricity as a default when asking its customers to choose between three different tariffs. In these natural experiments, the dependent variable is the proportion of customers choosing green electricity. We use the term "natural experiments" in the sense that we simply observe naturally occurring "treatments" without further manipulation (Harrison & List, 2004). A problem with observations such as these, however, is that they lack experimental control. For this reason, we added two laboratory experiments in which we exposed participants to hypothetical choices under varying conditions. This also allowed us to look into other dependent variables. We accept that choices in the laboratory lack real consequences, but we believe that the four studies together allow the testing of our hypothesis.

3.1. First Natural Experiment: A Green Default in the Real World

Schönau is a picturesque little town situated in the southern part of the Black Forest, an area that is politically dominated by the conservatives, especially in more rural areas. The influence of the Green Party (the German party that is commonly associated with the promotion of pro-environmental policies) is comparatively low: In the last elections for the German Parliament, the Party received approximately 5% of the ballots cast. We emphasize this to show that the area can hardly be described as the political centre of grass-roots environmentalism. In fact, the opposite might be true.

About 2,500 citizens inhabit Schönau. The unemployment rate is low. A quick glance at Schönau's Web site reveals that several small clubs are engaged in the cultivation of rustic folklore, including traditional costumes, dances, and songs. What makes Schönau interesting for our purposes is that in this town, green electricity is not the alternative but the default. Here is how it happened.

In the 1980s, a citizens' initiative was founded in Schönau as a reaction to the Chernobyl disaster. The objective of the group was activism against nuclear power. Campaigns like these were not uncommon in Germany in those days but it is remarkable that the activities of campaigners in Schönau resulted in proposals to take over the electricity grid in order to establish an environmentally friendly energy supply. Needless to say, this venture caused some conflict. Citizens had to decide if the initiative would be allowed to manage the Schönau grid. Before the vote, the Schönau city centre witnessed intense campaigns by both supporters and opponents of the proposal. Finally, the proposal was accepted by a very close margin (ca. 52% vs. 48%, turnout ca. 90%). Even more astonishingly, in 1997, the initiative managed to raise enough funds to buy the grid from its reluctant owner. Recall now

that the German electricity market was opened in 1998. Because the deal was clinched 1 year before, the EWS (i.e. the Schönau Power Company) became the incumbent utility in Schönau and it still is. EWS purchases mainly energy generated from renewables from newly built facilities and promotes solar energy. That is, EWS, also called 'Electricity Rebels', stands for a truly green approach.[3]

But as the heat surrounding the citizens' vote shows, the Schönau citizens were polarized with regard to the rebels' ideas. In fact, one of the managing directors of EWS told us: "We were really afraid because we did not know what would happen when the liberalization started." But those fears were unnecessary. In 2006 (about 8 years after the market opening), 1,669 out of 1,683 electricity meters[4] in Schönau were still supplied with electricity traded by EWS (data from EWS). Nearly every customer remained with the green default. Recall that the share of those participating in green electricity programs in other German towns, where there is usually a gray default, is approximately 1%.

3.2. Second Natural Experiment: A Utility-Induced Green Default

In the case of Schönau, switching away from the default requires searching for information about alternative options. In our second example, this effort is not necessary as it is the incumbent supplier itself providing a number of alternatives and asking their customers for a decision. The company published the data we will present. Wüstenhagen (2000, in German) previously used these data in a marketing analysis, but not to make the point we are making here.

In 1999, Energiedienst GmbH, a company supplying a grid area in southern Germany, diversified its services, offering three new tariffs where there had previously been only one. Letters were mailed to 150,000 private and business customers. Interesting here is the fact that a green (waterpower) tariff was used as the default: Customers wishing to be supplied with the green tariff did not need to respond. The green tariff was slightly cheaper than the previous tariff offered by the company. The other two options were a gray, even more economical tariff (ca. 8%

cheaper), and a more expensive green tariff (ca. 23% more expensive, including a higher share of electricity generated from new facilities). Customers preferring one of these two alternative tariffs had to reply.

Two months after the request was sent, 4.3% of the customers had decided to switch to the economical tariff, less than 1% had switched to the premium-priced green tariff, and .7% reacted by switching to a different supplier. About 94% of the customers remained with the default option.

It may be that by using a green default, the company intended to influence customers' behavior in such a way that they would choose the product the company wanted to distribute. We do not know. Our point is that here as well as in the Schönau natural experiment, the information presentation format had a dramatic effect on the electricity people used. More specifically, a green default means that most people use green electricity.

As already mentioned, natural experiments have their limitations. In the experiments reported here, (1) some people simply might not have known that they could switch, or how to do so; in this case, one cannot exactly say that those customers "chose" (although this argument applies more to the first experiment and less to the second one where the utility informed its customers about the opportunity to switch). (2) In the first experiment, the heated debate on the takeover of the grid might have had effects of its own that are difficult to judge; it may have, for example, made people more sensitive to the subject of preserving the environment. (3) We do not have data about offers from other suppliers in the two experiments, and this prevents us from disentangling the effect of default from that of price. (4) Related to this, both experiments looked at regions with above-average incomes. To address these limitations, we conducted two laboratory studies, which allowed more control and tested additional dependent variables.

3.3. First Laboratory Experiment: Choices

We designed a simple decision task that confronted people directly with the choice between different electricity suppliers. The control we gained by using a laboratory experiment was found in the random assignment of participants to conditions, the use of a 'neutral' condition, and the implementation of a trade-off (a more expensive green service vs. a cheaper gray service). We also asked participants to give reasons for their decisions. Our prediction was that more people would choose the more expensive green tariff when it was presented as the default option than when it was presented as an alternative to the lower priced gray tariff.

3.3.1. Method and procedure

Analyzing German marketing research, we found that younger adults, in general, know that they can choose their electricity supplier, because they are better informed, relocate more often, and are more familiar with modern registration procedures using the Internet. However, many older people are still unfamiliar with the task of choosing an electricity supplier. This is why our experimenters were instructed to address young adults (loosely defined as persons between the ages of 18 and 35 years).[5]

We gave participants a short questionnaire that consisted of two parts. The first part was a short vignette (see Appendix A). Participants were asked to imagine that they had moved to another town. In their new flat, they were confronted with the choice between two electricity suppliers: one advertising 'clean electricity' generated from environmentally benign renewable energy sources, and another offering a more economically priced tariff. For the latter option, no further information about the origin of the electricity was given. It was meant to represent a utility marketing gray energy (in standard electricity tariffs in Germany, a mix of fossil fuels and nuclear power is predominant). This design took into account the reality of marketing, namely, that suppliers distributing gray energy avoid discussing energy sources, for good reason; for instance, nuclear power is extremely controversial (we were not able to find a single utility that advertises cheap nuclear power). On the other hand, all utilities specializing in green energy explicitly highlight this information. A manipulation check (see below) ensured that

Table 37-1. Options in the First Laboratory Experiment

Company Name	Information Given	Monthly Costs
EcoEnergy	EcoEnergy sells clean electricity, generated from renewable energy sources. Contribute to climate protection and environmental protection!	€30 (ca. $39)
Aeon	We offer low-priced electricity tariffs—you cannot beat our prices. Save money with Acon!	€25 (ca. $32)

the participants interpreted the descriptions in such a way that the gray service appeared less environmentally benign than the green one.

The information given about the two companies and their tariffs is listed in Table 37-1. The prices are very close to what a small household in Germany actually pays for electricity per month. One of the two companies was introduced as the incumbent utility. The other utility was presented as a competitor that advertises its offers. To test for default effects, we used two different versions of the decision question. In the *green condition*, the green utility served as the default, and the gray one was the competitor. Roles were reversed in the *gray condition*. The prediction was that more people would choose the green option in the green condition.

Furthermore, we added a *neutral condition*. Here a choice had to be made between the two utilities without either of the two being the incumbent. Comparisons were planned between the gray condition as a benchmark (representing the usual situation in Germany) and the green and neutral conditions.

Participants were asked to give a short statement explaining the reasons for their decision. They also had to rate both utilities on 7-point scales (ranging from very negative to very positive), for both their environmental and pricing policy. Finally, participants had to rank five attributes (company reputation, environmental impact, location of provider, quality of service, price) according to their relevance for choosing an electricity supplier. The order of the attributes was randomized across participants. We also gathered demographic data. The completion of the questionnaire took approximately 5 min. Participants were rewarded with a bar of chocolate.

3.3.1.1. Participants. Participants were recruited in public places in Berlin and in the laboratory of the Max Planck Institute for Human Development while waiting to participate in other experiments. This resulted in a sample of 225 participants (126 female, 99 male). Mean age was 25 years (SD = 3.7). Persons younger than 18 years or older than 35 years were removed from the sample, which resulted in the exclusion of 8 persons. Excluding these cases from the analysis did not affect the results.

Most of the participants were students (63%). Participants were randomly assigned to one of the three conditions. A power analysis was conducted before the experiment to ensure that the selected sample size would result in a power of at least .80 for a medium effect size at a significance level of .05 (Cohen, 1988).

3.3.1.2. Manipulation checks. For environmental impact, participants rated the green utility (M = 4.9, SD = 1.1) better than the non-green utility (M = 3.3, SD = 1.1), $t(224) = 14.2$, $p = .001$. The price of the gray utility (M = 4.8, SD = 1.1) was considered to be better than that of the green one (M = 3.4, SD = 1.0), $t(224) = 14.49$, $p = .001$. Finally, for the ratings of the five attributes, price was the most important (M = 1.72, SD = .9), followed by environmental impact (M = 2.53, SD = 1.3), quality of service (M = 2.88, SD = 1.1), company reputation (M = 3.6, SD = 1.2), and local production (M = 4.24, SD = 1.0).

3.3.2. Results

3.3.2.1. Choices. The choices of the participants are displayed in Figure 37-1. In the gray condition, 31 of 75 participants (41%) chose the green utility, whereas 52 of 77 participants

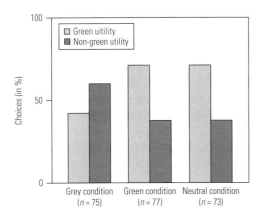

Figure 37-1. Choices of carrier across the three conditions.

Table 37-2. Frequencies of Mentioned Arguments

Argument	Mentioned (%)
Price considerations	71
Environmental considerations	62
Anticipated efforts caused by switching/laziness	15
Distrust/skepticism of a provider	12
Given insufficient information about energy sources or further conditions	9
Criticism of the default itself	2

[a]Excluded in neutral condition.

(68%) in the green condition chose the green utility. When the two options were presented in a neutral format (neutral condition), 67% chose green. A 3×2 χ^2 analysis shows that there was an overall effect of condition on participants' choices, $\chi^2 (2) = 13.94$, $p = .001$.

To assess which of the effects in the data are statistically significant, two separate 2×2 χ^2 tests were calculated. Supporting our hypothesis, more participants chose the green utility in the green condition as compared to participants from the gray condition, $\chi^2(1) = 10.52$, $p = .001$, with a medium effect size ($\Phi = .26$). Comparing participants' choices in the gray and the neutral condition, more participants chose the green utility in the neutral condition, $\chi^2(1) = 9.9$, $p = .002$, $\Phi = .26$.

3.3.2.2. Reasons. The reasons for the participants' choices were analyzed as follows. We tallied how often an attribute (such as price or environmental impact) was mentioned (in a positive or negative way). The most common reasons and their frequencies are displayed in Table 37-2. Two judges carried out the coding independently. As multiple codes could be assigned to a participant's statement, agreement between raters was calculated for each category separately. Interrater reliability was high (coefficient k ranged from .72 to .94). Disagreements were resolved by discussion.

The majority of the participants stated thoughts about the environment, the price, or both (44%) motivated their choice. We next wanted to analyze whether different conditions evoke different thoughts about the issues, but because there was high variability in the statements, we were not able to detect systematic differences as a function of the default. Still, some observations are interesting. First, 15% of the participants stated that anticipated effort (such as requesting a new contract) or laziness prevented them from switching, a tendency supporting the default option. Second, in the majority of cases, when distrust or skepticism of a provider was stated, it referred to the alternative, nondefault option (17 of 19 statements; neutral condition excluded). Third, in the cases where participants reported insufficient information, most of them wanted to learn more about the alternative option (12 out of 16), whereas fewer people stated that they would gather information about the default company (2 persons) or about both companies for comparison (2 persons; neutral condition excluded). Last, it is worth mentioning that only very few people (2%) criticized the default itself ("I do not like becoming a customer of a utility automatically; this is impertinent").

3.3.3. Discussion

The results of this experiment support the hypothesis that people are more likely to choose the green option when it is presented as the default than when it is presented as an alternative.

Moreover, a similar effect occurred between the gray default format and a neutral presentation format without any option being a default. (In reality, however, this situation is rare, as German energy law prescribes that incumbent utilities have to provide a 'basic supply'.)

The reasons the participants gave for their decisions provide some indication of why electricity defaults work. Expected inconvenience and uncertainty associated with switching might prevent people from doing so. Furthermore, distrust, skepticism, or complaints about insufficient information referred, in most cases, to the alternative option. Only a few participants seemed to assume that the default option had to be assessed or that there could be something wrong with it. Possibly, many people interpret the default option as an implicit recommendation in the sense that if there is a standard established by an authority, it cannot be (very) wrong.

We have to admit that this experiment is different in several ways from choosing an electricity supplier in reality. First, in reality, customers might not be directly confronted with the decision problem, as in the questionnaire. Second, in the questionnaire, the decision between the options can be made without any real transaction costs or search costs, and it has no real consequences. Third, in reality, some people might not even know that they can choose their electricity supplier. But all three arguments work *in favor* of the default in the real world. In fact, this might explain why substantially more participants switched in our study than in real life. The same tendency can be found in the organ donation study (Johnson & Goldstein, 2003). Our next experiment looks into the influence of defaults in the laboratory by investigating dependent variables other than choice.

3.4. Second Laboratory Experiment: Willingness to Pay and Accept

With this experiment we attempted to examine the influence of defaults in the choice of electricity not by directly testing how often the green utility is chosen but by asking for the monetary value people attach to the green utility. In decision-making research, there are two ways to measure this value: *willingness to pay* (WTP) and

willingness to accept (WTA). The main finding is that WTA > WTP, that is, to give up a good, people want to be given more money than they are willing to pay to acquire that good (Kahneman, Knetsch, & Thaler, 1991). This is called the endowment effect. In a sense, the endowment effect and the effect of defaults are related because the default is what people are *endowed* with. We thus hypothesize that peoples' WTA for green electricity will be higher than their WTP for green electricity (the corresponding hypothesis for gray electricity does not make much sense because people do not seem to be willing to pay any extra amount of money for gray electricity).

3.4.1. Method and procedure

We gave participants a short questionnaire. The first laboratory experiment showed that participants hesitated to switch from one company to another. Hence, in this second experiment, we stressed that no switching costs would be involved. Furthermore, because some participants criticized the lack of information in the first experiment, we added a short introductory explanation about electricity and its origins (see Appendix B). The explanation stressed that various opinions exist about the different forms of electricity supply (in Germany, not only is the energy from nuclear power controversial, but also the extension of wind power), so we wanted to survey customers' willingness to pay. We used a between-participants design with two conditions.

In the WTP condition, participants were asked if they were willing to switch to green electricity given that they currently have a gray tariff (see vignette in Appendix B). If so, they were asked to indicate what extra premium they would be willing to pay for this per month. Participants in the WTA condition were asked if they would be willing to switch to gray electricity given that they are supplied with green electricity by default. Participants willing to switch were asked to indicate how much cheaper the gray electricity tariff would have to be to make them switch.

In both cases, participants had the option to state that they would not switch by checking a "no" box. Following Irwin, Slovic, Lichtenstein, and McClelland (1993), WTP was assumed to be

0 for participants checking "no" in the WTP condition. The interpretation is that they are simply not willing to pay more for green electricity and thus their response is "0".

Participants not providing a value in the WTA condition were excluded from the WTP/WTA comparison (Irwin et al., 1993) because it is well known that participants in WTA conditions refuse to provide monetary values for decisions with moral connotations (Kahneman et al., 1991). Note that this behavior might be interpreted as "I am not willing to switch to gray energy, even if it is for free or for any compensation you offer". However, as this response indicates support for the green option, the frequency of these "protest answers" in the WTA condition is reported below.

Participants were also asked to make brief statements about their behavior. One more question checked whether participants knew what they were paying in reality. A short demographic section ended the questionnaire.

3.4.2. Participants

Eighty-eight participants (56 female, 32 male, age $M = 25.0$; SD = 3.2) completed a questionnaire in the laboratory while waiting for other experiments (and were given a bar of chocolate). Seventy-seven per cent of the participants were students. To select the sample size, a power analysis was carried out to ensure that the study had at least .80 power. We expected a substantial number of participants (in the WTA condition) to provide no values due to protest answers (see above), and therefore, potentially unequal group sizes were taken into account.

3.4.3. Participants not providing values in the WTA condition ("protest answers")

Twenty-three of the 47 participants (43%) in the WTA condition indicated that they were not willing to accept compensation for switching (see above). These participants were not included in the WTA/WTP comparison.

3.4.4. Willingness to pay and willingness to accept

For the remaining 65 participants, mean WTP and WTA were analyzed. Results are displayed in

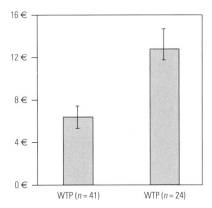

Figure 37-2. Stated willingness to pay and willingness to accept for green electricity in euros. Error bars display standard error.

Figure 37-2. The participants' WTP had a mean value of $M = €6.59$ (SD = €5.53, $n = 41$). The mean WTA was $M = €13.00$ (SD = €7.34, $n = 24$). A t-test revealed a significant difference, $t(63) = 4.02$, $p = .001$. Cohen's d was 1.03, representing a large effect (Cohen, 1988).

3.4.5. Switching behavior

An alternative interpretation is that people checking "no" (in both conditions) were not willing to switch to the alternative tariff. For this reason, we compared the share of potential switchers and nonswitchers. All 88 participants were included in the analysis. As reported above, 23 of the 47 participants (43%) in the WTA condition were under no means willing to switch, whereas 9 of 41 participants (22%) in the WTP condition refused to switch (i.e., WTP = 0). The share of "stayers" is higher in the WTA condition, $\chi^2(1) = 6.9$, $p = .009$.

3.4.6. Statements

We used the same procedure as in the first laboratory experiment, again with good interrater agreement (k ranging from .85 to .95). Statements about the environment (67% of the participants) or about the price difference (65%) were predominant, while 48% of the participants thought about both. But we were not able to detect any differences that could be attributed to the varying conditions.

The interpretation of the answers to the question of how much the participants were paying turned out to be difficult; most students live in shared flats, and many of them could not give a precise estimation of their share of the monthly bill (36% did not know what they were paying at all; others gave the sum for the whole shared flat). As a result, the variance of the sums was so high that we decided to omit further analysis.

3.4.7. Discussion

As hypothesized, participants were willing to pay a small premium for green electricity but demanded considerably more in compensation for giving up the green electricity supply. Note that only 57% of the participants in the WTA condition were included in the WTP/WTA analysis: the others stated that they would not switch no matter what the reduction might be. Overall, the findings support our hypothesis: once a green default is established, people are either reluctant to move away from this reference point or they demand a relatively large sum to do so (since WTA > WTP).

4. GENERAL DISCUSSION: CAN DEFAULTS PROMOTE PRO-ENVIRONMENTAL BEHAVIOUR?

We reported four studies that demonstrate a strong effect of information presentation format, specifically of the default used, on the choice of electricity utility. In electricity markets as currently organized, this effect leads to generation and consumption of energy from unsustainable sources. Changing the gray default—by establishing a green default or by just implementing a neutral choice situation—results in a significantly higher percentage of customers buying green electricity.

Although we suggested some explanations for why defaults in electricity marketing work and provided some exploratory analyses, we did not pursue this further here. We focused on showing that they work. More theoretical research is required, for example, on understanding better the recommendations that people perceive to be implicit in defaults (McKenzie et al., 2006). Another promising direction could investigate

the finding that people consider themselves far more responsible for their actions than for their omissions (Spranca, Minsk, & Baron, 1991).

At any rate, there may be opportunity for applications, especially at a local level. Imagine a community whose government plans to launch a new green electricity program to decrease the share of conventional power production from older plants. If this was a legally and politically feasible option, the community might enroll their citizens automatically in the program, thus establishing a default. Of course citizens would be free to opt out of the program any time they wish. Another example might be a block of flats that is supplied with green electricity when people move in. Finally, apart from making the more environmentally benign option the default, it may be worth trying the least intrusive option of abandoning defaults altogether.

We finish by urging for caution because the manipulation of defaults has its limits. There are technical issues, limitations of default effects, and moral issues. First, it may be that, from an engineering standpoint, the implementation of a green default is not possible. For example, it has been argued that the national energy supply of a country could not simply be replaced by renewable energy production from one day to the next even if all the consumers wanted to buy green power now. In the Netherlands, for example, suppliers had to stop advertising green power because it was sold out after 13% of the customers decided to buy green electricity (Bird et al., 2002). Perhaps, however, some imagination can be used to develop creative solutions (e.g., voluntary premiums), since the central issue is changing investment flows.

Second, note that even though the influence of defaults is strong, if price differences become too large, customers might react. For example, customers will not remain with a tariff when it costs $1,000 more each month regardless of whether it is the default or not. Also, when customers suspect that the vendor or the policy maker wants to force an option upon them, they might react (Brown & Krishna, 2004).

Third and finally, policy makers intentionally changing defaults may be accused of paternalistic manipulation (Berg & Gigerenzer, 2007; Klein,

2004; Sunstein & Thaler, 2003; Thaler & Sunstein, 2003). Of course, to some extent, institutions always provide starting points and defaults. And, from the environmental perspective, the existing default is not the most desirable. However, frequent opting out or switching might cause citizens to experience stress or unpleasantness. It is not so trivial to impose a default condition that conflicts with the fundamental values held by an individual as this might force a person to react. But when these ethical issues are taken into account, the manipulation of default rules actually might cause less excitement than expected.

Dealing with the "human factor" in sustainable development and pro-environmental behavior can yield theoretical and practical challenges (Gardner & Stern, 2002; Nickerson, 2003; Stern, 2000a, 2000b). Our specific findings demonstrate that in many cases, what we prefer depends on the context of choice and how the choice is presented (Bettman, Luce, & Payne, 1998; Payne et al., 1992); this has already been demonstrated for human behavior in areas such as health, finance, law, and marketing. When it comes to environmental issues, it is our conviction that a stronger consideration of insights from decision-making research will contribute to a better understanding and encouragement of pro-environmental behavior.

ACKNOWLEDGMENTS

We would like to thank Yaniv Hanoch, Mark Heitmann, Daniel Goldstein, Felix Warneken, Stefan Krauss, and the ABC Research Group for their comments and ideas.

NOTES

1. See the European Commission's White Paper on Renewable Energy Sources (1997) or the Directive on the Promotion of Electricity from Renewable Energy Sources (2001), available at http://ec.europa.eu/energy.
2. Brochure on the Internal Energy Market, available at http://ec.europa.eu/energy/gas/pubhcations/index_en.htm.
3. Simon (1956) used the term "environment" to label this collection of things but for the purposes of this paper we will call it *psychological environment* to differentiate it from the natural one.
4. The company's data records cover electricity meters that are largely, but not exactly related to the number of households or inhabitants.
5. The study took place in Berlin, and due to the availability of flats in this city, it is not unusual for 18-year-olds to live in their own flat. Persons younger than 18 have limited contractual capability in Germany. However, there is no strong rationale for choosing the age of 35 as the upper limit for "young adults," which is—in a way—arbitrary. If it is true that older people are less familiar with the task of choosing an electricity supplier or simply do not know that they can switch, an age effect can be predicted. We did not address this prediction in the present study.

APPENDIX A

Instructions in First Laboratory Experiment (translated from German)

Gray condition: "Imagine you have to relocate to another town. After you move into your new flat, you receive a letter from the electric power supplier, *Acon*. You are told that by moving into your new flat you became an *Acon* customer: "*Acon* is pleased to welcome you as a new customer. We are responsible for the basic electricity supply in this residential area. *We offer low-priced electricity tariffs—you cannot beat our prices. Save money with Acon!* Your monthly premium is €25." You are kindly asked to fill in some personal data on an attached document, which you do. A couple of days later a contract is sent to you.

Some weeks later you find a flyer in your mailbox, advertising offers from the electric power supplier *Eco-Energy*: "Switch to *Eco Energy*! Did you know that you can easily switch your electricity supplier? *Eco Energy sells clean electricity, generated from renewable energy sources. Contribute to climate protection and environmental protection!* Your monthly premium will be €30."

What do you do? (please check box)

☐ Stay with Acon
☐ Switch to Ecoenergy

Green condition: The vignette described the reverse situation; that is, the default company offered 'green' power and the advertisement was for cheaper electricity (see text). Although premiums for electricity vary according to individual consumption, participants were told by the experimenter to accept the premiums as given for the sake of simplicity.

Neutral condition: Here, the vignette had slightly different wording: "Imagine you have to relocate to another town. After you move into your new flat, your landlord kindly asks you to choose a power supplier. In this building, two electric power companies offer electricity. Here is some information about the two suppliers." Then the information about the two companies is given. To control for order effects, the order of the options was permutated randomly.

APPENDIX B

Instructions in second laboratory experiment (translated from German)

General information: "Electricity is produced in various ways. In Germany, conventionally produced electricity is—for the most part—generated by the burning of fossil fuels (e.g., coal) and atomic power. So-called green electricity is generated from renewable energy sources, such as water, wind, biomass, and to a small degree, the sun. In the majority of cases, green electricity is more expensive than conventional electricity. Renewable energy sources are considered to be more environmentally benign. By the way, the household electricity that is provided to customers via the grid is standardized and is technically homogeneous. Only the way it is generated and

fed into the grid might vary according to the contracted utility. We would like to emphasize that there are many different opinions about both conventional methods of electricity generation and renewable energies.

We have some questions about the electricity prices you are willing to pay. Please read the questions carefully first. We would like to encourage you to 'try' several numbers in your head before giving your final answer."

WTP condition: "There are cities in Germany whose inhabitants are supplied with conventionally produced electricity. Imagine you live in one of these cities. You are free to switch to green electricity, if you wish. Then you would pay a higher monthly premium. Would you be willing to switch?"

☐ NO.

☐ YES. If yes, what is the maximum additional amount you would be willing to pay each month?

_____euros

WTA condition: "There are German cities whose inhabitants are supplied with green electricity by default. Imagine you live in one of these cities. You are free to switch to conventionally produced electricity, if you wish. Then you would pay a lower monthly premium. Would you be willing to switch?"

☐ NO.

☐ YES. If yes, what is the minimum amount by which your monthly premium would have to be reduced?

_____euros

Introduction to Chapter 38

"If… ": Satisficing Algorithms for Mapping Conditional Statements onto Social Domains

The dazzling speed of daily communication through language is built on specialized evolved machinery able to make quick inferences about meaning. What is the nature of this machinery? Much of linguistics is preoccupied with syntax. Logical structure alone, however, is insufficient for understanding meaning. For instance, a father tells his 7-year-old daughter, "If you clean your room, we'll go to the movies." If the girl reduced his message to the logical form "if P, then Q," and reasoned logically, she would conclude that the statement does not imply "if not P, then not Q," because this would be committing a logical fallacy called "denial of the antecedent." Avoiding this logical fallacy, she would reason that her father is not implying that if she does not clean up her room, they will not go to the movies. Yet child and father both know in a blink that this is exactly what is meant.

A logical approach to meaning fails both descriptively and normatively: It does not describe how semantic inferences are drawn and even mistakes sound inferences for logical fallacies. This double failure is not hypothetical but has happened in the psychology of reasoning since the 1960s, when researchers presented conditional statements to participants and (mis)evaluated all answers that violated truth-table logic as reasoning errors, attributing them to cognitive limitations. Research on the four-card problem, also known as the Wason selection task, is a case in point (see Gigerenzer, 2000). This confusion between logical and semantic inferences is not restricted to conditionals, but presents a broader hindrance to progress in contemporary psychology, as illustrated by the "Linda problem" (see Gigerenzer, 2005; Hertwig, Benz, & Krauss, 2008; Hertwig & Gigerenzer, 1999).

That leaves us with the question of how the mind infers the meaning of a sentence, if not by logic. Let us narrow the question down to how the mind infers whether a conditional statement is a promise, a threat, a warning, or something else. Alejandro López-Rousseau and Timothy Ketelaar address how people intuitively make this inference based on a single, written sentence, with no further context, verbal signals, or facial expressions available. A view in line with Laplace's demon might assume a vast associate network that computes for each word—or each combination of words—in the conditional statement a probability distribution over the possible categories of meaning, such as threat and promise. The present article bets on a simpler solution, based on heuristics that work with only three surface cues. This approach is in the spirit of Grice's maxims. It takes a first step toward opening up a new perspective in the psycholinguistics of semantic inference.

CHAPTER 38

"If... ": Satisficing Algorithms for Mapping Conditional Statements onto Social Domains

Alejandro López-Rousseau and Timothy Ketelaar

Abstract: People regularly use conditional statements to communicate promises and threats, advice and warnings, permissions and obligations to other people. Given that all conditionals are formally equivalent—"if *P*, then *Q*"— the question is: When confronted with a conditional statement, how do people know whether they are facing a promise, a threat, or something else? In other words, what is the cognitive algorithm for mapping a particular conditional statement onto its corresponding social domain? This paper introduces the *pragmatic cues* algorithm and the *syntactic cue* algorithm as partial answers to this question. Two experiments were carried out to test how well these simple satisficing algorithms approximate the performance of the actual cognitive algorithm people use to classify conditional statements into social domains. Conditional statements for promises, threats, advice, warnings, permissions, and obligations were collected from people, and given to both other people and the algorithms for their classification. Their corresponding performances were then compared. Results revealed that even though these algorithms utilized a minimum number of cues and drew only a restricted range of inferences from these cues, they performed well above chance in the task of classifying conditional statements as promises, threats, advice, warnings, permissions, and obligations. Moreover, these simple satisficing algorithms performed comparable to actual people given the same task.

In the beginning was a warning, and the warning was "If you eat of the tree of knowledge, you will surely die" (Genesis 2:17). Since time immemorial people have used conditional statements like this to warn others of imminent dangers (e.g., "If you touch the fire, you will get burned"), promise them future rewards (e.g., "If you keep my secret, I will give you a gift"), permit them exceptional undertakings (e.g., "If you are strong enough, you can ride the horse"), and so on. Given that all conditional statements are formally equivalent—"if condition *P* obtains, then consequence *Q* ensues"—the question remains: When confronted with a conditional statement, how do people know whether they are facing a warning, a promise, a permission, or something else? Are there cognitive algorithms that map particular conditional statements onto their corresponding social domains? This paper introduces two algorithms as partial answers to this question.

THE PRAGMATICS OF CONDITIONAL STATEMENTS

Understanding the social content of conditionals in particular is an interesting and relevant step towards understanding the interpretation process of language in general in terms of adaptive reasoning algorithms. The study of how meaning is attached to verbal statements has been the province of a branch of cognitive psychology known as *pragmatics*. According to the pragmatics approach, arriving at the appropriate meaning of an utterance—be it a warning, a promise, or anything else—requires that the individual draws appropriate inferences. As such, the task of discerning the meaning of a statement turns out to be more of a process of utterance interpretation than utterance decoding (Sperber & Wilson, 1981, 1986). Consider the following utterances:

> Woman: I'm leaving you.
> Man: Who is he?

Most individuals interpret these utterances in the same way, that is, as statements occurring in a conversation between romantic lovers, one of whom wishes to end the relationship, while the other suspects infidelity. Yet, as pragmatics theorists quickly point out, none of these meanings can be directly recovered by decoding these utterances (see Sperber & Wilson, 1986). That is, there are no features (e.g., words) in these two utterances that directly translate into a clear statement of the nature of the relationship between the two speakers, their intentions, or an act of infidelity. Such meanings are not decoded from the words in an utterance; instead they are inferred from a variety of pragmatic (contextual) cues including the words in an utterance (Sperber & Wilson, 1986).

According to pragmatics theorists, individuals discern the meaning of an utterance by virtue of drawing certain inferences and not others. The sophistication of this human ability to draw appropriate inferences from utterances can be clearly seen in the case of irony (or sarcasm), where the individual correctly infers the speaker's meaning even though the literal meaning of the speaker's statement is the opposite of their intended meaning (e.g., "Fred is such an honest guy, he lies only twice an hour!").

Given the fact that (1) all conditional statements have the same logical form—"if *P*, then *Q*"— and (2) the claim from pragmatics that the intended meaning of a statement is inferred (rather than directly decoded) from pragmatic

cues, how then does an individual actually decide whether a particular conditional statement is, say, a threat or a promise? One intriguing possibility is that inferences about the appropriate social domain for a conditional statement may be triggered by the presence of particular cues (e.g., particular words) in the utterance. Although a simple heuristic process for categorizing statements into social domains (warnings, promises, permissions, etc.) would not necessarily provide the listener with the full meaning of the utterance, it could allow the recipient to achieve a quick and dirty approximation of the meaning of the statement.

DRAWING INFERENCES FROM CONDITIONAL STATEMENTS

There is a long tradition in psychology of studying the inferences that people draw about conditional statements, beginning with Wason's (1966) classic research on the *selection task* (e.g., Schaeken, Schroyens, & Dieussaert, 2001). In this task, participants are presented with four cards that have letters on one side and numbers on the other side (e.g., A, B, 1, 2), and then asked to select only those cards that need to be turned in order to test the conditional rule "If a card has a vowel on one side, then it has an even number on the other side." This rule is formally equivalent to a logical "if *P*, then *Q*" rule, where the four cards correspond to *P*, *not-P*, *not-Q*, and *Q*, respectively. The typical finding in this task is that most participants fail to select the necessary *not-Q* card (i.e., the 1-card). This failure has been interpreted as a difficulty in reasoning according to the logic of *modus tollens*—"if *P*, then *Q*"; "*not-Q*"; "therefore *not-P*"— and people have been thus depicted as bad logical reasoners.

Further studies have shown that when the original task is provided with social content, people do better (e.g., Griggs & Cox, 1982). For example, participants are presented with four cards representing people at a bar that have their drinks on one side and their ages on the other side (e.g., beer, cola, 16, 20), and then asked to select only those cards that need to be turned in order to test the conditional rule

"If a person is drinking beer, then she must be over 18 years old." This rule is also formally equivalent to a logical "if *P*, then *Q*" rule, but the typical finding now is that most participants do select the necessary *not-Q* card (i.e., the 16-card), apparently reasoning according to *modus tollens*. People have been thus depicted as good social reasoners.

Different theoretical explanations have been offered for this social content effect on the Wason selection task. For example, Cheng and Holyoak (1985; Cheng, Holyoak, Nisbett, & Oliver, 1986) suggest that people do not reason according to formal logic but to *pragmatic reasoning schemas* such as permissions and obligations. In a permission schema, when a given precondition is not satisfied (e.g., being over 18 years old), a given action must not be taken (e.g., drinking beer). Testing whether this holds amounts to selecting the *not-Q* card in any Wason selection task that maps onto a permission schema (e.g., the bar scenario).

Alternatively, Cosmides and Tooby (1992; Cosmides, 1989) suggest that people reason according to evolved *Darwinian algorithms* such as social contracts and threats. In a social contract, you must pay a given cost (e.g., being over 18 years old) to take a given benefit (e.g., drinking beer). Testing whether this holds amounts to detecting cheaters, and to now selecting the *not-Q* card in any Wason selection task that maps onto a social contract (e.g., the bar scenario).

Moreover, Gigerenzer and Hug (1992) suggest that cheating on a social contract depends on the *pragmatic perspective* of their participants. For example, whereas not working paid hours is cheating from the perspective of an employer, not paying worked hours is cheating from the perspective of an employee. Thus, this would lead to employers and employees selecting different cards to test the conditional rule "If an employee works some hours, then the employer must pay those hours." In particular, employees would select the *P* and *not-Q* cards, and employers would select the *Q* and *not-P* cards. In sum, whereas their explanations differ, all authors above agree that proper reasoning about conditionals is not done according to a general logical formalism but to specific psychological mechanisms.

However, although both the pragmatic schema and the evolved algorithm explanations account for reasoning about conditional statements, these explanations still beg a fundamental question: When confronted with a conditional statement, how do people know whether they are facing a permission and not an obligation, or a social contract and not a threat, or neither of these but something else? In other words, if discerning the appropriate meaning of a conditional statement entails employing the right schema or algorithm, what is the mechanism for mapping a particular conditional statement onto its corresponding schema or algorithm? This paper is an attempt to provide an ecologically valid answer to this question by studying conditional statements as used in natural language.

CONDITIONALS STATEMENTS AND DOMAIN SPECIFICITY

Linguists such as Fillenbaum (1975, 1976, 1977) have shown that everyday reasoning about conditional statements is *domain specific*. That is, reasoning about threats is not the same as reasoning about promises or other social domains. For example, whereas conditional threats (e.g., "If you hurt me, I'll beat you up") can be paraphrased as disjunctives (e.g., "Don't hurt me or I'll beat you up"), conditional promises (e.g., "If you help me, I'll take you out") cannot be paraphrased as disjunctives (e.g., "Don't help me or I'll take you out"). Moreover, domain-specific reasoning about conditionals is not necessarily logical. For example, conditionals (e.g., "If you order food, you must pay for it") invite for some inferences (e.g., "If I don't order food, I mustn't pay for it") that are logically invalid (i.e., "if *not-P*, then *not-Q*") but make perfect social sense nonetheless. Finally, domain-specific reasoning about conditional statements is not triggered by their general form—"if *P*, then *Q*"—but by their specific content and context. For example, although a conditional promise (e.g., "If you help me, I'll take you out") and a conditional threat (e.g., "If you hurt me, I'll beat you up") are formally equivalent, one is regarded as a promise and the other as a threat by virtue of their distinct consequences, namely, a benefit and a cost for the listener, respectively.

THE PRAGMATIC CUES APPROACH

Given the constraints of time and cognitive resources that typically confront individuals in the world, the cognitive algorithm for classifying conditional statements into social domains is assumed to be a *satisficing* algorithm: A simple serial procedure sufficing for satisfactory classifications in most cases (Gigerenzer, Todd, & the ABC Research Group, 1999; Simon, 1982). Take as an example a situation in which someone tells you "If you move, I'll kill you." You'd better know with accuracy and speed that this conditional is a threat to react appropriately. But exactly how do you know that this particular statement is a threat? Certainly the content and context of the conditional statement, as conveyed by linguistic cues (e.g., the word "kill" instead of the word "kiss") and nonlinguistic cues (e.g., a mean look instead of a nice smile), provide some guidance. Although the actual

cognitive algorithm that individuals employ when classifying conditional statements into social domains probably includes both kinds of cues, the first satisficing algorithm introduced here includes only linguistic cues for simplification. Moreover, although the actual cognitive algorithm probably includes syntactic, semantic, and pragmatic linguistic cues, this algorithm includes only pragmatic cues for the simple reason that social domains are essentially pragmatic. Finally, although the cognitive algorithm probably includes all social domains, this algorithm only includes six domains given their natural relevance and historical precedence in the literature (e.g., Cheng & Holyoak, 1985; Cosmides & Tooby, 1992; Fillenbaum, 1975). The domains are the following: *promises* (e.g., "If you help me, I'll take you out"), *threats* (e.g., "If you hurt me, I'll beat you up"), *advice* (e.g., "If you exercise, you'll be fit"), *warnings* (e.g., "If you smoke, you'll get sick"), *permissions* (e.g., "If you work now, you can rest later"), and *obligations* (e.g., "If you order food, you must pay for it"). In sum, a satisficing algorithm for classifying conditionals by pragmatic cues was

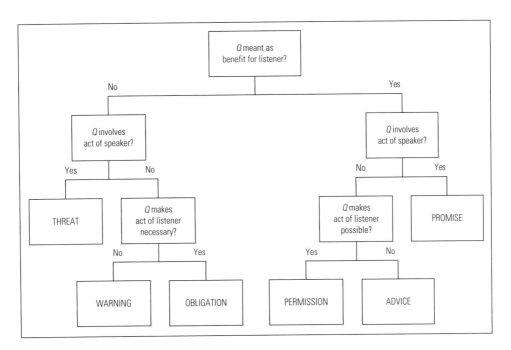

Figure 38-1. The pragmatic cues algorithm.

analytically derived, and consequently called the *pragmatic cues* algorithm.

The Pragmatic Cues Algorithm

The pragmatic cues algorithm is a binary decision tree based on three pragmatic cues that sequentially prune the tree until one of six social domains is left (see Figure 38-1). The cues are the following:

1. Is the conditional statement's consequent Q meant as a benefit for the listener? If it is meant as a benefit for the listener, the conditional statement represents a promise, an advice, or a permission. If it does not, the conditional statement represents a threat, a warning, or an obligation.
2. Does the conditional statement's consequent Q involve an act of the speaker? If it does involve an act of the speaker, the conditional statement represents a promise or a threat, depending on the first cue value. If it does not, the conditional statement represents an advice, a permission, a warning, or an obligation, depending on the first cue value.
3. Does the conditional statement's consequent Q make an act of the listener possible or necessary? If it does make an act of the listener possible or necessary, then the conditional statement represents a permission or an obligation, depending on the first two cue values. If it does not, the conditional statement represents an advice or a warning, depending on the first two cue values.

Take the example of the conditional statement "If you move, I'll kill you." The pragmatic cues algorithm would process this conditional statement by applying its first cue, and asking whether the conditional statement's consequent Q is meant as a benefit for the listener. Because being killed is not a benefit for the listener, the algorithm would follow its "no" branch to the second cue, and ask whether the conditional statement's consequent Q involves an act of the speaker. Because the killing is done by the speaker, the algorithm would follow its "yes" branch to the threat domain, and stop there. Thus, according to this algorithm, the conditional statement "If you move, I'll kill you" is a

threat. Different conditional statements are mapped onto different domains as can be verified by applying the algorithm to the following three examples: "If you smoke, you'll get sick," "If you work now, you can rest later," and "If you exercise, you'll be fit" (see Figure 38-1).

The pragmatic cues algorithm is meant to be simple by including the minimum possible of three cues to classify six domains. The algorithm is also meant to be serial by adopting the sequential form of a decision tree, which further simplifies the classification process by discarding already three domains from consideration after the first cue, and possibly two more domains after the second cue. And the algorithm is meant to be satisficing by producing correct classifications in most but not all cases. In this regard, the pragmatic cues algorithm could misclassify any conditional statement belonging to other (social) domains and/or depending on other (pragmatic) cues. For example, the algorithm would misclassify the conditional fact "If water boils, it evaporates," the conditional request "If you leave the room, please close the door," and the conditional promise "If I get a raise, I'll quit smoking" (see Figure 38-1). Still, the pragmatic cues algorithm would correctly classify most conditional promises, threats, advice, warnings, permissions, and obligations.

Overview of Experiment 1

Given that a vast number of complex and/or parallel and/or optimizing alternative algorithms could be used for this categorization task, an experiment was designed to empirically test how well the more parsimonious pragmatic cues algorithm approximates the performance of the actual cognitive algorithm that people use to classify conditionals statements into social domains. Briefly, conditional statements for promises, threats, advice, warnings, permissions, and obligations were collected from people, and given to both other people and the pragmatic cues algorithm for their classification. Their corresponding performances were then compared.

Evidently, it was expected that people would correctly classify all of other people's conditional statements except for obvious generation and/or interpretation errors. It was also expected that the pragmatic cues algorithm would correctly classify most conditional statements. And both people and the pragmatic cues algorithm were expected to perform far above chance. However, it was also expected that the pragmatic cues algorithm would perform somewhat worse than the actual cognitive algorithm that people use to classify conditionals statements into social domains. This is the case because the pragmatic cues algorithm was designed as a simple satisficing algorithm that draws only a restricted range of inferences from a minimum number of cues, whereas people might have access to a larger number of cues and inferences.

In sum, the pragmatic cues algorithm would have to perform both as badly as chance and far worse than people in order for it to be rejected as an approximation of the actual cognitive algorithm people use to classify conditionals statements into social domains. Here rests the power of this empirical test to discriminate between the proposed analytical-cues algorithm and any other random-cues algorithm.

EXPERIMENT 1

Method

Participants and materials. Sixty-two properly informed and protected students at the University of Munich volunteered for this experiment, originally in German. Typewritten booklets contained the instructions for the participants.

Design and procedure. This experiment had three conditions: the generation, evaluation, and algorithm conditions. In the generation condition, 50 participants separately provided each a written conditional promise, advice, permission, threat, warning, and obligation, for a total of 300 conditionals. The instructions were the following:

> We are interested in how you use *if–then* statements to communicate a promise, advice, permission, threat, warning, or obligation to someone else. Please write an example of each.
> Promise:
> If _____
> then _____.

For instance, one participant wrote the statement "If you don't study, then you'll fail the

exam" as an example of a warning. Thus, this conditional was one of the 50 warnings provided in the generation condition.

In the evaluation condition, three judges separately classified each of the 300 randomly ordered, nonlabelled conditionals as a promise, advice, permission, threat, warning, or obligation. The instructions were the following:

> This booklet contains 300 *if-then* statements. For each statement, please state if the speaker meant it as a promise (P), an advice (A), a permission (E), a threat (T), a warning (W), or an obligation (O) for the listener.
> 1. If you don't study,
> then you'll fail the exam. _____

Each conditional was then classified into the domain agreed upon by two out of the three judges. For example, the three judges wrote that the speaker meant the statement "If you don't study, then you'll fail the exam" as a warning (W) for the listener. Thus, this conditional was classified as a warning in the evaluation condition.

In the algorithm condition, nine judges separately provided the pragmatic cue values for each of the 300 randomly ordered, nonlabelled conditionals. There were three judges per cue. The instructions for the first cue were the following:

> This booklet contains 300 *if-then* statements. For each statement, please state if its *then*-part is meant as a benefit for the listener (Y), or not (N).
> 1. If you don't study,
> then you'll fail the exam. _____

The instructions for the second cue were: "This booklet contains 300 *if-then* statements. For each statement, please state if its *then*-part involves an act of the speaker (Y), or not (N)." Finally, the instructions for the third cue were: "This booklet contains 300 *if-then* statements. For each statement, please state if its *then*-part makes an act of the listener possible or necessary (Y), or not (N)."

Each conditional was then assigned the cue values agreed upon by two out of three judges per cue, and classified into the domain obtained following the pragmatic cues algorithm. For example, the three judges wrote that the *then*-part of the statement "If you don't study, then you'll fail the exam" is not meant as a benefit for the listener (N), does not involve an act of the speaker (N), and does not make an act of the listener possible or necessary (N).[1] Thus, following the pragmatic cues algorithm, this conditional was classified as a warning in the algorithm condition.

Participants were tested individually in all conditions.

Results and Discussion

Figure 38-2 shows the percentage of conditional promises, advice, permissions, threats, warnings, and obligations provided in the generation condition that were correctly classified as such in the evaluation and algorithm conditions.

Results show that people classified most conditional statements correctly across domains (average: 94%; range: 88% to 100%), and that the pragmatic cues algorithm did almost as well as people (average: 85%; range: 68% to 94%). Both the algorithm's and people's classifications were far better than chance (17%), and their misclassifications were randomly distributed across domains.[2] These findings indicate that the pragmatic cues algorithm approximates well the performance of the cognitive algorithm for mapping conditional statements onto social domains. The small difference is probably due to the additional cues the cognitive algorithm depends on. These findings thus suggest that the parsimoniously simple, serial, and satisficing pragmatic cues algorithm might be an integral part of the cognitive algorithm for classifying conditionals.

But what other cues and domains might also be integral parts of the cognitive algorithm? Besides pragmatic cues, the cognitive algorithm probably includes semantic, syntactic, and non-linguistic cues. Moreover, the cognitive algorithm probably includes orders, requests, and other social domains. The second satisficing algorithm introduced here explores the role of syntactic cues in the cognitive algorithm for classifying conditional statements.

THE SYNTACTIC CUES APPROACH

The inclusion of syntactic cues in the cognitive algorithm can be exemplified by means of conditional requests (e.g., "If you call, please send my regards"), which usually initiate their consequents with the word "please." This syntactic cue

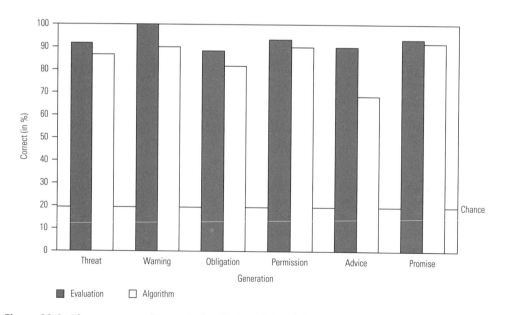

Figure 38-2. The percentage of correctly classified conditionals by condition.

signals a following request. Whether a request actually follows is then determined by additional pragmatic cues. Thus, the cognitive algorithm is here assumed to include syntactic cues as early detectors of social domains, which are later (dis) confirmed by pragmatic cues.

Take conditional threats as a less obvious example. Threats are typically used to induce people in doing something they are not doing (e.g., "If you don't pay, I'll break your arm"). Thus, conditional threats usually include the word "not" in their antecedents. This syntactic cue detects an imminent threat, which is then (dis)confirmed by the pragmatic cues proposed above (see pragmatic cues algorithm). In sum, to explore the role of syntactic cues in the cognitive algorithm for classifying conditional statements, a satisficing algorithm for detecting threats by syntactic cues was designed, and consequently called the *syntactic cue* algorithm.

The Syntactic Cue Algorithm

The syntactic cue algorithm is a binary decision tree based on just a single syntactic cue that prunes the tree into threats and nonthreats (see Figure 38-3). The cue is the following:

1. Does the conditional statement's antecedent *P* contain the word "not"? If it does contain the word "not," the conditional statement represents a threat. If it does not, the conditional statement represents no threat.

Take again as example the conditional statement "If you don't pay, I'll break your arm." The syntactic cue algorithm would process this

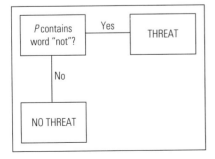

Figure 38-3. The syntactic cue algorithm.

conditional statement by applying its only cue, and asking whether the conditional statement's antecedent *P* contains the word "not." Because it does, the algorithm would follow its "yes" branch to the threat domain, and stop there. Thus, according to the algorithm, the conditional statement "If you don't pay, I'll break your arm" is a threat. Evidently, the syntactic cue algorithm would not detect any conditional threat excluding "not" from its antecedent (e.g., "If you testify, I'll cut out your tongue"), and would wrongly detect any conditional nonthreat including "not" in its antecedent (e.g., "If you don't mind, I'll invite you to dinner"). Still, the algorithm is expected to correctly detect most conditional threats.

[Experiment 2 reports that the syntactic cue algorithm correctly detects threats in 64% of all cases (chance = 17%)]

CONCLUSIONS

Are there cognitive algorithms that map particular conditional statements onto their corresponding social domains? Actual people no doubt have access to a vast number of cues and inferences that they can use to map conditional statements onto their social domains. The challenge in the current study was to determine whether relatively simple algorithms could perform as well as actual people. This was done by introducing two simple satisficing algorithms for classifying conditional statements into their appropriate social domains: the pragmatic cues and syntactic cue algorithms. Results revealed that even though these algorithms utilized a minimum number of cues and drew only a restricted range of inferences from these cues, they performed well above chance in the task of classifying conditional statements as promises, threats, advice, warnings, permissions, and obligations. Moreover, these simple satisficing algorithms performed comparable to actual people given the same task.

Gigerenzer (1995) has proposed that the psychological and linguistic approaches to studying reasoning about conditional statements could be integrated into a two-step research program. According to Gigerenzer, the first step would be to model the cognitive algorithm that maps conditional statements onto social domains. The second step would be to model the cognitive module that reasons and acts accordingly in each domain. This paper is an attempt to specify the first step of the proposed program by demonstrating how simple satisficing algorithms can approximate the performance of people.

ACKNOWLEDGMENTS

This research was supported by the Max Planck Society (MPG) and the German Research Council (DFG). Thanks are extended to Gerd Gigerenzer for theoretical inspiration, Alarcos Cieza and Julia Schmidt for data collection, Gregory Werner for computer assistance, and the Adaptive Behavior and Cognition (ABC) Research Group for constructive criticism.

NOTES

1. The last cue value was agreed upon by two out of the three judges.
2. Except for the algorithms' misclassifications of pieces of advice mostly as permissions (11 out of 16). For example, the advice "If you talk more, then you can solve your problems" was also misclassified as a permission. This is due to the algorithm's third cue (i.e., Does the conditional's consequent Q make an act of the listener possible or necessary?), where "possible" can broadly mean "plausible" or narrowly mean "permissible". A cue's rephrasing might better convey the intended narrow meaning (e.g., Does the conditional's consequent Q involve an authority making an act of the listener possible or necessary?).

Introduction to Chapter 39

Applying One Reason Decision-Making: The Prioritisation of Literature Searches

Searching for scientific articles is a bit like searching for mates (see Chapter 40). Of course, the object of desire is quite different. Nevertheless, in both cases, the search unfolds across alternatives, examined in a temporal sequence. We all know the dilemma. When turning to a new research topic, we do not know what are the relevant publications; the task is to spot them within a cloud of irrelevant articles. Fortunately, this task has been much simplified by electronic literature search systems, which after a few keystrokes spit out a list of publications that match our search terms. The default ordering of the articles, however, does not necessarily reflect their actual relevance, and therefore the user cannot help but peruse the articles (or abstracts) one by one.

How could one speed up this search? In this article, Michael Lee, Natasha Loughlin, and Ingrid Lundberg engineered two methods, one embodying one-reason decision-making, and the other using all available information. According to the complex Bayesian method, publications are ranked according to the probability that that they are relevant. To this end, the authors construct cues that, if present, indicate that an article is relevant. The validity of each cue is estimated on the basis of a reader's acceptance or rejection of previous articles, and is continuously updated. Based on the sum of all validity values associated with each cue, publications are prioritized, with the most relevant articles coming first. The one-reason method employs the same cues and ranks them according to the evidence that they provide in favor of an article being relevant. Validities and order of cues are continually updated with each newly read article. Starting with the most valid cue, a search is then made for unread articles that have a positive value on that cue. If an article is found, search is terminated; otherwise, the same process is repeated with the second-highest cue.

Lee and colleagues tested both methods against 10 actual literature searches, and measured the methods' performances against effort (i.e., the proportion of the articles read by the user) and accuracy (i.e., proportion of relevant articles found, with relevance inferred from people who have carried out the actual searches). The one-reason model is as good as or better than the Bayesian model, particularly in searches in which the proportion of relevant articles is small. Both methods are far from perfect, as the authors point out, because they need to look up all articles to identify the relevant ones. The likely reason is that some of the cues provided lack plausibility and are not used by people. The task ahead is to identify those cues that people actually use. On their basis, readers may soon enjoy intelligent literature search systems built on fast-and-frugal search methods.

CHAPTER 39

Applying One Reason Decision-Making: The Prioritisation of Literature Searches

Michael D. Lee, Natasha Loughlin, and Ingrid B. Lundberg

Abstract: The prioritization of literature searches aims to order the large numbers of articles returned by a simple search so that the ones most likely to be relevant are at the top of the list. Prioritization relies on having a good model of human decision-making that can learn from the articles users select as being relevant to make predictions about which of the remaining articles will be relevant. We develop and evaluate two psychological decision-making models for prioritization: A "rational" model that considers all of the available information, and a "one reason" model that uses limited information to make decisions. The models are evaluated in an experiment where users rate the relevance of every article returned by PsycINFO for a number of different research topics, with the results showing that both models achieve a level of prioritization that significantly improves upon the default ordering of PsycINFO. The one-reason model is shown to be superior to the rational model, especially when there are only a few relevant articles. The implications of the results for developing prioritization systems in applied settings are discussed, together with implications for the general modeling of human decision-making.

When a researcher first does a literature search, they usually are only able to supply general search criteria, such as one or two keywords, to indicate their broad topic of interest. Typically, these initial searches will return a large number of potentially relevant articles. Faced with this information overload, one option for the researcher is to refine their search, and hope that a more manageable list of articles is returned. Often, however, this refinement is difficult, because the researcher is unsure exactly what sorts of materials are available, and there is a need to "sample" or "explore" the large initial list of articles before a more detailed search can be constructed with any confidence.

Prioritization offers a different approach to dealing with the information overload. The basic idea is to begin presenting the articles, requiring the user to indicate whether or not that article is of interest. As each article is examined, prioritization acts to re-order the remaining articles so that the relevant ones are placed at the top of the list. If prioritization is effective, the problem of information overload is solved without the user ever having to construct a refined search. They only need to work from the top of the prioritized list until they reach the point where the articles are no longer of sufficient relevance to be worth pursuing.

While the prioritization problem has been tackled in a variety of information retrieval contexts using machine learning techniques (e.g., Balabanovic, 1998; Macskassy, Dayanik, & Hirsh

1999; Mehran, Dumais, Heckerman, & Horvitz, 1998), it has typically not been tackled from a cognitive modeling perspective. This is unfortunate, because prioritization rests on the ability to predict whether or not a user will evaluate an article as a relevant one, and so requires an effective model of human decision-making to be successful.

In this paper, we develop and evaluate two cognitive models for the prioritization of literature searches. One is a "rational" model, that performs exhaustive calculations, while the other is a "one reason" model, that requires only limited time by making assumptions about the nature of its environment. In the next section, we describe how literature searches are represented by these models, and how information about them is learned. We then describe the two models in detail, before presenting the results of an experiment where both are evaluated on real-world data. Finally, we draw some conclusions regarding the theoretical implications of the results for understanding human decision-making, and the applied implications for building a literature search prioritization system.

TWO MODELS OF DECISION-MAKING

Representation and Learning Assumptions

We follow Gigerenzer and Todd (1999), and a substantial body of other cognitive modeling (e.g., Medin & Schaffer, 1978; Tversky, 1977), in representing stimuli in terms of the presence or absence of a set of discrete features or properties, which we call cues. This means that each article is represented by information such as the authors of the article, the journal it appeared in, keywords in the title or the abstract, the language of publication, and so on.

As the user provides information, rating some articles as relevant and rejecting others, it is possible to learn how the individual cues are associated with the different judgments. At any stage, it is known how many times a cue has been associated with a previously presented article, and how many of those articles have been relevant. From these counts, it is possible to measure the

evidence the presence of a cue provides for a new article being relevant. In effect, the cues correspond to our representational assumptions, while the adjustment of evidence values associated with the cues correspond to our learning assumptions.

Following Lee, Chandrasena, and Navarro (2002), we adopt a Bayesian approach to learning. The basic idea is that we start with complete ignorance about how the cues relate to relevance, and each time a cue is observed to be associated with a relevant article, it comes to provide greater evidence that a new article with the cue will also be relevant. Similarly, as a cue is associated with more irrelevant articles, it provides greater evidence that a new article will also be irrelevant. The basic result from Bayesian statistics (Gelman, Carlin, Stern, & Rubin, 1995, p. 31) we use is that, if an event (such as a cue being associated with a relevant article) occurs k times out of n trials, the best estimate of its underlying probability is $(k + 1)/(n + 2)$. Lee, Chandrasena and Navarro (2002) provide a more detailed explanation of this Bayesian approach to learning, with a particular focus on its theoretical advantages over other methods.

The rational and one-reason models we consider both use cue representations and Bayesian evidence values, but differ in the way they calculate and combine the evidence values to reach a final decision. In this sense, the two models make the same assumptions regarding how people represent and learn about the articles, but make different assumptions regarding their decision processes in judging relevant articles.

The Rational Model

The "rational" approach assumes that people combine all of the available information in some (near) optimal way. This means that the evidence provided by all of the cues must be weighted and integrated to arrive at a final decision. Because it uses all of the data, the rational approach is of often regarded as a normative theory of decision-making, and is central to the decision and utility theoretic frameworks widely used in the physical sciences, and in behavioral sciences such as psychology and economics (see Doyle, 1999, for an overview).

Our version of a rational approach works by estimating the probability that an article is relevant, as opposed to irrelevant, on the basis of the cues it has. As it turns out, it is simpler to calculate this probability on a log-odds scale. This is a straightforward transformation: a probability of 0.75 means an event will occur three times out of four, which correspond to odds of 3:1, or log-odds of $\ln 3 \approx 1.10$. The log-odds scale has the advantages of being symmetric about the origin and additive: log-odds of zero mean that the probability of relevance is 0.5, and equal positive or negative increments represent equal amounts of evidence in favor of relevance or irrelevance. It should be emphasized, however, that making decisions based on the log-odds is identical to making decision based on the probabilities themselves.

Formally, the log-odds that an article is relevant (denoted G for "good"), as opposed to irrelevant (denoted B for "bad"), given their cue representations, is written as:

$$L_{GB} = \ln \frac{p(G|c_1,...,c_k)}{p(B|c_1,...,c_k)}.$$

Using Bayes' Theorem, this may be rewritten as:

$$L_{GB} = \ln \frac{p(G)}{p(B)} + \ln \frac{p(c_1,...,c_k|G)}{p(c_1,...,c_k|B)}.$$

The rational model we use here assumes that the evidence provided by each cue is independent when integrating them to give an estimate of the overall log-odds that an article is relevant, so the log-odds become:

$$L_{GB} \approx \ln \frac{p(G)}{p(B)} + \sum_{i=1}^{k} \ln \frac{p(c_i|G)}{p(c_i|B)}.$$

Given the log-odds for every article, prioritization involves simply sorting from the greatest log-odds value to the smallest. In this way, the articles most likely to be relevant are at the top, and those least likely to be relevant are at the bottom. Notice that, in doing this ordering, the prior odds, $p(G)/p(B)$ will be constant for every article, and so do not need to be calculated.

Prioritization is based entirely on the evidence provided by each of the cues associated with the articles.

The evidence values $p(c_i|G)/p(c_i|B)$ can be estimated on the basis of the user's acceptance or rejection of previous articles. In this way, the evidence values are continually learned from the user, starting at uninformative prior values, but evolving over time to reflect the preferences implicit in user decisions. Formally, suppose at a given point there have been g relevant articles, in which the i-th cue has been present x times, and b irrelevant articles, in which it has been present y times. Using the Bayesian approach to learning, we have:

$$\frac{p(c_i|G)}{p(c_i|B)} \approx \frac{(x+1)/(g+2)}{(y+1)/(b+2)}.$$

It is the sum of these evidence values, for each of the cues belonging to a new article, that gives a rational estimate of the log-odds that it is relevant.

The One-Reason Model

In developing their "fast-and-frugal" approach to modeling human decision-making, Gigerenzer and Todd (1999; see also Gigerenzer & Goldstein, 1996; Todd & Gigerenzer, 2000) challenge the rational approach. They argue that because human decision-making processes evolved in competitive environments, they need to be fast, and because they evolved in changeable environments, they need to have the robustness that comes from simplicity. Rational models usually do not meet these constraints, because they involve extensive and often complicated calculations in their decision-making processes.

The emphasis of fast-and-frugal modeling on the role of the environment follows ecological approaches[1] to psychology (e.g., Brunswik, 1943; Simon, 1956, 1982), and suggests that understanding human decision-making requires understanding not just mental processes, but also the external task environment, and its interaction with mental processes. As Gigerenzer and Todd (1999) argue, the fact that environments are not arbitrary means that they can play a role in supporting (or confounding) human decision-making. For example, in an environment where one piece of information in a stimulus is highly predictive of the remaining pieces of information, and the search for additional information is an effortful process, it is adaptive to consider only the first piece of information. Similarly, in an environment of diminishing returns, where each successive piece of information provides less information than previous pieces, it makes sense to base decisions on the first few pieces of information. Gigerenzer and Todd (1999) show that many real-world stimulus domains have these sorts of information structures, and develop a number of cognitive models that make inferences by assuming the presence of environmental regularities.

Unfortunately, none of these models is directly applicable to prioritization, and so we developed a new model using the basic fast-and-frugal approach. Gigerenzer and Todd (1999) argue that their models of human decision-making are based on simple mechanisms that answer three fundamental questions:

- How should a stimulus environment be searched for information?
- When should this search for information be terminated?
- Once the search has been terminated, what decision should be made given the available information?

In the context of finding relevant articles, as required for prioritization, it is not difficult to provide answers to these questions:

- Unread articles should be searched in terms of cues, looking for articles with cues that provide strong evidence that they are relevant.
- The search should be terminated as soon as a candidate relevant article has been identified. Since users read articles serially, there is no benefit in seeking to sort the unread articles beyond attempting to ensure that at any time the topmost article is the one most likely to be good.
- The best available article should be placed at the top of the list, as the next one to be read by the user.

These answers suggest a simple fast-and-frugal decision model for prioritization. The cues are ordered in terms of the evidence they provide in favor of an article being relevant. As with the rational model, these evidence values are easily estimated on the basis of the user's acceptance or rejection of previous articles, and so start at uninformative prior values, but are continually updated over time by learning from the cumulative information provided by all of the user decisions. Formally, if the i-th cue has been associated with n articles, k of which were relevant, then the ratio $(k + 1)/(n + 2)$, corresponding to what Gigerenzer and Todd (1999) call the validity of the cue, provides an appropriate measure. Starting with the highest validity cue, a search is made for an unread article with that cue. If this search is successful, the process terminates without considering any further cues. If no article is found, the search continues using the next best cue, and this process is repeated until an article is found. This model is closely related to take-the-best, and belongs to the class of what Gigerenzer and Todd (1999) term "one-reason decision-making" models. Only one reason, in the form of the presence of a high evidence cue, is ever required to find the next article for presentation.

EXPERIMENT

Data Collection

To compare the rational and one-reason models, we tested their ability to prioritize literature searches from the PsycINFO (2001) database. Our data set contained 10 different literature searches, done by people with experience in using the system, but without detailed knowledge of the models being evaluated. For each of the 10 searches, a topic was chosen, and a small set of keywords was chosen for an initial search. Every one of the articles returned by PsycINFO was then evaluated independently, assessing whether or not it was relevant to the topic.

Table 39-1 details the 10 literature searches, giving a description of the topic, the initial search keywords, the number of articles returned by the initial search, and the number of articles relevant to the topic found by exhaustive evaluation.

Table 39-1.   The Search Keywords, Topic, Number of Relevant Articles, and Total Number of Articles for the 10 Datasets

Initial Search	Topic	Relevant	Total
"drug abuse and delinquency"	The relationship between family and teenage delinquency or drug abuse	103	450
"effects of abuse"	Child physical and sexual abuse including incestuous and sibling abuse but not spousal abuse	127	342
"social facilitation"	Social intelligence in people with intellectual disabilities	59	606
"teamwork and teams"	Studies of teamwork and team training that operated in an adventure-based setting	3	327
"extroversion and introversion"	Differences between extroverted and introverted people's ability to deal with noise disturbances	7	464
"eyewitness testimony"	The use of line-ups for identifying suspects	9	379
	The use of polygraph procedures to determine the credibility of eyewitness testimony	4	379
"foreign policy"	The role of prime ministerial leadership styles in foreign policy decision-making	4	384
	Foreign policy using propaganda or the impact of propaganda on foreign policy	4	384
	Foreign policy with nuclear implications	17	384

The first five topics all relate to different keywords searches, while the remaining five relate to only two different searches. In this way, we are testing prioritization not just of different searches, but also of different topics within the same search. A range of topics are covered, most falling within the discipline of psychology, but with some (e.g., the foreign policy topics) extending into the social sciences more generally. All of the initial searches returned a large number of articles, ranging from 327 to 606. Importantly, the relative number of relevant articles varies significantly, ranging from a very small fraction (e.g., 3 out of 327), to a significant minority (e.g., 127 out of 342). This variation allows us to test the effectiveness of the two models for different base-rates of relevant articles.

Within the datasets, the returned articles were represented using cues defined by standard PsycINFO fields. For each field, the entire text entry for the article was considered, and common English words (such as "the" and "a") were removed using a stoplist. All of the remaining words were used to generate a cue by pairing it with the field name. For example, an article authored by Robert Goldstone would have the cues "Author = Robert" and "Author = Goldstone." The field within which a word appeared was regarded as establishing a different meaningful context for that word, and so distinct cues were created for repeated words in different fields. This means, for example, that if the word "study" appeared in both the title and the abstract of an article's entry, its representation would include both "Title = study" and "Abstract = study" cues. A complete list of the fields used to create cues is given in Table 39-2 together with a concrete example of a cue for each field. Across the 10 datasets, the number of cues used to represent all of the articles ranged from 4,346 to 10,712, with a mean of 7,447.

Results

Both the rational and one-reason models were applied to the datasets by simulating their impact on the order in which articles would have been presented to users. This was done by presenting the first article in the dataset, and then using the information regarding whether or not it was relevant to update the evidence values for

Table 39-2. The PsycINFO Fields Used to Define Cues, and an Example of a Cue from Each Field

Field	Sample Cue
Document Type	"Document Type = Journal-Article"
Title	"Title = conditioning"
Author	"Author = Jones"
Journal Name	"Journal Name = Psychonomic"
Language	"Language = English"
Abstract	"Abstract = findings"
Key Phrase	"Key Phrase = group"
Age Group	"Age Group = Adulthood"
Population	"Population = Human"
Population Location	"Population Location = US"
Publication Type	"Publication Type = Empirical-Study"

the cues. Using one or other of the decision models, the next prioritized article was then presented, its relevance noted, and evidence scores updated again. This process continued until all of the articles had been presented, and a record

was kept of the order in which they had been seen.

Figures 39-1 and 39-2 summarize the results of 50 independent applications of both models to all 10 datasets. They take the form of effort-reward graphs, relating hypothetical levels of effort (i.e., the proportion of the articles read by the user) to the resultant level of reward (i.e., the proportion of relevant articles found). Figure 39-1 shows the curve representing the mean performance of both models averaged over the datasets. For example, once a user has read the first 60% of the prioritized articles using the one-reason model, they have seen about 90% of the relevant articles. Because the models have a stochastic element, arising from breaking ties when two or more articles have equal evidence, the best- and worse-case performance is indicated by error bars (where large enough to be visible). The chance level of effort-reward performance, where each extra 10% of reading yields another 10% of the relevant articles, is shown by the thin solid line, and the performance obtained by reading the articles in the default reverse chronological order used by PsycINFO is shown by the thick

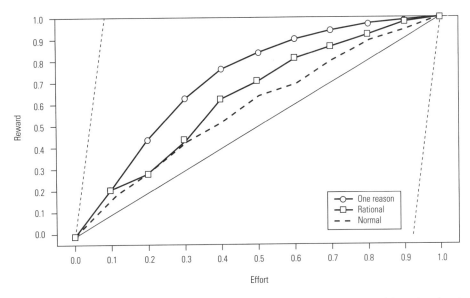

Figure 39-1. Effort-reward graph showing the average prioritization performance of the rational and one-reason models across all 10 datasets. Each dataset has been given equal weight in forming the average, and the error bars represent best-and worst-case performance across 50 independent applications of each model. The performance of the normal reverse chronological ordering, and chance performance, are also shown for comparison.

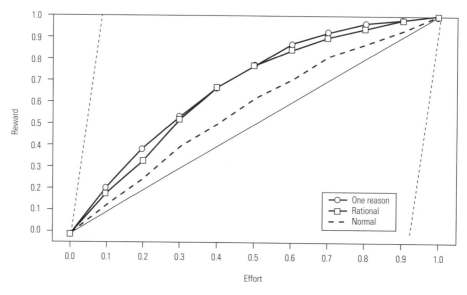

Figure 39-2. Effort-reward graph showing the average prioritization performance of the rational and one-reason models across all 10 datasets. Each dataset has been weighted according to the number of relevant articles in forming the average, and the error bars represent best- and worst-case performance across 50 independent applications of each model. The performance of the normal reverse chronological ordering, and chance performance, are also shown for comparison.

broken line. The thin broken lines show the best and worst possible performance corresponding, respectively, to the cases where all relevant articles are presented first, and all relevant articles are presented last.

It is clear from Figure 39-1 that the one-reason model outperforms the rational model, and that both approaches to prioritization are superior to either the default ordering or a random ordering. Using the one-reason model, for example, the first 30% of articles contain more than 60% of the relevant ones, compared to 40% for the rational model. It is also clear, however, that neither of the models achieves anything approaching the best possible performance, and that it is necessary to read all of the articles to guarantee finding all of the relevant ones.

Figure 39-2 shows the weighted average performance across all of the datasets, taking into account the number of relevant articles. This means, for example, that the dataset with nine relevant articles is weighted three times as much as the dataset with three relevant articles in forming the average performance curves. In effect, this aggregation treats all of the datasets as if they

were one large multifaceted search, whereas Figure 39-1 treats the datasets as a series of separate searches. Under the weighted average, Figure 39-2 shows the one-reason and rational models now have similar performance, and that they remain superior to both the default and random orderings. Once again, however, both models fall short of optimality, and all of the articles must be read to find the relevant ones.

The similar performance of the two models under a weighted average in Figure 39-2 suggests that the better performance of the one-reason model in Figure 39-1 is due to data sets with small numbers of relevant articles. To test this idea, we used a measure of prioritization effectiveness based on effort-reward performance that considered the level of the performance curve in relation to chance performance, averaged across all possible levels of effort. Geometrically, this measure is basically the area between a model's performance curve and the chance line on an effort-reward graph. After normalization, this measure takes the value one for best-case performance, zero for worst-case performance, and 0.5 for chance performance.

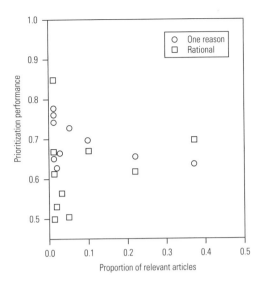

Figure 39-3. The prioritization performance of both models across all of the data sets, shown as a function of the proportion of relevant articles in the data sets.

Figure 39-3 shows the prioritization performance measure, for both rational and one-reason models, as a function of the proportion of relevant articles in the data set. This confirms that, for those data sets with a small proportional relevant articles, the prioritization performance of the one-reason model is generally superior to the rational model. Indeed, for many of these data sets, the rational model does not perform much better than chance. For data sets with a larger proportion of relevant articles, both the models seem to perform similarly, as would be suspected from Figure 39-2.

The prioritization performance measures shown in Figure 39-3 allow statistical inferences to be made about the differences between the rational and one-reason models. In particular, it is possible to examine whether the distribution of performance scores for the two models have significantly different means and/or variances. Most psychological research tackles these problems using Null-Hypothesis Significance Testing (NHST), despite long-standing and authoritative demonstrations (e.g., Edwards, Lindman, & Savage, 1963; Lindley, 1972) that it is an inconsistent, incoherent, and irrational methodology for statistical inference. Accordingly, we use the

Bayesian approach to model selection (e.g., Kass & Raftery, 1995; Lindley, 1972; Pitt, Myung, & Zhang, 2002; Sivia, 1996) to examine the two distributions, relying on the theory and software described in Lee (2002).

The basic idea behind the Bayesian analysis is to consider four possibilities for the two distributions: (a) that they have the same mean and the same variance (1m1v); (b) that they have different means but the same variance (2m1v); (c) that they have the same mean but different variances (1m2v); and (d) that they have different means and different variances (2m2v). The more complicated of these accounts, such as assuming different means and variances, will of course always fit the observed data better than a simpler account, such as assuming the same mean and same variance. Bayesian model selection, however, is not based on goodness-of-fit, but instead considers which model is *most likely* given the data, in a way that naturally balances goodness of fit with model complexity (Roberts & Pashler, 2000). In this way, the Bayes Factor between any two models can be can be estimated, quantifying how much more likely one is than the other (Kass & Raftery, 1995).

The results of applying these ideas to prioritization performance is summarised in Figure 39-4. The four top panels show the performance measures for both the rational (black dots) and one-reason (white dots) models. Each panel shows the best-fitting Gaussian distribution or distributions corresponding to the four possible assumptions about the equality of means and variances. Where different distributions are assumed, the darker lines correspond to the rational model, while the lighter lines correspond to the one-reason model. Under the Bayesian analysis, the most likely account was found to be the one that assumed different means and different variances (2m2v). The Bayes Factors of the other possibilities in relation to this account are shown in the bottom panel. It can be seen that the 1m2v, 2m1v and 1m1v accounts are, respectively, 1.5, 2.6, and 4.2 times less likely.

Within the Bayesian framework for statistical inference, what constitutes a "significant difference" is a question of the standard of scientific evidence for the problem at hand, and is not automated by reference to some critical value. Bayes Factors are naturally interpreted on a meaningful scale defined by betting, so that saying one account is twice as likely as another means that we should be willing to gamble twice as much money on the first account being correct. Against this background, we draw two basic conclusions from the analysis shown in Figure 39-4. The first is that there is considerable evidence the one-reason model has less variable (i.e., more consistent) performance, because those possibilities that assume the same variance (1m1v and 2m1v) are the least likely. The second is that there is some evidence the one-reason model has better prioritization performance, because this assumption (2m2v) is 1.5 times more likely than mean performance being the same (1m2v).

DISCUSSION

We start our discussion by considering the applied implications or our results, before turning to their message for modeling human

decision-making. Our experimental results demonstrate the potential of prioritization in applied settings, but also show that there is some way to go before a useful applied system can be developed. While both the one-reason and rational models clearly outperform the default ordering currently provided by PsycINFO, neither consistently manages to find all of the relevant articles before the user has had to do a significant amount of work. For an applied system, we suspect that something like 90% of the relevant articles would need to be found in the first 20–30% of those presented for almost every topic search. Our conclusion is that, while we believe we are on the right path, some improvement is necessary before the real-world problem of information overload is resolved without the need for refined searches.

This improvement must come from building better models of human decision-making, and it is here that our results have some clear lessons. Most importantly, the superior performance of the one-reason model over the rational model suggests that more complicated decision processes are probably not the answer. The one-reason

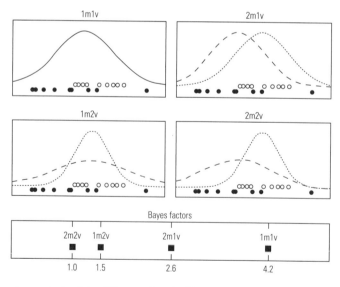

Figure 39-4. Bayesian analysis of the difference in prioritization performance between the rational (black dots, darker lines), and one-reason (white dots, lighter lines) models. The top four panels show the best-fitting distributions for the four possible Gaussian assumptions, and the bottom panel shows the estimated Bayes Factors in relation to the different means and different variances (2m 2v) account, which is the most likely given the data.

model uses a single piece of information about an article in deciding it is the best available, whereas the rational model considers every piece of information about every article to make the same decision. This makes the one-reason model much more computationally efficient, and so it has the potential to scale to the large volumes of information that characterize real-world problems. Given that statistical analysis of the prioritization performance measures showed the one-reason model is clearly more consistent and probably more effective than the rational model, it seems unlikely that adding more complications to the decision mechanisms will yield an improved model. In this sense, our results support Gigerenzer and Todd's (1999) claim that much of human decision-making is based on applying a simple heuristic to limited information. The relatively good performance of the one-reason model suggests that, at least for some articles, users based their decisions on a single piece of information.

ACKNOWLEDGMENTS

This research was supported by the Australian Defense Science and Technology Organization, and by the University of Adelaide Faculty of Health Sciences B3 Scheme. We thank an anonymous reviewer for helpful comments.

NOTES

1. The phrase "ecological approaches" is intended here to extend well beyond Gibsonian ideas of ecological optics, and encompasses more general psychological theorizing that emphasizes the role the environment plays in guiding cognitive processes.

Introduction to Chapter 40

Aggregate Age-at-Marriage Patterns from Individual Mate-Search Heuristics

When managers infer which customers are still active or magistrates infer which defendants are trustworthy, the set of objects is given (customers, defendants); the task is to search for cues to make the allocation. Most classes of heuristics in this book are designed for this situation. Yet there are situations in which the class of objects or persons itself needs to be found. Consider buying a house, or finding a partner for marriage. Here, one needs to search for the alternatives in the first place. Herbert Simon (1955, 1990) used the term *satisficing* for heuristics that solve this problem by relying on an aspiration level to stop search. Satisficing involves setting an (adjustable) aspiration level and ending the search for alternatives as soon as one is encountered that exceeds the aspiration level.

Mate choice presents such a situation in which a person encounters alternatives, that is, potential mates in a temporal sequence, without knowing much about the other alternatives waiting ahead. The structure of this search task requires choosing a prospect that fits one's criterion for success (aspiration level), given limited time for investigating each possible mate, and some risk that the prospective mate, doing his or her own search, will reject one's offer of union. Mate choice is a social domain in which numerous agents interact, thereby producing distinct marriage patterns in the aggregate. These patterns include unimodal age-at-first-marriage curves, high degree of homogamy (i.e., marriage of individuals who on some dimensions such as ethnicity, religion, attractiveness, or intelligence are similar to each other), and high degree of success (i.e., most people find a mate). Typically abstracting from the search and choice processes at work in the individual, demographers have documented these and other statistics of real human mating behavior.

This article—written by a psychologist (Peter Todd), a demographer (Francesco Billari), and a computer scientist (Jorge Simão)—unites individual heuristics and aggregate demographic data. The authors' ingenious methodological insight is that the aggregate data can be used to test whether or not individuals rely on a given heuristic. If, for instance, a particular heuristic cannot reproduce a distinct unimodal distribution of ages at which people first marry, which demographers have observed across a broad range of locations and historical periods, the heuristic is likely to be an unrealistic model of people's choice process. By testing various satisficing heuristics in terms of whether they give rise to emergent properties that match observed aggregate age-at-marriage patterns, the authors were able to winnow down the kind of psychological mechanisms that are likely to underlie human mate choice.

CHAPTER 40

Aggregate Age-at-Marriage Patterns from Individual Mate-Search Heuristics

Peter M. Todd, Francesco C. Billari, and Jorge Simão

Abstract: The distribution of age at first marriage shows well-known strong regularities across many countries and recent historical periods. We accounted for these patterns by developing agent-based models that simulate the aggregate behavior of individuals who are searching for marriage partners. Past models assumed fully rational agents with complete knowledge of the marriage market; our simulated agents used psychologically plausible simple heuristic mate search rules that adjust aspiration levels on the basis of a sequence of encounters with potential partners. Substantial individual variation must be included in the models to account for the demographically observed age-at-marriage patterns.

In modern Western societies, deciding when to get married seems like a highly personal and individual choice. Individuals may believe that they are considering options and weighing possibilities that nobody else has ever had to think about in quite the same way. Yet, much research has pointed out the societal and economic constraints that influence even these personal decisions (e.g., Lloyd & South, 1996). Indeed, when viewed from the aggregate level, the pattern of the age at which people first get married shows surprising regularity across populations (Coale, 1971). Somehow, what people are doing in the mating game at the individual level seems to be following systematic rules that generate distinct patterns at the population level. But how? And how can we find out?

The scientific study of marriage has done little to answer these questions because of a strong divi-sion in focus among fields. A long tradition of sociological and demographic research has gathered and analyzed data on aggregate population-level patterns, such as age at marriage and proportion ever marrying, in cohorts from different historical and geographic settings. But this top-down macro perspective has typically obscured (or has not considered) how each individual makes a choice. Psychologists and economists, on the other hand, have studied and modeled the (often heterogeneous and culturally varying) individual-level processes that can end in the decision to cohabit or marry. But this bottom-up micro view has omitted the patterns that emerge in a group of such deciding individuals. Given that the two perspectives, individual and group level, have data and hypotheses that can help to constrain and explain the other, we should find a way to bring them together to speak to each other.

One common language that could connect both perspectives is that of mathematics. Building mathematical models has been done with some success (see, e.g., Coale & McNeil, 1972; Diekmann, 1989), but with a certain degree of violence done to the assumptions at both the micro and macro levels. In particular, allowing for significant variation in the strategies used by individuals quickly makes the mathematical models of their interactions intractable. As we argue in this article, it is exactly such individual-level variation that may underlie the emergence of the observed patterns at the population level. Thus, in addition to being a challenging language in which to become fluent, mathematics may be inadequate for expressing the relationships that are crucial to understanding the micro/macro interactions in the marriage market.

Instead, we turn here to computer modeling as a lingua franca to foster communication between the top-down and bottom-up approaches. Agent-based simulation models that specify the mate-search and choice behavior of individual agents interacting in a group enabled us to capture and explore the impact of the vital variation that is often missing from mathematical models. We did so by controlling and monitoring the micro-level decision mechanisms of each agent and observing the patterns that emerged at the macro level as a consequence of their choices and interactions. This modeling approach is finding increasing application in the social sciences and beyond, enabling, as it does here, different previously separated research traditions to come together and illuminate each other (Epstein & Axtell, 1996; Gilbert & Troitzsch, 1999; Macy & Willer, 2002). Although agent-based modeling has not yet become widespread in demography, the study of demographic behavior could benefit significantly from this approach (Billari & Prskawetz, 2003).

In the rest of this article, we present our efforts to combine demographic and psychological approaches to marriage via agent-based modeling. Our aim is to explain the emergence of commonly observed patterns of age at first marriage (Coale, 1971) as an outcome of the interaction of many instances of individual decision-making behavior. While marriage-age patterns have been explored from other perspectives in the past, our explanation here is novel in that it aims to do more than just account for the demographic data—we also require our models to meet the additional constraints of being psychologically plausible and fitting to other data on individual mate-choice behavior. We start

with population-level empirical evidence on the distribution of ages at marriage and review existing explanations of the common invariant features of this distribution across cultures. We then take the bottom-up approach and simulate the behavior of a cohort of *satisficing* agents who are looking for (marriage) partners in situations of both one-sided and mutual-choice decision making. We find that plausible psychological mechanisms of choice that are suggested by the framework of *bounded rationality* need some refinements to be reconciled with the macro patterns of marriage choice. In particular, we show how population heterogeneity in strategies is compatible with observed macro patterns. As will become clear, the implications of our results open a wide space for future research developments, both on the side of empirical studies and on the side of agent-based modeling of social behavior.

THEORETICAL ACCOUNTS OF AGE PATTERNS OF MARRIAGE

The distribution of ages at which people first marry has been similar, at least in a qualitative way, across a broad range of geographic locations and historical periods (Coale, 1971; Coale & McNeil, 1972). After rising quickly from a minimum marriage age, this distribution follows a rough bell shape, with a long tail capturing people who marry late in life. Whereas Coale and McNeil studied this common pattern using the frequency distribution of age at marriage, here we use the more behaviorally relevant *hazard rate* of marriage. This rate, defined either in discrete or continuous time, is the probability of marriage (or density in the continuous-time case) conditional on the fact that an individual has not married before a certain exact age.

To illustrate the shape of these hazard rates for marriage, we show in Figure 40-1 the empirically observed functions[1] for men and women in three populations in the late twentieth century: Romania in 1998, and Norway in 1978 and 1998. In all the cases shown in the figure, notice that the rise of age-specific probabilities is faster than its decrease. Although the shape of the curve looks somewhat different for Norway in 1998,

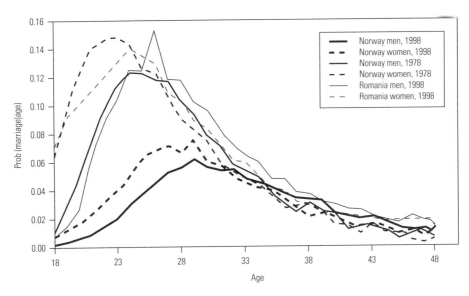

Figure 40-1. Hazard functions for marriage in European populations. (*Source:* Authors' elaborations on Eurostat, New Cronos database.)

where nonmarital cohabitation was widespread, it can still be described qualitatively in a similar way. In addition, hazard rates tend to converge to a level close to zero at later ages. This typical hazard-rate function can be observed for several other populations, and it is this overall pattern that we want to account for in our models.

Three main types of formal behavioral models have been proposed to explain these age patterns of marriage (Diekmann, 1989): latent-state (or compartment) models, diffusion models, and search models. Such models are usually applied to analyze the behavior of a cohort of individuals as they age. Latent-state models of first marriage, like Coale and McNeil's (1972) model, hypothesize that individuals in a cohort pass through various stages in early adult life before they get married and that the length of time this process takes is governed by a stochastic process. More precisely, Coale and McNeil proposed that the age at entry into the marriageable state is normally distributed and that there are three subsequent exponentially distributed delays (corresponding to life stages) before marriage. Although the Coale–McNeil model fits observed data for a complete cohort or population well, it performs less well in the case of forecasting the

behavior of a cohort by means of extrapolation (Goldstein & Kenney, 2001; Henz & Huinink, 1999), perhaps because of weakness in the behavioral assumptions of the model. The model has also been criticized for the absence of explicit assumptions regarding the workings of the search process (Burch, 1993; Coale & Trussell, 1996).

In diffusion models, mating happens by "contagion" from other people who are already mated. The model developed by Hernes (1972) is based on the idea that (first) marriages are influenced by two opposing forces that drive a cohort through a diffusion process. First, the pressure to marry increases with age because of the existence of social norms stating that "who marries late marries ill." Such norms are supposed to influence the threshold value for the acceptance of a partner, making this threshold fall with age. Second, as time (and age) goes by, the "marriageability" of individuals is reduced, so while each individual may become more eager to marry, he or she becomes less able to secure a willing partner. The combined effect of both these forces on the diffusion process produces a unimodal pattern for marriage hazard rates. The Hernes model has recently been applied to forecasting U.S. marriage patterns (Goldstein & Kenney, 2001). Similar patterns that fit observed first-marriage rates are produced by log-logistic diffusion models, where again the diffusion of behavior decreases with age (Billari, 2001; Brüderl & Diekmann, 1995).

Both latent-state and diffusion models fit observed demographic data well. Indeed, the difficulty of distinguishing these macro-level models on the basis of fit to data indicates a possible advantage for a third possibility: individual-based models, which provide different explanations of the observed marriage patterns that can be supported with individual-level behavioral data as well. In these models, typically based on economic job-search theory (e.g., Lippmann & McCall, 1976), agents act according to some search mechanism to seek mates in a reasonable (usually somehow optimal) manner (Burdett & Coles, 1999). Individuals who are represented in these models can select possible mates, for instance, by making and accepting offers, and the combined actions of these individuals over time yields distributions of age at marriage that can be compared to the demographically observed patterns.

Some individual-based search models of this kind are based on the assumption of perfectly rational agents performing optimal searches; they also typically assume that the agents are homogeneous in terms of their rational behavior. Keeley (1979), for example, adopted an optimal model from job-search theory in which individuals set a threshold financial value for the minimal (monetary) benefit they seek in a marriage; if an individual finds a partner with whom their combined income can exceed this threshold, then they marry. The cost-benefit analysis that is necessary to set such an optimal search threshold assumes full knowledge of the environment of potential mates and full rationality on the part of the individual, and thus this model is subject to the common criticisms of such unrealistic assumptions (Chase, Hertwig, & Gigerenzer, 1998; Oppenheimer, 1988): real human decision makers have only limited knowledge of the situation they face (here, the distribution of values of possible available mates and their own value on the marriage market),

limited ability to process whatever amount of information they do have, and limited time within which to make a decision. The presence of these limitations implies that we should build specific models of individual marriage-search processes starting from the assumption that individuals act according to *bounded* rationality, as we describe in the next section.[2]

MODELING SEQUENTIAL SEARCH PROCESSES

To construct an agent-based model to account for population-level demographic phenomena that are related to age at first marriage, we can create a set of simulated individuals who go about trying to marry (or mate) and monitor their success (or lack thereof) over time. Essentially, we want these agents to live out a life composed of the following steps: first, grow up until they reach the minimum marriageable age, possibly learning something along the way that will aid in their later marriage process; second, start to look for a marriage partner; third, if an acceptable (and agreeing) marriage partner is found, marry and leave the still-unmarried population, otherwise get a bit older, possibly learn something from the failed experience, and (if not too old) return to Step 2 to look again. We will record the age at which each individual first gets married (note that there are only first marriages in this version of the model) and the overall number of individuals who ever get married and then compare these data with the empirically observed facts to see how well this model fits. To be concrete, this model requires a specification of the way in which potential marriage partners are met and of how an individual searches through the potential partners. What are the possibilities that we should consider?

We start by specifying the nature of the environment in which the marriage process takes place—that is, how potential partners are encountered. One approach would be to say that all the potential partners are simultaneously available to an individual who is seeking to marry, and the individual must just compare them and choose the one who most closely matches some preference. This is the view of the marriage market proposed by some economists who are interested in how stable matchings can be made between men and women who have complete knowledge of all available partners (Bergstrom & Real, 2000). Although this full-knowledge assumption may apply to some small societies, it does not seem to match most of the cases of large populations for which demographers have collected age-at-marriage data. Instead, people who are seeking mates (or other things, such as houses, jobs, and even consumer products) often must choose between a set of options that they see not all at once, but one after another, sequentially. These situations are typically characterized by low (or zero) probability of being able to recall, or return to and choose, previously seen options once they have been passed by (e.g., individuals one has dated and broken up with in the past are probably not still interested in rekindling the relationship later). The problem then becomes one of deciding when to stop searching and to go with the currently available option.

Given this environment for marriage decisions, what kind of search mechanisms can people use to make their choices and stop their hunt? Again there are two main types of approaches. Inspired by the optimizing perspective of unbounded rationality mentioned in the last section, one could attempt to gather as much relevant information as possible about the distribution of available partners and then choose in a way that maximizes the chance of getting the best mate. For instance, one could attempt to compute the optimal point at which to stop searching, given the trade-off between time and other costs that accumulate with each alternative seen, and the chance that the next alternative that is checked will be better than those that were encountered previously. This approach could involve extensive calculations, such as Bayesian updating of probability estimates or assessments of the costs of forgone opportunities, and thus require considerable time and computational resources.

But to make choices in a useful amount of time, real agents must use a limited search across options because real decision makers have only a finite amount of time, knowledge, attention, or money to spend on a particular decision

(Todd, 2000). And indeed, there is considerable evidence that people who are faced with sequential search tasks use simple rules to make their choices (Dudey & Todd, 2002; Hey, 1982; Moon & Martin, 1990; Seale & Rapoport, 1997). As such, people are acting in accordance with what Simon (1990) called bounded, rather than unbounded, rationality—making decisions within the bounds of time, information, and computational ability that the task environment and human cognitive capacities impose on them. The notion of unbounded rationality, following the tenets of logic and probability theory, is a convenient fiction for constructing mathematical models of economic behavior, but to understand real human behavior, one should construct models of the actual bounded psychological processes that guide decision making. Moreover, the simple heuristics that people often use to make decisions with limited time and information not only are easier and faster to employ, they also can be surprisingly successful when applied in the proper task environments (Gigerenzer, Todd, & the ABC Research Group, 1999).

Simple search mechanisms require a quick and easy way to decide when to stop looking for options, that is, a stopping rule. What kinds of simple stopping rules are reasonable for a marriage model? For realistic search situations in which the distribution of available options (here, potential mates) is not known or well characterized and the costs of a search (here, the loss of all other opportunities) cannot be accurately assessed, traditional rational models cannot be readily applied and optimal stopping points cannot be calculated. Instead, for such decision problems, Simon (1990) proposed a *satisficing* approach to searches, in which individuals check successive alternatives until they find one that is good enough (rather than optimal) for their goals. This approach can be implemented by means of an aspiration level that individuals somehow set and then use in searching further, stopping that search as soon as an option is encountered that exceeds the aspiration level. Here, we assume that all potential marriage partners can be assessed on some unidimensional quality scale, so that the searchers can set a quality (or mate value) aspiration level for stopping a search upon finding a suitable aspiration-exceeding partner. The exact way in which the aspiration level is set depends on further details about the search situation that is encountered. (Of course, cultural norms and individual emotions exert strong influences on the search for and choice of a mate. Although we do not explore their roles here, both could operate in the search process as we present it, for instance, by affecting the aspiration level that is set and by indicating when an aspiration level has been met, as in falling in love.)

One way to conceive of the search for a marriage partner is as a shopping expedition in which potential mates are encountered one by one, choices must be made on the spot (no recall), and the final choice is made in a unilateral fashion by the searcher—the partner has no say in the marriage decision. Here, mate search can be characterized as one-sided, which is clearly a somewhat unrealistic simplification of the mate-search process for most (if not all) cultures, but which has proved useful as a starting point for mathematical modeling (cf. the *secretary* or *dowry problem* in probability theory; see Ferguson, 1989; Seale & Rapoport, 1997). Todd (1997; see also Todd & Miller, 1999) showed that a simple satisficing heuristic would do well at finding good partners in this situation: set an aspiration level at the highest-quality mate that one has seen during the first dozen or so potential partners, continue searching until a new partner is seen who exceeds that level, and select (marry) that person. Billari (2000) tested whether such a simple rule would produce the expected age-at-marriage patterns by recording how long the search would go on until a suitable partner was found and mapping that search length onto age.[3] He found that if all individuals used the same length of "learning time" to set their aspiration level (e.g., after seeing exactly 12 potential mates), age at first marriage peaked unnaturally immediately after the initial learning phase; only when variation in learning times was introduced did the typical right-skewed bell distribution appear.

Two-Sided (Mutual) Search Processes

The reason that one-sided mate searches, with one sex doing the searching and making the decisions, is an unrealistic model is that in many modern cultures, mate search is mutual: at the same time one sex is evaluating members of the other sex as prospective mates, they are themselves being evaluated in turn. If a particular man does not meet the standards of a particular woman in whom he is interested, for instance, then his courtship attempts are doomed to failure. Furthermore, in contrast to the solipsistic lone-searcher model (e.g., Todd, 1997), searching individuals interact in the real world, at a minimum because they are vying for the same set of potential mating partners. How can we model this more realistic two-sided mutual-choice situation?

To explore how different mate-search rules can work in a two-sided setting,[4] we start with a population containing two sets of searchers, 100 simulated men and 100 simulated women, each with a distinct mate value between 0.0 and 100.0 and all in competition with one another (within each sex) for the same set of possible mates. Each individual has the ability to assess accurately the mate values of members of the opposite sex, but (initially) lacks any knowledge of his or her own mate value. Each individual begins his or her simulated life by assessing and making (or not) practice marriage or mating offers to some specific number of members of the opposite sex during an "adolescence period" (akin to the learning phase in Billari, 2000). That is, for each potential partner an individual sees during adolescence, the individual judges whether the other's mate value is above his or her own aspiration level and, if so, makes an offer (which, however, cannot result in actual marriage during this initial period). Over this time, individuals can also adjust their aspiration level on the basis of whom they encounter and what happens during each encounter (e.g., offers or rejections).

After this adolescence period, the simulated men and women meet up in a further set of randomly assigned pairs, and they can either make a real proposal (an offer to mate) to their paired partner or decline to do so. If both individuals in a pair make an offer to each other, then this pair is deemed married and the two individuals are removed from the population. Otherwise, both individuals remain in the marriage pool to try again with someone else. This pairing-offering-marrying cycle is repeated until every individual is married or until every individual has had the opportunity to assess and propose to every member of the opposite sex exactly once.

With this simulation framework, we can test and compare different search and stopping mechanisms that the individuals use according to how many individuals in the population get married, how well matched the pairs end up being, and when the marriages occur. We can compare search rules along these dimensions not only against each other but also against sociological, demographic, and psychological data. On the first dimension, a worldwide effort to study (first) marriage patterns has shown that in most societies, 80% to 100% of adults marry (United Nations, 1990). (The exception is the emerging pattern of nonmarital cohabitation in some countries, but for our purposes, it can be considered equivalent to marriage.) Second, as we indicated earlier, a large body of research in sociology and psychology has demonstrated the high degree of homogamy that is evident in marriage patterns, along such dimensions as ethnicity, religion, socioeconomic status, attractiveness, intelligence, and height (Coltrane & Collins, 2001; Kalmijn, 1998). This degree of homogamy has been quantified in some cases in a way that provides useful data for vetting our models, such as the high correlation, between .4 and .6, of the physical attractiveness of people in married couples (Kalick & Hamilton, 1986). By taking attractiveness as a rough proxy for mate value (when other dimensions are held constant), we have a plausible numeric target (about .5) for the within-pair mate-value correlations that come out of our simulations. Finally, we have the age-at-first-marriage curves discussed earlier.

How do different search rules fare on these dimensions? First, trying to use a one-sided mate-search rule in the two-sided (and competitive) setting has disastrous results for most of the population. For instance, if everyone checks a dozen members of the opposite sex and sets an aspiration level equal to the highest mate value seen, then only 7% of the population will end up in mutually agreeing pairs (Todd & Miller, 1999). Furthermore, only the highest-valued

individuals end up mated with this rule (mostly in the top 10% of the population). This situation is certainly counter to human experience (as well as to that of other species in which mates select each other mutually, as in some monogamous animals), where the majority of individuals, across a wide range of relative mate values, are able to find mates. Clearly, a different kind of search rule must be used for mutual search.

An individual can achieve a much more successful two-sided mate search simply by using his or her own mate value (or slightly less) as the aspiration level for deciding which members of the opposite sex to propose to—assuming now that this mate value is known. With this approach, most of the population can succeed in finding and pairing up with mates of a similar value to their own (Miller & Todd, 1998; Todd & Miller, 1999). When we look at the hazard function for marriage, however, we see an unrealistic exponentially decreasing function (Figure 40-2a), similar to what appeared in Billari's (2000) one-sided search case. Thus, merely changing the search setting to two-sided choice does not, by itself, lead to a realistic distribution of marriage times. However, as Billari found, introducing variation in learning times (here, letting the adolescence period vary normally) proves to be a crucial factor that is sufficient to create the familiar unimodal hazard curve, as shown in Figure 40-2b.

But there is also a problem with this strategy: the accurate knowledge of one's own (relative) mate value that this strategy requires is not necessarily easy to come by. Individuals cannot be born with it because it is context sensitive (it depends on the others in one's social circle) and changes with age. Without this initial knowledge, then, people must somehow estimate their own mate value if they are to use it to form an aspiration level. What learning mechanisms could individuals use to arrive at aspirations that are in line with their own quality?

The one-sided learning rule presented earlier used only the information about the mate values of individuals who were encountered during the adolescent learning period, which does not reflect anything about the searcher's own mate value in our random-meeting environment.

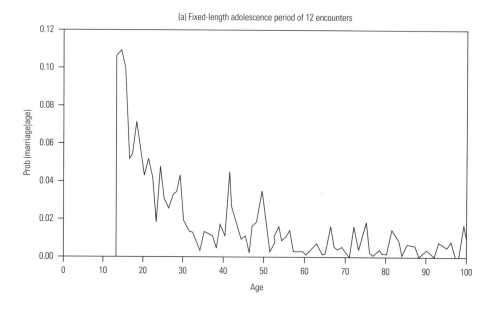

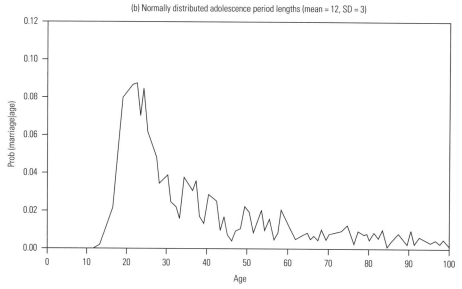

Figure 40-2. Hazard functions for marriage in a population of simulated agents who are searching for mates using aspiration levels close to their own mate value.

But there is more information available that can be used to infer one's own value: whether or not each encountered individual made a mating offer. In this case, the simulation model works as follows.

First, we set initial aspiration levels to an intermediate value of 50 for everyone, under a "no-knowledge" assumption (in these simulations, it does not make much difference if all individuals have the same initial aspiration level, whether 50 or otherwise, or if initial aspiration levels are randomly normally distributed). Next, each male A encounters a randomly chosen female B as the first step in each one's adolescent learning period. Male A can accurately see female B's mate value, and vice versa. If B's mate value is higher than A's aspiration level (currently 50), then A will make an offer to B; otherwise A will reject B. Similarly, B checks whether A's mate value is higher than her current aspiration level (also initially 50) and makes an offer to A or rejects him accordingly. A may then alter his aspiration level, for instance (depending on the learning rule he is using), adjusting it upward if he receives an offer from B and downward if he receives a rejection. B will do the same, depending on what she receives from A. So if A's mate value was 25 and B's mate value was 70, for example, then after this encounter, A may end up with a new aspiration level of 45 (following rejection by B), and B may end up with a new aspiration level of 55 (following an offer from A). Then A and B each go on to a second random encounter, using their new aspiration levels to determine whether to make an offer to or reject the next individual they encounter, and adjusting their aspiration levels further, depending on what they then receive in turn. This process of random encounters and aspiration-level adjustment continues through the adolescent learning phase for some predetermined number of encounters. Then the true mating phase begins, as described earlier, with the final aspiration levels from the adolescence period fixed and used to determine all further offers or rejections as the random encounters continue. During this mating phase, any pair who make offers to each other will be "married" and removed from the population, with their "age at marriage" recorded.

If agents employ a learning rule that uses only the data about offers or rejections received, adjusting their current aspiration level (and hence their self-perception of their own quality) up with every offer received and down with every rejection, as mentioned in the example of A and B, then less than half the population—and only those in the lower half of the mate-value distribution—ends up mating. This outcome arises because this learning rule acts in essentially a vain manner: above-average-quality individuals get more offers than rejections and hence raise their aspiration levels to be too high, while below-average individuals lower

their aspiration levels too far, but which also allows them to find other low-quality mates who are acceptable to them.

We can get around this problem by designing a learning rule that uses both sources of information: who made offers or not during adolescence, and what their quality was. By raising their aspiration levels with every proposal received from a higher-value member of the opposite sex and lowering the level every time a lower-value individual does not propose, members of both sexes can rapidly estimate their own mate value and use it to pair up with similarly valued mates. With such a rule, fewer than 20 encounters with members of the opposite sex are necessary for much of the population to form mated pairs of individuals with similar mate values (Todd & Miller, 1999).[5] In fact, setting an aspiration level by searching through many more individuals than this number during adolescence (out of a population of 100 possible mates) results in a decrease in the chance of finding an acceptable mate, pointing again to the benefits of a limited search within a bounded rationality approach.

How well does this mutual search heuristic, successful at the individual level, accord with the population-level demographic data on age at marriage? The hazard curve produced by this heuristic, when everyone has an adolescence period in which 12 potential partners are encountered, is once more a steeply declining function (Figure 40-3a). This function peaks at a marriage rate that is lower than that for two-sided search with knowledge of one's own value (Figure 40-2a), indicating the challenges of this competitive and initially ignorant mate-search situation. Given the shape of the hazard curve, the learning process that is necessary to set an appropriate aspiration level here is insufficient to generate a realistic distribution of mating times. But, as before, this insufficiency is overcome through the use of normally varying adolescence times (Figure 40-3b).

Adding a Courtship Period to the Matching Process

The foregoing models are, of course, simplifications of the real human courtship and marriage

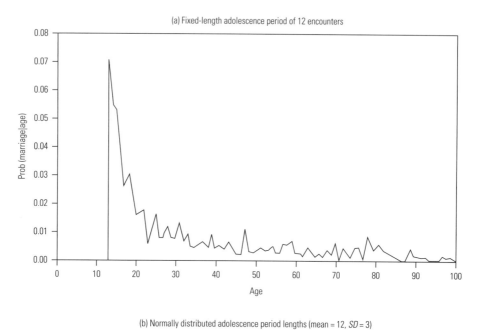

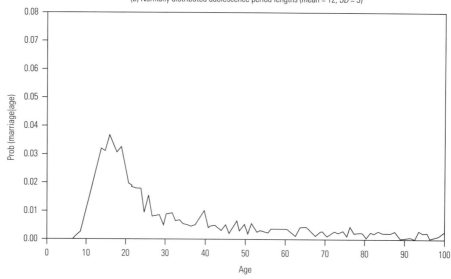

Figure 40-3. Hazard functions for marriage in a population of simulated agents who are searching for mates using aspiration levels learned based on offers and rejections received during an adolescence period.

process in many ways. Having learned from these initial simulations, we can continue to elaborate them to explore the importance and impact of other features of the courtship process in generating population-level marriage patterns. In particular, the models presented so far actually ignore the process of courtship itself, assuming that pairs of individuals somehow make an instantaneous decision whether or not to marry. Although whirlwind romances and Las Vegas weddings do occur, courtship in the real world is usually more extended than the hello–yes/no situation in our simulations. An extensive courtship period can serve a number of functions

(Simão & Todd, 2002): it can allow more information to be gathered about a potential partner, resulting in a better decision about his or her quality and potential match; it can enable an assessment of the potential partner's willingness to commit to a longer-term relationship (important in helping individuals to avoid the risk of abandonment, which can particularly affect women who are left with children to raise); and it can give both individuals the opportunity to keep monitoring other potential mates and possibly to switch to better partners before a long-term commitment is made. Thus, by including a courtship period in our models, we can more realistically account for the way that assortative mating based on multiple quality dimensions emerges. We have found that mate-search strategies that incorporate extended courtship and possible partner switching lead to most of a simulated population (over 95%) finding a mate with a similar overall quality (a within-pair correlation of about .5) after only a small number of courtships. These outcomes more closely match the statistics of real human populations than do the values that were produced by the models without courtship presented earlier (see Simão & Todd, 2002, for more details). Here, we are interested in whether the introduction of a lengthy courtship also influences the distribution of ages at which marriages occur (Simão & Todd, 2003)—that is, can adding the courtship period alone to our models account for the observed demographic data, or will there still be some missing necessary component?

In this new model, each individual has a specific minimum courtship time, which specifies how long it takes for the individual to commit fully to a relationship and become willing to marry. If two courting individuals "fall in love" with each other by continuously courting beyond this minimum duration, then they marry and do not consider further courtship opportunities. With this additional feature, the simulation proceeds as follows: at each time step, pairs of individuals may meet each other randomly at a certain specified rate (which can decline for the individuals the longer they have been involved in their current courtship, if any). In each new encounter, an individual decides what action to

perform on the basis of his or her current state: single individuals decide whether to try to start a relationship or wait to see if a better alternative becomes available. Courting individuals decide whether to continue to court their current partner or to try to switch to the newly encountered possibility. In either case, a new courtship can begin (leading to the termination of any old ones) only if both newly meeting parties agree.

These decisions are all made on the basis of aspiration levels, as in the previous models. However, in this case, there is no explicit adolescent aspiration-level learning period separate from the actual mating or marrying period. Rather, individuals (assumed to be roughly postadolescent at the start of the model) can immediately begin courtship, which may or may not lead to their ultimate marriage, and their aspiration levels can change throughout their lifetimes. Aspirations begin low (all individuals are undiscriminating) and rise or fall according to the mate quality of the partners that each individual courts. In addition, aspiration levels can be lowered whenever waiting for a higher-quality partner does not pay off because of lost reproductive lifetime. It is done simply by keeping track of the time a noncourting individual has been waiting for a partner and lowering his or her aspiration level when a waiting-time threshold is reached. Overall, this behavioral strategy can be interpreted, metaphorically, as individuals trying to climb up (and sometimes falling down) a ladder of partner qualities. When courting higher-quality partners, individuals tend to raise their aspiration level, and when rejected, or in any case with the passage of time, individuals tend to move their aspiration level down.

This courtship-based learning-and-switching process proves to be a better model of human mate search on a number of dimensions than the models described earlier, with most of its parameters having relatively little impact and the majority of its success arising from the introduction of courtship and switching. In particular, this model results in almost all individuals quickly finding and consequently marrying mates of similar levels of quality. But how quickly? In Figure 40-4 (the solid line), the distribution of ages at which individuals marry is an

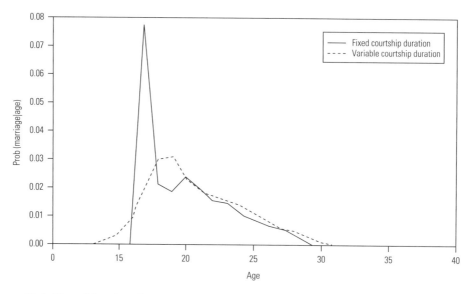

Figure 40-4. Hazard functions for marriage in a population of simulated agents using extended courtship. Shown are the results for individuals with a fixed five-year courtship duration before marriage (solid line) and individuals with a normally distributed courtship duration before marriage (mean = 5 years, SD = 3; dashed line).

unrealistically tight spike, generated by most of the high-quality individuals marrying quickly, coupled with a long tail produced by the low-quality individuals marrying over a much longer period. Although this outcome produces a testable prediction regarding the relation between mate quality and age at marriage that accords qualitatively with some observed data (cf. Kalick & Hamilton, 1986, whose model makes similar predictions), it differs from the expected age-at-first-marriage distribution much as did our first models. Thus, the courtship process alone does not appear to be sufficient to account for the population-level demographic patterns. Following our earlier finding that individual variation in learning time (adolescence) will lead to more realistic marriage-age distributions, we can test for a similar outcome in this case. Here, we do not have a separate learning phase to alter, but the courtship period serves a related function, allowing individuals a period within which to appraise their own quality and, if feasible, to switch to a better partner. If we introduce variation into the minimum courtship time, making it normally distributed across individuals instead

of fixed for everyone, the ages at marriage more closely follow the demographic patterns (Figure 40-4, the dashed line), again showing the importance of this simple manipulation of our models.

To summarize, what we have found so far in our explorations of mate-search mechanisms through a demographic lens is that various aspects of the individual search mechanism and task setting alone are insufficient to generate age-at-marriage distributions that reflect human patterns. Going from a noncompetitive one-sided search to a competitive two-sided (mutual) search did not create the expected skewed unimodal distribution or hazard function, nor did adding learning processes to the two-sided search, whether a nonmating adolescent trial period or an extended adult courtship period. Instead, we found that the introduction of variation across individuals in the population could lead to the appropriate patterns—but not just any type of variation. Only the inclusion of normal (or uniform) distributions of the length of learning periods (adolescence or courtship) resulted in the unimodal age-at-marriage curve;

varying the distribution of mate values (quality levels) or initial aspiration levels did not have an appreciable effect.

IMPLICATIONS AND CONCLUSIONS

Studying the problem of marriage timing by combining the top-down demographic approach with the bottom-up psychological modeling approach has enabled us to illuminate both perspectives. On the one hand, meeting the demographic constraints of the observed data on age at first marriage has required us to build realistic individual variation into our psychological models of mate search. On the other, looking at how individual search mechanisms can produce population-level outcomes has provided more psychologically satisfying (and satisficing) explanations of the demographic data, beyond merely pointing to latent stages or diffusion processes.

NOTES

1. More specifically, we graphed the age-specific conditional probabilities of first marriage, that is, the number of first marriages of people who attained a given age x in a year divided by the number of still-unmarried individuals of age $x - 1$ at the beginning of the year.
2. It is important to keep clear the distinction between the nature of the decision mechanisms that humans use and the way that these mechanisms came about. Individuals commonly rely on choice mechanisms with limited information use and processing, rather than employ complex optimizing processes to reach decisions. However, the mechanisms that humans use are themselves likely to have arisen through processes that are more akin to (constrained) optimization, namely, biological or cultural evolution (Macy & Flache, 1995). This evolutionary origin can result in our limited psychological mechanisms being nonetheless well fit to the situations and environments in which they are used, a match between mind and world termed *ecological rationality* (Gigerenzer & Todd, 1999).
3. Note that here choosing a mate is equated with marriage, and the number of potential partners seen is equated with age. The second mapping, from partners to age, is an assumption of this modeling work that needs to be tested against demographic data; alternatively, the simulations could be compared with data on the number of partners before, rather than age at, first marriage. But for now, given the difficulty of obtaining such data, we make the reasonable assumption that a linear relationship exists between age and number of partners.
4. See Todd and Miller (1999) and Dudey and Todd (2002) for further results regarding other search heuristics, and contact the authors for the Lisp code used.
5. However, the number of mated individuals hovered around an unrealistically low 50%, a problem that is addressed by the mating models with courtship presented in the following section.

REFERENCES

Numbers in parentheses indicate the chapters in which a reference is cited.

Chapter numbers in brackets indicate the chapters in which an alphabetic designator (also in brackets) was added to the year of publication; e.g., 2009a.

Abadie, A., & Gay S. (2006). The impact of presumed consent legislation on cadaveric organ donation: A cross-country study. *Journal of Health Economics, 25*, 599–620. (9)

Abelson, R. P., & Levi, A. (1985). Decision making and decision theory. In G. Lindzey & E. Aronson (Eds.), *Handbook of social psychology. Vol. I. Theory and method* (3rd ed., pp. 231–309). New York: Random House. (17)

Ackerman, P. L., Beier, M. E., & Boyle, M. O. (2002). Individual differences in working memory within a nomological network of cognitive and perceptual speed abilities. *Journal of Experimental Psychology, General, 131*, 567–589. (22)

Adams, J. A. (1961). Human tracking behavior. *Psychological Bulletin, 58*, 55–79. (33)

Addis, D. R., McIntosh, A. R., Moscovitch, M., Crawley, A. P., & McAndrews, M. P. (2004). Characterizing spatial and temporal features of autobiographical memory retrieval networks: A partial least squares approach. *Neuroimage, 23*, 1460–1471. (25)

Adhami, E., & Browne, D. P. (1996). Major crime enquiries: Improving expert support for detectives. *Police Research Group, Special Interest Series*, Paper 9. London: Home Office. (29)

Adorno, T. W., Frenkel-Brunswik, E., Levinson, D., & Sanford, N. (1950). *The authoritarian personality*. New York: Harper & Row. (9)

Aggleton, J. P., & Shaw, C. (1996). Amnesia and recognition memory: A re-analysis of psychometric data. *Neuropsychologia, 34*, 51–62. (25)

Aggleton, J. P., Van, S. D., Denby, C., Dix, S., Mayes, A. R., Roberts, N., et al. (2005). Sparing of the familiarity component of recognition memory in a patient with hippocampal pathology. *Neuropsychologia, 43*, 1810–1823. (25)

Aizpurua, J. M., Ichiishi, T., Nieto, J., & Uriarte, J. R. (1993). Similarity and preferences in the space of simple lotteries. *Journal of Risk and Uncertainty, 6*, 289–297. (8)

Akaike, H. (1973). Information theory as an extension of the maximum likelihood principle. In B. N. Petrov & F. Csaki (Eds.), *Proceedings of the Second International Symposium on Information Theory* (pp. 267–281). Budapest, Hungary: Akademiai Kiado. (11)

Alba, J. W., & Marmorstein, H. (1987). The effects of frequency knowledge on consumer decision making. *Journal of Consumer Research, 14*, 14–26. (2)

Albers, W. (2001). Prominence theory as a tool to model boundedly rational decisions. In G. Gigerenzer & R. Selten (Eds.), *Bounded rationality: The adaptive toolbox* (pp. 297–317). Cambridge, MA: MIT Press. (7, 8)

Ali, A. H. (2002). *The caged virgin: A Muslim woman's cry for reason*. London: Simon & Schuster. (9)

Allais, M. (1953). Le comportement de l'homme rationel devant le risque: Critique des postulats et axioms de l' école américaine [Rational man's behavior in face of risk: Critique of the American School's postulates and axioms]. *Econometrica, 21*, 503–546. (7)

Allais, M. (1979). Foundations of a positive theory of choice involving risk, and a criticism of the postulates and axioms of the American School. In M. Allais & O. Hagen (Eds.), *Expected utility hypothesis and the Allais paradox* (pp. 27–245). Dordrecht, the Netherlands: Reidel. (Original work published 1952) (8)

Allais, M. (1979). The so-called Allais paradox and rational decisions under uncertainty. In M. Allais & O. Hagen (Eds.), *Expected utility hypotheses and the Allais paradox* (pp. 437–681). Dordrecht, the Netherlands: Reidel. (7)

Allen, C. (2000). The evolution of rational demons. *Behavioral and Brain Sciences, 23,* 742. (17)

Allison, T., & Cicchetti, D. (1976). Sleep in mammals: Ecological and constitutional correlates. *Science, 174,* 732–734. (21)

Alpaydin, E. (2004). *Introduction to machine learning.* Cambridge, MA: MIT Press. (1)

Alter, A. L., & Oppenheimer, D. M. (2006). Predicting short-term stock fluctuations by using processing fluency. *Proceedings of the National Academy of Sciences of the United States of America, 103,* 9369–9372. (26)

Alter, A. L., & Oppenheimer, D. M. (2007). *Uniting the tribes of fluency into a metacognitive nation.* Manuscript submitted for publication. (26)

Altmann, E. M., & Gray, W. D. (2002). Forgetting to remember. *Psychological Science, 13,* 27–33. (4)

Amodio, D. M., & Frith, C. D. (2006). Meeting of minds: The medial prefrontal cortex and social cognition. *Nature Review Neuroscience, 7,* 268–277. (9)

Anderson, C.J. (2003). The psychology of doing nothing: Forms of decision avoidance result from reason and emotion. *Psychological Bulletin, 129,* 139–167. (37)

Anderson, J. R. (1990). *The adaptive character of thought.* Hillsdale, NJ: Erlbaum. (2, 5)

Anderson, J. R. (1991). The adaptive nature of human categorization. *Psychological Review, 98,* 409–429. (1, 14)

Anderson, J. R. (1991). Is human cognition adaptive? *Behavioral & Brain Sciences, 14,* 471–517. (1)

Anderson, J. R. (1993). *Rules of the mind.* Hillsdale, NJ: Erlbaum. (4)

Anderson, J. R. (2007). *How can the human mind occur in the physical universe?* Oxford, UK: Oxford University Press. (4)

Anderson, J. R., Bothell, D., Byrne, M. D., Douglass, S., Lebiere, C., & Qin, Y. (2004). An integrated theory of the mind. *Psychological Review, 111,* 1036–1060. (5, 26)

Anderson, J. R., Bothell, D., Lebiere, C., & Matessa, M. (1998). An integrated theory of list memory. *Journal of Memory and Language, 38,* 341–380. (4)

Anderson, J. R., & Lebiere, C. (1998). *The atomic components of thought.* Mahwah, NJ: Erlbaum. (4, 26)

Anderson, J. R., & Milson, R. (1989). Human memory: An adaptive perspective. *Psychological Review, 96,* 703–719. (4)

Anderson, J. R., & Schooler, L. J. (1991). Reflections of the environment in memory. *Psychological Science, 2,* 396–408. (4)

Anderson, J. R., & Schooler, L. J. (2000). The adaptive nature of memory. In E. Tulving & F. I. M. Craik (Eds.), *The Oxford handbook of memory* (pp. 557–570). New York: Oxford University Press. (4)

Anderson, N. H. (1981). *Foundations of information integration theory.* New York: Academic Press. (13)

Andersson, P., Edman, J., & Ekman, M. (2005). Predicting the World Cup 2002 in soccer: Performance confidence of experts and non-experts. *International Journal of Forecasting, 21,* 565–576. (31)

Andersson, P., Ekman, M., & Edman, J. (2003). *Forecasting the fast and frugal way: A study of performance and information-processing strategies of experts and non-experts when predicting the World Cup 2002 in soccer.* Unpublished manuscript, Center for Economic Psychology, Stockholm School of Economics. (27)

Angelillo, I. F., Ricciardi, G., Rossi, P., Pantisano, P., Langiano, E., & Pavia, M. (1999). Mothers and vaccination: Knowledge, attitude, and behavior in Italy. *Bulletin of the World Health Organization, 77,* 224–229. (35)

Arkes, H. R., & Ayton, P. (1999). The sunk cost and concorde effects: Are humans less rational than lower animals? *Psychological Bulletin, 125,* 591–600. (5)

Arkes, H. R., & Hammond, K. R. (1986). *Judgment and decision-making: An interdisciplinary reader.* New York: Cambridge University Press. (29)

Arkes, H. R., Wortmann, R. L., Saville, P. D., & Harkness, A. R. (1981). Hindsight bias among physicians weighting the likelihood of diagnoses. *Journal of Applied Psychology, 66,* 252–254. (10)

Armelius, B.-Å., & Armelius, K. (1974). The use of redundancy in multiple-cue judgments: Data from a suppressor-variable task. *American Journal of Psychology, 87,* 385–392. (13)

Arnauld, A., & Nicole, P. (1996). *Logic or the art of thinking.* Cambridge, UK: Cambridge University Press. (Original work published 1662). (7)

Arrow, K. J. (2004). Is bounded rationality unboundedly rational? Some ruminations. In M. Augier & J. G. March (Eds.), *Models of a man: Essays in memory of Herbert A. Simon* (pp. 47–55). Cambridge, MA: MIT Press. (9)

Ashby, F. G. (Ed.). (1992). *Multidimensional models of categorization.* Hillsdale, NJ: Erlbaum. (14)

Ashby, F. G., & Alfonso-Reese, L. A. (1995). Categorization as probability density estimation. *Journal of Mathematical Psychology, 39,* 216–233. (14)

Ashby, F. G., & Maddox, W. T. (2005). Human category learning. *Annual Review of Psychology, 56,* 149–178. (14)

Ashton, R. H. (1981). A descriptive study of information evaluation. *Journal of Accounting Research, 19,* 42–61. (13)

Atkinson, J. W. (1957). Motivational determinants of risk-taking behavior. *Psychological Review, 64,* 359–372. (7)

Atkinson, R. C., & Juola, J. F. (1974). Search and decision processes in recognition memory. In D. H. Krantz, R. C. Atkinson, R. D. Lucek, & P. Suppes (Eds.), *Contemporary developments in mathematical psychology* (Vol. 1, pp. 243–293). San Francisco: Freeman. (23)

Axelrod, R. (1984). *The evolution of cooperation.* New York: Basic Books. (1, 15)

Axelrod, R., & Hamilton, W. D. (1981). The evolution of cooperation. *Science, 211,* 1390–1396. (5)

Ayton, P., & Fisher, I. (2004). The hot hand fallacy and the gambler's fallacy: Two faces of subjective randomness? *Memory and Cognition, 32,* 1369–1378. (1)

Ayton, P., & Önkal, D. (1997). *Forecasting football fixtures: Confidence and judged proportion correct.* Unpublished manuscript, Department of Psychology, The City University of London. (3)

Ayton, P., & Önkal, D. (2004). *Effects of ignorance on judgmental forecasting.* Unpublished manuscript, Department of Psychology, The City University of London. (32)

Ayton, P., & Önkal, D. (2006). *Effects of ignorance and information on judgments and decisions.* Unpublished manuscript, City University, London. (31)

Balabanovic, M. (1998). Exploring versus exploiting when learning user models for text recommendation. *User Modeling and User-Adapted Interaction, 8,* 71–102. (39)

Balasubramanian, S., Gupta, S., Kamakura, W., & Wedel, M. (1998). Modeling large data sets in marketing. *Statistica Neerlandica, 52,* 303–324. (36)

Balda, R. P., & Kamil, A. C. (1992). Long-term spatial memory in Clark's nutcracker, *Nucifruga columbiana. Animal Behavior, 44,* 761–769. (5)

Balduzzi, P., & Lynch, A. W. (1999). Transaction costs and predictability: Some utility cost calculations. *Journal of Financial Economics, 52,* 47–78. (34)

Balkovsky, E., & Shraiman, B. I. (2002). Olfactory search at high Reynolds number. *Proceedings of the National Academy Sciences, U.S.A., 99,* 12589–12593. (5)

Ballweg, J. A., & Pagtolun-An, I. G. (1992). Parental underinvestment: A link in the fertility–mortality continuum. *Population Research and Policy Review, 11,* 73–89. (35)

Balota, D. A., & Chumbley, J. I. (1984). Are lexical decisions a good measure of lexical access? The role of word frequency in the neglected decision stage. *Journal of Experimental Psychology: Human Perception and Performance, 10,* 340–357. (23)

Baltes, P. B., & Baltes, M. M. (1990). Psychological perspectives on successful aging: The model of selective optimization with compensation. In P. B. Baltes & M. M. Baltes (Eds.), *Successful aging: Perspectives from the behavioral sciences* (pp. 1–34). New York: Cambridge University Press. (22)

Baltes, P. B., & Lindenberger, U. (1997). Emergence of a powerful connection between sensory and cognitive functions across the adult life span: A new window to the study of cognitive aging? *Psychology and Aging, 12,* 12–21. (22)

Baltes, P. B., Staudinger, U. M., & Lindenberger, U. (1999). Lifespan psychology: Theory and application to intellectual functioning. *Annual Review of Psychology, 50,* 471–507. (22)

Banks, W. P. (1970). Signal detection theory and human memory. *Psychological Bulletin, 74,* 81–99. (15)

Banks, W. P., & Coleman, M. J. (1981). Two subjective scales of number. *Perception & Psychophysics, 29,* 95–105. (7)

Barbey, A. K., & Sloman, S. A. (2007). Base-rate respect: From ecological rationality to dual processes. *Behavioral and Brain Sciences, 30,* 241–254. (1)

Bar-Eli, M., Avugos, S., & Raab, M. (2006). Twenty years of "hot hand" research: Review and critique. *Psychology of Sport and Exercise, 7,* 525–553. (32)

Barnett, S. A. (1963). *The rat: A study in behavior.* Chicago: Aldine. (3)

Barone, L. (2006). Bruno de Finetti, The Problem of "Full-Risk Insurances". *Journal of Investment Management, 4,* 19–43. (34)

Barreto, T. V., & Rodrigues, L. C. (1992). Factors influencing childhood immunization in an urban area of Brazil. *Journal of Epidemiology and Community Health, 46,* 357–361. (35)

Barry, C. B. (1974). Portfolio analysis under uncertain means, variances, and covariances. *Journal of Finance, 29,* 515–522. (34)

Barta, Z., Houston, A. I., McNamara, J. M., & Székely, T. (2002). Sexual conflict about parental care: The role of reserves. *American Naturalist, 159,* 687–705. (5)

Bartlett, F. C. (1995). *Remembering.* Cambridge, UK: Cambridge University Press. (Original work published 1932) (10)

Basolo, A. L., & Trainor, B. C. (2002). The confirmation of a female preference for a composite male trait in green swordtails. *Animal Behavior, 63,* 469–474. (5)

Batchelder, W. H., Riefer, D. M., & Hu, X. (1994). Measuring memory factors in source monitoring: Reply to Kinchla. *Psychological Review, 101,* 172–176. (4)

Bateson, M., Healy, S. D., & Hurly, T. A. (2003). Context-dependent foraging decisions in rufous hummingbirds. *Proceedings of the Royal Society of London, Series B: Biological Sciences, 270,* 1271–1276. (5)

Baucells, M., Carrasco, J. A., & Hogarth, R. M. (2008). Cumulative dominance and heuristic performance in binary multi-attribute choice. *Operations Research, 56,* 1289–1304. (8, 13, 14)

Baum, K. A., & Grant, W. E. (2001). Hummingbird foraging behavior in different patch types: Simulation of alternative strategies. *Ecological Modelling, 137,* 201–209. (5)

Baumeister, R. F., Vohs, K. D., & Funder, D. C. (2007). Psychology as the science of self-reports and finger movements. Whatever happened to actual behavior? *Perspectives on Psychological Science, 2,* 396–403. (9)

Bawa, V. S., Brown, S. J., & Klein, R. W. (1979). *Estimation risk and optimal portfolio choice.* Amsterdam: North Holland. (34)

Bayes, T. (1763). An essay towards solving a problem in the doctrine of chances. *Philosophical Transactions, 3,* 370–418. (6)

Beach, L. R., & Mitchell, T. R. (1978). A contingency model for the selection of decision strategies. *Academy of Management Review, 3,* 439–449. (1, 11, 17, 22)

Beall, A. C., & Loomis, J. M. (1997). Optic flow and visual analysis of the baseto-final turn. *International Journal of Aviation Psychology, 7,* 201–223. (33)

Becker, G. S. (1976). *The economic approach to human behavior.* Chicago: University of Chicago Press. (2)

Becker, G. S. (1991). *A treatise on the family.* Cambridge, MA: Harvard University Press. (35)

Becker, G. S. (1995). *The essence of Becker.* Stanford, CA: Hoover Institution Press. (9)

Becker, G. S., & Tomes, N. (1976). Child endowments and the quantity and quality of children. *Journal of Political Economy, 84,* 143–162. (35)

Becker, G. S., & Tomes, N. (1986). Human capital and the rise and fall of families. *Journal of Labor Economics, 4,* 1–39. (35)

Becker, M. H. (1974). The health belief model and personal health behavior. *Health Education Monographs, 2,* 324–508. (7)

Begg, I. M., Anas, A., & Farinacci, S. (1992). Dissociation of processes in belief: Source recollection, statement familiarity, and the illusion of truth. *Journal of Experimental Psychology: General, 121,* 446–458. (4)

Behrman, J. B., & Taubman, P. (1986). Birth order, schooling, and earnings. *Journal of Labor Economics, 4,* 121–145. (35)

Beilock, S. L., Bertenthal, B. I., McCoy, A. M., & Carr, T. H. (2004). Haste does not always make waste: Expertise, direction of attention, and speed versus accuracy in performing sensorimotor skills. *Psychonomic Bulletin and Review, 11,* 373–379. (1)

Beilock, S. L., Carr, T. H., MacMahon, C., & Starkes, J. L. (2002). When paying attention becomes counterproductive: Impact on divided versus skill-focused attention on novice and experienced performance of sensorimotor skills. *Journal of Experimental Psychology: Applied, 8,* 6–16. (1)

Bélisle, C., & Cresswell, J. (1997). The effects of a limited memory capacity on foraging behavior. *Theoretical Population Biology, 52,* 78–90. (5)

Bell, D. E. (1982). Regret in decision making under uncertainty. *Operations Research, 30,* 961–981. (7)

Bell, D. E. (1985). Disappointment in decision making under uncertainty. *Operations Research, 33,* 1–27. (7)

Benartzi, S., & Thaler, R. (2001). Naive diversification strategies in defined contribution saving plans. *American Economic Review, 91,* 79–98. (34, 35)

Benhamou, S. (1992). Efficiency of area-concentrated searching behaviour in a continuous patchy environment. *Journal of Theoretical Biology, 159,* 67–81. (5)

Benjamin, A. S., Bjork, R. A., & Hirshman, E. (1998). Predicting the future and reconstructing the past: A Bayesian characterization of the utility of subjective fluency. *Acta Psychologica, 98,* 267–290. (26)

Benjamin, A. S., Bjork, R. A., & Schwartz, B. L. (1998). The mismeasure of memory: When retrieval fluency is misleading as a metamnemonic index. *Journal of Experimental Psychology: General, 127,* 55–68. (26)

Bennell, C., & Canter, D. V. (2002). Linking commercial burglaries by modus operandi: Tests using regression and ROC analysis. *Science & Justice, 42,* 153–164. (29)

Bennis, W. M., Medin, D. L., & Bartels, D. M. (in press). The costs and benefits of calculation and moral rules. *Perspectives on Psychological Science, 5,* 187–202. (9)

Bennis, W. M., & Pachur, T. (2006). Fast and frugal heuristics in sports. *Psychology of Sport and Exercise, 7,* 611–629. (32)

Berg, N., & Gigerenzer, G. (2007). Psychology implies paternalism? Bounded rationality may reduce the rationale to regulate risk-taking. *Social Choice and Welfare, 28,* 337–359. (37)

Berger, K. S. (2000). *The developing person: Through childhood and adolescence.* New York: Worth. (35)

Bergert, F. B., & Nosofsky, R. M. (2007). A response-time approach to comparing generalized rational and take-the-best models of decision making. *Journal of Experimental Psychology: Learning, Memory, and Cognition, 33,* 107–129. (1, 20, 21, 24)

Bergstrom, C. T., & Real, L. A. (2000). Towards a theory of mutual mate choice: Lessons from two-sided matching. *Evolutionary Ecology Research, 2,* 493–508. (40)

Berk, L. E. (2000). *Child development* (5th ed.). Boston, MA: Allyn & Bacon. (35)

Bernoulli, D. (1954). Exposition of a new theory on the measurement of risk. *Econometrica, 22,* 23–36. (Original work published 1738) (7, 8)

Berretty, P. M., Todd, P. M., & Martignon, L. (1999). Categorization by elimination: Using few cues to choose. In G. Gigerenzer, P. M. Todd, & the ABC Research Group, *Simple heuristics that make us smart* (pp. 235–254). New York: Oxford University Press. (14)

Best, M. J., & Grauer, R. R. (1991). On the sensitivity of mean-variance-efficient portfolios to

changes in asset means: Some analytical and computational results. *The Review of Financial Studies, 4,* 315–342. (34)

Best, M. J., & Grauer, R. R. (1992). Positively weighted minimum-variance portfolios and the structure of asset expected returns. *Journal of Financial and Quantitative Analysis, 27,* 513–537. (34)

Betsch, T., & Haberstroh, S. (2005). Current research on routine decision making: Advances and prospects. In T. Betsch & S. Haberstroh (Eds.), *The routines of decision making* (pp. 359–376). Mahwah, NJ: Erlbaum. (21)

Betsch, T., & Haberstroh, S. (Eds.). (2005). *The routines of decision making.* Mahwah, NJ: Erlbaum. (17)

Bettman, J. R., Luce, M. F., & Payne, J. W. (1998). Constructive consumer choice processes. *Journal of Consumer Research, 25,* 187–217. (37)

Bhardwaj, R., & Brooks, L. (1992). The January anomaly: Effects of low share price, transaction costs, and bid-ask bias. *Journal of Finance, 47,* 553–575. (34)

Billari, F. C. (2000). Searching for mates using 'fast and frugal' heuristics: A demographic perspective. In G. Ballot & G. Weisbuch (Eds.), *Applications of simulation to social sciences* (pp. 63–65). Oxford, UK: Hermes Science. (40)

Billari, F. C. (2001). A log-logistic regression model for a transition rate with a starting threshold. *Population Studies, 55,* 15–24. (40)

Billari, F. C., & Prskawetz, A. (2003). *Agent-based computational demography.* Heidelberg, Germany: Physica Verlag. (40)

Binmore, K. (2009). *Rational decisions.* Princeton, NJ: Princeton University Press. (Introduction, 9)

Bird, L., Wüstenhagen, R., & Aabakken, J. (2002). A review of international green power markets: Recent experience, trends, and market drivers. *Renewable and Sustainable Energy Reviews, 6,* 513–536. (37)

Birn, R. M., Cox, R. W., & Bandettini, P. A. (2002). Detection versus estimation in event-related fMRI: Choosing the optimal stimulus timing. *Neuroimage, 15,* 252–264. (25)

Birnbaum, M. (2004). Causes of Allais common consequence paradoxes: An experimental dissection. *Journal of Mathematical Psychology, 48,* 87–106. (7, 8)

Birnbaum, M. (2008). Evaluation of the priority heuristic as a descriptive model of risky decision making: Comment on Brandstätter, Gigerenzer, and Hertwig (2006). *Psychological Review, 115,* 253–260. (1, 7)

Birnbaum, M., & Chavez, A. (1997). Tests of theories of decision making: Violations of branch independence and distribution independence. *Organizational Behavior and Human Decision Processes, 71,* 161–194. (7, 8)

Birnbaum, M., & Navarrete, J. (1998). Testing descriptive utility theories: Violations of stochastic dominance and cumulative independence. *Journal of Risk and Uncertainty, 17,* 49–78. (7)

Bishop, C. M. (1995). *Neural networks for pattern recognition.* Oxford, UK: Oxford University Press. (1)

Bishop, C. M. (2006). *Pattern recognition and machine learning.* New York: Springer. (1)

Bjork, E. L., & Bjork, R. A. (1988). On the adaptive aspects of retrieval failure in autobiographical memory. In M. M. Gruneberg, P. E. Morris, & R. N. Sykes (Eds.), *Practical aspects of memory: Current research and issues* (Vol II–1, pp. 283–286). Chichester, UK: Wiley. (4, 10)

Black, F., & Litterman, R. (1990). *Discussion paper. Asset allocation: Combining investor views with market equilibrium.* Goldman, Sachs & Co. (34)

Black, F., & Litterman, R. (1992). Global portfolio optimization. *Financial Analysts Journal, 48,* 28–43. (34)

Blake, J. (1981). Family size and the quality of children. *Demography, 18,* 421–442. (35)

Blake, J. (1989). *Family size and achievement.* Los Angeles: University of California Press. (35)

Blass, T. (1991). Understanding behavior in the Milgram obedience experiment: The role of personality, situations, and their interaction. *Journal of Personality and Social Psychology, 60,* 398–413. (9)

Blavatskyy, P. R. (2005). Back to the St. Petersburg paradox? *Management Science, 51,* 677–678. (8)

Blavatskyy, P. R., & Pogrebna, G. (2008). Risk aversion when gains are likely and unlikely: Evidence from a natural experiment with large stakes. *Theory and Decision, 64,* 395–420. (7)

Bless, H., Wänke, M., Bohner, G., Fellhauer, R. F., & Schwarz, N. (1994). Need for cognition: Eine Skala zur Erfassung von Engagement und Freude bei Denkaufgaben. *Zeitschrift für Sozialpsychologie, 25,* 147–154. (17)

Bloomfield, L. A. (1999, April). The flight of the Frisbee. *Scientific American, 280,* 132. (33)

Bloomfield, T., Leftwich R., & Long, J. (1977). Portfolio strategies and performance. *Journal of Financial Economics, 5,* 201–218. (34)

Bolger, F., & Wright, G. (1994). Assessing the quality of expert judgement: Issues and analysis. *Decision Support Systems, 11,* 1–24. (30)

Bolton, G. E., & Ockenfels, A. (2000). ERC: A theory of equity, reciprocity and competition. *American Economic Review, 90,* 166–193. (35)

Bolton, R. N. (1998). A dynamic model of the duration of the customer's relationship with a continuous service provider: The role of satisfaction. *Marketing Science, 17,* 45–65. (36)

Bonabeau, E. (2003). Don't trust your gut. *Harvard Business Review, 81,* 116–123. (36)

Bonduriansky, R. (2003). Layered sexual selection: A comparative analysis of sexual behaviour within an assemblage of piophilid flies. *Canadian Journal of Zoology, 81,* 479–491. (5)

Bookstaber R., & Langsam, J. (1985). On the optimality of coarse behavior rules. *Journal of Theoretical Biology, 116,* 161–193. (1, 5)

Boone, J. L., & Kessler, K. L. (1999). More status or more children? Social status, fertility reduction, and long-term fitness. *Evolution and Human Behavior, 20,* 257–277. (35)

Borgerhoff Mulder, M. (1998). Brothers and sisters: How sibling interactions affect optimal parental allocations. *Human Nature, 9,* 119–162. (35)

Börgers, T., & Sarin, R. (1997). Learning through reinforcement and replicator dynamics. *Journal of Economic Theory, 77,* 1–14. (11)

Borges, B., Goldstein, D. G., Ortmann, A., & Gigerenzer, G. (1999). Can ignorance beat the stock market? In G. Gigerenzer, P. M. Todd, & the ABC Research Group, *Simple heuristics that make us smart* (pp. 59–72). New York: Oxford University Press. (3, 15, 31)

Borkenau, P., & Ostendorf, F. (1993). *NEO-Fünf-Faktoren-Inventar (NEO-FFI).* Göttingen, Germany: Hogrefe. (17)

Borle, S., Singh, S., & Jain, D. (2008). Customer lifetime value measurement. *Management Science, 54,* 100–112. (36)

Boulier, B. L., & Stekler, H. O. (1999). Are sports seedings good predictors? An evaluation. *International Journal of Forecasting, 15,* 83–91. (31)

Boulier, B. L., & Stekler, H. O. (2003). Predicting the outcomes of National Football League games. *International Journal of Forecasting, 19,* 257–270. (31)

Bowlby, J. (1988). *Parent-child attachment and healthy human development.* New York: Basic Books. (35)

Boyd, M. (2001). On ignorance, intuition, and investing: A bear market test of the recognition heuristic. *Journal of Psychology and Financial Markets, 2,* 150–156. (31)

Boyd, R., & Richerson, P. J. (2005). *The origin and evolution of cultures.* New York: Oxford University Press. (1, 9)

Bozdogan, H. (2000). Akaike's information criterion and recent developments in information complexity. *Journal of Mathematical Psychology, 44,* 62–91. (11)

Bradbeer, J. W. (1988). *Seed dormancy and germination.* Glasgow, UK: Blackie. (5)

Brancazio, P. J. (1985). Looking into Chapman's homer: The physics of judging a fly ball. *American Journal of Physics, 53,* 849–855. (5, 33)

Brandstätter, E. (2004). *Choice behavior in risky gambles.* Unpublished raw data. (7)

Brandstätter, E., Gigerenzer, G., & Hertwig, R. (2006). The priority heuristic: Making choices without trade-offs. *Psychological Review, 113,* 409–432. (1, 8)

Brandstätter, E., Gigerenzer, G., & Hertwig, R. (2008). Risky choice with heuristics: Reply to Birnbaum (2008), Johnson, Schulte-Mecklenbeck, and Willemsen (2008), and Rieger and Wang (2008). *Psychological Review, 115,* 281–290. (1, 7)

Brandstätter, E., & Kühberger, A. (2005). *Outcome priority in risky choice.* Manuscript submitted for publication. (7)

Brandstätter, E., Kühberger, A., & Schneider, F. (2002). A cognitive-emotional account of the shape of the probability weighting function. *Journal of Behavioral Decision Making, 15,* 79–100. (7)

Brandt, M. W. (2007). Portfolio choice problems. In Y. Ait Sahalia & L. P. Hansen (Eds.), *Handbook of financial econometrics* (pp. 269–336). St. Louis, MO: Elsevier. (34)

Brandt, M. W., Santa-Clara, P., & Valkanov, R. (2007). *Parametric portfolio policies: Exploiting characteristics in the cross section of equity return.* Working Paper, UCLA. (34)

Brantingham, P. J., & Brantingham, P. L. (1981). *Environmental criminology.* Prospect Heights, IL: Waveland Press. (29)

Brase, G. L., & Richmond, J. (2004). The white-coat effect: Physician attire and perceived authority, friendliness, and attractiveness. *Journal of Applied Social Psychology, 34,* 2469–2481. (9)

Braybrooke, D. (2004). *Utilitarianism: Restorations; repairs; renovations.* Toronto, Canada: University of Toronto Press. (9)

Brehmer, A., & Brehmer, B. (1988). What have we learned about human judgment from thirty years

of policy capturing? In B. Brehmer & C. R. B. Joyce (Eds.), *Human judgment: The SJT view* (pp. 75–114). Amsterdam: North-Holland. (2, 28)

Brehmer, B. (1973). Note on the relation between single-cue probability learning and multiple-cue probability learning. *Organizational Behavior and Human Performance, 9,* 246–252. (21)

Brehmer, B. (1994). The psychology of linear judgement models. *Acta Psychologica, 87,* 137–154. (2, 13, 17, 24)

Brehmer, B., & Hagafors, R. (1986). Use of experts in complex decision making: A paradigm for the study of staff work. *Organizational Behavior and Human Decision Processes, 38,* 181–195. (13)

Brehmer, B., & Joyce, C. R. B. (Eds.). (1988). *Human judgment: The SJT view.* Amsterdam: North-Holland. (13)

Brehmer, B., & Kuylenstierna, J. (1980). Content and consistency in probabilistic inference tasks. *Organizational Behavior and Human Performance, 26,* 54–64. (13)

Breiman, L., Friedman, J. H., Olshen, R. A., & Stone, C. J. (1984). *Classification and regression trees.* New York: Chapman and Hall. (1, 2, 5, 12, 14)

Brewer, E. C. (1996). *Brewer's dictionary of phrase and fable* (15th ed.). London: Cassel. (5)

Brighton, H. (2006). Robust inference with simple cognitive models. In C. Lebiere & R. Wray, (Eds.), *AAAI Spring Symposium: Cognitive science principles meet AI-hard problems* (pp. 17–22). Menlo Park, CA: American Association for Artificial Intelligence. (1, 8, 9)

Brighton, H. (2007). *Ecological rationality and the bias/variance dilemma.* Unpublished manuscript: Max Planck Institute for Human Development, Berlin, Germany. (14)

Brighton, H., & Gigerenzer, G. (2008). Bayesian brains and cognitive mechanisms: Harmony or dissonance? In N. Chater & M. Oaksford (Eds.), *The probabilistic mind: Prospects for Bayesian cognitive science* (pp. 189–208). New York: Oxford University Press. (21)

Brighton, H., & Gigerenzer, G. (in press). How heuristics exploit uncertainty. In P. M. Todd, G. Gigerenzer, & the ABC Research Group, *Ecological rationality: Intelligence in the world.* New York: Oxford University Press. (1)

Brittain, A. W. (1992). The effect of parental age, birth order and other variables on early childhood mortality: A Caribbean example. *Social Science and Medicine, 35,* 1259–1271. (35)

Bröder, A. (2000a). A methodological comment on behavioral decision research. *Psychologische Beiträge, 42,* 645–662. (17, 24)

Bröder, A. (2000) [also: 2000b]. Assessing the empirical validity of the "take-the-best" heuristic as a model of human probabilistic inference. *Journal of Experimental Psychology: Learning, Memory, and Cognition, 26,* 1332–1346. (5, 7, 8, 11, 13, 14, [17], 18, 19, 22, 23, [24], 36)

Bröder, A. (2000c). *"Take the best – ignore the rest." Wann entscheiden Menschen begrenzt rational?* [When do people decide boundedly rationally?]. Lengerich, Germany: Pabst Science Publishers. (17)

Bröder, A. (2002). Take the best, Dawes' rule, and compensatory decision strategies: A regression-based classification method. *Quality and Quantity, 36,* 219–238. (17)

Bröder, A. (2003). Decision making with the "adaptive toolbox": Influence of environmental structure, intelligence, and working memory load. *Journal of Experimental Psychology: Learning, Memory, and Cognition, 29,* 611–625. (1, 5, 7, 8, 9, 11, 13, 14, 17, 22, 23, 24, 36)

Bröder, A. (2005). *Entscheiden mit der "adaptiven Werkzeugkiste": Ein empirisches Forschungsprogramm.* [Decision making with the "adaptive toolbox": An empirical research program]. Lengerich, Germany: Pabst Science Publishers. (17)

Bröder, A. (in press). The quest for take-the-best. In P. M. Todd, G. Gigerenzer, & the ABC Research Group, *Ecological rationality: Intelligence in the world.* New York: Oxford University Press. (1)

Bröder, A., & Eichler, A. (2001, April). *Individuelle Unterschiede in bevorzugten Entscheidungsstrategien.* [Individual differences in preferred decision strategies]. Poster presented at the 43rd "Tagung experimentell arbeitender Psychologen," Regensburg, Germany. (17)

Bröder, A., & Eichler, A. (2006). The use of recognition information and additional cues in inferences from memory. *Acta Psychologica, 121,* 275–284. (3, 23, 24, 26, 31)

Bröder, A., & Gaissmaier, W. (2007). Sequential processing of cues in memory-based multi-attribute decisions. *Psychonomic Bulletin & Review, 14,* 895–900. (1, 8, 17, 21)

Bröder, A., & Newell, B. R. (2008). Challenging some common beliefs about cognitive costs: Empirical work within the adaptive toolbox metaphor. *Judgment and Decision Making, 3,* 195–204. (11, 17)

Bröder, A., & Schiffer, S. (2003a). Bayesian strategy assessment in multi-attribute decision making. *Journal of Behavioral Decision Making, 16,* 193–213. (17, 20)

Bröder, A., & Schiffer, S. (2003) [also: 2003b]. "Take the best" versus simultaneous feature matching: Probabilistic inferences from memory and effects of representation format. *Journal of Experimental Psychology: General, 132,* 277–293. (5, 7, 8, 11, 13, [17], 19, [20], 24, 36)

Bröder, A., & Schiffer, S. (2006) [also: 2006a]. Adaptive flexibility and maladaptive routines in selecting fast and frugal decision strategies. *Journal of Experimental Psychology: Learning, Memory, and Cognition, 32,* 904–918. ([17], 21)

Bröder, A., & Schiffer, S. (2006) [also: 2006b]. Stimulus format and working memory in fast and frugal strategy selection. *Journal of Behavioral Decision Making, 19,* 361–380. ([17], 20, 24)

Brody, G. H., & Stoneman, Z. (1994). Sibling relationships and their association with parental differential treatment. In E. M. Hetherington, D. Reiss, & R. Plomin (Eds.), *Separate social worlds of siblings: The impact of nonshared environment on development* (pp. 129–142). Hillsdale, NJ: Erlbaum. (35)

Brody, G. H., Stoneman, Z., & Burke, M. (1987). Child temperaments, maternal differential behavior, and sibling relationships. *Developmental Psychology, 23,* 354–362. (35)

Brown, C. L., & Krishna, A. (2004). The skeptical shopper: A metacognitive account for effects of default options on choice. *Journal of Consumer Research, 31,* 529–539. (37)

Brown, G. W. (1951). Iterative solutions of games by fictitious play. In T. C. Koopmans (Ed.), *Activity analysis of production and allocation* (pp. 374–376). New York: Wiley. (11)

Brown, J., Lewis, V. J., & Monk, A. F. (1977). Memorability, word frequency and negative recognition. *Quarterly Journal of Experimental Psychology, 29,* 461–473. (3)

Brown, N. R., & Siegler, R. S. (1993). Metrics and mappings: A frame-work for understanding real-world quantitative estimation. *Psychological Review, 100,* 511 534. (2)

Brown, S. (1979). The effect of estimation risk on capital market equilibrium. *Journal of Financial and Quantitative Analysis, 14,* 215–20. (34)

Browne, M. W. (2000). Cross-validation methods. *Journal of Mathematical Psychology, 44,* 108–132. (11, 14)

Bruce, V., Green, P. R., & Georgeson, M. A. (1996). *Visual perception: Physiology, psychology, and ecology.* Hillsdale, NJ: Erlbaum. (33)

Brüderl, J., & Diekmann, A. (1995). The log-logistic rate model. Two generalizations with an application to demographic data. *Sociological Methods and Research, 24,* 158–186. (40)

Brunswik, E. (1943). Organismic achievement and environmental probability. *Psychological Review, 50,* 255–272. (10, 39)

Brunswik, E. (1952). The conceptual framework of psychology. In *International encyclopedia of unified science* (Vol. 1, No. 10, pp. 4–102). Chicago: University of Chicago Press. (10, 13)

Brunswik, E. (1955). Representative design and probabilistic theory in a functional psychology. *Psychological Review, 62,* 193–217. (2, 15)

Brunswik, E. (1957). Scope and aspects of the cognitive problem. In J. S. Bruner et al. (Eds.), *Contemporary approaches to cognition: A report of a symposium at the University of Colorado, May 12–14, 1955* (pp. 5–31). Cambridge, MA: Harvard University Press. (Introduction)

Bruss, F. T. (2000). Der Ungewissheit ein Schnippchen schlagen. *Spektrum der Wissenschaft, 6,* 106. (1)

Buchanan, L., & O'Connell A. (2006). A brief history of decision making. *Harvard Business Review, 84,* 32–41. (36)

Buck, A. J., Hakim, S., & Rengert, G. F. (1993). Burglar alarms and the choice behavior of burglars: A suburban phenomenon. *Journal of Criminal Justice, 21,* 497–507. (30)

Bukszar, E., & Connolly, T. (1988). Hindsight bias and strategic choice: Some problems in learning from experience. *Academy of Management Journal, 31,* 628–641. (10)

Bundesärztekammer (2008). *EU Bulletin, Nr. 9,* April 21, 2008. (9)

Buntine, W., & Caruana, R. (1992). *Introduction to IND Version 2.1 and recursive partitioning.* Moffet Field, CA: NASA Ames Research Centre. (5)

Burch, T. K. (1993). Theory, computers and the parameterization of demographic behavior. *Proceedings of the International Population Conference, Montreal, Canada* (Vol. 3, pp. 377–388). Liege, Belgium: International Union for the Scientific Study of Population. (40)

Burdett, K., & Coles, M. G. (1999). Long-term partnership formation: Marriage and employment. *Economic Journal, 109,* 307–334. (40)

Burger, J. M. (2009). Replicating Milgram: Would people still obey today? *American Psychologist, 64,* 1–11. (9)

Burke, D., & Fulham, B. J. (2003). An evolved spatial memory bias in a nectar-feeding bird? *Animal Behavior, 66,* 695–701. (5)

Burnham, K. P., & Anderson, D. R. (1998). *Model selection and inference: A practical information-theoretic approach.* New York: Springer. (11, 22)

Burns, B. D. (2004). Heuristics as beliefs and as behaviors: The adaptiveness of the "hot hand". *Cognitive Psychology, 48,* 295–311. (32)

Buschena, D., & Zilberman, D. (1995). Performance of the similarity hypothesis relative to existing models of risky choice. *Journal of Risk and Uncertainty, 11,* 233–262. (8)

Buschena, D., & Zilberman, D. (1999). Testing the effects of similarity on risky choice: Implications for violations of expected utility. *Theory and Decision, 46,* 251–276. (8)

Busemeyer, J. R. (1993). Violations of the speed-accuracy tradeoff relation: Decreases in decision accuracy with increases in decision time. In O. Svenson & A. J. Maule (Eds.), *Time pressure and stress in human judgment and decision making* (pp. 181–193). New York: Plenum Press. (11)

Busemeyer, J. R., & Myung, I. J. (1992). An adaptive approach to human decision making: Learning theory, decision theory, and human performance. *Journal of Experimental Psychology: General, 121,* 177–194. (11)

Busemeyer, J. R., & Townsend, J. T. (1993). Decision field theory: A dynamic-cognitive approach to decision making in an uncertain environment. *Psychological Review, 100,* 432–459. (7)

Bush, R. R., & Mosteller, F. (1955). *Stochastic models for learning.* New York: Wiley. (11)

Butler, R. (2003). *Cities and urban areas in United States with population over 100,000.* Retrieved July 10, 2008, from http://www.mongobay.com/cities_urban_01.htm (26)

Byron, M. (Ed.). (2004). *Satisficing and maximizing: Moral theorists on practical reason.* Cambridge, UK: Cambridge University Press. (9)

Caldwell, B. M., & Bradley, R. H. (1984). *Manual for the home observation for measurement of the environment* (Rev. ed.). Little Rock: University of Arkansas. (35)

Calkins, J. D., & Burley, N. T. (2003). Mate choice for multiple ornaments in the California quail, *Callipepla californica. Animal Behavior, 65,* 69–81. (5)

Camazine, S., Deneubourg, J.-L., Franks, N. R., Sneyd, J., Theraulaz, G., & Bonabeau, E. (2001).

Self-organization in biological systems. Princeton, NJ: Princeton University Press. (5)

Camerer, C. F. (1981). General conditions for the success of bootstrapping models. *Organizational Behavior and Human Performance, 27,* 411–422. (13)

Camerer, C. F. (1995). Individual decision making. In J. H. Kagel & A. E. Roth (Eds.), *The handbook of experimental economics* (pp. 587–703). Princeton, NJ: Princeton University Press. (7)

Camerer, C. F. (2000). Prospect theory in the wild: Evidence from the field. In D. Kahneman & A. Tversky (Eds.), *Choices, values, and frames* (pp. 288–298). Cambridge, UK: Cambridge University Press. (37)

Camerer, C. F., & Ho, T.-H. (1994). Violations of the betweenness axiom and nonlinearity in probability. *Journal of Risk and Uncertainty, 8,* 167–196. (8)

Camerer, C. F., & Ho, T.-H. (1999a). Experience-weighted attraction learning in games: Estimates from weak-link games. In David V. Budescu & I. Erev (Eds.), *Games and human behavior: Essays in honor of Amnon Rapoport* (pp. 31–51). Mahwah, NJ: Erlbaum. (11)

Camerer, C., & Ho, T.-H. (1999b). Experience-weighted attraction learning in normal form games. *Econometrica, 67,* 827–874. (11)

Camerer, C. F., & Johnson, E. J. (1991). The process performance paradox in expert judgment: How can experts know so much and predict so badly? In K. A. Ericsson & J. Smit (Eds.), *Toward a general theory of expertise: Prospects and limits* (pp. 195–217). Cambridge, UK: Cambridge University Press. (36)

Campbell, J. Y., & Viceira, L. M. (2002). *Strategic asset allocation.* New York: Oxford University Press. (34)

Candolin, U. (2003). The use of multiple cues in mate choice. *Biological Reviews, 78,* 575–595. (5)

Canter, D. V., Coffey, T., Huntley, M., & Missen, C. (2000). Predicting serial killers' home base using a decision support system. *Journal of Quantitative Criminology, 16,* 457–478. (29)

Canter, D. V., & Larkin, P. (1993). The environmental range of serial rapists. *Journal of Environmental Psychology, 13,* 63–69. (29)

Capone, D. L., & Nichols, W. W., Jr. (1975). Crime and distance: An analysis of offender behavior in space. *Proceedings of the Association of American Geographer, 7,* 45–49. (29)

Carhart, M. (1997). On the persistence in mutual fund performance. *Journal of Finance, 52,* 57–82. (34)

Carnap, R. (1947). On the application of inductive logic. *Philosophy and Phenonmenlogical Research, 8,* 133–148. (1)

Cavanna, A. E., & Trimble, M. R. (2006). The precuneus: A review of its functional anatomy and behavioural correlates. *Brain, 129,* 564–583. (25)

Chan, L. K., Karceski, C., & Lakonishok, J. (1999). On portfolio optimization: Forecasting covariances and choosing the risk model. *The Review of Financial Studies, 12,* 937–974. (34)

Chao, M. (2001). *The birth-order controversy: Within-family effects and their generalizability.* Unpublished honors thesis, University of California, Berkeley. (35)

Charnov, E. L. (1976). Optimal foraging, the marginal value theorem. *Theoretical Population Biology, 9,* 129–136. (5)

Chase, V. M. (1999). *Where to look to find out why: Rational information search in causal hypothesis testing.* Unpublished doctoral dissertation, University of Chicago. (6)

Chase, V. M., Hertwig, R., & Gigerenzer, G. (1998). Visions of rationality. *Trends in Cognitive Sciences, 2,* 206–214. (35, 40)

Chasseigne, G., Grau, S., Mullet, E., & Cama, V. (1999). How well do elderly people cope with uncertainty in a learning task? *Acta Psychologica, 103,* 229–238. (13)

Chasseigne, G., Ligneau, C., Grau, S., Le Gall, A., Roque, M., & Mullet, E. (2004). Aging and probabilistic learning in single-and multiple-cue tasks. *Experimental Aging Research, 30,* 23–45. (22)

Chasseigne, G., Mullet, E., & Stewart, T. R. (1997). Aging and multiple cue probability learning: The case of inverse relationships. *Acta Psychologica, 97,* 235–252. (13)

Chater, N. (2000). How smart can simple heuristics be? *Behavioral and Brain Sciences, 23,* 745–746. (11, 17)

Chater, N., & Oaksford, M. (1999). Ten years of the rational analysis of cognition. *Trends in Cognitive Sciences, 3,* 57–65. (5)

Chater, N., Oaksford, M., Nakisa, R., & Redington, M. (2003). Fast, frugal, and rational: How rational norms explain behavior. *Organizational Behavior and Human Decision Processes, 90,* 63–86. (1, 5, 18)

Chen, Y., & Sun, Y. (2003). Age differences in financial decision-making: Using simple heuristics. *Educational Gerontology, 29,* 627–635. (22)

Cheng, P. W., & Holyoak, K. J. (1985). Pragmatic reasoning schemas. *Cognitive Psychology, 17,* 391–416. (38)

Cheng, P. W., Holyoak, K. J., Nisbett, R. E., & Oliver, L. M. (1986). Pragmatic versus syntactic approaches to training deductive reasoning. *Cognitive Psychology, 18,* 293–328. (38)

Cheung, Y.-W., & Friedman, D. (1997). Individual learning in normal form games: Some laboratory results. *Games and Economic Behavior, 19,* 46–76. (11)

Cheverton, J., Kacelnik, A., & Krebs, J. R. (1985). Optimal foraging: Constraints and currencies. In B. Hölldobler & M. Lindauer (Eds.), *Experimental behavioral ecology* (pp. 109–126). Stuttgart: Fischer Verlag. (5)

Choi, J., Laibson, D., Madrian, B. C., & Metrick (2002). Defined contribution pensions: Plan rules, participant decisions, and the path of least resistance. In J. M. Poterba (Ed.), *Tax policy and the economy* (Vol. 16, pp. 67–114). Cambridge, MA: MIT Press. (37)

Chopra, V. K. (1993). Improving optimization. *Journal of Investing, 8,* 51–59. (34)

Christensen-Szalanski, J. J. J. (1978). Problem solving strategies: A selection mechanism, some implications, and some data. *Organizational Behavior & Human Performance, 22,* 307–323. (11, 17, 22)

Christensen-Szalanski, J. J. J., & Fobian Willham, C. (1991). The hindsight bias: A meta-analysis. *Organizational Behavior and Human Decision Processes, 48,* 147–168. (10)

Chu, P. C., & Spires, E. E. (2003). Perceptions of accuracy and effort of decision strategies. *Organizational Behavior & Human Decision Processes, 91,* 203–214. (17)

Clark, F. C., Kotchen, M. J., & Moore, M. R. (2003). Internal and external influences on pro-environmental behavior: Participation in a green electricity program. *Journal of Environmental Psychology, 23,* 237–246. (37)

Clark, S. E., & Gronlund, S. D. (1996). Global matching models of recognition memory: How the models match the data. *Psychonomic Bulletin and Review, 3,* 37–60. (23)

Clemen, R. T. (1989). Combining forecasts: A review and annotated bibliography. *International Journal of Forecasting, 5,* 559–583. (31)

Clutton-Brock, T. H. (1991). *The evolution of parental care.* Princeton, NJ: Princeton University Press. (35)

Clutton-Brock, T. H., & Albon, S. D. (1979). The roaring of red deer and the evolution of honest advertisement. *Behaviour, 69,* 145–170. (1)

Coale, A. J. (1971). Age patterns of marriage. *Population Studies, 25,* 193–214. (40)

Coale, A. J., & McNeil, D. R. (1972). The distribution by age of the frequency of first marriage in a female cohort. *Journal of the American Statistical Association, 67,* 743–749. (40)

Coale, A. J., & Trussell, J. (1996). The development and use of demographic models. *Population Studies, 50,* 469–484. (40)

Cohen, G., & Faulkner, D. (1983). Word recognition: Age differences in contextual facilitation effects. *British Journal of Psychology, 74,* 239–251. (22)

Cohen, J. (1960). A coefficient of agreement for nominal scales. *Educational and Psychological Measurement, 20,* 37–46. (29)

Cohen, J. (1988). *Statistical power analysis for the behavioral sciences* (2nd ed.). Hillsdale, NJ: Erlbaum. (10, 26, 37)

Cohen, J., Cohen, P., West, S. G., & Aiken, L. S. (2003). *Applied multiple regression/correlation analysis for the behavioral sciences.* Hillsdale, NJ: Erlbaum. (22)

Cokely, E. T., & Feltz, A. (2009). Adaptive variation in judgment and philosophical intuition. *Consciousness and Cognition, 18,* 355–357. (9)

Cole, M., & Cole, S. R. (1993). *The development of children* (2nd ed.). New York: Scientific American Library. (35)

Collett, T. S., & Land, M. F. (1975). Visual control of flight behaviour in the hoverfly, *Syritta pipiens* L. *Journal of Comparative Physiology, 99,* 1–66. (33)

Collett, T. S., & Land, M. F. (1978). How hoverflies compute interception courses. *Journal of Comparative Physiology, 125,* 191–204. (33)

Coltrane, S. L., & Collins, R. (2001). *Sociology of marriage and the family: Gender, love, and property.* Belmont, CA: Wadsworth. (40)

Commission of the European Communities (2007, May 30). *Organ donation and transplantation: policy actions at EU level. Impact assessment.* (Press Release No. IP/07/718). Retrieved from http://europa.eu/rapid/pressReleasesAction.do?reference=IP/07/718&format=HTML&aged=1&language=EN&guiLanguage=en (9)

Condorcet, N. C. (1785). *Essai sur l'application de l'analyse à la probabilité des décisions rendues à la pluralité des voix.* Paris. (27)

Conlisk, J. (1996). Why bounded rationality? *Journal of Economic Literature, 34,* 669–700. (8)

Cooksey, R. W. (1996). *Judgment analysis: Theory, methods, and applications.* San Diego, CA: Academic Press. (10, 12, 13)

Cooper, R. (2000). Simple heuristics could make us smart; but which heuristic do we apply when? *Behavioral and Brain Sciences, 23,* 746. (17)

Cosmides, L. (1989). The logic of social exchange: Has natural selection shaped how humans reason? Studies with the Wason selection task. *Cognition, 31,* 187–276. (38)

Cosmides, L., & Tooby, J. (1992). Cognitive adaptations for social exchange. In J. H. Barkow, L. Cosmides, & J. Tooby (Eds.), *The adapted mind: Evolutionary psychology and the generation of culture* (pp. 163–228). New York: Oxford University Press. (3, 38)

Cosmides, L., & Tooby, J. (1994). Beyond intuition and instinct blindness: Toward an evolutionarily rigorous cognitive science. *Cognition, 50,* 41–77. (3)

Cosmides, L., & Tooby, J. (1996). Are humans good intuitive statisticians after all? Rethinking some conclusions from the literature on judgment under uncertainty. *Cognition, 58,* 1–73. (28)

Cosmides, L., & Tooby, J. (2008). Can a general deontic logic capture the facts of humans' moral reasoning? How the mind interprets social exchange rules and detects cheaters. In W. Sinnott-Armstrong (Ed.), *Moral psychology: Vol 1. The evolution of morality: Adaptations and innateness* (pp. 53–119). Cambridge, MA: MIT Press. (9)

Costa, P. T., & McCrae, R. R. (1992). *The NEO personality inventory and NEO five factor inventory. Professional manual.* Odessa, FL: Psychological Assessment Resources. (17)

Costa, P. T., & McCrae, R. R. (1992). *NEO PI-R professional manual.* Odessa, FL: Psychological Assessment Resources. (35)

Costa-Gomes, M., Crawford, V. P., & Broseta, B. (2001). Cognition and behavior in normal form games: An experimental study. *Econometrica, 69,* 1193–1235. (11)

Cousins, N. (1989). *The biology of hope.* New York: E. P. Dutton. (6)

Cover, T., & Hart, P. (1967). Nearest neighbor pattern classification. *IEEE Transactions on Information Theory, 13,* 21–27. (1)

Coyle, T. R., Read, L. E., Gaultney, J. F., & Bjorklund, D. F. (1998). Giftedness and variability in strategic processing on a multitrial memory task: Evidence for stability in gifted cognition. *Learning & Individual Differences, 10,* 273–290. (22)

Craik, F. I. M., & McDowd, J. M. (1987). Age-differences in recall and recognition. *Journal of Experimental Psychology: Learning, Memory, and Cognition, 13,* 474–479. (3, 15)

Cresswell, W., Hilton, G. M., & Ruxton, G. D. (2000). Evidence for a rule governing the avoidance of superfluous escape flights. *Proceedings of the Royal Society of London, Series B: Biological Sciences, 267,* 733–737. (5)

Cross, F. R., & Jackson, R. R. (2005). Spider heuristics. *Behavioural Processes, 69,* 125–127. (5)

Curran, T. (2000). Brain potentials of recollection and familiarity. *Memory and Cognition, 28,* 923–938. (23)

Cutting, J. E., Springer, K., Braren, P. A., & Johnson, S. H. (1992). Wayfinding on foot from information in retinal, not optical, flow. *Journal of Experimental Psychology: General, 121,* 41–72. (33)

Cutting, J. E., & Wang, R. F. (2000). Heading judgments in minimal environments: The value of a heuristic when invariants are rare. *Perception & Psychophysics, 62,* 1146–1159. (33)

Czerlinski, J., Gigerenzer, G., & Goldstein, D. G. (1999). How good are simple heuristics? In G. Gigerenzer, P. M. Todd, & the ABC Research Group, *Simple heuristics that make us smart* (pp. 97–118). New York: Oxford University Press. (1, 2, 5, 9, 10, 12, 17, 18, 19)

Daly, M., & Wilson, M. I. (1988). The Darwinian psychology of discriminative parental solicitude. In D. W. Leger (Ed.), *Nebraska Symposium on Motivation: Vol. 35. Comparative perspectives in modern psychology* (pp. 91–144). Lincoln: University of Nebraska Press. (35)

Daly M., & Wilson, M. I. (1996). Violence against stepchildren. *Current Directions in Psychological Science, 5,* 77–81. (35)

Daniels, D., Dunn, J., Furstenberg, F. F., & Plomin, R. (1985). Environmental differences within the family and adjustment differences within pairs of siblings. *Child Development, 56,* 764–774. (35)

Daniels, D., & Plomin, R. (1985). Differential experiences of siblings in the same family. *Developmental Psychology, 21,* 747–760. (35)

Darwin, C. (1981). *The descent of man, and selection in relation to sex.* Princeton, NJ: Princeton University Press. (Original work published 1871) (9)

Darwin, C. (1965). *The expressions of the emotions in man and animal.* Chicago: University of Chicago Press. (Original work published 1872) (2)

Daston, L. J. (1988). *Classical probability in the Enlightenment.* Princeton, NJ: Princeton University Press. (2, 7, 8, 9)

Davie, R., Butler, N., & Goldstein, H. (1972). *From birth to seven: The second report of the national child development study (1958 cohort) with full statistical appendix.* London: Longman. (35)

Davies, C. (1971). Pre-trial imprisonment: A Liverpool study. *British Journal of Criminology, 11,* 32–48. (28)

Davies, M. F. (1987). Reduction of hindsight bias by restoration of foresight perspective: Effectiveness of foresight-encoding and hindsight-retrieval strategies. *Organizational Behavior and Human Decision Processes, 40,* 50–68. (10)

Davies, N. B., & Houston, A. I. (1981). Owners and satellites: The economics of territory defence in the pied wagtail, *Motacilla alba. Journal of Animal Ecology, 50,* 157–180. (5)

Davis, J. H. (1973). Group decision and social interaction: A theory of social decision schemes. *Psychological Review, 80,* 97–125. (27)

Davis, J. H. (1992). Some compelling intuitions about group consensus decisions, theoretical and empirical research, and interpersonal aggregation phenomena: Selected examples, 1950–1990. *Organizational Behavior and Human Decision Processes, 52,* 3–38. (27)

Davis, J. N. (1997). Birth order, sibship size, and status in modern Canada. *Human Nature, 8,* 205–230. (35)

Davis, J. N., & Todd, P. M. (1999). Parental investment by decision rules. In G. Gigerenzer, P. M. Todd, & the ABC Research Group, *Simple heuristics that make us smart* (pp. 309–324). New York: Oxford University Press. (35)

Davis, J. N., Todd, P. M., & Bullock, S. (1999). Environment quality predicts parental provisioning decisions. *Proceedings of the Royal Society of London, Series B: Biological Sciences, 266,* 1791–1797. (5, 35)

Dawes, R. M. (1979). The robust beauty of improper linear models in decision making. *American Psychologist, 34,* 571–582. (1, 2, 5, 7, 12, 13, 14, 20, 31)

Dawes, R. M., & Corrigan, B. (1974). Linear models in decision making. *Psychological Bulletin, 81,* 95–106. (1, 11, 12, 13)

Dawes, R. M., Faust, D., & Meehl, P. E. (1989). Clinical versus actuarial judgment. *Science, 243,* 1668–1674. (13)

Dawkins, R. (1982). *The extended phenotype.* San Francisco: Freeman. (5)

Dawkins, R. (1989). *The selfish gene* (2nd ed.). Oxford, UK: Oxford University Press. (1)

Dawkins, R. (2006). *The God delusion.* Boston, MA: Houghton Mifflin Harcourt. (9)

Deane, D. H., Hammond, K. R., & Summers, D. A. (1972). Acquisition and application of knowledge in complex inference tasks. *Journal of Experimental Psychology, 92,* 20–26. (13)

Deane, G. E. (1969). Cardiac activity during experimentally induced anxiety. *Psychophysiology, 6,* 17–30. (7)

de Finetti, B. (1979). A short confirmation of my standpoint. In M. Allais & O. Hagen (Eds.), *Expected utility hypotheses and the Allais paradox* (p. 161). Dordrecht, the Netherlands: Reidel. (7)

Dehn, D., & Erdfelder, E. (1998). What kind of bias is hindsight bias? *Psychological Research, 61,* 135–146. (10, 17)

Delbecq-Derousné, J., Beauvois, J. F., & Shallice, T. (1990). Preserved recall versus impaired recognition. *Brain, 113,* 1045–1074. (3)

DeMiguel, V., Garlappi, L., & Uppal, R. (2009). Optimal versus naive diversification: How inefficient is the $1/N$ portfolio strategy? *Review of Financial Studies, 22,* 1915–1953. (1, 9)

Deshpande, S. P., & Schoderbek, P. P. (1993). Pay-allocations by managers: A policy-capturing approach. *Human Relations, 46,* 465–479. (28)

Detrain, C., & Deneubourg, J.-L. (2002). Complexity of environment and parsimony of decision rules in insect societies. *Biological Bulletin, 202,* 268–274. (5)

Deutsch, M. (1975). Equity, equality, and need: What determines which value will be used as the basis of distributive justice? *Journal of Social Issues, 31,* 137–149. (9, 35)

de Vries, H., & Biesmeijer, J. C. (2002). Self-organization in collective honeybee foraging: Emergence of symmetry breaking, cross inhibition and equal harvest-rate distribution. *Behavioral Ecology and Sociobiology, 51,* 557–569. (5)

de Waal, F. (1982). *Chimpanzee politics.* London: Jonathan Cape. (3)

Dhami, M. K. (2002). Do bail information schemes really affect bail decisions? *Howard Journal of Criminal Justice, 41,* 245–262. (28)

Dhami, M. K. (2003). Psychological models of professional decision making. *Psychological Science, 14,* 175–180. (7, 9, 14)

Dhami, M. K., & Ayton, P. (1998). *Legal decision making the fast and frugal way*. Poster presented at the annual meeting of the Society for Judgment and Decision Making, Dallas, TX. (28)

Dhami, M. K., & Ayton, P. (2001). Bailing and jailing the fast and frugal way. *Journal of Behavioral Decision Making, 14,* 141–168. (14, 28, 30)

Dhami, M. K., & Harries, C. (2001). Fast and frugal versus regression models of human judgment. *Thinking & Reasoning, 7,* 5–27. (14, 28, 30)

Dhami, M. K., Hertwig, R., & Hoffrage, U. (2004). The role of representative design in an ecological approach to cognition. *Psychological Bulletin, 130,* 959–988. (15)

Die 100 grössten Unternehmen Deutschlands [The 100 biggest German companies]. (n.d.). Retrieved August 10, 2004, from http://www.sueddeutsche.de/imperia/md/content/pdf/wirtschaft/tabelle.pdf (26)

Dieckmann, A., & Rieskamp, J. (2007). The influence of information redundancy on probabilistic inferences. *Memory and Cognition, 35,* 1801–1813. (1, 9, 11, 22)

Dieckmann, A., & Todd, P. M. (2004). Simple ways to construct search orders. In K. Forbus, D. Gentner, & T. Regier (Eds.), *Proceedings of the 26th Annual Conference of the Cognitive Science Society* (pp. 309–314). Mahwah, NJ: Lawrence Erlbaum. (5)

Diekmann, A. (1989). Diffusion and survival models for the process of entry into marriage. *Journal of Mathematical Sociology, 14,* 31–44. (40)

DiFonzo, N. (1994). *Piggybacked syllogisms for investor behavior. Probabilistic mental modeling in rumor-based stock market trading*. Unpublished doctoral dissertation, Temple University, Philadelphia. (2)

Dobbins, I. G., Rice, H. J., Wagner, A. D., & Schacter, D. L. (2003). Memory orientation success: Separable neurocognitive components underlying episodic recognition. *Neuropsychologia, 41,* 318–333. (25)

Doherty, M. E. (Ed.). (1996). Social judgment theory [Special Issue]. *Thinking & Reasoning, 2,* 105–248. (10)

Doherty, M. E., Tweney, R. D., O'Connor, R. M., Jr., & Walker, B. (1988). *The role of data and feedback error in inference and prediction: Final report for ARI contract MDA903-85-K-0193*. Bowling Green, OH: Bowling Green State University. (13)

Domingos, P., & Pazzani, M. (1997). On the optimality of the simple Bayesian classifier under zero-one loss. *Machine Learning, 29,* 103–130. (1)

Donkers, B., Verhoef, P. C., & de Jong, M. (2007). Modeling CLV: A test of competing models in the insurance industry. *Quantitative Marketing and Economics, 5,* 163–190. (36)

Doris, J. M. (2002). *Lack of character*. New York: Cambridge University Press. (9)

Dougherty, M. R., Franco-Watkins, A. M., & Thomas, R. (2008). Psychological plausibility of the theory of probabilistic mental models and the fast and frugal heuristics. *Psychological Review, 115,* 199–213. (15, 21)

Dougherty, M. R. P., Gettys, C. F., & Ogden, E. E. (1999). Minerva-DM: A memory processes model for judgments of likelihood. *Psychological Review, 106,* 180–209. (11, 15, 26)

Downey, D. B. (1995). When bigger is not better: Family size, parental resources, and children's educational performance. *American Sociological Review, 60,* 746–761. (35)

Downey, D. B. (2001). Number of siblings and intellectual development: The resource dilution explanation. *American Psychologist, 56,* 497–504. (35)

Doyle, J. (1999). Rational decision-making. In R. A. Wilson & F. C. Keil (Eds.), *MIT encyclopedia of the cognitive sciences* (pp. 701–703). Cambridge, MA: MIT Press. (39)

Driessen, G., & Bernstein, C. (1999). Patch departure mechanisms and optimal host exploitation in an insect parasitoid. *Journal of Animal Ecology, 68,* 445–459. (5)

Dudey, T., & Todd, P. M. (2002). Making good decisions with minimal information: Simultaneous and sequential choice. *Journal of Bioeconomics, 3,* 195–215. (1, 40)

Dukas, R. (Ed.). (1998). *Cognitive ecology: The evolutionary ecology of information processing and decision making*. Chicago: University of Chicago Press. (5)

Dumas, B., & Jacquillat, B. (1990). Performance of currency portfolios chosen by a Bayesian technique: 1967–1985. *Journal of Banking and Finance, 14,* 539–558. (34)

Dunlosky, J., & Hertzog, C. (1998). Aging and deficits in associative memory: What is the role of strategy use? *Psychology and Aging, 13,* 597–607. (22)

Dunlosky, J., & Hertzog, C. (2000). Updating knowledge about encoding strategies: A componential analysis of learning about strategy effectiveness from task experience. *Psychology and Aging, 15,* 462–474. (22)

Dunn, J. F., & McGuire, S. (1994). Young children's nonshared experiences: A summary of studies in Cambridge and Colorado. In E. M. Hetherington, D. Reiss, & R. Plomin (Eds.), *Separate social worlds of siblings: The impact of nonshared environment on development* (pp. 111–128). Hillsdale, NJ: Erlbaum. (35)

Dunn, J. F., & Plomin, R. (1986). Determinants of maternal behavior toward three-year-old siblings. *British Journal of Developmental Psychology, 4,* 127–137. (35)

Dunn, J. F., Plomin, R., & Daniels, D. (1986). Consistency and change in mothers' behavior toward young siblings. *Child Development, 57,* 348–356. (35)

Dunn, J. F., Plomin, R., & Nettles, M. (1985). Consistency of mothers' behavior toward infant siblings. *Developmental Psychology, 21,* 1188–1195. (35)

Dusenbery, D. B. (2001). Performance of basic strategies for following gradients in two dimensions. *Journal of Theoretical Biology, 208,* 345–360. (5)

Ebbesen, E. B., & Konecni, V. J. (1975). Decision making and information integration in the courts: The setting of bail. *Journal of Personality and Social Psychology, 32,* 805–821. (28)

Ebbinghaus, H. (1964). *Memory: A contribution to experimental psychology.* Mineola, NY: Dover. (Original work published 1885) (4)

Ebbinghaus, H. (1966). *Über das Gedächtnis. Untersuchungen zur Experimentellen Psychologie* [About memory. Investgations in experimental psychology]. Amsterdam: E. J. Bonset. (Original work published 1885) (17)

Edgell, S. E., & Hennessey, J. E. (1980). Irrelevant information and utilization of event base rates in nonmetric multiple-cue probability learning. *Organizational Behavior and Human Performance, 26,* 1–6. (21)

Edwards, W. (1954). The theory of decision making. *Psychological Bulletin, 51,* 380–417. (7)

Edwards, W. (1962). Subjective probabilities inferred from decisions. *Psychological Review, 69,* 109–135. (7)

Edwards, W. (1968). Conservatism in human information processing. In B. Kleinmuntz (Ed.), *Formal representation of human judgment* (pp. 17–52). New York: Wiley. (7)

Edwards, W. (1972). N = 1: Diagnosis in unique cases. In J. A. Jacquez (Ed.), *Computer diagnosis and diagnostic methods* (pp. 139–151). Springfield, IL: Charles C Thomas. (29)

Edwards, W., Lindman, H., & Savage, L. J. (1963). Bayesian statistical inference for psychological research. *Psychological Review, 70,* 193–242. (39)

Ehrenberg, A. S. C. (1988). *Repeat-buying, theory and applications* (2nd ed.). London: Griffin. (36)

Einhorn, H. J. (1970). The use of nonlinear, non-compensatory models in decision making. *Psychological Bulletin, 73,* 221–230. (2, 3, 14, 17, 22, 24, 28)

Einhorn, H. J., & Hogarth, R. M. (1975). Unit weighting schemes for decision making. *Organizational Behavior and Human Performance, 13,* 171–192. (1, 2, 13)

Einhorn, H. J., & Hogarth, R. M. (1981). Behavioral decision theory: Processes of judgment and choice. *Annual Review of Psychology, 32,* 53–88. (3, 11)

Einhorn, H. J., Hogarth, R. M., & Klempner, E. (1977). Quality of group judgment. *Psychological Bulletin, 84,* 158–172. (21)

Einhorn, H. J., Kleinmuntz, D. N., & Kleinmuntz, B. (1979). Linear regression and process tracing models of judgment. *Psychological Review, 86,* 465–485. (11, 13)

Elder, G. H., Jr. (1974). *Children of the Great Depression: Social change in life experience.* Chicago: University of Chicago Press. (35)

Elder, G. H., Jr. (1998). The life course as developmental theory. *Child Development, 69,* 1–12. (35)

Ellsberg, D. (1961). Risk, ambiguity, and the Savage axioms. *Quarterly Journal of Economics, 75,* 643–699. (7)

Elman, J. L. (1993). Learning and development in neural networks: The importance of starting small. *Cognition, 48,* 71–99. (1)

Elrod, T., Johnson, R. D., & White, J. (2005). A new integrated model of noncompensatory and compensatory decision strategies. *Organizational Behavior and Human Decision Processes, 95,* 1–19. (23)

Elster, J. (1979). *Ulysses and the sirens: Studies in rationality and irrationality.* Cambridge, UK: Cambridge University Press. (2)

Elster, J. (1997). More than enough. *The University of Chicago Law Review, 64,* 749–764. (35)

Elwyn, G., Edwards, A., Eccles, M., & Rovner, D. (2001). Decision analysis in patient care. *The Lancet, 358,* 571–574. (18)

Eng, J. (n.d.). *ROC analysis: Web-based calculator for ROC curves.* Retrieved June 22, 2004, from http://www.jrocfit.org (26)

Engel, C., & Daston, L. J. (Eds.). (2006). *Is there value in inconsistency?* Baden-Baden, Germany: Nomos. (8)

Enquist, M., Leimar, O., Ljungberg, T., Mallner, Y., & Segerdahl, N. (1990). A test of the sequential assessment game: Fighting in the cichlid fish *Nannacara anomala*. *Animal Behavior, 40,* 1–14. (5)

Epstein, J. M., & Axtell, R. (1996). *Growing artificial societies: Social science from the bottom up.* Cambridge, MA: MIT Press. (40)

Erdfelder, E., & Buchner, A. (1998). Decomposing the hindsight bias: A multinomial processing tree model for separating recollection and reconstruction in hindsight. *Journal of Experimental Psychology: Learning, Memory, and Cognition, 24,* 387–414. (10)

Erev, I. (1998). Signal detection by human observers: A cutoff reinforcement learning model of categorization decisions under uncertainty. *Psychological Review, 105,* 280–298. (11)

Erev, I., Glozman, I., & Hertwig, R. (2008). What impacts the impact of rare events. *Journal of Risk and Uncertainty, 36,* 153–177. (8)

Erev, I., & Roth, A. E. (1998). Predicting how people play games: Reinforcement learning in experimental games with unique, mixed strategy equilibria. *American Economic Review, 88,* 848–881. (11)

Erev, I., & Roth, A. E. (2001). Simple reinforcement learning models and reciprocation in the prisoner's dilemma game. In G. Gigerenzer & R. Selten (Eds.), *Bounded rationality: The adaptive toolbox* (pp. 215–231). Cambridge, MA: MIT Press. (11)

Erev, I., Roth, A. E., Slonim, R. L., & Barron, G. (2002). *Combining a theoretical prediction with experimental evidence to yield a new prediction: An experimental design with a random sample of tasks.* Unpublished manuscript, Columbia University and Faculty of Industrial Engineering and Management, Techion, Haifa, Israel. (7, 8)

Erikson, E. H. (1968). *Identity: Youth and crisis.* New York: Norton. (35)

Ernst, C., & Angst, J. (1983). *Birth order: Its influence on personality.* Berlin, Germany: Springer Verlag. (35)

Estes, W. K. (1950). Toward a statistical theory of learning. *Psychological Review, 57,* 94–107. (11)

Estes, W. K. (1955). Statistical theory of spontaneous recovery and regression. *Psychological Review, 62,* 145–154. (4)

Estes, W. K. (1976). The cognitive side of probability learning. *Psychological Review, 83,* 37–64. (11)

Estes, W. K. (1994). *Classification and cognition.* New York: Oxford University Press. (28)

Ettenson, R., Shanteau, J., & Krogstad, J. (1987). Expert judgment: Is more information better? *Psychological Report, 60,* 227–238. (30)

Fader, P. S., & Hardie, B. G. S. (2001). Forecasting repeat sales at CDNOW: A Case Study. *Interfaces, 31,* 94–107. (36)

Fader, P. S., Hardie, B. G. S., & Lee, K. L. (2005a). Counting your customers the easy way: An alternative to the Pareto/NBD Model. *Marketing Science, 24,* 275–285. (36)

Fader, P. S., Hardie, B. G. S., & Lee, K. L. (2005b). RFM and CLV: Using iso-value curves for customer base analysis. *Journal of Marketing Research, 42,* 415–430. (36)

Fahrenberg, J., Hempel, R., & Selg, H. (1994). *Das Freiburger Persönlichkeits-Inventar FPI* (6th revised edition). Göttingen, Germany: Hogrefe. (17)

Fairhurst, S., Gallistel, C. R., & Gibbon, J. (2003). Temporal landmarks: Proximity prevails. *Animal Cognition, 6,* 113–120. (5)

Fama, E. F., & K. R. French. (1993). Common risk factors in the returns on stock and bonds. *Journal of Financial Economics, 33,* 3–56. (34)

Fantino, E. (1998). Judgement and decision making: Behavioral approaches. *The Behavioral Analyst, 21,* 203–218. (5)

Fantino, E., & Abarca, N. (1985). Choice, optimal foraging, and the delay-reduction hypothesis. *Behavioral Brain Sciences, 8,* 315–362. (5)

Farhar, B. C. (1999). *Willingness to pay for electricity from renewable resources: A review of utility market research.* Golden, CO: National Renewable Energy Laboratory. (37)

Fasolo, B., McClelland, G. H., & Todd, P. M. (2007). Escaping the tyranny of choice: When fewer attributes make choice easier. *Marketing Theory, 7,* 13–26. (37)

Fawcett, T. W. (2003). *Multiple cues and variation in mate-choice behaviour.* Unpublished doctoral dissertation, University of Cambridge. (5)

Fawcett, T. W., & Johnstone, R. A. (2003). Optimal assessment of multiple cues. *Proceeding of the Royal Society of London, Series B: Biological Sciences, 270,* 1637–1643. (5)

Fehr, E., & Schmidt, K. (1999). A theory of fairness, competition, and cooperation. *Quarterly Journal of Economics, 114,* 817–868. (1, 35)

Feltz, A., & Cokely, E. T. (2009). Do judgments about freedom and responsibility depend on who you are? Personality differences in intuitions about compatibilism and incompatibilism. *Consciousness and Cognition, 18,* 342–350. (9)

Ferguson, T. S. (1989). Who solved the secretary problem? *Statistical Science, 4,* 282–296. (40)

Ferstl, E. C., & von Cramon, D. Y. (2002). What does the frontomedian cortex contribute to language processing: Coherence or theory of mind? *Neuroimage, 17,* 1599–1612. (25)

Fiebach, C. J., & Friederici, A. D. (2002). Neural correlates of lexicality and word frequency in the auditory lexical decision task. In A. D. Friederici & D. Y. von Cramon (Eds.), *Annual report 2002* (pp. 28–29). Leipzig, Germany: Max Planck Institute for Human Cognitive and Brain Sciences. (25)

Fiebach, C. J., Friederici, A. D., Müller, K., & von Cramon, D. Y. (2002). fMRI evidence for dual routes to the mental lexicon in visual word recognition. *Journal of Cognitive Neuroscience, 14,* 11–23. (25)

Fiedler, K. (1983). On the testability of the availability heuristic. In R. W. Scholz (Ed.), *Decision making under uncertainty* (pp. 109–119). Amsterdam: North-Holland. (4)

Fiedler, K. (2000). Beware of samples! A cognitive-ecological sampling approach to judgment biases. *Psychological Review, 107,* 659–676. (6)

Fiedler, K., Brinkmann, B., Betsch, T., & Wild, B. (2000). A sampling approach to biases in conditional probability judgments: Beyond base rate neglect and statistical format. *Journal of Experimental Psychology: General, 129,* 399–418. (6)

Fildes, R., & Makridakis, S. (1995). The impact of empirical accuracy studies on time series analysis and forecasting. *International Statistical Review, 63,* 289–308. (31)

Fillenbaum, S. (1975). If: Some uses. *Psychological Research, 37,* 245–260. (38)

Fillenbaum, S. (1976). Inducements: On the phrasing and logic of conditional promises, threats, and warnings. *Psychological Research, 38,* 231–250. (38)

Fillenbaum, S. (1977). A condition on plausible inducements. *Language and Speech, 20,* 136–141. (38)

Finucane, M. L., Mertz, C. K., Slovic, P., & Schmidt, E. S. (2005). Task complexity and older adults' decision-making competence. *Psychology and Aging, 20,* 71–84. (22)

Finucane, M. L., Slovic, P., Hibbard, J., Peters, E., Mertz, C. K., & MacGregor, D. G. (2002). Aging and decision-making competence: An analysis of comprehension and consistency skills in older versus younger adults considering health-plan options. *Journal of Behavioral Decision Making, 15,* 141–164. (22)

Fischer, J. E., Steiner, F., Zucol, F., Berger, C., Martignon, L., Bossart, W., et al. (2002). Using simple heuristics to target macrolide prescription in children with community-acquired-pneumonia. *Archives of Pediatric and Adolescent Medicine, 156,* 1005–1008. (14)

Fischer Welt Almanach [Fischer World Almanac]. (1993). Frankfurt, Germany: Fischer. (2, 21)

Fischhoff, B. (1975). Hindsight ≠ foresight: The effect of outcome knowledge on judgment under uncertainty. *Journal of Experimental Psychology: Human Perception and Performance, 1,* 288–299. (10)

Fischhoff, B. (1977). Perceived informativeness of facts. *Journal of Experimental Psychology: Human Perception and Performance, 3,* 349–358. (2)

Fischhoff, B. (1982). Debiasing. In D. Kahneman, P. Slovic, & A. Tversky (Eds.), *Judgment under uncertainty: Heuristics and biases* (pp. 422–444). Cambridge, UK: Cambridge University Press. (10)

Fischhoff, B., & Beyth, R. (1975). "I knew it would happen." Remembered probabilities of once-future things. *Organizational Behavior and Human Performance, 13,* 1–16. (10)

Fishbein, M., & Ajzen, I. (1975). *Belief, attitude, intention, and behavior: An introduction to theory and research.* Reading, MA: Addison Wesley. (7)

Fishburn, P. C. (1974). Lexicographic orders, utilities and decision rules: A survey. *Management Science, 20,* 1442–1471. (1, 3, 8)

Fishburn, P. C. (1979). On the nature of expected utility. In M. Allais & O. Hagen (Eds.), *Expected utility hypotheses and the Allais paradox* (pp. 243–257). Dordrecht, the Netherlands: Reidel. (7)

Fishburn, P. C. (1988). *Nonlinear preference and utility theory.* Baltimore, MD: Johns Hopkins University Press. (2)

Fishburn, P. C. (1991). Nontransitive preferences in decision theory. *Journal of Risk and Uncertainty, 4,* 113–134. (2, 8)

Fishburn, P. C., & Kochenberger, G. A. (1979). Two–piece von Neumann-Morgenstern utility functions. *Decision Sciences, 10,* 503–518. (7)

Fiske, A. P. (1992). The four elementary forms of sociality: Framework for a unified theory of social relations. *Psychological Review, 99,* 689–723. (9)

Fleiss, J. L. (1981). *Statistical methods for rates and proportions.* New York: Wiley. (29)

Fletcher, P. C., Frith, C. D., Grasby, P. M., Shallice, T., Frackowiak, R. S., & Dolan, R. J. (1995). Brain systems for encoding and retrieval of auditory-verbal memory. An in vivo study in humans. *Brain, 118,* 401–416. (25)

Ford, J. K., Schmitt, N., Schechtman, L. S., Hults, B. M., & Doherty, M. L. (1989). Process tracing methods: Contributions, problems, and neglected research questions. *Organizational Behavior and Human Decision Processes, 43,* 75–117. (Introduction, 1, 8, 18, 22, 24)

Forman, S. D., Cohen, J. D., Fitzgerald, M., Eddy, W. F., Mintun, M. A., & Noll, D. C. (1995). Improved assessment of significant activation in functional magnetic resonance imaging (fMRI): Use of a cluster-size threshold. *Magnetic Resonance in Medicine, 33,* 636–647. (25)

Forrest, D., Goddard, J., & Simmons, R. (2005). Odds-setters as forecasters: The case of the football betting market. *International Journal of Forecasting, 21,* 552–564. (31)

Forrest, D., & Simmons, R. (2000). Forecasting sport: The behaviour and performance of football tipsters. *International Journal of Forecasting, 16,* 317–331. (31)

Fortin, D. (2003). Searching behavior and use of sampling information by free-ranging bison (*Bos bison*). *Behavioral Ecology and Sociobiology, 54,* 194–203. (5)

Foxall, G. R., & Goldsmith, R. E. (1988). Personality and consumer research: Another look. *Journal of the Market Research Society, 30,* 111–125. (17)

Fraenkel, G. S., & Gunn, D. L. (1940). *The orientation of animals: Kineses, taxes and compass reactions.* Oxford, UK: Oxford University Press. (5)

Fraisse, P. (1984). Perception and estimation of time. *Annual Review of Psychology, 35,* 1–36. (4, 26)

Frame, D., Hughson, E., & Leach, J. C. (2006). *Runs, regimes, and rationality: The hot hand strikes back.* Working paper. (32)

Frank, S. A. (1990). Sex allocation theory for birds and mammals. *Annual Review of Ecology and Systematics, 21,* 13–55. (35)

Franks, N. R., Mallon, E. B., Bray, H. E., Hamilton, M. J., & Mischler, T. C. (2003). Strategies for choosing between alternatives with different attributes: Exemplified by house-hunting ants. *Animal Behavior, 65,* 215–223. (5)

Friedman, M. (1953). *Essays in positive economics.* Chicago: Chicago University Press. (Introduction)

Friston, K. J., Fletcher, P., Josephs, O., Holmes, A., Rugg, M. D., & Turner, R. (1998). Event-related fMRI: Characterizing differential responses. *Neuroimage, 7,* 30–40. (25)

Friston, K. J., Frith, C. D., Turner, R., & Frackowiak, R. S. (1995). Characterizing evoked hemodynamics with fMRI. *Neuroimage, 2,* 157–165. (25)

Frosch, C., Beaman, C. P., & McCloy, R. (2007). A little learning is a dangerous thing: An experimental demonstration of ignorance-driven inference. *Quarterly Journal of Experimental Psychology, 60,* 1329–1336. (16)

Frost, P. A., & Savarino, J. E. (1986). An empirical bayes approach to efficient portfolio selection. *Journal of Financial and Quantitative Analysis, 21,* 293–305. (34)

Frost, P. A., & Savarino, J. E. (1988). For better performance constrain portfolio weights. *Journal of Portfolio Management, 15,* 29–34. (34)

Funder, D. (2001). Personality. *Annual Review of Psychology, 52,* 197–221. (9)

Galef, B. G. (1987). Social influences on the identification of toxic foods by Norway rats. *Animal Learning & Behavior, 15,* 327–332. (3, 5)

Galef, B. G., McQuoid, L. M., & Whiskin, E. E. (1990). Further evidence that Norway rats do not socially transmit learned aversions to toxic baits. *Animal Learning & Behavior, 18,* 199–205. (3, 5, 23)

Gallistel, C. R. (1990). *The organization of learning.* Cambridge, MA: MIT Press. (23)

Gambetta, D. (1996). *The Sicilian Mafia. The business of private protection.* Cambridge, MA: Harvard University Press. (9)

Gambetta, D., & Hamill, H. (2005). *Streetwise. How taxi drivers establish their customers' trustworthiness.* New York: Russel Sage. (21)

Garcia-Retamero, R., & Dhami, M. K. (2009). Take-the-best in expert-novice decision strategies for residential burglary. *Psychonomic Bulletin & Review, 16,* 163–169. (9, 30)

Garcia-Retamero, R., Hoffrage, U., & Dieckmann, A. (2007). When one cue is not enough: Combining fast and frugal heuristics with compound cue processing. *Quarterly Journal of Experimental Psychology, 60,* 1197–1215. (21)

Garcia-Retamero, R. & Rieskamp, J. (2008). Adaptive mechanisms for treating missing information: A simulation study. *The Psychological Record, 58,* 547–568. (21)

Garcia-Retamero, R., Takezawa, M., & Gigerenzer, G. (2008). Group communication and decision-making strategies. *Psicothema, 20,* 753–759. (30)

Gardner, G. T., & Stern, P. C. (2002). *Environmental problems and human behavior.* Boston, MA: Pearson Custom Publishing. (37)

Garey, M. R., & Johnson, D. S. (1979). *Computers and intractability: A guide to the theory of NP-completeness.* San Francisco: W. H. Freeman. (12)

Garlappi, L., Uppal, R., & Wang, T. (2007). Portfolio selection with parameter and model uncertainty: A multi-prior approach. *The Review of Financial Studies, 20,* 41–81. (34)

Geary, D. C. (2000). Evolution and proximate expression of human paternal investment. *Psychological Bulletin, 126,* 55–77. (35)

Geary, D. C., & Flinn, M. V. (2001). Evolution of human parental behavior and the human family. *Parenting: Science and Practice, 1,* 5–61. (35)

Geary, D. C., Frensch, P. A., & Wiley, J. G. (1993). Simple and complex mental subtraction: Strategy choice and speed-of-processing differences in younger and older adults. *Psychology and Aging, 8,* 242–256. (22)

Geary, D. C., & Wiley, J. G. (1991). Cognitive addition: Strategy choice and speed-of-processing differences in young and elderly adults. *Psychology and Aging, 6,* 474–483. (22)

Gelman, A., Carlin, J. B., Stern, H. S., & Rubin, D. B. (1995). *Bayesian data analysis.* London: Chapman and Hall. (39)

Geman, S., Bienenstock, E., & Doursat, R. (1992). Neural networks and the bias/variance dilemma. *Neural Computation, 4,* 1–58. (1, 9)

Gerson, R., & Damon, W. (1978). Moral understanding and children's conduct. In W. Damon (Ed.), *New directions for child development* (pp. 41–59). San Francisco: Jossey-Blass. (9)

Gibson, R. M. (1996). Female choice in sage grouse: the roles of attraction and active comparison. *Behavioral Ecology and Sociobiology, 39,* 55–59. (5)

Gigerenzer, G. (1981). *Messung und Modellbildung in der Psychologie* [Measurement and modelling in psychology]. Munich: Ernst Reinhard Verlag. (12)

Gigerenzer, G. (1991). From tools to theories: A heuristic of discovery in cognitive psychology. *Psychological Review, 98,* 254–267. (1, 9)

Gigerenzer, G. (1993). The bounded rationality of probabilistic mental models. In K. I. Manktelow & D. E. Over (Eds.), *Rationality: Psychological and philosophical perspectives* (pp. 284–313). London: Routledge. (2, 3)

Gigerenzer, G. (1994). Why the distinction between single-event probabilities and frequencies is important for psychology (and vice versa). In G. Wright & P. Ayton (Eds.), *Subjective probability* (pp. 129–161). Chichester, UK: Wiley. (2)

Gigerenzer, G. (1995). The taming of content: Some thoughts about domains and modules. *Thinking and Reasoning, 1,* 289–400. (38)

Gigerenzer, G. (1996). On narrow norms and vague heuristics: A reply to Kahneman and Tversky (1996). *Psychological Review, 103,* 592–596. (1, 3, 13)

Gigerenzer, G. (1998). Surrogates for theories. *Theory & Psychology, 8,* 195–204. (3)

Gigerenzer, G. (2000). *Adaptive thinking: Rationality in the real world.* New York: Oxford University Press. (Introduction, 1, 5, 17, 18, 29, 38)

Gigerenzer, G. (2001). The adaptive toolbox. In G. Gigerenzer & R. Selten (Eds.), *Bounded rationality* (pp. 37–50). Cambridge, MA: MIT Press. (15)

Gigerenzer, G. (2002). *Calculated risks: How to know when numbers deceive you.* New York: Simon & Schuster. (UK version: *Reckoning with risk: Learning to live with uncertainty,* London: Penguin). (6)

Gigerenzer, G. (2003). The adaptive toolbox and life span development: Common questions? In U. M. Staudinger & U. Lindenberger (Eds.), *Understanding human development: Life span psychology in exchange with other disciplines* (pp. 423–435). Dordrecht, The Netherlands: Kluwer. (22)

Gigerenzer, G. (2004). Fast and frugal heuristics: The tools of bounded rationality. In D. J. Koehler & N. Harvey (Eds.), *Blackwell handbook of judgment and decision making* (pp. 62–88). Oxford, UK: Blackwell. (5, 7, 8, 15, 32)

Gigerenzer, G. (2005). I think, therefore I err. *Social Research, 72,* 195–218. (8, 38)

Gigerenzer, G. (2006). Heuristics. In G. Gigerenzer & C. Engel (Eds.), *Heuristics and the law* (pp. 17–44). Cambridge, MA: MIT Press. (9)

Gigerenzer, G. (2007). *Gut feelings: The intelligence of the unconscious.* New York: Viking. (UK version: London: Allen Lane/Penguin). (1, 9, 30, 37)

Gigerenzer, G. (2008) [also: 2008a]. *Rationality for mortals.* New York: Oxford University Press. (1, [9], 21)

Gigerenzer, G. (2008b). Moral intuition = Fast and frugal heuristics? In W. Sinnott-Armstrong

(Ed.), *Moral psychology: Vol 2. The cognitive science of morality: Intuition and diversity* (pp. 1–26). Cambridge, MA: MIT Press. (9)

Gigerenzer, G., & Brighton, H. (2009). Homo heuristicus: Why biased minds make better inferences. *Topics in Cognitive Science, 1,* 107–143. (9, 32)

Gigerenzer, G., Czerlinski, J., & Martignon, L. (1999). How good are fast and frugal heuristics? In J. Shanteau, B. A. Mellers, & D. A. Schum (Eds.), *Decision science and technology: Reflections on the contributions of Ward Edwards* (pp. 81–104). Norwell, MA: Kluwer Academic Publishers. (12)

Gigerenzer, G., Dieckmann, A., & Gaissmaier, W. (in press). Heuristic search as a building block of cognition. In P. M. Todd, G. Gigerenzer, & the ABC Research Group, *Ecological Rationality: Intelligence in the world.* New York: Oxford University Press. (1)

Gigerenzer, G., & Engel, C. (2006). *Heuristics and the law.* Cambridge, MA: MIT Press. (28)

Gigerenzer, G., Gaissmaier, W., Kurz-Milcke, E., Schwartz, L. M., & Woloshin, S. (2007). Helping doctors and patients to make sense of health statistics. *Psychological Science in the Public Interest, 8,* 53–96. (6)

Gigerenzer G., & Goldstein, D. G. (1996). Reasoning the fast and frugal way: Models of bounded rationality. *Psychological Review, 103,* 650–669. (1, 3, 4, 5, 6, 7, 8, 10, 11, 12, 13, 14, 15, 17, 18, 19, 21, 22, 23, 24, 26, 28, 31, 32, 39)

Gigerenzer, G., & Goldstein, D. G. (1999). Betting on one good reason: The take the best heuristic. In G. Gigerenzer, P. M. Todd, & the ABC Research Group, *Simple heuristics that make us smart* (pp. 75–96). New York: Oxford University Press. (1, 3, 5, 15)

Gigerenzer, G., & Hoffrage, U. (1995). How to improve Bayesian reasoning without instruction: Frequency formats. *Psychological Review, 102,* 684–704. (2, 3, 6, 14)

Gigerenzer, G., & Hoffrage, U. (1999). Overcoming difficulties in Bayesian reasoning: A reply to Lewis & Keren and Mellers & McGraw. *Psychological Review, 106,* 425–430. (6)

Gigerenzer, G., Hoffrage, U., & Goldstein, D. G. (2008). Fast and frugal heuristics are plausible models of cognition: Reply to Dougherty, Franco-Watkins, & Thomas (2008). *Psychological Review, 115,* 230–239. (21)

Gigerenzer, G., Hoffrage, U., & Kleinbölting, H. (1991). Probabilistic mental models: A Brunswikian theory of confidence. *Psychological Review, 98,* 506–528. (2, 3, 10, 12, 15, 17, 23, 24)

Gigerenzer, G., & Hug, K. (1992). Domain specific reasoning: Social contracts, cheating, and perspective change. *Cognition, 43,* 127–171. (38)

Gigerenzer, G., & Kurz, E. (2001). Vicarious functioning reconsidered: A fast and frugal lens model. In K. R. Hammond & T. R. Stewart (Eds.), *The essential Brunswik: Beginnings, explications, applications* (pp. 342–347). New York: Oxford University Press. (7)

Gigerenzer, G., & Murray, D. J. (1987). *Cognition as intuitive statistics.* Hillsdale, N J: Erlbaum. (2, 7)

Gigerenzer, G., & Regier, T. (1996). How do we tell an association from a rule? Comment on Sloman (1996). *Psychological Bulletin, 119,* 23–26. (1)

Gigerenzer, G., & Richter, H. R. (1990). Context effects and their interaction with development: Area judgments. *Cognitive Development, 5,* 235–264. (8)

Gigerenzer, G., & Selten, R. (Eds.). (2001) [also: 2001a]. *Bounded rationality: The adaptive toolbox.* Cambridge, MA: MIT Press. (1, 3, 5, 8, [9], 14, 19, 21, 22, 25, 29)

Gigerenzer, G., & Selten, R. (2001) [also: 2001b]. Rethinking rationality. In G. Gigerenzer & R. Selten (Eds.), *Bounded rationality: The adaptive toolbox* (pp. 1–13). Cambridge, MA: MIT Press. ([9], 18)

Gigerenzer, G., Swijtink, Z., Porter, T., Daston, L., Beatty, J., & Krüger, L. (1989). *The empire of chance. How probability changed science and everyday life.* Cambridge, UK: Cambridge University Press. (2, 7)

Gigerenzer, G., & Todd, P. M. (1999). Fast and frugal heuristics: The adaptive toolbox. In G. Gigerenzer, P. M. Todd, & the ABC Research Group, *Simple heuristics that make us smart* (pp. 3–34). New York: Oxford University Press. (17, 18, 19, 39, 40)

Gigerenzer, G., Todd, P. M., & the ABC Research Group (1999). *Simple heuristics that make us smart.* New York: Oxford University Press. (1, 2, 3, 4, 5, 6, 7, 8, 9, 11, 12, 13, 14, 15, 17, 22, 23, 24, 26, 28, 29, 31, 32, 35, 36, 37, 38, 40)

Gigone, D., & Hastie, R. (1997). The impact of information on small group choice. *Journal of Personality and Social Psychology, 72,* 132–140. (27)

Gilbert, J. P., & Mosteller, F. (1966). Recognizing the maximum of a sequence. *American Statistical Association Journal, 61,* 35–73. (1)

Gilbert, N., & Troitzsch, K. G. (1999). *Simulation for the Social Scientist.* Buckingham, UK: Open University Press. (40)

Gilboa, A., Winocur, G., Grady, C. L., Hevenor, S. J., & Moscovitch, M. (2004). Remembering our past: Functional neuroanatomy of recollection of recent and very remote personal events. *Cerebral Cortex, 14,* 1214–1225. (25)

Gilbride, T. J., & Allenby, G. M. (2004). A choice model with conjunctive, disjunctive, and compensatory screening rules. *Marketing Science, 23,* 391–406. (8)

Gill, F. B. (1988). Trapline foraging by hermit hummingbirds: Competition for an undefended, renewable resource. *Ecology, 69,* 1933–1942. (5)

Gillund, G., & Shiffrin, R. M. (1984). A retrieval model for both recognition and recall. *Psychological Review, 91,* 1–67. (15)

Gilovich, T., & Griffin, D. W. (2002). Heuristics and biases then and now. In T. Gilovich, D. W. Griffin, & D. Kahneman (Eds.), *The psychology of intuitive judgment: Heuristic and biases* (pp. 1–18). Cambridge, UK: Cambridge University Press. (1)

Gilovich, T., Griffin, D. W., & Kahneman, D. (Eds.). (2002). *Heuristics and biases: The psychology of intuitive judgment.* New York: Cambridge University Press. (Introduction, 5)

Gilovich, T., Vallone, R., & Tversky, A. (1985). The hot hand in basketball: On the misperception of random sequences. *Cognitive Psychology, 17,* 295–314. (1, 32)

Gilpin, M. E. (1975). Limit cycles in competition communities. *The American Naturalist, 109,* 51–60. (2)

Ginzburg, L. R., Janson, C., & Ferson, S. (1996). Judgment under uncertainty: Evolution may not favor a probabilistic calculus. *Behavioral and Brain Sciences, 19,* 24–25. (10)

Glanzer, M., & Adams, J. K. (1985). The mirror effect in recognition memory. *Memory and Cognition, 13,* 8–20. (15)

Glanzer, M., Adams, J. K., Iverson, G. J., & Kim, K. (1993). The regularities of recognition memory. *Psychological Review, 100,* 546–567. (15)

Glaser, B. G., & Strauss, A. L. (1967). *The discovery of grounded theory: Strategies for qualitative research.* Chicago: Aldine. (29)

Gluck, M. A., & Bower, G. H. (1988). From conditioning to category learning: An adaptive network model. *Journal of Experimental Psychology. General, 117,* 227–247. (11)

Glucksberg, S., & McCloskey, M. (1981). Decisions about ignorance: Knowing that you don't know. *Journal of Experimental Psychology: Human Learning and Memory, 7,* 311–325. (3)

Gold, B. T., Balota, D. A., Kirchhoff, B. A., & Buckner, R. L. (2005). Common and dissociable activation patterns associated with controlled semantic and phonological processing: Evidence from fMRI adaptation. *Cerebral Cortex, 15,* 1438–1450. (25)

Goldberg, E., & Podell, K. (1999). Adaptive versus veridical decision making and the frontal lobes. *Consciousness and Cognition, 8,* 364–377. (25)

Goldberg, L. R. (1968). Simple Models or Simple Processes? Some Research on Clinical Judgments. *American Psychologist, 23,* 483–496. (36)

Goldberg, L. R. (1970). Man versus model of man: A rationale, plus some evidence, for a method of improving on clinical judgment. *Psychological Bulletin, 73,* 422–432. (13)

Goldfarb, D., & Iyengar, G. (2003). Robust portfolio selection problems. *Mathematics of Operations Research, 28,* 1–38. (34)

Goldstein, D. G. (1994). *The less-is-more effect in inference.* Unpublished master's thesis, University of Chicago. (2)

Goldstein, D. G. (1997). Models of bounded rationality for inference. *Dissertation Abstracts International, 58,* 435B. (3)

Goldstein, D. G. (2007). Getting attention for unrecognized brands. *Harvard Business Review, 85,* 24–28. (26)

Goldstein, D. G., & Gigerenzer, G. (1996). *Reasoning by recognition alone: How to exploit a lack of knowledge.* Unpublished manuscript. (2, 3)

Goldstein, D. G., & Gigerenzer, G. (1999). The recognition heuristic: How ignorance makes us smart. In G. Gigerenzer, P. M. Todd, & the ABC Research Group, *Simple heuristics that make us smart* (pp. 37–58). New York: Oxford University Press. (3, 4, 15, 16)

Goldstein, D. G., & Gigerenzer, G. (2002). Models of ecological rationality: The recognition heuristic. *Psychological Review, 109,* 75–90. (1, 2, 4, 5, 13, 15, 16, 19, 23, 24, 25, 26, 27, 31, 32)

Goldstein, D. G., Gigerenzer, G., Hogarth, R. M., Kacelnik, A., Kareev, Y., Klein, G., et al. (2001). Group report: Why and when do simple heuristics work? In G. Gigerenzer & R. Selten (Eds.), *Bounded rationality: The adaptive toolbox* (pp. 173–190). Cambridge, MA: MIT Press. (18)

Goldstein, H. (1971). Factors influencing the height of seven year old children – Results from the national child development study. *Human Biology, 43,* 92–111. (35)

Goldstein, J. R., & Kenney, C. T. (2001). Marriage delayed or marriage forgone? New cohort forecasts of first marriage for U.S. women. *American Sociological Review, 66,* 506–519. (40)

Gonzalez, C., Lerch, J. F., & Lebiere, C. (2003). Instance-based learning in dynamic decision making. *Cognitive Science, 27,* 591–635. (11)

Gonzalez-Vallejo, C., Sorum, P. C., Stewart, T. R., Chessare, J. B., & Mumpower, J. L. (1998). Physicians' diagnostic judgments and treatment decisions for acute otitis media in children. *Medical Decision Making, 18,* 149–162. (28)

Gonzalez, R., & Nelson, T. O. (1996). Measuring ordinal association in situations that contain tied scores. *Psychological Bulletin, 119,* 159–165. (15, 31)

Good, I. J. (1967). On the principle of total evidence. *The British Journal for the Philosophy of Science, 17,* 319–321. (1)

Gould, J. L., & Gould, C. G. (1988). *The honey bee.* New York: Scientific American Library. (5)

Gould, S. J. (1991). *Bully for brontosaurus: Reflections in natural history.* New York: W. W. Norton. (5)

Gould, S. J., & Lewontin, R. C. (1979). The spandrels of San Marco and the Panglossian paradigm: A critique of the adaptationist programme. *Proceedings of the Royal Society of London, Series B: Biological Sciences, 205,* 581–598. (5)

Goulson, D. (2000). Why do pollinators visit proportionally fewer flowers in large patches? *Oikos, 91,* 485–492. (5)

Grafen, A. (1990). Biological signals as handicaps. *Journal of Theoretical Biology, 144,* 517–546. (5)

Green, D. M., & Swets, J. A. (1966). *Signal detection theory and psychophysics.* New York: Wiley. (4, 23)

Green, L., & Mehr, D. R. (1997). What alters physicians' decisions to admit to the coronary care unit? *Journal of Family Practice, 45,* 219–226. (6, 14, 21)

Green, R. C., & Hollifield, B. (1992). When will mean-variance efficient portfolios be well diversified? *Journal of Finance, 47,* 1785–1809. (34)

Green, R. F. (1984). Stopping rules for optimal foragers. *American Naturalist, 123,* 30–40. (5)

Greene, J., & Haidt, J. (2002). How (and where) does moral judgment work? *TRENDS in Cognitive Sciences, 6,* 517–523. (9)

Greene, J. D., Sommerville, R. B., Nystrom, L. E., Darley, J. M., & Cohen, J. D. (2001). An fMRI investigation of emotional engagement in moral judgment. *Science, 293,* 2105–2108. (25)

Greenhouse, S. W., & Geisser, S. (1959). On methods in the analysis of profile data. *Psychometrika, 24,* 95–112. (21)

Grice, H. P. (1975). Logic and conversation. In P. Cole & J. Morgan (Eds.), *Syntax and semantics* (Vol. 3, pp. 41–58). New York: Academic Press. (24)

Griffin, D., & Tversky, A. (1992). The weighing of evidence and the determinants of confidence. *Cognitive Psychology, 24,* 411–435. (2)

Griffiths, T. L., & Tenenbaum, J. B. (2006). Optimal predictions in everyday cognition. *Psychological Science, 17,* 767–773. (1)

Griffore, R. J., & Bianchi, L. (1984). Effects of ordinal position on academic self-concept. *Psychological Reports, 55,* 263–268. (35)

Griggs, R. A., & Cox, J. R. (1982). The elusive thematic-materials effect in Wason's selection task. *British Journal of Psychology, 73,* 407–420. (3, 38)

Gröschner, C. & Raab. M. (2006). Wer wird Deutscher Meister? Deskriptive und normative Aspekte von Vorhersagemodellen im Sport. *Zeitschrift für Sportpsychologie, 13,* 23–36. (32)

Groffman, B., & Owen, G. (1986). Condorcet models, avenues for future research. In B. Groffman & G. Owen (Eds.), *Information pooling and group decision making* (pp. 93–102). Greenwich, CT: JAI Press. (27)

Gronlund, S. D., Ohrt, D. D., Dougherty, M. R. P., Perry, J. L., & Manning, C. A. (1998). Role of memory in air traffic control. *Journal of Experimental Psychology: Applied, 4,* 263–280. (15)

Gronlund, S. D., & Ratcliff, R. (1989). The time course of item and associative information: Implications for global memory models. *Journal of Experimental Psychology: Learning, Memory, and Cognition, 15,* 846–858. (23)

Gruber, H. E., & Vonèche, J. J. (1977). *The essential Piaget.* New York: Basic Books. (9)

Gupta, S., Lehmann, D. R., & Stuart, J. A. (2004). Valuing customers. *Journal of Marketing Research, 41,* 7–18. (36)

Gusnard, D. A., Akbudak, E., Shulman, G. L., & Raichle, M. E. (2001). Medial prefrontal cortex and self-referential mental activity: Relation to a default mode of brain function. *Proceedings of the National Academy of Sciences, U.S.A., 98,* 4259–4264. (25)

Guttman, L. (1944). A basis for scaling qualitative data. *American Sociological Review, 9,* 139–150. (1)

Hacking, I. (1975). *The emergence of probability.* Cambridge, UK: Cambridge University Press. (7, 9)

Haidt, J. (2001). The emotional dog and its rational tail: A social intuitionist approach to moral judgment. *Psychological Review, 108,* 814–834. (9)

Haidt, J., & Bjorklund, F. (2008). Social intuitionists answer six questions about moral psychology. In W. Sinnott-Armstrong (Ed.), *Moral Psychology, Vol. 2: The cognitive science of morality: Intuition and diversity* (pp. 181–217). Cambridge, MA: MIT Press. (9)

Ham-Rowbottom, K. A., Gifford, R., & Shaw, K. T. (1999). Defensible space theory and the police: Assessing the vulnerability of residents to burglary. *Journal of Environmental Psychology, 19,* 117–129. (30)

Hamilton, W. D. (1964a). The genetical evolution of social behavior. I. *Journal of Theoretical Biology, 7,* 1–16. (35)

Hamilton, W. D. (1964b). The genetical evolution of social behavior. II. *Journal of Theoretical Biology, 7,* 7–32. (35)

Hamm, S. (2002). AG-Spanne: Validierung eines deutschsprachigen Verfahrens zur Erfassung der Arbeitsgedächtnisspanne. [AG-Spanne: Validation of a technique for assessing the working memory span in the German language]. *Berichte aus dem Psychologischen Institut der Universität Bonn, 28*(2). (22)

Hammerstein, P. (2003). Why is reciprocity so rare in social animals? A protestant appeal. In P. Hammerstein (Ed.), *Genetic and cultural evolution of cooperation* (pp. 83–93). Cambridge, MA: MIT Press. (5, 9)

Hammond, K. R. (1955). Probabilistic functioning and the clinical method. *Psychological Review, 62,* 255–262. (10, 13)

Hammond, K. R. (1966). *The psychology of Egon Brunswik.* New York: Holt, Rinehart & Winston. (2)

Hammond, K. R. (1990). Functionalism and illusionism: Can integration be usefully achieved? In R. M. Hogarth (Ed.), *Insights in decision making* (pp. 227–261). Chicago: University of Chicago Press. (2)

Hammond, K. R. (1996). *Human judgment and social policy.* Oxford, UK: Oxford University Press. (3, 13)

Hammond, K. R. (2000). *Judgments under stress.* Oxford, UK: Oxford University Press. (30)

Hammond, K. R., Hursch, C. J., & Todd, F. J. (1964). Analyzing the components of clinical inference. *Psychological Review, 71,* 438–456. (2, 13)

Hammond, K. R., & Summers, D. A. (1965). Cognitive dependence on linear and nonlinear cues. *Psychological Review, 72,* 215–224. (13)

Hammond, K. R., Summers, D. A., & Deane, D. H. (1973). Negative effects of outcome-feedback in multiple-cue probability learning. *Organizational Behavior and Human Performance, 9,* 30–34. (13)

Hammond, K. R., Wilkins, M. M., & Todd, F. J. (1966). A research paradigm for the study of interpersonal learning. *Psychological Bulletin, 65,* 221–232. (13)

Hankinson, S. J., & Morris, M. R. (2003). Avoiding a compromise between sexual selection and species recognition: Female swordtail fish assess multiple species-specific cues. *Behavioral Ecology, 14,* 282–287. (5)

Hanushek, E. A. (1992). The trade-off between child quantity and quality. *Journal of Political Economy, 100,* 84–117. (35)

Harbort, S., & Mokros, A. (2001). Serial murderers in Germany from 1945 to 1995: A descriptive study. *Homicide Studies, 5,* 311–334. (29)

Harrison, G. W., & List, J. A. (2004). Field experiments. *Journal of Economic Literature, 42,* 1009–1055. (37)

Harvey, C. R., Liechty, J., Liechty, M., & Müller, P. (2003). *Portfolio selection with higher moments.* Working Paper, Duke University. (34)

Harvey, N., & Bolger, F. (2001). Collecting information: Optimizing outcomes, screening options, or facilitating discrimination. *Quarterly Journal of Experimental Psychology, 54A,* 269–301. (18)

Hasher, L., & Zacks, R. T. (1984). Automatic processing of fundamental information: The case of frequency of occurrence. *American Psychologist, 39,* 1372–1388. (6, 12)

Hasson, O. (1991). Sexual displays as amplifiers: Practical examples with an emphasis on feather decorations. *Behavioral Ecology, 2,* 189–197. (5)

Hastie, R., & Dawes, R. M. (2001). *Rational choice in an uncertain world.* London: Sage Publications. (29)

Hastie, R., & Kameda, T. (2005). The robust beauty of majority rules in group decisions. *Psychological Review, 112,* 494–508. (13, 21)

Hastie, R., & Park, B. (1986). The relationship between memory and judgment depends on whether the judgment task is memory based or online. *Psychological Review, 93,* 258–268. (18)

Hastie, T., Tibshirani, R., & Friedman, J. H. (2001). *The elements of statistical learning: Data mining, inference, and prediction.* New York: Springer. (1)

Hauert, C., & Stenull, O. (2002). Simple adaptive strategy wins the prisoner's dilemma. *Journal of Theoretical Biology, 218,* 261–272. (5)

Hauser, M. D. (2006). *Moral minds: How nature designed our universal sense of right and wrong.* New York: Ecco. (9)

Hausmann, D. (2004). *Informationssuche im Entscheidungsprozess* [Information search in the decision process]. Unpublished doctoral dissertation, University of Zürich, Switzerland. (17)

Hawkins, S. A., & Hastie, R. (1990). Hindsight: Biased judgment of the past events after the outcomes are known. *Psychological Bulletin, 107,* 311–327. (10)

Heald, J. E. (1991). Social judgment theory: Applications to educational decision making. *Educational Administration Quarterly, 27,* 343–357. (28)

Hebets, E. A. (2005). Attention-altering signal interactions in the multimodal courtship display of the wolf spider *Schizocosa uetzi. Behavioral Ecology, 16,* 75–82. (5)

Heckhausen, H. (1991). *Motivation and action.* Berlin, Germany: Springer-Verlag. (7, 8)

Heekeren, H. R., Wartenburger, I., Schmidt, H., Schwintowski, H. P., & Villringer, A. (2003). An fMRI study of simple ethical decision-making. *NeuroReport, 14,* 1215–1219. (25)

Heer, D. M. (1985). Effects of sibling number on child outcome. *Annual Review of Sociology, 11,* 27–47. (35)

Heer, D. M. (1986). Effect of number, order, and spacing of siblings on child and adult outcomes: An overview of current research. *Social Biology, 33,* 1–4. (35)

Henrich, J., & Boyd, R. (1998). The evolution of conformist transmission and the emergence of between-group differences. *Evolution and Human Behavior, 19,* 215–241. (5)

Hell, W., Gigerenzer, G., Gauggel, S., Mall, M., & Müller, M. (1988). Hindsight bias: An interaction of automatic and motivational factors? *Memory and Cognition, 16,* 533–538. (10)

Helsen, K., & Schmittlein, D. C. (1993). Analyzing duration times in marketing: Evidence for the effectiveness of hazard rate models. *Marketing Science, 12,* 395–414. (36)

Henson, R. (2005). A mini-review of fMRI studies of human medial temporal lobe activity associated with recognition memory. *Quarterly Journal of Experimental Psychology, Series B, Comparative and Physiological Psychology, 58,* 340–360. (25)

Henson, R. N. A., Rugg, M. D., Shallice, T., Josephs, O., & Dolan, R. J. (1999). Recollection and familiarity in recognition memory: An event-related functional magnetic resonance imaging study. *Journal of Neuroscience, 19,* 3962–3972. (25)

Henz, U., & Huinink, J. (1999). Problems concerning the parametric analysis of the age at first birth. *Mathematical Population Studies, 7,* 131–145. (40)

Herlihy, D. (1973). Three patterns of social mobility in medieval history. *Journal of Interdisciplinary History, 3,* 622–647. (35)

Hernes, G. (1972). The process of entry into first marriage. *American Sociological Review, 37,* 173–182. (40)

Hertwig, R., Barron, G., Weber, E. U., & Erev, I. (2004). Decision from experience and the effect of rare events. *Psychological Science, 15,* 534–539. (7)

Hertwig, R., Benz, B., & Krauss, S. (2008). The conjunction fallacy and the meanings of "and." *Cognition, 108,* 740–753. (38)

Hertwig, R., Davis, J. N., & Sulloway, F. (2002). Parental investment: How an equity motive can produce inequality. *Psychological Bulletin, 128,* 728–745. (9)

Hertwig, R., & Gigerenzer, G. (1999). The 'conjunction fallacy' revisited: How intelligent inferences look like reasoning errors. *Journal of Behavioral Decision Making, 12,* 275–305. (38)

Hertwig, R., Gigerenzer, G., & Hoffrage, U. (1997). The reiteration effect in hindsight bias. *Psychological Review, 104,* 194–202. (2, 4, 10)

Hertwig, R., Hoffrage, U., & the ABC Research Group (in press). *Simple heuristics in a social world.* New York: Oxford University Press. (35)

Hertwig, R., Hoffrage, U., Martignon, L., (1999). Quick estimation: Letting the environment do the work. In G. Gigerenzer, P. M. Todd, & the

ABC Research Group, *Simple heuristics that make us smart* (pp. 209–234). New York: Oxford University Press. (5)

Hertwig, R., & Ortmann, A. (2001). Experimental practices in economics. A methodological challenge for psychologists? *Behavioral and Brain Sciences, 24,* 383–451. (7)

Hertwig, R., Pachur, T., & Kurzenhäuser, S. (2005). Judgments of risk frequencies: Tests of possible cognitive mechanisms. *Journal of Experimental Psychology: Learning, Memory, and Cognition, 31,* 621–642. (4, 23, 26)

Hertwig, R., & Todd, P. M. (2003). More is not always better: The benefits of cognitive limits. In D. Hardman & L. Macchi (Eds.), *Thinking: Psychological perspectives on reasoning, judgment and decision making* (pp. 213–231). Chichester, UK: Wiley. (1, 4, 5, 24, 31)

Herzog, S. M. (2005). *The boundedly rational fluency heuristic: How ecologically valid is recognition speed?* Unpublished master's thesis, University of Basel, Basel, Switzerland. (23, 31)

Herzog, S. M., & Hertwig, R. (2009). The wisdom of many in one mind: Improving individual judgments with dialectical bootstrapping. *Psychological Science, 20,* 231–237. (35)

Hey, J. D. (1982). Search for rules for search. *Journal of Economic Behavior and Organization, 3,* 65–81. (40)

Hill, C. R., & Stafford, F. P. (1974). Allocation of time to preschool children and educational opportunity. *The Journal of Human Resources, 9,* 323–341. (35)

Hill, C. R., & Stafford, F. P. (1980). Parental care of children: Time diary estimates of quantity, predictability, and variety. *The Journal of Human Resources, 15,* 219–239. (35)

Hill, G. W. (1982). Group versus individual performance: Are N+1 heads better than one? *Psychological Bulletin, 91,* 517–539. (21)

Hill, J. A., Enstrom, D. A., Ketterson, E. D., Nolan, V., & Ziegenfus, C. (1999). Mate choice based on static versus dynamic secondary sexual traits in the dark-eyed junco. *Behavioral Ecology, 10,* 91–96. (5)

Hill, K., & Hurtado, A. M. (1996). *Ache life history: The ecology and demography of a foraging people.* New York: Aldine De Gruyter. (35)

Hills, T. T., & Adler, F. R. (2002). Time's crooked arrow: Optimal foraging and rate-biased time perception. *Animal Behavior, 64,* 589–597. (5)

Hilton, D. J. (1995). The social context of reasoning: Conversational inference and rational judgment. *Psychological Bulletin, 118,* 248–271. (24)

Hinsz, V. B., Tindale, R. S., & Vollrath, D. A. (1997). The emerging conceptualization of groups as information processors. *Psychological Bulletin, 121,* 43–64. (27)

Hintzman, D. L. (1988). Judgments of frequency and recognition memory in a multiple-trace memory model. *Psychological Review, 95,* 528–551. (11, 15)

Hintzman, D. L. (1990). Human learning and memory: Connections and dissociations. *Annual Review of Psychology, 41,* 109–139. (4)

Hintzman, D. L., & Curran, T. (1994). Retrieval dynamics of recognition and frequency judgments: Evidence for separate processes of familiarity and recall. *Journal of Memory and Language, 33,* 1–18. (23)

Hirshman, E. (1995). Decision processes in recognition memory: Criterion shifts and the list-strength paradigm. *Journal of Experimental Psychology: Learning, Memory, and Cognition, 21,* 302–313. (15)

Ho, T.-H., Park, Y.-H., & Zhou, Y. P. (2006). Incorporating satisfaction into customer value analysis: Optimal investment in lifetime value. *Marketing Science, 25,* 260–277. (36)

Hoch, S. J., & Lœwenstein, G. F. (1989). Outcome feedback: Hindsight and information. *Journal of Experimental Psychology: Learning, Memory, and Cognition, 15,* 605–619. (10)

Hodges, S. D., & Brealey, R.A. (1978). Portfolio selection in a dynamic and uncertain world. In J. H. Lorie & R. A. Brealey (Eds.), *Modern developments in investment management.* Hinsdale, IL: Dryden Press. (34)

Hoffman, P. J. (1960). The paramorphic representation of clinical judgment. *Psychological Bulletin, 57,* 116–131. (13, 28)

Hoffman, P. J., Earle, T. C., & Slovic, P. (1981). Multidimensional functional learning (MFL) and some new conceptions of feedback. *Organizational Behavior and Human Performance, 27,* 75–102. (13)

Hoffmann, R. (2000). Twenty years on: The evolution of cooperation revisited. *Journal of Artificial Societies and Social Simulation, 3.* (5)

Hoffrage, U. (1995). *Zur Angemessenheit subjektiver Sicherheits-Urteile. Eine Exploration der Theorie der probabilistischen mentalen Modelle,* [The adequacy of subjective confidence judgments: Studies concerning the theory of probabilistic mental models]. Doctoral dissertation, University of Salzburg, Austria. (2, 3, 10)

Hoffrage, U., & Hertwig, R. (1999). Hindsight bias: A price worth paying for fast and frugal memory. In G. Gigerenzer, P. M. Todd, & the ABC Research Group, *Simple heuristics that make us smart* (pp. 191–208). New York: Oxford University Press. (10)

Hoffrage, U., Hertwig, R., & Gigerenzer, G. (2000). Hindsight bias: A by-product of knowledge updating? *Journal of Experimental Psychology: Learning, Memory, and Cognition, 26,* 566–581. (5, 17)

Hoffrage, U., Martignon, L., & Hertwig, R. (1997, August). *Does "judgment policy capturing" really capture the policies?* Poster presented at Subjective Probability, Utility, and Decision Making, 16, Leeds, UK. (10)

Hogarth, R. M. (1978). A note on aggregating opinions. *Organizational Behavior and Human Performance, 21,* 40–46. (21, 31)

Hogarth, R. M. (1987). *Judgement and choice: The psychology of decision* (2nd ed.). Chichester, UK: Wiley. (3, 13, 29)

Hogarth, R. M. (in press). On ignoring scientific evidence: The bumpy road to enlightenment. In P. M. Todd, G. Gigerenzer, & the ABC Reseach Group, *Ecological rationality: Intelligence in the world.* New York: Oxford University Press. (1, 13)

Hogarth, R. M., Gibbs, B. J., McKenzie, C. R. M., & Marquis, M. A. (1991). Learning from feedback: Exactingness and incentives. *Journal of Experimental Psychology: Learning, Memory, and Cognition, 17,* 734–752. (13)

Hogarth, R. M., & Karelaia, N. (2005) [also: 2005a]. Ignoring information in binary choice with continuous variables: When is less "more"? *Journal of Mathematical Psychology, 49,* 115–124. (1, 7, [13], [14])

Hogarth, R. M., & Karelaia, N. (2005) [also: 2005b]. Simple models for multi-attribute choice with many alternatives: When it does and does not pay to face trade-offs with binary attributes. *Management Science, 51,* 1860–1872. (8, [13], [14])

Hogarth, R. M., & Karelaia, N. (2006) [also: 2006a]. Regions of rationality: Maps for bounded agents. *Decision Analysis, 3,* 124–144. ([13], 16)

Hogarth, R. M., & Karelaia, N. (2006) [also: 2006b]. "Take-the-best" and other simple strategies: Why and when they work "well" with binary cues. *Theory and Decision, 61,* 205–249. (1, 8, [13], 14)

Hogarth, R. M., & Karelaia, N. (2007). Heuristic and linear models of judgment: Matching rules and environments. *Psychological Review, 114,* 733–758. (14, 32)

Hogarth, R. M., & Reder, M. W. (Eds.). (1986). *Rational choice.* Chicago: University of Chicago Press. (7)

Holsti, O. R. (1969). *Content analysis for the social sciences and humanities.* Reading, MA: Addison-Wesley. (29)

Holte, R. C. (1993). Very simple classification rules perform well on most commonly used datasets. *Machine Learning, 3,* 63–91. (12)

Holzworth, R. J., & Doherty, M. E. (1976). Feedback effects in a metric multiple-cue probability learning task. *Bulletin of the Psychonomic Society, 8,* 1–3. (13)

Hooke, R., & Jeeves, T. A. (1961). "Direct search" solution of numerical and statistical problems. *Journal of the Association for Computing Machinery, 8,* 212–229. (19)

Horn, J. L., & Cattell, R. B. (1967). Age differences in fluid and crystallized intelligence. *Acta Psychologica, 26,* 107–129. (22)

Horton, S. (1988). Birth order and child nutritional status: Evidence from the Philippines. *Economic Development and Cultural Change, 36,* 341–354. (35)

Houston, A., Kacelnik, A., & McNamara, J. (1982). Some learning rules for acquiring information. In D. J. McFarland (Ed.), *Functional ontogeny* (pp. 140–191). London: Pitman. (5)

Howell, D. C. (2002). *Statistical methods for psychology* (5th ed.). Belmont, CA: Duxbury Press. (23)

Hoyer, W. D., & Brown, S. P. (1990). Effects of brand awareness on choice for a common, repeat-purchase product. *Journal of Consumer Research, 17,* 141–148. (5)

Hrdy, S. B. (1999). *Mother nature: A history of mothers, infants, and natural selection.* New York: Pantheon Books. (35)

Hsee, C. K. (1996). The evaluability hypothesis: An explanation for preference reversals between joint and separate evaluations of alternatives. *Organizational Behavior and Human Decision Processes, 67,* 247–257. (23)

IIsee, C. K., Loewenstein, G. F., Blount, S., & Bazerman, M. H. (1999). Preference reversals between joint and separate evaluation of options: A review and theoretical analysis. *Psychological Bulletin, 125,* 576–590. (23)

Hubbard Ashton, A., & Ashton, R. H. (1985). Aggregating subjective forecasts: Some empirical results. *Management Science, 31,* 1499–1508. (31)

Huber, O. (1980). The influence of some task variables on cognitive operations in an information-processing decision model. *Acta Psychologica, 45,* 187–196. (22)

Huber, O. (1982). *Entscheiden als Problemlösen* [Decision making as problem solving]. Bern, Switzerland: Hans Huber. (7)

Huber, O. (1989). Information-processing operators in decision making. In H. Montgomery & O. Svenson (Eds.), *Process and structure in human decision making* (pp. 3–21). New York: Wiley. (2)

Huberman, G., & Jiang, W. (2006). Offering vs. choice in 401(k) plans: Equity exposure and number of funds. *Journal of Finance, 61,* 763–801. (34)

Huettel, S. A., Mack, P. B., & McCarthy, G. (2002). Perceiving patterns in random series: Dynamic processing of sequence in prefrontal cortex. *Nature Neuroscience, 5,* 485–490. (32)

Hume, D. (1978). *A treatise of human nature.* Oxford, UK: Clarendon Press. (Original work published 1740) (26)

Hursch, C. J., Hammond, K. R., & Hursch, J. L. (1964). Some methodological considerations in multiple-probability studies. *Psychological Review, 71,* 42–60. (13)

Hutchinson, J. M. C., & Gigerenzer, G. (2005). Simple heuristics and rules of thumb: Where psychologists and behavioural biologists might meet. *Behavioural Processes, 69,* 97–124. (1, 2, 9)

Hutchinson, J. M. C., & Gigerenzer, G. (2005). Connecting behavioural biologists and psychologists: Clarifying distinctions and suggestions for further work. *Behavioural Processes, 69,* 159–163. (5)

Hutchinson, J. M. C., & Halupka, K. (2004). Mate choice when males are in patches: Optimal strategies and good rules of thumb. *Journal of Theoretical Biology, 231,* 129–151. (5)

Hutchinson, J. M. C., McNamara, J. M., & Cuthill, I. C. (1993). Song, sexual selection, starvation and strategic handicaps. *Animal Behavior, 45,* 1153–1177. (5)

Huttenlocher, J., Hedges, L., & Prohaska, V. (1988). Hierarchical organization in ordered domains: Estimating the dates of events. *Psychological Review, 95,* 471–484. (2)

Huttenlocher, P. R. (1994). Synaptogenesis in human cerebral cortex. In G. Dawson & K. W. Fischer (Eds.), *Human behavior and the developing brain* (pp. 35–54). New York: Guilford Press. (35)

Irwin, J. R., & Baron, J. (2001). Response mode effects and moral values. *Organizational Behavior and Human Decision Processes, 84,* 177–197. (37)

Irwin, J. R., Slovic, P., Lichtenstein, S., & McClelland, G. H. (1993). Preference reversals and the measurement of environmental values. *Journal of Risk and Uncertainty, 6,* 5–18. (37)

Ivey, P. K. (2000). Cooperative reproduction in Ituri Forest hunter-gatherers: Who cares for Efe infants? *Current Anthropology, 41,* 856–866. (35)

Iwasa, Y., Higashi, M., & Yamamura, N. (1981). Prey distribution as a factor determining the choice of optimal foraging strategy. *The American Naturalist, 117,* 710–723. (5)

Jablonski, P. G. (1999). A rare predator exploits prey escape behavior: The role of tail-fanning and plumage contrast in foraging of the painted redstart. *Behavioral Ecology, 10,* 7–14. (33)

Jacob, V. S., Gaultney, L. D., & Salvendy, G. (1986). Strategies and biases in human decision making and their implications for expert systems. *Behaviour and Information Technology, 5,* 119–140. (29)

Jacobsen, T., Schubotz, R. I., Hofel, L., & von Cramon, D. Y. (2006). Brain correlates of aesthetic judgment of beauty. *Neuroimage, 29,* 276–285. (25)

Jacoby, L. L. (1991). A process dissociation framework: Separating automatic from intentional uses of memory. *Journal of Memory and Language, 30,* 513–541. (23)

Jacoby, L. L., & Brooks, L. R. (1984). Nonanalytic cognition: Memory, perception and concept learning. In G. H. Bower (Ed.), *Psychology of learning and motivation* (pp. 1–47). New York: Academic Press. (4)

Jacoby, L. L., & Dallas, M. (1981). On the relationship between autobiographical memory and perceptual learning. *Journal of Experimental Psychology: General, 110,* 306–340. (1, 4, 26)

Jacoby, L. L., Kelley, C. M., Brown, J., & Jasechko, J. (1989). Becoming famous overnight: Limits on the ability to avoid unconscious influences of the past. *Journal of Personality and Social Psychology, 56,* 326–338. (3, 4, 23, 24)

Jacoby, L. L., & Whitehouse, K. (1989). An illusion of memory: False recognition influenced by unconscious perception. *Journal of Experimental Psychology: General, 118,* 126–135. (26)

Jacoby, L. L., Woloshyn, V., & Kelley, C. (1989). Becoming famous without being recognized: Unconscious influences of memory produced by dividing attention. *Journal of Experimental Psychology, 118,* 115–125. (3, 15)

Jagannathan, R., & Ma, T. (2003). Risk reduction in large portfolios: Why imposing the wrong constraints helps. *Journal of Finance, 58,* 1651–1684. (34)

Jäger, A. O., Süß, H.-M., & Beauducel, A. (1997). *Berliner Intelligenz-Struktur-Test.* Göttingen, Germany: Hogrefe. (17)

Jain, D., & Singh, S. S. (2002). Customer lifetime value research in marketing: A review and future directions. *Journal of Interactive Marketing, 16,* 34–47. (36)

James, W. (1890). *The principles of psychology* (Vol. 1). New York: Holt. (4)

James, W., & Stein, C. (1961). Estimation with quadratic loss. *Proceedings of the 4th Berkeley Symposium on Probability and Statistics 1.* Berkeley, CA: University of California Press. (34)

Janetos, A. C. (1980). Strategies of female mate choice: A theoretical analysis. *Behavioral Ecology and Sociobiology, 7,* 107–112. (5)

Janetos, A. C., & Cole, B. J. (1981). Imperfectly optimal animals. *Behavioral Ecology and Sociobiology, 9,* 203–209. (5)

Jarnecke, R. W., & Rudestam, K. E. (1976). Effects of amounts and units of information on the judgmental process. *Perceptual and Motor Skills, 13,* 823–829. (13)

Jedetski, J., Adelman, L., & Yeo, C. (2002). How web site decision technology affects consumers. *IEEE Internet Computing, 6,* 72–79. (8)

Jennions, M. D., & Petrie, M. (1997). Variation in mate choice and mating preferences: A review of causes and consequences. *Biological Reviews, 72,* 283–327. (5)

Jobson, J. D., & Korkie, R. (1980). Estimation for Markowitz efficient portfolios. *Journal of the American Statistical Association, 75,* 544–554. (34)

Jobson, J. D., & Korkie, R. (1981). Performance hypothesis testing with the sharpe and Treynor measures. *Journal of Finance, 36,* 889–908. (34)

Jobson, J. D., Korkie, R., & Ratti, V. (1979). Improved estimation for Markowitz portfolios using James-Stein type estimators. *Proceedings of the American Statistical Association, 41,* 279–292. (34)

Johnson, E. J., Bellman, S., & Lohse, G. L. (2002). Defaults, framing and privacy: Why opting in-opting out. *Marketing Letters, 13,* 5–15. (37)

Johnson, E. J., & Goldstein, D. G. (2003). Do defaults save lives? *Science, 302,* 1338–1339. (1, 9, 37)

Johnson, E. J., Hershey, J., Meszaros, J., & Kunreuther, H. (1993). Framing, probability distortions, and insurance decisions. *Journal of Risk and Uncertainty, 7,* 35–51. (9, 37)

Johnson, E. J., Meyer, R. J., & Ghose, S. (1989). When choice models fail: Compensatory models in negatively correlated environments. *Journal of Marketing Research, 26,* 255–270. (5)

Johnson, E. J., & Payne, J. W. (1985). Effort and accuracy in choice. *Management Science, 31,* 394–414. (11, 17)

Johnson, E. J., & Payne, J. W. (1986). The decision to commit a crime: An information processing analysis. In D. B. Cornish & R. V. Clarke (Eds.), *The reasoning criminal* (pp. 170–185). New York: Springer. (30)

Johnson, E. J., Payne, J. W., Schkade, D. A., & Bettman, J. R. (1991). *Monitoring information processing and decisions: The mouselab system.* Unpublished manuscript, Center for Decision Studies, Fuqua School of Business, Duke University. (19)

Johnson, E. J., Schulte-Mecklenbeck, M., & Willemsen, M. (2008). Process models deserve process data: Comment on Brandstätter, Gigerenzer, & Hertwig (2006). *Psychological Review, 115,* 263–272. (7)

Johnson, J. G., & Raab, M. (2003). Take the first: Option-generation and resulting choices. *Organizational Behavior and Human Decision Processes, 91,* 215–229. (1, 32)

Johnson, M. K., Hastroudi, S., & Lindsay, D. S. (1993). Source monitoring. *Psychological Bulletin, 114,* 3–28. (23)

Johnson, M. M. S. (1990). Age differences in decision making: A process methodology for examining strategic information processing. *Journal of Gerontology, 45,* 75–78. (22)

Johnson, M. M. S. (1993). Thinking about strategies during, before, and after making a decision. *Psychology and Aging, 8,* 231–241. (22)

Johnson, M. M. S., & Drungle, S. C. (2000). Purchasing over-the-counter medications: The impact of age differences in information processing. *Experimental Aging Research, 26,* 245–261. (22)

Johnson-Laird, P. N. (1983). *Mental models.* Cambridge, MA: Harvard University Press. (2)

Jolls, C., Sunstein, C. R., & Thaler, R. (1998). A behavioral approach to law and economics. *Stanford Law Review, 50,* 1471–1550. (1)

Jones, S., Juslin, P., Olsson, H., & Winman, A. (2000). *Algorithm, heuristic or exemplar: Process and representation in multiple cue judgment.* Paper presented at the Cognitive Science Society, Philadelphia. (18)

Jorion, P. (1985). International portfolio diversification with estimation risk. *Journal of Business, 58,* 259–278. (34)

Jorion, P. (1986). Bayes-Stein estimation for portfolio analysis. *Journal of Financial and Quantitative Analysis, 21,* 279–292. (34)

Jorion, P. (1991). Bayesian and CAPM estimators of the means: Implications for portfolio selection. *Journal of Banking and Finance, 15,* 717–727. (34)

Jorland, G. (1987). The Saint Petersburg paradox 1713–1937. In L. Krüger, G. Gigerenzer, & M. S. Morgan (Eds.), *The probabilistic revolution: Vol. 1. Ideas in the sciences* (pp. 157–190). Cambridge, MA: MIT Press. (8)

Juslin, P. (1993). An explanation of the hard-easy effect in studies of realism of confidence in one's general knowledge. *European Journal of Cognitive Psychology, 5,* 55–71. (2)

Juslin, P. (1994). The overconfidence phenomenon as a consequence of informal experimenter-guided selection of almanac items. *Organizational Behavior and Human Decision Processes, 57,* 226–246. (2)

Juslin, P., Jones, S., Olsson, H., & Winman, A. (2003). Cue abstraction and exemplar memory in categorization. *Journal of Experimental Psychology: Learning, Memory, and Cognition, 29,* 924–941. (11, 19)

Juslin, P., & Montgomery, H. (Eds.). (1999). *Judgment and decision making: New-Brunswikian and process-tracing approaches.* Hillsdale, NJ: Erlbaum. (28)

Juslin, P., Olsson, H., & Olsson, A. C. (2003). Exemplar effects in categorization and multiple-cue judgment. *Journal of Experimental Psychology: General, 132,* 133–156. (11, 19)

Juslin, P., & Persson, M. (2002). PROBabilities from EXemplars (PROBEX): A "lazy" algorithm for probabilistic inference from generic knowledge. *Cognitive Science, 26,* 563–607. (11, 13, 14, 18, 21)

Juslin, P., Winman, A., & Persson, T. (1995). Can overconfidence be used as an indicator of reconstructive rather than retrieval processes? *Cognition, 54,* 99–130. (2)

Kacelnik, A., & Todd, I. A. (1992). Psychological mechanisms and the Marginal Value Theorem: Effect of variability in travel time on patch exploitation. *Animal Behavior, 43,* 313–322. (5)

Kagan, J. (1987). Perspectives on infancy. In J. D. Osofsky (Ed.), *Handbook on infant development* (pp. 1150–1198). Oxford, UK: Wiley. (35)

Kahn, I., Davachi, L., & Wagner, A. D. (2004). Functional-neuroanatomic correlates of recollection: Implications for models of recognition memory. *Journal of Neuroscience, 24,* 4172–4180. (25)

Kahneman, D. (2000). Preface. In D. Kahneman & A. Tversky (Eds.), *Choices, values, and frames* (pp. ix–xvii). Cambridge, UK: Cambridge University Press. (7)

Kahneman, D. (2003). A perspective on judgement and choice: Mapping bounded rationality. *American Psychologist, 58,* 697–720. (8, 9)

Kahneman, D., Knetsch, J. L., & Thaler, R. H. (1991). Anomalies: The endowment effect, loss aversion, and status quo bias. *Journal of Economic Perspectives, 5,* 193–206. (37)

Kahneman, D., Slovic, P., & Tversky, A. (Eds.). (1982). *Judgment under uncertainty: Heuristics and biases.* Cambridge, UK: Cambridge University Press. (Introduction, 2, 4, 13, 29)

Kahneman, D., & Tversky, A. (1973). On the psychology of prediction. *Psychological Review, 80,* 237–251. (29)

Kahneman, D., & Tversky, A. (1979). Prospect theory: An analysis of decision under risk. *Econometrica, 47,* 263–291. (5, 7, 8, 37)

Kahneman, D., & Tversky, A. (1996). On the reality of cognitive illusions. *Psychological Review, 103,* 582–591. (1, 5, 13)

Kahneman, D., & Tversky, A. (Eds.). (2000). *Choices, values, and frames.* Cambridge, UK: Cambridge University Press. (7)

Kalick, S. M., & Hamilton, T. E. (1986). The matching hypothesis reexamined. *Journal of Personality and Social Psychology, 51,* 673–682. (40)

Kalmijn, M. (1998). Intermarriage and homogamy: Causes, patterns, trends. *Annual Review of Sociology, 24,* 395–421. (40)

Kamakura, W., Mela, C. F, Ansari, A., Bodapati, A., Fader, P., Iyengar, R., et al. (2005). Choice models and customer relationship management. *Marketing Letters, 16,* 279–291. (36)

Kameda, T., & Nakanishi, D. (2002). Cost-benefit analysis of social/cultural learning in a nonstationary uncertain environment: An evolutionary simulation and an experiment with human subjects. *Evolution and Human Behavior, 23,* 373–393. (21)

Kamil, A. C., & Sargent, T. D. (1981). *Foraging behavior: Ecological, ethological and psychological approaches.* New York: Garland STPM Press. (5)

Kan, R., & Zhou, G. (2007). Optimal portfolio choice with parameter uncertainty. *Journal of Financial and Quantitative Analysis, 42,* 621–656. (34)

Kane, M. J., & Engle, R. W. (2000). Working-memory capacity, proactive interference, and divided attention: Limits on long-term memory retrieval. *Journal of Experimental Psychology: Learning, Memory, and Cognition, 26,* 336–358. (22)

Kaplan, B. A., Mascie-Taylor, C. G. N., & Boldsen, J. (1992). Birth order and health status in a British national sample. *Journal of Biosocial Science, 24,* 25–33. (35)

Kaplan, H., Hill, K., Lancaster, J. B., & Hurtado, A. M. (2000). A theory of human life history evolution: Diet, intelligence, and longevity. *Evolutionary Anthropology, 9,* 156–185. (35)

Kaplan, H., Lancaster, J. B., & Anderson, K. G. (1998). Human parental investment and fertility: The life histories of men in Albuquerque. In A. Booth & N. Crouter (Eds.), *Men in families: When do they get involved? What difference does it make?* (pp. 55–111). New York: Erlbaum. (35)

Kareev, Y. (2000). Seven (indeed, plus or minus two) and the detection of correlations. *Psychological Review, 107,* 397–402. (4, 5)

Karelaia, N. (2006). Thirst for confirmation in multi-attribute choice: Does search for consistency impair decision performance? *Organizational Behavior and Human Decision Processes, 100,* 128–143. (1, 13)

Karelaia, N., & Hogarth, R. M. (2007). *Determinants of linear judgment: A meta-analysis of lens model studies (DEE Working Paper No. 1007).* Barcelona, Spain: Universitat Pompeu Fabra. (13)

Karsai, I., & Pénzes, Z. (2000). Optimality of cell arrangement and rules of thumb of cell initiation in *Polistes dominulus:* A modeling approach. *Behavioral Ecology, 11,* 387–395. (5)

Kass, R.E., & Raftery, A.E. (1995). Bayes factors. *Journal of the American Statistical Association, 90,* 773–795. (39)

Katsikopoulos, K. V., & Fasolo, B. (2006). New tools for decision analysts. *IEEE Transactions on Systems, Man, and Cybernetics: Systems and Humans, 36,* 960–967. (8, 14)

Katsikopoulos, K. V., & Gigerenzer, G. (2008). One-reason decision-making: Modeling viola-tions of expected utility theory. *Journal of Risk and Uncertainty, 37,* 35–56. (1)

Katsikopoulos, K. V., & Martignon, L. (2006). Naïve heuristics for paired comparisons: Some results on their relative accuracy. *Journal of Mathematical Psychology, 50,* 488–494. (1, 7, 8, 14, 19)

Katsikopoulos, K. V., Pachur, T., Machery, E., & Wallin, A. (2008). From Meehl (1954) to fast and frugal heuristics (and back): New insights into how to bridge the clinical-actuarial divide. *Theory and Psychology, 18,* 443–464. (14)

Katsikopoulos, K. V., Schooler, L. J., & Hertwig, R. (2008). *The robust beauty of mediocre information.* Unpublished manuscript, Max Planck Institute for Human Development, Berlin, Germany. (14)

Keasar, T., Rashkovich, E., Cohen, D., & Shmida, A. (2002). Bees in two-armed bandit situations: Foraging choices and possible decision mecha-nisms. *Behavioral Ecology, 13,* 757–765. (5)

Kee, F., Jenkins, J., McIllwaine, S., Patterson, C., Harper, S., & Shields, M. (2003). Fast and frugal models of clinical judgment in novice and expert physicians. *Medical Decision Making, 23,* 293–300. (14)

Keeley, M. C. (1979). An analysis of the age pattern of first marriage. *International Economic Review, 20,* 527–544. (40)

Keeney, R. L., & Raiffa, H. (1976). *Decisions with multiple objectives: Preferences and value trade-offs.* New York: Wiley. (13)

Keeney, R. L., & Raiffa, H. (1993). *Decisions with multiple objectives.* Cambridge, UK: Cambridge University Press. (Introduction, 1, 2, 3, 24)

Kelley, C. M., & Jacoby, L. L. (1998). Subjective reports and process dissociation: Fluency, knowing, and feeling. *Acta Psychologica, 98,* 127–140. (4, 26)

Kelley, C. M., & Lindsay, D. S. (1993). Remembering mistaken for knowing: Ease of retrieval as a basis for confidence in answers to general knowledge questions. *Journal of Memory and Language, 32,* 1–24. (26)

Kelling, G. L., & Coles, C. M. (1996). *Fixing broken windows: Restoring order and reducing crime in our communities.* New York: The Free Press. (9)

Kennedy, G. E. (1989). Middleborns' perceptions of family relationships. *Psychological Reports, 64,* 755–760. (35)

Kennedy, J. S. (1983). Zigzagging and casting as a programmed response to wind-borne odour: A review. *Physiological Entomology, 8,* 109–120. (5)

Kerr, N. L., & Tindale, R. S. (2004). Group performance and decision making. *Annual Review of Psychology, 55,* 623–655. (21)

Kessler, L., & Ashton, R. H. (1981). Feedback and prediction achievement in financial analysis. *Journal of Accounting Research, 19,* 146–162. (13)

Kidwell, J. S. (1981). Number of siblings, sibling spacing, sex, and birth order: Their effects on perceived parent–adolescent relationships. *Journal of Marriage and the Family, 43,* 315–332. (35)

Kidwell, J. S. (1982). The neglected birth order: Middleborns. *Journal of Marriage and the Family, 44,* 225–235. (35)

Kim, S., & Hasher, L. (2005). The attraction effect in decision making: Superior performance by older adults. *Quarterly Journal of Experimental Psychology, 58A,* 120–133. (22)

Kinchla, R. A. (1994). Comments on batchelder and riefer's multinomial model for source monitoring. *Psychological Review, 101,* 166–171. (4)

Klayman, J., & Ha, Y. (1987). Confirmation, disconfirmation, and information in hypothesis testing. *Psychological Review, 94,* 211–228. (2, 3, 28)

Klein, D. B. (2004). Status quo bias. *Econ Journal Watch, 1,* 260–271. (37)

Klein, G. A. (1998). *Sources of power. How people make decisions.* Cambridge, MA: MIT Press. (32)

Klein, G. A., Wolf, S., Militello, L. G., & Zsambok, C. E. (1995). Characteristics of skilled option generation in chess. *Organizational Behavior and Human Decision Processes, 62,* 63–69. (32)

Klein, R. W., & Bawa, V. S. (1976). The effect of estimation risk on optimal portfolio choice. *Journal of Financial Economics, 3,* 215–231. (34)

Kleinmuntz, B. (1990). Why we still use our heads instead of formulas: Toward an integrative approach. *Psychological Bulletin, 107,* 296–310. (13, 29)

Kleiter, G. D. (1994). Natural sampling. Rationality without base rates. In G. H. Fischer & D. Laming (Eds.), *Contributions to mathematical psychology, psychometrics, and methodology* (pp. 375–388). New York: Springer. (6)

Knight, F. (1921). *Risk, uncertainty, and profit.* Boston, MA: Houghton Mifflin. (34)

Knobe, J., & Nichols, S. (2008). An experimental philosophy manifesto. In J. Knobe & S. Nichols (Eds.), *Experimental Philosophy* (pp. 3–14). New York: Oxford University Press. (9)

Kobayashi, Y., & Amaral, D. G. (2003). Macaque monkey retrosplenial cortex: II. Cortical afferents. *Journal of Comparative Neurology, 466,* 48–79. (25)

Koch, H. L. (1960). The relation of certain formal attributes of siblings to attitudes held toward each other and toward their parents. *Monographs of the Society for Research in Child Development, 24*(78). (35)

Kocsis, R. N., & Irwin, H. J. (1997). An analysis of spatial patterns in serial rape, arson, and burglary: The utility of the circle theory of environmental range for psychological profiling. *Psychiatry, Psychology and Law, 4,* 195–206. (29)

Kodric-Brown, A., & Nicoletto, P. F. (2001). Female choice in the guppy (*Poecilia reticulata*): The interaction between male color and display. *Behavioral Ecology and Sociobiology, 50,* 346–351. (5)

Kohlberg, L. (1968). The child as a moral philosopher. *Psychology Today, 2,* 25–30. (9)

Körding, K. P., & Wolpert, D. M. (2004). Bayesian integration in sensorimotor learning. *Nature, 427,* 244–247. (5)

Koriat, A., Goldsmith, M., & Pansky, A. (2000). Toward a psychology of memory accuracy. *Annual Review of Psychology, 51,* 481–537. (4)

Koriat, A., Lichtenstein, S., & Fischhoff, B. (1980). Reasons for confidence. *Journal of Experimental Psychology: Human Learning and Memory, 6,* 107–118. (2)

Koriat, A., & Ma'ayan, H. (2005). The effects of encoding fluency and retrieval fluency on judgments of learning. *Journal of Memory and Language, 52,* 478–492. (26)

Kovalchik, S., Camerer, C. F., Grether, D. M., Plott, C. R., & Allman, J. M. (2005). Aging and decision making: A comparison between neurologically healthy elderly and young individuals. *Journal of Economic Behavior & Organization, 58,* 79–94. (22)

Krafft, M. (2002). *Kundenbindung und Kundenwert.* Heidelberg, Germany: Physica-Verlag. (36)

Krause, B. J., Schmidt, D., Mottaghy, F. M., Taylor, J., Halsband, U., Herzog, H., et al. (1999). Episodic retrieval activates the precuneus irrespective of the imagery content of word pair associates. A PET study. *Brain, 122,* 255–263. (25)

Krauss, S., Martignon, L., Hoffrage, U., & Gigerenzer, G. (2001). *Bayesian reasoning and natural frequencies: A generalization to complex situations.* Unpublished paper, Max Planck Institute for Human Development, Berlin, Germany. (6)

Krebs, J. R., & Davies, N. B. (1987). *An introduction to behavioral ecology* (2nd ed.). Oxford, UK: Blackwell. (2)

Krebs, J. R., Erichsen, J. T., Webber, M. I., & Charnov, E. L. (1977). Optimal prey selection in the great tit (*Parus major*). *Animal Behavior, 25,* 30–38. (5)

Krebs, J. R., Stephens, D. W., & Sutherland, W. J. (1983). Perspectives in optimal foraging. In A. H. Bush & G. A. Clark (Eds.), *Perspectives in ornithology: Essays presented for the centennial of the American ornithologists' union* (pp. 165–221). Cambridge, UK: Cambridge University Press. (5)

Krippendorff, K. (1980). *Content analysis: An introduction to its methodology.* Beverly Hills, CA: Sage. (29)

Kruschke, J. K. (1992). ALCOVE: An exemplar-based connectionist model of category learning. *Psychological Review, 99,* 22–44. (11)

Kuhl, J. (1994). Action versus state orientation: Psychometric properties of the Action Control Scale (ACS-90). In J. Kuhl & J. Beckmann (Eds.), *Volition and personality. Action versus state orientation* (pp. 47–59). Göttingen, Germany: Hogrefe & Huber. (17)

Künzler, R., & Bakker, T. C. M. (2001). Female preferences for single and combined traits in computer animated stickleback males. *Behavioral Ecology, 12,* 681–685. (5)

Kuo, H.-H. D., & Hauser, R. M. (1996). Gender, family configuration, and the effect of family background on educational attainment. *Social Biology, 43,* 98–131. (35)

Kurz, E., & Martignon, L. (1999). Weighing, then summing: The triumph and tumbling of a modeling practice in psychology. In L. Magnani, N. Nersessian, & P. Thagard (Eds.), *Model-based reasoning in scientific discovery* (pp. 26–31). Pavia, Italy: Cariplo. (12)

Laboratory for Energy and the Environment (2005). *A survey of public attitudes towards energy and environment in Great Britain.* Cambridge, MA: Massachusetts Institute of Technology, Laboratory for Energy and the Environment. (37)

Lafon, P., Chasseigne, G., & Mullet, E. (2004). Functional learning among children, adolescents, and young adults. *Journal of Experimental Child Psychology, 88,* 334–347. (13)

Lages, M., Hoffrage, U., & Gigerenzer, G. (1999). *How heuristics produce intransitivity and how intransitivity can discriminate between heuristics.* Unpublished manuscript, Max Planck Institute for Human Development, Berlin, Germany. (12)

Lamberts, K. (1995). Categorization under time pressure. *Journal of Experimental Psychology: General, 124,* 161–180. (14)

Lamberts, K. (2000). Information-accumulation theory of speeded categorization. *Psychological Review, 107,* 227–260. (11, 14)

Lanchester, B. S., & Mark, R. F. (1975). Pursuit and prediction in the tracking of moving food by a teleost fish (*Acanthaluteres spilomelanurus*). *Journal of Experimental Biology, 63,* 627–645. (33)

Laughlin, P. R., & Ellis, A. L. (1986). Demonstrability and social combination processes on mathematical intellective tasks. *Journal of Experimental Social Psychology, 22,* 177–189. (27)

Lawler, E. L., Lenstra, J. K., Rinnooy-Kan, A. H. G., & Shmoys, D. B. (Eds.). (1985). *The traveling salesman problem.* New York: Wiley. (5)

Ledoit, O., & Wolf, M. (2004a). Honey, I shrunk the sample covariance matrix: Problems in mean-variance optimization. *Journal of Portfolio Management, 30,* 110–119. (34)

Ledoit, O., & Wolf, M. (2004b). A well-conditioned estimator for large-dimensional covariance matrices. *Journal of Multivariate Analysis, 88,* 365–411. (34)

Lee, J.-W., & Yates, J. F. (1992). How quantity judgment changes as the number of cues increases: An analytical framework and review. *Psychological Bulletin, 112,* 363–377. (13)

Lee, M. D. (2002). *Are these two groups of scores significantly different? A Bayesian approach.* Unpublished manuscript. (39)

Lee, M. D., Chandrasena, L. H., & Navarro, D. J. (2002). Using cognitive decision models to prioritize e-mails. In W. G. Gray & C. D. Schunn (Eds.), *Proceedings of the 24th Annual Conference of the Cognitive Science Society* (pp. 478–483). Mahwah, NJ: Erlbaum. (19, 39)

Lee, M. D., & Corlett, E. Y. (2003). Sequential sampling model of human text classification. *Cognitive Science, 27,* 159–193. (14)

Lee, M. D., & Cummins, T. D. R. (2004). Evidence accumulation in decision making: Unifying the 'take the best' and the 'rational' models. *Psychonomic Bulletin & Review, 11,* 343–352. (14, 17, 19, 21, 24, 36)

Lee, M. D., Loughlin, N., & Lundberg, I. B. (2002). Applying one reason decision-making: The prioritization of literature searches. *Australian Journal of Psychology, 54,* 137–143. (1)

Lee, R. B. (1979). *The Kung San: Men, women and work in a foraging society.* Cambridge, UK: Cambridge University Press. (35)

Leeflang, P., Wittink, D. R., Wedel, M., & Naert, P. A. (2000). *Building models for marketing decisions*. Boston, MA: Kluwer Academic. (36)

Legendre, G., Raymond, W., & Smolensky, P. (1993). Analytic typology of case marking and grammatical voice. *Proceedings of the Berkeley Linguistics Society, 19,* 464–478. (2)

Leibowitz, A. (1974a). Education and home production. *American Economic Review, 64,* 243–250. (35)

Leibowitz, A. (1974b). Home investments in children. *Journal of Political Economy, 82,* 111–131. (35)

Leibowitz, A. (1977). Parental inputs and children's achievement. *The Journal of Human Resources, 12,* 242–251. (35)

Leland, J. W. (1994). Generalized similarity judgments: An alternative explanation for choice anomalies. *Journal of Risk and Uncertainty, 9,* 151–172. (7, 8)

Leland, J. W. (2002). Similarity judgments and anomalies in intertemporal choice. *Economic Inquiry, 40,* 574–581. (8)

Lemaire, P., Arnaud, L., & Lecacheur, M. (2004). Adults' age-related differences in adaptivity of strategy choices: Evidence from computational estimation. *Psychology and Aging, 10,* 467–481. (22)

Lemaire, P., & Siegler, R. S. (1995). Four aspects of strategic change: Contributions to children's learning of multiplication. *Journal of Experimental Psychology: General, 124,* 83–97. (22)

Lerner, J. S., & Tetlock, P. E. (1999). Accounting for the effects of accountability. *Psychological Bulletin, 125,* 255–275. (11)

Lesmond, D. A., Ogden, J. P., & Trzcinka, C. A. (1999). A new estimate of transaction costs. *The Review of Financial Studies, 12,* 1113–1141. (34)

Levine, N., & Associates. (2000). *Crimestat: A spatial statistics program for the analysis of crime incident locations* (version 1.1). Washington, DC: National Institute of Justice. (29)

Levy, M., & Levy, H. (2002). Prospect theory: Much ado about nothing? *Management Science, 48,* 1334–1349. (7)

Lewis, S. A., & Britton, J. R. (1998). Measles infection, measles vaccination and the effect of birth order in the aetiology of hay fever. *Clinical and Experimental Allergy, 28,* 1493–1500. (35)

Lewontin, R. C. (1968). Evolution of complex genetic systems. In M. Gerstenhaber (Ed.), *Some mathematical questions in biology* (pp.

62–87). Providence, RI: American Mathematical Society. (2)

Li, J., & Taylor, B. (1993). Factors affecting uptake of measles, mumps, and rubella immunization. *British Medical Journal, 307,* 168–171. (35)

Li, S. (1995). Survival Analysis. *Marketing Research, 7,* 17–23. (36)

Li, S.-C., Lindenberger, U., Hommel, B., Aschersleben, G., Prinz, W., & Baltes, P. B. (2004). Lifespan transformations in the couplings of mental abilities and underlying cognitive processes. *Psychological Science, 15,* 155–163. (22)

Lifjeld, J. T., & Slagsvold, T. (1988). Female pied flycatchers *Ficedula hypoleuca* choose male characteristics in homogeneous habitats. *Behavioral Ecology and Sociobiology, 22,* 27–36. (5)

Lilly, G. (1994). Bounded rationality: A Simon-like explication. *Journal of Economic Dynamics and Control, 18,* 105–230. (8)

Lima, S. L. (1994). Collective detection of predatory attack by birds in the absence of alarm signals. *Journal of Avian Biology, 25,* 319–326. (5)

Lindell, M. K. (1976). Cognitive and outcome feedback in multiple-cue probability learning tasks. *Journal of Experimental Psychology: Human Learning and Memory, 2,* 739–745. (13)

Lindenberger, U., Mayr, U., & Kliegl, R. (1993). Speed and intelligence in old age. *Psychology and Aging, 8,* 207–220. (22)

Lindenberger, U., & Pötter, U. (1998). The complex nature of unique and shared effects in hierarchical linear regression: Implications for developmental psychology. *Psychological Methods, 3,* 218–230. (22)

Lindert, P. H. (1977). Sibling position and achievement. *The Journal of Human Resources, 12,* 198–219. (35)

Lindley, D.V. (1972). *Bayesian statistics: A review.* Philadelphia, PA: Society for Industrial and Applied Mathematics. (39)

Lippmann, S.A., & McCall, J. J. (1976). The economics of job search: A survey (part I). *Economic Inquiry, 14,* 155–189. (40)

Lipsey, R. G. (1956). The general theory of the second best. *Review of Economic Studies, 24,* 11–32. (9)

Lipshitz, R. (2000). Two cheers for bounded rationality [Commentary]. *Behavioral and Brain Sciences, 23,* 756. (11, 17, 28)

Litterman, R. (2003). *Modern investment management: An equilibrium approach.* New York: Wiley. (34)

Lloyd, K. M., & South, S. J. (1996). Contextual influences on young men's transition to first marriage. *Social Forces, 74,* 1097–1119. (40)

Loewenstein, G. F., Weber, E. U., Hsee, C. K., & Welch, N. (2001). Risk as a feeling. *Psychological Bulletin, 127,* 267–286. (7, 8)

Logan, G. D. (1988). Toward an instance theory of automatization. *Psychological Review, 95,* 492–527. (11)

Logan, G. D. (2002). An instance theory of attention and memory. *Psychological Review, 109,* 376–400. (11)

Logue, A. W. (1988). Research on self-control: An integrating framework. *Behavioral Brain Sciences, 11,* 665–704. (5)

Lohmann, G., Müller, K., Bosch, V., Mentzel, H., Hessler, S., Chen, L., et al. (2001). LIPSIA – A new software system for the evaluation of functional magnetic resonance imaging of the human brain. *Computerized Medical Imaging and Graphics, 25,* 449–457. (25)

Lombardi, W. J., Higgins, E. T., & Bargh, J. A. (1987). The role of consciousness in priming effects on categorization: Assimilation versus contrast as a function of awareness of the priming task. *Personality and Social Psychology Bulletin, 13,* 411–429. (26)

Long, W. J., Grith, J. L., Selker, H. P., & D'Agostino, R. B. (1993). A comparison of logistic regression to decision-tree induction in a medical domain. *Computers in Biomedical Research, 26,* 74–97. (14)

Loomes, G., Starmer, C., & Sugden, R. (1991). Observing violations of transitivity by experimental methods. *Econometrica, 59,* 425–439. (7)

Loomes, G., & Sugden, R. (1982). Regret theory: An alternative theory of rational choice under uncertainty. *The Economic Journal, 92,* 805–824. (7)

Loomes, G., & Sugden, R. (1986). Disappointment and dynamic consistency in choice under uncertainty. *Review of Economic Studies, 53,* 271–282. (7)

Loomes, G., & Sugden, R. (1987). Testing for regret and disappointment in choice under uncertainty. *The Economic Journal, 97,* 118–129. (8)

Lopes, L. L. (1987). Between hope and fear: The psychology of risk. Advances in *Experimental Social Psychology, 20,* 255–295. (7)

Lopes, L. L. (1991). The rhetoric of irrationality. *Theory and Psychology, 1,* 65–82. (3)

Lopes, L. L. (1992). Three misleading assumptions in the customary rhetoric of the bias literature. *Theory and Psychology, 2,* 231–236. (2)

Lopes, L. L. (1995). Algebra and process in the modeling of risky choice. In J. R. Busemeyer, R. Hastie, & D. Medin (Eds.), *Decision making from the perspective of cognitive psychology.* New York: Academic Press. (2, 7, 8)

Lopes, L. L., & Oden, G. C. (1991). The rationality of intelligence. In E. Eels & T. Maruszewski (Eds.), *Poznan studies in the philosophy of the sciences and the humanities* (Vol. 21, pp. 225–249). Amsterdam: Rodopi. (4)

Lopes, L. L., & Oden, G. C. (1999). The role of aspiration level in risky choice: A comparison of cumulative prospect theory and SP/A theory. *Journal of Mathematical Psychology, 43,* 286–313. (7, 8)

Louvière, J. J. (1988). *Analyzing decision making: Metric conjoint analysis.* Thousand Oaks, CA: Sage. (13)

Lovie, A. D., & Lovie, P. (1986). The fiat maximum effect and linear scoring models for prediction. *Journal of Forecasting, 5,* 159–168. (2)

Luce, M. F., Payne, J. W., & Bettman, J. R. (1999). Emotional trade-off difficulty and choice. *Journal of Marketing Research, 36,* 143–159. (13)

Luce, R. D. (1956). Semiorders and a theory of utility discrimination. *Econometrica, 24,* 178–191. (Introduction, 7, 8)

Luce, R. D. (1959). *Individual choice behavior.* New York: Wiley. (11)

Luce, R. D. (1990). Rational versus plausible accounting equivalences in preference judgments. *Psychological Science, 1,* 225–234. (8)

Luce, R. D. (2000). Fast, frugal, and surprisingly accurate heuristics. *Behavioral and Brain Sciences, 23,* 757–758. (17)

Luce, R. D., & von Winterfeldt, D. (1994). What common ground exists for descriptive, prescriptive, and normative utility theories? *Management Science, 40,* 263–279. (8)

Luchins, A. S., & Luchins, E. H. (1959). *Rigidity of behavior: A variational approach to the effect of Einstellung.* Oxford, UK: University of Oregon Press. (17)

Luchins, A. S., & Luchins, E. H. (1994). The water jar experiments and Einstellung effects: I. Early history and surveys of textbook citations. *Gestalt Theory, 16,* 101–121. (2)

Lundrigan, S., & Canter, D. (2001). Spatial patterns of serial murder: An analysis of disposal site location choice. *Behavioral Sciences and the Law, 19,* 595–610. (29)

Luria, A. R. (1968). *The mind of a mnemonist.* New York: Basic Books. (1, 4)

Luttbeg, B. (1996). A comparative Bayes tactic for mate assessment and choice. *Behavioral Ecology, 7*, 451–460. (5)

Lynch, K. A., & Greenhouse, J. B. (1994). Risk factors for infant mortality in nineteenth-century Sweden. *Population Studies, 48*, 117–133. (35)

Macchi, L., & Mosconi, G. (1998). Computational features vs frequentist phrasing in the base-rate fallacy. *Swiss Journal of Psychology, 57*, 79–85. (6)

Maccoby, E. E., & Martin, J. A. (1983). Socialization in the context of the family: Parent-child interaction. In P. H. Mussen & E. M. Hetherington (Eds.), *Handbook of child psychology: Vol. 4. Socialization, personality, and social development* (pp. 1–110). New York: Wiley. (35)

MacCrimmon, K. R. (1968). Descriptive and normative implications of the decision-theory postulate. In K. H. Borch & J. Mossin (Eds.), *Risk and uncertainty* (pp. 3–23). New York: St. Martin's Press. (7, 8)

MacKay, D. J. C. (1992). Bayesian interpolation. *Neural Computation, 4*, 415–447. (5)

MacKay, D. J. C. (1995). Probable networks and plausible predictions – A review of practical Bayesian methods for supervised neural networks. *Network: Computation in Neural Systems, 6*, 469–505. (7)

MacKinlay, A. C., & Pástor, L. (2000). Asset pricing models: Implications for expected returns and portfolio selection. *The Review of Financial Studies, 13*, 883–916. (34)

Macskassy, S. A., Dayanik, A. A., & Hirsh, H. (1999). EmailValet: Learning user preferences for wireless email. *Proceedings of Learning About Users Workshop, IJCAI'99*. (39)

Macy, M. W., & Flache, A. (1995). Beyond rationality in models of choice. *Annual Review of Sociology, 21*, 73–91. (40)

Macy, M. W., & Willer, R. (2002). From factors to actors: Computational sociology and agent-based modeling. *Annual Review of Sociology, 28*, 143–166. (40)

Madrian, B., & Shea, D. (2001). The power of suggestion: Inertia in 401(k) participation and savings behavior. *Quarterly Journal of Economics, 116*, 11–49. (37)

Maeshima, S., Ozaki, F., Masuo, O., Yamaga, H., Okita, R., & Moriwaki, H. (2001). Memory impairment and spatial disorientation following a left retrosplenial lesion. *Journal of Clinical Neuroscience, 8*, 450–451. (25)

Maguire, E. A., Frith, C. D., & Morris, R. G. (1999). The functional neuroanatomy of comprehension and memory: The importance of prior knowledge. *Brain, 122*, 1839–1850. (25)

Makridakis, S., Anderson, N. H., Carbone, R., Fildes, M., Hibon, R., Lewdowski, J., et al. (1982). The accuracy of extrapolation (time series) methods: Results of a forecasting competition. *Journal of Forecasting, 1*, 111–153. (31)

Makridakis, S., Chatfield, C., Hibon, M., Lawrence, M., Mills, T., Ord, K., et al. (1993). The M2-competition: A real-time judgmentally based forecasting study. *International Journal of Forecasting, 9*, 5–22. (31)

Makridakis, S., & Hibon, M. (1979). Accuracy of forecasting: An empirical investigation. *Journal of the Royal Statistical Society, 142*, 97–145. (31)

Makridakis, S., & Hibon, M. (2000). The M3-competition: Results, conclusions, and implications. *International Journal of Forecasting, 16*, 451–476. (9, 31)

Makridakis, S., & Winkler, R. L. (1983). Averages of forecasts: Some empirical results. *Management Science, 29*, 987–996. (31)

Mallon, E. B., & Franks, N. R. (2000). Ants estimate area using Buffon's needle. *Proceedings of the Royal Society of London, Series B: Biological Sciences, 267*, 765–770. (5)

Malmberg, K. J. (2002). On the form of ROCs constructed from confidence ratings. *Journal of Experimental Psychology: Learning, Memory, and Cognition, 28*, 380–387. (4)

Malthouse, E., & Blattberg, R. (2005). Can we predict customer lifetime value? *Journal of Interactive Marketing, 19*, 2–16. (36)

Mandler, G. (1980). Recognizing: The judgment of previous occurrence. *Psychological Review, 87*, 252–271. (23)

Marchetti, K. (1998). The evolution of multiple male traits in the yellow-browed leaf warbler. *Animal Behavior, 55*, 361–376. (5)

Marewski, J. N., Gaissmaier, W., Dieckmann, A., Schooler, L. J., & Gigerenzer, G. (2005, August). *Ignorance-based reasoning? Applying the recognition heuristic to elections.* Paper presented at the 20th Biennial Conference on Subjective Probability, Utility and Decision Making, Stockholm, Sweden. (23, 24, 31)

Marewski, J. N., Gaissmaier, W., Schooler, L. J., Goldstein, D. G., & Gigerenzer, G. (2010). From recognition to decisions: Extending and testing recognition-based models for multi-alternative inference. *Psychonomic Bulletin and Review, 17*, 287–309. (1, 24)

Marewski, J. N., & Schooler, L. J.(2010). *Cognitive niches: An ecological model of emergent strategy selection.* Unpublished manuscript. (1, 26)

Marjoribanks, K. (1988). Sibling, family environment and ability correlates of adolescents' aspirations: Ethnic group differences. *Journal of Biosocial Science, 20,* 203–209. (35)

Marjoribanks, K. (1989). Ethnicity, sibling, and family correlates of young adults' status attainment: A follow-up study. *Social Biology, 36,* 23–31. (35)

Marjoribanks, K. (1991). The sibling resource dilution theory: An analysis. *The Journal of Psychology, 125,* 337–346. (35)

Markowitz, H. M. (1952). Portfolio selection. *Journal of Finance, 7,* 77–91. (34)

Markowitz, H. M. (1952). The utility of wealth. *Journal of Political Economy, 60,* 151–158. (7)

Markowitz, H. M. (1956). The optimization of a quadratic function subject to linear constraints. *Naval Research Logistics Quarterly, 3,* 111–133. (34)

Markowitz, H. M. (1959). *Portfolio selection: Efficient diversification of investments.* New York: Wiley. (34)

Marley, A. A. J., & Luce, R. D. (2005). Independence properties vis-à-vis several utility representations. *Theory and Decision, 58,* 77–143. (8)

Marr, D. (1982). *Vision.* San Francisco: Freeman. (5, 14)

Martignon, L. (2001). Comparing fast and frugal heuristics and optimal models. In G. Gigerenzer & R. Selten (Eds.), *Bounded rationality: The adaptive toolbox* (pp. 147–171). Cambridge, MA: MIT Press. (19)

Martignon, L., & Hoffrage, U. (1999). Why does one-reason decision making work? A case study in ecological rationality. In G. Gigerenzer, P. M. Todd, & the ABC Research Group, *Simple heuristics that make us smart* (pp. 119–140). New York: Oxford University Press. (1, 6, 12, 13, 14, 17, 18, 19, 29)

Martignon, L., & Hoffrage, U. (2002). Fast, frugal, and fit: Simple heuristics for paired comparison. *Theory and Decision, 52,* 29–71. (1, 5, 7, 8, 12, 13, 14, 17, 21, 32)

Martignon, L., Katsikopoulos, K. V., & Woike, J. (2008). Categorization with limited resources: A family of simple heuristics. *Journal of Mathematical Psychology, 52,* 352–361. (1, 6)

Martignon, L., & Laskey, K. B. (1999). Bayesian benchmarks for fast and frugal heuristics. In G. Gigerenzer, P. M. Todd, & the ABC Research Group, *Simple heuristics that make us smart* (pp. 169–188). New York: Oxford University Press. (5, 10, 11)

Martignon, L., & Schmitt, M. (1999). Simplicity and robustness of fast and frugal heuristics. *Minds and machines, 9,* 565–593. (12)

Martignon, L., Vitouch, O., Takezawa, M., & Forster, M. (2003). Naïve and yet enlightened: From natural frequencies to fast and frugal decision trees. In D. Hardman & L. Macchi (Eds.), *Thinking: Psychological perspectives on reasoning, judgment, and decision making* (pp. 189–211). Chichester, UK: Wiley. (8, 14)

Mata, R., Schooler, L. J., & Rieskamp, J. (2007). The aging decision maker: Cognitive aging and the adaptive selection of decision strategies. *Psychology and Aging, 22,* 796–810. (9, 24, 30)

Mather, M. (2006). A review of decision making processes: Weighing the risks and benefits of aging. In L. L. Carstensen & C. R. Hartel (Eds.), *When I'm 64* (pp. 145–173). Washington, DC: National Academy Press. (22)

Matheson, D. (2006). Bounded rationality, epistemic externalism and the enlightenment picture of cognitive virtue. In R. Stainton (Ed.), *Contemporary debates in cognitive science* (pp. 134–144). Oxford, UK: Blackwell. (9)

Maynard Smith, J. (1982). *Evolution and the theory of games.* Cambridge, UK: Cambridge University Press. (5)

McBeath, M. K., Shaffer, D. M., & Kaiser, M. K. (1995a). How baseball outfielders determine where to run to catch fly balls. *Science, 268,* 569–573. (33)

McBeath, M. K., Shaffer, D. M., & Kaiser, M. K. (1995b). Play ball! *Science, 268,* 1683–1685. (33)

McBeath, M. K., Shaffer, D. M., & Kaiser, M. K. (1996). On catching fly balls. *Science, 273,* 258–260. (33)

McBeath, M. K., Shaffer, D. M., & Sugar, T. G. (2002). Catching baseball pop flies: Individual differences in aggressiveness and handedness. *Abstracts of the Psychonomic Society, 7,* 103. (33)

McBeath, M. K., Shaffer, D. M., Sugar, T. G., & Roy, W. L. (2002). *What is a straight line?: Support for the linear optical trajectory heuristic for interception of balls in flight.* Manuscript submitted for publication. (33)

McClelland, A. G. R., & Bolger, F. (1994). The calibration of subjective probabilities: Theories and models 1980–1994. In G. Wright & P. Ayton, *Subjective probability* (pp. 453–482). New York: Wiley. (2, 17)

McClennen, E. E. (1990). *Rationality and dynamic choice.* Cambridge, UK: Cambridge University Press. (2)

McCloskey, D. N. (1985). *The rhetoric of economics.* Madison: University of Wisconsin Press. (2)

McCloskey, M., & Zaragoza, M. (1985). Misleading postevent information and memory for events: Arguments and evidence against memory impairment hypotheses. *Journal of Experimental Psychology: General, 114,* 1–6. (10)

McCloy, R., Beaman, C. P., Frosch, A., & Goddard, K. (2010). Fast and frugal framing effects? *Journal of Experimental Psychology: Learning, Memory, and Cognition, 36,* 1043–1052. (16)

McCloy, R., Beaman, C. P., & Smith, P. T. (2008). The relative success of recognition-based inference in multichoice decisions. *Cognitive Science, 32,* 1037–1048. (32)

McCrae, R. R., & Costa, P. T., Jr. (1987). Validation of the five-factor model of personality across instruments and observers. *Journal of Personality and Social Psychology, 52,* 81–90. (35)

McDonald, G. C., & Schwing, R. C. (1973). Instabilities of regression estimated relating air pollution to mortality. *Technometrics, 15,* 463–482. (21)

McElree, B., Dolan, P. O., & Jacoby, L. L. (1999). Isolating the contributions of familiarity and source information to item recognition: A time course analysis. *Journal of Experimental Psychology: Learning, Memory, and Cognition, 25,* 563–582. (23)

McGeoch, J. A. (1932). Forgetting and the law of disuse. *Psychological Review, 39,* 352–370. (4)

McGinley, M. A., & Charnov, E. L. (1988). Multiple resources and the optimal balance between size and number of offspring. *Evolutionary Ecology, 2,* 77–84. (35)

McGrath, R. E. (2008). Predictor combination in binary decision-making situations. *Psychological Assessment, 20,* 195–205. (13)

McHale, S. M., & Pawletko, T. M. (1992). Differential treatment of siblings in two family contexts. *Child Development, 63,* 68–81. (35)

McKenna, P., & Warrington, E. K. (1980). Testing for nominal dysphasia. *Journal of Neurology, Neurosurgery and Psychiatry, 43,* 781–788. (3)

McKenzie, C. R. M., Liersch, M. J., & Finkelstein, S. R. (2006). Recommendations implicit in policy defaults. *Psychological Science, 17,* 414–420. (37)

McLeod, P., & Dienes, Z. (1993). Running to catch the ball. *Nature, 362,* 23. (33)

McLeod, P., & Dienes, Z. (1996). Do fielders know where to go to catch the ball or only how to get there? *Journal of Experimental Psychology: Human Perception and Performance, 22,* 531–543. (5, 32, 33)

McLeod, P., Reed, N., & Dienes, Z. (2001). Toward a unified fielder theory: What we do not yet know about how people run to catch a ball. *Journal of Experimental Psychology: Human Perception and Performance, 27,* 1347–1355. (33)

McNamara, J. M., & Houston, A. I. (1985). Optimal foraging and learning. *Journal of Theoretical Biology, 117,* 231–249. (5)

McNamara, J. M., & Houston, A. I. (1987a). Partial preferences and foraging. *Animal Behavior, 35,* 1084–1099. (5)

McNamara, J. M., & Houston, A. I. (1987b). Memory and the efficient use of information. *Journal of Theoretical Biology, 125,* 385–395. (5)

McNamara, J. M., & Houston, A. I. (2009). Integrating function and mechanism. *Trends in Ecology and Evolution, 24,* 670–675. (5)

Medin, D. L., Altom, M. W., & Murphy, T. D. (1984). Given versus induced category representations: Use of prototype and exemplar information in classification. *Journal of Experimental Psychology: Learning, Memory, and Cognition, 10,* 333–352. (11)

Medin, D. L., & Schaffer, M. M. (1978). Context theory of classification learning. *Psychological Review, 85,* 207–238. (11, 14, 39)

Meehl, P. E. (1954). *Clinical versus statistical prediction: A theoretical analysis and a review of the evidence.* Minnesota: University of Minnesota Press. (13, 29)

Meehl, P. E., & Rosen, A. (1955). Antecedent probability and the efficiency of psychometric signs, patterns or cutting scores. *Psychological Bulletin, 52,* 194–216. (29)

Mehran, S., Dumais, S., Heckerman, D., & Horvitz, E. (1998). *A Bayesian approach to filtering junk e-mail.* AAAI-98 Workshop on Learning for Text Categorization. (39)

Mekos, D., Hetherington, E. M., & Reiss, D. (1996). Sibling differences in problem behavior and parental treatment in nondivorced and remarried families. *Child Development, 67,* 2148–2165. (35)

Mellers, B. A. (2000). Choice and the relative pleasure of consequences. *Psychological Bulletin, 126,* 910–924. (7)

Mellers, B. A., & Biagini, K. (1994). Similarity and choice. *Psychological Review, 101*, 505–518. (7)

Mellers, B. A., Chang, S., Birnbaum, M. H., & Ordòñez, L. D. (1992). Preferences, prices, and ratings in risky decision making. *Journal of Experimental Psychology: Human Perception and Performance, 18*, 347–361. (7)

Memmel, C. (2003). Performance hypothesis testing with the sharpe ratio. *Finance Letters, 1*, 21–23. (34)

Menger, C. (1990). *Grundsätze der Volkswirtschaftslehre* [Principles of economics]. Düsseldorf, Germany: Wirtschaft und Finanzen. (Original work published 1871) (7)

Menzel, R. (2001). Searching for the memory trace in a mini-brain, the honeybee. *Learning and Memory, 8*, 53–62. (5)

Menzel, R., & Giurfa, M. (2001). Cognitive architecture of a mini-brain: The honeybee. *Trends in Cognitive Sciences, 5*, 62–71. (5)

Menzel, R., Greggers, U., & Hammer, M. (1993). Functional organization of appetitive learning and memory in a generalist pollinator the honey bee. In D. R. Papaj & A. C. Lewis (Eds.), *Insect learning: Ecological and evolutionary perspectives* (pp. 79–125). New York: Chapman and Hall. (5)

Messick, D. M. (1993). Equality as a decision heuristic. In B. A. Mellers & J. Baron (Eds.), *Psychological perspectives on justice* (pp. 11–31). New York: Cambridge University Press. (9, 35)

Messick, D. M., & Schell, T. (1992). Evidence for an equality heuristic in social decision making. *Acta Psychologica, 80*, 311–323. (35)

Metz, C. E., Shen, J. H., Wang, P. L., & Kronman, H. B. (1994). *ROCFIT software, Technical Report.* Chicago: University of Chicago. (26)

Michaels, C. F., & Oudejans, R. R. D. (1992). The optics and actions of catching fly balls: Zeroing out optical acceleration. *Ecological Psychology, 4*, 199–222. (33)

Michaud, R. O. (1989). The markowitz optimization enigma: Is optimized optimal? *Financial Analysts Journal, 45*, 31–42. (34)

Michaud, R. O. (1998). *Efficient asset management.* Boston, MA: Harvard Business School Press. (34)

Miezin, F. M., Maccotta, L., Ollinger, J. M., Petersen, S. E., & Buckner, R. L. (2000). Characterizing the hemodynamic response: Effects of presentation rate, sampling procedure, and the possibility of ordering brain activity based on relative timing. *Neuroimage, 11*, 735–759. (25)

Milgram, S. (1974). *Obedience to authority: An experimental view.* New York: Harper and Row. (Introduction, 9)

Miller, G. F., & Todd, P. M. (1998). Mate choice turns cognitive. *Trends in Cognitive Sciences, 2*, 190–98. (40)

Mischel, W. (1968). *Personality and assessment.* New York: Wiley. (9)

Mischel, W. (December, 2008). The toothbrush problem. *Observer, 21.* (4)

Mischel, W., & Shoda, Y. (1995). A cognitive-affective system theory of personality: Reconceptualizing situations, dispositions, dynamics, and invariance in personality structure. *Psychological Review, 102*, 246–268. (24)

Mitchell, A. (2005). Who knows the relative worth of customers? *Precision Marketing, 17*, 12. (36)

Mitchell, T. M. (1997). *Machine learning.* New York: McGraw-Hill. (14)

Modin, B. (2002). Birth order and mortality: A lifelong follow-up of 14,200 boys and girls born in early 20th century Sweden. *Social Science & Medicine, 54*, 1051–1064. (35)

Moll, J., de Oliveira-Souza, R., Eslinger, P. J., Bramati, I. E., Mourao-Miranda, J., Andreiuolo, P. A., et al. (2002). The neural correlates of moral sensitivity: A functional magnetic resonance imaging investigation of basic and moral emotions. *The Journal of Neuroscience, 22*, 2730–2736. (25)

Montgomery, H. (1983). Decision rules and the search for a dominance structure: Towards a process model of decision making. In P. C. Humphreys, O. Svenson, & A. Vari (Eds.), *Analyzing and aiding decision processes* (pp. 343–369). Amsterdam: North-Holland. (13, 18)

Montgomery, H., & Willén, H. (1999). Decision making and action: The search for good structure. In P. Juslin & H. Montgomery (Eds.), *Judgment and decision making: Neo-Brunswikian and process-tracing approaches* (pp.147–174). Mahwah, NJ: LEA. (18)

Moon, P., & Martin, A. (1990). Better heuristics for economic search: Experimental and simulation evidence. *Journal of Behavioral Decision Making, 3*, 175–193. (40)

MORI. (1996). *Green energy: A survey of public opinions by MORI.* London: The Parliamentary Renewable and Sustainable Energy Group. (37)

Morrison, D. F. (1990). *Multivariate statistical methods.* New York: McGraw-Hill. (34)

Morwitz, V. G., & Schmittlein, D. C. (1998). Testing new direct marketing offerings: The interplay of management judgment and statistical models. *Management Science, 44,* 610–628. (36)

Mosteller, F., & Nogee, P. (1951). An experimental measurement of utility. *The Journal of Political Economy, 59,* 371–404. (7)

Moyer, R. S., & Landauer, T. K. (1967). Time required for judgements of numerical inequality. *Nature, 215,* 1519–1520. (5)

Muchinsky, P. M., & Dudycha, A. L. (1975). Human inference behavior in abstract and meaningful environments. *Organizational Behavior and Human Performance, 13,* 377–391. (13)

Mugford, S. T., Mallon, E. B., & Franks, N. R. (2001). The accuracy of Buffon's needle: A rule of thumb used by ants to estimate area. *Behavioral Ecology, 12,* 655–658. (1, 5)

Mulhern, F. (1999). Customer profitability analysis: Measurement, concentration, and research directions. *Journal of Interactive Marketing, 13,* 25–40. (36)

Müller, M., & Wehner, R. (1988). Path integration in desert ants, *Cataglyphis fortis. Proceedings of the National Academy of Sciences, USA, 85,* 5287–5290. (5)

Murdock, B. B. (1997). Context and mediators in a theory of distributed associative memory (TODAM2). *Psychological Review, 104,* 839–862. (15)

Musch, J., Brockhaus, R., & Bröder, A. (2002). Ein Inventar zur Erfassung von zwei Faktoren sozialer Erwünschtheit. *Diagnostica, 48,* 121–129. (17)

Myung, I. J., Forster, M., & Browne, M. W. (Eds.). (2000). A special issue on model selection. *Journal of Mathematical Psychology, 44,* 1–231. (14)

Myung, I. J., & Pitt, M. A. (1997). Applying Occam's razor in modelling cognition: A Bayesian approach. *Psychonomic Bulletin & Review, 4,* 79–95. (11)

Nagel, T. (1993). Moral luck. In D. Statman (Ed.), *Moral luck* (pp. 57–71). Albany, NY: State University of New York Press. (9)

Naghavi, H. R., & Nyberg, L. (2005). Common fronto-parietal activity in attention, memory, and consciousness: Shared demands on integration? *Consciousness and Cognition, 14,* 390–425. (25)

Nakata, K., Ushimaru, A., & Watanabe, T. (2003). Using past experience in web relocation decisions enhances the foraging efficiency of the spider *Cyclosa argenteoalba. Journal of Insect Behavior, 16,* 371–380. (5)

Narvaez, D., & Lapsley, D. (2005). The psychological foundations of everyday morality and moral expertise. In D. Lapsley & C. Power (Eds.), *Character psychology and character education* (pp. 140–165). Notre Dame, IN: University of Notre Dame Press. (9)

Narveson, J. (2004). Maximizing life on a budget; or, if you would maximize, then satisfice! In M. Byron (Ed.), *Satisficing and maximizing: Moral theorists on practical reason* (pp. 59–70). Cambridge, UK: Cambridge University Press. (9)

Nee, C., & Meenaghan, A. (2006). Expert decision making in burglars. *British Journal of Criminology, 46,* 935–949. (30)

Nee, C., & Taylor, M. (2000). Examining burglars' target selection: Interview, experiment, or ethnomethodology? *Psychology, Crime, and Law, 6,* 45–59. (30)

Neiderhiser, J. M., Reiss, D., Hetherington, E. M., & Plomin, R. (1999). Relationships between parenting and adolescent adjustment over time: Genetic and environmental contributions. *Developmental Psychology, 35,* 680–692. (35)

Neilson, W., & Stowe, J. (2002). A further examination of cumulative prospect theory parameterizations. *The Journal of Risk and Uncertainty, 24,* 31–46. (8)

Neiman, S. (2008). *Moral clarity: A guide for grownup idealists.* New York: Harcourt. (9)

Neisser, U. (1981). John Dean's memory: A case study. *Cognition, 9,* 1–22. (10)

Nelder, J. A., & Mead, R. (1965). A simplex method for function minimization. *Computer Journal, 7,* 308–313. (11)

Nellen, S. (2003). *The use of the "Take The Best" heuristic under different conditions, modeled with ACT-R.* Paper presented at the Fifth International Conference on Cognitive Modeling, Bamberg, Germany. (4)

Nelson, T. O. (2003). Relevance of unjustified strong assumptions when utilizing signal detection theory. *Behavioral & Brain Sciences, 26,* 351. (15)

Newell, A. (1973). You can't play 20 questions with nature and win: Projective comments on the papers of this symposium. In W. C. Chase (Ed.), *Visual information processing* (pp. 283–308). New York: Academic Press. (4)

Newell, B. R. (2005). Re-visions of rationality? *Trends in Cognitive Sciences, 9,* 11–15. (1, 17, 19, 23, 26)

Newell, B. R., & Fernandez, D. (2006). On the binary quality of recognition and the inconsequentiality of further knowledge: Two critical tests of the recognition heuristic. *Journal of Behavioral Decision Making, 19,* 333–346. (24, 26, 31)

Newell, B. R., Lagnado, D. A., & Shanks, D. R. (2007). *Straight choices: The psychology of decision making.* Hove, UK: Psychology Press. (21)

Newell, B. R., Rakow, T., Weston, N. J., & Shanks, D. R. (2004). Search strategies in decision making: The success of success. *Journal of Behavioral Decision Making, 17,* 117–137. (17, 18, 19, 21, 24, 36)

Newell, B. R., & Shanks, D. R. (2003). Take the best or look at the rest? Factors influencing "one-reason" decision making. *Journal of Experimental Psychology: Learning, Memory, and Cognition, 29,* 53–65. (1, 5, 11, 13, 14, 17, 18, 19, 21, 22, 23, 24, 36)

Newell, B. R., & Shanks, D. R. (2004). On the role of recognition in decision making. *Journal of Experimental Psychology: Learning, Memory, and Cognition, 30,* 923–935. (3, 19, 23, 24, 31)

Newell, B. R., Weston, N. J., & Shanks, D. R. (2003). Empirical tests of a fast-and-frugal heuristic: Not everyone "takes-the-best." *Organizational Behavior and Human Decision Processes, 91,* 82–96. (1, 7, 11, 13, 14, 17, 18, 24, 36)

Newport, E. L. (1990). Maturational constraints on language learning. *Cognitive Science, 14,* 11–28. (1)

Newstead, S. E. (2000). What is an ecologically rational heuristic? *Behavioral and Brain Sciences, 23,* 759–760. (17)

Nicholas, S., Kershaw, C., & Walker, A. (2007). *Crime in England and Wales 2006/07.* London: Home Office. (30)

Nichols, T., Brett, M., Andersson, J., Wager, T., & Poline, J. B. (2005). Valid conjunction inference with the minimum statistic. *Neuroimage, 25,* 653–660. (25)

Nickerson, R. S. (2003). *Psychology and environmental change.* Mahwah, NJ: Lawrence Erlbaum Associates. (37)

Nisbett, R. E., & Ross, L. (1980). *Human inference: Strategies and shortcomings of social judgment.* Englewood Cliffs, NJ: Prentice-Hall. (28)

Nordic Energy Regulators (2005). *Supplier switching in the Nordic countries: Current practices and recommendations for the future development.* Available from http://www.energiamarkkinavirasto.fi (37)

Norris, D. G. (2000). Reduced power multislice MDEFT imaging. *Journal of Magnetic Resonance Imaging, 11,* 445–451. (25)

Northoff, G., & Bermpohl, F. (2004). Cortical midline structures and the self. *Trends in Cognitive Sciences, 8,* 102–107. (25)

Nosofsky, R. M. (1984). Choice, similarity, and the context theory of classification. *Journal of Experimental Psychology: Learning, Memory, and Cognition, 10,* 104–114. (14)

Nosofsky, R. M. (1986). Attention, similarity, and the identification-categorization relationship. *Journal of Experimental Psychology: General, 115,* 39–57. (11)

Nosofsky, R. M. (1988). Similarity, frequency, and category representations. *Journal of Experimental Psychology: Learning, Memory, and Cognition, 14,* 54–65. (11)

Nosofsky, R. M. (1990). Relations between exemplar similarity and likelihood models of classification. *Journal of Mathematical Psychology, 34,* 393–418. (1)

Nosofsky, R. M., & Bergert, F. B. (2007). Limitations of exemplar models of multi-attribute probabilistic inference. *Journal of Experimental Psychology: Learning, Memory, and Cognition, 33,* 999–1019. (1, 8, 19, 21)

Nosofsky, R. M., & Johansen, M. K. (2000). Exemplar-based accounts of "multiple-system" phenomena in perceptual categorization. *Psychonomic Bulletin & Review, 7,* 375–402. (11)

Nosofsky, R. M., Kruschke, J. K., & McKinley, S. C. (1992). Combining exemplar-based category representations and connectionist learning rules. *Journal of Experimental Psychology: Learning, Memory, and Cognition, 18,* 211–233. (11)

Nosofsky, R. M., & Palmeri, T. J. (1997). An exemplar-based random-walk model of speeded classification. *Psychological Review, 104,* 266–300. (14)

Nosofsky, R. M., & Palmeri, T. J. (1998). A rule-plus-exception model for classifying objects in continuous-dimension spaces. *Psychonomic Bulletin and Review, 5,* 345–369. (14)

Oaksford, M. (2000). Speed, frugality, and the empirical basis of take-the-best. *Behavioral and Brain Sciences, 23,* 760–761. (17)

Oaksford, M., & Chater, N. (1998). *Rational models of cognition.* Oxford, UK: Oxford University Press. (1)

Oaksford, M., & Chater, N. (2007). *Bayesian rationality: The probabilistic approach to human reasoning.* Oxford, UK: Oxford University Press. (32)

O'Brien, D. P. (1993). Mental logic and human irrationality: We can put a man on the moon, so why can't we solve those logical-reasoning problems? In K. I. Manktelow & D. E. Over (Eds.), *Rationality: Psychological and philosophical perspectives* (pp. 110–135). London: Routledge. (17)

Ochsner, K. N., Knierim, K., Ludlow, D. H., Hanelin, J., Ramachandran, T., Glover, G., et al. (2004). Reflecting upon feelings: An fMRI study of neural systems supporting the attribution of emotion to self and other. *Journal of Cognitive Neuroscience, 16,* 1746–1772. (25)

O'Connor, M., Remus, W., & Lim, K. (2005). Improving judgmental forecasts with judgmental bootstrapping and task feedback support. *Journal of Behavioral Decision Making, 18,* 246–260. (13)

Ogilvie, J. R., & Schmitt, N. (1979). Situational influences on linear and nonlinear use of information. *Organizational Behavior and Human Performance, 23,* 292–306. (28)

Ohtsubo, Y., & Kameda, T. (1998). The function of equality heuristic in distributive bargaining: Negotiated allocation of costs and benefits in a demand revelation context. *Journal of Experimental Social Psychology, 34,* 90–108. (35)

Olberg, R. M., Worthington, A. H., & Venator, K. R. (2000). Prey pursuit and interception in dragonflies. *Journal of Comparative Physiology A, 186,* 155–162. (33)

Oppenheimer, D. M. (2003). Not so fast! (and not so frugal!): Rethinking the recognition heuristic. *Cognition, 90,* B1–B9. (3, 23, 24, 25, 26)

Oppenheimer, D. M. (2004). Spontaneous discounting of availability in frequency judgment tasks. *Psychological Science, 15,* 100–105. (23, 24)

Oppenheimer, V. K. (1988). A theory of marriage timing. *American Journal of Sociology, 94,* 563–591. (40)

Organisation for Economic Co-operation and Development/International Energy Agency. (2006). *World energy outlook 2006.* International Energy Agency. (37)

Oskarsson, A. T., Van Boven, L., McClelland, G. H., & Hastie, R. (2009). What's next? Judging sequences of binary events. *Psychological Bulletin, 135,* 262–285. (32)

Oudejans, R. R. D., Michaels, C. F., Bakker, F. C., & Davids, K. (1999). Shedding some light on catching in the dark: Perceptual mechanisms for catching fly balls. *Journal of Experimental Psychology: Human Perception and Performance, 25,* 531–542. (5)

Pachur, T. (2010). Recognition-based inference: When is less more in the real world? *Psychonomic Bulletin and Review, 17,* 589–598. (16, 32)

Pachur, T., & Biele, G. (2007). Forecasting from ignorance: The use and usefulness of recognition in lay predictions of sports events. *Acta Psychologica, 125,* 99–116. (16, 23, 24, 26, 31, 32)

Pachur, T., Bröder, A., & Marewski, J. N. (2008). The recognition heuristic in memory-based inference: Is recognition a non-compensatory cue? *Journal of Behavioral Decision Making, 21,* 183–210. (1, 26)

Pachur, T., & Hertwig, R. (2006). On the psychology of the recognition heuristic: Retrieval primacy as a key determinant of its use. *Journal of Experimental Psychology: Learning, Memory, and Cognition, 32,* 983–1002. (24, 25, 26)

Pachur, T., Mata, R., & Schooler, L. J. (2009). Cognitive aging and the adaptive use of recognition in decision making. *Psychology and Aging, 24,* 901–915. (22, 23, 24)

Pachur, T., Todd, P. M., Gigerenzer, G., Schooler, L. J., & Goldstein, D. G. (in press). When is the recognition heuristic an adaptive tool? In: P. Todd, G. Gigerenzer, & the ABC Research Group, *Ecological rationality: Intelligence in the world.* New York: Oxford University Press. (25)

Packer, H. L. (1968). *The limits of the criminal sanction.* Stanford, CA: Stanford University Press. (28)

Page, E. B., & Grandon, G. M. (1979). Family configuration and mental ability: Two theories contrasted with U.S. data. *American Educational Research Journal, 16,* 257–272. (35)

Parducci, A. (1965). Category judgment: A range-frequency model. *Psychological Review, 72,* 407–418. (8)

Park, C. W., Youl Jun, S., & MacInnis, D. J. (2000). Choosing what I want versus rejecting what I do not want: An application of decision framing to product option choice decisions. *Journal of Marketing Research, 43,* 187–202. (37)

Partan, S., & Marler, P. (1999). Communication goes multimodal. *Science, 283,* 1272–1273. (5)

Pascal, B. (1962). *Pensées.* Paris: Editions du Seuil. (Original work published 1669) (9)

Pástor, L. (2000). Portfolio selection and asset pricing models. *Journal of Finance, 55,* 179–223. (34)

Pástor, L., & Stambaugh, R. F. (2000). Comparing asset pricing models: An investment perspective. *Journal of Financial Economics, 56,* 335–381. (34)

Patricelli, G. L., Uy, J. A. C., & Borgia, G. (2003). Multiple male traits interact: Attractive bower decorations facilitate attractive behavioural displays in satin bowerbirds. *Proceedings of the Royal Society of London, Series B: Biological Sciences, 270,* 2389–2395. (5)

Paulhus, D. L. (1984). Two-component models of socially desirable responding. *Journal of Personality and Social Psychology, 46,* 598–609. (17)

Paulhus, D. L., Trapnell, P. D., & Chen, D. (1999). Birth order effects on personality and achievement within families. *Psychological Science, 10,* 482–488. (35)

Payne, J. W. (1973). Alternative approaches to decision making under risk: Moments vs. risk dimensions. *Psychological Bulletin, 80,* 439–453. (7)

Payne, J. W. (1976). Task complexity and contingent processing in decision making: An information search and protocol analysis. *Organizational Behavior and Human Performance, 16,* 366–387. (17, 18, 22)

Payne, J. W., & Bettman, J. R. (2001). Preferential choice and adaptive strategy use. In G. Gigerenzer & R. Selten (Eds.), *Bounded rationality: The adaptive toolbox* (pp. 123–145). Cambridge, MA: MIT Press. (19)

Payne, J. W., Bettman, J. R., & Johnson, E. J. (1988). Adaptive strategy selection in decision making. *Journal of Experimental Psychology: Learning, Memory, and Cognition, 14,* 534–552. (11, 17, 19, 22)

Payne, J. W., Bettman, J. R., & Johnson, E. J. (1992). Behavioral decision research: A constructive processing perspective. *Annual Review of Psychology, 43,* 87–131. (37)

Payne, J. W., Bettman, J. R., & Johnson, E. J. (1993). *The adaptive decision maker.* New York: Cambridge University Press. (Introduction, 1, 2, 3, 5, 7, 8, 9, 11, 13, 14, 17, 19, 21, 22, 23, 26, 28, 35)

Payne, J. W., Bettman, J. R., & Luce, M. F. (1996). When time is money: Decision behavior under opportunity-cost time pressure. *Organizational Behavior and Human Decision Processes, 66,* 131–152. (7)

Payne, J. W., & Braunstein, M. L. (1971). Preferences among gambles with equal underlying distributions. *Journal of Experimental Psychology, 87,* 13–18. (7)

Payne, R. W., & Preece, D. A. (1980). Identification keys and diagnostic tables: A review. *Journal of Royal Statistical Society A, 143,* 253–292. (14)

Payne, S. J., Richardson, J., & Howes, A. (2000). Strategic use of familiarity in display-based problem solving. *Journal of Experimental Psychology: Learning, Memory, and Cognition, 26,* 1685–1701. (23)

Pearl, L. (1988). *Probabilistic reasoning in intelligent systems.* San Francisco: Morgan Kaufmann. (6)

Pennington, D. C. (1981). The British fireman's strike of 1977/78: An investigation of judgments in foresight and hindsight. *British Journal of Social Psychology, 20,* 89–96. (10)

Perlich, C., Provost, F., & Simonoff, J. S. (2003). Tree-induction vs. logistic regression: A learning curve analysis. *Journal of Machine Learning Research, 4,* 211–255. (1)

Persijn, G. (1997). Public education and organ donation. *Transplantation Proceedings, 29,* 1614–1617. (9)

Peters, E., Finucane, M. L., MacGregor, D. G., & Slovic, P. (2000). The bearable lightness of aging: Judgment and decision processes in older adults. In National Research Council, P. C. Stern, & L. L. Carstensen (Eds.), *The aging mind: Opportunities in cognitive research* (Appendix C, pp. 144–165). Washington, DC: National Academy Press. (22)

Peterson, S., & Simon, T. J. (2000). Computational evidence for the subitizing phenomenon as an emergent property of the human cognitive architecture. *Cognitive Science, 24,* 93–122. (4)

Petrie, M., & Halliday, T. (1994). Experimental and natural changes in the peacock's (Pavo cristatus) train can affect mating success. *Behavioral Ecology and Sociobiology, 35,* 213–217. (1)

Pfanzagl, J. (1974). *Allgemeine Methodenlehre der Statistik.* Berlin, Germany: De Gruyter. (24)

Phelps, R. H., & Shanteau, J. (1978). Livestock judges: How much information can an expert use? *Organizational Behavior and Human Performance, 21,* 209–219. (28)

Pichert, D., & Katsikopoulos, K. V. (2008). Green defaults: Information presentation and pro-environmental behavior. *Journal of Environmental Psychology, 28,* 63–73. (1, 9)

Pippin, R. B. (2009). Natural & normative. *Daedalus, Summer 2009,* 35–43. (9)

Pitt, M. A., & Myung, I. J. (2002). When a good fit can be bad. *Trends in Cognitive Sciences, 6,* 421–425. (11)

Pitt, M. A., Myung, I. J., & Zhang, S. (2002). Toward a method of selecting among computational models of cognition. *Psychological Review, 109,* 472–491. (11, 39)

Pitz, G. F., & Sachs, N. J. (1984). Judgment and decision: Theory and applications. *Annual Review of Psychology, 35,* 139–163. (11)

Plomin, R., & Daniels, D. (1987). Why are children in the same family so different from one another? *Behavioral and Brain Sciences, 10,* 1–16. (35)

Pohl, R. (2006). Empirical tests of the recognition heuristic. *Journal of Behavioral Decision Making, 19,* 251–271. (1, 3, 15, 16, 23, 24, 25, 26, 31)

Pohl, R. F, & Eisenhauer, M. (1997). SARA: An associative model for anchoring and hindsight bias. In M. G. Shafto & P. Langley (Eds.), *Proceedings of the Nineteenth Annual Conference of the Cognitive Science Society* (p. 1103). Mahwah. NJ: Erlbaum. (10)

Pollack, H. N. (1995). Play ball! *Science, 268,* 1681. (33)

Popper, K. R. (1959). *The logic of scientific inquiry.* London: Hutchinson. (17)

Poses, R. M., Bekes, C., Winkler, R. L., Scott, E., & Copare, F. J. (1990). Are two (inexperienced) heads better than one (experienced) head? Averaging house officers' prognostic judgments for critically ill patients. *Archives of Internal Medicine, 150,* 1874–1878. (31)

Powell, B., & Steelman, L. C. (1989). The liability of having brothers: Paying for college and the sex composition of the family. *Sociology of Education, 62,* 134–147. (35)

Powell, B., & Steelman, L. C. (1993). The educational benefits of being spaced out: Sibship density and educational progress. *American Sociological Review, 58,* 367–381. (35)

Pozen, M. W., D'Agostino, R. B., & Mitchell, J. B. (1980). The usefulness of a predictive instrument to reduce inappropriate admissions to the coronary care unit. *Annals of Internal Medicine, 92,* 238–242. (14)

Pozen, M. W., D'Agostino, R. B., Selker, H. P., Sytkowski, P. A., & Hood, W. B. (1984). A predictive instrument to improve coronary-care-unit admission practices in acute ischemic heart disease. *New England Journal of Medicine, 310,* 1273–1278. (6)

Pratt, S. C., Mallon, E. B., Sumpter, D. J. T., & Franks, N. R. (2002). Quorum sensing, recruitment, and collective decision-making during colony emigration by the ant *Leptothorax albipennis. Behavioral Ecology and Sociobiology, 52,* 117–127. (5)

Prelec, D. (1998). The probability weighting function. *Econometrica, 66,* 497–527. (8)

Preston, M. G., & Baratta, P. (1948). An experimental study of the auction value of an uncertain outcome. *American Journal of Psychology, 61,* 183–193. (7)

Price, J. (1969). Personality differences within families: Comparisons of adult brothers and sisters. *Journal of Biosocial Science, 1,* 117–205. (35)

Prince, A., & Smolensky, P. (1991). *Notes on connectionism and harmony theory in linguistics.* Boulder, CO: University of Colorado, Department of Computer Science. (2)

Proctor, C. J., Broom, M., & Ruxton, G. D. (2001). Modelling antipredator vigilance and flight response in group foragers when warning signals are ambiguous. *Journal of Theoretical Biology, 211,* 409–417. (5)

PsycINFO. (2001). Norwood, MA: SilverPlatter International. (39)

Puto, C. P. (1987). The framing of buying decisions. *Journal of Consumer Research, 14,* 301–315. (37)

Quiggin, J. (1982). A theory of anticipated utility. *Journal of Economic Behavior and Organization, 3,* 323–343. (7)

Quinlan, J. R. (1993). *C4.5: Programs for machine learning.* San Mateo, CA: Morgan Kaufmann. (1, 5)

Raab, M., Gula, B., & Gigerenzer, G. (2009). *The hot hand exists and is used for allocation.* Manuscript submitted for publication. (32)

Raaijmakers, J. G. W. (2003). Spacing and repetition effects in human memory: Application of the SAM model. *Cognitive Science, 27,* 431–452. (4)

Raaijmakers, J. G. W., & Shiffrin, R. M. (2002). Models of memory. In H. Pashler & D. Medin (Eds.), *Stevens' Handbook of experimental psychology: Vol 2. Memory and cognitive processes* (pp. 43–76). New York: Wiley. (15)

Rachlinski, J. J. (1996). Gains, losses, and the psychology of litigation. *Southern California Law Review, 70,* 113–119. (7)

Raguso, R. A., & Willis, M. A. (2002). Synergy between visual and olfactory cues in nectar feeding by naïve hawkmoths, *Manduca sexta. Animal Behavior, 64,* 685–695. (5)

Rakow, T., Hinvest, N., Jackson, E., & Palmer, M. (2004). Simple heuristics from the adaptive toolbox: Can we perform the requisite learning? *Thinking and Reasoning, 10,* 1–29. (21)

Rakow, T., Newell, B. R. R., Fayers, K., & Hersby, M. (2005). Evaluating three criteria for establishing cue-search hierarchies in inferential judgment. *Journal of Experimental Psychology: Learning, Memory, and Cognition, 31,* 1088–1104. (11)

Ranganath, C., Yonelinas, A. P., Cohen, M. X., Dy, C. J., Tom, S. M., & D'Esposito, M. (2003). Dissociable correlates of recollection and familiarity within the medial temporal lobes. *Neuropsychologia, 42,* 2–13. (25)

Ratcliff, R., Clark, S. E., & Shiffrin, R. M. (1990). List-strength effect: Data and discussion. *Journal of Experimental Psychology: Learning, Memory, and Cognition, 16,* 163–178. (15)

Ratcliff, R., Gronlund, S. D., & Sheu, C. F. (1992). Testing global memory models using ROC curves. *Psychological Review, 99,* 518–535. (15)

Ratcliff, R., & McKoon, G. (1989). Similarity information versus relational information: Differences in the time course of retrieval. *Cognitive Psychology, 21,* 139–155. (23)

Ratcliff, R., Shiffrin, M. R., & Clark, S. E. (1990). List-strength: I. Data and discussion. *Journal of Experimental Psychology: Learning, Memory, and Cognition, 16,* 163–178. (4)

Ratcliff, R., & Smith, P. L. (2004). A comparison of sequential sampling models for two-choice reaction time. *Psychological Review, 111,* 333–367. (23)

Real, L. A. (1990a). Predator switching and the interpretation of animal choice behavior: The case for constrained optimization. In R. N. Hughes (Ed.), *Behavioural mechanisms of food selection* (Vol. G 20, pp. 1–21). Berlin, Germany: Springer. (5)

Real, L. (1990b). Search theory and mate choice. I. Models of single-sex discrimination. *American Naturalist, 136,* 376–404. (5)

Real, L. A. (1992). Information processing and the evolutionary ecology of cognitive architecture. *American Naturalist, 140,* S108–S145. (5)

Reber, R., Schwarz, N., & Winkielman, P. (2004). Processing fluency and aesthetic pleasure: Is beauty in the perceiver's processing experience? *Personality and Social Psychology Review, 8,* 364–382. (26)

Rechten, C., Avery, M., & Stevens, A. (1983). Optimal prey selection: Why do great tits show partial preferences? *Animal Behavior, 31,* 576–584. (5)

Regier, T. (1996). *The human semantic potential: Spatial language and constrained connectionism.* Cambridge, MA: MIT Press. (3)

Reichardt, W., & Poggio, T. (1976). Visual control of orientation behaviour in the fly. *Quarterly Reviews of Biophysics, 9,* 311–438. (33)

Reimer, T., & Hoffrage, U. (2003). Information aggregation in groups: The approach of simple group heuristics (SIGH). In R. Alterman & D. Kirsch (Eds.), *Proceedings of the Twenty-Fifth Annual Conference of the Cognitive Science Society* (pp. 982–987). Boston, MA: Cognitive Science Society. (27)

Reimer, T., & Katsikopoulos, K. V. (2004). The use of recognition in group decision-making. *Cognitive Science, 28,* 1009–1029. (5, 16, 23, 26)

Reinartz, W. J., & Kumar, V. (2000). On the profitability of long-life customers in a noncontractual setting: An empirical investigation and implications for marketing. *Journal of Marketing, 64,* 17–35. (36)

Reinartz, W. J., & Kumar, V. (2003). The impact of customer relationship characteristics on profitable lifetime duration. *Journal of Marketing, 67,* 77–99. (36)

Reiss, D., Hetherington, E. M., Plomin, R., Howe, G. W., Simmens, S. J., Henderson, S. H., et al. (1995). Genetic questions for environmental studies: Differential parenting of siblings and its association with depression and antisocial behavior in adolescents. *Archives of General Psychiatry, 52,* 925–936. (35)

Rengert, G., Piquero, A. R., & Jones, P. R. (1999). Distance decay re-examined. *Criminology, 37,* 427–445. (29)

Richardson, H. S. (2004). Satisficing: Not good enough. In M. Byron (Ed.), *Satisficing and maximizing: Moral theorists on practical reason* (pp. 106–130). Cambridge, UK: Cambridge University Press. (9)

Richter, J., Richter, G., Eisemann, M., & Mau, R. (1997). Sibship size, sibship position, parental rearing, and psychopathological manifestations in adults: Preliminary analysis. *Psychopathology, 30,* 155–162. (35)

Richter, T., & Späth, P. (2006). Recognition is used as one cue among others in judgment and decision making. *Journal of Experimental Psychology: Learning, Memory, and Cognition, 32,* 150–162. (1, 3, 23, 24, 26, 31)

Rieger, M. O., & Wang, M. (2008). What is behind the priority heuristic? A mathematical analysis and comment on Brandstätter, Gigerenzer, and Hertwig (2006). *Psychological Review, 115,* 274–280. (7)

Rieskamp, J. (1998). *Die Verwendung von Entscheidungsstrategien unter verschiedenen Bedingungen: Der Einfluß von Zeitdruck und Rechtfertigung.* [The use of decision strategies in different conditions: Influence of time pressure and accountability]. Unpublished diploma thesis, Technical University of Berlin, Germany. (17)

Rieskamp, J. (2006). Perspectives of probabilistic inferences: Reinforcement learning and an adaptive network compared. *Journal of Experimental Psychology. Learning, Memory, and Cognition, 32*, 1355–1370. (22, 36)

Rieskamp, J., Busemeyer, J. R., & Laine, T. H. (2003). How do people learn to allocate resources? Comparing two learning theories. *Journal of Experimental Psychology: Learning, Memory, and Cognition, 29*, 1066–1081. (11)

Rieskamp, J., Busemeyer, J. R., & Mellers, B. A. (2006). Extending the bounds of rationality: Evidence and theories of preferential choice. *Journal of Economic Literature, 44*, 631–661. (11)

Rieskamp, J., & Hoffrage, U. (1999). When do people use simple heuristics, and how can we tell? In G. Gigerenzer, P. M. Todd, & the ABC Research Group, *Simple heuristics that make us smart* (pp. 141–167). New York: Oxford University Press. (5, 7, 8, 11, 13, 17, 18, 19, 22, 24, 28, 36)

Rieskamp, J., & Hoffrage, U. (2008). Inferences under time pressure: How opportunity cost affect strategy selection. *Acta Psychologica, 127*, 258–276. (1, 11, 18, 21, 22)

Rieskamp, J., & Otto, P. E. (2006). SSL: A theory of how people learn to select strategies. *Journal of Experimental Psychology: General, 135*, 207–236. (1, 4, 5, 8, 9, 17, 19, 21, 22, 24, 26, 30, 36)

Riggle, E. D. B., & Johnson, M. M. S. (1996). Age differences in political decision making: Strategies for evaluating political candidates. *Political Behavior, 18*, 99–118. (22)

Rissanen, J. (1978). Modeling by shortest data description. *Automatica, 14*, 465–471. (19)

Rivest, R. J. (1987). Learning decision lists. *Machine Learning, 2*, 229–246. (12)

Robert Koch Institute (2001). *Epidemiologisches Bulletin* [Epidemiological Bulletin] (Vol. 20). Berlin, Germany: Author. (23)

Roberts, P. (2005). *The end of oil: On the edge of a perilous new world.* New York: Bloomsbury. (37)

Roberts, S., & Pashler, H. (2000). How persuasive is a good fit? A comment on theory testing. *Psychological Review, 107*, 358–367. (1, 7, 8, 11, 17, 39)

Rodgers, J. L. (2001). What causes birth order-intelligence patterns? The admixture hypoth-

esis, revived. *American Psychologist, 56*, 505–510. (35)

Rodgers, J. L., Cleveland, H. H., van den Oord, E., & Rowe, D. C. (2000). Resolving the debate over birth order, family size, and intelligence. *American Psychologist, 55*, 599–612. (35)

Roe, B., Teisl, M. F., Levy, A., & Russell, M. (2001). US consumers' willingness to pay for green electricity. *Energy Policy, 29*, 917–925. (37)

Roe, B., Teisl, M. F., Rong, H., & Levy, A. S. (2001). Characteristics of consumer preferred labeling policies: Experimental evidence from price and environmental disclosure for deregulated electricity service. *Journal of Consumer Affairs, 35*, 1–2. (37)

Rohde, P. A., Andres, A. A., Atzwanger, K., Butovskaya, M., Lampert, A., Mysterud, L., et al. (2002). *Perceived parental favoritism, closeness to kin, and the rebel of the family: The effects of birth order and sex.* Unpublished manuscript. (35)

Roitberg, B. D., Reid, M. L., & Li, C. (1993). Choosing hosts and mates: The value of learning. In D. R. Papaj & A. C. Lewis (Eds.), *Insect learning: Ecological and evolutionary perspectives* (pp. 174–194). New York: Chapman and Hall. (5)

Römer, H., & Krusch, M. (2000). A gain-control mechanism for processing of chorus sounds in the afferent auditory pathway of the bush-cricket *Tettigonia viridissima* (Orthoptera; Tettigoniidae). *Journal of Comparative Physiology A, 186*, 181–191. (5)

Rommelfanger, H., & Unterharnscheid, D. (1985). Entwicklung einer Hierarchie gewichteter Bonitätskriterien [Development of a hierarchy of weighted credit-worthiness criteria]. *Österreichisches Bankarchiv, 12*, 419–427. (11)

Rosander, K., & von Hofsten, C. (2002). Development of gaze tracking of small and large objects. *Experimental Brain Research, 146*, 257–264. (5)

Roscoe, S. N. (1968). Airborne displays for flight and navigation. *Human Factors, 10*, 321–332. (33)

Rose, Charlie (Executive Producer). (2009, February 11). *The Charlie Rose Show* [Television show]. New York: PBS. (33)

Rosenbaum, J. E. (2009). Patient teenagers? A comparison of the sexual behavior of virginity pledgers and matched nonpledgers. *Pediatrics, 123*, 110–120. (9)

Rosenheim, J. A., Nonacs, P., & Mangel, M. (1996). Sex ratios and multifaceted parental investment. *American Naturalist, 148*, 501–535. (35)

Rosseel, Y. (2002). Mixture models of categorization. *Journal of Mathematical Psychology, 46,* 178–210. (14)

Rossmo, D. K. (1993). Multivariate spatial profiles as a tool in crime investigation. In C. R. Block, M. Dabdoub, & S. Fregley (Eds.), *Crime analysis through computer mapping* (pp. 65–97). Washington, DC: Police Executive Research Forum. (29)

Rossmo, D. K. (2000). *Geographic profiling.* Boca Raton, FL: CRC Press. (29)

Rossmo, D. K. (2005). Geographic heuristics or shortcuts to failure? Response to Snook et al. *Applied Cognitive Psychology, 19,* 651–654. (29)

Rothstein, H. G. (1986). The effects of time pressure on judgment in multiple cue probability learning. *Organizational Behavior and Human Decision Processes, 37,* 83–92. (13)

Rotter, J. B. (1954). *Social learning and clinical psychology.* Englewood Cliffs, NJ: Prentice Hall. (7)

Rowe, C. (1999). Receiver psychology and the evolution of multicomponent signals. *Animal Behavior, 58,* 921–931. (5)

Rowe, C., & Skelhorn, J. (2004). Avian psychology and communication. *Proceedings of the Royal Society of London, Series B: Biological Sciences, 271,* 1435–1442. (5)

Roy, A. D. (1952). Safety first and the holding of assets. *Econometrica, 20,* 431–49. (34)

Royden, C. S., & Hildreth, E. C. (1996). Human heading judgments in the presence of moving objects. *Perception & Psychophysics, 58,* 836–856. (33)

Rubinstein, A. (1988). Similarity and decision-making under risk (Is there a utility theory resolution to the Allais-paradox?). *Journal of Economic Theory, 46,* 145–153. (7, 8)

Rubinstein, A. (2003). Economics and psychology? The case of hyperbolic discounting. *International Economic Review, 44,* 1207–1216. (7)

Rugg, M. D., & Yonelinas, A. P. (2003). Human recognition memory: A cognitive neuroscience perspective. *Trends in Cognitive Sciences, 7,* 313–319. (25)

Rumelhart, D. E., Hinton, G. E., & Williams, R. J. (1986). Learning internal representations by error propagation. In D. E. Rumelhart & J. L. McClelland (Eds.), *Parallel distributed processing: Explorations in the microstructure of cognition* (pp. 318–362). Cambridge, MA: MIT Press. (1)

Rumelhart, D. E., & Todd, P. M. (1993). Learning and connectionist representations. In D. E.

Meyer & S. Kornblum (Eds.), *Attention and performance XIV* (pp. 3–30). Cambridge, MA: MIT Press. (3)

Rust, R., & Chung, T. S. (2006). Marketing models of service and relationships. *Marketing Science, 25,* 560–580. (36)

Sainfort, F. C., Gustafson, D. H., Bosworth, K., & Hawkins, R. (1990). Decision support systems effectiveness: Conceptual framework and empirical evaluation. *Organizational Behavior and Human Decision Processes, 45,* 232–252. (29)

Salmon, C. A. (1998). The evocative nature of kin terminology in political rhetoric. *Politics and the Life Sciences, 17,* 51–57. (35)

Salmon, C. A. (1999). On the impact of sex and birth order on contact with kin. *Human Nature, 10,* 183–197. (35)

Salmon, C. A., & Daly, M. (1998). Birth order and familial sentiment: Middleborns are different. *Evolution and Human Behavior, 19,* 299–312. (35)

Salthouse, T. A. (1991). *Theoretical perspectives on cognitive aging.* Hillsdale, NJ: Erlbaum. (22)

Samuelson, W., & Zeckhauser, R. (1988). Status quo bias in decision making. *Journal of Risk and Uncertainty, 1,* 7–59. (37)

Sanfey, A. G., & Hastie, R. (1999). Judgment and decision making across the adult life span. In D. Park & N. Schwarz (Eds.), *Cognitive aging: A primer.* Philadelphia, PA: Psychology Press. (22)

Santrock, J. W. (2002). *Life-span development* (8th ed.). Boston, MA: McGraw-Hill. (35)

Sargent, T. J. (1993). *Bounded rationality in macroeconomics.* New York: Oxford University Press. (8)

Sato, Y., Saito, Y., & Sakagami, T. (2003). Rules for nest sanitation of a social spider mite, *Schizotetranychus miscanthi* Saito (Acari: Tetranychidae). *Ethology, 109,* 713–724. (5)

Savage, L. J. (1954). *The foundations of statistics.* New York: Wiley. (Introduction, 7, 8, 9, 12)

Saxe, R. (2006). Uniquely human social cognition. *Current Opinion in Neurobiology, 16,* 235–239. (9)

Scarborough, D. L., Cortese, C., & Scarborough, H. (1977). Frequency and repetition effects in lexical memory. *Journal of Experimental Psychology: Human Perception and Performance, 3,* 1–17. (23)

Scarr, S., & Salapatek, P. (1970). Patterns of fear development during infancy. *Merrill-Palmer Quarterly, 16,* 53–90. (23)

Schachter, F. F., Gilutz, G., Shore, E., & Adler, M. (1978). Sibling deidentification judged by mothers: Cross-validation and developmental studies. *Child Development, 49,* 543–546. (35)

Schacter, D. L., & Tulving, E. (1994). What are the memory systems of 1994? In D. L. Schacter & E. Tulving (Eds.), *Memory systems* (pp. 1–38). Cambridge, MA: MIT Press. (3)

Schaeken, W., Schroyens, W., & Dieussaert, K. (2001). Conditional assertions, tense, and explicit negatives. *European Journal of Cognitive Psychology, 4,* 433–450. (38)

Scheibehenne, B., & Bröder, A. (2007). Predicting Wimbledon 2005 tennis results by mere player name recognition. *International Journal of Forecasting, 3,* 415–426. (1, 24, 31, 32)

Scheper-Hughes, N. (1992). *Death without weeping: The violence of everyday life in Brazil.* Berkeley, CA: University of California Press. (35)

Scherer, B. (2002). Portfolio resampling: Review and critique. *Financial Analysts Journal, 58,* 98–109. (34)

Schkade, D. A., & Johnson, E. J. (1989). Cognitive processes in preference reversals. *Organizational Behavior and Human Decision Processes, 44,* 203–231. (7)

Schmidt, F. L. (1971). The relative efficiency of regression and simple unit weighting predictor weights in applied differential psychology. *Educational and Psychological Measurement, 31,* 699–714. (1)

Schmidtz, D. (2004). Satisficing as a humanly rational strategy. In M. Byron (Ed.), *Satisficing and maximizing: Moral theorists on practical reason* (pp. 30–58). Cambridge, UK: Cambridge University Press. (9)

Schmitt, M., & Martignon, L. (2006). On the complexity of learning lexicographic strategies. *Journal of Machine Learning Research, 7,* 55–83. (1)

Schmittlein, D. C., Morrison, D. G., & Colombo, R. (1987). Counting your customers: Who are they and what will they do next? *Management Science, 33,* 1–24. (36)

Schmittlein, D. C., & Peterson, R. A. (1994). Customer base analysis: An industrial purchase process application. *Marketing Science, 13,* 41–67. (36)

Schneider, B. H., Atkinson, L., & Tardif, C. (2001). Child-parent attachment and children's peer relations: A quantitative review. *Developmental Psychology, 37,* 86–100. (35)

Schonfield, D., & Robertson, B. (1966). Memory storage and aging. *Canadian Journal of Psychology, 20,* 228–236. (3)

Schooler, C. (1972). Birth order effects: Not here, not now! *Psychological Bulletin, 78,* 161–175. (35)

Schooler, L. J., & Anderson, J. R. (1997). The role of process in the rational analysis of memory. *Cognitive Psychology, 32,* 219–250. (4)

Schooler, L. J., & Hertwig, R. (2005). How forgetting aids heuristic inference. *Psychological Review, 112,* 610–628. (1, 5, 15, 24, 26, 32)

Schuck-Paim, C., Pompilio, L., & Kacelnik, A. (2004). State-dependent decisions cause apparent violations of rationality in animal choice. *PLoS Biology, 2,* e402. (5)

Schunk, D., & Betsch, C. (2006). Explaining heterogeneity in utility functions by individual differences in decision modes. *Journal of Economic Psychology, 27,* 386–401. (24)

Schunn, C. D., & Anderson, J. R. (1998). Scientific discovery. In J. R. Anderson & C. Lebiere (Eds.), *The atomic components of thought* (pp. 255–296). Mahwah, NJ: Erlbaum. (4)

Schunn, C. D., & Reder, L. M. (2001). Another source of individual differences: Strategy adaptivity to changing rates of success. *Journal of Experimental Psychology: General, 130,* 59–76. (22)

Schwartz, B., Ward, A., Monterosso, J., Lyubomirsky, S., White, K., & Lehman, D. R. (2002). Maximizing versus satisficing: Happiness is a matter of choice. *Journal of Personality and Social Psychology, 83,* 1178–1197. (9)

Schwarz, G. (1978). Estimating the dimension of a model. *Annals of Statistics, 6,* 461–464. (19)

Schwarz, N. (1999). Self-reports: How the questions shape the answers. *American Psychologist, 54,* 93–105. (8)

Schwarz, N. (2004). Metacognitive experiences in consumer judgment and decision making. *Journal of Consumer Psychology, 14,* 332–348. (26)

Schwarz, N., Bless, H., Strack, F., Klumpp, G., Rittenauer-Schatka, H., & Simons, A. (1991). Ease of retrieval as information: Another look at the availability heuristic. *Journal of Personality and Social Psychology, 61,* 195–202. (23, 24, 26)

Schwarz, N., Hippler, H.-J., Deutsch, B., & Strack, F. (1985). Response categories: Effects on behavioral reports and comparative judgments. *Public Opinion Quarterly, 49,* 388–395. (8)

Schwarz, N., & Wänke, M. (2002). Experiential and contextual heuristics in frequency judgments: Ease of recall and response scales. In P. Sedlmeier & T. Betsch (Eds.), *Etc.: Frequency processing and cognition* (pp. 89–108). New York: Oxford University Press. (26)

Schwarzer, R., & Jerusalem, M. (Eds.). (1999). *Skalen zur Erfassung von Lehrer- und Schülermerkmalen.* Berlin, Germany: Free University Berlin. (17)

Scrimshaw, S. C. M. (1978). Infant mortality and behavior in the regulation of family size. *Population and Developmental Review, 4,* 383–403. (35)

Scrimshaw, S. C. M. (1984). Infanticide in human populations. In G. Hausfater & S. B. Hrdy (Eds.), *Infanticide: Comparative and evolutionary perspectives* (pp. 439–462). New York: Aldine. (35)

Seale, D. A., & Rapoport, A. (1997). Sequential decision making with relative ranks: An experimental investigation of the secretary problem. *Organizational Behavior and Human Decision Processes, 69,* 221–236. (40)

Sedlmeier, P., Hertwig, R., & Gigerenzer, G. (1998). Are judgments of the positional frequencies of letters systematically biased due to availability? *Journal of Experimental Psychology: Learning, Memory, and Cognition, 24,* 754–770. (1, 4, 26)

Seeley, T. D. (1995). *The wisdom of the hive.* Cambridge, MA: Harvard University Press. (5)

Seeley, T. D. (2001). Decision making in superorganisms: How collective wisdom arises from the poorly informed masses? In G. Gigerenzer & R. Selten (Eds.), *Bounded rationality: The adaptive toolbox* (pp. 249–262). Cambridge, MA: MIT Press. (18)

Seeley, T. D. (2003). Consensus building during nest-site selection in honey bee swarms: The expiration of dissent. *Behavioral Ecology and Sociobiology, 53,* 417–424. (5)

Seeley, T. D., & Visscher, P. K. (2003). Choosing a home: How scouts in a honey bee swarm perceive the completion of their group decision making. *Behavioral Ecology and Sociobiology, 54,* 511–520. (5)

Seeley, T. D., & Visscher, P. K. (2004). Quorum sensing during nest-site selection by honeybee swarms. *Behavioral Ecology and Sociobiology, 56,* 594–601. (5)

Selten, R. (2001). What is bounded rationality? In G. Gigerenzer & R. Selten (Eds.), *Bounded rationality: The adaptive toolbox* (pp. 13–36). Cambridge, MA: MIT Press. (1, 7, 8)

Semenza, C., & Sgaramella, T. M. (1993). Production of proper names: A clinical case study of the effects of phonemic cueing. In G.

Cohen & D. M. Burke (Eds.), *Memory for proper names* (pp. 265–280). Hove, UK: Erlbaum. (3)

Semenza, C., & Zettin, M. (1989). Evidence from aphasia for the role of proper names as pure referring expressions. *Nature, 342,* 678–679. (3)

Serwe, S., & Frings, C. (2006). Who will win Wimbledon? The recognition heuristic in predicting sports events. *Journal of Behavioral Decision Making, 19,* 321–332. (1, 23, 24, 26, 31, 32)

Shaffer, D. M., Krauchunas, S. M., Eddy, M., & McBeath, M. K. (2004). How dogs navigate to catch Frisbees. *Psychological Science, 15,* 437–441. (1, 5, 9, 32)

Shaffer, D. M., & McBeath, M. K. (2002). Baseball outfielders maintain a linear optical trajectory when tracking uncatchable fly balls. *Journal of Experimental Psychology: Human Perception and Performance, 28,* 335–348. (33)

Shafir, E., Simonson, I., & Tversky, A. (1993). Reason-based choice. *Cognition, 49,* 11–36. (8)

Shafir, S., Waite, T. A., & Smith, B. H. (2002). Context-dependent violations of rational choice in honeybees (*Apis mellifera*) and gray jays (*Perisoreus canadensis*). *Behavioral Ecology and Sociobiology, 51,* 180–187. (5)

Shah, A. K., & Oppenheimer, D. M. (2008). Heuristics made easy: An effort-reduction framework. *Psychological Bulletin, 137,* 207–222. (1)

Shanks, D. R. (1991). Categorization by a connectionist network. *Journal of Experimental Psychology: Learning, Memory, and Cognition, 17,* 433–443. (11)

Shanks, D. R., & Lagnado, D. (2000). Sub-optimal reasons for rejecting optimality. *Behavioral and Brain Sciences, 23,* 761–762. (17)

Shannon, C. (1948). A mathematical theory of communication. *Bell Systems Technical Journal, 27,* 379–423, 623–656. (12)

Shanteau, J. (1988). Psychological characteristics and strategies of expert decision makers. *Acta Psychologica, 68,* 203–215. (30)

Shanteau, J. (1992a). Competence in experts: The role of task characteristics. *Organizational Behavior and Human Decision Processes, 53,* 254–266. (30)

Shanteau, J. (1992) [also: 1992b]. How much information does an expert use? Is it relevant? *Acta Psychologica, 81,* 75–86. (9, [30])

Shanteau, J., Grier, M., Johnson, J., & Berner, E. (1991). Teaching decision-making skills to student nurses. In J. Baron & R. V. Brown

(Eds.), *Teaching decision-making to adolescents* (pp. 105–200). Hillsdale, NJ: Erlbaum. (30)

Shanteau, J., & Thomas, R. P. (2000). Fast and frugal heuristics: What about unfriendly environments? *Behavioral and Brain Sciences, 23,* 762–763. (5, 7, 29)

Shapiro, N. (Executive Producer). (2000, April 12). *Dateline* [Television broadcast]. New York: National Broadcasting Company Inc. (29)

Sharma, S. (1996). *Applied multivariate techniques.* New York: Wiley. (36)

Shaw, J. S., III. (1996). Increases in eyewitness confidence resulting from postevent questioning. *Journal of Experimental Psychology: Applied, 2,* 126–146. (26)

Shaw, J. S., McClure, K. A., & Wilkens, C. E. (2001). Recognition instructions and recognition practice can alter the confidence–response time relationship. *Journal of Applied Psychology, 86,* 93–103. (26)

Shaw, K. T., & Gifford, R. (1994). Residents' and burglars' assessment of burglary risk from defensible space cues. *Journal of Environmental Psychology, 14,* 177–194. (30)

Shepard, R. N. (1967) [also: 1967a]. On subjectively optimum selections among multi-attribute alternatives. In W. Edwards & A. Tversky (Eds.), *Decision making* (pp. 257–283). Harmondsworth, UK: Penguin Books. (2, [3])

Shepard, R. N. (1967) [also: 1967b]. Recognition memory for words, sentences, and pictures. *Journal of Verbal Learning and Verbal Behavior, 6,* 156–163. ([3], 15)

Shepard, R. N. (1974). Representation of structure in similarity data: Problems and prospects. *Psychometrika, 39,* 373–421. (1)

Shepard, R. N. (1987). Towards a universal law of generalization for psychological science. *Science, 237,* 1317–1323. (1, 17)

Shepard, R. N. (1990). *Mind sights.* New York: Freeman. (12)

Sherden, W. A. (1998). *The fortune sellers: The big business of buying and selling predictions.* New York: Wiley. (29)

Shettleworth, S. J. (1998). *Cognition, evolution and behavior.* New York: Oxford University Press. (5)

Shettleworth, S. J. (2005). Taking the best for learning. *Behavioural Processes, 69,* 147–149. (5)

Shiffrin, R. M., Huber, D. E., & Marinelli, K. (1995). Effects of category length and strength on familiarity in recognition. *Journal of Experimental Psychology: Learning, Memory, and Cognition, 21,* 267–287. (15)

Shiffrin, R. M., & Steyvers, M. (1997). A model for recognition memory: REM-retrieving effectively from memory. *Psychonomic Bulletin and Review, 4,* 145–166. (15)

Shiloh, S., Koren, S., & Zakay, D. (2001). Individual differences in compensatory decision-making style and need for closure as correlates of subjective decision complexity and difficulty. *Personality and Individual Differences, 30,* 699–710. (17)

Shine, R., Phillips, B., Waye, H., LeMaster, M., & Mason, R. T. (2003). The lexikon of love: What cues cause size-assortative courtship by male garter snakes. *Behavioral Ecology and Sociobiology, 53,* 234–237. (5)

Shortliffe, E. H. (1976). *Computer-based medical consultations: MYCIN.* New York: Elsevier. (29)

Shweder, R. A., Much, N. C., Mahaptra, M., & Park, L. (1997). The "big three" of morality (autonomy, community, and divinity), and the "big three" explanations of suffering, as well. In A. Brandt & P. Rozin (Eds.), *Morality and health* (pp. 119–169). New York: Routledge. (9)

Sieck, W. R., & Yates, J. F. (2001). Overconfidence effects in category learning: A comparison of connectionist and exemplar memory models. *Journal of Experimental Psychology: Learning, Memory, and Cognition, 27,* 1003–1021. (11)

Siegel, S., & Castellan, N. J. (1988). *Nonparametric statistics for the behavioral sciences* (2nd ed.). New York: McGraw-Hill. (18)

Simão, J., & Todd, P. M. (2002). Modeling mate choice in monogamous mating systems with courtship. *Adaptive Behavior, 10,* 113–136. (5, 40)

Simão, J., & Todd, P. M. (2003). Emergent patterns of mate choice in human populations. *Artificial Life, 9,* 403–417. (40)

Simmons, J. A., Fenton, M. B., & O'Farrell, M. J. O. (1979). Echolocation and pursuit of prey by bats. *Science, 203,* 16–21. (33)

Simon, H. A. (1945). *Administrative behavior. A study of decision-making processes in administrative organization.* New York: Free Press. (2)

Simon, H. A. (1955). A behavioral model of rational choice. *Quarterly Journal of Economics, 69,* 99–118. (Introduction, 1, 8, 9, 24, 40)

Simon, H. A. (1956). Rational choice and the structure of the environment. *Psychological Review, 63,* 129–138. (2, 5, 8, 13, 15, 18, 19, 22, 29, 37, 39)

Simon, H. A. (1957). *Models of man*. New York: Wiley. (Introduction, 7)

Simon, H. A. (1976). From substantive to procedural rationality. In S. J. Latsis (Ed.), *Method and appraisal in economics* (pp. 129–148). New York: Cambridge University Press. (19)

Simon, H. A. (1977). On judging the plausibility of theories. In H. A. Simon (Ed.), *Models of discovery* (pp. 25–45). Dordrecht, the Netherlands: Reidel. (7)

Simon, H. A. (1982). *Models of bounded rationality*. Cambridge, MA: MIT Press. (2, 10, 38, 39)

Simon, H. A. (1983). *Reason in human affairs*. Stanford, CA: Stanford University Press. (7)

Simon, H. A. (1990). Invariants of human behavior. *Annual Review of Psychology, 41,* 1–19. (Introduction, 2, 5, 9, 15, 40)

Simon, H. A. (1991). *Models of my life*. New York: Basic Books. (1)

Simon, H. A. (1992). *Economics, bounded rationality, and the cognitive revolution*. Aldershot, UK: Elgar. (2)

Simon, H. A. (1992). What is an "explanation" of behavior? *Psychological Science, 3,* 150–161. (1)

Simon, H. A. (1996). *The sciences of the artificial* (3rd ed.). Cambridge, MA: MIT Press. (9)

Simon H. A. (1999). [Endorsement of the book: Gigerenzer, G., Todd, P. M., & the ABC Research Group (1999). *Simple heuristics that make us smart*. New York: Oxford University Press.] (Introduction)

Simpson, G. G., Genadall, A. R., & Dean, C. (1999). When to switch to flowering. *Annual Review of Cell and Developmental Biology, 99,* 519–550. (5)

Simpson, J. A., & Weiner, E. S. C. (Eds.). (1989). *The Oxford English dictionary* (2nd ed.). Oxford, UK: Clarendon Press. (35)

Sirot, E. (2001). Mate-choice copying by females: The advantages of a prudent strategy. *Journal of Evolutionary Biology, 14,* 418–423. (5)

Sivia, D. S. (1996). *Data analysis: A Bayesian tutorial*. Oxford, UK: Clarendon Press. (39)

Skinner, W. G. (1992). Seek a loyal subject in a filial son: Family roots of political orientation in Chinese society. In Institute of Modern History, Academia Sinica (Eds.), *Family process and political process in modern Chinese history* (pp. 943–993). Taipei, People's Republic of China: Academia Sinica. (35)

Slegers, D. W., Brake, G. L., & Doherty, M. E. (2000). Probabilistic mental models with continuous predictors. *Organizational Behavior and Human Decision Processes, 81,* 98–114. (12, 15, 18)

Sloman, S. A. (1996). The empirical case for two systems of reasoning. *Psychological Bulletin, 119,* 3–22. (1)

Slote, M. (2004). Two views of satisficing. In M. Byron (Ed.), *Satisficing and maximizing: Moral theorists on practical reason* (pp. 14–29). Cambridge, UK: Cambridge University Press. (9)

Slovic, P. (1995). The construction of preference. *American Psychologist, 60,* 364–371. (37)

Slovic, P., Finucane, M., Peters, E., & MacGregor, D. G. (2002). The affect heuristic. In T. Gilovich, D. Griffin & D. Kahneman (Eds.), *Heuristics and biases: The psychology of intuitive judgment* (pp. 397–420). New York: Cambridge University Press. (13)

Slovic, P., & Fischhoff, B. (1977). On the psychology of experimental surprise. *Journal of Experimental Psychology: Human Perception and Performance, 3,* 544–551. (10)

Slovic, P., Griffin, D., & Tversky, A. (1990). Compatibility effects in judgment and choice. In R. M. Hogarth (Ed.), *Insights in decision making: A tribute to Hillel J. Einhorn* (pp. 5–27). Chicago: University of Chicago Press. (7, 8)

Slovic, P., & Lichtenstein, S. (1968). Relative importance of probabilities and payoffs in risk taking. *Journal of Experimental Psychology Monographs, 78,* 1–18. (7)

Slovic, P., & Lichtenstein, S. (1971). Comparison of Bayesian and regression approaches to the study of information processing in judgment. *Organizational Behavior and Human Performance, 6,* 649–744. (17)

Smith, A. (1761). *The theory of moral sentiments*. London: Millar. (9)

Smith, L., & Gilhooly, K. (2006). Fast and frugal versus regression models of decision-making: The case of prescribing for depression. *Applied Cognitive Psychology, 20,* 265–274. (14)

Smith, V. L., & Walker, J. M. (1993). Monetary rewards and decision cost in experimental economics. *Economic Inquiry, 31,* 245–261. (11)

Sniezek, J. A., & Buckley, T. (1993). Becoming more or less uncertain. In N. J. Castellan (Ed.), *Individual and group decision making* (pp. 87–108). Hillsdale, NJ: Erlbaum. (2)

Snook, B., Canter, D. V., & Bennell, C. (2002). Predicting the home location of serial offenders: A preliminary comparison of the accuracy of human judges with a geographic profiling system. *Behavioral Sciences and the Law, 20,* 1–10. (29)

Snook, B., & Cullen, R. M. (2006). Recognizing national hockey league greatness with an ignorance-based heuristic. *Canadian Journal of Experimental Psychology, 60,* 33–43. (15, 16, 24, 31, 32)

Snook, B., Zito, M., Bennell, C., & Taylor, P. J. (2005). On the complexity and accuracy of geographic profiling strategies. *Journal of Quantitative Criminology, 21,* 1–26. (29)

Sorkin, R. D., West, R., & Robinson, D. E. (1998). Group performance depends on the majority rule. *Psychological Science, 9,* 456–463. (27)

Sperber, D., Cara, E., & Girotto, V. (1995). Relevance theory explains the selection task. *Cognition, 57,* 31–95. (2)

Sperber, D., & Wilson, D. (1981). Pragmatics. *Cognition, 10,* 281–286. (38)

Sperber, D., & Wilson, D. (1986). *Relevance: Communication and cognition.* Cambridge, MA: Harvard University Press. (38)

Spranca, M., Minsk, E., & Baron, J. (1991). Omissions and commissions in judgement and choice. *Journal of Experimental Social Psychology, 27,* 76–105. (37)

Squire, L. R. (1994). Declarative and non-declarative memory: Multiple brain systems supporting learning and memory. In D. L. Schacter & E. Tulving (Eds.), *Memory systems* (pp. 203–231). Cambridge, MA: MIT Press. (25)

Squire, L. R., Knowlton, B., & Musen, G. (1993). The structure and organization of memory. *Annual Review of Psychology, 44,* 453–495. (3)

Squire, L. R., Ojemann, J. G., Miezin, F. M., Petersen, S. E., Videen, T. O., & Raichle, M. E. (1992). Activation of the hippocampus in normal humans: A functional anatomical study of memory. *Proceedings of the National Academy of Sciences, U.S.A., 89,* 1837–1818. (25)

Squire, L. R., Stark, C. E. L., & Clark, R. E. (2004). The medial temporal lobe. *Annual Review of Neuroscience, 27,* 279–306. (25)

Stahl, D. O. (1996). Boundedly rational rule learning in a guessing game. *Games and Economic Behavior, 16,* 303–330. (11)

Stahl, D. O. (2000). Rule learning in symmetric normal-form games: Theory and evidence. *Games and Economic Behavior, 32,* 105–138. (11)

Stahlberg, D., & Maass, A. (1998). Hindsight bias: Impaired memory of biased reconstruction? In W. Stroebe & M. Hewstone (Eds.), *European review of social psychology* (Vol. 8, pp. 106–132). New York: Wiley. (10)

Standing, L. (1973). Learning 10,000 pictures. *Quarterly Journal of Experimental Psychology, 25,* 207–222. (3, 15)

Starmer, C. (2000). Developments in non-expected utility theory: The hunt for a descriptive theory of choice under risk. *Journal of Economic Literature, 38,* 332–382. (8)

Statman, D. (1993). *Moral luck.* Albany, NY: State University of New York Press. (9)

Steelman, L. C. (1985). A tale of two variables: The intellectual consequences of sibship size and birth order. *Review of Educational Research, 55,* 353–386. (35)

Steelman, L. C., & Powell, B. (1989). Acquiring capital for college: The constraints of family configuration. *American Sociological Review, 54,* 844–855. (35)

Stein, C. (1955). Inadmissibility of the usual estimator for the mean of a multivariate normal distribution. In *3rd Berkeley Symposium on Probability and Statistics 1* (pp. 197–206). Berkeley, CA: University of California Press. (34)

Steinmann, D. O. (1974). Transfer of lens model learning. *Organizational Behavior and Human Performance, 12,* 1–16. (13)

Steinmann, D. O., & Doherty, M. E. (1972). A lens model analysis of a bookbag and poker chip experiment: A methodological note. *Organizational Behavior and Human Performance, 8,* 450–455. (13)

Stephens, D. W. (2002). Discrimination, discounting and impulsivity: A role for an informational constraint. *Philosophical Transaction of the Royal Society of London, Series B: Biological Sciences, 357,* 1527–1537. (5)

Stephens, D. W., & Anderson, D. (2001). The adaptive value of preference for immediacy: When shortsighted rules have farsighted consequences. *Behavioral Ecology, 12,* 330–339. (5)

Stephens, D. W., & Krebs, J. R. (1986). *Foraging theory.* Princeton, NJ: Princeton University Press. (2)

Stern, P. C. (2000b). Information, incentives, and proenvironmental consumer behavior. *Journal of Consumer Policy, 22,* 461–478. (37)

Stern, P. C. (2000a). Toward a coherent theory of environmentally significant behavior. *Journal of Social Issues, 56,* 407–424. (37)

Sternberg, R. J. (2000). Damn it, I still don't know what to do! *Behavioral and Brain Sciences, 23,* 764. (29)

Stevens, J. R., & Hauser, M. D. (2004). Why be nice? Psychological constraints on the evolution of cooperation. *TRENDS in Cognitive Sciences, 8,* 60–65. (9)

Stewart, T. (1988). Judgment analysis: Procedures. In B. Brehmer & C. R. B. Joyce (Eds.), *Human judgment: The SJT view* (pp. 41–74). Amsterdam: North-Holland. (28)

Stigler, G. J. (1961). The economics of information. *Journal of Political Economy, 69,* 213–225. (1, 8)

Stoll, H., & Whaley, R. (1983). Transaction costs and the small firm effect. *Journal of Financial Economics, 12,* 57–79. (34)

Stone, G. O. (1986). An analysis of the delta rule and the learning of statistical associations. In D. Rumelhart, J. McClelland, & the PDP Research Group (Eds.), *Parallel distributed processing: Explorations in the microstructure of cognition* (pp. 444–459). Cambridge, MA: MIT Press. (2)

Stone, M. (1974). Cross-validatory choice and assessment of statistical predictions. *Journal of the Royal Statistical Society B, 36,* 111–147. (1)

Strack, F., & Bless, H. (1994). Memory for nonoccurrences: Metacognitive and presuppositional strategies. *Journal of Memory and Language, 33,* 203–217. (3)

Stumpf, H., Angleitner, A., Wieck, T., Jackson, D. N., & Beloch-Till, H. (1984). *Deutsche Personality Research Form (PRF).* Göttingen, Germany: Hogrefe. (17)

Sugar, T. G., & McBeath, M. K. (2001). Robotic modeling of mobile catching as a tool for understanding biological interceptive behavior. *Behavior and Brain Sciences, 24,* 1078–1080. (33)

Sulloway, F. J. (1996). *Born to rebel: Birth order, family dynamics, and creative lives.* New York: Pantheon Books. (35)

Sulloway, F. J. (1999). Birth order. In M. A. Runco & S. R. Pritzken (Eds.), *Encyclopedia of creativity* (Vol. 1, pp. 189–202). San Diego, CA: Academic Press. (35)

Sulloway, F. J. (2001a). Birth order, sibling competition, and human behavior. In H. R. Holcomb III (Ed.), *Conceptual challenges in evolutionary psychology: Innovative research strategies* (pp. 39–83). Dordrecht, the Netherlands: Kluwer Academic. (35)

Sulloway, F. J. (2001b). *Study on birth order and personality.* Unpublished data. (35)

Suluh, A., Sugar, T. G., & McBeath, M. K. (2001). Spatial navigational principles: Applications to mobile robots. *Proceedings of the 2001 IEEE International Conference on Robotics and Automation, 2,* 1689–1694. (33)

Summers, S. A., Summers, R. C., & Karkau, V. T. (1969). Judgments based on different functional relationships between interacting cues and a criterion. *American Journal of Psychology, 82,* 203–211. (13)

Sunstein, C. R. (Ed.). (2000). *Behavioral law and economics.* Cambridge, UK: Cambridge University Press. (1)

Sunstein, C. R. (2003). Terrorism and probability neglect. *Journal of Risk and Uncertainty, 26,* 121–136. (7, 8)

Sunstein, C. R. (2005). Moral heuristics. *Behavioral and Brain Sciences, 28,* 531–542. (9)

Sunstein, C. R., & Thaler, R. H. (2003). Libertarian paternalism is not an oxymoron. *University of Chicago Law Review, 70,* 1159–1202. (37)

Sutton, R. S., & Barto, A. G. (1998). *Reinforcement learning: An introduction.* Cambridge, MA: MIT Press. (11)

Svenson, O. (1979). Process descriptions of decision making. *Organizational Behavior & Human Performance, 23,* 86–112. (22)

Svenson, O. (1992). Differentiation and consolidation theory of human decision making: A frame of reference for the study of pre and postdecision processes. *Acta Psychologica, 80,* 143–168. (11, 18)

Svenson, O. (1996). Decision making and the search for fundamental psychological regularities: What can be learned from a process perspective? *Organizational Behavior and Human Decision Processes, 65,* 252–267. (18)

Svenson, O., & Maule, J. A. (Eds.). (1993). *Time pressure and stress in human judgment and decision making.* London: Plenum Press. (22)

Swanton, C. (2004). Satisficing and perfectionism in virtue ethics. In M. Byron (Ed.), *Satisficing and maximizing: Moral theorists on practical reason* (pp. 176–189). Cambridge, UK: Cambridge University Press. (9)

Swets, J. A., Dawes, R. M., & Monahan, J. (2000). Psychological science can improve diagnostic decisions. *Psychological Science in the Public Interest, 1,* 1–26. (29)

Swets, J. A., Tanner, W. P., Jr., & Birdsall, T. G. (1961). Decision processes in perception. *Psychological Review, 68,* 301–340. (4)

Talairach, P., & Tournoux, J. (1988). *Co-planar stereotactic atlas of the human brain.* Stuttgart, Germany: Thieme. (25)

Tamura, M., & Suzuki, M. (1997). Criminal profiling research on serial arson: Examinations of circle hypothesis estimating offender's residential area. *Research on Prevention of Crime and Delinquency, 38,* 13–25. (29)

Taubman, P., & Behrman, J. B. (1986). Effect of number and position of siblings on child and adult outcomes. *Social Biology, 33,* 22–34. (35)

Tauber, M. J., & Tauber, C. A. (1976). Insect seasonality: Diapause maintenance, termination, and postdiapause development. *Annual Review of Entomology, 21,* 81–107. (5)

Taylor, P. J. (2002). A partial order scalogram analysis of communication behaviour in crisis negotiation with the prediction of outcome. *International Journal of Conflict Management, 13,* 4–37. (29)

Taylor, P. J., Bennell, C., & Snook, B. (2002). Problems of classification in investigative psychology. In K. Jajuga, A. Sokolowski, & H.-H. Bock (Eds.), *Classification, clustering, and data analysis: Recent advances and applications* (pp. 479–487). Heidelberg, Germany: Springer. (29)

Taylor, P. J., Bennell, C., & Snook, B. (2008). The bounds of cognitive heuristic performance on the geographic profiling task. *Applied Cognitive Psychology, 22,* 410–430. (29)

Thaler, R. H. (1991). *Quasi rational economics.* New York: Russell Sage Foundation. (Introduction)

Thaler, R. H., & Sunstein, C. R. (2003). Libertarian paternalism. *American Economic Review, 93,* 175–179. (37)

Thaler, R. H., & Sunstein, C. R. (2008). *Nudge: Improving decisions about health, wealth, and happiness.* New Haven, CT: Yale University Press. (9)

The best-paid athletes. (2004, June 24). Retrieved July 28, 2004, from http://www.forbes.com/2004/06/23/04athletesland.html (26)

The world's richest people. (2004). Retrieved July, 29, 2004, from http://www.forbes.com/2004/02/25/bill04land.html (26)

Thirion, J. P. (1998). Image matching as a diffusion process: An analogy with Maxwell's demons. *Medical Image Analysis, 2,* 243–260. (25)

Thompson, K., & Grime, J. P. (1983). A comparative study of germination responses to diurnally-fluctuating temperatures. *Journal of Applied Ecology, 20,* 141–156. (5)

Thomson, J. D. (1996). Trapline foraging by bumblebees: I. Persistence of flight-path geometry. *Behavioral Ecology, 7,* 158–164. (5)

Thorngate, W. (1980). Efficient decision heuristics. *Behavioral Science, 25,* 219–225. (7)

Thornton, W. J. L., & Dumke, H. (2005). Age differences in everyday problem solving and decision making effectiveness: A meta-analytic review. *Psychology and Aging, 20,* 85–99. (22)

Thuijsman, F., Peleg, B., Amitai, M., & Shmida, A. (1995). Automata, matching and foraging behavior of bees. *Journal of Theoretical Biology, 175,* 305–316. (5)

Thurstone, L. L. (1930). The learning function. *Journal of General Psychology, 3,* 469–493. (11)

Timmermans, D. (1993). The impact of task complexity on information use in multi-attribute decision making. *Journal of Behavioral Decision Making, 6,* 95–111. (18)

Tinbergen, N. (1958). *Curious naturalists.* London: Country Life. (1, 5)

Toates, F. M. (1975). *Control theory in biology and experimental psychology.* London: Hutchinson Educational. (33)

Todd, I. A., & Kacelnik, A. (1993). Psychological mechanisms and the Marginal Value Theorem: Dynamics of scalar memory for travel time. *Animal Behavior, 46,* 765–775. (5)

Todd, P. M. (1997). Searching for the next best mate. In R. Conte, R. Hegselmann, & P. Terna (Eds.), *Simulating social phenomena* (pp. 419–436). Berlin, Germany: Springer. (40)

Todd, P. M. (1999). Simple inference heuristics versus complex decision machines. *Minds & Machines, 9,* 461–477. (5)

Todd, P. M. (2000). Fast and frugal heuristics for environmentally bounded minds. In G. Gigerenzer & R. Selten (Eds.), *Bounded rationality: The adaptive toolbox* (pp. 51–70). Cambridge, MA: MIT Press. (40)

Todd, P. M., & Dieckmann, A. (2005). Heuristics for ordering cue search in decision making. In L. K. Saul, Y. Weiss, & L. Bottou (Eds.), *Advances in neural information processing systems* (Vol. 17, pp. 1393–1400). Cambridge, MA: MIT Press. (5, 21)

Todd, P. M., & Dieckmann, A. (in press). Simple rules for ordering cues in one-reason decision making. In P. M. Todd, G. Gigerenzer, & the ABC Research Group, *Ecological rationality: Intelligence in the world.* New York: Oxford University Press. (21)

Todd, P. M., & Gigerenzer, G. (2000). Precis of "Simple heuristics that make us smart". *Behavioral and Brain Sciences, 23,* 727–780. (3, 39)

Todd, P. M., & Gigerenzer, G. (2001). Shepard's mirrors or Simon's scissors? *Behavioral and Brain Sciences, 24,* 704–705. (9)

Todd, P. M., Gigerenzer, G., & the ABC Research Group. (in press). *Ecological rationality: Intelligence in the world.* New York: Oxford University Press. (1, 14)

Todd, P. M., & Goodie, A. S. (2002). Testing the ecological rationality of base rate neglect. In B. Hallam, D. Floreano, J. Hallam, G. Hayes, & J.-A. Meyer (Eds.), *From animals to animats 7: Proceedings of the Seventh International Conference on Simulation of Adaptive Behavior* (pp. 215–223). Cambridge, MA: MIT Press/Bradford Books. (17)

Todd, P. M., & Kirby, S. (2001). I like what I know: How recognition-based decisions can structure the environment. In J. Kelemen & P. Sosik (Eds.), *Advances in artificial life: Sixth European conference.* Heidelberg, Germany: Springer-Verlag. (4)

Todd, P. M., & Miller, G. F. (1999). From pride and prejudice to persuasion: Satisficing in mate search. In G. Gigerenzer, P. M. Todd, & the ABC Research Group, *Simple heuristics that make us smart* (pp. 287–308). New York: Oxford University Press. (1, 5, 40)

Todorov, A. (2001). *Predicting real outcomes: When heuristics are as smart as statistical models.* Unpublished manuscript. (32)

Tolstoy, L. (1982). *War and peace.* London: Penguin Classics. (Original work published 1869) (10)

Tomasello, M. (2000). *The cultural origins of human cognition.* Cambridge, MA: Harvard University Press. (9)

Top artists. (2003). Retrieved July 10, 2008, from http://web.archive.org/web/20040216195220/http://www.ria.com/gp/bestsellers/topartists.asp (26)

Toscani, O. (1997). *Die Werbung ist ein lächelndes Aas* [Advertisement is a beast that smiles at us]. Frankfurt, Germany: Fischer. (3)

Toth, J. P., & Daniels, K. A. (2002). Effects of prior experience on judgments of normative word frequency: Automatic bias and correction. *Journal of Memory and Language, 46,* 845–874. (4)

Travis, R., & Kohli, V. (1995). The birth order factor: Ordinal position, social strata, and educational achievement. *Journal of Social Psychology, 135,* 499–507. (35)

Trivers, R. L. (1972). Parental investment and sexual selection. In B. Campbell (Ed.), *Sexual selection and the descent of man: 1871–1971* (pp. 136–179). Chicago: Aldine. (35)

Trivers, R. L. (1974). Parent-offspring conflict. *American Zoologist, 14,* 249–264. (35)

Truffer, B., Markard, J., & Wüstenhagen, R. (2001). Eco-labeling of electricity: Strategies and tradeoffs in the definition of environmental standards. *Energy Policy, 29,* 885–897. (37)

Tucker, L. R. (1964). A suggested alternative formulation in the developments by Hursch, Hammond, and Hursch and by Hammond, Hursch, and Todd. *Psychological Review, 71,* 528–530. (13)

Tucker, W. (1987). Where do the homeless come from? *National Review, 39,* 34–44. (21)

Turner, S. (1969). Delinquency and distance. In T. Sellin & M. E. Wolfgang (Eds.), *Delinquency: Selected studies* (pp. 11–26). New York: Wiley. (29)

Tversky, A. (1969). Intransitivity of preferences. *Psychological Review, 76,* 31–48. (7, 8, 11)

Tversky, A. (1972). Elimination by aspects: A theory of choice. *Psychological Review, 79,* 281–299. (Introduction, 1, 5, 7, 19, 24)

Tversky, A. (1977). Features of similarity. *Psychological Review, 84,* 327–352. (1, 39)

Tversky, A., & Fox, C. R. (1995). Weighing risk and uncertainty. *Psychological Review, 102,* 269–283. (7, 8)

Tversky, A., & Gilovich, T. (1989). The cold facts about the "hot hand" in basketball. *Chance, 2,* 16–21. (32)

Tversky, A., & Kahneman, D. (1973). Availability: A heuristic for judging frequency and probability. *Cognitive Psychology, 5,* 207–232. (1, 4, 13, 26)

Tversky, A., & Kahneman, D. (1974). Judgment under uncertainty: Heuristics and biases. *Science, 185,* 1124–1131. (1, 3, 10, 26)

Tversky, A., & Kahneman, D. (1983). Extensional versus intuitive reasoning: The conjunction fallacy in probability judgment. *Psychological Review, 90,* 293–315. (13)

Tversky, A., & Kahneman, D. (1992). Advances in prospect theory: Cumulative representation of uncertainty. *Journal of Risk and Uncertainty, 5,* 297–323. (7, 8)

Tversky, A., Sattath, S., & Slovic, P. (1988). Contingent weighting in judgment and choice. *Psychological Review, 95,* 371–384. (7)

Tweney, R. D., & Doherty, M. E. (1983). Rationality and the psychology of inference. *Synthese, 57,* 139–161. (31)

Tweney, R. D., & Walker, B. J. (1990). Science education and the cognitive psychology of science. In B. F. Jones & L. Idol (Eds.), *Dimensions of thinking and cognitive instruction* (pp. 291–310). Hillsdale, NJ: Erlbaum. (2)

Ugurbil, K., Garwood, M., Ellermann, J., Hendrich, K., Hinke, R., Hu, X. P., et al. (1993). Imaging at high magnetic fields: Initial experiences at 4 T. *Magnetic Resonance Quarterly, 9,* 259–277. (25)

United Nations. (1990). *Patterns of first marriage: Timing and prevalence.* New York: United Nations. (40)

Unkelbach, C. (2007). Reversing the truth effect: Learning the interpretation of processing fluency in judgments of truth. *Journal of Experimental Psychology: Learning, Memory, and Cognition, 33,* 219–230. (26)

Valenstein, E., Bowers, D., Verfaellie, M., Heilman, K. M., Day, A., & Watson, R. T. (1987). Retrosplenial amnesia. *Brain, 110,* 1631–1646. (25)

van Alphen, J. J. M., Bernstein, C., & Driessen, G. (2003). Information acquisition and time allocation in insect parasitoids. *Trends in Ecology and Evolution, 18,* 81–87. (5)

Vandell, D. L., & Beckwith, S. (1989, April). *Maternal styles of interaction with infant twins.* Paper presented at the meeting of the Society for Research in Child Development, Kansas City, MO. (35)

van Raaij, W. F. (1983). Techniques for process tracing in decision making. In L. Sjöberg, T. Tyszka, & J. Wise (Eds.), *Human decision making* (pp. 179–196). Bodafors, Sweden: Doxa. (17)

Verhoef, P. C., Spring, P. N., Hoekstra, J. C., & Leeflang, P. S. H. (2002). The commercial use of segmentation and predictive modeling techniques for database marketing in the Netherlands. *Decision Support Systems, 34,* 471–481. (36)

Vicario, D. S., Naqvi, N. H., & Raksin, J. N. (2001). Sex differences in discrimination of vocal communication signals in a songbird. *Animal Behavior, 61,* 805–817. (5)

Viscusi, W. K. (1989). Prospective reference theory: Toward an explanation of the paradoxes. *Journal of Risk and Uncertainty, 2,* 235–264. (8)

Vishton, P. M., & Cutting, J. E. (1995). Wayfinding, displacements, and mental maps: Velocity fields are not typically used to determine one's aimpoint. *Journal of Experimental Psychology: Human Perception and Performance, 21,* 978–995. (33)

Vollrath, F. (1987). Altered geometry of webs in spiders with regenerated legs. *Nature, 328,* 247–248. (5)

Volz, K. G., Schooler, L. J., Schubotz, R. I., Raab, M., Gigerenzer, G., & von Cramon, D. Y. (2006). Why you think Milan is larger than Modena: Neural correlates of the recognition heuristic. *Journal of Cognitive Neuroscience, 18,* 1924–1936. (1, 5, 15, 23, 24, 26)

von Helversen, B., & Rieskamp, J. (2008). The mapping model: A cognitive theory of quantitative estimation. *Journal of Experimental Psychology: General, 137,* 73–96. (6)

von Neumann, J., & Morgenstern, O. (1947). *Theory of games and economic behavior.* Princeton, NJ: Princeton University Press. (7)

von Wangenheim, F., & Lentz, P. (2005). *Customer portfolio analysis: Applying financial risk and volatility measures to customer segmentation and risk-adjusted lifetime value determination.* Retrieved August 17, 2007, from http://ssrn.com/abstract=782064 (36)

Vroom, V. H. (1964). *Work and motivation.* New York: Wiley. (7)

Vulkan, N. (2000). An economist's perspective on probability matching. *Journal of Economic Surveys, 14,* 101–118. (23)

Wade, B. (1988). *Mileage points can fly away.* Retrieved January 14, 2008, from http://query.nytimes.com/gst/fullpage.html?res=940DE1DC1F3DF933A15752C1A96E948260 (36)

Wagenmakers, E. J. M., Zeelenberg, R., Steyvers, M., Shiffrin, R. M., & Raaijmakers, J. G. W. (2004). Nonword repetition in lexical decision: Support for two opposing processes. *Quarterly Journal of Experimental Psychology, 57A,* 1191–1210. (23)

Wagner, A. D., Shannon, B. J., Kahn, I., & Buckner, R. L. (2005). Parietal lobe contributions to episodic memory retrieval. *Trends in Cognitive Sciences, 9,* 445–453. (25)

Wainer, H. (1976). Estimating coefficients in linear models: It don't make no nevermind. *Psychological Bulletin, 83,* 213–217. (11, 13)

Wajnberg, E., Fauvergue, X., & Pons, O. (2000). Patch leaving decision rules and the Marginal Value Theorem: An experimental analysis and a simulation model. *Behavior and Ecology, 11,* 577–586. (5)

Wajnberg, E., Gonsard, P.-A., Tabone, E., Curty, C., Lezcano, N., & Colazza, S. (2003). A comparative analysis of patch-leaving decision rules in a parasitoid family. *Journal of Animal Ecology, 72,* 618–626. (5)

Wald, A. (1947). *Sequential analysis.* New York: Wiley. (5)

Waller, W. S. (1988). Brunswikian research in accounting and auditing. In B. Brehmer & C. R. B. Joyce (Eds.), *Human judgment: The SJT view* (pp. 247–272). Amsterdam: North-Holland. (28)

Wallis, G., & Bülthoff, H. (1999). Learning to recognize objects. *Trends in Cognitive Sciences, 3,* 22–31. (23)

Wallraff, H. G. (2001). Navigation by homing pigeons: Updated perspective. *Ethology Ecology and Evolution, 13,* 1–48. (5)

Wallsten, T. S. (1996). An analysis of judgment research analyses. *Organizational Behavior & Human Decision Processes, 65,* 220–226. (15)

Wallsten, T. S., Erev, I., & Budescu, D. V. (2000). The importance of theory: Response to Brenner (2000). *Psychological Review, 107,* 947–949. (15)

Wang, Z. (2005). A shrinkage approach to model uncertainty and asset allocation. *The Review of Financial Studies, 18,* 673–705. (34)

Ward, B. D. (2000). *Simultaneous inference for fMRI data.* Retrieved January 6, 2006, from afni.nimh. nih.gov/afni/doc/manual/AlphaSim (25)

Warrington, E. K., & McCarthy, R. A. (1988). The fractionation of retrograde amnesia. *Brain and Cognition, 7,* 184–200. (3)

Wason, P. C. (1966). Reasoning. In B. M. Foss (Ed.), *New horizons in psychology* (pp. 135–151). Harmondsworth, UK: Penguin. (38)

Watkins, M. J. (1984). Models as toothbrushes. *The Behavioural and Brain Sciences, 7,* 86. (4)

Watts, R. G., & Bahill, T. A. (1990). *Keep your eye on the ball.* New York: W. H. Freeman. (33)

Webb, B., & Reeve, R. (2003). Reafferent or redundant: Integration of phonotaxis and optomotor behavior in crickets and robots. *Adaptive Behavior, 11,* 137–158. (5)

Weber, E. U., Böckenholt, U., Hilton, D. J., & Wallace, B. (1993). Determinants of diagnostic hypothesis generation: Effects of information, base rates, and experience. *Journal of Experimental Psychology: Learning, Memory, and Cognition, 19,* 1151–1164. (2)

Wechsler, D. (1981). *Wechsler Adult Intelligence Scale: Revised Manual (WAIS-R).* New York: Psychological Corporation. (22)

Weininger, O. (1903). Geschlecht und Charakter [Sex and character]. Vienna: Wilhelm Braumüller. (9)

Weisberg, S. (1985). *Applied linear regression.* New York: Wiley. (1, 21)

Weldon, E., & Gargano, G. M. (1985). Cognitive effort in additive task groups: The effects of shared responsibility on the quality of multiattribute judgments. *Organizational Behavior and Human Decision Processes, 36,* 348–361. (28)

Wells, M. S. (1988). Effects of body size and resource value on fighting behaviour in a jumping spider. *Animal Behavior, 36,* 321–326. (5)

Wheeler, M. E., & Buckner, R. L. (2003). Functional dissociation among components of remembering: Control, perceived oldness, and content. *Journal of Neuroscience, 23,* 3869–3880. (25)

Whittlesea, B. W. A. (1993). Illusions of familarity. *Journal of Experimental Psychology: Learning, Memory, and Cognition, 19,* 1235–1253. (4, 26)

Whittlesea, B. W. A. (1997). Production, evaluation, and preservation of experiences: Constructive processing in remembering and performance tasks. In D. L. Medin (Ed.), *The psychology of learning and motivation* (Vol. 37, pp. 211–264). San Diego, CA: Academic Press. (23)

Whittlesea, B. W. A., & Leboe, J. P. (2003). Two fluency heuristics (and how to tell them apart). *Journal of Memory and Language, 49,* 62–79. (26)

Wickens, T. D. (1992). *Engineering psychology and human performance.* New York: Harper Collins. (33)

Wickens, T. D. (1989). *Multiway contingency tables analysis for the social sciences.* Hillsdale, NJ: Erlbaum. (11)

Wickens, T. D. (2002). *Elementary signal detection theory.* Oxford, UK: Oxford University Press. (15)

Wiegmann, D. D., & Mukhopadhyay, K. (1998). The fixed sample search rule and use of an indicator character to evaluate mate quality. *Journal of Theoretical Biology, 193,* 709–715. (5)

Wiegmann, D. D., Real, L. A., Capone, T. A., & Ellner, S. (1996). Some distinguishing features of models of search behavior and mate choice. *American Naturalist, 147,* 188–204. (5)

Wigfield, A., & Eccles, J. S. (1992). The development of achievement task values: A theoretical analysis. *Developmental Review, 12,* 265–310. (7)

Wigton, R. S. (1996). Social judgment theory and medical judgment. *Thinking and Reasoning, 2,* 175–190. (28)

Wilke, A., Hutchinson, J. M. C., & Todd, P. M. (2004). Testing simple rules for human foraging in patchy environments. In K. Forbus, D. Gentner, & T. Regier (Eds.), *Proceedings of the 26th Annual Conference of the Cognitive Science Society* (p. 1656). Mahwah, NJ: Erlbaum. (5)

Williams, A. C. (1966). Attitudes toward speculative risks as an indicator of attitudes toward pure risks. *Journal of Risk and Insurance, 33,* 577–586. (7)

Williams, B. (1981). *Moral luck.* Cambridge, UK: Cambridge University Press. (9)

Williams, C. M. (1956). Physiology of insect diapause. X. An endocrine mechanism for the influence of temperature on the diapausing pupa of the cecropia silkworm. *Biological Bulletin, 110,* 201–218. (5)

Wilson, D. S. (2002). *Darwin's cathedral: Evolution, religion, and the nature of society.* Chicago: University of Chicago Press. (9)

Wilson, R. S., Beckett, L. A., Barnes, L. L., Schneider, J. A., Bach, J., Evans, D. A., et al. (2002). Individual differences in rates of change in cognitive abilities of older persons. *Psychology and Aging, 17,* 179–193. (22)

Wiltschko, R., & Wiltschko, W. (2003). Avian navigation: From historical to modern concepts. *Animal Behavior, 65,* 257–272. (5)

Wimsatt, W. C. (1976). Reductionism, levels of organization, and the mind-body problem. In G. G. Globus, G. Maxwell, & I. Savodnik (Eds.), *Consciousness and the brain: A scientific and philosophical inquiry* (pp. 199–267). New York: Plenum. (2)

Winkielman, P., Schwarz, N., Fazendeiro, T. A., & Reber, R. (2003). The hedonic marking of processing fluency: Implications for evaluative judgment. In J. Musch & K. C. Klauer (Eds.), *The psychology of evaluation: Affective processes in cognition and emotion* (pp. 189–217). Mahwah, NJ: Erlbaum. (26)

Winkler, R. L., & Makridakis, S. (1983). The combination of forecasts. *Journal of the Royal Statistical Society, Series A, 146,* 150–157. (31)

Winman, A., Juslin, P., & Björkman, M. (1998). The confidence-hindsight mirror effect in judgment: An accuracy-assessment model for the knew-it-all-along phenomenon. *Journal of Experimental Psychology: Learning, Memory, and Cognition, 24,* 415–431. (10)

Wohlstetter, R. (1962). *Pearl Harbor: Warning and decision.* Stanford, CA: Stanford University Press. (10)

Wood, S., Busemeyer, J., Koling, A., Cox, C. R., & Davis, H. (2005). Older adults as adaptive decision makers: Evidence from the Iowa Gambling Task. *Psychology and Aging, 20,* 220–225. (22)

Woodley, W. L., Simpson, J., Biondini, R., & Berkeley, J. (1977). Rainfall results 1970–75: Florida area cumulus experiment. *Science, 195,* 735–742. (21)

Worsley, K. J., & Friston, K. J. (1995). Analysis of fMRI time-series revisited-again. *Neuroimage, 2,* 173–181. (25)

Wottawa, H. (1987). Hypotheses Agglutination (HYPAG): A method for configuration-based analysis of multivariate data. *Methodika, 1,* 68–92. (14)

Wright, R., Logie, R. H., & Decker, S. H. (1995). Criminal expertise and offender decision making: An experimental study of the target-selection process in residential burglary. *Journal of Research in Crime & Delinquency, 32,* 39–54. (30)

Wu, G., & Gonzalez, R. (1996). Curvature of the probability weighting function. *Management Science, 42,* 1676–1690. (8)

Wübben, M., & von Wangenheim, F. (2008). Instant customer base analysis: Managerial heuristics often "get it right". *Journal of Marketing, 72,* 82–93. (1, 9)

Wüstenhagen, R. (2000). *Ökostrom - von der Nische zum Massenmarkt. Entwicklungsperspektiven und Marketingstrategien für eine zukunftsfähige Elektrizitätsbranche.* Zürich, Switzerland: vdf-Hochschulverlag. (37)

Yaari, M. E. (1987). The dual theory of choice under risk. *Econometrica, 55,* 95–115. (7)

Ydenberg, R. C. (1982). Great tits and giving-up times: Decision rules for leaving patches. *Behaviour, 90,* 1–24. (5)

Yee, M., Dahan, E., Hauser, J. R., & Orlin, J. B. (2007). Greedoid-based non-compensatory two-stage consideration-then-choice inference. *Marketing Science, 26,* 532–549. (1, 8)

Yonelinas, A. P. (2001). Consciousness, control, and confidence: The 3 Cs of recognition memory. *Journal of Experimental Psychology: General, 130,* 361–379. (26)

Yonelinas, A. P. (2002). The nature of recollection and familiarity: A review of 30 years of research. *Journal of Memory and Modern Language, 46,* 441–517. (23)

Yonelinas, A. P., Kroll, N. E., Quamme, J. R., Lazzara, M. M., Sauve, M. J., Widaman, K. F., et al. (2002). Effects of extensive temporal lobe damage or mild hypoxia on recollection and familiarity. *Nature Neuroscience, 5,* 1236–1241. (25)

Yonelinas, A. P., Otten, L. J., Shaw, K. N., & Rugg, M. D. (2005). Separating the brain regions involved in recollection and familiarity in recognition memory. *The Journal of Neuroscience, 25,* 3002–3008. (25)

York, K. M., Doherty, M. E., & Kamouri, J. (1987). The influence of cue unreliability in a multiple cue probability learning task. *Organizational Behavior and Human Decision Processes, 39,* 303–317. (13)

Youmans, R. J., & Stone, E. R. (2005). To thy own self be true: Finding the utility of cognitive information feedback. *Journal of Behavioral Decision Making, 18,* 319–341. (13)

Zajonc, R. B. (2001). The family dynamic of intellectual development. *American Psychologist, 56,* 490–496. (35)

Zajonc, R. B., & Markus, G. B. (1975). Birth order and intellectual development. *Psychological Review, 82,* 74–88. (35)

Zajonc, R. B., Markus, H., & Markus, G. B. (1979). The birth order puzzle. *Journal of Personality and Social Psychology, 37,* 1325–1341. (35)

Zakay, D. (1990). The role of personal tendencies in the selection of decision-making strategies. *Psychological Record, 40,* 207–213. (17, 24)

Zdrahal-Urbanek, J., & Vitouch, O. (2004). *Would you vote for Saddam? Recognition, valence, and choice in low-information decision settings.* Poster presented at the Risk, Decision, and Human Error Conference, Trento, Italy. (27)

Zerssen, D. (1994). Persönlichkeitszüge als Vulnerabilitätsindikatoren - Probleme ihrer Erfassung. *Fortschritt der Neurologie, Psychiatrie und ihrer Grenzgebiete, 62,* 1–13. (17)

Zervas, L. J., & Sherman, M. F. (1994). The relationship between perceived parental favoritism and self-esteem. *The Journal of Genetic Psychology, 155,* 25–33. (35)

Zimbardo, P. (2007). *The Lucifer effect: Understanding how good people turn to evil.* New York: Random House. (9)

Zuk, M., Ligon, J. D., & Thornhill, R. (1992). Effects of experimental manipulation of male secondary sex characters on female mate preference in red jungle fowl. *Animal Behavior, 44,* 999–1006. (5)

AUTHOR INDEX

Note: Page references followed by "*f*" and "*t*" denote figures and tables, respectively.

SUBJECT INDEX

Note: Page numbers followed by "*f*" and "*t*" denote figures and tables, respectively.